Saint Thomas A

Commentary on Metaphysics
Books 1–6

Translated by John P. Rowan

Aristotle Commentaries

Volume 50
Latin/English Edition of the Works of St. Thomas Aquinas

AQUINAS INSTITUTE
GREEN BAY, WI

EMMAUS ACADEMIC
STEUBENVILLE, OH

We would like to thank Kevin Bergdorf, Patricia Lynch, Josh and Holly Harnisch, Fr. Brian McMaster, Dr. Brian Cutter, and the Studentate Community of the Dominican Province of St. Albert the Great, USA, for their support. This series is dedicated to Marcus Berquist, Rose Johanna Trumbull, John and Mary Deignan, Thomas and Eleanor Sullivan, Ann C. Arcidi, the Very Rev. Romanus Cessario, OP, STM, and Fr. John T. Feeney and his sister Mary.

Published with the ecclesiastical approval of
The Most Reverend David L. Ricken, DD, JCL
Bishop of Green Bay
Given on May 13, 2020

LIBRARY OF CONGRESS CATALOGING-IN-PUBLICATION DATA

Names: Thomas, Aquinas, Saint, 1225?-1274, author. | Rowan, John Patrick, translator. |
  Thomas, Aquinas, Saint, 1225?-1274. In duodecim libros Metaphysicorum Aristotelis expositio. |
  Thomas, Aquinas, Saint, 1225?-1274. In duodecim libros Metaphysicorum Aristotelis expositio. English.

Title: Commentary on Metaphysics : Aristotle commentaries / Saint Thomas Aquinas ; translated by John P. Rowan.

Description: Steubenville : Emmaus Academic, 2019. |
  Series: Latin/English edition of the works of St. Thomas Aquinas; volumes 50-51 |
  Contents: [v. 1.] Books 1-6 -- [v. 2.] Books 7-12. |
  Latin and English translation in parallel columns. |
  Summary: "Foundational in its consideration of being and the transcendentals, the Metaphysics of Aristotle is a dense and difficult work on its own. This volume contains the first half of St. Thomas's commentary on the Metaphysics, beginning with discussing the views of Aristotle's predecessors and moving towards a discussion of being"-- Provided by publisher.

Identifiers: LCCN 2019022578 (print) | LCCN 2019022579 (ebook) | ISBN 9781623400507 (v. 1 : hardcover) | ISBN 9781623400514 (v. 2 : hardcover) | ISBN 9781623401504 (ebook)

Subjects: LCSH: Aristotle. Metaphysics. | Metaphysics--Early works to 1800.

Classification: LCC B434 .T53 2019 (print) | LCC B434 (ebook) | DDC 110--dc23 |
  LC record available at https://lccn.loc.gov/2019022578 |
  LC ebook record available at https://lccn.loc.gov/2019022579

Notes on the Text

Latin Text of St. Thomas

Thomas's commentaries on Aristotle were written around 1266–1272, and his commentary on the *Metaphysics* was likely completed after Thomas had returned to Paris to teach again, between 1271–1272. Thomas seems to have used multiple Latin translations of Aristotle in working on his commentary, and although he was clearly aware of the existence of books 13 and 14 of the *Metaphysics*, he does not comment on them directly. As of yet, there is no critical edition of Thomas's commentary on the *Metaphysics*; the Latin text used in this edition is thus based on the 1964 Marietti edition, the work of M. R. Cathala, OP, and Raymund M. Spiazzi, OP. The text has been edited and revised by The Aquinas Institute.

Greek Text of Aristotle

The Greek text of Aristotle is taken from the edition of W. D. Ross (Oxford, 1970). Ross's edition makes use of an important manuscript not taken into account by Bekker, and he pays special attention to punctuation, which is useful in comprehending the Greek text. Ross's text is presented here largely untouched, albeit with a few important emendations.

English Translation of Aristotle and St. Thomas

The English translation, originally published by the Henry Regnery Company in 1961, is the work of John P. Rowan, who was a professor of philosophy at Duquesne University. In Rowan's words, "This translation does not pretend to be a transliteration of the original. Since strict adherence to this method very often results in the use of latinisms and word structures that are foreign to the English reader, it seemed advisable, if the thought of the original was to be presented in as accurate and readily understandable a form as possible, to render the Latin as idiomatically and meaningfully as current English usage permits. . . . Throughout the whole translation the aim has been to produce as faithful and accurate a rendition of St. Thomas's work as circumstances permit." Rowan's translation has been edited and revised by The Aquinas Institute.

The Aquinas Institute requests your assistance in the continued perfection of these texts.
If you discover any errors, please send us a note by email: editor@aquinasinstitute.org

DEDICATED WITH LOVE TO
OUR LADY OF MT. CARMEL

Contents

COMMENTARY ON METAPHYSICS 1–6

PROLOGUE

Sicut docet Philosophus in *Politicis* suis, quando aliqua plura ordinantur ad unum, oportet unum eorum esse regulans, sive regens, et alia regulata, sive recta. Quod quidem patet in unione animae et corporis; nam anima naturaliter imperat, et corpus obedit. Similiter etiam inter animae vires: irascibilis enim et concupiscibilis naturali ordine per rationem reguntur. Omnes autem scientiae et artes ordinantur in unum, scilicet ad hominis perfectionem, quae est eius beatitudo. Unde necesse est, quod una earum sit aliarum omnium rectrix, quae nomen sapientiae recte vindicat. Nam sapientis est alios ordinare.

Quae autem sit haec scientia, et circa qualia, considerari potest, si diligenter respiciatur quomodo est aliquis idoneus ad regendum. Sicut enim, ut in libro praedicto Philosophus dicit, homines intellectu vigentes, naturaliter aliorum rectores et domini sunt: homines vero qui sunt robusti corpore, intellectu vero deficientes, sunt naturaliter servi: ita scientia debet esse naturaliter aliarum regulatrix, quae maxime intellectualis est. Haec autem est, quae circa maxime intelligibilia versatur.

Maxime autem intelligibilia tripliciter accipere possumus.

Primo quidem ex ordine intelligendi. Nam ex quibus intellectus certitudinem accipit, videntur esse intelligibilia magis. Unde, cum certitudo scientiae per intellectum acquiratur ex causis, causarum cognitio maxime intellectualis esse videtur. Unde et illa scientia, quae primas causas considerat, videtur esse maxime aliarum regulatrix.

Secundo ex comparatione intellectus ad sensum. Nam, cum sensus sit cognitio particularium, intellectus per hoc ab ipso differre videtur, quod universalia comprehendit. Unde et illa scientia maxime est intellectualis, quae circa principia maxime universalia versatur. Quae quidem sunt ens, et ea quae consequuntur ens, ut unum et multa, potentia et actus.

Huiusmodi autem non debent omnino indeterminata remanere, cum sine his completa cognitio de his, quae sunt propria alicui generi vel speciei, haberi non possit. Nec iterum in una aliqua particulari scientia tractari debent: quia cum his unumquodque genus entium ad sui cognitionem indigeat, pari ratione in qualibet particulari scientia tractarentur. Unde restat quod in una communi scientia huiusmodi tractentur; quae cum maxime intellectualis sit, est aliarum regulatrix.

When several things are ordained to one thing, one of them must rule or govern and the rest be ruled or governed, as the Philosopher teaches in the *Politics*. This is evident in the union of soul and body, for the soul naturally commands and the body obeys. The same thing is true of the soul's powers, for the concupiscible and irascible appetites are ruled in a natural order by reason. Now all the sciences and arts are ordained to one thing, namely, to man's perfection, which is happiness. Hence one of these sciences and arts must be the mistress of all the others, and this rightly lays claim to the name of wisdom. For it is the office of the wise man to direct others.

We can discover which science this is and the sort of things with which it deals by carefully examining the qualities of a good ruler. For just as men of superior intelligence are naturally the rulers and masters of others, whereas those of great physical strength and little intelligence are naturally slaves (as the Philosopher says in the aforementioned book), in a similar way, the science that is intellectual in the highest degree should be naturally the ruler of the others. This science is the one that treats of the most intelligible objects.

Now "most intelligible objects" can be understood in three ways.

First, from the viewpoint of the order of knowing: those things from which the intellect derives certitude seem to be more intelligible. Therefore, since the certitude of science is acquired by the intellect knowing causes, a knowledge of causes seems to be intellectual in the highest degree. Hence that science that considers first causes also seems to be the ruler of the others in the highest degree.

Second, by comparing the intellect with the senses. While sensory perception is a knowledge of particulars, the intellect seems to differ from sense by reason of the fact that it comprehends universals. Hence that science is preeminently intellectual which deals with the most universal principles. These principles are being and those things that follow being, such as unity and plurality, potency and act.

Now such principles should not remain entirely undetermined, since without them complete knowledge of the principles that are proper to any genus or species cannot be had. Nor again should they be dealt with in any one particular science, for, since a knowledge of each genus of beings stands in need of such principles, they would with equal reason be investigated in every particular science. It follows, then, that such principles should be treated by one common science, which, since it is intellectual in the highest degree, is the mistress of the others.

Tertio ex ipsa cognitione intellectus. Nam cum una-quaeque res ex hoc ipso vim intellectivam habeat, quod est a materia immunis, oportet illa esse maxime intelligibilia, quae sunt maxime a materia separata. Intelligibile enim et intellectum oportet proportionata esse, et unius generis, cum intellectus et intelligibile in actu sint unum. Ea vero sunt maxime a materia separata, quae non tantum a signata materia abstrahunt, sicut formae naturales in universali acceptae, de quibus tractat scientia naturalis, sed omnino a materia sensibili. Et non solum secundum rationem, sicut mathematica, sed etiam secundum esse, sicut Deus et intelligentiae. Unde scientia, quae de istis rebus considerat, maxime videtur esse intellectualis, et aliarum princeps sive domina.

Haec autem triplex consideratio, non diversis, sed uni scientiae attribui debet. Nam praedictae substantiae separatae sunt universales et primae causae essendi. Eiusdem autem scientiae est considerare causas proprias alicuius generis et genus ipsum: sicut naturalis considerat principia corporis naturalis. Unde oportet quod ad eamdem scientiam pertineat considerare substantias separatas, et ens commune, quod est genus, cuius sunt praedictae substantiae communes et universales causae.

Ex quo apparet, quod quamvis ista scientia praedicta tria consideret, non tamen considerat quodlibet eorum ut subiectum, sed ipsum solum ens commune. Hoc enim est subiectum in scientia, cuius causas et passiones quaerimus, non autem ipsae causae alicuius generis quaesiti. Nam cognitio causarum alicuius generis, est finis ad quem consideratio scientiae pertingit. Quamvis autem subiectum huius scientiae sit ens commune, dicitur tamen tota de his quae sunt separata a materia secundum esse et rationem. Quia secundum esse et rationem separari dicuntur, non solum illa quae nunquam in materia esse possunt, sicut Deus et intellectuales substantiae, sed etiam illa quae possunt sine materia esse, sicut ens commune. Hoc tamen non contingeret, si a materia secundum esse dependerent.

Secundum igitur tria praedicta, ex quibus perfectio huius scientiae attenditur, sortitur tria nomina. Dicitur enim scientia divina sive theologia, inquantum praedictas substantias considerat. Metaphysica, inquantum considerat ens et ea quae consequuntur ipsum. Haec enim transphysica inveniuntur in via resolutionis, sicut magis communia post minus communia. Dicitur autem prima philosophia, inquantum primas rerum causas considerat.

Third, from the viewpoint of the intellect's own knowledge. Since each thing has intellective power by virtue of being free from matter, those things that are altogether separate from matter must be intelligible in the highest degree. For the intellect and the intelligible object must be proportionate to each other and must belong to the same genus, since the intellect and the intelligible object are one in act. Now those things are separate from matter in the highest degree that abstract not only from signate matter, as the natural forms taken universally of which the philosophy of nature treats, but from sensible matter altogether. These are separate from matter not only in their intelligible constitution, as the objects of mathematics, but also in being, as God and the intelligences. Therefore, the science that considers such things seems to be the most intellectual and the ruler or mistress of the others.

Now this threefold consideration should be assigned to one and the same science and not to different sciences, because the aforementioned separate substances are the universal and first causes of being. Moreover, it pertains to one and the same science to consider both the proper causes of some genus and the genus itself. (For example, the philosophy of nature considers the principles of a natural body.) Therefore, it must be the office of one and the same science to consider the separate substances and being in general, which is the genus of which the aforementioned substances are the common and universal causes.

From this it is evident that although this science studies the three things mentioned above, it does not investigate any one of them as its subject, but only being in general. For the subject of a science is the genus whose causes and properties we seek, and not the causes themselves of the particular genus studied; a knowledge of the causes of some genus is the goal to which the investigation of a science attains. Now, although the subject of this science is being in general, the whole of it is predicated of those things that are separate from matter both in their intelligible constitution and in being. For it is not only those things that can never exist in matter that are said to be separate from matter in their intelligible constitution and being, such as God and the intellectual substances, but also those that can exist without matter, as being in general. This could not be the case, however, if their existence depended on matter.

Therefore, in accordance with the three things mentioned above from which this science derives its perfection, three names arise. It is called "divine science" or "theology" inasmuch as it considers the aforementioned substances. It is called "metaphysics" inasmuch as it considers being and the attributes that naturally accompany being (for things that transcend the physical order are discovered by the process of analysis, as the more common are discovered after the less common). And it is called "first philosophy" inasmuch as it considers the first causes of things.

Sic igitur patet quid sit subiectum huius scientiae, et qualiter se habeat ad alias scientias, et quo nomine nominetur.

Therefore, it is evident what the subject of this science is, and how it is related to the other sciences, and by what names it is designated.

Book 1

History of Metaphysical Inquiry

Lecture 1

The dignity and object of this science

980a21 Omnes homines natura scire desiderant. [2]

Signum autem est sensuum dilectio. Praeter enim utilitatem, propter seipsos diliguntur, et maxime aliorum, qui est per oculos. Non enim solum ut agamus, sed et nihil agere debentes, ipsum videre prae omnibus (ut dicam) aliis eligimus. Causa autem est, quod hic maxime sensuum nos cognoscere facit, et multas diiferentias demonstrat.

980a27 Animalia quidem igitur natura sensum habentia fiunt. [9]

980a28 Ex sensibus autem quibusdam quidem ipsorum memoria non fit, quibusdam vero fit. Et propter hoc alia quidem prudentia sunt, alia vero disciplinabiliora non possibilibus memorari. Prudentia quidem sunt sine addiscere, quaecumque sonos audire non potentia sunt, ut apes, et utique si aliquod aliud huiusmodi est animalium genus. Addiscunt autem quaecumque cum memoria et hunc habent sensum. [10]

980b25 Alia quidem igitur imaginationibus et memoriis vivunt, experimenti autem parum participant: hominum autem genus arte et rationibus. [14]

980b28 Fit autem ex memoria hominibus experimentum. Eiusdem namque rei multae memoriae unius experientiae potentiam faciunt. Et fere videtur scientiae simile experimentum esse, et arti. [17]

981a2 Hominibus autem scientia et ars per experientiam evenit. *Experientia quidem*

πάντες ἄνθρωποι τοῦ εἰδέναι ὀρέγονται φύσει.

σημεῖον δ’ ἡ τῶν αἰσθήσεων ἀγάπησις: καὶ γὰρ χωρὶς τῆς χρείας ἀγαπῶνται δι’ αὐτάς, καὶ μάλιστα τῶν ἄλλων ἡ διὰ τῶν ὀμμάτων. οὐ γὰρ μόνον ἵνα πράττωμεν ἀλλὰ καὶ μηθὲν {25} μέλλοντες πράττειν τὸ ὁρᾶν αἱρούμεθα ἀντὶ πάντων ὡς εἰπεῖν τῶν ἄλλων. αἴτιον δ’ ὅτι μάλιστα ποιεῖ γνωρίζειν ἡμᾶς αὕτη τῶν αἰσθήσεων καὶ πολλὰς δηλοῖ διαφοράς.

φύσει μὲν οὖν αἴσθησιν ἔχοντα γίγνεται τὰ ζῷα,

ἐκ δὲ ταύτης τοῖς μὲν αὐτῶν οὐκ ἐγγίγνεται μνήμη, τοῖς δ’ ἐγγίγνεται. {980b21} καὶ διὰ τοῦτο ταῦτα φρονιμώτερα καὶ μαθητικώτερα τῶν μὴ δυναμένων μνημονεύειν ἐστί, φρόνιμα μὲν ἄνευ τοῦ μανθάνειν ὅσα μὴ δύναται τῶν ψόφων ἀκούειν (οἷον μέλιττα κἂν εἴ τι τοιοῦτον ἄλλο γένος ζῴων ἔστι), μανθάνει {25} δ’ ὅσα πρὸς τῇ μνήμῃ καὶ ταύτην ἔχει τὴν αἴσθησιν.

τὰ μὲν οὖν ἄλλα ταῖς φαντασίαις ζῇ καὶ ταῖς μνήμαις, ἐμπειρίας δὲ μετέχει μικρόν: τὸ δὲ τῶν ἀνθρώπων γένος καὶ τέχνῃ καὶ λογισμοῖς.

γίγνεται δ’ ἐκ τῆς μνήμης ἐμπειρία τοῖς ἀνθρώποις: αἱ γὰρ πολλαὶ μνῆμαι τοῦ αὐτοῦ πράγματος μιᾶς ἐμπειρίας δύναμιν ἀποτελοῦσιν. {981a1} καὶ δοκεῖ σχεδὸν ἐπιστήμῃ καὶ τέχνῃ ὅμοιον εἶναι καὶ ἐμπειρία,

ἀποβαίνει δ’ ἐπιστήμῃ καὶ τέχνη διὰ τῆς ἐμπειρίας τοῖς ἀνθρώποις: ἡ μὲν

All men naturally desire to know.

A sign of this is the delight we take in the senses; for apart from their usefulness they are loved for themselves, and most of all the sense that operates through the eyes. For not only that we may act, but even when we intend to do nothing, we prefer sight (as we may say) to all the other senses. The reason is that of all the senses this most enables us to know and reveals many differences between things.

Animals by nature, then, are born with sensory power.

Now in some animals memory arises from the senses, but in others it does not; for this reason the former are prudent and more capable of being taught than those that are unable to remember. Those that cannot hear sounds are prudent but unable to learn, as the bee and any other similar type of animal there may be. But any that have this sense together with memory are able to learn.

Thus other animals live by imagination and memory and share little in experience, whereas the human race lives by art and reasoning.

Now in men experience comes from memory, for many memories of the same thing produce the capacity of a single experience. And experience seems to be somewhat like science and art.

But in men science and art come from experience, for *experience causes art and*

enim *artem fecit*, sicut ait Polus recte dicens, *sed inexperientia casum.* Fit autem ars cum ex multis experimentalibus conceptionibus una fit universalis, velut de similibus, acceptio. [18]

981a7 Acceptionem quidem enim habere, quod Calliae et Socrati hac aegritudine laborantibus hoc contulit, et ita multis singularium, experimenti est: quod autem omnibus huiusmodi secundum unam speciem determinatis, hac aegritudine laborantibus contulit, ut phlegmaticis, aut cholericis, aut aestu febricitantibus, artis est. [19]

981a12 Ad agere quidem igitur experientia quidem nihil ab arte differre videtur. Sed expertos magis proficere videmus, sine experientia rationem habentibus. Causa autem est, quia experientia quidem singularium est cognitio: ars vero universalium. Actus autem et generationes omnes circa singularia sunt. Non enim medicus sanat hominem nisi secundum accidens: sed Calliam, aut Socratem, aut aliquem sic dictorum, cui esse hominem accidit. Si igitur sine experimento quis rationem habeat, et universale quidem cognoscat, in hoc autem singulare ignoret, multotiens quidem peccabit. Singulare namque magis curabile est. [20]

981a24 Sed tamen scire et obviare, magis arte quam experimento esse arbitramur: et artifices expertis sapientiores esse opinamur: tamquam magis sit scire sapientiam sequentem omnia. [23]

981a28 Hoc autem est quia hi quidem causam sciunt, illi vero non. Experti quidem enim ipsum sciunt quia, sed propter quid nesciunt; hi autem propter quid, et causam cognoscunt. [24]

981a30 Unde et architectores circa quodlibet quidem huiusmodi honorabiliores, et magis scire manu artificibus putamus, et sapientiores, quia factorum causas sciunt. [25]

Illi vero sicut quaedam inanimatorum faciunt quidem, non scientia autem faciunt quae faciunt, ut ignis quidem exurit. Inanimata quidem igitur natura

γὰρ ἐμπειρία τέχνην ἐποίησεν, ὡς φησὶ Πῶλος, ἡ {5} δ' ἀπειρία τύχη. γίγνεται δὲ τέχνη ὅταν ἐκ πολλῶν τῆς ἐμπειρίας ἐννοημάτων μία καθόλου γένηται περὶ τῶν ὁμοίων ὑπόληψις.

τὸ μὲν γὰρ ἔχειν ὑπόληψιν ὅτι Καλλίᾳ κάμνοντι τηνδὶ τὴν νόσον τοδὶ συνήνεγκε καὶ Σωκράτει καὶ καθ' ἕκαστον οὕτω πολλοῖς, ἐμπειρίας ἐστίν· {10} τὸ δ' ὅτι πᾶσι τοῖς τοιοῖσδε κατ' εἶδος ἓν ἀφορισθεῖσι, κάμνουσι τηνδὶ τὴν νόσον, συνήνεγκεν, οἷον τοῖς φλεγματώδεσιν ἢ χολώδεσι [ἢ] πυρέττουσι καύσῳ, τέχνης.

πρὸς μὲν οὖν τὸ πράττειν ἐμπειρία τέχνης οὐδὲν δοκεῖ διαφέρειν, ἀλλὰ καὶ μᾶλλον ἐπιτυγχάνουσιν οἱ ἔμπειροι τῶν ἄνευ τῆς ἐμπειρίας {15} λόγον ἐχόντων (αἴτιον δ' ὅτι ἡ μὲν ἐμπειρία τῶν καθ' ἕκαστόν ἐστι γνῶσις ἡ δὲ τέχνη τῶν καθόλου, αἱ δὲ πράξεις καὶ αἱ γενέσεις πᾶσαι περὶ τὸ καθ' ἕκαστόν εἰσιν· οὐ γὰρ ἄνθρωπον ὑγιάζει ὁ ἰατρεύων ἀλλ' ἢ κατὰ συμβεβηκός, ἀλλὰ Καλλίαν ἢ Σωκράτην ἢ τῶν ἄλλων τινὰ {20} τῶν οὕτω λεγομένων ᾧ συμβέβηκεν ἀνθρώπῳ εἶναι· ἐὰν οὖν ἄνευ τῆς ἐμπειρίας ἔχῃ τις τὸν λόγον, καὶ τὸ καθόλου μὲν γνωρίζῃ τὸ δ' ἐν τούτῳ καθ' ἕκαστον ἀγνοῇ, πολλάκις διαμαρτήσεται τῆς θεραπείας· θεραπευτὸν γὰρ τὸ καθ' ἕκαστον):

ἀλλ' ὅμως τό γε εἰδέναι καὶ τὸ ἐπαΐειν τῇ {25} τέχνῃ τῆς ἐμπειρίας ὑπάρχειν οἰόμεθα μᾶλλον, καὶ σοφωτέρους τοὺς τεχνίτας τῶν ἐμπείρων ὑπολαμβάνομεν, ὡς κατὰ τὸ εἰδέναι μᾶλλον ἀκολουθοῦσαν τὴν σοφίαν πᾶσι:

τοῦτο δ' ὅτι οἱ μὲν τὴν αἰτίαν ἴσασιν οἱ δ' οὔ. οἱ μὲν γὰρ ἔμπειροι τὸ ὅτι μὲν ἴσασι, διότι δ' οὐκ ἴσασιν· οἱ δὲ τὸ διότι {30} καὶ τὴν αἰτίαν γνωρίζουσιν.

διὸ καὶ τοὺς ἀρχιτέκτονας περὶ ἕκαστον τιμιωτέρους καὶ μᾶλλον εἰδέναι νομίζομεν τῶν χειροτεχνῶν καὶ σοφωτέρους, {981b1} ὅτι τὰς αἰτίας τῶν ποιουμένων ἴσασιν

(τοὺς δ', ὥσπερ καὶ τῶν ἀψύχων ἔνια ποιεῖ μέν, οὐκ εἰδότα δὲ ποιεῖ ἃ ποιεῖ, οἷον καίει τὸ πῦρ· τὰ μὲν οὖν ἄψυχα φύσει τινὶ ποιεῖν τούτων ἕκαστον τοὺς

inexperience causes luck, as Polus rightly states. Art comes into being when from many conceptions acquired by experience a single universal judgment is formed about similar things.

For to judge that this [medicine] has been beneficial to Callias and Socrates and many other individuals who suffer from this disease is a matter of experience; but to judge that it has been beneficial to all individuals of a particular kind (such as the phlegmatic, the bilious, or the feverish) who suffer from this disease is a matter of art.

In practical matters, then, experience seems to differ in no way from art. But we see that men of experience are more proficient than those who have theory without experience. The reason is that experience is a knowledge of singulars, whereas art is a knowledge of universals. But all actions and processes of generation are concerned with singulars. For the physician heals man only incidentally, but he heals Socrates, or Callias, or some individual that can be named, to whom the nature of man happens to belong. Therefore, if anyone has theory without experience, and knows the universal but not the singulars contained in this, he will very often make mistakes. For it is only the individual man who can be cured.

Yet we think that to know and to refute objections belong to art rather than to experience, and we are of the opinion that those who are proficient in art are wiser than men of experience, as it is more to know if one's wisdom pursues all things.

Now this is because the former know the cause whereas the latter do not. For those who have experience know that something is so but do not know why, whereas the others know the why and the cause.

For this reason, too, we think that the architects in each art are more honorable, and that they know more and are wiser than the manual laborers, because they understand the causes of the things done.

Indeed, we think that the latter resemble certain inanimate things, which act but do not know what they do, like a fire which burns. Therefore, inanimate things

quadam unumquodque faciunt horum, sed manu artifices propter consuetudinem faciunt, tamquam non secundum practicos esse sapientiores sint, sed secundum quod rationes habent ipsi, et causas cognoscunt.

δὲ χειροτέχνας {5} δι᾽ ἔθος), ὡς οὐ κατὰ τὸ πρακτικοὺς εἶναι σοφωτέρους ὄντας ἀλλὰ κατὰ τὸ λόγον ἔχειν αὐτοὺς καὶ τὰς αἰτίας γνωρίζειν.

perform each of their actions as a result of a certain natural disposition, whereas manual laborers perform theirs through habit, implying that some men are wiser not insofar as they are practical, but insofar as they themselves have the theories and know the causes.

981b7 Et omnino signum scientis est posse docere, et ob hoc magis artem experimento scientiam esse existimamus. Possunt enim hi docere, illi autem docere non possunt. [29]

ὅλως τε σημεῖον τοῦ εἰδότος καὶ μὴ εἰδότος τὸ δύνασθαι διδάσκειν ἐστίν, καὶ διὰ τοῦτο τὴν τέχνην τῆς ἐμπειρίας ἡγούμεθα μᾶλλον ἐπιστήμην εἶναι: δύνανται γάρ, οἱ δὲ οὐ δύνανται διδάσκειν.

In general, a sign of scientific knowledge is the ability to teach, and for this reason we think that art rather than experience is science. For those who have an art are able to teach, whereas the others are not.

981b10 Amplius autem sensuum, nec unum sapientiam esse ponimus, cum et his singularium cognitiones maxime sint propriae. Sed propter quid de nullo dicunt: ut propter quid ignis calidus, sed quia calidus solum sit. [30]

ἔτι δὲ τῶν αἰσθήσεων οὐδεμίαν ἡγούμεθα εἶναι σοφίαν: καίτοι κυριώταταί γ᾽ εἰσὶν αὗται τῶν καθ᾽ ἕκαστα γνώσεις: ἀλλ᾽ οὐ λέγουσι τὸ διὰ τί περὶ οὐδενός, οἷον διὰ τί θερμὸν τὸ πῦρ, ἀλλὰ μόνον ὅτι θερμόν.

Furthermore, we do not hold that any one of the senses is wisdom, since the cognition of singular things belongs especially to the senses. However, these do not tell us why a thing is so; for example, they do not tell us why fire is hot but only that it is so.

981b13 Primum quidem igitur conveniens est quamlibet artem invenientem ultra communes sensus, ab hominibus mirari, non solum propter aliquam inventorum utilitatem, sed sicut sapientem, et ab aliis distinguentem. Pluribus autem repertis artibus, et aliis quidem ad necessaria, aliis vero ad introductionem existentibus: semper tales illis sapientiores esse arbitrandum est propter id, quod illorum scientiae ad usum non sunt. [31]

τὸ μὲν οὖν πρῶτον εἰκὸς τὸν ὁποιανοῦν εὑρόντα τέχνην παρὰ τὰς κοινὰς αἰσθήσεις θαυμάζεσθαι {15} ὑπὸ τῶν ἀνθρώπων μὴ μόνον διὰ τὸ χρήσιμον εἶναί τι τῶν εὑρεθέντων ἀλλ᾽ ὡς σοφὸν καὶ διαφέροντα τῶν ἄλλων: πλειόνων δ᾽ εὑρισκομένων τεχνῶν καὶ τῶν μὲν πρὸς τἀναγκαῖα τῶν δὲ πρὸς διαγωγὴν οὐσῶν, ἀεὶ σοφωτέρους τοὺς τοιούτους ἐκείνων ὑπολαμβάνεσθαι διὰ τὸ μὴ πρὸς {20} χρῆσιν εἶναι τὰς ἐπιστήμας αὐτῶν.

It is only fitting, then, that the one who discovered any art whatsoever that went beyond the common perceptions of men should be admired by men, not only because of some usefulness of his discoveries, but as one who is wise and as distinguishing from others. And as more of the arts were discovered, some to supply the necessities of life, and others to introduce us [to the sciences], those who discovered the latter were always considered to be wiser than those who discovered the former, because their sciences were not for the sake of utility.

Unde omnibus talibus rebus iam partis, quae non ad voluptatem, nec ad necessitatem scientiarum repertae sunt. Et primum in his locis ubi vacabant. Unde circa Aegyptum mathematicae artes primum substiterunt. Ibi namque gens sacerdotum vacare dimissa est.

ὅθεν ἤδη πάντων τῶν τοιούτων κατεσκευασμένων αἱ μὴ πρὸς ἡδονὴν μηδὲ πρὸς τἀναγκαῖα τῶν ἐπιστημῶν εὑρέθησαν, καὶ πρῶτον ἐν τούτοις τοῖς τόποις οὗ πρῶτον ἐσχόλασαν: διὸ περὶ Αἴγυπτον αἱ μαθηματικαὶ πρῶτον τέχναι συνέστησαν, ἐκεῖ γὰρ ἀφείθη σχολάζειν {25} τὸ τῶν ἱερέων ἔθνος.

Hence, after all such arts had already been developed, those sciences were discovered which are pursued for the sake of neither pleasure nor necessity. This happened first in those places where men had leisure. Hence the mathematical arts originated in Egypt, for there the priestly class was permitted leisure.

981b25 In moralibus quidem igitur, quae sit artis et scientiae differentia et similium generum, dictum est. [34]

εἴρηται μὲν οὖν ἐν τοῖς ἠθικοῖς τίς διαφορὰ τέχνης καὶ ἐπιστήμης καὶ τῶν ἄλλων τῶν ὁμογενῶν:

(The difference between art and science and similar mental states has been stated in the *Nicomachean Ethics*.)

981b27 Cuius autem gratia nunc sermonem facimus, hoc est, quia denominatam sapientiam circa primas causas et principia existimant omnes versari. Quare sicut dictum est prius, expertus quidem quemcumque sensum habentibus sapientior esse videtur, artifex autem expertis, architector autem manu artifice, speculativi autem magis activis.

οὗ δ᾽ ἕνεκα νῦν ποιούμεθα τὸν λόγον τοῦτ᾽ ἐστίν, ὅτι τὴν ὀνομαζομένην σοφίαν περὶ τὰ πρῶτα αἴτια καὶ τὰς ἀρχὰς ὑπολαμβάνουσι πάντες: ὥστε, καθάπερ εἴρηται πρότερον, {30} ὁ μὲν ἔμπειρος τῶν ὁποιανοῦν ἐχόντων αἴσθησιν εἶναι δοκεῖ σοφώτερος, ὁ δὲ τεχνίτης τῶν ἐμπείρων, χειροτέχνου δὲ ἀρχιτέκτων, αἱ δὲ θεωρητικαὶ τῶν ποιητικῶν μᾶλλον.

Now the reason for undertaking this investigation is that all men think that the science that is called wisdom deals with the primary causes and principles of things. Hence, as we have said before (981a24–981a28), the man of experience is considered to be wiser than one who has any of the senses; the artist wiser than the man of experience; the architect wiser

Quod quidem igitur sapientia et circa quasdam causas et principia sit scientia, manifestum est. [35]

{982a1} ὅτι μὲν οὖν ἡ σοφία περί τινας ἀρχὰς καὶ αἰτίας ἐστὶν ἐπιστήμη, δῆλον.

than the manual laborer; and speculative knowledge wiser than practical knowledge. It is quite evident, then, that wisdom is a science of certain causes and principles.

---

1. Huic autem scientiae Aristoteles prooemium praemittit, in quo duo tradit.

Primo quidem ostendit circa quid haec scientia versetur.

Secundo qualis sit ista scientia, ibi, *quia vero non activa*.

Circa primum duo facit.

Primo ostendit, quod huius scientiae, quae sapientia dicitur, est considerare causas.

Secundo quales vel quas causas considerat, ibi, *quoniam autem scientiam hanc*.

Circa primum praemittit quaedam ex quibus ad propositum arguit.

Secundo ex praedictis rationem sumit, ibi, *cuius autem gratia nunc*.

Circa primum duo facit.

Primo ostendit in communi scientiae dignitatem.

Secundo, ostendit cognitionis ordinem, ibi, *animalia quidem igitur* et cetera.

Scientiae autem dignitatem ostendit per hoc quod naturaliter desideratur ab omnibus tamquam finis. Unde circa hoc duo facit.

Primo proponit intentum.

Secundo probat, ibi, *signum autem*.

Proponit igitur primo, quod omnibus hominibus naturaliter desiderium inest ad sciendum.

2. Cuius ratio potest esse triplex: primo quidem, quia unaquaeque res naturaliter appetit perfectionem sui. Unde et materia dicitur appetere formam, sicut imperfectum appetit suam perfectionem. Cum igitur intellectus, a quo homo est id quod est, in se consideratus sit in potentia omnia, nec in actum eorum reducatur nisi per scientiam, quia nihil est eorum quae sunt, ante intelligere, ut dicitur in tertio *De anima*: sic naturaliter unusquisque desiderat scientiam sicut materia formam.

3. Secundo, quia quaelibet res naturalem inclinationem habet ad suam propriam operationem: sicut calidum ad calefaciendum, et grave ut deorsum moveatur. Propria autem operatio hominis inquantum homo, est intelligere. Per hoc enim ab omnibus aliis differt. Unde naturaliter desiderium hominis inclinatur ad intelligendum, et per consequens ad sciendum.

4. Tertio, quia unicuique rei desiderabile est, ut suo principio coniungatur; in hoc enim uniuscuiusque per-

1. Aristotle first sets down an introduction to this science, in which he treats of two things.

First [2], he points out with what this science is concerned.

Second [53], he explains what kind of science it is, at *that this is not a practical science* (982b11).

In regard to the first he does two things.

First, he shows that the office of this science, which is called wisdom, is to consider the causes of things.

Second [36], he explains with what causes or kinds of causes it is concerned, at *but since we are in search* (982a4).

In regard to the first, he prefaces certain preliminary considerations from which he argues in support of his thesis.

Second [35], he draws a conclusion from these considerations, at *now the reason for undertaking* (981b27).

In regard to the first he does two things.

First, he makes clear the dignity of scientific knowledge in general.

Second [9], he explains the hierarchy in knowing, at *animals by nature* (980a27).

Now he establishes the dignity of scientific knowledge from the fact that it is naturally desired as an end by all men. Hence, in regard to this he does two things.

First, he states his intention.

Second [2], he proves it, at *a sign of this* (980a21).

Accordingly, he first says that the desire to know belongs by nature to all men.

2. Three reasons can be given for this. The first is that each thing naturally desires its own perfection. Hence matter is also said to desire form as any imperfect thing desires its perfection. Therefore, since the intellect, by which man is what he is, considered in itself is all things potentially, and becomes them actually only through knowledge, because the intellect is none of the things that exist before it understands them, as is stated in *On the Soul* 3, so each man naturally desires knowledge just as matter desires form.

3. The second reason is that each thing has a natural inclination to perform its proper operation, as something hot is naturally inclined to heat, and something heavy to be moved downwards. Now the proper operation of man as man is to understand, for by reason of this he differs from all other things. Hence the desire of man is naturally inclined to understand and therefore to possess scientific knowledge.

4. The third reason is that it is desirable for each thing to be united to its source, since it is in this that the perfection

fectio consistit. Unde et motus circularis est perfectissimus, ut probatur octavo *Physicorum*, quia finem coniungit principio. Substantiis autem separatis, quae sunt principia intellectus humani, et ad quae intellectus humanus se habet ut imperfectum ad perfectum, non coniungitur homo nisi per intellectum: unde et in hoc ultima hominis felicitas consistit. Et ideo naturaliter homo desiderat scientiam.

Nec obstat si aliqui homines scientiae huic studium non impendant; cum frequenter qui finem aliquem desiderant, a prosecutione finis ex aliqua causa retrahantur, vel propter difficultatem perveniendi, vel propter alias occupationes. Sic etiam licet omnes homines scientiam desiderent, non tamen omnes scientiae studium impendunt, quia ab aliis detinentur, vel a voluptatibus, vel a necessitatibus vitae praesentis, vel etiam propter pigritiam vitant laborem addiscendi.

Hoc autem proponit Aristoteles ut ostendat, quod quaerere scientiam non propter aliud utilem, qualis est haec scientia, non est vanum, cum naturale desiderium vanum esse non possit.

5. Deinde ostendit quod proposuerat, per signum: quia cum sensus ad duo nobis deserviant; scilicet ad cognitionem rerum, et ad utilitatem vitae; diliguntur a nobis propter seipsos, inquantum cognoscitivi sunt, et etiam propter hoc, quod utilitatem ad vitam conferunt. Et hoc patet ex hoc, quod ille sensus maxime ab omnibus diligitur, qui magis cognoscitivus est, qui est visus, quem diligimus non solum ad agendum aliquid, sed etiam si nihil agere deberemus. Cuius causa est, quia iste sensus, scilicet visus, inter omnes magis facit nos cognoscere, et plures differentias rerum nobis demonstrat.

6. In quo manifestum est quod duas praeeminentias visus in cognoscendo ad alios sensus ponit.

Unam quidem quia perfectius cognoscit. Quod quidem visui accidit, eo quod spiritualior est inter omnes sensus. Quanto enim aliqua vis cognoscitiva est immaterialior, tanto est perfectior in cognoscendo. Quod autem visus sit immaterialior, patet si consideretur eius immutatio, qua ab obiecto immutatur. Nam, cum omnia alia sensibilia immutent organum et medium sensus secundum aliquam materialem immutationem, sicut tactus obiectum calefaciendo et infrigidando, obiectum vero gustus, afficiendo sapore aliquo organum gustus mediante saliva, obiectum autem auditus per motum corporalem, obiectum autem odoratus per fumalem evaporationem, solum obiectum visus non immutat nec organum nec medium nisi spirituali immutatione. Non enim pupilla nec aer coloratur, sed solum speciem coloris recipiunt secundum esse spirituale. Quia igitur sensus in actu consistit in actuali immutatione sensus

of each thing consists. This is also the reason why circular motion is the most perfect motion, as is proved in *Physics* 8, because its terminus is united to its starting point. Now it is only by means of his intellect that man is united to the separate substances, which are the source of the human intellect and to which the human intellect is related as something imperfect to something perfect. It is for this reason, too, that the ultimate happiness of man consists in this union. Therefore, man naturally desires to know.

The fact that some men do not devote any study to this science does not disprove this thesis. For those who desire some end are often prevented from pursuing it for some reason or other, either because of the difficulty of attaining it or because of other occupations. And in this way, too, even though all men desire knowledge, still not all devote themselves to the pursuit of it because they are held back by other things such as pleasures or the needs of the present life—or they may even avoid the effort that learning demands because they are lazy.

Now Aristotle makes this statement in order to show that it is not pointless to search for a science that is not useful for anything else (such as this science), since a natural desire cannot exist in vain.

5. Then he establishes his thesis by means of an example. Since our senses serve us in two respects—in knowing things and in meeting the needs of life—we love them for themselves inasmuch as they enable us to know and also assist us to live. This is evident from the fact that all men take the greatest delight in the sense that is most knowing, the sense of sight. We value it not merely so we can do things, but even when we are not required to act at all. This is because this sense of sight is the most knowing of all our senses and makes us aware of many differences between things.

6. In this part, it is clear that he gives two reasons why sight is superior to the other senses in knowing.

The first is that it knows in a more perfect way, and this belongs to it because it is the most spiritual of all the senses. For the more immaterial a power is, the more perfectly it knows. And evidently sight is a more immaterial sense if we consider the modification produced in it by its object. All other sensible objects change both the organ and medium of a sense by a material modification: for example, the object of touch by heating and cooling, the object of taste by affecting the organ of taste with some flavor through the medium of saliva, the object of hearing by means of motion in the body, and the object of smell by means of the evaporation of vaporous elements. But the object of sight changes the organ and medium of sight only by a spiritual modification. Neither the pupil of the eye nor the air becomes colored, but they only receive the form of color in a spiritual mode of being. Therefore, because actual sensation consists in the actual modification of a sense by

ab obiecto, manifestum est illum sensum spiritualiorem esse in sua operatione, qui immaterialius et spiritualius immutatur. Et ideo visus certius et perfectius iudicat de sensibilibus inter alios sensus.

7. Aliam autem praeeminentiam ponit, quia nobis plura demonstrat. Quod quidem accidit ex ratione sui obiecti. Tactus enim et gustus, et similiter odoratus et auditus sunt cognoscitivi illorum accidentium, in quibus distinguuntur inferiora corpora a superioribus. Visus autem est cognoscitivus illorum accidentium, in quibus communicant inferiora corpora cum superioribus. Nam visibile actu est aliquid per lucem, in qua communicant inferiora corpora cum superioribus, ut dicitur secundo *De anima*; et ideo corpora caelestia solo visu sunt sensibilia.

8. Est autem alia ratio, quia visus plures differentias rerum demonstrat; quia sensibilia corpora praecipue per visum et tactum cognoscere videmur, et adhuc magis per visum. Cuius ratio ex hoc sumi potest: quod alii tres sensus sunt cognoscitivi eorum quae a corpore sensibili quodammodo effluunt, et non in ipso consistunt: sicut sonus est a corpore sensibili, ut ab eo fluens et non in eo manens: et similiter fumalis evaporatio cum qua et ex qua odor diffunditur. Visus autem et tactus percipiunt illa accidentia quae rebus ipsis immanent, sicut color et calidum et frigidum. Unde iudicium tactus et visus extenditur ad res ipsas, iudicium autem auditus et odoratus ad ea quae a rebus ipsis procedunt, non ad res ipsas. Et inde est quod figura et magnitudo et huiusmodi, quibus ipsa res sensibilis disponitur, magis percipitur visu et tactu, quam aliis sensibus. Et adhuc amplius magis visu quam tactu, tum propter hoc quod visus habet maiorem efficaciam ad cognoscendum, ut dictum est, tum propter hoc, quod quantitas et ea quae ad ipsam sequuntur, quae videntur esse sensibilia communia, proximius se habent ad obiectum visus quam ad obiectum tactus. Quod ex hoc patet, quod obiectum visus omne corpus habens aliquam quantitatem aliquo modo consequitur, non autem obiectum tactus.

9. Deinde cum dicit *animalia quidem* prosequitur de ordine cognitionis.

Et primo quantum ad bruta animalia.

Secundo quantum ad homines, ibi, *alia quidem igitur* et cetera.

Circa vero bruta animalia tangit primo quidem id in quo omnia animalia communicant.

Secundo id in quo animalia differunt, et seinvicem excedunt, ibi, *ex sensibus.*

Communicant autem omnia animalia in hoc quod naturaliter sensus habent. Nam ex hoc animal est animal, quod habet animam sensitivam, quae natura est

its object, it is evident that that sense which is changed in a more immaterial and spiritual way is more spiritual in its operation. Hence sight judges about sensible objects in a more certain and perfect way than the other senses do.

7. The other reason which he gives for the superiority of sight is that it gives us more information about things. This is attributable to the nature of its object, for touch and taste, and likewise smell and hearing, perceive those accidents by which lower bodies are distinguished from higher ones. But sight perceives those accidents that lower bodies have in common with higher ones. For a thing is actually visible by means of light, which is common both to lower and higher bodies, as is said in *On the Soul* 2. Hence the celestial bodies are perceptible only by means of sight.

8. There is also another reason. Sight informs us of many differences between things, for we seem to know sensible things best by means of sight and touch, but especially by means of sight. The reason for this can be drawn from the fact that the other three senses perceive those accidents that in a way flow from a sensible body and do not remain in it. Thus sound comes from a sensible body inasmuch as it flows away from it and does not remain in it. The same thing is true of the evaporation of volatile elements, with which and by which odor is diffused. But sight and touch perceive those accidents that remain in sensible bodies, such as color, warmth, and coldness. Hence the judgment of sight and touch is extended to things themselves, whereas the judgment of hearing and smell is extended to those accidents that flow from things and not to things themselves. It is for this reason that figure and size and the like, by which a sensible being itself is disposed, are perceived more by sight and touch than by the other senses. And they are perceived more by sight than by touch, both because sight knows more efficaciously, as has been pointed out [6], and also because quantity and those [accidents] which naturally follow from it (which are seen to be the common sensibles) are more closely related to the object of sight than to that of touch. This is clear from the fact that the object of sight belongs in some degree to every body having some quantity, whereas the object of touch does not.

9. *Animals by nature, then* (980a27). Here he considers the hierarchy in knowledge.

He first does this [9] with respect to brute animals;

and then [14], with respect to men, at *thus other animals* (980b25).

With respect to brute animals he mentions first what all animals have in common;

second [10], that by which they differ and surpass one another, at *now in some animals* (980a28).

Now all animals are alike in the respect that they possess by nature the power of sensation. For an animal is an animal by reason of the fact that it has a sentient soul,

animalis, sicut forma unicuique propria est natura eius. Quamvis autem omnia animalia sensum habeant naturaliter, non tamen omnia habent omnes sensus, sed solum perfecta. Omnia vero habent sensum tactus. Ipse enim est quodammodo fundamentum omnium aliorum sensuum. Non autem habent omnia sensum visus, quia sensus visus est omnibus aliis perfectior in cognoscendo, sed tactus magis necessarius. Est enim cognoscitivus eorum, ex quibus animal constat, scilicet calidi, frigidi, humidi et sicci. Unde sicut visus inter omnes est perfectior in cognoscendo, ita tactus est magis necessarius, utpote primus existens in via generationis. Ea enim quae sunt perfectiora, secundum hanc viam, sunt posteriora respectu illius individui, quod de imperfecto ad perfectionem movetur.

10. Deinde cum dicit *ex sensibus* ponit diversitatem cognitionis, quae est in brutis: et tangit etiam tres gradus cognitionis in huiusmodi animalibus. Quaedam enim sunt, quae licet sensum habeant, non tamen habent memoriam, quae ex sensu fit. Memoria enim sequitur phantasiam, quae est motus factus a sensu secundum actum, ut habetur in secundo *De anima*. In quibusdam vero animalibus ex sensu non fit phantasia, et sic in eis non potest esse memoria: et huiusmodi sunt animalia imperfecta, quae sunt immobilia secundum locum, ut conchilia. Cum enim animalibus cognitio sensitiva sit provisiva ad vitae necessitatem et ad propriam operationem, animalia illa memoriam habere debent, quae moventur ad distans motu progressivo: nisi enim apud ea remaneret per memoriam intentio praeconcepta, ex qua ad motum inducuntur, motum continuare non possent quousque finem intentum consequerentur. Animalibus vero immobilibus sufficit ad proprias operationes, praesentis sensibilis acceptio, cum ad distans non moveantur; et ideo sola imaginatione confusa habent aliquem motum indeterminatum, ut dicitur tertio *De anima*.

11. Ex hoc autem, quod quaedam animalia memoriam habent, et quaedam non habent, sequitur quod quaedam sunt prudentia et quaedam non. Cum enim prudentia ex praeteritorum memoria de futuris provideat (unde secundum Tullium in secundo *Rhetoricae*, partes eius ponuntur memoria, intelligentia, et providentia), in illis animalibus prudentia esse non potest, qui memoria carent. Illa vero animalia, quae memoriam habent, aliquid prudentiae habere possunt. Dicitur autem prudentia aliter in brutis animalibus, et aliter hominibus inesse. In hominibus quidem est prudentia secundum quod ex ratione deliberant quid eos oporteat agere; unde dicitur sexto *Ethicorum*, quod prudentia est recta ratio agibilium. Iudicium autem de rebus agendis

which is the nature of an animal in the sense in which the distinctive form of each thing is its nature. But even though all animals are naturally endowed with sensory power, not all animals have all the senses, but only perfect animals. All have the sense of touch, for this sense in a way is the basis of all the other senses. However, not all have the sense of sight, because this sense knows in a more perfect way than all the other senses. But touch is more necessary, for it perceives the elements of which an animal is composed (the hot, cold, moist and dry). Hence, just as sight knows in a more perfect way than the other senses, in a similar way touch is more necessary inasmuch as it is the first to exist in the process of generation. For those things that are more perfect according to this process come later in the development of the individual, which is moved from a state of imperfection to one of perfection.

10. *Now in some animals* (980a28). Here he indicates the different kinds and three levels of knowing found among brute animals. For there are certain animals that have sensation, although they do not have memory, which comes from sensation. For memory accompanies imagination, which is a movement caused by the senses in their act of sensing, as we find in *On the Soul* 2. But in some animals imagination does not accompany sensation, and therefore memory cannot exist in them. This is found verified in imperfect animals, which are incapable of local motion, such as shellfish. Since sensory cognition enables animals to make provision for the necessities of life and to perform their characteristic operations, those animals that move toward something at a distance by means of local motion must have memory. If the anticipated goal by which they are induced to move did not remain in them through memory, they could not continue to move toward the intended goal which they pursue. But in the case of immobile animals, the reception of a present sensible quality is sufficient for them to perform their characteristic operations, since they do not move toward anything at a distance. Hence these animals have an indefinite movement as a result of vague imagination alone, as is said in *On the Soul* 3.

11. Again, from the fact that some animals have memory and some do not, it follows that some are prudent and some not. For, since prudence makes provision for the future from memory of the past (hence Cicero makes memory, understanding, and foresight parts of prudence in *Rhetoric* 2), prudence cannot be had by those animals that lack memory. Now those animals that have memory can have some prudence, although prudence has one meaning in the case of brute animals and another in the case of man. Men are prudent inasmuch as they deliberate rationally about what they ought to do. Hence *Ethics* 6 says that prudence is a rationally regulated plan of things to be done. But the judgment about things to be done that is not a result of any rational deliberation, but of some natural instinct, is

non ex rationis deliberatione, sed ex quodam naturae instinctu, prudentia in aliis animalibus dicitur. Unde prudentia in aliis animalibus est naturalis aestimatio de convenientibus prosequendis, et fugiendis nocivis, sicut agnus sequitur matrem et fugit lupum.

12. Inter ea vero, quae memoriam habent, quaedam habent auditum et quaedam non. Quaecumque autem auditum non habent, ut apes, vel si quod aliud huiusmodi animal est, licet prudentiam habere possint, non tamen sunt disciplinabilia, ut scilicet per alterius instructionem possint assuescere ad aliquid faciendum vel vitandum: huiusmodi enim instructio praecipue recipitur per auditum: unde dicitur in libro *De sensu et sensato*, quod auditus est sensus disciplinae. Quod autem dicitur apes auditum non habere, non repugnat ei, quod videntur ex quibusdam sonis exterreri. Nam sicut sonus vehemens occidit animal, et scindit lignum, ut in tonitruo patet, non propter sonum, sed propter commotionem aeris vehementem in quo est sonus: ita animalia, quae auditu carent, iudicium de sonis non habendo possunt per sonos aereos exterreri. Illa vero animalia, quae memoriam et auditum habent, et disciplinabilia et prudentia esse possunt.

13. Patet igitur tres esse gradus cognitionis in animalibus.

Primus est eorum, quae nec auditum nec memoriam habent: unde nec disciplinabilia sunt, nec prudentia.

Secundus est eorum quae habent memoriam, sed non auditum; unde sunt prudentia, et non disciplinabilia.

Tertius est eorum, quae utrumque habent, et sunt prudentia et disciplinabilia.

Quartus autem modus esse non potest, ut scilicet sit aliquod animal, quod habeat auditum, et non habeat memoriam. Sensus enim, qui per exterius medium suum sensibile apprehendunt, inter quos est auditus, non sunt nisi in animalibus quae moventur motu progressivo, quibus memoria deesse non potest, ut dictum est.

14. Deinde cum dicit *alia quidem* ostendit gradus cognitionis humanae. Et circa hoc duo facit.

Primo namque ostendit in quo cognitio humana excedit praedictorum cognitionem.

Secundo ostendit quomodo humana cognitio per diversos gradus distribuatur, ibi, *fit autem ex memoria.*

Dicit ergo in prima parte, quod vita animalium regitur imaginatione et memoria: imaginatione quidem, quantum ad animalia imperfecta; memoria vero quan-

called prudence in other animals. Hence in other animals prudence is a natural estimate about the pursuit of what is fitting and the avoidance of what is harmful, as a lamb follows its mother and runs away from a wolf.

12. But among those animals that have memory, some have hearing and some do not. And all those that cannot hear (as the bee or any other such animal) are still incapable of being taught even though they have prudence; that is, they cannot be habituated to the doing or avoiding of something through someone else's instruction, because such instruction is received chiefly by means of hearing. Hence in *On Sense and Sense Perception* it is stated that hearing is the sense by which we receive instruction. Furthermore, the statement that bees do not have hearing is not opposed in any way to the observation that they are frightened by certain sounds. For just as a very loud sound kills an animal and splits wood, as is evident in the case of thunder, not because of the sound but because of the violent motion of the air in which the sound is present, in a similar fashion those animals that lack hearing can be frightened by the sounding air even though they have no perception of sound. However, those animals that have both memory and hearing can be both prudent and teachable.

13. It is evident, then, that there are three levels of knowing in animals.

The first level is that had by animals that have neither hearing nor memory, which are therefore neither capable of being taught nor of being prudent.

The second level is that of animals that have memory but are unable to hear, which are therefore prudent but incapable of being taught.

The third level is that of animals that have both of these faculties, and which are therefore prudent and capable of being taught.

Moreover, there cannot be a fourth level, so that there would be an animal that had hearing but lacked memory. For those senses that perceive their sensible objects by means of an external medium—and hearing is one of these—are found only in animals that have locomotion and which cannot do without memory, as has been pointed out [10].

14. *Thus other animals* (980b25). Here he explains the levels of human knowing. In regard to this he does two things.

First [14], he explains how human knowing surpasses the knowing of the abovementioned animals.

Second [17], he shows how human knowing is divided into different levels, at *now in men* (980b28).

Accordingly, in the first part (980b25), he says that the life of animals is ruled by imagination and memory: by imagination in the case of imperfect animals, and by

tum ad animalia perfecta. Licet enim et haec imaginationem habeant, tamen unumquodque regi dicitur ab eo quod est principalius in ipso. Vivere autem hic non accipitur secundum quod est esse viventis, sicut accipitur in secundo *De anima*: cum dicitur, *vivere viventibus est esse*. Nam huiusmodi vivere animalis non est ex memoria et imaginatione, sed praecedit utrumque. Accipitur autem vivere pro actione vitae, sicut et conversationem hominum vitam dicere solemus. In hoc vero, quod cognitionem animalium determinat per comparationem ad regimen vitae, datur intelligi quod cognitio inest ipsis animalibus non propter ipsum cognoscere, sed propter necessitatem actionis.

15. Supra memoriam autem in hominibus, ut infra dicetur, proximum est experimentum, quod quaedam animalia non participant nisi parum. Experimentum enim est ex collatione plurium singularium in memoria receptorum. Huiusmodi autem collatio est homini propria, et pertinet ad vim cogitativam, quae ratio particularis dicitur: quae est collativa intentionum individualium, sicut ratio universalis intentionum universalium. Et, quia ex multis sensibus et memoria animalia ad aliquid consuescunt prosequendum vel vitandum, inde est quod aliquid experimenti, licet parum, participare videntur. Homines autem supra experimentum, quod pertinet ad rationem particularem, habent rationem universalem, per quam vivunt, sicut per id quod est principale in eis.

16. Sicut autem se habet experimentum ad rationem particularem, et consuetudo ad memoriam in animalibus, ita se habet ars ad rationem universalem. Ideo sicut perfectum vitae regimen est animalibus per memoriam adiuncta assuefactione ex disciplina, vel quomodolibet aliter, ita perfectum hominis regimen est per rationem arte perfectam. Quidam tamen ratione sine arte reguntur; sed hoc est regimen imperfectum.

17. Deinde cum dicit *fit autem* ostendit diversos gradus humanae cognitionis. Et circa hoc duo facit.

Primo comparat experimentum ad artem quidem.
Secundo comparat artem speculativam ad activam, ibi, *primum igitur conveniens* et cetera.
Circa primum duo facit.
Primo ostendit generationem artis et experimenti.
Secundo praeeminentiam unius ad alterum, ibi, *ad agere quidem igitur* et cetera.
Circa primum duo facit.
Primo proponit utriusque praedictorum generationem.
Secundo manifestat per exemplum, ibi, *acceptionem quidem enim* et cetera.

memory in the case of perfect animals. For even though the latter also have imagination, still each thing is said to be ruled by that [power] which holds the highest place within it. Now in this discussion life does not mean the being of a living thing, as it is understood in *On the Soul* 2, when he says that *for living things to live is to be*; for the life of an animal in this sense is not a result of memory or imagination but is prior to both of these. But "life" is taken to mean "vital activity," just as we are also accustomed to speak of association as the life of men. But by the fact that he establishes the truth about the cognition of animals with reference to the management of life, we are given to understand that knowing belongs to these animals not for the sake of knowing, but because of the need for action.

15. Now, as is stated below [18], in men the next thing above memory is experience, which some animals have only to a small degree. For an experience arises from the association of many singular [intentions] received in memory. And this kind of association is proper to man, and pertains to the cogitative power (also called particular reason), which associates particular intentions just as universal reason associates universal ones. Now since animals are accustomed to pursue or avoid certain things as a result of many sensations and memory, they seem to share something of experience, even though it be slight. But above experience, which belongs to particular reason, men have as their chief power a universal reason by means of which they live.

16. And just as experience is related to particular reason [in men], and customary activity to memory in animals, in a similar way art is related to universal reason. Therefore, just as the life of animals is ruled in a perfect way by memory together with activity that has become habitual through training, or in any other way whatsoever, in a similar way man is ruled perfectly by reason perfected by art. Some men, however, are ruled by reason without art; but this rule is imperfect.

17. *Now in men* (980b28). Here he explains the different levels of human knowing. And in regard to this he does two things.

First [17], he compares art with experience;
second [31], he compares speculative art with practical art, at *it is only fitting* (981b13).

He treats the first point in two ways.
First, he explains how art and experience originate.
Second [20], he explains how one is superior to the other, at *in practical matters* (981a12).

In regard to the first, he does two things.
First, he explains how each of the above originates.

Second [19], he makes this clear by means of an example, at *for to judge* (981a7).

Circa primum duo facit.

Primo ponit generationem experimenti.

Secundo artis generationem ibi, *hominibus autem* et cetera.

Dicit ergo primo, quod ex memoria in hominibus experimentum causatur. Modus autem causandi est iste: quia ex multis memoriis unius rei accipit homo experimentum de aliquo, quo experimento potens est ad facile et recte operandum. Et ideo quia potentiam recte et faciliter operandi praebet experimentum, videtur fere esse simile arti et scientiae. Est enim similitudo eo quod utrobique ex multis una acceptio alicuius rei sumitur. Dissimilitudo autem, quia per artem accipiuntur universalia, per experimentum singularia, ut postea dicetur.

18. Deinde cum dicit *hominibus autem* ponit generationem artis: et dicit, quod ex experientia in hominibus fit scientia et ars: et probat per auctoritatem Poli, qui dicit, quod *experientia facit artem, sed inexperientia casum.* Quando enim aliquis inexpertus recte operatur, a casu est. Modus autem, quo ars fit ex experimento, est idem cum modo praedicto, quo experimentum fit ex memoria. Nam sicut ex multis memoriis fit una experimentalis scientia, ita ex multis experimentis apprehensis fit universalis acceptio de omnibus similibus. Unde plus habet hoc ars quam experimentum: quia experimentum tantum circa singularia versatur, ars autem circa universalia.

19. Quod consequenter per exempla exponit, cum dicit, *acceptionem quidem* et cetera: quia cum homo accepit in sua cognitione quod haec medicina contulit Socrati et Platoni tali infirmitate laborantibus, et multis aliis singularibus, quidquid sit illud, hoc ad experientiam pertinet: sed, cum aliquis accipit, quod hoc omnibus conferat in tali specie aegritudinis determinata, et secundum talem complexionem, sicut quod contulit febricitantibus et phlegmaticis et cholericis, id iam ad artem pertinet.

20. Deinde cum dicit *ad agere* comparat artem ad experimentum per modum praeeminentiae. Et secundum hoc duo facit.

Primo comparat quantum ad actionem.

Secundo quantum ad cognitionem, ibi, *sed tamen scire* et cetera.

Dicit ergo, quod quantum ad actum pertinet, experientia nihil videtur differre ab arte. Cum enim ad actionem venitur, tollitur differentia, quae inter experimentum et artem erat per universale et singulare: quia sicut experimentum circa singularia operatur, ita et ars; unde praedicta differentia erat in cognoscendo tantum. Sed quamvis in modo operandi ars et experimentum non differant, quia utraque circa singularia operatur, dif-

In regard to the first, he does two things.

First, he describes how experience originates;

and second [18], how art originates, at *but in men science* (981a2).

He says first, then, that in men experience is caused by memory. This is the way in which it is caused: from several memories of a single thing a man acquires experience about some matter, and by means of this experience he is able to act easily and correctly. Therefore, because experience provides us with the ability to act easily and correctly, it seems to be almost the same as science and art. For they are alike inasmuch as in either case from many instances a single view of a thing is obtained. But they differ inasmuch as universals are grasped by art and singular things by experience, as is stated later [18].

18. *But in men science and art* (981a2). Here he describes the way in which art arises. He says that in men science and art come from experience, and he proves this on the authority of Polus, who says that *experience causes art and inexperience causes luck.* For when an inexperienced person acts correctly, this happens by chance. Furthermore, the way in which art arises from experience is the same as the way spoken of above in which experience arises from memory. Just as one experiential cognition comes from many memories of a thing, so does one universal judgment about all similar things come from the apprehension of many experiences. Hence art has this more than does experience, because experience is concerned only with singulars while art is concerned with universals.

19. Next, he makes this clear by means of examples, at *for to judge* (981a7). When a man has learned that this medicine has been beneficial to Socrates, and to Plato, and to many other individuals who were suffering from some particular disease (whatever it may be), this is a matter of experience. But when a man learns that this particular treatment is beneficial to men who have some particular kind of disease and some particular kind of physical constitution, as it has benefited the feverish, the phlegmatic, and the bilious, it is now a matter of art.

20. *In practical matters* (981a12). He compares art to experience from the viewpoint of preeminence; and in regard to this he does two things.

First, he compares them from the viewpoint of action;

second [23], from the viewpoint of knowledge, at *yet we think* (981a24).

He says, then, that in practical matters experience seems to differ in no way from art: when it comes to acting, the difference between experience and art (which is a difference between the universal and the singular) disappears, because art operates with reference to singulars just as experience does. Therefore, the aforesaid difference pertains only to the way in which they come to know. But even though art and experience do not differ in the way

ferunt tamen in efficacia operandi. Nam experti magis proficiunt in operando illis qui habent rationem universalem artis sine experimento.

21. Cujus causa est, quia actiones sunt circa singularia, et singularium sunt omnes generationes. Universalia enim non generantur nec moventur nisi per accidens, inquantum hoc singularibus competit. Homo enim generatur hoc homine generato. Unde medicus non sanat hominem nisi per accidens; sed per se sanat Platonem aut Socratem, aut aliquem hominem singulariter dictum, cui convenit esse hominem, vel accidit inquantum est curatus. Quamvis enim esse hominem per se conveniat Socrati, tamen curato et medicato per accidens convenit: haec est enim per se, Socrates est homo: quia si Socrates definiretur, poneretur homo in eius definitione, ut in quarto dicetur. Sed haec est per accidens, curatus vel sanatus est homo.

22. Unde cum ars sit universalium, experientia singularium, si aliquis habet rationem artis sine experientia, erit quidem perfectus in hoc quod universale cognoscat; sed quia ignorat singulare cum experimento careat, multotiens in curando peccabit: quia curatio magis pertinet ad singulare quam ad universale, cum ad hoc pertineat per se, ad illud per accidens.

23. Deinde cum dicit *sed tamen* comparat experimentum ad artem quantum ad cognitionem. Et circa hoc duo facit.

Primo ponit praeeminentiam artis ad experimentum.

Secundo probat, ibi, *hoc autem est quia hi quidem* et cetera.

Proponit autem praeeminentiam artis et scientiae quantum ad tria.

Scilicet quantum ad scire, quod quidem magis arbitramur esse per artem quam per experimentum.

Item quantum ad obviare, quod in disputationibus accidit. Nam habens artem potest disputando obviare his quae contra artem dicuntur, non autem habens experimentum.

Item quantum ad hoc quod artifices plus accedunt ad finem sapientiae, quam experti, *tamquam magis sit*, idest contingat, *scire sapientiam sequentem omnia*, idest dum sequitur universalia. Ex hoc enim artifex sapientior iudicatur, quam expertus quia universalia considerat.

in which they act, because both act on singular things, nevertheless they differ in the effectiveness of their action. For men of experience act more effectively than those who have the universal knowledge of an art but lack experience.

21. This is because actions have to do with singular things, and all processes of generation belong to singular things. For universals are neither generated nor moved except accidentally, inasmuch as this belongs to singular things. For man is generated when this man is generated. Hence a physician heals man only accidentally, but properly he heals Plato or Socrates, or some man that can be individually named, to whom the nature of man belongs—or rather to whom it is accidental inasmuch as he is the one healed. For even though the nature of man belongs to Socrates *per se*, still it belongs only accidentally to the one healed or cured. The proposition "Socrates is a man" is an *per se* one, because, if Socrates were defined, man would be given in his definition, as will be said below in book 4. But the proposition "What is healed or cured is man" is an accidental one.

22. Hence, since art has to do with universals and experience with singulars, if anyone has the theoretical knowledge of an art but lacks experience, he will be perfect insofar as he knows the universal, but since he does not know the singular (since he lacks experience), he will very often make mistakes in healing. For healing belongs to the realm of the singular rather than to that of the universal, because it belongs to the former *per se* and to the latter accidentally.

23. *Yet we think* (981a24). Here he compares art with experience from the viewpoint of knowing. In regard to this he does two things.

First, he states how art is superior to experience;

and second [24], he proves this at *now this is because* (981a28).

He claims that art and science are superior to experience in three respects.

First, they are superior from the viewpoint of scientific knowledge, which we think is attained by art rather than by experience.

Second, they are superior from the viewpoint of meeting objections, which occurs in disputes. For in a dispute the one who has an art is able to meet the objections raised against that art, but one who has only experience cannot do this.

Third, they are superior from this point of view. Those who have an art come nearer to the goal of wisdom than men of experience, *as it is*, that is, it happens to be, *more to know if one's wisdom pursues all things*, insofar as it pursues universals. For one who has an art is judged wiser than one who has experience, because he considers universals.

Vel aliter. *Tamquam magis sit scire secundum sapientiam omnia sequentem*, idest universalia.

Alia litera, *tamquam magis secundum scire sapientia omnia sequente*: quasi dicat: *tamquam sapientia sequente omnia* idest consequente ad unumquodque, *magis sit secundum scire*, quam secundum operari: ut scilicet dicantur sapientes magis qui magis sciunt, non qui magis sunt operativi.

Unde alia litera hunc sensum habet planiorem, qui sic dicit: *tamquam secundum illud quod est scire magis, omnes sequuntur sapientiam.*

24. Consequenter cum dicit *hoc autem* probat praedictam praeeminentiam tripliciter.

Prima probatio talis est. Illi, qui sciunt causam et propter quid, scientiores sunt et sapientiores illis qui ignorant causam, sed solum sciunt quia. Experti autem sciunt quia, sed nesciunt propter quid. Artifices vero sciunt causam, et propter quid, et non solum quia: ergo sapientiores et scientiores sunt artifices expertis.

25. Primo primam probat cum dicit, *unde et architectores* et cetera. Probatio talis est. Illi qui sciunt causam et propter quid comparantur ad scientes tantum quia, sicut architectonicae artes ad artes artificum manu operantium. Sed architectonicae artes sunt nobiliores: ergo et illi qui sciunt causas et propter quid, sunt scientiores et sapientiores scientibus tantum quia.

26. Huius probationis prima ex hoc apparet, quia architectores sciunt causas factorum. Ad cuius intellectum sciendum est, quod architector dicitur quasi principalis artifex: ab archos quod est princeps, et techne quod est ars. Dicitur autem ars principalior illa, quae principaliorem operationem habet. Operationes autem artificum hoc modo distinguuntur: quia quaedam sunt ad disponendum materiam artificii, sicut carpentarii secando ligna et complanando disponunt materiam ad formam navis. Alia est operatio ad inductionem formae; sicut cum aliquis ex lignis dispositis et praeparatis navem compaginat. Alia est operatio in usum rei iam constitutae; et ista est principalissima. Prima autem est infima, quia prima ordinatur ad secundam, et secunda ad tertiam. Unde navisfactor est architector respectu eius qui praeparat ligna. Gubernator autem, qui utitur navi iam facta, est architector respectu navis factoris.

27. Et, quia materia est propter formam, et talis debet esse materia quae formae competat, ideo navisfactor scit causam, quare ligna debeant esse sic disposita; quod

Or in another version: *as it is more according to wisdom to know as one pursuing all things*, that is, universals.

Another reading has: *as more conformable to knowing, since wisdom pursues all things*, as if to say: *as more dependent upon knowing* than upon doing, *since wisdom pursues all things*, that is, it seeks to reach each single thing, so that those are rather called wise who are more knowing, not those who are more men of action.

Hence another reading expresses this meaning more clearly, saying: *as all pursue wisdom more with respect to knowing*.

24. *Now this is because* (981a28). Then he proves the superiority of art and science mentioned above, and he does this by means of three arguments.

The first runs thus. Those who know the cause and reason why a thing is so are more knowing and wiser than those who merely know that it is so but do not know why. Now men of experience know that something is so but do not know the reason, whereas men who have an art not only know that something is so but also know its cause and reason. Hence those who have an art are wiser and more knowing than those who have experience.

25. *For this reason, too* (981a30). Here he proves the first aspect of superiority, and this runs as follows. Those who know the cause and reason why a thing is so are compared to those who merely know that it is as the architectonic arts are to the arts of manual laborers. But the architectonic arts are nobler. In a similar way, then, those who know the causes and reasons of things are more knowing than those who merely know that things are so.

26. The first part of this proof becomes clear from the fact that architects know the causes of the things that are done. In order to understand this we must note that architect means chief artist, from ἄρχος meaning chief, and τέχνη meaning art. Now that art is said to be a chief art which performs a more important operation. Indeed, the operations of artists are distinguished in this way, for some operations are directed to disposing the material of the artifact. Carpenters, for example, by cutting and planing the wood, dispose matter for the form of a ship. Another operation is directed to introducing this form into the matter—for example, when someone builds a ship out of wood that has been disposed and prepared. A third operation is directed to the use of the finished product, and this is the highest operation. But the first operation is the lowest because it is directed to the second and the second to the third. Hence the shipbuilder is a superior artist compared with the one who prepares the wood; the navigator, who uses the completed ship, is a superior artist compared with the shipbuilder.

27. Further, since matter exists for the sake of form, and ought to be such as to befit the form, the shipbuilder knows the reason why the wood should be shaped in some

nesciunt illi qui praeparant ligna. Similiter, cum tota navis sit propter usum ipsius, ille qui navi utitur, scit quare talis forma debeat esse; ad hoc enim debet talis esse, ut tali usui conveniens sit. Et sic patet, quod ex forma artificii sumitur causa operationum, quae sunt circa dispositionem materiae. Et ex usu sumitur causa operationum, quae sunt circa formam artificiati.

28. Et sic manifestum est, quod architectores factorum causas sciunt. Illos vero, scilicet manu artifices, iudicamus vel denominamus, sicut quaedam inanimatorum. Et hoc non ideo quia faciunt operationes artificiales, sed quia quae faciunt, incognita faciunt. Sciunt enim quia, sed causas non cognoscunt; sicut etiam ignis exurit absque aliqua cognitione. Est igitur quantum ad hoc similitudo inter inanimata et manu artifices, quod sicut absque causae cognitione inanimata operantur ut ordinata ab aliquo superiori intellectu in proprium finem, ita et manu artifices. Sed in hoc est differentia: quia inanimata faciunt unumquodque suorum operum per naturam, sed manu artifices per consuetudinem: quae licet vim naturae habeat inquantum ad unum inclinat determinate, tamen a natura differt in hoc, quod est circa ea quae sunt ad utrumlibet secundum humanam cognitionem. Naturalia enim non consuescimus, sicut dicitur in secundo *Ethicorum*. Nec etiam cognitione carentium est consuescere. Haec autem quae dicta sunt, sic sunt consideranda tamquam ex eis appareat, quod aliqui non sunt sapientiores secundum quod est *practicos*, id est operatores esse, quod convenit expertis; sed secundum quod aliqui habent rationem de agendis, et cognoscunt causas agendorum, ex quibus rationes sumuntur: quod convenit architectoribus.

29. Deinde cum dicit *et omnino* ponit secundam rationem: quae talis est. Signum scientis est posse docere: quod ideo est, quia unumquodque tunc est perfectum in actu suo, quando potest facere alterum sibi simile, ut dicitur quarto *Meteororum*. Sicut igitur signum caliditatis est quod possit aliquid calefacere, ita signum scientis est, quod possit docere, quod est scientiam in alio causare.

Artifices autem docere possunt, quia cum causas cognoscant, ex eis possunt demonstrare: demonstratio autem est syllogismus faciens scire, ut dicitur primo *Posteriorum*. Experti autem non possunt docere, quia non possunt ad scientiam perducere cum causam ignorent. Et si ea quae experimento cognoscunt aliis tradant, non recipientur per modum scientiae, sed per modum

particular way; but those who prepare the wood do not know this. And in a similar way, since the completed ship exists in order to be used, the one who uses the ship knows why it should have some particular form; for the form should be one that befits its use. Thus it is evident that the reason for the operations that dispose the matter is taken from the design of the product in the artist's mind, and the reason for the operations that produce the form of the artifact is taken from its use.

28. It is evident, then, that the architects know the causes of the things that are done. In fact, we judge and speak about the others—the manual laborers—as we do about certain inanimate things. This is not because they do not perform artful operations, but because they do things without knowing the cause; they know that something is to be done but not why it is, just as fire burns without knowing why. Hence there is a likeness between inanimate things and manual laborers from this point of view: just as inanimate things act without knowing the causes, inasmuch as they are directed to their proper end by a superior intellect, so also do manual laborers. But they differ in this respect: inanimate things perform each of their operations as a result of their nature, whereas manual laborers perform theirs through habit. And while habit is practically the same as nature inasmuch as it is inclined to one definite effect, still habit differs from nature inasmuch as it is open to opposites by reason of human knowledge. For we do not habituate natural bodies, as is stated in *Ethics* 2. Indeed, it is impossible to cause habits in things that lack knowledge. Now the statements that have been made—as is evident from the statements themselves—must be interpreted as meaning that some men are wiser not insofar as they are *practical* men of action, as befits men of experience. Rather, they are wiser insofar as they have a plan for things to be done and know their causes, which are the basis of such a plan, as befits architects.

29. *In general, a sign of scientific knowledge* (981b7). Here he gives the second argument, which is as follows: a sign of knowledge is the ability to teach, and this is so because each thing is perfect in its activity when it can produce another thing similar to itself, as is said in *Meteorology* 4. Therefore, just as the possession of heat is indicated by the fact that a thing can heat something else, the possession of knowledge is indicated by the fact that one can teach (that is, cause knowledge in another).

But men who have an art can teach, for since they know causes they can demonstrate from these; and demonstration is a syllogism that produces knowledge, as is said in *Posterior Analytics* 1. But men who have experience alone cannot teach; since they do not know the causes, they cannot cause knowledge in someone else. And if they do teach others the things that they know by experience, these

opinionis vel credulitatis. Unde patet quod artifices sunt magis sapientes et scientes expertis.

30. Deinde cum dicit *amplius autem* ponit tertiam rationem; quae talis est. Cognitiones singularium magis sunt propriae sensibus quam alicui alteri cognitioni, cum omnis cognitio singularium a sensu oriatur. Sed tamen, *nec unum*, idest nullum sensum dicimus sapientiam, scilicet propter hoc quod licet aliquis sensus cognoscat quia, tamen, non propter quid cognoscit. Tactus enim iudicat quod ignis calidus est, non tamen apprehendit propter quid: ergo experti qui habent singularium cognitionem causam ignorantes, sapientes dici non possunt.

31. Deinde cum dicit *primum quidem* comparat artem activam speculativae. Et circa hoc duo facit.

Primo ostendit, quod ars speculativa magis est sapientia quam activa.

Secundo respondet cuidam obiectioni, ibi, *in moralibus*.

Ostendit autem quod primo dictum est, tali ratione. In quibuscumque scientiis vel artibus invenitur id propter quod homines scientes prae aliis hominibus in admiratione vel honore habentur, illae scientiae sunt magis honorabiles, et magis dignae nomine sapientiae. Quilibet autem inventor artis habetur in admiratione, propter hoc quod habet sensum et iudicium et discretionem causae ultra aliorum hominum sensum, et non propter utilitatem illorum quae invenit: sed magis admiramur, *sicut sapientem et ab aliis distinguentem*. Sapientem quidem, quantum ad subtilem inquisitionem causarum rei inventae: distinguentem vero, quantum ad investigationem differentiarum unius rei ad aliam. Vel aliter, *ab aliis distinguentem*, ut passive legatur, quasi in hoc ab aliis distinguatur. Unde alia litera habet, *differentem*. Ergo scientiae aliquae sunt magis admirabiles et magis dignae nomine sapientiae propter eminentiorem sensum, et non propter utilitatem.

32. Cum igitur plures artes sint repertae quantum ad utilitatem, quarum quaedam sunt ad vitae necessitatem, sicut mechanicae; quaedam vero ad introductionem in aliis scientiis, sicut scientiae logicales: illi artifices dicendi sunt sapientiores, quorum scientiae non sunt ad utilitatem inventae, sed propter ipsum scire, cuiusmodi sunt scientiae speculativae.

33. Et quod speculativae scientiae non sint inventae ad utilitatem, patet per hoc signum: quia, *iam partis*, id est acquisitis vel repertis omnibus huiusmodi, quae possunt esse ad introductionem in scientiis, vel ad necessitatem vitae, vel ad voluptatem, sicut artes quae sunt

things are not learned after the manner of scientific knowledge, but after that of opinion or belief. Hence, it is clear that men who have an art are wiser and more knowing than those who have experience.

30. *Furthermore, we do not hold* (981b10). Here he gives the third argument, which is as follows. Knowing singular things is proper to the senses rather than to any other type of knowing, since our entire knowledge of singular things originates with the senses. Yet we do not hold that *any one* (that is, any one of the senses) is wisdom, because even though each sense knows that a thing is so, it does not know why it is so. Touch judges that fire is hot but does not know why it is hot. Therefore, men of experience, who have a knowledge of singular things but do not know their causes, cannot be called wise men.

31. *It is only fitting* (981b13). Here he compares practical art with speculative art; and in regard to this he does two things.

First [31], he shows that a speculative art is wisdom to a greater degree than a practical art.

Second [34], he answers an objection, at *the difference* (981b25).

He proves his first statement by this argument. In any of the sciences or arts we find that men with scientific knowledge are more admired and are held in higher esteem than all other men, because their knowledge is held to be nobler and more worthy of the name of wisdom. Now the discoverer of any art at all is admired because he perceives, judges, and discerns a cause beyond the perceptions of other men, and not because of the usefulness of his discoveries. We admire him rather *as one who is wise and as distinguishing from others*. As being wise, indeed, in the subtle way in which he investigates the causes of his discoveries, and as distinguishing from others insofar as he investigates the ways in which one thing differs from another. Or, according to another interpretation, *as distinguishing from others* is to be read passively, as being distinguished in this respect from others. Hence another text has *one who is different*. Some sciences, then, are more admirable and worthy of the name of wisdom because their observations are more outstanding, not because they are useful.

32. Therefore, since many useful arts have been discovered (some to provide the necessities of life, as the mechanical arts, and others to introduce us to the sciences, as the logical disciplines), those artists must be said to be wiser whose sciences were discovered not for the sake of utility but merely for the sake of knowing. These are the speculative sciences.

33. That the speculative sciences were not discovered for the sake of utility is made clear by this fact: after all sciences *had already been developed* (that is, acquired or discovered) which can serve as introductions to the other sciences, or provide the necessities of life, or give pleasure

ordinatae ad hominum delectationem: speculativae non sunt propter huiusmodi repertae, sed propter seipsas. Et quod non sint ad utilitatem inventae, patet ex loco quo inventae sunt. In locis enim illis primo repertae sunt, ubi primo homines studuerunt circa talia.

Alia litera habet, *et primum his locis ubi vacabant*, id est ab aliis occupationibus quiescentes studio vacabant quasi necessariis abundantes. Unde et circa Aegyptum primo inventae sunt artes mathematicae, quae sunt maxime speculativae, a sacerdotibus, qui sunt concessi studio vacare, et de publico expensas habebant, sicut etiam legitur in Genesi.

34. Sed quia usus nomine artis fuerat et sapientiae et scientiae quasi indifferenter, ne aliquis putet haec omnia esse nomina synonyma idem penitus significantia hanc opinionem removet, et remittit ad librum moralium, idest ad sextum *Ethicorum*, ubi dictum est, in quo differant scientia et ars et sapientia et prudentia et intellectus. Et ut breviter dicatur, sapientia et scientia et intellectus sunt circa partem animae speculativam, quam ibi scientificum animae appellat. Differunt autem, quia intellectus est habitus principiorum primorum demonstrationis. Scientia vero est conclusionis ex causis inferioribus. Sapientia vero considerat causas primas. Unde ibidem dicitur caput scientiarum. Prudentia vero et ars est circa animae partem practicam, quae est ratiocinativa de contingentibus operabilibus a nobis. Et differunt: nam prudentia dirigit in actionibus quae non transeunt ad exteriorem materiam, sed sunt perfectiones agentis: unde dicitur ibi quod prudentia est recta ratio agibilium. Ars vero dirigit in factionibus, quae in materiam exteriorem transeunt, sicut aedificare et secare: unde dicitur quod ars est recta ratio factibilium.

35. Deinde cum dicit *cuius autem* ostendit ex praehabitis principale propositum; quod scilicet sapientia sit circa causas. Unde dicit quod hoc est cuius gratia *nunc sermonem facimus*, idest ratiocinationem praedictam: quia scientia illa quae denominatur sapientia, videtur esse circa primas causas, et circa prima principia. Quod quidem patet ex praehabitis. Unusquisque enim tanto sapientior est, quanto magis accedit ad causae cognitionem: quod ex praehabitis patet; quia expertus est sapientior eo qui solum habet sensum sine experimento. Et artifex est sapientior experto quocumque. Et inter artifices architector est sapientior manu artifice. Et inter artes etiam et scientias, speculativae sunt magis scientiae quam activae. Et haec omnia ex praedictis patent. Unde relinquitur quod illa scientia, quae simpliciter est sapientia, est circa causas. Et est similis modus arguendi, sicut si diceremus: illud quod est magis calidum, est ma-

(as those arts whose object is to delight man), the speculative sciences were discovered not for this kind of end, but for their own sake. The fact that they were not discovered for the sake of utility becomes evident from the place in which they were discovered. For they originated in those places where men first applied themselves to such things.

Another version reads, *and first in those places where men had leisure*, that is, they had time for study because they were released from other occupations as a result of the abundance of necessary things. Hence the mathematical arts, which are speculative in the highest degree, were first discovered in Egypt by the priests, who were given time for study, and whose expenses were defrayed by the community, as we also read in Genesis 47:22.

34. But because the names "wisdom," "science," and "art" have been used indifferently, lest someone should think that these terms are synonymous, he excludes this opinion and refers to *Ethics* 6, where he has explained the difference between art, wisdom, science, prudence, and understanding. To give the distinction briefly, wisdom, science, and understanding pertain to the speculative part of the soul, which he speaks of in that work as the scientific part of the soul. But they differ in that understanding is the habit of the first principles of demonstration, whereas science has to do with conclusions drawn from subordinate causes, and wisdom with first causes. This is the reason it is spoken of there as the chief science. But prudence and art belong to the practical part of the soul, which reasons about our contingent courses of action. And these also differ, for prudence directs us in actions that do not pass over into some external matter but are perfections of the one acting—this is why prudence is defined in that work as the right reason of things to be done. But art directs us in those productive actions, such as building and cutting, which pass over into external matter—this is why art is defined as the right reason of things to be made.

35. *Now the reason* (981b27). From what has been said he proves his major thesis: wisdom deals with the causes of things. He says that the reason *for undertaking this investigation*, that is, the above piece of reasoning, is that the science which is called wisdom seems to be about first causes and principles. This is evident from the foregoing, for the more a man attains to a knowledge of the cause, the wiser he is. This is also evident from the foregoing because the man of experience is wiser than one who has sensation alone without experience; because the artist is wiser than any man of experience; and because among artists the architect is wiser than the manual laborer. And similarly among the arts and sciences the speculative are more scientific than the practical. All these things are clear from the foregoing remarks. It follows, then, that that science which is wisdom in an absolute sense is concerned with the causes of things. The method of arguing would be

gis igneum: unde quod simpliciter est ignis, est calidum simpliciter.

similar if we were to say that that which is hotter is more afire, and therefore that that which is afire in an absolute sense is hot in an absolute sense.

LECTURE 2

What wisdom considers

982a4 Quoniam autem scientiam hanc quaerimus, circa quales causas et circa qualia principia sapientia et scientia sit, hoc utique considerandum erit. Si itaque accipiat aliquis existimationes, quas de sapiente habemus, fortassis ex his manifestum erit. Primum itaque sapientem scire omnia maxime, sicut decet, accipimus non singularem scientiam eorum habentem. [36]

ἐπεὶ δὲ ταύτην τὴν ἐπιστήμην ζητοῦμεν, τοῦτ᾽ ἂν εἴη {5} σκεπτέον, ἡ περὶ ποίας αἰτίας καὶ περὶ ποίας ἀρχὰς ἐπιστήμη σοφία ἐστίν. εἰ δὴ λάβοι τις τὰς ὑπολήψεις ἃς ἔχομεν περὶ τοῦ σοφοῦ, τάχ᾽ ἂν ἐκ τούτου φανερὸν γένοιτο μᾶλλον. ὑπολαμβάνομεν δὴ πρῶτον μὲν ἐπίστασθαι πάντα τὸν σοφὸν ὡς ἐνδέχεται, μὴ καθ᾽ ἕκαστον ἔχοντα ἐπιστήμην {10} αὐτῶν:

But since we are in search of this science, it will therefore be necessary to consider with what kind of causes and principles wisdom or science deals. This will perhaps become evident if we take the opinions that we have about the wise man. First of all, then, we think that the wise man is one who knows all things in the highest degree, as becomes him, without having a knowledge of them individually.

982a10 Postea difficilia cognoscere potentem, nec levia homini noscere, hunc sapientem dicimus. Sentire enim omnibus est commune, quare facile et non sophon. [37]

εἶτα τὸν τὰ χαλεπὰ γνῶναι δυνάμενον καὶ μὴ ῥάδια ἀνθρώπῳ γιγνώσκειν, τοῦτον σοφόν (τὸ γὰρ αἰσθάνεσθαι πάντων κοινόν, διὸ ῥάδιον καὶ οὐδὲν σοφόν):

Next, we say that that man is wise who is capable of knowing things that are difficult and not easy for man to understand. For sensory perception is common to all, and is therefore easy and not a matter of wisdom.

982a12 Adhuc certiorem. [38]

ἔτι τὸν ἀκριβέστερον

Again, [we consider him wise who is] more certain.

982a13 Et magis causas docentem, sapientiorem circa omnem esse scientiam. [39]

καὶ τὸν διδασκαλικώτερον τῶν αἰτιῶν σοφώτερον εἶναι περὶ πᾶσαν ἐπιστήμην:

And in every branch of science we say that he is wiser who is more capable of teaching us about the causes of things.

982a14 Sed et hanc scientiarum quae sui ipsius causa est, et sciendi gratia eligibilis est, magis est sapientia, quam quae contingentium gratia. [40]

καὶ τῶν ἐπιστημῶν δὲ τὴν {15} αὑτῆς ἕνεκεν καὶ τοῦ εἰδέναι χάριν αἱρετὴν οὖσαν μᾶλλον εἶναι σοφίαν ἢ τὴν τῶν ἀποβαινόντων ἕνεκεν,

Again, among the sciences we think that that science which exists for itself and is desirable for the sake of knowledge is wisdom to a greater degree than one that is desirable for the sake of contingent effects.

982a16 Et hanc sapientiam magis famulante antiquiorem esse. Non enim ordinari, sed sapientem ordinare oportet; neque hunc ab altero, sed ab hoc minus sapientem suaderi. Tales quidem igitur aestimationes et tot de sapientia et sapientibus habemus. [41]

καὶ τὴν ἀρχικωτέραν τῆς ὑπηρετούσης μᾶλλον σοφίαν: οὐ γὰρ δεῖν ἐπιτάττεσθαι τὸν σοφὸν ἀλλ᾽ ἐπιτάττειν, καὶ οὐ τοῦτον ἑτέρῳ πείθεσθαι, ἀλλὰ τούτῳ τὸν ἧττον σοφόν. τὰς μὲν οὖν ὑπολήψεις τοιαύτας καὶ τοσαύτας ἔχομεν περὶ τῆς σοφίας καὶ τῶν σοφῶν:

And we think that a superior science which is rather the more venerable comes nearer to wisdom than a subordinate science. For a wise man must not be directed but must direct, and he must not obey another but must be obeyed by one who is less wise. Such then and so many are the opinions that we have about the wise and about wisdom.

982a21 Istorum autem, haec quidem omnia scire, universalem scientiam maxime habenti inesse necesse est: hic autem novit omnia aliqualiter subiecta. [44]

τούτων δὲ τὸ μὲν πάντα ἐπίστασθαι τῷ μάλιστα ἔχοντι τὴν καθόλου ἐπιστήμην ἀναγκαῖον ὑπάρχειν (οὗτος γὰρ οἶδέ πως πάντα τὰ ὑποκείμενα),

Now of these attributes, that of knowing all things necessarily belongs to him who has universal knowledge in the highest degree, because he knows which are subordinate.

982a23 Sed fere autem et difficillima sunt ea hominibus ad cognoscendum, quae maxime sunt universalia. Nam a sensibus sunt remotissima. [45]

σχεδὸν δὲ καὶ χαλεπώτατα ταῦτα γνωρίζειν τοῖς ἀνθρώποις, τὰ μάλιστα {25} καθόλου (πορρωτάτω γὰρ τῶν αἰσθήσεών ἐστιν),

But the things that are just about the most difficult for man to understand are also those that are most universal; for they are farthest removed from the senses.

982a25 Scientiarum vero certissimae sunt, quae maxime priorum sunt. Nam quae

ἀκριβέσταται δὲ τῶν ἐπιστημῶν αἵ μάλιστα τῶν πρώτων εἰσίν (αἱ γὰρ ἐξ

Again, the most certain of the sciences are those that are most concerned with

sunt ex paucioribus, certiores sunt ex additione dictis ut Arithmetica Geometria. [47]

ἐλαττόνων ἀκριβέστεραι τῶν ἐκ προσθέσεως λεγομένων, οἷον ἀριθμητικὴ γεωμετρίας):

primary things. For sciences based on fewer principles are more certain than those that have additional principles, as arithmetic is more certain than geometry.

982a28 Est et doctrinalis quae causarum est speculatrix magis. Hi namque docent qui causas de singulis dicunt. [48]

ἀλλὰ μὴν καὶ διδασκαλική γε ἡ τῶν αἰτιῶν θεωρητικὴ μᾶλλον (οὗτοι γὰρ διδάσκουσιν, οἱ τὰς {30} αἰτίας λέγοντες περὶ ἑκάστου),

Moreover, that science which speculates about the causes of things is more instructive. For those who teach us are those who assign the causes of every single thing.

982a30 Et noscere, et scire sui gratia maxime inest ei, quae maxime scibilis scientia: nam qui quidem scire propter se desiderat, ipsam maxime scientiam maxime desiderabit: talis autem est, quae maxime scibilis. [49]

τὸ δ᾽ εἰδέναι καὶ τὸ ἐπίστασθαι αὐτῶν ἕνεκα μάλισθ᾽ ὑπάρχει τῇ τοῦ μάλιστα ἐπιστητοῦ ἐπιστήμη (ὁ γὰρ τὸ ἐπίστασθαι δι᾽ αὐτὸ αἱρούμενος τὴν μάλιστα ἐπιστήμην μάλιστα αἱρήσεται, {982b1} τοιαύτη δ᾽ ἐστὶν ἡ τοῦ μάλιστα ἐπιστητοῦ),

Again, to understand and to know for their own sake are found most in the science of what is most knowable. For one who desires scientific knowledge for itself will desire in the highest degree science in the highest degree, and such a science is of what is most knowable.

Maxime autem scibilia prima principia et causae. Nam propter haec et ex his alia dignoscuntur, sed non haec per subiecta.

μάλιστα δ᾽ ἐπιστητὰ τὰ πρῶτα καὶ τὰ αἴτια (διὰ γὰρ ταῦτα καὶ ἐκ τούτων τἆλλα γνωρίζεται ἀλλ᾽ οὐ ταῦτα διὰ τῶν ὑποκειμένων),

Now first principles and causes are most knowable, for it is by reason of these and from these that other things are known, but these are not known through things subordinate to them.

982b4 Maxime vero principalis scientiarum, et maxime principalis subserviente, quae cognoscit cuius causa sunt agenda singula: hoc autem est bonum uniuscuiusque, totaliter autem optimum in natura omni. [50]

ἀρχικωτάτη δὲ τῶν ἐπιστημῶν, καὶ {5} μᾶλλον ἀρχικὴ τῆς ὑπηρετούσης, ἡ γνωρίζουσα τίνος ἕνεκέν ἐστι πρακτέον ἕκαστον: τοῦτο δ᾽ ἐστὶ τἀγαθὸν ἑκάστου, ὅλως δὲ τὸ ἄριστον ἐν τῇ φύσει πάσῃ.

But that science is highest and superior to subordinate sciences which knows the reason why each single thing must be done. This is the good of every single thing, and viewed universally it is the greatest good in the whole of nature.

982b7 Ex omnibus ergo quae dicta sunt, in eamdem cadit scientiam quaesitum nomen. Oportet enim hanc primorum principiorum et causarum esse speculativam: etenim bonum et quod cuius gratia una causarum est. [51]

ἐξ ἁπάντων οὖν τῶν εἰρημένων ἐπὶ τὴν αὐτὴν ἐπιστήμην πίπτει τὸ ζητούμενον ὄνομα: δεῖ γὰρ ταύτην τῶν πρώτων ἀρχῶν καὶ αἰτιῶν εἶναι θεωρητικήν: {10} καὶ γὰρ τἀγαθὸν καὶ τὸ οὗ ἕνεκα ἐν τῶν αἰτίων ἐστίν.

In view of everything that has been said, then, the term that we are investigating evidently falls to the same science. For this science must speculate about first principles and causes, because the good, or that for the sake of which something is done, is also one of the causes.

---

36. Postquam Philosophus ostendit quod sapientia sit quaedam scientia circa causas existens, hic vult ostendere circa quales causas et circa qualia principia sit. Ostendit autem quod est circa causas maxime universales et primas; et argumentatur a definitione sapientiae. Unde circa hoc tria facit.

Primo colligit definitionem sapientiae ex his quae homines de homine sapiente et sapientia opinantur.

Secundo ostendit quod omnia ista conveniunt universali scientiae, quae considerat causas primas et universales, ibi, *istorum autem* et cetera.

Tertio concludit propositum, ibi, *ex omnibus ergo* et cetera.

Circa primum ponit sex opiniones hominum communes quae de sapientia habentur.

36. Having shown that wisdom is a knowledge of causes, the Philosopher's aim here is to establish with what kinds of causes and what kinds of principles it is concerned. He shows that it is concerned with the most universal and primary causes, and he argues this from the definition of wisdom. In regard to this he does three things.

First, he formulates a definition of wisdom from the different opinions that men have about the wise man and about wisdom.

Second [44], he shows that all of these are proper to that universal science which considers first and universal causes, at *now of these* (982a21).

Third [51], he draws the conclusion at which he aims, at *in view of everything* (982b7).

In regard to the first he gives six common opinions which men have entertained about wisdom.

Primam, ibi, *primum itaque* et cetera. Quae talis est: quod communiter omnes accipimus sapientem maxime scire omnia, sicut eum decet, non quod habeat notitiam de omnibus singularibus. Hoc enim est impossibile, cum singularia sint infinita, et infinita intellectu comprehendi non possint.

37. Deinde cum dicit *postea difficilia* secundam ponit: et est ista, quod illum sapientem ponimus esse, qui est potens ex virtute sui intellectus cognoscere difficilia, et illa quae non sunt levia communiter hominibus ad sciendum; quia *commune est omnibus sentire*, idest sensibilia cognoscere. Unde hoc est *facile, et non est sophon*, idest aliquid sapientis et ad sapientem pertinens: et sic patet, quod id quod proprie ad sapientem pertinet, non leviter ab omnibus cognoscitur.

38. Deinde cum dicit *adhuc certiorem* tertiam ponit: et est, quod nos dicimus illum sapientem esse qui de his quae scit, habet certitudinem magis quam alii communiter habeant.

39. Deinde cum dicit *et magis* quartam ponit: et est talis. Illum dicimus magis sapientem in omni scientia, qui potest assignare causas cuiuslibet quaesiti, et per hoc docere.

40. Deinde cum dicit *sed et hanc* quintam ponit: et est, quod illa de numero scientiarum est sapientia, quae per se est magis eligibilis et voluntaria, idest volita gratia scientiae, et propter ipsum scire, quam illa scientia, quae est causa quorumque aliorum contingentium quae possunt ex scientia generari; cuiusmodi est necessitas vitae, delectatio et huiusmodi alia.

41. Deinde cum dicit *et hanc* sextam ponit: et est talis, quod istam sapientiam, de qua facta est mentio, oportet esse vel dicimus esse *magis antiquiorem*, idest digniorem, *famulante scientia*. Quod quidem ex praehabitis intelligi potest. Nam in artibus mechanicis famulantes sunt illae, quae exequuntur manu operando praecepta superiorum artificum, quos supra architectores et sapientes nominavit.

42. Et quod magis conveniat ratio sapientiae scientiis imperantibus quam famulantibus, probat per duo.

Primo, quia scientiae famulantes ordinantur a superioribus scientiis. Artes enim famulantes ordinantur in finem superioris artis, sicut ars equestris ad finem militaris. Sed sapientem secundum omnem opinionem non decet ordinari ab alio, sed ipsum potius alios ordinare.

Item inferiores architectores persuadentur a superioribus, inquantum credunt superioribus artificibus circa operanda vel fienda. Credit enim navisfactor gubernatori docenti qualis debet esse forma navis. Sapienti autem

He states the first where he says, *but since we are in search* (982a4). This opinion is that in general we all consider those especially to be wise who know all things, as befits them, without having a knowledge of every singular thing. For this is impossible since singular things are infinite in number, and an infinite number of things cannot be comprehended by the intellect.

37. *Next, we say that* (982a10). Here he gives the second opinion, which is this: we hold that man to be wise who is capable, by reason of his intellect, of knowing difficult things and those that are not easy for ordinary men to understand. For *sensory perception*, that is, the knowing of sensible things, *is common to all*, and is therefore *easy and not a matter of wisdom*. That is to say, it is neither a mark nor the office of a wise man. Thus it is clear that whatever pertains properly to wisdom is not easily known by all.

38. *Again, [we consider]* (982a12). Here he gives the third opinion: we say that he is wise who, regarding what he knows, is more certain than other men generally are.

39. *And in every branch* (982a13). Here he gives the fourth opinion. That man is said to be wiser in every science who can give the causes of anything that is brought into question, and can teach by means of this.

40. *Again, among the sciences* (982a14). Here he gives the fifth opinion. Among the many sciences, that science which is more desirable and willed for its own sake (that is, chosen for the sake of knowledge and for knowledge itself alone), is more of the nature of wisdom than one that is for the sake of any of the other contingent effects that can be caused by knowledge (such as the necessities of life, pleasure, and so forth).

41. *And we think* (982a16). Here he gives the sixth opinion, namely, that this wisdom, of which mention has been made, must be or is said to be *rather the more venerable*, that is, nobler, *than a subordinate science*. This can be understood from the foregoing. For in the field of the mechanical arts, subordinate artists are those who execute by manual operations the commands of superior artists, whom he referred to above as architects and wise men.

42. He proves by two arguments that the notion of wisdom belongs to sciences that give orders rather than to those that take them.

The first is that subordinate sciences are directed to superior sciences. For subordinate arts are directed to the end of a superior art, as the art of horsemanship to the end of the military art. But in the opinion of all it is not fitting that a wise man should be directed by someone else, but that he should direct others.

The second is that inferior artists are induced to act by superior artists inasmuch as they rely upon superior artists for the things that they must do or make. Thus the shipbuilder relies upon the instructions of the navigator for

non convenit ut ab alio persuadeatur, sed quo ipse aliis persuadeat suam scientiam.

43. Istae igitur sunt tales opiniones, quas homines accipiunt de sapientia et sapiente. Ex quibus omnibus potest quaedam sapientiae descriptio formari: ut ille sapiens dicatur, qui scit omnia etiam difficilia per certitudinem et causam, ipsum scire propter se quaerens, alios ordinans et persuadens. Et sic patet quasi maior syllogismi. Nam omnem sapientem oportet talem esse; et e converso, quicumque est talis, sapiens est.

44. Deinde cum dicit *istorum autem* ostendit quod omnia praedicta conveniunt ei qui cognoscit primas causas et universales; et eo ordine prosequitur quo supra posuit. Unde primo posuit quod habenti scientiam universalem maxime insit omnia scire; quod erat primum. Quod sic patet. Quicumque enim scit universalia, aliquo modo scit ea quae sunt subiecta universalibus, quia scit ea in illa: sed his quae sunt maxime universalia sunt omnia subiecta, ergo ille qui scit maxime universalia, scit quodammodo omnia.

45. Deinde cum dicit *sed fere autem* ostendit eidem inesse secundum, tali ratione. Illa quae sunt maxime a sensibilibus remota, difficilia sunt hominibus ad cognoscendum; nam sensitiva cognitio est omnibus communis, cum ex ea omnis humana cognitio initium sumat. Sed illa quae sunt maxime universalia, sunt sensibilibus remotissima, eo quod sensus singularium sunt: ergo universalia sunt difficillima hominibus ad cognoscendum. Et sic patet quod illa scientia est difficillima, quae est maxime de universalibus.

46. Sed contra hoc videtur esse quod habetur primo *Physicorum*. Ibi enim dicitur quod magis universalia sunt nobis primo nota. Illa autem quae sunt primo nota, sunt magis facilia. Sed dicendum, quod magis universalia secundum simplicem apprehensionem sunt primo nota, nam primo in intellectu cadit ens, ut Avicenna dicit, et prius in intellectu cadit animal quam homo. Sicut enim in esse naturae quod de potentia in actum procedit prius est animal quam homo, ita in generatione scientiae prius in intellectu concipitur animal quam homo. Sed quantum ad investigationem naturalium proprietatum et causarum, prius sunt nota minus communia; eo quod per causas particulares, quae sunt unius generis vel speciei, pervenimus in causas universales.

Ea autem quae sunt universalia in causando, sunt posterius nota quo ad nos, licet sint prius nota secundum

the kind of form that a ship ought to have. However, it does not befit a wise man that he should be persuaded to act by someone else, but that he should use his knowledge to persuade others to act.

43. These, then, are the kind of opinions that men have of wisdom and the wise. From all of these a description of wisdom can be formulated, so that the wise man is described as one who knows everything (even difficult matters) with certitude and through their cause, seeking this knowledge for its own sake, and directing and persuading others to act. And in this way the major premise of the syllogism becomes evident. For every wise man must be such, and conversely whoever is such is wise.

44. *Now of these* (982a21). Here he shows that all of the above attributes come together in the man who knows the first and universal causes of things, following the same order as he did above. Thus he held first that knowledge of all things in the highest degree belongs to him who has universal knowledge. This was the first opinion, and it is made clear in this way. Whoever knows universals knows in some respect the things that are subordinate to universals, because he knows the universal in them. But all things are subordinate to those that are most universal. Therefore, the one who knows the most universal things in a sense knows everything.

45. *But the things* (982a23). Here he proves that the second attribute belongs to the same person by the following argument. Those things that are farthest removed from the senses are difficult for men to know, for sensory perception is common to all men (since all human knowledge originates with this). But those things that are most universal are farthest removed from sensible things, because the senses have to do with singular things. Hence universals are the most difficult for men to know. Thus it is clear that that science is the most difficult which is most concerned with universals.

46. But the statement that appears in *Physics* 1 seems to contradict this. For it is said there that more universal things are known first by us, and those things that are known first are those which are easier. Yet it must be said that those things that are more universal according to simple apprehension are known first, for being is the first thing that comes into the intellect (as Avicenna says), and animal comes into the intellect before man does. Just as in the order of nature, which proceeds from potency to act, animal is prior to man, so too in the genesis of knowledge the intellect conceives animal before it conceives man. But with respect to the investigations of natural properties and causes, less universal things are known first, because we discover universal causes by means of the particular causes that belong to one genus or species.

Now those things that are universal in causing are known subsequently by us (notwithstanding the fact that

naturam, quamvis universalia per praedicationem sint aliquo modo prius quo ad nos nota quam minus universalia, licet non prius nota quam singularia; nam cognitio sensus qui est cognoscitivus singularium, in nobis praecedit cognitionem intellectivam quae est universalium. Facienda est etiam vis in hoc quod maxime universalia non dicit simpliciter esse difficillima, sed *fere*. Illa enim quae sunt a materia penitus separata secundum esse, sicut substantiae immateriales, sunt magis difficilia nobis ad cognoscendum, quam etiam universalia: et ideo ista scientia, quae sapientia dicitur, quamvis sit prima in dignitate, est tamen ultima in addiscendo.

47. Deinde cum dicit *scientiarum vero* ostendit tertium eidem inesse, tali ratione. Quanto aliquae scientiae sunt priores naturaliter, tanto sunt certiores: quod ex hoc patet, quia illae scientiae, quae dicuntur ex additione ad alias, sunt minus certae scientiis quae pauciora in sua consideratione comprehendunt ut arithmetica certior est geometria, nam ea quae sunt in geometria, sunt ex additione ad ea quae sunt in arithmetica. Quod patet si consideremus quid utraque scientia considerat ut primum principium scilicet unitatem et punctum. Punctus enim addit supra unitatem situm: nam ens indivisibile rationem unitatis constituit: et haec secundum quod habet rationem mensurae, fit principium numeri. Punctus autem supra hoc addit situm.

Sed scientiae particulares sunt posteriores secundum naturam universalibus scientiis, quia subiecta earum addunt ad subiecta scientiarum universalium: sicut patet, quod ens mobile de quo est naturalis philosophia, addit supra ens simpliciter, de quo est metaphysica, et supra ens quantum de quo est mathematica: ergo scientia illa quae est de ente, et maxime universalibus, est certissima. Nec illud est contrarium, quia dicitur esse ex paucioribus, cum supra dictum sit, quod sciat omnia. Nam universale quidem comprehendit pauciora in actu, sed plura in potentia. Et tanto aliqua scientia est certior, quanto ad sui subiecti considerationem pauciora actu consideranda requiruntur. Unde scientiae operativae sunt incertissimae, quia oportet quod considerent multas singularium operabilium circumstantias.

48. Deinde cum dicit *est et doctrinalis* ostendit quartum eidem inesse, tali ratione. Illa scientia est magis doctrix vel doctrinalis, quae magis considerat causas: illi enim soli docent, qui causas de singulis dicunt; quia scire per causam est, et docere est scientiam in aliquo causare. Sed illa scientia quae universalia considerat,

they are things that are primarily knowable according to their nature), although things that are universal by predication are known to us in some way before the less universal (notwithstanding the fact that they are not known prior to singular things). In us, sensory knowledge, which is cognitive of singular things, precedes intellective knowledge, which is about universals. And some importance must also be attached to the fact that he does not say that the most universal things are the most difficult absolutely, but *just about*. For those things that are entirely separate from matter in being, as immaterial substances, are more difficult for us to know than universals. Therefore, even though this science which is called wisdom is the first in dignity, it is still the last to be learned.

47. *Again, the most certain* (982a25). Here he shows that the third attribute belongs to the same science. This is his argument: the more any sciences are prior by nature, the more certain they are. This is clear from the fact that those sciences which are said to originate as a result of adding something to the other sciences are less certain than those which take fewer things into consideration; for example, arithmetic is more certain than geometry because the objects considered in geometry are a result of adding to those considered in arithmetic. This becomes evident if we consider what these two sciences take as their first principle, namely, the point and the unit. For the point adds to the unit the notion of position, because undivided being constitutes the intelligible structure of the unit; insofar as this has the function of a measure it becomes the principle of number. And the point adds to this the notion of position.

However, particular sciences are subsequent in nature to universal sciences, because their subjects add something to the subjects of universal sciences. For example, it is evident that mobile being (with which the philosophy of nature deals) adds to simple being (with which metaphysics is concerned), and to quantified being (with which mathematics is concerned). Hence that science which treats of being and the most universal things is the most certain. Moreover, the statement here that this science deals with fewer principles is not opposed to the one made above, that it knows all things. For the universal takes in fewer inferiors actually, but many potentially. And the more certain a science is, the fewer actual things it has to consider in investigating its subject matter. Hence the practical sciences are the least certain, because they must consider the many circumstances attending individual effects.

48. *Moreover, that science* (982a28). Here he proves that the fourth attribute belongs to the same science by this argument. That science is more instructive (or better able to teach) which is concerned to a greater degree with causes. For only those teach who assign the causes of every single thing, because scientific knowledge comes about through

causas primas omnium causarum considerat: unde patet quod ipsa est maxime doctrix.

49. Deinde cum dicit *et noscere* ostendit quintum eidem inesse, tali ratione. Illarum scientiarum maxime est scire et cognoscere earum causa, idest propter seipsas et non propter alias, quae sunt de maxime scibilibus: sed illae scientiae quae sunt de primis causis, sunt de maxime scibilibus: igitur illae scientiae maxime sui gratia desiderantur.

Primam sic probat. Qui desiderat scire propter scire, magis desiderat scientiam: sed maxima scientia est de maxime scibilibus: ergo illae scientiae sunt magis desideratae propter seipsas quae sunt de magis scibilibus.

Secundam probat sic. Illa, ex quibus et propter quae alia cognoscuntur, sunt magis scibilia his quae per ea cognoscuntur: sed per causas et principia alia cognoscuntur et non e converso, et cetera.

50. Deinde cum dicit *maxime vero* ostendit sextum inesse eidem: et est ratio talis. Illa scientia se habet ad alias ut principalis, sive ut architectonica ad servilem sive ad famulantem, quae considerat causam finalem, cuius causa agenda sunt singula; sicut apparet in his, quae supra diximus. Nam gubernator, ad quem pertinet usus navis, qui est finis navis, est quasi architector respectu navisfactoris, qui ei famulatur. Sed praedicta scientia maxime considerat causam finalem rerum omnium. Quod ex hoc patet, quia hoc cuius causa agendo sunt singula, *est bonum uniuscuiusque*, idest particulare bonum. Finis autem bonum est in unoquoque genere. Id vero, quod est finis omnium, idest ipsi universo, est hoc quod est optimum in tota natura: et hoc pertinet ad considerationem praedictae scientiae: ergo praedicta est principalis, sive architectonica omnium aliarum.

51. Deinde cum dicit *ex omnibus* concludit ex praedictis conclusionem intentam; dicens, quod ex omnibus praedictis apparet, quod in eamdem scientiam cadit nomen sapientiae, quod quaerimus; scilicet in illam scientiam, quae est theorica, idest speculativa primorum principiorum et causarum. Hoc autem manifestum est quantum ad sex primas conditiones, quae manifeste pertinent consideranti universales causas. Sed, quia sexta conditio tangebat finis considerationem, quae apud antiquos non manifeste ponebatur esse causa, ut infra dicetur; ideo specialiter ostendit, quod haec conditio est

some cause, and to teach is to cause knowledge in another. But that science which considers universals considers the first of all the causes. Hence it is evidently the best fitted to teach.

49. *Again, to understand* (982a30). Here he proves that the fifth attribute belongs to the same science by this argument. It is most properly the office of the sciences about the most knowable things to know and understand for their own sake—that is, for the sake of those sciences themselves and not for something else. But it is the sciences that deal with first causes which consider the most knowable things. Therefore, those sciences are desired most for their own sake.

He proves the first premise thus. One who most desires knowledge for the sake of knowledge most desires scientific knowledge. But the highest kind of knowledge is concerned with things that are most knowable. Therefore, those sciences are desired most for their own sake which have to do with things that are most knowable.

He proves the second premise thus. Those things from which and by reason of which other things are known are more knowable than the things that are known by means of them. But these other things are known through causes and principles, and not vice versa, and so on.

50. *But that science* (982b4). Here he proves that the sixth attribute belongs to the same science by the following argument. That science which considers the final cause (or that for the sake of which particular things are done) is related to the other sciences as a chief or master science is to a subordinate or ancillary one, as is evident from the foregoing remarks. For the navigator, to whom the use, or end, of the ship belongs, is a kind of architect in relation to the shipbuilder who serves him. But the aforesaid science is concerned most with the final cause of all things. This is clear when we consider how that for the sake of which all particular things are done *is the good of every single thing*, that is, a particular good. But the end in any genus of things is a good, and that which is the end of all things (that is, of the universe itself) is the greatest good in the whole of nature. Now this belongs to the consideration of the science in question, and therefore it is the chief or architectonic science with reference to all the others.

51. *In view of everything* (982b7). Here he draws from the foregoing arguments his intended conclusion, saying that it is clear from everything that has been said that the name "wisdom" which we are investigating belongs to the same science that considers or speculates about first principles and causes. This is evident from the six primary conditions which clearly pertain to the science that considers universal causes. But because the sixth condition touched on the consideration of the end, which was not clearly held to be a cause among the ancient philosophers, as will be said below [1177], he therefore shows in a special way that

eiusdem scientiae, quae scilicet est considerativa primarum causarum; quia videlicet ipse finis, qui est bonum, et cuius causa fiunt alia, est una de numero causarum. Unde scientia, quae considerat primas et universales causas, oportet etiam quod consideret universalem finem omnium, quod est optimum in tota natura.

this condition belongs to the same science, namely, the one which considers first causes. For the end, which is a good and that for the sake of which other things are done, is one of the many causes. Hence the science that considers first and universal causes must also be the one that considers the universal end of all things, which is the greatest good in the whole of nature.

LECTURE 3

Metaphysics' nature and goal

982b11 Quia vero non activa, palam ex primis philosophantibus. Nam propter admirari homines nunc et primum incoeperunt philosophari: a principio quidem pauciora dubitabilium mirantes, deinde paulatim procedentes, et de maioribus dubitantes, ut de lunae passionibus, et de his quae circa solem et astra, etiam de universi generatione. Qui vero dubitat et admiratur, ignorare videtur. Quare et philomythes, philosophus aliqualiter est. Fabula namque ex miris constituitur. Quare, si ad ignorantiam effugiendam philosophati sunt, palam quia propter scire, studere persecuti sunt, et non usus alicuius causa. [53]

ὅτι δ' οὐ ποιητική, δῆλον καὶ ἐκ τῶν πρώτων φιλοσοφησάντων· διὰ γὰρ τὸ θαυμάζειν οἱ ἄνθρωποι καὶ νῦν καὶ τὸ πρῶτον ἤρξαντο φιλοσοφεῖν, ἐξ ἀρχῆς μὲν τὰ πρόχειρα τῶν ἀτόπων θαυμάσαντες, εἶτα κατὰ μικρὸν οὕτω προϊόντες {15} καὶ περὶ τῶν μειζόνων διαπορήσαντες, οἷον περί τε τῶν τῆς σελήνης παθημάτων καὶ τῶν περὶ τὸν ἥλιον καὶ ἄστρα καὶ περὶ τῆς τοῦ παντὸς γενέσεως. ὁ δ' ἀπορῶν καὶ θαυμάζων οἴεται ἀγνοεῖν (διὸ καὶ ὁ φιλόμυθος φιλόσοφός πώς ἐστιν· ὁ γὰρ μῦθος σύγκειται ἐκ θαυμασίων)· ὥστ' εἴπερ διὰ {20} τὸ φεύγειν τὴν ἄγνοιαν ἐφιλοσόφησαν, φανερὸν ὅτι διὰ τὸ εἰδέναι τὸ ἐπίστασθαι ἐδίωκον καὶ οὐ χρήσεώς τινος ἕνεκεν.

That this is not a practical science is evident from those who first philosophized. For it is because of wonder that men both now and formerly began to philosophize, about less important matters, and then progressing little by little, they raised questions about more important ones, such as the phases of the moon and the courses of the sun and the stars and the generation of the universe. But one who raises questions and wonders seems to be ignorant. Hence the philosopher is also to some extent a lover of myth, for myths are composed of wonders. If they philosophized, then, in order to escape from ignorance, they pursued their studies for the sake of knowledge and not for any utility.

982b22 Testatur autem hoc accidens. Nam fere cunctis existentibus, quae sunt necessariorum, et ad pigritiam et eruditionem, talis prudentia inquiri coepit. Palam igitur, quia propter nullam ipsam quaerimus aliam necessitatem. [57]

μαρτυρεῖ δὲ αὐτὸ τὸ συμβεβηκός· σχεδὸν γὰρ πάντων ὑπαρχόντων τῶν ἀναγκαίων καὶ πρὸς ῥᾳστώνην καὶ διαγωγὴν ἡ τοιαύτη φρόνησις ἤρξατο ζητεῖσθαι. δῆλον οὖν ὡς δι' {25} οὐδεμίαν αὐτὴν ζητοῦμεν χρείαν ἑτέραν,

And what has happened bears witness to this. For when nearly all the things necessary for life, pastimes, and learning were acquired, this kind of prudence began to be sought. It is evident, then, that we do not seek this knowledge for the sake of any other necessity.

982b25 Sed ut dicimus, homo liber, qui suimet, et non alterius causa est, sic et haec sola libera est scientiarum: sola namque haec suimet causa est. [58]

ἀλλ' ὥσπερ ἄνθρωπος, φαμέν, ἐλεύθερος ὁ αὑτοῦ ἕνεκα καὶ μὴ ἄλλου ὤν, οὕτω καὶ αὐτὴν ὡς μόνην οὖσαν ἐλευθέραν τῶν ἐπιστημῶν· μόνη γὰρ αὕτη αὑτῆς ἕνεκέν ἐστιν.

But just as we say that a man is free who exists for himself and not for another, in a similar fashion this is the only free science, because it alone exists for itself.

982b28 Propter quod et iuste non humana eius putetur possessio. Multipliciter enim hominum natura serva est. [60]

διὸ καὶ δικαίως ἂν οὐκ ἀνθρωπίνη νομίζοιτο αὐτῆς ἡ κτῆσις· πολλαχῇ γὰρ ἡ φύσις δούλη τῶν {30} ἀνθρώπων ἐστίν,

For this reason, too, it might rightly be thought that this science is not a human possession, since in many respects human nature is servile.

982b30 Quare secundum Simonidem, *solus quidem Deus hunc habet honorem*. Virum vero non dignum non quaerere quae secundum se est scientiam. Sic autem dicunt aliqui poetae, quia divinum natum est invidere: et in hoc contingere maxime verisimile, et infortunatos omne imperfectos esse. Sed nec divinum invidum esse convenit: sed secundum proverbium: *multa mentiuntur poetae*. [61]

κατὰ Σιμωνίδην "θεὸς ἂν μόνος τοῦτ' ἔχοι γέρας", ἄνδρα δ' οὐκ ἄξιον μὴ οὐ ζητεῖν τὴν καθ' αὑτὸν ἐπιστήμην. εἰ δὴ λέγουσί τι οἱ ποιηταὶ καὶ πέφυκε φθονεῖν τὸ θεῖον, {983a1} ἐπὶ τούτου συμβῆναι μάλιστα εἰκὸς καὶ δυστυχεῖς {2} εἶναι πάντας τοὺς περιττούς. ἀλλ' οὔτε τὸ θεῖον φθονερὸν ἐνδέχεται εἶναι, ἀλλὰ κατὰ τὴν παροιμίαν πολλὰ ψεύδονται ἀοιδοί,

Hence, according to Simonides, *only God has this honor*, and it is unfitting that man should not seek knowledge that befits him. Some poets accordingly say that the deity is naturally envious. It is most likely that it should happen in this case, and that all those who are imperfect are unfortunate. But it is not fitting that the deity should be envious, for as the proverb says: *the poets tell many lies.*

983a4 Nec ea aliam honora iliorem oportet existimare. Nam maxime divina, et maxime honoranda. Tails autem dupliciter

οὔτε τῆς τοιαύτης ἄλλην χρὴ νομίζειν τιμιωτέραν. {5} ἡ γὰρ θειοτάτη καὶ τιμιωτάτη· τοιαύτη δὲ διχῶς ἂν εἴη μόνη·

Nor must we think that any other science is more honorable than this. For what is most divine is most honorable. But then

utique erit solum. Quam enim maxime Deus habet, dea scientiarum est: et utique si qua sit divinorum. [64]

ἥν τε γὰρ μάλιστ᾿ ἂν ὁ θεὸς ἔχοι, θεία τῶν ἐπιστημῶν ἐστί, κἂν εἴ τις τῶν θείων εἴη.

it alone will be such, and in two ways. For of all knowledge that which God most properly has is divine; if there is any such knowledge, it is concerned with divine matters.

Sola autem ista, ambo haec sortita est. Deus autem videtur causa omnibus esse, et principium quoddam: et talem aut solus, aut maxime Deus habet. Necessariores quidem igitur omnes ipsa, dignior vero nulla.

μόνη δ᾿ αὕτη τούτων ἀμφοτέρων τετύχηκεν: ὅ τε γὰρ θεὸς δοκεῖ τῶν αἰτίων πᾶσιν εἶναι καὶ ἀρχή τις, καὶ τὴν τοιαύτην ἢ μόνος ἢ μάλιστ᾿ {10} ἂν ἔχοι ὁ θεός. ἀναγκαιότεραι μὲν οὖν πᾶσαι ταύτης, ἀμείνων δ᾿ οὐδεμία.

But this science alone has both of these characteristics, for God seems to be a cause and in some sense a principle according to all men, and such [knowledge as this] God either alone has, or has in the highest degree. Therefore, all the other sciences are more necessary, but none is more excellent.

983a11 Oportet vero aliqualiter constituere ordinem ipsius ad contrarium nobis earum quae a principio quaestionum. Incipiunt quidem homines, ut diximus, omnes ab admirari, si ita habent quemadmodum mirabilium automata, nondum speculantibus causam, aut circa solis conversiones, aut diametri non commensurationem. [66]

δεῖ μέντοι πως καταστῆναι τὴν κτῆσιν αὐτῆς εἰς τοὐναντίον ἡμῖν τῶν ἐξ ἀρχῆς ζητήσεων. ἄρχονται μὲν γάρ, ὥσπερ εἴπομεν, ἀπὸ τοῦ θαυμάζειν πάντες εἰ οὕτως ἔχει, καθάπερ <περὶ> τῶν θαυμάτων ταὐτόματα [τοῖς μήπω τεθεωρηκόσι {15} τὴν αἰτίαν] ἢ περὶ τὰς τοῦ ἡλίου τροπὰς ἢ τὴν τῆς διαμέτρου ἀσυμμετρίαν

But it is necessary in a sense to bring to a halt the progression of this science at the contrary of our original questions. Indeed, as we have said, all men begin by wondering whether things are like strange chance occurrences to those who do not yet know the cause, or by wondering about reversals in the course of the sun, or about the incommensurability of the diagonal [of a square].

Mirum enim videtur esse omnibus, si quid numerorum non mensuratur. Oportet autem in contrarium, et ad dignius, iuxta proverbium, proficere, quemadmodum et in his cum didicerint: nihil enim ita mirabitur vir geometricus, quam si diameter commensurabilis fiat.

(θαυμαστὸν γὰρ εἶναι δοκεῖ πᾶσι <τοῖς μήπω τεθεωρηκόσι τὴν αἰτίαν> εἴ τι τῷ ἐλαχίστῳ μὴ μετρεῖται): δεῖ δὲ εἰς τοὐναντίον καὶ τὸ ἄμεινον κατὰ τὴν παροιμίαν ἀποτελευτῆσαι, καθάπερ καὶ ἐν τούτοις ὅταν μάθωσιν: οὐθὲν γὰρ {20} ἂν οὕτως θαυμάσειεν ἀνὴρ γεωμετρικὸς ὡς εἰ γένοιτο ἡ διάμετρος μετρητή.

For it would seem wonderful to all if something having the nature of number were immeasurable. But it is necessary to advance to the contrary state and, as the proverb says, the worthier one, as also happens in a sense in these matters when men have learned them. For nothing would surprise a geometrician more than if the diagonal [of a square] were commensurable [with its side].

Quae quidem igitur natura scientiae quaesitae dictum est, et quae sit intentio, qua oportet adipisci quaestionem et totam methodum.

τίς μὲν οὖν ἡ φύσις τῆς ἐπιστήμης τῆς ζητουμένης, εἴρηται, καὶ τίς ὁ σκοπὸς οὗ δεῖ τυγχάνειν τὴν ζήτησιν καὶ τὴν ὅλην μέθοδον.

It has been stated, then, what the nature is of the science that we are seeking and what its goal is for which our search and whole method must be undertaken.

---

52. Ostenso circa quae versatur consideratio huius scientiae, ostendit qualis sit scientia ista. Et circa hoc duo facit.

Primo ostendit dignitatem huius scientiae.

Secundo ostendit ad quem terminum ista scientia pervenire conetur, ibi, *oportet vero aliqualiter* et cetera.

Circa primum facit quatuor.

Primo ostendit quod non est scientia activa, sed speculativa.

Secundo, quod ipsa est libera maxime, ibi, *sed ut dicimus* et cetera.

Tertio, quod non est humana, ibi, *propter quod et iuste*.

Quarto, quod est honorabilissima, ibi, *nec ea aliam*.

52. Having indicated the things with which this science deals, Aristotle now shows what kind of science it is. In regard to this he does two things.

First (982b11; [53]), he reveals the dignity of this science; second (983a11; [66]), the goal which it attempts to reach, at *but it is necessary*.

In regard to the first he does four things.

First, he shows that this is not a practical science but a speculative one;

second (982b25; [58]), that it is free in the highest degree, at *but just as we say*;

third (982b28; [60]), that it is not human, at *for this reason*;

fourth (983a4; [64]), that it is the most honorable science, at *nor must we think that*.

Primum ostendit dupliciter.

Primo per rationem.

Secundo per signum, ibi, *testatur autem hoc* et cetera.

53. Primo ergo ponit talem rationem. Nulla scientia in qua quaeritur ipsum scire propter seipsum, est scientia activa, sed speculativa: sed illa scientia, quae sapientia est, vel philosophia dicitur, est propter ipsum scire: ergo est speculativa et non activa. Minorem hoc modo manifestat. Quicumque quaerit fugere ignorantiam sicut finem, tendit ad ipsum scire propter seipsum: sed illi, qui philosophantur, quaerunt fugere ignorantiam sicut finem: ergo tendunt in ipsum scire propter seipsum.

54. Quod autem ignorantiam fugere quaerant, patet ex hoc, quia illi, qui primo philosophati sunt, et qui nunc philosophantur, incipiunt philosophari propter admirationem alicuius causae: aliter tamen a principio, et modo: quia a principio admirabantur dubitabilia pauciora, quae magis erant in promptu, ut eorum causae cognoscerentur: sed postea ex cognitione manifestorum ad inquisitionem occultorum paulatim procedentes incoeperunt dubitare de maioribus et occultioribus, sicut *de passionibus lunae*, videlicet de eclypsi eius, et mutatione figurae eius, quae variari videtur, secundum quod diversimode se habet ad solem. Et similiter dubitaverunt de his quae sunt circa solem, ut de eclypsi eius, et motu ipsius, et magnitudine eius. Et de his quae sunt circa astra, sicut de quantitate ipsorum, et ordine, et aliis huiusmodi, et de totius universi generatione. Quod quidam dicebant esse generatum casu, quidam intellectu, quidam amore.

55. Constat autem, quod dubitatio et admiratio ex ignorantia provenit. Cum enim aliquos manifestos effectus videamus, quorum causa nos latet, eorum tunc causam admiramur. Et ex quo admiratio fuit causa inducens ad philosophiam, patet quod philosophus est aliqualiter *philomythes*, idest amator fabulae, quod proprium est poetarum. Unde primi, qui per modum quemdam fabularem de principiis rerum tractaverunt, dicti sunt poetae theologizantes, sicut fuit Perseus, et quidam alii, qui fuerunt septem sapientes. Causa autem, quare philosophus comparatur poetae, est ista, quia uterque circa miranda versatur. Nam fabulae, circa quas versantur poetae, ex quibusdam mirabilibus constituuntur. Ipsi etiam philosophi ex admiratione moti sunt ad philosophandum. Et quia admiratio ex ignorantia provenit, patet quod ad hoc moti sunt ad philosophandum ut ignorantiam effugarent. Et sic deinde patet, quod scientiam, *persecuti sunt*, idest studiose quaesierunt, solum ad cognoscendum, et non causa alicuius *usus* idest utilitatis.

56. Notandum est autem, quod cum prius nomine sapientiae uteretur, nunc ad nomen philosophiae

He proves the first in two ways.

First, by an argument;

second (982b22; [57]), by an example, at *and what has happened.*

53. First, he gives this argument. No science in which knowledge itself is sought for its own sake is a practical science, but a speculative one. But that science which is wisdom, or philosophy as it is called, exists for the sake of knowledge itself. Hence it is speculative and not practical. He proves the minor premise in this way. Whoever seeks as an end to escape from ignorance tends toward knowledge for itself. But those who philosophize seek as an end to escape from ignorance. Therefore, they tend toward knowledge for itself.

54. That they seek to escape from ignorance is made clear from the fact that those who first philosophized and who now philosophize did so from wonder about some cause, although they did this at first differently from now. For at first they wondered about less important problems, which were more obvious, in order that they might know their cause; but later on, progressing little by little from the knowledge of more evident matters to the investigation of obscure ones, they began to raise questions about more important and hidden matters, such as *the phases of the moon*, such as its eclipse, and its change of shape, which seems to vary inasmuch as it stands in different relations to the sun. And similarly they raised questions about the phenomena of the sun (such as its eclipse, its movement, and its size), and about the phenomena of the stars (such as their size, arrangement, and so forth), and about the origin of the whole universe, which some said was produced by chance, others by an intelligence, and others by love.

55. Further, he points out that perplexity and wonder arise from ignorance. For when we see certain obvious effects whose cause we do not know, we wonder about their cause. And since wonder was the motive which led men to philosophy, it is evident that the philosopher is, in a sense, *a lover of myth*, that is, a lover of myth, as is characteristic of the poets. Hence the first men to deal with the principles of things in a mythical way, such as Perseus and certain others who were the seven sages, were called the theologizing poets. Now the reason why the philosopher is compared to the poet is that both are concerned with wonders. For the myths with which the poets deal are composed of wonders, and the philosophers themselves were moved to philosophize as a result of wonder. And since wonder stems from ignorance, they were obviously moved to philosophize in order to escape from ignorance. It is accordingly evident from this that *they pursued* knowledge, or diligently sought it, only for itself and not for any *utility* or usefulness.

56. Now we must note that, while this science was first designated by the name "wisdom," this was later changed to

se transfert. Nam pro eodem accipiuntur. Cum enim antiqui studio sapientiae insistentes sophistae, idest sapientes vocarentur, Pythagoras interrogatus quid se esse profiteretur, noluit se sapientem nominare, sicut sui antecessores, quia hoc praesumptuosum videbatur esse; sed vocavit se philosophum, idest amatorem sapientiae. Et exinde nomen sapientis immutatum est in nomen philosophi, et nomen sapientiae in nomen philosophiae. Quod etiam nomen ad propositum aliquid facit. Nam ille videtur sapientiae amator, qui sapientiam non propter aliud, sed propter seipsam quaerit. Qui enim aliquid propter alterum quaerit, magis hoc amat propter quod quaerit, quam quod quaerit.

57. Deinde cum dicit **testatur autem** probat idem per signum; dicens, quod hoc quod dictum est, scilicet quod sapientia vel philosophia non sit propter aliquam utilitatem quaesita, sed propter ipsam scientiam, testatur, **accidens**, idest eventus, qui circa inquisitores philosophiae provenit. Nam cum eis cuncta fere existerent, quae sunt ad necessitatem vitae, et quae sunt **ad pigritiam**, idest ad voluptatem, quae in quadam vitae quiete consistit, et quae sunt etiam ad eruditionem necessaria, sicut scientiae logicales, quae non propter se quaeruntur, sed ut introductoriae ad alias artes, tunc primo incoepit quaeri talis prudentia, idest sapientia. Ex quo patet, quod non quaeritur propter aliquam necessitatem aliam a se, sed propter seipsam: nullus enim quaerit hoc quod habetur. Unde, quia omnibus aliis habitis ipsa quaesita est, patet quod non propter aliquid aliud ipsa quaesita est, sed propter seipsam.

58. Deinde cum dicit **sed ut dicimus** hic probat secundum, scilicet quod ipsa sit libera; et utitur tali ratione. Ille homo proprie dicitur liber, qui non est alterius causa, sed est causa sui ipsius. Servi enim dominorum sunt, et propter dominos operantur, et eis acquirunt quicquid acquirunt. Liberi autem homines sunt sui ipsorum, utpote sibi acquirentes et operantes. Sola autem haec scientia est propter seipsam: ergo ipsa sola est libera inter scientias.

59. Et notandum, quid hoc potest dupliciter intelligi. Uno modo quod hoc quod dicitur **haec sola** demonstret in genere omnem scientiam speculativam. Et tunc verum est quod solum hoc genus scientiarum propter seipsum quaeritur. Unde et illae solae artes liberales dicuntur, quae ad sciendum ordinantur: illae vero quae ordinantur ad aliquam utilitatem per actionem habendam, dicuntur mechanicae sive serviles.

Alio modo, ut demonstret specialiter istam philosophiam, sive sapientiam, quae est circa altissimas causas; quia inter causas altissimas etiam est finalis causa, ut

the name "philosophy," since they mean the same thing. For while the ancients who pursued the study of wisdom were called sophists (that is, wise men), Pythagoras, when asked what he professed himself to be, refused to call himself a wise man as his predecessors had done because he thought this was presumptuous, but called himself a philosopher (that is, a lover of wisdom). And from that time the name "wise man" was changed to "philosopher," and "wisdom" to "philosophy." This name also contributes something to the point under discussion, for that man seems to be a lover of wisdom who seeks wisdom, not for some other reason, but for itself alone. For he who seeks one thing on account of something else has greater love for that on whose account he seeks than for that which he seeks.

57. **And what has happened** (982b22). Here he proves the same point by means of an example. He says that the statement that wisdom or philosophy is not sought for any utility but for knowledge itself is proved by **what has happened**, that is, by what has occurred in the case of those who have pursued philosophy. For when nearly everything was discovered which is necessary for life, **pastimes** (that is, for the pleasure which consists in a life of ease), and learning, such as the logical sciences which are not sought for themselves but as introductions to the other arts, then man began for the first time to seek this kind of prudence, namely, wisdom. And from this it is clear that wisdom is not sought because of any necessity other than itself but for itself alone, for no one seeks something which he already possesses. Hence, because wisdom was sought after all other knowledge had been discovered, it is evident that it was not sought for some reason other than itself, but for itself.

58. **But just as** (982b25). Here he proves the second attribute—namely, that wisdom is free—and he uses the following argument. That man is properly said to be free who does not exist for someone else but for himself. For slaves exist for their masters, work for them, and acquire for them whatever they acquire. But free men exist for themselves inasmuch as they acquire things for themselves and work for themselves. But only this science exists for itself. Therefore, among all the sciences only this science is free.

59. Now we must note that this can be understood in two ways. In one way, the expression **this is the only** may indicate every speculative science as a genus. And then it is true that only this genus of science is sought for itself. Hence, only those arts which are directed to knowing are called liberal arts, whereas those which are directed to some useful end attained by action are called mechanical or servile arts.

Understood in another way, the expression may specifically indicate this philosophy or wisdom which deals with the highest causes, for the final cause is also one of the high-

supra dictum est. Unde oportet, quod haec scientia consideret ultimum et universalem finem omnium. Et sic omnes aliae scientiae in eam ordinantur sicut in finem; unde sola ista maxime propter se est.

60. Deinde cum dicit *propter quod* hic probat tertium scilicet quod non sit humana. Et circa hoc duo facit.

Primo ostendit propositum.

Secundo excludit quorumdam errorem, ibi, *quare secundum Simonidem* et cetera.

Ostendit autem propositum suum tali ratione. Scientia, quae est maxime libera, non potest esse ut possessio naturae illius, quae multipliciter est ministra vel ancilla: humana autem natura *in multis*, idest quantum ad multa est ministra: ergo praedicta scientia non est humana possessio. Dicitur autem humana natura ministra, inquantum multipliciter necessitatibus subditur. Ex quo provenit, quod quandoque praetermittit id quod est secundum se quaerendum, propter ea quae sunt necessaria vitae; sicut dicitur in tertio *Topicorum*, quod philosophari melius est quam ditari, licet ditari quandoque sit magis eligendum, puta indigenti necessariis. Ex quo patet, quod illa sapientia tantum propter seipsam quaeritur, quae non competit homini ut possessio. Illud enim habetur ab homine ut possessio, quod ad nutum habere potest, et quo libere potest uti. Ea autem scientia, quae propter se tantum quaeritur, homo non potest libere uti, cum frequenter ab ea impediatur propter vitae necessitatem. Nec etiam ad nutum subest homini, cum ad eam perfecte homo pervenire non possit. Illud tamen modicum quod ex ea habetur, praeponderat omnibus quae per alias scientias cognoscuntur.

61. Deinde cum dicit *quare secundum* hic excludit errorem cuiusdam Simonidis poetae, qui dicebat, quod soli Deo competit hunc honorem habere, quod velit illam scientiam, quae est propter seipsam quaerenda, et non propter aliud. Sed *non est dignum viro quod non quaerat illam scientiam quae est secundum suam conditionem*, quae scilicet ordinatur ad necessaria vitae, quibus homo indiget.

62. Iste autem error Simonidis proveniebat ex aliquorum poetarum errore, qui dicebant, quod res divina invidet, et ex invidia ea quae ad honorem suum pertinent non vult Deus ab omnibus acceptari. Et si in aliis Deus hominibus invidet, multo magis est iustum in hoc, scilicet in scientia propter se quaesita, quae est honorabilissima inter omnia. Et secundum eorum opinionem, sequitur, quod omnes imperfecti sunt infortunati. Fortunatos enim esse homines dicebant ex providentia deorum, qui eis bona sua communicabant. Unde ex invidia deorum sua bona communicare nolentium, sequitur,

est causes, as was stated above [51]. Therefore, this science must consider the highest and universal end of all things. And in this way all the other sciences are subordinated to it as an end. Hence only this science exists in the highest degree for itself.

60. *For this reason* (982b28). Here he proves the third attribute, namely, that this science is not human. In regard to this he does two things.

First, he proves his thesis.

Second [61], he criticizes an erroneous view held by certain men, at *hence, according to Simonides* (982b30).

He proves his thesis by the following argument. A science which is free in the highest degree cannot be a possession of that nature which is servile and subordinate in many respects. But human nature is servile *in many respects*, that is, in many ways. Therefore, this science is not a human possession. Now human nature is said to be servile insofar as it stands in need of many things. And on this account it happens that man sometimes neglects what should be sought for its own sake because of the things necessary for life. Thus it is said in *Topics* 3 that it is better to philosophize than to become wealthy, although sometimes becoming wealthy is more desirable—that is, to one lacking life's necessities. From this it is clear that the wisdom which is sought for itself alone does not belong to man as his proper possession. For man has as his possession what he can have at his command and use freely. But man cannot use freely that science which is sought for itself alone, since he is often kept from it because of the necessities of life. Nor again is it subject to man's command, because man cannot acquire it perfectly. Yet that very small part of it which he does have outweighs all the things known through the other sciences.

61. *Hence, according to Simonides* (982b30). Here he rejects the error of a certain poet, Simonides, who said that it is proper to God alone to have the honor of desiring that knowledge which ought to be sought for its own sake and not for the sake of something else. But *it is unfitting that man should not seek knowledge that befits him*, namely, that which is directed to the necessities of life required by man.

62. Now Simonides' error came from that of certain poets who said that the deity is envious, and that since he is envious he does not desire that the things that pertain to his honor should be shared by all. And if God is envious of men in other things, he is rightly more so in this case—that is, in the case of the science which is sought for its own sake, which is the most honorable of all the sciences. And according to the opinion of these men it follows that all who are imperfect are unfortunate, for they said that men are fortunate as a result of the providence of the gods, who communicate their goods to men. Hence as a result

quod homines extra perfectionem huius scientiae remanentes sint infortunati.

63. Sed radix huius opinionis est falsissima; quia non est conveniens, quod aliqua res divina invideat. Quod ex hoc patet, quia invidia est tristitia de prosperitate alicuius. Quod quidem accidere non potest, nisi quia bonum alterius aestimatur ab invido ut proprii boni diminutio. Deo autem non convenit esse tristem, cum non sit alicui malo subiectus. Nec etiam per bonum alterius eius bonum diminui potest; quia ex eius bonitate, sicut ex indeficienti fonte, omnia bona effluunt. Unde etiam Plato dixit, quod a Deo est omnis relegata invidia. Sed poetae non solum in hoc, sed in multis aliis mentiuntur, sicut dicitur in proverbio vulgari.

64. Deinde cum dicit *nec ea aliam* ostendit quartum, scilicet quod haec scientia sit honorabilissima, tali ratione. Illa scientia est maxime honorabilis, quae est maxime divina, sicut etiam Deus honorabilior est rebus omnibus: sed ista scientia est maxime divina: ergo est honorabilissima.

Minor sic probatur. Aliqua scientia dicitur esse divina dupliciter; et haec sola scientia utroque modo divina dicitur. Uno modo scientia divina dicitur quam Deus habet. Alio modo, quia est de rebus divinis. Quod autem haec sola habeat utrumque, est manifestum; quia, cum haec scientia sit de primis causis et principiis, oportet quod sit de Deo; quia Deus hoc modo intelligitur ab omnibus, ut de numero causarum existens, et ut quoddam principium rerum. Item talem scientiam, quae est de Deo et de primis causis, aut solus Deus habet, aut si non solus, ipse tamen maxime habet. Solus quidem habet secundum perfectam comprehensionem. Maxime vero habet, inquantum suo modo etiam ab hominibus habetur, licet ab eis non ut possessio habeatur, sed sicut aliquid ab eo mutuatum.

65. Ex his autem ulterius concludit, quod omnes aliae scientiae sunt necessariae magis quam ista ad aliquam vitae utilitatem: minus enim sunt propter se quaesitae. Sed nulla aliarum dignior ista potest esse.

66. Deinde cum dicit *oportet vero* hic ponit terminum, in quem proficit ista scientia; et dicit quod ordo eius consistit vel terminatur ad contrarium eius quod erat in illis qui prius istam scientiam quaerebant. Sicut etiam in generationibus naturalibus et motibus accidit. Nam unusquisque motus terminatur ad contrarium eius a quo motus incipit. Unde, cum inquisitio sit motus quidam ad scientiam, oportet quod terminetur ad contrarium eius a quo incipit.

Initiata est autem (ut praedictum est) inquisitio huius scientiae ab admiratione de omnibus: quia pri-

of the envy of the gods, who are unwilling to communicate their goods, it follows that men, who remain outside the perfection of this science, are unfortunate.

63. But the basis of this opinion is most false, because it is not fitting that any divinity should be envious. This is evident from the fact that envy is sadness at someone else's prosperity. But this can occur only because the one who is envious thinks that someone else's good diminishes his own. Now it is impossible that God should be sad, because he is not subject to evil of any kind. Nor can his goodness be diminished by someone else's goodness, since every good flows from his goodness as from an unfailing spring. Hence Plato also said that there is no envy of any kind in God. But the poets have lied not only in this matter but in many others, as is stated in the common proverb.

64. *Nor must we think* (983a4). Here he proves the fourth attribute—namely, that this is the most honorable science—by the following argument. That science which is most divine is most honorable, just as God himself is also the most honorable of all things. But this science is the most divine, and is therefore the most honorable.

The minor premise is proved in this way: a science is said to be divine in two ways, and only this science is said to be divine in both ways. First, the science which God has is said to be divine; second, the science which is about divine matters is said to be divine. But it is evident that only this science meets both of these requirements, because, since this science is about first causes and principles, it must be about God, for God is understood in this way by all inasmuch as he is one of the causes and a principle of things. Again, either God alone has such a science which is about God and first causes, or, if not he alone, at least he has it in the highest degree. Indeed, he alone has it in a perfectly comprehensive way. And he has it in the highest degree inasmuch as it is also had by men in their own way, although it is not had by them as a human possession, but as something borrowed from him.

65. From these considerations he draws the further conclusion that all other sciences are more necessary than this science for use in practical life, for these sciences are sought least of all for themselves. But none of the other sciences can be more excellent than this one.

66. *But it is necessary* (983a11). He now gives the goal toward which this science moves. He says that its progression comes to rest, or is terminated, in the contrary of what was previously found in those who first sought this science, as also happens in the case of natural generations and motions. For each motion is terminated in the contrary of that from which the motion begins. Hence, since investigation is a kind of movement towards knowledge, it must be terminated in the contrary of that from which it begins.

But, as was stated above [53], the investigation of this science began with man's wonder about all things, because

mi admirabantur pauciora, posteriores vero occultiora. Quae quidem admiratio erat, si res ita se haberet sicut *automata mirabilia*, idest quae videntur mirabiliter a casu accidere.

Automata enim dicuntur quasi per se accidentia. Admirantur enim homines praecipue quando aliqua a casu eveniunt hoc modo, ac si essent praevisa vel ex aliqua causa determinata. Casualia enim non a causa sunt determinata, et admiratio est propter ignorantiam causae. Et ideo cum homines nondum poterant speculari causas rerum, admirabantur omnia quasi quaedam casualia. Sicut admirantur *circa conversiones solis*, quae sunt duae; scilicet duos tropicos, hyemalem et aestivalem.

Nam in tropico aestivali incipit sol converti versus meridiem, cum prius versus septemtrionem tenderet. In tropico autem hyemali e converso. Et etiam circa hoc quod diameter non est commensurabilis lateri quadrati. Cum enim non mensurari videatur esse solius indivisibilis, sicut sola unitas est quae non mensuratur a numero, sed ipsa omnes numeros mensurat, mirum videtur si aliquid quod non est indivisibile non mensuratur; ac per hoc id quod non est minimum non mensuratur. Constat autem, quod diametrum quadrati et latus eius non sunt indivisibilia, sive minima. Unde mirum videtur si non sunt commensurabilia.

67. Cum ergo philosophiae inquisitio ab admiratione incipiat, oportet ad contrarium finire vel proficere; et ad id proficere quod est dignius, ut proverbium vulgare concordat, quo dicitur, quod semper proficere est in melius. Quid enim sit illud contrarium et dignius, patet in praedictis mirabilibus; quia quando iam homines discunt causas praedictorum, non mirantur. Ut geometer non admiratur si diameter sit incommensurabilis lateri. Scit enim causam huius; quia scilicet proportio quadrati diametri ad quadratum lateris non est sicut proportio numeri quadrati ad numerum quadratum, sed sicut proportio duorum ad unum. Unde relinquitur, quod proportio lateris ad diametrum non sit sicut proportio numeri ad numerum. Et ex hoc patet quod commensurari non possunt. Illae enim solae lineae sunt commensurabiles, quarum proportio ad invicem est sicut proportio numeri ad numerum. Erit ergo finis huius scientiae in quem proficere debemus, ut causas cognoscentes, non admiremur de earum effectibus.

68. Patet igitur ex praedictis quae sit natura huius scientiae, quia est speculativa, libera, non humana, sed divina: et quae est eius intentio, qua oportet habere quaestionem et totam methodum et totam hanc artem.

the first philosophers wondered about less important matters and subsequent philosophers about more hidden ones. And the object of their wonder was whether the case was like that of *strange chance occurrences*, that is, things that seem to happen mysteriously by chance.

For things that happen as if by themselves are called chance occurrences. Hence men wonder most of all when things happen by chance in this way, supposing that they were foreseen or determined by some cause. For chance occurrences are not determined by a cause, and wonder results from ignorance of a cause. Therefore, when men were not yet able to recognize the causes of things, they wondered about all things as if they were chance occurrences, just as they wondered *about reversals in the course of the sun*, which are two in number (namely, the solstices of winter and of summer).

For at the summer solstice the sun begins to decline toward the south, after previously declining toward the north. But at the winter solstice the opposite occurs. And they wondered also that the diagonal of a square is not commensurable with a side. For, since to be immeasurable seems to belong to the indivisible alone (just as unity alone is what is not measured by number but itself measures all numbers), it seems to be a matter of wonder that something which is not indivisible is immeasurable, and consequently that what is not a smallest part is immeasurable. Now it is evident that the diagonal of a square and its side are neither indivisible nor smallest parts. Hence it seems a matter of wonder if they are not commensurable.

67. Therefore, since philosophical investigation began with wonder, it must end in or arrive at the contrary of this, and this is to advance to the worthier view, as the common proverb agrees which states that one must always advance to the better. For it is evident in the above wonders what that opposite and worthier view is, because when men have already learned the causes of these things they do not wonder. Thus the geometrician does not wonder if the diagonal is incommensurable with a side. For he knows the reason for this—namely, that the proportion of the square of the diagonal to the square of a side is not as the proportion of the square of a number to the square of a number, but as the proportion of two to one. Hence it follows that the proportion of a side to the diagonal is not as the proportion of number to number. And from this it is evident that they cannot be made commensurable. For only those lines are commensurable which are proportioned to each other as number to number. Hence the goal of this science to which we should advance will be that, in knowing the causes of things, we do not wonder about their effects.

68. From what has been said, then, it is evident what the nature of this science is. It is speculative and free, and it is not a human possession but a divine one. It is also evident what its aim is, for which the whole inquiry, method, and

Intendit enim circa primas et universales rerum causas, de quibus etiam inquirit et determinat. Et propter harum cognitionem ad praedictum terminum pervenit, ut scilicet non admiretur cognitis causis.

art must be conducted. For its goal is the first and universal causes of things, about which it also makes investigations and establishes the truth. And by reason of the knowledge of these it reaches this goal, namely, that there should be no wonder because the causes of things are known.

LECTURE 4

Opinions about the material cause

983a24 Quoniam autem manifestum est, quod earum, quae a principio causarum oportet sumere scientiam; tunc enim scire dicimus unumquodque, quando primam causam cognoscere putamus: causae vero quadrupliciter dicuntur: quarum quidem unam causam dicimus esse substantiam, et quod quid erat esse, reducitur enim ipsum quare primum, ad rationem ultimam, causa autem et principium, ipsum quare primum, unam vero materiam et subiectum; tertiam autem unde principium motus: quartam vero causam ei oppositam, et quod est cuius causa et bonum. Finis igitur generationis et motus omnis hic est; sufficienter quidem igitur de his speculatum est in his, quae de natura. [70]

ἐπεὶ δὲ φανερὸν ὅτι τῶν ἐξ ἀρχῆς αἰτίων δεῖ λαβεῖν {25} ἐπιστήμην (τότε γὰρ εἰδέναι φαμὲν ἕκαστον, ὅταν τὴν πρώτην αἰτίαν οἰώμεθα γνωρίζειν), τὰ δ᾽ αἴτια λέγεται τετραχῶς, ὧν μίαν μὲν αἰτίαν φαμὲν εἶναι τὴν οὐσίαν καὶ τὸ τί ἦν εἶναι (ἀνάγεται γὰρ τὸ διὰ τί εἰς τὸν λόγον ἔσχατον, αἴτιον δὲ καὶ ἀρχὴ τὸ διὰ τί πρῶτον), ἑτέραν δὲ τὴν ὕλην {30} καὶ τὸ ὑποκείμενον, τρίτην δὲ ὅθεν ἡ ἀρχὴ τῆς κινήσεως, τετάρτην δὲ τὴν ἀντικειμένην αἰτίαν ταύτῃ, τὸ οὗ ἕνεκα καὶ τἀγαθόν (τέλος γὰρ γενέσεως καὶ κινήσεως πάσης τοῦτ᾽ ἐστίν), τεθεώρηται μὲν οὖν ἱκανῶς περὶ αὐτῶν ἡμῖν ἐν τοῖς περὶ φύσεως,

It is evident, then, that one must acquire scientific knowledge of those causes which stand at the beginning, for we say that we have scientific knowledge of each thing when we think we comprehend its first cause. Now causes are spoken of in four ways. Of these we say that one is the substance or quiddity[1] of a thing, for the first "why" of a thing is reduced to its ultimate intelligible structure, and the first why of a thing is a cause or principle. Another is the matter or subject. A third is the source of motion. A fourth is the cause which is opposite to this, namely, that for the sake of which, or the good; for this is the goal of every generation and motion. There has been sufficient consideration of these in our works on nature.

983b1 Accipiemus tamen et nobis priores ad entium perscrutationem venientes, et de veritate philosophantes: palam enim, quia dicunt illi principia quaedam et causas. Supervenientibus igitur, erit aliquid prae opere methodo quae nunc. Aut enim aliud aliquod causae genus inveniemus, aut modo dictis magis credemus. [72]

ὅμως δὲ παραλάβωμεν καὶ τοὺς πρότερον ἡμῶν εἰς ἐπίσκεψιν τῶν ὄντων ἐλθόντας καὶ φιλοσοφήσαντας περὶ τῆς ἀληθείας. δῆλον γὰρ ὅτι κἀκεῖνοι λέγουσιν ἀρχάς τινας καὶ αἰτίας: ἐπελθοῦσιν οὖν ἔσται τι προὔργου τῇ μεθόδῳ τῇ νῦν: {5} ἢ γὰρ ἕτερόν τι γένος εὑρήσομεν αἰτίας ἢ ταῖς νῦν λεγομέναις μᾶλλον πιστεύσομεν.

However, let us examine those who have undertaken an investigation of existing things and have philosophized about the truth before us. For evidently they too speak of certain principles and causes. Therefore, to us who come later [their views] will serve as an introduction to the study which we are now making, for we shall either discover some other genus of cause, or be more convinced of those which have just been expounded.

983b6 Primum igitur philosophantium plurimi sola ea, quae in materiae specie, putaverunt omnium esse principia. Nam ex quo sunt omnia entia, et ex quo fiunt primo, et in quod corrumpuntur ultimo, substantia quidem manente, in passionibus vero mutata, hoc elementum et id principium dicunt esse eorum quae sunt. [73]

τῶν δὴ πρώτων φιλοσοφησάντων οἱ πλεῖστοι τὰς ἐν ὕλης εἴδει μόνας ᾠήθησαν ἀρχὰς εἶναι πάντων: ἐξ οὗ γὰρ ἔστιν ἅπαντα τὰ ὄντα καὶ ἐξ οὗ γίγνεται πρώτου καὶ εἰς ὃ φθείρεται τελευταῖον, τῆς μὲν {10} οὐσίας ὑπομενούσης τοῖς δὲ πάθεσι μεταβαλλούσης, τοῦτο στοιχεῖον καὶ ταύτην ἀρχήν φασιν εἶναι τῶν ὄντων,

Most of those who first philosophized thought that only the things that belong to the species of matter are the principles of all things. For that of which all things are composed, from which they first come to be, and into which they are finally dissolved while their substance remains (although it is changed in its attributes)—this they call the element and principle of existing things.

983b11 Et propter hoc nec generari aliquid putant, nec corrumpi, quasi tali natura semper conservata: sicut nec dicimus Socratem generari simpliciter, quando fit bonus aut musicus, nec cor-

καὶ διὰ τοῦτο οὔτε γίγνεσθαι οὐθὲν οἴονται οὔτε ἀπόλλυσθαι, ὡς τῆς τοιαύτης φύσεως ἀεὶ σῳζομένης, ὥσπερ οὐδὲ τὸν Σωκράτην φαμὲν οὔτε γίγνεσθαι ἁπλῶς ὅταν γίγνηται καλὸς ἢ μουσι-

And for this reason they thought that nothing is either generated or corrupted, as if such a reality always remained in existence. And just as we do not say that Socrates comes to be in an unqualified

---

1. Throughout the text, *quod quid erat esse* is translated as "quiddity" or "essence," except where a more literal rendering of the phrase is required.

rumpi, quando deponit habitus istos, propterea quod subiectum maneat Socrates ipse: sic nec aliorum nihil: oportet enim esse aliquam materiam, aut unam, aut plures una, ex quibus fiunt alia, illa conservata. Pluralitatem tamen et speciem talis principii, non eamdem omnes dicunt. [75]

κὸς {15} οὔτε ἀπόλλυσθαι ὅταν ἀποβάλλῃ ταύτας τὰς ἕξεις, διὰ τὸ ὑπομένειν τὸ ὑποκείμενον τὸν Σωκράτην αὐτόν, οὕτως οὐδὲ τῶν ἄλλων οὐδέν: ἀεὶ γὰρ εἶναί τινα φύσιν ἢ μίαν ἢ πλείους μιᾶς ἐξ ὧν γίγνεται τἆλλα σωζομένης ἐκείνης. τὸ μέντοι πλῆθος καὶ τὸ εἶδος τῆς τοιαύτης ἀρχῆς οὐ τὸ αὐτὸ {20} πάντες λέγουσιν,

sense when he becomes good or musical, or is corrupted when he loses these states, because the subject Socrates himself remains, in the same way they say that nothing else is generated or corrupted. For there must be some matter, either one or more than one, from which other things come to be, and which itself remains in existence. However, they do not all speak in the same way about the number and nature of such a principle.

983b20 Thales quidem talis philosophiae princeps, aquam ait esse. Unde et terram esse super aquam asserebat. [77]

ἀλλὰ Θαλῆς μὲν ὁ τῆς τοιαύτης ἀρχηγὸς φιλοσοφίας ὕδωρ φησὶν εἶναι (διὸ καὶ τὴν γῆν ἐφ᾽ ὕδατος ἀπεφήνατο εἶναι),

Thales, the originator of this kind of philosophy, says that this principle is water; this is why he also claimed that the earth rests upon water.

983b22 Forsan enim hanc opinionem accipiens, quia cunctorum nutrimentum humidum videbat esse, et ipsum calidum ex hoc factum, et animal vivere: ex quo fit vero, hoc est principium omnium. Propter hoc igitur eam est accipiens aestimationem. [79]

λαβὼν ἴσως τὴν ὑπόληψιν ταύτην ἐκ τοῦ πάντων ὁρᾶν τὴν τροφὴν ὑγρὰν οὖσαν καὶ αὐτὸ τὸ θερμὸν ἐκ τούτου γιγνόμενον καὶ τούτῳ ζῶν (τὸ δ᾽ ἐξ οὗ γίγνεται, τοῦτ᾽ ἐστὶν {25} ἀρχὴ πάντων)—διά τε δὴ τοῦτο τὴν ὑπόληψιν λαβὼν ταύτην

For presumably he took this position because he saw that the nutriment of all things is moist, that heat itself is generated from this, and that animal life comes from this. But that from which each thing comes to be is a principle of all things. He bases his opinion on this, then,

983b26 Et quia cunctorum spermata naturam haben humidam: aqua vero natura principium est humidis. [80]

καὶ διὰ τὸ πάντων τὰ σπέρματα τὴν φύσιν ὑγρὰν ἔχειν, τὸ δ᾽ ὕδωρ ἀρχὴν τῆς φύσεως εἶναι τοῖς ὑγροῖς.

and on the fact that the seeds of all things have a moist nature, and water is by nature the principle of moist things.

983b27 Sunt autem aliqui antiquiores et multum ante eam, quae nunc est, generationem, et primo theologizantes sic putant de natura existimandum. Oceanum enim et Thetin generationis parentes fecerunt, sacramentumque deorum aquam Stygem ab ipsis poetis vocatam. Honorabilius enim, quod antiquius. Sacramentum autem honorabilius. Si quidem igitur antiquior aliqua ista et senior fuit de natura opinio, forsan utique incertum est. Thales quidem secundum hunc modum pronunciasse dicitur de prima causa. Hypponem quidem enim non utique aliquis significabit posuisse cum his, propter sui intellectus parvitatem. [82]

εἰσὶ δέ τινες οἳ καὶ τοὺς παμπαλαίους καὶ πολὺ πρὸ τῆς νῦν γενέσεως καὶ πρώτους θεολογήσαντας οὕτως οἴονται περὶ τῆς φύσεως {30} ὑπολαβεῖν: Ὠκεανόν τε γὰρ καὶ Τηθὺν ἐποίησαν τῆς γενέσεως πατέρας, καὶ τὸν ὅρκον τῶν θεῶν ὕδωρ, τὴν καλουμένην ὑπ᾽ αὐτῶν Στύγα [τῶν ποιητῶν]: τιμιώτατον μὲν γὰρ τὸ πρεσβύτατον, ὅρκος δὲ τὸ τιμιώτατόν ἐστιν. {984a} εἰ μὲν οὖν ἀρχαία τις αὕτη καὶ παλαιὰ τετύχηκεν οὖσα περὶ τῆς φύσεως {1} ἡ δόξα, τάχ᾽ ἂν ἄδηλον εἴη, Θαλῆς μέντοι λέγεται οὕτως ἀποφήνασθαι περὶ τῆς πρώτης αἰτίας (Ἵππωνα γὰρ οὐκ ἄν τις ἀξιώσειε θεῖναι μετὰ τούτων διὰ τὴν εὐτέλειαν {5} αὐτοῦ τῆς διανοίας):

But there are some who think that the ancients who lived long before the present generation and were the first to speculate about the gods held this view about the nature of things. For they made Oceanus and Tethys the parents of generation, and held the oath of the gods to be by a body of water, to which the poets gave the name Styx. For what is oldest is most honorable, and what is most honorable is that by which one swears. Whether this view of nature is in fact the ancient and primary one is perhaps uncertain. Thales is said to have expressed himself in this way about the first cause, but no one could say that Hippo is to be included in this group, because of the weakness of his understanding.

984a5 Anaximenes autem et Diogenes aurem priorem aqua, et maxime principium simplicium corporum ponunt. [86]

Ἀναξιμένης δὲ ἀέρα καὶ Διογένης πρότερον ὕδατος καὶ μάλιστ᾽ ἀρχὴν τιθέασι τῶν ἁπλῶν σωμάτων,

Anaximenes and Diogenes hold that air is prior to water and is the most fundamental of the simple bodies.

984a7 Hippasus autem Metapontinus, et Heraclitus Ephesius, ignem. [87]

Ἵππασος δὲ πῦρ ὁ Μεταποντῖνος καὶ Ἡράκλειτος ὁ Ἐφέσιος, Ἐμπεδοκλῆς δὲ τὰ τέτταρα,

Hippasus of Metopontium and Heraclitus of Ephesus hold that fire [is the primary principle].

984a8 Empedocles vero quatuor, cum dictis terram quartum addens. Eam namque dixit semper manere et non fieri nisi

πρὸς τοῖς εἰρημένοις γῆν προστιθεὶς τέταρτον (ταῦτα γὰρ ἀεὶ διαμένειν καὶ οὐ {10} γίγνεσθαι ἀλλ᾽ ἢ πλήθει καὶ ὀλι-

Empedocles holds that there are four [simple bodies], since he adds a fourth—earth—to those already mentioned. For

pluralitate et paucitate congregata, et disgregatione in unum et ex uno. [88]

γότητι, συγκρινόμενα καὶ διακρινόμενα εἰς ἕν τε καὶ ἐξ ἑνός):

he says that these always remain and only become many or few in number by being combined into a unity and separated out of a unity.

984a11 Anaxagoras vero Clazomenius, isto quidem aetate prior, factis vero posterior, infinita dixit esse principia. Nam fere omnia corpora partium consimilium, ut ignem aut aquam, ita generari et corrumpi ait congregatione et disgregatione solum: aliter autem nec generari nec corrumpi, sed permanere semper sempiterna. Ex his quidem igitur solam quis causam intelliget eam, quae in materiae specie dicitur. [90]

Ἀναξαγόρας δὲ ὁ Κλαζομένιος τῇ μὲν ἡλικίᾳ πρότερος ὢν τούτου τοῖς δ' ἔργοις ὕστερος ἀπείρους εἶναί φησι τὰς ἀρχάς: σχεδὸν γὰρ ἅπαντα τὰ ὁμοιομερῆ καθάπερ ὕδωρ ἢ πῦρ οὕτω γίγνεσθαι καὶ {15} ἀπόλλυσθαί φησι, συγκρίσει καὶ διακρίσει μόνον, ἄλλως δ' οὔτε γίγνεσθαι οὔτ' ἀπόλλυσθαι ἀλλὰ διαμένειν ἀίδια. ἐκ μὲν οὖν τούτων μόνην τις αἰτίαν νομίσειεν ἂν τὴν ἐν ὕλης εἴδει λεγομένην:

Anaxagoras of Clazomenae, who was prior to Empedocles in years but later in his speculations, says that the principles of things are infinite in number. For he says that nearly all bodies which are made up of parts like themselves, such as fire or water, are generated or corrupted merely by combining and separating; but that otherwise they are neither generated nor corrupted but always remain in existence. From these views, then, one might think that the only cause is the one which is said to belong to the species of matter.

---

69. Posito prooemio, in quo ostendit intentionem huius scientiae et dignitatem et terminum, incipit prosequi scientiam praefatam: et dividitur in duas partes.

Primo ostendit quid priores philosophi de causis rerum tradiderunt.

Secundo veritatem huius scientiae incipit prosequi in secundo libro, ibi, *de veritate quidem theoria* et cetera.

Prima autem pars dividitur in duas.

Primo ponit opiniones philosophorum de causis rerum.

Secundo improbat eas quantum ad hoc quod male dixerunt ibi, *ergo quicumque* et cetera.

Circa primum duo facit.

Primo resumit enumerationem causarum, quam in secundo *Physicorum* diffusius fuerat prosecutus.

Secundo prosequitur opinionem philosophorum, ibi, *accipiemus tamen* et cetera.

70. Dicit ergo, quod quia hoc manifestum est, scilicet quod sapientia est causarum speculatrix, debemus incipere a causis rerum scientiam sumendo. Quod etiam ex ratione scientiae congruum videtur; quia tunc unumquodque scire dicimus aliquem, quando putamus non ignorare causam.

Causae autem quadrupliciter dicuntur: quarum una est ipsa causa formalis, quae est ipsa substantia rei, per quam scitur quid est unaquaeque res. Constat enim, ut dictum est secundo *Physicorum*, quod non dicimus aliquid esse alicuius naturae priusquam acceperit formam. Et quod forma sit causa, patet; quia quaestionem qua dicitur quare est aliquid, reducimus tamquam ad rationem ultimam ad causam formalem, incipiendo a formis proximis et procedendo usque ad ultimam. Patet autem, quod quare quaerit de causa et principio. Unde patet quod forma est causa. Alia vero causa est materialis.

69. Having set forth a preface in which he indicates the aim of this science, its dignity and goal, Aristotle begins to deal with this science; and this is divided into two parts.

In the first [70], he explains what the first philosophers had to say about the causes of things.

In the second [274], he begins to pursue the truth of this science. He does this in book 2, at *theoretical or speculative knowledge* (993a30).

The first part is divided into two members.

First, he gives the opinions of the philosophers about the causes of things.

Second [181], he criticizes them insofar as their statements are unsatisfactory, at *therefore, all those* (988b22).

In regard to the first he does two things.

First, he takes up again the enumeration of causes which was treated in greater detail in *Physics* 2.

Second [72], he presents the opinions of the philosophers, at *however, let us examine* (983b1).

70. Accordingly, he first says that, since it is evident that wisdom speculates about causes, we ought to begin by acquiring knowledge from the causes of things. This also seems to be in keeping with the intelligible structure of science, because we say that we know each thing scientifically when we think we are not ignorant of its cause.

Now causes are spoken of in four ways. One of these is the formal cause, which is the very substance of a thing by which we know what each thing is. For it is well known, as is stated in *Physics* 2, that we do not say that anything has a nature before it has received a form. Now it is clear that a form is a cause, because to answer the question "Why is something so?" we go back to its formal cause as its ultimate explanation, beginning with proximate forms and proceeding to the ultimate form. But evidently the "why" asks about a cause and principle. Hence it is evident that a form is a cause. A second cause is the material cause. A

Tertia vero causa est efficiens, quae est unde principium motus. Quarta causa est finalis, quae opponitur causae efficienti secundum oppositionem principii et finis. Nam motus incipit a causa efficiente, et terminatur ad causam finalem. Et hoc est etiam cuius causa fit aliquid, et quae est bonum uniuscuiusque naturae.

71. Sic igitur causam finalem per tria notificat; scilicet quia est terminus motus, et per hoc opponitur principio motus, quod est causa efficiens: et quia est primum in intentione, ratione cuius dicitur cuius causa: et quia est per se appetibile, ratione cuius dicitur bonum. Nam bonum est quod omnia appetunt.

Unde exponens quo modo causa finalis efficienti opponatur, dicit quod est finis generationis et motus, quorum principium est causa efficiens. Per quae duo videtur duplicem finem insinuare. Nam finis generationis est forma ipsa, quae est pars rei. Finis autem motus est aliquid quaesitum extra rem quae movetur. De his dicit sufficienter se tractasse in libro *Physicorum*, ne ab eo ad praesens diffusior expositio causarum quaereretur.

72. Deinde cum dicit *accipiemus tamen* hic ponit opinionem philosophorum de causis. Et circa hoc duo facit.

Primo assignat rationem, quare hoc faciendum sit.

Secundo incipit prosequi suam intentionem, ibi, *primum igitur* et cetera.

Dicit ergo, quod quamvis de causis tractatum sit in *Physicis*, tamen nunc accipiendum est opiniones philosophorum, qui prius venerunt ad perscrutandum naturam entium, qui prius philosophati sunt de veritate quam Aristoteles; quia et ipsi causas et principium ponunt. Nobis igitur, qui eis supervenimus, considerare eorum opiniones, erit aliquid *prius*, idest aliquod praeambulum, *methodo*, idest in arte, quae nunc a nobis quaeritur.

Unde et litera Boetii habet, *accedentibus igitur ad opus scientiae prae opere viae quae nunc est aliquid erit*: alia litera habet, *supervenientibus igitur quae nunc est aliquid erit vitae opus via*, et legenda est sic, *nobis igitur supervenientibus ei, quae nunc est via*, idest in praesenti methodo et arte, consideranda erit horum opinio, *quasi aliquod vitae opus*, idest necessarium sicut opera quae sunt ad vitae conservationem, ut intelligatur quasi quadam metaphora uti in loquendo, per *vitae opus*, quodlibet necessarium accipiens.

Utilitas autem est illa, quia aut ex praedictis eorum inveniemus aliud genus a causis praenumeratis, aut ma-

third is the efficient cause, which is the source of motion. A fourth is the final cause, which is opposite to the efficient cause as a goal is to a starting-point, for motion begins with the efficient cause and terminates with the final cause. This cause is also that for the sake of which a thing comes to be, and the good of each nature.

71. He makes the final cause known by three considerations. It is the goal of motion, and thus is opposite to the source of motion, which is the efficient cause. It is first in intention, and for this reason is said to be that for the sake of which. And it is desirable of itself, and for this reason is called a good, for the good is what all desire.

Hence, in explaining how the final cause is opposite to the efficient cause, he says that it is the end of every process of generation and motion, whose starting point is the efficient cause. By these two types of change he seems to imply that there is a twofold goal. For the goal of a process of generation is the form itself, which is a part of a thing. But the goal of motion is something sought for outside the thing moved. He says that he has treated these causes at sufficient length in the *Physics*, lest he should be asked to make a more extensive treatment of them.

72. *However, let us examine* (983b1). Here he states what the philosophers had to say about the causes; and in regard to this he does two things.

First, he gives the reasons why this must be done;

and, second (983b6; [73]), he begins to carry out his plan, at *most of those*.

Accordingly, he says that even though there is a treatise on the causes in the *Physics* it is still necessary to consider the opinions of the philosophers who first undertook an investigation of the natures of existing things, and have philosophized about the truth before him; because they too set down causes and principles. Therefore, for us who have come later, a consideration of their opinions will be *first*, or a preamble, *in the study*, that is, to the art which we are now seeking.

Hence the text of Boethius also says: *therefore, as we enter upon the task of this science, their opinions will constitute a preamble to the road that is now to be traveled.* Another text has: *therefore, as we enter upon our present course it will be a certain work of life in the investigation that now confronts us*, and it must be read in this way: *therefore, as we enter upon our present course*, that is, upon the present study and art, it will be necessary to consider the opinion of these men *as a work of life*, that is to say, as necessary, like works which are done for the preservation of life, so that this reading is interpreted as a metaphorical way of speaking, meaning by *work of life* anything necessary.

Now this is useful, because from the opinions of these men we will either discover another genus of causes over

gis credemus his, quae modo diximus de causis, quod, scilicet sint quatuor.

73. Deinde cum dicit *primum igitur* hic incipit antiquorum philosophorum opiniones prosequi; et circa hoc duo facit.

Primo recitat aliorum opiniones.

Secundo reprobat, ibi, *ergo quicumque*.

Circa primum duo facit.

Primo recitat singulorum opinionem de causis.

Secundo colligit in summa quae dicta sunt, ibi, *breviter igitur* et cetera.

Prima pars dividitur in duas.

Prima ponit opiniones praetermittentium causam formalem.

Secundo ponit opinionem Platonis, qui primo causam formalem posuit, ibi, *post dictas vero philosophias* et cetera.

Circa primum duo facit.

Primo ponit opinionem illorum, qui posuerunt principia aliquas res manifestas.

Secundo illorum, qui adinvenerunt extrinseca principia, ibi, *Leucippus* et cetera.

Circa primum duo facit.

Primo tangit opiniones antiquorum de causa materiali.

Secundo de causa efficiente, ibi, *procedentibus autem sic*.

Circa primum duo facit.

Primo ponit quid senserunt de causa materiali. Et primo ponit opiniones ponentium causam materialem in generali.

Secundo prosequitur eorum opiniones in speciali, ibi, *Thales* et cetera.

Circa primum duo facit.

Primo ponit quid senserunt de causa materiali.

Secundo quid senserunt de rerum generatione, quod ex primo sequebatur, ibi, *et propter hoc nec generari* et cetera.

74. Dicit ergo primo, quod plurimi eorum qui primo philosophati sunt de rerum naturis, posuerunt principia omnium esse sola illa, quae reducuntur ad speciem causae materialis. Et ad hoc dicendum accipiebant quatuor conditiones materiae, quae ad rationem principii pertinere videntur.

Nam id ex quo res est, principium rei esse videtur: huiusmodi autem est materia; nam ex materia dicimus materiatum esse, ut ex ferro cultellum.

and above those already enumerated, or be more convinced of the things that have just been stated about the causes, namely, that there are four of them.

73. *Most of those* (983b6). Here he begins to deal with the opinions of the ancient philosophers; and in regard to this he does two things.

First (983b6), he states their opinions;

second (988b22; [181]), he finds fault with them, at *therefore, all those*.

In regard to the first he does two things.

First, he states the opinions which each one of the philosophers held about the causes.

Second (988a18; [171]), he summarizes the discussion, at *we have examined*.

The first part is divided into two parts.

In the first (983b6; [74]), he gives the opinions of those who omitted the formal cause.

In the second (987a29; [151]), he gives the opinion of Plato, who was the first to posit a formal cause, at *after the philosophies*.

In regard to the first he does two things.

First, he gives the opinion of those who claimed that certain evident things are principles.

Second (985b4; [112]), he gives the opinions of those who devised extrinsic principles, at *Leucippus and his colleague*.

In regard to the first he does two things.

First, he touches on the opinions which the ancient philosophers held about the material cause;

second (984a18; [93]), on their opinions about the efficient cause, at *but as men*.

In regard to the first he does two things.

First, he states in a general way the views of those who posited a material cause.

Second (983b20; [77]), he examines their views in detail, at *Thales, the originator*.

In regard to the first he does two things.

First, he states their opinions about the material cause.

Second (983b11; [75]), he states their opinions about the generation of things, which follow from the first, at *and for this reason*.

74. Accordingly, he says first (983b6) that most of those who first philosophized about the natural world held that the principles of all things are merely those which are referred to the species of material cause. In regard to this, it must be said that they took the four conditions of matter which seem to belong to the notion of a principle.

For that of which a thing is composed seems to be a principle of that thing. But matter is such a thing, for we say that a thing that has matter is "of" its matter, as a knife is of iron.

Item illud ex quo fit aliquid, cum sit et principium generationis rei, videtur esse causa rei, quia res per generationem procedit in esse. Ex materia autem primo res fit, quia materia rerum factioni praeexistit. Et ex ipsa etiam non per accidens aliquid fit. Nam ex contrario vel privatione aliquid per accidens dicitur fieri, sicut dicimus quod ex nigro sit album.

Tertio illud videtur esse rerum principium, in quod finaliter omnia per corruptionem resolvuntur. Nam sicut principia sunt prima in generatione, ita sunt ultima in resolutione. Et hoc etiam materiae manifeste contingit.

Quarto, cum principia oportet manere, id videtur esse principium, quod in generatione et corruptione manet. Materia autem, quam dicebant esse substantiam rei, manet in omni transmutatione; sed passiones mutantur, ut forma, et omnia quae adveniunt supra substantiam materiae. Et ex his omnibus concludebant, quod materia est elementum et principium omnium eorum quae sunt.

75. Deinde cum dicit *et propter* hic ponit secundarium quod ponebant quasi ex praecedentibus sequens, scilicet nihil simpliciter generari vel corrumpi in entibus.

Nam quando fit aliqua mutatio circa passiones substantia manente, non dicimus aliquid esse generatum vel corruptum simpliciter, sed solum secundum quid: sicut cum Socrates fit bonus aut musicus, non dicitur fieri simpliciter, sed fieri hoc. Et similiter quando deponit huiusmodi habitum, non dicitur corrumpi simpliciter sed secundum quid. Materia autem quae est rerum substantia secundum eos, semper manet. Omnis autem mutatio fit circa aliqua quae adveniunt ei, ut passiones.

Et ex hoc concludebant quod nihil generatur vel corrumpitur simpliciter, sed solum secundum quid.

76. Quamvis autem sic convenirent in ponendo causam materialem, tamen differebant in eius positione quantum ad duo: scilicet quantum ad pluralitatem: quia quidam ponebant unam, quidam plures: et quantum ad speciem, quia quidam ponebant ignem, quidam aquam et cetera. Similiter ponentium plura, quidam haec, quidam illa principia materialia rebus attribuebant.

77. Deinde cum dicit *Thales quidem*. Hic incipit recitare opiniones singulorum, de causa materiali.

That from which a thing comes to be (which is also a principle of the process of generation of that thing) seems to be one of its causes, because a thing comes into being by way of generation. But a thing first comes to be from matter, because the matter of things precedes their production. And a thing does not come from matter in an accidental way, for a thing is generated in an accidental way from its contrary or privation, as when we say that white comes from black.

Third, that into which all things are ultimately dissolved by corruption seems to be a principle of things. For just as principles are first in the process of generation, in a similar way they are last in the process of dissolution. Obviously this too pertains to matter.

Fourth, since a principle must remain in existence, then that which remains throughout the process of generation and corruption seems to be a principle. Now the matter which they said is the substance of a thing remains throughout every transmutation, although its attributes, such as its form and everything that accrues to it over and above its material substance, are changed. From all these considerations they concluded that matter is the element and principle of all beings.

75. *And for this reason* (983b11). Then he gives, as a secondary point, what they held as following from the above—namely, that in the world nothing is generated or corrupted in an absolute sense.

For when some change occurs with regard to a thing's attributes, and its substance remains unchanged, we do not say that it is generated or corrupted in an absolute sense, but only in a qualified one. For example, when Socrates becomes good or musical, we do not say that he simply comes to be, but comes to be this. And similarly when he loses a state of this kind, we do not say that he is corrupted in an absolute sense, but only in a qualified one. But matter (which is the substance of things according to them) always remains, and every change affects some of a thing's accidents, such as its attributes.

From this they concluded that nothing is generated or corrupted in an absolute sense, but only in a qualified one.

76. Yet even though they all agreed in positing a material cause, nevertheless they differed in their position in two respects: first, with respect to the number of material causes, because some held that there is one, and others many; second, with respect to its nature, because some held that it is fire, others water, and so on. Similarly, among those who posited many material causes, some assigned certain ones as the material principles of things, and some the others.

77. *Thales, the originator* (983b20). Here he begins to give the opinions of each of the philosophers about the material cause.

Et primo ponit opinionem ponentium unam causam materialem.

Secundo ponentium plures, ibi, *Empedocles vero*.

Circa primum tria facit.

Quia primo ponit opinionem ponentium aquam esse principium omnium.

Secundo ponentium aerem, ibi, *Anaximenes* et cetera.

Tertio ponentium ignem, ibi, *Hyppasus* et cetera.

Circa primum duo facit.

Primo ponit opinionem Thaletis, qui dicebat aquam esse rerum principium.

Secundo ponit opinionis probationem, ibi, *forsan enim* et cetera.

Dicit ergo, quod Thales princeps *talis philosophiae*, idest speculativae, dixit aquam esse primum rerum principium. Dicitur autem Thales speculativae philosophiae princeps fuisse, quia inter septem sapientes, qui post theologos poetae fuerunt, ipse solus ad considerandum rerum causas se transtulit, aliis sapientibus circa moralia occupatis.

Nomina septem sapientum sunt ista. Primus Thales Milesius tempore Romuli, et apud Hebraeos tempore Achaz regis Israel. Secundus fuit Pittacus Mitylenaeus, apud Hebraeos regnante Sedechia, et apud Romanos Tarquinio Prisco. Alii quinque fuerunt Solon Atheniensis, Chilon Lacedaemonius, Periander Corinthius, Cleobulus Lydius, Bias Priennensis, qui fuerunt omnes tempore Babylonicae captivitatis.

Quia igitur inter hos solus Thales rerum naturas scrutatus est, suasque disputationes literis mandans emicuit, ideo hic princeps huius scientiae dicitur.

78. Nec debet inconveniens videri, si opiniones hic tangit eorum, qui solum de scientia naturali tractaverunt; quia secundum antiquos qui nullam substantiam cognoverunt nisi corpoream et mobilem, oportebat quod prima philosophia esset scientia naturalis, ut in quarto dicetur. Ex hac autem positione ulterius procedebat ad hoc, quod terra esset super aquam fundata, sicut principiatum supra suum principium.

79. Deinde cum dicit *forsan enim* hic ponit rationes quibus Thales potuit induci ad praedictam positionem.

Et primo ostendit quomodo ad hoc inducebatur ratione.

Secundo quomodo inducebatur primorum auctoritate, ibi, *sunt et aliqui antiquiores* et cetera.

Inducebatur autem duplici ratione.

First, he gives the opinions of those who posited one material cause;

second [88], the opinions of those who posited many, at *Empedocles* (984a8).

In regard to the first he does three things.

First, he gives the opinions of those who claimed that water is the principle of all things;

second [86], he gives the opinion of those who made air the principle of things, at *Anaximenes* (984a5);

and third [87], the opinion of those who claimed that fire is the principle of things, at *Hippasus* (984a7).

In regard to the first he does two things.

First, he gives the opinion of Thales, who said that water is the principle of things;

second [79], the reason for this opinion (*for presumably*).

He says then that Thales, the originator *of this kind of philosophy*, speculative philosophy, said that water is the first principle of all things. Thales is said to have been the originator of speculative philosophy because he was the only one of the seven wise men who came after the theological poets to make an investigation into the causes of things, the other sages being concerned with moral matters.

The names of the seven wise men are as follows. The first was Thales of Miletus, who lived during the time of Romulus and when Achaz, King of Israel, was reigning over the Hebrews. The second was Pittacus of Mitylene, who lived when Sedecias was reigning over the Hebrews and when Tarquinius Priscus was reigning over the Romans. The other five sages were Solon of Athens, Chilo of Lacedaemon, Periander of Corinth, Cleobulus of Lydia, and Bias of Prienne, all of whom lived during the period of the Babylonian captivity.

Hence, since Thales alone among these men investigated the natures of things and distinguished himself by committing his arguments to writing, he is described here as the originator of this science.

78. Nor should it be thought unfitting if he touches here on the opinions of those who have treated only the philosophy of nature, because, according to the ancients, who knew no other substance except the bodily and mobile, it was necessary that first philosophy be the philosophy of nature, as is stated in book 4. And from this position Thales next adopted this one, that the earth rests upon water, as anything having a principle is based on its principle.

79. *For presumably he took* (983b22). Here he gives the reasons by which Thales could be led to the above position.

First, he shows how he was led to this position by his own reasoning;

and second [82], by the authority of his predecessors, at *but there are some* (983b27).

Now he was led by two lines of reasoning.

Una quae sumitur ex consideratione causae ipsius rei.

Alia quae sumitur ex consideratione generationis rerum, ibi, *et quia cunctorum* et cetera.

Haec ergo media sunt ordinata. Nam ex primo sequitur secundum. Quod enim est aliis principium essendi, est etiam primum principium ex quo res generantur. Tertium sequitur ex secundo. Nam unumquodque per corruptionem resolvitur in id ex quo generatum est. Quartum autem sequitur ex secundo et tertio. Nam quod praecedit generationem rerum, et remanet post corruptionem, oportet esse semper manens.

80. Primo modo utebatur tribus signis ad ostendendum aquam esse principium essendi rebus:

quorum primum est, quia nutrimentum viventium oportet esse humidum. Ex eodem autem viventia nutriuntur et sunt; et sic humor videtur esse principium essendi.

Secundum signum est, quia esse cuiuslibet rei corporeae, et maxime viventis, per proprium et naturalem calorem conservatur: calor autem ex humore fieri videtur, cum ipse humor sit quasi caloris materia: unde ex hoc videtur quod humor sit rebus principium essendi.

Tertium signum est, quia vita animalis in humido consistit. Unde propter desiccationem naturalis humidi, animal moritur, et per eius conservationem, animal sustentatur. Vivere autem viventibus est esse. Unde ex hoc etiam patet quod humor sit rebus principium essendi.

Et haec etiam tria signa seinvicem consequuntur. Ideo enim animal humido nutritur, quia calor naturalis humido sustentatur; et ex his duobus sequitur, quod vivere animalis sit semper per humidum. Id autem ex quo aliquid fit, idest ex quo aliquid esse consequitur, est principium omnibus quae ex illo esse habent. Et propter hoc accepit hanc opinionem quod humor esset omnibus principium.

81. Similiter etiam accepit signum ex rerum generatione, quia generationes viventium, quae sunt nobilissima in entibus, fiunt ex seminibus. Semina autem sive spermata omnium viventium habent humidam naturam. Unde ex hoc etiam apparet, quod humor est generationis rerum principium. Si autem omnibus praedictis coniungatur quod aqua est humiditatis principium, sequitur quod aqua sit primum rerum principium.

82. Deinde cum dicit *sunt autem* hic ostendit quomodo Thales inducebatur ad praedictam positionem per auctoritates antiquorum. Et dicit quod aliqui fuerunt antiquiores Thalete et multum ante generationem hominum qui erant tempore Aristotelis, qui fuerunt primo

One is taken from the cause itself of a thing.

The other is taken from a consideration of the generation of things, at *and on the fact* (983b22).

Therefore, these premises are related. For the second follows from the first, because that which is a principle of being of other things is also the first principle from which things are generated. The third follows from the second, because by corruption each thing is dissolved into that from which it was generated. The fourth follows from the second and the third; for that which precedes the generation of things and remains after they have been corrupted must always remain in being.

80. In the first line of reasoning he uses three indications to show that water is the principle of being of things.

The first of these is that the nutriment of living things must be moist. But living things derive nourishment and being from the same principle; thus moisture appears to be the principle of being of things.

The second indication is that the being of any physical thing, and especially of a living one, is conserved by its proper and natural heat. But heat seems to be generated from moisture, since moisture itself is in a sense the matter of heat. Hence from this it appears that moisture is a principle of being of things.

The third indication is that animal life depends on moisture. Hence an animal dies as a result of its natural moisture being dried up, and is kept in existence as a result of its moisture being preserved. But in living things, to live is to be. Hence it is also evident from this that moisture is a principle of being of things.

These three indications also have a natural connection with one another. For an animal is nourished by moisture, because its natural heat is sustained by moisture. And from these two it follows that animal life is always due to moisture. But that from which a thing comes to be (that is, from which a thing gets its being) is a principle of everything that derives being from it. And for this reason he adopted this opinion that moisture is the principle of all things.

81. In a similar way, he also draws an indication of this from the generation of things, because the processes of generation of living things, which are the noblest of beings, come from seed. But the seed or spermata of all living things has a moist nature. Hence from this it also appears that moisture is a principle of generation of things. Again, if we add to all of the above points the fact that water is the principle of moisture, it follows that water is the first principle of things.

82. *But there are some* (983b27). Here he shows how Thales was led to the above position by the authority of the ancients. He says that prior to Thales and many years before the men of Aristotle's time there were some men, the first to speculate about the gods, who seem to have held this

theologizantes, qui visi sunt hanc opinionem de natura habuisse, scilicet quod aqua est principium omnium.

83. Ad cuius evidentiam sciendum est, quod apud Graecos primi famosi in scientia fuerunt quidam poetae theologi, sic dicti, quia de divinis carmina faciebant. Fuerunt autem tres, Orpheus, Museus et Linus, quorum Orpheus famosior fuit. Fuerunt autem tempore, quo iudices erant in populo Iudaeorum. Unde patet, quod diu fuerunt ante Thaletem, et multo magis ante Aristotelem qui fuit tempore Alexandri. Isti autem poetae quibusdam aenigmatibus fabularum aliquid de rerum natura tractaverunt. Dixerunt enim quod Oceanus, ubi est maxima aquarum aggregatio, et Thetis, quae dicitur dea aquarum, sunt parentes generationis: ex hoc sub fabulari similitudine dantes intelligere aquam esse generationis principium.

84. Hanc sententiam alia fabulosa narratione velaverunt, dicentes, quod sacramentum vel iuramentum deorum erat per aquam quamdam, quam poetae dicunt Stygem, et dicunt eam esse paludem infernalem. Ex hoc autem quod deos dicebant iurare per aquam, dederunt intelligere, quod aqua erat nobilior ipsis deis, quia sacramentum vel iuramentum fit id quod est honorabilius. Hos autem quod est prius, est honorabilius. Perfectum enim praecedit imperfectum natura et tempore simpliciter, licet in uno aliquo imperfectio perfectionem praecedat tempore. Unde per hoc patet quod aquam existimabant priorem esse ipsis diis, quos intelligebant esse corpora caelestia. Et quia isti antiquissimi aquam dixerunt esse rerum principium, si aliqua opinio fuit prior ista de naturalibus, non est nobis manifesta. Sic igitur patet quid Thales de prima causa rerum dicitur existimasse.

85. Quidam autem philosophus, qui vocatur Hyppon, non fuit dignatus aliquid superaddere his propter suae scientiae vel intelligentiae imperfectionem. Unde in libro *De anima* ponitur inter grossiores, ubi dicitur quod posuit aquam esse animam et principium rerum, sumens argumentum ex rerum seminibus, ut hic dictum est de Thalete. Unde patet quod nihil addit supra Thaletis sententiam. Vel potest intelligi quod quia imperfecte dixit, non reddidit se dignum, ut eius sententia hic contineretur cum aliis.

86. Deinde cum dicit *Anaximenes autem* hic ponuntur opiniones ponentium aerem esse principium, qui fuerunt Diogenes et Anaximenes ponentes aerem priorem aqua esse naturaliter, et principium omnium simplicium corporum, scilicet quatuor elementorum, et per consequens omnium aliorum. Fuit autem Anaximenes tertius a Thalete. Fuit autem discipulus Anaximandri,

opinion about nature, namely, that water is the principle of all things.

83. With a view to making this clear, we must bear in mind that among the Greeks the first who were famous for their learning were certain theological poets, so called because of the songs that they wrote about the gods. These poets, who were three in number—Orpheus, Museus, and Linus (of whom Orpheus was the more famous)—lived during the time when the judges ruled over the Jewish people. Hence it is clear that they lived long before Thales and much longer before Aristotle, who lived during the time of Alexander. These poets dealt to some extent with the nature of things by means of certain figurative representations in myths. For they said that Oceanus, where the greatest aggregation of waters is found, and Tethys, which is the name they gave to the goddess of the waters, are the parents of generation, implying under the form of a myth that water is the principle of generation.

84. They cloaked this view in another fabulous story, saying that the oath or vow of the gods was by a certain body of water, which the poets call Styx and describe as an underground swamp. And when they said that the gods swore by water, they implied that water was nobler than the gods themselves, because an oath or vow is taken on what is most honorable. Now that which is prior is more honorable, for the perfect is prior absolutely to the imperfect, both in nature and in time, although in a particular being imperfection is prior temporally to perfection. Hence, from this it is evident that they thought that water is prior to the gods themselves, whom they thought to be celestial bodies. And since these earliest thinkers said that water is the principle of things, if there was any opinion about natural bodies prior to theirs, we do not know what it was. Thus, what Thales is said to have thought about the first cause of things is now clear.

85. A certain philosopher named Hippo was not credited with adding anything to those mentioned because of the imperfection of his knowledge or understanding. Hence, in *On the Soul*, Hippo is placed among the ruder thinkers; for in that work it is stated that Hippo, basing his argument on the seeds of things (as was said here of Thales), held water to be the soul and principle of things. Hence it is clear that he adds nothing to Thales' view. Or the statement can mean that, since he spoke imperfectly, he did not make himself worthy to have his doctrine included here with the others.

86. *Anaximenes and Diogenes* (984a5). Here he gives the opinions of those who held that air is the principle of things. These were Diogenes and Anaximenes, who held that air is naturally prior to water and is the principle of all simple bodies, that is, of the four elements, and thus of all other things. Anaximenes is the third philosopher after Thales and the disciple of Anaximander, who was the

qui fuit discipulus Thaletis. Diogenes vero discipulus Anaximenis fuisse dicitur. Haec tamen differentia fuit inter opinionem Diogenis et Anaximenis: quia Anaximenes aerem simpliciter posuit principium rerum, Diogenes autem dixit quod aer rerum principium esse non posset, nisi quia compos erat divinae rationis. Ex quo provenit opinio quae tangitur primo *De anima*. Ratio autem quare aerem ponebat rerum principium, potuit sumi ex respiratione, per quam vita animalium reservatur; et quia ex immutatione aeris videntur variari generationes et corruptiones rerum.

87. Deinde cum dicit *Hyppasus autem* hic ponit quod duo philosophi Hyppasus et Heraclitus posuerunt ignem esse primum principium ut materiam. Et potuerunt moveri ex eius subtilitate, sicut infra dicetur.

88. Deinde cum dicit *Empedocles vero* hic ponit opiniones ponentium plura principia materialia.

Et primo Empedoclis, qui posuit plura finita.

Secundo Anaxagorae, qui posuit plura infinita, ibi, *Anaxagoras vero* et cetera.

Ponit ergo primo, opinionem Empedoclis quantum ad hoc quod tria praedicta elementa, scilicet aquam, aerem et ignem dicit esse rerum principia, addens eis quartum, scilicet terram.

89. Secundo quantum ad hoc, quod ista etiam elementa dixit semper manere et non generari nec corrumpi, sicut illi qui posuerunt unam causam materialem; sed per congregationem horum et divisionem secundum multitudinem et paucitatem dixit ex eis alia generari et corrumpi, inquantum ista quatuor per concretionem in unum et disgregationem ex uno dividuntur.

90. Deinde cum dicit *Anaxagoras vero* hic ponit opinionem Anaxagorae, qui fuit alter discipulus Anaximenis, qui fuit condiscipulus Diogenis: patria quidem Clazomenius, prior aetate quam Empedocles, sed factis sive operibus posterior, vel quia posterius philosophari incoepit, quia in numero principiorum minus bene dixit quam Empedocles. Dixit enim principia materialia esse infinita, cum sit dignius finita principia et pauciora accipere, quod fecit Empedocles, ut dicitur in primo *Physicorum*.

Non enim solum dixit principia rerum esse ignem et aquam et alia elementa, sicut Empedocles; sed omnia quae sunt consimilium partium, ut caro, os, medulla et similia, quorum infinitas minimas partes principia rerum posuit, ponens in unoquoque infinitas partes singulorum inesse propter id quod in inferioribus unum ex alio generari posse invenit, cum generationem rerum

disciple of Thales; Diogenes is said to have been the disciple of Anaximenes. Yet there is this difference between the opinion of Diogenes and that of Anaximenes: Anaximenes held that air is the principle of things in an absolute sense, whereas Diogenes said that air could be the principle of things only if it possessed a divine nature. From this comes the opinion which is touched on in *On the Soul* 1. Now the reason why he held that air is the principle of things could be taken from the process of respiration, by which the life of animals is conserved, and because the processes whereby things are generated and corrupted seem to be modified as a result of changes in the air.

87. *Hippasus of Metopontium* (984a7). Here he states that two philosophers, Hippasus and Heraclitus, held that fire is the material principle of things. And they could have been influenced by its subtleness, as is said below.

88. *Empedocles* (984a8). Here he gives the opinions of those who posited many material principles.

First, he gives the opinion of Empedocles, who held that there are a limited number of such principles;

second [90], that of Anaxagoras, who held that there are an infinite number, at *Anaxagoras* (984a11).

First (984a8), he gives Empedocles' opinion regarding the three elements mentioned above (water, air, and fire), which he says are the principles of things, adding to them a fourth, earth.

89. Second, he gives Empedocles' opinion about the permanence of these elements; like those who hold that there is one material cause, he holds that these elements always remain and are neither generated nor corrupted. However, he said that other things are generated from and divided into these elements according as a greater or smaller number of them are combined or separated out (that is, inasmuch as these four are united by the process of combination and lose their unity by the process of separation).

90. *Anaxagoras* (984a11). Here he gives the opinion of Anaxagoras, who was the other disciple of Anaximenes and the classmate of Diogenes. A native of Clazomenae, he was prior to Empedocles in years but later in his activity or work, either because he began to philosophize later, or because his explanation of the number of principles is less satisfactory than that of Empedocles. For he said that there are an infinite number of material principles, whereas it is better to take a limited and smaller number, as Empedocles did, as is stated in *Physics* 1.

For Anaxagoras not only said that fire, water, and the other elements are the principles of things, as Empedocles did, but also claimed that all things having like parts, such as flesh, bones, marrow and so forth, whose smallest parts are infinite in number, are the principles of things. For he claimed that in each being there are an infinite number of parts of each type of thing, because he found that in the

non diceret esse nisi per separationem a mixto, ut planius explicavit primo *Physicorum*.

91. Secundo etiam Anaxagoras convenit cum Empedocle in hoc, scilicet quod generatio et corruptio rerum non est nisi per concretionem et discretionem partium praedictarum infinitarum, et quod aliter nec generari nec corrumpi contingit aliquid. Sed huiusmodi rerum principia infinita, ex quibus rerum substantiae efficiuntur, permanere dixit sempiterna.

92. Concludit ergo Aristoteles quod ex praedictis philosophorum opinionibus aliquis cognoscet solam causam, quae continetur sub specie causae materialis.

case of inferior things one of these can be generated from another. He said, in fact, that things could be generated only by being separated out from a mixture, as Aristotle has explained more fully in *Physics* 1.

91. Second, Anaxagoras also agrees with Empedocles on this point: things are generated and corrupted only insofar as the parts of these infinite principles are combined or separated out, and that if this were not the case nothing would be generated or corrupted. But he said that the infinite number of principles of this kind, from which the substances of things are produced, always remain in being.

92. From the opinions of these philosophers, then, Aristotle concludes that the only cause which these men recognized was the one which belongs to the species of material cause.

LECTURE 5

Opinions about the efficient cause

984a18 Procedentibus autem sic, res ipsa viam fecit similiter et quaerere coegit. Si enim quam maxime omnis generatio et corruptio ex aliquo uno aut pluribus est, qualiter hoc accidit et quae causa? Non enim utique facit ipsum subiectum transmutare seipsum. Dico autem veluti neque lignum, neque aes, alterutrum ipsorum permutandi est causa: neque lignum facit lectum, neque aes statuam, sed aliquid aliud permutationis est causa. Hoc autem quaerere, est aliud principium quaerere, ut si dicatur unde principium motus. [93]

προϊόντων δ᾽ οὕτως, αὐτὸ τὸ πρᾶγμα ὡδοποίησεν αὐτοῖς καὶ συνηνάγκασε ζητεῖν· εἰ γὰρ ὅτι μάλιστα {20} πᾶσα γένεσις καὶ φθορὰ ἔκ τινος ἑνὸς ἢ καὶ πλειόνων ἐστίν, διὰ τί τοῦτο συμβαίνει καὶ τί τὸ αἴτιον; οὐ γὰρ δὴ τό γε ὑποκείμενον αὐτὸ ποιεῖ μεταβάλλειν ἑαυτό· λέγω δ᾽ οἷον οὔτε τὸ ξύλον οὔτε ὁ χαλκὸς αἴτιος τοῦ μεταβάλλειν ἑκάτερον αὐτῶν, οὐδὲ ποιεῖ τὸ μὲν ξύλον κλίνην ὁ δὲ χαλκὸς ἀνδριάντα, {25} ἀλλ᾽ ἕτερόν τι τῆς μεταβολῆς αἴτιον. τὸ δὲ τοῦτο ζητεῖν ἐστι τὸ τὴν ἑτέραν ἀρχὴν ζητεῖν, ὡς ἂν ἡμεῖς φαίημεν, ὅθεν ἡ ἀρχὴ τῆς κινήσεως.

But as men proceeded in this way, reality itself again opened up a path and forced them to make investigations. For if every process of generation and corruption is from some one thing or more than one, why does this occur, and what is the cause? For certainly the subject itself does not cause itself to change. I mean, for example, that neither wood nor bronze is the cause of the change undergone by either one of them; for wood does not produce a bed, or bronze a statue, but something else is the cause of the change. But to seek this is to seek another principle, as if one were to say that from which the beginning of motion comes.

984a25 Igitur omnino qui talem viam a principio tetigerunt, et unum esse subiectum dixerunt, nihil difficultatis sibimet fecerunt, unum quidem omne dicentes, et quasi ab ea quaestione devicti, ipsum esse immobile dicunt, et naturam totam non solum secundum generationem et corruptionem (hoc etenim antiquum est, et quod omnes esse confessi sunt) verum et secundum aliam mutationem omnem esse: et hoc eorum est proprium. [94]

οἱ μὲν οὖν πάμπαν ἐξ ἀρχῆς ἁψάμενοι τῆς μεθόδου τῆς τοιαύτης καὶ ἓν φάσκοντες εἶναι τὸ ὑποκείμενον οὐθὲν ἐδυσχέραναν ἑαυτοῖς, ἀλλ᾽ ἔνιοί {30} γε τῶν ἓν λεγόντων, ὥσπερ ἡττηθέντες ὑπὸ ταύτης τῆς ζητήσεως, τὸ ἓν ἀκίνητόν φασιν εἶναι καὶ τὴν φύσιν ὅλην οὐ μόνον κατὰ γένεσιν καὶ φθοράν (τοῦτο μὲν γὰρ ἀρχαῖόν τε καὶ πάντες ὡμολόγησαν) ἀλλὰ καὶ κατὰ τὴν ἄλλην μεταβολὴν πᾶσαν· καὶ τοῦτο αὐτῶν ἴδιόν ἐστιν.

Now in general those who have taken such a course from the very beginning, and who said that the subject is one, created no difficulty for themselves when they said that everything is one. Some, being baffled, so to speak, by this question, say that this [one subject] and the whole of nature is immobile not only with respect to generation and corruption (for this is an ancient opinion and one which all men confess to be true), but also with respect to every other change. This opinion is peculiar to them.

Unum ergo solum dicentium ipsum esse, nulli talem intelligere causam convenit, nisi forte Parmenidi: et hoc intantum, quia non solum unam, sed etiam duas aliqualiter ponit causas esse. Plura vero facientibus, magis contingit dicere: ut ipsum calidum et frigidum, aut ignem et terram. Utuntur enim quasi motivam materiam habentem naturam igne; aqua vero et terra et huiusmodi, contrario.

{984b1} τῶν μὲν οὖν ἓν φασκόντων εἶναι τὸ πᾶν οὐθενὶ συνέβη τὴν τοιαύτην συνιδεῖν αἰτίαν πλὴν εἰ ἄρα Παρμενίδῃ, καὶ τούτῳ κατὰ τοσοῦτον ὅσον οὐ μόνον ἓν ἀλλὰ καὶ δύο πως τίθησιν αἰτίας εἶναι· {5} τοῖς δὲ δὴ πλείω ποιοῦσι μᾶλλον ἐνδέχεται λέγειν, οἷον τοῖς θερμὸν καὶ ψυχρὸν ἢ πῦρ καὶ γῆν· χρῶνται γὰρ ὡς κινητικὴν ἔχοντι τῷ πυρὶ τὴν φύσιν, ὕδατι δὲ καὶ γῇ καὶ τοῖς τοιούτοις τοὐναντίον.

Hence, of those who said that the [universe] itself is one, it occurred to none of them to conceive of such a cause, except perhaps Parmenides, and to him only insofar as he claims that there is not one cause but also in a sense two causes. But for those who make the elements of things many, such as the hot and cold, or fire and earth, a better explanation is possible, because they use fire as if it were a material principle which is active in nature, but water and earth and the like they use in the opposite way.

984b8 Post hos autem et talia principia tamquam non sufficientia existentium generare naturam, iterum ab ipsa veritate (velut aiebamus) coacti habitum quaesierunt principium: ipsis enim et bene hoc quidem eorum, quae sunt, habe-

μετὰ δὲ τούτους καὶ τὰς τοιαύτας ἀρχάς, ὡς οὐχ ἱκανῶν οὐσῶν γεννῆσαι τὴν τῶν ὄντων φύσιν, πάλιν {10} ὑπ᾽ αὐτῆς τῆς ἀληθείας, ὥσπερ εἴπομεν, ἀναγκαζόμενοι τὴν ἐχομένην ἐζήτησαν ἀρχήν. τοῦ γὰρ εὖ καὶ καλῶς τὰ μὲν ἔχειν τὰ δὲ

After these men and such principles, as if they were insufficient to generate the natures of existing things, men were again compelled, as we said (984a18), by the truth itself to seek for the next principle. For perhaps it is unlikely that either

re, ilia vero fieri, forsan nec ignem, nec terram, neque aliud talium nihil, verisimile causam esse: neque illos conveniens existimare: neque iterum ipsi automato et fortunae tantam committere rem bene habere. [97]

984b15 Dicens et aliquis inesse intellectum unum, quemadmodum animalibus: et in natura causam et mundi et ordinis totius, et excitans, apparuit purificans priores praeter convenientia dicentes. Palam quidem igitur, Anaxagoram scimus hos sermones tetigisse, attamen habet prius Hermotimus Clazomenius causam dicendi. Sic quidem igitur opinantes, similiter ipsius bene causam, principium existentium esse posuerunt: et tale unde motus existentibus inest. [100]

984b23 Suspicatus est autem utique aliquis Hesiodum quaesivisse primum huiusmodi, et utique si aliquis alius amorem aut desiderium in existentibus quasi principium posuisset, ut Parmenides. Etenim hic tentans monstrare universi generationem, primum quidem ait *deorum Amorem fore providentem omnibus*. Hesiodus vero *omnium primum chaos fuisse, deinde terram latam, et Amorem qui omnia condocet immortalia*: quasi necessarium sit in existentibus esse causam, quae res ipsas moveat et congreget. His quidem igitur quomodo distribuere de hoc oporteat quis primus, liceat iudicare posterius. [101]

γίγνεσθαι τῶν ὄντων ἴσως οὔτε πῦρ οὔτε γῆν οὔτ' ἄλλο τῶν τοιούτων οὐθὲν οὔτ' εἰκὸς αἴτιον εἶναι οὔτ' ἐκείνους οἰηθῆναι· οὐδ' αὖ τῷ αὐτομάτῳ καὶ τύχη τοσοῦτον ἐπιτρέψαι {15} πρᾶγμα καλῶς εἶχεν.

νοῦν δή τις εἰπὼν ἐνεῖναι, καθάπερ ἐν τοῖς ζῴοις, καὶ ἐν τῇ φύσει τὸν αἴτιον τοῦ κόσμου καὶ τῆς τάξεως πάσης οἷον νήφων ἐφάνη παρ' εἰκῇ λέγοντας {18} τοὺς πρότερον. φανερῶς μὲν οὖν Ἀναξαγόραν ἴσμεν ἁψάμενον τούτων τῶν λόγων, αἰτίαν δ' ἔχει πρότερον Ἑρμότιμος {20} ὁ Κλαζομένιος εἰπεῖν. οἱ μὲν οὖν οὕτως ὑπολαμβάνοντες ἅμα τοῦ καλῶς τὴν αἰτίαν ἀρχὴν εἶναι τῶν ὄντων ἔθεσαν, καὶ τὴν τοιαύτην ὅθεν ἡ κίνησις ὑπάρχει τοῖς οὖσιν.

ὑποπτεύσειε δ' ἄν τις Ἡσίοδον πρῶτον ζητῆσαι τὸ τοιοῦτον, κἄν εἴ τις ἄλλος ἔρωτα ἢ ἐπιθυμίαν ἐν τοῖς οὖσιν ἔθηκεν {25} ὡς ἀρχήν, οἷον καὶ Παρμενίδης· καὶ γὰρ οὗτος κατασκευάζων τὴν τοῦ παντὸς γένεσιν πρώτιστον μέν (φησιν) ἔρωτα θεῶν μητίσατο πάντων Ἡσίοδος δὲ πάντων μὲν πρώτιστα χάος γένετ', αὐτὰρ ἔπειτα γαῖ' εὐρύστερνος. ἠδ' ἔρος, ὃς πάντεσσι μεταπρέπει ἀθανάτοισιν, ὡς δέον ἐν τοῖς {30} οὖσιν ὑπάρχειν τιν' αἰτίαν ἥτις κινήσει καὶ συνάξει τὰ πράγματα. τούτους μὲν οὖν πῶς χρὴ διανεῖμαι περὶ τοῦ τίς πρῶτος, ἐξέστω κρίνειν ὕστερον·

fire or earth or anything else of this kind should be the cause of the good dispositions of things that are or come to be; nor was it consistent that they should think this to be the case. Nor again would it be right to attribute so important a matter to chance occurrence and fortune.

And when someone said that there is one intellect present in nature as in animals, and that this is the cause of the world and the arrangement of the whole, he seemed to atone for the untenable statements made by his predecessors. We know that Anaxagoras expressed these views, although Hermotimus of Clazomenae was the first to speak of such a cause. Those, therefore, who held these opinions likewise posited a principle in existing things, which is the cause of their goodness, and that sort of cause that is the source of motion in the world.

Now someone might have suspected that Hesiod was the first to have investigated this sort of cause, or anyone else who held that love or desire is a principle in existing things, as Parmenides did. For in the place where he attempts to explain the generation of the universe, he says that *Love, the first of all the gods, was made.* And Hesiod says that *the first of all things to be made was chaos, then broad earth, and Love, who is pre-eminent among the immortals*—as though there must be in the world some cause which moves things and brings them together. Which of these thinkers is prior will be decided later on.

---

93. Postquam posuit opinionem de causa materiali, hic ponit opinionem de causa efficiente: quae est unde principium motus. Et dividitur in duas.

Primo ponit opiniones eorum, qui simpliciter assignaverunt causam motus et generationis.

Secundo prosequitur opinionem illorum, qui posuerunt causam efficientem, quae est etiam principium boni et mali in rebus, ibi, *post hos* et cetera.

Circa primum duo facit.

Primo ponit rationem cogentem ad ponendum causam moventem.

Secundo ostendit qualiter ad positionem diversi diversimode se habuerunt, ibi, *igitur omnino qui talem* et cetera.

93. Having given the philosophers' opinions about the material cause, Aristotle now gives their opinions about the efficient cause, which is the source of motion. This is divided into two parts.

First, he gives the opinion of those who assigned without qualification a cause of motion and generation.

Second [97], he examines the opinion of those who posited an efficient cause, which is also the principle of good and evil in the world, at *after these men* (984b8).

In regard to the first he does two things.

First, he gives the reasoning which compelled them to posit an efficient cause.

Second [94], he shows the different positions which different men have held regarding this, at *now in general* (984a25).

Dicit ergo: quidam philosophi sic processerunt in causa materiali ponenda; sed et ipsa rei evidens natura dedit eis viam ad veritatis cognitionem vel inventionem, et coegit eos quaerere dubitationem quamdam quae inducit in causam efficientem, quae talis est.

Nulla res vel subiectum transmutat seipsum, sicut lignum non transmutat seipsum ut ex eo lectus fiat: nec aes est sibi causa transmutandi, ut ex eo fiat statua: sed oportet aliquid aliud esse quod est eis mutationis causa, quod est artifex. Sed ponentes causam materialem unam vel plures, dicebant ex ea sicut ex subiecto fieri generationem et corruptionem rerum: ergo oportet quod sit aliqua alia causa mutationis; et hoc est quaerere aliud genus principii et causae, quod nominatur, unde principium motus et cetera.

94. Deinde cum dicit *igitur omnino* hic ostendit quod ad praedictam rationem tripliciter philosophi se habuerunt. Illi enim, qui istam viam a principio tetigerunt, et dixerunt unam causam materialem, non multum se gravabant in solutione huius quaestionis: erant enim contenti ratione materiae, causam motus penitus negligentes.

95. Alii vero dicentes omnia unum esse, quasi per praedictam rationem devicti, non valentes pervenire ad assignandam causam motus, negaverunt totaliter motum. Unde dixerunt, quod totum universum est unum ens immobile.

In quo differebant a primis naturalibus, qui dicebant unam causam esse omnium rerum substantiam, quae tamen movetur per rarefactionem et condensationem, ut sic ex uno plura quodammodo fierent: licet non dicerent quod mutaretur secundum generationem et corruptionem simpliciter: hoc enim quod nihil simpliciter generaretur vel corrumperetur fuit antiqua opinio ab omnibus confessa, ut ex supradictis patet.

Sed istis posterioribus proprium fuit differentiae quod totum est unum immobile, sicut omni motu carens. Hi fuerunt Parmenides et Melissus, ut infra dicetur.

Ergo patet quod illis, qui dicunt totum unum immobile, non contigerit intelligere eos *talem causam* scilicet causam motus, quia ex quo motum subtrahunt, frustra quaerunt causam motus nisi tantum Parmenides: quia iste etsi poneret unum secundum rationem, ponebat tamen plura secundum sensum, ut infra dicetur.

Unde inquantum plura ponebat, conveniebat ei ponere plures causas, quarum una esset movens, et alia mota: quia sicut pluralitatem secundum sensum pone-

He says (984a18), then, that some philosophers have proceeded in this way in positing a material cause, but that the very nature of reality clearly provided them with a course for understanding or discovering the truth, and compelled them to investigate a problem which led them to the efficient cause. This problem is as follows.

No thing or subject changes itself—for example, wood does not change itself so that a bed comes from it, nor does bronze cause itself to be changed in such a way that a statue comes from it—but there must be some other principle which causes the change they undergo, and this is the artist. But those who posited a material cause, whether one or more than one, said that the generation and corruption of things come from this cause as a subject. Therefore, there must be some other cause of change, and to seek this is to seek another genus of principle and cause, which is called the source of motion.

94. *Now in general* (984a25). He shows here that the philosophers have adopted three positions with respect to the foregoing issue. For those who adopted this course from the very beginning, and said that there is one material cause, were not greatly concerned with the solution of this problem. For they were content with their view of matter and neglected the cause of motion altogether.

95. But others, who said that all things are one, being defeated (as it were) by this issue since they were unable to go so far as to assign a cause of motion, denied motion altogether. Hence they said that the whole universe is one immobile being.

In this respect, they differed from the first philosophers of nature, who said that one cause is the substance of all things although it is moved by rarefaction and condensation, so that in this way many things come to be in some measure from one principle. However, they did not say that this principle is subject to generation and corruption in an absolute sense. For the view that nothing was generated or corrupted without qualification is an ancient one admitted by all of them, as is clear from what was said above [75].

But it was peculiar to these later thinkers to say that the whole of reality is one immobile being, devoid of every kind of motion. These men were Parmenides and Melissus, as will be explained below [138].

Hence it is evident that it was impossible for those who said that the whole is one immobile being to conceive of *such a cause*, that is, a cause of motion. By the very fact that they did away with motion, they sought in vain for a cause of motion. An exception was Parmenides, for even though he held that there is only one thing according to reason, he held that there are many things according to the senses, as will be stated below [101].

Hence, inasmuch as Parmenides held that there are many things, it was in keeping with his position to hold that there are many causes, one of which would be a mover

bat, ei oportebat quod poneret motum secundum sensum. Nam ex uno subiecto non potest intelligi pluralitas constituta, nisi per aliquem modum motus.

96. Tertii fuerunt qui plures facientes rerum substantias, consenserunt praedictae rationi ponentes causam motus. Ponebant enim calidum vel frigidum causas, vel ignem et terram: quorum igne utebantur ut habente mobilem, idest motivam naturam; aqua vero et terra et aere contrario, vel ut habentibus naturam passivam: et sic ignis erat ut causa efficiens, alia vero ut causa materialis.

97. Deinde cum dicit *post hos* hic ponit opiniones ponentium causam efficientem non solum ut principium motus, sed etiam ut principium boni vel mali in rebus. Et circa hoc duo facit.

Primo narrat eorum opiniones.

Secundo ostendit in quo in ponendo causas defecerunt, ibi, *isti quidem.*

Circa primum duo facit.

Primo ponit opinionis rationes, ex quibus movebantur ad ponendum aliam causam a praedictis.

Secundo ostendit quomodo diversimode causam posuerunt, ibi, *dicens et aliquis* et cetera.

Dicit ergo primo, quod post praedictos philosophos qui solum unam causam materialem posuerunt, vel plures corporales, quarum una erat activa, alia ut passiva: et post alia prima principia ab eis posita, iterum fuerunt ab ipsa veritate coacti, *ut aiebamus,* idest sicut supra dictum est, ut quaererent principium, *habitum* idest consequenter se habens ad praedicta, scilicet causam boni, quae quidem est causa finalis, licet ab eis non poneretur nisi per accidens, ut infra patebit. Ponebatur enim ab eis solum causa boni per modum causae efficientis. Et ad hoc cogebantur, quia praemissa principia non sufficiebant ad generandum naturam entium, in qua quidem inveniuntur aliqua bene se habere. Quod demonstrat conservatio corporum in propriis locis, extra quae corrumpuntur. Et ulterius utilitates, quae proveniunt ex partibus animalium, quae hoc modo dispositae inveniuntur secundum quod congruit ad bonum esse animalis.

98. Huiusmodi autem bonae dispositionis vel habitudinis, quam quaedam res iam habent, quaedam vero adipiscuntur per aliquam factionem, non sufficienter ponitur causa vel ignis, vel terra, vel aliquod talium corporum: quia ista corpora determinate agunt ad unum secundum necessitatem propriarum formarum, sicut ignis calefacit et tendit sursum, aqua vero infrigidat et

and the others something moved. For just as he held that there are many things according to the senses, in a similar way it was necessary for him to hold that there is motion according to the senses, because a plurality of things can be understood to be produced from one subject only by some kind of motion.

96. Third, there were those who, in making the substances of things many, assented to the aforesaid reasoning by positing a cause of motion. For they maintained that the hot or the cold (that is, fire or earth) are causes; and of these they used fire as having a mobile (that is, an active) nature, but water, earth, and air they used in the opposite way, as having a passive nature. Thus fire was a sort of efficient cause, but the others a sort of material cause.

97. *After these men* (984b8). Here he gives the opinion of those who posited an efficient cause, not only as a principle of motion, but also as a principle of good and evil in things. In regard to this he does two things.

First, he expounds their views.

Second [107], he shows in what respect they failed in assigning the causes of things, at *these thinkers* (985a10).

In regard to the first he does two things.

First, he gives the reasons for their position by which they were induced to posit another cause besides the foregoing one.

Second [100], he shows how they posited this kind of cause in different ways, at *and when someone* (984b15).

He says first, then, that after the foregoing philosophers who held that there is only one material cause, or many bodies, one of which was active and the others passive, and after the other first principles given by them, men were again compelled by the truth itself, *as we said,* as was stated above [93], to seek the *next* principle (the one which naturally follows the foregoing one), namely, the cause of good. This is really the final cause, although it was held by them only accidentally, as will be seen below [177]. For they held that there is a cause of goodness in things only after the manner of an efficient cause. They were compelled to do this because the foregoing principles were not sufficient to account for the generation of the natural world, in which some things are found to be well disposed. The fact that bodies are conserved in their proper places and are corrupted outside of them proves this. So do the benefits resulting from the parts of animals, which are found to be disposed in this manner according as this is in keeping with an animal's good state of being.

98. But neither fire nor earth nor any such bodies were held to be adequate causes of this kind of good disposition or state of being, which some things already have but others acquire by some kind of production. For these bodies act in one definite way according to the necessity of their proper forms, as fire heats things and tends upward, and water cools things and tends downward. But the aforesaid

tendit deorsum. Praedictae autem utilitates, et bonae dispositiones rerum exigunt habere causam non determinatam ad unum tantum, cum in diversis animalibus diversimode inveniantur partes dispositae, et in unoquoque secundum congruentiam ipsorum naturae.

99. Unde non est conveniens, quod ignis vel terra vel aliquod huiusmodi sit causa praedictae bonae habitudinis rerum: nec fuit conveniens, quod ipsi hoc aestimaverint: nec iterum bene se habet dicere, quod sint automata idest per se evenientia et casualia, et quod a fortuna tantum immutetur eorum causalitas: licet aliqui eorum hoc dixerint, ut Empedocles et quicumque posuerunt causam materialem tantum: sicut patet secundo *Physicorum*.

Quod tamen patet etiam esse falsum, per hoc quod huiusmodi bonae dispositiones inveniuntur vel semper, vel in maiori parte. Ea autem quae sunt a casu vel a fortuna, non sunt sicut semper, sed nec sicut frequenter, sed ut raro. Et propter hoc necessarium fuit alterum invenire principium bonae dispositionis rerum, praeter quatuor elementa. Alia litera habet, *nec ipsi automato et fortunae*; et est idem sensus quod prius.

100. Deinde cum dicit *dicens et* hic ponit in speciali opiniones de praedicto principio.

Et primo ponit opiniones ponentium unam causam.

Secundo ponentium duas, ibi, *quoniam vero contraria bonis* et cetera.

Circa primum duo facit.

Primo ponit opiniones ponentium causam primam efficientem intellectum.

Secundo ponentium amorem, ibi, *suspicatus est autem* et cetera.

Dicit ergo quod post praedictam rationem apparuit aliquis dicens intellectum esse in tota natura, sicut est in animalibus, et ipsum esse causam mundi et ordinis totius, idest universi, in quo ordine consistit bonum totius, et uniuscuiusque. Et hic purificavit priores philosophos, ad puram veritatem eos reducens qui inconvenientia dixerunt, huiusmodi causam non tangentes. Hanc autem sententiam manifeste tangit Anaxagoras, licet causam huiusmodi sententiam proferendi dederit ei primo quidam alius philosophus, scilicet Hermotimus Clazomenius. Unde patet quod illi qui sunt opinati sic, simul posuerunt idem rebus esse principium, quod bene haberent se, et quod esset unde principium motus est.

benefits and good states of the being of things must have a cause which is not limited to one effect only, since the parts of different animals are found to be disposed in different ways, and in each one insofar as it is in keeping with its nature.

99. Hence, it is not reasonable that fire or earth or the like should be the cause of the aforesaid good state of being which things have, nor was it reasonable that these men should have thought this to be the case. Nor again would it be reasonable to say that these things are chance occurrences—that is, that they are accidental or come about by chance, and that their causality is changed only fortuitously—although some of these thinkers had said this, as Empedocles and all those who posited a material cause, as is evident in *Physics* 2.

However, this is also seen to be false because good dispositions of this kind are found either always or for the most part, whereas things that come about by chance or fortune do not occur always or for the most part, but seldom. For this reason, then, it was necessary to discover besides the four elements some other principle which would account for the good dispositions of things. Another text has *nor again would it be right to attribute so important a matter to chance occurrence and fortune*, but this means the same as the above.

100. *And when someone said* (984b15). Here he gives in detail the opinions about the aforesaid principle.

First, he gives the opinions of those who held that there is one efficient cause;

second [104], the opinions of those who held that there are two such causes, at *but since there would seem* (984b32).

In regard to the first he does two things.

First, he gives the views of those who held that the first efficient cause is an intellect;

second [101], the opinions of those who held that it is love, at *now someone might* (984b23).

He says, then, that after the foregoing doctrine someone appeared who said that there is an intellect present in nature at large, just as there is in animals, and that this is the cause of the world and the order of the whole (that is, of the universe), in which order the good of the entire universe and that of every single part consists. And this man atoned for the first philosophers by reducing to pure truth those who said unreasonable things and did not mention this kind of cause. Now Anaxagoras clearly stated this doctrine, although another philosopher—Hermotimus of Clazomenae—first gave him the idea of proposing this opinion. Hence it is evident that those who held this opinion claimed at the same time that the principle by which things are well disposed and the one which is the source of motion in things are one and the same.

101. Deinde cum dicit *suspicatus est* ponit opinionem ponentium amorem esse principium primum; quem tamen non ita expresse vel plane, posuerunt. Et ideo dicit, quod suspicio fuit apud aliquos, quod Hesiodus quaesivisset huiusmodi principium bonae habitudinis rerum, vel quicumque alius posuit amorem vel desiderium in rebus. Cum enim Parmenides universi generationem monstrare tentaret, dixit, quod amor deorum providit omnibus, ut mundus constitueretur.

Nec est contra sensum eius, qui posuit unum ens immobile, quod hic dicit; quia hic ponebat plura secundum sensum, licet unum secundum rationem, ut supra dictum est, et infra dicetur. Deos autem corpora caelestia appellabat, vel forte aliquas substantias separatas.

102. Sed Hesiodus dixit quod primo omnium fuit chaos, et deinde facta est terra latior, ut esset receptaculum aliorum: posuerunt enim receptaculum et locum principium esse, ut dicitur quarto *Physicorum*. Et posuit rerum principium amorem, qui condocet omnia immortalia. Et hoc ideo, quia communicatio bonitatis ex amore provenire videtur. Nam beneficium est signum et effectus amoris. Unde, cum ex rebus immortalibus huiusmodi corruptibilia esse habeant, et omnem bonam dispositionem, oportet hoc amori immortalium attribuere. Immortalia autem posuit vel ipsa corpora caelestia, vel ipsa principia materialia. Sic autem posuit chaos et amorem, quasi necessarium sit in rerum existentiis esse non solum materiam motuum, sed et ipsam causam agentem, quae res moveat et congreget; quod videtur ad amorem pertinere. Nam et in nobis amor ad actiones movet, et quia est omnium affectionum principium. Nam et timor et tristitia et spes, non nisi ex amore procedunt. Quod autem amor congreget, ex hoc patet; quia ipse amor est unio quaedam amantis et amati, dum amans amatum quasi se reputat. Iste autem Hesiodus ante philosophorum tempora fuit in numero poetarum.

103. Quis autem horum sit *prior*, idest potior in scientia, utrum ille qui dixit amorem esse primum principium, vel qui dixit intellectum, *posterius* poterit iudicari, scilicet ubi agetur de Deo. Et hoc iudicium distributionem vocat: quia per hoc unicuique suus gradus attribuitur dignitatis. Alia translatio planius habet: *hos quidem igitur quomodo congruat transire, et quis de hoc sit prior, posterius poterit iudicari.*

101. *Now someone might* (984b23). Here he gives the opinion of those who claimed that love is the first principle, although they did not hold this very explicitly or clearly. Accordingly, he says that some suspected that Hesiod had sought for such a principle to account for the good disposition of things, or anyone else who posited love or desire in nature. For when Parmenides attempted to explain the generation of the universe, he said that in the establishing of the universe, love, the first of all the gods, was made.

Nor is this opposed to his doctrine that there is one immobile being, of which Aristotle speaks here, because this man held that there are many things according to the senses, although there is only one thing according to reason, as was stated above and will be stated below. Moreover, he called the celestial bodies (or perhaps certain separate substances) gods.

102. But Hesiod said that first of all there was chaos, and then broad earth was made to be the receptacle of everything else; for it is evident that the receptacle and place are principles, as is stated in *Physics* 4. And he also held that love, which instructs all the immortals, is a principle of things. He did this because the communication of goodness seems to spring from love, for a good deed is a sign and effect of love. Hence, since corruptible things derive their being and every good disposition from immortal beings of this kind, this must be attributed to the love of the immortals. Furthermore, he held that the immortals are either the celestial bodies themselves or material principles themselves. Thus he posited chaos and love as though there had to be in existing things not only a material cause of their motions, but also an efficient cause which moves and unites them, which seems to be the office of love. For love moves us to action because it is the source of all the emotions, since fear, sadness and hope proceed only from love. That love unites things is clear from this: love itself is a certain union between the lover and the thing loved, seeing that the lover regards the beloved as himself. This man Hesiod is to be numbered among the poets who lived before the time of the philosophers.

103. Now, as to which one of these thinkers is *prior*, that is, more competent in knowledge, whether the one who said that love is the first principle, or the one who said that intellect is, can be decided *later on*, that is, where God is discussed. He calls this decision an arrangement, because the degree of excellence belonging to each man is allotted to him in this way. Another translation states this more clearly: *therefore, in what order it is fitting to go over these thinkers, and who in this order is prior, can be decided later on.*

LECTURE 6

Love and hate as causes

984b32 Quoniam vero contraria bonis videbantur esse in natura, et non solum ordinatio et bonum, sed inordinatio et turpe, pluraque mala melioribus, et prava bonis; sic alius aliquis amorem induxit et litem, singula singulorum causam horum. [104]

ἐπεὶ δὲ καὶ τἀναντία τοῖς ἀγαθοῖς ἐνόντα ἐφαίνετο ἐν τῇ φύσει, καὶ οὐ μόνον τάξις καὶ τὸ καλὸν ἀλλὰ καὶ ἀταξία καὶ τὸ αἰσχρόν, {985a1} καὶ πλείω τὰ κακὰ τῶν ἀγαθῶν καὶ τὰ φαῦλα τῶν καλῶν, οὕτως ἄλλος τις φιλίαν εἰσήνεγκε καὶ νεῖκος, ἑκάτερον ἑκατέρων αἴτιον τούτων.

But since there would seem to be in nature things that are contrary to those that are good, and not only order and good but also disorder and what is base, and evil things more numerous than good ones, and base things more numerous than noble ones, for this reason another thinker introduced love and strife as causes, each of its own type of effects.

Siquis enim assequatur et accipiat ad intellectum, et non ad ea quae balbutiendo Empedocles dixit, inveniet amorem quidem esse causam aggregatorum, litem vero malorum.

εἰ γάρ τις ἀκολουθοίη καὶ λαμβάνοι πρὸς τὴν διάνοιαν {5} καὶ μὴ πρὸς ἃ ψελλίζεται λέγων Ἐμπεδοκλῆς, εὑρήσει τὴν μὲν φιλίαν αἰτίαν οὖσαν τῶν ἀγαθῶν τὸ δὲ νεῖκος τῶν κακῶν·

For if anyone grasps what Empedocles said, taking it according to its meaning rather than according to its faltering expression, he will find that love is the cause of things that come to be by aggregation, and strife the cause of evil things.

Quare siquis dixerit et quodammodo dicere et primum dicere Empedoclem bonum et malum principia, forsan bene dicet, si bonorum omnium bonum est causa, et malorum malum.

ὥστ' εἴ τις φαίη τρόπον τινὰ καὶ λέγειν καὶ πρῶτον λέγειν τὸ κακὸν καὶ τὸ ἀγαθὸν ἀρχὰς Ἐμπεδοκλέα, τάχ' ἂν λέγοι καλῶς, εἴπερ τὸ τῶν ἀγαθῶν ἁπάντων αἴτιον {10} αὐτὸ τἀγαθόν ἐστι [καὶ τῶν κακῶν τὸ κακόν].

Hence, if anyone were to say that Empedocles, in a sense, both said and was the first to say that good and evil are principles, he would perhaps speak correctly, that is, if the cause of all good things is good and that of all evil things is evil.

985a10 Isti quidem igitur (sicut diximus) et usque ad hoc duas causas tetigerunt, quas in *Physicis* determinavimus, materiam, et id unde motus: obscure quidem, et non manifeste, sed qualiter in bellis ineruditi faciunt. Etenim illi circumducti saepe bonas plagas faciunt, at nec illi ex scientia, nec isti visi sunt scientes dicere quod dicunt. His etenim fere usi nihil videntur nisi parum. [107]

οὗτοι μὲν οὖν, ὥσπερ λέγομεν, καὶ μέχρι τούτου δυοῖν αἰτίαν ὧν ἡμεῖς διωρίσαμεν ἐν τοῖς περὶ φύσεως ἡμμένοι φαίνονται, τῆς τε ὕλης καὶ τοῦ ὅθεν ἡ κίνησις, ἀμυδρῶς μέντοι καὶ οὐθὲν σαφῶς ἀλλ' οἷον ἐν ταῖς μάχαις οἱ ἀγύμναστοι ποιοῦσιν· καὶ γὰρ ἐκεῖνοι περιφερόμενοι {15} τύπτουσι πολλάκις καλὰς πληγάς, ἀλλ' οὔτε ἐκεῖνοι ἀπὸ ἐπιστήμης οὔτε οὗτοι ἐοίκασιν εἰδέναι ὅ τι λέγουσιν· σχεδὸν γὰρ οὐθὲν χρώμενοι φαίνονται τούτοις ἀλλ' ἢ κατὰ μικρόν.

These thinkers, then, as we have said, to this extent have touched on two of the causes which we established in the *Physics*—matter and the source of motion—though only obscurely and with no clarity, much as untrained men conduct themselves in battle. For the latter, though encircled, often deal telling blows, but without science. In the same way these thinkers do not seem to be aware of what they are saying. For it seems that they almost never make use of the causes except to a small degree.

985a18 Anaxagoras autem artificialiter ad mundi generationem utitur intellectu. Nam quando dubitat quae causa ex necessitate est, tunc attrahit ipsum. In aliis vero omnia magis causantur eorum quae fiunt, quam intellectu. [108]

Ἀναξαγόρας τε γὰρ μηχανῇ χρῆται τῷ νῷ πρὸς τὴν κοσμοποιίαν, καὶ ὅταν ἀπορήσῃ διὰ τίν' αἰτίαν {20} ἐξ ἀνάγκης ἐστί, τότε παρέλκει αὐτόν, ἐν δὲ τοῖς ἄλλοις πάντα μᾶλλον αἰτιᾶται τῶν γιγνομένων ἢ νοῦν,

Anaxagoras uses "intellect" in an artificial way in generating the world. For when he is in difficulty as to what is necessarily the cause of something, he drags in this intellect; but in other cases he makes everything but intellect the cause of what comes to be.

985a21 Et Empedocles plus quidem hic utitur causis; sed tamen nec sufficienter, neque in his invenitur quod confessum est. A multis igitur arguitur in locis apud ipsum: amor secernat, lis autem concernat. Nam cum in elementa quidem ipsum esse a lite distrahitur, tunc

καὶ Ἐμπεδοκλῆς ἐπὶ πλέον μὲν τούτου χρῆται τοῖς αἰτίοις, οὐ μὴν οὔθ' ἱκανῶς, οὔτ' ἐν τούτοις εὑρίσκει τὸ ὁμολογούμενον. πολλαχοῦ γοῦν αὐτῷ ἡ μὲν φιλία διακρίνει τὸ δὲ νεῖκος συγκρίνει. {25} ὅταν μὲν γὰρ εἰς τὰ στοιχεῖα διίστηται τὸ πᾶν ὑπὸ τοῦ νεῖκους, τότε τὸ πῦρ

Empedocles, it is true, makes greater use of causes than Anaxagoras, though not sufficiently; nor does one find in his use of them what he professed. In many places he argues that love separates things, and that strife brings them together. For when being itself is separated

ignis in unum et aliorum elementorum singula concernuntur. Cum autem iterum in unum ab amore conveniunt, necesse rursum, ut ex singulis particulae secernantur. [109]

εἰς ἓν συγκρίνεται καὶ τῶν ἄλλων στοιχείων ἕκαστον· ὅταν δὲ πάλιν ὑπὸ τῆς φιλίας συνίωσιν εἰς τὸ ἕν, ἀναγκαῖον ἐξ ἑκάστου τὰ μόρια διακρίνεσθαι πάλιν.

into its elements by strife, then fire and each of the other elements are brought together into a unity. But when they are united by love, the particles must again be separated out from each element.

985a29 Empedocles quidem, praeter priores, primus hanc causam dividens induxit, non unum faciens motus principium, sed diversa et contraria. [111]

Ἐμπεδοκλῆς μὲν οὖν παρὰ τοὺς πρότερον πρῶτος {30} τὸ τὴν αἰτίαν διελεῖν εἰσήνεγκεν, οὐ μίαν ποιήσας τὴν τῆς κινήσεως ἀρχὴν ἀλλ᾽ ἑτέρας τε καὶ ἐναντίας,

In contrast to the first philosophers, then, Empedocles was the first to introduce this cause, dividing it in such a way as to make the source of motion not a single principle, but different and contrary ones.

Amplius autem quae in materiae specie dicuntur elementa quatuor primus dixit, non tamen utitur quatuor, sed ut duobus existentibus, solmn quidem igne secundum se: oppositis vero quasi una natura terra, aere et aqua: sumet autem utique aliquis id speculans ex elementis.

ἔτι δὲ τὰ ὡς ἐν ὕλης εἴδει λεγόμενα στοιχεῖα τέτταρα πρῶτος εἶπεν (οὐ μὴν χρῆταί γε τέτταρσιν ἀλλ᾽ ὡς δυσὶν οὖσι μόνοις, {985b1} πυρὶ μὲν καθ᾽ αὑτὸ τοῖς δ᾽ ἀντικειμένοις ὡς μιᾷ φύσει, γῇ τε καὶ ἀέρι καὶ ὕδατι· λάβοι δ᾽ ἄν τις αὐτὸ θεωρῶν ἐκ τῶν ἐπῶν)·

Moreover, he was the first to claim that the elements, which are said to belong to the species of matter, are four in number, although he does not use them as four but as two, taking fire by itself alone, and its opposites—earth, air, and water—as a single nature (984a25). But anyone may see this by studying his basic sayings.

Hic quidem ergo, sicut diximus, sic et tot dixit principia.

οὗτος μὲν οὖν, ὥσπερ λέγομεν, οὕτω τε καὶ τοσαύτας εἴρηκε τὰς ἀρχάς·

This philosopher, then, as we have said, has spoken in this way about the principles of things and their number.

---

104. Hic ponit opinionem ponentium contrarietatem in huiusmodi, et rationem eos moventem, quae talis erat.

In rerum natura videbantur aliqua esse contraria bonis, quia in natura non solum invenitur ordinatum et bonum, sed aliquando inordinatum et turpe: non potest autem dici quod mala non habeant causam, sed accidant a casu: quia mala sunt plura melioribus, et prava sunt plura bonis simpliciter: quae autem sunt a casu sine causa determinata non sunt ut in pluribus, sed ut in paucioribus.

Unde, cum contrariorum sint contrariae causae, oportet non solum causam rerum ponere amorem, ex quo proveniunt ordinationes et bona: sed et odium, ex quo proveniunt inordinationes et turpia vel mala: ut sic singula mala et bona proprias causas habeant.

105. Et quod ista fuerit ratio movens Empedoclem patet, si quis assequatur sententiam eius, et accipiat sententiam, quam dicere voluit, et non ad verba, quae imperfecte et quasi balbutiendo dixit.

Dixit enim quod amoris est congregare, odii disgregare: sed quia ex congregatione est rerum generatio, ex qua rebus est esse et bonum: per segregationem vero est corruptio, quae est via ad non esse et malum, iam patet

104. Here Aristotle gives the opinion of those who posited contrariety in beings of this kind, and the reason which moved them, which is as follows.

There would seem to be in nature things that are contrary to those that are good, because in nature one finds not only things that are ordered and good, but sometimes things that are disordered and base. Now it cannot be said that evil things have no cause but happen by chance, because evil things are more numerous than good ones, and base things more numerous than those which are unqualifiedly noble. But those things that come to be by chance without a definite cause do not occur for the most part, but in the smaller number of cases.

Hence, since contrary effects have contrary causes, it was necessary to hold as a cause of things not only love, from which the order and good in things originate, but also hate, which is the source of disorder and baseness or evil in things, so that in this way particular instances of evil and good have their own type of causes.

105. That this was the reason which moved Empedocles is evident if anyone grasps what he says, taking his statement according to its meaning rather than according to the words which he used imperfectly and as though he were stammering.

For he said that it is the office of love to bring the elements together, and of hate to separate them. But since the generation of things is a result of the coming together of the elements (by reason of which there is being and good

quod voluit amorem esse causam aggregatorum, idest bonorum, et odium esse causam malorum.

Et ita si quis dicat, quod Empedocles fuit primus, qui dixit bonum et malum esse principia, forsitan bene dixit.

106. Si tamen secundum Empedoclem fuit hoc quod bonum est causa omnium bonorum, et malum omnium malorum. Quod enim aliquorum malorum posuit causam malam, scilicet corruptionis, et aliquorum bonorum bonum, scilicet generationis, manifestum est: sed quia non sequebatur quod omnia bona essent per amicitiam, nec omnia mala per odium, cum distinctio partium mundi adinvicem esset per odium, et confusio per amicitiam, ideo non usquequaque posuit bonum causam bonorum, et malum causam malorum.

107. Deinde cum dicit *isti quidem* hic ostendit, quod in ponendo praedictas causas deficiebant.

Et primo loquitur generaliter de eis.
Secundo specialiter, ibi, *Anaxagoras autem* et cetera.

Dicit ergo primo, quod praedicti philosophi, scilicet Anaxagoras et Empedocles, usque ad hoc pervenerunt, quod posuerunt duas causas illarum quatuor, quae sunt determinatae in *Physicis*, scilicet materiam et causam motus; sed obscure et non manifeste tradiderunt, quia non exprimebant quod illa, quae causas esse ponebant, ad ista causarum genera reducerentur. Sed in hoc quod de causis posuerunt duas, convenienter assimilabantur bellatoribus non eruditis, qui ab adversariis circumducti faciunt aliquando bonos ictus, sed non per artem, sed a casu. Quod ex hoc patet, quia etsi aliquando accidit eis, non tamen semper aut frequenter. Similiter etiam praedicti philosophi non sunt usi dicere quod dicunt, nec usi sunt scientibus, idest sicut scientes.

Unde alia translatio habet, *sed nec illi scientiam, nec hi assimilati sunt scientibus dicere quod dicunt*. Quod ex hoc patet, quia cum praedictas causas posuissent, fere non sunt eis usi, quia in paucis utebantur. Unde videtur quod non ex arte, sed quadam inducti necessitate eas casualiter induxerunt.

108. Deinde cum dicit *Anaxagoras autem* hic ostendit in quo specialiter eorum uterque defecerit.

Et primo de Anaxagora.
Secundo de Empedocle, ibi, *et Empedocles*.

in things), and their corruption a result of the separation of the elements (which is the way to non-being and evil), it is now evident that he wanted love to be the cause of things that come to be by aggregation, that is, of good things, and hate the cause of evil things.

Thus if one were to say that Empedocles was the first to maintain that good and evil are principles, he would perhaps speak correctly.

106. That is to say, this would follow if Empedocles did hold that good is the cause of all good things, and evil the cause of all evil things. For it is evident that he posited evil as the cause of some evil things, namely, of corruption, and good as the cause of some good things, namely, of generation. But because it would not follow that all good things would be caused by friendship or all evil things by hate, since the parts of the world would be differentiated by hate and fused together by friendship, therefore he did not always hold that good is the cause of good things, and evil the cause of evil things.

107. *These thinkers* (985a10). Here he shows that in giving these causes the philosophers treated them inadequately.

First, he mentions them in a general way.
Second [108], he treats each one individually, at *Anaxagoras* (985a18).

He says first, then, that these philosophers—Anaxagoras and Empedocles—arrived at a doctrine of two of the causes which have been established in the *Physics*, namely matter and the cause of motion, although they treated these obscurely and with no clarity because they did not explain that those principles which they held to be the causes of things could be reduced to these genera of causes. But insofar as they posited two of these causes, they may be likened to untrained warriors who, though encircled by the enemy, sometimes strike good blows, not by art but by chance. This is evident because even though they happen to do this sometimes, this does not occur always or for the most part. In like manner, too, these philosophers were not accustomed to express themselves accurately, nor was it their custom to speak knowingly, that is, as men who know.

Hence another translation has: *but these men neither have science, nor are they to be compared with men who realize what they are saying*. This is shown by the fact that, although they had proposed these causes, they hardly ever used them, because they employed them in few instances. Hence it seems that they introduced them not as a result of art, but by accident, because they were moved to do so by necessity.

108. *Anaxagoras* (985a18). Here he shows in what particular respect the view of each is unsatisfactory.

First, he speaks of Anaxagoras;
second [109], of Empedocles, at *Empedocles* (985a21).

Dicit ergo primo, quod Anaxagoras utitur intellectu ad mundi generationem; in quo videtur artificialiter loqui, non dubitans de causis generationis mundi, ex necessitate attrahit, idest producit ipsum intellectum, non valens reducere mundi generationem in aliquam aliam causam distinguentem res, nisi in aliquod in se distinctum et immixtum, cuiusmodi est intellectus. Sed in omnibus aliis assignat causas magis ex omnibus aliis, quam ex intellectu, sicut in specialibus rerum naturis.

109. Deinde cum dicit *et Empedocles* hic ostendit in quo deficiat Empedocles. Et circa hoc duo facit.

Primo ostendit in quo deficit.

Secundo quid proprium prae aliis dixit, ibi, *Empedocles igitur*.

Dicit ergo primo, quod Empedocles in determinando de particularibus rerum naturis, *plus utitur causis* a se positis, scilicet quatuor elementis, et odio et amore, quam Anaxagoras, quia singulorum generationem et corruptionem in praedictas causas reducit, non autem Anaxagoras in intellectum. Sed in duobus deficit.

Primo, quia non sufficienter huiusmodi causas tradit. Utitur enim eis quasi dignitatibus per se notis, quae non sunt per se nota, ut dicitur primo *Physicorum*: dum scilicet supponebat quasi per se notum, quod lis determinato tempore dominabatur in elementis, et alio tempore determinato amor.

110. Secundo, quia in his quae quaerit, non invenitur illud quod est ab eo confessum, idest suppositum quasi principium, scilicet quod amor congreget et odium disgreget; quia in multis locis oportet quod e contrario amor *secernat*, idest dividat, et odium *concernat*, idest congreget; quia quando ipsum universum in partes suas per odium, *distrahitur*, idest deiicitur, quod est in generatione mundi, tunc omnes partes ignis in unum conveniunt, et similiter singulae partes aliorum elementorum, *concernunt*, idest adinvicem coniunguntur. Sic igitur odium, non solum partes ignis dividit a partibus aeris, sed etiam partes ignis coniungit adinvicem. E contrario autem, cum elementa in unum conveniunt per amorem, quod accidit in destructione universi, tunc necesse est ut partes ignis adinvicem separentur, et similiter singulorum partes adinvicem secernantur. Non enim posset ignis commisceri aeri nisi partes ignis adinvicem separarentur, et similiter partes aeris nisi invicem se elementa praedicta penetrarent, ut sic amor sicut coniungit

He says first, then, that Anaxagoras uses "intellect" to generate the world, and in so doing he seems to speak of it in an artificial way. For when he inquires about the causes of the world's generation, he drags it in of necessity—that is, he invents this intelligence only because he is unable to attribute the generation of the world to any other cause which would differentiate things except to one which is essentially distinct and unmixed, and intellect is a thing of this kind. But in all other cases he draws his causes from any other source rather than intellect, as in the case of the particular natures of things.

109. *Empedocles* (985a21). Here he shows in what respect Empedocles' doctrine is inadequate, and in regard to this he does two things.

First, he shows in what respect Empedocles' doctrine is inadequate.

Second [111], he explains what Empedocles himself held in contrast to the other philosophers, at *in contrast* (985a29).

He says, first (985a21), that Empedocles, in dealing with the particular natures of things, *makes greater use of causes* posited by him (the four elements, and love and hate) than Anaxagoras did, because he reduced the generation and corruption of particular things to these causes, and not to intelligence as Anaxagoras did. But Empedocles failed in two ways.

First, he failed because he does not treat causes of this kind adequately enough; for he uses things that are not self-evident as though they were self-evident axioms, as is stated in *Physics* 1, insofar as he assumed that they are self-evident, because at one definite time strife has dominion over the elements and at another does love.

110. Second, he failed because in the matters which he investigates, one does not find what he has professed (that is, what he held as a principle)—namely, that love combines things and that strife separates them, because in many places love must on the contrary separate or divide things, and strife *bring them together* or unite them. For when the universe itself *is separated out*, or divided into its parts, by hate, as occurs when the world is generated, all particles of fire are then combined into one whole, and so also are the individual particles of the other elements *brought together*, or joined to each other. Hence, strife not only separates the particles of fire from those of air, but also brings together the particles of fire. But, on the other hand, when the elements come together through love, which occurs when the universe is destroyed, the particles of fire must then be separated from each other, and so also must the particles of the other elements. For fire can be mixed with air only if the particles of fire are separated from each other. And the same is true of the particles of air only if these elements

extranea, ita dividat similia, secundum quod sequitur ex eius positione.

111. Deinde cum dicit *Empedocles quidem* hic ostendit quomodo Empedocles prae aliis philosophis proprium posuit. Et dicit quod duo prae aliis posuit.

Unum est quod causam unde motus divisit in duas contrarias partes.

Aliud est quod causam materialem dixit esse quatuor elementa: non quod utatur quatuor elementis ut quatuor, sed ut duobus, quia ignem comparat aliis tribus dicens, quod ignis habet naturam activam, et alia passivam.

Et hoc potest aliquis sumere ex elementis rerum ab ipso traditis, vel *elementis* principiis suae doctrinae quae posuit.

Alia litera habet *ex versibus*, quia dicitur metrice suam philosophiam scripsisse. Et huic concordat alia translatio quae dicit, *ex rationibus*. Hic igitur, ut dictum est et sic tot primus posuit principia, quia quatuor, et ea quae dicta sunt.

penetrate one another, so that love not only unites unlike things but also separates like things, according to what follows from his position.

111. *In contrast* (985a29). Here he shows in what respect Empedocles' own doctrine differs from that of the other philosophers. He says that Empedocles maintained two things in contrast to the others.

First, he divided the cause which is the source of motion into two contrary parts.

Second, he held the material cause to be constituted of four elements—not that he uses the four elements as four, but rather as two, because he contrasts fire with the other three, saying that fire is active in nature and the others passive in nature.

Anyone can gather this from the elements of things treated by him, or from his *basic sayings* in the sense of the rudiments of the doctrine which he propounded.

Another version reads *from his verses*, because he is said to have written his philosophy in meters. And still another version, which says *from his statements*, agrees with this. As has been stated, then, this philosopher was the first to stipulate in this way that the principles of things are four in number, and to speak of those which have been mentioned.

LECTURE 7

Atomists' and Pythagoreans' opinions

985b4 Leucippus et collega eius Democritus, elementa quidem plenum et inane dicunt esse: dicentes velut hoc quidem ens, illud vero non ens; horum autem planum quidem et solidum ens, inane vero non ens. Propter quod et nihil magis ens non ente dicunt esse; quia neque inane corpore. Causas autem entium haec ut materiam. [112]

Λεύκιππος δὲ καὶ ὁ ἑταῖρος {5} αὐτοῦ Δημόκριτος στοιχεῖα μὲν τὸ πλῆρες καὶ τὸ κενὸν εἶναί φασι, λέγοντες τὸ μὲν ὂν τὸ δὲ μὴ ὄν, τούτων δὲ τὸ μὲν πλῆρες καὶ στερεὸν τὸ ὄν, τὸ δὲ κενὸν τὸ μὴ ὄν (διὸ καὶ οὐθὲν μᾶλλον τὸ ὂν τοῦ μὴ ὄντος εἶναί φασιν, ὅτι οὐδὲ τοῦ κενοῦ τὸ σῶμα), αἴτια δὲ τῶν ὄντων ταῦτα ὡς {10} ὕλην.

Leucippus and his colleague Democritus say that the elements of things are the full and the void, calling the one being and the other non-being. For this reason they say that the full or solid is being, and the void is non-being. For this reason too they say that being no more is than non-being, because the void no more is than body; and they hold that these are the material causes of things.

985b10 Et quemadmodum qui unum faciunt substantiam subiectam, alia passionibus eius generant, rarum et spissum principia passionum ponentes, eodem modo et hi differentes causas aliorum esse dicunt. Has vero tres dicunt esse, figuram, ordinem et positionem. Differre autem aiunt ens rhysmo et diathygi et tropi solum. Horum autem rhysmus figura est et diathyge ordo, et trope positio. Differt enim A, ab N, figura: AN autem a NA, ordine: Z autem ab N, positione. [115]

καὶ καθάπερ οἱ ἓν ποιοῦντες τὴν ὑποκειμένην οὐσίαν τἆλλα τοῖς πάθεσιν αὐτῆς γεννῶσι, τὸ μανὸν καὶ τὸ πυκνὸν ἀρχὰς τιθέμενοι τῶν παθημάτων, τὸν αὐτὸν τρόπον καὶ οὗτοι τὰς διαφορὰς αἰτίας τῶν ἄλλων εἶναί φασιν. ταύτας μέντοι τρεῖς εἶναι λέγουσι, σχῆμά τε καὶ τάξιν καὶ {15} θέσιν: διαφέρειν γάρ φασι τὸ ὂν ῥυσμῷ καὶ διαθιγῇ καὶ τροπῇ μόνον: τούτων δὲ ὁ μὲν ῥυσμὸς σχῆμά ἐστιν ἡ δὲ διαθιγὴ τάξις ἡ δὲ τροπὴ θέσις: διαφέρει γὰρ τὸ μὲν A τοῦ N σχήματι τὸ δὲ AN τοῦ NA τάξει τὸ δὲ Z τοῦ H θέσει.

And just as those who make the underlying substance one generate other things from this by means of its attributes, holding that rarity and density are the principles of these attributes, in the same way these men say that the differences of the atoms are the causes of different things. These differences, they say, are three: shape, arrangement, and position. For they claim that what exists differs only by rhythm, inter-contact, and turning; of these, rhythm means shape, inter-contact arrangement, and turning position. For A differs from N in shape, and Z from N in position.

De motu vero unde aut quomodo inest habentibus, et hi aliis consimiliter, negligenter dimiserunt. De duabus igitur causis (ut diximus) in tantum videtur quaesitum esse prius.

περὶ δὲ κινήσεως, ὅθεν ἢ πῶς ὑπάρξει τοῖς οὖσι, καὶ {20} οὗτοι παραπλησίως τοῖς ἄλλοις ῥαθύμως ἀφεῖσαν. περὶ μὲν οὖν τῶν δύο αἰτιῶν, ὥσπερ λέγομεν, ἐπὶ τοσοῦτον ἔοικεν ἐζητῆσθαι παρὰ τῶν πρότερον.

But with regard to motion, from whence it comes or how it is present in things, these men carelessly dismissed this question as the other thinkers did. As we have said before, then, these two types of causes seem to have been investigated to this extent by the first thinkers.

985b23 In his autem et ante hos vocati Pythagorici mathematica tangentes primi ea pro uxerunt, et in eis nutriti, horum principia omnia esse putaverunt. [119]

ἐν δὲ τούτοις καὶ πρὸ τούτων οἱ καλούμενοι Πυθαγόρειοι τῶν μαθημάτων ἁψάμενοι πρῶτοι ταῦτά τε προήγαγον, καὶ {25} ἐντραφέντες ἐν αὐτοῖς τὰς τούτων ἀρχὰς τῶν ὄντων ἀρχὰς ᾠήθησαν εἶναι πάντων.

But during the time of these and prior to them lived those called the Pythagoreans who dealt with mathematics and were the first to develop it; having been reared in mathematics, they thought that their principles were the principles of all things.

Horum autem quoniam natura numeri primi, et in numeris speculari multas similitudines inexistentibus et factis magis quam in igne et terra: quia talis numerorum passio, iustitia: illa vero talis, anima et intellectus: alia vero, tempus: et aliorum (ut est dicere) unumquodque similiter.

ἐπεὶ δὲ τούτων οἱ ἀριθμοὶ φύσει πρῶτοι, ἐν δὲ τούτοις ἐδόκουν θεωρεῖν ὁμοιώματα πολλὰ τοῖς οὖσι καὶ γιγνομένοις, μᾶλλον ἢ ἐν πυρὶ καὶ γῇ καὶ ὕδατι, ὅτι τὸ μὲν τοιονδὶ τῶν ἀριθμῶν πάθος δικαιοσύνη {30} τὸ δὲ τοιονδὶ ψυχή τε καὶ νοῦς ἕτερον δὲ καιρὸς καὶ τῶν ἄλλων ὡς εἰπεῖν ἕκαστον ὁμοίως,

But since among these principles numbers are naturally first, they thought they saw in numbers, more than in fire and earth, many resemblances to things that are and come to be, because this attribute of numbers is justice, another is soul and mind, and still another is time, and similarly, so to speak, with each thing.

985b31 Amplius autem harmoniarum in numeris speculantes passiones et rationes, quoniam et alia quidem numeris secundum naturam omnem videbantur assimilata esse, et numeri sunt omnes natura primi: elementa numerorum existentium, elementa cunctorum esse existimabant, et totum caelum harmoniam esse et numerum, et quaecumque habebant confessa monstrare, et in numeris, et in harmoniis, et ad caeli passiones et partes, et ad ornatum totum ea colligentes adaptabant. Et si quil alicubi deficiebat, advocabant continuatum ipsis esse negotium. Dico autem quoniam perfectus denarius esse videtur, et omnem comprehendere numerorum naturam, et quae secundum caelum feruntur decem quidem esse dicuntur: solum autem novem existentibus manifestis, et ideo antictonam decimam faciunt. De his autem certius est a nobis in aliis determinatum. [121]

ἔτι δὲ τῶν ἁρμονιῶν ἐν ἀριθμοῖς ὁρῶντες τὰ πάθη καὶ τοὺς λόγους, ἐπεὶ δὴ τὰ μὲν ἄλλα τοῖς ἀριθμοῖς ἐφαίνοντο τὴν φύσιν ἀφωμοιῶσθαι πᾶσαν, οἱ δ᾽ ἀριθμοὶ πάσης τῆς φύσεως πρῶτοι, {986a1} τὰ τῶν ἀριθμῶν στοιχεῖα τῶν ὄντων στοιχεῖα πάντων ὑπέλαβον εἶναι, καὶ τὸν ὅλον οὐρανὸν ἁρμονίαν εἶναι καὶ ἀριθμόν· καὶ ὅσα εἶχον ὁμολογούμενα ἔν τε τοῖς ἀριθμοῖς καὶ ταῖς ἁρμονίαις πρὸς {5} τὰ τοῦ οὐρανοῦ πάθη καὶ μέρη καὶ πρὸς τὴν ὅλην διακόσμησιν, ταῦτα συνάγοντες ἐφήρμοττον. κἂν εἴ τί που διέλειπε, προσεγλίχοντο τοῦ συνειρομένην πᾶσαν αὐτοῖς εἶναι τὴν πραγματείαν· λέγω δ᾽ οἷον, ἐπειδὴ τέλειον ἡ δεκὰς εἶναι δοκεῖ καὶ πᾶσαν περιειληφέναι τὴν τῶν ἀριθμῶν φύσιν, {10} καὶ τὰ φερόμενα κατὰ τὸν οὐρανὸν δέκα μὲν εἶναί φασιν, ὄντων δὲ ἐννέα μόνον τῶν φανερῶν διὰ τοῦτο δεκάτην τὴν ἀντίχθονα ποιοῦσιν. διώρισται δὲ περὶ τούτων ἐν ἑτέροις ἡμῖν ἀκριβέστερον.

Moreover, since they considered the attributes and ratios of harmonies in terms of numbers, and since other things in their whole nature seemed to be likened to numbers, and since numbers are the first things in the whole of nature, they thought that the elements of numbers are the elements of all things, and that the whole heaven is a harmony and number. And whatever they had revealed in the case of numbers and harmonies which they could show to be in agreement with the motions and parts of the heavens, and its whole arrangement, they collected and adapted to these. And if anything was lacking anywhere, they called it in order that their undertaking might be complete. I mean that since the number ten seems to be the perfect number and to comprise the whole nature of numbers, they said that the bodies which move in the heavens are ten in number; but as only nine are observable they therefore invented a tenth, the counter-earth. These things have been dealt with more exactly in another work.[2]

---

112. Hic incipit ponere positiones eorum, qui posuerunt de principiis positiones extraneas non manifestas.

Et primo illorum qui posuerunt plura principia rerum.

Secundo illorum, qui posuerunt tantum unum ens, ibi, *sunt autem aliqui* et cetera.

Circa primum duo facit.

Primo ponit opinionem Leucippi et Democriti, qui posuerunt principia rerum corporea.

Secundo ponit opinionem Pythagoricorum, qui posuerunt principia rerum incorporea, ibi, *in his autem* et cetera.

Circa primum duo facit.

Primo ponit opinionem Democriti et Leucippi de causa materiali rerum.

Secundo de causa diversitatis, quomodo scilicet ex materia plures res diversificantur, in quo etiam apparet causa generationis et corruptionis rerum: in quo etiam cum antiquis philosophis conveniebant, ibi, *et quemadmodum in unum* et cetera.

Dicit ergo, quod duo philosophi, qui amici dicuntur, quia in omnibus se sequebantur, scilicet Democritus et Leucippus, posuerunt rerum principia plenum et inane,

112. Here he begins to give the positions of those who held strange and obscure views about the principles of things.

First, he gives the position of those who held that there are many principles of things;

and second [134] the position of those who held that there is only one being, at *but there are some* (983b27).

In regard to the first he does two things.

First, he gives the opinion of Leucippus and Democritus, who held that the principles of things are bodily.

Second [119], he gives the opinion of the Pythagoreans, who held that the principles of things are incorporeal entities, at *but during the time* (985b23).

In regard to the first he does two things.

First, he gives the opinion of Democritus and Leucippus about the material cause of things;

and second [115], their opinion about the cause of diversity, that is, how matter is differentiated into many things. In this discussion, the cause of the generation and corruption of things also becomes evident; this is a point on which these men agreed with the ancient philosophers, at *and just as those who* (985b10).

He says, then, that two philosophers, Democritus and Leucippus, who are called friends because they followed each other in all things, held that the principles of things

---

2. *De caelo* 2.13.

sive vacuum; quorum plenum est ens, et vacuum sive inane non ens.

113. Ad huius autem opinionis evidentiam recolendum est hoc quod Philosophus dicit in primo *De generatione*, ubi diffusius eam tradit. Cum enim quidam philosophi posuissent omnia esse unum ens continuum, immobile: quia nec motus sine vacuo esse potest, ut videtur, nec etiam rerum distinctio, ut dicebant, cum continuitatis privationem, ex qua oportet intelligere corporum diversitatem, nisi per vacuum non possent comprehendere, vacuum autem nullo modo esse ponerent, supervenit Democritus, qui eorum rationi consentiens, diversitatem autem et motum a rebus auferre non valens, vacuum esse posuit, et omnia corpora ex quibusdam indivisibilibus corporibus esse composita: propter hoc, quia non videbatur sibi quod ratio posset assignari quare ens universum magis in una parte esset divisum quam in alia;

ne poneret totum esse continuum, praeelegit ponere ubique totum et totaliter esse divisum; quod esse non posset si remaneret aliquod divisibile indivisum. Huiusmodi autem indivisibilia corpora invicem coniungi non possunt, nec esse ut ponebat, nisi vacuo mediante: quia nisi vacuum inter duo eorum interveniret, oporteret ex eis duobus unum esse continuum quod ratione praedicta non ponebat. Sic igitur uniuscuiusque corporis magnitudinem constitutam dicebat ex illis indivisibilibus corporibus implentibus indivisibilia spatia, et ex quibusdam spatii vacuis ipsis indivisibilibus corporibus interiacentibus, quae quidem poros esse dicebat.

114. Ex quo patet quod cum vacuum sit non ens, et plenum sit ens, non magis ponebat rei constitutionem ens quam non ens: quia nec corpora magis quam vacuum, nec vacuum magis quam corpora; sed ex duobus simul dicebat, ut dictum est corpus constitui. Unde praedicta duo ponebat rerum causas sicut materiam.

115. Deinde cum dicit *et quemadmodum* hic ostendit in quo conveniebant praedicti philosophi cum antiquis philosophis, qui ponebant unam tantum materiam. Ostendit autem quod conveniebant cum eis in duobus.

Primo quidem, quia sicut sunt ponentes unam materiam, et ex illa materia una generabant aliam secundum diversas materiae passiones, quae sunt rarum et densum, quae accipiebant ut principia omnium aliarum passionum; ita et isti, scilicet Democritus et Leucippus, dicebant, quod causae differentes erant *aliorum*, scilicet corporum constitutorum ex indivisibilibus, videlicet quod per aliquas differentias illorum indivisibilium corporum et pororum diversa entia constituebantur.

are the full and the void or "empty," of which the full is being, and the void or empty is non-being.

113. Now in order to clarify this opinion we must recall what the Philosopher says in *On Generation and Corruption* 1, where he treats it more fully. For certain philosophers had held that everything is one continuous immobile being, because it seems that there cannot be motion without a void, or any distinction between things, as they said. And though they could not comprehend the privation of continuity (by reason of which bodies must be understood to be differentiated) except by means of a void, they claimed that the void existed in no way. Democritus, who came after them, and who agreed with their reasoning but was unable to exclude diversity and motion from things, held that the void existed, and that all bodies are composed of certain indivisible bodies. He did this because it seemed to him that no reason could be given why the whole of being should be divided in one part rather than another.

And lest he should hold that the whole of being is continuous, he therefore chose to maintain that this whole is divided everywhere and in its entirety; this could not be the case if anything divisible remained undivided. And according to him indivisible bodies of this kind can neither exist nor be joined together except by means of the void. For if the void did not come between any two of them, one continuous whole would result from the two, which he did not hold for the above reason. Hence he said that the continuous quantity of each body is constituted both of those indivisible bodies filling indivisible spaces and of certain empty spaces, which he called pores, coming between these indivisible bodies.

114. And since the void is non-being and the full is being, it is evident from this that he did not hold that a thing was constituted by being rather than non-being, because the bodies did not constitute things more than the void or the void more than bodies, but he said that a body is composed at once of these two things, as is clear in the text. Hence he held that these two things are the causes of things as their matter.

115. *And just as those* (985b10). Here he shows in what respect these philosophers agreed with the ancients who claimed that there is only one matter. He indicates agreement in two respects.

First, just as the ancient philosophers held that there is one matter, and from that one matter generated something else according to the different attributes of matter (namely, the rare and dense, which they accepted as the principles of all other attributes), in a similar way Democritus and Leucippus said that there were different causes *of different things* (namely, of the bodies composed of these indivisible bodies)—that is, that different beings were produced as a result of certain differences of these indivisible bodies and their pores.

116. Eas autem differentias dicebant esse, unam secundum figuram, quae attenditur ex hoc quod aliquid est angulatum, circulare et rectum:

aliam secundum ordinem quae est secundum prius et posterius:

aliam secundum positionem, quae est secundum ante et retro, dextrum et sinistrum, sursum et deorsum. Et sic dicebant quod unum ens differt ab alio vel *rhysmo* idest figura, vel *diathyge* idest ordine, vel *trope* idest positione.

117. Et hoc probat per exemplum in literis Graecis, in quibus una litera differt ab alia figura: sicut et in nostris differt una ab altera: A enim differt ab N, figura; AN vero et NA, differunt secundum ordinem, nam una ante aliam ordinatur. Una etiam differt ab altera positione, ut Z ab N, sicut et apud nos videmus quod semivocales post liquidas poni non possunt ante quas ponuntur mutae in eadem syllaba.

Sicut ergo propter triplicem diversitatem in literis ex eisdem literis diversimode se habentibus fit tragoedia et comoedia, ita ex eisdem corporibus indivisibilibus diversimode habentibus fiunt diversae species rerum.

118. Aliud vero in quo conveniebant isti philosophi cum antiquis est, quod sicut antiqui neglexerunt ponere causam ex qua motus inest rebus, ita et isti, licet illa indivisibilia corpora dicerent esse per se mobilia. Sic ergo patet quod per praedictos philosophos nihil dictum est nisi de duabus causis, scilicet de causa materiali ab omnibus, et de causa movente a quibusdam.

119. Deinde cum dicit *in his autem* hic ponit opiniones Pythagoricorum ponentium numeros esse substantias rerum. Et circa hoc duo facit.

Primo ponit opiniones de rerum substantia.

Secundo de rerum principiis, ibi, *sed cuius gratia advenimus.*

Circa primum ponit duo, ex quibus inducebantur ad ponendum numeros esse rerum substantias.

Secundum ponit ibi, *amplius autem harmoniarum* et cetera.

Dicit ergo quod Pythagorici philosophi fuerunt, *in his*, idest, contemporanei aliquibus dictorum philosophorum, *et ante hos*, quia fuerunt quidam quibusdam priores.

Sciendum est autem duo fuisse philosophorum genera. Nam quidam vocabantur Ionici, qui morabantur in illa terra, quae nunc Graecia dicitur: et isti sumpserunt principium a Thalete, ut supra dictum est. Alii philo-

116. Now they said that these differences are first differences in shape, because things are angular, circular, and square;

second, differences in arrangement, that is, insofar as the indivisible bodies are prior or subsequent;

third, differences in position, insofar as these bodies are in front or behind, right or left, or above and below. Hence they said that one being differs from another either *by rhythm*, which is shape, or *by inter-contact*, which is arrangement, or *by turning*, which is position.

117. He illustrates this by using the letters of the Greek alphabet, which differ from each other in shape just as in our alphabet one letter also differs from another; for A differs from N in shape. Again, AN differs from NA in arrangement, because one letter is placed before the other. And one letter also differs from another in position, as Z from N, just as in our language we also see that semivowels cannot stand after liquids preceded by mutes in the same syllable.

Therefore, just as "license" and "silence" come from the same letters as a result of the letters being disposed in different ways because of this threefold difference, in a similar fashion different species of things are produced from the same indivisible bodies as a result of the latter being disposed in different ways.

118. The second respect in which these philosophers agreed with the ancients is this. Just as the ancient philosophers neglected to posit a cause which accounts for motion in things, so also did these men, although they would say that these indivisible bodies are capable of self-motion. Thus it is evident that these philosophers mentioned only two of the causes: all of them spoke of the material cause, and some of the efficient cause.

119. *But during the time of these* (985b23). Here he gives the opinions of the Pythagoreans, who held that numbers are the substances of things. In regard to this he does two things.

First, he gives their opinions about the substance of things;

and second [124], their opinions about the principles of things, at *but the reason* (986a13).

In regard to the first he gives two reasons by which they were led to assert that numbers are the substances of things.

He gives the second reason [121] where he says, *moreover, since they considered* (985b31).

He says that the Pythagoreans were philosophers who lived *during the time of these*, that is, they were contemporaries of some of the foregoing philosophers; *and prior to them*, because they preceded some of them.

Now it must be understood that there were two groups of philosophers. One group was called the Ionians, who inhabited the land which is now called Greece. This group originated with Thales, as was pointed out above [77].

sophi fuerunt Italici, in illa parte Italiae quae quondam Magna Graecia dicebatur, quae nunc Apulia et Calabria dicitur: quorum philosophorum princeps fuit Pythagoras natione Samius, sic dictus a quadam Calabriae civitate. Et haec duo philosophorum genera simul concurrerunt. Et propter hoc dicit quod fuerunt, *in his et ante hos.*

120. Isti autem Italici philosophi, qui et Pythagorici dicuntur, primi produxerunt quaedam mathematica, ut ea rerum sensibilium substantias et principia esse dicerent. Dicit ergo, *primi*, quia Platonici eos sunt secuti. Ex hoc autem moti sunt ut mathematica introducerent, quia erant nutriti in eorum studio. Et ideo principia mathematicorum credebant esse principia omnium entium. Consuetum est enim apud homines, quod per ea quae noverunt, de rebus iudicare velint. Et quia inter mathematica numeri sunt priores, ideo conati sunt speculari similitudines rerum naturalium, et quantum ad esse et quantum ad fieri, magis in numeris quam in sensibilibus elementis, quae sunt terra et aqua et huiusmodi.

Sicut enim praedicti philosophi passiones rerum sensibilium adaptant passionibus rerum naturalium, per quamdam similitudinem ad proprietates ignis et aquae et huiusmodi corporum: ita mathematici adaptabant proprietates rerum naturalium ad numerorum passiones, quando dicebant quod aliqua passio numerorum est causa iustitiae, et aliqua causa animae et intellectus, et aliqua causa temporis, et sic de aliis. Et sic passiones numerorum intelliguntur esse rationes et principia quaedam omnium apparentium in rebus sensibilibus, et quantum ad res voluntarias, quod designatur per iustitiam, et quantum ad formas substantiales rerum naturalium, quod designatur per intellectum et animam: et quantum ad accidentia, quod designatur per tempus.

121. Deinde cum dicit *amplius autem* hic ponit secundum motivum. Considerabant enim passiones harmoniarum, consonantiarum musicalium et earum rationes, scilicet proportiones, ex natura numerorum. Unde cum soni consonantes sint quaedam sensibilia, eadem ratione sunt conati et cetera alia sensibilia secundum rationem et secundum totam naturam assimilare numeris, ita quod numeri sunt primi in tota natura.

122. Et propter hoc etiam aestimaverunt quod principia numerorum essent principia omnium entium existentium, et totum caelum nihil aliud esse dicebant nisi quamdam naturam et harmoniam numerorum, idest proportionem quamdam numeralem, similem proportioni, quae consideratur in harmoniis. Unde quaecumque habebant *confessa*, idest manifesta, quae poterant adaptare numeris et harmoniis adaptabant, et

The other group of philosophers were the Italians, who lived in that part of Italy which was once called Greater Greece and is now called Apulia and Calabria. The leader of these philosophers was Pythagoras, a native of Samos, so called from a certain city of Calabria. These two groups of philosophers lived at the same time, and this is why he says that they lived *during the time of these and prior to them*.

120. These Italian philosophers, also called Pythagoreans, were the first to develop certain mathematical entities, so that they said that these are the substances and principles of sensible things. He says that they were *the first* because the Platonists were their successors. They were moved to bring in mathematics because they were brought up in the study of these sciences, and therefore they thought that the principles of mathematics are the principles of all existing things. For men are wont to judge about things in terms of what they already know. And since among mathematical entities numbers are first, these men therefore tried to see resemblances of natural things, both as regards their being and generation, in numbers rather than in the sensible elements (earth, water, and the like).

For just as the foregoing philosophers adapted the attributes of sensible things to those of natural things because of a certain resemblance which they bear to the properties of fire, water, and bodies of this kind, in a similar fashion these mathematicians adapted the properties of natural things to the attributes of numbers when they said that some one attribute of number is the cause of justice, another the cause of soul and intellect, and still another the cause of opportunity, and so on for other things. And in this way the attributes of numbers are understood to be the intelligible structures and principles of all things appearing in the sensible world, both in the realm of voluntary matters (signified by justice), and in that of the substantial forms of natural things (signified by soul and intellect), and in that of accidents (signified by opportunity).

121. *Moreover, since they* (985b31). Here he gives the second reason which motivated them. For they thought of the attributes of harmonies—musical consonants and their ratios or proportions—in terms of the nature of numbers. Hence, since harmonious sounds are certain sensible things, they attempted by the same reasoning to liken all other sensible things (both in their intelligible structure and in their whole nature) to numbers, so that numbers are the first things in the whole of nature.

122. For this reason too they thought that the principles of numbers are the principles of all existing things, and they said that the whole heaven is merely a kind of nature and harmony of numbers, a kind of numerical proportion similar to the proportion found in harmonies. Hence, whatever they had *revealed*, or had shown, which they could adapt to numbers and harmonies, they also adapted both to the changes undergone by the heavens (as its motion, eclipses,

quantum ad caeli passiones, sicut sunt motus et eclypses et huiusmodi et quantum ad partes, sicut sunt diversi orbes: et quantum ad totum caeli ornatum, sicut sunt diversae stellae et diversae figurae in constellationibus.

123. Et si aliquid deficiebat in rebus manifestis quod non videretur numeris adaptari, *advocabant*, idest ipsi de novo ponebant *continuatum esse eis omne negotium*, idest ad hoc quod totum negotium eorum quod erat adaptare sensibilia ad numeros, continuaretur, dum omnia sensibilia numeris adaptarent, sicut patet in uno exemplo. In numeris enim denarius videtur esse perfectus, eo quod est primus limes, et comprehendit in se omnium numerorum naturam: quia omnes alii numeri non sunt nisi quaedam repetitio denarii. Propter quod Plato usque ad decem faciebat numerum, ut dicitur quarto *Physicorum*.

Unde et Pythagoras, sphaeras, quae moventur in caelo, dixit decem, quamvis novem solum harum sint apparentes: quia deprehenduntur septem motibus planetarum, octava ex motu stellarum fixarum, nona vero ex motu diurno, qui est motus primus.

Sed et Pythagoras addit decimam quae esset *antictona* idest in contrarium mota in inferioribus sphaeris, et per consequens in contrarium sonans. Dicebat enim ex motu caelestium corporum fieri quamdam harmoniam: unde sicut harmonia fit ex proportione sonorum contrariorum, scilicet gravis et acuti, ita ponebat quod in caelo erat unus motus in oppositam partem aliis motibus, ut fieret harmonia. Et secundum hanc positionem motus diurnus pertinebat ad decimam sphaeram, quae est ab oriente in occidentem, aliis sphaeris revolutis e contrario ab occidente in orientem. Nona vero secundum eum esse poterat, quae primo revolvebat omnes sphaeras inferiores in contrarium primi motus. De his autem quae ad opinionem istam Pythagorae pertinent, determinatum est diffusius et certius in ultimis libris huius scientiae.

and the like), and to its parts (as the different orbs), and to the whole arrangement of the heavens (as the different stars and different figures in the constellations).

123. And if anything was lacking in the observable order of things that did not seem to be adapted to numbers, *they called it in*, that is, they invented something new *in order that their whole undertaking*, which was to adapt sensible things to numbers, *might be made complete*, until they had adapted all sensible things to numbers, as is evident in one example. For the number ten seems to be the perfect number, because it constitutes the first limit and contains within itself the nature of all numbers; for all other numbers are merely a kind of repetition of the number ten. This is why Plato counted up to ten, as Aristotle says in *Physics* 4.

Hence Pythagoras also said that the spheres which move in the heavens are ten in number, although only nine of these are observable; we observe seven in the motions of the planets, an eighth in the motion of the fixed stars, and a ninth in the daily motion, which is the first motion.

But Pythagoras adds a tenth sphere, which was that of the *counter-earth*, that is, which is moved in the opposite direction to the motion in the lower spheres and therefore produces a contrary sound. For he said that a kind of harmony results from the motion of the celestial bodies, so that just as a harmony is produced from a proportion of contrary sounds of low and high notes, in a similar way he claimed that in the heavens there was a single motion in the opposite direction to that of the other motions in order that a harmony might result. According to this position, the daily motion belonged to the tenth sphere, which moves from east to west, the other spheres being revolved in the opposite direction from west to east. In fact, according to him, it could have been the ninth sphere which first revolved all the lower spheres in the opposite direction to the first motion. The things that pertain to this opinion of Pythagoras are considered more extensively and more definitely in the last books of this science.

LECTURE 8

The Pythagoreans' doctrine of contraries

986a13 Sed cuius gratia advenimus, hoc est, ut accipiamus et de his quae ponunt esse principia, et quomodo in dictas cadunt causas. Videntur autem igitur et hi numerum putare principium esse quasi materiam existentibus, et quasi passiones et habitus. [124]

ἀλλ᾽ οὐ δὴ χάριν ἐπερχόμεθα, τοῦτό ἐστιν ὅπως λάβωμεν καὶ παρὰ τούτων τίνας εἶναι τιθέασι τὰς {15} ἀρχὰς καὶ πῶς εἰς τὰς εἰρημένας ἐμπίπτουσιν αἰτίας. φαίνονται δὴ καὶ οὗτοι τὸν ἀριθμὸν νομίζοντες ἀρχὴν εἶναι καὶ ὡς ὕλην τοῖς οὖσι καὶ ὡς πάθη τε καὶ ἕξεις,

But the reason we have come [to examine these philosophers] is that we may also learn from them what they hold the principles of things to be, and how these principles fall under the causes already described. Now these men also seem to think that number is the principle of existing things both as their matter and as their attributes and states.

Numeri vero elementa par et impar; et quidem hoc finitum, illud vero infinitum. Unum autem ex his utrisque esse; etenim par esse et impar; numerum vero ex uno. Numerus autem, sicut dictum est, totum caelum.

τοῦ δὲ ἀριθμοῦ στοιχεῖα τό τε ἄρτιον καὶ τὸ περιττόν, τούτων δὲ τὸ μὲν πεπερασμένον τὸ δὲ ἄπειρον, τὸ δ᾽ ἓν ἐξ ἀμφοτέρων εἶναι τούτων {20} (καὶ γὰρ ἄρτιον εἶναι καὶ περιττόν), τὸν δ᾽ ἀριθμὸν ἐκ τοῦ ἑνός, ἀριθμοὺς δέ, καθάπερ εἴρηται, τὸν ὅλον οὐρανόν.

According to them, the elements of number are the even and odd; of these the latter is limited and the former is unlimited. The unit is composed of both of these, since it is both even and odd, and number is derived from the unit. And number, as has been stated (985b31), constitutes the whole heaven.

986a22 Eorumdem autem alii decem dicunt esse principia secundum coelementationem dicta, finitum et infinitum, par et impar, unum et plura, dextrum et sinistrum, masculinum et femininum, quiescens et motum, rectum et curvum, lucem et tenebras, malum et bonum, quadrangulare et longius altera parte. [127]

ἕτεροι δὲ τῶν αὐτῶν τούτων τὰς ἀρχὰς δέκα λέγουσιν εἶναι τὰς κατὰ συστοιχίαν λεγομένας, πέρας [καὶ] ἄπειρον, περιττὸν [καὶ] ἄρτιον, ἓν [καὶ] πλῆθος, δεξιὸν [καὶ] ἀριστερόν, ἄρρεν {25} [καὶ] θῆλυ, ἠρεμοῦν [καὶ] κινούμενον, εὐθὺ [καὶ] καμπύλον, φῶς [καὶ] σκότος, ἀγαθὸν [καὶ] κακόν, τετράγωνον [καὶ] ἑτερόμηκες·

But other members of the same school say that the principles of things are ten in number, which they give as co-elements: the limited and unlimited, even and odd, one and many, right and left, masculine and feminine, rest and motion, straight and curved, light and darkness, good and evil, the quadrangular and rectangular.

986a27 Quemadmodum videtur Alcmaeon Crotoniates suscipere, et aut hic ab illis, aut illi ab hoc hunc sermonem acceperunt. Etenim fuit aetate Alcmaeon sene existente Pythagora. Is vero consimiliter enuntiavit. [131]

ὅνπερ τρόπον ἔοικε καὶ Ἀλκμαίων ὁ Κροτωνιάτης ὑπολαβεῖν, καὶ ἤτοι οὗτος παρ᾽ ἐκείνων ἢ ἐκεῖνοι παρὰ τούτου παρέλαβον τὸν λόγον τοῦτον· καὶ γὰρ [ἐγένετο τὴν ἡλικίαν] Ἀλκμαίων {30} [ἐπὶ γέροντι Πυθαγόρᾳ,] ἀπεφήνατο [δὲ] παραπλησίως τούτοις·

Alcmaeon of Croton seems to have formed his opinion in the same way, and either he derived the theory from them or they from him; for Alcmaeon (who had reached maturity when Pythagoras was an old man) expressed views similar to those of the Pythagoreans.

Nam ait esse duo, multas humanorum dicens contrarietates, non sicut hi determinatas, sed quascumque fortuna contingentes: ut album nigrum, dulce amarum, bonum malum, parvum magnum. Hic quidem indeterminate proiecit de ceteris. Pythagorici vero et quot et quae contrarietates enunciaverunt.

φησὶ γὰρ εἶναι δύο τὰ πολλὰ τῶν ἀνθρωπίνων, λέγων τὰς ἐναντιότητας οὐχ ὥσπερ οὗτοι διωρισμένας ἀλλὰ τὰς τυχούσας, οἷον λευκὸν μέλαν, γλυκὺ πικρόν, ἀγαθὸν κακόν, μέγα μικρόν. οὗτος μὲν οὖν ἀδιορίστως ἀπέρριψε περὶ τῶν λοιπῶν, {986b1} οἱ δὲ Πυθαγόρειοι καὶ πόσαι καὶ τίνες αἱ ἐναντιώσεις ἀπεφήναντο.

For he says that many things in human affairs are in twos, calling them contrarieties, not distinguished as these men had distinguished them, but such as are taken at random, for example, white and black, sweet and bitter, good and evil, small and great. It is true that this philosopher threw out vague remarks about the other contrarieties, but the Pythagoreans have declared both what the contrarieties are and how many there are.

986b2 Ab his igitur ambobus tantum est accipere, quia contraria sunt existentium principia: quot vero ab aliis, et quia haec sint. Qualiter autem ad dictas cau-

παρὰ μὲν οὖν τούτων ἀμφοῖν τοσοῦτον ἔστι λαβεῖν, ὅτι τἀναντία ἀρχαὶ τῶν ὄντων· τὸ δ᾽ ὅσαι παρὰ τῶν ἑτέρων, καὶ τίνες αὗταί εἰσιν. πῶς μέντοι πρὸς {5}

From both of these, then, we can gather this much, that contraries are the principles of existing things; but how many they are and that they are these we must

sas conducere contingit plura, plane quidem non est articulatum ab illis. Videtur autem ut in materiae specie elementa ordinare. Ex his enim ut ex his quae insunt, constitui et plasmari dicunt substantiam. [132]

τὰς εἰρημένας αἰτίας ἐνδέχεται συνάγειν, σαφῶς μὲν οὐ διήρθρωται παρ᾽ ἐκείνων, ἐοίκασι δ᾽ ὡς ἐν ὕλης εἴδει τὰ στοιχεῖα τάττειν: ἐκ τούτων γὰρ ὡς ἐνυπαρχόντων συνεστάναι καὶ πεπλάσθαι φασὶ τὴν οὐσίαν.

gather from other thinkers. The way in which many principles can be brought together under the causes described is not clearly expressed by them, although they seem to allot their elements to the species of matter; for they say that substance is composed and molded out of these as something inherent.

Antiquorum quidem igitur elementa naturae plura dicentium, ex his sufficiens est intellectui speculari.

τῶν μὲν οὖν παλαιῶν καὶ πλείω λεγόντων τὰ στοιχεῖα τῆς φύσεως ἐκ τούτων ἱκανόν {10} ἐστι θεωρῆσαι τὴν διάνοιαν:

From these remarks, then, it is possible to get an adequate understanding of the ancient philosophers' meaning who said that the elements of things are many.

---

124. Hic ponit opinionem Pythagoricorum de principiis. Et circa hoc duo facit.

Primo ostendit quid circa rerum principia aestimabant.

Secundo ad quod genus causae principia ab eis posita reducuntur, ibi, *ab his igitur ambobus* et cetera.

Ponit autem circa primum tres opiniones.

Secunda incipit ibi, *eorumdem autem alii* et cetera.

Tertia ibi, *quemadmodum videtur.*

Dicit ergo primo, quod huius gratia venit ad opiniones Pythagoricorum recitandas, ut ostenderet per eorum opiniones, quae sunt rerum principia, et quomodo rerum principia ab eis posita incidunt in causas suprapositas. Videntur enim Pythagorici ponere numerum esse principium entium sicut numerum, et passiones numeri esse sicut passiones entium, et sicut habitus; ut per passiones intelligamus accidentia cito transeuntia, per habitus accidentia permanentia. Sicut ponebant quod passio alicuius numeri secundum quam dicitur aliquis numerus par, erat iustitia propter aequalitatem divisionis, quia talis numerus aequaliter per media dividitur usque ad unitatem, sicut octonarius in duos quaternarios, quaternarius vero in duos binarios, et binarius in duas unitates. Et simili modo alia accidentia rerum assimilabant accidentibus numerorum.

125. Principia vero numerorum dicebant esse par et impar, quae sunt primae numerorum differentiae. Paremque numerum dicebant esse principium infinitatis, imparem vero principium finitatis, sicut exponitur in tertio *Physicorum*: quia infinitum in rebus praecipue videtur sequi divisionem continui. Par autem est numerus aptus divisioni. Impar enim sub se numerum parem concludit addita unitate, quae indivisionem causat.

Probat etiam hoc, quia numeri impares per ordinem sibi additi semper retinent figuram quadrati, pares autem figuram variant. Ternarius enim unitati quae est

124. Here he states what the Pythagoreans had to say about the principles of things. In regard to this he does two things.

First, he expounds their opinions about the principles of things;

second [132], he indicates to what genus of cause the principles laid down by them are reduced, at *from both of these* (986b2).

In regard to the first he gives three opinions.

The second [127] begins at the words, *but other members* (986a22);

and the third [131] at *Alcmaeon of Croton* (986a27).

He says first (986a13), then, that the reason he came to examine the opinions of the Pythagoreans is that he might show from their opinions what the principles of things are and how the principles laid down by them fall under the causes given above. For the Pythagoreans seem to hold that number is the principle of existing things as matter, and that the attributes of number are the attributes and states of existing things. By "attributes" we mean transient accidents, and by "states," permanent accidents. They also held that evenness of number is justice, because of the equality of division. Such a number is evenly divided into two parts right down to the unit: for example, the number eight is divided into two fours, the number four into two twos, and the number two into two units. And in a similar way they likened the other accidents of things to the accidents of numbers.

125. In fact, they said that the even and odd, which are the first differences of numbers, are the principles of numbers. And they said that even number is the principle of unlimitedness and odd number the principle of limitation, as is shown in the *Physics* 3; but in reality the unlimited seems to result chiefly from the division of the continuous. An even number is capable of division, but an odd number includes within itself an even number plus a unit, and this makes it indivisible.

He also proves this as follows. When odd numbers are added to each other successively, they always retain the figure of a square, whereas even numbers change their

principium numerorum additus facit quaternarium, qui primus est quadratus. Nam bis duo quatuor sunt. Rursus quaternario quinarius additus, qui est impar, secundum novenarium constituit, qui est etiam quadratus: et sic de aliis.

Si vero binarius qui est primus par, unitati addatur, triangularem numerum constituit, scilicet ternarium. Cui si addatur quaternarius, qui est secundus par, constituit heptangulum numerum, qui est septenarius. Et sic deinceps numeri pares sibi invicem additi, figuram non eamdem servant. Et hac ratione infinitum attribuebant pari, finitum vero impari. Et quia finitum est ex parte formae, cui competit vis activa, ideo pares numeros dicebant esse feminas, impares vero masculos.

126. Ex his vero duobus, scilicet pari et impari, finito et infinito, non solum numerum constituebant, sed etiam ipsum unum, idest unitatem. Unitas enim et par est virtute et impar. Omnes enim differentiae numeri unitati conveniunt in virtute, quia quaecumque differentiae numeri in unitate resolvuntur. Unde in ordine imparium primum invenitur unitas. Et similiter in ordine parium et quadratorum et perfectorum numerorum, et sic de aliis numeri differentiis: quia unitas licet non sit actu aliquis numerus, est tamen omnis numerus virtute. Et sicut unum dicebat componi ex pari et impari, ita numerum ex unitatibus: caelum vero et omnia sensibilia ex numeris. Et hic erat ordo principiorum quem ponebant.

127. Deinde cum dicit *eorumdem autem* hic ponit aliam opinionem Pythagoricorum de principiis; dicens, quod de numero eorumdem Pythagoricorum fuerunt aliqui, qui non posuerunt unam tantum contrarietatem in principiis, sicut praedicti; sed posuerunt decem principia *secundum coelementationem dicta*, idest accipiendo unumquodque illorum cum suo coelemento, idest cum suo contrario.

Et huius positionis ratio fuit, quia non solum accipiebant prima principia, sed etiam proxima principia singulis rerum generibus attributa. Ponebant ergo primo finitum et infinitum, sicut et illi qui praedicti sunt; et consequenter par et impar, quibus finitum et infinitum attribuitur. Et quia par et impar sunt prima rerum principia, et primo ex eis causantur numeri, ponebant tertio differentiam numerorum, scilicet unum et plura, quae duo ex pari et impari causabantur. Et quia ex numero constituebantur magnitudines, secundum quod in numeris positionem accipiebant (nam secundum eos punctus nihil aliud erat quam unitas positionem habens, et linea dualitas positionem habens), ideo consequenter

figure. For when the number three is added to the unit, which is the principle of numbers, the number four results, which is the first square, because two times two equals four. Again, when the number five, which is an odd number, is added to the number four, the number nine results, which is also a square number. And so on with the others.

But if the number two, which is the first even number, is added to the number one, a triangular number results—the number three. And if the number four, which is the second even number, is added to the number three, there results a septangular number—the number seven. And when even numbers are added to each other successively in this way, they do not retain the same figure. This is why they attributed the unlimited to the even and the limited to the odd. And since limitedness pertains to form, to which active power belongs, they therefore said that even numbers are feminine, and odd numbers masculine.

126. From these two (namely, the even and odd, the limited and unlimited), they produced not only number but also the unit itself—unity. For unity is virtually both even and odd, because all differences of number are virtually contained in the unit, all being reduced to the unit. Hence, in the list of odd numbers the unit is found to be the first. And the same is true in the list of even numbers, square numbers, and perfect numbers. This is also the case with the other differences of number, because even though the unit is not actually a number, it is still virtually all numbers. And just as the unit is said to be composed of the even and odd, in a similar way number is composed of units. Indeed, the heavens and all sensible things are composed of numbers. This was the sequence of principles which they gave.

127. *But other members* (986a22). Here he gives another opinion which the Pythagoreans held about the principles of things. He says that among these same Pythagoreans there were some who claimed that there is not just one contrariety in principles, as the foregoing did, but ten principles, *which they give as co-elements*, that is, by taking each of these principles with its co-principle, or contrary.

The reason for this position was that they took not only the first principles but also the proximate principles attributed to each genus of things. Hence, they posited first the limited and the unlimited (as did those who have just been mentioned), and subsequently the even and the odd (to which the limited and unlimited are attributed). And because the even and odd are the first principles of things, and numbers are first produced from them, they posited third a difference of numbers—namely, the one and the many, both of which are produced from the even and the odd. Again, because continuous quantities are composed of numbers, inasmuch as they understood numbers to have position (for, according to them, the point was

ponebant principia positionum dextrum et sinistrum. Dextrum enim invenitur perfectum, sinistrum autem imperfectum. Et ideo dextrum erat ex parte imparis, sinistrum ex parte paris. Quia vero naturalia super magnitudines mathematicas addunt virtutem activam et passivam, ideo ulterius ponebant principia masculum et feminam. Masculum enim ad virtutem activam pertinet, femineum ad passivam: quorum masculum pertinet ad imparem, femineum vero ad parem numerum, ut dictum est.

128. Ex virtute autem activa et passiva sequitur in rebus motus et quies: quorum motus quia deformitatem habet et alteritatem, in ordine infiniti et paris ponitur, quies vero in ordine finiti et imparis. Differentiae autem motuum primae sunt circulare et rectum. Et ideo consequenter rectum ad parem numerum pertinet; unde et lineam rectam dualitatem esse dicebant. Curvum vero sive circulare ratione uniformitatis pertinet ad imparem, qui indivisionem ex forma unitatis retinet.

129. Nec solum ponebant principia rerum quantum ad actiones naturales et motus, sed etiam quantum ad actiones animales. Et quantum quidem ad cognitionem ponebant lucem et tenebras: quantum vero ad appetitum, bonum et malum. Nam lux est cognitionis principium, tenebra vero ignorantiae ascribitur. Bonum etiam est in quod appetitus tendit, malum vero a quo recedit.

130. Diversitas autem perfectionis et imperfectionis non solum in naturalibus et voluntariis virtutibus et motibus invenitur, sed etiam in magnitudine et figuris. Quae quidem figurae intelliguntur ut supervenientes substantiis magnitudinum, sicut virtutes motus et actiones substantiis rerum naturalium. Et ideo quantum ad hoc ponebant principium *quadrangulare*, idest quadratum, et altera parte longius. Dicitur autem quadratum figura constans ex quatuor lateribus aequalibus, cuius quatuor anguli sunt recti; et provenit talis figura ex ductu alicuius lineae in seipsam. Unde cum ex ipsa unitate causetur, ad numerum imparem pertinet. Figura vero altera parte longior dicitur, cuius omnes anguli sunt recti, et latera vicissim sibi opposita sunt aequalia, non tamen omnia latera sunt aequalia omnibus. Unde patet quod sicut quadratum consurgit ex ductu unius lineae in seipsam, ita figura altera parte longior, ex ductu duarum linearum in unam. Et sic pertinet ad numerum parem, qui primus est dualitas.

131. Deinde cum dicit *quemadmodum* hic ponit tertiam opinionem Pythagoricorum, dicens, quod Alc-

merely the unit having position, and the line the number two having position), they therefore claimed next that the principles of positions are the right and left, for the right is found to be perfect and the left imperfect. Therefore, the right is determined from the aspect of oddness, and the left from the aspect of evenness. But because natural bodies have both active and passive powers in addition to mathematical extensions, they therefore next maintained that masculine and feminine are principles. For masculine pertains to active power, and feminine to passive power; of these, masculine pertains to odd number and feminine to even number, as has been stated [125].

128. Now it is from active and passive power that motion and rest originate in the world. Of these, motion is placed in the class of the unlimited and even, because it partakes of irregularity and otherness, and rest in the class of the unlimited and odd. Furthermore, the first differences of motions are the circular and straight, so that as a consequence of this the straight pertains to even number. Hence they said that the straight line is the number two, but that the curved or circular line, by reason of its uniformity, pertains to odd number, which retains its undividedness because of the form of unity.

129. And they posited principles not only to account for the natural operations and motions of things, but also to account for the operations of living things. In fact, they held that light and darkness are principles of knowing, but that good and evil are principles of appetite. For light is a principle of knowing, whereas darkness is ascribed to ignorance; good is that to which appetite tends, whereas evil is that from which it turns away.

130. Again, they said that the difference of perfection and imperfection is found not only in natural things and in voluntary powers and motions, but also in continuous quantities and figures. These figures are understood to be something over and above the substances of continuous quantities, just as the powers responsible for motions and operations are something over and above the substances of natural bodies. Therefore, with reference to this they held that what is *quadrangular* (that is, the square and the rectangle) is a principle. Now a square is said to be a figure of four equal sides whose four angles are right angles, and such a figure is produced by multiplying a line by itself. Therefore, since it is produced from the unit itself, it belongs to the odd numbers. But a rectangle is defined as a figure whose angles are all right angles and whose opposite sides alone, not all sides, are equal to each other. Hence it is clear that, just as a square is produced by multiplying one line by itself, in a similar way a rectangle is produced by multiplying one line by another. Hence it pertains to the even numbers, of which the first is the number two.

131. *Alcmaeon of Croton* (986a27). Here he gives the third opinion of the Pythagoreans, saying that Alcmaeon

maeon Crotoniates, sic dictus a civitate unde oriundus fuit, videtur suscipere quantum ad aliquid idem quod praedicti Pythagorici dixerunt, scilicet quod plura contraria sint principia. Aut enim accepit a Pythagoricis, aut illi ab isto. Et quod utrumque esse potuerit, patet per hoc quod fuit contemporaneus Pythagoricorum: ita tamen quod incoepit philosophari Pythagora sene existente.

Sed qualitercumque fuerit, multum similiter enunciavit Pythagoricis. Dixit enim multa quae sunt *humanorum* idest multa rerum sensibilium esse in quadam dualitate constituta, intelligens per dualitatem opposita contrarie. Sed tamen in hoc differt a praedictis, quia Pythagorici dicebant determinatas contrarietates esse rerum principia. Sed ille proiecit quasi inordinate ponens quascumque contrarietates, quae a fortuna ad mentem suam deveniebant, esse rerum principia: sicut album nigrum, dulce amarum, et sic de aliis.

132. Deinde cum dicit *ab his igitur* hic colligit ex praedictis quid Pythagorici de principiis senserunt, et quomodo principia ab eis posita ad aliquod genus causae reducantur. Dicit ergo quod ex ambobus praedictis, scilicet Alcmaeone et Pythagoricis una communis opinio accipi potest, scilicet quod principia entium sunt contraria; quod non est ab aliis dictum. Quod intelligendum est circa causam materialem.

Nam circa causam efficientem posuit Empedocles contrarietatem. Antiqui vero naturales, contraria posuerunt principia, ut rarum et densum; contrarietatem tamen ex parte formae assignantes. Empedocles vero etsi principia materialia posuerit quatuor elementa, non tamen posuit ea principia prima materialia ratione contrarietatis, sed propter eorum naturas et substantiam: isti vero contrarietatem ex parte materiae posuerunt.

133. Quae etiam sint ista contraria quae isti posuerunt, patet ex dictis. Sed quomodo praedicta principia contraria ab eis posita possunt *conduci* idest reduci ad praedictas species causarum, non est manifeste *articulatum,* idest distincte expressum ab eis. Tamen videtur quod huiusmodi principia ordinentur secundum speciem causae materialis. Dicunt enim quod substantia rerum constituitur et plasmatur ab istis principiis, sicut ex his quae insunt: quod est ratio causae materialis. Materia enim est ex qua fit aliquid cum insit. Quod quidem dicitur ad differentiam privationis, ex qua etiam dicitur aliquid fieri, non tamen inest, sicut dicitur musicum fieri ex non musico.

of Croton, so named from the city in which he was raised, seems to maintain somewhat the same view as that expressed by these Pythagoreans, namely, that many contraries are the principles of things. For either he derives the theory from the Pythagoreans, or they from him. That either of these might be true is clear from the fact that he was a contemporary of the Pythagoreans, granted that he began to philosophize when Pythagoras was an old man.

But whichever happens to be true, he expressed views similar to those of the Pythagoreans. For he said that many of the things *in the realm of human affairs* (that is, many of the attributes of sensible things) are arranged in pairs, understanding by pairs opposites which are contrary. Yet in this matter he differs from the foregoing philosophers, because the Pythagoreans said that determinate contraries are the principles of things. But he throws them in, as it were, without any order, holding that any of the contraries which he happened to think of are the principles of things, such as white and black, sweet and bitter, and so on.

132. *From both of these* (986b2). Here he gathers together from the above remarks what the Pythagoreans thought about the principles of things, and how the principles which they posited are reduced to some genus of cause. He says, then, that from both of those mentioned above (namely, Alcmaeon and the Pythagoreans), it is possible to draw one common opinion not expressed by earlier thinkers: the principles of existing things are contraries. This must be understood with reference to the material cause.

For Empedocles posited contrariety in the case of the efficient cause, and the ancient philosophers of nature posited contrary principles, such as rarity and density, although they attributed contrariety to form. But even though Empedocles held that the four elements are material principles, he still did not claim that they are the first material principles by reason of contrariety, but because of their natures and substance. These men, however, attributed contrariety to matter.

133. The nature of the contraries posited by these men is evident from the foregoing discussion. But how the aforesaid contrary principles posited by them can be *brought together under* (or reduced to) the types of causes described is not clearly *expressed* (or distinctly stated) by them. Yet it seems that such principles are allotted to the species of material cause, for they say that the substance of things is composed and molded out of these principles as something inherent, and this is the notion of a material cause. For matter is that from which a thing comes to be as something inherent. This is added to distinguish it from privation, from which something also comes to be but which is not inherent, as the musical is said to come from the non-musical.

LECTURE 9

Eleatics and Pythagoreans' opinions

986b10 Sunt autem aliqui, qui de omni quasi existente una natura enuntiaverunt, modo vero non eodem omnes, neque ipsius bene, neque ipsius secundum naturam. [134]

εἰσὶ δέ τινες οἳ περὶ τοῦ παντὸς ὡς μιᾶς οὔσης φύσεως ἀπεφήναντο, τρόπον δὲ οὐ τὸν αὐτὸν πάντες οὔτε τοῦ καλῶς οὔτε τοῦ κατὰ τὴν φύσιν.

But there are some who spoke of the whole as if it were a single nature, although the statements which they made are not all alike with regard to either their acceptableness or their conformity with nature.

986b12 Igitur ad praesentem causarum perscrutationem nullatenus congruit de ipsis sermo. Non enim ut philosophorum quidam, qui unum posuerunt ipsum ens, tamen generant ex materia quasi ex uno. Sed alio dicunt hi modo. Illi namque motum apponunt ipsum omne generantes, hi vero immobile dicunt esse. [135]

εἰς μὲν οὖν τὴν νῦν σκέψιν τῶν αἰτίων οὐδαμῶς συναρμόττει περὶ αὐτῶν ὁ λόγος (οὐ γὰρ ὥσπερ ἔνιοι τῶν φυσιολόγων ἓν ὑποθέμενοι {15} τὸ ὂν ὅμως γεννῶσιν ὡς ἐξ ὕλης τοῦ ἑνός, ἀλλ᾽ ἕτερον τρόπον οὗτοι λέγουσιν· ἐκεῖνοι μὲν γὰρ προστιθέασι κίνησιν, γεννῶντές γε τὸ πᾶν, οὗτοι δὲ ἀκίνητον εἶναί φασιν):

Therefore, a consideration of these men pertains in no way to the present investigation of causes. For they do not, like certain of the philosophers who supposed being to be one, still generate it from the one as matter; but they speak of this in another way. For the others assume motion when they generate this whole, whereas these thinkers say it is immobile.

986b17 Sed quidem secundum tantum praesenti proprium est inquisitioni. Parmenides enim videtur unum secundum rationem tangere. Melissus vero ipsum secundum materiam. Quare et hic quidem finitum, ille vero infinitum id esse ait. Xenophanes vero primus horum unum dixit. Parmenides enim, qui huius dicitur fuisse discipulus, nihil explanavit. Neque de natura horum neuter visus est tangere; sed ad totum caelum respiciens, ipsum unum dicit esse Deum. [137]

οὐ μὴν ἀλλὰ τοσοῦτόν γε οἰκεῖόν ἐστι τῇ νῦν σκέψει. Παρμενίδης μὲν γὰρ ἔοικε τοῦ κατὰ τὸν λόγον ἑνὸς ἅπτεσθαι, Μέλισσος {20} δὲ τοῦ κατὰ τὴν ὕλην (διὸ καὶ ὁ μὲν πεπερασμένον ὁ δ᾽ ἄπειρόν φησιν εἶναι αὐτό): Ξενοφάνης δὲ πρῶτος τούτων ἑνίσας (ὁ γὰρ Παρμενίδης τούτου λέγεται γενέσθαι μαθητής) οὐθὲν διεσαφήνισεν, οὐδὲ τῆς φύσεως τούτων οὐδετέρας ἔοικε θιγεῖν, ἀλλ᾽ εἰς τὸν ὅλον οὐρανὸν ἀποβλέψας τὸ ἓν εἶναί φησι τὸν {25} θεόν.

Yet their opinion is relevant to the present investigation to some extent; for Parmenides seems to touch on unity according to concept and Melissus on unity according to matter. This is why the former says that it is limited, and the latter that it is unlimited. Xenophanes, the first of those to speak of the one (for Parmenides is said to have been his disciple), made nothing clear, nor does he seem to come up to these men. But with regard to the whole heaven he says that the one is God.

986b25 Igitur ii (sicut diximus) praetermittendi sunt ad praesentem inquisitionem. Duo quidem, et penitus, tamquam existentes parum agrestiores, Xenophanes et Melissus. [142]

οὗτοι μὲν οὖν, καθάπερ εἴπομεν, ἀφετέοι πρὸς τὴν νῦν ζήτησιν, οἱ μὲν δύο καὶ πάμπαν ὡς ὄντες μικρὸν ἀγροικότεροι, Ξενοφάνης καὶ Μέλισσος:

As we have stated, then, these men must be dismissed for the purposes of the present inquiry. In fact, two of them—Xenophanes and Melissus—are to be disregarded altogether as being a little too rustic.

Parmenides autem magis videns visus est dicere. Praeter enim ens, non ens, nihil dignatur esse; unde ex necessitate opinatur unum esse ens, et aliud nihil: de quo in *Physicis* manifestius diximus.

Παρμενίδης δὲ μᾶλλον βλέπων ἔοικέ που λέγειν: παρὰ γὰρ τὸ ὂν τὸ μὴ ὂν οὐθὲν ἀξιῶν εἶναι, ἐξ ἀνάγκης ἓν οἴεται εἶναι, τὸ ὄν, καὶ {30} ἄλλο οὐθέν (περὶ οὗ σαφέστερον ἐν τοῖς περὶ φύσεως εἰρήκαμεν),

Parmenides, however, seems to speak with more insight, for he thought that besides being there is only non-being, and this is thought to be nothing. This is why he thinks that being is necessarily one and nothing else. We have discussed this point more clearly in the *Physics*.

Coactus vero apparentia sequi, et quid unum quidem secundum rationem, plura vero secundum sensum opinatus esse, duas causas et duo principia rursus ponit, calidum et frigidum, ut ignem et terram dicens. Horum autem

ἀναγκαζόμενος δ᾽ ἀκολουθεῖν τοῖς φαινομένοις, καὶ τὸ ἓν μὲν κατὰ τὸν λόγον πλείω δὲ κατὰ τὴν αἴσθησιν ὑπολαμβάνων εἶναι, δύο τὰς αἰτίας καὶ δύο τὰς ἀρχὰς πάλιν τίθησι, θερμὸν καὶ ψυχρόν, οἷον πῦρ καὶ γῆν λέγων: {987a1}

But being compelled to follow the observed facts, and having assumed that what is one from the viewpoint of reason is many from the viewpoint of the senses, he postulates in turn two principles (that is, two causes), the hot and cold, calling

quod quidem est secundum ens, calidum ordinat, alterum vero secundum non ens.

987a2 Igitur ex dictis et a sapientibus iam rationi consentientibus ea accepimus. A primis quidem igitur principium esse corporeum. Aqua namque et ignis et consimilia corpora sunt; et ab his quidem unum, ab aliis vero plura principia corporea. Utrisque tamen ea ut in materiae specie ponentibus, [145]

et a quibusdam cum hac illam unde motus. Et hanc ab his quidem unam, ab aliis vero duas. Igitur usque ad Italicos, et absque illis mediocrius dixerunt alii de ipsis. Attamen (ut diximus) duabus sunt causis usi, et harum alteram, hi quidem unam, alii vero duas faciunt illam, unde motus.

987a13 Pythagorici vero duo quidem principia dixerunt secundum eumdem modum, tantum autem addiderunt, quod et proprium est eorum, quia finitum et infinitum et unum, et non alias aliquas putaverunt esse naturas, ut ignem aut terram, aut aliud aliquid tale: sed infinitum ipsum et unum ipsum horum esse substantiam, de quibus praedicantur. Qua propter et numerum esse substantiam omnium. [147]

De his igitur secundum hunc enunciaverunt modum, et de ipso quid est, dicere et definire coeperunt. Valde autem simpliciter tractaverunt. Superficialiter enim definierunt, et cui primo inerat dictus terminus, hoc esse substantiam rei putaverunt. Ut si quis existimet ratione idem esse duplum ac dualitatem, eo quod primo i est duobus duplum.

Sed forsitan duplo et dualitati non idem est esse. Si autem non, multa ipsum unum erit, quod et illis accidit. De prio-

---

τούτων δὲ κατὰ μὲν τὸ ὂν τὸ θερμὸν τάττει θάτερον δὲ κατὰ τὸ μὴ ὄν.

ἐκ μὲν οὖν τῶν εἰρημένων καὶ παρὰ τῶν συνηδρευκότων ἤδη τῷ λόγῳ σοφῶν ταῦτα παρειλήφαμεν, παρὰ μὲν τῶν πρώτων σωματικήν τε τὴν ἀρχήν (ὕδωρ γὰρ καὶ {5} πῦρ καὶ τὰ τοιαῦτα σώματά ἐστιν), καὶ τῶν μὲν μίαν τῶν δὲ πλείους τὰς ἀρχὰς τὰς σωματικάς, ἀμφοτέρων μέντοι ταύτας ὡς ἐν ὕλης εἴδει τιθέντων,

παρὰ δέ τινων ταύτην τε τὴν αἰτίαν τιθέντων καὶ πρὸς ταύτῃ τὴν ὅθεν ἡ κίνησις, καὶ ταύτην παρὰ τῶν μὲν μίαν παρὰ τῶν δὲ δύο. μέχρι μὲν {10} οὖν τῶν Ἰταλικῶν καὶ χωρὶς ἐκείνων μορυχώτερον εἰρήκασιν οἱ ἄλλοι περὶ αὐτῶν, πλὴν ὥσπερ εἴπομεν δυοῖν τε αἰτίαιν τυγχάνουσι κεχρημένοι, καὶ τούτων τὴν ἑτέραν οἱ μὲν μίαν οἱ δὲ δύο ποιοῦσι, τὴν ὅθεν ἡ κίνησις:

οἱ δὲ Πυθαγόρειοι δύο μὲν τὰς ἀρχὰς κατὰ τὸν αὐτὸν εἰρήκασι τρόπον, τοσοῦτον {15} δὲ προσεπέθεσαν ὃ καὶ ἴδιόν ἐστιν αὐτῶν, ὅτι τὸ πεπερασμένον καὶ τὸ ἄπειρον [καὶ τὸ ἓν] οὐχ ἑτέρας τινὰς ᾠήθησαν εἶναι φύσεις, οἷον πῦρ ἢ γῆν ἤ τι τοιοῦτον ἕτερον, ἀλλ' αὐτὸ τὸ ἄπειρον καὶ αὐτὸ τὸ ἓν οὐσίαν εἶναι τούτων ὧν κατηγοροῦνται, διὸ καὶ ἀριθμὸν εἶναι τὴν οὐσίαν πάντων.

περί τε {20} τούτων οὖν τοῦτον ἀπεφήναντο τὸν τρόπον, καὶ περὶ τοῦ τί ἐστιν ἤρξαντο μὲν λέγειν καὶ ὁρίζεσθαι, λίαν δ' ἁπλῶς ἐπραγματεύθησαν. ὡρίζοντό τε γὰρ ἐπιπολαίως, καὶ ᾧ πρώτῳ ὑπάρξειεν ὁ λεχθεὶς ὅρος, τοῦτ' εἶναι τὴν οὐσίαν τοῦ πράγματος ἐνόμιζον, ὥσπερ εἴ τις οἴοιτο ταὐτὸν εἶναι διπλάσιον καὶ τὴν {25} δυάδα διότι πρῶτον ὑπάρχει τοῖς δυσὶ τὸ διπλάσιον.

ἀλλ' οὐ ταὐτὸν ἴσως ἐστὶ τὸ εἶναι διπλασίῳ καὶ δυάδι: εἰ δὲ μή, πολλὰ τὸ ἓν ἔσται, ὃ κἀκείνοις συνέβαινεν. παρὰ

---

the one fire and the other earth. Of these he ranks the hot with being and the cold with non-being.

From what has been said, then, and from the wise men who have already agreed with this reasoning, we have acquired these things. From the first philosophers we have learned that the principle of all things is bodily, because water and fire and the like are bodies; and from some we have learned that there is one bodily principle, and from others, many (although both suppose that these belong to the species of matter).

And from others we have learned that in addition to this cause there is the source from which motion begins, which some claim to be one and others two. Down to the Italian philosophers, then, and independent of them, others have spoken of these things in a more trivial way, except that, as we have said, they have used two kinds of causes, and one of these—the source of motion—some thinkers consider as one and others as two.

Now the Pythagoreans have spoken of these two principles in the same way, but added this much (which is peculiar to them)—they did not think that the limited, unlimited, and one are different natures, like fire or earth or anything else of this kind, but that the unlimited itself and the one itself are the substance of the things of which they are predicated. And this is why they considered number as the substance of all things.

These thinkers, then, have expressed themselves thus with regard to these things, and they began to discuss and define the "what" itself of things, although they treated it far too simply. For they defined things superficially and thought that the substance of a thing is that to which a given definition first applies—just as if one supposed that double and two are the same because that to which the double first belongs is the number two.

But perhaps "to be double" is not the same as "to be two"; and if it is not, then the one itself will be many. This, indeed,

ribus quidem igitur et aliis tot est accipere.

μὲν οὖν τῶν πρότερον καὶ τῶν ἄλλων τοσαῦτα ἔστι λαβεῖν.

is the conclusion which they reached. From the first philosophers and others, then, this much can be learned.

---

134. Hic ponit opiniones philosophorum de toto universo, sicut de uno ente; et circa hoc duo facit.

Primo ponit eorum opiniones in communi.

Secundo ostendit quomodo consideratio huius opinionis ad praesentem tractatum pertineat, et quomodo non, ibi, *igitur ad praesentem* et cetera.

Dicit ergo quod aliqui alii philosophi a praedictis fuerunt, qui enuntiaverunt, *de omni*, idest de universo quasi de una natura, idest quasi totum universum esset unum ens vel una natura. Quod tamen non eodem modo omnes posuerunt, sicut infra patebit. Ipso tamen modo, quo diversificati sunt, nec bene dixerunt, nec naturaliter. Nullus enim eorum naturaliter locutus est, quia motum rebus subtrahunt. Nullus etiam bene locutus est, quia positionem impossibilem posuerunt, et per rationes sophisticas: sicut patet primo *Physicorum*.

135. Deinde cum dicit *igitur ad* hic ostendit quomodo consideratio huius positionis ad praesentem tractatum pertinet, et quomodo non.

Et primo ostendit quod non pertinet, si consideretur eorum positio.

Secundo ostendit quod pertinet, si consideretur positionis ratio, vel positionis modus, ibi, *sed quidem secundum causam* et cetera.

Dicit ergo, quod quia isti philosophi posuerunt tantum unum ens, et unum non potest sui ipsius esse causa, patet, quod ipsi non potuerunt invenire causas. Nam positio, idest pluralitas, causarum diversitatem in rebus exigit. Unde, quantum ad praesentem perscrutationem quae est de causis, non congruit ut sermo de eis habeatur.

Secus autem est de antiquis naturalibus, qui tantum ens posuerunt esse unum, de quibus debet hic sermo haberi. Illi enim ex illo uno generant multa, sicut ex materia, et sic ponunt causam et causatum. Sed isti de quibus nunc agitur, alio modo dicunt. Non enim dicunt quod sint omnia unum secundum materiam, ita quod ex uno omnia generentur; sed dicunt quod simpliciter sunt unum.

136. Et ratio huius diversitatis est, quod antiqui naturales apponebant motum illis, qui ponebant unum principium et unum ens, dicentes ipsum esse mobile. Et ideo per aliquem modum motus, sicut per rarefactionem et condensationem poterant ex illo uno diversa generari. Et per hunc modum dicebant generari totum

134. Here he gives the opinions of those philosophers who spoke of the whole universe as one being; and in regard to this he does two things.

First, he gives the opinion which they held in common; and second [135], he shows how a consideration of this opinion is relevant to the present treatise, and how it is not, at *therefore, a consideration* (986b12).

He says, then, that there were certain philosophers, other than those just mentioned, who spoke *of the whole*, that is, of the universe, as if it were of one nature—as if the whole universe were a single being or a single nature. However, not all maintained this position in the same way, as he will make clear below [138–49]. Yet in the way in which they differ their statements are neither acceptable nor in conformity with nature. None of their statements are in conformity with nature, because they did away with motion in things. And none of them are acceptable, because they held an impossible position and used sophistical arguments, as is clear in *Physics* 1.

135. *Therefore, a consideration* (986b12). Here he shows how a consideration of this position pertains to the present investigation and how it does not.

He shows, first, that it has no bearing on this investigation if we consider their position itself;

second [137], that it does have a bearing on this investigation if the reasoning or method behind their position is considered, at *yet their opinion* (986b17).

He says, then, that since these philosophers held that there is only one being, and a single thing cannot be its own cause, it is clear that they could not discover the causes. For the position that there is a plurality of things demands a diversity of causes in the world. Hence, a consideration of their statements is of no value for the purposes of the present study, which deals with causes.

But the situation is different in the case of the ancient philosophers of nature, who held that there is only one being, and whose statements must be considered here. For they generated many things from that one principle as matter, and thus posited both cause and effect. But these men with whom we are now dealing speak of this in a different way. For they do not say that all things are one materially, so that all things are generated from one matter, but that all things are one in an absolute sense.

136. The reason for this difference is that the ancient philosophers of nature added motion to the view of those who posited one being and one principle, and said that this one being is mobile; therefore, different things could be generated from that one principle by a certain kind of motion (that is, by rarefaction and condensation). And they

universum secundum diversitatem, quae in partibus eius invenitur. Et tamen quia non ponebant variationem secundum substantiam, nisi secundum accidentia, ut supra dictum est, ideo relinquebatur quod totum universum esset unum secundum substantiam, diversificatum tamen secundum accidentia. Sed isti dicebant illud quod ponebant esse unum penitus immobile. Et ideo ex illo uno non poterat aliqua diversitas rerum causari. Et propter hoc nec secundum substantiam nec secundum accidentia pluralitatem in rebus ponere poterant.

137. Deinde cum dicit *sed quidem* hic ostendit quomodo eorum opinio pertineat ad praesentem perscrutationem.

Et primo generaliter de omnibus.

Secundo specialiter de Parmenide, ibi, *igitur ii.*

Dicit ergo primo, quod licet diversitatem rebus auferrent, et per consequens causalitatem, tamen eorum opinio est propria praesenti inquisitioni, secundum tantum quantum dicetur: quantum scilicet ad modum ponendi, et quantum ad rationem positionis.

138. Parmenides enim qui fuit unus ex eis, videtur tangere unitatem *secundum rationem,* idest ex parte formae. Argumentatur enim sic. Quicquid est praeter ens, est non ens: et quicquid est non ens, est nihil: ergo quicquid est praeter ens est nihil. Sed ens est unum. Ergo quicquid est praeter unum, est nihil. In quo patet quod considerabat ipsam rationem essendi quae videtur esse una, quia non potest intelligi quod ad rationem entis aliquid superveniat per quod diversificetur: quia illud quod supervenit enti, oportet esse extraneum ab ente. Quod autem est huiusmodi, est nihil.

Unde non videtur quod possit diversificare ens. Sicut etiam videmus quod differentiae advenientes generi diversificant ipsum, quae tamen sunt praeter substantiam eius. Non enim participant differentiae genus, ut dicitur quarto *Topicorum.* Aliter genus esset de substantia differentiae, et in definitionibus esset nugatio, si posito genere, adderetur differentia, si de eius substantia esset genus, sicut esset nugatio si species adderetur. In nullo etiam differentia a specie differret. Ea vero quae sunt praeter substantiam entis, oportet esse non ens, et ita non possunt diversificare ens.

139. Sed in hoc decipiebantur, quia utebantur ente quasi una ratione et una natura sicut est natura alicuius generis; hoc enim est impossibile. Ens enim non est genus, sed multipliciter dicitur de diversis. Et ideo in primo *Physicorum* dicitur quod haec est falsa, *ens est unum*: non enim habet unam naturam sicut unum genus vel una species.

said that the whole universe with respect to the diversity found in its parts is generated in this way. Yet, since they held that the only change affecting substance is accidental, as was stated above [75], the conclusion then followed that the whole universe is one thing substantially but many things accidentally. But these thinkers said that the one being which they posited is immobile in an absolute sense; therefore, a diversity of things could not be produced from that one being. Since this being is immobile, they could not posit any plurality in the world, either substantial or accidental.

137. *Yet their opinion* (986b17). Here he shows how their opinion is relevant to the present inquiry.

First, he deals with all of these thinkers in general;

second [142], with Parmenides in particular, at *as we have stated* (986b25).

He says first that, although they did away with diversity in the world (and consequently with causality), nevertheless their opinion is relevant to the present study so far as regards the method by which they establish their position and the reason for their position.

138. Parmenides, who was a member of this group, seems to touch on unity *according to concept,* or according to form, for he argued as follows. Besides being there is only non-being, and non-being is nothing. Therefore, besides being there is nothing. But being is one. Therefore, besides the one there is nothing. In this argument he clearly considered the concept itself of being, which seems to be one, because nothing can be understood to be added to the concept of being by which it might be diversified. For whatever is added to being must be other than being. But anything such as this is nothing.

Hence it does not seem that this can diversify being, just as we also see that differences added to a genus diversify it, even though these differences are outside the substance of that genus. For differences do not participate in a genus, as is stated in the *Topics* 4—otherwise a genus would have the substance of a difference. And definitions would be nonsense if when a genus is given the difference were added, granted that the genus were the substance of the difference, just as it would be nonsense if the species were added. Moreover, a difference would not differ in any way from a species. But those things that are outside the substance of being must be non-being, and thus cannot diversify being.

139. But they were mistaken in this matter, because they used being as if it were one in intelligible structure and in nature, like the nature of any genus. But this is impossible. For being is not a genus but is predicated of different things in many ways. Therefore, in *Physics* 1, it is said that the statement *being is one* is false. For being does not have one nature like one genus or one species.

140. Sed Melissus considerabat ens ex parte materiae. Argumentabatur enim unitatem entis, ex eo quod ens non generatur ex aliquo priori, quod proprie pertinet ad materiam quae est ingenita.

Arguebat enim sic: quod est generatum, habet principium; ens non est generatum, ergo non habet principium. Quod autem caret principio, et fine caret; ergo est infinitum. Et si est infinitum, est immobile: quia infinitum non habet extra se quo moveatur. Quod autem ens non generetur, probat sic. Quia si generatur, aut generatur ex ente, aut ex non ente; atqui nec ex non ente, quia non ens est nihil, et ex nihilo nihil fit. Nec ex ente; quia sic aliquid esset antequam fieret; ergo nullo modo generatur.

In qua quidem ratione patet quod tetigit ens ex parte materiae; quia non generari ex aliquo prius existente materiae est. Et quia finitum pertinet ad formam, infinitum vero ad materiam, Melissus qui considerabat ens ex parte materiae, dixit esse unum ens infinitum. Parmenides vero, qui considerabat ens ex parte formae, dixit ens esse finitum. Sic igitur inquantum consideratur ens ratione materiae et formae, tractare de his pertinet ad praesentem considerationem, quia materia et forma in numero causarum ponuntur.

141. Xenophanes vero qui fuit primus inter dicentes omnia esse unum, unde etiam Parmenides fuit eius discipulus, non explanavit qua ratione diceret omnia esse unum, nec sumendo rationem aliquam ex parte materiae, nec ex parte formae. Et sic de neutra natura scilicet neque de materia neque de forma visus est *tangere* hos id est pertingere et adaequare eos irrationalitate dicendi; sed respiciens ad totum caelum dixit esse ipsum unum Deum. Antiqui enim dicebant ipsum mundum esse Deum. Unde videns omnes partes mundi in hoc esse similes, quia corporeae sunt, iudicavit de eis quasi omnia essent unum. Et sicut praedicti posuerunt unitatem entium per considerationem eorum quae pertinent ad formam vel ad materiam, ita iste respiciens ad ipsum compositum.

142. Deinde cum dicit *igitur ii* his specialiter intendit dicere quomodo opinio Parmenidis ad perscrutationem praesentem pertineat; concludens ex praedictis, quod quia diversitatem ab entibus auferebant, et per consequens causalitatem, quantum ad praesentem quaestionem pertinet, omnes praetermittendi sunt. Sed duo eorum, scilicet Xenophanes et Melissus, sunt penitus praetermittendi, quia aliquantulum fuerunt, *agrestiores*, idest minus subtiliter procedentes. Sed Parmenides visus est dicere suam opinionem, *magis videns*, idest quasi

140. But Melissus considered being in terms of matter. For he argued that being is one by reason of the fact that being is not generated from something prior, and this characteristic pertains properly to matter, which is ungenerated.

For he argued in this way. Whatever is generated has a starting-point. But being is not generated and therefore does not have a starting-point. But whatever lacks a starting-point lacks an end and therefore is unlimited. And if it is unlimited, it is immobile, because what is unlimited has nothing outside itself by which it is moved. That being is not generated he proves thus. If being were generated, it would be generated either from being or from non-being. But it is not generated from non-being, because non-being is nothing and from nothing nothing comes. Nor is it generated from being, because then a thing would be before it came to be. Therefore, it is not generated in any way.

In this argument he obviously treats being as matter, because it is of the very nature of matter not to be generated from something prior. And since limitation pertains to form, and unlimitedness to matter, Melissus, who considered being under the aspect of matter, said that there is one unlimited being. But Parmenides, who considered being under the aspect of form, said that being is limited. Hence, insofar as being is considered under the aspect of form and matter, a study of these men is relevant to the present investigation, because matter and form are included among the causes.

141. But Xenophanes, who was the first of those to say that everything is one (and therefore Parmenides was his disciple), did not explain by what reasoning he maintained that all things are one by arguing either from the viewpoint of matter or from that of form. Hence, with respect to neither nature—that is, neither matter nor form—does he seem *to come up to these men*, that is, to reach and equal them in their irrational manner of arguing. But concerning the whole heaven he says that the one is God. For the ancients said that the world itself is God. Hence, seeing that all parts of the universe are alike insofar as they are bodies, he came to think of them as if they were all one. And just as the foregoing philosophers held that beings are one by considering those things that pertain either to matter or to form, in a similar way these philosophers maintained this position regarding the composite itself.

142. *As we have stated* (986b25). His aim here is to explain in a special way how the opinion of Parmenides pertains to the present investigation. He concludes from the foregoing that, since these men did away with diversity in the world (and therefore with causality), all of them must be disregarded so far as the present study is concerned. Two of them—Xenophanes and Melissus—must be disregarded altogether, because they are *a little too rustic*, that is, they proceeded with less accuracy. But Parmenides seems to have expressed his views *with more insight*, that is, with

plus intelligens. Utitur enim tali ratione. Quicquid est praeter ens, est non ens: quicquid est non ens, *dignatur esse nihil* idest dignum reputat esse nihil. Unde ex necessitate putat sequi quod ens sit unum, et quicquid est aliud ab ente, sit nihil. De qua quidem ratione manifestius dictum est primo *Physicorum*.

143. Licet autem Parmenides ista ratione cogatur ad ponendum omnia esse unum; tamen quia sensui apparebat multitudinem esse in rebus, coactus sequi ea quae apparent, voluit in sua positione utrique satisfacere, et apparentiae sensus et rationi.

Unde dixit quod omnia sunt unum secundum rationem, sed sunt plura secundum sensum. Et inquantum ponebat pluralitatem secundum sensum, potuit in rebus ponere causam et causatum. Unde posuit duas causas, scilicet calidum et frigidum: quorum unum attribuebat igni, aliud terrae. Et unum videbatur pertinere ad causam efficientem, scilicet calidum et ignis; aliud ad causam materialem, scilicet frigidum et terra. Et ne eius positio suae rationi videretur esse opposita, qua concludebat quod quicquid est praeter unum, est nihil: dicebat quod unum praedictorum, scilicet calidum, erat ens: alterum vero quod est praeter illud unum ens, scilicet frigidum, dicebat esse non ens secundum rationem et rei veritatem, sed esse ens solum secundum apparentiam sensus.

144. In hoc autem aliquo modo ad veritatem appropinquat. Nam principium materiale non est ens in actu cui attribuebat terram; similiter etiam alterum contrariorum est ut privatio, ut dicitur primo *Physicorum*. Privatio autem ad rationem non entis pertinet. Unde et frigidum quodammodo est privatio calidi, et sic est non ens.

145. Deinde cum dicit *igitur ex* hic recolligit ea, quae dicta sunt de opinionibus antiquorum; et circa hoc duo facit.

Primo recolligit ea quae dicta sunt de opinionibus antiquorum naturalium.

Secundo quae dicta sunt de opinionibus Pythagoricorum qui mathematicam introduxerunt, ibi, *Pythagorici* et cetera.

Concludit ergo primo ex dictis, quod ex his praedictis, qui idem considerabant, scilicet esse causam materialem rerum substantiam, et qui iam incipiebant per rationem sapere causas rerum inquirendo ipsas, accepimus eas quae dictae sunt. *A primis namque philosophis acceptum est quod principium omnium rerum est corpo-*

greater understanding. For he employs the following argument. Besides being there is only non-being, and whatever is non-being *is thought to be nothing*—that is, he considers it worthy to be nothing. Hence he thought that it necessarily followed that being is one, and that whatever is other than being is nothing. This argument has been treated more clearly in *Physics* 1.

143. But even though Parmenides was compelled by this argument to hold that all things are one, yet, because there appeared to the senses to be many things in reality, and because he was compelled to accept what appeared to the senses, it was his aim to make his position conform to both of these—that is, to what is apprehended both by the senses and by reason.

Hence he said that all things are one according to reason but many according to the senses. And inasmuch as he held that there is a plurality of things according to the senses, he was able to hold that there is in the world both cause and effect. Hence he posited two causes, the hot and the cold, one of which he ascribed to fire, and the other to earth. And one of these (the hot or fire) seemed to pertain to the efficient cause, and the other (cold or earth) to the material cause. And lest his position should seem to contradict the conclusion of his own argument that whatever is besides being is nothing, he said that one of these causes (the hot) is being, and that the other cause (the one besides being, or the cold) is non-being, according to both reason and the truth of the thing itself, and is a being only according to sensory perception.

144. Now in this matter he comes very close to the truth; for the material principle, which he held to be earth, is not an actual being. And in a similar way, too, one of two contraries is a privation, as is said in *Physics* 1. But privation does not belong to the intelligible constitution of being. Hence in a sense cold is the privation of heat, and thus is non-being.

145. *From what has been said* (987a2). Here he summarizes the remarks which have been made about the doctrines of the ancient philosophers, and in regard to this he does two things.

First, he summarizes the remarks made about the doctrines of the ancient philosophers of nature;

second [147], those made about the doctrines of the Pythagoreans, who introduced mathematics, at *now the Pythagoreans* (987a13).

Therefore, from the above remarks he concludes first that we learn the causes which have been mentioned from the foregoing philosophers, who adopted the same opinion that the material cause is the substance of things, and who were already beginning by the use of reason to know the causes of things by investigating them. For *from the first*

reum. Quod patet per hoc, quod aqua et huiusmodi quae principia rerum ponebant, quaedam corpora sunt.

In hoc autem differebant, quod quidam ponebant illud principium corporeum esse unum tantum, sicut Thales, Diogenes, et similes. Quidam vero ponebant esse plura, sicut Anaxagoras, Democritus et Empedocles. Utrique tamen, tam isti qui ponebant unum, quam illi qui ponebant plura esse, huiusmodi corporea principia ponebat in specie causae materialis. Quidam vero eorum non solum causam materialem posuerunt, sed cum ea addiderunt causam unde principium motus: quidam eam unam ponentes, sicut Anaxagoras intellectum, et Parmenides amorem: quidam vero duas, sicut Empedocles amorem et odium.

146. Unde patet quod praedicti philosophi qui fuerunt usque ad Italicos, scilicet Pythagoram, *et absque illis* idest separatam opinionem habentes de rebus non communicando opinionibus Pythagoricorum, obscurius dixerunt de principiis, quia non assignabant ad quod genus causae huiusmodi principia reducerentur: et tamen utebantur duabus causis, scilicet principio motus et materia; et alteram istarum, scilicet ipsam unde principium motus, quidam fecerunt unam, ut dictum est, quidam duas.

147. Deinde cum dicit *Pythagorici vero* hic recolligit quae dicta sunt a Pythagoricis, et quantum ad id quod erat commune cum praedictis, et quantum ad id quod erat eis proprium. Commune tamen fuit aliquibus praedictorum et Pythagoricorum, quod ponerent duo principia aliqualiter eodem modo cum praedictis. Sicut enim Empedocles ponebat duo principia contraria, quorum unum erat principium bonorum, et aliud principium malorum, ita et Pythagorici: ut patet ex coordinatione principiorum contrariorum supposita a Pythagoricis.

148. In hoc tamen non eodem modo, quia Empedocles illa principia contraria ponebat in specie causae materialis, ut supra dictum est. Pythagorici autem addiderunt quod erat eis proprium supra opinionem aliorum; primo quidem quia dicebant quod hoc quod dico unum finitum et infinitum non erant accidentia aliquibus aliis naturis, sicut igni aut terrae, aut alicui huiusmodi. Sed hoc quod dico unum finitum et infinitum, erant substantiae eorumdem, de quibus praedicabantur. Et ex hoc concludebant quod numerus, qui ex unitatibus constituitur, sit substantia rerum omnium. Alii vero naturales, licet ponerent unum et finitum, seu infinitum, tamen attribuebant ista alicui alteri naturae,

philosophers we have learned that the principle of all things is bodily. This is evident from the fact that water and the like, which are given as the principles of things, are bodies.

However, they differed in this respect: some (such as Thales, Diogenes, and similar thinkers) claimed that there is only one bodily principle, whereas others (such as Anaxagoras, Democritus, and Leucippus) held that there are several bodily principles. Yet both groups (that is, both those who posited one principle and those who posited many) placed such bodily principles in the species of material cause. And some of them not only posited a material cause but added to this the cause from which motion begins. Some held it to be one (as Anaxagoras did in positing intellect, and Parmenides did in positing love), and others to be two (as Empedocles did in positing love and hate).

146. Hence, it is clear that these philosophers who lived down to the time of the Italians, or Pythagoreans, *and [were] independent of them*—that is, who had their own opinions about reality and were unaware of those of the Pythagoreans—spoke obscurely about the principles of things, for they did not designate to what genus of cause such principles might be reduced. Yet they made use of two causes, the source from which motion begins and matter. Some said that the former (the source from which motion begins) is one, and others two, as has been pointed out [145].

147. *Now the Pythagoreans* (987a13). Here he summarizes the opinions expressed by the Pythagoreans, both what they held in common with the foregoing philosophers and what was peculiar to themselves. Now the opinion common to some of the foregoing philosophers and to the Pythagoreans was this: that they posited, in a sense, two principles in the same way as the foregoing philosophers did. For Empedocles held that there are two contrary principles, one being the principle of good things, and the other the principle of evil things, and the Pythagoreans did the same thing, as is clear from the coordination of contrary principles which they posited.

148. However, they did not do this in the same way, because Empedocles placed these contrary principles in the species of material cause, as was stated above [111], but the Pythagoreans added their own opinion to that of the other thinkers. The first thing that they added is this: they said that what I call the "one," the "limited," and the "unlimited" are not accidents of any other natures, such as fire or earth or the like, but claimed that what I call the "one," the "limited," and the "unlimited" constitute the substance of the same things of which they are predicated. From this they concluded that number, which is constituted of units, is the substance of all things. But while the other philosophers of nature posited the one, the limited, and the unlimited,

sicut accidentia attribuuntur subiecto, ut igni, vel aquae, vel alicui huiusmodi.

149. Secundo addiderunt super alios philosophos, quia inceperunt dicere et definire de *ipso quid est*, scilicet substantia et rerum quidditate. Sed tamen valde simpliciter de hoc tractaverunt, superficialiter definientes. Non enim attendebant in assignandis definitionibus nisi unum tantum. Dicebant enim quod si aliquis terminus dictus inesset alicui primo, quod erat substantia illius rei; sicut si aliquis aestimet quod proportio dupla sit substantia dualitatis: quia talis proportio primo in numero binario invenitur. Et quia ens primo inveniebatur in uno quam in multis, nam multa ex uno constituuntur, ideo dicebant quod ens est ipsa substantia unius.

Sed haec eorum determinatio non erat conveniens: quia licet dualitas sit dupla, non tamen idem est esse dualitatis et dupli, ita quod sint idem secundum rationem, sicut definitio et definitum.

Si autem etiam esset verum quod illi dicebant, sequeretur quod multa essent unum. Contingit enim aliqua multa primo inesse alicui uni, sicut dualitati primo inest paritas et proportio dupla. Et sic sequitur quod par et duplum sint idem: similiter quod cuicumque inest duplum sit idem dualitati, ex quo duplum est dualitatis substantia. Quod quidem etiam et Pythagoricis contingebat. Nam multa et diversa assignabant quasi unum essent, sicut proprietates numerales dicebant idem esse cum proprietatibus naturalium rerum.

150. Sic igitur concludit quod tot est accipere a prioribus philosophis, qui posuerunt tantum unum principium materiale, et ab aliis posterioribus qui posuerunt plura principia.

they nevertheless attributed these to another nature, as accidents are attributed to a subject—for example, to fire or water or something of this kind.

149. The second addition which they made to the views of the other philosophers is this: they began to discuss and to define *the "what" itself*, that is, the substance and quiddity of things, although they treated this far too simply by defining things superficially. For in giving definitions they paid attention only to one thing, because they said that if any given definition were to apply primarily to some thing, this would be the substance of that thing—just as if one were to suppose that the ratio "double" is the substance of the number two, because such a ratio is found first in the number two. And since being was found first in the one rather than in the many (for the many is composed of ones), they therefore said that being is the substance itself of the one.

But this conclusion of theirs is not acceptable, for although the number two is double, the essence of two-ness is not the same as that of the double in such a way that they are the same conceptually, as the definition and the thing defined.

But even if their statements were true, it would follow that the many would be one. For some plurality can belong primarily to something one: for example, evenness and the ratio double belong first to the number two. Hence it would follow that the even and the double are the same. And it would likewise follow that that to which the double belongs is the same as the number two, so long as the double is the substance of the number two. This, indeed, is also the conclusion which the Pythagoreans drew, for they attributed plurality and diversity to things as if they were one, just as they said that the properties of numbers are the same as the properties of natural beings.

150. Hence, Aristotle concludes that it is possible to learn this much from the early philosophers, who posited only one material principle, and from the later philosophers, who posited many principles.

LECTURE 10

The Platonic theory of ideas

987a29 Post dictas vero philosophias, Platonis supervenit negotium, in multis quidem hos sequens, aliam vero et propriam praeter Italicorum philosophiam habens. Nam ex novo conveniens Cratyli et Heracliti opinionibus, quasi sensibilibus omnibus semper defluentibus et scientia de his non existente, hoc quidem et posterius ita suscepit. Socrate vero circa moralia negociante et de tota natura nihil, in his tamen universale quaerente et de definitionibus intellectum firma te, illum recipiens propter huiusmodi susceperat, quasi de aliis hoc eveniens et non de sensibilium aliquo. [151]

Impossibile namque est communem rationem esse alicuius sensibilium semper transmutantium. Sic itaque talia quidem existentium ideas et species appellavit; sensibilia vero propter hoc et secundum hoc dici omnia. Nam secundum participationem esse multa univocorum speciebus: participationem vero secundum nomen transmutavit. Pythagorici quidem existentia dicunt esse numerorum imitatione. Plato vero participatione, nomen transmutans. Participationem tamen aut imitationem, quae sit utique specierum, dimiserunt in communi quaerere.

μετὰ δὲ τὰς εἰρημένας φιλοσοφίας ἡ Πλάτωνος ἐπεγένετο {30} πραγματεία, τὰ μὲν πολλὰ τούτοις ἀκολουθοῦσα, τὰ δὲ καὶ ἴδια παρὰ τὴν τῶν Ἰταλικῶν ἔχουσα φιλοσοφίαν. ἐκ νέου τε γὰρ συνήθης γενόμενος πρῶτον Κρατύλῳ καὶ ταῖς Ἡρακλειτείοις δόξαις, ὡς ἁπάντων τῶν αἰσθητῶν ἀεὶ ῥεόντων καὶ ἐπιστήμης περὶ αὐτῶν οὐκ οὔσης, ταῦτα μὲν καὶ ὕστερον οὕτως ὑπέλαβεν· {987b1} Σωκράτους δὲ περὶ μὲν τὰ ἠθικὰ πραγματευομένου περὶ δὲ τῆς ὅλης φύσεως οὐθέν, ἐν μέντοι τούτοις τὸ καθόλου ζητοῦντος καὶ περὶ ὁρισμῶν ἐπιστήσαντος πρῶτου τὴν διάνοιαν, ἐκεῖνον ἀποδεξάμενος διὰ τὸ τοιοῦτον {5} ὑπέλαβεν ὡς περὶ ἑτέρων τοῦτο γιγνόμενον καὶ οὐ τῶν αἰσθητῶν:

ἀδύνατον γὰρ εἶναι τὸν κοινὸν ὅρον τῶν αἰσθητῶν τινός, ἀεί γε μεταβαλλόντων. οὗτος οὖν τὰ μὲν τοιαῦτα τῶν ὄντων ἰδέας προσηγόρευσε, τὰ δ' αἰσθητὰ παρὰ ταῦτα καὶ κατὰ ταῦτα λέγεσθαι πάντα: κατὰ μέθεξιν γὰρ εἶναι τὰ {10} πολλὰ ὁμώνυμα τοῖς εἴδεσιν. τὴν δὲ μέθεξιν τοὔνομα μόνον μετέβαλεν: οἱ μὲν γὰρ Πυθαγόρειοι μιμήσει τὰ ὄντα φασὶν εἶναι τῶν ἀριθμῶν, Πλάτων δὲ μεθέξει, τοὔνομα μεταβαλών. τὴν μέντοι γε μέθεξιν ἢ τὴν μίμησιν ἥτις ἂν εἴη τῶν εἰδῶν ἀφεῖσαν ἐν κοινῷ ζητεῖν.

After the philosophies described came the system of Plato, which followed them in many respects, but also had other theses of its own in addition to the philosophy of the Italians. For Plato, agreeing at the very beginning with the opinions of Cratylus (1010a7) and Heraclitus that all sensible things are always in a state of flux, and that there is no scientific knowledge of them, also accepted this doctrine in later years. However, when Socrates, concerning himself with moral matters and neglecting nature as a whole, sought for the universal in these matters and fixed his thought on definition, Plato accepted him because of this kind of investigation, and assumed that this consideration refers to other entities and not to sensible ones.

For, according to him, it is impossible that there should be a common definition of any one of these sensible things that are always changing. Such entities, then, he called ideas or forms, and he said that all sensible things exist because of them and in conformity with them, for there are many individuals of the same name because of participation in these forms. With regard to participation, he changed the name, for while the Pythagoreans say that things exist by imitation of numbers, Plato says that they exist by participation, changing the name. Yet what this participation or imitation of forms is they commonly neglected to investigate.

987b14 Amplius autem praeter sensibilia et species, mathematica rerum intermedia dicit esse. Et differentia a sensibilibus quidem: quia sempiterna sunt et immobilia. A speciebus autem eo quod haec quidem multa similia sunt, species autem ipsum unum unaquaeque solum. [157]

ἔτι δὲ παρὰ τὰ αἰσθητὰ {15} καὶ τὰ εἴδη τὰ μαθηματικὰ τῶν πραγμάτων εἶναί φησι μεταξύ, διαφέροντα τῶν μὲν αἰσθητῶν τῷ ἀΐδια καὶ ἀκίνητα εἶναι, τῶν δ' εἰδῶν τῷ τὰ μὲν πόλλ' ἄττα ὅμοια εἶναι τὸ δὲ εἶδος αὐτὸ ἓν ἕκαστον μόνον.

Further, he says that besides sensible things and ideas there are the objects of mathematics, which are an intermediate genus. These differ from sensible things in being eternal and immobile; from the ideas in that there are many alike, whereas each idea is itself only one.

987b18 Quoniam autem species causae sunt aliis, illarum elementa omnium putaverunt existentium elementa esse: ut quidem igitur materiam, magnum et parvum esse principia: ut autem sub-

ἐπεὶ δ' αἴτια τὰ εἴδη τοῖς ἄλλοις, τἀκείνων στοιχεῖα πάντων ᾠήθη τῶν ὄντων εἶναι {20} στοιχεῖα. ὡς μὲν οὖν ὕλην τὸ μέγα καὶ τὸ μικρὸν εἶναι ἀρχάς, ὡς δ' οὐσίαν τὸ ἕν: ἐξ ἐκείνων γὰρ κατὰ

And since the forms are the causes of other things, he thought that the elements of these are the elements of all existing things. Hence, according to him, the great and small are principles as mat-

stantiam, unum: ex illis enim secundum participationes unius, species esse numeros. [159]

987b22 Unum tamen substantiam, et non aliquod aliud ens dici unum, consimiliter Pythagoricis dixit; et numeros esse causas merae substantiae similiter ut illi. [160]

987b25 Pro infinito vero et uno, dualitatem facere et infinitum ex magno et parvo: hoc proprium. Amplius hic quidem numeros praeter sensibilia, illi vero numeros esse dicunt res ipsas, et mathematica intermedia horum non ponunt. [162]

987b29 Unum igitur et numeros praeter res facere et non ut Pythagorici, et specierum introductio, propter eam quae in rationibus perscrutationem evenit. Priores enim non participaverunt dialectica. [164]

987b33 Dualitatem autem facere alteram naturam, quia numeri extra priores omnes naturaliter ex ea generantur, velut ex aliquo echimagio. [165]

988a1 Attamen e contrario contingit. Non enim rationabile ita: nunc enim ex materia multa faciunt, species vero semel generat solum. [166]

988a3 Videtur autem ex una materia una mensura. Speciem autem, quam inducit unus existens, multa facit. Similiter quoque se habet masculus ad feminam. Haec enim ab uno impletur motu, ille vero multas implet. Et tales mutationes principiorum illorum sunt. Plato quidem igitur de quaesitis ita definit. [167]

988a8 Palam autem est ex dictis, quia duabus causis solum est usus: ipsaque est eius quod quid est, et ipsa materia. Species enim eius quod quid est causae sunt aliis, speciebus vero unum. [169]

Et quae materia subiecta de qua species: haec quidem in sensibilibus,

μέθεξιν τοῦ ἑνὸς [τὰ εἴδη] εἶναι τοὺς ἀριθμούς.

τὸ μέντοι γε ἓν οὐσίαν εἶναι, καὶ μὴ ἕτερόν γέ τι ὂν λέγεσθαι ἕν, παραπλησίως τοῖς Πυθαγορείοις ἔλεγε, καὶ τὸ τοὺς ἀριθμοὺς αἰτίους εἶναι τοῖς ἄλλοις {25} τῆς οὐσίας ὡσαύτως ἐκείνοις·

τὸ δὲ ἀντὶ τοῦ ἀπείρου ὡς ἑνὸς δυάδα ποιῆσαι, τὸ δ' ἄπειρον ἐκ μεγάλου καὶ μικροῦ, τοῦτ' ἴδιον· καὶ ἔτι ὁ μὲν τοὺς ἀριθμοὺς παρὰ τὰ αἰσθητά, οἱ δ' ἀριθμοὺς εἶναί φασιν αὐτὰ τὰ πράγματα, καὶ τὰ μαθηματικὰ μεταξὺ τούτων οὐ τιθέασιν.

τὸ μὲν οὖν τὸ ἓν καὶ τοὺς {30} ἀριθμοὺς παρὰ τὰ πράγματα ποιῆσαι, καὶ μὴ ὥσπερ οἱ Πυθαγόρειοι, καὶ ἡ τῶν εἰδῶν εἰσαγωγὴ διὰ τὴν ἐν τοῖς λόγοις ἐγένετο σκέψιν (οἱ γὰρ πρότεροι διαλεκτικῆς οὐ μετεῖχον),

τὸ δὲ δυάδα ποιῆσαι τὴν ἑτέραν φύσιν διὰ τὸ τοὺς ἀριθμοὺς ἔξω τῶν πρώτων εὐφυῶς ἐξ αὐτῆς γεννᾶσθαι ὥσπερ ἔκ τινος ἐκμαγείου.

καίτοι συμβαίνει γ' ἐναντίως· οὐ γὰρ εὔλογον οὕτως. οἱ μὲν γὰρ ἐκ τῆς ὕλης πολλὰ ποιοῦσιν, τὸ δ' εἶδος ἅπαξ γεννᾷ μόνον,

φαίνεται δ' ἐκ μιᾶς ὕλης μία τράπεζα, ὁ δὲ τὸ εἶδος ἐπιφέρων εἷς ὢν πολλὰς ποιεῖ. {5} ὁμοίως δ' ἔχει καὶ τὸ ἄρρεν πρὸς τὸ θῆλυ· τὸ μὲν γὰρ ὑπὸ μιᾶς πληροῦται ὀχείας, τὸ δ' ἄρρεν πολλὰ πληροῖ· καίτοι ταῦτα μιμήματα τῶν ἀρχῶν ἐκείνων ἐστίν. Πλάτων μὲν οὖν περὶ τῶν ζητουμένων οὕτω διώρισεν·

φανερὸν δ' ἐκ τῶν εἰρημένων ὅτι δυοῖν αἰτίαν μόνον κέχρηται, τῇ τε {10} τοῦ τί ἐστι καὶ τῇ κατὰ τὴν ὕλην (τὰ γὰρ εἴδη τοῦ τί ἐστιν αἴτια τοῖς ἄλλοις, τοῖς δ' εἴδεσι τὸ ἕν),

καὶ τίς ἡ ὕλη ἡ ὑποκειμένη καθ' ἧς τὰ εἴδη μὲν ἐπὶ τῶν αἰσθητῶν τὸ δ' ἓν ἐν

ter, and the one as substance. For it is from these by participation in the one that the ideas are numbers.

Yet Plato said that the one is substance and that no other being is to be called one, just as the Pythagoreans did. Also like them, he said that numbers are the causes of real substance.

But to posit a dyad in place of the indeterminate one, and to produce the unlimited out of the great and small, is peculiar to him. Moreover, he says that numbers exist apart from sensible things, whereas they say that things themselves are numbers. Further, they do not maintain that the objects of mathematics are an intermediate class.

Therefore, his making the one and numbers to exist apart from things and not in things (as Pythagoreans did), and his introducing the separate forms, was due to his investigation into the ideas of things. For the earlier philosophers were ignorant of dialectic.

But his making the dyad to be a different nature was due to the fact that all numbers, with the exception of prime numbers, are naturally generated from the number two as a matrix.

Yet what happens is the contrary of this. For this view is not a reasonable one, because the Platonists produce many things from matter but their form generates only once.

And from one matter one measure seems to be produced, whereas he who induces the form, even though he is one, produces many measures. The male is also related to the female in a similar way, for the latter is impregnated by one act, but the male impregnates many females. And such are the changes in these principles. Concerning the causes under investigation, then, Plato defines them thus.

From the foregoing account it is evident that Plato used only two causes: one being the whatness of a thing, and the other, matter. For the forms are the cause of the whatness in other things, and the one is the cause of the whatness in the forms.

It is also evident what the underlying matter is of which the forms are predi-

unum vero in speciebus dicitur: quia ea dualitas est, magnum et parvum.

τοῖς εἴδεσι λέγεται, ὅτι αὕτη δυάς ἐστι, τὸ μέγα καὶ τὸ μικρόν,

cated in the case of sensible things, and the one in the case of the forms—it is this duality, the great and small.

Amplius boni et mali causam dedit elementis singulis singularem. Quod magis dicimus primorum investigate quosdam philosophorum velut Empedoclis et Anaxagorae.

ἔτι δὲ τὴν τοῦ εὖ καὶ τοῦ κακῶς αἰτίαν τοῖς στοιχείοις {15} ἀπέδωκεν ἑκατέροις ἑκατέραν, ὥσπερ φαμὲν καὶ τῶν προτέρων ἐπιζητῆσαί τινας φιλοσόφων, οἶον Ἐμπεδοκλέα καὶ Ἀναξαγόραν.

Moreover, he assigned the cause of good and evil to these two elements, one to each of them, which is rather a problem, as we say (984b15) that some of the first philosophers (such as Empedocles and Anaxagoras) have attempted to investigate.

---

151. Positis opinionibus antiquorum de causa materiali et efficiente, hic tertio ponit opinionem Platonis, qui primo manifeste induxit causam formalem. Et dividitur in partes duas.

Primo enim ponit opinionem Platonis.

Secundo colligit ex omnibus praedictis quid de quatuor generibus causarum ab aliis philosophis sit positum, ibi, *breviter et recapitulariter* et cetera.

Circa primum duo facit.

Primo ponit opinionem Platonis de rerum substantiis.

Secundo de rerum principiis, ibi, *quoniam autem species* et cetera.

Circa primum duo facit.

Primo ponit opinionem Platonis quantum ad hoc quod posuit ideas.

Secundo quantum ad hoc quod posuit substantias medias, scilicet mathematica separata, ibi, *amplius autem praeter sensibilia.*

Dicit ergo primo, quod post omnes praedictos philosophos supervenit negocium Platonis, qui immediate Aristotelem praecessit. Nam Aristoteles eius discipulus fuisse perhibetur. Plato siquidem in multis secutus est praedictos philosophos naturales, scilicet Empedoclem, Anaxagoram et alios huiusmodi, sed alia quaedam habuit propria praeter illos praedictos philosophos, propter philosophiam Italicorum Pythagoricorum. Nam ipse ut studiosus erat ad veritatis inquisitionem, ubique terrarum philosophos quaesivit, ut eorum dogmata sciret. Unde in Italiam Tarentum venit, et ab Archita Tarentino Pythagorae discipulo de opinionibus Pythagoricis est instructus.

152. Cum enim naturales philosophos, qui in Graecia fuerunt, sequi videret, et intra eos aliqui posteriores ponerent omnia sensibilia semper esse in fluxu, et quod scientia de eis esse non potest, quod posuerunt Heraclitus et Cratylus, huiusmodi positionibus tamquam novis Plato consuetus, et cum eis conveniens in hac positione

151. Having given the opinion of the ancient philosophers about the material and efficient cause, he gives a third opinion, that of Plato, who was the first to clearly introduce the formal cause. This is divided into two parts.

First, he gives Plato's opinion.

Second [171], from all of the foregoing remarks he makes a summary of the opinions which the other philosophers expressed about the four genera of causes, at *we have examined* (988a18).

In regard to the first he does two things.

First, he gives Plato's opinion about the substances of things;

second [159], his opinion about the principles of things, at *and since the forms* (987b18).

In regard to the first he does two things.

First, he gives Plato's opinion insofar as he posited ideas;

and second [157], insofar as he posited intermediate substances, the separate mathematical entities, at *further, he says* (987b14).

He first says that after all the foregoing philosophers came the system of Plato, who immediately preceded Aristotle; for Aristotle is considered to have been his disciple. And even if Plato followed in many respects the natural philosophers who preceded him, such as Empedocles, Anaxagoras, and the like, he nevertheless had certain other doctrines of his own in addition to those of the preceding philosophers, because of the philosophy of the Italians, or Pythagoreans. For insofar as he was devoted to the study of truth he sought out the philosophers of all lands in order to learn their teachings. Hence he came to Tarentum in Italy, and was instructed in the teachings of the Pythagoreans by Archytas of Tarentum, a disciple of Pythagoras.

152. Now Plato would seem to follow the natural philosophers who lived in Greece; of this group some of the later members held that all sensible things are always in a state of flux, and that there can be no scientific knowledge of them (which was the position of Heraclitus and Cratylus). And since Plato became accustomed to positions of

ipse posterius ita esse suscepit, unde dixit particularium scibilium scientiam esse relinquendam.

Socrates etiam, qui fuit magister Platonis, et discipulus Archelai, qui fuit auditor Anaxagorae, propter hanc opinionem, quae suo tempore surrexerat, quod non potest esse de sensibilibus scientia, noluit aliquid de rerum naturis perscrutari, sed solum circa moralia negociatus est. Et ipse prius incepit in moralibus quaerere quid esset universale, et insistere ad definiendum.

153. Unde et Plato tamquam eius auditor, *recipiens* Socratem, idest sequens suscepit hoc ad inquirendum in rebus naturalibus, quasi in eis hoc posset evenire, ut universale in eis acciperetur de quo definitio traderetur, ita quod definitio non daretur de aliquo sensibilium, quia cum sensibilia sint semper *transmutantium*, idest transmutata, non potest alicuius eorum communis ratio assignari.

Nam omnis ratio oportet quod et omni et semper conveniat, et ita aliquam immutabilitatem requirit. Et ideo huiusmodi entia universalia, quae sunt a rebus sensibilibus separata, de quibus definitiones assignantur, nominavit ideas et species existentium sensibilium: *ideas* quidem, idest formas, inquantum ad earum similitudinem sensibilia constituebantur: species vero inquantum per earum participationem esse substantiale habebant. Vel ideas inquantum erant principium essendi, species vero inquantum erant principium cognoscendi.

Unde et sensibilia omnia habent esse propter praedictas et secundum eas. Propter eas quidem inquantum ideae sunt sensibilibus causae essendi. *Secundum eas* vero inquantum sunt eorum exemplaria.

154. Et quod hoc sit verum, patet ex eo, quod singulis speciebus attribuuntur *multa individua univocorum*, idest multa individua univocae speciei praedicationem suscipientia et hoc secundum participationem; nam species, vel idea est ipsa natura speciei, qua est existens homo per essentiam.

Individuum autem est homo per participationem, inquantum natura speciei in hac materia designata participatur. Quod enim totaliter est aliquid, non participat illud, sed est per essentiam idem illi. Quod vero non totaliter est aliquid habens aliquid aliud adiunctum, proprie participare dicitur.

Sicut si calor esset calor per se existens, non diceretur participare calorem, quia nihil esset in eo nisi calor. Ignis

this kind from the very beginning, and agreed with these men in this position, which he acknowledged to be true in later years, he therefore said that scientific knowledge of particular sensible things must be abandoned.

And Socrates (who was Plato's master and the disciple of Archelaus, a pupil of Anaxagoras), because of this position which arose in his time—that there can be no science of sensible things—was unwilling to make any investigation into the nature of physical things, but busied himself only with moral matters. And in this field he first began to investigate what the universal is, and to insist upon the need for definition.

153. Hence, Plato, being Socrates' pupil, *accepted* Socrates, that is, followed him, and adopted this method for the purpose of investigating natural beings. He did so believing that in their case the universal in them could successfully be grasped and a definition be assigned to it, with no definition being given for any sensible thing. For, since sensible things are always *changing*, or being changed, no common intelligible structure can be assigned to any of them.

Every definition must conform to each thing defined and must always do so, and thus each requires some kind of immutability. Hence universal entities of this kind, which are separate from sensible things and that to which definitions are assigned, he called the ideas or forms of sensible things. He called them *ideas*, or exemplars, inasmuch as sensible things are made in likeness to them; and he called them forms inasmuch as sensible things have substantial being by participating in them. Or he called them ideas inasmuch as they are principles of being, and forms inasmuch as they are principles of knowledge.

Hence all sensible things have being because of them and in conformity with them. They have being because of the ideas insofar as the ideas are the causes of the being of sensible things, and *in conformity with them* insofar as they are the exemplars of sensible things.

154. The truth of this is clear from the fact that *many individuals of the same name* are attributed to one form alone—that is, there are many individuals which have the same form predicated of them, and predicated by participation. For the form or idea of man is the specific nature itself by which there exists man essentially.

But an individual is man by participation inasmuch as the specific nature is participated in by this designated matter. For that which is something in its entirety does not participate in it but is essentially identical with it, whereas that which is not something in its entirety but has this other thing joined to it is said properly to participate in that thing.

Thus, if heat were a self-subsistent heat, it would not be said to participate in heat, because it would contain nothing

vero quia est aliquid aliud quam calor, dicitur participare calorem.

155. Similiter autem cum idea hominis separata nihil aliud habeat nisi ipsam naturam speciei, est essentialiter homo. Et propterea ab eo vocabatur per se homo. Socrates vero vel Plato, quia habet praeter naturam speciei principium individuans quod est materia signata, ideo dicitur secundum Platonem participare speciem.

156. Hoc autem nomen participationis Plato accepit a Pythagora. Sed tamen transmutavit ipsum. Pythagorici enim dicebant numeros esse causas rerum sicut Platonici ideas, et dicebant quod huiusmodi existentia sensibilia erant quasi quaedam imitationes numerorum. Inquantum enim numeri qui de se positionem non habent, accipiebant positionem, corpora causabant. Sed quia Plato ideas posuit immutabiles ad hoc quod de eis possent esse scientiae et definitiones, non conveniebat et in ideis uti nomine imitationis. Sed loco eius usus est nomine participationis. Sed tamen est sciendum, quod Pythagorici, licet ponerent participationem, aut imitationem, non tamen perscrutati sunt qualiter species communis participetur ab individuis sensibilibus, sive ab eis imitetur, quod Platonici tradiderunt.

157. Deinde cum dicit *amplius autem* hic ponit opinionem Platonis de mathematicis substantiis: et dicit quod Plato posuit alias substantias praeter species et praeter sensibilia, idest mathematica; et dixit quod huiusmodi entia erant media trium substantiarum, ita quod erant supra sensibilia et infra species, et ab utrisque differebant.

A sensibilibus quidem, quia sensibilia sunt corruptibilia et mobilia, mathematica vero sempiterna et immobilia. Et hoc accipiebant ex ipsa ratione scientiae mathematicae, nam mathematica scientia a motu abstrahit.

Differunt vero mathematica a speciebus, quia in mathematicis inveniuntur differentia secundum numerum, similia secundum speciem: alias non salvarentur demonstrationes mathematicae scientiae. Nisi enim essent duo trianguli eiusdem speciei, frustra demonstraret geometra aliquos triangulos esse similes; et similiter in aliis figuris.

Hoc autem in speciebus non accidit. Nam cum in specie separata nihil aliud sit nisi natura speciei, non potest esse singularis species nisi una. Licet enim alia sit species hominis, alia asini, tamen species hominis non est nisi una, nec species asini, et similiter de aliis.

but heat. But since fire is something other than heat, it is said to participate in heat.

155. In a similar way, since the separate idea of man contains nothing but the specific nature itself, it is man *per se*; and for this reason it was called by him man-in-itself. But since Socrates and Plato have in addition to their specific nature an individuating principle, which is designated matter, they are therefore said to participate in a form, according to Plato.

156. Now Plato took this term "participation" from Pythagoras, although he made a change in the term. For the Pythagoreans said that numbers are the causes of things, just as the Platonists said that the ideas are, and claimed that sensible things of this kind exist as certain imitations of numbers. For inasmuch as numbers, which have no position of themselves, received positions, they caused bodies. But because Plato held that the ideas are unchangeable in order that there might be scientific knowledge of them, he did not agree that the term "imitation" could be used of the ideas, but in place of it he used the term "participation." However, it must be noted that even though the Pythagoreans posited participation or imitation, they still did not investigate the way in which a common form is participated in by individual sensible things or imitated by them. But the Platonists have treated of this.

157. *Further, he says* (987b14). Here he gives Plato's opinion about the mathematical substances. He says that Plato posited other substances—the objects of mathematics—in addition to the forms and sensible things. Moreover, he said that beings of this kind were an intermediate genus among the three kinds of substances, or that they were above sensible substances and below the forms, and differed from both.

The mathematical substances differed from sensible substances because sensible substances are corruptible and changeable, whereas the mathematical substances are eternal and immobile. The Platonists got this idea from the way in which mathematical science conceives its objects, for mathematical science abstracts from motion.

The mathematical substances also differed from the forms, because the objects of mathematics are found to be numerically different and specifically the same—otherwise the demonstrations of mathematics would prove nothing. For unless two triangles belonged to the same species, geometry would attempt in vain to demonstrate that some triangles are similar; and the same thing is true of other figures.

But this does not happen in the case of the forms. For, since a form is just the specific nature itself of a thing, each form can only be unique. Even though the form of man is one thing, and the form of ass another thing, nevertheless the form of man is unique, and so is the form of ass; the same thing is true of other things.

158. Patet autem diligenter intuenti rationes Platonis, quod ex hoc in sua positione erravit, quia credidit, quod modus rei intellectae in suo esse sit sicut modus intelligendi rem ipsam.

Et ideo quia invenit intellectum nostrum dupliciter abstracta intelligere, uno modo sicut universalia intelligimus abstracta a singularibus, alio modo sicut mathematica abstracta a sensibilibus, utrique abstractioni intellectus posuit respondere abstractionem in essentiis rerum: unde posuit et mathematica esse separata et species.

Hoc autem non est necessarium. Nam intellectus etsi intelligat res per hoc, quod similis est eis quantum ad speciem intelligibilem, per quam fit in actu; non tamen oportet quod modo illo sit species illa in intellectu quo in re intellecta: nam omne quod est in aliquo, est per modum eius in quo est.

Et ideo ex natura intellectus, quae est alia a natura rei intellectae, necessarium est quod alius sit modus intelligendi quo intellectus intelligit, et alius sit modus essendi quo res existit. Licet enim id in re esse oporteat quod intellectus intelligit, non tamen eodem modo.

Unde quamvis intellectus intelligat mathematica non cointelligendo sensibilia, et universalia praeter particularia, non tamen oportet quod mathematica sint praeter sensibilia, et universalia praeter particularia.

Nam videmus quod etiam visus percipit colorem sine sapore, cum tamen in sensibilibus sapor et color simul inveniantur.

159. Deinde cum dicit *quoniam autem* hic ponit opinionem Platonis de rerum principiis: et circa hoc duo facit.

Primo ponit quae principia rebus Plato assignavit.

Secundo ad quod genus causae reducuntur, ibi, *palam autem ex dictis* et cetera.

Circa primum duo facit.

Primo ponit cuiusmodi principia Plato assignaverit.

Secundo ostendit quomodo Plato cum Pythagoricis communicet, et in quo differat ab eis, ibi, *unum tamen substantiam.*

Dicit ergo primo, quod quia secundum Platonem species separatae sunt causae omnibus aliis entibus, ideo elementa specierum putaverunt esse elementa omnium

158. Now to one who carefully examines Plato's arguments it is evident that Plato's opinion was false, because he believed that the mode of being which the thing known has in reality is the same as the one which it has in the act of being known.

Therefore, since he found that our intellect understands abstractions in two ways—in one way as we understand universals abstracted from singulars, and in another way as we understand the objects of mathematics abstracted from sensible things—he claimed that for each abstraction of the intellect there is a corresponding abstraction in the essences of things. Hence he held that both the objects of mathematics and the forms are separate.

But this is not necessary. For even though the intellect understands things insofar as it becomes assimilated to them through the intelligible form by which it is put into act, it still is not necessary that a form should have the same mode of being in the intellect that it has in the thing known. For everything that exists in something else exists there according to the mode of the recipient.

Therefore, considering the nature of the intellect (which is other than the nature of the thing known) the mode of understanding by which the intellect understands must be one kind of mode, and the mode of being by which things exist must be another. For although the object which the intellect understands must exist in reality, it does not exist there according to the same mode.

Hence, even though the intellect understands mathematical entities without simultaneously understanding sensible substances, and understands universals without understanding particulars, it is not therefore necessary that the objects of mathematics should exist apart from sensible things, or that universals should exist apart from particulars.

For we also see that sight perceives color apart from flavor, even though flavor and color are found together in sensible substances.

159. *And since the forms* (987b18). Here he gives Plato's opinion concerning the principles of things; and in regard to this he does two things.

First, he states the principles which Plato assigned to things;

second [169], the genus of cause to which they are reduced, at *from the foregoing* (988a8).

In regard to the first he does two things.

First, he tells us what kind of principles Plato had assigned to things.

Second [160], he shows in what respect Plato agreed with the Pythagoreans, and in what respect he differed from them, at *yet Plato* (987b22).

He first says that since the forms are the causes of all other beings according to Plato, the Platonists therefore thought that the elements of the forms are the elements of

entium. Et ideo assignabant rebus pro materia magnum et parvum, et quasi *substantiam* rerum, idest formam dicebant esse unum. Et hoc ideo, quia ista ponebant esse principia specierum. Dicebant enim quod sicut species sunt sensibilibus formae, ita unum est forma specierum.

Et ideo sicut sensibilia constituuntur ex principiis universalibus per participationem specierum, ita species, quas dicebat esse numeros, constituuntur secundum eum, *ex illis*, scilicet magno et parvo. Unitas enim diversas numerorum species constituit per additionem et subtractionem, in quibus consistit ratio magni et parvi.

Unde cum unum opinaretur esse substantiam entis, quia non distinguebat inter unum quod est principium numeri, et unum quod convertitur cum ente, videbatur sibi quod hoc modo multiplicarentur diversae species separatae ex una quae est communis substantia, sicut ex unitate diversae species numerorum multiplicantur.

160. Deinde cum dicit *unum tamen* hic comparat opinionem Platonis Pythagorae.

Et primo ostendit in quo conveniebant.

Secundo in quo differebant, ibi, *pro infinito*.

Conveniebant autem in duabus positionibus. Quarum prima est quod unum sit substantia rerum. Dicebant enim Platonici, sicut etiam Pythagorici, quod hoc quod dico unum non probatur de aliquo alio ente, sicut accidens de subiecto, sed hoc signat substantiam rei. Et hoc ideo, quia, ut dictum est, non distinguebant inter unum quod convertitur cum ente, et unum quod est principium numeri.

161. Secunda positio sequitur ex prima. Dicebant enim Platonici (similiter ut Pythagorici) numeros esse causas substantiae omnibus entibus. Et hoc ideo quia numerus nihil aliud est quam unitates collectae. Unde si unitas est substantia, oportet quod etiam numerus.

162. Deinde cum dicit *pro infinito* hic ostendit in quo differebant. Et circa hoc duo facit.

Primo enim ponit differentiam inter eos.

Secundo differentiae causam, ibi, *unum igitur et numeros* et cetera.

Est autem ista differentia in duobus. Primo quantum ad hoc Pythagorici ponebant (ut dictum est) duo principia, ex quibus constituebantur, scilicet finitum et infinitum: quorum unum, scilicet infinitum, se habet ex parte materiae.

Plato vero loco huius unius quod Pythagoras posuit, scilicet infiniti, fecit dualitatem, ponens ex parte materiae magnum et parvum. Et sic infinitum quod Pythagoras posuit unum principium, Plato posuit consistere ex

all beings. Hence, they assigned as the material principle of things the great and small, and said that *the substance* of things (that is, their form) is the one. They did this because they held these to be the principles of the forms. For they said that just as the forms are the formal principles of sensible things, in a similar way the one is the formal principle of the forms.

Therefore, just as sensible things are constituted of universal principles by participation in the forms, in a similar way the forms (which he said are numbers) are constituted *from these*, that is of the great and small. For the unit constitutes different species of numbers by addition and subtraction, in which the notion of the great and small consists.

Hence, since the one was thought to be the substance of being (because he did not distinguish between the one which is the principle of number and the one which is convertible with being), it seemed to him that a plurality of different forms might be produced from the one, which is their common substance, in the same way that a plurality of different species of numbers is produced from the unit.

160. *Yet Plato* (987b22). Here he compares the position of Plato with that of Pythagoras.

First, he shows in what respect they agreed;

second [162], in what respect they differed, at *but to posit* (987b25).

Now they agreed in two positions. The first is that the one is the substance of things. For the Platonists, like the Pythagoreans, said that what I call the one is not predicated of some other being as an accident is of a subject, but signifies a thing's substance. They said this, as we have pointed out [159], because they did not distinguish between the one which is convertible with being and the one which is the principle of number.

161. The second position follows from the first, for the Platonists, like the Pythagoreans, said that numbers are the causes of the substance of all beings; they held this because number is just a collection of units. Hence if the one is substance, number must also be such.

162. *But to posit* (987b25). Here he shows in what respect they differed. In regard to this he does two things.

First, he states how they differed.

Second [164], he gives the reason for this difference, at *therefore, his making* (987b29).

Now this difference involves two things. First, the Pythagoreans, as has already been stated, posited two principles of which things are constituted—the limited and the unlimited—of which one, the unlimited, has the character of matter.

But in place of this one principle, the unlimited, which the Pythagoreans posited, Plato created a dyad, holding that the great and small have the character of matter. Hence the unlimited, which Pythagoras claimed to be one princi-

magno et parvo. Et hoc est proprium opinionis suae in comparatione ad Pythagoram.

163. Secunda differentia est, quia Plato posuit numeros praeter sensibilia, et hoc dupliciter. Ipsas enim species, numeros esse dicebat, sicut supra habitum est. Et iterum inter species et sensibilia posuit mathematica (ut supra dictum est) quae secundum suam substantiam numeros esse dicebat.

Sed Pythagorici dicunt ipsas res sensibiles esse numeros, et non ponunt mathematica media inter species et sensibilia, nec iterum ponunt species separatas.

164. Deinde cum dicit **unum igitur** hic ostendit causam differentiae.

Et primo secundae.

Secundo causas differentiae primae, ibi, **dualitatem autem facere** et cetera.

Dicit ergo quod ponere unum et numeros praeter res sensibiles, et non in ipsis sensibilibus, sicut Pythagorici fecerunt, et iterum introducere species separatas, evenit Platonicis propter scrutationem, **quae est in rationibus**, idest propter hoc quod perscrutati sunt de definitionibus rerum, quas credebant non posse attribui rebus sensibilibus, ut dictum est. Et hac necessitate fuerunt coacti ponere quasdam res quibus definitiones attribuuntur. Sed Pythagorici qui fuerunt priores Platone, non participaverunt dialecticam, ad quam pertinet considerare definitiones et universalia huiusmodi, quarum consideratio induxit ad introductionem idearum.

165. Deinde cum dicit **dualitatem autem** hic ostendit causam alterius differentiae, quae scilicet ex parte materiae est.

Et primo ponit causam huiusmodi differentiae.

Secundo ostendit Platonem non rationabiliter motum esse, ibi, **attamen e contrario**.

Dicit ergo quod ideo Platonici fecerunt dualitatem esse numerum, qui est alia natura a speciebus, quia omnes numeri naturaliter generantur ex dualitate praeter numeros primos. Dicuntur autem numeri primi, quos nullus numerat, sicut ternarius, quinarius, septenarius, undenarius, et sic de aliis. Hi enim a sola unitate constituuntur immediate. Numeri vero, quos aliquis alius numerus numerat, non dicuntur primi, sed compositi, sicut quaternarius, quem numerat dualitas; et universaliter omnis numerus par a dualitate numeratur. Unde numeri pares materiae attribuuntur, cum eis attribuatur infinitum, quod est materia, ut supra dictum est. Hac ratione posuit dualitatem, ex qua sicut **aliquo echimagio**,

ple, Plato claimed to consist of the great and small. This is his own opinion in contrast with that of Pythagoras.

163. The second difference is that Plato held that numbers are separate from sensible things, and this in two ways. For he said that the forms themselves are numbers, as was pointed out above [159]. He also held, as was stated above [157], that the objects of mathematics are an intermediate genus between the forms and sensible things, and that they are numbers by their very essence.

But the Pythagoreans said that sensible things themselves are numbers, and did not make the objects of mathematics an intermediate species between the forms and sensible things. Nor again did they hold that the forms are separate from things.

164. **Therefore, his making** (987b29). Here he gives the reason for the difference.

First, he gives the reason for the second difference; second [165], the reason for the first difference, at **but his making** (987b33).

He says, then, that the Platonists adopted the position that both the one and numbers exist apart from sensible things and not in sensible things, as the Pythagoreans claimed. They also introduced separate forms because of the investigation **into the ideas of things**, that is, because of their investigation of the definitions of things, which they thought could not be attributed to sensible substances, as has been stated [150]. This is the reason they were compelled to hold that there are certain things to which definitions are assigned. But the Pythagoreans, who came before Plato, were ignorant of dialectic, whose office it is to investigate definitions and universals of this kind, the study of which led to the introduction of the ideas.

165. **But his making** (987b33). Here he gives the reason for the other difference, the one concerning matter.

First, he gives the reason for such a difference.

Second [166], he shows that Plato was not reasonably motivated, at **yet what happens is the contrary** (988a1).

He accordingly says that the Platonists made the dyad to be a number of a different nature than the forms, because all numbers with the exception of prime numbers are produced from it. They called prime numbers those which are not measured by any other number (such as three, five, seven, eleven, and so on), for these are produced immediately from unity alone. But numbers which are measured by some other number are not called prime numbers, but composite ones (for example, the number four, which is measured by the number two). And in general every even number is measured by the number two. Hence even numbers are attributed to matter, since unlimitedness, which belongs to matter, is attributed to them, as has been stated

idest ex aliquo exemplari omnes alii numeri pares generantur.

166. Deinde cum dicit *attamen e contrario* hic ostendit Platonem irrationabiliter posuisse. Et circa hoc duo facit.

Primo enim ex ratione naturali ostendit hoc.

Secundo etiam ponit rationem naturalem, quae Platonem movebat ad suam opinionem, ibi, *videtur autem ex una materia*.

Dicit ergo quod quamvis Plato poneret dualitatem ex parte materiae, tamen e converso contingit, sicut attestantur opiniones omnium aliorum philosophorum naturalium, qui posuerunt contrarietatem ex parte formae, et unitatem ex parte materiae, sicut patet primo *Physicorum*. Ponebant enim rerum materiam aerem, vel aquam, aliquid huiusmodi, ex quo diversitatem rerum constituebant per rarum et densum, quae ponebant quasi principia formalia. Non enim est rationabile ponere sicut Plato posuit.

Et hoc ideo quia ex materia viderunt philosophi multa fieri per successionem formarum in ipsa. Illa enim materia, quae modo substat uni formae, post modum substare poterit pluribus, uno corrupto et alio generato.

Sed una species sive una forma solum *semel generat*, idest constituit aliquid generatum. Cum enim aliquid generatur accipit formam quidem, quae forma eadem numero non potest alteri generatio advenire, sed esse desinit generato corrupto. In quo manifeste apparet quod una materia ad multas formas se habet, et non e converso una forma ad multas materias se habet.

Et sic videtur rationabilius ponere ex parte materiae unitatem, sed dualitatem sive contrarietatem ex parte formae, sicut posuerunt naturales, quam e converso, sicut posuit Plato.

167. Deinde cum dicit *videtur autem* hic ponit rationem e converso ex his sensibilibus acceptam secundum opinionem Platonis. Videbat enim Plato quod unumquodque recipitur in aliquo secundum mensuram recipientis. Unde diversae receptiones videntur provenire ex diversis mensuris recipientium. Una autem materia est una mensura recipiendi. Vidit etiam quod agens, qui inducit speciem, facit multas res speciem habentes, cum sit unus, et hoc propter diversitatem quae est in materiis. Et huius exemplum apparet in masculo et femina. Nam masculus se habet ad feminam sicut agens et imprimens speciem ad materiam. Femina autem impraegnatur ab una actione viri. Sed masculus unus potest impraegnare multas feminas. Et inde est quod posuit unitatem ex parte speciei, et dualitatem ex parte materiae.

above [125]. This is why he posited the dyad, from which as *a matrix*, or exemplar, all other even numbers are produced.

166. *Yet what happens* (988a1). Here he proves that Plato made unreasonable assumptions; in regard to this he does two things.

First, he proves this by an argument from nature.

Second [167], he gives the argument based on the nature of things, which led Plato to adopt this position, at *and from one matter* (988a3).

He says that although Plato posited a dyad on the part of matter, still what happens is the contrary of this, as the opinions of all the other natural philosophers testify; for they claimed that contrariety pertains to form and unity to matter, as is clear in *Physics* 1. For they held that the material principle of things is air or water or something of this kind, from which the diversity of things is produced by rarefaction and condensation, which they regarded as formal principles. For Plato's position is not a reasonable one.

Now the natural philosophers adopted this position because they saw that many things are generated from matter as a result of a succession of forms in matter. For that matter which now supports one form may afterward support many forms as a result of one form being corrupted and another being generated.

But one species or form *generates only once*, that is, constitutes the thing which is generated. For when something is generated it receives a form, and the same form numerically cannot become the form of another thing that is generated, but ceases to be when that which was generated undergoes corruption. In this argument it is clearly apparent that one matter is related to many forms, and not the reverse (one form to many matters).

Thus it seems more reasonable to hold that unity pertains to matter but duality or contrariety to form, as the philosophers of nature claimed. This is the opposite of what Plato held.

167. *And from one matter* (988a3). Here he gives an opposite argument taken from sensible things according to the opinion of Plato. For Plato saw that each thing is received in something else according to the measure of the recipient. Hence receptions seem to differ according as the capacities of recipients differ. But one matter is one capacity for reception. And Plato also saw that the agent who induces the form, although he is one, causes many things to have this form; this comes about because of diversity on the part of matter. An example of this is evident in the case of male and female, for a male is related to a female as an agent and one who impresses a form on matter. But a female is impregnated by one action of a male, whereas one male can impregnate many females. This is why he held that unity pertains to form and duality to matter.

168. Est autem attendendum quod haec diversitas inter Platonem et naturales accidit propter diversam de rebus considerationem.

Naturales enim considerant tantum quae sunt sensibilia, prout sunt subiecta transmutationi, in qua unum subiectum successive accipit contraria. Et ideo posuerunt unitatem ex parte materiae, et contrarietatem ex parte formae. Sed Plato ex consideratione universalium deveniebat ad ponendum principia sensibilium rerum. Unde, cum diversitatis multorum singularium sub uno universali causa sit divisio materiae, posuit diversitatem ex parte materiae, et unitatem ex parte formae. *Et tales sunt mutationes illorum principiorum*, quae posuit Plato, idest participationes, vel ut ita dicam influentias in causata: sic enim nomen immutationis Pythagoras accipit. Vel immutationes dicit inquantum Plato mutavit opinionem de principiis, quam primi naturales habuerunt, ut ex praedictis patet. Et sic patet ex praedictis, quod Plato de causis quaesitis a nobis ita definivit.

169. Deinde cum dicit *palam autem* hic ostendit ad quod genus causae principia a Platone posita reducantur. Dicit ergo, ex dictis palam esse quod Plato usus est solum duobus generibus causarum. Causa enim *ipsa*, idest causa, quae est causa ei, *quod quid est*, idest quidditatis rei, scilicet causa formalis, per quam rei quidditas constituitur: et etiam usus est ipsa materia. Quod ex hoc patet, quia species quas posuit *sunt aliis*, idest sensibilibus causae eius *quod quid est*, idest causae formales:

ipsis vero speciebus causa formalis est hoc quod dico unum, et illa videtur substantia de qua sunt species: sicut ens unum ponit causam formalem specierum: ita magnum et parvum ponit earum causam quasi materialem, ut supra dictum est. Et hae quidem causae, scilicet formalis et materialis, non solum sunt respectu specierum, sed etiam respectu sensibilium, quia unum dicitur *in speciebus*: idest id quod hoc modo se habet ad sensibilia, sicut unum ad speciem, est ipsa species, quia ea dualitas quae respondet sensibilibus pro materia est magnum et parvum.

170. Ulterius Plato assignavit causam eius quod est bonum et malum in rebus, et singulis elementis ab eo positis. Nam causam boni ascribebat speciei, causam vero mali materiae. Sed tamen causam boni et mali conati sunt investigare quidam primorum philosophorum, scilicet Anaxagoras et Empedocles, qui ad hoc specialiter aliquas causas in rebus constituerunt, ut ab eis possent assignare principia boni et mali. In hoc autem quod boni causas et mali tetigerunt, aliquo modo accedebant ad

168. Now we must note that this difference between Plato and the philosophers of nature is a result of the fact that they considered things from different points of view.

For the philosophers of nature considered sensible things only insofar as they are subject to change, in which one subject successively acquires contrary qualities. Hence they attributed unity to matter and contrariety to form. But Plato, because of his investigation of universals, went on to give the principles of sensible things. Therefore, since the cause of the diversity of the many singular things that come under one universal is the division of matter, he held that diversity pertains to matter and unity to form. *And such are the changes in these principles* which Plato posited—that is, participations, or, as I may say, influences in the things generated. For Pythagoras understands the word "change" in this way. Or Aristotle says "changes" inasmuch as Plato changed the opinion which the first philosophers of nature had about principles, as is evident from the foregoing. Hence it is evident from the foregoing that Plato dealt thus with the causes which we are investigating.

169. *From the foregoing* (988a8). Here he shows to what genus of cause the principles given by Plato are referred. He says that it is evident from the foregoing that Plato used only two kinds of causes. For he used as *one* cause of a thing the cause of its *whatness* (that is, its quiddity, or its formal cause, which determines its quiddity), and he also used matter itself. This is also evident from the fact that the forms which he posited are *the cause of the whatness in other things*, that is, the causes of the *whatness* of sensible things (namely, their formal causes).

But the formal cause of the forms themselves is what I call the one, which seems to be the substance of which the forms are composed. And just as he holds that the one is the formal cause of the forms, in a similar fashion he holds that the great and small are their material cause, as was stated above [159]. And these causes—the formal and the material cause—are referred not only to the forms but also to sensible substances, because there is some subject of which the one is predicated *in the forms*. That is to say, that which is related to sensible substances in the same way as the one is to the forms is itself a form, because that duality which relates to sensible things as their matter is the great and small.

170. Furthermore, Plato indicated the cause of good and evil in the world, and he did this with reference to each of the elements which he posited. For he made form the cause of good and matter the cause of evil. However, some of the first philosophers attempted to investigate the cause of good and evil, such as Anaxagoras and Empedocles, who established certain causes in the world with end of giving the principles of good and evil by means of these causes. And in touching upon these causes of good and evil they

ponendum causam finalem, licet non per se, sed per accidens eam ponerent, ut infra dicetur.

came very close to positing the final cause, although they did not posit this cause directly, but only indirectly, as is stated below [177].

LECTURE 11

Summary of ancient opinions

988a18 Breviter igitur et capitulariter quid et quomodo de principiis et veritate dixerunt pertransivimus. Attamen ab eis tantum habemus, quia dicentium de principio et causa, nullus praeter ea quae sunt in *Physicis* a nobis determinata, dixit. [171]

988a22 Sed omnes obscure quidem, verumtamen illis appropinquavere. [172]

988a23 Illi namque ut materiam principium dicunt, sive unam sive plures supponant, et sive corpus, sive incorporeum hoc ponant, ut Plato quidem magnum et parvum dicens, Italici vero infinitum, Empedocles ignem, terram, aquam, et a rem, Anaxagoras autem similium partium infinitatem. Et hi omnes sunt talem causam tangentes. Et amplius quicumque a rem aut ignem, aut aquam, aut igne spissius, aere autem subtilius. Etenim quoddam tale primum elementum dixerunt. Hi quidem igitur hanc causam solum tetigerunt. [173]

988a32 Alii vero quidem unde principium motus, ut quicumque amicitiam et litem et intellectum, aut amorem, aut extra haec principium faciunt. [174]

988a34 Quod quid erat esse vero, et substantiam plane nullus dedit. Maxime vero hi dicunt qui species et eas in speciebus rationes ponunt. [175]

Neque enim ut materiam sensibilibus species, et quae sunt in speciebus: neque ut huic principium motus proveniens existimant: immobilitatis autem causas magis, et eius quod est in quiete esse dicunt. Sed quod quid erat esse aliorum, singulis species praestant, speciebus autem unum.

988b6 Cuius vero causa actus et transmutationes et motus modo quodam dicunt

συντόμως μὲν οὖν καὶ κεφαλαιωδῶς ἐπεληλύθαμεν τίνες τε καὶ πῶς τυγχάνουσιν εἰρηκότες περί τε τῶν ἀρχῶν {20} καὶ τῆς ἀληθείας· ὅμως δὲ τοσοῦτόν γ᾿ ἔχομεν ἐξ αὐτῶν, ὅτι τῶν λεγόντων περὶ ἀρχῆς καὶ αἰτίας οὐθεὶς ἔξω τῶν ἐν τοῖς περὶ φύσεως ἡμῖν διωρισμένων εἴρηκεν,

ἀλλὰ πάντες ἀμυδρῶς μὲν ἐκείνων δέ πως φαίνονται θιγγάνοντες.

οἱ μὲν γὰρ ὡς ὕλην τὴν ἀρχὴν λέγουσιν, ἄν τε μίαν ἄν τε πλείους {25} ὑποθῶσι, καὶ ἐάν τε σῶμα ἐάν τε ἀσώματον τοῦτο τιθῶσιν (οἷον Πλάτων μὲν τὸ μέγα καὶ τὸ μικρὸν λέγων, οἱ δ᾿ Ἰταλικοὶ τὸ ἄπειρον, Ἐμπεδοκλῆς δὲ πῦρ καὶ γῆν καὶ ὕδωρ καὶ ἀέρα, Ἀναξαγόρας δὲ τὴν τῶν ὁμοιομερῶν ἀπειρίαν· οὗτοί τε δὴ πάντες τῆς τοιαύτης αἰτίας ἡμμένοι εἰσί, καὶ ἔτι ὅσοι {30} ἀέρα ἢ πῦρ ἢ ὕδωρ ἢ πυρὸς μὲν πυκνότερον ἀέρος δὲ λεπτότερον· καὶ γὰρ τοιοῦτόν τινες εἰρήκασιν εἶναι τὸ πρῶτον στοιχεῖον)· οὗτοι μὲν οὖν ταύτης τῆς αἰτίας ἥψαντο μόνον,

ἕτεροι δέ τινες ὅθεν ἡ ἀρχὴ τῆς κινήσεως (οἷον ὅσοι φιλίαν καὶ νεῖκος ἢ νοῦν ἢ ἔρωτα ποιοῦσιν ἀρχήν)·

τὸ δὲ τί ἦν εἶναι {35} καὶ τὴν οὐσίαν σαφῶς μὲν οὐθεὶς ἀποδέδωκε, {988b1} μάλιστα δ᾿ οἱ τὰ εἴδη τιθέντες λέγουσιν

(οὔτε γὰρ ὡς ὕλην τοῖς αἰσθητοῖς τὰ εἴδη καὶ τὸ ἓν τοῖς εἴδεσιν οὔθ᾿ ὡς ἐντεῦθεν τὴν ἀρχὴν τῆς κινήσεως γιγνομένην ὑπολαμβάνουσιν—ἀκινησίας γὰρ αἴτια μᾶλλον καὶ τοῦ ἐν ἠρεμίᾳ εἶναι φασιν—ἀλλὰ τὸ τί ἦν εἶναι {5} ἑκάστῳ τῶν ἄλλων τὰ εἴδη παρέχονται, τοῖς δ᾿ εἴδεσι τὸ ἕν)·

τὸ δ᾿ οὗ ἕνεκα αἱ πράξεις καὶ αἱ μεταβολαὶ καὶ αἱ κινήσεις τρόπον μέν τινα λέ-

We have examined, then, in a brief and summary way those philosophers who have spoken about the principles of things and about the truth, and the way in which they did this. Yet we have learned from them this much: none of those who have discussed principle and cause have said anything beyond the points established by us in the *Physics*.

Yet all have approached these causes obscurely.

For some speak of the principle as matter, whether they suppose it to be one or many, and whether they assume it to be a body or something incorporeal, as Plato speaks of the great and small; the Italians of the unlimited; Empedocles of fire, earth, water, and air; and Anaxagoras of an infinite number of like parts. All these have touched on this kind of cause, and so also have those who make the first principle air or fire or water or something denser than fire or rarer than air. For they have said that some such body is the primary element. These thinkers, then, have touched only on this cause.

But others have introduced the source of motion. For example, those who make friendship and strife, or intellect, or love, or something besides these, a principle of things.

But the quiddity or substance no one has presented clearly. Those who express it best are those who posit the ideas and the intelligible natures inherent in the ideas.

For they do not think of the ideas and the things inherent in them as the matter of sensible things; nor do they think of them as the source from which motion originates, for they say that these things are the causes rather of immobility and of that which is at rest. But the forms are responsible for the quiddity of all other things, and the one for the quiddity of the forms.

That for the sake of which there are actions and changes and motions they af-

causam, ita vero non dicunt, nec quo vere est. [177]

Nam intellectum quidem dicentes, aut amorem, ut bonum quidem has ponunt causas non ut gratia horum, aut existens, aut factum aliquid entium, sed ut ab his horum motum dicunt. Similiter autem et unum aut ens dicentes esse talem naturam, substantiae quidem causam dicunt esse, non tamen huius causa, aut esse aut fieri. Quare dicere et non dicere aliqualiter accidit eis bonum esse causam. Non enim simpliciter, sed secundum accidens dicunt.

988b16 Quod quidem igitur recte determinatum est de causis et quot et quae, testimonium praebere nobis videntur et hi omnes aliam causam tangere non valentes. Adhuc autem quia quaerenda sunt principia aut sic omnia, aut horum aliquo modo palam. Quomodo etiam unusquisque horum dixit, et quomodo habent de principiis contingentes dubitationes, post hoc pertranseamus de ipsis. [180]

γουσιν αἴτιον, οὕτω δὲ οὐ λέγουσιν οὐδ᾽ ὅνπερ πέφυκεν.

οἱ μὲν γὰρ νοῦν λέγοντες ἢ φιλίαν ὡς ἀγαθὸν μὲν ταύτας τὰς αἰτίας τιθέασιν, οὐ μὴν ὡς {10} ἕνεκά γε τούτων ἢ ὂν ἢ γιγνόμενόν τι τῶν ὄντων ἀλλ᾽ ὡς ἀπὸ τούτων τὰς κινήσεις οὔσας λέγουσιν: ὡς δ᾽ αὕτως καὶ οἱ τὸ ἓν ἢ τὸ ὂν φάσκοντες εἶναι τὴν τοιαύτην φύσιν τῆς μὲν οὐσίας αἴτιόν φασιν εἶναι, οὐ μὴν τούτου γε ἕνεκα ἢ εἶναι ἢ γίγνεσθαι, ὥστε λέγειν τε καὶ μὴ λέγειν πως συμβαίνει αὐτοῖς {15} τἀγαθὸν αἴτιον: οὐ γὰρ ἁπλῶς ἀλλὰ κατὰ συμβεβηκὸς λέγουσιν.

ὅτι μὲν οὖν ὀρθῶς διώρισται περὶ τῶν αἰτίων καὶ πόσα καὶ ποῖα, μαρτυρεῖν ἐοίκασιν ἡμῖν καὶ οὗτοι πάντες, οὐ δυνάμενοι θιγεῖν ἄλλης αἰτίας, πρὸς δὲ τούτοις ὅτι ζητητέαι αἱ ἀρχαὶ ἢ οὕτως ἅπασαι ἢ τινὰ τρόπον τοιοῦτον, δῆλον: {20} πῶς δὲ τούτων ἕκαστος εἴρηκε καὶ πῶς ἔχει περὶ τῶν ἀρχῶν, τὰς ἐνδεχομένας ἀπορίας μετὰ τοῦτο διέλθωμεν περὶ αὐτῶν.

firm in some way to be a cause, but not in the way we are determining causes, or in the way in which it is truly a cause.

For while those who speak of intellect or love posit these causes as good, they do not say that anything exists or comes to be because of them, but claim that the motion of things stems from them. In like manner, those who say that the one or being is such a reality say that it is the cause of substance, but not that things either are or come to be for the sake of this. Hence, it happens to them that in a way they both say and do not say that the good is a cause, for they do not speak of it in its principal aspect but in a secondary one.

Therefore, all these philosophers, being unable to touch on any other cause, seem to bear witness to the fact that we have dealt correctly with the causes, as to both their number and their kinds. Moreover, it is evident that all principles must be sought in this way or in some similar one. As to the way in which each of these philosophers has spoken, and how they have raised possible problems about the principles of things, let us discuss these points next.

---

171. Hic recolligit omnia quae ab antiquis de causis sunt dicta: et circa hoc tria facit.

Primo ostendit, quod priores philosophi nullam causam de quatuor generibus causarum ab eis suprapositis addere potuerunt.

Secundo ostendit qualiter praedictas causas tetigerunt, ibi, *sed omnes obscure* et cetera.

Tertio concludit conclusionem principaliter intentam, ibi, *quod quidem igitur recte* et cetera.

Dicit ergo, quod breviter et sub quodam capitulo sive compendio pertranseundo dictum est, qui philosophi, et quomodo locuti sunt de principiis rerum et de veritate, quantum ad ipsam rerum substantiam. Sed ex eorum dictis tantum haberi potest, quod nullus eorum, qui de causis et principiis rerum dixerunt, potuit dicere aliquas causas praeter illas, quae distinctae sunt secundo *Physicorum*.

172. Deinde cum dicit *sed omnes* hic ponit qualiter illas causas posuerunt.

Et primo in generali.

Secundo in speciali, ibi, *illi namque* et cetera.

171. Here he makes a summary of everything that the early philosophers have said about causes, and in regard to this he does three things.

First (988a18; [171]), he shows that the early philosophers were unable to add another kind of cause to the four genera of causes given above (983a24; [70]).

Second (988a22; [172]), he indicates the way in which they touched upon these causes, at *yet all*.

Third (988b16; [180]), he draws the conclusion at which he chiefly aims, at *therefore, all these*.

He first says (988a18) that in giving this brief and summary account he has stated who the philosophers are, and how they have spoken of the principles of things and of what is true of the substance itself of things. And from their statements this much can be learned: none of those who have spoken about causes and principles were able to mention any causes other than those distinguished in *Physics* 2.

172. *Yet all* (988a22). Here he gives the way in which they dealt with each of the causes.

He does this first (988a22) in a general way,

and second (988a23; [172]), in a special way, at *for some speak*.

Dicit ergo primo, quod non solum nihil addiderunt, sed quo modo appropinquaverunt, et hoc non manifeste, sed obscure. Non enim assignaverunt secundum quod genus causae principia ab eis posita rerum causae essent; sed solum posuerunt illa, quae ad aliquod genus causae adaptari possunt.

173. Deinde cum dicit *illi namque* hic ostendit in speciali quomodo singulas causas tetigerunt.

Et primo quomodo tetigerunt causam materialem.

Secundo quomodo causam efficientem, ibi, *alii vero*.

Tertio quomodo causam formalem, ibi, *quod quid erat esse vero* et cetera.

Quarto quomodo causam finalem, ibi, *cuius vero causa* et cetera.

Dicit ergo primo, quod illi, scilicet priores philosophi, omnes in hoc conveniunt, quod dant rebus aliquod principium quasi materiam. Differunt tamen in duobus.

Primo, quia quidam posuerunt unam materiam, sicut Thales et Diogenes et similes: quidam plures, sicut Empedocles.

Secundo, quia quidam posuerunt rerum materiam esse aliquod corpus, sicut praedicti philosophi. Quidam incorporeum, sicut Plato qui posuit dualitatem.

Posuit enim Plato magnum et parvum, quae non dicunt aliquod corpus. Italici vero, idest Pythagorici posuerunt infinitum, quod iterum non est corpus. Empedocles vero quatuor elementa quae sunt corpora. Similiter Anaxagoras posuit *infinitatem similium partium* idest infinitas partes consimiles principia esse.

Et hi omnes tetigerunt *talem causam*, scilicet materialem. Et etiam illi qui dixerunt aerem aut aquam aut ignem esse principium, vel aliquod medium inter haec elementa, scilicet igne spissius, aere subtilius; omnes enim tales praedicti tale corpus posuerunt esse primum elementum.

Et sic patet quod dicit, quod philosophi quantum ad haec, quae praedicta sunt, posuerunt solam causam materialem.

174. Deinde cum dicit *alii quidem* hic ponit opiniones de causa efficiente, dicens, quod alii praedictorum philosophorum posuerunt cum causa materiali causam unde principium motus: sicut quicumque posuerunt causam rerum amorem, odium, et intellectum; aut qui faciunt aliqua principia agentia praeter haec, sicut Parmenides qui posuit ignem quasi causam agentem.

175. Deinde cum dicit *quod quid* hic ponit opiniones de causa formali; et dicit quod causa, per quam scitur

Accordingly he says first that they not only have not added anything, but in the way in which they approached these causes they proceeded obscurely and not clearly. For they have not stated to what genus of cause the principles posited by them would belong, but they gave as principles things that can be adapted to some genus of cause.

173. *For some speak* (988a23). Here he shows in a special way how they touched on each of these causes.

He shows first (988a23) how they touched on the material cause;

second (988a32; [174]), on the efficient cause, at *but others*;

third (988a34; [175]), on the formal cause, at *but the quiddity*;

fourth (988b6; [177]), on the final cause, at *that for the sake of which*.

He says first (988a23) that those philosophers, the early ones, all agree insofar as they assign some material cause to things. Yet they differ in two respects.

First, they differ in that some, such as Thales, Diogenes, and the like, held that the material principle is one, whereas others, such as Empedocles, claimed that it is many.

Second, they differ in that some, such as the first group above, held that the material principle of things is a body, whereas others, such as Plato who posited a dyad, claimed that it is something incorporeal.

For Plato posited the great and small, which the Platonists do not speak of as a body. The Italians, or Pythagoreans, posited the unlimited, but neither is this a body. Empedocles, on the other hand, posited the four elements, which are bodies; Anaxagoras also posited *an infinite number of like parts*, or that the principles of things are an infinite number of like parts.

All of these thinkers have touched on *this kind of cause*, or the material cause, and so also have those who said that the principle of things is air or water or fire or something midway between these elements (that is, what is denser than fire and rarer than air). For all philosophers such as those just mentioned have claimed that some kind of body is the first element of things.

Thus Aristotle's statement is evident: in the light of the foregoing remarks these philosophers have posited only the material cause.

174. *But others* (988a32). Here he gives their opinions about the efficient cause. He says that some of the foregoing philosophers have posited, in addition to the material cause, a cause from which motion begins—for example, those who made love or hate or intellect a cause of things, or those who introduced some other active principle distinct from these, as Parmenides, who made fire an efficient cause.

175. *But the quiddity* (988a34). Here he gives their opinions about the formal cause. He says that no one attributed

quid est rei substantia, idest causam formalem, nullus manifeste rebus attribuit, et si aliquid tangerent antiqui philosophi quod pertineret ad causam formalem, sicut Empedocles qui posuit os et carnem habere aliquam rationem per quam sunt huiusmodi; non tamen hoc quod pertinet ad causam formalem ponebant per modum causae.

176. Sed inter alios maxime appropinquaverunt ad ponendum causam formalem qui posuerunt species, et eas rationes qui ad species pertinent, sicut unitatem et numerum et alia huiusmodi.

Species enim et ea quae sunt modo praedicto in speciebus, ut unitas et numerus, non suscipiuntur vel ponuntur ab eis ut materia rerum sensibilium, cum potius ex parte rerum sensibilium materiam ponant. Nec ponunt eas ut causas unde motus proveniat rebus, immo magis sunt rebus causa immobilitatis.

Quicquid enim necessarium in sensibilibus invenitur, hoc ex speciebus causari dicebant, et ipsas, scilicet species, dicebant esse absque motu. Ad hoc enim ab eis ponebantur, ut dictum est, quod immobiles existentes uniformiter se haberent, ita quod de eis possent dari definitiones et fieri demonstrationes. Sed secundum eorum opinionem species rebus singulis praestant quidditatem per modum causae formalis, et unitas hoc ipsum praestat speciebus.

177. Deinde cum dicit *cuius vero* hic ponit opiniones quorumdam de causa finali, dicens quod philosophi quodammodo finem cuius causa motus et transmutationes et actiones fiunt, dicunt esse causam, et quodammodo non dicunt, nec dicunt eodem modo, quo vera causa est. Illi enim qui dicunt causam esse intellectum vel amorem, ponunt eas causas quasi bonum. Dicebant enim huiusmodi esse causas ut res bene se habeant. Boni enim causa esse non potest nisi bonum.

Unde sequitur quod ponerent intellectum et amorem esse causam, sicut bonum est causa. Bonum autem potest intelligi dupliciter. Uno modo sicut causa finalis, inquantum aliquid fit gratia alicuius boni. Alio modo per modum causae efficientis, sicut dicimus quod bonus homo facit bonum.

Isti ergo philosophi non dixerunt praedictas causas esse bonas, quasi horum causa aliquod entium sit aut fiat, quod pertinet ad rationem causae finalis; sed quia a praedictis, scilicet intellectu et amore, procedebat motus quidam ad esse et fieri rerum, quod pertinet ad rationem causae efficientis.

the cause through which a thing's substance is known (that is, the formal cause) to things with any clarity. And if the ancient philosophers touched on something that might pertain to the formal cause (as Empedocles did when he claimed that bone and flesh contain some proportion of the elements by which they are things of this kind), nevertheless they did not treat what belongs to the formal cause after the manner of a cause.

176. But among the other philosophers, those who posited the forms and those intelligible aspects which belong to the forms (such as unity, number, and the like) came closest to positing the formal cause.

For the forms and everything that belongs to the forms in the aforesaid way, such as unity and number, are not acknowledged or assumed by them to be the matter of sensible things, since they place matter rather on the side of sensible things; nor do they claim that the forms are the causes from which motion originates in the world, but rather that they are the cause of immobility in things.

For they said that whatever is found to be necessary in sensible things is caused by the forms, and that these, the forms, are immobile. For they claimed that the forms, because immobile, are uniform in being, as has been said (987a29; [156]), so that definitions can be given of them and demonstrations made about them. But according to the opinion of these men the forms are responsible for the quiddity of particular things after the manner of a formal cause, and the one is responsible for the quiddity of the forms.

177. *That for the sake of which* (988b6). Here he gives the opinions of certain thinkers about the final cause. He says that in one sense the philosophers say that the goal for the sake of which motions, changes, and activities occur is a cause, and in another sense they do not. And they neither speak of it in the same way, nor in the way in which it is a true cause. For those who affirm that intellect or love is a cause posit these causes as good. For they said that things of this kind are the causes of things being well disposed, since the cause of good can only be good.

Hence it follows that they could make intellect and love to be causes, just as the good is a cause. But good can be understood in two ways: in one way as a final cause in the sense that something comes to be for the sake of some good, and in another way as an efficient cause, as we say that the good man does good.

Now these philosophers did not say that the foregoing causes are good in the sense that they are the reason for the existence or coming to be of some beings, which pertains to the intelligibility of the final cause, but in the sense that there proceeds from these causes—intellect and will— a kind of motion toward the being and coming-to-be of things. And this pertains to the intelligibility of the efficient cause.

178. Similiter autem Pythagorici et Platonici qui dixerunt rerum substantiam esse ipsum unum et ens, uni etiam et enti attribuebant bonitatem. Et sic dicebant talem naturam, scilicet bonum, esse rebus sensibilibus causam substantiae, vel per modum causae formalis, sicut Plato posuit, vel per modum materiae sicut Pythagorici.

Non tamen dicebant quod esse rerum aut fieri esset huius causa, scilicet unius et entis, quod pertinet ad rationem causae finalis.

Et sic sicut naturales posuerunt bonum esse causam, non per modum causae formalis, sed per modum causae efficientis: ita Platonici posuerunt bonum esse causam per modum causae formalis et non per modum causae finalis: Pythagorici vero per modum causae materialis.

179. Unde patet quod accidebat eis quodammodo dicere bonum esse causam, et quodammodo non dicere. Non enim simpliciter dicebant bonum esse causam, sed per accidens. Bonum enim secundum propriam rationem est causa per modum causae finalis. Quod ex hoc patet, quod bonum est, quod omnia appetunt. Id autem, in quod tendit appetitus, est finis: bonum igitur secundum propriam rationem est causa per modum finis.

Illi igitur ponunt bonum simpliciter esse causam, qui ponunt ipsum esse causam finalem. Qui autem attribuunt bono alium modum causalitatis, ponunt ipsum esse causam, et hoc per accidens, quia non ex ratione boni, sed ratione eius cui accidit esse bonum, ut ex hoc quod est esse activum vel perfectivum. Unde patet quod isti philosophi causam finalem non ponebant nisi per accidens, quia scilicet ponebant pro causa, id cui convenit esse finem, scilicet bonum; non tamen posuerunt ipsum esse causam per modum finalis causae, ut dictum est.

180. Deinde cum dicit *quod quidem* hic concludit conclusionem principaliter intentam, scilicet quod determinatio facta superius de causis quae et quot sint, recta fuit. Huius enim testimonium videntur praebere praedicti philosophi, nullum genus causae valentes addere supra praedicta. Et haec utilitas provenit ex praedictarum opinionum recitatione.

Alia autem utilitas est, quia inde palam est, quod principia rerum sunt quaerenda in ista scientia, ut omnia quae antiqui posuerunt, et quae superius sunt determinata, aut aliquod horum. Maxime enim haec scientia considerat causam formalem et finalem et aliquo modo etiam moventem. Nec solum oportet praedictas opiniones recitasse; sed post haec transeundo dicendum est quomodo quilibet horum dixerit, et in quo bene, et in

178. In a similar way, the Pythagoreans and Platonists, who said that the substance of things is the one itself or being, also attributed goodness to the one or being. Thus they said that such a reality, the good, is the cause of the substance of sensible things, either in the manner of a formal cause (as the Platonists maintained), or in the manner of a material cause (as the Pythagoreans claimed).

However, they did not say that the being and coming-to-be of things exists for the sake of this (that is, the one or being); this is something that pertains to the intelligibility of the final cause.

Hence, just as the philosophers of nature claimed that the good is a cause in the manner of an efficient cause and not in that of a formal cause, in a similar way the Platonists claimed that the good is a cause in the manner of a formal cause, and not in that of a final cause. The Pythagoreans, on the other hand, considered it to be a cause in the manner of a material cause.

179. It is evident, then, that in one sense they happened to speak of the good as a cause and in another not. For they did not speak of it as a cause in its principal aspect, but in a secondary one, because according to its proper intelligible structure the good is a cause in the manner of a final cause. This is clear from the fact that the good is what all desire. Now that to which an appetite tends is a goal. Therefore, according to its proper intelligible structure the good is a cause in the manner of a goal.

Hence those who make the good a cause in its principal aspect claim that it is a final cause. But those who attribute a different mode of causality to the good claim that the good is a cause but only accidentally, because they do not hold that it is such by reason of being good, but by reason of that to which good happens to belong by reason of its being active or perfective. Hence it is clear that those philosophers posited a final cause only accidentally, because they posited as a cause something that is fitting to be an end—namely, the good. However, they did not claim that it is a cause in the manner of a final cause, as has been stated.

180. *Therefore, all these* (988b16). Here he draws the conclusion at which he chiefly aims: the things established about the causes, both as to their number and their kinds, are correct. For the foregoing philosophers seem to bear witness to this in being unable to add another genus of cause to those discussed above. This is one of the useful things resulting from the account of the foregoing views.

Another is that evidently the principles of things must be investigated in this science, either all or some of those which the ancient philosophers posited and which have been established above. For this science considers chiefly the formal and final cause, and also in a sense the efficient cause. Now it is not only necessary that the above views be discussed, but after this examination it is also necessary to describe the way in which each of these men has spoken

quo male; et quomodo ea quae dicuntur de principiis habent aliquam dubitationem.

(both in what sense their statements are acceptable and in what sense not), and how the statements which have been made about the principles of things contain a problem.

LECTURE 12

The number of material principles

988b22 Ergo quicumque unum ipsum omne, et unam esse quamdam naturam quasi materiam ponunt, et eam corpoream et mensuram habentem, palam quod multipliciter delinquunt. Corporum enim elementa ponunt solum, incorporeorum vero non, tamquam non existentibus incorporeis. [181]

ὅσοι μὲν οὖν ἕν τε τὸ πᾶν καὶ μίαν τινὰ φύσιν ὡς ὕλην τιθέασι, καὶ ταύτην σωματικὴν καὶ μέγεθος ἔχουσαν, δῆλον ὅτι πολλαχῶς ἁμαρτάνουσιν. τῶν γὰρ σωμάτων τὰ {25} στοιχεῖα τιθέασι μόνον, τῶν δ᾽ ἀσωμάτων οὔ, ὄντων καὶ ἀσωμάτων.

Therefore, all those who hold that the whole is one and say that there is a certain single nature as matter, and that this is bodily and has measure, are clearly at fault in many ways. For they give only the elements of bodies and not those of incorporeal things, as if incorporeal things did not exist.

988b26 De generatione quoque et corruptione causam dicere conantes, et de omnibus physice tractantes, motus causam auferunt. [182]

καὶ περὶ γενέσεως καὶ φθορᾶς ἐπιχειροῦντες τὰς αἰτίας λέγειν, καὶ περὶ πάντων φυσιολογοῦντες, τὸ τῆς κινήσεως αἴτιον ἀναιροῦσιν.

And in attempting to state the cause of generation and corruption, and in treating all things according to the method of natural philosophy, they do away with the cause of motion.

988b28 Amplius autem substantiam nullius posuerunt causam, neque quod quid est. [183]

ἔτι δὲ τῷ τὴν οὐσίαν μηθενὸς αἰτίαν τιθέναι μηδὲ τὸ τί ἐστι,

Furthermore, they did not claim that the substance or whatness of a thing is a cause of anything.

988b29 Et ad hoc quodlibet simplicium corporum esse principium quodcumque, praeter terram, non considerantes ea, quae ex invibem generationem aliqualiter faciunt. [184]

καὶ πρὸς τούτοις τῷ ῥᾳδίως τῶν {30} ἁπλῶν σωμάτων λέγειν ἀρχὴν ὁτιοῦν πλὴν γῆς, οὐκ ἐπισκεψάμενοι τὴν ἐξ ἀλλήλων γένεσιν πῶς ποιοῦνται,

And they were wrong in holding that any of the simple bodies except earth is a principle, without considering how they are generated from each other.

Dico autem ignem, terram, aquam et aerem: haec quidem enim concretione, illa vero discretione invicem fiunt. Haec autem ad prius esse et posterius plurimum differunt.

λέγω δὲ πῦρ καὶ ὕδωρ καὶ γῆν καὶ ἀέρα. τὰ μὲν γὰρ συγκρίσει τὰ δὲ διακρίσει ἐξ ἀλλήλων γίγνεται, τοῦτο δὲ πρὸς τὸ πρότερον εἶναι καὶ ὕστερον διαφέρει πλεῖστον.

I mean fire, earth, water and air; for some of these are generated from each other by combination and others by separation. Now it makes the greatest difference as to which of these is prior and which subsequent.

Aliqualiter enim utique videbitur maxime elementum esse omnium ex quo primo fit congregatione primum. Tale vero est quod minutissimae partis et subtilissimum corporum. Unde quicumque ponunt ignem principium, maxime confessae rationi huic dicunt: tale vero et aliorum unusquisque confitetur elementum esse quoddam corporum.

τῇ μὲν γὰρ ἂν {35} δόξειε στοιχειωδέστατον εἶναι πάντων ἐξ οὗ γίγνονται συγκρίσει πρώτου, {989a1} τοιοῦτον δὲ τὸ μικρομερέστατον καὶ λεπτότατον ἂν εἴη τῶν σωμάτων (διόπερ ὅσοι πῦρ ἀρχὴν τιθέασι, μάλιστα ὁμολογουμένως ἂν τῷ λόγῳ τούτῳ λέγοιεν· τοιοῦτον δὲ καὶ τῶν ἄλλων ἕκαστος ὁμολογεῖ τὸ στοιχεῖον εἶναι τὸ τῶν σωμάτων:

For in one way it would seem that the most basic element of all is that from which a thing first comes to be by combination. But such an element will be one which has the smallest parts and is the subtlest of bodies. Hence all those who posit fire as the first principle make statements that conform most closely to this theory. But each of the other thinkers admits that the primary element of bodies is something of this kind.

989a5 Nullus enim posteriorum et unum dicentium, terram esse elementum voluit: palam quia propter magnitudinem partialitatis. Quodlibet autem trium elementorum iudicem quemdam accepit. Hi namque ignem, illi vero aquam, alii aerem hoc esse dicunt. Sed quare non terram dicunt, quemadmodum hominum multi? Omnia namque ter-

οὐθεὶς γοῦν ἠξίωσε τῶν ἓν λεγόντων γῆν εἶναι στοιχεῖον, δηλονότι διὰ τὴν μεγαλομέρειαν, τῶν δὲ τριῶν ἕκαστον στοιχείων εἴληφέ τινα κριτήν, οἱ μὲν γὰρ πῦρ οἱ δ᾽ ὕδωρ οἱ δ᾽ ἀέρα τοῦτ᾽ εἶναί φασιν· καίτοι διὰ τί ποτ᾽ οὐ καὶ τὴν γῆν λέγουσιν, ὥσπερ οἱ πολλοὶ τῶν ἀνθρώπων; πάντα {10} γὰρ εἶναί φασι γῆν, φησὶ δὲ καὶ Ἡσίοδος τὴν

For none of the later thinkers, and none of those who spoke about the one, wanted earth to be an element, evidently because of the size of its particles. But each of the other three elements finds some supporter, for some say that this primary element is fire, others water, and others air. But why do they not say that it is earth, as in a sense most men do? For they say

ram esse dicunt. Dicit autem Hesiodus terram primam corporum factam esse: sic enim antiquam et publicam contingit existimationem esse. Secundum hanc igitur rationem nec siquis horum aliquid dicit praeter ignem, nec siquis aere quidem spissius hoc ponit, aqua autem subtilius, non recte utique dicet.

γῆν πρώτην γενέσθαι τῶν σωμάτων: οὕτως ἀρχαίαν καὶ δημοτικὴν συμβέβηκεν εἶναι τὴν ὑπόληψιν): κατὰ μὲν οὖν τοῦτον τὸν λόγον οὔτ᾽ εἴ τις τούτων τι λέγει πλὴν πυρός, οὔτ᾽ εἴ τις ἀέρος μὲν πυκνότερον τοῦτο τίθησιν ὕδατος δὲ {15} λεπτότερον, οὐκ ὀρθῶς ἂν λέγοι:

that everything is earth. And Hesiod says that earth is the first of bodies to be generated; for this happens to be the ancient and common view. Therefore, according to this theory, if anyone says that any of these bodies with the exception of fire is the primary element of things, or if anyone holds that it is something denser than air but rarer than water, he will not speak the truth.

989a15 Si vero est, quod est generatione posterius, natura prius, et quod est densatum et concretum posterius generatione, horum erit contrarium; aqua quidem aere prior, et terra aqua. De ponentibus quidem igitur unam causam qualem diximus, sint haec dicta. [187]

εἰ δ᾽ ἔστι τὸ τῇ γενέσει ὕστερον τῇ φύσει πρότερον, τὸ δὲ πεπεμμένον καὶ συγκεκριμένον ὕστερον τῇ γενέσει, τοὐναντίον ἂν εἴη τούτων, ὕδωρ μὲν ἀέρος πρότερον γῆ δὲ ὕδατος. περὶ μὲν οὖν τῶν μίαν τιθεμένων αἰτίαν οἵαν εἴπομεν, ἔστω ταῦτ᾽ εἰρημένα:

However, if that which is later in generation is prior in nature, and if that which is condensed and compounded is later in generation, then the reverse will be true—water will be prior to air, and earth to water. Let these points suffice, then, regarding those who posit one cause such as we have described.

989a19 Idem quoque et si quis haec plura ponit, velut Empedocles, quatuor dicit esse corpora materiam. Etenim huic haec quidem eadem, alia vero propria accidere est necesse. Ex adinvicem enim generata cernimus, quasi non semper igne et terra eodem corpora permanente. Dictum est autem de his in *Physicis*. [190]

τὸ δ᾽ {20} αὐτὸ κἂν εἴ τις ταῦτα πλείω τίθησιν, οἷον Ἐμπεδοκλῆς τέτταρά φησιν εἶναι σώματα τὴν ὕλην. καὶ γὰρ τούτῳ τὰ μὲν ταὐτὰ τὰ δ᾽ ἴδια συμβαίνειν ἀνάγκη. γιγνόμενά τε γὰρ ἐξ ἀλλήλων ὁρῶμεν ὡς οὐκ ἀεὶ διαμένοντος πυρὸς καὶ γῆς τοῦ αὐτοῦ σώματος (εἴρηται δὲ ἐν τοῖς περὶ φύσεως περὶ αὐτῶν),

The same consequence will also be true if anyone posits many elements, as Empedocles says that the four bodies are the matter of things. For these same consequences must befall this man, as well as some which are peculiar to himself. For we see things being generated from each other in such a way that the same body does not always remain fire or earth. But we have spoken of these matters in our physical treatises.

989a25 Et de moventium causa, utrum unum aut plura ponendum, nec recte nec rationabiliter putandum est omnino dictum esse. [192]

καὶ περὶ τῆς τῶν κινουμένων αἰτίας, πότερον ἓν ἢ δύο θετέον, οὔτ᾽ ὀρθῶς οὔτε εὐλόγως οἰητέον εἰρῆσθαι παντελῶς.

And concerning the cause of things in motion, whether one or more than one must be posited, it must not be thought that what has been said is either entirely correct or reasonable.

989a26 Et ex toto alterationem auferre est necesse sic dicentibus. Non enim ex calido frigidum, nec ex frigido calidum erit. Quod enim ea patietur contraria, et quae est una natura, quae sit ignis et aqua? Quod ille non ponit. [193]

ὅλως τε ἀλλοίωσιν ἀναιρεῖσθαι ἀνάγκη τοῖς οὕτω λέγουσιν: οὐ γὰρ ἐκ θερμοῦ ψυχρὸν οὐδὲ ἐκ ψυχροῦ θερμὸν ἔσται. τί γὰρ αὐτὰ ἂν πάσχοι τἀναντία, καὶ τίς εἴη ἂν μία φύσις ἡ γιγνομένη {30} πῦρ καὶ ὕδωρ, ὃ ἐκεῖνος οὔ φησιν.

And in general those who speak thus must do away with alteration, because the cold will not come from the hot, nor the hot from the cold. For what is it that undergoes these contraries and what is the one nature which becomes fire and water? Such a thing Empedocles does not admit.

989a30 Anaxagoram vero siquis susceperit, duo elementa dicere, suscipiant maxime secundum rationem, quam ille quidem non articulavit: secutus tamen est ex necessitate dicentes eam. [194]

Ἀναξαγόραν δ᾽ εἴ τις ὑπολάβοι δύο λέγειν στοιχεῖα, μάλιστ᾽ ἂν ὑπολάβοι κατὰ λόγον, ὃν ἐκεῖνος αὐτὸς μὲν οὐ διήρθρωσεν, ἠκολούθησε μέντ᾽ ἂν ἐξ ἀνάγκης τοῖς ἐπάγουσιν αὐτόν.

But if anyone were to maintain that Anaxagoras speaks of two elements, they would acknowledge something fully in accord with a theory which he himself has not stated articulately, although he would have been forced to follow those who express this view.

989a33 Nam absurdo existente taliter dicere permixta esse a principio omnia, et quia oportet accipere quod impermixta praeexistant, et quia non aptum cuili-

ἀτόπου γὰρ ὄντος καὶ ἄλλως τοῦ φάσκειν μεμῖχθαι τὴν ἀρχὴν πάντα, {989b1} καὶ διὰ τὸ συμβαίνειν ἄμικτα δεῖν προϋπάρχειν καὶ διὰ τὸ μὴ πε-

For to say, as he did, that in the beginning all things are mixed together is absurd, both because it would be necessary to understand that things previously existed

bet permisceri quodlibet. Adhuc autem quia passiones et accidenda separantur a substantiis: eorumdem enim permixtio est et separatio. [195]

Tamen si quis exequitur articulans quod vult dicere, forte apparebit mirabilius dicens. Quando namque nihil erat discretum, palam quia nihil erat verum dicere de substanda illa. Dico autem quia neque album, neque nigrum, aut fuscum aut alium colorem: sed neque colorata erat ex necessitate: horum enim colorem aliquem haberet.

Similiter autem et sine humoribus. Eadem quoque ratione, neque aliud similium. Nihil enim neque quale aliquod id possibile est esse, neque quantum, neque quid. Aliqua enim dictarum in parte specierum inessent utique ei, sed hoc palam impossibile permixtis omnibus. Iam enim discreta essent. Dixit autem permixta esse omnia praeter intellectum. Hunc autem impermixtum solum et purum.

Ex his autem accidet eidem dicere duo principia intellectum ipsum: hoc enim simpliciter impermixtum et alterum quale ponimus indeterminatum antequam determinetur et quadam specie participet. Quare quod dicit quidem, neque recte, neque plane. Vult tamen aliquid posterius dicentibus propinquum et nunc apparentibus magis. Verum hi quidem his qui circa generationem sermonibus et corruptionem et motum proprii sunt solum. Fere namque circa talis substantiae principia et causas quaerunt solum.

φυκέναι τῷ τυχόντι μίγνυσθαι τὸ τυχόν, πρὸς δὲ τούτοις ὅτι τὰ πάθη καὶ τὰ συμβεβηκότα χωρίζοιτ᾽ ἂν τῶν οὐσιῶν (τῶν γὰρ αὐτῶν μῖξίς ἐστι καὶ χωρισμός),

ὅμως εἴ τις ἀκολουθήσειε {5} συνδιαρθρῶν ἃ βούλεται λέγειν, ἴσως ἂν φανείη καινοπρεπεστέρως λέγων. ὅτε γὰρ οὐθὲν ἦν ἀποκεκριμένον, δῆλον ὡς οὐθὲν ἦν ἀληθὲς εἰπεῖν κατὰ τῆς οὐσίας ἐκείνης, λέγω δ᾽ οἷον ὅτι οὔτε λευκὸν οὔτε μέλαν ἢ φαιὸν ἢ ἄλλο χρῶμα, ἀλλ᾽ ἄχρων ἦν ἐξ ἀνάγκης: εἶχε γὰρ ἄν τι τούτων {10} τῶν χρωμάτων:

ὁμοίως δὲ καὶ ἄχυμον τῷ αὐτῷ λόγῳ τούτῳ, οὐδὲ ἄλλο τῶν ὁμοίων οὐδέν: οὔτε γὰρ ποιόν τι οἷόν τε αὐτὸ εἶναι οὔτε ποσὸν οὔτε τί. τῶν γὰρ ἐν μέρει τι λεγομένων εἰδῶν ὑπῆρχεν ἂν αὐτῷ, τοῦτο δὲ ἀδύνατον μεμιγμένων γε πάντων: ἤδη γὰρ ἂν ἀπεκέκριτο, φησὶ δ᾽ {15} εἶναι μεμιγμένα πάντα πλὴν τοῦ νοῦ, τοῦτον δὲ ἀμιγῆ μόνον καὶ καθαρόν.

ἐκ δὴ τούτων συμβαίνει λέγειν αὐτῷ τὰς ἀρχὰς τό τε ἕν (τοῦτο γὰρ ἁπλοῦν καὶ ἀμιγές) καὶ θάτερον, οἷον τίθεμεν τὸ ἀόριστον πρὶν ὁρισθῆναι καὶ μετασχεῖν εἴδους τινός, ὥστε λέγει μὲν οὔτ᾽ ὀρθῶς οὔτε σαφῶς, βούλεται μέντοι {20} τι παραπλήσιον τοῖς τε ὕστερον λέγουσι καὶ τοῖς νῦν φαινομένοις μᾶλλον. ἀλλὰ γὰρ οὗτοι μὲν τοῖς περὶ γένεσιν λόγοις καὶ φθορὰν καὶ κίνησιν οἰκεῖοι τυγχάνουσι μόνον (σχεδὸν γὰρ περὶ τῆς τοιαύτης οὐσίας καὶ τὰς ἀρχὰς καὶ τὰς αἰτίας ζητοῦσι μόνης):

in an unmixed state, and because it is not fitting that anything should be mixed with just anything. Also because properties and accidents could be separated from substances (for there is both mixture and separation of the same things).

Yet, if anyone were to follow him up and articulate what he means, his statement would perhaps appear more astonishing. For when nothing was distinct from anything else, evidently nothing would be truly predicated of that substance. I mean that it would be neither white nor black nor tawny, nor have any color, but would necessarily be colorless; otherwise it would have one of these colors.

Similarly, it would be without humors. And for the same reason it would have no other similar attribute. For it could not have any quality or quantity or whatness, because, if it had, some of the attributes described as formal principles would inhere in it. But this is obviously impossible, since all things are mixed together; they would already be distinct from each other. But he said that all things are mixed together except intellect, and that this alone is unmixed and pure.

Now from these statements it follows for him that there are two principles, one being the intellect itself (for this is unmixed in an absolute sense), and the other being the kind of thing we suppose the indeterminate to be before it is limited and participates in a form. Hence, what he says is neither correct nor clear, although he intends something similar to what later thinkers said and what is now more apparent. But these thinkers are concerned only with theories proper to generation, corruption and motion, for usually it is only of this kind of substance that these men seek the principles and causes.

---

181. Postquam recitavit opiniones philosophorum de principiis, hic incipit eas improbare. Et dividitur in duas partes.

Primo improbat singulas opiniones.

Secundo recolligit ea quae dicta sunt, et continuat se ad sequentia, ibi, **quoniam ergo dictas causas** et cetera.

Prima dividitur in duas partes.

181. Having stated the opinions which the philosophers held about the principles of things, Aristotle begins here to criticize them. This is divided into two parts.

First, he criticizes each opinion.

Second [272], he summarizes his discussion and links it up with what follows, at **from the foregoing** (993a11).

The first is divided into two parts.

Primo reprobat opiniones eorum qui naturaliter locuti sunt.

Secundo reprobat opiniones illorum qui non naturaliter sunt locuti, scilicet Pythagorae et Platonis, eo quod altiora principia posuerunt quam naturales, ibi, *quicumque vero* et cetera.

Circa primum duo facit.

Primo improbat opiniones eorum qui posuerunt unam causam materialem.

Secundo eorum qui posuerunt plures, ibi, *idem quoque et si quis*.

Circa primum duo facit.

Primo improbat opiniones praedictas in generali.

Secundo in speciali, ibi, *et ad hoc* et cetera.

Improbat autem in generali triplici ratione.

Prima ratio talis est. Quia in rebus non solum sunt corporea, sed etiam quaedam incorporea, ut patet ex libro *De anima*. Sed ipsi non posuerunt principia nisi corporea: quod ex hoc patet, quia ipsi ponebant, *unum omne* idest universum esse unum secundum substantiam, et esse unam naturam quasi materiam, et eam esse corpoream, et habentem *mensuram* idest dimensionem: corpus autem non potest esse causa rei incorporeae; ergo patet quod in hoc deliquerunt insufficienter rerum principia tradentes. Et non solum in hoc, sed in multis, ut ex sequentibus rationibus apparet.

182. Deinde cum dicit *de generatione* hic ponit secundam rationem quae talis est. Quicumque habet necesse determinare de motu, oportet quod ponat causam motus: sed praedicti philosophi habebant necesse tractare de motu: quod ex duobus patet: tum quia ipsi conabantur dicere causas generationis et corruptionis rerum, quae sine motu non sunt: tum etiam quia de rebus omnibus naturaliter tractare volebant:

naturalis autem consideratio requirit motum, eo quod natura est principium motus et quietis, ut patet secundo *Physicorum*: ergo debebant tractare de causa, quae est principium motus. Et ita cum illam auferrent causam, nihil de ea dicendo, patet etiam quod in hoc deliquerunt.

183. Deinde cum dicit *amplius autem* hic ponit tertiam rationem. Quaelibet enim res naturalis habet *substantiam*, idest formam partis, *et quod quid est*, idest quidditatem quae est forma totius. Formam dicit, inquantum est principium subsistendi: et quod quid est,

First, he criticizes the opinions of those who have treated things according to the method of natural philosophy.

Second [201], he criticizes the opinions of those, Pythagoras and Plato, who have not treated things according to the method of natural philosophy because they posited higher principles than the natural philosophers did, at *but all those* (989b24).

In regard to the first part he does two things.

First, he criticizes the opinions of those who posited one material cause;

and second [190], the opinions of those who posited many, at *the same consequence* (989a19).

In regard to the first he does two things.

First, he criticizes the foregoing opinions in a general way;

second [184], in a special way, at *and they were wrong* (988b29).

He criticizes these opinions in a general way by means of three arguments.

The first (988b22) is this: in the world there are not only bodies but also certain incorporeal things, as is clear from *On the Soul*. But these men posited only bodily principles, which is clear from the fact that they maintained that *the whole is one*, that is, that the universe is one thing substantially, and that there is a single nature as matter, and that this is bodily and has *measure*, or dimension. But a body cannot be the cause of an incorporeal thing. Therefore, it is evident that they were at fault in this respect that they treated the principles of things inadequately. And they were at fault not only in this respect but in many others, as is clear from the following arguments.

182. *And in attempting* (988b26). Here he gives the second argument, which runs thus: whoever feels obliged to establish the truth about motion must posit a cause of motion. But these philosophers felt obliged to treat motion, which is clear for two reasons: first, because they tried to state the causes of generation and corruption in the world, which do not occur without motion; second, because they wanted to treat things according to the method of natural philosophy.

But since a treatment of things according to this method involves motion (because nature is a principle of motion and rest, as is clear in *Physics* 2), they should therefore have dealt with that cause which is the source of motion. And since they did away with the cause of motion by saying nothing about it, obviously they were also at fault in this respect.

183. *Furthermore, they did not* (988b28). Here he gives the third argument: every natural being has *a substance*, that is, a form of the part, and *whatness*, or quiddity, which is the form of the whole. He says "form" inasmuch as it is a principle of subsistence, and "whatness" inasmuch as it is

inquantum est principium cognoscendi, quia per eam scitur quid est res: sed praedicti philosophi formam non ponebant esse alicuius causam: ergo insufficienter de rebus tractabant, in hoc etiam delinquentes, quod causam formalem praetermittebant.

184. Deinde cum dicit *nullus enim* hic reprobat opiniones eorum in speciali: et hoc dupliciter.

Primo quantum ad hoc quod ponebant elementa praeter ignem esse principia.

Secundo quantum ad hoc quod praetermittebant terram, ibi, *si vero est, quod est generatione* et cetera.

Primo ergo resumit eorum positionem, qui videlicet ponebant esse elementum quodlibet simplicium corporum praeter terram. Et rationem opinionis ostendit, quia ipsi videbant simplicia corpora ex invicem generari, ita quod quaedam fiunt ex illis per concretionem sive per inspissationem, sicut grossiora ex subtilioribus.

185. Ostendit etiam modum procedendi contra eorum opiniones ex eorum rationibus. Ponebant enim hac ratione aliquod istorum esse principium, quia ex eo generabantur alia concretione vel discretione. Qui duo modi multum differunt quantum ad prioritatem vel posterioritatem eius ex quo aliquid generatur. Nam secundum unum modum videtur esse prius id ex quo generatur aliquid per concretionem. Et hanc rationem primo ponit. Secundum vero alium modum videtur esse prius illud, ex quo generatur aliquid per rarefactionem; et ex hoc sumit secundam rationem.

186. Quod enim illud ex quo generatur aliquid per concretionem sit primum, hoc attestatur opinioni, quae nunc habetur, quod illud sit elementum maxime omnium, ex quo alia fiunt per concretionem. Quod quidem patet per rationem, et eorum positiones. Per rationem quidem: quia id ex quo fiunt alia per concretionem est hoc quod est subtilissimum inter corpora, minutissimas partes habens. Et hoc esse videtur simplicius. Unde si simplex est prius composito, videtur quod hoc sit primum. Per eorum vero positiones: quia quicumque posuerunt ignem esse principium, posuerunt ipsum primum esse principium, quia est subtilissimum corporum. Similiter autem alii visi sunt hanc rationem sequi, existimantes tale esse elementum corporum, quod est subtiles partes habens. Quod ex hoc patet, quod nullus posteriorum prosecutus est poetas theologos, qui dixerunt terram esse elementum. Et manifestum est quod hoc renuerunt ponere, *propter magnitudinem partialitatis* idest propter grossitiem partium. Constat autem quod quodlibet aliorum trium elementorum ac-

a principle of knowing, because "what a thing is" is known by means of this. But the foregoing philosophers did not claim that form is a cause of anything. They treated things inadequately, then, and were also at fault in neglecting the formal cause.

184. *For none of the later* (989a5). Here he criticizes their opinions in a special way; and he does this with respect to two things.

First, he criticizes them for maintaining that all the elements with the exception of fire are the principles of things.

Second [187], he criticizes them for omitting earth, at *however, if* (989a15).

First (989a5), he takes up once more the position of those who claimed that each of the simple bodies except earth is the primary element of things. The reason which he gives for this position is that these men saw that the simple bodies are generated from each other in such a way that some come from others by combination or compacting, as grosser things come from more refined ones.

185. He also explains how to proceed against their opinions from their own arguments. For they claimed that one of these elements is the principle of things by arguing that other things are generated from it either by combination or by separation. Now it makes the greatest difference as to which of these two ways is prior and which subsequent, for on this depends the priority or posteriority of that from which something is generated. For, on the one hand, that seems to be prior from which something is produced by combination. And he gives this argument first. Yet, on the other hand, that seems to be prior from which something is produced by rarefaction. And he bases his second argument on this.

186. For the fact that the primary element is that from which something is produced by combination supports the opinion which is now held, that the most basic element is that from which other things are produced by combination. This in fact is evident both from reason and from the things that they held. It is evident from reason because that from which other things are produced by combination is the most refined type of body, and the one having the smallest parts: this seems to be the simpler body. Hence, if the simple is prior to the composite, this body seems to be first. It is also evident from the things that they held, because all those who posited fire as the principle of things asserted that it is the first principle. Similarly, others have been seen to follow this argument, for they thought that the primary element of bodies is the one having the finest parts. This is evident from the fact that none of the later philosophers followed the theological poets, who said that earth is the primary element of things. Evidently they refused to do this *because of the size of its parts*, that is, because of the coarseness of its parts. However, it is a fact that each

cepit aliquem philosophorum, qui iudicavit ipsum esse principium. Sed quia non dixerunt terram principium esse, ideo non potest dici quod hoc non dixerunt, quia esset contra communem opinionem. Nam multitudo hominum hoc existimabat, quod terra esset substantia omnium. Et Hesiodus etiam, qui fuit unus de theologicis poetis, dixit quod inter alia corpora primum facta est terra. Et sic patet quod opinio quod terra esset principium, fuit antiqua, quia ab ipsis poetis theologicis posita, qui fuerunt ante naturales philosophos: et publica, quia in eam consenserunt plures. Unde restat quod hac sola ratione posteriores naturales evitaverunt ponere terram esse principium, propter grossitiem partium. Sed constat quod terra habet grossiores partes quam aqua, et aqua quam aer, et aer quam ignis, et si quid est medium inter ea grossius est quam ignis. Unde patet, sequendo hanc rationem, quod nullus eorum recte dixit, nisi qui posuit ignem esse principium. Nam ex quo ratione subtilitatis aliquid ponitur principium, necessarium est illud poni primum principium quod est omnium subtilissimum.

187. Deinde cum dicit *si vero* hic ponit aliam rationem, per quam e converso videtur quod terra sit maxime elementum. Constat enim quod illud quod est in generatione posterius, est prius secundum naturam; eo quod natura in finem generationis tendit, sicut in id quod est primum in eius intentione. Sed quanto aliquid est magis densum et compositum, tanto est etiam posterius generatione: quia in via generationis ex simplicibus proceditur ad composita, sicut ex elementis fiunt mixta, et ex mixtis humores et membra: ergo illud quod est magis compositum et spissum illud est prius secundum naturam. Et sic sequitur contrarium eius quod prima ratio concludebat, scilicet quod aqua sit prior aere, et terra prior aqua quasi primum principium.

188. Est autem attendendum quod differt quaerere illud quod est prius in uno et eodem, et illud quod est prius simpliciter. Si enim quaeratur quid est prius simpliciter, oportet perfectum esse prius imperfecto, sicut et actum potentia. Nihil enim reducitur de imperfecto ad perfectum, vel de potentia in actum, nisi per aliquod perfectum ens actu. Et ideo, si loquamur de primo universi, oportet ipsum esse perfectissimum.

Sed respectu unius particularis, quod procedit de potentia in actum perfectum, potentia est prius tempore actu, licet posterius natura. Constat etiam quod primum omnium oportet esse simplicissimum, eo quod composita dependent a simplici et non e converso. Necessarium ergo erat antiquis naturalibus quod utrumque

of the other three elements finds some philosopher who judges it to be the principle of things. But their refusal to make earth a principle is not to be explained by a refusal to reject a common opinion, for many men thought that earth is the substance of things. Hesiod, who was one of the theological poets, also said that earth is the first of all bodies to come into being. Thus the opinion that earth is the principle of things is evidently an ancient one, because it was maintained by the theological poets, who preceded the philosophers of nature. It was also the common opinion, because many men accepted it. It follows, then, that the later philosophers avoided the position that earth is a principle only because of the coarseness of its parts. But it is certain that earth has coarser parts than water, and water than air, and air than fire; if there is any intermediate element, it is evident that it is grosser than fire. Hence by following this argument it is clear that none of them spoke correctly, except he who held that fire is the first principle. For as soon as some element is held to be a principle by reason of its minuteness, the most minute element must be held to be the first principle of things.

187. **However, if that which** (989a15). Here he gives another argument, and according to it the opposite seems to be true, namely, that earth is the most basic element of things. For it is evident that whatever is subsequent in generation is prior in nature, because nature tends to the goal of generation as the first thing in its intention. But the denser and more composite something is, the later it appears in the process of generation; for the process of generation proceeds from simple things to composite ones, just as mixed bodies come from the elements, and the humors and members of a living body from mixed bodies. Hence, whatever is more composite and condensed is prior in nature. In this way a conclusion is reached which is the opposite of that following from the first argument: water is now prior to air and earth to water as the first principle of things.

188. It should be noted, however, that it is a different thing to look for what is prior in one and the same entity and for what is prior without qualification. For if one seeks what is prior without qualification, the perfect must be prior to the imperfect, just as act is prior to potency. For a thing is brought from a state of imperfection to one of perfection, or from potency to act, only by something completely actual. Therefore, if we speak of what is first in the whole universe, it must be the most perfect thing.

But in the case of one particular thing which goes from potency to complete act, potency is prior to act in time, although it is subsequent in nature. It is also clear that the first of all things must be one that is simplest, for the composite depends on the simple, and not the reverse. It was necessary, then, that the ancient philosophers should

attribuerent primo principio totius universi, scilicet cum summa simplicitate maximam perfectionem.

Haec autem duo non possunt simul attribui alicui principio corporali. Nam in corporibus generabilibus et corruptibilibus sunt simplicissima imperfecta; ideo cogebantur quasi rationibus contrariis diversa principia ponere. Praeeligebant autem rationem simplicitatis, quia non considerabant res nisi secundum modum, secundum quem aliquid exit de potentia in actum; in cuius ordine non oportet id quod est principium esse perfectius. Huiusmodi autem contrarietatis dissolutio haberi non potest, nisi ponendo primum entium principium incorporeum: quia hoc erit simplicissimum, ut de eo inferius Aristoteles probabit.

189. Concludit autem in fine quod de positionibus eorum, qui dixerunt unam causam materialem, ea sufficiant quae ad praesens dicta.

190. Deinde cum dicit *idem quoque* hic ponit rationes contra ponentes plures causas materiales.

Et primo contra Empedoclem.

Secundo contra Anaxagoram, ibi, *Anaxagoram* et cetera.

Dicit ergo primo, quod idem accidit Empedocli qui posuit quatuor corpora esse materiam, quia patiebatur eamdem difficultatem ex praedicta contrarietate. Nam ex ratione simplicitatis, ignis videbatur esse maxime principium, alia vero ratione terra, ut dictum est.

Quaedam etiam inconvenientia accidunt Empedocli eadem cum praedictis. Sicut de hoc quod non posuit causam formalem, et de praedicta contrarietate simplicitatis et perfectionis in corporalibus, licet contra eum non sit ratio de ablatione causae moventis. Sed quaedam alia inconvenientia accidunt ei, propria praeter ea quae accidunt ponentibus unam causam materialem.

191. Et hoc patet tribus rationibus. Quarum prima talis est. Quia prima principia non generantur ex invicem, eo quod principia semper oportet manere, ut dictum est primo *Physicorum*. Sed ad sensum videmus quod quatuor elementa ex invicem generantur, unde et de eorum generatione in scientia naturali determinatur. Ergo inconvenienter posuit quatuor elementa prima rerum principia.

192. Deinde cum dicit *et de moventium* hic ostendit secundum inconveniens quod pertinet ad causam moventem. Ponere enim plures causas moventes et contrarias non omnino dictum est recte, nec omnino rationabiliter. Si enim causae moventes accipiantur proxime,

attribute both of these properties (the greatest perfection along with the greatest simplicity) to the first principle of the whole universe.

However, these two properties cannot be attributed simultaneously to any bodily principle, for in bodies subject to generation and corruption the simplest entities are imperfect. They were compelled, then, as by contrary arguments, to posit different principles. Yet they preferred the argument of simplicity, because they considered things only insofar as something passes from potency to act, and in this order it is not necessary that anything which is a principle should be more perfect. But this kind of opposition can be resolved only by maintaining that the first principle of things is incorporeal, because this principle will be the simplest one, as Aristotle will prove below [2548].

189. Last of all he concludes that for the purpose of the present discussion enough has been said about the positions of those who affirm one material cause.

190. *The same consequence* (989a19). Here he gives the arguments against those who posited many material causes.

First, he argues against Empedocles;

second [194], against Anaxagoras, *but if anyone* (989a30).

First (989a19), he says that the same consequence faces Empedocles, who held that the four bodies are the matter of things, because he experienced the same difficulty with regard to the above contrariety. For according to the argument of simplicity fire would seem to be the most basic principle of bodies; according to the other argument, earth would seem to be such, as has been stated [187].

And while Empedocles faced some of the same absurd conclusions as the preceding philosophers (namely, he did not posit either a formal cause or the aforesaid contrariety of simplicity and perfection in bodily things), there is no argument against him for doing away with the cause of motion. But he did face certain other absurd conclusions besides those that confronted the philosophers who posited one material cause.

191. This is shown by three arguments, of which the first is as follows. First principles are not generated from each other, because a principle must always remain in existence, as is pointed out in *Physics* 1. But we perceive that the four elements are generated from each other, and for this reason their generation is dealt with in natural philosophy. Hence his position that the four elements are the first principles of things is untenable.

192. *And concerning the cause* (989a25). Here he gives the second absurdity, which has to do with the cause of motion. For to posit many and contrary causes of motion is not at all correct or reasonable; because if the causes of motion are understood to be proximate ones, they must

oportet eas esse contrarias, cum earum effectus contrarii appareant. Si autem accipiatur prima causa, tunc oportet esse unum, sicut apparet in duodecimo huius scientiae, et in octavo *Physicorum*. Cum igitur ipse intendat ponere primas causas moventes, inconvenienter posuit eas contrarias.

193. Deinde cum dicit *et ex toto* hic ponit tertiam rationem quae ducit ad inconveniens, et est talis. In omni alteratione oportet esse idem subiectum quod patitur contraria. Et hoc ideo, quia ex uno contrario non fit alterum, ita quod unum contrarium in alterum convertatur, sicut ex calido non fit frigidum, ita quod ipse calor fiat frigus vel e converso, licet ex calido fiat frigidum suppositum uno subiecto tantum, inquantum unum subiectum quod suberat calori, postea subest frigori. Empedocles vero non posuit unum subiectum contrariis, immo contraria in diversis subiectis posuit, sicut calidum in igne, et frigidum in aqua. Nec iterum posuit istis duobus unam naturam subiectam; ergo nullo modo potuit alterationem ponere. Et hoc est inconveniens quod alteratio totaliter auferatur.

194. Deinde cum dicit *Anaxagoram vero* hic prosequitur de opinione Anaxagorae: et circa hoc duo facit.

Primo ostendit qualiter opinio Anaxagorae est suscipienda quasi vera, et quomodo quasi falsa in generali.

Secundo explicat utrumque in speciali, ibi, *nam absurdo existente* et cetera.

Dicit ergo primo quod si quis vult suscipere opinionem Anaxagorae veram de eo quod posuit duo principia, scilicet materiam et causam agentem, accipiat eam secundum rationem quam videtur ipse secutus, quasi quadam necessitate veritatis coactus, ut sequeretur eos, qui hanc rationem exprimunt. Ipse vero *non articulavit eam*, idest non expresse distinxit. Eius ergo opinio est vera quantum ad hoc quod non expressit, falsa quantum ad hoc quod expressit.

195. Et hoc in speciali patet sic. Quia si totaliter accipiatur eius opinio secundum quod in superficie apparebat ex eius dictis, apparebit maior absurditas propter quatuor rationes.

Primo, quia hoc ipsum quod est, omnia in principio mundi fuisse permixta, est absurdum, cum distinctio partium mundi aestimetur secundum sententiam Aristotelis sempiterna.

Secunda ratio est, quia impermixtum se habet ad permixtum sicut simplex ad compositum: sed simplicia praeexistunt compositis, et non e converso: ergo im-

be contraries, since their effects seem to be contraries. But if the first cause is understood, then it must be unique, as is apparent in book 12 [2492] of this work, and in *Physics* 8. Therefore, since he intends to posit the first causes of motion, his position that they are contraries is untenable.

193. *And in general* (989a26). Here he gives the third argument which leads to an absurdity: in every process of alteration it must be the same subject which undergoes contraries. This is true because one contrary does not come from another in such a way that one is converted into the other. For example, the cold does not come from the hot in such a way that heat itself becomes cold or the reverse, although the cold does come from the hot when the underlying subject is one only inasmuch as the single subject which is now the subject of heat is afterwards the subject of cold. But Empedocles did not hold that contraries have one subject. In fact, he held that they are found in different subjects, as heat in fire and cold in water. Nor again did he hold that there is one nature underlying these two. Therefore, he could not posit alteration in any way. Yet it is absurd that alteration should be done away with altogether.

194. *But if anyone* (989a30). Here he deals with Anaxagoras' opinion, and in regard to this he does two things.

First, he shows in general in what respect Anaxagoras' opinion should be accepted as true, and in what respect not.

Second, he explains each of these in particular, at *for to say* (989a33).

He says, first, that if anyone wishes to maintain that Anaxagoras' opinion is true insofar as he posited two principles—the material and the efficient cause—let him understand this according to the reasoning which Anaxagoras himself seems to have followed, as if compelled by some need for truth, inasmuch as he would have followed those who expressed this theory, which he himself *has not stated articulately*, that is, he has not expressed it distinctly. Therefore, with reference to what he has not expressly stated, his opinion is true; but with reference to what he has expressly stated his opinion is false.

195. This is made clear in particular as follows. If his opinion is taken in its entirety according to a superficial understanding of his statements, a greater absurdity will appear *for four reasons*.

First, his opinion that all things were mixed together at the beginning of the world is absurd, for in Aristotle's opinion the distinction between the parts of the world is thought to be eternal.

The second reason is that what is unmixed is related to what is mixed as the simple to the composite. But simple bodies are prior to composite ones, and not the reverse.

permixta oportet praeexistere mixtis, cuius contrarium Anaxagoras dicebat.

Tertia ratio est, quia non quodlibet natum est misceri cuilibet in corporibus; sed illa sola nata sunt adinvicem misceri, quae nata sunt adinvicem transire per aliquam alterationem, eo quod mixtio est miscibilium alteratorum unio. Anaxagoras vero ponebat quodlibet esse mixtum cuilibet.

Quarta ratio est, quia eorumdem est permixtio et separatio: non enim dicuntur misceri nisi illa quae apta nata sunt separata existere: sed passiones et accidentia sunt permixta substantiis, ut Anaxagoras dicebat: ergo sequeretur quod passiones et accidentia possent a substantiis separari, quod est manifeste falsum. Istae igitur absurditates apparent, si consideretur opinio Anaxagorae superficialiter.

196. Tamen si quis exequatur *articulariter*, idest distincte et manifeste perquirat quod Anaxagoras *vult dicere*, idest ad quod eius intellectus tendebat, licet exprimere nesciret, apparebit eius dictum mirabilius et subtilius praecedentium philosophorum dictis. Et hoc propter duo.

Primo, quia magis accessit ad veram materiae cognitionem. Quod ex hoc patet, quia in illa permixtione rerum quando nihil erat ab alio discretum, sed omnia erant permixta, de illa substantia sic permixta, quam ponebat rerum materiam, nihil vere poterat de ea praedicari, ut patet de coloribus; non enim poterat de ea praedicari aliquis specialis color, ut diceretur esse alba, vel nigra, vel secundum aliquem alium colorem colorata; quia secundum hoc oporteret illum colorem non esse aliis permixtum. Et similiter color in genere non poterat de ea praedicari, ut diceretur esse colorata; quia de quocumque praedicatur genus, necesse est aliquam eius speciem praedicari, sive sit praedicatio univoca sive denominativa. Unde si illa substantia esset colorata, de necessitate haberet aliquem determinatum colorem, quod est contra praedicta. Et similis ratio est de *humoribus* idest saporibus, et de omnibus aliis huiusmodi.

Unde nec ipsa genera prima poterant de ipso praedicari, ut scilicet esse qualis vel quanta vel aliquid huiusmodi. Si enim genera praedicarentur, oportet quod aliqua specierum particularium inesset ei; quod est impossibile, si ponantur omnia esse permixta; quia iam ista species, quae de illa substantia diceretur, esset ab aliis distincta.

Et haec est vera natura materiae, ut scilicet non habeat actu aliquam formam, sed sit in potentia ad omnes; quia et ipsum mixtum non habet actu aliquid eorum quae in eius mixtionem conveniunt, sed potentia tan-

Therefore, what is unmixed must be prior to what is mixed. This is the opposite of what Anaxagoras said.

The third reason is this: in the case of bodies not anything at all is naturally disposed to be mixed with anything else, but only those things are naturally disposed to be mixed which are naturally inclined to pass over into each other by some kind of alteration. For a mixture is a union of the altered things that are capable of being mixed. But Anaxagoras held that anything is mixed with just anything.

The fourth reason is this: there is both mixture and separation of the same things, for only those things are said to be mixed which are naturally disposed to exist apart. But properties and accidents are mixed with substances, as Anaxagoras said. Therefore, it follows that properties and accidents can exist apart from substances. This is evidently false. These absurdities appear then, if Anaxagoras' opinion is considered in a superficial way.

196. Yet if anyone were to follow him up *and articulate*, that is, investigate clearly and distinctly, the things that Anaxagoras *means*, or his intellect held, although he did not know how to express this, his statement would appear to be more astonishing and subtler than those of the preceding philosophers. This will be so for two reasons.

First, he came closer to a true understanding of matter. This is clear from the fact that in that mixture of things, when nothing was distinguished from anything else but all things were mixed together, nothing could be truly predicated of that substance which is so mixed, which he held to be the matter of things. This is clear in the case of colors, for no special color could be predicated of it so that it might be said to be white or black or have some other color, because, according to this, that color would necessarily be unmixed with other things. Similarly, neither could color in general be predicated of it so that it might be said to be colored, because everything of which a generic term is predicated must also have a specific term predicated of it, whether the predication be univocal or denominative. Hence, if that substance were colored, it would necessarily have some special color. But this is opposed to the foregoing statement. And the argument is similar with respect to *humors* (that is, flavors), and to all other things of this kind.

Hence the primary genera themselves could not be predicated of it in such a way that it would have quality or quantity or some attribute of this kind. For if these genera were predicated of it, some particular species would necessarily belong to it. But this is impossible, if all things are held to be mixed together. For this species which would be predicated of that substance would already be distinguished from the others.

And this is the true nature of matter: it does not have any form actually but is in potency to all forms. For the mixed body itself does not have actually any of the things that combine in its mixture, but has them only potentially.

tum. Et propter hanc similitudinem materiae primae ad mixtum, videtur posuisse mixtionem praedictam, licet aliqua differentia sit inter potentiam materiae et potentiam mixti.

Nam miscibilia, etsi sint in potentia in mixto, tamen non sunt in eo in potentia pure passiva. Manent enim virtute in mixto. Quod ex hoc potest patere, quia mixtum habet motum et operationes ex virtute corporum miscibilium; quod non potest dici de his, quae sunt in potentia in materia prima.

Est et alia differentia: quia mixtum etsi non sit actu aliquod miscibilium, est tamen aliquid actu: quod de materia prima dici non potest. Sed hanc differentiam videtur removere Anaxagoras ex hoc, quod non posuit particularem aliquam mixtionem, sed universalem omnium.

197. Secundo, subtilius caeteris dixit, quia magis accessit ad verum cognitionem primi principii agentis. Dixit enim omnia esse permixta praeter intellectum; et hunc dixit solum esse impermixtum et purum.

198. Ex quibus patet, quod ipse posuit duo esse principia, et ipsum intellectum posuit esse unum, secundum quod ipse est simplex et impermixtus; et alterum principium posuit materiam primam, quam ponimus sicut indeterminatam, antequam determinetur, et antequam aliquam speciem participet. Materia enim, cum sit infinitarum formarum, determinatur per formam, et per eam consequitur aliquam speciem.

199. Patet igitur quod Anaxagoras secundum illa quae exprimit, nec dixit recte, nec plene. Tamen videbatur directe dicere aliquid propinquius opinionibus posteriorum, quae sunt veriores, scilicet opinioni Platonis et Aristotelis qui recte de materia prima senserunt, quae quidem opiniones tunc erant magis apparentes.

200. Ultimo excusat se Aristoteles a perscrutatione diligentiori harum opinionum, quia sermones dictorum philosophorum sunt proprii sermonibus naturalibus, ad quos pertinet tractare de generatione et corruptione. Ipsi enim fere posuerunt principia et causas talis substantiae, scilicet materialis et corruptibilis. Dicit autem *fere*, quia de aliis substantiis non tractabant, quamvis quaedam principia ab eis posita possent ad alia etiam extendere, ut patet de intellectu maxime. Quia igitur non posuerunt principia communia omnibus substantiis, quod pertinet ad istam scientiam, sed principia solum substantiarum corruptibilium, quod pertinet ad scientiam naturalem; ideo diligens inquisitio de praedictis opinionibus magis pertinet ad scientiam naturalem quam ad istam.

And it is because of this likeness between prime matter and what is mixed that he seems to have posited the above mixture, although there is some difference between the potency of matter and that of a mixture.

For even though the elements which constitute a mixture are present in the mixture potentially, they are still not present in a state of pure passive potency, for they remain virtually in the mixture. This can be shown from the fact that a mixture has motion and operations as a result of the bodies of which the mixture is composed. But this cannot be said of the things that are present potentially in prime matter.

And there is also another difference, namely, that even though a mixture is not actually any of the mixed bodies which it contains, yet it is something actual. This cannot be said of prime matter. But Anaxagoras seems to do away with this difference, because he has not posited any particular mixture but the universal mixture of all things.

197. The second reason is this: he spoke more subtly than the others because he came closer to a true understanding of the first active principle. For he said that all things are mixed together except intellect, and that this alone is unmixed and pure.

198. From these things it is clear that he posited two principles: one of these he claimed to be the intellect itself, insofar as it is simple and unmixed with other things; the other is prime matter, which we claim is like the indeterminate before it is limited and participates in a form. For since prime matter is the subject of an infinite number of forms, it is limited by a form and acquires some species by means of it.

199. It is clear, then, that, in regard to the things that he stated expressly, Anaxagoras neither spoke correctly nor clearly. Yet he would seem to say something directly which comes closer to the opinions of the later philosophers, which are truer (namely, to those of Plato and Aristotle, whose judgments about prime matter were correct) and which were then more apparent.

200. In concluding, Aristotle excuses himself from a more diligent investigation of these opinions, because the statements of these philosophers belong to the realm of physical discussions, which treat of generation and corruption. For these men usually posited principles and causes of this kind of substance (that is, of material and corruptible substance). He says *usually* because, while they did not treat other substances, certain of the principles laid down by them can also be extended to other substances. This is most evident in the case of intellect. Therefore, since they have not posited principles common to all substances, which pertains to this science, but only principles of corruptible substances, which pertains to the philosophy of nature, a diligent study of the foregoing opinions belongs rather to the philosophy of nature than to this science.

LECTURE 13

Critique of the Pythagoreans' opinions

989b24 Quicumque vero de omnibus existentibus faciunt theoricam, existentium autem haec quidem sensibilia, illa vero insensibilia ponunt, palam autem quia de utrisque generibus perscrutationem faciunt. Propter quod magis utique immorabitur aliquis de eis quod bene aut non bene dicunt, ad praesentem nobis propositorum perscrutationem. [201]

989b29 Ergo qui Pythagorici sunt vocati, principiis et elementis extraneae a physiologis sunt usi. Causa vero, quia acceperunt ea ex non sensibilibus. Nam mathematica existentium sine motu sunt, extra ea quae sunt circa astrologiam. Disputant tamen et tractant omnia de natura. Generant enim caelum, et quod circa huius partes et passiones et operationes accidit observant. Et principia et causas in hoc dispensant, uasi aliis physiologis consentientes. Quia ens hoc est quodcumque sensibile est, et comprehendit vocatum caelum. Causas vero et principia (sicut diximus) dicunt sufficientia pertingere usque ad ea quae sunt entium superiora et magis quam de natura rationibus convenientia. [202]

990a8 Ex quo tamen modo motus inerit, finito et infinito solum suppositis pari et impari, non dicunt. Quomodo autem possibile sine motu et transmutatione, generationem et corruptionem esse, aut eorum quae geruntur opera circa caelum? [204]

990a12 Amplius autem sive quis det ex eis esse magnitudinem, sive hoc ostendatur, tamen quomodo erunt haec corporum levia, ilia vero gravitatem habentia? Ex quibus enim supponunt et dicunt, nihil magis de mathematicis corporibus dicunt quam de sensibilibus. Unde de igne et terra et aliis huiusmodi corporibus nihil dixerunt, sicut nihil de sen-

ὅσοι δὲ περὶ μὲν ἁπάντων τῶν ὄντων ποιοῦνται {25} τὴν θεωρίαν, τῶν δ᾽ ὄντων τὰ μὲν αἰσθητὰ τὰ δ᾽ οὐκ αἰσθητὰ τιθέασι, δῆλον ὡς περὶ ἀμφοτέρων τῶν γενῶν ποιοῦνται τὴν {27} ἐπίσκεψιν· διὸ μᾶλλον ἄν τις ἐνδιατρίψειε περὶ αὐτῶν, τί καλῶς ἢ μὴ καλῶς λέγουσιν εἰς τὴν τῶν νῦν ἡμῖν προκειμένων σκέψιν.

οἱ μὲν οὖν καλούμενοι Πυθαγόρειοι ταῖς μὲν {30} ἀρχαῖς καὶ τοῖς στοιχείοις ἐκτοπωτέροις χρῶνται τῶν φυσιολόγων (τὸ δ᾽ αἴτιον ὅτι παρέλαβον αὐτὰς οὐκ ἐξ αἰσθητῶν· τὰ γὰρ μαθηματικὰ τῶν ὄντων ἄνευ κινήσεώς ἐστιν ἔξω τῶν περὶ τὴν ἀστρολογίαν), διαλέγονται μέντοι καὶ πραγματεύονται περὶ φύσεως πάντα· γεννῶσί τε γὰρ τὸν οὐρανόν, {990a1} καὶ περὶ τὰ τούτου μέρη καὶ τὰ πάθη καὶ τὰ ἔργα διατηροῦσι τὸ συμβαῖνον, καὶ τὰς ἀρχὰς καὶ τὰ αἴτια εἰς ταῦτα καταναλίσκουσιν, ὡς ὁμολογοῦντες τοῖς ἄλλοις φυσιολόγοις ὅτι τό γε ὂν τοῦτ᾽ ἐστὶν ὅσον αἰσθητόν ἐστι καὶ περιείληφεν ὁ {5} καλούμενος οὐρανός. τὰς δ᾽ αἰτίας καὶ τὰς ἀρχάς, ὥσπερ εἴπομεν, ἱκανὰς λέγουσιν ἐπαναβῆναι καὶ ἐπὶ τὰ ἀνωτέρω τῶν ὄντων, καὶ μᾶλλον ἢ τοῖς περὶ φύσεως λόγοις ἁρμοττούσας.

ἐκ τίνος μέντοι τρόπου κίνησις ἔσται πέρατος καὶ ἀπείρου μόνων ὑποκειμένων καὶ περιττοῦ καὶ ἀρτίου, οὐθὲν {10} λέγουσιν, ἢ πῶς δυνατὸν ἄνευ κινήσεως καὶ μεταβολῆς γένεσιν εἶναι καὶ φθορὰν ἢ τὰ τῶν φερομένων ἔργα κατὰ τὸν οὐρανόν.

ἔτι δὲ εἴτε δοίη τις αὐτοῖς ἐκ τούτων εἶναι μέγεθος εἴτε δειχθείη τοῦτο, ὅμως τίνα τρόπον ἔσται τὰ μὲν κοῦφα τὰ δὲ βάρος ἔχοντα τῶν σωμάτων; ἐξ ὧν γὰρ ὑποτίθενται {15} καὶ λέγουσιν, οὐθὲν μᾶλλον περὶ τῶν μαθηματικῶν λέγουσι σωμάτων ἢ τῶν αἰσθητῶν· διὸ περὶ πυρὸς ἢ γῆς ἢ τῶν ἄλλων τῶν τοιούτων σωμάτων οὐδ᾽ ὁτιοῦν εἰρήκασιν, ἅτε

But all those who make a study of all existing things, and who claim that some are sensible and others not, evidently make a study of both genera. And for this reason one should dwell at greater length on the statements they have made, whether they be acceptable or not, for the purposes of the present study which we now propose to make.

Therefore, those who are called Pythagoreans used principles and elements which are foreign to the physicists. The reason is that they did not take them from sensible things. For the objects of mathematics, with the exception of those that pertain to astronomy, are devoid of motion. Nevertheless, they discuss and treat everything that has to do with the physical world, for they generate the heavens and observe what happens in regard to its parts, passions, and operations. And in doing this they use up their principles and causes, as though they agreed with the others (that is, the physicists) that whatever exists is sensible and is contained by the so-called heavens. But, as we have stated, the causes and principles are sufficient to extend even to a higher genus of beings, and are better suited to these than to their theories about the physical world.

Yet how there will be motion if only the limited and unlimited and even and odd are posited as principles, they do not say. But how can there be generation or corruption, or the activities of those bodies which traverse the heavens, if there is no motion or change?

And further, whether one grants them that continuous quantities come from these things, or whether this is demonstrated, how is it that some bodies are light and others heavy? For from what they suppose and state, they say nothing more about mathematical bodies than they do about sensible ones. Hence they have said nothing about fire, earth, and

sibilibus existimant dicentes proprium. [205]

990a18 Amplius autem quomodo oportet accipere eas quidem esse numen passiones, et numerum in caelo existentium et factorum et ab initio et nunc? Numerum vero ullum esse praeter numerum hunc, ex quo consistit mundus? [206]

Nam cum in hac parte opinio et tempus sit eis, parum vero desuper aut subtus iniustitia et discredo, aut et permixtio, demonstrationem autem dicant, quia horum unumquodque numerus est: accidit autem secundum hunc locum iam pluralitatem esse constitutarum magnitudinum, quia passiones hae sequuntur singula loca: utrum idem est hic numerus qui in coelo est, quem oportet accipere, quia unumquodque est, aut praeter hunc alius?

Plato namque ait alium esse. Existimat quidem etiam et ille numeros haec esse et horum causas: sed illos quidem intellectuales causas, hos vero sensibiles.

De Pythagoricis quidem dimittatur ad praesens, sufficit enim ipsa tangere tantum.

οὐθὲν περὶ τῶν αἰσθητῶν οἶμαι λέγοντες ἴδιον.

ἔτι δὲ πῶς δεῖ λαβεῖν αἴτια μὲν εἶναι τὰ τοῦ ἀριθμοῦ πάθη καὶ τὸν ἀριθμὸν {20} τῶν κατὰ τὸν οὐρανὸν ὄντων καὶ γιγνομένων καὶ ἐξ ἀρχῆς καὶ νῦν, ἀριθμὸν δ' ἄλλον μηθένα εἶναι παρὰ τὸν ἀριθμὸν τοῦτον ἐξ οὗ συνέστηκεν ὁ κόσμος;

ὅταν γὰρ ἐν τῳδὶ μὲν τῷ μέρει δόξα καὶ καιρὸς αὐτοῖς ᾖ, μικρὸν δὲ ἄνωθεν ἢ κάτωθεν ἀδικία καὶ κρίσις ἢ μῖξις, ἀπόδειξιν δὲ λέγωσιν ὅτι {25} τούτων μὲν ἕκαστον ἀριθμός ἐστι, συμβαίνει δὲ κατὰ τὸν τόπον τοῦτον ἤδη πλῆθος εἶναι τῶν συνισταμένων μεγεθῶν διὰ τὸ τὰ πάθη ταῦτα ἀκολουθεῖν τοῖς τόποις ἑκάστοις, πότερον οὗτος ὁ αὐτός ἐστιν ἀριθμός, ὁ ἐν τῷ οὐρανῷ, ὃν δεῖ λαβεῖν ὅτι τούτων ἕκαστόν ἐστιν, ἢ παρὰ τοῦτον ἄλλος;

ὁ μὲν γὰρ {30} Πλάτων ἕτερον εἶναί φησιν· καίτοι κἀκεῖνος ἀριθμοὺς οἴεται καὶ ταῦτα εἶναι καὶ τὰς τούτων αἰτίας, ἀλλὰ τοὺς μὲν νοητοὺς αἰτίους τούτους δὲ αἰσθητούς.

περὶ μὲν οὖν τῶν Πυθαγορείων ἀφείσθω τὰ νῦν (ἱκανὸν γὰρ αὐτῶν ἅψασθαι τοσοῦτον):

other bodies of this kind, since they have nothing to say that is proper to sensible things.

Further, how are we to understand that the attributes of number and number itself are the causes of what exists and comes to pass in the heavens, both from the beginning and now? And how are we to understand that there is no other number except that of which the world is composed?

For when they place opportunity and opinion in one part of the heavens, and a little above or below them injustice and separation or mixture, and when they state as proof of this that each of these is a number, and claim that there already happens to be in this place a plurality of quantities constituted of numbers, because these attributes of number correspond to each of these places, we may ask whether this number which is in the heavens is the same as that which we understand each sensible thing to be, or whether there is another kind of number in addition to this?

For Plato says there is another. In fact, he also thinks that both these things and their causes are numbers, but that some are intellectual causes and others sensible ones.

Regarding the Pythagoreans, then, let us dismiss them for the present, for it is enough to have touched upon them to the extent that we have.

---

201. Hic disputat contra opiniones Pythagorae et Platonis, qui altera principia posuerunt quam naturalia. Et circa hoc duo facit.

Primo ostendit quod consideratio harum opinionum magis pertinet ad scientiam praesentem, quam praedictarum.

Secundo incipit contra eas disputare, ibi, *ergo qui Pythagorici sunt vocati.*

Dicit ergo primo, quod illi qui *faciunt theoricam*, idest considerationem de omnibus entibus, et ponunt, quod entium quaedam sunt sensibilia, quaedam insensibilia, perscrutantur de utroque genere entium. Unde investigare de opinionibus eorum, qui bene et qui non bene dixerunt, magis pertinet ad perscrutationem quam proponimus tradere in hac scientia. Nam haec scientia est de omnibus entibus, non de aliquo particulari genere

201. Here he argues dialectically against the opinions of Pythagoras and Plato, who posited different principles from those which pertain to the philosophy of nature. In regard to this he does two things.

First, he shows that a study of these opinions rather than those mentioned above belongs to the present science.

Second [202], he begins to argue dialectically against these opinions, at *therefore, those who* (989b29).

He first says (989b24), then, that those who *make a study* (or an investigation) of all existing things, and hold that some are sensible and others non-sensible, make a study of both genera of beings. Hence an investigation of the opinions of those who spoke either correctly or incorrectly belongs rather to the study which we now propose to make in this science. For this science deals with all beings and not with some particular genus of being. Hence,

entis. Et sic illa quae pertinent ad omnia entis genera, magis sunt hic consideranda quam illa quae pertinent ad aliquod particulare genus entis et cetera.

202. Deinde cum dicit *ergo qui* hic disputat contra opiniones praedictorum philosophorum.

Et primo contra Pythagoram.

Secundo contra Platonem, ibi, *qui vero ideas.*

Circa primum duo facit.

Primo ostendit in quo Pythagoras conveniebat cum naturalibus, et in quo ab eis differebat.

Secundo disputat contra eius opinionem, ibi, *ex quo tamen modo motus* et cetera.

Sciendum est ergo, quod Pythagorici in uno conveniebant cum naturalibus, in alio ab eis differebant.

Differebant quidem in positione principiorum; usi sunt enim principiis rerum extraneo modo a naturalibus. Cuius causa est, quia principia rerum non acceperunt ex sensibilibus sicut naturales, sed ex mathematicis, quae sunt sine motu, unde non sunt naturalia.

Quod autem mathematica dicuntur esse sine motu, referendum est ad illas scientias, quae sunt pure mathematicae, sicut arithmetica et geometria. Astrologia enim considerat motum, quia astrologia est media scientia inter mathematicam et naturalem. Principia enim sua astrologia et aliae mediae applicant ad res naturales, ut patet secundo *Physicorum.*

203. Conveniebat autem Pythagoras cum naturalibus quantum ad ea quorum principia quaerebat. Disputabat enim et tractabat de omnibus naturalibus. Tractabat enim de generatione caeli, et observabat omnia quae accidunt circa partes caeli, quae dicuntur diversae sphaerae, vel etiam diversae stellae: et quae accidunt circa passiones vel circa eclipses luminarium, et quae accidunt circa operationes et circa motus corporum caelestium, et circa eorum effectus in rebus inferioribus; et singulis huiusmodi dispensabat causas, adaptando scilicet unicuique propriam causam. Et videbatur etiam in hoc consentire aliis naturalibus, quod solum sit illud ens, quod est sensibile, quod comprehenditur a caelo quod videmus. Non enim ponebat aliquod corpus sensibile infinitum, sicut alii naturales posuerunt. Nec iterum ponebat plures mundos, sicut posuit Democritus.

Ideo autem videbatur aestimare quod nulla entia essent nisi sensibilia, quia non assignabat principia et causas nisi talibus substantiis. Nihilominus tamen causae et principia, quae assignabat, non erant propria et determinata sensibilibus, sed erant sufficientia ascendere

the things that pertain to every genus of being are to be considered here rather than those which pertain to some particular genus of being.

202. *Therefore, those who* (989b29). Here he argues against the opinions of the foregoing philosophers.

First (989b29), he argues against Pythagoras;

second [208], against Plato, at *but those who posited ideas* (990a34).

In regard to the first he does two things.

First, he shows in what way Pythagoras agreed with the philosophers of nature, and in what way he differed from them.

Second [204], he argues against Pythagoras' position, at *yet how* (990a8).

We must understand (989b29), then, that in one respect the Pythagoreans agreed with the philosophers of nature, and in another respect they differed from them.

They differed from them in their position regarding principles, because they employed principles of things in a way foreign to the philosophers of nature. The reason is that they did not take the principles of things from sensible beings, as the natural philosophers did, but from the objects of mathematics, which are devoid of motion, and are therefore not physical.

And the statement that the objects of mathematics are devoid of motion must be referred to those sciences which are purely mathematical, such as arithmetic and geometry. Astronomy considers motion because astronomy is a science midway between mathematics and natural philosophy. For astronomy and other intermediate sciences apply their principles to natural things, as is clear in *Physics* 2.

203. Now Pythagoras agreed with the philosophers of nature concerning the things whose principles he sought, for he discussed and treated all natural beings. He dealt with the generation of the heavens and observed everything that happens to the parts of the heavens (by which are meant the different spheres, or also the different stars). He also considered what happens to its passions, or to the eclipses of the luminous bodies; and what happens to the operations and motions of the heavenly bodies, and their effects on lower bodies. And he used up causes on particular things of this kind by applying to each one its proper cause. He also seemed to agree with the other philosophers of nature in thinking that that alone has being which is sensible and is contained by the heavens which we see. For he did not posit an infinite sensible body, as the other philosophers of nature did. Nor again did he hold that there are many worlds, as Democritus did.

He therefore seemed to think that there are no beings except sensible ones, because he assigned principles and causes only to such substances. However, the causes and principles which he laid down are not proper or limited to sensible things, but are sufficient for ascending to higher

ad superiora entia, idest ad entia intellectualia. Et erant adhuc magis convenientia quam rationes naturalium, quae non poterant extendi ultra sensibilia, quia ponebant principia corporea. Pythagoras vero, quia ponebat principia incorporea, scilicet numeros, quamvis non poneret principia nisi corporum sensibilium, ponebat tamen entium intelligibilium, quae non sunt corpora, principia pene, sicut et Plato posterius fecit.

204. Deinde cum dicit *ex quo tamen* hic ponit tres rationes contra opinionem Pythagorae:

quarum prima talis est. Pythagoras non poterat assignare, quomodo motus adveniat rebus, quia non ponebat principia nisi finitum et infinitum, par et impar, quae ponebat principia sicut substantia, sive materialia principia. Sed oportebat eum concedere motum rebus inesse. Quomodo enim esset possibile sine motu et transmutatione esse generationem et corruptionem in corporibus, et operationes eorum, quae geruntur circa caelum, quae per motus quosdam fiunt? Patet quod nullo modo. Unde cum Pythagoras consideravit de generatione et corruptione, et eis quae geruntur circa caelum, patet quod insufficienter posuit non assignans aliqua principia motus.

205. Deinde cum dicit *amplius autem* hic ponit secundam rationem. Pythagoras enim ponebat ex numeris componi magnitudines. Sed sive hoc probet, sive concedatur, non poterat ex numeris assignare causam, quare quaedam sunt gravia, quaedam levia. Quod ex hoc patet, quia rationes numerorum non magis adaptantur corporibus sensibilibus quam mathematicis quae sunt non gravia et levia. Unde patet, quod ipsi nihil dixerunt plus de corporibus sensibilibus, quam de mathematicis.

Et sic patet, quod cum corpora sensibilia, ut ignis et terra et huiusmodi, inquantum talia, addant aliquid supra mathematica, nihil proprium de istis sensibilibus dixerunt secundum veram aestimationem. Et sic iterum patet, quod insufficienter posuerunt, praetermittentes assignare causas eorum, quae sunt propria sensibilibus.

206. Deinde cum dicit *amplius autem* hic ostendit tertiam rationem, quae procedit ex hoc, quod Pythagoras videbatur ponere duo contraria.

Ponebat enim ex una parte, quod numerus et numeri passiones sunt causa eorum quae sunt in caelo, et omnium generabilium et corruptibilium a principio mundi:

ex alia vero ponebat, quod non erat aliquis alius numerus praeter istum numerum ex quo constituitur mundi substantia, numerum enim substantiam rerum

beings, that is, intellectual ones. And they were better fitted to these than the theories of the natural philosophers which could not be extended beyond sensible things, because these philosophers claimed that principles are bodily. But since Pythagoras posited incorporeal principles (namely, numbers), although he posited only principles of sensible bodies, he came very close to positing principles of intelligible beings, which are not bodies, as Plato did later.

204. *Yet how* (990a8). Here he gives three arguments against the opinion of Pythagoras.

The first is this. Pythagoras could not explain how motion originates in the world, because he posited as principles only the limited and unlimited and the even and odd, which he held to be principles as substance, or material principles. But he had to admit that there is motion in the world. For how could there be generation and corruption in bodies, and how could there be any activities of the heavenly bodies, which occur as a result of certain kinds of motion, unless motion and change existed? Evidently they could not exist in any way. Hence, since Pythagoras considered generation and corruption and the operations of the heavenly bodies without assigning any principle of motion, his position is clearly unsatisfactory.

205. *And further* (990a12). Here he gives the second argument. For Pythagoras claimed that continuous quantities are composed of numbers. But whether he proves this or takes it for granted, he could not give any reason on the part of numbers as to why some things are heavy and others light. This is clear from the fact that his arguments about numbers are no more adapted to sensible bodies than they are to the objects of mathematics, which are neither heavy nor light. Hence they obviously said nothing more about sensible bodies than they did about the objects of mathematics.

Therefore, since sensible bodies (such as earth and fire and the like) considered in themselves add something over and above the objects of mathematics, it is evident that they said nothing proper in any true sense about these sensible bodies. Thus it is also evident that the principles which they laid down are not sufficient, since they neglected to give the causes of those attributes which are proper to sensible bodies.

206. *Further, how are we* (990a18). Here he gives the third argument, which is based on the fact that Pythagoras seemed to hold two contrary positions.

For, on the one hand, he held that number and the attributes of number are the cause both of those events which occur in the heavens and of all generable and corruptible things from the beginning of the world.

Yet, on the other hand, he held that there is no other number besides that of which the substance of things is composed; for he held that number is the substance of

posuit. Hoc autem quomodo est accipere, cum idem non sit causa sui ipsius?

Nam Pythagoras ex hoc dicit demonstrari, quod unumquodque horum sensibilium est numerus secundum substantiam suam, quia in hac parte universi sunt entia contingentia, de quibus est opinio, et quae subsunt tempori inquantum aliquando sunt et aliquando non sunt. Si autem generabilia et corruptibilia essent partim supra aut subtus, in ordine universi esset inordinatio, vel per modum iniustitiae, dum, scilicet, aliqua res sortiretur nobiliorem locum vel minus nobilem quam sibi debeatur: aut per modum discretionis, inquantum corpus si poneretur extra locum suum, divideretur a corporibus similis naturae: vel per modum mixtionis et confusionis, dum corpus extra suum locum positum oportet permisceri alteri corpori, sicut si aliqua pars aquae esset in aliquo loco aeris, vel in loco terrae.

Et videtur in hoc tangere duplicem convenientiam corporis naturalis ad suum locum. Unam ex ordine situs, secundum quod nobiliora corpora sortiuntur altiorem locum, in quo videtur quaedam iustitia. Aliam autem ex similitudine vel dissimilitudine corporum locatorum adinvicem, cui contrariatur discretio et permixtio.

Quia igitur res secundum quod determinatum situm habent, in universo convenienter se habent, quia situs in modico mutaretur sequeretur inconveniens, ut dictum et manifestum est, quod omnes partes universi sunt ordinatae secundum determinatam proportionem; omnis enim determinata proportio est secundum numeros. Unde ostendebat Pythagoras, quod omnia entia essent numerus.

Sed ex alia parte videmus quod magnitudines constitutae in diversis locis sunt plures et diversae, quia singula loca universi consequuntur propriae passiones, quibus corpora diversificantur. Nam aliae sunt passiones corporis existentis sursum et deorsum.

Cum igitur Pythagoras ratione praedicta dicat omnia sensibilia numerum, et videamus accidere diversitatem in sensibilibus secundum diversa loca, utrum sit idem et unus numerus tantum, qui est, *in caelo*, idest in toto corpore sensibili quod in caelo includatur, de quo oportet accipere quod est substantia uniuscuiusque sensibilis? Aut praeter hunc numerum qui est substantia rerum sensibilium, est alius numerus qui est eorum causa?

Plato autem dixit alium numerum, qui est substantia sensibilium, et qui est causa. Et quia ipse Plato existimavit sicut Pythagoras, numeros esse ipsa corpora

things. But how is this to be understood, since one and the same thing is not the cause of itself?

For Pythagoras says that the former position may be demonstrated from the fact that each one of these sensible things is numerical in substance, because in this part of the universe there are contingent beings, about which there is opinion and which are subject to time inasmuch as they sometimes are and sometimes are not. But if generable and corruptible things were partly above or partly below, there would be disorder in the order of the universe, either after the manner of injustice (insofar as some being would receive a nobler or less noble place than it ought to have); or after the manner of separation (in the sense that, if a body were located outside its own place, it would be separated from bodies of a like nature); or after the manner of mixture and mingling, provided that a body located outside its proper place must be mixed with some other body (for example, if some part of water occupied a place belonging to air or to earth).

In this discussion he seems to touch on two ways in which a natural body conforms to its proper place. One pertains to the order of position, according to which nobler bodies receive a higher place, in which there seems to be a kind of justice. The other pertains to the similarity or dissimilarity between bodies in place, to which separation and mingling may be opposed.

Therefore, insofar as things have a definite position, they are fittingly situated in the universe. For if their position were fitting it would result that all parts of the universe are arranged in a definite proportion, as it has been stated and shown; for every definite proportion is numerical. And it was from this that Pythagoras showed that all things would be numbers.

But, on the other hand, we see that the continuous quantities established in different places are many and different, because the particular places in the universe correspond to the proper attributes by which bodies are differentiated. For the attributes of bodies which are above differ from those which are below.

Hence, since Pythagoras affirms that all sensible things are numbers by means of the above argument, and we see that the difference in sensible bodies is attributable to difference in place, the question arises whether the number which exists *in the heavens* (that is, in the whole visible body which comprises the heavens) is merely the same as that which must be understood to be the substance of each sensible thing, or whether besides this number which constitutes the substance of sensible things there is another number which is their cause.

Now Plato said that there is one kind of number which is the substance of sensible things, and another which is their cause. And while both Plato himself and Pythagoras

sensibilia et causas eorum, sed numeros intellectuales aestimavit causas insensibilium, numeros vero sensibiles causas esse et formas sensibilium. Quid quia Pythagoras non fecit, insufficienter posuit.

207. Concludit autem in fine quod ista sufficiant de Pythagoricis opinionibus, nam eas tetigisse sufficit.

thought that numbers are both sensible bodies themselves and their causes, Plato alone considered intellectual numbers to be the causes of things that are not sensible, and sensible numbers to be the causes and forms of sensible things. And since Pythagoras did not do this, his position is unsatisfactory.

207. In concluding, Aristotle says that these remarks about the Pythagoreans' opinions will suffice; for it is enough to have touched upon them to this extent.

LECTURE 14

Critique of the Platonic Ideas

990a34 Qui vero ideas posuerunt, primum quidem horum existentium accipere causas quaerentes, alia his aequalia numero attulerunt: ut si quis numerare volens paucioribus quidem existentibus putet non posse, plures vero facientes numeret. [208]	οἱ δὲ τὰς ἰδέας αἰτίας τιθέμενοι πρῶτον μὲν ζητοῦντες τωνδὶ τῶν ὄντων λαβεῖν τὰς αἰτίας ἕτερα τούτοις ἴσα τὸν ἀριθμὸν ἐκόμισαν, ὥσπερ εἴ τις ἀριθμῆσαι βουλόμενος ἐλαττόνων μὲν ὄντων οἴοιτο μὴ δυνήσεσθαι, πλείω δὲ ποιήσας ἀριθμοίη	But those who posited ideas, and were the first to seek an understanding of the causes of sensible things, introduced other principles equal in number to these—as though one who wishes to count things thinks that this cannot be done when they are few, but believes that he can count them after he has increased their number.
Nam fere aequales aut non pauciores his sunt species, de quibus quaerentes causas ab his ad illas pervenerunt.	(σχεδὸν γὰρ ἴσα—ἢ οὐκ {5} ἐλάττω—ἐστὶ τὰ εἴδη τούτοις περὶ ὧν ζητοῦντες τὰς αἰτίας ἐκ τούτων ἐπ᾽ ἐκεῖνα προῆλθον:	For the separate forms are almost equal to, or not fewer than, these sensible things in the search for whose causes these thinkers have proceeded from sensible things to the forms.
Secundum unumquodque enim aequivocum homogeneum aliquid est, et circa substantias aliorum est in multis unum et in his et in sempiternis.	καθ᾽ ἕκαστον γὰρ ὁμώνυμόν τι ἔστι καὶ παρὰ τὰς οὐσίας, τῶν τε ἄλλων ἔστιν ἓν ἐπὶ πολλῶν, καὶ ἐπὶ τοῖσδε καὶ ἐπὶ τοῖς ἀϊδίοις):	For to each thing there corresponds some homogeneous entity bearing the same name, and with regard to the substances of other things there is a one-in-many, both in the case of these sensible things and in those which are eternal.
990b8 Amplius autem secundum quos modos ostendimus quia sunt species, secundum nullum videntur horum. Ex quibusdam enim non est necesse fieri syllogismum; ex quibusdam vero ita; et non quorum putamus, horum fiunt species. [210]	ἔτι δὲ καθ᾽ οὓς τρόπους δείκνυμεν ὅτι ἔστι τὰ εἴδη, κατ᾽ οὐθένα φαίνεται τούτων: {10} ἐξ ἐνίων μὲν γὰρ οὐκ ἀνάγκη γίγνεσθαι συλλογισμόν, ἐξ ἐνίων δὲ καὶ οὐχ ὧν οἰόμεθα τούτων εἴδη γίγνεται.	Furthermore, the forms do not become evident from any of the ways in which we prove that they exist. From some, no syllogism necessarily follows, but from others there does. According to these, there are forms of things of which we do not think there are forms.
990b11 Quia secundum rationes eas, quae fiunt ex scientiis, omnium erunt species quorumcumque sunt scientiae, et secundum unum in multis et in negationibus. [211]	κατά τε γὰρ τοὺς λόγους τοὺς ἐκ τῶν ἐπιστημῶν εἴδη ἔσται πάντων ὅσων ἐπιστῆμαί εἰσι, καὶ κατὰ τὸ ἓν ἐπὶ πολλῶν καὶ τῶν ἀποφάσεων,	According to those arguments from the sciences, there will be forms of all things of which there are sciences; according to the argument of the one-in-many there will also be forms of negations.
990b13 Et secundum quod intelligitur aliquid corrumpi corruptibilium: phantasma enim aliquid horum est. [212]	κατὰ δὲ τὸ νοεῖν τι φθαρέντος τῶν φθαρτῶν: φάντασμα {15} γάρ τι τούτων ἔστιν.	Again, according to the argument that there is some understanding of corruption, there will be forms of corruptible things; for of these there is some sensible image.
990b15 Amplius autem rationum certissimae, aliae, quidem eorum quae ad aliquid ideas faciunt, quorum non dicunt esse secundum se genus, aliae vero tertium hominem dicunt. [213]	ἔτι δὲ οἱ ἀκριβέστεροι τῶν λόγων οἱ μὲν τῶν πρός τι ποιοῦσιν ἰδέας, ὧν οὔ φαμεν εἶναι καθ᾽ αὑτὸ γένος, οἱ δὲ τὸν τρίτον ἄνθρωπον λέγουσιν.	Again, according to the most certain arguments, some establish forms of relations, of which they deny there is any essential genus; but others lead to the third man.
990b17 Et omnino quae sunt de speciebus rationes, auferunt ea quae magis esse volunt dicentes species esse, quam ipsas ideas esse. Accidit autem ei dualitatem	ὅλως τε ἀναιροῦσιν οἱ περὶ τῶν εἰδῶν λόγοι ἃ μᾶλλον εἶναι βουλόμεθα [οἱ λέγοντες εἴδη] τοῦ τὰς ἰδέας εἶναι: συμβαίνει γὰρ μὴ {20} εἶναι τὴν δυάδα πρώτην	And in general the arguments for the forms do away with the existence of the things that those who speak of the forms are more anxious to retain than the forms

non esse primam, sed numerum: et ad aliquid, ipso quod secundum se. [217]

Et omnia quaecumque aliquid de speciebus opiniones sequentes opposuerunt principiis.

990b22 Amplius autem ad existimationem quidem secundum quam dicimus ideas non solum esse substantiarum species, sed et multorum aliorum. Etenim intelligentia una non solum circa substantias, sed et de aliis est. Et scientiae non solum sunt ipsius substantiae, sed aliorum. Accidunt autem et mille talia alia. [219]

990b27 Secundum vero necessitatem et opiniones de ideis, si sunt participabiles species, substantiarum necesse ideas esse solum. [220]

Non enim secundum accidens participantur; sed oportet hanc in unoquoque participare, inquantum non de subiecto dicuntur.

Dico autem ut si quid per se duplo participat, hoc et sempiterno participat, sed secundum accidens; accidit enim duplo sempiternum esse. Quare substantia erit species.

990b34 Haec vero substantiam esse hic significat et illic. Quare necesse est apparere quid praeter eas unum in multis. Et si quidem eadem species idearum, et participantium aliquid erit commune. [221]

Quid enim magis incorruptibilibus dualitatibus, et dualitatibus multis quidem, sed sempiternis dualitas unum et idem, quam in hac et aliqua? Si vero non eadem species, aequivocatio est et simpliciter, ut siquis vocat hominem Calliam et lignum, nullam illarum communitatem inspiciens.

ἀλλὰ τὸν ἀριθμόν, καὶ τὸ πρός τι τοῦ καθ᾽ αὑτό,

καὶ πάνθ᾽ ὅσα τινὲς ἀκολουθήσαντες ταῖς περὶ τῶν ἰδεῶν δόξαις ἠναντιώθησαν ταῖς ἀρχαῖς.

ἔτι κατὰ μὲν τὴν ὑπόληψιν καθ᾽ ἣν εἶναί φαμεν τὰς ἰδέας οὐ μόνον τῶν οὐσιῶν ἔσται εἴδη ἀλλὰ πολλῶν καὶ ἑτέρων (καὶ γὰρ τὸ {25} νόημα ἓν οὐ μόνον περὶ τὰς οὐσίας ἀλλὰ καὶ κατὰ τῶν ἄλλων ἐστί, καὶ ἐπιστῆμαι οὐ μόνον τῆς οὐσίας εἰσὶν ἀλλὰ καὶ ἑτέρων, καὶ ἄλλα δὲ μυρία συμβαίνει τοιαῦτα):

κατὰ δὲ τὸ ἀναγκαῖον καὶ τὰς δόξας τὰς περὶ αὐτῶν, εἰ ἔστι μεθεκτὰ τὰ εἴδη, τῶν οὐσιῶν ἀναγκαῖον ἰδέας εἶναι μόνον.

οὐ {30} γὰρ κατὰ συμβεβηκὸς μετέχονται ἀλλὰ δεῖ ταύτῃ ἑκάστου μετέχειν ᾗ μὴ καθ᾽ ὑποκειμένου λέγεται

(λέγω δ᾽ οἷον, εἴ τι αὐτοδιπλασίου μετέχει, τοῦτο καὶ ἀϊδίου μετέχει, ἀλλὰ κατὰ συμβεβηκός:

συμβέβηκε γὰρ τῷ διπλασίῳ ἀϊδίῳ εἶναι), ὥστ᾽ ἔσται οὐσία τὰ εἴδη: ταὐτὰ δὲ ἐνταῦθα οὐσίαν σημαίνει κἀκεῖ {991a1} ἢ τί ἔσται τὸ εἶναί τι παρὰ ταῦτα, τὸ ἓν ἐπὶ πολλῶν; καὶ εἰ μὲν ταὐτὸ εἶδος τῶν ἰδεῶν καὶ τῶν μετεχόντων, ἔσται τι κοινόν

(τί γὰρ μᾶλλον ἐπὶ τῶν φθαρτῶν δυάδων, καὶ τῶν πολλῶν μὲν ἀϊδίων δέ, τὸ {5} δυὰς ἓν καὶ ταὐτόν, ἢ ἐπί τ᾽ αὐτῆς καὶ τῆς τινός;): εἰ δὲ μὴ τὸ αὐτὸ εἶδος, ὁμώνυμα ἂν εἴη, καὶ ὅμοιον ὥσπερ ἂν εἴ τις καλοῖ ἄνθρωπον τόν τε Καλλίαν καὶ τὸ ξύλον, μηδεμίαν κοινωνίαν ἐπιβλέψας αὐτῶν.

---

themselves. For it happens that the dyad is not first, but that number is, and that the relative is prior to that which exists of itself.

And all the other conclusions which some reach by following up the opinions about the ideas are opposed to the principles of the theory.

Again, according to the opinion whereby we claim that there are ideas, there will be forms not only of substances but also of many other things. For there is one concept not only of substances, but also of other things; and there are sciences not only of substance itself but also of other things. And a thousand other such difficulties face them.

But according to logical necessity and the opinions about the ideas, if the forms are participated in, there must be ideas only of substances.

For they are not participated in according to what is accidental. But things must participate in each form in this respect: insofar as each form is not predicated of a subject.

I mean that if anything participates in doubleness itself, it also participates in the eternal, but only accidentally; for it is an accident of doubleness to be eternal. Hence the forms will be substances.

But these things signify substance both here and in the ideal world; otherwise, why is it necessary that a one-in-many appear in addition to these sensible things? Indeed, if the form of the ideas and that of the things that participate in them are the same, there will be something in common.

For why should duality be one and the same in the case of corruptible twos and in those which are many but eternal, rather than in the case of this idea of duality and a particular two? But if the form is not the same, there will be pure equivocation; just as if one were to call both Callias and a piece of wood man, without observing any common attribute which they might have.

---

208. Hic disputat contra opinionem Platonis: et dividitur in duas partes.

208. Here he argues disputatively against Plato's opinion. This is divided into two parts.

Primo disputat contra eius opinionem, quantum ad hoc quod ponebat de rerum substantiis.

Secundo quantum ad hoc quod de rerum principiis, ibi, *omnino autem sapientia.*

Prima dividitur in duas partes.

Primo enim disputat contra hoc quod ponebat substantias species.

Secundo quantum ad hoc quod ponebat de mathematicis, ibi, *amplius si sunt numeri.*

Circa primum duo facit.

Primo enim disputat contra ipsam positionem Platonis.

Secundo contra rationem ipsius, ibi, *amplius autem secundum quos* et cetera.

Dicit ergo primo, quod Platonici ponentes ideas esse quasdam substantias separatas, in hoc videntur deliquisse, quia cum ipsi quaerentes causas horum sensibilium entium, praetermissis sensibilibus, adinvenerunt quaedam alia nova entia aequalia numeris sensibilibus.

Et hoc videtur inconveniens: quia qui quaerit causas aliquarum rerum, debet ipsas certificare, non alias res addere, ex quarum positione accrescat necessitas inquisitionis: hoc enim simile est ac si aliquis vellet numerare res aliquas, quas non putet se posse numerare sicut pauciores, sed vult eas numerare multiplicando eas per additionem aliquarum rerum.

Constat enim quod talis stulte movetur, quia in paucioribus est via magis plana, quia melius et facilius certificantur pauca quam multa. Et numerus tanto est certior quanto est minor, sicut propinquior unitati, quae est mensura certissima. Sicut autem numeratio est quaedam rerum certificatio quantum ad numerum, ita inquisitio de causis rerum est quaedam certa mensura ad certificationem naturae rerum. Unde sicut numeratae pauciores res facilius certificantur quantum ad earum numerum, ita pauciores res facilius certificantur quantum ad earum naturam.

Unde cum Plato ad notificandum res sensibiles tantum, multiplicaverit rerum genera, adiunxit difficultates, accipiens quod est difficilius ad manifestationem facilioris, quod est inconveniens.

209. Et quod ideae sint aequales numero, aut non pauciores sensibilibus, de quibus Platonici inquirunt causas (quibus Aristoteles se connumerat, quia Platonis discipulus fuit) et determinaverunt procedentes de his sensibilibus ad praedictas species, manifestum est si consideretur, qua ratione Platonici ideas induxerunt:

First [208], he argues against Plato's opinion with reference to his position about the substances of things;

second [217], with reference to his position about the principles of things, at *and in general* (990b17).

The first is divided into two parts.

First, he argues against Plato's position that the forms are substances;

second (991b9; [239]), against the things that he posited about the objects of mathematics, at *further, if the forms.*

In regard to the first he does two things.

First, he argues against this position of Plato;

second [210], against the reasoning behind it, *furthermore, the forms* (990b8).

He first says (990a34) that the Platonists, in holding that the ideas are certain separate substances, seemed to be at fault in that when they sought for the causes of these sensible beings, they neglected sensible beings and invented certain other new entities equal in number to sensible beings.

This seems to be absurd, because one who seeks the causes of certain things ought to make these evident and not add other things, the premising of which only adds to the number of points which have to be investigated. For it would be similar if a man who wished to count certain things, which he did not think he was able to count because they are few, believed that he could count them by increasing their number through the addition of certain other things.

But it is evident that such a man acts foolishly, because the path is clearer when there are fewer things; it is better and easier to make certain of fewer things than of many. And the smaller a number is, the more certain it is to us, inasmuch as it is nearer to the unit, which is the most accurate measure. And just as the process of counting things is the measure we use to make certain of their number, in a similar fashion an investigation of the causes of things is the accurate measure for making certain of their natures. Therefore, just as the number of fewer numerable things is made certain of more easily, in a similar way the nature of fewer things is made certain of more easily.

Hence, when Plato increased the genera of beings to the extent that he did with a view to explaining sensible things, he added to the number of difficulties by taking what is more difficult in order to explain what is less difficult. This is absurd.

209. That the ideas are equal in number to, or not fewer than, sensible things, whose causes the Platonists seek (and Aristotle includes himself among their number because he was Plato's disciple), and which they established by going from sensible things to the aforesaid forms, becomes evident if one considers by what reasoning the Platonists

hac, scilicet, quia videbant in omnibus univocis unum esse in multis.

Unde id unum ponebant esse speciem separatam. Videmus tamen, quod circa omnes substantias rerum aliarum ab ideis invenitur unum in multis per modum univocae praedicationis, inquantum inveniuntur multa unius speciei. Et hoc non solum in sensibilibus corruptibilibus, sed etiam in mathematicis, quae sunt sempiterna: quia et in eis multa sunt unius speciei, ut supra dictum est.

Unde relinquitur quod omnibus speciebus rerum sensibilium respondeat aliqua idea. Quaelibet igitur earum est quoddam aequivocum cum istis sensibilibus, quia communicat in nomine cum eis. Sicut enim Socrates dicitur homo, ita et illa. Tamen differunt ratione. Ratio enim Socratis est cum materia. Ratio vero hominis idealis est sine materia. Vel secundum aliam literam, unaquaeque species dicitur esse aliquid univocum, inquantum scilicet est unum in multis, et convenit cum illis de quibus praedicatur, quantum ad rationem speciei.

Ideo autem dicit aequales, aut non pauciores, quia ideae vel ponuntur solum specierum, et sic erunt aequales numero istis sensibilibus, si numerentur hic sensibilia secundum diversas species, et non secundum diversa individua quae sunt infinita. Vel ponuntur ideae non solum specierum, sed etiam generum; et sic sunt plures ideae quam species sensibilium, quia ideae tunc erunt species omnes, et praeter haec omnia et singula genera.

Et propter hoc dicit aut non pauciores quidem, sed plures. Vel aliter, ut dicantur esse aequales, inquantum ponebat eas esse sensibilium; non pauciores autem sed plures, inquantum ponebat eas non solum species sensibilium, sed etiam mathematicorum.

210. Deinde cum dicit *amplius autem* hic disputat contra Platonem quantum ad rationem suae positionis. Et circa hoc duo facit.

Primo tangit modos in generali, quibus rationes Platonis deficiebant.

Secundo exponit illos in speciali, ibi, *quia secundum rationes* scientiarum.

Dicit ergo primo, quod secundum nullum illorum modorum videntur species esse, secundum quos nos Platonici ostendimus species esse. Et hoc ideo quia ex quibusdam illorum modorum non necessarium est *fieri syllogismum*, idest quasdam rationes Platonis, quia scilicet non de necessitate possunt syllogizare species esse: ex quibusdam vero modis fit syllogismus, sed non ad

introduced the ideas. Now they reasoned thus: they saw that there is a one-in-many for all things having the same name. Hence they claimed that this one-in-many is a form.

Yet with respect to all substances of things other than the ideas, we see that there is found to be a one-in-many which is predicated of them univocally inasmuch as there are found to be many things that are specifically one. This occurs not only in the case of sensible things but also in that of the objects of mathematics, which are eternal; because among these there are also many things that are specifically one, as was stated above [157].

Hence it follows that some idea corresponds to each species of sensible things; and therefore each idea is something having the same name as these sensible things, because the ideas agree with them in name. For just as Socrates is called man, so also is the idea of man. Yet they differ conceptually; for the intelligible structure of Socrates contains matter, whereas that of the ideal man is devoid of matter. Or, according to another reading, each form is said to be something having the same name as these sensible things inasmuch as it is a one-in-many and agrees with the things of which it is predicated so far as the intelligible structure of the species is concerned.

Therefore he says that they are equal to, or not fewer than, these things. For either there are held to be ideas only of species, and then they would be equal in number to these sensible things (granted that things are counted here insofar as they differ specifically and not individually, for the latter difference is infinite); or there are held to be ideas not only of species but also of genera, and then there would be more ideas than there are species of sensible things, because all species would be ideas and in addition to these each and every genus would be an idea.

This is why he says that they are either not fewer than or more. Or, in another way, they are said to be equal inasmuch as he claimed that they are the forms of sensible things. And he says not "fewer than" but "more" inasmuch as he held that they are the forms not only of sensible things but also of the objects of mathematics.

210. *Furthermore, the forms* (990b8). Here he argues dialectically against the reasoning behind Plato's position; in regard to this he does two things.

First, he gives a general account of the ways in which Plato's arguments fail.

Second [211], he explains them in detail, at *according to those arguments* (990b11).

He says, first, that with regard to the ways in which we Platonists prove the existence of the forms, according to none of these are the forms seen to exist. The reason is that *no syllogism follows* necessarily from some of these ways—that is, from certain arguments of Plato—because they cannot demonstrate with necessity the existence of the ideas. However, from other arguments a syllogism does

propositum Platonis: quia per quasdam suas rationes ostenditur, quod species separatae sunt quarumdam rerum, quarum esse species Platonici non putaverunt similiter, sicut et illarum quarum putaverunt, esse species.

211. Deinde cum dicit *quia secundum* hic prosequitur istos modos in speciali.

Et primo prosequitur secundum, ostendendo quod sequitur per rationem Platonis species esse aliquorum, quorum species non ponebat.

Secundo prosequitur primum, ostendens quod rationes Platonis non sunt sufficientes ad ostendendum esse ideas, ibi, *omnium autem dubitabit aliquis* et cetera.

Circa primum ponit septem rationes: quarum prima talis est. Una rationum inducentium Platonem ad ponendum ideas sumebatur ex parte scientiae: quia videlicet scientia cum sit de necessariis, non potest esse de his sensibilibus, quae sunt corruptibilia, sed oportet quod sit de entibus separatis incorruptibilibus. Secundum igitur hanc rationem ex scientiis sumptam, sequitur quod species sint omnium quorumcumque sunt scientiae. Scientiae autem non solum sunt de hoc quod est esse unum in multis, quod est per affirmationem, sed etiam de negationibus: quia sicut sunt aliquae demonstrationes concludentes affirmativam propositionem, ita sunt etiam demonstrationes concludentes negativam propositionem: ergo oportet etiam negationum ponere ideas.

212. Deinde cum dicit *et secundum* hic ponit secundam rationem. In scientiis enim non solum intelligitur quod quaedam semper se eodem modo habent, sed etiam quod quaedam corrumpuntur; aliter tolleretur scientia naturalis, quae circa motum versatur. Si igitur oportet esse ideas omnium illorum quae in scientiis intelliguntur, oportet esse ideas corruptibilium inquantum corruptibilia, hoc est inquantum sunt haec sensibilia singularia; sic enim sunt corruptibilia.

Non autem potest dici secundum rationem Platonis, quod scientiae illae, quibus intelligimus corruptiones rerum, intelligantur corruptiones horum sensibilium; quia horum sensibilium non est intellectus, sed imaginatio vel phantasia, quae est motus factus a sensu secundum actum, secundum quod dicitur in secundo *De anima*.

213. Deinde cum dicit *amplius autem* hic ponit tertiam rationem, quae continet duas conclusiones, quas certissimis rationibus dicit concludi.

Una est, quia si ideae sunt omnium, quorum sunt scientiae, scientiae autem non solum sunt de absolutis,

follow, although it does not support Plato's thesis; for by certain of his arguments there are proved to be forms of certain things of which the Platonists did not think there are forms, just as there are proved to be forms of those things of which they think there are forms.

211. *According to those arguments* (990b11). Here he examines in detail the arguments by which the Platonists establish ideas.

First, he examines the second argument, and he does this by showing that from Plato's argument it follows that there are forms of some things for which the Platonists did not posit forms.

Second [225], he examines the first argument, and he does this by showing that Plato's arguments are not sufficient to prove that ideas exist, at *but the most* (991a8).

In regard to the first member of this division he gives seven arguments. The first is this. One of the arguments that induced Plato to posit ideas is taken from scientific knowledge. For, since science is concerned with necessary things, it cannot be concerned with sensible things, which are corruptible, but must be concerned with separate entities, which are incorruptible. According to the argument taken from the sciences, then, it follows that there are forms of every sort of thing of which there are sciences. Now there are sciences not only of that which is one-in-many, which is affirmative, but also of negations; for just as there are some demonstrations which conclude with an affirmative proposition, in a similar way there are demonstrations which conclude with a negative proposition. Hence it is also necessary to posit ideas of negations.

212. *Again, according to the argument* (990b13). Here he gives the second argument. In the sciences it is understood not only that some things always exist in the same way, but also that some things are destroyed; otherwise, the philosophy of nature, which deals with motion, would be destroyed. Therefore, if there must be ideas of all the things that are comprehended in the sciences, there must be ideas of corruptible things insofar as they are such, that is, insofar as these are singular sensible things; for thus are things corruptible.

But according to Plato's theory, it cannot be said that those sciences by which we understand the processes of corruption in the world attain any understanding of the processes of corruption in sensible things, for there is no comprehension of these sensible things, but only imagination or phantasy, which is a motion produced by the senses in their act of sensing, as is pointed out in *On the Soul* 2.

213. *Again, according to the most* (990b15). Here he gives the third argument, which contains two conclusions that he says are drawn from the most certain arguments of Plato.

One conclusion is this: if there are ideas of all things of which there are sciences, and there are sciences not only

sed etiam sunt de his quae dicuntur ad aliquid, sequitur hac ratione faciente quod ideae sunt etiam eorum quae sunt ad aliquid: quod est contra opinionem Platonis; quia cum ideae separatae sint secundum se existentes, quod est contra rationem eius quod est ad aliquid, non ponebat Plato eorum quae sunt ad aliquid, aliquod esse genus idearum, quia secundum se dicuntur.

214. Alia conclusio est quae ex aliis rationibus certissimis sequitur, quod scilicet sit tertius homo. Quod quidem tripliciter potest intelligi.

Uno modo quod intelligatur, quod homo idealis sit tertius a duobus hominibus sensibilibus, qui communis hominis praedicationem suscipiunt. Sed haec non videtur eius esse intentio, licet non tangatur secundo *Elenchorum*: haec enim est positio contra quam disputat: unde ad hoc non duceret quasi ad inconveniens.

215. Alio modo potest intelligi, ut dicatur tertius homo, scilicet qui sit communis et homini ideali et homini sensibili.

Cum enim homo sensibilis et homo idealis conveniant in ratione, sicut duo homines sensibiles, et sicut homo idealis ponitur tertius praeter duos homines sensibiles, ita alius homo debet poni tertius praeter hominem idealem et hominem sensibilem.

Et hoc etiam non videtur hic esse eius intentio, quia ad hoc inconveniens statim alia ratione ducet: unde esset superfluum hic ad idem inconveniens ducere.

216. Tertio modo potest intelligi, quia Plato ponebat in quibusdam generibus tria, quaedam scilicet sensibilia, mathematica et species, sicut in numeris et lineis et omnibus huiusmodi.

Non est autem maior ratio quare in quibusdam rebus ponantur media quam in aliis; ergo oportebat etiam in specie hominis ponere hominem medium, qui erit tertius inter hominem sensibilem et idealem: et hanc etiam rationem in posterioribus libris Aristoteles ponit.

217. Deinde cum dicit **et omnino** hic ponit quartam rationem quae talis est. Quicumque per suam rationem removet aliqua, quae sunt apud eum magis nota quam ipsa positio, inconvenienter ponit. Sed istae rationes, quas Plato posuit, de speciebus separatis, auferunt quaedam principia, quae Platonici dicentes esse species magis volunt esse vera quam hoc ipsum quod est, ideas esse: ergo Plato inconvenienter posuit.

of absolutes but also of things predicated relatively, then in giving this argument it follows that there are also ideas of relations. This is opposed to Plato's view. For, since the separate ideas are things that exist of themselves, which is opposed to the intelligibility of a relation, Plato did not hold that there is a genus of ideas of relations, because the ideas are said to exist of themselves.

214. The second conclusion is one which follows from other most certain arguments, namely, that there is a third man. This phrase can be understood in three ways.

First, it can mean that the ideal man is a third man distinct from two men perceived by the senses, who have the common name "man" predicated of both of them. But this does not seem to be what he has in mind, granted that it is not mentioned in the *Sophistical Refutations* 2, because he argues against the position. Hence, according to this, it would not lead to an absurdity.

215. The second way in which this expression can be understood is this: the third man means one that is common to the ideal man and to one perceived by the senses.

For, since both a man perceived by the senses and the ideal man have a common intelligible structure (like two men perceived by the senses), then just as the ideal man is held to be a third man in addition to two men perceived by the senses, in a similar way there should be held to be another third man in addition to the ideal man and one perceived by the senses.

But neither does this seem to be what he has in mind here, because he leads us immediately to this absurdity by means of another argument. Hence it would be pointless to lead us to the same absurdity here.

216. The third way in which this expression can be understood is this. Plato posited three kinds of entities in certain genera of things, namely, sensible substances, the objects of mathematics, and the forms. He does this, for example, in the case of numbers, lines, and the like.

But there is no reason why intermediate things should be held to exist in certain genera rather than in others. Hence in the species of man it was also necessary to posit an intermediate man, who will be a third man midway between the man perceived by the senses and the ideal man. Aristotle also gives this argument in the later books of this work [2160].

217. *And in general* (990b17). Here he gives the fourth argument, which runs as follows. Whoever by his own reason does away with certain principles which are better known to him than the ones which he posits adopts an absurd position. But these theories about the forms which Plato held do away with certain principles whose reality the Platonists (when they said that there are ideas) were more convinced of than the existence of the ideas. Therefore, Plato's position is absurd.

Minorem autem sic manifestat. Ideae secundum Platonem sunt priores rebus sensibilibus et mathematicis: sed ipsae ideae sunt numeri secundum eum, et magis numeri impares quam pares, quia numerum imparem attribuebat formae, parem autem materiae. Unde et dualitatem dixit esse materiam. Sequitur ergo quod alii numeri sunt priores dualitate, quam ponebat sicut materiam sensibilium, ponens magnum et parvum. Cuius contrarium Platonici maxime asserebant, scilicet dualitatem esse primam in genere numeri.

218. Item si, sicut per superiorem rationem probatum est, oportet esse aliquas ideas relationum, quae sint secundum se ad aliquid, et ipsa idea est prior eo quod participat ideam, sequitur quod hoc ipsum quod est ad aliquid est prius absoluto quod secundum se dicitur. Nam huiusmodi substantiae sensibiles, quae participant ideas, absolute dicuntur. Et similiter de omnibus est quaecumque illi qui sequuntur opinionem de ideis dicunt opposita principiis per se notis, quae etiam ipsi maxime concedebant.

219. Deinde cum dicit *amplius autem* hic ponit quintam rationem, quae talis est. Ideae ponebantur a Platone, ut eis competerent rationes sive definitiones positae in scientiis, ut etiam de eis scientiae esse possent.

Sed *intelligentia una*, idest simplex et indivisibilis, qua scitur de unoquoque quid est, non solum est circa substantias *sed etiam de aliis*, scilicet accidentibus. Et similiter scientiae non solum sunt substantiae, et de substantia, sed etiam inveniuntur scientiae *aliorum*, scilicet accidentium: ergo patet quod ad aestimationem, secundum quam vos Platonici esse dicitis ideas, sequitur quod species non solum essent substantiarum, sed etiam multorum aliorum, scilicet accidentium.

Et hoc idem sequitur non solum propter definitiones et scientias, sed etiam accidunt multa *alia talia*, scilicet plurima, ex quibus oportet ponere ideas accidentium secundum rationes Platonis. Sicut quia ponebat ideas principia essendi et fieri rerum, et multorum huiusmodi, quae conveniunt accidentibus.

220. Sed ex alia parte secundum quod Plato opinabatur de ideis, et secundum necessitatem, qua sunt necessariae sensibilibus *inquantum* scilicet sunt participabiles a sensibilibus, est necessarium ponere quod ideae sint solum substantiarum.

Quod sic patet. Ea quae sunt secundum accidens non participantur: sed ideam oportet participari in unoquoque inquantum non dicitur de subiecto.

The minor premise is proved in this way. According to Plato the ideas are prior both to sensible things and to the objects of mathematics. But according to him the ideas themselves are numbers, and they are odd numbers rather than even ones, because he attributed odd number to form and even number to matter. Hence he also said that the dyad is matter. Therefore, it follows that other numbers are prior to the dyad, which he held to be the matter of sensible things, and identified with the great and small. Yet the Platonists asserted the very opposite of this, namely, that the dyad is first in the genus of number.

218. Again, if, as has been proved by the above argument [213], there must be ideas of relations, which are self-subsistent relations, and if the idea itself is prior to whatever participates in the idea, it follows that the relative is prior to the absolute, which is said to exist of itself. For sensible substances of this kind, which participate in ideas, are said to be in an unqualified sense. And in like manner whatever those who follow the opinion about the ideas say of all things is opposed to self-evident principles which even they themselves are most ready to acknowledge.

219. *Again, according to the opinion* (990b22). Here he gives the fifth argument, which is as follows. Ideas were posited by Plato in order that the intelligible structures and definitions of things given in the sciences might correspond to them, and in order that there could be sciences of them.

But there is *one concept*, a simple and indivisible concept, by which the quiddity of each thing is known—that is, not only the quiddity of substances *but also of other things*, namely, of accidents. And in a similar way there are sciences not only of substance and about substance, but there are also found to be sciences *of other things*, namely, of accidents. Hence, according to the opinion by which you, Platonists, acknowledge the existence of ideas, it evidently follows that there will be forms not only of substances but also of many other things, namely, of accidents.

This same conclusion follows not only because of definitions and the sciences, but there also happen to be many *other such*, or very many, reasons why it is necessary to posit ideas of accidents according to Plato's arguments. For example, he held that the ideas are the principles of being and of becoming in the world, and of many such aspects which apply to accidents.

220. But, on the other hand, according to Plato's opinion about the ideas and according to logical necessity, insofar as the ideas are indispensable to sensible things—namely, *insofar* as they are capable of being participated in by sensible things—it is necessary to posit ideas only of substances.

This is proved thus. Things that are accidental are not participated in. But an idea must be participated in by each thing insofar as it is not predicated of a subject.

Quod sic patet. Quia si aliquod sensibile participat *per se duplo*, idest duplo separato (sic enim appellabat Plato omnia separata, scilicet per se entia): oportet quod participet sempiterno; non quidem per se, quia tunc sequeretur quod dupla sensibilia essent sempiterna, sed per accidens: inquantum scilicet ipsum per se duplum quod participatur est sempiternum.

Ex quo patet quod participatio non est eorum quae accidentia sunt, sed solummodo substantiarum. Unde secundum opinionem Platonis non erat aliquod accidens species separata, sed solum substantia: et tamen secundum rationem sumptam ex scientiis oportebat quod esset species etiam accidentium, ut dictum est.

221. Deinde cum dicit *haec vero* hic ponit sextam rationem, quae talis est. Istae res sensibiles substantiam significant in rebus quae videntur et similiter illic, ut in rebus intelligibilibus, quae substantiam significant, quia tam intelligibilia quam sensibilia substantiam ponebant: ergo necesse est ponere praeter utrasque substantias, scilicet intelligibiles et sensibiles, aliquid commune eis quod sit unum in multis: ex hac enim ratione Platonici ideas ponebant, quia inveniebant unum in multis, quod credebant esse praeter illa multa.

222. Et quod hoc ponere sit necessarium, scilicet aliquod unum praeter substantias sensibiles et praeter species, sic ostendit. Aut enim ideae et sensibilia quae participant ideas sunt unius speciei aut non. Si sunt unius speciei, omnium autem multorum in specie convenientium oportet ponere secundum positionem Platonis unam speciem separatam communem, oportebit igitur aliquid ponere commune sensibilibus et ipsis ideis, quod sit separatum ab utroque.

Non potest autem responderi ad hanc rationem quod ideae quae sunt incorporales et immateriales non indigent aliis speciebus superioribus; quia similiter mathematica quae ponuntur a Platone media inter sensibilia et species, sunt incorporea et immaterialia: et tamen, quia plura eorum inveniuntur unius speciei, Plato posuit eorum speciem communem separatam, qua etiam participant non solum mathematica, sed etiam sensibilia.

Si igitur est una et eadem dualitas, quae est species vel idea dualitatis, quae quidem est etiam in dualitatibus sensibilibus quae sunt corruptibiles, sicut exemplar est in exemplato et in dualitatibus etiam mathematicis quae sunt multae unius speciei, sed tamen sunt sempiternae, eadem ratione in eadem dualitate, scilicet quae est idea et in alia quae est mathematica, vel sensibilis, erit alia

This becomes clear as follows. If any sensible thing participates in **doubleness itself**, that is, in a separate doubleness (for Plato spoke of all separated things in this way, namely, as self-subsisting things), it must participate in the eternal. But it does not do this *per se* (because then it would follow that any double perceived by the senses would be eternal), but accidentally, insofar as doubleness itself, which is participated in, is eternal.

And from this it is evident that there is no participation in things that are accidental, but only in substances. Hence, according to Plato's position a separate form was not an accident but only a substance. Yet according to the argument taken from the sciences there must also be forms of accidents, as was stated above [219].

221. *But these things* (990b34). Then he gives the sixth argument, which runs thus. These sensible things signify substance both in the case of things perceived by the senses and in that of those in the ideal world, namely, in the case of intelligible things, which signify substance (because they held that both intelligible things and sensible ones are substance). Therefore, it is necessary to posit in addition to both of these substances—intelligible and sensible ones— some common entity which is a one-in-many. For the Platonists maintained that the ideas exist on the grounds that they found a one-in-many which they believed to be separate from the many.

222. The need for positing a one apart from both sensible substances and the forms he proves thus. The ideas and the sensible things that participate in them either belong to one species or not. If they belong to one species, and it is necessary to posit, according to Plato's position, one common separate form for all things having a common nature, then it will be necessary to posit some entity common to both sensible things and the ideas themselves which exists apart from both.

Now one cannot answer this argument by saying that the ideas, which are incorporeal and immaterial, do not stand in need of any higher forms. For the objects of mathematics, which Plato places midway between sensible substances and the forms, are similarly incorporeal and immaterial. Yet since many of them are found to belong to one species, Plato held that there is a common form for these things, in which not only the objects of mathematics participate but also sensible substances.

Therefore, if the two-ness which is the form or idea of two-ness is identical with that found in sensible twos, which are corruptible (just as a pattern is found in the things fashioned after it), and with that found in mathematical twos, which are many in one species (but are nevertheless eternal), then for the same reason in the case of the same two-ness (the idea two) and in that of the other

dualitas separata. Non enim potest reddi propter quid illud sit, et hoc non sit.

223. Si autem detur alia pars, scilicet sensibilia quae participant ideas non sunt eiusdem speciei cum ideis: sequitur quod nomen quod dicitur de ideis et de substantia sensibili dicatur omnino aequivoce. Illa enim dicuntur aequivoce, quorum solum nomen commune est, ratione speciei existente diversa. Nec solum sequitur quod sint quocumque modo aequivoca, sed simpliciter aequivoca, sicut illa quibus imponitur unum nomen sine respectu ad aliquam communicationem, quae dicuntur aequivoca a casu. Sicut si aliquem hominem aliquis vocaret Calliam et aliquod lignum.

224. Hoc autem ideo addidit Aristoteles quia posset aliquis dicere quod non omnino aequivoce aliquod nomen praedicatur de idea et de substantia sensibili, cum de idea praedicetur essentialiter, de substantia vero sensibili per participationem. Nam idea hominis secundum Platonem dicitur per se homo, hic autem homo sensibilis dicitur per participationem. Sed tamen talis aequivocatio non est pura; sed nomen quod per participationem praedicatur, dicitur per respectum ad illud quod praedicatur per se, quod non est pura aequivocatio, sed multiplicitas analogiae. Si autem essent omnino aequivoca a casu idea et substantia sensibilis, sequeretur quod per unum non posset cognosci aliud, sicut aequivoca non se invicem notificant.

two-ness (which is either mathematical or sensible), there will be another separate two-ness. For no reason can be given why the former should exist and the latter should not.

223. But if the other alternative is admitted—that sensible things, which participate in the ideas, do not have the same form as the ideas—it follows that the name which is predicated of both the ideas and sensible substances is predicated in a purely equivocal way. For those things are said to be equivocal which have only a common name and differ in their intelligible structure. And it follows that they are not only equivocal in every way but equivocal in an absolute sense, like those things on which one name is imposed without regard for any common attribute, which are said to be equivocal by chance—for example, if one were to call both Callias and a piece of wood man.

224. Now Aristotle added this because someone might say that a name is not predicated of an idea and of a sensible substance in a purely equivocal way, since a name is predicated of an idea *per se* and of a sensible substance by participation. For, according to Plato, the idea of man is called man in himself, whereas this man whom we apprehend by the senses is said to be a man by participation. However, such an equivocation is not pure equivocation. But a name which is predicated by participation is predicated with reference to something that is predicated *per se*; this is not pure equivocation, but the multiplicity of analogy. However, if an idea and a sensible substance were altogether equivocal by chance, it would follow that one could not be known through the other, as one equivocal thing cannot be known through another.

LECTURE 15

The destruction of the Platonists' arguments for the ideas

991a8 Omnium autem dubitabit aliquis maxime, quid conferunt species sempiternis sensibilium, aut his quae fiunt et corrumpuntur. [225]

πάντων δὲ μάλιστα διαπορήσειεν ἄν τις τί ποτε συμβάλλεται τὰ εἴδη τοῖς {10} ἀϊδίοις τῶν αἰσθητῶν ἢ τοῖς γιγνομένοις καὶ φθειρομένοις:

But the most important problem of all that one might raise is what the forms contribute to sensible things, either to those which are eternal or to those which are generated and corrupted.

991a11 Nec enim motus, nec transmutationis ullius sunt causa in eis. [226]

οὔτε γὰρ κινήσεως οὔτε μεταβολῆς οὐδεμιᾶς ἐστὶν αἴτια αὐτοῖς.

For they are not the cause of motion or of any change whatever in these things.

991a12 Sed nec ad scientiam nihil auxiliantur eis, quia est aliorum nec enim illae horum substantia: nam essent in eis. [227]

ἀλλὰ μὴν οὔτε πρὸς τὴν ἐπιστήμην οὐθὲν βοηθεῖ τὴν τῶν ἄλλων (οὐδὲ γὰρ οὐσία ἐκεῖνα τούτων: ἐν τούτοις γὰρ ἂν ἦν),

Nor are they of any assistance in knowing other things, for they are not the substance of other things, because if they were they would exist in them.

Nec ad esse cum non participantibus insint. Sic enim forsan causa videbitur esse album permixtum albo.

οὔτε εἰς τὸ εἶναι, μὴ ἐνυπάρχοντά γε τοῖς μετέχουσιν: οὕτω μὲν {15} γὰρ ἂν ἴσως αἴτια δόξειεν εἶναι ὡς τὸ λευκὸν μεμιγμένον τῷ λευκῷ,

Nor do they contribute anything to the being of other things, for they are not present in the things that participate in them. For if they were they would perhaps seem to be causes, as whiteness mixed with some white thing.

Sed haec quidem ratio valde mobilis est, quam Anaxagoras prius, et Hesiodus posterius et alii quidam dixerunt. Facile namque colligere est multa et impossibilia ad talem opinionem. At vero nec ex speciebus sunt alia secundum ullum modum consuetorum.

ἀλλ᾽ οὗτος μὲν ὁ λόγος λίαν εὐκίνητος, ὃν Ἀναξαγόρας μὲν πρῶτος Εὔδοξος δ᾽ ὕστερον καὶ ἄλλοι τινὲς ἔλεγον (ῥᾴδιον γὰρ συναγαγεῖν πολλὰ καὶ ἀδύνατα πρὸς τὴν τοιαύτην δόξαν):

But this theory, which was first stated by Anaxagoras and later by Hesiod and certain other thinkers, is easily disposed of. For it is easy to bring many absurd conclusions against such a view. In fact, other things are not derived from the forms in any of the customary ways.

991a19 Dicere vero exemplaria esse et eis alia participare, vaniloquium est, et metaphoras dicere poeticas. [231]

ἀλλὰ μὴν οὐδ᾽ ἐκ τῶν εἰδῶν ἐστὶ τἆλλα {20} κατ᾽ οὐθένα τρόπον τῶν εἰωθότων λέγεσθαι. τὸ δὲ λέγειν παραδείγματα αὐτὰ εἶναι καὶ μετέχειν αὐτῶν τἆλλα κενολογεῖν ἐστὶ καὶ μεταφορὰς λέγειν ποιητικάς.

Again, to say that they are exemplars, and that other things participate in them, is to speak with empty talk and to utter poetic metaphors.

991a22 Nam quid est opus ad ideas respiciens? Contingit enim et esse et fieri simile aliquod, et non simile illi. Quare existente Socrate et non existente fiet qualis Socrates. [232]

τί γάρ ἐστι τὸ ἐργαζόμενον πρὸς τὰς ἰδέας ἀποβλέπον; ἐνδέχεταί τε καὶ εἶναι καὶ γίγνεσθαι ὅμοιον ὁτιοῦν καὶ μὴ εἰκαζόμενον {25} πρὸς ἐκεῖνο, ὥστε καὶ ὄντος Σωκράτους καὶ μὴ ὄντος γένοιτ᾽ ἂν οἷος Σωκράτης:

For what is the work which looks toward the ideas? For one thing may both be and become similar to another thing and not be like it. So whether Socrates exists or not, a man like Socrates might come to be.

991a26 Similiter autem palam, quia etiam si sit Socrates sempiternus, erunt eiusdem exemplaria plura, quare et species: ut hominis animal et bipes: similiter autem et autosanthropos. [234]

ὁμοίως δὲ δῆλον ὅτι κἂν εἰ ἦν ὁ Σωκράτης ἀΐδιος. ἔσται τε πλείω παραδείγματα τοῦ αὐτοῦ, ὥστε καὶ εἴδη, οἷον τοῦ ἀνθρώπου τὸ ζῷον καὶ τὸ δίπουν, ἅμα δὲ καὶ τὸ αὐτοάνθρωπος.

Similarly, it is evident that this will be the case even if Socrates is eternal. And there will be many exemplars of the same thing, and for this reason many forms, as animal and two-footed and man-in-himself will be the form of man.

991a29 Amplius autem non solum sensibilium species exemplaria, sed etiam ipsarum, ut genus specierum; quare idem erit exemplar et imago. [235]

ἔτι οὐ μόνον τῶν αἰσθητῶν {30} παραδείγματα τὰ εἴδη ἀλλὰ καὶ αὐτῶν, οἷον τὸ γένος, ὡς γένος εἰδῶν: ὥστε τὸ αὐτὸ ἔσται παράδειγμα καὶ εἰκών.

Further, the forms will be the exemplars not only of sensible things but also of the forms themselves, as the genus of the species. Hence the same thing will be both an exemplar and a copy.

991b1 Amplius opinabitur utique impossibile esse separatim substantiam, et cuius est substantia. Quare quomodo ideae substantiae rerum existentes separatim erunt? [236]

ἔτι δόξειεν ἂν ἀδύνατον εἶναι χωρὶς τὴν οὐσίαν καὶ οὗ ἡ οὐσία· ὥστε πῶς ἂν αἱ ἰδέαι οὐσίαι τῶν πραγμάτων οὖσαι χωρὶς εἶεν;

Again, it is thought to be impossible that the substance of a thing and that of which it is the substance should exist apart. Hence, if the forms are the substances of things, how will they exist apart from them?

991b3 In Phaedone vero sic dicitur quod ipsius esse et fieri causae sint species, et etiam existentibus speciebus, tamen non fiunt participantia nisi sit quod movit. [237]

ἐν δὲ τῷ Φαίδωνι οὕτω λέγεται, ὡς καὶ τοῦ εἶναι καὶ τοῦ γίγνεσθαι αἴτια τὰ εἴδη ἐστίν· καίτοι τῶν εἰδῶν {5} ὄντων ὅμως οὐ γίγνεται τὰ μετέχοντα ἂν μὴ ᾖ τὸ κινῆσον,

But in the *Phaedo* it is stated that the forms are the causes both of being and of coming to be. Yet even if the forms do exist, still the things that participate in them will not come to be unless there is something which produces motion.

991b6 Et multa fiunt alia ut domus et anulus, quorum non dicimus esse species: quare palam quia contingit et alias et esse et fieri, et propter tales causas quales et nunc dictas. [238]

καὶ πολλὰ γίγνεται ἕτερα, οἷον οἰκία καὶ δακτύλιος, ὧν οὔ φαμεν εἴδη εἶναι· ὥστε δῆλον ὅτι ἐνδέχεται καὶ τἆλλα καὶ εἶναι καὶ γίγνεσθαι διὰ τοιαύτας αἰτίας οἵας καὶ τὰ ῥηθέντα νῦν.

And many other things come to be, such as a house and a ring, of which we do not say that there are any forms. It is evident, then, that other things can exist and come to be because of such causes as those responsible for the things just mentioned.

---

225. Hic improbat opinionem Platonis quantum ad hoc quod non concludebat quod concludere intendebat. Intendebat enim Plato concludere ideas esse per hoc, quod sunt necesse sensibilibus rebus secundum aliquem modum. Unde Aristoteles ostendens quod ideae ad nihil possunt sensibilibus utiles esse, destruit rationes Platonis de positione idearum: et ideo dicit, quod inter omnia dubitabilia, quae sunt contra Platonem, illud est maximum, quod species a Platone positae non videntur aliquid conferre rebus sensibilibus, nec sempiternis, sicut sunt corpora caelestia: nec his, quae fiunt et corrumpuntur, sicut corpora elementaria. Quod sigillatim de omnibus ostendit propter quae Plato ponebat ideas, cum dicit *nec enim*.

226. Ibi incipit quinque ostendere.
Primo quod non prosunt ad motum.

Secundo quod non prosunt ad scientias, ibi, *sed nec ad scientiam*.

Tertio quod non prosunt exemplaria, ibi, *dicere vero exemplaria* et cetera.

Quarto quod non prosunt sicut substantiae, ibi, *amplius opinabitur*.

Quinto quod non prosunt sicut causae fiendi, ibi, *in Phaedone vero* et cetera.

Dicit ergo primo, quod species non possunt conferre sensibilibus, ita quod sint eis causa motus vel transmutationis alicuius. Cuius rationem hic non dicit, sed superius tetigit, quia videlicet ideae non introducebantur propter motum, sed magis propter immobilitatem. Quia enim Platoni videbatur quod omnia sensibilia semper essent in motu, voluit aliquid ponere extra sensibilia

225. Here Aristotle attacks the opinion of Plato insofar as he did not draw the conclusion which he intended to draw. For Plato intended to conclude that there are ideas by this argument that they are necessary in some way for sensible things. Hence, Aristotle, by showing that the ideas cannot contribute anything to sensible things, destroys the arguments by which Plato posits ideas. Thus he says (991a8) that of all the objections which may be raised against Plato the foremost is that the forms which Plato posited do not seem to contribute anything to sensible things, either to those which are eternal, as the celestial bodies, or to those which are generated and corrupted, as the elemental bodies. He shows that this criticism applies to each of the arguments by which Plato posited ideas, at *for they are not* (991a11).

226. Here (991a11) he begins to present five objections.

He argues, first [226], that they are useless in explaining motion;

second [227], that they are useless in explaining our knowledge of sensible things, at *nor are they* (991a12);

third [231], that they are of no value as exemplars, at *again, to say* (991a19);

fourth [236], that they are of no value as the substances of things, at *again, it is thought* (991b1);

and fifth [237] that they are of no value as causes of generation, at *but in the Phaedo* (991b3).

Accordingly, he says, first (991a11), that the forms cannot contribute anything to sensible things in such a way as to be the cause of motion or of any kind of change in them. He does not give the reason for this here but mentioned it above [237], because it is clear that the ideas were not introduced to explain motion but rather to explain immutability. For, since it seemed to Plato that all

fixum et immobile, de quo posset esse certa scientia. Unde species non poterant ab eo poni sicut principia sensibilia motus, sed potius sicut immobiles, et immobilitatis principia: ut scilicet si aliquid fixum et eodem modo se habens in rebus sensibilibus invenitur, hoc sit secundum participantiam idearum, quae per se sunt immobiles.

227. Deinde cum dicit *sed nec ad* ostendit secundo, quod species non prosunt sensibilibus ad scientiam, tali ratione. Cognitio uniuscuiusque perficitur per cognitionem suae substantiae, et non per cognitionem aliquarum substantiarum extrinsecarum: sed substantiae separatae quas dicebant species, sunt omnino aliae ab istis substantiis sensibilibus: ergo earum cognitio non auxiliatur ad scientiam illorum sensibilium.

228. Nec potest dici quod illae species sunt substantiae istorum sensibilium: nam cuiuslibet rei substantia est in eo cuius est substantia. Si igitur illae species essent substantiae rerum sensibilium, essent in his sensibilibus: quod est contra Platonem.

229. Nec iterum potest dici quod illae species adsint istis substantiis sensibilibus, sicut participantibus eas. Hoc enim modo Plato opinabatur aliquas species horum sensibilium causas esse. Sicut nos intelligeremus ipsum album per se existens, ac si esset quoddam album separatum, permisceri albo quod est in subiecto, et albedinem participare, ut sic etiam dicamus quod homo iste, qui est separatus, permisceatur huic homini qui componitur ex materia et natura speciei, quam participat. Sed haec ratio est valde *mobilis*, idest destructibilis: hanc enim rationem primo tetigit Anaxagoras qui posuit etiam formas et accidentia permisceri rebus. Et secundo tetigit Hesiodus et alii quidam. Et ideo dico quod est valde mobilis, scilicet quia facile est colligere multa impossibilia contra talem opinionem. Sequitur enim, sicut supra dixit contra Anaxagoram, quod accidentia et formae possunt esse sine substantiis. Nam ea sola nata sunt misceri quae possunt separatim existere.

230. Sic igitur non potest dici quod species sic conferant ad scientiam sensibilium ut eorum substantiae, nec quod sint eis principia existendi per modum participandi. Nec etiam potest dici quod ex speciebus sicut ex principiis *sunt alia*, scilicet sensibilia secundum ullum eorum modum qui consueverunt dici.

Unde si eadem sunt principia essendi et cognoscendi, oportet quod species non conferant ad scientias, cum

sensible things are always in motion, he wanted to posit something separate from sensible things that is fixed and immobile, of which there can be certain knowledge. Hence, according to him, the forms could not be held to be sensible principles of motion, but rather to be immutable things and principles of immutability; so that, undoubtedly, whatever is found to be fixed and constant in sensible things will be due to participation in the ideas, which are immutable in themselves.

227. *Nor are they of any assistance* (991a12). Second, he shows that the forms do not contribute anything to the knowledge of sensible things by the following argument. Knowledge of each thing is acquired by knowing its own substance, and not by knowing certain substances which are separate from it. But these separate substances, which they call forms, are altogether other than sensible substances. Therefore, a knowledge of them is of no assistance in knowing other sensible things.

228. Nor can it be said that the forms are the substances of these sensible things; for the substance of each thing is present in the thing whose substance it is. Therefore, if then forms were the substances of sensible things, they would be present in sensible things. This is opposed to Plato's opinion.

229. Nor again can it be said that the forms are present in these sensible substances as in things that participate in them (for Plato thought that some forms are the causes of sensible things in this way). Just as we might understand whiteness itself existing of itself as a certain separate whiteness to be mingled with the whiteness in a subject, and to participate in whiteness, in a similar way we might say that man, who is separate, is mingled with this man who is composed of matter and the specific nature in which he participates. But this argument is easily *disposed of*, or destroyed; Anaxagoras, who also held that forms and accidents are mingled with things, was the first to state it. Hesiod and certain other thinkers were the second to mention it. Therefore, I say that it is easily disposed of, because it is easy to bring many absurd conclusions against such an opinion. For it would follow, as he pointed out above [194] against Anaxagoras, that accidents and forms could exist without substances. For only those things can exist separately which are naturally disposed to be mixed with other things.

230. It cannot be said, then, that the forms contribute in any way to our knowledge of sensible things as their substances. Nor can it be said that they are the principles of being in these substances by way of participation. Nor again can it be said that from these forms as principles *other things*—sensible ones—come to be in any of the ways in which we are accustomed to speak.

Therefore, if principles of being and principles of knowledge are the same, the forms cannot possibly make

principia essendi esse non possint. Ideo autem dicit **secundum ullum modum consuetorum** dici, quia Plato invenerat novos modos aliquid ex alio cognoscendi.

231. Deinde cum dicit **dicere vero** hic tertio ostendit, quod species non conferant sensibilibus sicut exemplaria.

Et primo proponit intentum.
Secundo probat, ibi, **nam quid opus est** et cetera.

Dicit ergo primo, quod dicere species esse exemplaria sensibilium et mathematicorum eo quod huiusmodi causas participent, est dupliciter inconveniens. Uno modo, quia vanum et nulla utilitas est huiusmodi exemplaria ponere, sicut ostendet. Alio modo quia est simile metaphoris quas poetae inducunt, quod ad philosophum non pertinet. Nam philosophus ex propriis docere debet.

Ideo autem hoc dicit esse metaphoricum, quia Plato productionem rerum naturalium assimilavit factioni rerum artificialium, in quibus artifex ad aliquid exemplar respiciens, operatur aliquid simile suae arti.

232. Deinde cum dicit **nam quid est** hic probat propositum tribus rationibus.

Hoc enim videtur esse opus exemplaris, idest utilitas, quod artifex respiciens ad exemplar inducat similitudinem formae in suo artificio. Videmus autem in operatione naturalium rerum, quod similia ex similibus generantur, sicut ex homine generatur homo. Aut ergo similitudo ista provenit in rebus generatis propter respectum alicuius agentis ad exemplar, aut non. Si non, quid erat **opus**, idest utilitas quod aliquod agens sic respiciens ad ideas sicut ad exemplaria? Quasi dicat, nullum. Si autem similitudo provenit ex respectu ad exemplar separatum, tunc non poterit dici quod causa huius similitudinis in genito sit forma inferioris generantis. Fiet enim aliquid simile propter respectum ad hoc exemplar separatum, et non per respectum ad agens hoc sensibile. Et hoc est quod dicit **et non simile illi**, idest agenti sensibili. Ex quo sequitur hoc inconveniens quod aliquis generetur similis Socrati, sive posito, sive remoto Socrate. Quod videmus esse falsum; quia nisi Socrates agat in generatione, nunquam generabitur aliquis similis Socrati. Si igitur hoc est falsum, quod non similitudo generatorum dependeat a proximis generantibus, vanum et superfluum est ponere aliqua exemplaria separata.

any contribution to scientific knowledge, since they cannot be principles of knowing. Hence he says **in any of the customary ways** of speaking, because Plato invented new ways of deriving knowledge of one thing from something else.

231. **Again, to say** (991a19). Here he gives the third objection against the arguments for separate forms. He says that the forms are of no value to sensible things as their exemplars.

First (991a19), he states his thesis;

second [232], he proves it, at **for what is the work** (991a22).

Accordingly he says, first (991a19), that to say that the forms are the exemplars both of sensible things and the objects of mathematics (because the latter participate in causes of this kind) is untenable for two reasons. First, because it is vain and useless to posit exemplars of this kind, as he will show; second, because this manner of speaking is similar to the metaphors which the poets introduce, which do not pertain to the philosopher. For the philosopher ought to teach by using proper causes.

Hence he says that this manner of speaking is metaphorical, because Plato likened the generation of natural substances to the making of works of art, in which the artisan, by looking at some exemplar, produces something similar to his artistic idea.

232. **For what is the work** (991a22). Here he proves his thesis by three arguments.

For the work (or use) of an exemplar seems to be this: the artisan by looking at an exemplar induces a likeness of the form in his own artifact. But in the operations of natural beings we see that like things are generated by like, as man is generated by man. Therefore, this likeness arises in things that are generated, either because some agent looks toward an exemplar or not. If not, then what is **the work**, or utility, of the agent's so looking toward the ideas as exemplars? This is as if to say, none. But if the likeness results from looking at a separate exemplar, then it cannot be said that the cause of this likeness in the thing generated is the form of an inferior agent. For something similar would come into being with reference to this separate exemplar and not with reference to this sensible agent. And this is what he means when he says **and not be like it**, that is, like the sensible agent. From this the following absurdity results: someone similar to Socrates will be generated whether Socrates is held to exist or not. This we see is false, for unless Socrates plays an active part in the process of generation, no one similar to Socrates will ever be generated. Therefore, if it is false that the likeness of things that are generated does not depend on proximate agents, it is pointless and superfluous to posit separate exemplars of any kind.

233. Sciendum autem quod illa ratio, etsi destruat exemplaria separata a Platone posita, non tamen removet divinam scientiam esse rerum omnium exemplarem.

Cum enim res naturales naturaliter intendant similitudines in res generatas inducere, oportet quod ista intentio ad aliquod principium dirigens reducatur, quod est in finem ordinans unumquodque. Et hoc non potest esse nisi intellectus cuius sit cognoscere finem et proportionem rerum in finem. Et sic ista similitudo effectuum ad causas naturales reducitur, sicut in primum principium, in intellectum aliquem. Non autem oportet quod in aliquas alias formas separatas: quia ad similitudinem praedictam sufficit praedicta directio in finem, qua virtutes naturales diriguntur a primo intellectu.

234. Deinde cum dicit *similiter autem* hic ponit secundam rationem, quae talis est. Sicut Socrates ex eo quod est Socrates addit aliquid supra hominem, ita etiam homo addit aliquid supra animal: et sicut Socrates participat hominem, ita homo participat animal. Sed si praeter istum Socratem sensibilem poneretur alius Socrates sempiternus, quasi exemplaris, sequeretur quod huius Socratis sensibilis essent plura exemplaria, scilicet Socrates sempiternus et idea hominis: ergo et eadem ratione species hominis habet plura exemplaria. Erit enim exemplar eius et animal et bipes et iterum *autosanthropos*, idest idea hominis. Hoc autem est inconveniens quod unius exemplati sint plura exemplaria: ergo inconveniens est ponere huiusmodi sensibilium exemplaria.

235. Deinde cum dicit *amplius autem* hic ponit tertiam rationem, quae talis est. Sicut se habet species ad individuum, ita se habet genus ad speciem. Si igitur species sunt exemplaria sensibilium individuorum, ut Plato ponit, ipsarum etiam specierum erunt aliqua exemplaria, scilicet genus specierum: quod est inconveniens: quia tunc sequeretur quod idem, scilicet species, erit exemplum alterius, scilicet individui sensibilis, et imago ab alio exemplata, scilicet a genere; quod videtur esse inconveniens.

236. Deinde cum dicit *amplius opinabitur* hic quarto ostendit quod species non conferunt rebus sensibilibus sicut earum substantiae vel causae formales, quia hic *opinabitur*, idest hoc est opinativum (ut impersonaliter ponatur), quod impossibile est separari substantiam ab eo cuius est substantia. Sed hae separantur ab eo cuius sunt ideae, idest a sensibilibus: ergo non sunt substantiae sensibilium.

237. Deinde cum dicit *in Phaedone* hic ostendit quod non conferunt species sensibilibus ad eorum fieri,

233. However, it should be noted that, even though this argument does away with the separate exemplars postulated by Plato, it still does not do away with the fact that God's knowledge is the exemplar of all things.

For, since things in the physical world are naturally inclined to induce their likeness in things that are generated, this inclination must be traced back to some directing principle which ordains each thing to its end. This can only be the intellect of that being who knows the end and the relationship of things to the end. Therefore, this likeness of effects to their natural causes is traced back to an intellect as their first principle. But it is not necessary that this likeness should be traced back to any other separate forms; because in order to have the above-mentioned likeness this direction of things to their end, according to which natural powers are directed by the first intellect, is sufficient.

234. *Similarly, it is evident* (991a26). Here he gives the second argument, which runs as follows. Just as Socrates adds something to man because he is Socrates, in a similar way man adds something to animal. And just as Socrates participates in man, so does man participate in animal. But if besides this Socrates whom we perceive there is held to be another Socrates who is eternal, as his exemplar, it will follow that there are several exemplars of this Socrates whom we perceive, namely, the eternal Socrates and the form man. And by the same reasoning the form man will have several exemplars; for its exemplar will be both animal and two-footed and also *man-in-himself*, or the idea of man. But that there should be several exemplars of a single thing made in likeness to an exemplar is untenable. Therefore, it is absurd to hold that things of this kind are the exemplars of sensible things.

235. *Further, the forms* (991a29). Here he gives the third argument, which runs thus. Just as a form is related to an individual, so also is a genus related to a species. Therefore, if the forms are the exemplars of individual sensible things, as Plato held, there will be also certain exemplars of these forms, namely, their genus. But this is absurd, because then it would follow that one and the same thing, form, would be an exemplar of one thing (namely, of the individual whom we perceive by the senses), and a copy made in likeness to something else (namely, a genus). This seems to be absurd.

236. *Again, it is thought* (991b1). Here he proves his fourth objection: the forms contribute nothing to sensible things as their substances or formal causes. For *it is thought* by him, that is to say, it is a matter of opinion (to put this impersonally), that it is impossible for a thing's substance to exist apart from the thing whose substance it is. But the forms exist apart from the things of which they are the forms, that is, apart from sensible things. Therefore, they are not the substances of sensible things.

237. *But in the Phaedo* (991b3). Here he shows that the forms are of no value in accounting for the coming to be

quamvis Plato dixerit *in Phaedone*, idest in quodam suo libro, quod species sunt causae rebus sensibilibus essendi et fiendi. Sed hoc improbat duabus rationibus:

quarum prima talis est. Posita causa ponitur effectus: sed existentibus speciebus non propter hoc fiunt entia particularia sive individua participantia species, nisi sit aliquid motivum quod moveat ad speciem. Quod ex hoc patet, quia species semper eodem modo sunt secundum Platonem.

Si igitur eis positis essent vel fierent individua participantia eas, sequeretur quod semper essent huiusmodi individua, quod patet esse falsum: ergo non potest dici quod species sint causae fieri et esse rerum; et praecipue cum non poneret species causas esse motivas, ut supra dictum est.

Sic enim a substantiis separatis immobilibus ponit Aristoteles procedere et fieri et esse inferiorum, inquantum illae substantiae sunt motivae caelestium corporum, quibus mediantibus causatur generatio et corruptio in istis inferioribus.

238. Deinde cum dicit *et multa* hic ponit secundam rationem, quae talis est. Sicut se habent artificialia ad causas artificiales, ita se habent naturalia ad causas naturales. Sed videmus quod multa alia a naturalibus, ut domus et annulus, fiunt in istis inferioribus, quorum Platonici species non ponebant: ergo *et alias*, scilicet naturalia contingit esse et fieri propter tales causas proximas, quales contingit esse nunc dictas, scilicet artificiales; ut scilicet sicut res artificiales fiunt a proximis agentibus, ita et res naturales.

of sensible things, although Plato said *in the Phaedo* (that is, in one of his works), that the forms are the causes both of the being and of the coming to be of sensible things. But Aristotle disproves this by two arguments.

The first is as follows: to posit the cause is to posit the effect. However, even if the forms exist, the particular or individual things that participate in the forms will come into being only if there is some agent which moves them to acquire form. This is evident from Plato's opinion that the forms are always in the same state.

Therefore, assuming that these forms exist, if individuals were to exist or come into being by participating in them, it would follow that individual substances of this kind would always be. This is clearly false. Therefore, it cannot be said that the forms are the causes of both the coming to be and the being of sensible things. The chief reason is that Plato did not hold that the forms are efficient causes, as was stated above [226].

For Aristotle holds that the being and coming to be of lower substances proceeds from immobile separate substances, inasmuch as these substances are the movers of the celestial bodies, by means of which generation and corruption are produced in these lower substances.

238. *And many other* (991b6). Here he gives the second argument, which runs thus. Just as artifacts are related to artificial causes, so are natural bodies to natural causes. But we see that many other things besides natural bodies come into being in the realm of these lower bodies, such as a house and a ring, for which the Platonists did not posit any forms. Therefore, *other things* (namely, natural things) can both be and come to be because of such proximate causes as those just mentioned (that is, artificial ones). Thus, just as artificial things come to be as a result of proximate agents, so also do natural things.

LECTURE 16

The ideas are not numbers

991b9 Amplius si sunt numeri species, quomodo causae erunt? Utrum quia alii numeri sunt ipsa existentia, ut hic quidem numerus homo, ille vero Socrates et alius Callias? Quid igitur his sunt causae illi? Nec enim si hi sunt sempiterni, illi vero non, differunt. [239]

ἔτι εἴπερ εἰσὶν ἀριθμοὶ τὰ εἴδη, πῶς αἴτιοι ἔσονται; {10} πότερον ὅτι ἕτεροι ἀριθμοί εἰσι τὰ ὄντα, οἷον ὁδὶ μὲν <ὁ> ἀριθμὸς ἄνθρωπος ὁδὶ δὲ Σωκράτης ὁδὶ δὲ Καλλίας; τί οὖν ἐκεῖνοι τούτοις αἴτιοί εἰσιν; οὐδὲ γὰρ εἰ οἱ μὲν ἀΐδιοι οἱ δὲ μή, οὐδὲν διοίσει.

Further, if the forms are numbers, in what way will they be causes? Will it be because existing things are other numbers, so that this number is man, another Socrates, and still another Callias? In what respect, then, are the former the cause of the latter? For it will make no difference if the former are eternal and the latter are not.

Si vero quia rationes numerorum et hic, ut symphonia, palam quia est unum quidem, quorum sunt rationes. Si itaque haec materia, manifestum quia et ipsi numeri et aliquae rationes sunt aliud ad aliud. Dico autem ut si est Callias ratio in numeris ignis, aquae, terrae et aeris et autosanthropos, sive numerus quis existens, sive non, tamen est ratio in numeris quorumdam et non numerus; et non erit quis numerus praeter ea.

εἰ δ᾽ ὅτι λόγοι ἀριθμῶν τἀνταῦθα, οἷον ἡ συμφωνία, δῆλον ὅτι ἐστὶν ἕν γέ τι ὧν εἰσι λόγοι. εἰ δή {15} τι τοῦτο, ἡ ὕλη, φανερὸν ὅτι καὶ αὐτοὶ οἱ ἀριθμοὶ λόγοι τινὲς ἔσονται ἑτέρου πρὸς ἕτερον. λέγω δ᾽ οἷον, εἰ ἔστιν ὁ Καλλίας λόγος ἐν ἀριθμοῖς πυρὸς καὶ γῆς καὶ ὕδατος καὶ ἀέρος, καὶ ἄλλων τινῶν ὑποκειμένων ἔσται καὶ ἡ ἰδέα ἀριθμός· καὶ αὐτοάνθρωπος, εἴτ᾽ ἀριθμός τις ὢν εἴτε μή, ὅμως ἔσται λόγος {20} ἐν ἀριθμοῖς τινῶν καὶ οὐκ ἀριθμός, οὐδ᾽ ἔσται τις διὰ ταῦτα ἀριθμός.

But if it is because the things here are ratios of numbers, like a harmony, then clearly there will be one kind of thing of which they are the ratios. And if this is matter, evidently the numbers themselves will be certain ratios of one thing to something else. I mean that, if Callias is a numerical ratio of fire, water, earth, and air, his idea will also be a ratio of certain things, and man-in-himself, whether it be a number or not, will still be a numerical ratio of certain things and not just a number. Nor will it be any number besides these.

991b22 Amplius ex multis numeris fit unus numerus: ex speciebus autem una species qualiter vel quomodo? [244]

ἔτι ἐκ πολλῶν ἀριθμῶν εἷς ἀριθμὸς γίγνεται, ἐξ εἰδῶν δὲ ἓν εἶδος πῶς;

Again, one number will come from many numbers, but how or in what way can one form come from many forms?

991b23 Sed si nec ex eis, sed ex unis, ut in millenario, quomodo se habent unitates? Sive enim eiusdem speciei, multa inconvenientia accidunt, sive non eiusdem speciei. Nec enim eaedem sibi sunt invicem, nec aliae omnes omnibus. [245]

εἰ δὲ μὴ ἐξ αὐτῶν ἀλλ᾽ ἐκ τῶν ἐν τῷ ἀριθμῷ, οἷον ἐν τῇ μυριάδι, πῶς ἔχουσιν αἱ μονάδες; εἴτε γὰρ ὁμοειδεῖς, πολλὰ συμβήσεται ἄτοπα, εἴτε μὴ ὁμοειδεῖς, {25} μήτε αὐταὶ ἀλλήλαις μήτε αἱ ἄλλαι πᾶσαι πάσαις·

But if one number is not produced from them but from the units which they contain, as the units in the number ten thousand, how are the units related? For if they are specifically the same, many absurdities will follow; and if they are not, neither will they be the same as one another nor all the others the same as all.

991b26 Quomodo namque different impassibiles existentes? Nec enim rationabilia haec, nec intelligentiae confessa. [247]

τίνι γὰρ διοίσουσιν ἀπαθεῖς οὖσαι; οὔτε γὰρ εὔλογα ταῦτα οὔτε ὁμολογούμενα τῇ νοήσει.

For in what way will they differ, if they have no attributes? For these statements are neither reasonable nor in accord with our understanding.

991b27 Amplius autem aliud aliquod genus numeri facere est necesse, circa quod fit arithmetica. [248]

ἔτι δ᾽ ἀναγκαῖον ἕτερον γένος ἀριθμοῦ κατασκευάζειν περὶ ὃ ἡ ἀριθμητική,

Further, if the forms are numbers, it is necessary to set up some other genus of number: that with which arithmetic deals.

Et omnia intermedia dicta, ex quibus simpliciter, aut ex quibus sunt princi-

καὶ πάντα τὰ μεταξὺ λεγόμενα ὑπό τινων, ἃ πῶς ἢ ἐκ τίνων {30} ἐστὶν

And all the things that are said to be intermediate, from what things or what

piis, aut quale inter praesentia erunt et eas?

ἀρχῶν; ἢ διὰ τί μεταξὺ τῶν δεῦρό τ᾽ ἔσται καὶ αὐτῶν;

principles in an absolute sense will they come, or why will they be an intermediate class between the things at hand and those ideas?

991b31 Amplius autem unitates, quae sunt in dualitate, utraque est ex aliqua priori dualitate: quamvis impossibile. [250]

ἔτι αἱ μονάδες αἱ ἐν τῇ δυάδι ἑκατέρα ἔκ τινος προτέρας δυάδος· καίτοι ἀδύνατον.

Again, each of the units which are contained in the number two will come from a prior two. But this is impossible.

992a1 Amplius quare numerus ex his collectus est? [251]

ἔτι διὰ τί ἓν ὁ ἀριθμὸς συλλαμβανόμενος;

Further, why is a number something composed of these?

992a2 Amplius autem cum dictis, si sint differentes unitates, oportebit ita dicere, quemadmodum et quicumque elementa quatuor, aut duo dicunt. Et enim horum quilibet non commune dicit elementum, ut corpus, sed ignem et terram: sive sit corpus commune ipsum, sive non. Nunc autem dicimus quod uno existente quemadmodum igne aut aqua, similium partium. Si vero sic, non erunt substantiae numeri. Sed palam, quia si commune est aliquod unum ipsum, et hoc est principium: quare multipliciter dicitur ipsum unum, aliter est impossibile. [252]

ἔτι δὲ πρὸς τοῖς εἰρημένοις, εἴπερ εἰσὶν αἱ μονάδες διάφοροι, ἐχρῆν οὕτω λέγειν ὥσπερ καὶ ὅσοι τὰ στοιχεῖα τέτταρα ἢ δύο λέγουσιν· καὶ γὰρ τούτων ἕκαστος οὐ {5} τὸ κοινὸν λέγει στοιχεῖον, οἷον τὸ σῶμα, ἀλλὰ πῦρ καὶ γῆν, εἴτ᾽ ἔστι τι κοινόν, τὸ σῶμα, εἴτε μή. νῦν δὲ λέγεται ὡς ὄντος τοῦ ἑνὸς ὥσπερ πυρὸς ἢ ὕδατος ὁμοιομεροῦς· εἰ δ᾽ οὕτως, οὐκ ἔσονται οὐσίαι οἱ ἀριθμοί, ἀλλὰ δῆλον ὅτι, εἴπερ ἐστί τι ἓν αὐτὸ καὶ τοῦτό ἐστιν ἀρχή, πλεοναχῶς λέγεται τὸ ἕν· ἄλλως {10} γὰρ ἀδύνατον.

And, again, in addition to what has been said, if the units are different, it will be necessary to speak of them in the same way as do those who say that the elements are four or two. For none of them designates as an element what is common (namely, body), but fire and earth, whether body is something in common or not. But now we are speaking of the one as if it were one thing made up of like parts, as fire or water. But if this is the case, numbers will not be substances. Yet it is evident that, if the one itself is something common and a principle, then the one is used in different senses; otherwise, this will be impossible.

992a10 Volentes autem substantias ad principia reducere, longitudines quidem enim ponimus ex producto et brevi, et ex aliquo parvo et magno: et planum ex lato et arcto: corpus vero ex profundo et humili. [254]

βουλόμενοι δὲ τὰς οὐσίας ἀνάγειν εἰς τὰς ἀρχὰς μήκη μὲν τίθεμεν ἐκ βραχέος καὶ μακροῦ, ἔκ τινος μικροῦ καὶ μεγάλου, καὶ ἐπίπεδον ἐκ πλατέος καὶ στενοῦ, σῶμα δ᾽ ἐκ βαθέος καὶ ταπεινοῦ.

Now when we wish to reduce substances to their principles, we claim that lengths come from the long and short (that is, from a kind of great and small), and the plane from the wide and narrow, and body from the deep and shallow.

992a13 Attamen quomodo habebit aut planum lineam, aut solidum lineam et planum? Aliud enim est genus et latum et arctum et profundum et humile. Quemadmodum ergo nec numerus est in eis, quia multum et paucum ab his alterum, palam quia nec aliud nihil superiorum inerit inferioribus. At vero nec genus profundi latum. Erit enim planum aliquod corpus. [255]

καίτοι πῶς ἕξει ἢ τὸ ἐπίπεδον γραμμὴν ἢ τὸ στερεὸν γραμμὴν καὶ ἐπίπεδον; ἄλλο {15} γὰρ γένος τὸ πλατὺ καὶ στενὸν καὶ βαθὺ καὶ ταπεινόν· ὥσπερ οὖν οὐδ᾽ ἀριθμὸς ὑπάρχει ἐν αὐτοῖς, ὅτι τὸ πολὺ καὶ ὀλίγον ἕτερον τούτων, δῆλον ὅτι οὐδ᾽ ἄλλο οὐθὲν τῶν ἄνω ὑπάρξει τοῖς κάτω.

Yet how will a surface contain a line, or a solid a line or surface? For the wide and narrow is a different genus from the deep and shallow. Hence, just as number is not present in these, because the many and few differ from these, it is evident that no one of the other higher genera will be present in the lower. And the broad is not in the genus of the deep, for then the solid would be a kind of surface.

992a19 Amplius puncta ex quo existunt? Huic quidem generi et Plato oppugnabat tamquam existente geometrice dogmate, sed lineae principium vocabat. Hic autem multoties indivisibiles lineas posuit, quamvis necesse est aliquid horum esse. Quare ex qua ratione linea est, et punctum est. [257]

ἀλλὰ μὴν οὐδὲ γένος τὸ πλατὺ τοῦ βάθεος· ἦν γὰρ ἂν ἐπίπεδόν τι τὸ σῶμα. ἔτι αἱ στιγμαὶ ἐκ {20} τίνος ἐνυπάρξουσιν; τούτῳ μὲν οὖν τῷ γένει καὶ διεμάχετο Πλάτων ὡς ὄντι γεωμετρικῷ δόγματι, ἀλλ᾽ ἐκάλει ἀρχὴν γραμμῆς—τοῦτο δὲ πολλάκις ἐτίθει—τὰς ἀτόμους γραμμάς. καίτοι ἀνάγκη τούτων εἶναί τι πέρας· ὥστ᾽ ἐξ οὗ λόγου γραμμὴ ἔστι, καὶ στιγμὴ ἔστιν.

Further, from what will points derive being? Plato was opposed to this genus of objects as a geometrical fiction, but he called them the principle of a line. And he often holds that there are indivisible lines. Yet these must have some limit. Therefore, any argument that proves the existence of the line also proves the existence of the point.

239. Hic improbat opinionem Platonis de speciebus inquantum ponebat eas esse numeros. Et circa hoc duo facit.

Primo disputat contra ea quae posita sunt ab ipso de numeris.

Secundo contra ea quae posita sunt ab ipso de aliis mathematicis, ibi, *volentes autem substantias* et cetera.

Circa primum ponit sex rationes:

quarum prima talis est. Eorum quae sunt idem secundum substantiam, unum non est causa alterius: sed sensibilia secundum substantiam sunt numeri secundum Platonicos et Pythagoricos: si igitur species sunt etiam numeri, non poterunt species esse causae sensibilium.

240. Si autem dicatur quod alii numeri sunt species, et alii sunt sensibilia, sicut ad literam Plato ponebat: ut si dicamus quod hic numerus est homo, et ille alius numerus est Socrates et alius numerus est Callias, istud adhuc non videtur sufficere: quia secundum hoc sensibilia et species conveniunt in ratione numeri: et eorum, quae sunt idem secundum rationem, unum non videtur esse causa alterius: ergo species non erunt causae horum sensibilium.

241. Non iterum potest dici quod sunt causae; quia illi numeri, si sunt species, sunt sempiterni. Illa enim differentia non sufficit ad hoc quod quaedam ponantur causae aliorum; quia aliqua differunt per sempiternum et non sempiternum secundum esse suum absolute consideratum; sed per causam et causatum differunt secundum habitudinem unius ad alterum: ergo diversa numero non differunt per causam et causatum per hoc, quod quaedam sunt sempiterna, et quaedam non sempiterna.

242. Si autem dicatur quod haec sensibilia sunt quaedam *rationes*, idest proportiones numerorum, et per hunc modum numeri sunt causae horum sensibilium, sicut videmus in *symphoniis*, idest in musicis consonantiis, quia numeri dicuntur esse causae consonantiarum, inquantum proportiones numerales, quae applicantur sonis, consonantias reddunt: palam est quod oportebat praeter ipsos numeros in sensibilibus ponere aliquod unum secundum genus, cui applicantur proportiones numerales: ut scilicet eorum, quae sunt illius generis proportiones, sensibilia constituant; sicut praeter proportiones numerales in consonantiis inveniuntur soni.

Si autem illud, cui applicatur illa proportio numeralis in sensibilibus est materia, manifestum est quod oportebat dicere, quod ipsi numeri separati qui sunt species, sint proportiones alicuius unius, scilicet ad ali-

239. Here he destroys Plato's opinion about the forms inasmuch as Plato claimed that they are numbers. In regard to this he does two things.

First, he argues dialectically against Plato's opinion about numbers,

and second [254], against his opinion about the other objects of mathematics, at *now when we wish* (992a10).

In regard to the first part he gives six arguments.

The first (991b9) is this. In the case of things that are substantially the same, one thing is not the cause of another. But sensible things are substantially numbers, according to the Platonists and Pythagoreans. Therefore, if the forms themselves are numbers, they cannot be the cause of sensible things.

240. But if it is said that some numbers are forms and others are sensible things, as Plato literally held (as though we were to say that this number is man and another is Socrates and still another is Callias), even this would not seem to be sufficient. For, according to this view, the intelligible structure of number will be common both to sensible things and the forms. But in the case of things that have the same intelligible structure, one does not seem to be the cause of another. Therefore, the forms will not be the causes of sensible things.

241. Nor again can it be said that they are causes for the reason that, if those numbers are forms, they are eternal. For this difference—namely, that some things differ from others in virtue of being eternal and non-eternal in their own being considered absolutely—is not sufficient to explain why some things are held to be the causes of others. Indeed, things differ from each other as cause and effect rather because of the relationship which one has to the other. Therefore, things that differ numerically do not differ from each other as cause and effect because some are eternal and some are not.

242. Again, it is said that sensible things are certain *ratios* or proportions of numbers, and that numbers are the causes of these sensible things, as we also observe to be the case in *harmonies*, that is, in the combinations of musical notes. For numbers are said to be the causes of harmonies insofar as the numerical proportions applied to sounds yield harmonies. Now if the above is true, then just as in harmonies there are found to be sounds in addition to numerical proportions, in a similar way it was obviously necessary to posit in addition to the numbers in sensible things something generically one to which the numerical proportions are applied, so that the proportions of those things that belong to that one genus would constitute sensible things.

However, if that to which the numerical proportion in sensible things is applied is matter, evidently those separate numbers, which are forms, had to be termed proportions of some one thing to something else. For this particular

quod aliud. Oportet enim dicere quod hic homo, qui est Callias vel Socrates, est similis homini ideali qui dicitur *autosanthropos* idest per se homo. Si igitur Callias non est numerus tantum, sed magis est ratio quaedam vel proportio in numeris elementorum, scilicet ignis, terrae, aquae et aeris; et ipse homo idealis erit quaedam ratio vel proportio in numeris aliquorum; et non erit homo idealis numerus per suam substantiam.

Ex quo sequitur, quod nullus numerus erit *praeter ea*, id est praeter res numeratas. Si enim numerus specierum est maxime separatus, et ille non est separatus a rebus, sed est quaedam proportio rerum numeratarum, nunc nullus alius numerus erit separatus: quod est contra Platonicos.

243. Sequitur autem, quod homo idealis sit proportio aliquorum numeratorum, sive ponatur esse numerus, sive non: tam enim secundum ponentes substantias esse numeros, quam secundum naturales, qui numeros substantias esse non dicebant, oportet quod in rerum substantiis aliquae proportiones numerales inveniantur: quod patet praecipue ex opinione Empedoclis, qui ponebat unamquamque rerum sensibilium constitui per quamdam harmoniam et proportionem.

244. Deinde cum dicit *amplius ex* hic ponit secundam rationem, quae talis est. Ex multis numeris fit unus numerus. Si igitur species sunt numeri, ex multis speciebus fiet una species, quod est impossibile.

Nam si ex multis diversarum specierum aliquid unum in specie constituatur, hoc fit per mixtionem, in qua non salvantur species eorum quae miscentur, sicut ex quatuor elementis fit lapis.

Et iterum ex huiusmodi diversis secundum speciem non fit aliquod unum ratione specierum, quia ipsae species non coniunguntur ad aliquod unum constituendum, nisi secundum rationem individuorum, qui alterantur, ut possint permisceri: ipsae autem species numerorum binarii et ternarii simul coniunctae numerum constituunt quinarium, ita quod in quinario uterque numerus remanet et salvatur.

245. Sed quia ad hanc rationem posset responderi ex parte Platonis, quod ex multis numeris non fit unus numerus, sed quilibet numerus immediate constituitur ex unitatibus, ideo consequenter cum dicit *sed si nec* excludit etiam hanc responsionem. Si enim dicitur quod aliquis numerus maior, ut millenarius, non constituatur *ex eis*, scilicet ex duobus vel pluribus numeris minoribus, sed constituitur *ex unis*, idest ex unitatibus, remanebit quaestio quomodo se habent unitates adinvicem, ex

man, called Callias or Socrates, must be said to be similar to the ideal man, called *man-in-himself*, or humanity. Hence, if Callias is not merely a number, but is rather a kind of ratio or numerical proportion of the elements (that is, of fire, earth, water, and air), and if the ideal man-in-himself is a kind of ratio or numerical proportion of certain things, the ideal man will not be a number by reason of its own substance.

From this it follows that there will be no number *besides these*, that is, besides the things numbered. For if the number which constitutes the forms is separate in the highest degree, and if it is not separate from things but is a kind of proportion of numbered things, no other number will now be separate. This is opposed to Plato's view.

243. It also follows that the ideal man is a proportion of certain numbered things, whether it is held to be a number or not. For according to those who held that substances are numbers, and according to the philosophers of nature, who denied that numbers are substances, some numerical proportions must be found in the substances of things. This is most evident in the case of the opinion of Empedocles, who held that each one of these sensible things is composed of a certain harmony or proportion of the elements.

244. *Again, one number* (991b22). Here he gives the second argument which runs thus: one number is produced from many numbers. Therefore, if the forms are numbers, one form is produced from many forms. But this is impossible.

For if from many things that differ specifically something specifically one is produced, this comes about by mixture, in which the natures of the things mixed are not preserved (just as a stone is produced from the four elements).

Again, from things of this kind which differ specifically, one thing is not produced by reason of the forms, because the forms themselves are combined in such a way as to constitute a single thing only in accordance with the intelligible structure of individual things, which are altered in such a way that they can be mixed together. And when the forms themselves of the numbers two and three are combined, they give rise to the number five, so that each number remains and is retained in the number five.

245. But since someone could answer this argument, in support of Plato, by saying that one number does not come from many numbers, but each number is immediately constituted of units, Aristotle is therefore logical in rejecting this answer, at *but if one number* (991b23). For if it is said that some greater number, such as ten thousand, is not produced *from them* (namely, from twos or many smaller numbers), but *from the units* (or ones), this question will follow: how are the units of which numbers are composed

quibus numeri constituuntur? Aut enim oportet, quod omnes unitates sint conformes adinvicem, aut quod sint difformes adinvicem.

246. Sed primo modo sequuntur multa inconvenientia, et praecipue quantum ad ponentes species esse numeros; quia sequitur quod diversae species non differant secundum substantiam, sed solum secundum excessum unius speciei super aliam. Inconveniens etiam videtur, quod unitates nullo modo differant; et tamen sunt multae, cum diversitas multitudinem consequatur.

247. Si vero non sint conformes, hoc potest esse dupliciter.

Uno modo, quia unitates unius numeri sunt differentes ab unitatibus alterius numeri, sicut unitates binarii ab unitatibus ternarii; et tamen unitates unius et eiusdem numeri sibi invicem sunt conformes.

Alio modo ut unitates eiusdem numeri non sibi invicem, nec unitatibus alterius numeri conformes existant. Hanc divisionem significat, cum dicit, *nec eaedem sibi invicem*, idest quae ad eumdem numerum pertinent, *nec aliae omnes* et cetera, scilicet quae pertinent ad diversos numeros.

Quocumque autem modo ponatur difformitas inter unitates, videtur inconveniens. Nam omnis difformitas est per aliquam formam vel passionem; sicut videmus quod corpora difformia differunt calido et frigido, albo et nigro, et huiusmodi passionibus: unitates autem huiusmodi passionibus carent, cum sint impassibiles secundum Platonicos; ergo non poterit inter ea poni talis difformitas vel differentia, quae causatur ab aliqua passione. Et sic patet quod ea quae Plato ponit de speciebus et numeris, nec sunt *rationabilia*, sicut illa quae per certam rationem probantur, nec sunt *intelligentiae confessa*, sicut ea quae sunt per se nota, et solo intellectu certificantur, ut prima demonstrationis principia.

248. Deinde cum dicit *amplius autem* hic ponit tertiam rationem contra Platonem, quae talis est. Omnia mathematica, quae a Platone sunt dicta intermedia sensibilium et specierum, sunt ex numeris, aut simpliciter, sicut ex propriis principiis, aut sicut ex primis. Et hoc ideo dicit, quia secundum unam viam videtur quod numeri sint immediata principia aliorum mathematicorum; nam unum dicebant constituere punctum, binarium lineam, ternarium superficiem, quaternarium corpus. Secundum vero aliam viam videntur resolvi mathematica in numeros, sicut in prima principia et non in proxima. Nam corpora dicebant componi ex superficiebus, superficies ex lineis, lineas ex punctis, puncta autem ex unitatibus, quae constituunt numeros. Utroque

related to each other? For all units must either conform with each other or not.

246. But many absurd conclusions follow from the first alternative, especially for those who claim that the forms are numbers. For it will follow that different forms do not differ substantially but only insofar as one form surpasses another. It also seems absurd that units should differ in no way and yet be many, since difference is a result of multiplicity.

247. But if they do not conform, this can happen in two ways.

First, they can lack conformity because the units of one number differ from those of another number, as the units of the number two differ from those of the number three, although the units of one and the same number will conform with each other.

Second, they can lack conformity insofar as the units of one and the same number do not conform with each other or with the units of another number. He indicates this distinction when he says, *neither will they be the same as one another* (991b26), namely, the units which comprise the same number, *nor all the others the same as all*, namely, those which belong to different numbers.

Indeed, in whatever way there is held to be lack of conformity between units an absurdity is apparent. For every instance of non-conformity involves some form or attribute, just as we see that bodies which lack conformity differ insofar as they are hot and cold, white and black, or in terms of similar attributes. Now units lack qualities of this kind, because they have no qualities, according to Plato. Hence it will be impossible to hold that there is any non-conformity or difference between them of the kind caused by a quality. Thus it is evident that Plato's opinions about the forms and numbers are neither *reasonable* (for example, those proved by an apodictic argument) nor *in accord with our understanding* (for example, those things that are self-evident and verified by intellect alone, as the first principles of demonstration).

248. *Further, if the forms* (991b27). Here he gives the third argument against Plato, which runs thus. All objects of mathematics, which Plato affirmed to be midway between the forms and sensible substances, are derived unqualifiedly from numbers, either as proper principles, or as first principles. He says this because in one sense numbers seem to be the immediate principles of the other objects of mathematics. For the Platonists said that the number one constitutes the point, the number two the line, the number three surface, and the number four the solid. But in another sense the objects of mathematics seem to be reduced to numbers as first principles and not as proximate ones. For the Platonists said that solids are composed of surfaces, surfaces of lines, lines of points, and points of units, which

autem modo sequebatur numeros esse principia aliorum mathematicorum.

249. Sicut igitur alia mathematica erant media inter sensibilia et species, ita necessarium est facere aliquod genus numeri, quod sit aliud a numeris qui sunt species, et a numeris qui sunt substantia sensibilium:

et quod de huiusmodi numero sit arithmetica, sicut de proprio subiecto, quae est una mathematicarum, sicut geometria de magnitudinibus mathematicis.

Hoc autem ponere videtur superfluum esse. Nam nulla ratio poterit assignari quare sunt numeri medii *inter praesentia*, idest sensibilia *et eas* scilicet species, cum tam sensibilia quam species sint numeri.

250. Deinde cum dicit *amplius autem* hic ponit quartam rationem, quae talis est. Ea quae sunt in sensibilibus et in mathematicis sunt causata ex speciebus: si igitur aliqua dualitas in sensibilibus et in mathematicis invenitur, oportet quod utraque unitas huius posterioris dualitatis sit causata ex priori dualitate, quae est species dualitatis.

Et hoc est *impossibile*, scilicet quod unitas ex dualitate causetur. Hoc enim praecipue oportet dicere, si unitates unius numeri sint alterius speciei ab unitatibus alterius, quia tunc a specie ante illius numeri unitates, species sortientur. Et sic oportet quod unitates posterioris dualitatis sint causatae ex priori dualitate.

251. Deinde cum dicit *amplius quare* hic ponit quintam rationem, quae talis est. Multa non conveniunt ad unum constituendum, nisi propter aliquam causam, quae potest accipi vel extrinseca, sicut aliquod agens quod coniungit, vel intrinseca, sicut aliquod vinculum uniens. Vel si aliqua uniuntur per seipsa, oportet ut unum sit ut potentia, et aliud ut actus. Nullum autem horum potest dici in unitatibus *quare numerus* idest ex qua causa numerus erit quoddam comprehensum, idest congregatum ex pluribus unitatibus: quasi dicat: non erit hoc assignare.

252. Deinde cum dicit *amplius autem* hic ponit sextam rationem, quae talis est. Si numeri sunt species et substantiae rerum, oportet, sicut praemissum est, dicere vel quod unitates sint differentes, aut convenientes. Si autem differentes, sequitur quod unitas, inquantum unitas, non sit principium. Quod patet per similitudinem sumptam a naturalium positione. Naturales enim aliqui posuerunt quatuor corpora esse principia. Quamvis autem commune sit ipsis hoc quod est esse corpus, non tamen ponebant corpus commune esse principium, sed

constitute numbers. But in either way it followed that numbers are the principles of the other objects of mathematics.

249. Therefore, just as the other objects of mathematics constituted an intermediate genus between sensible substances and the forms, in a similar way it was necessary to devise some genus of number which is other than the numbers that constitute the forms and other than those that constitute the substance of sensible things.

And arithmetic, which is one of the mathematical sciences, evidently deals with this kind of number as its proper subject, just as geometry deals with mathematical extensions.

However, this position seems to be superfluous, for no reason can be given why number should be midway *between the things at hand*, or sensible things, *and those in the ideal world*, or the forms, since both sensible things and the forms are numbers.

250. *Again, each of the units* (991b31). Here he gives the fourth argument, which runs thus. Those things that exist in the sensible world and those which exist in the realm of mathematical entities are caused by the forms. Therefore, if some number two is found both in the sensible world and in the realm of the objects of mathematics, each unit of this subsequent two must be caused by a prior two, which is the form of two-ness.

But it is *impossible* that unity should be caused by duality. For it would be most necessary to say this if the units of one number were of a different species than those of another number, because then these units would acquire their species from a form which is prior to the units of that number. And thus the units of a subsequent two would have to be produced from a prior two.

251. *Further, why is* (992a1). Here he gives the fifth argument, which runs thus: many things combine so as to constitute one thing only by reason of some cause, which can be considered to be either extrinsic, as some agent which unites them, or intrinsic, as some unifying bond. Or if some things are united of themselves, one of them must be potential and another actual. However, in the case of units none of these reasons can be said to be the one reason *why a number* (that is, the cause by which a number) will be a certain combination, or collection of many units. That is to say: it will be impossible to give any reason for this.

252. *And, again, in addition* (992a2). Here he gives the sixth argument, which runs thus. If numbers are the forms and substances of things, it will be necessary to say, as has been stated before [245], either that units are different, or that they conform. But if they are different, it follows that unity as unity will not be a principle. This is clarified by a similar case drawn from the position of the natural philosophers. For some of these thinkers held that the four elemental bodies are principles. But even though being a body is common to these elements, these philosophers

magis ignem, terram, aquam et aerem, quae sunt corpora differentia. Unde, si unitates sint differentes, quamvis omnes conveniant in ratione unitatis, non tamen erit dicendum, quod ipsa unitas inquantum huiusmodi sit principium; quod est contra positionem Platonicorum. Nam nunc ab eis dicitur, quod unum sit principium, sicut primo de naturalibus dicitur quod ignis aut aqua aut aliquod corpus similium partium principium sit. Sed si hoc est verum quod conclusum est contra positionem Platonicorum, scilicet quod unum inquantum unum non sit principium et substantia rerum, sequeretur quod numeri non sunt rerum substantia. Numerus enim non ponitur esse rerum substantia, nisi inquantum constituitur ex unitatibus, quae dicuntur esse rerum substantiae. Quod iterum est contra positionem Platonicorum, quam nunc prosequitur, qua scilicet ponitur, quod numeri sint species.

253. Si autem dicas quod omnes unitates sunt indifferentes, sequitur *quod omne*, idest universum totum sit aliquid unum et idem, ex quo substantia rei cuiuslibet est ipsum unum, quod est commune indifferens. Et ulterius sequitur, quod idem illud sit unum principium omnium: quod est impossibile ratione ipsius rationis, quae de se est inopinabilis, ut scilicet sint omnia unum secundum rationem substantiae; tum quia includit contradictionem ex eo quod ponit unam esse substantiam rerum, et tamen ponit illud unum esse principium. Nam unum et idem non est sui ipsius principium: nisi forte dicatur quod unum multipliciter dicitur, ut distincto uno ponantur omnia esse unum genere, et non specie vel numero.

254. Volentes autem substantias hic disputat contra positionem Platonis quantum ad hoc quod posuit de magnitudinibus mathematicis.

Et primo ponit eius positionem.

Secundo obiicit contra ipsam, ibi, *attamen quomodo habebit* et cetera.

Dicit ergo primo, quod Platonici volentes rerum substantias reducere ad prima principia, cum ipsas magnitudines dicerent esse substantias rerum sensibilium, lineam, superficiem et corpus, istorum principia assignantes, putabant se rerum principia invenisse. Assignando autem magnitudinum principia, dicebant *longitudines*, idest lineas componi ex producto et brevi, eo quod principia rerum omnium ponebant esse contraria. Et quia linea est prima inter quantitates continuas, ei per prius attribuebant magnum et parvum, ut per hoc quod haec duo sunt principia lineae, sint etiam principia aliarum magnitudinum. Dicit autem *ex aliquo parvo et magno*, quia parvum et magnum etiam in speciebus ponebantur, ut dictum est, sed secundum quod per situm determinatur et quodammodo particulari ad genus ma-

did not maintain that a common body is a principle, but rather fire, earth, water, and air, which are different bodies. Therefore, if units are different, even though all have in common the intelligible constitution of unity, it will not be said that unity itself as such is a principle. This is contrary to the Platonists' position; for they now say that the unit is the principle of things, just as the natural philosophers say that fire or water or some body with like parts is the principle of things. But if our conclusion against the Platonists' theory is true—that unity as such is not the principle and substance of things—it will follow that numbers are not the substances of things. For number is held to be the substance of things only insofar as it is constituted of units, which are said to be the substances of things. This is also contrary to the Platonists' position which is now being examined, namely, that numbers are forms.

253. But if you say that all units are undifferentiated, it follows that *the whole*, that is, the entire universe, is a single entity, since the substance of each thing is the one itself, and this is something common and undifferentiated. Further, it follows that the same entity is the principle of all things. But this is impossible by reason of the notion involved, which is inconceivable in itself—namely, that all things should be one according to the aspect of substance. For this view contains a contradiction, since it claims that the one is the substance of all things, yet maintains that the one is a principle. For one and the same thing is not its own principle, unless, perhaps, it is said that "the one" is used in different senses, so that when the senses of the one are differentiated all things are said to be generically one and not numerically or specifically one.

254. *Now when we wish* (992a10). Here he argues against Plato's position with reference to his views about mathematical extensions.

First (992a10), he gives Plato's position;

second [255], he advances an argument against it, at *yet how will* (992a13).

He says, first, that the Platonists, wishing to reduce the substances of things to their first principles, when they say that continuous quantities themselves are the substances of sensible things, thought they had discovered the principles of things when they assigned line, surface, and solid as the principles of sensible things. But in giving the principles of continuous quantities they said that *lengths*, or lines, are composed of the long and short, because they held that contraries are the principles of all things. And since the line is the first of continuous quantities, they first attributed to it the great and small, for inasmuch as these two are the principles of the line, they are also the principles of other continuous quantities. He says *from a kind of great and small* because the great and small are also placed among the forms, as has been stated [217]. But insofar as they are

gnitudinum, constituunt primo lineam, et deinde alias magnitudines. *Planum* autem, idest superficiem eadem ratione dicebant componi ex lato et arcto, et corpus ex profundo et humili.

255. Deinde cum dicit *attamen quomodo* hic obiicit contra praedictam positionem duabus rationibus:

quarum prima talis est. Quorum principia sunt diversa, ipsa etiam sunt diversa; sed principia dictarum magnitudinum secundum praedictam positionem sunt diversa. Latum enim et arctum, quae ponuntur principia superficiei, sunt alterius generis quam profundum et humile, quae ponuntur principia corporis. Et similiter potest dici de longo et brevi quod differunt ab utroque; ergo etiam linea et superficies et corpus erunt adinvicem distincta. Quomodo ergo poterat dici quod superficies haberet in se lineam, et quod corpus habeat lineam et superficiem?

Et ad huius rationis confirmationem inducit simile de numero. Multum enim et paucum, quae simili ratione ponuntur principia rerum, sunt alterius generis a longo et brevi, lato et stricto, profundo et humili. Et ideo numerus non continetur in his magnitudinibus, sed est separatus per se. Unde et eadem ratione nec superius inter praedicta erit etiam in inferioribus, sicut linea non in superficie, nec superficies in corpore.

256. Sed quia posset dici, quod quaedam praedictorum contrariorum sunt genera aliorum, sicut quod longum esset lati genus, et latum genus profundi; hoc removet tali ratione. Sicut habent se principia adinvicem, et principiata: si igitur latum est genus profundi, et superficies erit genus corporis. Et ita corpus erit aliquod planum, idest aliqua species superficiei: quod patet esse falsum.

257. Deinde cum dicit *amplius puncta* hic ponit secundam rationem, quae sumitur ex punctis; circa quam Plato videtur dupliciter deliquisse.

Primo quidem, quia cum punctus sit terminus lineae, sicut linea superficiei, et superficies corporis; sicut posuit aliqua principia, ex quibus componuntur praedicta, ita debuit aliquid ponere ex quo existerent puncta; quod videtur praetermisisse.

258. Secundo, quia circa puncta videbatur diversimode sentire. Quandoque enim contendebat totam doctrinam geometricam de hoc genere existere, scilicet de punctis, inquantum scilicet puncta ponebat principia et substantiam omnium magnitudinum. Et hoc non solum implicite, sed etiam explicite punctum vocabat principium lineae, sic ipsum definiens. Multoties vero dicebat,

limited by position, and are thus particularized in the genus of continuous quantities, they constitute first the line and then other continuous quantities. And for the same reason they said that *surface* is composed of the wide and narrow, and body of the deep and shallow.

255. *Yet how will a surface* (992a13). Here he argues against the foregoing position by means of two arguments.

The first is as follows. Things whose principles are different are themselves different. But the principles of continuous quantities mentioned above are different, according to the foregoing position, for the wide and narrow, which are posited as the principles of surface, belong to a different genus than the deep and shallow, which are held to be the principles of body. The same thing can be said of the long and short, which differ from each of the above. Therefore, line, surface, and body all differ from each other. How then will one be able to say that a surface contains a line, and a body a line and a surface?

In confirmation of this argument he introduces a similar case involving number. For the many and few, which are held to be principles of things for a similar reason, belong to a different genus than the long and short, the wide and narrow, and the deep and shallow. Therefore, number is not contained in these continuous quantities but is *per se* separate. Hence, for the same reason, the higher of the above mentioned things will not be contained in the lower—for example, a line will not be contained in a surface or a surface in a body.

256. But because it could be said that certain of the foregoing contraries are the genera of the others—for example, that the long is the genus of the broad, and the broad the genus of the deep—he destroys this objection by the following argument. Things composed of principles are related to each other in the same way as their principles are. Therefore, if the broad is the genus of the deep, surface will also be the genus of body. Hence a solid will be a kind of plane—that is, a species of surface. This is clearly false.

257. *Further, from what will* (992a19). Here he gives the second argument, which involves points. In regard to this Plato seems to have made two errors.

First, Plato claimed that a point is the limit of a line, just as a line is the limit of a surface and a surface the limit of a body. Therefore, just as he posited certain principles of which the latter are composed, so too he should have posited some principle from which points derive their being. But he seems to have omitted this.

258. The second error is this. Plato seems to have held different opinions about points. For sometimes he maintained that the whole science of geometry treats this genus of things (namely, points), inasmuch as he held that points are the principles and substance of all continuous quantities. And he not only implied this but even explicitly stated that a point is the principle of a line, defining it

quod lineae indivisibiles essent principia linearum, et aliarum magnitudinum; et hoc genus esse, de quo sit geometria, scilicet lineae indivisibiles. Et tamen per hoc quod ponit ex lineis indivisibilibus componi omnes magnitudines, non evadit quin magnitudines componantur ex punctis, et quin puncta sint principia magnitudinum. Linearum enim indivisibilium necessarium esse aliquos terminos, qui non possunt esse nisi puncta. Unde ex qua ratione ponitur linea indivisibilis principium magnitudinum, ex eadem ratione et punctum principium magnitudinis ponitur.

in this way. But many times he said that indivisible lines are the principles of lines and other continuous quantities, and that this is the genus of things with which geometry deals (namely, indivisible lines). Yet by reason of the fact that he held that all continuous quantities are composed of indivisible lines, he did not avoid the consequence that continuous quantities are composed of points, and that points are the principles of continuous quantities. For indivisible lines must have some limits, and these can only be points. Hence, by whatever argument indivisible lines are held to be the principles of continuous quantities, by the same argument too the point is held to be the principle of continuous quantity.

LECTURE 17

The ideas are not principles

992a24 Omnino autem sapientia de manifestis causam inquirente hoc quidem praetermisimus. Nihil enim de causa dicimus unde principium est transmutationis. Horum autem substantiam dicere putantes ipsorum, alias quidem substantias dicimus esse. Quomodo vero illae substantiae horum, est supervacuus. Nam et participare, sicut prius diximus, nihil est. [259]

ὅλως δὲ ζητούσης τῆς σοφίας περὶ {25} τῶν φανερῶν τὸ αἴτιον, τοῦτο μὲν εἰάκαμεν (οὐθὲν γὰρ λέγομεν περὶ τῆς αἰτίας ὅθεν ἡ ἀρχὴ τῆς μεταβολῆς), τὴν δ᾽ οὐσίαν οἰόμενοι λέγειν αὐτῶν ἑτέρας μὲν οὐσίας εἶναί φαμεν, ὅπως δ᾽ ἐκεῖναι τούτων οὐσίαι, διὰ κενῆς λέγομεν· τὸ γὰρ μετέχειν, ὥσπερ καὶ πρότερον εἴπομεν, οὐθέν ἐστιν.

And, in general, even though wisdom investigates the causes of apparent things, we have neglected this study. For we say nothing about the cause from which motion originates. And while we think that we are stating the substance of these sensible things, we introduce other substances. But the way in which we explain how the latter are the substances of the former is empty talk, for to participate, as we have said before (991a20), signifies nothing.

Nec quam in scientiis videmus existens causa, propter quam omnis intellectus et omnis natura facit, nec hanc causam quam modo dicimus esse unum principiorum, nihil tangunt species. Sed facta est mathematica praesentibus philosophia dicentibus aliorum gratia ea oportere tractari.

οὐδὲ δὴ ὅπερ ταῖς {30} ἐπιστήμαις ὁρῶμεν ὂν αἴτιον, δι᾽ ὃ καὶ πᾶς νοῦς καὶ πᾶσα φύσις ποιεῖ, οὐδὲ ταύτης τῆς αἰτίας, ἥν φαμεν εἶναι μίαν τῶν ἀρχῶν, οὐθὲν ἅπτεται τὰ εἴδη, ἀλλὰ γέγονε τὰ μαθήματα τοῖς νῦν ἡ φιλοσοφία, φασκόντων ἄλλων χάριν αὐτὰ δεῖν πραγματεύεσθαι.

Moreover, that which we see to be the cause in the sciences—that by reason of which all intellect and all nature operates—on that cause which we say is one of the principles, the forms do not touch in any way. But mathematics has been turned into philosophy by present-day thinkers (1028b16), although they say that mathematics must be treated for the sake of other things.

992b1 Amplius autem substantiam subiectam ut materiam, magis mathematicam aliquis suscipiat, et magis praedicari et differentiam esse substantiae et materiei, ut magnum et parvum: sicut physiologi aiunt rarum et spissum primas subiecti dicentes esse differentias has. Haec autem superabundantiae sunt quaedam et defectio. [260]

ἔτι δὲ τὴν ὑποκειμένην οὐσίαν ὡς ὕλην μαθηματικωτέραν ἄν τις ὑπολάβοι, καὶ μᾶλλον κατηγορεῖσθαι καὶ διαφορὰν εἶναι τῆς οὐσίας καὶ τῆς ὕλης ἢ ὕλην, οἷον τὸ μέγα καὶ τὸ μικρόν, ὥσπερ καὶ οἱ φυσιολόγοι {5} φασὶ τὸ μανὸν καὶ τὸ πυκνόν, πρώτας τοῦ ὑποκειμένου φάσκοντες εἶναι διαφορὰς ταύτας· ταῦτα γάρ ἐστιν ὑπεροχή τις καὶ ἔλλειψις.

Further, one might suppose that the underlying substance which they consider as matter is too mathematical, and that it is rather a predicate and difference of substance and matter, like the great and small. This is just as the philosophers of nature speak of the rare and dense (985b10), which they say are the primary differences of the underlying subject, for these are a kind of excess and defect.

992b7 Et de motu. Si quidem haec erit motus, palam quia moventur species: sin autem, unde venit? Tota namque de natura aufertur perscrutatio. [261]

περί τε κινήσεως, εἰ μὲν ἔσται ταῦτα κίνησις, δῆλον ὅτι κινήσεται τὰ εἴδη· εἰ δὲ μή, πόθεν ἦλθεν; ὅλη γὰρ ἡ περὶ φύσεως ἀνήρηται σκέψις.

And with regard to motion, if these entities are motion, evidently the forms are moved; but if they are not, from what does motion come? For if it has no cause, the whole study of nature is destroyed.

992b9 Et quod videtur facile esse monstrare, quod unum omnia non sint. Ex positione enim omnia unum non fiant. Sed si aliquid unum siquis dicat omnia, et nec hoc si non dat genus universale esse. Hoc autem in quibusdam impossibile. [262]

ὅ τε δοκεῖ ῥάδιον {10} εἶναι, τὸ δεῖξαι ὅτι ἓν ἅπαντα, οὐ γίγνεται· τῇ γὰρ ἐκθέσει οὐ γίγνεται πάντα ἓν ἀλλ᾽ αὐτό τι ἕν, ἂν διδῷ τις πάντα· καὶ οὐδὲ τοῦτο, εἰ μὴ γένος δώσει τὸ καθόλου εἶναι· τοῦτο δ᾽ ἐν ἐνίοις ἀδύνατον.

And what seems easy to show is that all things are not one, for from their position all things do not become one. But if someone should assert that all things are some one thing, not even this is true unless one grants that the universal is a genus. In certain other cases this is impossible.

992b13 Nullam namque rationem habent, nec quae sunt post numeros longitudines, latitudines, solida: nec quae modo sunt

οὐθένα δ᾽ ἔχει λόγον οὐδὲ τὰ μετὰ τοὺς ἀριθμοὺς μήκη τε καὶ ἐπίπεδα καὶ στερεά, οὔτε ὅπως ἔστιν ἢ {15} ἔσται

For they do not have any theory about the lengths, widths, and solids which come after the numbers, either as to how they

aut futura sunt, nec si aliquam habent potestatem. Haec enim nec species possibile esse, non enim sunt numeri. Nec intermedia; sunt enim illa mathematica. Nec corruptibilia: sed rursum quartum videtur hoc aliquod genus. [264]

οὔτε τίνα ἔχει δύναμιν: ταῦτα γὰρ οὔτε εἴδη οἷόν τε εἶναι (οὐ γάρ εἰσιν ἀριθμοί) οὔτε τὰ μεταξύ (μαθηματικὰ γὰρ ἐκεῖνα) οὔτε τὰ φθαρτά, ἀλλὰ πάλιν τέταρτον ἄλλο φαίνεται τοῦτό τι γένος.

now exist or will exist, or what importance they have. For it is impossible that they should be forms (since they are not numbers), or intermediate things (for those are the objects of mathematics), or corruptible things. On the contrary, it seems that they form a fourth genus.

992b18 Et omnino existentium quaerere elementa, non dividentem multipliciter dicta, invenire impossibile est. [265]

ὅλως τε τὸ τῶν ὄντων ζητεῖν στοιχεῖα μὴ διελόντας, πολλαχῶς λεγομένων, ἀδύνατον εὑρεῖν,

And, in general, to look for the elements of existing things without distinguishing the different senses in which things are said to be makes it impossible to discover them.

Et aliter secundum hunc modum quaerentes ex quibus sunt elementis. Ex quibus enim facere aut pati, aut ipsum rectum non est accipere.

ἄλλως {20} τε καὶ τοῦτον τὸν τρόπον ζητοῦντας ἐξ οἵων ἐστὶ στοιχείων. ἐκ τίνων γὰρ τὸ ποιεῖν ἢ πάσχειν ἢ τὸ εὐθύ, οὐκ ἔστι δήπου λαβεῖν,

And their view is unsatisfactory in another way—namely, in the way in which they seek for the elements of which things are composed. For it is impossible to understand of what things action or passion or straightness is composed.

Sed siquidem substantiarum solum esse contingit, tunc quidem existentium omnium elementa quaerere aut putare habere, non est verum.

ἀλλ᾽ εἴπερ, τῶν οὐσιῶν μόνον ἐνδέχεται: ὥστε τὸ τῶν ὄντων ἁπάντων τὰ στοιχεῖα ἢ ζητεῖν ἢ οἴεσθαι ἔχειν οὐκ ἀληθές.

But if this is possible only in the case of substances, then to look for the elements of all existing things, or to think that we have found them, is a mistake.

992b24 Quomodo autem aliquis discet omnium elementa? Palam enim quia non est possibile praeexistere cognoscentem prius. Sicut enim geometrizare discentem, alia quidem oportet praescire, quorum autem scientia, et de quibus futuris est discere, non praenoscit, ita et in aliis. [268]

πῶς δ᾽ ἄν τις καὶ μάθοι τὰ τῶν πάντων στοιχεῖα; {25} δῆλον γὰρ ὡς οὐθὲν οἷόν τε προϋπάρχειν γνωρίζοντα πρότερον. ὥσπερ γὰρ τῷ γεωμετρεῖν μανθάνοντι ἄλλα μὲν ἐνδέχεται προειδέναι, ὧν δὲ ἡ ἐπιστήμη καὶ περὶ ὧν μέλλει μανθάνειν οὐθὲν προγιγνώσκει, οὕτω δὴ καὶ ἐπὶ τῶν ἄλλων,

But how will one acquire knowledge of the elements of all things? For it is clearly impossible to have prior knowledge of anything. For just as one acquiring knowledge of geometry must have a prior knowledge of other things, but not of the things that this science investigates and which he is to learn, so it is in the case of the other sciences.

Quare si qua est omnium scientia, et de quibus oportet, ut quidam aiunt, nihil utique hic praeexistit cognoscens.

ὥστ᾽ εἴ τις τῶν πάντων ἔστιν ἐπιστήμη, οἵαν δή τινές φασιν, {30} οὐθὲν ἂν προϋπάρχοι γνωρίζων οὗτος.

Hence, if there is a science of all things as some say (and there must be a science of these), the one learning this science does not have any prior knowledge of it.

Quamvis sit omnis disciplina per praecognita, aut omnia, aut quaedam, aut per demonstrationem, aut per definitiones.

καίτοι πᾶσα μάθησις διὰ προγιγνωσκομένων ἢ πάντων ἢ τινῶν ἐστί, καὶ ἡ δι᾽ ἀποδείξεως <καὶ> ἡ δι᾽ ὁρισμῶν

But all learning proceeds from things previously known, either all or some of them, whether the learning be by demonstration or by definitions.

Oportet enim ex quibus est definitio praescire et esse nota: similiter autem et quae per inductionem.

(δεῖ γὰρ ἐξ ὧν ὁ ὁρισμὸς προειδέναι καὶ εἶναι γνώριμα): ὁμοίως δὲ καὶ ἡ δι᾽ ἐπαγωγῆς.

For the parts of which definitions are composed must already be known beforehand and be evident. The same thing is true in the case of things discovered by induction.

992b33 Sed si est existens connaturalis, mirum quomodo obliviscimur habentes potissimam scientiarum. [269]

ἀλλὰ μὴν εἰ καὶ τυγχάνοι σύμφυτος οὖσα, {993a1} θαυμαστὸν πῶς λανθάνομεν ἔχοντες τὴν κρατίστην τῶν ἐπιστημῶν.

But if this science were connatural, it is a wonder how we could be unconscious of having the most important of the sciences.

993a2 Amplius autem quomodo aliquis cognoscit ex quibus est, et quomodo est manifestum? Etenim hoc habet dubitationem. Ambiget enim aliquis quemad-

ἔτι πῶς τις γνωριεῖ ἐκ τίνων ἐστί, καὶ πῶς ἔσται δῆλον; καὶ γὰρ τοῦτ᾽ ἔχει ἀπορίαν: ἀμφισβητήσειε γὰρ ἄν τις ὥσπερ καὶ περὶ ἐνίας {5} συλλαβάς: οἱ μὲν γὰρ

Again, how is anyone to know the elements of which things are composed, and how is this to be made evident? For this also presents a difficulty, because one

modum et circa quasdam syllabas. Hi namque SMA ex S, M et A dicunt: alii vero quemdam sonum alium dicunt esse et cognitorum nullum. [270]

τὸ ζα ἐκ τοῦ ς καὶ δ καὶ α φασὶν εἶναι, οἱ δέ τινες ἕτερον φθόγγον φασὶν εἶναι καὶ οὐθένα τῶν γνωρίμων.

might argue in the same way as one does about certain syllables. For some say that SMA is made up of S, M, and A, whereas others say that it is a totally different sound and not any of those which are known to us.

993a7 Amplius autem et quorum est sensus, haec quomodo aliquis non habens sensum cognoscet? Quamvis oporteat, si omnium sunt elementa, ex quibus, quemadmodum compositae sunt voces ex elementis propriis. [271]

ἔτι δὲ ὧν ἐστιν αἴσθησις, ταῦτα πῶς ἄν τις μὴ ἔχων τὴν αἴσθησιν γνοίη; καίτοι ἔδει, εἴγε πάντων ταὐτὰ στοιχεῖά ἐστιν ἐξ ὧν, ὥσπερ αἱ σύνθετοι φωναί εἰσιν ἐκ τῶν {10} οἰκείων στοιχείων.

Again, how could one know the things of which a sense is cognizant without having that sense? Yet this will be necessary if sensible things are the elements of which all things are composed, just as spoken words are composed of their proper elements.

993a11 Quoniam ergo dictas causas in *Physicis* quaerere visi sunt omnes et extra has nullam habemus dicere, palam ex prius dictis. Sed obscure haec et modo quodam omnes prius dictae sunt, modo vero quodam nullatenus. [272]

ὅτι μὲν οὖν τὰς εἰρημένας ἐν τοῖς φυσικοῖς αἰτίας ζητεῖν ἐοίκασι πάντες, καὶ τούτων ἐκτὸς οὐδεμίαν ἔχοιμεν ἄν εἰπεῖν, δῆλον καὶ ἐκ τῶν πρότερον εἰρημένων· ἀλλ᾽ ἀμυδρῶς ταύτας, καὶ τρόπον μέν τινα πᾶσαι πρότερον εἴρηνται τρόπον {15} δέ τινα οὐδαμῶς.

From the foregoing, then, it is evident that they all seem to seek the causes mentioned in the *Physics*, and that we cannot state any other in addition to these. But they understood these obscurely, and while in one sense all causes have been mentioned before, in another sense they have not been mentioned at all.

Balbutiens vero visa prima philosophia de omnibus, velut nova existens circa principium et primum. Quoniam et Empedocles ossi dicit inesse rationes: hoc autem est quod quid erat esse et substantia rei.

ψελλιζομένη γὰρ ἔοικεν ἡ πρώτη φιλοσοφία περὶ πάντων, ἅτε νέα τε καὶ κατ᾽ ἀρχὰς οὖσα [καὶ τὸ πρῶτον], ἐπεὶ καὶ Ἐμπεδοκλῆς ὀστοῦν τῷ λόγῳ φησὶν εἶναι, τοῦτο δ᾽ ἐστὶ τὸ τί ἦν εἶναι καὶ ἡ οὐσία τοῦ πράγματες.

Indeed, the earliest philosophy seems to speak in a faltering way about all subjects inasmuch as it was new as regards principles and the first of its kind. For even Empedocles says that ratios are present in bone, and that this is the quiddity or substance of a thing.

At vero similiter necessarium et carnis et aliorum singulorum esse rationem, aut nihil. Propter hoc enim et caro et os est et aliorum unumquodque et non propter materiam, quam ille dicit ignem, et terram, et aerem, et aquam. Sed hoc alio dicente quidem similiter dixit ex necessitate, manifeste vero non dixit. De talibus quidem igitur prius est ostensum. Quaecumque vero de ipsis his dubitabit aliquis, resumamus iterum: nam forsan ex ipsis aliquid investigabimus ad posteriores dubitationes.

ἀλλὰ μὴν ὁμοίως ἀναγκαῖον καὶ σάρκας καὶ τῶν ἄλλων {20} ἕκαστον εἶναι τὸν λόγον, ἢ μηδὲ ἕν· διὰ τοῦτο γὰρ καὶ σὰρξ καὶ ὀστοῦν ἔσται καὶ τῶν ἄλλων ἕκαστον καὶ οὐ διὰ τὴν ὕλην, ἣν ἐκεῖνος λέγει, πῦρ καὶ γῆν καὶ ὕδωρ καὶ ἀέρα. ἀλλὰ ταῦτα ἄλλου μὲν λέγοντος συνέφησεν ἄν ἐξ ἀνάγκης, σαφῶς δὲ οὐκ εἴρηκεν. περὶ μὲν οὖν τούτων δεδήλωται καὶ {25} πρότερον· ὅσα δὲ περὶ τῶν αὐτῶν τούτων ἀπορήσειεν ἄν τις, {26} ἐπανέλθωμεν πάλιν· τάχα γὰρ ἄν ἐξ αὐτῶν εὐπορήσαιμέν τι πρὸς τὰς ὕστερον ἀπορίας.

But if this is true, there must likewise be a ratio of flesh and of every other thing, or of nothing. For it is because of this that flesh and bone and every other thing exists, and not because of their matter, which he says is fire, earth, air, and water. But if someone else had said this, he would have been forced to agree to the same thing. But he has not said this. Such things as these, then, have been explained before. So let us return again to whatever problems one might raise about the same subject, for perhaps in the light of these we shall be able to make some investigation into subsequent problems.

---

259. Hic improbat positionem Platonis quantum ad hoc, quod ponebat de rerum principiis.

Et primo quantum ad hoc quod ponebat principia essendi.

Secundo quantum ad hoc quod ponebat principia cognoscendi, ibi, *quomodo autem aliquis* et cetera.

Circa primum ponit sex rationes;

quarum prima sumitur ex hoc, quod genera causarum praetermittebat. Unde dicit quod *omnino sapientia*,

259. Here Aristotle destroys Plato's opinion about the principles of things.

First, he destroys Plato's opinion about principles of being;

second [268], his opinion about principles of knowledge, at *but how will one* (992b24).

In regard to the first part he gives six arguments.

The first is based on the fact that Plato neglected to deal with the genera of causes. Thus he says that *in general, wis-*

scilicet philosophia habet inquirere causas *de manifestis*, idest de his, quae sensui apparent. Ex hoc enim homines inceperunt philosophari, quod causas inquisiverunt, ut in prooemio dictum est. Platonici autem, quibus se connumerat, rerum principia praetermiserunt, quia nihil dixerunt de causa efficiente, quae est principium transmutationis. Causam vero formalem putaverunt se assignare ponentes ideas.

Sed, dum ipsi putaverunt se dicere substantiam eorum, scilicet sensibilium, dixerunt quasdam esse alias substantias separatas ab istis diversas. Modus autem, quo assignabant illa separata esse substantias horum sensibilium, *est supervacuus*, idest efficaciam non habens nec veritatem. Dicebant enim quod species sunt substantiae eorum inquantum ab istis participantur. Sed hoc quod de participatione dicebant, nihil est, sicut ex supradictis patet.

Item species, quas ipsi ponebant, non tangunt causam finalem, quod tamen videmus in aliquibus scientiis, quae demonstrant per causam finalem, et propter quam causam omne agens per intellectum et agens per naturam operatur, ut secundo *Physicorum* ostensum est.

Et sicut ponendo species non tangunt causam quae dicitur finis, ita nec causam quae dicitur principium, scilicet efficientem, quae fini quasi opponitur.

Sed Platonicis praetermittentibus huiusmodi causas facta sunt naturalia, ac si essent mathematica sine motu, dum principium et finem motus praetermittebant. Unde et dicebant quod mathematica debent tractari non solum propter seipsa, sed aliorum gratia, idest naturalium, inquantum passiones mathematicorum sensibilibus attribuebant.

260. Deinde cum dicit *amplius autem* hic ponit secundam rationem, quae talis est. Illud, quod ponitur tamquam rei materia, magis est substantia rei et praedicabile de re, quam illud quod est separatum a re: sed species est separata a rebus sensibilibus: ergo secundum Platonicorum opinionem magis aliquid suscipiet substantiam subiectam, ut materiam, esse substantiam mathematicorum quam speciem separatam. Magis etiam suscipiet eam praedicari de re sensibili quam speciem praedictam. Platonici enim ponebant magnum et parvum esse differentiam substantiae et materiei. Haec enim duo principia ponebant ex parte materiae, sicut naturales ponentes rarum et densum esse primas differentias *subiecti* idest materiae, per quas scilicet materia transmutabatur, dicentes eas quodammodo scilicet

dom, or philosophy, has as its aim to investigate the causes *of apparent things*, that is, things apparent to the senses. For men began to philosophize because they sought for the causes of things, as was stated in the prologue [53]. But the Platonists, among whom he includes himself, neglected the principles of things, because they said nothing about the efficient cause, which is the source of change. And by positing the ideas they thought they had given the formal cause of things.

But while they thought that they were speaking of the substance of sensible things, they posited the existence of certain other separate substances which differ from these. However, the way in which they assigned these separate substances as the substances of sensible things *is empty talk*, that is, it proves nothing and is not true. For they said that the forms are the substances of sensible things inasmuch as they are participated in by sensible things. But what they said about participation is meaningless, as is clear from what was said above [225].

Furthermore, the forms which they posited have no connection with the final cause, although we see that this is a cause in certain sciences which demonstrate by means of the final cause, and that it is by reason of this cause that every intellectual agent and every natural one operates, as has been shown in the *Physics* 2.

And just as they do not touch on that cause which is called an end when they postulate the existence of the forms [169], neither do they treat of that cause which is called the source of motion (namely, the efficient cause, which is like the opposite of the final cause).

But the Platonists, by omitting causes of this kind (since they did omit a starting-point and end of motion), have dealt with natural things as if they were objects of mathematics, which lack motion. Hence they said that the objects of mathematics should be studied not only for themselves but for the sake of other things (namely, natural bodies), inasmuch as they attributed the properties of the objects of mathematics to sensible bodies.

260. *Further, one might* (992b1). Here he gives the second argument, which runs thus: that which is posited as the matter of a thing is the substance of a thing, and is predicable of a thing to a greater degree than something which exists apart from it. But a form exists apart from sensible things. Therefore, according to the opinion of the Platonists, one might suppose that the underlying substance as matter is the substance of the objects of mathematics rather than a separate form. Furthermore, he admits that it is predicated of a sensible thing rather than the above form. For the Platonists held that the great and small is a difference of substance or matter, for they referred these two principles to matter just as the philosophers of nature [115] held that rarity and density are the primary differences of *the underlying subject*, or matter, by which matter is

magnum et parvum. Quod ex hoc patet, quia rarum et densum sunt quaedam superabundantia et defectio. Spissum enim est quod habet multum de materia sub eisdem dimensionibus. Rarum quod parum. Et tamen Platonici substantiam rerum sensibilium magis dicebant species quam mathematica, et magis praedicari.

261. Deinde cum dicit *et de motu* hic ponit tertiam rationem, quae talis est. Si ea, quae sunt in sensibilibus, causantur a speciebus separatis, necessarium est dicere quod sit in speciebus idea motus, aut non. Si est ibi aliqua species et idea motus, etiam constat quod non potest esse motus sine eo quod movetur, necesse erit quod species moveantur; quod est contra Platonicorum opinionem, qui ponebant species immobiles.

Si autem non sit idea motus, ea autem quae sunt in sensibilibus causantur ab ideis, non erit assignare causam, unde motus veniat ad ista sensibilia. Et sic aufertur tota perscrutatio scientiae naturalis, quae inquirit de rebus mobilibus.

262. Deinde cum dicit *et quod* hic ponit quartam rationem, quae talis est. Si unum esset substantia rerum omnium sicut Platonici posuerunt, oporteret dicere quod omnia sint unum, sicut et naturales, qui ponebant substantiam omnium esse aquam, et sic de elementis aliis. Sed facile est monstrare, quod omnia non sunt unum: ergo positio quae ponit substantiam omnium esse unum, est improbabilis.

263. Si autem aliquis dicat quod ex positione Platonis non sequitur quod omnia sint unum simpliciter, sed aliquod unum, sicut dicimus aliqua esse unum secundum genus, vel secundum speciem; si quis velit dicere sic omnia esse unum, nec hoc etiam poterit sustineri, nisi hoc quod dico unum, sit genus, vel universale omnium. Per hunc enim modum possemus dicere omnia esse unum specialiter, sicut dicimus hominem et asinum esse animal substantialiter. Hoc autem quibusdam videtur impossibile, scilicet quod sit unum genus omnium; quia oporteret, quod differentia divisiva huius generis non esset una, ut in tertio dicetur, ergo nullo modo potest poni quod substantia rerum omnium sit unum.

264. Deinde cum dicit **nullam namque** hic ponit quintam rationem, quae talis est. Plato ponebat post numeros, longitudines et latitudines et soliditates esse substantias rerum sensibilium, ex quibus scilicet corpora componerentur. Hoc autem secundum Platonis positionem nullam rationem habere videtur, quare debeant poni nec in praesenti, nec in futuro. Nec etiam videtur

changed, and spoke of them in a sense as the great and small. This is clear from the fact that rarity and density are a kind of excess and defect. For the dense is what contains a great deal of matter under the same dimensions, and the rare is what contains very little matter. Yet the Platonists said that the forms are the substance of sensible things rather than the objects of mathematics, and that they are predicable of them to a greater degree.

261. *And with regard* (992b7). Here he gives the third argument, which runs thus. If those attributes which exist in sensible things are caused by separate forms, it is necessary to say either that there is an idea of motion among the forms or that there is not. If there is a form or idea of motion among the forms, and there cannot be motion without something that is moved, it also follows that the forms must be moved. But this is opposed to the Platonists' opinion, for they claimed that the forms are immobile.

On the other hand, if there is no idea of motion, and these attributes which exist in sensible things are caused by the ideas, it will be impossible to assign a cause for the motion which occurs in sensible things. Thus the entire investigation of natural philosophy, which studies mobile things, will be destroyed.

262. *And what seems easy* (992b9). Then he gives the fourth argument, which runs thus. If unity were the substance of all things, as the Platonists assumed, it would be necessary to say that all things are one, just as the philosophers of nature also did in claiming that the substance of all things is water, and so on for the other elements. But it is easy to show that all things are not one. Hence the position that unity is the substance of all things is not held in high repute.

263. But let us assume that someone might say that it does not follow, from Plato's position, that all things are one in an unqualified sense but in a qualified sense, just as we say that some things are one generically or specifically. And if someone wished to say that all things are one in this way, even this could be held only if what I call the one were a genus or universal predicate of all things. For then we could say that all things are one specifically, just as we say that both a man and an ass are animal substantially. But in certain cases it seems impossible that there should be one genus of all things, because the difference dividing this genus would necessarily not be one, as will be said in book 3 [432]. Therefore, in no way can it be held that the substance of all things is one.

264. *For they do not have* (992b13). Here he gives the fifth argument, which runs thus. Plato placed lengths, widths, and solids after numbers as the substances of sensible things, namely, as that of which they are composed. But, according to Plato's position, there seems to be no reason why they should be held to exist either now or in the future. Nor does this notion seem to have any efficacy

habere aliquam potestatem ad hoc quod sint sensibilium causae. Per praesentia enim hic oportet intelligi immobilia, quia semper eodem modo se habent. Per *futura* autem corruptibilia et generabilia, quae esse habent post non esse.

Quod sic patet. Plato enim ponebat tria genera rerum; scilicet sensibilia, et species, et mathematica quae media sunt. Huiusmodi autem lineae et superficies, ex quibus componuntur corpora sensibilia, non est possibile esse species, quia species sunt numeri essentialiter. Huiusmodi autem sunt post numeros. Nec iterum potest dici quod sunt intermedia inter species et sensibilia. Huiusmodi enim sunt entia mathematica, et a sensibilibus separata: quod non potest dici de illis lineis et superficiebus ex quibus corpora sensibilia componuntur. Nec iterum possunt esse sensibilia. Nam sensibilia sunt corruptibilia; huiusmodi autem incorruptibilia sunt, ut infra probabitur in tertio. Ergo vel ista nihil sunt, vel sunt quartum aliquod genus entium, quod Plato praetermisit.

265. Deinde cum dicit *et omnino* hic ponit sextam rationem, quae talis est. Impossibile est invenire principia alicuius multipliciter dicti, nisi multiplicitas dividatur. Ea enim quae solo nomine convenientia sunt et differunt ratione, non possunt habere principia communia, quia sic haberent rationem eamdem, cum rei cuiuscumque ratio ex suis principiis sumatur. Distincta autem principia his, quibus solum nomen commune est, assignari impossibile est, nisi his quorum principia sunt assignanda adinvicem diversis. Cum igitur ens multipliciter dicatur et non univoce de substantia et aliis generibus, inconvenienter assignat Plato principia existentium, non dividendo abinvicem entia.

266. Sed quia aliquis posset aliquibus ratione differentibus, quibus nomen commune est, principia assignare, singulis propria principia coaptando, sine hoc quod nominis communis multiplicitatem distingueret, hoc etiam Platonici non fecerunt. Unde *et aliter*, idest alia ratione inconvenienter rerum principia assignaverunt quaerentes ex quibus elementis sunt entia, secundum hunc modum, quo quaesierunt, ut scilicet non omnibus entibus sufficientia principia assignarent. Non enim ex eorum dictis est accipere ex quibus principiis est agere aut pati, aut curvum aut rectum, aut alia huiusmodi accidentia. Assignabant enim solum principia substantiarum, accidentia praetermittentes.

267. Sed si aliquis defendendo Platonem dicere vellet, quod tunc contingit omnium entium elementa esse

to establish them as the causes of sensible things. For things that exist now must mean immobile things (because these always exist in the same way), whereas things that *will exist* must mean those which are capable of generation and corruption, which acquire being after non-being.

This becomes clear in this way. Plato posited three genera of things: sensible things, the forms, and the objects of mathematics (which are an intermediate genus). But such lines and surfaces as those of which sensible bodies are composed cannot be forms, for the forms are essentially numbers, whereas these things come after numbers. Nor can such lines and surfaces be said to be an intermediate genus between the forms and sensible things. For the things in this intermediate genus are the objects of mathematics, and exist apart from sensible things, but this cannot be said of the lines and surfaces of which sensible bodies are composed. Nor again can such lines and surfaces be sensible things, for the latter are corruptible, but these lines and surfaces are incorruptible, as will be proved below in book 3 [466]. Therefore, either these things are nothing at all or they constitute a fourth genus of things, which Plato omitted.

265. *And, in general* (992b18). Here he gives the sixth argument, which runs thus. It is impossible to discover the principles of anything that is spoken of in many senses, unless these many senses are distinguished. Now those things that agree in name only and differ in their intelligible structure cannot have common principles, otherwise they would have the same intelligible structure, since the intelligible structure of a thing is derived from its own principles. But it is impossible to assign distinct principles for those things that have only the name in common, unless it be those whose principles must be indicated to differ from each other. Therefore, since being is predicated both of substance and of the other genera in different senses and not in the same sense, Plato assigned inadequate principles for things by failing to distinguish beings from each other.

266. But, since someone could assign principles to things that differ in their intelligible structure and have a common name by adjusting proper principles to each without distinguishing the many senses of the common name, and since the Platonists have not done this, then *in another way*, or by another argument, they assigned inadequate principles to things when they looked for the elements of which things are made—namely, in the way in which they sought for them, inasmuch as they did not assign principles which are sufficient for all things. For from their statements it is impossible to understand the principles of which either action and passion or curvature and straightness (or other such accidents) are composed. For they indicated only the principles of substances and neglected accidents.

267. But if in defense of Plato someone wished to say that it is possible for the elements of all things to have been

acquisita aut inventa, quando contingit solarum substantiarum principia habita esse vel inventa, hoc opinari non est verum. Nam licet principia substantiarum etiam quodammodo sint principia accidentium, tamen accidentia propria principia habent. Nec sunt omnibus modis omnium generum eadem principia, ut ostendetur infra, undecimo vel duodecimo huius.

268. Deinde cum dicit *quomodo autem* disputat contra Platonem quantum ad hoc, quod ponebat ideas esse principia scientiae in nobis.

Et ponit quatuor rationes: quarum prima est. Si ex ipsis ideis scientia in nobis causatur, non continget addiscere rerum principia. Constat autem quod addiscimus. Ergo ex ipsis ideis scientia non causatur in nobis.

Quod autem non contingeret aliquid addiscere sic probat. Nullus enim praecognoscit illud quod addiscere debet; sicut geometra, etsi praecognoscat alia quae sunt necessaria ad demonstrandum, tamen ea quae debet addiscere non debet praecognoscere. Et similiter est in aliis scientiis.

Sed si ideae sunt causa scientiae in nobis, oportet quod omnium scientiam habeant, quia ideae sunt rationes omnium scibilium: ergo non possumus aliquid addiscere, nisi aliquis dicatur addiscere illud quod prius praecognovit.

Unde si ponatur quod aliquis addiscat, oportet quod non praeexistat cognoscens illa quae addiscit, sed quaedam alia cum quibus fiat disciplinatus, idest addiscens praecognita *omnia*, idest universalia *aut quaedam*, idest singularia. Universalia quidem, sicut in his quae addiscuntur per demonstrationem et definitionem; nam oportet sicut in demonstrationibus, ita in definitionibus esse praecognita ea, ex quibus definitiones fiunt, quae sunt universalia; singularia vero oportet esse praecognita in his quae discuntur per inductionem.

269. Deinde cum dicit *sed si est* hic ponit secundam rationem, quae talis est. Si ideae sunt causa scientiae, oportet nostram scientiam esse nobis connaturalem. Sensibilia enim per haec naturam propriam adipiscuntur, quia ideas participant secundum Platonicos. Sed potissima disciplina sive cognitio est illa quae est nobis connaturalis, nec eius possumus oblivisci, sicut patet in cognitione primorum principiorum demonstrationis, quae nullus ignorat: ergo nullo modo possumus omnium scientiam ab ideis in nobis causatam oblivisci.

acquired or discovered at the moment when the principles of substances alone happen to have been acquired or discovered, this opinion would not be true. For even if the principles of substances are also in a sense the principles of accidents, nevertheless accidents have their own principles. Nor are the principles of all genera the same in all respects, as will be shown below in book 11 [2173] and book 12 [2455] of this work.

268. *But how will one* (992b24). Here he argues dialectically against Plato's position that the ideas are the principles of our scientific knowledge.

He gives four arguments, of which the first is this. If our scientific knowledge is caused by the ideas themselves, it is impossible for us to acquire knowledge of the principles of things. But it is evident that we do acquire knowledge. Therefore, our knowledge is not caused by the ideas themselves.

That it would be impossible to acquire knowledge of anything, he proves thus. No one has any prior knowledge of that object of which he ought to acquire knowledge. For example, even though in the case of geometry one has prior knowledge of other things that are necessary for demonstration, nevertheless the objects of which he ought to acquire knowledge he must not know beforehand. The same thing is also true in the case of the other sciences.

But if the ideas are the cause of our knowledge, men must have knowledge of all things, because the ideas are the intelligible structures of all knowable things. Therefore, we cannot acquire knowledge of anything unless one might be said to acquire knowledge of something which he already knew.

If it is held, then, that someone acquires knowledge, he must not have any prior knowledge of the thing which he comes to know, but only of certain other things through which he becomes instructed; that is, one acquires knowledge through things previously known, either of *all*, that is, of universals, *or some of them*, that is, of singular things. One learns through universals in the case of those things that are discovered by demonstration and definition, for in the case of demonstrations and definitions the things of which definitions or universals are composed must be known first. And in the case of things that are discovered by induction singular things must be known first.

269. *But if this science* (992b33). Here he gives the second argument, which runs thus. If the ideas are the cause of our knowledge, it must be connatural to us, for men grasp sensible things through this proper nature, because sensible things participate in ideas (according to the Platonists). But the most important knowledge or science is one that is connatural to us and which we cannot forget, as is evident of our knowledge of the first principles of demonstration, of which no one is ignorant. Hence there is no way in which we can forget the knowledge of all things caused in us by

Quod est contra Platonicos, qui dicebant quod anima ex unione ad corpus obliviscitur scientiae, quam naturaliter in omnibus habet: et postea per disciplinam addiscit homo illud quod est prius notum, quasi addiscere nihil sit nisi reminisci.

270. Deinde cum dicit *amplius autem* hic ponit tertiam rationem, quae talis est. Ad rerum cognitionem requiritur, quod homo non solum cognoscat formas rerum, sed etiam principia materialia, ex quibus componitur. Quod ex hoc patet, quia de his interdum contingit esse dubitationem, sicut de hac syllaba SMA, quidam dubitant utrum sit composita ex tribus literis scilicet S, M, A, aut sit una litera praeter omnes praedictas habens proprium sonum. Sed ex ideis non possunt cognosci nisi principia formalia, quia ideae sunt formae rerum: ergo non sunt sufficientes causae cognitionis rerum principiis materialibus remanentibus ignotis.

271. Deinde cum dicit *amplius autem* hic ponit quartam rationem, quae talis est. Ad cognitionem rerum oportet de sensibilibus notitiam habere, quia sensibilia sunt manifesta elementa materialia omnium rerum, ex quibus componuntur, sicut voces compositae, ut syllabae et dictiones componuntur ex propriis elementis. Si igitur per ideas scientia in nobis causatur, oportet quod per ideas causetur in nobis cognitio sensibilium. Cognitio autem in nobis causata ex ideis sine sensu est accepta, quia per sensum non habemus habitudinem ad ideas. In cognoscendo ergo sequitur quod aliquis non habens sensum possit cognoscere sensibilia, quod patet esse falsum. Nam caecus natus non potest habere scientiam de coloribus.

272. Deinde cum dicit *quoniam ergo* hic colligit ea, quae ab antiquis de principiis dicta sunt; dicens quod ex prius dictis est manifestum, quod antiqui philosophi conati sunt quaerere causas a nobis in libro *Physicorum* determinatas, et quod per dicta eorum non habemus aliquam causam extra causas ibi declaratas.

Has autem causas obscure dixerunt, et quodammodo omnes ab eis sunt tactae, quodammodo vero nullam earum tetigerunt. Sicut enim pueri de novo loqui incipientes imperfecte et balbutiendo loquuntur, ita philosophia priorum philosophorum nova existens, visa est balbutiendo et imperfecte de omnibus loqui circa principia. Quod in hoc patet quod Empedocles primo dixit quod ossa habent quamdam rationem idest commixtionem proportionis, quae quidem ratio est quod quid est et substantia rei. Sed similiter necessarium est de carne et de singulis aliorum, aut de nullo. Omnia enim ista ex elementis commixta sunt. Et propter hoc patet quod caro et os et omnia huiusmodi non sunt id quod sunt,

the ideas. But this is contrary to the Platonists' opinion, who said that the soul forgets the knowledge which it has of all things by nature as a result of its union with the body, and that by teaching a man acquires knowledge of something that he previously knew, as though the process of acquiring knowledge were merely one of remembering.

270. *Again, how is anyone* (993a2). Here he gives the third argument, which runs thus. In order to know things, a man must acquire knowledge not only of the forms of things but also of the material principles of which they are composed. This is evident from the fact that occasionally questions arise regarding these. For example, with regard to the syllable SMA, some raise the question whether it is composed of the three letters S, M, and A, or whether it is one letter which is distinct from these and has its own sound. But only the formal principles of things can be known through the ideas, because the ideas are the forms of things. Hence the ideas are not a sufficient cause of our knowledge of things when material principles remain unknown.

271. *Again, how could* (993a7). Here he gives the fourth argument, which runs thus. In order to know reality, we must know sensible things, because sensible things are the apparent material element of which all things are composed, just as complex sounds (such as syllables and words) are composed of their proper elements. If, then, knowledge is caused in us by the ideas, our knowledge of sensible things must be caused by the ideas. But the knowledge which is caused in us by the ideas is grasped without the senses, because we have no connection with the ideas through the senses. Therefore, in the act of perception it follows that anyone who does not have a sense can apprehend the object of that sense. This is clearly false, for a man born blind cannot have any knowledge of colors.

272. *From the foregoing* (993a11). Here he summarizes the statements made by the ancient philosophers. He says that from what has been said above it is evident that the ancient philosophers attempted to investigate the cause which he dealt with in the *Physics*, and that in their statements we find no cause in addition to those established in that work.

However, these men discussed these causes obscurely, and while in a sense they have mentioned all of these causes, in another sense they have not mentioned any of them. For just as young children at first speak imperfectly and in a stammering way, in a similar fashion this philosophy, since it was new, seems to speak imperfectly and in a stammering way about the principles of all things. This is borne out by the fact that Empedocles was the first to say that bones have a certain ratio, or proportional mixture, and that this is a thing's quiddity or substance. But the same thing must also be true of flesh and of every other single thing or of none of them, for all of these things are mixtures of the elements. And for this reason it is evident that flesh

propter materiam quae ab eo ponitur quatuor elementa, sed propter hoc principium, scilicet formale.

Hoc autem Empedocles quasi ex necessitate veritatis coactus posuit aliquo alio expressius ista dicente, sed ipse manifeste non expressit.

Et sicut expresse non manifestaverunt naturam formae, ita nec materiae, ut supra de Anaxagora dictum est. Et similiter nec alicuius alterius principii.

De talibus ergo quae ab aliis imperfecte dicta sunt, dictum est prius. Iterum autem in tertio libro recapitulabimus de istis quaecumque circa hoc potest aliquis dubitare ad unam partem vel ad aliam. Ex talibus enim dubitationibus forsitan investigabimus aliquid utile ad dubitationes, quas posterius per totam scientiam prosequi et determinare oportet.

and bone and all things of this kind are not what they are because of their matter, which he identified with the four elements, but because of this principle—their form.

Empedocles, however, compelled as it were by necessity of truth, would have maintained this view if it had been expressed more clearly by someone else, but he did not express it clearly.

And just as the ancient philosophers have not clearly expressed the nature of form, neither have they clearly expressed the nature of matter, as was said above about Anaxagoras [90]. Nor have they clearly expressed the nature of any other principles.

Therefore, we have spoken before [190] concerning such things as have been stated imperfectly. And with regard to these matters we will restate again in book 3 [423] whatever difficulties can be raised on both sides of the question. For perhaps from such difficulties we will discover some useful information for dealing with the problems which must be examined and solved later on throughout this whole science.

Book 2

The Search for Truth and Causes

Lecture 1

The acquisition of truth

993a30 De veritate quidem theoria, id est contemplatio, sic difficilis est, sic vero facilis. [274]

ἡ περὶ τῆς ἀληθείας θεωρία τῇ μὲν χαλεπῇ τῇ δὲ ῥαδία.

Theoretical or speculative knowledge of truth is in one sense difficult, and in another easy.

993a31 Signum autem, nec digne nullus adipisci ipsam posse, nec omnes fallere, sed unumquemque aliquid de natura dicere. [275]

σημεῖον δὲ τὸ μήτ᾽ ἀξίως μηδένα δύνασθαι θιγεῖν αὐτῆς μήτε πάντας ἀποτυγχάνειν, {993b1} ἀλλ᾽ ἕκαστον λέγειν τι περὶ τῆς φύσεως,

An indication of this is found in the fact that, while no one can attain an adequate knowledge of it, all men together do not fail, because each one is able to say something true about nature.

993b2 Et secundum unumquemque quidem nihil aut parum ei immittere, de omnibus autem coarticulatis fieri magnitudinem aliquam. [276]

καὶ καθ᾽ ἕνα μὲν ἢ μηθὲν ἢ μικρὸν ἐπιβάλλειν αὐτῇ, ἐκ πάντων δὲ συναθροιζομένων γίγνεσθαί τι μέγεθος·

And while each one individually contributes nothing or very little to the truth, still as a result of the combined efforts of all a great amount of truth becomes known.

993b4 Quare si videtur habere, ut proverbialiter dicimus, *In foribus quis delinquet?* Sic quidem utique erit facilis. [277]

ὥστ᾽ εἴπερ ἔοικεν ἔχειν καθάπερ τυγχάνομεν παροιμιαζόμενοι, {5} τίς ἂν θύρας ἁμάρτοι; ταύτῃ μὲν ἂν εἴη ῥαδία, τὸ δ᾽ ὅλον τι ἔχειν καὶ μέρος μὴ δύνασθαι δηλοῖ τὸ χαλεπὸν αὐτῆς.

Therefore, if the situation in the case of truth seems to be like the one which we speak of in the proverb "Who will miss a door?," then in this respect it will be easy to know the truth.

993b6 Habere autem totum et partem non posse, difficultatem eius ostendit. [278]

ἴσως δὲ καὶ τῆς χαλεπότητος οὔσης κατὰ δύο τρόπους, οὐκ ἐν τοῖς πράγμασιν ἀλλ᾽ ἐν ἡμῖν τὸ αἴτιον αὐτῆς·

But the fact that we cannot simultaneously grasp a whole and its parts shows the difficulty involved.

993b7 Forsan autem et difficultate secundum duos existente modos, non in rebus, sed in nobis est eius causa. Sicut enim nycticoracum oculi ad lucem diei se habent, sic et animae nostrae intellectus ad ea quae sunt omnium naturae manifestissima. [279]

ὥσπερ γὰρ τὰ τῶν νυκτερίδων ὄμματα πρὸς τὸ {10} φέγγος ἔχει τὸ μεθ᾽ ἡμέραν, οὕτω καὶ τῆς ἡμετέρας ψυχῆς ὁ νοῦς πρὸς τὰ τῇ φύσει φανερώτατα πάντων.

However, since the difficulty is twofold, perhaps its cause is not in things but in us. For just as the eyes of owls are to the light of day, so is our soul's intellective power to those things that are by nature the most evident of all.

993b11 Non solum autem his habere gratiam iustum est, quorum aliquis opiniombus communicaverit; sed his qui adhuc superficialiter enuntiaverunt. Etenim conferunt aliquid. Nam habitum nostrum praeexercuerunt. [287]

οὐ μόνον δὲ χάριν ἔχειν δίκαιον τούτοις ὧν ἄν τις κοινώσαιτο ταῖς δόξαις, ἀλλὰ καὶ τοῖς ἐπιπολαιότερον ἀποφηναμένοις· καὶ γὰρ οὗτοι συνεβάλοντό τι· τὴν γὰρ ἕξιν προήσκησαν ἡμῶν·

Now it is only right that we should be grateful not merely to those with whose views we agree but also to those who until now have spoken in a superficial way, for they too have made some contribution because they have made use of the habit which we now exercise.

Nam si Timotheus non fuisset, multam melodiam non haberemus. Si autem non Phrynis, Timotheus non fuisset.

{15} εἰ μὲν γὰρ Τιμόθεος μὴ ἐγένετο, πολλὴν ἂν μελοποιίαν οὐκ εἴχομεν· εἰ δὲ μὴ Φρῦνις, Τιμόθεος οὐκ ἂν ἐγένετο.

Thus if there had been no Timotheus, we would not have a great part of our music; and if there had been no Phrynis, there would have been no Timotheus.

Eodem vero modo et de enuntiantibus veritatem. A quibusdam enim opiniones quasdam accepimus, sed alii, ut hi forent, causa fuerunt.

τὸν αὐτὸν δὲ τρόπον καὶ ἐπὶ τῶν περὶ τῆς ἀληθείας ἀποφηναμένων· παρὰ μὲν γὰρ ἐνίων παρειλήφαμέν τινας δόξας, οἱ δὲ τοῦ γενέσθαι τούτους αἴτιοι γεγόνασιν.

The same is true of those who have made statements about the truth, for we have accepted certain opinions from some of them, and others have been the cause of them attaining their knowledge as they have been the cause of us attaining ours.

---

273. Postquam Philosophus reprobavit opiniones antiquorum philosophorum de primis principiis rerum, circa quae versatur principaliter philosophi primi intentio, hic accedit ad determinandum veritatem. Aliter autem se habet consideratio philosophiae primae circa veritatem, et aliarum particularium scientiarum. Nam unaquaeque particularis scientia considerat quamdam particularem veritatem circa determinatum genus entium, ut geometria circa rerum magnitudines, arithmetica circa numeros. Sed philosophia prima considerat universalem veritatem entium. Et ideo ad hunc philosophum pertinet considerare, quomodo se habeat homo ad veritatem cognoscendam.

274. Dividitur ergo ista pars in partes duas.

In prima parte determinat ea quae pertinent ad considerationem universalis veritatis.

In secunda incipit inquirere veritatem de primis principiis et omnibus aliis, ad quae extenditur huius philosophiae consideratio; et hoc in tertio libro, qui incipit, *necesse est nobis acquisitam scientiam* et cetera.

Prima autem pars dividitur in partes tres.

In prima dicit qualiter se habet homo ad considerationem veritatis.

In secunda ostendit ad quam scientiam principaliter pertineat cognitio veritatis, ibi, *vocari vero philosophiam veritatis* et cetera.

In tertia parte ostendit modum considerandae veritatis, ibi, *contingunt autem auditiones* et cetera.

Circa primum tria facit.

Primo ostendit facilitatem existentem in cognitione veritatis.

Secundo ostendit causam difficultatis, ibi, *forsan autem et difficultate* et cetera.

Tertio ostendit quomodo homines se invicem iuvant ad cognoscendum veritatem, ibi, *non solum autem his dicere* et cetera.

Circa primum duo facit.

273. Having criticized the ancient philosophers' opinions about the first principles of things, with which first philosophy is chiefly concerned, the Philosopher now begins to establish what is true. First philosophy considers truth in a different way from the particular sciences do. Each of the particular sciences considers a particular truth out a definite genus of beings—for example, geometry deals with the continuous quantities of bodies, and arithmetic with numbers—but first philosophy considers what is universally true of things. Therefore, it pertains to this science to consider in what respects man is capable of knowing the truth.

274. This part is divided into two sections.

In the first (993a30; [274]), he deals with the things that belong to a universal consideration of truth.

In the second (995a24; [338]) he begins to investigate what is true of first principles and of everything else with which this philosophy deals. He does this in book 3, which begins with the words *with a view to the science under investigation*.

The first part is again divided into three parts.

In the first of these he explains in what respects man is capable of knowing the truth.

In the second (993b19; [290]) he indicates to what science the knowledge of truth principally belongs, at *it is only right to call*.

In the third (994b32; [331]) he explains the method by which truth is investigated, at *the way in which people are affected*.

In regard to the first he does three things.

First, he shows in what respect it is easy to know the truth.

Second (993b7; [279]), he gives the reason for the difficulty involved, at *however, since the difficulty is twofold*.

Third (993b11; [287]), he shows how men assist each other to know the truth, at *now it is only right*.

In regard to the first he does two things.

Primo proponit intentum, dicens, quod *theoria*, idest consideratio vel speculatio de veritate *quodammodo est facilis, et quodammodo difficilis.*

275. Secundo ibi *signum autem* manifestat propositum.

Et primo quantum ad facilitatem.

Secundo quantum ad difficultatem, ibi, *habere autem totum et partem* et cetera.

Facilitatem autem in considerando veritatem ostendit tripliciter.

Primo quidem hoc signo, quod licet nullus homo veritatis perfectam cognitionem adipisci possit, tamen nullus homo est ita expers veritatis, quin aliquid de veritate cognoscat. Quod ex hoc apparet, quod unusquisque potest enuntiare de veritate et natura rerum, quod est signum considerationis interioris.

276. Secundum signum ponit ibi *et secundum* dicens quod licet id quod unus homo potest immittere vel apponere ad cognitionem veritatis suo studio et ingenio, sit aliquid parvum per comparationem ad totam considerationem veritatis, tamen illud, quod aggregatur ex *omnibus coarticulatis*, idest exquisitis et collectis, fit aliquid magnum, ut potest apparere in singulis artibus, quae per diversorum studia et ingenia ad mirabile incrementum pervenerunt.

277. Tertio manifestat idem per quoddam exemplum vulgaris proverbii, ibi *quare si* concludens ex praemissis, quod ex quo unusquisque potest cognoscere de veritate, licet parum, ita se habere videtur in cognitione veritatis, sicut proverbialiter dicitur: in *foribus*, idest in ianuis domorum, *quis delinquet?* Interiora enim domus difficile est scire, et circa ea facile est hominem decipi:

sed sicut circa ipsum introitum domus qui omnibus patet et primo occurrit, nullus decipitur, ita etiam est in consideratione veritatis: nam ea, per quae intratur in cognitionem aliorum, nota sunt omnibus, et nullus circa ea decipitur:

huiusmodi autem sunt prima principia naturaliter nota, ut non esse simul affirmare et negare, et quod omne totum est maius sua parte, et similia.

Circa conclusiones vero, ad quas per huiusmodi, quasi per ianuam, intratur, contingit multoties errare. Sic igitur cognitio veritatis est facilis inquantum scilicet ad minus istud modicum, quod est principium, per se

First, he states what he intends to prove. He says that *theoretical knowledge*, that is, the contemplative or speculative understanding of truth, *is in one sense difficult, and in another easy*.

275. Second, at *an indication of this* (993a31), he explains what he intends to prove:

first, in what sense it is easy to know the truth;

second [278], in what sense it is difficult, at *but the fact* (993b6).

He shows in what sense it is easy to know the truth by giving three indications.

The first is this: while no man can attain a complete knowledge of the truth, still no man is so completely devoid of truth that he knows nothing about it. This is shown by the fact that anyone can make a statement about the truth and the nature of things, which is a sign of interior consideration.

276. *And while each one individually* (993b2). Here he gives the second indication. He says that while the amount of truth that one man can discover or contribute to the knowledge of truth by his own study and talents is small compared with a complete knowledge of truth, nevertheless what is known as a result of *the combined efforts of all*—that is, what is discovered and collected into one whole—becomes quite extensive. This can be seen in the case of the particular arts, which have developed in a marvelous manner as a result of the studies and talents of different men.

277. *Therefore, if the situation* (993b4). Third, he shows that the same thing is true by citing a common proverb. He concludes from the foregoing that *if* anyone can attain some knowledge of the truth, even though it be little, the situation in the case of knowledge is like the one that we speak of in the proverb, *who will miss a door?* that is, the outer door of a house. For it is difficult to know what the interior of a house is like, and a man is easily deceived in such matters.

But just as no one is mistaken about the entrance of a house, which is evident to all and is the first thing that we perceive, so too this is the case with regard to the knowledge of truth, for those truths through which we enter into a knowledge of others are known to all, and no man is mistaken about them.

Those first principles which are naturally apprehended are truths of this sort—for example, it is impossible to both affirm and deny something at the same time, and every whole is greater than each of its parts, and so on.

On the other hand, there are many ways in which error may arise with respect to the conclusions into which we enter through such principles as through an outer door. Therefore, it is easy to know the truth if we consider that

notum, per quod intratur ad veritatem, est omnibus per se notum.

278. Deinde cum dicit *habere autem* manifestat difficultatem; dicens, quod hoc ostendit difficultatem quae est in consideratione veritatis, quia non possumus habere circa veritatem totum et partem. Ad cuius evidentiam considerandum est, quod hoc dixit omnibus esse notum, per quod in alia introitur. Est autem duplex via procedendi ad cognitionem veritatis.

Una quidem per modum resolutionis, secundum quam procedimus a compositis ad simplicia, et a toto ad partem, sicut dicitur in primo *Physicorum*, quod confusa sunt prius nobis nota. Et in hac via perficitur cognitio veritatis, quando pervenitur ad singulas partes distincte cognoscendas.

Alia est via compositionis, per quam procedimus a simplicibus ad composita, qua perficitur cognitio veritatis cum pervenitur ad totum. Sic igitur hoc ipsum, quod homo non potest in rebus perfecte totum et partem cognoscere, ostendit difficultatem considerandae veritatis secundum utramque viam.

279. Deinde cum dicit *forsan autem* ostendit causam praemissae difficultatis. Ubi similiter considerandum est, quod in omnibus, quae consistunt in quadam habitudine unius ad alterum, potest impedimentum dupliciter vel ex uno vel ex alio accidere: sicut si lignum non comburatur, hoc contingit vel quia ignis est debilis, vel quia lignum non est bene combustibile; et similiter oculus impeditur a visione alicuius visibilis, aut quia est debilis aut quia visibile est tenebrosum. Sic igitur potest contingere quod veritas sit difficilis ad cognoscendum, vel propter defectum qui est in ipsis rebus, vel propter defectum qui est in intellectu nostro.

280. Et quod quantum ad aliquas res difficultas contingat in cognoscendo veritatem ipsarum rerum ex parte earum, patet. Cum enim unumquodque sit cognoscibile inquantum est ens actu, ut infra in nono huius dicetur, illa quae habent esse deficiens et imperfectum, sunt secundum seipsa parum cognoscibilia, ut materia, motus et tempus propter esse eorum imperfectionem, ut Boetius dicit in libro *De duabus naturis*.

281. Fuerunt autem aliqui philosophi, qui posuerunt difficultatem cognitionis veritatis totaliter provenire ex parte rerum, ponentes nihil esse fixum et stabile in rebus, sed omnia esse in continuo fluxu ut infra in quarto huius dicetur. Sed hoc excludit Philosophus, dicens, quod quamvis difficultas cognoscendae veritatis forsan possit secundum aliqua diversa esse dupliciter, videlicet

small amount of it which is comprised of self-evident principles, through which we enter into other truths, because this much is evident to all.

278. *But the fact that we cannot* (993b6). Here he explains in what sense it is difficult to know the truth. He says that our inability to grasp the whole truth and a part of it shows the difficulty involved in the search for truth. In support of this we must consider his statement that the truth through which we gain admission to other truths is known to all. Now there are two ways in which we attain knowledge of the truth.

The first is the method of analysis, by which we go from what is complex to what is simple or from a whole to a part, as it is said in *Physics* 1 that the first objects of our knowledge are confused wholes. Now our knowledge of the truth is perfected by this method when we attain a distinct knowledge of the particular parts of a whole.

The other method is that of synthesis, by which we go from what is simple to what is complex; we attain knowledge of truth by this method when we succeed in knowing a whole. Thus the fact that man is unable to know perfectly a whole and a part in things shows the difficulty involved in knowing the truth by both of these methods.

279. *However, since the difficulty is twofold* (993b7). He gives the reason for this difficulty. Here too it must be noted that in all cases in which there is a certain relationship between two things, an effect can fail to occur in two ways, because of either one of the things involved. For example, if wood does not burn, this may happen either because the fire is not strong enough or because the wood is not combustible enough. And in a similar way, the eye may be prevented from seeing a visible object either because the eye is weak or because the visible object is in the dark. Therefore, in like manner, it may be difficult to know the truth about things either because things themselves are imperfect in some way or because of some weakness on the part of our intellect.

280. Now it is evident that we experience difficulty in knowing the truth about some things because of the things themselves, for, since each thing is knowable insofar as it is an actual being, as will be stated below in book 9 [1894] of this work, then those things that are deficient and imperfect in being are less knowable by their very nature. For example, matter, motion, and time are less knowable because of the imperfect being which they have, as Boethius says in his book *The Two Natures*.

281. Now there were some philosophers who claimed that the difficulty experienced in knowing the truth is wholly attributable to things themselves, because they maintained that nothing is fixed and stable in nature but that everything is in a state of continual change, as will be stated in book 4 [683] of this work. But the Philosopher denies this, saying that even though the difficulty

ex parte nostra, et ex parte rerum; non tamen principalis causa difficultatis est ex parte rerum, sed ex parte nostra.

282. Et hoc sic probat. Quia, si difficultas esset principaliter ex parte rerum, sequeretur, quod illa magis cognosceremus, quae sunt magis cognoscibilia secundum suam naturam: sunt autem maxime cognoscibilia secundum naturam suam, quae sunt maxime in actu, scilicet entia immaterialia et immobilia, quae tamen sunt maxime nobis ignota. Unde manifestum est, quod difficultas accidit in cognitione veritatis, maxime propter defectum intellectus nostri. Ex quo contingit, quod intellectus animae nostrae hoc modo se habet ad entia immaterialia, quae inter omnia sunt maxime manifesta secundum suam naturam, sicut se habent oculi nycticoracum ad lucem diei, quam videre non possunt, quamvis videant obscura. Et hoc est propter debilitatem visus eorum.

283. Sed videtur haec similitudo non esse conveniens. Sensus enim quia est potentia organi corporalis, corrumpitur ex vehementia sensibilis. Intellectus autem, cum non sit potentia alicuius organi corporei, non corrumpitur ex excellenti intelligibili. Unde post apprehensionem alicuius magni intelligibilis, non minus intelligimus minus intelligibilia, sed magis, ut dicitur in tertio *De anima*.

284. Dicendum est ergo, quod sensus impeditur a cognitione alicuius sensibilis dupliciter. Uno modo per corruptionem organi ab excellenti sensibili; et hoc locum non habet in intellectu. Alio modo ex defectu proportionis ipsius virtutis sensitivae ad obiectum. Potentiae enim animae non sunt eiusdem virtutis in omnibus animalibus; sed sicuti homini hoc in sua specie convenit, quod habeat pessimum olfactum, ita nycticoraci, quod habeat debilem visum, quia non habet proportionem ad claritatem diei cognoscendam.

285. Sic igitur, cum anima humana sit ultima in ordine substantiarum intellectivarum, minime participat de virtute intellectiva; et sicut ipsa quidem secundum naturam est actus corporis, eius autem intellectiva potentia non est actus organi corporalis, ita habet naturalem aptitudinem ad cognoscendum corporalium et sensibilium veritatem, quae sunt minus cognoscibilia secundum suam naturam propter eorum materialitatem, sed tamen cognosci possunt per abstractionem sensibilium a phantasmatibus. Et quia hic modus cognoscendi veritatem convenit naturae humanae animae secundum quod est forma talis corporis; quae autem sunt naturalia semper manent; impossibile est, quod anima humana huiusmodi corpori unita cognoscat de veritate rerum, nisi quantum potest elevari per ea quae abstrahendo a

experienced in knowing the truth can perhaps be twofold because of different things (that is, our intellect and things themselves), still the principal source of the difficulty is not things, but our intellect.

282. He proves this in the following way. If this difficulty were attributable principally to things, it would follow that we would know best those things that are most knowable by nature. But those things that are most knowable by nature are those which are most actual, namely, immaterial and unchangeable things, yet we know these least of all. Obviously, then, the difficulty experienced in knowing the truth is due principally to some weakness on the part of our intellect. From this it follows that our soul's intellectual power is related to those immaterial beings which are by nature the most knowable of all as the eyes of owls are to the light of day, which they cannot see because their power of vision is weak, although they do see dimly lighted things.

283. But it is evident that this simile is not adequate, for, since a sense is a power of a bodily organ, it is made inoperative as a result of its sensible object being too intense. But the intellect is not a power of a bodily organ and is not made inoperative as a result of its intelligible object being too intelligible. Therefore, after understanding objects that are highly intelligible, our ability to understand less intelligible objects is not decreased but increased, as is stated in *On the Soul* 3.

284. Therefore, it must be said that a sense is prevented from perceiving some sensible object for two reasons. First, because a sensory organ is rendered inoperative as a result of its sensible object being too intense. This does not occur in the case of the intellect. Second, because of some deficiency in the ability of a sensory power to perceive its object, for the powers of the soul in all animals do not have the same efficacy. Thus, just as it is proper to man by nature to have the weakest sense of smell, in a similar way it is proper to an owl to have the weakest power of vision, because it is incapable of perceiving the light of day.

285. Therefore, since the human soul occupies the lowest place in the order of intellective substances, it has the least intellective power. As a matter of fact, just as it is by nature the act of a body, although its intellective power is not the act of a bodily organ, in a similar way it has a natural capacity to know the truth about bodily and sensible things. These are less knowable by nature because of their materiality, although they can be known by abstracting sensible forms from phantasms. And since this process of knowing truth befits the nature of the human soul insofar as it is the form of this kind of body (and whatever is natural always remains so), it is possible for the human soul, which is united to this kind of body, to know the truth about things only insofar as it can be elevated to the level of the things that it understands by abstracting from

phantasmatibus intelligit. Per haec autem nullo modo potest elevari ad cognoscendum quidditates immaterialium substantiarum, quae sunt improportionatae istis substantiis sensibilibus. Unde impossibile est quod anima humana huiusmodi corpori unita, apprehendat substantias separatas cognoscendo de eis quod quid est.

286. Ex quo apparet falsum esse quod Averroes hic dicit in *Commento*, quod Philosophus non demonstrat hic, res abstractas intelligere esse impossibile nobis, sicut impossibile est vespertilioni inspicere solem. Et ratio sua, quam inducit, est valde derisibilis. Subiungit enim, quoniam si ita esset, natura otiose egisset, quia fecit illud quod in se est naturaliter intelligibile, non esse intellectum ab aliquo; sicut si fecisset solem non comprehensum ab aliquo visu. Deficit enim haec ratio.

Primo quidem in hoc, quod cognitio intellectus nostri non est finis substantiarum separatarum, sed magis e converso. Unde non sequitur, quod, si non cognoscantur substantiae separatae a nobis, quod propter hoc sint frustra. Frustra enim est, quod non consequitur finem ad quem est.

Secundo, quia etsi substantiae separatae non intelliguntur a nobis secundum suas quidditates, intelliguntur tamen ab aliis intellectibus; sicut solem etsi non videat oculus nycticoracis, videt tamen eum oculus aquilae.

287. Deinde cum dicit **non solum** ostendit quomodo se homines adinvicem iuvant ad considerandum veritatem. Adiuvatur enim unus ab altero ad considerationem veritatis dupliciter. Uno modo directe. Alio modo indirecte.

Directe quidem iuvatur ab his qui veritatem invenerunt: quia, sicut dictum est, dum unusquisque praecedentium aliquid de veritate invenit, simul in unum collectum, posteriores introducit ad magnam veritatis cognitionem.

Indirecte vero, inquantum priores errantes circa veritatem, posterioribus exercitii occasionem dederunt, ut diligenti discussione habita, veritas limpidius appareret.

288. Est autem iustum ut his, quibus adiuti sumus in tanto bono, scilicet cognitione veritatis, gratias agamus. Et ideo dicit, quod **iustum est gratiam habere**, non solum his, quos quis existimat veritatem invenisse, quorum opinionibus aliquis communicat sequendo eas; sed etiam illis, qui superficialiter locuti sunt ad veritatem investigandam, licet eorum opiniones non sequamur; quia isti etiam aliquid conferunt nobis. Praestiterunt enim nobis quoddam exercitium circa inquisitionem veritatis.

phantasms. However, by this process it cannot be elevated to the level of knowing the quiddities of immaterial substances because these are not on the same level as sensible substances. Therefore, it is impossible for the human soul, which is united to this kind of body, to apprehend separate substances by knowing their quiddities.

286. For this reason the statement which Averroes makes at this point in his *Commentary* is evidently false, namely, that the Philosopher does not prove here that it is just as impossible for us to understand abstract substances as it is for a bat to see the sun. The argument that he gives is wholly ridiculous, for he adds that if this were the case, nature would have acted in vain because it would have made something that is naturally knowable in itself to be incapable of being known by anything else. It would be the same as if it had made the sun incapable of being seen. This argument is not satisfactory for two reasons.

First, the end of separate substances does not consist in being understood by our intellect, but rather the converse. Therefore, if separate substances are not known by us, it does not follow that they exist in vain, for only that exists in vain which fails to attain the end for which it exists.

Second, even though the quiddities of separate substances are not understood by us, they are understood by other intellects. The same is true of the sun, for even though it is not seen by the eye of the owl, it is seen by the eye of the eagle.

287. **Now it is only right** (993b11). He shows how men assist each other to know the truth. One man assists another to consider the truth in two ways: directly and indirectly.

One is assisted directly by those who have discovered the truth, because, as has been pointed out, when each of our predecessors has discovered something about the truth (which is gathered together into one whole), he also introduces his followers to a more extensive knowledge of truth.

One is assisted indirectly insofar as those who have preceded us and who were wrong about the truth have bequeathed to their successors the occasion for exercising their mental powers, so that by diligent discussion the truth might be seen more clearly.

288. Now it is only fitting that we should be grateful to those who have helped us attain so great a good as knowledge of the truth. Therefore, he says that **it is only right that we should be grateful** not merely to those whom we think have found the truth and with whose views we agree by following them, but also to those who, in the search for truth, have made only superficial statements, even though we do not follow their views. For these men too have given us something because they have shown us

Et ponit exemplum de inventoribus musicae. Si enim non *fuisset Timotheus* qui multa de arte musicae invenit, non haberemus ad praesens multa, quae scimus circa melodias. Et si non praecessisset quidam philosophus nomine *Phrynis*, Timotheus non fuisset ita instructus in musicalibus. Et similiter est dicendum de philosophis qui enuntiaverunt universaliter veritatem rerum. A quibusdam enim praedecessorum nostrorum accepimus aliquas opiniones de veritate rerum, in quibus credimus eos bene dixisse, alias opiniones praetermittentes. Et iterum illi, a quibus nos accepimus, invenerunt aliquos praedecessores, a quibus acceperunt, quique fuerunt eis causa instructionis.

instances of actual attempts to discover the truth. By way of an example he mentions the founders of music, for if there *had been no Timotheus*, who discovered a great part of the art of music, we would not have many of the facts that we know about melodies. But if Timotheus had not been preceded by a wise man named *Phrynis*, he would not have been as well off in the subject of music. The same thing must be said of those philosophers who made statements of universal scope about the truth of things, for we accept from certain of our predecessors whatever views about the truth of things we think are true and disregard the rest. Again, those from whom we accept certain views had predecessors from whom they in turn accepted certain views and who were the source of their information.

LECTURE 2

The supreme science of truth

993b19 Vocari vero philosophiam, veritatis scientiam recte habet. Nam theoricae finis est veritas, et practicae opus. Etenim si quo modo se habet, intendunt, non tamen secundum se, sed ut ad aliquid et nunc speculantur practici. [290]

ὀρθῶς δ᾽ ἔχει καὶ τὸ καλεῖσθαι {20} τὴν φιλοσοφίαν ἐπιστήμην τῆς ἀληθείας. θεωρητικῆς μὲν γὰρ τέλος ἀλήθεια πρακτικῆς δ᾽ ἔργον· καὶ γὰρ ἂν τὸ πῶς ἔχει σκοπῶσιν, οὐ τὸ ἀΐδιον ἀλλ᾽ ὃ πρός τι καὶ νῦν θεωροῦσιν οἱ πρακτικοί.

It is only right to call philosophy the science of truth. For the end of theoretical knowledge is truth, whereas that of practical knowledge is action, for even when practical men investigate the way in which something exists, they do not consider it in itself but in relation to some particular thing and to the present moment.

993b23 Nescimus autem verum sine causa. [291]

οὐκ ἴσμεν δὲ τὸ ἀληθὲς ἄνευ τῆς αἰτίας·

But we know a truth only by knowing its cause.

Unumquodque vero maxime id ipsum aliorum dicitur, secundum quod et in aliis inest univocatio. Puta ignis calidissimus, etenim est causa aliis hic caloris.

ἕκαστον δὲ μάλιστα αὐτὸ τῶν ἄλλων καθ᾽ ὃ καὶ {25} τοῖς ἄλλοις ὑπάρχει τὸ συνώνυμον (οἷον τὸ πῦρ θερμότατον· καὶ γὰρ τοῖς ἄλλοις τὸ αἴτιον τοῦτο τῆς θερμότητος):

Now anything which is the basis of a univocal predication about other things has that attribute in the highest degree. Thus fire is hottest and is actually the cause of heat in other things.

Quare et verissimum quod posterioribus est causa ut sint vera. Quapropter semper existentium principia esse verissima necesse est. Non enim quandoque vera, quandoque non vera;

ὥστε καὶ ἀληθέστατον τὸ τοῖς ὑστέροις αἴτιον τοῦ ἀληθέσιν εἶναι. διὸ τὰς τῶν ἀεὶ ὄντων ἀρχὰς ἀναγκαῖον ἀεὶ εἶναι ἀληθεστάτας

Therefore, that is also true in the highest degree which is the cause of all subsequent things being true. For this reason the principles of things that always exist must be true in the highest degree, because they are not sometimes true and sometimes not true.

nec illis causa aliqua est ut sint, sed illa aliis. Quare unumquodque sicut se habet ut sit, ita et ad veritatem.

(οὐ γάρ ποτε ἀληθεῖς, οὐδ᾽ ἐκείναις αἴτιόν τί ἐστι τοῦ {30} εἶναι, ἀλλ᾽ ἐκεῖναι τοῖς ἄλλοις), ὥσθ᾽ ἕκαστον ὡς ἔχει τοῦ εἶναι, οὕτω καὶ τῆς ἀληθείας.

Nor is there any cause of their being, but they are the cause of the being of other things. Therefore, insofar as each thing has being, to that extent it is true.

994a1 At vero quod sit principium quoddam et non infinitae causae existentium, nec in directum, nec secundum speciem, palam. Neque enim ut ex materia hoc ex hoc in infinitum progredi est possibile, et velut carnem quidem ex terra, terram vero ex aere, aerem autem ex igne, et hoc non stare. Nec unde principium motus; ut hominem ab aere moveri, et hunc a sole, et solem a lite, et huiusmodi nullum esse finem. [299]

ἀλλὰ μὴν ὅτι γ᾽ ἔστιν ἀρχή τις καὶ οὐκ ἄπειρα τὰ αἴτια τῶν ὄντων οὔτ᾽ εἰς εὐθυωρίαν οὔτε κατ᾽ εἶδος, δῆλον. οὔτε γὰρ ὡς ἐξ ὕλης τόδ᾽ ἐκ τοῦδε δυνατὸν ἰέναι εἰς ἄπειρον (οἷον σάρκα μὲν ἐκ γῆς, γῆν δ᾽ ἐξ ἀέρος, ἀέρα δ᾽ ἐκ πυρός, {5} καὶ τοῦτο μὴ ἵστασθαι), οὔτε ὅθεν ἡ ἀρχὴ τῆς κινήσεως (οἷον τὸν μὲν ἄνθρωπον ὑπὸ τοῦ ἀέρος κινηθῆναι, τοῦτον δ᾽ ὑπὸ τοῦ ἡλίου, τὸν δὲ ἥλιον ὑπὸ τοῦ νείκους, καὶ τούτου μηδὲν εἶναι πέρας):

Further, it is evident that there is a principle, and that the causes of existing things are not infinite either in series or in species. For it is impossible that one thing should come from something else as from matter in an infinite regress—for example, flesh from earth, earth from air, air from fire, and so on to infinity. Nor can the causes from which motion originates proceed to infinity, as though man were moved by the air, the air by the sun, the sun by strife, and so on to infinity.

Similiter autem nec id, cuius causa, in infinitum ire est possibile. Iter quidem sanitatis causa, illam vero felicitatis, et felicitatem alterius, et ita semper aliud

ὁμοίως δὲ οὐδὲ τὸ οὗ ἕνεκα εἰς ἄπειρον οἷόν τε ἰέναι, βάδισιν μὲν ὑγιείας ἕνεκα, ταύτην δ᾽ εὐδαιμονίας, τὴν δ᾽ εὐδαιμονίαν {10} ἄλλου, καὶ οὕτως ἀεὶ ἄλλο

Again, neither can there be an infinite regress in the case of the reason for which something is done, as though walking were for the sake of health, health for

alterius causam esse. Et in quod quid erat esse similiter.

ἄλλου ἕνεκεν εἶναι: καὶ ἐπὶ τοῦ τί ἦν εἶναι δ᾽ ὡσαύτως.

the sake of happiness, and happiness for the sake of something else, so that one thing is always being done for the sake of something else. The same is true in the case of the quiddity.

---

289. Postquam Philosophus ostendit qualiter se habet homo ad considerationem veritatis, hic ostendit quod cognitio veritatis maxime ad philosophiam primam pertineat. Et circa hoc duo facit.

Primo ostendit, quod ad philosophiam primam maxime pertineat cognitio veritatis.

Secundo excludit quamdam falsam opinionem, per quam sua probatio tolleretur, ibi, *at vero quod sit principium*.

Circa primum duo facit.

Primo ostendit, quod ad philosophiam primam pertineat cognitio veritatis.

Secundo quod maxime ad ipsam pertineat, ibi, *nescimus autem verum sine causa* et cetera.

Haec autem duo ostendit ex duobus, quae supra probata sunt in prooemio libri: scilicet quod sapientia sit non practica, sed speculativa: et quod sit cognoscitiva causarum primarum.

290. Ex primo autem horum sic argumentatur ad primam conclusionem. Theorica, idest speculativa, differt a practica secundum finem: nam finis speculativae est veritas: hoc enim est quod intendit, scilicet veritatis cognitionem. Sed finis practicae est opus, quia etsi *practici*, hoc est operativi, intendant cognoscere veritatem, quomodo se habeat in aliquibus rebus, non tamen quaerunt eam tamquam ultimum finem. Non enim considerant causam veritatis secundum se et propter se, sed ordinando ad finem operationis, sive applicando ad aliquod determinatum particulare, et ad aliquod determinatum tempus. Si ergo huic coniunxerimus, quod sapientia sive philosophia prima non est practica, sed speculativa, sequetur quod recte debeat dici scientia veritatis.

291. Sed quia multae sunt scientiae speculativae, quae veritatem considerant, utpote geometria et arithmetica, fuit necessarium consequenter ostendere, quod philosophia prima *maxime* consideret veritatem, propter id quod supra ostensum est, scilicet quod est considerativa primarum causarum. Et ideo argumentatur sic. Scientia de vero non habetur nisi per causam: ex quo apparet, quod eorum verorum, de quibus est scientia aliqua, sunt aliquae causae, quae etiam veritatem habent. Non enim potest sciri verum per falsum, sed per aliud verum. Unde et demonstratio, quae facit scientiam, ex veris est, ut dicitur in primo *Posteriorum*.

289. Having shown how man is disposed for the study of truth, the Philosopher now shows that the knowledge of truth belongs preeminently to first philosophy. Regarding this he does two things.

First (993b19; [290]), he shows that knowledge of the truth belongs preeminently to first philosophy.

Second (994a1; [299]), he rejects a false doctrine that would render his proof untenable, at *further, it is evident*.

In regard to the first, he does two things.

First, he shows that knowledge of the truth belongs to first philosophy.

Second [290], that it belongs in the highest degree to this science, at *but we know a truth* (993b23).

He proves these two propositions from two things established above in the prologue of this book, namely, that wisdom is not a practical but a speculative science [53], and that it knows first causes [48].

290. He argues from the first of these to the first conclusion in this way. Theoretical or speculative knowledge differs from practical knowledge by its end, for the end of speculative knowledge is truth, because it has knowledge of the truth as its objective. But the end of practical knowledge is action, because, even though *practical men*, that is, men of action, attempt to understand the truth as it belongs to certain things, they do not seek this as an ultimate end. For they do not consider the cause of truth in and for itself as an end, but in relation to action, by applying it either to some definite individual or to some definite time. Therefore, if we add to the above the fact that wisdom or first philosophy is not practical but speculative, it follows that first philosophy is most fittingly called the science of truth.

291. But since there are many speculative sciences which consider the truth, such as geometry and arithmetic, therefore it was necessary to show that first philosophy considers truth *in the highest degree* inasmuch as it has been shown above that it considers first causes [48]. Hence he argues as follows. We have knowledge of truth only when we know a cause. This is apparent from the fact that the true things about which we have some knowledge have causes which are also true, because we cannot know what is true by knowing what is false, but only by knowing what is true. This is also the reason why demonstration, which causes science, begins with what is true, as is stated in *Posterior Analytics* 1.

292. Deinde adiungit quamdam universalem propositionem, quae talis est. *Unumquodque inter alia maxime* dicitur, ex quo causatur in aliis aliquid univoce praedicatum de eis; sicut ignis est causa caloris in elementatis. Unde, cum calor univoce dicatur et de igne et de elementatis corporibus, sequitur quod ignis sit calidissimus.

293. Facit autem mentionem de univocatione, quia quandoque contingit quod effectus non pervenit ad similitudinem causae secundum eamdem rationem speciei, propter excellentiam ipsius causae. Sicut sol est causa caloris in istis inferioribus: non tamen inferiora corpora possunt recipere impressionem solis aut aliorum caelestium corporum secundum eamdem rationem speciei, cum non communicent in materia. Et propter hoc non dicimus solem esse calidissimum sicut ignem, sed dicimus solem esse aliquid amplius quam calidissimum.

294. Nomen autem veritatis non est proprium alicui speciei, sed se habet communiter ad omnia entia. Unde, quia illud quod est causa veritatis, est causa communicans cum effectu in nomine et ratione communi, sequitur quod illud, quod est posterioribus causa ut sint vera, sit verissimum.

295. Ex quo ulterius concludit quod principia eorum, quae sunt semper, scilicet corporum caelestium, necesse est esse verissima. Et hoc duplici ratione.

Primo quidem, quia non sunt *quandoque vera et quandoque non*, et per hoc transcendunt in veritate generabilia et corruptibilia, quae quandoque sunt et quandoque non sunt.

Secundo, quia nihil est eis causa, sed ipsa sunt causa essendi aliis. Et per hoc transcendunt in veritate et entitate corpora caelestia: quae etsi sint incorruptibilia, tamen habent causam non solum quantum ad suum moveri, ut quidam opinati sunt, sed etiam quantum ad suum esse, ut hic Philosophus expresse dicit.

296. Et hoc est necessarium: quia necesse est ut omnia composita et participantia, reducantur in ea, quae sunt per essentiam, sicut in causas. Omnia autem corporalia sunt entia in actu, inquantum participant aliquas formas. Unde necesse est substantiam separatam, quae est forma per suam essentiam, corporalis substantiae principium esse.

297. Si ergo huic deductioni adiungamus, quod philosophia prima considerat primas causas, sequitur ut prius habitum est, quod ipsa considerat ea, quae sunt maxime vera. Unde ipsa est maxime scientia veritatis.

298. Ex his autem infert quoddam corollarium. Cum enim ita sit, quod ea, quae sunt aliis causa essendi, sint maxime vera, sequitur quod unumquodque sicut se habet ad hoc quod sit, ita etiam se habet ad hoc quod

292. Then he adds the following universal proposition. When a univocal predicate is applied to several things, in each case *anything which is the basis of a univocal predication about other things has that attribute in the highest degree*. Thus fire is the cause of heat in compounds. Therefore, since heat is predicated univocally both of fire and of compound bodies, it follows that fire is hottest.

293. Now he says "univocal" because sometimes it happens that an effect does not become like its cause so as to have the same specific nature, because of the excellence of that cause. For example, the sun is the cause of heat in these lower bodies, but the form which these lower bodies receive cannot be of the same specific nature as that possessed by the sun or any of the celestial bodies, since they do not have a common matter. This is why we do not say that the sun is hottest, as we say fire is, but that it is something superior to the hottest.

294. Now the term "truth" is not proper to one species of beings only, but is applied universally to all beings. Therefore, since the cause of truth is one having the same name and intelligible structure as its effect, it follows that whatever causes subsequent things to be true is itself most true.

295. From this he again concludes that the principles of things that always exist, namely, the celestial bodies, must be most true. He does this for two reasons.

First, they are not *sometimes true and sometimes not true*, and therefore surpass the truth of things subject to generation and corruption, which sometimes exist and sometimes do not.

Second, these principles have no cause, but are the cause of the being of other things. And for this reason they surpass the celestial bodies in truth and in being, and even though the latter are incorruptible, they have a cause not only of their motion, as some men thought, but also of their being, as the Philosopher clearly states in this place.

296. Now this is necessary because everything that is composite in nature and participates in being must ultimately have as its causes those things that have existence by their very essence. But all bodily things are actual beings insofar as they participate in certain forms. Therefore, a separate substance which is a form by its very essence must be the principle of bodily substance.

297. If we add to this conclusion the fact that first philosophy considers first causes, it then follows, as was said above [291], that first philosophy considers those things that are most true. Consequently, this science is preeminently the science of truth.

298. From these conclusions he draws a corollary: since those things that cause the being of other things are true in the highest degree, it follows that each thing is true insofar as it is a being. For things that do not always have being in

habeat veritatem. Ea enim, quorum esse non semper eodem modo se habet, nec veritas eorum semper manet. Et ea quorum esse habet causam, etiam veritatis causam habent. Et hoc ideo, quia esse rei est causa verae existimationis quam mens habet de re. Verum enim et falsum non est in rebus, sed in mente, ut dicetur in sexto huius.

299. Deinde cum dicit *at vero* removet quoddam, per quod praecedens probatio posset infringi: quae procedebat ex suppositione huius, quod philosophia prima considerat causas primas. Hoc autem tolleretur si causae in infinitum procederent. Tunc enim non essent aliquae primae causae. Unde hoc hic removere intendit: et circa hoc duo facit.

Primo proponit intentum.

Secundo probat propositum, ibi, *mediorum enim extra quae est aliquid* et cetera.

Dicit ergo primo: palam potest esse ex his, quae dicentur, quod sit aliquod principium esse et veritatis rerum; et quod causae existentium non sunt infinitae, nec procedendo in directum secundum unam aliquam speciem causae, puta in specie causarum efficientium; nec etiam sunt infinitae secundum speciem, ita quod sint infinitae species causarum.

300. Exponit autem quod dixerat causas infinitas esse in directum.

Primo quidem in genere causae materialis. Non enim possibile est procedere in infinitum in hoc, quod aliquid fiat ex aliquo, sicut ex materia, puta ut caro fiat ex terra, terra vero ex aere, aer ex igne, et hoc non stet in aliquo primo, sed procedat in infinitum.

Secundo exemplificat in genere causae efficientis; dicens, quod nec possibile est ut causa, quae dicitur unde principium motus, in infinitum procedat: puta cum dicimus hominem moveri ad deponendum vestes ab aere calefacto, aerem vero calefieri a sole, solem vero moveri ab aliquo alio, et hoc in infinitum.

Tertio exemplificat in genere causarum finalium; et dicit, quod similiter non potest procedere in infinitum illud quod est *cuius causa*, scilicet causa finalis; ut si dicamus quod iter sive ambulatio est propter sanitatem, sanitas autem propter felicitatem, felicitas autem propter aliquid, et sic in infinitum.

Ultimo facit mentionem de causa formali: et dicit quod similiter non potest procedi in infinitum in hoc quod est *quod quid erat esse*, idest in causa formali quam significat definitio. Sed exempla praetermittit, quia sunt manifesta, et probatum est in primo *Posteriorum*, quod non proceditur in infinitum in praedicatis,

the same way do not always have truth in the same way, and those which have a cause of their being also have a cause of their truth. The reason for this is that a thing's being is the cause of any true judgment which the mind makes about a thing, for truth and falsity are not in things, but in the mind, as will be said in book 6 [1230] of this work.

299. At *further, it is evident* (994a1), he rejects a position that would render the above proof untenable, for this proof proceeded on the supposition that first philosophy considers first causes. But if there were an infinite regress in causes, this proof would be destroyed, for then there would be no first cause. So his aim here is to refute this position. Concerning this he does two things.

First (994a1), he points out what he intends to prove.

Second [301], he proceeds to do so, at *for intermediate things* (994a11).

He says, first, that from what has been said it can clearly be shown that there is some first principle of the being and truth of things. He states that the causes of existing things are not infinite in number because we cannot proceed to infinity in a series of causes belonging to one and the same species (for example, the species of efficient causes). Nor again are causes infinite in species, as though the species of causes were infinite in number.

300. Then he explains his statement about an infinite number of causes in a series.

He first does this in regard to the genus of material causes. For it is impossible to have an infinite series in the sense that one thing always comes from something else as its matter (for example, that flesh comes from earth, earth from air, and air from fire), and that this does not terminate in some first entity but goes on to infinity.

Second, he gives an example of this in the genus of efficient cause. He says that it is impossible to have an infinite series in the genus of cause which we define as the source of motion—for example, when we say that a man is moved to put aside his clothing because the air becomes warm, the air having been heated in turn by the sun, the sun having been moved by something else, and so on to infinity.

Third, he gives an example of this in the genus of final causes. He says that it is also impossible to proceed to infinity **in the case of the reason for which** something is done (that is, the final cause)—for example, if we were to say that a journey or a walk is undertaken for the sake of health, health for the sake of happiness, happiness for the sake of something else, and so on to infinity.

Finally, he mentions the formal cause. He says that it is also impossible to proceed to infinity in the case of the *quiddity*, or the formal cause, which the definition signifies. However, he omits examples because these are evident, and because it was shown in *Posterior Analytics* 1 that it is impossible to proceed to infinity in the matter of predication,

puta quod animal praedicetur de homine in eo quod quid est, et vivum de animali, et sic in infinitum.

as though animal were predicated quidditatively of man, living of animal, and so on to infinity.

LECTURE 3

The existence of first efficient and material causes

994a11 Mediorum enim extra quae est aliquid ultimum et primum, necesse est esse quod prius est causa ipsorum post se. Nam si dicere nos oporteat unum trium causam, quod primum est dicemus, [301]

τῶν γὰρ μέσων, ὧν ἐστί τι ἔσχατον καὶ πρότερον, ἀναγκαῖον εἶναι τὸ πρότερον αἴτιον τῶν μετ᾽ αὐτό. εἰ γὰρ εἰπεῖν ἡμᾶς δέοι τί τῶν τριῶν αἴτιον, τὸ πρῶτον ἐροῦμεν:

For intermediate things in a series limited by some first and last thing must have as their cause the first member of the series, which they follow, because if we had to say which one of these three is the cause of the others, we would say that it is the first.

non enim quod est ultimum. Nullius enim quod finale est. Sed nec medium, nam unius. Nihil enim differt unum aut plura esse, nec infinita aut finita.

οὐ γὰρ δὴ τό γ᾽ ἔσχατον, οὐδενὸς γὰρ τὸ {15} τελευταῖον: ἀλλὰ μὴν οὐδὲ τὸ μέσον, ἑνὸς γάρ (οὐθὲν δὲ διαφέρει ἓν ἢ πλείω εἶναι, οὐδ᾽ ἄπειρα ἢ πεπερασμένα).

What is last is not the cause, since what is last is not a cause of anything. Neither is the intermediate the cause, because it is the cause of only one; for it makes no difference whether one or several intermediates exist, or an infinite or finite number.

Infinitorum vero secundum modum istum et omnino infiniti partes omnes mediae sunt, similiter autem usque modo. Quare si nihil est ex toto aliquid primum, nec ex toto causa nulla est.

τῶν δ᾽ ἀπείρων τοῦτον τὸν τρόπον καὶ ὅλως τοῦ ἀπείρου πάντα τὰ μόρια μέσα ὁμοίως μέχρι τοῦ νῦν: ὥστ᾽ εἴπερ μηδέν ἐστι πρῶτον, ὅλως αἴτιον οὐδέν ἐστιν.

Indeed, in series that are infinite in this way or in the infinite in general, all parts are intermediates to the same degree right down to the present one. Therefore, if there is nothing first in the whole series, nothing in the series is a cause.

994a19 At vero nec in deorsum est possibile in infinitum procedere, ipso sursum habente principium; ut ex igne quidem aquam, ex aqua vero terram, et ita semper aliquod aliud fieri genus. [305]

ἀλλὰ μὴν οὐδ᾽ ἐπὶ τὸ κάτω {20} οἷόν τε εἰς ἄπειρον ἰέναι, τοῦ ἄνω ἔχοντος ἀρχήν, ὥστ᾽ ἐκ πυρὸς μὲν ὕδωρ, ἐκ δὲ τούτου γῆν, καὶ οὕτως ἀεὶ ἄλλο τι γίγνεσθαι γένος.

Neither is it possible to proceed to infinity in a downward direction, where there is a starting point in an upward direction, so that water comes from fire, earth from water, and some other genus of things always being generated in this way.

994a22 Dupliciter autem fit hoc ex hoc, non ut hoc dicitur post hoc, ut ex isthmiis olympia, sed ut ex puero mutato fieri vir, aut ex aqua aer. [308]

διχῶς γὰρ γίγνεται τόδε ἐκ τοῦδε—μὴ ὡς τόδε λέγεται μετὰ τόδε, οἷον ἐξ Ἰσθμίων Ὀλύμπια, ἀλλ᾽ ἢ ὡς ἐκ παιδὸς ἀνὴρ μεταβάλλοντος ἢ ὡς ἐξ ὕδατος ἀήρ.

Now there are two ways in which one thing comes from another. I do not mean "from" in the sense of "after," as the Olympian games are said to come from the Isthmian, but as a man comes from a boy as a result of a boy changing, or as air comes from water.

994a25 Ergo sic ex puero fieri virum dicimus, quomodo ex eo quod fit, quod factum est, aut ex eo quod perficitur, perfectum. [310]

ὡς μὲν οὖν ἐκ παιδὸς ἄνδρα γίγνεσθαί φαμεν, ὡς ἐκ τοῦ γιγνομένου τὸ γεγονὸς ἢ ἐκ τοῦ ἐπιτελουμένου τὸ τετελεσμένον

We say, then, that a man comes from a boy in the sense that what has come into being comes from what is coming into being, or in the sense that what has been completed comes from what is being completed.

Semper enim est medium inter esse et non esse, generatio; ita et quod fit, existentis et non existentis.

(ἀεὶ γάρ ἐστι μεταξύ, ὥσπερ τοῦ εἶναι καὶ μὴ εἶναι γένεσις, οὕτω καὶ τὸ γιγνόμενον τοῦ ὄντος καὶ μὴ ὄντος:

For generation is always midway between being and non-being, and thus whatever is coming into being is midway between what is and what is not.

Est autem addiscens qui fit sciens; et hoc est quod dicitur, quod fit ex ad-

ἔστι γὰρ ὁ μανθάνων γιγνόμενος ἐπιστήμων, καὶ τοῦτ᾽ ἐστὶν ὃ λέγε-

Now a learner is one who is becoming learned, and this is the meaning of the

discente sciens: hoc veto ex aere aqua, corrupto altero.

ται, {30} ὅτι γίγνεται ἐκ μανθάνοντος ἐπιστήμων): τὸ δ᾽ ὡς ἐξ ἀέρος ὕδωρ, φθειρομένου θατέρου.

statement that the man of science comes from the learner. But water comes from air in the sense that it comes into being when the latter ceases to be.

994a31   Propter quod ilia quidem non reflectuntur adinvicem, nec fit ex viro puer. Non enim fit ex generatione quod fit, sed est post generationem. [311]

διὸ ἐκεῖνα μὲν οὐκ ἀνακάμπτει εἰς ἄλληλα, {994b1} οὐδὲ γίγνεται ἐξ ἀνδρὸς παῖς (οὐ γὰρ γίγνεται ἐκ τῆς γενέσεως τὸ γιγνόμενον ἀλλ᾽ <ὃ> ἔστι μετὰ τὴν γένεσιν:

This is why changes of the former kind are not reversible, and thus a boy does not come from a man. The reason is that what has come into being does not come from generation, but exists after generation.

Sic enim est dies ex aurora, quia post hanc: propter quod nec aurora ex die. Altera vero reflectuntur.

οὕτω γὰρ καὶ ἡμέρα ἐκ τοῦ πρωῒ, ὅτι μετὰ τοῦτο: διὸ οὐδὲ τὸ πρωῒ ἐξ ἡμέρας): θάτερα δὲ ἀνακάμπτει.

This is the way in which the day comes from the dawn, namely, in the sense that it exists after the dawn: because of this the dawn cannot come from the day. On the other hand, changes of the latter sort are reversible.

994b3   Utroque autem modo impossibile est in infinitum ire: existentium vero intermediorum necesse est finem esse. Quaedam vero adinvicem reflectuntur. Alterius enim corruptio, alterius est generatio. [312]

ἀμφοτέρως δὲ ἀδύνατον εἰς ἄπειρον ἰέναι: τῶν μὲν γὰρ ὄντων μεταξὺ {5} ἀνάγκη τέλος εἶναι, τὰ δ᾽ εἰς ἄλληλα ἀνακάμπτει: ἡ γὰρ θατέρου φθορὰ θατέρου ἐστὶ γένεσις.

Now in neither way is it possible to proceed to infinity; for existing intermediaries must have some end, and one thing may be changed into the other because the corruption of one is the generation of the other.

994b6   Simul autem impossibile primum sempiternum corrumpi. Quoniam enim non est infinita generatio in sursum, necesse ex quo corrupto primo aliquid factum est, non sempiternum esse. [314]

ἅμα δὲ καὶ ἀδύνατον τὸ πρῶτον ἀΐδιον ὂν φθαρῆναι: ἐπεὶ γὰρ οὐκ ἄπειρος ἡ γένεσις ἐπὶ τὸ ἄνω, ἀνάγκη ἐξ οὗ φθαρέντος πρώτου τι ἐγένετο μὴ ἀΐδιον εἶναι.

At the same time it is impossible that an eternal first cause should be corrupted, for, since generation is not infinite in an upward direction, then a first principle by whose corruption something else is produced could not be eternal.

---

301. Postquam Philosophus praemisit quod causae entium non sunt infinitae, hic probat propositum.

Et primo, quod non sint infinitae in directum.

Secundo, quod non sint infinitae secundum speciem, ibi, *sed si infinitae essent* et cetera.

Circa primum quatuor facit.

Primo ostendit propositum in causis efficientibus vel moventibus.

Secundo in causis materialibus, ibi, *at vero nec in deorsum*.

Tertio in causis finalibus, ibi, *amplius autem quod est cuius causa* et cetera.

Quarto in causis formalibus, ibi, *sed nec quod quid erat esse* et cetera.

Circa primum sic procedit.

Primo proponit quamdam propositionem: scilicet, quod in omnibus his, quae sunt media inter duo extrema, quorum unum est ultimum, et aliud primum, necesse est quod illud quod est primum, sit causa posteriorum, scilicet medii et ultimi.

302. Et hanc propositionem manifestat per divisionem: quia, si oporteat nos dicere quid sit causa inter

301. Having assumed above that the causes of beings are not infinite in number, the Philosopher now proves this.

First (994a11; [301]), he proves that there are not an infinite number of causes in a series;

and second (994b27; [330]), that the species of causes are not infinite in number, at *again, if the species of causes*.

In regard to the first he does four things.

First, he proves his assumption in the case of efficient or moving causes;

second (994a19; [305]), in the case of material causes, at *neither is it possible*;

third (994b9; [316]), in the case of final causes, at *again, that for the sake of which*;

and fourth (994b16; [320]), in the case of formal causes, at *nor can the quiddity*.

In regard to the first he proceeds as follows.

First, he lays down this premise. In the case of all those things that lie between two extremes, one of which is last and the other first, the first is necessarily the cause of those which come after it (namely, what is intermediate and what is last).

302. Then he proves this premise by a process of division. For if we had to say which of the three—that is,

aliqua tria, quae sunt primum, medium et ultimum, ex necessitate dicemus causam esse id quod est primum. Non enim possumus dicere id quod est ultimum, esse causam omnium, quia nullius est causa; alioquin non est ultimum, cum effectus sit posterior causa. Sed nec possumus dicere quod medium sit causa omnium; quia nec est causa nisi unius tantum, scilicet ultimi.

303. Et ne aliquis intelligat, quod medium nunquam habeat post se nisi unum, quod est ultimum, quod tunc solum contingit, quando inter duo extrema est unum medium tantum, ideo ad hoc excludendum concludit quod nihil ad propositum differt, utrum sit unum tantum medium, vel plura: quia omnia plura media accipiuntur loco unius, inquantum conveniunt in ratione medii.

Et similiter non differt utrum sint media finita vel infinita; quia dummodo habeant rationem medii, non possunt esse prima causa movens.

Et quia ante omnem secundam causam moventem requiritur prima causa movens, requiritur quod ante omnem causam mediam sit causa prima, quae nullo modo sit media, quasi habens aliam causam ante se.

Sed, si praedicto modo ponantur causae moventes procedere in infinitum, sequitur, quod omnes causae sunt mediae. Et sic universaliter oportet dicere, quod cuiuslibet infiniti, sive in ordine causae, sive in ordine magnitudinis, omnes partes sint mediae: si enim esset aliqua pars quae non esset media, oporteret, quod vel esset prima vel ultima: et utrumque repugnat rationi infiniti, quod excludit omnem terminum et principium et finem.

304. Est autem et ad aliud attendendum: quod, si alicuius finiti sint plures partes mediae, non omnes partes simili ratione sunt mediae. Nam quaedam magis appropinquant primo, quaedam magis appropinquant ultimo. Sed in infinito quod non habet primum et ultimum, nulla pars potest magis appropinquare vel minus principio aut ultimo. Et ideo usque ad quamcumque partem, quam modo signaveris, omnes partes similiter sunt mediae. Sic igitur, si causae moventes procedant in infinitum, nulla erit causa prima: sed causa prima erat causa omnium: ergo sequeretur, quod totaliter omnes causae tollerentur: sublata enim causa tolluntur ea quorum est causa.

305. Deinde cum dicit *at vero* ostendit, quod non est possibile procedere in infinitum in causis materialibus.

Et primo proponit quod intendit.

the first, the intermediate, or the last—is the cause of the others, we would have to say that the first is the cause. We could not say that what is last is the cause of all the others, because it is not a cause of anything. For in other respects what is last is not a cause, since an effect follows a cause. Nor could we say that the intermediate is the cause of all the others, because it is the cause of only one of them, namely, what is last.

303. And lest someone should think that an intermediate is followed by only one thing, namely, what is last (for this occurs only when there is a single thing between two extremes), in order to exclude this interpretation he adds that it makes no difference to the premise given above whether there is only one intermediate or several, because all intermediates are taken together as one insofar as they have in common the character of an intermediate.

Nor again does it make any difference whether there are a finite or infinite number of intermediates, because so long as they have the nature of an intermediate they cannot be the first cause of motion.

Further, since there must be a first cause of motion prior to every secondary cause of motion, then there must be a first cause prior to every intermediate cause, which is not an intermediate in any sense, as though it had a cause prior to itself.

But if we were to hold that there is an infinite series of moving causes in the above way, then all causes would be intermediate ones. Thus we would have to say without qualification that all parts of any infinite thing, whether of a series of causes or of continuous quantities, are intermediate ones. For if there were a part that was not an intermediate one, it would have to be either a first or a last, and both of these are opposed to the nature of the infinite, which excludes every limit, whether it be a starting point or a terminus.

304. Now there is another point that must be noted—namely, that if there are several intermediate parts in any finite thing, not all parts are intermediate to the same degree, for some are closer to what is first, and some to what is last. But in the case of some infinite thing in which there is neither a first nor a last part, no part can be closer to or farther away from either what is first or what is last. Therefore, all parts are intermediates to the same degree right down to the one you designate now. Consequently, if the causes of motion proceed to infinity in this way, there will be no first cause. But a first cause is the cause of all things. Therefore, it will follow that all causes are eliminated, for when a cause is removed the things of which it is the cause are also removed.

305. *Neither is it possible* (994a19). He shows that it is impossible to proceed to infinity in the case of material causes.

First (994a19; [300]), he states what he intends to prove.

Secundo probat propositum, ibi, *dupliciter enim fit hoc ex hoc* et cetera.

Circa primum considerandum est, quod patiens subiicitur agenti: unde procedere in agentibus est sursum ire, procedere autem in patientibus est in deorsum ire.

Sicut autem agere attribuitur causae moventi, ita pati attribuitur materiae. Unde processus causarum moventium est in sursum, processus autem causarum materialium est in deorsum.

Quia ergo ostenderat, quod non est in infinitum procedere in causis moventibus quasi in sursum procedendo, subiungit, quod nec possibile est ire in infinitum in deorsum, secundum scilicet processum causarum materialium, supposito, quod sursum ex parte causarum moventium inveniatur aliquod principium.

306. Et exemplificat de processu naturalium, qui est in deorsum: ut si dicamus quod ex igne fit aqua, et ex aqua terra, et sic in infinitum. Et utitur hoc exemplo secundum opinionem antiquorum naturalium, qui posuerunt unum aliquod elementorum esse principium aliorum quodam ordine.

307. Potest autem et aliter exponi, ut intelligamus, quod in causis moventibus manifesti sunt ad sensum ultimi effectus, qui non movent: et ideo non quaeritur, si procedatur in infinitum in inferius secundum illud genus, sed si procedatur in superius.

Sed in genere causarum materialium e converso supponitur unum primum, quod sit fundamentum et basis aliorum; et dubitatur utrum in infinitum procedatur in deorsum secundum processum eorum quae generantur ex materia.

Et hoc sonat exemplum propositum: non enim dicit ut ignis ex aqua, et hoc ex alio, sed e converso, ex igne aqua et ex hoc aliud: unde supponitur prima materia, et quaeritur, an sit processus in infinitum in his quae generantur ex materia.

308. Deinde cum dicit *dupliciter autem* probat propositum: et circa hoc quatuor facit.

Primo distinguit duos modos, quibus fit aliquid ex aliquo.

Secundo ostendit duplicem differentiam inter illos duos modos, ibi, *ergo sic ex puero.*

Second (994a22; [308]), he proceeds with his proof, at *now there are two ways.*

In regard to the first, it must be noted that a patient is subjected to the action of an agent. Therefore, to pass from agent to agent is to proceed in an upward direction, whereas to pass from patient to patient is to proceed in a downward direction.

Now just as action is attributed to the cause of motion, so is undergoing action attributed to matter. Therefore, among the causes of motion the process is in an upward direction, whereas among material causes the process is in a downward direction.

Consequently, since he showed among moving causes that it is impossible to proceed to infinity in an upward direction (as it were), he adds that it is impossible to proceed to infinity in a downward direction (that is, in the process of material causes), granted that there is a starting point in an upward direction among the causes of motion.

306. He illustrates this by way of the process of natural bodies, which proceeds in a downward direction, as if we were to say that water comes from fire, earth from water, and so on to infinity. He uses this example in accordance with the opinion of the ancient philosophers of nature, who held that one of these elements is the source of the others in a certain order.

307. However, this can also be explained in another way, inasmuch as we understand that in the case of moving causes there are evident to the senses certain ultimate effects which do not move anything else. Therefore, we do not ask if there is an infinite regress in the lower members of that genus, but if there is an infinite regress in the higher ones.

But in regard to the genus of material causes, he assumes that there is one first cause which is the foundation and basis of the others; and he inquires whether there is an infinite regress in a downward direction in the process of those things that are generated from matter.

The example which he gives illustrates this, because he does not say that fire comes from water and this in turn from something else, but the converse, namely, that water comes from fire, and something else again from this. For this reason first matter is held to exist, and he asks whether the things that are generated from matter proceed to infinity.

308. *Now there are two ways in which* (994a22). He proves his original thesis. Concerning this he does four things.

First (994a22; [308]), he distinguishes between the two ways in which one thing comes from something else.

Second (994a25; [310]), he shows that these two ways differ in two respects, at *we say, then, that a man.*

Tertio ostendit quod secundum neutrum eorum contingit procedere in infinitum, ibi, *utroque autem modo impossibile est* et cetera.

Quarto ostendit secundum quem illorum modorum ex primo materiali principio alia fiant, ibi, *simul autem impossibile* et cetera.

Dicit ergo primo, quod duobus modis fit aliquid ex aliquo proprie et per se. Et utitur isto modo loquendi, ut excludat illum modum, quo dicitur improprie aliquid fieri ex aliquo ex hoc solo, quod fit post illud: ut si dicamus, quod quaedam festa Graecorum, quae dicebantur Olympia, fiunt ex quibusdam aliis festis, quae dicebantur Isthmia, puta si nos diceremus quod festum Epiphaniae fit ex festo Natalis. Hoc autem non proprie dicitur, quia fieri est quoddam mutari: in mutatione autem non solum requiritur ordo duorum terminorum, sed etiam subiectum idem utriusque: quod quidem non contingit in praedicto exemplo: sed hoc dicimus, secundum quod imaginamur tempus esse ut subiectum diversorum festorum.

309. Sed oportet proprie dicere aliquid fieri ex aliquo, quando aliquod subiectum mutatur de hoc in illud. Et hoc dupliciter. Uno modo sicut dicimus, quod ex puero fit vir, inquantum scilicet puer mutatur de statu puerili in statum virilem: alio modo sicut dicimus, quod ex aqua fit aer per aliquam transmutationem.

310. Deinde cum dicit *ergo sic* ostendit duas differentias inter praedictos modos.

Quarum prima est, quia dicimus ex puero fieri virum, sicut ex eo quod est in fieri, fit illud quod iam est factum; aut ex eo quod est in perfici, fit illud quod iam est perfectum. Illud enim quod est in fieri et in perfici, est medium inter ens et non ens, sicut generatio est medium inter esse et non esse.

Et ideo, quia per medium venitur ad extremum, dicimus, quod ex eo quod generatur fit illud quod generatum est, et ex eo quod perficitur, fit illud quod perfectum est. Et sic dicimus, quod ex puero fit vir, vel quod ex addiscente fit sciens, quia addiscens se habet ut in fieri ad scientem.

In alio autem modo, quo dicimus ex aere fieri aquam, unum extremorum non se habet ut via vel medium ad alterum, sicut fieri ad factum esse; sed magis ut terminus a quo recedit, ut ad alium terminum perveniatur. Et ideo ex uno corrupto fit alterum.

311. Deinde cum dicit *propter quod* concludit ex praemissa differentia, aliam differentiam. Quia enim in primo modo unum se habet ad alterum ut fieri ad factum esse, et medium ad terminum, patet, quod habent

Third (994b3; [312]), he shows that it is impossible to proceed to infinity in either of these ways, at *now in neither way*.

Fourth (994b6; [314]), he shows in which of these ways other things come from the first material principle, at *at the same time*.

He says, first, that one thing comes from another properly and *per se* in two ways. He speaks thus in order to exclude that way in which something is said in an improper sense to come from something else only by reason of the fact that it comes after it, as when it is said that certain feasts of the Greeks called the Olympian come from those called the Isthmian, or as if we were to say that the feast of Epiphany comes from the Nativity. But this is an improper use of the word, because the process of coming to be is a change, and in a change it is necessary not only that an order exist between the two limits of the change but also that both limits have the same subject. Now this is not the case in the above example, but we speak in this way insofar as we think of time as the subject of different feasts.

309. Now, properly speaking, it is necessary to say that one thing comes from something else when some subject is changed from this into that. This occurs in two ways: first, as when we say that a man comes from a boy in the sense that a boy is changed from boyhood to manhood; second, as when we say that air comes from water as a result of substantial change.

310. *We say, then, that a man* (994a25). He explains the twofold sense in which these two ways differ.

First, we say that a man comes from a boy in the sense that what has already come into being comes from what is coming into being, or in the sense that what has already been completed comes from what is being completed. For anything in a state of becoming and of being completed is midway between being and non-being, just as generation is midway between existence and nonexistence.

Therefore, since we reach an extreme through an intermediate, we say that what has been generated comes from what is being generated, and that what has been completed comes from what is being completed. Now this is the sense in which we say that a man comes from a boy, or a man of science from a learner, because a learner is one who is becoming a man of science.

But in the other sense—the one in which we say that water comes from fire—one of the limits of the change is not related to the other as a passage or intermediate, as generation is to being, but rather as the limit from which a thing starts in order to reach another limit. Therefore, one comes from the other when the other is corrupted.

311. *This is why changes* (994a31). He infers another difference from the foregoing one. Since, in the first way, one thing is related to the other as generation is to being, and as an intermediate to a limit, it is evident that one

ordinem naturaliter adinvicem. Et ideo non reflectuntur adinvicem, ut indifferenter unum fiat ex altero. Unde non dicimus quod ex viro fiat puer sicut dicimus e converso.

Cuius ratio est, quia illa duo ex quorum uno secundum istum modum dicitur alterum fieri, non se habent adinvicem sicut duo termini mutationis alicuius; sed sicut ea, quorum unum est post alterum.

Et hoc est quod dicit, quod illud *quod fit*, idest terminus generationis, scilicet esse, non fit ex generatione, quasi ipsa generatio mutetur in esse; sed est post generationem, quia naturali ordine consequitur ad generationem, sicut terminus est post viam, et ultimum post medium.

Unde, si consideramus ista duo, scilicet generationem et esse, non differunt ab illo modo quem exclusimus, in quo consideratur ordo tantum; sicut cum dicimus, quod dies fit ex aurora, quia est post auroram. Et propter istum naturalem ordinem, non dicimus e converso, quod aurora fit *ex die*, idest post diem. Et ex eadem ratione non potest esse, quod puer fiat ex viro.

Sed secundum alterum modum, quo aliquid fit ex altero, invenitur reflexio. Sicut enim aqua generatur ex aere corrupto, ita aer generatur ex aqua corrupta. Et hoc ideo, quia ista duo non se habent adinvicem secundum naturalem ordinem, scilicet ut medium ad terminum; sed sicut duo extrema quorum utrumque potest esse et primum et ultimum.

312. Deinde cum dicit *utroque autem* ostendit quod non sit procedere in infinitum secundum utrumque istorum modorum.

Et primo secundum primum, prout dicimus ex puero fieri virum. Illud enim ex quo dicimus aliquid fieri, sicut ex puero virum, se habet ut medium inter duo extrema, scilicet inter esse et non esse: sed positis extremis impossibile est esse infinita media: quia extremum infinitati repugnat: ergo secundum istum modum non convenit procedere in infinitum.

313. Similiter etiam nec secundum alium; quia in alio modo invenitur reflexio extremorum adinvicem, propter hoc quod alterius corruptio est alterius generatio, ut dictum est.

Ubicumque autem est reflexio, reditur ad primum, ita scilicet quod id quod fuit primo principium, postea sit terminus. Quod in infinitis non potest contingere, in

is naturally ordained to the other. Therefore, they are not reversible so that one comes from the other indifferently. Consequently, we do not say that a boy comes from a man, but the reverse.

The reason for this is that those two things, of which one is said to come from the other in this way, are not related to each other in the same way as the two limits of a change, but as two things one of which comes after the other in sequence.

And this is what he means when he says that *what has come into being* (that is, the terminus of generation or being) does not come from generation as though generation itself were changed into being, but is that which exists after generation, because it follows generation in a natural sequence. This is in the same way that one's destination comes after a journey, and as what is last comes after what is intermediate.

Therefore, if we consider these two things—generation and being—the way in which they are related does not differ from the one we have excluded in which sequence alone is considered, as when we say that the day comes from the dawn because it comes after the dawn. Moreover, this natural sequence prevents us from saying in an opposite way that the dawn comes *from the day*, that is, after the day. For the same reason, a boy cannot come from a man.

But in the other sense in which one thing comes from another, the process is reversible; just as water is generated by reason of air being corrupted, in a similar way air is generated by reason of water being corrupted. The reason is that these two are not related to each other in a natural sequence as an intermediate to a limit, but as two limits, either one of which can be first or last.

312. *Now in neither way* (994b3). He shows that it is impossible to proceed to infinity in either of these ways.

First, in the way in which we say that a man comes from a boy. For the thing from which we say something else comes as a man comes from a boy has the position of an intermediary between two limits (that is, between being and non-being). But an infinite number of intermediates cannot exist when certain limits are held to exist, since limits are opposed to infinity. Therefore, it is impossible to have an infinite series in this way.

313. In like manner, it is impossible to have an infinite series in the other way, for in that way one limit is converted into the other because the corruption of one is the generation of the other, as has been explained.

Now, wherever a reversible process exists, there is a return to some first thing in the sense that what was at first a starting-point is afterwards a terminus. This cannot

quibus non est principium et finis. Ergo nullo modo ex aliquo potest aliquid fieri in infinitum.

314. Deinde cum dicit *simul autem* ostendit quod praedictorum modorum ex prima materia aliquid fiat. Ubi considerandum est, quod Aristoteles utitur hic duabus communibus suppositionibus, in quibus omnes antiqui naturales conveniebant:

quarum una est, quod sit aliquod primum principium materiale, ita scilicet quod in generationibus rerum non procedatur in infinitum ex parte superiori, scilicet eius ex quo generatur.

Secunda suppositio est, quod prima materia est sempiterna. Ex hac igitur secunda suppositione statim concludit, quod ex prima materia non fit aliquid secundo modo, scilicet sicut ex aere corrupto fit aqua, quia scilicet illud quod est sempiternum, non potest corrumpi.

315. Sed quia posset aliquis dicere, quod primum principium materiale non ponitur a philosophis sempiternum, propter hoc quod unum numero manens sit sempiternum, sed quia est sempiternum per successionem, sicut si ponatur humanum genus sempiternum: hoc excludit ex prima suppositione, dicens, quod, quia generatio non est infinita in sursum, sed devenitur ad aliquod primum principium materiale, necesse est quod, si aliquid sit primum materiale principium, ex quo fiunt alia per eius corruptionem, quod non sit illud sempiternum de quo philosophi dicunt. Non enim posset esse illud primum materiale principium sempiternum, si eo corrupto alia generarentur, et iterum ipsum ex alio corrupto generaretur. Unde manifestum est, quod ex primo materiali principio fit aliquid, sicut ex imperfecto et in potentia existente, quod est medium inter purum non ens et ens actu; non autem sicut aqua ex aere fit corrupto.

occur in the case of things that are infinite, in which there is neither a starting-point nor a terminus. Consequently, there is no way in which one thing can come from another in an infinite regress.

314. *At the same time it is impossible* (994b6). He shows in which of these ways something comes from first matter. Now it must be noted that in this place Aristotle uses two common suppositions accepted by all of the ancient philosophers.

First, that there is a primary material principle, and therefore that in the process of generation there is no infinite regress on the part of the higher, namely, of that from which a thing is generated.

Second, that matter is eternal. Therefore, from this second supposition he immediately concludes that nothing comes from first matter in the second way—that is, in the way in which water comes from air as a result of the latter's corruption, because what is eternal cannot be corrupted.

315. But since someone could say that the philosophers did not hold that the first material principle is eternal because it remains numerically one eternally, but because it is eternal by succession (as if the human race were held to be eternal), he therefore excludes this from the first supposition. He says that since generation is not infinite in an upward direction but stops at a first material principle, then if there is a first material principle by reason of whose corruption other things come into being, it must not be the eternal principle of which the philosophers speak. The reason is that the first material principle cannot be eternal if other things are generated by reason of its corruption and it in turn is generated by the corruption of something else. It is evident, then, that a thing comes from this first material principle as something imperfect and potential which is midway between pure non-being and actual being, but not as water comes from air by reason of the latter's corruption.

LECTURE 4

The existence of first final and formal causes

994b9 Amplius autem quod est cuius causa, finis est. Tale autem quod non alicuius causa, sed alia illius. [316]

ἔτι δὲ τὸ οὗ ἕνεκα τέλος, τοιοῦτον δὲ ὃ μὴ ἄλλου {10} ἕνεκα ἀλλὰ τἆλλα ἐκείνου,

Again, that for the sake of which something comes to be is an end. Now such a thing is not for the sake of something else, but other things are for its sake.

Quare, si quidem fuerit tale ipsum ultimum, non erit infinitum; si vero nihil tale, non erit cuius causa.

ὥστ᾽ εἰ μὲν ἔσται τοιοῦτόν τι ἔσχατον, οὐκ ἔσται ἄπειρον, εἰ δὲ μηθὲν τοιοῦτον, οὐκ ἔσται τὸ οὗ ἕνεκα,

Therefore, if there is such a thing as an ultimate end, there will not be an infinite regress; but if there is no ultimate end, there will be no reason for which things come to be.

994b12 Sed qui infinitum faciunt, latet auferentes boni naturam. [317]

ἀλλ᾽ οἱ τὸ ἄπειρον ποιοῦντες λανθάνουσιν ἐξαιροῦντες τὴν τοῦ ἀγαθοῦ φύσιν

Now those who posit infinity do away with the nature of the good without realizing it.

994b13 Et nullus conabitur aliquid facere ad terminum non futurus venire. [318]

(καίτοι οὐθεὶς ἂν ἐγχειρήσειεν οὐδὲν πράττειν μὴ μέλλων ἐπὶ πέρας ἥξειν):

But no one will attempt to do anything unless he thinks he can carry it through to its term.

994b14 Neque utique erit intellectus in talibus. Nam causa alicuius semper facit qui intellectum habet: hic enim terminus finis est rei. [319]

οὐδ᾽ ἂν εἴη νοῦς ἐν {15} τοῖς οὖσιν: ἕνεκα γάρ τινος ἀεὶ πράττει ὅ γε νοῦν ἔχων, τοῦτο δέ ἐστι πέρας: τὸ γὰρ τέλος πέρας ἐστίν.

Nor will there be any intelligence in such matters, because one who has intelligence always acts for the sake of something, since this limit is the end of a thing.

994b16 Sed nec quod quid erat esse convenit reduci ad aliquam definitionem multiplicantem rationem. [320]

ἀλλὰ μὴν οὐδὲ τὸ τί ἦν εἶναι ἐνδέχεται ἀνάγεσθαι εἰς ἄλλον ὁρισμὸν πλεονάζοντα τῷ λόγῳ:

Nor can the quiddity be reduced to a definition which adds to the defining notes.

994b18 Semper enim quae ante est, magis est, et quae posterior non est. Cuius autem primum non est, nec erit quod habitum est. [322]

ἀεί τε γὰρ ἔστιν ὁ ἔμπροσθεν μᾶλλον, ὁ δ᾽ ὕστερος οὐκ ἔστιν, οὗ δὲ τὸ πρῶτον μὴ ἔστιν, οὐδὲ {20} τὸ ἐχόμενον:

For a prior definition is always more of a definition, whereas a subsequent one is not. Where the first does not apply, neither does a later one.

994b20 Amplius scire destruunt qui ita dicunt. Non enim possibile scire priusquam ad individua perveniatur. [323]

ἔτι τὸ ἐπίστασθαι ἀναιροῦσιν οἱ οὕτως λέγοντες, οὐ γὰρ οἷόν τε εἰδέναι πρὶν εἰς τὰ ἄτομα ἐλθεῖν:

Again, those who speak in this way do away with science, because it is impossible to have science until we reach what is undivided.

994b21 Et cognoscere non est. Nam quae sic sunt infinita, quomodo contingit intelligere? [326]

καὶ τὸ γιγνώσκειν οὐκ ἔστιν, τὰ γὰρ οὕτως ἄπειρα πῶς ἐνδέχεται νοεῖν;

Nor will knowledge itself exist; for how can one understand things that are infinite in this way?

994b23 Non enim simile in linea, quae secundum divisiones non stat: intelligere enim non est non statuentem. Propter quod non enumerabit sectiones, quae per infinita procedunt. [327]

οὐ γὰρ ὅμοιον ἐπὶ τῆς γραμμῆς, ἣ κατὰ τὰς διαιρέσεις μὲν οὐχ ἵσταται, νοῆσαι δ᾽ οὐκ ἔστι μὴ στήσαντα (διόπερ {25} οὐκ ἀριθμήσει τὰς τομὰς ὁ τὴν ἄπειρον διεξιών),

This case is not like that of a line, whose divisibility has no limit, for it would be impossible to understand a line if it had no limits. This is why no one will count the sections, which proceed to infinity.

994b25 Sed materiam in eo quod movetur intelligere est necesse, et infinito nihil est, esse autem non. Si vero non est infinitum, quod est esse infinito? [328]

ἀλλὰ καὶ τὴν ὕλην οὐ κινουμένῳ νοεῖν ἀνάγκη. καὶ ἀπείρῳ οὐδενὶ ἔστιν εἶναι: εἰ δὲ μή, οὐκ ἄπειρόν γ᾽ ἐστὶ τὸ ἀπείρῳ εἶναι.

But it is necessary to understand that there is matter in everything that is moved, and that the infinite involves nothingness, but essence does not. But if there is no infinite, what essence does the infinite have?

994b27 Sed si infinitae essent pluralitate species causarum, non esset nec ita cognoscere. Tunc enim scire putamus, cum causas ipsas noverimus. Infinitum vero secundum adiectionem non est pertransire in finito tempore. [330]

ἀλλὰ μὴν καὶ εἰ ἄπειρά γ' ἦσαν πλήθει τὰ εἴδη τῶν αἰτίων, οὐκ ἂν ἦν οὐδ' οὕτω τὸ γιγνώσκειν· τότε γὰρ εἰδέναι οἰόμεθα {30} ὅταν τὰ αἴτια γνωρίσωμεν· τὸ δ' ἄπειρον κατὰ τὴν πρόσθεσιν οὐκ ἔστιν ἐν πεπερασμένῳ διεξελθεῖν.

Again, if the species of causes were infinite in number, it would also be impossible to know anything. For we think that we have scientific knowledge when we know the causes themselves of things, but what is infinite by addition cannot be traversed in a finite period of time.

---

316. Postquam probavit Philosophus, quod in causis moventibus et materialibus non proceditur in infinitum, hic ostendit idem in causa finali, quae nominatur *cuius causa* fit aliquid. Et ostendit propositum quatuor rationibus:

quarum prima talis est. Id, quod est cuius causa, habet rationem finis. Sed finis est id quod non est propter alia, sed alia sunt propter ipsum. Aut ergo est aliquid tale, aut nihil: et si quidem fuerit aliquid tale, ut scilicet omnia sint propter ipsum, et ipsum non sit propter alia, ipsum erit ultimum in hoc genere; et ita non procedetur in infinitum: si autem nihil inveniatur tale, non erit finis. Et ita tolletur hoc genus causae, quod dicitur cuius causa.

317. Secundam rationem ponit ibi, *sed qui*, quae derivatur ex praemissa ratione. Ex prima enim ratione conclusum est quod qui ponunt infinitatem in causis finalibus, removeant causam finalem. Remota autem causa finali, removetur natura et ratio boni: eadem enim ratio boni et finis est; nam bonum est quod omnia appetunt, ut dicitur in primo *Ethicorum*. Et ideo illi qui ponunt infinitum in causis finalibus, auferunt totaliter naturam boni, licet ipsi hoc non percipiant.

318. Tertiam rationem ponit ibi, *et nullus*, quae talis est. Si sit infinitum in causis finalibus, nullus poterit pervenire ad ultimum terminum, quia infinitorum non est ultimus terminus: sed nullus conatur ad aliquid faciendum nisi per hoc, quod se existimat venturum ad aliquid, sicut ad ultimum terminum: ergo ponentes infinitum in causis finalibus excludunt omnem conatum ad operandum, etiam naturalium rerum: nullius enim rei motus naturalis est nisi ad id ad quod nata est pervenire.

319. Quartam rationem ponit ibi *neque utique* quae talis est. Qui ponit infinitum in causis finalibus, excludit terminum, et per consequens excludit finem cuius causa fit aliquid. Sed omne agens per intellectum agit causa alicuius finis: ergo sequetur quod inter causas operativas non sit intellectus, et ita tolletur intellectus practicus. Quae cum sint inconvenientia, oportet removere pri-

316. Having shown that there is no infinite regress either among the causes of motion or among material causes, the Philosopher now shows that the same thing is true of the final cause, which is called *that for the sake of which* something comes to be (994b9). He proves this by four arguments.

The first is as follows. That for the sake of which something comes to be has the character of an end. But an end does not exist for the sake of other things, but others exist for its sake. Now such a thing either exists or not. If there is something of such a kind that all things exist for its sake and not it for the sake of something else, it will be the last thing in this order; and thus there will not be an infinite regress. However, if no such thing exists, no end will exist; thus the genus of final cause will be eliminated.

317. *Now those who posit infinity* (994b12). He gives the second argument, which is derived from the foregoing one, for from the first argument he concluded that those who posit an infinite regress in final causes do away with the final cause. Now when the final cause is removed, so also is the nature and notion of the good, because "good" and "end" have the same meaning, since the good is that which all desire, as is said in *Ethics* 1. Therefore, those who hold that there is an infinite regress in final causes do away completely with the nature of the good, although they do not realize this.

318. *But no one will attempt* (994b13). He gives the third argument, which is as follows. If there were an infinite number of final causes, no one could reach a last terminus, because there is no last terminus in an infinite series. But no one will attempt to do anything unless he thinks he is able to accomplish something as a final goal. Therefore, those who hold that final causes proceed to infinity do away with every attempt to operate and even with the activities of natural bodies, for a thing's natural movement is only toward something which it is naturally disposed to attain.

319. *Nor will there be* (994b14). He states the fourth argument, which is as follows. One who posits an infinite number of final causes does away with a limit, and therefore with the end for the sake of which a cause acts. But every intelligent agent acts for the sake of some end. Therefore, it would follow that there is no intellect among causes which are productive. Thus the practical intellect

mum, id scilicet ex quo sequuntur, scilicet infinitum a causis finalibus.

320. Deinde cum dicit *sed nec* ostendit quod non sit infinitum in causis formalibus: et circa hoc duo facit.

Primo proponit quod intendit.

Secundo probat propositum, ibi: *semper enim* et cetera.

Circa primum considerandum est quod unumquodque constituitur in specie per propriam formam. Unde definitio speciei maxime significat formam rei. Oportet ergo accipere processum in formis secundum processum in definitionibus. In definitionibus enim una pars est prior altera, sicut genus est prius differentia, et differentiarum una est prior altera. Idem ergo est quod in infinitum procedatur in formis et quod in infinitum procedatur in partibus definitionis.

Et ideo volens ostendere quod non sit procedere in infinitum in causis formalibus, proponit non esse infinitum in partibus definitionis. Et ideo dicit quod non convenit hoc quod est quod quid erat esse, in infinitum reduci ad aliam definitionem, ut sic semper multiplicetur ratio. Puta qui definit hominem in definitione eius ponit animal. Unde definitio hominis reducitur ad definitionem animalis, quae ulterius reducitur ad definitionem alicuius alterius, et sic multiplicatur ratio definitiva. Sed hoc non convenit in infinitum procedere.

321. Non autem hoc dicimus quasi in uno et eodem individuo multiplicentur formae secundum numerum generum et differentiarum, ut scilicet in homine sit alia forma a qua est homo, et alia a qua est animal, et sic aliis; sed quia necesse est ut in rerum natura tot gradus formarum inveniantur, quod inveniuntur genera ordinata et differentiae. Est enim in rebus invenire aliquam formam, quae est forma, et non est forma corporis; et aliquam quae est forma corporis, sed non est forma animati corporis; et sic de aliis.

322. Deinde cum dicit *semper enim* probat propositum quatuor rationibus.

Quarum prima talis est. In multitudine formarum vel rationum semper illa quae est prius *est magis*. Quod non est intelligendum quasi sit completior; quia formae specificae sunt completae. Sed dicitur esse magis, quia est in plus quam illa quae est posterior, quae non est ubicumque est prior. Non enim ubicumque est ratio animalis, est ratio hominis. Ex quo argumentatur, quod si primum non est, *nec habitum* idest consequens est. Sed si in infinitum procedatur in rationibus et formis, non erit prima ratio vel forma definitiva; ergo excludentur omnes consequentes.

is eliminated. But since these things are absurd, we must reject the first position, from which they follow—namely, that there is an infinite number of final causes.

320. *Nor can the quiddity* (994b16). He shows that there is not an infinite number of formal causes. In regard to this he does two things.

First (994b16; [320]), he states what he intends to prove.

Second (994b18; [322]), he proves it, at *for a prior definition.*

Regarding the first we must understand that each thing derives its particular species from its proper form, and this is why the definition of a species signifies chiefly a thing's form. Therefore, we must understand that a procession of forms is consequent upon a procession of definitions, for one part of a definition is prior to another just as genus is prior to difference and one difference is prior to another. Therefore, an infinite regress in forms and an infinite regress in the parts of a definition are one and the same.

Now since Aristotle wishes to show that it is impossible to proceed to infinity in the case of formal causes, he holds that it is impossible to proceed to infinity in the parts of a definition. Hence he says that it is impossible for a thing's quiddity to be reduced to another definition, and so on to infinity, so that the defining notes are always increased in number. For example, one who defines man gives animal in his definition, and therefore the definition of man is reduced to that of animal, and this in turn to the definition of something else, thereby increasing the defining notes. But to proceed to infinity in this way is absurd.

321. Now we do not mean by this that there are the same number of forms in each individual as there are genera and differences (so that in man there is one form by which he is man, another by which he is animal, and so on), but we mean that there must be as many grades of forms in reality as there are orders of genera and differences in knowledge. For we find in reality one form which is not the form of a body, another which is the form of a body but not of an animated body, and so on.

322. *For a prior definition* (994b18). He proves his premise by four arguments.

The first is this. Wherever there are a number of forms or defining notes, a prior definition is always *more of a definition.* This does not mean that a prior form is more complete (for specific forms are complete), but that a prior form belongs to more things than a subsequent form, which is not found wherever a prior form is found (for example, the definition of man is not found wherever that of animal is found). From this he argues that if the first thing does not fit the thing defined, *neither does a later one.* But if there were an infinite regress in definitions and forms, there would be no first definition or definitive form. Hence all subsequent definitions and forms would be eliminated.

323. Secundam rationem ponit ibi *amplius scire* quae talis est. Impossibile est aliquid sciri prius quam perveniatur ad individua. Non autem accipitur hic individuum singulare, quia scientia non est de singularibus.

Sed individuum potest dici uno modo ipsa ratio speciei specialissimae, quae non dividitur ulterius per essentiales differentias. Et secundum hoc intelligitur quod non habetur perfecta scientia de re, quousque perveniatur ad speciem specialissimam; quia ille qui scit aliquid in genere, nondum habet perfectam scientiam de re.

Et secundum hanc expositionem oportet dicere, quod sicut prima ratio concludebat, quod in causis formalibus non proceditur in infinitum in sursum, ita haec ratio concludit, quod non proceditur in infinitum in deorsum. Sic enim non esset devenire ad speciem specialissimam. Ergo ista positio destruit perfectam scientiam.

324. Sed quia formalis divisio non solum est secundum quod genus dividitur per differentias, per cuius divisionis privationem species specialissima potest dici individuum, sed etiam est secundum quod definitum dividitur in partes definitionis, ut patet in primo *Physicorum*; ideo individuum potest hic dici, cuius definitio non resolvitur in aliqua definientia.

Et secundum hoc, supremum genus est individuum. Et secundum hoc erit sensus, quod non potest haberi scientia de re per aliquam definitionem, nisi deveniatur ad suprema genera, quibus ignoratis impossibile est aliquod posteriorum sciri. Et secundum hoc concludit ratio, quod in causis formalibus non procedatur in infinitum in sursum, sicut et prius.

325. Vel ad idem concludendum potest aliter exponi individuum, ut scilicet propositio immediata dicatur individuum. Si enim procedatur in infinitum in definitionibus in sursum, nulla erit propositio immediata. Et sic universaliter tolletur scientia, quae est de conclusionibus deductis ex principiis immediatis.

326. Deinde cum dicit *et cognoscere* tertiam rationem ponit quae procedit non solum ad scientiam excludendam, sed ad excludendum simpliciter omnem cognitionem humanam. Et circa hanc rationem duo facit.

Primo ponit rationem.

Secundo excludit obiectionem quamdam, ibi, *non enim simile* et cetera.

323. *Again, those who speak* (994b20). He gives the second argument, which is as follows. It is impossible to have scientific knowledge of anything until we come to what is undivided. Now in this place "undivided" cannot mean the singular, because there is no science of the singular.

However, it can be understood in two other ways. First, it can mean the definition itself of the last species, which is not further divided by essential differences. In this sense his statement can mean that we do not have complete knowledge of a thing until we reach its last species, for one who knows the genus to which a thing belongs does not yet have a complete knowledge of that thing.

According to this interpretation, we must say that just as the first argument concluded that it is impossible to have an infinite regress in an upward direction among formal causes, in a similar fashion this second argument concludes that it is impossible to have an infinite regress in a downward direction, otherwise it would be impossible to reach a last species. Therefore, this position destroys any complete knowledge.

324. Now a formal division exists not only when a genus is divided by differences (and when such division is no longer possible the last species can be said to be undivided), but also when the thing defined is divided into its definitive parts, as is evident in *Physics* 1. Therefore, in this place "undivided" can also mean a thing whose definition cannot be resolved into any definitive parts.

Now, according to this the supreme genus is undivided, and from this point of view his statement can mean that we cannot have scientific knowledge of a thing by definition unless we reach its supreme genera, because when these remain unknown it is impossible to know its subsequent genera. And according to this, the second argument concludes (as the former one did) that it is impossible to proceed to infinity in an upward direction among formal causes.

325. Or, in order to reach the same conclusion, "undivided" can be explained in another way, namely, in the sense that an immediate proposition is undivided. For if it were possible to proceed to infinity in an upward direction in the case of definitions, there would be no immediate proposition, and thus science as such (which is about conclusions derived from immediate principles) would be destroyed.

326. *Nor will knowledge* (994b21). He gives the third argument, which proceeds to show that such an infinite regress would destroy not only science but any kind of human knowing whatsoever. In regard to this argument he does two things.

First (994b21; [326]), he gives his argument.

Second (994b23; [327]), he refutes an objection raised against it, at *this case is not like*.

Ratio autem talis est. Unumquodque cognoscitur per intellectum suae formae: sed si in formis procedatur in infinitum, non poterunt intelligi; quia infinitum inquantum huiusmodi, non comprehenditur intellectu: ergo ista positio universaliter destruit cognitionem.

327. Deinde cum dicit **non enim** excludit quamdam obviationem. Posset enim aliquis dicere, quod illud quod habet infinitas formas, potest cognosci, sicut et linea, quae in infinitum dividitur. Sed hoc excludit, dicens, quod non est simile de linea, cuius divisiones non stant, sed in infinitum procedunt. Impossibile enim est quod aliquid intelligatur nisi in aliquo stetur; unde linea, inquantum statuitur ut finita in actu propter suos terminos, sic potest intelligi; secundum vero quod non statur in eius divisione, non potest sciri. Unde nullus potest numerare divisiones lineae secundum quod in infinitum procedunt.

Sed infinitum in formis est infinitum in actu, et non in potentia, sicut est infinitum in divisione lineae; et ideo, si essent infinitae formae, nullo modo esset aliquid scitum vel notum.

328. Deinde cum dicit **sed materiam** ponit quartam rationem, quae talis est. In omni eo quod movetur necesse est intelligere materiam. Omne enim quod movetur est in potentia: ens autem in potentia est materia: ipsa autem materia habet rationem infiniti, et ipsi infinito, quod est materia, convenit ipsum nihil, quia materia secundum se intelligitur absque omni forma. Et, cum ei quod est infinitum, conveniat hoc quod est nihil, sequitur per oppositum, quod illud per quod est esse, non sit infinitum, et quod **infinito**, idest materiae, non sit esse infinitum. Sed esse est per formam: ergo non est infinitum in formis.

329. Est autem hic advertendum quod hic ponit nihil esse de ratione infiniti, non quod privatio sit de ratione materiae, sicut Plato posuit non distinguens privationem a materia; sed quia privatio est de ratione infiniti. Non enim ens in potentia habet rationem infiniti, nisi secundum quod est sub ratione privationis, ut patet in tertio *Physicorum*.

330. Deinde cum dicit **sed si infinitae** ostendit quod non sunt infinitae species causarum, tali ratione. Tunc putamus nos scire unumquodque quando cognoscimus omnes causas eius: sed, si sunt infinitae causae secundum adiunctionem unius speciei ad aliam, non erit pertransire istam infinitatem, ita quod possint omnes causae cognosci: ergo etiam per istum modum excluditur cognitio rerum.

The argument is as follows. We know each thing by understanding its form. But if there were an infinite regress in forms, these forms could not be understood, because the intellect is incapable of understanding the infinite as infinite. Therefore, this position destroys knowing in its entirety.

327. *This case is not like* (994b23). He disposes of an objection, for someone could say that a thing having an infinite number of forms can be understood in the same way as a line which is divided to infinity. But he denies this. He says that this case is not the same as that of a line, whose divisions do not stop but go on to infinity. For it is impossible to understand anything unless some limit is set to it. Therefore, a line can be understood inasmuch as some actual limit is given to it by reason of its extremes. However, it cannot be understood insofar as its division does not terminate. Hence no one can count the divisions of a line insofar as they are infinite.

But as applied to forms "infinite" means actually infinite, and not potentially infinite as it does when applied to the division of a line. Therefore, if there were an infinite number of forms, there would be no way in which a thing could be known either scientifically or in any way at all.

328. *But it is necessary* (994b25). He gives the fourth argument, which runs thus. Matter must be understood to exist in everything that is moved, for whatever is moved is in potency, and what is in potency is matter. But matter itself has the character of the infinite, and nothingness belongs to the infinite in the sense of matter, because matter taken in itself is understood without any of kind of form. And since nothingness belongs to the infinite, it follows contrariwise that the principle by which the infinite is a being is itself not infinite, and that it does not belong to *the infinite* (or to matter) to be infinite in being. But things are by virtue of their form. Hence there is no infinite regress among forms.

329. However, it must be noted that in this place Aristotle holds that the infinite involves the notion of nothingness, not because matter involves the notion of privation (as Plato claimed when he failed to distinguish between privation and matter), but because the infinite involves the notion of privation. For a potential being contains the notion of the infinite only insofar as it comes under the nature of privation, as is evident in *Physics* 3.

330. *Again, if the species* (994b27). He shows that the species of causes are not infinite in number, and he uses the following argument. We think that we have scientific knowledge of each thing when we know all its causes. But if there were an infinite number of causes in the sense that one species of cause may be added to another continuously, it would be impossible to traverse this infinity in such a way that all causes could be known. Hence in this way too the knowing of things would be destroyed.

LECTURE 5

The method of metaphysics

994b32 Contingunt autem auditiones secundum consuetudinem entibus. Nam ut consuevimus ita dignamur dici: et quae praeter ea, non similia videntur, sed praeter consuetudinem minus nota et magis extranea. Nam consuetum notius. [331]

αἱ δ᾽ ἀκροάσεις κατὰ τὰ ἔθη συμβαίνουσιν: ὡς γὰρ εἰώθαμεν οὕτως ἀξιοῦμεν λέγεσθαι, {995a1} καὶ τὰ παρὰ ταῦτα οὐχ ὅμοια φαίνεται ἀλλὰ διὰ τὴν ἀσυνήθειαν ἀγνωστότερα καὶ ξενικώτερα: τὸ γὰρ σύνηθες γνώριμον.

The way in which people are affected by what they hear depends upon the things to which they are accustomed. For it is in terms of such things that we judge statements to be true, and anything over and above these does not seem similar, but less intelligible and more remote. For it is the things to which we are accustomed that are better known.

995a3 Quantam vero vim habeat quod consuetum est, leges ostendunt, in quibus fabularia et puerilia magis valent cognitione de eis propter cosuetudinem. [333]

ἡλίκην δὲ ἰσχὺν ἔχει τὸ σύνηθες οἱ νόμοι δηλοῦσιν, ἐν οἷς τὰ μυθώδη καὶ {5} παιδαριώδη μεῖζον ἰσχύει τοῦ γινώσκειν περὶ αὐτῶν διὰ τὸ ἔθος.

The great force which custom has is shown by the laws, in which legendary and childish elements prevail over our knowledge of them, because of custom.

995a6 Alii vero, si non mathematice quis dicat, non recipiunt dicentes. Alii vero si non exemplariter. Et hi testem induci dignantur poetam. [334]

οἱ μὲν οὖν ἐὰν μὴ μαθηματικῶς λέγῃ τις οὐκ ἀποδέχονται τῶν λεγόντων, οἱ δ᾽ ἂν μὴ παραδειγματικῶς, οἱ δὲ μάρτυρα ἀξιοῦσιν ἐπάγεσθαι ποιητήν.

Now some men will not accept what a speaker says unless he speaks in mathematical terms; others, unless he gives examples; while others expect him to quote a poet as an authority.

Et illi quidem omnia certe. His vero flebilis est certitude aut propter impotentiam complectendi, aut propter micrologiam: habet autem quod certum est tale.

καὶ οἱ μὲν πάντα ἀκριβῶς, τοὺς δὲ λυπεῖ τὸ ἀκριβὲς ἢ διὰ τὸ μὴ δύνασθαι {10} συνείρειν ἢ διὰ τὴν μικρολογίαν: ἔχει γάρ τι τὸ ἀκριβὲς τοιοῦτον,

Again, some want everything stated with certitude, while others find certitude annoying, either because they are incapable of comprehending anything or because they consider exact inquiry to be quibbling—for there is some similarity.

Unde quemadmodum in symbolis et rationibus non liberum esse quibusdam videtur.

ὥστε, καθάπερ ἐπὶ τῶν συμβολαίων, καὶ ἐπὶ τῶν λόγων ἀνελεύθερον εἶναί τισι δοκεῖ.

Hence it seems to some men that just as liberality is lacking when a fee is charged for a banquet, so also is it lacking in arguments.

995a12 Propter quod oportet erudiri quomodo singula sunt recipienda; et absurdum est simul quaerere scientiam et modum sciendi. Est autem neutrum facile accipere. [335]

διὸ δεῖ πεπαιδεῦσθαι πῶς ἕκαστα ἀποδεκτέον, ὡς ἄτοπον ἅμα ζητεῖν ἐπιστήμην καὶ τρόπον ἐπιστήμης: ἔστι δ᾽ οὐδὲ θάτερον ῥάδιον λαβεῖν.

For this reason one must be trained how to meet every kind of argument, and it is absurd to search simultaneously for knowledge and for the method of acquiring it. Neither of these is easily attained.

995a14 Acribologia vero mathematica non in omnibus est expetenda, sed in non habentibus materiam. Propter quod non naturalis est modus: omnis enim forsan natura materiam habet. Ideo primum perscrutandum quid est natura. Ita namque et de quibus est physica, manifestum est. Et si unius scientiae aut plurium est causas et principia considerare. [336]

τὴν {15} δ᾽ ἀκριβολογίαν τὴν μαθηματικὴν οὐκ ἐν ἅπασιν ἀπαιτητέον, ἀλλ᾽ ἐν τοῖς μὴ ἔχουσιν ὕλην. διόπερ οὐ φυσικὸς ὁ τρόπος: ἅπασα γὰρ ἴσως ἡ φύσις ἔχει ὕλην. διὸ σκεπτέον πρῶτον τί ἐστιν ἡ φύσις: οὕτω γὰρ καὶ περὶ τίνων ἡ φυσικὴ δῆλον ἔσται [καὶ εἰ μιᾶς ἐπιστήμης ἢ πλειόνων τὰ αἴτια καὶ {20} τὰς ἀρχὰς θεωρῆσαί ἐστιν].

But the exactness of mathematics is not to be expected in all cases, but only in those which have no matter. This is why its method is not that of natural philosophy; for perhaps the whole of nature contains matter. Hence we must first investigate what nature is, for in this way it will become evident what the things are with which natural philosophy deals, and whether it belongs to one science or to several to consider the causes and principles of things.

331. Postquam Philosophus ostendit, quod consideratio veritatis partim est difficilis et partim facilis, et quod maxime pertinet ad primum philosophum, hic ostendit, quis sit modus conveniens ad considerandum veritatem: et circa hoc duo facit.

Primo enim ponit diversos modos, quos homines sequuntur in consideratione veritatis.

Secundo ostendit quis sit modus conveniens, ibi, *propter quod oportet erudiri* et cetera.

Circa primum duo facit.

Primo ostendit efficaciam consuetudinis in consideratione veritatis.

Secundo concludit diversos modos, quibus homines utuntur in consideratione, propter diversas consuetudines, ibi, *alii vero si non mathematicae* et cetera.

Circa primum duo facit.

Primo ostendit virtutem consuetudinis in consideratione veritatis.

Secundo manifestat per signum, ibi, *quantam vero vim habeat* et cetera.

Dicit ergo primo, quod auditiones contingunt in hominibus de his quae sunt secundum consuetudines. Ea enim, quae sunt consueta, libentius audiuntur et facilius recipiuntur. Dignum enim videtur nobis, ut ita dicatur de quocumque, sicut consuevimus audire. Et si qua dicantur nobis praeter ea quae consuevimus audire, non videntur nobis similia in veritate his quae consuevimus audire. Sed videntur nobis minus nota et magis extranea a ratione, propter hoc quod sunt inconsueta. Illud enim quod est consuetum, est nobis magis notum.

332. Cuius ratio est, quia consuetudo vertitur in naturam; unde et habitus ex consuetudine generatur, qui inclinat per modum naturae. Ex hoc autem quod aliquis habet talem naturam vel talem habitum, habet proportionem determinatam ad hoc vel illud. Requiritur autem ad quamlibet cognitionem determinata proportio cognoscentis ad cognoscibile. Et ideo secundum diversitatem naturarum et habituum accidit diversitas circa cognitionem. Videmus enim, quod hominibus secundum humanam naturam sunt innata prima principia; et secundum habitum virtutis apparet unicuique bonum, quod convenit illi virtuti: sicut et gustui videtur aliquid conveniens, secundum eius dispositionem. Sic igitur, quia consuetudo causat habitum consimilem naturae, contingit quod ea quae sunt consueta sint notiora.

333. Deinde cum dicit *quantam vero* manifestat quod dixerat per quoddam signum; ostendens, quod leges ab hominibus positae ostendunt per experientiam, quantam vim habeat consuetudo: in quibus quidem le-

331. Having shown that the study of truth is in one sense difficult and in another easy, and that it belongs preeminently to first philosophy, the Philosopher now exposes the proper method of investigating the truth. In regard to this he does two things.

First (994b32; [331]), he gives the different methods which men follow in the study of truth.

Second (995a12; [335]), he shows which method is the proper one, at *for this reason one must*.

In regard to the first he does two things.

First, he shows how powerful custom is in the study of truth.

Second (995a6; [334]), he concludes that the different methods which men employ in the study of truth depend on the different things to which they are accustomed, at *now some men*.

In regard to the first he does two things.

First, he shows how powerful custom is in the study of truth.

Second (995a3; [333]), he makes this clear by an example, at *the great force*.

He first says that the way in which people are affected by what they hear depends upon the things to which they are accustomed, because such things are more willingly heard and more easily understood. For things spoken of in a manner to which we are accustomed seem to us to be acceptable; and if any things are said to us over and above what we have been accustomed to hear, these do not seem to have the same degree of truth. As a matter of fact they seem less intelligible to us and further removed from reason just because we are not accustomed to them. For it is the things that we are accustomed to hear that we know best of all.

332. Now the reason for this is that things that are customary become natural. Hence a habit, which disposes us in a way similar to nature, is also acquired by customary activity. And from the fact that someone has some special sort of nature or special kind of habit, he has a definite relationship to one thing or another. But in every kind of cognition there must be a definite relationship between the knower and the object of cognition. Therefore, to the extent that natures and habits differ, there are diverse kinds of cognition. For we see that there are innate first principles in men because of their human nature, and that what is proper to some special virtue appears good to one who has this habit of virtue. Again, something appears palatable to the sense of taste because of its disposition. Therefore, since custom produces a habit which is similar to nature, it follows that what is customary is better known.

333. *The great force* (995a3). Here he makes his previous statement clear by giving a concrete case. He says that the laws which men pass are positive evidence of the force of custom, for the legendary and childish elements in these

gibus propter consuetudinem magis valent fabulariter et pueriliter dicta, ad hoc quod eis assentiatur, quam cognitio veritatis.

Loquitur autem hic Philosophus de legibus ab hominibus adinventis, quae ad conservationem civilem sicut ad ultimum finem ordinantur; et ideo quicumque invenerunt eas, aliqua quibus hominum animi retraherentur a malis et provocarentur ad bona secundum diversitatem gentium et nationum in suis legibus tradiderunt, quamvis multa eorum essent vana et frivola, quae homines a pueritia audientes magis approbabant quam veritatis cognitionem. Sed lex divinitus data ordinat hominem ad veram felicitatem cui omnis falsitas repugnat. Unde in lege Dei nulla falsitas continetur.

334. Deinde cum dicit *alii vero* hic ostendit quomodo homines in consideratione veritatis propter consuetudinem diversos modos acceptant: et dicit, quod quidam non recipiunt quod eis dicitur, nisi dicatur eis per modum mathematicum. Et hoc quidem convenit propter consuetudinem his, qui in mathematicis sunt nutriti.

Et quia consuetudo est similis naturae, potest etiam hoc quibusdam contingere propter indispositionem: illis scilicet, qui sunt fortis imaginationis, non habentes intellectum multum elevatum.

Alii vero sunt, qui nihil volunt recipere nisi proponatur eis aliquod exemplum sensibile, vel propter consuetudinem, vel propter dominium sensitivae virtutis in eis et debilitatem intellectus.

Quidam vero sunt qui nihil reputent esse dignum ut aliquid eis inducatur absque testimonio poetae, vel alicuius auctoris. Et hoc etiam est vel propter consuetudinem, vel propter defectum iudicii, quia non possunt diiudicare utrum ratio per certitudinem concludat; et ideo quasi non credentes suo iudicio requirunt iudicium alicuius noti.

Sunt etiam aliqui qui omnia volunt sibi dici per certitudinem, idest per diligentem inquisitionem rationis. Et hoc contingit propter bonitatem intellectus iudicantis, et rationes inquirentis; dummodo non quaeratur certitudo in his, in quibus certitudo esse non potest.

Quidam vero sunt qui tristantur, si quid per certitudinem cum diligenti discussione inquiratur. Quod quidem potest contingere dupliciter.

Uno modo propter impotentiam complectendi: habent enim debilem rationem, unde non sufficiunt ad considerandum ordinem complexionis priorum et posteriorum.

Alio modo propter micrologiam, idest parvorum ratiocinationem. Cuius similitudo quaedam est in cer-

laws are more effective in winning assent than is knowledge of the truth.

Now the Philosopher is speaking here of the laws devised by men, which have as their ultimate end the preservation of the political community. Therefore, the men who have established these laws have handed down in them (in keeping with the diversity of peoples and nations involved) certain directives by which human souls might be drawn away from evil and persuaded to do good, although many of them, which men had heard from childhood and of which they approved more readily than of what they knew to be true, were empty and foolish. (But the law given by God directs men to that true happiness to which everything false is opposed. Therefore, there is nothing false in the divine law.)

334. *Now some men* (995a6). Here he shows how men as a result of custom use different methods in the study of truth. He says that some men listen to what is said to them only if it is mathematical in character, and this is acceptable to those who have been educated in mathematics because of the habits which they have.

Now, since custom is like nature, the same thing can also happen to certain men because they are poorly disposed in some respect, such as those who have a strong imagination but little intelligence.

Then there are others who do not wish to accept anything unless they are given a concrete example, either because they are accustomed to this or because their sensory powers dominate and their intellect is weak.

Again, there are some who think that nothing is convincing enough unless a poet or some authority is cited. This is also a result either of custom or of poor judgment, because they cannot decide for themselves whether the conclusion of an argument is certain; therefore, having no faith in their own judgment, as it were, they require the judgment of some recognized authority.

Again, there are others who want everything said to them with certitude, that is, by way of careful rational investigation. This occurs because of the superior intelligence of the one making the judgment and the arguments of the one conducting the investigation, provided that one does not look for certitude where it cannot be had.

On the other hand, there are some who are annoyed if some matter is investigated in an exact way by means of a careful discussion. This can occur for two reasons.

First, they lack the ability to comprehend anything; since their reasoning power is poor, they are unable to understand the order in which premises are related to conclusions.

Second, it occurs because of quibbling—that is, reasoning about the smallest matters— which bears some resem-

titudinali inquisitione, quae nihil indiscussum relinquit usque ad minima. Imaginantur autem quidam, quod sicut in symbolis conviviorum non pertinet ad liberalitatem, quod debeant etiam minima computari in ratiocinio, ita etiam sit quaedam importunitas et illiberalitas, si homo velit circa cognitionem veritatis etiam minima discutere.

335. Deinde cum dicit *propter quod* ostendit quis sit modus conveniens ad inquirendum veritatem; et circa hoc duo facit.

Primo enim ostendit, quomodo homo possit cognoscere modum convenientem in inquisitione veritatis.

Secundo ostendit, quod ille modus qui est simpliciter melior, non debet in omnibus quaeri, ibi, *acribologia vero* et cetera.

Dicit ergo primo, quod quia diversi secundum diversos modos veritatem inquirunt; ideo oportet quod homo instruatur per quem modum in singulis scientiis sint recipienda ea quae dicuntur. Et quia non est facile quod homo simul duo capiat, sed dum ad duo attendit, neutrum capere potest; absurdum est, quod homo simul quaerat scientiam et modum qui convenit scientiae. Et propter hoc debet prius addiscere logicam quam alias scientias, quia logica tradit communem modum procedendi in omnibus aliis scientiis. Modus autem proprius singularum scientiarum, in scientiis singulis circa principium tradi debet.

336. Deinde cum dicit *acribologia vero* ostendit quod ille modus, qui est simpliciter optimus, non debet in omnibus quaeri; dicens quod *acribologia* idest diligens et certa ratio, sicut est in mathematicis, non debet requiri in omnibus rebus, de quibus sunt scientiae; sed debet solum requiri in his, quae non habent materiam. Ea enim quae habent materiam, subiecta sunt motui et variationi: et ideo non potest in eis omnibus omnimoda certitudo haberi. Quaeritur enim in eis non quid semper sit et ex necessitate; sed quid sit ut in pluribus.

Immaterialia vero secundum seipsa sunt certissima, quia sunt immobilia. Sed illa quae in sui natura sunt immaterialia, non sunt certa nobis propter defectum intellectus nostri, ut praedictum est. Huiusmodi autem sunt substantiae separatae. Sed mathematica sunt abstracta a materia, et tamen non sunt excedentia intellectum nostrum: et ideo in eis est requirenda certissima ratio. Et quia tota natura est circa materiam, ideo iste modus certissimae rationis non pertinet ad naturalem philosophum. Dicit autem *forsan* propter corpora caelestia, quia non habent eodem modo materiam sicut inferiora.

337. Et, quia in scientia naturali non convenit iste certissimus rationis modus, ideo in scientia naturali ad

blance to the search for certitude since it leaves nothing undiscussed down to the smallest detail. Then there are some who think that, just as liberality is lacking when the smallest details are taken into account in computing the fee for a banquet, in a similar way there is a lack of civility and liberality when a man also wishes to discuss the smallest details in the search for truth.

335. *For this reason one must be trained* (995a12). He exposes the proper method of investigating the truth. Concerning this he does two things.

First [335], he shows how a man can discover the proper method of investigating the truth.

Second [336], he explains that the method which is absolutely the best should not be demanded in all matters, at *but the exactness of mathematics* (995a14).

He first says that since different men use different methods in the search for truth, one must be trained in the method which the particular sciences must use to investigate their subject. And since it is not easy for a man to undertake two things at once (indeed, so long as he tries to do both he can succeed in neither), it is absurd for a man to try to acquire a science and at the same time to acquire the method proper to that science. This is why a man should learn logic before any of the other sciences, because logic considers the general method of procedure in all the other sciences. Moreover, the method appropriate to the particular sciences should be considered at the beginning of these sciences.

336. *But the exactness of mathematics* (995a14). He shows that the method which is absolutely the best should not be demanded in all the sciences. He says that the *exactness* (namely, the careful and certain demonstrations) found in mathematics should not be demanded in the case of all things of which we have science, but only in the case of those things that have no matter. For things that have matter are subject to motion and change, and therefore in their case complete certitude cannot be had. In the case of these things, we do not look for what exists always and of necessity, but only for what exists in the majority of cases.

Now immaterial things are most certain by their very nature because they are unchangeable, although they are not certain to us because our intellectual power is weak, as was stated above [279]. The separate substances are things of this kind. But while the things with which mathematics deals are abstracted from matter, they do not surpass our understanding; therefore, in their case most certain reasoning is demanded. Again, because the whole of nature involves matter, this method of most certain reasoning does not belong to natural philosophy. However, he says *perhaps* because of the celestial bodies, since they do not have matter in the same sense that lower bodies do.

337. Now since this method of most certain reasoning is not the method proper to natural science, in order to know

cognoscendum modum convenientem illi scientiae, primo perscrutandum est quid sit natura: sic enim manifestum erit de quibus sit scientia naturalis. Et iterum considerandum est, *si unius scientiae*, scilicet naturalis, sit omnes causas et principia considerare, aut sit diversarum scientiarum. Sic enim poterit scire quis modus demonstrandi conveniat naturali. Et hunc modum ipse observat in secundo *Physicorum*, ut patet diligenter intuenti.

which method is proper to that science we must investigate first what nature is. In this way, we will discover the things that natural philosophy studies. Further, we must investigate **whether it belongs to one science** (that is, to natural philosophy) or to several sciences to consider all causes and principles. In this way we will be able to learn which method of demonstration is proper to natural philosophy. He deals with this method in *Physics* 2, as is obvious to anyone who examines it carefully.

Book 3

Metaphysical Problems

Lecture 1

Necessity of considering all difficulties

995a24 Necesse est ad quaesitam scientiam nos aggredi primum de quibus dubitare primum oportet. Haec autem sunt quaecumque de ipsis aliter susceperunt quidam, et si quid praeter hoc est praetermissum. [338]

ἀνάγκη πρὸς τὴν ἐπιζητουμένην ἐπιστήμην ἐπελθεῖν ἡμᾶς {25} πρῶτον περὶ ὧν ἀπορῆσαι δεῖ πρῶτον: ταῦτα δ᾽ ἐστὶν ὅσα τε περὶ αὐτῶν ἄλλως ὑπειλήφασί τινες, κἂν εἴ τι χωρὶς τούτων τυγχάνει παρεωραμένον.

With a view to the science under investigation we must attack first those subjects which must first be investigated. These are all the subjects about which some men have entertained different opinions, and any other besides these which has been omitted.

995a27 Inest autem investigare volentibus prae opere bene dubitare. Posterius enim investigatio priorum est solutio dubitatorum. Solvere enim non est ignorantis vinculum. [339]

ἔστι δὲ τοῖς εὐπορῆσαι βουλομένοις προὔργου τὸ διαπορῆσαι καλῶς: ἡ γὰρ ὕστερον εὐπορία λύσις τῶν πρότερον ἀπορουμένων ἐστί, λύειν δ᾽ οὐκ {30} ἔστιν ἀγνοοῦντας τὸν δεσμόν,

Now for those who wish to investigate the truth it is worth the while to ponder these difficulties well. For the subsequent study of truth is nothing else than the solution of earlier problems. For it is impossible to untie a knot without knowing it.

Sed mentis dubitatio, hoc de re demonstrat: inquantum enim dubitat, intantum similiter ligatis est passus. Impossibile enim utrisque procedere ad quod est ante. Propter quod oportet difficultates speculari omnes prius, et horum causas.

ἀλλ᾽ ἡ τῆς διανοίας ἀπορία δηλοῖ τοῦτο περὶ τοῦ πράγματος: ᾗ γὰρ ἀπορεῖ, ταύτῃ παραπλήσιον πέπονθε τοῖς δεδεμένοις: ἀδύνατον γὰρ ἀμφοτέρως προελθεῖν εἰς τὸ πρόσθεν. διὸ δεῖ τὰς δυσχερείας τεθεωρηκέναι πάσας πρότερον,

But a perplexity on the part of the mind makes this evident in regard to the matter at hand. Insofar as the mind is perplexed, to that extent it experiences something similar to men who are bound—in both cases it is impossible to move forward. For this reason, then, it is first necessary to consider all the difficulties and the reasons for them.

995a34 Et quia quaerentes sine dubitatione primo, similes quo oportet ire ignorantibus. [340]

τούτων τε χάριν καὶ διὰ τὸ τοὺς {35} ζητοῦντας ἄνευ τοῦ διαπορῆσαι πρῶτον ὁμοίους εἶναι τοῖς ποῖ δεῖ βαδίζειν ἀγνοοῦσι,

This is also necessary for another reason, namely, that those who make investigations without first recognizing the problem are like those who do not know where they ought to go.

995a35 Et adhuc neque quando quaesitum invenit, cognoscit. Finis enim huic est non manifestus. Praedubitanti autem manifestus. [341]

καὶ πρὸς τούτοις οὐδ᾽ εἴ ποτε τὸ ζητούμενον εὕρηκεν ἢ μὴ γιγνώσκειν: {995b1} τὸ γὰρ τέλος τούτῳ μὲν οὐ δῆλον τῷ δὲ προηπορηκότι δῆλον.

Again, one would not even know when he finds the thing which he is seeking, for the goal is not evident to such a man, but it is evident to one who previously discussed the difficulties.

995b2 Amplius autem melius necesse est se habere ad iudicandum eum qui audivit velut adversariorum et dubitantium omnes rationes. [342]

ἔτι δὲ βέλτιον ἀνάγκη ἔχειν πρὸς τὸ κρῖναι τὸν ὥσπερ ἀντιδίκων καὶ τῶν ἀμφισβητούντων λόγων ἀκηκοότα πάντων.

Furthermore, one who has heard all the arguments of the litigants, as it were, and of those who argue the question, is necessarily in a better position to pass judgment.

338. Postquam Philosophus in secundo libro ostendit modum considerandae veritatis, hic procedit ad veritatis considerationem.

Et primo procedit modo disputativo, ostendens ea quae sunt dubitabilia circa rerum veritatem.

Secundo incipit determinare veritatem. Et hoc in quarto libro, qui incipit ibi, *est scientia quaedam quae speculatur.*

Prima autem pars dividitur in partes duas.

In prima dicit de quo est intentio,

in secunda exequitur propositum, ibi, *est autem dubitatio prima quod* et cetera.

Circa primum duo facit.

Primo enim dicit de quo est intentio.

Secundo rationem assignat suae intentionis, ibi, *inest autem investigare volentibus* et cetera.

Dicit ergo primo, quod ad hanc scientiam, quam quaerimus de primis principiis, et universali veritate rerum, necesse est ut primum aggrediamur ea de quibus oportet, dubitare, antequam veritas determinetur.

Sunt autem huiusmodi dubitabilia propter duas rationes. Vel quia antiqui philosophi aliter susceperunt opinionem de eis quam rei veritas habeat, vel quia omnino praetermiserunt de his considerare.

339. Deinde cum dicit *inest autem* assignat quatuor rationes suae intentionis:

et primo dicit quod volentibus investigare veritatem contingit *prae opere*, idest ante opus *bene dubitare*, idest bene attingere ad ea quae sunt dubitabilia. Et hoc ideo quia posterior investigatio veritatis, nihil aliud est quam solutio prius dubitatorum. Manifestum est autem in solutione corporalium ligaminum, quod ille qui ignorat vinculum, non potest solvere ipsum. Dubitatio autem de aliqua re hoc modo se habet ad mentem, sicut vinculum corporale ad corpus, et eumdem effectum demonstrat. Inquantum enim aliquid dubitat, intantum patitur aliquid simile his qui sunt stricte ligati. Sicut enim ille qui habet pedes ligatos, non potest in anteriora procedere secundum viam corporalem, ita ille qui dubitat, quasi habens mentem ligatam, non potest ad anteriora procedere secundum viam speculationis. Et ideo sicut ille qui vult solvere vinculum corporale, oportet quod prius inspiciat vinculum et modum ligationis, ita ille qui vult solvere dubitationem, oportet quod prius speculetur omnes difficultates et earum causas.

340. Deinde cum dicit *et quia quaerentes* secundam rationem ponit; et dicit quod illi qui volunt inquirere veritatem non considerando prius dubitationem, assimilantur illis qui nesciunt quo vadant. Et hoc ideo, quia sicut terminus viae est illud quod intenditur ab ambu-

338. Having indicated in book 2 [331] the method of considering the truth, the Philosopher now proceeds with his study of the truth.

First, he proceeds disputatively, indicating those points which are open to question so far as the truth of things is concerned.

Second [529], he begins to establish what is true, and he does this in book 4, which begins: *there is a certain science* (1003a21).

The first part is divided into two sections.

In the first, he states what he intends to do.

In the second [346], he proceeds to do it, at *the first problem* (995b4).

In regard to the first he does two things.

First, he states what he intends to do.

Second [339], he gives the reasons for this, at *now for those* (995a27).

He first says, then, that with a view to this science which we are seeking about first principles and what is universally true of things, we must first attack those subjects about which it is necessary to raise questions before the truth is established.

Now there are disputed points of this kind for two reasons: either because the ancient philosophers entertained a different opinion about these things than is really true, or because they completely neglected to consider them.

339. *Now for those* (995a27). Here he gives four arguments in support of this thesis:

first, he says that for those who wish to investigate the truth it is *worth the while*, that is, worth the effort, *to ponder these difficulties well*, that is, to examine carefully those matters which are open to question. This is necessary because the subsequent study of truth is nothing else than the solution of earlier difficulties. Now in loosening a physical knot it is evident that one who is unacquainted with this knot cannot loosen it. But a difficulty about some subject is related to the mind as a physical knot is to the body, and manifests the same effect. For insofar as the mind is puzzled about some subject, it experiences something similar to those who are tightly bound. For just as one whose feet are tied cannot move forward on an earthly road, in a similar way one who is puzzled, and whose mind is bound, as it were, cannot move forward on the road of speculative knowledge. Therefore, just as one who wishes to loosen a physical knot must first of all inspect the knot and the way in which it is tied, in a similar way one who wants to solve a problem must first survey all the difficulties and the reasons for them.

340. *This is also necessary* (995a34). Here he gives the second argument. He says that those who wish to investigate the truth without first considering the problem are like those who do not know where they are going. This is true for this reason: just as the end of a journey is the goal

lante, ita exclusio dubitationis est finis qui intenditur ab inquirente veritatem. Manifestum est autem quod ille qui nescit quo vadat, non potest directe ire, nisi forte a casu: ergo nec aliquis potest directe inquirere veritatem, nisi prius videat dubitationem.

341. Deinde cum dicit *et adhuc* tertiam rationem ponit; et dicit, quod sicut ex hoc quod aliquis nescit quo vadat, sequitur quod quando pervenit ad locum quem intendebat nescit utrum sit quiescendum vel ulterius eundum, ita etiam quando aliquis non praecognoscit dubitationem, cuius solutio est finis inquisitionis, non potest scire quando invenit veritatem quaesitam, et quando non; quia nescit finem suae inquisitionis, qui est manifestus ei qui primo dubitationem cognovit.

342. *Et quia* quartam rationem ponit, quae sumitur ex parte auditoris. Auditorem enim oportet iudicare de auditis. Sicut autem in iudiciis nullus potest iudicare nisi audiat rationes utriusque partis, ita necesse est eum, qui debet audire philosophiam, melius se habere in iudicando si audierit omnes rationes quasi adversariorum dubitantium.

343. Est autem attendendum, quod propter has rationes consuetudo Aristotelis fuit fere in omnibus libris suis, ut inquisitioni veritatis vel determinationi praemitteret dubitationes emergentes. Sed in aliis libris singillatim ad singulas determinationes praemittit dubitationes: hic vero simul praemittit omnes dubitationes, et postea secundum ordinem debitum determinat veritatem. Cuius ratio est, quia aliae scientiae considerant particulariter de veritate: unde et particulariter ad eas pertinet circa singulas veritates dubitare: sed ista scientia sicut habet universalem considerationem de veritate, ita etiam ad eam pertinet universalis dubitatio de veritate; et ideo non particulariter, sed simul universalem dubitationem prosequitur.

344. Potest etiam et alia esse ratio; quia dubitabilia, quae tangit, sunt principaliter illa, de quibus philosophi aliter opinati sunt. Non autem eodem ordine ipse procedit ad inquisitionem veritatis, sicut et alii philosophi. Ipse enim incipit a sensibilibus et manifestis, et procedit ad separata, ut patet infra in septimo.

Alii vero intelligibilia et abstracta voluerunt sensibilibus applicare. Unde, quia non erat eodem ordine determinaturus, quo ordine processerunt alii philosophi, ex quorum opinionibus dubitationes sequuntur; ideo

intended by one who travels on foot, in a similar way the solution of a problem is the goal intended by one who is seeking the truth. But it is evident that one who does not know where he is going cannot go there directly, except perhaps by chance. Therefore, neither can one seek the truth directly unless he first sees the problem.

341. *Again, one would* (995a35). Here he gives the third argument. He says that just as one who is ignorant of where he is going does not know whether he should stop or go further when he reaches his appointed goal, in a similar way one who does not know beforehand the problem whose solution marks the terminus of his search cannot know when he finds the truth which he is seeking and when not. For he does not know what the goal of his investigations is. But this is evident to one who knew the problem beforehand.

342. *Furthermore* (995b2). He gives the fourth argument, which is taken from the viewpoint of a judge. For a judge must pass judgment on the things that he hears. But just as one can pass judgment in a lawsuit only if he hears the arguments on both sides, in a similar way one who has to pass judgment on a philosophy is necessarily in a better position to do so if he will hear all the arguments, as it were, of the disputants.

343. Now it must be noted that it was for these reasons that Aristotle was accustomed, in nearly all his works, to set forth the problems which emerge before investigating and establishing what is true. But while in other works Aristotle sets down the problems one at a time in order to establish the truth about each one, in this work he sets forth all the problems at once, and afterwards in the proper order establishes the things that are true. The reason for this is that other sciences consider the truth in a particular way, and therefore it belongs to them to raise problems of a particular kind about individual truths. But just as it belongs to this science to make a universal study of truth, so also does it belong to it to discuss all the problems which pertain to the truth. Therefore, it does not discuss its problems one at a time, but all at once.

344. There can also be another reason for this—namely, that those problems on which he touches are chiefly those about which the philosophers have held different opinions. However, he does not proceed to investigate the truth in the same order as the other philosophers did. For he begins with things that are sensible and evident and proceeds to those which are separate from matter, as is evident below in book 7 [1566].

But the other philosophers wanted to apply intelligible and abstract principles to sensible things. Hence, because he did not intend to establish the truth in the same order as that followed by the other philosophers, and from whose

praeelegit primo ponere dubitationes omnes seorsum, et postea suo ordine dubitationes determinare.

345. Tertiam assignat Averroes dicens hoc esse propter affinitatem huius scientiae ad logicam, quae tangitur infra in quarto. Et ideo dialecticam disputationem posuit quasi partes principales huius scientiae.

views these problems arise, he therefore decided to give first all the problems in a separate section, and afterwards to solve these problems in their proper order.

345. Averroes gives another reason. He says that Aristotle proceeds in this way because of the relationship of this science to logic, which will be touched on below in book 4 [588]. Therefore, he made dialectical discussion a principal part of this science.

LECTURE 2

Questions on metaphysical method

995b4 Est autem dubitatio prima quidem quibus prooemialiter dictis dubitavimus, utrum unius scientiae aut multarum est scientiarum causas speculari. [346]

995b6 Et utrum substantiae principia est scientiae huius scire solum, aut de principiis de quibus ostendunt omnes: ut utrum contingit unum et idem simul dicere et negare, aut non, et de aliis talibus. [347]

Et si est circa substantiam, utrum una circa omnes, aut plures sunt. Sed, si plures, utrum omnes cognatae, aut earum hae quidem sapientiae, illae vero aliquid aliud dicendae sunt.

995b13 Et hoc idem quoque necessarium est quaerere, utrum sensibiles substantiae esse solum dicendae sunt, aut praeter has aliae; [350]

et utrum unicae sunt, aut plura genera sunt substantiarum, ut facientes species et mathematica inter ista et sensibilia dixerunt. De his igitur, ut diximus, perscrutandum est.

995b18 Et utrum circa substantias solum speculatio, aut circa quae accidunt secundum se substantiis. Adhuc de eodem et diverso, simili et dissimili et contrarietate, priore et posteriore et aliis omnibus talibus de quibus dialectici intendere tentant, ex probabilibus solum perscrutationem facientes, quorum theorica est de omnibus. Amplius autem his eisdem quaecumque secundum se accidunt, et non solum quid est horum unumquodque. Sed utrum unum est uni contrarium. [352]

ἔστι δ' ἀπορία πρώτη {5} μὲν περὶ ὧν ἐν τοῖς πεφροιμιασμένοις διηπορήσαμεν, πότερον μιᾶς ἢ πολλῶν ἐπιστημῶν θεωρῆσαι τὰς αἰτίας:

καὶ πότερον τὰς τῆς οὐσίας ἀρχὰς τὰς πρώτας ἐστὶ τῆς ἐπιστήμης ἰδεῖν μόνον ἢ καὶ περὶ τῶν ἀρχῶν ἐξ ὧν δεικνύουσι πάντες, οἷον πότερον ἐνδέχεται ταὐτὸ καὶ ἓν ἅμα φάναι καὶ ἀποφάναι {10} ἢ οὔ, καὶ περὶ τῶν ἄλλων τῶν τοιούτων:

εἴ τ' ἐστι περὶ τὴν οὐσίαν, πότερον μία περὶ πάσας ἢ πλείονές εἰσι, κἂν εἰ πλείονες πότερον ἅπασαι συγγενεῖς ἢ τὰς μὲν σοφίας τὰς δὲ ἄλλο τι λεκτέον αὐτῶν.

καὶ τοῦτο δ' αὐτὸ τῶν ἀναγκαίων ἐστὶ ζητῆσαι, πότερον τὰς αἰσθητὰς οὐσίας εἶναι {15} μόνον φατέον ἢ καὶ παρὰ ταύτας ἄλλας,

καὶ πότερον μοναχῶς ἢ πλείονα γένη τῶν οὐσιῶν, οἷον οἱ ποιοῦντες τά τε εἴδη καὶ τὰ μαθηματικὰ μεταξὺ τούτων τε καὶ τῶν αἰσθητῶν. περί τε τούτων οὖν,

καθάπερ φαμέν, ἐπισκεπτέον, καὶ πότερον περὶ τὰς οὐσίας ἡ θεωρία μόνον ἐστὶν ἢ καὶ περὶ {20} τὰ συμβεβηκότα καθ' αὑτὰ ταῖς οὐσίαις, πρὸς δὲ τούτοις περὶ ταὐτοῦ καὶ ἑτέρου καὶ ὁμοίου καὶ ἀνομοίου καὶ ἐναντιότητος, καὶ περὶ προτέρου καὶ ὑστέρου καὶ τῶν ἄλλων ἁπάντων τῶν τοιούτων περὶ ὅσων οἱ διαλεκτικοὶ πειρῶνται σκοπεῖν ἐκ τῶν ἐνδόξων μόνων ποιούμενοι τὴν σκέψιν, τίνος {25} ἐστὶ θεωρῆσαι περὶ πάντων: ἔτι δὲ τούτοις αὐτοῖς ὅσα καθ' αὑτὰ συμβέβηκεν, καὶ μὴ μόνον τί ἐστι τούτων ἕκαστον ἀλλὰ καὶ ἆρα ἓν ἑνὶ ἐναντίον:

The first problem concerns the things about which we raised questions in our introductory statements, namely, whether it belongs to one science or to many to speculate about the causes.

And there is also the problem of whether it belongs to this science to know only the principles of substance, or also the principles on which all sciences base their demonstrations (for example, whether it is possible to affirm and deny one and the same thing at the same time or not, and other such principles).

And if this science deals with substance, there is the question of whether one science deals with all substances, or many sciences. And if many, whether all are cognate, or whether some should be called wisdom and others something else.

It is also necessary to inquire whether sensible substances alone must be said to exist, or whether there are other substances in addition to these.

Also, whether they are unique, or whether there are many kinds of substances, as was said by those who put forms and mathematical objects between these and sensible things. As we said, then, this must be examined.

There is also the problem of whether this speculation has to do with substances alone or also with the proper accidents of substances. And we must inquire about sameness and difference, likeness and unlikeness, contrariety, priority and posteriority, and all other such things that the dialecticians attempt to treat (basing their investigations only on probabilities). For to them too it belongs to theorize about all these things. Furthermore, we must investigate all those *per se* accidents of these same things, and not only what each one of them is, but also whether there is one contrary for each one.

346. Secundum ea quae praedixit Philosophus, incipit praemittere dubitationes determinationi veritatis; et dividit in duas partes.

In prima ponit dubitationes.

In secunda causas dubitationum, inducendo rationes ad singulas dubitationes, ibi, *primum ergo de quibus in primis dicimus* et cetera.

Dictum est autem in secundo libro, quod prius oportet quaerere modum scientiae, quam ipsam scientiam.

Et ideo primo ponit dubitationes pertinentes ad modum considerationis huius scientiae.

Secundo ponit dubitationes pertinentes ad prima principia, de quibus est ista scientia, ut in primo libro dictum est; et hoc ibi, *et utrum principia et elementa* et cetera.

Ad modum autem scientiae huius duo pertinent, ut in secundo dictum est: scilicet consideratio causarum, ex quibus scientia demonstrat; et iterum res de quibus scientia considerat.

Unde circa primum duo facit.

Primo movet dubitationem pertinentem ad considerationem causarum.

Secundo movet multas dubitationes pertinentes ad ea de quibus est scientia, ibi, *et utrum substantiae principia* et cetera.

Dicit ergo quod prima dubitatio est quam dubitando proposuimus in fine secundi libri, qui est quasi prooemium ad totam scientiam, scilicet utrum consideratio causarum quatuor, secundum quatuor genera, pertineat ad unam scientiam, vel ad multas et diversas. Et hoc est quaerere utrum unius scientiae, et praecipue huius, sit demonstrare ex omnibus causis, vel magis diversae scientiae ex diversis demonstrent.

347. Deinde cum dicit *et utrum* movet dubitationes de his, de quibus considerat ista scientia.

Et primo inquirit de quibus considerat ista scientia sicut de substantiis.

Secundo de quibus considerat ista scientia sicut de accidentibus, ibi, *et utrum circa substantias* et cetera.

Circa primum duo facit.

Primo multiplicat, quaestiones ex parte ipsius scientiae, quae est de substantia.

Secundo ex parte substantiarum ipsarum, ibi, *et hoc idem quoque* et cetera.

Circa primum ponit tres quaestiones.

Supposito enim ex his quae in primo libro dicta sunt, quod ista scientia consideret principia prima, prima quaestio hic erit utrum ad hanc scientiam solum pertineat cognoscere prima principia substantiae, aut etiam ad hanc scientiam pertineat considerare de primis principiis demonstrationis, ex quibus omnes scientiae de-

346. Following his announced plan, the Philosopher begins to set down the problems which are encountered in establishing the truth. He divides this into two parts.

In the first, he gives these problems;

and in the second [369], he gives the reasons for these problems, by indicating the arguments on either side of the question, at *therefore, let us discuss* (996a18).

Now it was stated in book 2 [335] that it is necessary to seek the method of a science before seeking the science itself.

Therefore, he first gives the problems which pertain to this science's method of investigation.

Second [355], he gives the problems which pertain to the first principles with which this science deals, as has been stated in book 1 [36]; and this is at *and we must inquire* (995b27).

Now a science is concerned with two things, as was said in book 2 [336], namely, a study of the causes by which it demonstrates and the things with which it deals.

Hence in regard to the first point he does two things.

First, he presents a problem concerning the investigation of causes.

Second [347], he presents several problems concerning the things with which this science deals, at *and there is also the problem* (995b6).

He says, then, that the first problem is one which we proposed in the issues raised at the end of book 2 [336], which is, so to speak, the prologue to the whole of science. It is whether a study of the four causes in their four genera belongs to one science or to many different sciences And this is to ask whether it belongs to one science, and especially to this science, to demonstrate by means of all the causes, or rather whether some sciences demonstrate by one cause and some by another.

347. *And there is also the problem* (995b6). Here he raises problems about the things that this science considers.

First, he inquires about the things that this science considers about substances;

second, about the things that this science considers about accidents, at *there is also* (995b18).

Concerning the first he does two things.

First, he raises questions about the science itself, which is about substance;

second [350], about substances themselves, at *it is also necessary* (995b13).

In regard to the first he raises three questions.

For if it is supposed, from what was said in book 1 [35], that this science considers first principles, the first question here will be whether it belongs to this science only to know the first principles of substances, or also to consider the first principles of demonstration, by means of which all sciences demonstrate. For example, should this science

monstrant; ut puta quod haec scientia consideret utrum contingat unum et idem simul affirmare et negare, vel non: et similiter de aliis demonstrationis principiis primis et per se notis.

348. Secunda quaestio est, si ista scientia est considerativa substantiae sicut primi entis, utrum sit una scientia considerans omnes substantias, vel sint plures scientiae de diversis substantiis. Videtur enim quod de pluribus substantiis debeant esse plures scientiae.

349. Tertia quaestio est, si sint plures scientiae de pluribus substantiis, utrum omnes sint *cognatae*, idest unius generis, sicut geometria et arithmetica sunt in genere mathematicae scientiae, vel non sint unius generis, sed quaedam earum sint in genere sapientiae, quaedam vero in aliquo alio genere, puta in genere scientiae naturalis, vel mathematicae. Videtur enim secundum primum aspectum, quod non sint unius generis, cum substantiae materiales et immateriales non eodem modo cognoscantur.

350. Deinde cum dicit *et hoc idem* multiplicat quaestiones ex parte substantiae; et ponit duas quaestiones:

quarum prima est, utrum dicendum sit, quod sint solum substantiae sensibiles, ut antiqui naturales posuerunt, vel etiam praeter substantias sensibiles sint aliae substantiae immateriales et intelligibiles, ut posuit Plato.

351. Secunda quaestio est, si sunt aliquae substantiae separatae a sensibilibus, utrum *sint unicae*, idest unius generis tantum, aut sint plura genera talium substantiarum, sicut quidam attendentes duplicem abstractionem, scilicet universalis a particulari, et formae mathematicae a materia sensibili, posuerunt utrumque genus subsistere. Et ita ponebant substantias separatas quae sunt universalia abstracta subsistentia, inter quae et substantias sensibiles particulares posuerunt mathematica subsistentia separata, scilicet numeros, magnitudines et figuras.

De istis igitur quaestionibus sicut nunc moventur, perscrutandum est inferius;

primo quidem disputative,

secundo determinando veritatem.

352. Deinde cum dicit *et utrum circa* inquirit utrum consideratio huius scientiae de accidentibus sit. Et ponit tres quaestiones.

Quarum prima est, utrum speculatio huius scientiae sit solum circa substantias, propter hoc quod dicitur philosophia substantiae: aut etiam sit circa ea quae per se substantiis accidunt, eo quo ad eamdem scientiam

consider whether it is possible to affirm and deny one and the same thing at the same time or not? And the same thing applies to the other first and self-evident principles of demonstration.

348. And if this science considers substance as the primary kind of being, the second question is whether there is one science which considers all substances, or whether there are many sciences which consider different substances. For it seems that there should be many sciences which consider many substances.

349. And if there are many sciences which consider many substances, the third question is whether all are *cognate*, that is, whether all belong to one genus, as geometry and arithmetic belong to the genus of mathematical science, or whether they do not, but some to the genus of wisdom and some to another genus (for example, to the genus of natural philosophy or to that of mathematical science). For, according to the first point of view, it seems that they do not belong to one genus, since material and immaterial substances are not known by the same method.

350. *It is also necessary* (995b13). Here he adds to the number of questions about substance, and he does this by raising two questions.

The first question is whether sensible substances alone must be held to exist, as the philosophers of nature claimed, or whether there are in addition to sensible substances other immaterial and intelligible substances, as Plato claimed.

351. And if there are some substances separate from sensible things, the second question is whether *they are unique*, that is, whether they belong only to one genus, or whether there are many genera of such substances. For certain men, understanding that there is a twofold abstraction (namely, of the universal from the particular, and of the mathematical form from sensible matter) held that each genus is self-subsistent. Thus they held that there are separate substances which are subsisting abstract universals, and between these and particular sensible substances they placed the objects of mathematics—numbers, continuous quantities, and figures—which they regarded as separate subsisting things.

Concerning the questions which have now been raised, then, it is necessary to investigate them below.

He does this first by arguing both sides of the question, and second by determining its truth.

352. *There is also the problem* (995b18). Here he asks whether this science's investigations extend to accidents, and he raises three questions.

The first is whether this science, seeing that it is called the philosophy of substance, speculates about substance alone, or whether it also speculates about the proper accidents of substance. For it seems to be the office of the same

pertinere videtur ut consideret subiectum et per se accidentia subiecti.

353. Secunda quaestio est, utrum haec scientia consideret de quibusdam quae videntur esse per se accidentia entis, et consequi omnia entia: scilicet de eodem et diverso, simili et dissimili, et de contrarietate, et de priori et posteriori, et omnibus aliis huiusmodi, de quibus dialectici tractant, qui habent considerationem de omnibus. Sed tamen de huiusmodi perscrutantur, non ex necessariis, sed ex probabilibus. Ex una enim parte videtur quod cum sint communia, pertineant ad philosophum primum. Ex alia parte videtur quod ex quo dialectici ista considerant, quorum est ex probabilibus procedere, quod non pertineat ad considerationem ipsius philosophi cuius est demonstrare.

354. Tertia quaestio est, cum ad ista communia accidentia entis quaedam per se consequantur, utrum ad philosophum pertineat circa unumquodque horum solum considerare quid est, aut etiam illa quae consequuntur ad ipsa, puta utrum unum uni sit contrarium.

science to consider a subject and the proper accidents of that subject.

353. The second question is whether this science considers certain things that seem to be proper accidents of being and which belong to all beings, namely, sameness and difference, likeness and unlikeness, contrariety, priority and posteriority, and all others of this kind which are treated by the dialecticians, who deal with all things. However, they do not examine such things according to necessary premises but according to probable ones. For from one point of view it seems that, since these accidents are common ones, they pertain to first philosophy. But from another point of view it seems that, since they are considered by the dialecticians (whose office it is to argue from probabilities), an examination of them does not belong to the consideration of the philosopher (whose office it is to demonstrate).

354. And since certain proper attributes naturally flow from these common accidents of being, the third question is whether it is the function of the philosopher to consider in regard to the common accidents only their quiddity, or also their properties (for example, whether there is one opposite for each one).

LECTURE 3

Questions on metaphysics' object

995b27 Et utrum principia et elementa genera sunt, aut in quae dividitur existentium singulum. Et si genera, utrum quaecumque dicuntur de individuis finalia, aut prima. Et utrum animal aut homo principium et magis est quam singulare. [355]

καὶ πότερον αἱ ἀρχαὶ καὶ τὰ στοιχεῖα τὰ γένη ἐστὶν ἢ εἰς ἃ διαιρεῖται ἐνυπάρχοντα ἕκαστον· καὶ εἰ τὰ γένη, πότερον ὅσα ἐπὶ τοῖς ἀτόμοις λέγεται {30} τελευταῖα ἢ τὰ πρῶτα, οἷον πότερον ζῷον ἢ ἄνθρωπος ἀρχή τε καὶ μᾶλλον ἔστι παρὰ τὸ καθ᾽ ἕκαστον.

And we must inquire whether it is genera that constitute the principles and elements of things, or the parts into which each existing thing is divided. And if it is genera, whether it is those that are predicated of individuals first or last. And we must also inquire whether animal or man is a principle, and exists more truly than the singular.

995b31 Maxime vero quaerendum est et tractandum, utrum est aliquid praeter materiam causa secundum se, aut non. Et hoc separabile, aut non: et utrum unum aut plura numero. [357]

μάλιστα δὲ ζητητέον καὶ πραγματευτέον πότερον ἔστι τι παρὰ τὴν ὕλην αἴτιον καθ᾽ αὑτὸ ἢ οὔ, καὶ τοῦτο χωριστὸν ἢ οὔ, καὶ πότερον ἓν ἢ πλείω τὸν ἀριθμόν,

But most of all it is necessary to investigate and treat the question of whether, besides matter, there is any cause in the proper sense or not, whether it is separable or not, and whether it is numerically one or many.

995b34 Et utrum est aliquid praeter synolon (dico autem synolon quando praedicatur aliquid materia) aut nihil, aut horum quidem, horum vero non. [360]

καὶ πότερον ἔστι τι παρὰ τὸ {35} σύνολον (λέγω δὲ τὸ σύνολον, ὅταν κατηγορηθῇ τι τῆς ὕλης) ἢ οὐθέν, ἢ τῶν μὲν τῶν δ᾽ οὔ, καὶ ποῖα τοιαῦτα τῶν ὄντων.

And we must ask whether there is anything besides the *synolon* (and by *synolon* I mean matter when something is predicated of it), or nothing; or whether this is true of some things but not of others.

996a1 Amplius autem utrum principia numero aut specie determinata et quae in rationibus et in subiecto. [361]

ἔτι αἱ ἀρχαὶ πότερον ἀριθμῷ ἢ εἴδει ὡρισμέναι, καὶ αἱ ἐν τοῖς λόγοις καὶ αἱ ἐν τῷ ὑποκειμένῳ;

Further, we must inquire whether the principles of things are limited in number or in kind, both those in the intelligible structures of things and those in the underlying subject.

Et utrum corruptibilium et incorruptibilium eadem, aut diversa. Et utrum corruptibilia omnia, aut corruptibilium corruptibilia.

καὶ πότερον τῶν φθαρτῶν καὶ ἀφθάρτων αἱ αὐταὶ ἢ ἕτεραι, καὶ πότερον ἄφθαρτοι πᾶσαι ἢ τῶν φθαρτῶν φθαρταί;

Also, whether the principles of corruptible and of incorruptible things are the same or different. Also, whether they are all incorruptible, or whether those of corruptible things are corruptible.

Amplius autem quod omnium difficillimum est et plurimam habet dubitationem, utrum unum et ens, quemadmodum Pythagorici dicunt et Plato, non aliquid alterum esse supra existentium substantiam, aut non: sed alterum aliquid ipsum subiectum, ut Empedocles amorem dicit, alius vero ignem, alius aquam, alius aerem. Et utrum principia sint universalia, aut singularia rerum.

ἔτι δὲ τὸ πάντων {5} χαλεπώτατον καὶ πλείστην ἀπορίαν ἔχον, πότερον τὸ ἓν καὶ τὸ ὄν, καθάπερ οἱ Πυθαγόρειοι καὶ Πλάτων ἔλεγεν, οὐχ ἕτερόν τί ἐστιν ἀλλ᾽ οὐσία τῶν ὄντων; ἢ οὔ, ἀλλ᾽ ἕτερόν τι τὸ ὑποκείμενον, ὥσπερ Ἐμπεδοκλῆς φησὶ φιλίαν ἄλλος δέ τις πῦρ ὁ δὲ ὕδωρ ἢ ἀέρα· καὶ πότερον αἱ ἀρχαὶ {10} καθόλου εἰσὶν ἢ ὡς τὰ καθ᾽ ἕκαστα τῶν πραγμάτων,

And the most difficult question of all, and the most disputed one, is whether unity and being are not something different from the substances of existing things, as the Pythagoreans and Plato say, or whether this is not the case, but the underlying subject is something different, as Empedocles holds of love, another thinker of fire, another of water, and another of air. And we must inquire whether the principles of things are universals or singular things.

996a10 Et potestate aut actu. Amplius utrum aliter aut secundum motum. Haec enim dubitationem praestant magnam. [365]

καὶ δυνάμει ἢ ἐνεργείᾳ· ἔτι πότερον ἄλλως ἢ κατὰ κίνησιν· καὶ γὰρ ταῦτα ἀπορίαν ἂν παράσχοι πολλήν.

Again, we must inquire whether they exist potentially or actually. And also whether they are principles of things in reference to motion or in some other way. For these questions present great difficulty.

996a12 Adhuc autem utrum numeri, aut longitudines et figurae et puncta, substantiae sunt quaedam, aut non. Et si substantiae, utrum separatae a sensibilibus, aut in eis. De his etenim omnibus non solum difficile veritatem inquirere, sed nec dubitatur facile bene. [366]

πρὸς δὲ τούτοις πότερον οἱ ἀριθμοὶ καὶ τὰ μήκη καὶ τὰ σχήματα καὶ αἱ στιγμαὶ οὐσίαι τινές εἰσιν ἢ οὔ, κἂν εἰ οὐσίαι πότερον {15} κεχωρισμέναι τῶν αἰσθητῶν ἢ ἐνυπάρχουσαι ἐν τούτοις; περὶ γὰρ τούτων ἁπάντων οὐ μόνον χαλεπὸν τὸ εὐπορῆσαι τῆς ἀληθείας ἀλλ᾽ οὐδὲ τὸ διαπορῆσαι τῷ λόγῳ ῥάδιον καλῶς.

And in addition to these questions we must inquire whether numbers or lengths and points are somehow substances or not. And if they are substances, whether they are separate from sensible things or are found in them. Concerning all these matters, not only is it difficult to discover what is true, but it is not even easy to state the problems well.

---

355. Postquam Philosophus movit quaestiones pertinentes ad modum considerandi huius scientiae, hic movet quaestiones pertinentes ad res de quibus ista scientia considerat. Et quia ista scientia considerat de principiis primis, ut in primo dictum est, ideo movet hic quaestiones de principiis rerum. Prima autem rerum principia ponebantur et species et mathematica.

Unde primo movet quaestiones pertinentes ad species.

Secundo quaestiones pertinentes ad mathematica, ibi, *adhuc autem utrum numeri, aut longitudines* et cetera.

Circa primum duo facit.

Primo quaerit quae sunt principia.

Secundo qualia sunt, ibi, *amplius autem utrum principia numero aut specie determinata* et cetera.

Quia vero principia ponebantur universalia separata, primo quaeritur utrum universalia sint principia.

Secundo utrum res separatae sint principia, ibi, *maxime vero quaerendum est* et cetera.

Circa primum ponit duas quaestiones;

quarum prima est, utrum genera sint principia et elementa rerum, aut ea in quae sicut in ultima dividitur quodcumque singulare existens. Et ratio huius dubitationis est, quia elementum est ex quo primo componitur res, et in quod ultimo dividitur.

Invenimus autem duplicem modum compositionis et divisionis:

unum scilicet secundum rationem, prout species resolvuntur in genera. Et secundum hoc videntur genera esse principia et elementa, ut Plato posuit.

Alio modo secundum naturam sicut corpora naturalia componuntur ex igne et aere et aqua et terra, et

355. Having raised questions pertaining to the method of investigation which this science uses, the Philosopher now raises questions pertaining to the things that this science considers. And since this science considers first principles, as has been stated in book 1 [35], he therefore raises here questions pertaining to the principles of things. Now both the forms and the objects of mathematics were held to be the first principles of things.

Therefore, first he raises questions concerning species;

second [366], concerning the objects of mathematics, at *and in addition to these* (996a12).

In regard to the first he does two things.

First, he asks what things are principles;

second [361], what sort of beings they are, at *further, we must inquire* (996a1).

And since separate universals were held to be the principles of things, he asks first whether universals are the principles of things;

second [357], whether separate entities are the principles of things, at *but most of all* (995b31).

Concerning the first he asks two questions.

The first is whether genera constitute the principles and elements of things, or the ultimate parts into which each individual thing is divided. This question arises because an element is that of which a thing is first composed and into which it is ultimately divided.

Now we find a twofold mode of composition and dissolution.

One has to do with the intelligible constitution, in which species are resolved into genera, and according to this mode genera seem to be the principles and elements of things, as Plato claimed.

The other mode of composition and dissolution has to do with the real order. For example, natural bodies are

in haec resolvuntur. Et propter hoc naturales posuerunt esse prima principia elementa.

356. Secunda quaestio est, supposito quod genera sint principia rerum, utrum principia sint universalia dicta de individuis, scilicet species specialissimae, quas genera appellat secundum Platonicorum consuetudinem, quia continent sub se plura individua, sicut genera plures species;

aut magis sint principia prima generalissima, ut puta quid sit magis principium, utrum animal vel homo, qui est principium quoddam secundum Platonicos, et magis vere existens quam singulare.

Oritur autem haec dubitatio propter duas divisiones rationis. Quarum una est secundum quam genera dividimus in species. Alia vero est secundum quam species resolvimus in genera. Semper enim videtur illud quod est ultimus terminus divisionis esse primum principium et elementum in componendo.

357. Deinde cum dicit *maxime vero* quaerit de principiis ex parte separationis: et movet quatuor quaestiones,

quarum prima est, cum primi naturales posuerint solum causam materialem, utrum aliquid aliud praeter materiam sit causa secundum se, aut non.

358. Secunda quaestio est, supposito quod aliquid praeter materiam sit causa, utrum illud sit separabile a materia, sicut posuit Plato, aut sicut posuit Pythagoras.

359. Tertia quaestio est, si est aliquid separabile a materia, utrum sit unum tantum, sicut posuit Anaxagoras, aut plura numero sicut posuit Plato et ipse Aristoteles.

360. Quarta quaestio est, *utrum aliquid sit praeter synolon*, id est simul totum, aut nihil; aut in quibusdam sit aliquid, et in quibusdam non: et qualia sint in quibus sunt et qualia in quibus non. Exponit autem quid sit *synolon* vel simul totum, scilicet quando *praedicatur aliquid de materia*.

Ad cuius intellectum considerandum est quod Plato posuit hominem et equum et ea quae sic praedicantur, esse quasdam formas separatas. Per hoc autem homo praedicatur de Socrate vel Platone, quod materia sensibilis participat formam separatam. Socrates ergo vel Plato dicitur synolon vel simul totum, quia constituitur per hoc quod materia participat formam separatam. Et est quasi quoddam praedicatum de materia.

composed of fire, air, water, and earth, and are dissolved into these. It was for this reason that the natural philosophers claimed that the elements constitute the first principles of things.

356. And assuming that genera are the principles of things, the second question is whether the principles of things are to be identified with the universals which are predicated of individual things (that is, the lowest species, which he calls genera, after the usage of the Platonists), because the lowest species contain under themselves many individuals, just as genera contain many species.

Or is it rather the first and most common genera that constitute principles? For example, which of the two is more of a principle, animal or man? For man is a principle according to the Platonists, and is more real than any singular man.

Now this problem arises because of two divisions which reason makes. One of these is that whereby we divide genera into species, and the other is that whereby we resolve species into genera. For it seems that whatever is the last term in a process of division is always the first principle and element in a process of composition.

357. *But most of all* (995b31). Here he inquires whether separate entities are the principles of things, and he raises four questions.

Since the first philosophers of nature posited only a material cause, the first question is whether, besides matter, there is anything else that is a cause in the proper sense or not.

358. And granted that there is some other cause besides matter, the second question is whether it is separable from matter, as Plato or Pythagoras held.

359. And if there is something separable from matter, the third question is whether it is a single thing, as Anaxagoras claimed, or many, as Plato and Aristotle himself claimed.

360. The fourth question is *whether there is anything besides the synolon* (that is, the concrete whole), or nothing; or whether there is something in certain cases and not in others; and what kind of things they are in those cases in which there is something else, and what kind of things they are in those in which there is not. And he explains what a *synolon*, or concrete whole, is. Namely, it is *matter when something is predicated of it*.

Now in order to understand this, we must note that Plato claimed that man and horse (and universals which are predicated in this way) are certain separate forms; and that man is predicated of Socrates or Plato by reason of the fact that sensible matter participates in a separate form. Hence Socrates or Plato is called a *synolon*, or concrete whole, because each is constituted as a result of matter participating in a separate form. And each is, as it were, a kind of predicate of matter.

Quaerit ergo Philosophus hic utrum quod quid est individui, sit aliquid aliud praeter ipsum individuum, vel non: aut etiam in quibusdam est aliud et in quibusdam non aliud. Quam quidem quaestionem Philosophus determinabit in septimo.

361. Deinde cum dicit *amplius autem* movet quaestiones circa modum existendi principiorum.

Et quia ens dividitur per unum et multa, per actum et potentiam, primo quaerit quomodo sint principia secundum unitatem et multitudinem.

Secundo quomodo sint secundum actum et potentiam, ibi, *et potestate aut actu.*

Circa primum movet quatuor quaestiones:

quarum prima est, utrum principia sint determinata secundum numerum, aut secundum speciem. Puta quia dicimus tria esse principia naturae. Potest autem intelligi, vel quia sunt determinata secundum numerum, ita scilicet quod sola una numero forma sit principium naturae, et sola una numero materia et privatio. Et potest intelligi quod sit determinata secundum speciem, ita, scilicet, quod sint multa principia materialia quae conveniant in specie materialis principii, et sic de aliis. Et quia quidam philosophorum assignabant causas formales, sicut Platonici, quidam autem solas materiales, sicut antiqui naturales, addit quod ista quaestio habet locum *in rationibus*, idest in causis formalibus, *et in subiecto*, idest in causis materialibus.

362. Secunda quaestio est, utrum corruptibilium et incorruptibilium sint eadem principia aut diversa. Et si sint diversa, utrum omnia sint incorruptibilia, vel corruptibilium principia sint corruptibilia et incorruptibilium incorruptibilia.

363. Tertia quaestio est, utrum unum et ens significent ipsam substantiam rerum et non aliquid aliud additum supra substantiam rerum, sicut dicebant Pythagorici et Platonici, vel non significent ipsam substantiam rerum, sed sit aliquid aliud subiectum unitati et entitati, scilicet ignis aut aer, aut aliquid aliud huiusmodi, ut antiqui naturales posuerunt. Hanc autem quaestionem dicit esse difficillimam et maxime dubitabilem, quia ex ista quaestione dependet tota opinio Platonis et Pythagorae, qui ponebant numeros esse substantiam rerum.

364. Quarta quaestio est, utrum principia rerum sint sicut quaedam *universalia, vel sicut aliqua singularia*, idest utrum ea quae ponuntur esse principia habeant rationem principii secundum rationem universalem, vel secundum quod unumquodque eorum est aliquid et singulare.

Hence the Philosopher asks here whether the whatness of the individual thing is something else in addition to the individual thing itself, or not; or also whether it is something else in the case of some things and not in that of others. The Philosopher will answer this question in book 7 [7356].

361. *Further, we must inquire* (996a1). Here he raises questions about the way in which principles exist.

And since being is divided by the one and many, and by act and potency, he asks first whether these principles are one or many.

Second [365], whether they are actual or potential, at *again, we must inquire* (996a10).

In regard to the first he asks four questions,

the first of which is whether the principles are limited according to number or to kind. We say, for example, that there are three principles of nature. Now the statement that they are limited in number can mean that the principle of nature is numerically a single form and a single matter and privation. And the statement that they are limited in kind can mean that there are many material principles which have in common the specific nature of material principle, and so on for the rest. Since some of the philosophers, such as the Platonists, attributed formal causes to things, while others, such as the ancient natural philosophers, attributed only material causes to things, he adds that this question is applicable both *in the intelligible structures*, that is, in formal causes, *and in the underlying subject*, that is, in material causes.

362. The second question is whether the principles of corruptible and of incorruptible things are the same or different. And if they are different, whether all are incorruptible, or whether the principles of corruptible things are corruptible and those of incorruptible things are incorruptible.

363. The third question is whether unity and being signify the very substance of things and not something added to the substance of things (as the Pythagoreans and Platonists claimed), or whether they do not signify the substance of things, but something else is the subject of unity and being (for example, fire or air or something else of this kind, as the ancient philosophers of nature held). Now he says that this question is the most difficult and most puzzling one, because on this question depends the entire thought of Plato and Pythagoras, who held that numbers are the substance of things.

364. The fourth question is whether the principles of things are somehow *universals or singular things*, that is, whether those things that are held to be principles have the character of a principle in the sense of a universal intelligible nature, or according as each is a particular and singular thing.

365. Deinde cum dicit *et potestate* quaerit utrum principia sint secundum potentiam vel secundum actum. Et haec quaestio maxime videtur pertinere ad principia materialia. Potest enim esse dubitatio, utrum primum materiale principium sit aliquod corpus in actu, ut ignis aut aer, ut antiqui naturales posuerunt, aut aliquid existens in potentia tantum, ut Plato posuit. Et quia motus est actus existentis in potentia, et est quodammodo medium inter potentiam et actum, ideo adiungit aliam quaestionem, utrum principia sint causae rerum solum secundum motum, sicut naturales posuerunt sola principia motus, vel materialia, vel efficientia: vel etiam sint principia aliter quam per motum, sicut Plato posuit per quamdam participationem huius sensibilia ab immaterialibus causari. Has autem quaestiones ideo se movisse dicit, quia magnam dubitationem habent, ut patet ex discordia philosophorum circa eas.

366. Deinde cum dicit *adhuc autem* movet quaestiones pertinentes ad mathematica, quae quidem principia rerum ponuntur: et movet duas quaestiones.

Quarum prima est, utrum numeri et longitudines et figurae et puncta sint quaedam substantiae, ut Pythagorici vel Platonici posuerunt; vel non, sicut posuerunt naturales.

367. Secunda quaestio est, si sunt substantiae, utrum sint separatae a sensibilibus, ut posuerunt Platonici, aut in sensibilibus, ut Pythagorici.

368. Moventur autem quaestiones istae tamquam disputandae infra et determinandae: quia in his non solum difficile est veritatem inquirere, sed etiam non est facile bene dubitare de eis, inveniendo scilicet probabiles rationes dubitationis.

365. *Again, we must inquire* (996a10). Here he asks whether these principles exist potentially or actually. This question seems to refer especially to material principles, for it can be a matter of dispute whether the first material principle is some actual body, such as fire or air, as the ancient philosophers of nature held, or something which is only potential, as Plato held. And since motion is the actualization of something in potency, and is, in a sense, midway between potency and act, he therefore also asks whether the principles of things are causes only in reference to motion (as the philosophers of nature posited only material or efficient principles of motion), or whether they are principles which act also in some other way than by motion (as Plato claimed that sensible things are caused by immaterial entities by a certain participation in these). Furthermore, he says that these questions have been raised because they present the greatest difficulty, as is clear from the manner in which the philosophers have disagreed about them.

366. *And in addition to these* (996a12). Here he raises questions concerning the objects of mathematics, which are posited as the principles of things. He raises two questions.

The first is whether numbers, lengths, figures, and points are somehow substances, as the Pythagoreans or Platonists held, or whether they are not, as the philosophers of nature held.

367. And if they are substances, the second question is whether they are separate from sensible things, as the Platonists held, or exist in sensible things, as the Pythagoreans held.

368. Now these questions are raised as problems which must be debated and settled below, because in these matters, not only is it difficult to discover the truth, but it is not even easy to debate the matter adequately by finding probable arguments for either side of the question.

Lecture 4

How many sciences study all causes?

996a18   Primum ergo de quibus in primis diximus, utrum unius aut plurium scientiarum sint speculanda omnia genera causarum. [369]

πρῶτον μὲν οὖν περὶ ὧν πρῶτον εἴπομεν, πότερον μιᾶς ἢ πλειόνων ἐστὶν ἐπιστημῶν θεωρῆσαι πάντα τὰ γένη τῶν {20} αἰτίων.

Therefore, let us discuss first the problem about which we first spoke (995b4): whether it is the office of one science or of many to study all the genera of causes.

996a20   Unius enim scientiae quomodo erit non contraria principia existentia, cognoscere? [370]

μιᾶς μὲν γὰρ ἐπιστήμης πῶς ἂν εἴη μὴ ἐναντίας οὔσας τὰς ἀρχὰς γνωρίζειν;

For how will it be the office of one science to come to principles since they are not contrary?

996a21   Amplius autem multis existentium non insunt omnia. Quo namque modo possibile est motus principium esse in omnibus immobilibus, aut boni naturam? [372]

ἔτι δὲ πολλοῖς τῶν ὄντων οὐχ ὑπάρχουσι πᾶσαι: τίνα γὰρ τρόπον οἷόν τε κινήσεως ἀρχὴν εἶναι τοῖς ἀκινήτοις ἢ τὴν τἀγαθοῦ φύσιν,

Furthermore, in the case of many existing things not all the principles are present. How can a principle of motion be present in all immobile things, or how can the nature of the good be found there?

Siquidem omne, quod bonum est, secundum se et propter suam naturam finis est, et ita causa, quod illius causa et fiunt et sunt cetera. Finis autem, et cuius causa, actus cuiusdam est finis.

εἴπερ ἅπαν ὃ ἂν ᾖ ἀγαθὸν καθ᾽ αὑτὸ καὶ διὰ τὴν αὑτοῦ φύσιν τέλος ἐστὶν {25} καὶ οὕτως αἴτιον ὅτι ἐκείνου ἕνεκα καὶ γίγνεται καὶ ἔστι τἆλλα, τὸ δὲ τέλος καὶ τὸ οὗ ἕνεκα πράξεώς τινός ἐστι τέλος,

For everything which is a good in itself and by reason of its own nature is an end and thus a cause, because it is for its sake that other things come to be and exist. Further, the end and that for the sake of which something comes to be is the terminus of some action.

Sed actus omnes cum motu: quare in immobilibus non continget hoc esse principium, neque esse aliquid autoagathon, idest per se bonum.

αἱ δὲ πράξεις πᾶσαι μετὰ κινήσεως; ὥστ᾽ ἐν τοῖς ἀκινήτοις οὐκ ἂν ἐνδέχοιτο ταύτην εἶναι τὴν ἀρχὴν οὐδ᾽ εἶναί τι αὐτοαγαθόν.

But all actions involve motion. Therefore, it would be impossible for this principle to be present in immobile things, nor could there be an *autoagathon*, that is, a good in itself.

Unde et in mathematicis nihil per hanc ostenditur causam, neque est demonstratio ulla, eo quod melius aut deterius. Sed nec omnino ullus talium alicuius reminiscitur. Quapropter et Sophistarum quidam, ut Aristippus, ipsas praeneglexit. In aliis enim artibus et illiberalibus, ut tectonica et coriaria, eo quod melius aut deterius dici omnia; mathematicas vero nullam de bonis aut de malis rationem facere.

διὸ καὶ ἐν τοῖς μαθήμασιν οὐθὲν δείκνυται διὰ {30} ταύτης τῆς αἰτίας, οὐδ᾽ ἔστιν ἀπόδειξις οὐδεμία διότι βέλτιον ἢ χεῖρον, ἀλλ᾽ οὐδὲ τὸ παράπαν μέμνηται οὐθεὶς οὐθενὸς τῶν τοιούτων, ὥστε διὰ ταῦτα τῶν σοφιστῶν τινες οἷον Ἀρίστιππος προεπηλάκιζεν αὐτάς· ἐν μὲν γὰρ ταῖς ἄλλαις τέχναις, καὶ ταῖς βαναύσοις, οἷον ἐν τεκτονικῇ καὶ σκυτικῇ, διότι {35} βέλτιον ἢ χεῖρον λέγεσθαι πάντα, τὰς δὲ μαθηματικὰς οὐθένα ποιεῖσθαι λόγον περὶ ἀγαθῶν καὶ κακῶν.

Hence in mathematics too nothing is proved by means of this cause, nor is there any demonstration on the grounds that a thing is better or worse. Nor does anyone make any mention at all of anything of this kind. And for this reason some of the Sophists, for example, Aristippus, disregarded these. For in the other arts, even in the servile ones, such as the art of building and cobbling, all things are to be explained on the grounds that they are better or worse; but the mathematical sciences give no account of things that are good or evil.

996b1   At vero, si scientiae causarum sunt plures, et altera alterius principia, quae earum est dicenda quae quaeritur? Aut quis maxime res quaesitas est eas sciens habentium? [376]

ἀλλὰ μὴν εἴ γε πλείους ἐπιστῆμαι τῶν αἰτίων εἰσὶ καὶ ἑτέρα ἑτέρας ἀρχῆς, τίνα τούτων φατέον εἶναι τὴν ζητουμένην, ἢ τίνα μάλιστα τοῦ πράγματος τοῦ ζητουμένου ἐπιστήμονα τῶν ἐχόντων {5} αὐτάς;

But on the other hand, if there are many sciences of the causes, and different sciences for different principles, which of these must be said to be the one that is being sought, or which one of those who have them is best informed about the subject under investigation?

996b5   Contingit enim eidem omnes modos causarum inesse; ut domus, unde qui-

ἐνδέχεται γὰρ τῷ αὐτῷ πάντας τοὺς τρόπους τοὺς τῶν αἰτίων ὑπάρχειν, οἷον

For it is possible for the same thing to have all the kinds of causes. For example,

dem motus, ars et aedificator: cuius vero causa, opus et materia terra et lapides: species vero ratio. [377]

οἰκίας ὅθεν μὲν ἡ κίνησις ἡ τέχνη καὶ ὁ οἰκοδόμος, οὗ δ᾿ ἕνεκα τὸ ἔργον, ὕλη δὲ γῆ καὶ λίθοι, τὸ δ᾿ εἶδος ὁ λόγος.

in the case of a house the source of motion is the art and the builder, the final cause is its function, the matter is earth and stones, and the form is the plan.

996b8 Igitur ex dudum determinatis, quem decet vocare scientiarum sapientiam? [378]

ἐκ μὲν οὖν τῶν πάλαι διωρισμένων τίνα χρὴ καλεῖν τῶν ἐπιστημῶν σοφίαν

Therefore, from the things established a little while ago (982a4–982b7; [36–51]), which of the sciences should be called wisdom?

Habet enim rationem quamlibet appellari inquantum senior et principalior, cui veluti servientes non contradicere scientias alias certum est, quae finis et boni talis est. Huius enim causa sunt cetera.

ἔχει λόγον ἑκάστην {10} προσαγορεύειν: ἢ μὲν γὰρ ἀρχικωτάτη καὶ ἡγεμονικωτάτη καὶ ἧ ὥσπερ δούλας οὐδ᾿ ἀντειπεῖν τὰς ἄλλας ἐπιστήμας δίκαιον, ἡ τοῦ τέλους καὶ τἀγαθοῦ τοιαύτη (τούτου γὰρ ἕνεκα τἄλλα),

For there is a reason for calling each one of them such. For inasmuch as wisdom takes precedence and is a more authoritative science, and one which the others, like slaves, have no right to contradict, then the science that deals with the end and the good is such a science, because other things are for the sake of this.

996b13 Inquantum vero primarum causarum et maxime scibilis definita est esse, substantiae utique erit talis. Multis enim modis rationem scientibus, magis quidem scire dicimus eum, qui novit in ipso esse quid ipsa res, quam in non esse; [379]

ἢ δὲ τῶν πρώτων αἰτίων καὶ τοῦ μάλιστα ἐπιστητοῦ διωρίσθη εἶναι, ἡ τῆς οὐσίας ἂν εἴη τοιαύτη: πολλαχῶς γὰρ {15} ἐπισταμένων τὸ αὐτὸ μᾶλλον μὲν εἰδέναι φαμὲν τὸν τῷ εἶναι γνωρίζοντα τί τὸ πρᾶγμα ἢ τῷ μὴ εἶναι,

But insofar as wisdom has been defined (982a30; [49]) as the science of first causes and of what is most knowable, such a science will be about substance. For while a subject may be known in many ways, we say that he who knows what a thing is in its being knows it better than he who knows it in its non-being.

et horum eorumdem aliud alio magis; et maxime quid est et non quantum, aut quale, aut aliquid facere aut pati apta nata est. Amplius autem et in aliis scire singula et quorum demonstrationes sunt, tunc putamus existere, quando scimus quid est: ut quid est tetragonizare? Quia mediae inventio. Similiter autem et in aliis.

αὐτῶν δὲ τούτων ἕτερον ἑτέρου μᾶλλον, καὶ μάλιστα τὸν τί ἐστιν ἀλλ᾿ οὐ τὸν πόσον ἢ ποῖον ἢ τί ποιεῖν ἢ πάσχειν πέφυκεν. ἔτι δὲ καὶ ἐν τοῖς ἄλλοις τὸ εἰδέναι ἕκαστον καὶ ὧν ἀποδείξεις {20} εἰσί, τότ᾿ οἰόμεθα ὑπάρχειν ὅταν εἰδῶμεν τί ἐστιν (οἷον τί ἐστι τὸ τετραγωνίζειν, ὅτι μέσης εὕρεσις: ὁμοίως δὲ καὶ ἐπὶ τῶν ἄλλων),

And in the former case one knows better than another, especially he who knows what a thing is, and not how great it is or of what sort it is or anything that it is naturally disposed to do or to undergo. Further, in the case of other things, too, we think that we know every single thing (and those of which there are demonstrations) when we know what each is—for example, what squaring is, because it is finding the middle term. The same thing is true in other cases.

996b22 Circa generationes vero et actus et circa omnem transmutationem opinamur nos perfecte cognoscere, quando cognoscimus principium motus: hoc autem alterum et oppositum fini. Quapropter videtur alterius esse scientiae causarum harum singulas speculari. [382]

περὶ δὲ τὰς γενέσεις καὶ τὰς πράξεις καὶ περὶ πᾶσαν μεταβολὴν ὅταν εἰδῶμεν τὴν ἀρχὴν τῆς κινήσεως: τοῦτο δ᾿ ἕτερον καὶ ἀντικείμενον τῷ τέλει, ὥστ᾿ ἄλλης ἂν {25} δόξειεν ἐπιστήμης εἶναι τὸ θεωρῆσαι τῶν αἰτίων τούτων ἕκαστον.

But with regard to processes of generation and actions and every change, we think that we know these perfectly when we know the principle of motion. But this differs from and is opposite to the end of motion. And for this reason it seems to be the province of a different science to speculate about each one of these causes.

---

369. Postquam Philosophus movit quaestiones, quae faciunt dubitationem in ista scientia, hic incipit de eis disputare; et dividitur in tres partes.

In prima disputat de quaestionibus pertinentibus ad considerationem huius scientiae.

369. Having raised the questions which cause difficulty in this science, Aristotle begins here to treat them dialectically. This is divided into three parts.

In the first part, he treats the questions which pertain to the method of investigation of this science.

In secunda de quaestionibus pertinentibus ad substantias, ibi, *amplius autem utrum sensibiles substantiae* et cetera.

In tertia parte de quaestionibus pertinentibus ad principia substantiarum, ibi, *et de principiis utrum oporteat genera et elementa* et cetera.

Circa primum tria facit.

Primo enim disputat de consideratione huius scientiae quantum ad causas per quas demonstratur.

Secundo quantum ad prima demonstrationis principia, ibi, *at vero de principiis demonstrationis* et cetera.

Tertio quantum ad ipsas substantias, ibi, *totaliter quae substantiarum utrum una est* et cetera.

Circa primum duo facit.

Primo enim resumit quaestionem de qua disputare intendit, concludens ex ipso enumerationis ordine, quod primo disputandum est de istis, de quibus primum dictum est in enumeratione quaestionum, utrum scilicet ad unam scientiam vel ad plures pertineat speculari omnia genera causarum; ut sic ordo disputationis ordini quaestionum motarum respondeat.

370. Secundo ibi *unius enim* ponit rationes ad quaestionem; et circa hoc tria facit.

Primo enim ponit rationem ad ostendendum, quod considerare omnia genera causarum non pertineat ad unam scientiam.

Secundo movet alteram quaestionem: supposito quod ad diversas scientias pertineat diversa genera causarum considerare, cuius causae consideratio pertinet ad philosophum primum. Et disputat ad diversas quaestionis partes; et hoc, ibi, *at vero si scientiae causarum sunt plures* et cetera.

Tertio ex hac disputatione secunda concludit conclusionem primarum rationum, ibi, *quapropter videtur alterius esse scientiae* et cetera.

Circa primum ponit duas rationes;

dicens, quod cum unius scientiae sit considerare contraria, quomodo erit unius scientiae considerare principia, cum non sint contraria? Quae quidem ratio si secundum superficiem consideretur, nullius videtur esse momenti. Videtur enim procedere ex destructione antecedentis, ac si sic argumentaretur: si principia sunt contraria, sunt unius scientiae: ergo, si non sunt contraria, non sunt unius scientiae.

371. Posset ergo dici, quod Philosophus in his disputationibus non solum probabilibus rationibus utitur, sed etiam interdum sophisticis, ponens rationes quae ab aliis inducebantur. Sed non videtur esse rationabile, quod in tanta re tantus Philosophus tam frivolam et parum apparentem rationem induxisset. Unde aliter dicendum

In the second [403], he treats the questions which pertain to substances, at *furthermore, there is* (997a34).

In the third [423], he treats the questions which pertain to the principles of substances, at *concerning the principles* (998a21).

In regard to the first he does three things.

First, he argues dialectically about this science's method of investigation, with reference to the causes by means of which it demonstrates;

second [379], with reference to the first principles of demonstration, at *but insofar* (996b13);

third [393], with reference to substances themselves, at *and there is the problem* (997a15).

In regard to the first he does two things.

First, he takes up again the question about which he plans to argue dialectically, concluding from the order in which the questions have been listed that it is necessary first to debate those issues which were stated first in the list of questions—namely, whether it is the function of one science or of many to investigate all the genera of causes. In this way the order of argument corresponds to the order in which the questions have been raised.

370. *For how will it be* (996a20). Second, he gives the arguments relating to this question, and in regard to this he does three things.

First (996a20), he gives an argument for the purpose of showing that it is not the office of a single science to consider all the genera of causes.

Second (996b1; [376]), assuming that it belongs to different sciences to consider the different genera of causes, he asks which genus of cause it is that is investigated by first philosophy. He argues on both sides of this question, at *but on the other hand*.

Third (996b22; [382]), he draws from this second dispute the conclusion of the first arguments, at *but with regard to*.

In regard to the first (996a20) he gives two arguments.

He asks, since it belongs to one science to consider contraries, how it will belong to one science to consider principles, since they are not contrary? This view, if it is considered superficially, seems to be of no importance, for it appears to follow from the destruction of the antecedent, as if one were to argue thus. If principles are contraries, they belong to one science; therefore, if they are not contraries, they do not belong to one science.

371. Therefore, it can be said that in these disputes the Philosopher not only uses probable arguments, but sometimes also uses sophistical ones when he gives arguments introduced by others. But it does not seem reasonable that in such an important matter so great a Philosopher would have introduced an argument which is both trifling and

est, quod si quis recte consideret naturam diversorum, quae ad eamdem scientiam pertinent, quaedam pertinent ad unam scientiam secundum sui diversitatem, quaedam vero secundum quod reducuntur ad aliquod unum. Multa quidem igitur alia diversa inveniuntur pertinere ad unam scientiam, secundum quod reducuntur ad aliquod unum; puta, ut ad unum totum, vel ad unam causam, vel ad unum subiectum. Sed contraria et quaelibet opposita pertinent ad unam scientiam secundum se ipsa, eo quod unum est ratio cognoscendi alterum. Et ex hoc efficitur ista propositio probabilis, quod omnia diversa, quae sunt contraria, pertineant ad unam scientiam. Unde sequeretur, si principia sunt diversa et non sunt contraria, quod non pertineant ad unam scientiam.

372. Deinde cum dicit *amplius autem* secundam rationem ponit, quae talis est. Diversorum pertinentium ad unam scientiam, quaecumque scientia considerat unum considerat et aliud, ut patet in contrariis, quorum diversitas secundum se pertinet ad unam scientiam non per reductionem ad aliquid aliud unum: sed non quaecumque scientia considerat unam causam considerat omnes causas: ergo consideratio omnium causarum non pertinet ad unam scientiam.

373. Minorem probat per hoc, quod diversae scientiae sunt de diversis entibus; et multa entia sunt, quibus non possunt attribui omnes causae. Quod primo manifestat in causa, quae dicitur, unde principium motus: non enim videtur, quod possit esse principium motus in rebus immobilibus. Ponuntur autem quaedam entia immobilia, et praecipue secundum Platonicos ponentes numeros et substantias separatas. Unde, si qua scientia de his considerat, non potest considerare de causa quae est unde principium motus.

374. Secundo manifestat idem de causa finali, quae habet rationem boni. Boni enim natura non videtur posse inveniri in rebus immobilibus, si hoc concedatur, quod omne quod est bonum secundum se et propter suam naturam, est finis. Et hoc modo causa est, inquantum propter ipsam et causa eius omnia fiunt et sunt.

Dicit autem, *quod est bonum secundum se et propter suam naturam*, ad excludendum bonum utile, quod non dicitur de fine, sed magis de eo quod est ad finem. Unde quae sic solum dicuntur bona inquantum sunt utilia ad aliud, non sunt bona secundum se et propter suam naturam. Sicut potio amara non est secundum se bona, sed solum secundum quod ordinatur ad finem sanitatis, quae est secundum se bona: finis autem, et cuius causa fit aliquid, videtur esse terminus alicuius actus: omnes autem actiones videntur esse cum motu.

Ergo videtur sequi, quod in rebus immobilibus non possit esse hoc principium, scilicet causa finalis, quae

insignificant. Hence a different explanation must be given, namely, that if one rightly considers the nature of the various things that belong to the same science, some belong to a single science insofar as they are different, but others insofar as they are reduced to some one thing. Hence many other different things are found to belong to one science insofar as they are reduced to one thing (for example, to one whole, one cause, or one subject). But contraries and all opposites belong essentially to one science by reason of the fact that one is the means of knowing the other. And from this comes this probable proposition that all different things that are contraries belong to one science. Therefore, if principles were different and were not contraries, it would follow that they would not belong to one science.

372. *Furthermore, in the case* (996a21). Here he gives the second argument, which runs thus. In the case of different things that belong to one science, whatever science considers one also considers another. This is evident in the case of contraries, which are different and belong essentially to one science without being reduced to some other unity. But not every science which considers one cause considers all causes. Therefore, the study of all the causes does not belong to a single science.

373. He proves the minor premise thus. Different sciences deal with different beings, and there are many beings to which all the causes cannot be assigned. He makes this clear, first, with regard to that cause which is called the source of motion, for it does not seem that there can be a principle of motion in immobile things. Now certain immobile things are posited, especially by the Platonists, who claim that numbers and substances are separate entities. Hence, if any science considers these, it cannot consider the cause which is the source of motion.

374. Second, he shows that the same thing is true of the final cause, which has the character of good. For it does not seem that the character of goodness can be found in immobile things, if it is conceded that everything which is good in itself and by reason of its own nature is an end. And it is a cause in the sense that all things come to be and exist because of it and for its sake.

However, he says *everything which is a good in itself and by reason of its own nature* in order to exclude the useful good, which is not predicated of the end, but of the means to the end. Hence those things that are said to be good only in the sense that they are useful for something else are not good in themselves and by reason of their own nature. For example, a bitter medicine is not good in itself, but only insofar as it is directed to the end, health, which is a good in itself. But an end, or that for the sake of which something comes to be, seems to be the terminus of an action. But all actions seem to involve motion.

Therefore, it seems to follow that this principle—that is, the final cause, which has the character of goodness—

habet rationem boni. Et quia quae sunt per se existentia absque materia, necesse est quod sint immobilia, ideo non videtur esse possibile, quod sit aliquid **autoagathon**, idest per se bonum, ut Plato ponebat. Omnia enim immaterialia et non participata vocabat per se existentia, sicut ideam hominis vocabat hominem per se, quasi non participatum in materia. Unde et per se bonum dicebat id quod est sua bonitas non participata, scilicet primum principium omnium.

375. Et ad hanc rationem confirmandam inducit quoddam signum. Ex hoc enim quod finis non potest esse in rebus immobilibus, videtur procedere quod in scientiis mathematicis, quae abstrahunt a materia et motu, nihil probatur per hanc causam, sicut probatur in scientia naturali, quae est de rebus mobilibus, aliquid per rationem boni. Sicut cum assignamus causam quare homo habet manus, quia per eas melius potest exequi conceptiones rationis.

In mathematicis autem nulla demonstratio fit hoc modo, quod hoc modo sit quia melius est sic esse, aut deterius si ita non esset. Puta si diceretur quod angulus in semicirculo est rectus, quia melius est quod sic sit quam quod sit acutus vel obtusus. Et quia posset forte aliquis esse alius modus demonstrandi per causam finalem, puta si diceretur, si finis erit, necesse est id quod est ad finem praecedere: ideo subiungit, quod nullus omnino in mathematicis facit mentionem alicuius talium pertinentium ad bonum vel ad causam finalem.

Propter quod quidam sophistae, ut Aristippus, qui fuit de secta Epicureorum, omnino neglexit demonstrationes quae sunt per causas finales, reputans eas viles ex hoc quod in artibus illiberalibus sive mechanicis, ut in arte **tectonica**, idest aedificatoria, et **coriaria**, omnium rationes assignantur ex hoc quod est aliquid melius vel deterius. In mathematicis vero, quae sunt nobilissimae et certissimae scientiae, nulla fit mentio de bonis et malis.

376. Deinde cum dicit **at vero** interponit aliam quaestionem:

et primo proponit eam. Et habet duas partes.

Prima enim pars quaestionis est. Si diversae causae considerentur a pluribus scientiis, ita quod altera scientia sit alterius causae considerativa, quae illarum debet dici scientia **quae quaeritur**? Idest philosophia prima? Utrum scilicet illa quae considerat causam formalem, aut quae considerat causam finalem, vel quae considerat aliquam aliarum?

cannot exist in immobile things. Further, since those things that exist of themselves apart from matter must be immobile, it therefore does not seem possible that **an autoagathon** (or a good-in-itself) exists, as Plato held. For he called all immaterial and unparticipated things entities which exist of themselves, just as he called the idea of man "man-in-himself," as though not something participated in matter. Hence he also called the good-in-itself that which is its own goodness unparticipated—namely, the first principle of all things.

375. Moreover, with a view to strengthening this argument he introduces an example. From the fact that there cannot be an end in the case of immobile things, it seems to follow that, in the mathematical sciences (which abstract from matter and motion), nothing is proved by means of this cause, as in the science of nature (which deals with mobile things) something is proved by means of the notion of good. For example, we may give as the reason why man has hands that by them he is more capable of executing the things that reason conceives.

But in the mathematical sciences no demonstration is made by saying that something is so because it is better for it to be so, or worse if it were not so—as if one were to say that the angle in a semi-circle is a right angle because it is better that it should be so than be acute or obtuse. And because there can be, perhaps, another way of demonstrating by means of the final cause (for example, if one were to say that if an end is to be, then what exists for the sake of an end must first be), he therefore adds that in the mathematical sciences no one makes any mention at all of any of those things that pertain to the good or to the final cause.

And for this reason certain sophists, as Aristippus, who belonged to the Epicurean school, completely disregarded any demonstrations which employ final causes, considering them to be worthless in view of the fact that in the servile or mechanical arts, for example, in the **art of building**, that is, in carpentry, and in that of **cobbling**, all things are explained on the grounds that something is better or worse. But in the mathematical sciences, which are the noblest and most certain of the sciences, no mention is made of things good and evil.

376. **But on the other hand** (996b1). Here he interjects another question.

First, he states this question, which has two parts.

The first part of the question is this. If different causes are considered by many sciences, so that a different science considers a different cause, then which of these sciences should be called the one **that is being sought**, that is, first philosophy? Is it the one which considers the formal cause, or the one which considers the final cause, or the one which considers one of the other causes?

Secunda pars quaestionis est, si aliquae res sint quae habeant plures causas, quis maxime cognoscit rem illam eorum qui considerant illas causas?

377. Secundo cum dicit *contingit enim* manifestat partem secundam quaestionis per hoc, quod una et eadem res invenitur, quae habet omnes modos causarum: sicut domus causa unde principium motus, est ars et aedificator. Id vero cuius causa vel finis causa domus *est opus*, idest usus eius, qui est habitatio. Causa vero sicut materia est terra, ex qua fiunt lateres et lapides. Causa vero sicut species vel forma, est ipsa ratio domus, quam artifex praeconceptam mente in materia ponit.

378. Tertio ibi *igitur ex* reassumit quaestionem, scilicet quam dictarum scientiarum possumus vocare sapientiam, secundum ea quae de sapientia prius determinavimus in principio libri: utrum scilicet illam, quae considerat causam formalem, vel quae considerat causam finalem, vel aliquam aliarum causarum.

Et ponit consequenter rationes ad singulas trium causarum: dicens, quod ratio quaedam videtur de *qualibet* scientia, idest quae est per quamcumque causam, quod appelletur nomine sapientiae.

Et primo quantum ad scientiam quae est per causam finalem. Dictum est enim in principio libri, quod ista scientia, quae sapientia dicitur, est maxime principalis et ordinativa aliarum, quasi subditarum.

Sic igitur inquantum sapientia *est senior*, idest prior ordine dignitatis, et principalior quadam auctoritate ordinandi alias, quia non est iustum quod aliae scientiae contradicant ei, sed ab ea accipiant sua principia, sicut ei servientes; videtur quod illa scientia, *quae est finis et boni*, idest quae procedit per causam finalem, sit digna nomine sapientiae. Et hoc ideo, quia omnia alia sunt propter finem, unde finis est quodammodo causa omnium aliarum causarum.

Et sic scientia, quae procedit per causam finalem, est principalior. Cuius signum est, quod artes illae, ad quas pertinent fines, principantur et praecipiunt aliis artibus, sicut gubernatoria navifactivae. Unde, si sapientia est principalis et praeceptiva respectu aliarum, maxime videtur quod procedat per causam finalem.

379. Deinde cum dicit *inquantum vero* inducit rationem de causa formali. Dictum est enim in prooemio libri, quod sapientia est primarum causarum, et eius quod est maxime scibile, et quod est maxime certum.

The second part of the question is this. If there are some things that have many causes, which one of those who consider those causes knows that subject best?

377. *For it is possible* (996b5). He clarifies the second part of the question by the fact that one and the same thing is found to have every type of cause. For example, in the case of a house, the source of motion is the art and the builder; the reason for which, or the final cause of the house, *is its function*, or its use, which is habitation; its material cause is the earth, from which the walls and floor are made; and its species or form is the plan of the house, which the architect, after first conceiving it in his mind, gives to matter.

378. *Therefore, from the things* (996b8). Here he takes up again the question as to which of the aforesaid sciences we can call wisdom on the basis of the points previously established about wisdom at the beginning of this work (982a4; [36])—namely, whether it is the science which considers the formal cause, or the one which considers the final cause, or the one which considers one of the other causes.

And he gives, in order, arguments relating to each of the three causes, saying that there seems to be some reason why *each one* of the sciences (that is, any one which proceeds by means of any cause at all) should be called by the name of wisdom.

First, he speaks of that science which proceeds by means of the final cause. For it was stated at the beginning of this work that this science, which is called wisdom, is the most authoritative one, and the one which directs others as subordinates.

Therefore, inasmuch as wisdom *takes precedence*, or is prior in the order of dignity and more influential in its authoritative direction of the other sciences (because it is not right that the others should contradict it but they should take their principles from it as its servants), it seems that that science *that deals with the end and the good*, that is, the one which proceeds by means of the final cause, is worthy of the name of wisdom. And this is true because everything else exists for the sake of the end, so that in a sense the end is the cause of all the other causes.

Thus the science which proceeds by means of the final cause is the most important one. This is indicated by the fact that those arts which are concerned with ends are more important than and prior to the other arts. For example, the art of navigation is more important than and prior to the art of ship-building. Hence, if wisdom is preeminent and regulative of the other sciences, it seems that it proceeds especially by means of the final cause.

379. *But insofar as wisdom* (996b13). Here he introduces the arguments relating to the formal cause. For it was said in the prologue of this work (982b7; [51]) that wisdom is concerned with first causes and with whatever is most knowable and most certain.

Et secundum hoc videtur quod sit *substantiae*, idest per causam formalem: quia inter diversos modos sciendi, magis dicimus scire illum qui scit aliquid esse, quam qui scit aliquid non esse.

Unde et in *Posterioribus* Philosophus probat, quod demonstratio affirmativa est potior quam negativa. Inter eos autem, qui sciunt aliquid affirmare, unum alio magis dicimus scire.

Sed inter omnes maxime dicimus scire illum, qui cognoscit quid est res, non autem qui scit quanta est, vel qualis, et quid possit facere vel pati. Sic igitur in cognoscendo ipsam rem absolute perfectissimum est scire quid est res, quod est scire substantiam rei. Sed etiam in aliis cognoscendis, puta proprietatibus rei, magis dicimus scire singula, de quibus sunt demonstrationes, quando etiam de ipsis accidentibus vel proprietatibus scimus quod quid est; quia quod quid est non solum invenitur in substantiis, sed etiam in accidentibus.

380. Et ponit exemplum de tetragonismo, idest quadratura superficiei aeque distantium laterum non quadratae, quam quadrare dicimur, cum invenimus quadratum ei aequale. Cum autem omnis superficies aeque distantium laterum et rectorum angulorum ex duabus lineis contineatur, quae rectum continent angulum, ita, quod totalis superficies nihil est aliud quam ductus unius earum in alia, tunc invenimus quadratum aequale superficiei praedictae, quando invenimus lineam quae sit media in proportione inter duas lineas praedictas. Puta, si linea A, ad lineam B se habet sicut linea B ad lineam C, quadratum lineae B est aequale superficiei, quae continetur in A et A, ut probatur in sexto Euclidis.

381. Et apparet manifeste in numeris. Sex enim est medium in proportione inter novem et quatuor. Novem enim se habet ad sex in proportione sesquialtera, et similiter sex ad quatuor. Quadratum autem senarii est trigintasex. Quod etiam perficitur ex ductu quaternarii in novenarium. Quater enim novem sunt trigintasex. Et simile est in omnibus aliis.

382. Deinde ponit rationem de causa movente *circa generationes* videmus enim quod circa generationes et actiones, et circa omnem transmutationem maxime dicimur aliquid scire quando cognoscimus principium motus, et quod motus nihil est aliud quam actus mobilis a movente, ut dicitur in tertio *Physicorum*. Praetermittit autem de causa materiali, quia illa imperfectissime se habet ad hoc quod sit principium cognoscendi: non enim fit cognitio per id quod est in potentia, sed per id quod est in actu, ut infra in nono dicetur.

And according to this it seems to be concerned with *substance*; that is, it proceeds by means of the formal cause. For among the different ways of knowing things, we say that he who knows that something exists knows more perfectly than he who knows that it does not exist.

Hence in the *Posterior Analytics* the Philosopher proves that an affirmative demonstration is preferable to a negative demonstration. And among those who know something affirmatively, we say that one knows more perfectly than another.

But we say that he knows more perfectly than any of the others who knows what a thing is, and not he who knows how great it is, or what it is like, or what it can do or undergo. Therefore, to know a thing itself in the most perfect way absolutely is to know what it is, and this is to know its substance. But even in knowing other things (for example, a thing's properties), we say that we know best every single thing about which there are demonstrations when we also know the whatness of their accidents and properties. For whatness is found not only in substance but also in accidents.

380. He gives the example of squaring—that is, squaring a surface of equally distant sides which is not square but which we say is squared when we find a square equal to it. But since every rectangular surface of equally distant sides is contained by the two lines which contain the right angle, so that the total surface is simply the product of the multiplication of one of these lines by the other, then we find a square equal to this surface when we find a line which is the proportional mean between these two lines. For example, if line A is to line B as line B is to line C, the square of line B is equal to the surface contained by C and A, as is proved in Euclid's *Elements* 6.

381. This becomes quite evident in the case of numbers. For six is the proportional mean between nine and four; for nine is related to six in the ratio of one to one and a half, and so also is six to four. Now the square of six is thirty-six, which is also produced by multiplying four by nine, for four times nine equals thirty-six. And it is similar in all other cases.

382. *But with regard to processes* (996b22). Here he gives an argument pertaining to the cause of motion. For in processes of generation and actions and in every change, we can say we know a thing when we know its principle of motion, and that motion is nothing else than the act of something mobile produced by a mover, as is stated in *Physics* 3. He omits the material cause, however, because that cause is a principle of knowing in the most imperfect way, for the act of knowing is not caused by what is potential but by what is actual, as is stated below in book 9 (1051a21; [1894]).

383. His igitur positis ad secundam quaestionem pertinentibus, inducit rationem ex eisdem rationibus supra positis ad primam quaestionem, scilicet quod alterius scientiae sit considerare omnes istas causas, eo quod in diversis rebus diversae causae videntur habere principalitatem, sicut in mobilibus principium motus, in scibilibus quod quid est, finis autem in his quae ordinantur ad finem.

384. Hanc autem quaestionem Aristoteles in sequentibus expresse solvere non invenitur: potest tamen eius solutio ex his quae ipse inferius in diversis locis determinat, colligi. Determinat enim in quarto, quod ista scientia considerat ens inquantum est ens; unde et eius est considerare primas substantias, non autem scientiae naturalis, quia supra substantiam mobilem sunt aliae substantiae. Omnis autem substantia vel est ens per seipsam, si sit forma tantum; vel si sit composita ex materia et forma, est ens per suam formam;

unde inquantum haec scientia est considerativa entis, considerat maxime causam formalem. Primae autem substantiae non cognoscuntur a nobis ut sciamus de eis quod quid est, ut potest aliqualiter haberi ex his quae in nono determinantur: et sic in earum cognitione non habet locum causa formalis. Sed quamvis ipsae sint immobiles secundum seipsas, sunt tamen causa motus aliorum per modum finis;

et ideo ad hanc scientiam, inquantum est considerativa primarum substantiarum, praecipue pertinet considerare causam finalem, et etiam aliqualiter causam moventem. Causam autem materialem secundum seipsam nullo modo, quia materia non convenienter causa est entis, sed alicuius determinati generis, scilicet substantiae mobilis. Tales autem causae pertinent ad considerationem particularium scientiarum, nisi forte considerentur ab hac scientia inquantum continentur sub ente. Sic enim ad omnia suam considerationem extendit.

385. His autem visis, rationes inductas facile est solvere.

Primo enim nihil prohibet diversas causas ad hanc scientiam pertinere unam existentem, licet non sint contraria, quia reducuntur ad unum, scilicet ad ens commune, sicut dictum est.

Similiter nihil prohibet, etsi non quaelibet scientia consideret omnes causas, quin aliqua scientia possit considerare omnes vel plures earum inquantum reducuntur ad aliquid unum. Sed specialiter descendendo, dicendum est, quod nihil prohibet in immobilibus considerari et principium motus, et finem sive bonum; in

383. Then after having given those arguments which pertain to the second question, he introduces an argument which is based on the same reasons as were given above (996a20; [370]) in reference to the first question—namely, that it is the office of a different science to consider all these causes, because in different subject matters different causes seem to have the principal role. For example, the source of motion has this in mobile things, the quiddity in demonstrable things, and the end in things directed to an end.

384. However, we do not find that Aristotle explicitly solves this question later on, though his solution can be ascertained from the things that he establishes below in different places. For in book 4 [533] he establishes that this science considers being as being, and therefore that it also belongs to it (and not to the philosophy of nature) to consider first substances, for there are other substances besides mobile ones. But either every substance is a being of itself (granted that it is only a form) or it is a being by its form (granted that it is composed of matter and form).

Hence inasmuch as this science considers being, it considers the formal cause before all the rest. But the first substances are not known by us in such a way that we know what they are, as can be understood in some way from the things established in book 9 [1904]. Thus in our knowledge of them the formal cause has no place. But even though they are immobile in themselves, they are nevertheless the cause of motion in other things after the manner of an end.

Hence inasmuch as this science considers first substances, it belongs to it especially to consider the final cause, and also in a way the efficient cause. But to consider the material cause in itself does not belong to it in any way, because matter is not properly a cause of being, but of some definite kind of being, namely, of mobile substance. However, such causes belong to the consideration of the particular sciences, unless perhaps they are considered by this science inasmuch as they are contained under being. For it extends its analysis to all things in this way.

385. Now when these things are seen it is easy to answer the arguments which have been raised.

First, nothing prevents the different causes in this science from belonging to a single existing thing, even though they are not contraries, because they are reducible to one thing—being in general—as has been stated [384].

And in a similar way, even though not every science considers all of the causes, still nothing prevents one science from being able to consider all of the causes or several of them insofar as they are reducible to some one thing. But to be more specific, it must be said that in the case of immobile things nothing prevents the source of motion

immobilibus inquam quae sunt tamen moventia sicut sunt primae substantiae:

in his autem quae neque moventur nec movent, non est consideratio principii motus, nec finis sub ratione finis motus, quamvis possit considerari finis sub ratione finis alicuius operationis sine motu.

Sicut si ponantur esse substantiae intelligentes non moventes, ut Platonici posuerunt, nihilominus tamen inquantum habent intellectum et voluntatem oportet ponere in eis finem et bonum, quod est obiectum voluntatis. Mathematica autem non moventur, nec movent, nec habent voluntatem. Unde in eis non consideratur bonum sub nomine boni et finis. Consideratur tamen in eis id quod est bonum, scilicet esse et quod quid est. Unde falsum est, quod in mathematicis non sit bonum, sicut ipse infra in nono probat.

386. Ad quaestionem vero secundam iam patet responsio; quia ad hanc scientiam pertinet consideratio trium causarum, de quibus rationes inducit.

and the end or good from being investigated. By immobile things I mean here those which are still causes of motion, as the first substances.

However, in the case of those things that are neither moved nor cause motion, there is no investigation of the source of motion, or of the end in the sense of the end of motion, although an end can be considered as the goal of some operation which does not involve motion.

For if there are held to be intellectual substances which do not cause motion, as the Platonists claimed, still insofar as they have an intellect and a will it is necessary to hold that they have an end and a good which is the object of their will. However, the objects of mathematics neither are moved nor cause motion nor have a will. Hence in their case the good is not considered under the name of good and end, although in them we do consider what is good (namely, their being and what they are). Hence the statement that the good is not found in the objects of mathematics is false, as he proves below in book 9 [1888].

386. The reply to the second question is already clear, for a study of the three causes, about which he argued dialectically, belongs to this science.

LECTURE 5

How many sciences study the principles of demonstration and substance?

996b26 At vero et de principiis demonstrationis utrum unius scientiae est aut plurium, dubitatio est. Dico autem demonstrativa communes opiniones ex quibus demonstrant, ut quoniam omne necessarium est aut dicere aut negare, et impossibile simul esse et non esse, et quaecumque tales propositiones. [387]

ἀλλὰ μὴν καὶ περὶ τῶν ἀποδεικτικῶν ἀρχῶν, πότερον μιᾶς ἐστὶν ἐπιστήμης ἢ πλειόνων, ἀμφισβητήσιμόν ἐστιν (λέγω {28} δὲ ἀποδεικτικὰς τὰς κοινὰς δόξας ἐξ ὧν ἅπαντες δεικνύουσιν) οἷον ὅτι πᾶν ἀναγκαῖον ἢ φάναι ἢ ἀποφάναι, καὶ {30} ἀδύνατον ἅμα εἶναι καὶ μὴ εἶναι, καὶ ὅσαι ἄλλαι τοιαῦται προτάσεις,

But with respect to the principles of demonstration there is also the problem of whether they are studied by one science or by many. By principles of demonstration I mean the common opinions from which demonstrations proceed—for example, everything must either be either affirmed or be denied, and it is impossible both to be and not to be at the same time, and all other such propositions.

Utrum harum una scientia et substantiae, aut alia? Et si non una est, quam oportet appellare, quae nunc est quaesita?

πότερον μία τούτων ἐπιστήμη καὶ τῆς οὐσίας ἢ ἑτέρα, κἂν εἰ μὴ μία, ποτέραν χρὴ προσαγορεύειν τὴν ζητουμένην νῦν.

Is there one science which deals with these principles and with substance, or are there different sciences? And, if not one, which of the two must be called the one that is now being sought?

996b33 Unius igitur esse non est rationabile. Quid enim magis Geometriae quam qualiscumque de his est proprium audire? Si igitur similiter qualiscumque sit, omnium vero non contingit, sicut nec aliarum, ita neque ipsas substantias cognoscentes proprium est de ipsis cognoscere. [388]

μιᾶς μὲν οὖν οὐκ εὔλογον εἶναι· τί γὰρ μᾶλλον γεωμετρίας ἢ ὁποιασοῦν περὶ τούτων ἐστὶν ἴδιον τὸ ἐπαΐειν; {35} εἴπερ οὖν ὁμοίως μὲν ὁποιασοῦν ἐστίν, ἁπασῶν δὲ μὴ ἐνδέχεται, {997a1} ὥσπερ οὐδὲ τῶν ἄλλων οὕτως οὐδὲ τῆς γνωριζούσης τὰς οὐσίας ἴδιόν ἐστι τὸ γιγνώσκειν περὶ αὐτῶν.

Now it would be unreasonable that these things should be studied by one science. For why should the study of these be proper to geometry rather than to any other science? In a similar way, then, if this study pertains to any science but cannot pertain to all, an understanding of these principles is no more proper to the science which studies substance than it is to any other science.

997a2 Simul autem quomodo erit ipsorum scientia? Quid enim et unumquodque harum existit ens et nunc novimus. Utuntur ergo eis ut notis artes aliae. Si autem de his demonstratio, oportebit aliquod igitur esse subiectum, et haec quidem passiones, illa vero dignitates eorum. Namque de omnibus esse demonstrationem est impossibile. Necesse enim ex aliquo esse et circa aliquid et aliquorum demonstrationem: quare accidit esse unum genus aliquid monstratorum. Omnes enim demonstrativae dignitatibus utuntur. [389]

ἅμα δὲ καὶ τίνα τρόπον ἔσται αὐτῶν ἐπιστήμη; τί μὲν γὰρ ἕκαστον τούτων τυγχάνει ὂν καὶ νῦν γνωρίζομεν (χρῶνται γοῦν ὡς γιγνωσκομένοις {5} αὐτοῖς καὶ ἄλλαι τέχναι)· εἰ δὲ ἀποδεικτικὴ περὶ αὐτῶν ἐστί, δεήσει τι γένος εἶναι ὑποκείμενον καὶ τὰ μὲν πάθη τὰ δ᾽ ἀξιώματ᾽ αὐτῶν (περὶ πάντων γὰρ ἀδύνατον ἀπόδειξιν εἶναι), ἀνάγκη γὰρ ἔκ τινων εἶναι καὶ περί τι καὶ τινῶν τὴν ἀπόδειξιν· ὥστε συμβαίνει πάντων εἶναι γένος ἕν {10} τι τῶν δεικνυμένων, πᾶσαι γὰρ αἱ ἀποδεικτικαὶ χρῶνται τοῖς ἀξιώμασιν.

But at the same time, how will there be a science of these principles? For we already know what each one of them is; therefore, the other arts use them as something known. However, if there is demonstration of them, there will have to be some subject genus, and some of the principles will have to be properties and others axioms. For there cannot be demonstration of all things, since demonstration must proceed from something, and be about something, and be demonstration of certain things. It follows, then, that there is a single genus of demonstrable things, for all demonstrative sciences use axioms.

997a11 At vero si alia quae substantiae et quae de his, quae earum principalior et prior est? Universaliter enim maxime omnium principia sunt dignitates. Et si non est philosophi, cuius erit alterius

ἀλλὰ μὴν εἰ ἑτέρα ἡ τῆς οὐσίας καὶ ἡ περὶ τούτων, ποτέρα κυριωτέρα καὶ προτέρα πέφυκεν αὐτῶν; καθόλου γὰρ μάλιστα καὶ πάντων ἀρχαὶ τὰ ἀξιώματά ἐστιν, εἴ τ᾽ ἐστὶ μὴ τοῦ φιλοσόφου, τίνος

But on the other hand, if the science which considers substance differs from the one which considers axioms, which of these sciences is the more important and prior one? For axioms are most universal

determinare veritatem et falsitatem? [391]

ἔσται περὶ αὐτῶν ἄλλου τὸ {15} θεωρῆσαι τὸ ἀληθὲς καὶ ψεῦδος;

and are the principles of all things. And if it does not belong to the philosopher to establish truth and falsity, to what other person will it belong?

---

387. Postquam disputavit de prima quaestione quae erat de consideratione causarum, hic intendit disputare de consideratione principiorum demonstrationis, ad quam scientiam pertineat; et circa hoc tria facit.

Primo movet quaestionem.

Secundo disputat ad unam partem, ibi, *unius igitur esse* et cetera.

Tertio disputat ad aliam partem, ibi, *at vero si alia* et cetera.

Dicit ergo primo, quod dubitatio est *de principiis demonstrationis, utrum considerare de his pertineat ad unam scientiam vel ad plures*. Et exponit quae sunt demonstrationis principia. Et dicit, quod sunt *communes* conceptiones omnium ex quibus procedunt omnes demonstrationes, inquantum scilicet singula principia propriarum conclusionum demonstratarum habent firmitatem virtute principiorum communium. Et exemplificat de primis principiis maxime sicut quod necesse est de unoquoque aut affirmare aut negare. Et aliud principium est quod impossibile est idem simul esse et non esse. Est ergo haec quaestio, utrum haec principia et similia pertineant ad unam scientiam vel ad plures. Et si ad unam, utrum pertineant ad scientiam quae est considerans substantiam, vel ad aliam. Et si ad aliam, quam earum oportet nominare sapientiam vel philosophiam primam quam nunc quaerimus.

388. Deinde cum dicit *unius igitur* obiicit ad unam partem quaestionis, scilicet ad ostendendum quod non est unius scientiae considerare principia omnia, supple demonstrationis, et substantiam.

Et ponit duas rationes: quarum prima talis est. Cum omnes scientiae utantur praedictis principiis demonstrationis; nulla ratio esse videtur quare magis pertineat ad unam quam ad aliam: nec etiam videtur rationabile, quod eorum consideratio pertineat ad omnes scientias, quia sic sequeretur quod idem tractaretur in diversis scientiis, quod esset superfluum. Videtur igitur relinqui, quod nulla scientia consideret de principiis istis: ergo per quam rationem non pertinet ad aliquam aliarum scientiarum tradere cognitionem de huiusmodi demonstrationis principiis, per eamdem rationem non pertinet ad scientiam cuius est considerare de substantia.

389. Secunda ratio ponitur ibi *simul autem*, quae talis est. Modus de quo est cognitio in scientiis est duplex. Unus modus secundum quod de unoquoque cognosci-

387. Having debated the first question which had to do with the study of causes, Aristotle's intention here is to argue dialectically about the science which is concerned with the study of the first principles of demonstration; in regard to this he does three things.

First, he raises the question.

Second (996b33; [388]), he argues one side of the question, at *now it would be unreasonable*.

Third (997a11; [391]), he argues on the other side of the question, at *but on the other hand*.

Accordingly, he first states the problem relating *to the principles of demonstration* (996b26), namely, *whether they are studied by one science or by many*. Further, he explains what the principles of demonstration are, saying that they are the *common* conceptions of all men on which all demonstrations are based—that is, inasmuch as the particular principles of the proper demonstrated conclusions derive their stability from these common principles. And he gives an example of first principles, especially this one: everything must either be affirmed or be denied. Another principle which he mentions is that it is impossible for the same thing both to be and not to be at the same time. Hence the question arises as to whether these principles and similar ones pertain to one science or to many. And if they pertain to one science, whether they pertain to the science which investigates substance or to another science. And if to another science, then which of these must be called wisdom, or first philosophy, which we now seek.

388. *Now it would be* (996b33). Here he argues one side of the question with a view to showing that it is not the office of one science to consider all first principles, that is, the first principles of demonstration and substance.

He gives two arguments, of which the first runs thus. Since all sciences employ these principles of demonstration, there seems to be no reason why the study of them should pertain to one science rather than to another. Nor again does it seem reasonable that they should be studied by all sciences, because then it would follow that the same thing would be treated in different sciences, which would be superfluous. Hence it seems to follow that no science considers these principles. Therefore, for the very same reason that it does not belong to any of the other sciences to give us a knowledge of such principles, for this reason too it follows that it does not belong to the science whose function it is to consider substance.

389. *But at the same time* (997a2). Here he gives the second argument, which runs thus. In the sciences there are two methods by which knowledge is acquired. One is

tur quid est. Alius modus secundum quod cognitio per demonstrationem acquiritur. Primo autem modo non pertinet ad aliquam scientiam tradere cognitionem de principiis demonstrationis, quia talis cognitio principiorum praesupponitur ante omnes scientias. Quod enim *unumquodque horum sit ens ex nunc novimus*, idest statim a principio cognoscimus quid significent haec principia, per quorum cognitionem statim ipsa principia cognoscuntur. Et, quia talis cognitio principiorum inest nobis statim a natura, concludit, quod omnes artes et scientiae, quae sunt de quibusdam aliis cognitionibus, utuntur praedictis principiis tamquam naturaliter notis.

390. Similiter autem probatur, quod praedictorum principiorum cognitio non traditur in aliqua scientia per demonstrationem; quia si esset aliqua demonstratio de eis, oporteret tria tunc principia considerari; scilicet genus subiectum, passiones, et dignitates. Et ad huius manifestationem, subdit, quod impossibile est de omnibus esse demonstrationem: non enim demonstrantur subiecta, sed de subiectis passiones. De subiectis vero oportet praecognoscere an est et quid est, ut dicitur in primo *Posteriorum*.

Et hoc ideo, quia necesse est demonstrationem esse ex aliquibus, sicut ex principiis, quae sunt dignitates, et circa aliquod, quod est subiectum, et aliquorum, quae sunt passiones. Ex hoc autem statim manifestum est ex uno horum trium, quod dignitates non demonstrantur; quia oporteret quod haberent aliquas dignitates priores, quod est impossibile. Unde praetermisso hoc modo procedendi tamquam manifesto, procedit ex parte subiecti. Cum enim una scientia sit unius generis subiecti, oporteret quod illa scientia, quae demonstraret dignitates, haberet unum subiectum. Et sic oporteret, quod omnium scientiarum demonstrativarum esset unum genus subiectum, quia omnes scientiae demonstrativae utuntur huiusmodi dignitatibus.

391. Deinde cum dicit *at vero* obiicit ad aliam partem. Si enim dicatur, quod alia scientia sit, quae est de huiusmodi principiis, et alia, quae est de substantia, remanebit dubitatio quae ipsarum sit principalior et prior.

Ex una enim parte dignitates sunt maxime universales, et principia omnium, quae traduntur in quibuscumque scientiis. Et secundum hoc videtur quod scientia, quae est de huiusmodi principiis, sit principalissima. Ex alia vero parte, cum substantia sit primum et principale ens; manifestum est, quod prima philosophia est scientia substantiae. Et si non est eadem scientia substantiae et dignitatum non erit de facili dicere cuius alterius sit

that by which the whatness of each thing is known, and the other is that by which knowledge is acquired through demonstration. But it does not belong to any science to give us a knowledge of the principles of demonstration by means of the first method, because such knowledge of principles is assumed to be prior to all the sciences. *For we already know what each one of them is*; that is, we know from the very beginning what these principles signify, and by knowing this, the principles themselves are immediately known. And since such knowledge of principles belongs to us immediately, he concludes that all the arts and sciences which are concerned with other kinds of cognitions make use of these principles as things naturally known by us.

390. But it is proved in the same way that a knowledge of these principles is not presented to us in any science by means of demonstration, because if there was demonstration of them, then three principles would have to be considered: namely, the subject genus, its properties, and the axioms. In order to clarify this he adds that there cannot be demonstration of all things, for subjects are not demonstrated but properties are demonstrated of subjects. Concerning subjects, however, it is necessary to know beforehand whether they exist and what they are, as is stated in *Posterior Analytics* 1.

The reason is that demonstration must proceed from certain things as principles, which are the axioms, and be about something, which is the subject, and be demonstrative of certain things, which are properties. Now according to this it is immediately evident of one of these three, the axioms, that they are not demonstrated. Otherwise there would have to be certain axioms prior to the axioms, which is impossible. Therefore, having dismissed this method of procedure as obvious, he proceeds to consider the subject genus. For since one science has one subject genus, then that science which would demonstrate axioms would have one subject genus. Thus there would have to be one subject genus for all demonstrative sciences, because all demonstrative sciences use axioms of this kind.

391. *But on the other hand* (997a11). Here he argues the other side of the question. For if it is said that there is one science which deals with such principles and another which deals with substance, the problem will remain as to which of these sciences is the more important and prior one.

For, on the one hand, since the axioms are most universal and are the principles of everything that is treated in any of the sciences, it seems that the science which deals with such principles is the most important one. Yet, on the other hand, since substance is the first and principal kind of being, it is evident that first philosophy is the science of substance. And if it is not the same science which deals with substance and with the axioms, it will not be easy to

considerare veritatem et falsitatem circa dignitates, si non est primi philosophi qui considerat substantiam.

392. Hanc autem quaestionem determinat Philosophus in quarto huius; et dicit, quod ad philosophum potius pertinet consideratio dignitatum, inquantum ad ipsum pertinet consideratio entis in communi, ad quod per se pertinent huiusmodi principia prima, ut maxime apparet in eo quod est maxime primum principium, scilicet quod impossibile est idem esse et non esse. Unde omnes scientiae particulares utuntur huiusmodi principiis sicut utuntur ipso ente, quod tamen principaliter considerat philosophus primus. Et per hoc solvitur ratio prima.

Secunda autem ratio solvitur per hoc, quod philosophus non considerat huiusmodi principia tamquam faciens ea scire definiendo vel absolute demonstrando; sed solum elenchice, idest contradicendo disputative negantibus ea, ut in quarto dicetur.

state to which of the other sciences it belongs to consider the truth and falsity of these axioms if it does not belong to first philosophy, which considers substance.

392. The Philosopher answers this question in book 4 [590] of this work. He says that the study of the axioms belongs chiefly to the philosopher inasmuch as it pertains to him to consider being in general, to which first principles of this kind belong *per se*, as is most evident in the case of the very first principle: it is impossible for the same thing both to be and not to be [at the same time]. Hence all the particular sciences use principles of this kind just as they use being itself, although it is the first philosopher who is chiefly concerned with this. And the first argument is solved in this way.

But the second argument is solved thus: the philosopher does not consider principles of this kind in such a way as to make them known by defining them or by demonstrating them in an absolute sense, but by refutation, that is, by arguing disputatively against those who deny them, as is stated in book 6 [608].

LECTURE 6

Are all substances considered by one science or by many?

997a15	Totaliterque substantiarum utrum una omnium sit aut plures scientiae. [393]	ὅλως τε τῶν οὐσιῶν πότερον μία πασῶν ἐστιν ἢ πλείους ἐπιστῆμαι;	And there is the problem of whether there is one science or many sciences which deal with all substances.
997a16	Siquidem ergo non una, cuius substantiae ponenda est scientia? [394]	εἰ μὲν οὖν μὴ μία, ποίας οὐσίας θετέον τὴν ἐπιστήμην ταύτην;	If there is not one science, then with what substances must this science deal?
997a17	Unam vero omnium non est rationabile. Etenim demonstrativa una de omnibus erit utique per se accidentibus. Siquidem demonstrativa omnis circa aliquod subiectum speculatur per se accidentia ex communibus opinionibus. [395]	τὸ δὲ μίαν πασῶν οὐκ εὔλογον· καὶ γὰρ ἂν ἀποδεικτικὴ μία περὶ πάντων εἴη τῶν συμβεβηκότων, εἴπερ πᾶσα ἀποδεικτικὴ περὶ {20} τι ὑποκείμενον θεωρεῖ τὰ καθ᾽ αὑτὰ συμβεβηκότα ἐκ τῶν κοινῶν δοξῶν.	But it is unreasonable that there should be one science of all substances, for then one science would demonstrate all *per se* accidents (if it is true that every demonstrative science speculates about the *per se* accidents of some subject by proceeding from common opinions).
	Et circa idem igitur genus accidentia per se eiusdem est speculari ex eisdem opinionibus.	περὶ οὖν τὸ αὐτὸ γένος τὰ συμβεβηκότα καθ᾽ αὑτὰ τῆς αὐτῆς ἐστι θεωρῆσαι ἐκ τῶν αὐτῶν δοξῶν.	Hence it is the office of the same science to study the *per se* accidents of the same subject genus by proceeding from the same opinions.
	Nam circa ipsum quia, unius; et ex quibus, unius, sive eiusdem, sive alterius.	περί τε γὰρ ὃ μιᾶς καὶ ἐξ ὧν μιᾶς, εἴτε τῆς αὐτῆς εἴτε ἄλλης,	For it belongs to one science to consider that something is so, and it belongs to one science (whether to the same science or to another) to consider the principles.
	Quare et accidentia, sive hae speculentur, aut ex his, una.	ὥστε καὶ τὰ συμβεβηκότα, εἴθ᾽ αὗται θεωροῦσιν εἴτ᾽ {25} ἐκ τούτων μία.	Hence it belongs to one science to consider accidents, whether they are studied by these sciences or by one derived from them.
997a25	Amplius autem utrum circa substantiam solum theoria est, aut circa ipsas et accidentia. [399]	ἔτι δὲ πότερον περὶ τὰς οὐσίας μόνον ἡ θεωρία ἐστὶν ἢ καὶ περὶ τὰ συμβεβηκότα ταύταις;	Further, there is the problem of whether this science is concerned only with substances, or also with accidents.
	Dico autem ut si solidum quaedam substantia est et linea et superficies, utrum eiusdem scientiae est eadem cognoscere, et accidentia circa unumquodque genus, de quibus mathematicae ostendunt, aut alterius.	λέγω δ᾽ οἷον, εἰ τὸ στερεὸν οὐσία τίς ἐστι καὶ γραμμαὶ καὶ ἐπίπεδα, πότερον τῆς αὐτῆς ταῦτα γνωρίζειν ἐστὶν ἐπιστήμης καὶ τὰ συμβεβηκότα περὶ ἕκαστον γένος περὶ ὧν αἱ μαθηματικαὶ {30} δεικνύουσιν, ἢ ἄλλης.	I mean, for example, that if a solid is a kind of substance, and also lines and surfaces, the question arises as to whether it is the function of the same science to know these and also the accidents of each genus of things about which the mathematical sciences make demonstrations, or whether it is the concern of a different science.
997a30	Nam si eiusdem demonstrativa quaedam esset, et quae substantiae est. Non autem videtur eius quod quid est demonstratio. [400]	εἰ μὲν γὰρ τῆς αὐτῆς, ἀποδεικτική τις ἂν εἴη καὶ ἡ τῆς οὐσίας, οὐ δοκεῖ δὲ τοῦ τί ἐστιν ἀπόδειξις εἶναι·	For if it is the concern of the same science, a particular one will undertake these demonstrations and this will be the one which deals with substance. However, there does not seem to be any demonstration of the quiddity.
997a32	Si vero diversae, quae erit speculans circa substantiam accidentia? Hoc enim reddere est valde difficile. [401]	εἰ δ᾽ ἑτέρας, τίς ἔσται ἡ θεωροῦσα περὶ τὴν οὐσίαν τὰ συμβεβηκότα; τοῦτο γὰρ ἀποδοῦναι παγχάλεπον.	But if it is the concern of a different science, which science will it be that studies the accidents of substances? For to solve this is very difficult.

393. Postquam disputavit duas quaestiones pertinentes ad considerationem huius scientiae, hic disputat tertiam, quae est de consideratione substantiarum et accidentium.

Et dividitur in partes duas, secundum quod circa hoc duas quaestiones disputat.

Secunda incipit ibi, *amplius autem utrum sensibiles substantiae* et cetera.

Circa primum tria facit.

Primo movet quaestionem, quae est, utrum omnium substantiarum sit una scientia, aut plures scientiae considerent diversas substantias.

394. Secundo ibi *siquidem ergo* obiicit ad primam partem; scilicet ad ostendendum quod una scientia sit de omnibus substantiis: quia si non esset una de omnibus substantiis, non posset assignari, ut videtur, cuius substantiae sit considerativa haec scientia, eo quod substantia, in quantum substantia, est principaliter ens. Unde non videtur quod magis pertineat ad considerationem principalis scientiae una substantia quam alia.

395. Tertio ibi *unam vero* obiicit in contrarium, dicens quod non est rationabile ponere unam esse scientiam omnium substantiarum. Sequeretur enim quod esset una scientia demonstrativa de omnibus per se accidentibus. Et hoc ideo, quia omnis scientia demonstrativa aliquorum accidentium, speculatur per se accidentia circa aliquod subiectum: et hoc ex aliquibus conceptionibus communibus. Quia igitur scientia demonstrativa non speculatur accidentia nisi circa subiectum aliquod, sequitur quod ad eamdem scientiam pertineat considerare aliquod genus subiectum, ad quam pertineat considerare per se accidentia illius generis, et e converso, dummodo demonstratio fiat ex eisdem principiis.

396. Sed quandoque contingit quod demonstrare quia ita est, per aliqua principia, pertinet ad aliquam scientiam, et demonstrare principia ex quibus demonstrabatur quia ita est, pertinet ad unam scientiam, quandoque quidem ad eamdem, quandoque vero ad aliam.

Ad eamdem quidem, sicut geometria demonstrat, quod triangulus habet tres angulos aequales duobus rectis, per hoc quod angulus exterior trianguli est aequalis duobus interioribus sibi oppositis, quod tantum demonstrare pertinet ad geometriam.

Ad aliam vero scientiam, sicut musicus probat quod tonus non dividitur in duo semitonia aequalia, per hoc quod proportio sesquioctava cum sit superparticularis, non potest dividi in duo aequalia. Sed hoc probare non pertinet ad musicum sed ad arithmeticum. Sic ergo patet, quod quandoque accidit diversitas in scientiis

393. Having debated two questions which pertain to the scope of investigation of this science, he now treats the third question which is about the study of substances and accidents.

This is divided into two parts inasmuch as he discusses two questions on this point.

The second (997a34; [403]) begins where he says, *furthermore, there is*.

In regard to the first he does three things.

First, he raises the question of whether there is one science that considers all substances, or whether there are many sciences that consider different substances.

394. *If there is not* (997a16). Second, he argues the first side of the question with a view to showing that there is one science of all substances. For if there were not one science of all substances, then apparently it would be impossible to designate the substance which this science considers, because substance as substance is the primary kind of being. Hence it does not seem that one substance rather than another belongs to the consideration of the basic science.

395. *But it is unreasonable* (997a17). Third, he argues the other side of the question, saying that it is unreasonable to hold that there is one science of all substances. For it would follow that there would be one demonstrative science of all *per se* accidents. And this is true because every science which demonstrates certain accidents speculates about the *per se* accidents of some particular subject, and it does this from certain common conceptions. Therefore, since a demonstrative science considers the accidents only of some particular subject, it follows that the study of some subject genus belongs to the same science that is concerned with the study of the *per se* accidents of that genus, and vice versa, so long as demonstrations proceed from the same principles.

396. But sometimes it happens to be the function of some science to demonstrate from certain principles that a thing is so, and sometimes it happens to be the function of some science to demonstrate the principles from which it was demonstrated that a thing is so. This sometimes belongs to the same science and sometimes to a different one.

An example of its being the function of the same science is seen in the case of geometry, which demonstrates that a triangle has three angles equal to two right angles in virtue of the principle that the exterior angle of a triangle is equal to the two interior angles opposite to it. For to demonstrate this belongs to geometry alone.

An example of its being the function of a different science is seen in the case of music, which proves that a tone is not divided into two equal semitones because a ratio of nine to eight (which is superparticular) cannot be divided into two equal parts. But to prove this does not pertain to the musician, but to the arithmetician. It is

propter diversitatem principiorum, dum una scientia demonstrat principia alterius scientiae per quaedam altiora principia.

397. Sed supposita identitate principiorum non potest esse diversitas in scientiis, dummodo sint eadem accidentia et idem genus subiectum, quasi una scientia consideret subiectum, et eadem accidentia. Unde sequitur, quod scientia quae considerat substantiam consideret etiam accidentia; ita quod si sint plures scientiae considerantes substantias, erunt considerantes accidentia. Si vero una earum sola sit quae consideret substantias, una sola erit quae considerabit accidentia. Hoc autem est impossibile; quia sic sequeretur non esse nisi unam scientiam, cum nulla scientia sit quae non demonstret accidentia de aliquo subiecto: non ergo ad unam scientiam pertinet considerare omnes substantias.

398. Haec autem quaestio determinatur in quarto huius, ubi ostenditur quod ad primam scientiam, ad quam pertinet considerare de ente inquantum est ens, pertinet considerare de substantia inquantum est substantia: et sic considerat omnes substantias secundum communem rationem substantiae; et per consequens ad eam pertinet considerare communia accidentia substantiae. Particularia vero accidentia quarumdam substantiarum pertinet considerare ad particulares scientias, quae sunt de particularibus substantiis; sicut ad scientiam naturalem pertinet considerare accidentia substantiae mobilis. Verumtamen in substantiis est etiam ordo: nam primae substantiae sunt substantiae immateriales. Unde et earum consideratio pertinet proprie ad philosophum primum. Sicut si non essent aliae substantiae priores substantiis mobilibus corporalibus, scientia naturalis esset philosophia prima, ut dicitur infra in sexto.

399. Deinde cum dicit *amplius autem* ponit aliam quaestionem de consideratione substantiae et accidentis. Et circa hoc etiam tria facit.

Primo movet quaestionem, quae est, utrum consideratio huius scientiae sit solum circa substantiam, aut etiam circa ea quae accidunt substantiis. Puta si dicamus quod lineae, superficies et solida sint quaedam substantiae, ut quidam posuerunt, quaeritur utrum eiusdem scientiae sit considerare ista, et per se accidentia horum, quae demonstrantur in scientiis mathematicis; aut alterius.

400. Secundo ibi *nam si* obiicit ad unam partem. Si enim eiusdem scientiae est considerare accidentia et substantias; cum scientia quae considerat accidentia sit demonstrativa accidentium, sequitur quod scientia quae considerat substantiam, sit demonstrativa substan-

evident, then, that sometimes sciences differ because their principles differ, so long as one science demonstrates the principles of another science by means of certain higher principles.

397. But if it is assumed that the principles are identical, sciences could not differ so long as the accidents are the same and the subject genus is the same, as if one science considered the subject and another its accidents. Hence it follows that that science which considers a substance will also consider its accidents, so that if there are many sciences which consider substances, there will be many sciences which consider accidents. But if there is only one science which considers substances, there will be only one science which considers accidents. But this is impossible, because it would then follow that there would be only one science, since there is no science which does not demonstrate the accidents of some subject. Therefore, it is not the function of one science to consider all substances.

398. This is treated in book 4 [546] of this work, where it is shown that the examination of substance as substance belongs to the first science, whose province it is to consider being as being. Thus it considers all substances according to the common aspect of substance. Therefore, it belongs to this science to consider the common accidents of substance. But it belongs to the particular sciences, which deal with particular substances, to consider the particular accidents of substances, just as it belongs to the science of nature to consider the accidents of mobile substance. However, among substances there is also a hierarchy, for the first substances are immaterial ones. Hence the study of them belongs properly to first philosophy, just as the philosophy of nature would be first philosophy if there were no other substances prior to mobile bodily substances, as is stated below in book 6 [1170].

399. *Further, there is the problem* (997a25). Here he raises another question regarding the study of substance and accidents. Concerning this he does three things.

First, he raises the question of whether the investigation of this science is concerned with substance alone or also with the attributes that are accidents of substances. For example, if we say that lines, surfaces, and solids are substances of some sort, as some held, the question arises whether it belongs to the same science to consider such things and also their proper accidents, which are demonstrated in the mathematical sciences, or whether it belongs to another science.

400. *For if it is the concern* (997a30). Second, he argues one side of the question. For if it belongs to the same science to consider accidents and substances, then, since a science which considers accidents demonstrates accidents, it follows that a science which considers substance demon-

tiarum: quod est impossibile: cum definitio declarans substantiam, quae significat quod quid est, non demonstretur. Sic ergo non erit eiusdem scientiae substantias considerare et accidentia.

401. Tertio ibi *si vero* obiicit in contrarium: quia si diversae scientiae considerant substantiam et accidens, non erit assignare quae scientia speculetur accidentia circa substantiam, quia talis scientia considerabit utrumque, cum tamen hoc videatur ad omnes scientias pertinere: quia omnis scientia considerat per se accidentia circa subiectum, ut dictum est.

402. Hanc autem quaestionem determinat Philosophus in quarto huius; dicens, quod ad eam scientiam, ad quam pertinet considerare de substantia et ente, pertinet etiam considerare de per se accidentibus substantiae et entis. Non tamen sequetur quod eodem modo consideret utrumque, scilicet demonstrando substantiam, sicut demonstrat accidens; sed definiendo substantiam et demonstrando accidens inesse vel non inesse, ut plenius habetur in fine noni huius.

strates substances. But this is impossible, for the definition of a substance, which expresses the quiddity, is indemonstrable. Hence it will not belong to the same science to consider substances and accidents.

401. *But if it is the concern* (997a32). Third, he argues the other side of the question. If different sciences consider substance and accident, it will not be possible to state which science it is that speculates about the accidents of substance, because the science which would do this would consider both, although this would seem to pertain to all sciences. For every science considers the *per se* accidents of its subject, as has been explained.

402. The Philosopher answers this question in book 4 [570] of this work, saying that it is also the office of that science which is concerned with the study of substance and being to consider the proper accidents of substance and being. Yet it does not follow that it would consider each in the same way, that is, by demonstrating substance as it demonstrates accidents, but by defining substance and by demonstrating that accidents either belong to or do not belong to it. This is explained more fully at the end of book 9 [1895] of this work.

LECTURE 7

Are there substances separate from sensible things?

997a34 Amplius autem utrum sensibiles substantiae solae causae sint dicendae, aut praeter eas aliae. Et utrum unum genus, aut plura genera substantiarum sunt, ut dicentes species et intermedia, circa quae mathematicas dicunt esse scientias. [403]

997b3 Quomodo ergo dicimus species causasque et substantias secundum se, dictum est in prioribus de omnibus ipsis sermonibus. [406]

997b5 Multis autem modis habentibus difficultatem, nullo minus absurdum dicere quidem alias aliquas esse naturas praeter eas quae in caelo sunt, has autem easdem dicere sensibilibus, nisi quia haec quidem sempiterna, illa vero corruptibilia. [407]

Nam per se hominem dicunt hominem esse et equum et sanitatem, aliud autem nihil simile facientes deos esse ostendentibus et humanae speciei esse. Nihil enim aliud illi fecerunt quam homines sempiternos, nec hi species nisi sensibiles sempiternas.

997b12 Amplius autem siquis praeter species et sensibilia intermedia ponat, multas habebit dubitationes. Palam enim quia similiter lineae praeter ipsas sensibiles erunt, et unumquodque aliorum generum. [410]

Igitur quoniam astrologia una harum est, erit quoddam caelum praeter sensibile caelum, et sol et luna et alia similiter caelestia. Et quomodo his credere oportet?

Neque enim immobile rationabile esse, mobile vero impossibile omnino. Similiter autem et de quibus perspectiva tractat et in mathematicis harmoni-

ἔτι δὲ πότερον τὰς αἰσθητὰς οὐσίας μόνας εἶναι {35} φατέον ἢ καὶ παρὰ ταύτας ἄλλας, καὶ πότερον μοναχῶς ἢ πλείω γένη τετύχηκεν ὄντα τῶν οὐσιῶν, {997b1} οἷον οἱ λέγοντες τά τε εἴδη καὶ τὰ μεταξύ, περὶ ἃ τὰς μαθηματικὰς εἶναί φασιν ἐπιστήμας;

ὡς μὲν οὖν λέγομεν τὰ εἴδη αἴτιά τε καὶ οὐσίας εἶναι καθ᾽ ἑαυτὰς εἴρηται ἐν τοῖς πρώτοις λόγοις περὶ {5} αὐτῶν:

πολλαχῇ δὲ ἐχόντων δυσκολίαν, οὐθενὸς ἧττον ἄτοπον τὸ φάναι μὲν εἶναί τινας φύσεις παρὰ τὰς ἐν τῷ οὐρανῷ, ταύτας δὲ τὰς αὐτὰς φάναι τοῖς αἰσθητοῖς πλὴν ὅτι τὰ μὲν ἀΐδια τὰ δὲ φθαρτά.

αὐτὸ γὰρ ἄνθρωπόν φασιν εἶναι καὶ ἵππον καὶ ὑγίειαν, ἄλλο δ᾽ οὐδέν, παραπλήσιον {10} ποιοῦντες τοῖς θεοὺς μὲν εἶναι φάσκουσιν ἀνθρωποειδεῖς δέ: οὔτε γὰρ ἐκεῖνοι οὐδὲν ἄλλο ἐποίουν ἢ ἀνθρώπους ἀϊδίους, οὔθ᾽ οὗτοι τὰ εἴδη ἀλλ᾽ ἢ αἰσθητὰ ἀΐδια.

ἔτι δὲ εἴ τις παρὰ τὰ εἴδη καὶ τὰ αἰσθητὰ τὰ μεταξὺ θήσεται, πολλὰς ἀπορίας ἕξει: δῆλον γὰρ ὡς ὁμοίως γραμμαί τε παρά τ᾽ αὐτὰς καὶ {15} τὰς αἰσθητὰς ἔσονται καὶ ἕκαστον τῶν ἄλλων γενῶν:

ὥστ᾽ ἐπείπερ ἡ ἀστρολογία μία τούτων ἐστίν, ἔσται τις καὶ οὐρανὸς παρὰ τὸν αἰσθητὸν οὐρανὸν καὶ ἥλιός τε καὶ σελήνη καὶ τἆλλα ὁμοίως τὰ κατὰ τὸν οὐρανόν. καίτοι πῶς δεῖ πιστεῦσαι τούτοις;

οὐδὲ γὰρ ἀκίνητον εὔλογον εἶναι, κινούμενον δὲ {20} καὶ παντελῶς ἀδύνατον: ὁμοίως δὲ καὶ περὶ ὧν ἡ ὀπτικὴ πραγματεύεται καὶ ἡ ἐν τοῖς μαθήμασιν

Furthermore, there is the problem whether sensible substances alone must be said to exist, or others besides these. And whether there is one genus or many genera of substances, as is held by those who speak of the forms and the intermediate entities with which they say the mathematical sciences deal.

Now the way in which we say that the forms are both causes and substances in themselves has been treated in our first discussions concerning all of these things (987a29).

But while they involve difficulty in many respects, it is no less absurd to say that there are certain other natures besides those which exist in the heavens, and that these are the same as sensible things, except that the former are eternal whereas the latter are corruptible.

For they say nothing more or less than that there is a man-in-himself and horse-in-himself and health-in-itself, which differ in no respect from their sensible counterparts. In this they act like those who say that there are gods and that they are of human form. For just as the latter made nothing else than eternal men, in a similar way the former make the forms nothing else than eternal sensible things.

Furthermore, if anyone holds that there are intermediate entities in addition to the forms and sensible substances, he will face many problems. For evidently there will be, in like manner, lines in addition to ordinary sensible lines, and the same will be true of other genera of things.

Therefore, since astronomy is one of these mathematical sciences, there will be a heaven in addition to the one we perceive, and a sun and moon, and the same will be true of the other celestial bodies. And how are we to accept these things?

For it is unreasonable that a heaven should be immobile, but that it should be mobile is altogether impossible. The same thing is true of the things with

ca. Etenim hoc impossibile esse praeter sensibilia propter easdem causas.

ἁρμονική· καὶ γὰρ ταῦτα ἀδύνατον εἶναι παρὰ τὰ αἰσθητὰ διὰ τὰς αὐτὰς αἰτίας·

which the science of perspective is concerned, and of harmonics in mathematics, because for the same reasons it is also impossible that these should exist apart from sensible things.

Nam si sunt sensibilia intermedia et sensus, palam et manifestum, quia et animalia erunt intermedia et ipsorum et corruptibilium.

εἰ γὰρ ἔστιν αἰσθητὰ μεταξὺ καὶ αἰσθήσεις, δῆλον ὅτι καὶ ζῷα ἔσονται μεταξὺ αὐτῶν τε καὶ τῶν φθαρτῶν.

For if there are intermediate sensible objects and senses, evidently there will be intermediate animals between animals-in-themselves and those which are corruptible.

997b25 Dubitabit autem aliquis et circa quae existentium quaerere oportet has scientias. [413]

ἀπορήσειε δ᾽ ἄν τις καὶ περὶ ποῖα τῶν ὄντων δεῖ ζητεῖν ταύτας τὰς ἐπιστήμας.

Again, one might also raise the question as to what things these sciences must investigate.

Nam si in hoc differt geometria idest ars mensurandi terram, a geodaesia idest ab arte dividendi terram solum, quia haec quidem horum est quae sentimus, illa vero non sensibilium, palam vero quod praeter medicinam et alia erit scientia, et praeter unamquamque aliarum, inter ipsam medicinalem et hanc medicinalem.

εἰ γὰρ τούτῳ διοίσει τῆς γεωδαισίας ἡ γεωμετρία μόνον, ὅτι ἡ μὲν τούτων ἐστὶν ὧν αἰσθανόμεθα ἡ δ᾽ οὐκ αἰσθητῶν, δῆλον ὅτι καὶ παρ᾽ ἰατρικὴν ἔσται τις ἐπιστήμη καὶ παρ᾽ ἑκάστην τῶν ἄλλων μεταξὺ αὐτῆς τε ἰατρικῆς {30} καὶ τῆσδε τῆς ἰατρικῆς·

For if geometry, the art of measuring the earth, differs from geodesy, the art of dividing the earth, only in that the latter deals with things that we sense, whereas the former deals with what is not sensible, evidently there will be, besides the science of medicine, another science between the science of medicine itself and this particular science of medicine; and this will be true of the other sciences.

Sed quomodo hoc possibile? Etenim salubria quaedam utique erunt praeter sensibilia et etiam sanum.

καίτοι πῶς τοῦτο δυνατόν; καὶ γὰρ ἂν ὑγιείν᾽ ἄττα εἴη παρὰ τὰ αἰσθητὰ καὶ αὐτὸ τὸ ὑγιεινόν.

But how is this possible? For then there will be certain healthy things besides those which are sensible and besides health-in-itself.

997b32 Similiter autem nec hoc videtur quod geodaesia sensibilium sit magnitudinum et corruptibilium; corrupta enim esset utique corruptis. [414]

ἅμα δὲ οὐδὲ τοῦτο ἀληθές, ὡς ἡ γεωδαισία τῶν αἰσθητῶν ἐστὶ μεγεθῶν καὶ φθαρτῶν· ἐφθείρετο γὰρ ἂν φθειρομένων.

Similarly, neither does it seem that geodesy is concerned with continuous quantities which are sensible and corruptible. For in this case it would be destroyed when they are destroyed.

997b34 At vero nec sensibilium erit magnitudinum, nec circa caelum haec astrologia. Nec enim sensibiles lineae sunt tales, quales dicit geometria; nihil enim rectum sensibilium, ita nec rotundum. [416]

ἀλλὰ μὴν οὐδὲ τῶν αἰσθητῶν ἂν εἴη μεγεθῶν {35} οὐδὲ περὶ τὸν οὐρανὸν ἡ ἀστρολογία τόνδε. {998a1} οὔτε γὰρ αἱ αἰσθηταὶ γραμμαὶ τοιαῦταί εἰσιν οἵας λέγει ὁ γεωμέτρης (οὐθὲν γὰρ εὐθὺ τῶν αἰσθητῶν οὕτως οὐδὲ στρογγύλον·

Nor again will astronomy deal with sensible continuous quantities, or with this heaven. For the lines we perceive by the senses are not such as those of which geometry speaks, since none of the things perceived by the senses are straight or round in this way.

Tangit enim regulam non secundum punctum circulus, sed ut Protagoras ait geometras redarguens. Nec motus, nec revolutiones caeli similes de quibus astrologia sermones dicit, nec astris puncta naturam habent eamdem.

ἅπτεται γὰρ τοῦ κανόνος οὐ κατὰ στιγμὴν ὁ κύκλος ἀλλ᾽ ὥσπερ Πρωταγόρας ἔλεγεν ἐλέγχων τοὺς γεωμέτρας), οὔθ᾽ αἱ κινήσεις καὶ {5} ἕλικες τοῦ οὐρανοῦ ὅμοιαι περὶ ὧν ἡ ἀστρολογία ποιεῖται τοὺς λόγους, οὔτε τὰ σημεῖα τοῖς ἄστροις τὴν αὐτὴν ἔχει φύσιν.

For the circle does not touch the rule at a point, but in the way in which Protagoras spoke in arguing against the geometricians. Neither are the motions or revolutions of the heavens similar to the things of which geometry speaks, nor do points have the same nature as the stars.

998a7 Sunt autem et aliqui, qui dicunt esse quidem intermedia haec infra species et sensibilia, non extra sensibilia, sed in his. Quibus accidentia impossibilia omnia quidem maioris est orationis per-

εἰσὶ δέ τινες οἵ φασιν εἶναι μὲν τὰ μεταξὺ ταῦτα λεγόμενα τῶν τε εἰδῶν καὶ τῶν αἰσθητῶν, οὐ μὴν χωρίς γε τῶν αἰσθητῶν ἀλλ᾽ ἐν τούτοις· οἷς τὰ συμβαίνοντα ἀδύνατα πάντα {10} μὲν πλείονος

However, there are also some who say that these intermediate entities, which are below the forms and above sensible things, do not exist outside of sensible things, but in them. But to enumerate all

transire: sufficit enim et talia speculari. [417]

the impossible consequences which follow from this theory would require too long a discussion. It will be sufficient to propose the following consideration.

998a11 Non enim talibus congruum est habere sic sic solum, sed palam quia et species contingit in sensibilibus esse. Eiusdem enim rationis utraque ea sunt. [418]

It is unreasonable that this should be so only in the case of such things, but evidently it is also possible for the forms to exist in sensible things, because both of these views depend on the same argument.

998a13 Amplius autem duo solida in eodem necesse loco esse. [419]

Furthermore, it would be necessary for two solids to occupy the same place.

998a14 Et non esse immobilia in motis existentia sensibilibus. [420]

And the objects of mathematics would not be immobile, since they exist in sensible things, which are moved.

998a15 Totaliter autem cuius causa quis ponet esse quidem ipsa, esse autem in sensibilibus. Eadem enim contingunt inconvenientia eis quae dicta sunt. Erit enim caelum aliquod praeter caelum, non tamen extra, sed in eodem loco: quod est magis impossibile. [421]

Moreover, on the whole, to what end would anyone hold that they exist but exist in sensible things? For the same absurdities as those described will apply to these suppositions. For there will be a heaven in addition to the one which we perceive, although it will not be separate, but in the same place. But this is quite impossible.

De his ergo dubitatio multa, quomodo oportet positam habere veritatem.

In these matters, then, it is difficult to see how it is possible to have any positive truth.

---

403. Postquam disputavit Philosophus quaestiones pertinentes ad considerationem huius scientiae, hic disputat quaestiones pertinentes ad ipsas substantias, de quibus principaliter considerat ista scientia. Et circa hoc tria facit.

Primo movet quaestiones.

Secundo ostendit unde accipi possint rationes ad unam partem, ibi, *quomodo ergo dicimus* et cetera.

Tertio obiicit ad partem contrariam, ibi, *multis autem modis habentibus difficultatem* et cetera.

Circa primum movet duas quaestiones:

quarum prima est, utrum in universitate rerum solae substantiae sensibiles inveniantur, sicut aliqui antiqui naturales dixerunt, aut etiam inveniantur quaedam aliae substantiae, praeter sensibiles, sicut posuerunt Platonici.

404. Secunda quaestio est, supposito quod sint aliquae substantiae, praeter sensibiles, utrum illae substantiae sint unius generis, aut magis sint plura genera harum substantiarum. Utramque enim opinionem recipit. Quidam enim posuerunt praeter substantias sensibiles esse solas species separatas, idest per se hominem immaterialem, et per se equum: et sic de aliis speciebus.

403. Having debated the questions which pertain to the scope of this science, the Philosopher now treats dialectically the questions which pertain to the substances themselves with which this science is chiefly concerned. In regard to this he does three things.

First, he raises the questions.

Second (997b3; [406]), he indicates the source from which arguments can be drawn in support of one side of the question, at *now the way*.

Third (997b5; [407]), he argues on the other side of the question, at *but while they involve*.

In regard to the first part of this division he raises two questions.

The first question is whether sensible substances alone are found in the universe, as certain of the ancient philosophers of nature claimed, or whether besides sensible substances there are certain others, as the Platonists claimed.

404. And assuming that besides sensible substances there are certain others, the second question is whether these substances belong to one genus, or whether there are many genera of substances. For he considers both opinions. For some thinkers held that, in addition to sensible substances, there are only separate forms: an immaterial man-in-himself and horse-in-itself and so on for the other

Alii vero posuerunt quasdam alias intermedias substantias inter species et sensibilia, scilicet mathematica, de quibus dicebant esse mathematicas scientias.

405. Et huius ratio est, quia ponebant duplicem abstractionem rerum: puta abstractionem intellectus, qui dicitur abstrahere uno modo universale a particulari, iuxta quam abstractionem ponebant species separatas per se subsistentes.

Alio modo formas quasdam a materia sensibili, in quarum scilicet definitione non ponitur materia sensibilis, sicut circulus abstrahitur ab aere. Iuxta quam ponebant mathematica abstracta, quae dicebant media inter species et sensibilia, quia conveniunt cum utrisque.

Cum speciebus quidem, inquantum sunt separata a materia sensibili; cum sensibilibus autem, inquantum inveniuntur plura ex eis in una specie, sicut plures circuli et plures lineae.

406. Deinde cum dicit *quomodo ergo* ostendit quomodo ad unam partem argumentari possit; et dicit quod hoc dictum est *in primis sermonibus*, idest in primo libro, quomodo species ponantur causae rerum sensibilium, et substantiae quaedam per se subsistentes. Unde ex his quae ibi dicta sunt in recitatione opinionis Platonis, accipi possunt rationes ad partem affirmativam.

407. Deinde cum dicit *multis autem* obiicit ad partem negativam.

Et primo ad ostendendum quod non sunt species separatae a sensibilibus.

Secundo ad ostendendum quod non sunt mathematica separata, ibi, *amplius autem siquis praeter species* et cetera.

Supra autem in primo libro multas rationes posuit contra ponentes species: et ideo illis rationibus praetermissis ponit quamdam rationem, quae videtur efficacissima; et dicit, quod cum positio ponentium species separatas, multas habeat difficultates, illud quod nunc dicetur non continet minorem absurditatem aliquo aliorum, scilicet quod aliquis dicat quasdam esse naturas praeter naturas sensibiles, quae sub caelo continentur. Nam caelum est terminus corporum sensibilium, ut in primo *De caelo et mundo* probatur. Ponentes autem species, non ponebant eas esse infra caelum, nec extra, ut dicitur in tertio *Physicorum*.

Et ideo convenienter dicit, quod ponebant quasdam naturas praeter eas quae sunt in caelo. Dicebant autem contrarias naturas esse easdem secundum speciem et

species of things, whereas others held that there are certain other substances midway between the forms and sensible things, namely, the objects of mathematics, with which they said the mathematical sciences deal.

405. The reason for this view is that they posited on the part of the intellect a twofold process of abstracting things: one whereby the intellect is said to abstract the universal from the particular, and according to this mode of abstraction they posited separate forms, which subsist of themselves.

They posited another whereby the intellect is said to abstract from sensible matter certain forms whose definition does not include sensible matter, as a circle is abstracted from brass. And according to this mode of abstraction they posited separate objects of mathematics, which they said are midway between the forms and sensible substances, because they have something in common with both:

with the forms inasmuch as they are separate from sensible matter, and with sensible substances inasmuch as many of them are found in one species, as many circles and many lines.

406. *Now the way in which* (997b3). Then he shows how it is possible to argue one side of the question, saying that it has been stated *in our first discussions*, that is, in book 1 (987a29; [151]), how the forms are held to be both the causes of sensible things and substances which subsist of themselves. Hence, from the things that have been said there in presenting the views of Plato, arguments can be drawn in support of the affirmative side of the question.

407. *But while they involve* (997b5). Here he advances reasons for the negative side.

He does this first (997b5) for the purpose of showing that the forms are not separate from sensible things;

second (997b12; [410]), for the purpose of showing that the objects of mathematics are not separate, at *furthermore, if anyone*.

Now above in book 1 (990a12; [208]) he gave many arguments against those who posited separate forms; therefore, passing over those arguments, he gives the line of reasoning which seems most effective. He says (997b5) that while the position of those who posit separate forms contains many difficulties, the position of those which is now given is no less absurd than any of the others—namely, that someone should say that there are certain natures in addition to the sensible ones which are contained beneath the heavens. For the heavens constitute the limit of sensible bodies, as is proved in *On the Heavens* 1. But those who posited the forms did not place them below the heavens or outside of it, as is stated in *Physics* 3.

Hence, in accordance with this, he says that they posited certain other natures in addition to those which exist in the heavens. And they said that these contrary natures are

rationem, et in istis sensibilibus: quinimmo dicebant illas naturas esse species horum sensibilium;

puta quod homo separatus est humanitas hominis huius sensibilis, et quod homo sensibilis est homo participatione illius hominis. Hanc tamen differentiam ponebant inter ea, quia illae naturae immateriales sunt sempiternae, istae vero sensibiles sunt corruptibiles.

408. Et quod ponerent illas naturas easdem istis patet per hoc, quod sicut in istis sensibilibus invenitur homo, equus, et sanitas, ita in illis naturis ponebant **hominem per se**, idest sine materia sensibili, et similiter equum et sanitatem;

et nihil aliud ponebant in substantiis separatis, nisi quod erant materialiter in sensibilibus. Quae quidem positio videtur esse similis positioni ponentium deos esse humanae speciei, quae fuit positio Epicureorum, ut Tullius dicit in libro *De natura deorum*. Sicut enim qui ponebant deos humanae speciei, nihil aliud fecerunt quam ponere homines sempiternos secundum suam naturam, ita et illi qui ponebant species nihil aliud faciunt quam ponunt res sensibiles sempiternas, ut equum, bovem, et similia.

409. Est autem valde absurdum, quod id quod secundum suam naturam est corruptibile, sit eiusdem speciei cum eo, quod per suam naturam est incorruptibile: quin potius corruptibile et incorruptibile differunt specie, ut infra dicetur in decimo huius. Potest tamen contingere quod id quod secundum suam naturam est corruptibile, virtute divina perpetuo conservetur in esse.

410. Deinde cum dicit **amplius autem** obiicit contra ponentes mathematica media inter species et sensibilia.

Et primo contra illos, qui ponebant mathematica media, et a sensibilibus separata.

Secundo contra illos, qui ponebant mathematica, sed in sensibilibus esse, ibi, **sunt autem et aliqui qui dicunt** et cetera.

Circa primum duo facit.

Primo ponit rationes contra primam opinionem,

secundo obiicit pro ea, ibi, **at vero nec sensibilium** et cetera.

Contra primum obiicit tribus viis:

quarum prima est, quod sicut scientia quaedam mathematica est circa lineam, ita etiam sunt quaedam mathematicae scientiae circa alia subiecta. Si igitur sunt quaedam lineae praeter lineas sensibiles, de quibus geo-

the same as these sensible things both in kind and in their intelligible constitution, and that they exist in these sensible things—or rather, they said that those natures are the forms of these sensible things.

For example, they said that a separate man constitutes the humanity of this particular man who is perceived by the senses, and that a man who is perceived by the senses is a man by participating in that separate man. Yet they held that these differ in this respect: those immaterial natures are eternal, whereas these sensible natures are corruptible.

408. That they hold those natures to be the same as these sensible things is clear from the fact that just as man, horse, and health are found among sensible things, in a similar way they posited among these natures **a man-in-himself**, or one lacking sensible matter. They did the same with regard to horse and health.

Moreover, they claimed that nothing else existed in separate substances except the counterpart of what existed materially in the sensible world. This position seems to be similar to that of those who held that the gods are of human form, which was the position of the Epicureans, as Cicero states in *The Nature of the Gods*. For just as those who held that the gods are of human form did nothing else than make men eternal in nature, in a similar way those who claimed that there are forms do nothing else than hold that there are eternal sensible things, such as horse, ox, and the like.

409. But it is altogether absurd that what is naturally corruptible should be specifically the same as what is naturally incorruptible. It is rather the opposite that is true, namely, that corruptible and incorruptible things differ in kind to the greatest degree, as is said below in book 10 (1058b26; [2137]) of this work. Yet it can happen that what is naturally corruptible is kept in being perpetually by divine power.

410. **Furthermore, if anyone** (997b12). Then he argues against those who claimed that the objects of mathematics are midway between the forms and sensible things.

First (997b12; [410]), he argues against those who held that the objects of mathematics are intermediate entities and are separate from sensible things;

second (998a7; [417]), against those who held that the objects of mathematics exist but exist in sensible things, at **however, there are**.

In regard to the first, he does two things.

First, he introduces arguments against the first position.

Second (997b34; [416]), he argues in support of this position, at **nor again**.

He brings up three arguments against the first position.

The first argument is this. Just as there is a mathematical science about the line, in a similar way there are certain mathematical sciences about other subjects. If, then, there are certain lines in addition to the sensible ones with which

metra tractat, pari ratione in omnibus aliis generibus, de quibus aliae scientiae mathematicae tractant, erunt quaedam praeter sensibilia. Sed hoc ponere ostendit esse inconveniens in duabus scientiis mathematicis.

411. Primo quidem in astrologia, quae est una scientiarum mathematicarum, cuius subiectum est caelum et caelestia corpora. Sequetur ergo secundum praedicta, quod sit aliud caelum praeter caelum sensibile, et similiter alius sol et alia luna, et similiter de aliis corporibus caelestibus. Sed hoc est incredibile: quia illud aliud caelum, aut est mobile, aut immobile. Si est immobile, hoc videtur esse irrationabile, cum videamus naturale esse caelo quod semper moveatur. Unde et astrologus aliquid considerat circa motum caeli. Dicere vero quod caelum sit separatum, et sit mobile, est impossibile, eo quod nihil separatum a materia potest esse mobile.

412. Deinde ostendit idem esse inconveniens in aliis scientiis mathematicis, scilicet in perspectiva, quae considerat lineam visualem, et *in harmonica* idest musica, quae considerat proportiones sonorum audibilium.

Impossibile est autem haec esse intermedia inter species et sensibilia; quia si ista sensibilia sint intermedia, scilicet soni et visibilia, sequetur etiam quod sensus sunt intermedii. Et cum sensus non sint nisi in animali, sequetur quod etiam animalia sint intermedia inter species et corruptibilia; quod est omnino absurdum.

413. Deinde cum dicit *dubitabit autem* secunda via talis est. Si in illis generibus, de quibus sunt scientiae mathematicae, invenitur triplex gradus rerum; scilicet sensibilia, species, et intermedia; cum de omnibus speciebus et omnibus sensibilibus videatur esse similis ratio, videtur sequi quod inter quaelibet sensibilia et suas species sunt aliqua media:

unde remanet dubitatio ad quae rerum genera se extendant scientiae mathematicae. Si enim scientia mathematica, puta geometria, differt a geodaesia, quae est scientia de mensuris sensibilibus, in hoc solum quod geodaesia est de mensuris sensibilibus, geometria vero de intermediis non sensibilibus, pari ratione praeter omnes scientias, quae sunt de sensibilibus, erunt secundum praedicta quaedam scientiae mathematicae de intermediis: puta si scientia medicinalis est de quibusdam sensibilibus, erit quaedam alia scientia praeter scientiam medicinalem, et praeter unamquamque similem scien-

geometry deals, by the same token there will be certain things in addition to those perceived by the senses in all other genera of things with which the other mathematical sciences deal. But he shows that it is impossible to hold this with regard to two of the mathematical sciences.

411. He does this first in the case of astronomy, which is one of the mathematical sciences and which has as its subject the heavens and the celestial bodies. Hence, according to what has been said, it follows that there is another heaven besides the one perceived by the senses, and similarly another sun and another moon, and so on for the other celestial bodies. But this is incredible, because that other heaven would be either mobile or immobile. If it were immobile, this would seem to be unreasonable, since we see that it is natural for the heavens to be always in motion. Hence the astronomer also makes some study of the motions of the heavens. But to say that a heaven should be both separate and mobile is impossible, because nothing separate from matter can be mobile.

412. Then he shows that the same view is unacceptable in the case of other mathematical sciences (for example, in that of perspective, which considers visible lines, and in *harmonics*, that is, in that of music, which studies the ratios of audible sounds).

Now it is impossible that there should be intermediate entities between the forms and sensible things. For if these sensible things—sounds and visible lines—were intermediate entities, it would also follow that there are intermediate senses. And since senses exist only in an animal, it would follow that there are also intermediate animals between the form animal and corruptible animals. But this is altogether absurd.

413. *Again, one might* (997b25). The second argument is as follows. If in those genera of things with which the mathematical sciences deal there are three degrees of things—sensible substances, forms, and intermediate entities—then, since the intelligible structure of all sensible things and of all forms seems to be the same, it appears to follow that there are intermediate entities between any sensible things at all and their forms.

Hence there remains the problem as to what genera of things are included in the scope of the mathematical sciences. For if a mathematical science such as geometry differs from geodesy (the science of sensible measurements) only in the respect that geodesy deals with sensible measurements while geometry deals with intermediate things that are not sensible, there will be in addition to all the sciences which consider sensible things certain other mathematical sciences which deal with these intermediate entities. For example, if the science of medicine deals with certain sensible bodies, there will be in addition to

tiam, quae erit media inter medicinalem quae est de sensibilibus, et medicinalem quae est de speciebus.

Sed hoc est impossibile; quia cum medicina sit circa *salubria*, idest circa sanativa, si medicina est media, sequitur quod etiam sanativa sint media praeter sensibilia sanativa et praeter autosanum, idest per se sanum, quod est species sani separati: quod est manifeste falsum.

Relinquitur ergo, quod istae scientiae mathematicae non sunt circa aliqua quae sunt media inter sensibilia et species separatas.

414. Deinde cum dicit *similiter autem* tertiam viam ponit, per quam destruitur quoddam, quod praedicta positio ponebat; quod scilicet esset aliqua scientia circa sensibiles magnitudines: et sic si inveniretur alia scientia circa magnitudines, ex hoc haberetur quod essent magnitudines mediae. Unde dicit, quod hoc non est verum quod geodaesia sit scientia sensibilium magnitudinum, quia sensibiles magnitudines sunt corruptibiles. Sequeretur ergo quod geodaesia esset de magnitudinibus corruptibilibus. Sed scientia videtur corrumpi corruptis rebus de quibus est. Socrate enim non sedente, iam non erit vera opinio qua opinabamur eum sedere. Sequeretur ergo quod geodaesia vel geosophia, ut alii libri habent, corrumpatur corruptis magnitudinibus sensibilibus; quod est contra rationem scientiae, quae est necessaria et incorruptibilis.

415. Posset tamen haec ratio ad oppositum induci: ut dicatur quod per hanc rationem intendit probare, quod nullae scientiae sunt de sensibilibus. Et ita oportet quod omnes scientiae vel sint de rebus mediis, vel sint de speciebus.

416. Deinde cum dicit *at vero* obiicit pro praedicta positione in hunc modum. De ratione scientiae est, quod sit verorum. Hoc autem non esset, nisi esset de rebus prout sunt. Oportet igitur res, de quibus sunt scientiae, tales esse, quales traduntur in scientiis.

Sed sensibiles lineae non sunt tales, quales dicit geometra. Et hoc probat per hoc, quod geometria probat, quod circulus tangit *regulam*, idest rectam lineam solum in puncto, ut patet in tertio Euclidis. Hoc autem non invenitur verum in circulo et linea sensibilibus. Et hac ratione usus fuit Protagoras, destruens certitudines scientiarum contra geometras.

the science of medicine (and any like science) some other science which will be intermediate between the science of medicine which deals with sensible bodies and the science of medicine which deals with the forms.

But this is impossible, for since medicine is about *healthy things* (or things that are conducive to health), then it will also follow, if there is an intermediate science of medicine, that there will be intermediate health-giving things in addition to the health-giving things perceived by the senses and absolute health (or health-in-itself), which is the form of health separate from matter. But this is clearly false.

Hence it follows that these mathematical sciences do not deal with certain things that are intermediate between sensible things and the separate forms.

414. *Similarly, neither* (997b32). Then he gives the third argument, and here one of the points in the foregoing position is destroyed. Namely, this is that there would be a science of continuous quantities which are perceptible; thus, if there were another science of continuous quantities, it would follow from this that there would be intermediate continuous quantities. Hence he says that it is not true that geodesy is a science of perceptible continuous quantities, because such continuous quantities are corruptible. It would follow, then, that geodesy is concerned with corruptible continuous quantities. But it seems that a science is destroyed when the things with which it deals are destroyed, for when Socrates is not sitting, our present knowledge that he is sitting will not be true. Therefore, it would follow that geodesy (or geosophics, as other readings say) is destroyed when sensible continuous quantities are destroyed. But this is contrary to the character of science, which is necessary and incorruptible.

415. Yet this argument can be brought in on the opposite side of the question, inasmuch as one may say that he intends to prove by this argument that there are no sciences of sensible things, so that all sciences must be concerned with either the intermediate entities or the forms.

416. *Nor again will* (997b34). Here he argues in support of this position as follows. It belongs to the very notion of science that it should be concerned with what is true. But this would not be the case unless it were about things as they are. Therefore, the things about which there are sciences must be the same in themselves as they are shown to be in the sciences.

But sensible lines are not such as geometry says they are. He proves this on the grounds that geometry demonstrates that a circle touches *the rule*, that is, a straight line, only at a point, as is shown in Euclid's *Elements* 3. But this is not found to be true of a circle and a line in sensible things. Protagoras used this argument when he destroyed the certainties of the sciences against the geometricians.

Similiter etiam motus et revolutiones caelestes non sunt tales, quales astrologus tradit. Videtur enim naturae repugnare, quod ponantur motus corporum caelestium per excentricos, et epicyclos, et alios diversos motus, quos in caelo describunt astrologi.

Similiter etiam nec quantitates corporum caelestium sunt tales, sicut describunt eas astrologi. Utuntur enim astris ut punctis, cum tamen sint corpora magnitudinem habentia.

Unde videtur quod nec geometria sit de sensibilibus magnitudinibus, nec astrologia de caelo sensibili. Relinquitur igitur, quod sint de aliquibus aliis mediis.

417. Deinde cum dicit **sunt autem** obiicit contra aliam positionem.

Et primo ponit intentum.

Secundo inducit rationes ad propositum, ibi, **non enim in talibus** et cetera.

Dicit ergo primo, quod quidam ponunt esse quasdam naturas medias inter species et sensibilia, et tamen non dicunt ea esse separata a sensibilibus, sed quod sunt in ipsis sensibilibus. Sicut patet de opinione illorum, qui posuerunt dimensiones quasdam per se existentes, quae penetrant omnia corpora sensibilia, quas quidam dicunt esse locum corporum sensibilium, ut dicitur in quarto *Physicae*, et ibidem improbatur. Unde hic dicit, quod prosequi omnia impossibilia, quae sequuntur ad hanc positionem, maioris est negocii. Sed nunc aliqua breviter tangere sufficit.

418. Deinde cum dicit **non enim** inducit quatuor rationes contra praedictam positionem:

quarum prima talis est. Eiusdem rationis videtur esse quod praeter sensibilia ponantur species et mathematica media, quia utrumque ponitur propter abstractionem intellectus: si igitur ponuntur mathematica esse in sensibilibus, congruum est quod non solum ita se habeant in eis, sed etiam quod species ipsae sint in sensibilibus, quod est contra opinionem ponentium species. Ponunt enim eas esse separatas: et non esse alicubi.

419. Secundam rationem ponit ibi, **amplius autem** quae talis est. Si mathematica sunt alia a sensibilibus, et tamen sunt in eis, cum corpus sit quoddam mathematicum, sequitur quod corpus mathematicum simul est in eodem cum corpore sensibili: ergo **duo solida**, idest duo corpora erunt in eodem loco; quod est impossibile, non solum de duobus corporibus sensibilibus, sed etiam de corpore sensibili et mathematico: quia utrumque habet

Similarly, the movements and revolutions of the heavens are not such as the astronomers describe them, for it seems to be contrary to nature to explain the movements of the celestial bodies by means of eccentrics and epicycles and other different movements which the astronomers describe in the heavens.

Similarly, neither are the quantities of the celestial bodies such as the astronomers describe them to be, for they use stars as points even though they are still bodies having extension.

It seems, then, that geometry does not deal with perceptible continuous quantities, and that astronomy does not deal with the heaven which we perceive. Hence it remains that these sciences are concerned with certain other things, which are intermediate.

417. *However, there are* (998a7). Here he argues against another position.

First, he states the point at issue.

Second (998a11; [418]), he brings in arguments to his purpose, at *it is unreasonable*.

Accordingly, he says, first (998a7), that some thinkers posit natures midway between the forms and sensible things, yet they do not say that these natures are separate from sensible things, but exist in sensible things themselves. This is clear regarding the opinion of those who held that there are certain self-subsistent dimensions which penetrate all sensible bodies, which some thinkers identify with the place of sensible bodies, as is stated in *Physics* 4 and is disproved there. Hence he says here that to pursue all the absurd consequences of this position is a major undertaking, but that it is now sufficient to touch on some points briefly.

418. *It is unreasonable* (998a11). Then he brings four arguments against this position.

The first runs as follows. It seems to be for the same reason that in addition to sensible things the forms and objects of mathematics are posited, because both are held by reason of abstraction on the part of the intellect. If, then, the objects of mathematics are held to exist in sensible things, it is fitting that not only they but also the forms themselves should exist there. But this is contrary to the opinion of those who posit the existence of the forms. For they hold that these are separate, and not that they exist anywhere in particular.

419. *Furthermore, it would be* (998a13). Here he gives the second argument, which runs thus. If the objects of mathematics differ from sensible things yet exist in them, since a body is an object of mathematics, it follows that a mathematical body exists simultaneously with a sensible body in the same subject. Therefore, *two solids*, or two bodies, will exist in the same place. This is impossible not only for two sensible bodies but also for a sensible body

dimensiones, ratione quarum duo corpora prohibentur esse in eodem loco.

420. Tertiam rationem ponit ibi, *et non esse* moto enim aliquo movetur id quod in eo est: sed sensibilia moventur: si igitur mathematica sunt in sensibilibus, sequetur quod mathematica moveantur: quod est contra rationem mathematicorum, quae non solum abstrahunt a materia, sed etiam a motu.

421. Quartam rationem ponit ibi *totaliter autem* quae talis est. Nihil rationabiliter ponitur nisi propter aliquam causarum; et praecipue si ex tali positione maius inconveniens sequatur. Sed ista positio ponitur sine causa. Eadem enim inconvenientia sequentur ponentibus mathematica esse media et in sensibilibus, quae sequuntur ponentibus ea non esse in sensibilibus, et adhuc quaedam alia propria et maiora, ut ex praedictis patet. Haec igitur positio est irrationabilis. Ultimo autem concludit quod praedictae quaestiones habent multam dubitationem, quomodo se habeat veritas in istis.

422. Has autem quaestiones pertractat Philosophus infra, duodecimo, tertiodecimo et quartodecimo huius, ostendens non esse mathematicas substantias separatas, nec etiam species. Et ratio quae movebat ponentes mathematica et species sumpta ab abstractione intellectus, solvitur in principio decimitertii. Nihil enim prohibet aliquid quod est tale, salva veritate considerari ab intellectu non inquantum tale; sicut homo albus potest considerari non inquantum albus:

et hoc modo intellectus potest considerare res sensibiles, non inquantum mobiles et materiales, sed inquantum sunt quaedam substantiae vel magnitudines; et hoc est intellectum abstrahere a materia et motu.

Non autem sic abstrahit secundum intellectum, quod intelligat magnitudines et species esse sine materia et motu. Sic enim sequeretur quod vel esset falsitas intellectus abstrahentis, vel quod ea quae intellectus abstrahit, sint separata secundum rem.

and a mathematical one, because each has dimensions, by reason of which two bodies are prevented from being in the same place.

420. *And the objects of mathematics* (998a14). Here he gives the third argument. For when something is moved, anything that exists within it is moved. But sensible things are moved. Therefore, if the objects of mathematics exist in sensible things, it follows that the objects of mathematics are moved. But this is contrary to the intelligible constitution of mathematical objects, which abstract not only from matter but also from motion.

421. Then he gives the fourth argument, at *moreover, on the whole* (998a15), which runs thus. No position is thought to be reasonable unless it is based on one of the causes, and especially if a more untenable conclusion follows from such a position. But this position is held without a cause. For the same absurdities face those who hold the objects of mathematics to be intermediate entities and to exist in sensible things as face those who hold that they do not exist in sensible things, as well as certain other peculiar and greater difficulties, as is clear from what has been said above. Hence, this position is an unreasonable one. In concluding, he states that the questions mentioned above involve much difficulty as to what is true in these matters.

422. Now the Philosopher treats these questions below in books 12, 13, and 14 of this work, where he shows that there are neither separate mathematical substances nor forms. The reasoning which moved those who posited the objects of mathematics and the forms, which are derived from an abstraction of the intellect, is given at the beginning of book 13. For nothing prevents a thing which has some particular attribute from being considered by the intellect without its being viewed under this aspect, and yet being considered truly, just as a white man can be considered without white being considered.

Thus the intellect can consider sensible things not inasmuch as they are mobile and material, but inasmuch as they are substances or continuous quantities. This is to abstract the thing known from matter and motion.

However, so far as the thing known is concerned, the intellect does not abstract in such a way that it understands continuous quantities and forms to exist without matter and motion. For then it would follow either that the intellect of the one abstracting is false or that the things that the intellect abstracts are separate in reality.

LECTURE 8

Are genera principles of things?

998a21   Et de principiis, utrum oporteat genera elementa et principia suscipere, aut magis ex quibus, cum insint, est unumquodque primis. [423]

998a23   Ut vocis elementa et principia videntur esse ex quibus componuntur voces omnes primum, sed non commune vox. Et diagrammatum ea dicimus elementa, quorum demonstrationes insunt in aliorum demonstrationibus, aut omnium aut plurimorum. [424]

998a28   Amplius autem corporum qui dicunt esse plura elementa, et qui unum, ex quibus componuntur et constant principia dicunt esse: ut Empedocles ignem et aquam et quae sunt insimul, haec elementa dicit esse, ex quibus sunt entia quae sunt, sed non ut genera dicit ea eorum quae sunt. [425]

998a32   Adhuc autem et aliorum siquis vult naturam speculari, ut lectum ex quibus partibus et quomodo compositus, cognoscet eius naturam. Et ex his quidem rationibus non sunt principia genera existentium. [426]

998b4   Quod si cognoscimus unumquodque per definitiones, et principia definitorum sunt ipsa genera, necesse et definitorum principia esse genera. [427]

998b6   Et si est eorum quae sunt accipere scientiam, accipienda est scientia specierum, secundum quas dicuntur esse entia. Specierum autem principia sunt genera. [428]

998b9   Videntur autem quidam dicentium elementa existentium unum, aut ens, aut magnum, aut parvum, ut generibus eis uti. [429]

καὶ περὶ τῶν ἀρχῶν πότερον δεῖ τὰ γένη στοιχεῖα καὶ ἀρχὰς ὑπολαμβάνειν ἢ μᾶλλον ἐξ ὧν ἐνυπαρχόντων ἐστὶν ἕκαστον πρώτων,

οἷον φωνῆς στοιχεῖα καὶ ἀρχαὶ δοκοῦσιν εἶναι ταῦτ' ἐξ ὧν σύγκεινται αἱ φωναὶ {25} πρώτων, ἀλλ' οὐ τὸ κοινὸν ἡ φωνή· καὶ τῶν διαγραμμάτων ταῦτα στοιχεῖα λέγομεν ὧν αἱ ἀποδείξεις ἐνυπάρχουσιν ἐν ταῖς τῶν ἄλλων ἀποδείξεσιν ἢ πάντων ἢ τῶν πλείστων,

ἔτι δὲ τῶν σωμάτων καὶ οἱ πλείω λέγοντες εἶναι στοιχεῖα καὶ οἱ ἕν, ἐξ ὧν σύγκειται καὶ ἐξ ὧν συνέστηκεν ἀρχὰς λέγουσιν {30} εἶναι, οἷον Ἐμπεδοκλῆς πῦρ καὶ ὕδωρ καὶ τὰ μετὰ τούτων στοιχεῖά φησιν εἶναι ἐξ ὧν ἐστὶ τὰ ὄντα ἐνυπαρχόντων, ἀλλ' οὐχ ὡς γένη λέγει ταῦτα τῶν ὄντων.

πρὸς δὲ τούτοις καὶ τῶν ἄλλων εἴ τις ἐθέλει τὴν φύσιν ἀθρεῖν, {998b1} οἷον κλίνην ἐξ ὧν μορίων συνέστηκε καὶ πῶς συγκειμένων, τότε γνωρίζει τὴν φύσιν αὐτῆς. ἐκ μὲν οὖν τούτων τῶν λόγων οὐκ ἂν εἴησαν αἱ ἀρχαὶ τὰ γένη τῶν ὄντων·

εἰ δ' ἕκαστον μὲν {5} γνωρίζομεν διὰ τῶν ὁρισμῶν, ἀρχαὶ δὲ τὰ γένη τῶν ὁρισμῶν εἰσίν, ἀνάγκη καὶ τῶν ὁριστῶν ἀρχὰς εἶναι τὰ γένη.

κἂν {7} εἰ ἔστι τὴν τῶν ὄντων λαβεῖν ἐπιστήμην τὸ τῶν εἰδῶν λαβεῖν καθ' ἃ λέγονται τὰ ὄντα, τῶν γε εἰδῶν ἀρχαὶ τὰ γένη εἰσίν.

φαίνονται δέ τινες καὶ τῶν λεγόντων στοιχεῖα τῶν ὄντων τὸ {10} ἕν ἢ τὸ ὂν ἢ τὸ μέγα καὶ μικρὸν ὡς γένεσιν αὐτοῖς χρῆσθαι.

Concerning the principles of things there is the problem of whether genera must be regarded as the elements and principles of things, or rather the first things of which each thing is composed inasmuch as they are intrinsic.

Just as the elements and principles of a word seem to be those things of which all words are first composed, but not word in common. And just as we say that the elements of diagrams are those things whose demonstrations are found in the demonstrations of others, either of all or of most of them.

Furthermore, those who say that the elements of bodies are many, and those who say that they are one, call the things of which bodies are composed and constituted their principles, as Empedocles says that fire and water and those things that are included with these are the elements from which existing things derive their being. But he does not speak of them as the genera of existing things.

And again if anyone wished to speculate about the nature of other things, in finding out in regard to each (a bed, for example) of what parts it is made and how it is put together, he will come to know its nature. And according to these arguments, genera are not the principles of existing things.

But if we know each thing through definitions, and genera are the principles of definitions, genera must be the principles of the things defined.

And if in order to acquire scientific knowledge of existing things it is necessary to acquire scientific knowledge of their species, according to which they are said to be beings, then genera are the principles of species.

Moreover, some of those who say that the elements of existing things are the one or being or the great and small seem to use these as genera.

998b11 Sed non possibile dicere utrobique principia ipsa. Ratio namque substantiae est una. Diversa ergo erit quae est per genera definitio et quae dicit ex quibus est quae insunt. [430]

ἀλλὰ μὴν οὐδὲ ἀμφοτέρως γε οἷόν τε λέγειν τὰς ἀρχάς. ὁ μὲν γὰρ λόγος τῆς οὐσίας εἷς· ἕτερος δ᾽ ἔσται ὁ διὰ τῶν γενῶν ὁρισμὸς καὶ ὁ λέγων ἐξ ὧν ἔστιν ἐνυπαρχόντων.

But it is not possible to speak of principles in both ways; for the meaning of substance is one. Therefore, a definition by means of genera will differ from one which gives the intrinsic constituents.

998b14 Adhuc autem, si maxime principia sunt genera, utrum prima generum oportet existimare principia, aut ultima praedicata de individuis? Etenim hoc dubitationem habet. [431]

πρὸς δὲ τούτοις εἰ καὶ ὅτι μάλιστα ἀρχαὶ τὰ γένη εἰσί, {15} πότερον δεῖ νομίζειν τὰ πρῶτα τῶν γενῶν ἀρχὰς ἢ τὰ ἔσχατα κατηγορούμενα ἐπὶ τῶν ἀτόμων; καὶ γὰρ τοῦτο ἔχει ἀμφισβήτησιν.

Again, if genera are the principles of things in the fullest sense, there is the question of whether the first genera must be thought to be principles, or those which are lowest and are predicated of individual things. For this also raises a problem.

998b17 Nam siquidem universalia sunt magis principia, palam quia suprema generum: ea namque maxime dicuntur de omnibus existentibus: tot igitur erunt entium principia, quot et prima genera: quare erit ens et unum principia et substantiae: ea namque de omnibus maxime dicuntur existentibus. Non est autem possibile genus entium esse unum, neque unum, neque ens. Nam necesse est differentias cuiusque generis et esse, et unam esse quamlibet. Impossibile autem praedicari aut species de propriorum generum differentiis, aut genus sine suis speciebus. Quare si unum genus aut ens, nulla differentia neque unum neque ens erit. Sed si non genera, nec principia erunt, si principia genus. [432]

εἰ μὲν γὰρ ἀεὶ τὰ καθόλου μᾶλλον ἀρχαί, φανερὸν ὅτι τὰ ἀνωτάτω τῶν γενῶν· ταῦτα γὰρ λέγεται κατὰ πάντων. τοσαῦται οὖν ἔσονται ἀρχαὶ τῶν ὄντων ὅσαπερ {20} τὰ πρῶτα γένη, ὥστ᾽ ἔσται τό τε ὂν καὶ τὸ ἓν ἀρχαὶ καὶ οὐσίαι· ταῦτα γὰρ κατὰ πάντων μάλιστα λέγεται τῶν ὄντων. οὐχ οἷόν τε δὲ τῶν ὄντων ἓν εἶναι γένος οὔτε τὸ ἓν οὔτε τὸ ὄν· ἀνάγκη μὲν γὰρ τὰς διαφορὰς ἑκάστου γένους καὶ εἶναι καὶ μίαν εἶναι ἑκάστην, ἀδύνατον δὲ κατηγορεῖσθαι ἢ τὰ εἴδη τοῦ {25} γένους ἐπὶ τῶν οἰκείων διαφορῶν ἢ τὸ γένος ἄνευ τῶν αὐτοῦ εἰδῶν, ὥστ᾽ εἴπερ τὸ ἓν γένος ἢ τὸ ὄν, οὐδεμία διαφορὰ οὔτε ὂν οὔτε ἓν ἔσται. ἀλλὰ μὴν εἰ μὴ γένη, οὐδ᾽ ἀρχαὶ ἔσονται, εἴπερ ἀρχαὶ τὰ γένη.

For if universals are the principles of things to a greater degree, evidently these must be the highest genera, because it is most properly these which are predicated of all existing things. Therefore, there will be as many principles of existing things as there are first genera. Hence being and unity will be principles and substances, for it is these especially which are predicated of all existing things. It is impossible, however, that unity or being should be a single genus of existing things, for it is necessary both that the differences of each genus exist and that each be one. But if unity and being are not genera, neither will they be principles, if genera are principles.

998b28 Amplius autem quae sunt intermedia et coaccepta cum differentiis erunt genera usque ad individua. Nunc autem haec quidem videntur, illa autem non videntur. Adhuc magis differentiae sunt principia quam genera; et si hae sunt principia, infinita (ut ita dicatur) erunt principia. Aliter et si primum quidem genus principium ponat. [434]

ἔτι καὶ τὰ μεταξὺ συλλαμβανόμενα μετὰ τῶν διαφορῶν ἔσται γένη μέχρι τῶν ἀτόμων {30} (νῦν δὲ τὰ μὲν δοκεῖ τὰ δ᾽ οὐ δοκεῖ)· πρὸς δὲ τούτοις ἔτι μᾶλλον αἱ διαφοραὶ ἀρχαὶ ἢ τὰ γένη· εἰ δὲ καὶ αὗται ἀρχαί, ἄπειροι ὡς εἰπεῖν ἀρχαὶ γίγνονται, ἄλλως τε κἂν τις τὸ πρῶτον γένος ἀρχὴν τιθῇ.

Further, those things that are intermediate and are taken along with differences will be genera down to individuals. But some seem to be such, whereas others do not. Again, differences are principles to a greater degree than genera. If they are principles, principles will be infinite in number, so to speak. And this will appear in another way also if one holds that the first genus is a principle.

999a1 At vero et si magis principium speciale sit unum, unum autem indivisibile, indivisibile vero omne sive secundum quantitatem, sive secundum speciem, et prius quod secundum speciem: genera vero divisibilia in species: magis utique erit unum ultimum praedicatum. Non enim est genus homo aliquorum hominum. [436]

ἀλλὰ μὴν καὶ εἰ μᾶλλόν γε ἀρχοειδὲς τὸ ἕν ἐστιν, ἓν δὲ τὸ ἀδιαίρετον, ἀδιαίρετον δὲ ἅπαν ἢ κατὰ τὸ ποσὸν ἢ κατ᾽ εἶδος, πρότερον δὲ τὸ κατ᾽ εἶδος, τὰ δὲ γένη διαιρετὰ εἰς εἴδη, μᾶλλον ἂν ἓν τὸ {5} ἔσχατον εἴη κατηγορούμενον· οὐ γάρ ἐστι γένος ἄνθρωπος τῶν τινῶν ἀνθρώπων.

But, on the other hand, if unity is a specific principle to a greater degree, and unity is indivisible, and everything indivisible is such either in quantity or in species, and what is indivisible in species is prior, and genera are divisible into species, then it will be rather the lowest predicate which is one. For man is not the genus of particular men.

999a6 Amplius in quibus et prius et posterius est, non est possibile in his aliquid esse praeter ea. [437]

ἔτι ἐν οἷς τὸ πρότερον καὶ ὕστερόν ἐστιν, οὐχ οἷόν τε τὸ ἐπὶ τούτων εἶναί τι παρὰ ταῦτα

Further, in the case of those things to which prior and subsequent apply, it is not possible in their case that there should be something which exists apart from them.

Ut si prima numerorum est dualitas, non erit numerus aliquis praeter speciem numerorum; similiter autem nec figura aliqua, praeter species figurarum.

(οἷον εἰ πρώτη τῶν ἀριθμῶν ἡ δυάς, οὐκ ἔσται τις ἀριθμὸς παρὰ τὰ εἴδη τῶν ἀριθμῶν· ὁμοίως δὲ οὐδὲ σχῆμα παρὰ τὰ εἴδη {10} τῶν σχημάτων·

For example, if the number two is the first of numbers, there will not be any number apart from the species of numbers, nor, likewise, any figure apart from the species of figures.

Si autem non horum, schola aliorum genera erunt praeter species. Horum enim maxime videntur esse genera. In individuis vero non hoc est primum et aliud posterius.

εἰ δὲ μὴ τούτων, σχολῇ τῶν γε ἄλλων ἔσται τὰ γένη παρὰ τὰ εἴδη· τούτων γὰρ δοκεῖ μάλιστα εἶναι γένη)· ἐν δὲ τοῖς ἀτόμοις οὐκ ἔστι τὸ μὲν πρότερον τὸ δ' ὕστερον.

But if the genera of these things do not exist apart from the species, then in the case of other things the teaching will be that there are genera apart from the species; for of these things there seem especially to be genera. But among individual things one is not prior and another subsequent.

999a13 Amplius autem ubi hoc quidem melius, illud autem vilius, semper quod est melius, prius. Quare nihil horum erit genus. Ex his igitur magis videntur quae de individuis sunt praedicata, esse generum principia. [439]

ἔτι ὅπου τὸ μὲν βέλτιον τὸ δὲ χεῖρον, ἀεὶ τὸ βέλτιον πρότερον· ὥστ' οὐδὲ τούτων ἂν εἴη γένος. ἐκ μὲν οὖν τούτων {15} μᾶλλον φαίνεται τὰ ἐπὶ τῶν ἀτόμων κατηγορούμενα ἀρχαὶ εἶναι τῶν γενῶν·

Further, where one thing is better and another worse, that which is better is always prior; so that there will be no genus of these things. From these considerations, then, it seems that it is the terms predicated of individuals, rather than genera, which are principles.

999a16 Iterum autem quomodo oportet suscipere principia, dicere facile non est. Principium enim et causam oportet esse praeter res quarum est principium, et possibile, ab eis separatum esse. Tale vero aliquid praeter singularia esse, quare aliquis suscipit, nisi quia universaliter et de omnibus praedicatur? Sed si propter hoc, magis universalia, magis ponenda sunt principia. Quare principia erunt genera prima. [441]

πάλιν δὲ πῶς αὖ δεῖ ταύτας ἀρχὰς ὑπολαβεῖν οὐ ῥάδιον εἰπεῖν. τὴν μὲν γὰρ ἀρχὴν δεῖ καὶ τὴν αἰτίαν εἶναι παρὰ τὰ πράγματα ὧν ἀρχή, καὶ δύνασθαι εἶναι χωριζομένην αὐτῶν· τοιοῦτον δέ τι παρὰ τὸ καθ' ἕκαστον {20} εἶναι διὰ τί ἄν τις ὑπολάβοι, πλὴν ὅτι καθόλου κατηγορεῖται καὶ κατὰ πάντων; ἀλλὰ μὴν εἰ διὰ τοῦτο, τὰ μᾶλλον καθόλου μᾶλλον θετέον ἀρχάς· ὥστε ἀρχαὶ τὰ πρῶτ' ἂν εἴησαν γένη.

But again it is not easy to state how one must conceive these to be the principles of things. For a principle or cause must be distinct from the things of which it is the principle or cause, and must be able to exist apart from them. But why should one think that anything such as this exists apart from singular things, except that it is predicated universally and of all things? But if this is the reason, then the more universal things are, the more they must be held to be principles. Hence the first genera will be principles of things.

---

423. Postquam Philosophus disputavit de quaestionibus motis de substantiis, hic disputat de quaestionibus motis de principiis. Et dividitur in partes duas.

In prima disputat de quaestionibus, quibus quaerebatur quae sunt principia.

Secundo de quaestionibus quibus quaerebatur qualia sint principia, et hoc ibi, *adhuc autem utrum substantia.*

Circa primum disputat de duabus quaestionibus.

Primo utrum universalia sint principia.

423. Having debated the questions which were raised about substances, the Philosopher now treats dialectically the questions which were raised about principles. This is divided into two parts.

In the first, he discusses the questions which asked what the principles of things are;

in the second (1044b29; [456]), the questions which asked what kind of things the principles are, at *again, there is the problem*.

In the first part of this division he discusses two questions:

first, whether universals are the principles of things;

Secundo utrum sint aliqua principia a materia separata, ibi, *est autem habita de his disputatio* et cetera.

Circa primum disputat duas quaestiones:

quarum prima est, utrum genera sint principia;

secunda, quae genera, utrum scilicet prima genera, vel alia, ibi, *ad hoc autem si maxime principia sunt genera* et cetera.

Circa primum duo facit.

Primo movet quaestionem.

Secundo disputat. Secunda ibi, *ut vocis elementa* et cetera.

Est ergo quaestio prima de principiis, utrum oportet recipere vel opinari quod ipsa genera, quae de pluribus praedicantur, sint elementa et principia rerum, vel magis sint dicenda principia et elementa ea, ex quibus unumquodque est, sicut ex partibus.

Sed addit duas conditiones: quarum una est *cum insint*, quod ponitur ad differentiam contrarii et privationis. Dicitur enim album fieri ex nigro, vel non albo, quae tamen non insunt albo. Unde non sunt eius elementa.

Alia conditio est qua dicit *primis*, quod ponitur ad differentiam secundorum componentium. Sunt enim corpora animalium ex carnibus et nervis quae insunt animali non tamen dicuntur animalis elementa, quia non sunt haec prima ex quibus animal componitur, sed magis ignis, aer, aqua et terra, ex quibus etiam existunt carnes et nervi.

424. Deinde cum dicit *ut vocis* disputat ad hanc quaestionem: et circa hoc tria facit.

Primo ostendit, quod ea, ex quibus primis aliquid componitur, sint principia et elementa.

Secundo obiicit ad partem contrariam, ibi, *inquantum autem cognoscimus unumquodque* et cetera.

Tertio excludit quamdam responsionem qua posset dici, quod utraque sunt principia et elementa, ibi, *at vero nec utrobique* et cetera.

Circa primum primo ponit tres rationes:

quarum prima procedit ex naturalibus, in quibus manifestat propositum secundum duo exempla:

quorum primum est de voce dearticulata, cuius principium et elementum non dicitur esse commune, quod est vox, sed magis illa, ex quibus primis componuntur omnes voces, quae dicuntur literae.

Secundum exemplum ponit in diagrammatibus idest in demonstrativis descriptionibus figurarum geometricarum. Dicuntur enim horum diagrammatum esse

second (999a24; [443]), whether any principles are separate from matter, at *but there is a problem*.

In regard to the first he discusses two questions,

of which the first is whether genera are the principles of things.

The second (998b14; [431]) asks which genera these are, whether the first genera or the others, at *again, if genera*.

In regard to the first he does two things:

first, he raises the question;

second (998a23; [424]), he treats it dialectically, at *just as the elements*.

The first question has to do with the principles of things. Is it necessary to accept or believe that those genera which are predicated of many things are the elements and principles of things, or rather that those parts of which every single thing is composed must be called the elements and principles of things?

But he adds two conditions, one of which is *inasmuch as they are intrinsic*, which is given in order to distinguish these parts from a contrary and a privation. For white is said to come from black or the non-white, although these are not intrinsic to white. Hence they are not its elements.

The other condition is what he calls *the first things*, which is given in order to distinguish them from secondary components. For the bodies of animals are composed of flesh and nerves, which exist within the animal, yet these are not called the elements of animals, because they are not the first things of which an animal is composed, but rather fire, air, water, and earth, from which flesh and nerves derive their being.

424. *Just as the elements* (998a23). Here he treats this question dialectically, and in regard to this he does three things.

First, he shows that the first things of which anything is composed are its principles and elements.

Second (998b4; [427]), he argues the opposite side of the question, at *but if we know*.

Third (998b11; 430), he rejects one answer by which it could be said that both of these[3] are the principles and elements of things, at *but it is not*.

In regard to the first he gives three arguments.

The first of these proceeds from natural phenomena, in which he makes his thesis evident by two examples.

He first gives the example of a word, whose principle and element is not said to be the common term "word," but rather the first constituents of which all words are composed, which are called letters.

He gives diagrams (the demonstrative descriptions of geometrical figures) as a second example. For the elements of these diagrams are not said to be the common term

---

3. Namely, genera and constituent parts.

elementa non hoc commune quod est diagramma, sed magis illa theoremata, quorum demonstrationes insunt demonstrationibus aliorum theorematum geometralium, aut omnium, aut plurimorum; quia scilicet aliae demonstrationes procedunt ex suppositione primarum demonstrationum. Unde et liber Euclidis dicitur liber elementorum, quia scilicet in eo demonstrantur prima geometriae theoremata, ex quibus aliae demonstrationes procedunt.

425. Secundam rationem ponit ibi *amplius autem* quae procedit in rebus naturalibus. Et dicit quod illi, qui ponunt elementa corporum vel plura vel unum, illa dicunt esse principia et elementa corporum, ex quibus componuntur et constant tamquam in eis existentibus.

Sicut Empedocles dicit, elementa corporum naturalium esse ignem et aquam, et alia huiusmodi, quae simul cum his elementa rerum dicit, ex quibus primis cum insint corpora naturalia constituuntur. Ponebant autem praeter haec duo, alia quatuor principia, scilicet aerem et terram, litem et amicitiam, ut in primo dictum est. Non autem dicebat, nec Empedocles nec alii naturales philosophi, quod genera rerum essent earum principia et elementa.

426. Tertiam rationem ponit ibi *adhuc autem* quae procedit in artificialibus: et dicit quod siquis velit *speculari naturam*, idest definitionem indicantem essentiam aliorum corporum a corporibus naturalibus, scilicet artificialium, puta si vult cognoscere lectum, oportet considerare ex quibus partibus componitur et modum compositionis earum, et sic cognoscet naturam lecti. Et post hoc concludit quod genera non sunt principia entium.

427. Deinde cum dicit *quod si cognoscimus* obiicit ad partem contrariam:

et ponit tres rationes, quarum prima talis est. Unumquodque cognoscitur per suam definitionem. Si igitur idem est principium essendi et cognoscendi, videtur, quod id quod est principium definitionis sit principium rei definitae. Sed genera sunt principia definitionum, quia ex eis primo definitiones constituuntur: ergo genera sunt principia rerum quae definiuntur.

428. Secundam rationem ponit ibi *et si est* quae talis est. Per hoc accipitur scientia de unaquaque re, quod scitur species eius secundum quam res est: non enim potest cognosci Socrates nisi per hoc quod scitur quod est homo. Sed genera sunt principia specierum, quia species constituuntur ex genere et differentia: ergo genera sunt principia eorum quae sunt.

"diagram," but rather those theorems whose demonstrations are found in the demonstrations of other geometrical theorems, either of all or of most of them, because the other demonstrations proceed from the supposition of the first demonstrations. Hence Euclid's book is called *The Elements*, because the first theorems of geometry, from which the other demonstrations proceed, are demonstrated therein.

425. *Furthermore, those who* (998a28). Here he gives the second argument, which also employs certain examples drawn from nature. He says that those who hold that the elements of bodies are either one or many say that the principles and elements of bodies are those things of which bodies are composed and made up as intrinsic constituents.

Thus Empedocles says that the elements of natural bodies are fire and water and other things of this kind, which along with these he calls the elements of things. Natural bodies are constituted of these first things inasmuch as they are intrinsic. Moreover, the early philosophers held that in addition to these two principles there are four others—air, earth, strife, and friendship—as was stated in book 1 (984b32; [104]). But neither Empedocles nor the other philosophers of nature said that the genera of things are the principles and elements of these natural bodies.

426. *And again if anyone* (998a32). Here he gives the third argument, which involves things made by art. He says that if someone wished to *speculate about the nature*, that is, about the definition which indicates the essence of other bodies than natural ones (namely, of bodies made by human art)—for example, if one wished to know a bed—it would be necessary to consider of what parts it is made and how they are put together. In this way he would know the nature of a bed. And after this he concludes that genera are not the principles of existing things.

427. *But if we know* (998b4). Here he argues the other side of the question.

He gives three arguments, the first of which is as follows. Each thing is known through its definition. Therefore, if a principle of being is the same as a principle of knowing, it seems that anything which is a principle of definition is also a principle of the thing defined. But genera are principles of definitions, because definitions are first composed of them. Hence genera are the principles of the things defined.

428. *And if in order to* (998b6). Here he gives the second argument, which runs thus. Scientific knowledge of each thing is acquired by knowing the species from which it gets its being, for Socrates can be known only by understanding that he is man. But genera are principles of species, because the species of things are composed of genera and differences. Therefore, genera are the principles of existing things.

429. Tertiam rationem ponit ibi *videntur autem* et sumitur ex auctoritate Platonicorum, qui posuerunt unum et ens esse principia, et magnum et parvum, quibus utuntur ut generibus: ergo genera sunt principia.

430. Deinde cum dicit *sed non possibile* excludit quamdam responsionem, qua posset dici quod utraque sunt principia; dicens quod non est possibile dicere utrobique esse *principia*, ut elementa, id est partes ex quibus componitur aliquid, et genera. Et hoc probat tali ratione.

Unius rei una est ratio definitiva manifestans eius substantiam, sicut et una est substantia uniuscuiusque: sed non est eadem ratio definitiva quae datur per genera et quae datur per partes ex quibus aliquid componitur: ergo non potest esse utraque definitio indicans substantiam rei. Ex principiis autem rei potest sumi ratio definitiva significans substantiam eius. Impossibile est ergo quod principia rerum sint simul genera, et ea ex quibus res componuntur.

431. Deinde cum dicit *adhuc autem* disputat secundam quaestionem.

Et primo movet eam.

Secundo ad eam rationes inducit ibi, *nam siquidem universalia* et cetera.

Dicit ergo quod si ponamus quod genera sint maxime principia, quae oportet existimare magis esse principia? Utrum prima de numero *generum*, scilicet communissima, aut etiam infima, quae proxima praedicantur de individuis, scilicet species specialissimas. Hoc enim habet dubitationem, sicut ex sequentibus patet.

432. Deinde cum dicit *nam siquidem* obiicit ad propositam quaestionem: et circa hoc tria facit.

Primo enim inducit rationes ad ostendendum quod prima genera non possunt esse principia.

Secundo inducit rationes ad ostendendum, quod species ultimae magis debent dici principia, ibi, *at vero et si magis*.

Tertio obiicit ad propositum, ibi, *iterum autem* et cetera.

Circa primum ponit tres rationes: quarum prima talis est. Si genera sunt magis principia quanto sunt universalia oportet quod illa quae sunt maxime universalia, quae scilicet dicuntur de omnibus, sint prima inter genera et maxime principia. Tot ergo erunt rerum principia, quod sunt huiusmodi genera communissima. Sed communissima omnium sunt unum et ens, quae de

429. *Moreover, some of those* (998b9). Here he gives a third argument, which is based on the authority of the Platonists, who held that the one and being are the principles of things, and also the great and small, which are used as genera. Therefore, genera are the principles of things.

430. *But it is not possible* (998b11). Here he excludes one answer which would say that both of these are principles. He says that it is impossible to say that both of these are *principles*, that is, both the elements (or the parts of which something is composed) and genera. He proves this by the following argument.

Of each thing there is one definite concept which manifests its substance, just as there is also one substance of each thing. But the definitive concept which involves genera is not the same as the one which involves the parts of which a thing is composed. Hence it cannot be true that each definition indicates a thing's substance. But the definitive concept which indicates a thing's substance cannot be taken from its principles. Therefore, it is impossible that both genera and the parts of which things are composed should be simultaneously the principles of things.

431. *Again, if genera* (998b14). Then he treats the second question dialectically.

First, he raises the question;

second (998b17; [432]), he brings up arguments relative to this question, at *for if universals*.

Accordingly, he asks: if we hold that genera are the principles of things in the fullest sense, which of these genera should be considered to be the principles of things to a greater degree? Must we consider those *genera* which are first in number (namely, the most common), or also the lowest genera, which are proximately predicated of the individual (namely, the lowest species)? For this is open to question, as is clear from what follows.

432. *For if universals* (998b17). Here he argues about the question which was proposed, and in regard to this he does three things.

First, he introduces arguments to show that the first genera cannot be principles.

Second (999a1; [436]), he introduces arguments to show that the last species should rather be called the principles of things, at *but, on the other hand*.

Third (999a16; [441]), he debates the proposed question, at *but again it is*.

In regard to the first (998b17) he gives three arguments, of which the first runs thus. If genera are principles to the extent that they are more universal, then those which are most universal (namely, those which are predicated of all things) must be the first genera and the principles of things in the highest degree. Hence there will be as many principles of things as there are most common genera of

omnibus praedicantur: ergo unum et ens erunt principia et substantiae omnium rerum.

Sed hoc est impossibile; quia non possunt omnium rerum esse genus, unum et ens: quia, cum ens et unum universalissima sint, si unum et ens essent principia generum, sequeretur quod principia non essent genera. Sic ergo positio, qua ponitur communissima generum esse principia, est impossibilis, quia sequitur ex ea oppositum positi, scilicet quod principia non sunt genera.

433. Quod autem ens et unum non possint esse genera, probat tali ratione. Quia cum differentia addita generi constituat speciem, de differentia praedicari non poterit nec species sine genere, nec genus sine speciebus. Quod autem species de differentia praedicari non possit, patet ex duobus.

Primo quidem, quia differentia in plus est quam species, ut Porphyrius tradit.

Secundo, quia cum differentia ponatur in definitione speciei, non posset species praedicari per se de differentia, nisi intelligeretur quod differentia esset subiectum speciei, sicut numerus est subiectum paris, in cuius definitione ponitur. Hoc autem non sic se habet; sed magis differentia est quaedam forma speciei. Non ergo posset species praedicari de differentia, nisi forte per accidens.

Similiter etiam nec genus per se sumptum, potest praedicari de differentia praedicatione per se. Non enim genus ponitur in definitione differentiae, quia differentia non participat genus, ut dicitur in quarto *Topicorum*. Nec etiam differentia ponitur in definitione generis: ergo nullo modo per se genus praedicatur de differentia. Praedicatur tamen de eo quod habet **differentiam**, idest de specie, quae habet differentiam in actu.

Et ideo dicit, quod de propriis differentiis generis non praedicatur species, nec genus sine speciebus, quia scilicet genus praedicatur de differentiis secundum quod sunt in speciebus. Nulla autem differentia potest accipi de qua non praedicetur ens et unum, quia quaelibet differentia cuiuslibet generis est ens et est una, alioquin non posset constituere unam aliquam speciem entis. Ergo impossibile est quod unum et ens sint genera.

434. Deinde cum dicit **amplius autem** secundam rationem ponit, quae talis est. Si genera dicuntur principia quia sunt communia et praedicantur de pluribus, oportebit quod omnia quae pari ratione erunt principia, quia sunt communia, et praedicata de pluribus, sint genera. Sed omnia quae sunt media inter prima genera et individua, quae scilicet sunt coaccepta cum differentiis aliquibus, sunt communia praedicata de pluribus: ergo sunt principia et sunt genera: quod patet esse falsum. Quaedam enim eorum sunt genera, sicut species su-

this kind. But the most common of all genera are unity and being, which are predicated of all things. Therefore, unity and being will be the principles and substances of all things.

But this is impossible, because unity and being cannot be genera of all things. For, since unity and being are most universal, if they were principles of genera, it would follow that genera would not be the principles of things. Hence the position which maintains that the most common genera are principles is an impossible one, because from it there follows the opposite of what was held, namely, that genera are not principles.

433. That being and unity cannot be genera he proves by this argument. Since a difference added to a genus constitutes a species, a species cannot be predicated of a difference without a genus, or a genus without a species. That it is impossible to predicate a species of a difference is clear for two reasons.

First, because a difference applies to more things than a species, as Porphyry says.

Second, since a difference is given in the definition of a species, a species can be predicated *per se* of a difference only if a difference is understood to be the subject of a species, as number is the subject of evenness, in whose definition it is given. This, however, is not the case; but a difference is rather a formal principle of a species. Therefore, a species cannot be predicated of a difference except, perhaps, in an incidental way.

Similarly too neither can a genus, taken in itself, be predicated of a difference by *per se* predication. For a genus is not given in the definition of a difference, because a difference does not share in a genus, as is stated in *Topics* 4. Nor again is a difference given in the definition of a genus. Therefore, a genus is not predicated *per se* of a difference in any way. Yet it is predicated of that which has *a difference*, namely, of a species, which actually contains a difference.

Hence he says that a species is not predicated of the proper differences of a genus, nor is a genus independently of its species, because a genus is predicated of its differences inasmuch as they inhere in a species. But no difference can be conceived of which unity and being are not predicated, because any difference of any genus is a one and a being, otherwise it could not constitute any one species of being. It is impossible, then, that unity and being should be genera.

434. *Further, those things* (998b28). Then he gives the second argument, which runs thus. If genera are called principles because they are common and predicated of many things, then for a like reason all those things that are principles because they are common and predicated of many will have to be genera. But all things that are intermediate between the first genera and individuals (namely, those which are considered together with some differences) are common predicates of many things. Hence they are both principles and genera. But this is evidently false. For

balternae; quaedam vero non sunt genera, sicut species specialissimae. Non ergo verum est, quod prima genera sive communia sint principia prima.

435. Praeterea. Si prima genera sunt principia, quia sunt principia cognitionis specierum, multo magis differentiae sunt principia, quia differentiae sunt principia formalia specierum. Forma autem et actus est maxime principium cognoscendi. Sed differentias esse principia rerum est inconveniens, quia secundum hoc erunt quasi infinita principia. Sunt enim, ut ita dicatur, infinitae rerum differentiae; non quidem infinitae secundum rerum naturam, sed quoad nos. Et quod sint infinitae, patet dupliciter. Uno modo siquis consideret multitudinem ipsam differentiarum secundum se. Alio modo siquis accipiat primum genus quasi primum principium. Manifestum enim est quod sub eo continentur innumerabiles differentiae. Non ergo prima genera sunt principia.

436. Deinde cum dicit *at vero* ostendit, quod species specialissimae sunt magis principia quam genera; et ponit tres rationes, quarum prima talis est.

Unum secundum Platonicos maxime videtur habere *speciem*, idest rationem principii. Unum vero habet rationem indivisibilitatis, quia unum nihil est aliud quam ens indivisum. Dupliciter est autem aliquid indivisibile: scilicet secundum quantitatem, et secundum speciem. Secundum quantitatem, quidem, sicut punctus et unitas: et hoc indivisibile opponitur divisioni quantitatis. Secundum speciem autem, sicut quod non dividitur in multas species. Sed inter haec duo indivisibilia prius et principalius est quod est indivisibile secundum speciem, sicut et species rei est prior quam quantitas eius; ergo illud quod est indivisibile secundum speciem, est magis principium eo quod est indivisibile secundum quantitatem. Et quidem secundum quantitatis numeralis divisionem videtur esse magis indivisibile genus, quia multarum specierum est unum genus: sed secundum divisionem speciei magis est indivisibilis una species. Et sic ultimum praedicatum de pluribus quod non est genus plurium specierum, scilicet species specialissima, est magis unum secundum speciem quam genus. Sicut homo et quaelibet alia species specialissima, non est genus aliquorum hominum. Est ergo magis principium species quam genus.

437. Deinde cum dicit *amplius in quibus* secundam rationem ponit, quae procedit ex quadam positione Platonis;

qui quando aliquid unum de pluribus praedicatur, non secundum prius et posterius, posuit illud unum separatum, sicut hominem praeter omnes homines.

some of them are genera, like subaltern species, whereas others are not, as the lowest species. It is not true, then, that the first or common genera are the principles of things.

435. Further, if the first genera are principles, because they are the principles by which we know species, then differences will be principles to a greater degree, because differences are the formal principles of species, and form or act is chiefly the principle of knowing. But it is unfitting that differences should be the principles of things, because in that case there would be an infinite number of principles, so to speak. For the differences of things are infinite, in a way—not infinite in reality but to us. That they are infinite in number is revealed in two ways: in one way if we consider the multitude of differences in themselves; in another way if we consider the first genus as a first principle, for evidently innumerable differences are contained under it. The first genera, then, are not the principles of things.

436. *But, on the other hand* (999a1). Then he shows that the lowest species are principles to a greater degree than genera. He gives three arguments, of which the first runs thus.

According to the Platonists it is the one which seems to have *the species*, or character, of a principle to the greatest degree. Indeed, unity has the character of indivisibility, because a one is merely an undivided being. But a thing is indivisible in two ways, namely, in quantity and in species. In quantity, as the point and unit, and this is a sort of indivisibility opposed to the division of quantity; in species, as what is not divided into many species. But of these two types of indivisibility the first and more important one is indivisibility in species, just as the species of a thing is prior to its quantity. Therefore, that which is indivisible in species is more of a principle because it is indivisible in quantity. And in the division of quantity the genus seems to be more indivisible, because there is one genus of many species, but in the division of species one species is more indivisible. Hence the last term which is predicated of many which is not a genus of many species (namely, the lowest species) is one to a greater degree in species than a genus— for example, man or any other lowest species is not the genus of particular men. Therefore, a species is a principle to a greater degree than a genus.

437. *Further, in the case* (999a6). Then he gives the second argument, which is based on a certain position of Plato.

At one time Plato held that there is some one thing which is predicated of many things without priority and posteriority, and that this is a separate unity, as man is

Quando vero aliquid praedicatur de pluribus secundum prius et posterius, non ponebat illud separatum.

Et hoc est quod dicit quod *in quibus prius et posterius est*, scilicet quando unum eorum de quibus aliquod commune praedicatur est altero prius, non est possibile in his aliquid esse separatum, praeter haec multa de quibus praedicatur.

Sicut si numeri se habent secundum ordinem, ita quod dualitas est prima species numerorum, non invenitur idea numeri praeter omnes species numerorum. Eadem ratione non invenitur figura separata, praeter omnes species figurarum.

438. Et huius ratio esse potest, quia ideo aliquod commune ponitur separatum, ut sit quoddam primum quod omnia alia participent. Si igitur unum de multis sit primum, quod omnia alia participent, non oportet ponere aliquod separatum, quod omnia participant. Sed talia videntur omnia genera; quia omnes species generum inveniuntur differre secundum perfectius et minus perfectum. Et, per consequens, secundum prius et posterius secundum naturam.

Si igitur eorum quorum unum est prius altero, non est accipere aliquod commune separatum, si genus praeter species inveniatur, erunt *schola aliorum*, idest erit eorum alia doctrina et regula, et non salvabitur in eis praedicta regula.

Sed manifestum est quod inter individua unius speciei, non est unum primum et aliud posterius secundum naturam, sed solum tempore. Et ita species secundum scholam Platonis est aliquid separatum. Cum igitur communia sint principia inquantum sunt separata, sequitur quod sit magis principium species quam genus.

439. Deinde cum dicit *amplius autem* tertiam rationem ponit quae sumitur ex meliori et peiori: quia in quibuscumque invenitur unum alio melius, semper illud quod est melius, est prius secundum naturam. Sed horum quae sic se habent non potest poni unum genus commune separatum: ergo eorum quorum unum est melius et aliud peius non potest poni unum genus separatum. Et sic redit in idem quod prius. Haec enim ratio inducitur quasi confirmatio praecedentis, ad ostendendum, quod in speciebus cuiuslibet generis invenitur prius et posterius.

440. Et ex tribus his rationibus concludit propositum; scilicet quod species specialissimae quae immediate de individuis praedicantur, magis videntur esse

separate from all men. At another time he held that there is some one thing which is predicated of many things according to priority and posteriority, and that this is not a separate unity.

This is what Aristotle means when he says *in the case of those things to which prior and subsequent apply*—in other words, when one of the things of which a common term is predicated is prior to another, it is impossible in such cases that there should be anything separate from the many things of which this common term is predicated.

For example, if numbers stand in such a sequence that two is the first species of number, no separate idea of number will be found to exist apart from all species of numbers. And on the same grounds no separate figure will be found to exist apart from all species of figures.

438. The reason for this can be that a common attribute is held to be separate so as to be some first entity in which all other things participate. If, then, this first entity is a one applicable to many in which all other things participate, it is not necessary to hold that there is some separate entity in which all things participate. But all genera seem to be things of this kind, because all types of genera are found to differ insofar as they are more or less perfect, and thus insofar as they are prior and subsequent in nature.

Hence, if in those cases in which one thing is prior to another, it is impossible to regard anything common as a separate entity on the supposition that there is a genus apart from species, then *in the case of other things the teaching* will differ—there will be another doctrine and rule concerning them, and the foregoing rule will not apply to them.

But considering the individuals of one species, it is evident that one of these is not prior and another subsequent in nature, but only in time. And thus according to Plato's teaching a species is separate. Since, then, these common things are principles inasmuch as they are separate, it follows that a species is a principle to a greater degree than a genus.

439. *Further, where one thing* (999a13). Here he gives the third argument, which uses the notions "better or worse." For in all those cases where one thing is better than another, that which is better is always prior in nature. But there cannot be held to be one common genus of those things that exist in this way. Hence there cannot be held to be one separate genus in the case of those things in which one is better and another worse. Thus the conclusion is the same as the above. For this argument is introduced to strengthen the preceding one, so to speak, with a view to showing that there is priority and posteriority among the species of any genus.

440. And from these three arguments he draws the conclusion in which he is chiefly interested: the lowest species, which are predicated immediately of individuals,

principia quam genera. Ponitur enim genitivus generum loco ablativi more Graecorum. Unde litera Boetii planior est, quae expresse concludit huiusmodi praedicata magis esse principia quam genera.

441. Deinde cum dicit *iterum autem* obiicit in contrarium tali ratione. Principium et causa est praeter res quarum est principium et causa, et possibile est ab eis esse separatum. Et hoc ideo quia nihil est causa sui ipsius. Et loquitur hic de principiis et causis extrinsecis, quae sunt causae totius rei. Sed aliquid esse praeter singularia non ponitur, nisi quia est commune et universaliter de omnibus praedicatum: ergo quanto aliquid est magis universale, tanto magis est separatum, et magis debet poni principium. Sed genera prima sunt maxime universalia: ergo genera prima sunt maxime principia.

442. Harum autem quaestionum solutio innuitur ex hac ultima ratione. Secundum hoc enim genera vel species universalia principia ponebantur, inquantum ponebantur separata. Quod autem non sint separata et per se subsistentia ostendetur in septimo huius. Unde et Commentator in octavo ostendet quod principia rerum sunt materia et forma, ad quorum similitudinem se habent genus et species. Nam genus sumitur a materia, differentia vero a forma, ut in eodem libro manifestabitur.

Unde, cum forma sit magis principium quam materia, secundum hoc etiam erunt species magis principia quam genera. Quod vero contra obiicitur ex hoc quod genera sunt principia cognoscendi speciem et definitiones ipsius, eodem modo solvitur sicut et de separatione. Quia enim separatim accipitur a ratione genus sine speciebus, est principium in cognoscendo. Et eodem modo esset principium in essendo, si haberet esse separatum.

seem to be the principles of things to a greater degree than genera. Here he use the genitive case in the place of the ablative, as is the Greek custom. Thus Boethius' rendition is more clear, which expressly concludes that lowest species are more principles than genera.

441. *But again it is not* (999a16). Here he argues the opposite side of the question as follows. A principle and a cause are distinct from the things of which they are the principle and cause, and are capable of existing apart from them. And this is true, because nothing is its own cause. He is speaking here of extrinsic principles and causes, which are causes of a thing in its entirety. But the only thing that is held to exist apart from singular things is what is commonly and universally predicated of all things. Therefore, the more universal a thing is, the more separate it is, and the more it should be held to be a principle. But the first genera are most universal. Therefore, the first genera are the principles of things in the highest degree.

442. Now the solution to these questions is implied in this last argument. For, according to this argument, genera or species are held to be universal principles inasmuch as they are held to be separate. But the fact that they are not separate and self-subsistent is shown in book 7 [1592] of this work. Hence the Commentator also shows, in book 8, that the principles of things are matter and form, to which genus and species bear some likeness. For a genus is derived from matter and difference from form, as will be shown in the same book [720].

Hence, since form is more of a principle than matter, species will consequently be principles more than genera. But the objection which is raised against this, on the grounds that genera are the principles of knowing a species and its definitions, is answered in the same way as the objection raised about their separateness. For, since a genus is understood separately by the mind without understanding its species, it is a principle of knowing. And in the same way it would be a principle of being, supposing that it had a separate being.

LECTURE 9

Are there universals separate from singular things?

999a24 Est autem habita his dubitatio et omnium difficillima et ad considerandum maxime necessaria, de qua ratio nunc existit. [443]

ἔστι δ' ἐχομένη τε τούτων ἀπορία καὶ πασῶν χαλεπωτάτη {25} καὶ ἀναγκαιοτάτη θεωρῆσαι, περὶ ἧς ὁ λόγος ἐφέστηκε νῦν.

But there is a problem connected with these things, which is the most difficult of all and the most necessary to consider, with which our analysis is now concerned.

999a26 Nam si non est aliquid praeter singularia, singularia vero infinita, quomodo accipere contingit scientiam? [444]

εἴτε γὰρ μὴ ἔστι τι παρὰ τὰ καθ' ἕκαστα, τὰ δὲ καθ' ἕκαστα ἄπειρα, τῶν δ' ἀπείρων πῶς ἐνδέχεται λαβεῖν ἐπιστήμην;

For if there is nothing apart from singular things, and singular things are infinite in number, how is it possible to acquire scientific knowledge of them?

Nam inquantum unum aliquid et idem, et inquantum universale aliquid est, intantum omnia cognoscimus.

ἢ γὰρ ἕν τι καὶ ταὐτόν, καὶ ἣ καθόλου τι ὑπάρχει, ταύτῃ πάντα γνωρίζομεν.

For insofar as there is something that is one and the same, and insofar as there is something universal which relates to singular things, to that extent we acquire knowledge of them.

999a29 At vero si hoc est necesse, et oportet aliquid esse praeter singularia, erit necesse esse genera praeter singularia, aut ultima, aut prima. Hoc autem quia impossibile, nunc dubitavimus. [445]

ἀλλὰ μὴν εἰ τοῦτο {30} ἀναγκαῖόν ἐστι καὶ δεῖ τι εἶναι παρὰ τὰ καθ' ἕκαστα, ἀναγκαῖον ἂν εἴη τὰ γένη εἶναι παρὰ τὰ καθ' ἕκαστα, ἤτοι τὰ ἔσχατα ἢ τὰ πρῶτα· τοῦτο δ' ὅτι ἀδύνατον ἄρτι διηπορήσαμεν.

But if this is necessary, and there must be something apart from singular things, it will be necessary that genera exist apart from singular things, and they will be either the last or the first. But the impossibility of this has already appeared from our discussion.

999a32 Amplius autem, si quam maxime et aliquid praeter simul totum, quando praedicatur aliquid de materia, utrum si est aliquid praeter omnia oportet aliquid esse, aut praeter quaedam esse et praeter quaedam non esse, aut praeter nihil. [447]

ἔτι εἰ ὅτι μάλιστα ἔστι τι παρὰ τὸ σύνολον ὅταν κατηγορηθῇ τι τῆς ὕλης, πότερον, εἰ ἔστι, παρὰ πάντα δεῖ εἶναί τι, ἢ παρὰ μὲν ἔνια εἶναι παρὰ δ' ἔνια μὴ εἶναι, ἢ παρ' οὐδέν;

Further, if there is something apart from the concrete whole (which is most disputable)—as when something is predicated of matter—if there is such a thing, the problem arises of whether it must exist apart from all concrete wholes, or apart from some and not from others, or apart from none.

999b1 Si igitur nihil est praeter singularia, nihil est intelligibile, sed omnia sensibilia et scientia nullius, nisi quis dicat sensum esse scientiam. [448]

εἰ μὲν οὖν μηδέν ἐστι παρὰ τὰ καθ' ἕκαστα, οὐθὲν ἂν εἴη νοητὸν ἀλλὰ πάντα αἰσθητὰ καὶ ἐπιστήμη οὐδενός, εἰ μή τις εἶναι λέγει τὴν αἴσθησιν ἐπιστήμην.

If, then, there is nothing apart from singular things, nothing will be intelligible, but all things will be sensible, and there will be no science of anything, unless one might say that sensory perception is science.

999b3 Amplius autem neque sempiternum est aliquid, nec immobile. Nam sensibilia omnia corrumpuntur et in motu sunt. [449]

ἔτι δ' οὐδ' ἀΐδιον οὐθὲν οὐδ' ἀκίνητον (τὰ γὰρ αἰσθητὰ {5} πάντα φθείρεται καὶ ἐν κινήσει ἐστίν)·

Further, neither will anything be eternal or immobile; for all sensible things perish and are subject to motion.

999b5 At vero si sempiternum nihil est, nec generationem possibile est esse. Necesse enim est aliquid esse quod factum est et ex quo fit; et horum ultimum ingenitum, si stat, et ex non ente generari impossibile. [450]

μὴν εἴ γε ἀΐδιον μηθέν ἐστιν, οὐδὲ γένεσιν εἶναι δυνατόν. ἀνάγκη γὰρ εἶναί τι τὸ γιγνόμενον καὶ ἐξ οὗ γίγνεται καὶ τούτων τὸ ἔσχατον ἀγένητον, εἴπερ ἵσταταί τε καὶ ἐκ μὴ ὄντος γενέσθαι ἀδύνατον·

But if there is nothing eternal, neither can there be generation, for there must be something which has come to be and something from which it comes to be; and the last of these must be ungenerated, since the process of generation must have a limit, and since it is impossible for anything to come to be from non-being.

999b8 Amplius autem cum sit generatio et motus, finem esse necesse est. Motus enim nullus est infinitus, sed omnis est finitus. Generarique impossibile, quod est impossibile factum esse. Quod autem generatum est, esse necesse est, quando primo factum est. [451]

ἔτι δὲ γενέσεως οὔσης καὶ κινήσεως ἀνάγκη καὶ πέρας εἶναι (οὔτε {10} γὰρ ἄπειρός ἐστιν οὐδεμία κίνησις ἀλλὰ πάσης ἔστι τέλος, γίγνεσθαί τε οὐχ οἷόν τε τὸ ἀδύνατον γενέσθαι:

Further, since generation and motion exist, there must be a terminus. For no motion is infinite, but every motion has a terminus. And that which is incapable of coming to be cannot be generated. But that which has come to be must exist as soon as it has come to be.

999b12 Amplius autem, si materia est, quia est ingenita, multo rationabilius est esse substantiam, quando haec aliquando fit esse. Nam si nec haec erit, nec illa, nihil erit omnino. Sed si hoc est impossibile, necesse est aliquid esse praeter synolon, scilicet formam et speciem. [453]

τὸ δὲ γεγονὸς ἀνάγκη εἶναι ὅτε πρῶτον γέγονεν): ἔτι δ᾽ εἴπερ ἡ ὕλη ἔστι διὰ τὸ ἀγένητος εἶναι, πολὺ ἔτι μᾶλλον εὔλογον εἶναι τὴν οὐσίαν, ὅ ποτε ἐκείνη γίγνεται: εἰ γὰρ μήτε τοῦτο ἔσται {15} μήτε ἐκείνη, οὐθὲν ἔσται τὸ παράπαν, εἰ δὲ τοῦτο ἀδύνατον, ἀνάγκη τι εἶναι παρὰ τὸ σύνολον, τὴν μορφὴν καὶ τὸ εἶδος.

Further, if matter exists because it is ungenerated, it is much more reasonable that substance should exist, since that is what matter eventually comes to be. For if neither the one nor the other exists, nothing at all will exist. But if this is impossible, there must be something besides the *synolon*, and this is the form or species.

999b16 Sed si hoc iterum quis ponit, dubitatio est, in quibus hos ponet et in quibus non. Nam quia in omnibus non, existimatur manifestum. Non enim ponemus domum aliquam praeter domus aliquas. [454]

εἰ δ᾽ αὖ τις τοῦτο θήσει, ἀπορία ἐπὶ τίνων τε θήσει τοῦτο καὶ ἐπὶ τίνων οὔ. ὅτι μὲν γὰρ ἐπὶ πάντων οὐχ οἷόν τε, φανερόν: οὐ γὰρ ἂν θείημεν εἶναί τινα οἰκίαν παρὰ τὰς τινὰς {20} οἰκίας.

But again if anyone holds this to be true, the problem arises concerning in what cases one may hold this and in what not. For evidently this is not thought to be so in all cases. For we do not hold that there is a house apart from particular houses.

---

443. Postquam Philosophus disputavit quaestionem de universalibus, utrum sint principia, hic consequenter movet quaestionem de separatis, utrum scilicet aliquid sit separatum a sensibilibus, quod sit eorum principium. Et circa hoc pertractat duas quaestiones:

quarum prima est, an universalia sint separata a singularibus.

Secunda est, an sit aliquid formale separatum ab his quae sunt composita ex materia et forma, ibi, *amplius autem si quam maxime* et cetera.

Circa primum tria facit.

Primo describit dubitationem.

Secundo obiicit ad unam partem, ibi, *nam si non est* et cetera.

Tertio obiicit ad partem aliam, ibi, *at vero* et cetera.

Est ergo haec dubitatio de eo quod tactum est in ultima ratione praecedentis quaestionis, utrum scilicet universale sit separatum a singularibus, sicut praemissa ratio supponebat. Et hoc est quod dicit, *de qua ratio nunc existit*, idest de qua immediate praecedens ratio praecessit. De hac autem dubitatione ita dicit:

primo quod *est habita*, idest consequenter se habens ad praemissa: quia sicut iam dictum est, ex hoc dependet consideratio praecedentis quaestionis. Nam si universalia non sunt separata, non sunt principia: si autem sunt separata, sunt principia.

Secundo dicit de ea, quod est difficillima omnium dubitationum huius scientiae. Quod ostenditur ex hoc

443. Having debated the question of whether universals are the principles of things, the Philosopher now raises a question about their separability, namely, whether there is anything separate from sensible things as their principle. In regard to this he considers two questions.

The first (999a24; [443]) of these is whether universals are separate from singular things.

The second (999a32; [447]) is whether there is any formal principle separate from things that are composed of matter and form, at *further, if there is something*.

In regard to the first he does three things.

First, he describes the problem.

Second (999a26; [444]), he argues one side of the question, at *for if there is nothing*.

Third (999a29; [445]), he argues the other side of the question, at *but if this is*.

Accordingly, this problem arises with regard to a point mentioned in the last argument of the preceding question, namely, whether a universal is separate from singular things, as the aforesaid argument supposed. He describes this problem as the one *with which our analysis is now concerned* (999a24), that is, the one which immediately preceded the foregoing argument. And he speaks of it in this way:

first, that it is *connected with* (or is a consequence of) the foregoing one, because the consideration of the preceding question depends on this, as has already been stated. For if universals are not separate, they are not principles; if they are separate, they are principles.

Second, he speaks of this problem as the most difficult of all the problems in this science. This is shown by the

quod eminentissimi philosophi de ea diversimode senserunt. Nam Platonici posuerunt universalia esse separata, aliis philosophis contra ponentibus.

Tertio dicit de ea quod est maxime necessaria ad considerandum, quia scilicet ex ea dependet tota cognitio substantiarum tam sensibilium quam immaterialium.

444. Deinde cum dicit *nam si non* obiicit ad ostendendum, quod universalia sint separata a singularibus. Singularia enim sunt infinita: infinita autem cognosci non possunt. Unde singularia omnia cognosci non possunt nisi inquantum reducuntur ad aliquid unum, quod est universale. Sic igitur scientia de rebus singularibus non habetur, nisi inquantum sciuntur universalia. Sed scientia non est nisi verorum et existentium: ergo universalia sunt aliqua per se existentia praeter singularia.

445. Deinde cum dicit *at vero si* obiicit in contrarium hoc modo. Si necesse est universalia esse aliquid praeter singularia, oportet quod genera sint praeter singularia, vel prima generum, vel etiam ultima, quae sunt immediate ante singularia. Sed hoc est impossibile, ut ex praecedenti dubitatione patet; ergo universalia non sunt a singularibus separata.

446. Hanc autem dubitationem solvit Philosophus in septimo huius, ubi ostendit multipliciter universalia non esse substantias per se subsistentes. Nec oportet, sicut multoties dictum est, quod aliquid eumdem modum essendi habeat in rebus, per quem modum ab intellectu scientis comprehenditur. Nam intellectus immaterialiter cognoscit materialia: et similiter naturas rerum, quae singulariter in rebus existunt, intellectus cognoscit universaliter, idest absque consideratione principiorum et accidentium individualium.

447. Deinde cum dicit *amplius autem* prosequitur de alia quaestione: utrum scilicet aliquid sit separatum a compositis ex materia et forma: et circa hoc duo facit.

Primo movet quaestionem.
Secundo prosequitur eam, ibi, *si igitur* et cetera.

Circa primum considerandum est, quod primo movet quaestionem, utrum universale sit separatum a singularibus.

Contingit autem aliquod singulare esse compositum ex materia et forma: non tamen omne singulare ex materia et forma est compositum, nec secundum rei veritatem: quia substantiae separatae sunt quaedam particulares substantiae, quia per se stantes et per se operantes; nec etiam secundum opinionem Platonicorum, qui ponebant etiam in mathematicis separatis esse quaedam particularia, ponendo plura ex eis in una specie. Et

fact that the most eminent philosophers have held different opinions about it. For the Platonists held that universals are separate, whereas the other philosophers held the contrary.

Third, he says that this problem is one which it is most necessary to consider, because the entire knowledge of substances, both sensible and immaterial, depends on it.

444. *For if there is nothing* (999a26). Here he advances an argument to show that universals are separate from singular things. For singular things are infinite in number, and what is infinite cannot be known. Hence all singular things can be known only insofar as they are reduced to some kind of unity which is universal. Therefore, there is science of singular things only inasmuch as universals are known. But science is only about things that are true and which exist. Therefore, universals are things that exist of themselves apart from singular things.

445. *But if this is* (999a29). Then he argues the other side of the question in this way. If it is necessary that universals be something apart from singular things, it is necessary that genera exist apart from singular things, either the first genera or also the last, which are immediately prior to singular things. But this is impossible, as is clear from the preceding discussion. Therefore, universals are not separate from singular things.

446. The Philosopher solves this problem in book 7 (1039a24; [1592]) of this work, where he shows in many ways that universals are not substances which subsist of themselves. Nor is it necessary, as has often been said, that a thing should have the same mode of being in reality that it has when understood by the intellect of a knower. For the intellect knows material things immaterially, and in a similar way it knows universally the natures of things that exist as singulars in reality, without considering the principles and accidents of individuals.

447. *Further, if there is something* (999a32). Here he raises another question, namely, whether anything is separate from things composed of matter and form; in regard to this he does two things.

First, he raises the question.

Second (999b1; [448]), he proceeds to deal with it, at *if, then, there is*.

In regard to the first, it should be observed that he first raises the question of whether a universal is separate from singular things.

Now it happens to be the case that some singular things are composed of matter and form. But not all singular things are so composed, either according to the real state of affairs, since separate substances are particular because existing and operating of themselves, or even according to the opinion of the Platonists, who held that even among separate mathematical entities there are particulars inasmuch as they held that there are many of them in a single

quamvis dubitari possit, utrum etiam in his quae non sunt composita ex materia et forma, sit aliquid separatum sicut universale a singulari, tamen hoc maxime habet dubitationem in rebus compositis ex materia et forma.

Et ideo dicit, quod maxime est dubitabile, utrum sit aliquid, *praeter simul totum* et cetera, idest praeter rem compositam ex materia et forma. Et quare dicatur simul totum compositum, exponit subdens, ut *quando praedicatur aliquid de materia*. Ponebat enim Plato quod sensibilis materia participabat universalia separata. Et ex hoc erat quod universalia praedicantur de singularibus. Et ipsae participationes universalium formarum in materialibus sensibilibus constituunt simul totum, quasi universalis forma per modum participationis cuiusdam sit de materia praedicata.

In his autem quaestionem trimembrem proponit: utrum scilicet praeter omnia huiusmodi sit aliquid separatum, aut praeter quaedam eorum et non praeter alia, aut praeter nihil eorum.

448. Deinde cum dicit *si igitur* prosequitur praedictam dubitationem: et circa hoc duo facit.

Primo obiicit contra hoc, quod poni posset nihil separatum esse ab his quae sunt composita ex materia et forma.

Secundo obiicit ad oppositum, ibi, *sed si hoc* et cetera.

Circa primum, obiicit duplici via.

Primo quidem ex hoc, quod ea quae sunt composita ex materia et forma sunt sensibilia: unde proponit quod ea quae sunt composita ex materia et forma sunt singularia. Singularia autem non sunt intelligibilia, sed sensibilia. Si igitur nihil est praeter singularia composita ex materia et forma nihil erit intelligibile, sed omnia entia erunt sensibilia.

Scientia autem non est nisi intelligibilium: ergo sequitur quod nullius rei sit scientia: nisi aliquis dicat quod sensus et scientia sunt idem, ut antiqui naturales posuerunt: sicut dicitur in primo *De anima*.

Utrumque autem horum est inconveniens: scilicet vel quod non sit scientia, vel quod scientia sit sensus: ergo et primum est inconveniens, scilicet quod nihil sit praeter singularia composita ex materia et forma.

449. Deinde cum dicit *amplius autem* secundo obiicit ex hoc quod composita ex materia et forma sunt mobilia. Inducit talem rationem. Omnia sensibilia composita ex materia et forma corrumpuntur et in motu

species. And while it is open to dispute whether there is anything separate in the case of those things that are not composed of matter and form, as the universal is separate from the particular, the problem is chiefly whether there is anything separate in the case of things that are composed of matter and form.

Hence he says that the point which causes most difficulty is whether there is something *apart from the concrete whole*, that is, apart from the thing composed of matter and form. The reason why a composite thing is called a concrete whole he explains by adding *as when something is predicated of matter*. For Plato held that sensible matter participates in separate universals, and that for this reason universals are predicated of singular things. These participations in universal forms by material sensible things constitute a concrete whole inasmuch as a universal form is predicated of matter through some kind of participation.

Now in regard to these things he raises a question which has three parts, namely, whether there is anything that exists apart from all things of this kind, or apart from some and not from others, or apart from none.

448. *If, then, there is* (999b1). Here he proceeds to deal with this problem; and concerning it he does two things.

First, he argues against the position that nothing can be held to be separate from things composed of matter and form.

Second (999b16; [454]), he argues the other side of the question, at *but again if anyone holds this*.

In regard to the first (999b1), he advances two arguments.

First, he argues from the principle that those things that are composed of matter and form are sensible things; therefore, he proposes that those things that are composed of matter and form are singulars. However, singular things are not intelligible, but sensible. Therefore, if there is nothing, apart from singular things that are composed of matter and form, nothing will be intelligible, but all beings will be sensible.

But there is science only of things that are intelligible. Therefore, it follows that there will be no science of anything, unless one were to say that sensory perception and science are the same, as the ancient philosophers of nature held, as is stated in *On the Soul* 1.

But both of these conclusions are untenable, namely, that there is no science and that science is sensory perception. Therefore, the first position is also untenable, namely, that nothing exists except singular things that are composed of matter and form.

449. *Further, neither will anything* (999b3). Second, he argues on the grounds that things composed of matter and form are mobile. He gives the following argument. All sensible things composed of matter and form perish

sunt: si igitur nihil sit praeter huiusmodi entia, sequetur quod nihil sit sempiternum nec immobile.

450. Deinde cum dicit *at vero* ostendit esse inconveniens, scilicet quod nihil sit sempiternum et immobile:

et primo ex parte materiae.

Secundo ex parte formae, ibi, *amplius autem cum sit* et cetera.

Dicit ergo primo, quod si nihil est sempiternum, non est possibile esse generationem alicuius rei. Et hoc probat sic. Quia in omni generatione necesse est aliquid quod fit, et aliquid ex quo fit. Si ergo id ex quo fit aliquid, iterum generatur, oportet quod ex aliquo generetur.

Aut ergo necesse est quod in infinitum procedatur in materiis, aut quod stet processus in aliquo primo, quod sit aliquod primum materiale principium non generatum: nisi forte dicatur quod generetur ex non ente, quod est impossibile. Si autem in infinitum procederetur, numquam posset compleri generatio, quia infinita non est transire:

ergo vel oportet ponere aliquid ingenitum materiale principium, aut impossibile est esse aliquam generationem.

451. Deinde cum dicit *amplius autem* ostendit idem ex parte causae formalis: et ponit duas rationes: quarum prima talis est.

Omnis generatio et motus necesse est quod habeat aliquem finem. Et hoc probat, quia nullus motus est infinitus, sed cuiuslibet motus est aliquis finis. Hoc autem planum est in illis motibus, qui finiuntur in suis terminis. Sed videtur habere instantiam in motu circulari, qui potest esse perpetuus et infinitus, ut probatur in octavo *Physicorum*. Et quamvis supposita sempiternitate motus, tota continuitas circularis motus sit infinita, secundum quod circulatio succedit circulationi, tamen quaelibet circulatio secundum speciem suam, completa et finita est. Quod autem ei succedat alia circulatio, hoc accidit quantum ad circulationis speciem.

452. Et quod dixerat de motu universaliter, specialiter ostendit de generatione: non enim potest esse aliqua generatio una infinita, quia non potest aliquid generari quod impossibile est pervenire ad finem generationis, cuius finis est factum esse. Et quod factum esse sit terminus generationis, ex hoc patet: quia quod generatum est, necesse est esse *quando primo factum est*, id est quando primo terminatur generatio eius.

Oportet igitur quod cum forma secundum quam aliquid est, sit terminus generationis, quod non sit pro-

and are subject to motion. Therefore, if there is nothing apart from beings of this kind, it will follow that nothing is eternal or immobile.

450. *But if there is* (999b5). Here he shows that this conclusion is untenable, namely, that nothing is eternal and immobile.

He does this first with respect to matter;

second (999b8; [451]) with respect to form, at *further, since generation*.

Accordingly, he says first (999b5) that if nothing is eternal, it is impossible for anything to be generated. He proves this as follows. In every process of generation there must be something which comes to be and something from which it comes to be. Therefore, if that from which a thing comes to be is itself generated, it must be generated from something.

Hence either there must be an infinite regress in material principles or the process must stop with some first thing which is a first material principle that is ungenerated, unless it might be said, perhaps, that it is generated from non-being; but this is impossible. Now if the process were to go on to infinity, generation could never be completed, because what is infinite cannot be traversed.

Therefore, it is necessary to hold either that there is some material principle which is ungenerated or that it is impossible for any generation to take place.

451. *Further, since generation* (999b8). Here he proves the same thing with respect to the formal cause, and he gives two arguments, the first of which is as follows.

Every process of generation and motion must have some terminus. He proves this on the grounds that no motion is infinite, but that each motion has some terminus. This is clear in the case of other motions which are completed in their termini. But it seems that a contrary instance is had in the case of circular motion, which can be perpetual and infinite, as is proved in *Physics* 8. And even though motion is assumed to be eternal, so that the entire continuity of circular motion is infinite insofar as one circular motion follows another, still each circular motion is both complete in its species and finite. That one circular motion should follow another is accidental so far as the specific nature of circular motion is concerned.

452. The things that he said about motion in general he proves specially in regard to generation; for no process of generation can be infinite, because that thing cannot be generated whose process of generation cannot come to an end, since the end of generation is to have been made. That its being made is the terminus of generation is clear from the fact that what has been generated must exist *as soon as it has come to be*, that is, as soon as its generation is first terminated.

Therefore, since the form whereby something is, is the terminus of generation, it must be impossible to have an

cedere in infinitum in formis, sed quod sit aliqua forma ultima, cuius non sit aliqua generatio. Omnis enim generationis finis est forma, ut dictum est. Et sic videtur quod sicut materiam, ex qua aliquid generatur, oportet esse ingenitam, ex eo quod non proceditur in infinitum, ita etiam quod formam aliquam oportet esse ingenitam, ex hoc quod in infinitum non procedatur in formis.

453. Deinde cum dicit *amplius autem* secundam rationem ponit quae talis est.

Si materia aliqua est prima quia est ingenita, multo rationabilius est quod sit substantia, idest forma ingenita, cum per formam res habeat esse; materia vero magis sit subiectum generationis et transmutationis. Si vero neutrum eorum sit ingenitum, nihil omnino erit ingenitum; cum omne quod est, pertineat ad rationem materiae vel formae, vel sit compositum ex utroque. Hoc autem est impossibile, ut nihil sit ingenitum, sicut probatum est. Ergo relinquitur quod necesse est aliquid esse *praeter synolon*, idest simul totum, idest praeter singulare compositum ex materia et forma.

Et hoc dico aliquid quod sit forma et species. Materia enim per se non potest esse separata a singularibus, quia non habet esse nisi per aliud. De forma vero hoc magis videtur, per quam est esse rerum.

454. Deinde cum dicit *sed si hoc* obiicit in contrarium. Si enim aliquis ponat aliquam formam esse separatam praeter singularia composita ex materia et forma, erit dubitatio in quibus hoc sit ponendum et in quibus non. Manifestum enim est quod hoc non est ponendum in omnibus, praecipue in artificialibus. Non enim est possibile quod sit aliqua domus praeter hanc domum sensibilem compositam ex materia et forma.

455. Hanc autem dubitationem solvit Aristoteles partim quidem in duodecimo huius: ubi ostendit esse quasdam substantias a sensibilibus separatas, quae sunt secundum seipsas intelligibiles: partim vero in septimo huius, ubi ostendit formas et species rerum sensibilium non esse a materia separatas.

Non tamen sequitur, quod de rebus sensibilibus non possit haberi scientia, vel quod scientia sit sensus. Non enim oportet, quod eumdem modum essendi habeant res in seipsis, quem habent in consideratione scientis. Quae enim seipsis materialia sunt, ab intellectu immaterialiter cognoscuntur, ut etiam supra dictum est. Nec etiam oportet, si forma non est separata a materia, quod

infinite regress in the case of forms, and there must be some last form of which there is no generation. For the end of every generation is a form, as we have said. Thus it seems that, just as the matter from which a thing is generated must itself be ungenerated because it is impossible to have an infinite regress, in a similar way there must be some form which is ungenerated because it is impossible to have an infinite regress in the case of forms.

453. *Further, if matter exists* (999b12). He gives the second argument, which runs thus.

If there is some first matter which is ungenerated, it is much more reasonable that there should be some substance, that is, some form, which is ungenerated, since a thing has being through its form, whereas matter is rather the subject of generation and transmutation. But if neither of these is ungenerated, then absolutely nothing will be ungenerated, since everything which exists has the character of matter or form or is composed of both. But it is impossible that nothing should be ungenerated, as has been proved (999b8; [452]). Therefore, it follows that there must be something else *besides the synolon*, or concrete whole—that is, besides the singular thing which is composed of matter and form.

And by something else I mean the form or species. For matter in itself cannot be separated from singular things, because it has being only by reason of something else. But this seems to be true rather of form, by which things have being.

454. *But again if anyone* (999b16). Here he argues the other side of the question. For if one holds that there is some form separate from singular things that are composed of matter and form, the problem arises as to in which cases this must be admitted and in which not. For obviously this must not be held to be true in the case of all things, especially in that of those made by art. For it is impossible that there should be a house apart from this sensible house, which is composed of matter and form.

455. Now Aristotle solves this problem partly in book 12 [2488] of this work, where he shows that there are certain substances separate from sensible things and intelligible in themselves, and partly in book 7 [1503], where he shows that the forms or species of sensible things are not separate from matter.

However, it does not follow that no science of sensible things can be had or that science is sensory perception. For it is not necessary that things have in themselves the same mode of being which they have in the intellect of one who knows them. For those things that are material in themselves are known in an immaterial way by the intellect, as has also been stated above [446]. And even though a

generetur: quia formarum non est generatio, sed compositorum, ut in septimo huius ostendetur.

Patet ergo in quibus oportet ponere separatas formas, et in quibus non. Nam omnium eorum quae sunt secundum suam naturam sensibilia, formae non sunt separatae. Sed illa quae sunt secundum naturam suam intelligibilia, sunt a materia separata. Non enim substantiae separatae sunt naturae horum sensibilium, sed sunt altioris naturae, alium habentes ordinem in rebus.

form is not separate from matter, it is not therefore necessary that it should be generated, for it is not forms that are generated, but composites, as will be shown in book 7 [1417] of this work.

It is clear, then, in what cases it is necessary to posit separate forms and in what not. For the forms of all things that are sensible by nature are not separate from matter, whereas the forms of things that are intelligible by nature are separate from matter. For the separate substances do not have the nature of sensible things, but are of a higher nature and belong to another order of existing things.

LECTURE 10

Do all things have a single substance?

999b20 Adhuc autem utrum substantia una est omnium, ut hominum. [456]

πρὸς δὲ τούτοις πότερον ἡ οὐσία μία πάντων ἔσται, οἷον τῶν ἀνθρώπων;

Again, there is the problem of whether all things (for example, all men) have a single substance.

999b21 Sed impossibile est. Non enim unum omnia quorum substantia una, sed multa et differentia. Sed hoc extra rationem est. [457]

ἀλλ᾽ ἄτοπον: ἓν γὰρ πάντα ὧν ἡ οὐσία μία. ἀλλὰ πολλὰ καὶ διάφορα; ἀλλὰ καὶ τοῦτο ἄλογον.

But this is absurd; for not all things whose substance is one are themselves one, but are many and different. But this too is untenable.

999b23 Simul autem et quomodo sit materia horum singulum, et synolon. [458]

ἅμα δὲ καὶ πῶς γίγνεται ἡ ὕλη τούτων ἕκαστον καὶ ἔστι τὸ σύνολον ἄμφω ταῦτα;

And at the same time there is the problem of how matter becomes each of the many things and a concrete whole.

999b24 Amplius autem et de principiis hoc dubitabit aliquis. Nam si specie sunt unum, nihil erit numero unum. Nec unum iterum unum ipsum et ens. Et scire quomodo erit, nisi quid unum fuerit in omnibus? [460]

ἔτι δὲ περὶ τῶν ἀρχῶν {25} καὶ τόδε ἀπορήσειεν ἄν τις. εἰ μὲν γὰρ εἴδει εἰσὶν ἕν, οὐθὲν ἔσται ἀριθμῷ ἕν, οὐδ᾽ αὐτὸ τὸ ἓν καὶ τὸ ὄν: καὶ τὸ ἐπίστασθαι πῶς ἔσται, εἰ μή τι ἔσται ἓν ἐπὶ πάντων;

And again one might also raise this problem about principles. For if they are specifically one, there will be nothing that is numerically one. Nor again will unity itself and being be one. And how will there be science unless there is some unity in all things?

999b27 At vero si numero unum et unum quodlibet principiorum et non quemadmodum in sensibilibus alia aliorum, ut in hac syllaba, BA specie existente et principia specie eadem: etenim ea sunt numero diversa. [464]

ἀλλὰ μὴν εἰ ἀριθμῷ ἓν καὶ μία ἑκάστη τῶν ἀρχῶν, καὶ μὴ ὥσπερ ἐπὶ τῶν αἰσθητῶν ἄλλαι ἄλλων (οἷον τῆσδε τῆς συλλαβῆς {30} τῷ εἴδει τῆς αὐτῆς οὔσης καὶ αἱ ἀρχαὶ εἴδει αἱ αὐταί: καὶ γὰρ αὗται ὑπάρχουσιν ἀριθμῷ ἕτεραι),

But, on the other hand, if they are numerically one, each of the principles will also be one, and not, as in the case of sensible things, different for different things; for example, if the syllable BA is taken as a species, its principles in every case are specifically the same, for they are numerically different.

Quod si non ita, sed quae sunt entium principia numero unum sunt, non erunt praeter elementa quippiam aliud. Nam dicere numero unum, aut singulare, nihil differt. Sic enim dicimus unumquodque numero unum.

εἰ δὲ μὴ οὕτως ἀλλ᾽ αἱ τῶν ὄντων ἀρχαὶ ἀριθμῷ ἕν εἰσιν, οὐκ ἔσται παρὰ τὰ στοιχεῖα οὐθὲν ἕτερον: τὸ γὰρ ἀριθμῷ ἓν ἢ τὸ καθ᾽ ἕκαστον λέγειν διαφέρει οὐθέν: οὕτω γὰρ λέγομεν τὸ καθ᾽ ἕκαστον, τὸ ἀριθμῷ ἕν,

However, if this is not so, but the things that are the principles of beings are numerically one, there will be nothing else besides the elements. For it makes no difference whether we say "numerically one" or "singular," because it is in this way that we say each thing is numerically one.

Universale vero quod in his est. Ut si vocis elementa numero essent determinata, tot literas esse necesse esset, quot elementa. Duobus quidem eisdem non existentibus, nec pluribus.

καθόλου δὲ τὸ ἐπὶ τούτων. {1000a1} ὥσπερ οὖν εἰ τὰ τῆς φωνῆς ἀριθμῷ ἦν στοιχεῖα ὡρισμένα, ἀναγκαῖον ἦν ἂν τοσαῦτα εἶναι τὰ πάντα γράμματα ὅσαπερ τὰ στοιχεῖα, μὴ ὄντων γε δύο τῶν αὐτῶν μηδὲ πλειόνων.

But the universal is what exists in these. For example, if the elements of a word were limited in number, there would have to be as many letters as there are elements. Indeed, no two of them would be the same, nor would more than two.

---

456. Postquam Philosophus inquisivit quae sunt principia, et utrum sint aliqua a materia separata, hic inquirit qualia sint principia.

Et primo inquirit de unitate et multitudine ipsorum.

Secundo inquirit, utrum sint in potentia vel in actu, ibi, *his autem affine est quaerere* et cetera.

456. Having asked what the principles are, and whether some are separate from matter, the Philosopher now asks what the principles are like.

First (999b20; [456]), he asks whether the principles are one or many;

second (1002b32; [519]), whether they exist potentially or actually, at *and connected with these problems*;

Tertio utrum principia sint universalia vel singularia, ibi, *et utrum universalia sint* et cetera.

Circa primum duo facit.

Primo inquirit qualiter principia se habeant ad unitatem.

Secundo qualiter ipsum unum se habeat ad rationem principii, ibi, *omnium autem* et cetera.

Circa primum tria facit.

Primo inquirit specialiter de principio formali, utrum sit unum omnium existentium in una specie.

Secundo inquirit idem de omnibus generaliter principiis, ibi, *amplius autem* et cetera.

Tertio inquirit, utrum eadem sint principia aut diversa corruptibilium et incorruptibilium, ibi, *non minor autem* et cetera.

Circa primum duo facit.

Primo movet dubitationem.

Secundo obiicit ad quaestionem, ibi, *sed impossibile est*.

Est ergo dubitatio, utrum sit una substantia, idest forma omnium existentium in una specie, puta hominum.

457. Deinde cum dicit *sed impossibile* obiicit ad unam partem quaestionis: scilicet ad ostendendum quod non sit una forma omnium existentium in una specie: et hoc duabus rationibus,

quarum prima talis est. Ea quae sunt in una specie, sunt multa et differentia: si igitur omnium in una specie existentium sit una substantia, sequetur quod ea quorum substantia est una, sint multa et differentia: quod est irrationabile.

458. Deinde cum dicit *simul autem* hic ponit secundam rationem, quae talis est. Illud, quod est in se unum et indivisum, non componitur cum aliquo diviso ad constitutionem multorum. Sed manifestum est quod materia dividitur in diversis singularibus. Si igitur substantia formalis esset una et eadem, non esset assignare quomodo singulum horum singularium sit materia habens talem substantiam, quae est una et indivisa, ita quod singulariter sit simul totum habens haec duo, scilicet materia et formam substantialem, quae est una et indivisa.

459. In contrarium autem non obiicit, quia rationes, quae ad sequentem quaestionem proponuntur ad oppositum praedictarum rationum, sunt etiam illae quae sunt propositae supra de separatione universalium. Nam si sit universale separatum, necesse est ponere unam numero substantiam eorum quae conveniunt in specie, quia universale est substantia singularium. Huius autem quaestionis veritas determinatur in septimo huius, ubi ostendetur, quod quid est, idest essentiam cuiuslibet rei

third (1003a6; [523]), whether they are universals or singular things, at *and there is also the problem*.

In regard to the first, he does two things.

First (999b20; [456]), he inquires how the principles stand with respect to unity;

second (1001a4; [488]), what relationship unity has to the notion of principle, at *but the most difficult*.

In regard to the first he does three things.

First, he inquires specially about the formal principle, asking whether all things that are specifically the same have a single form.

Second (999b24; [460]), he asks the same question of all principles in general, at *and again one might*.

Third (1000a5; [466]), he asks whether corruptible and incorruptible things have the same principles or different ones, at *again, there is a problem*.

In regard to the first he does two things.

First, he introduces the problem.

Second (999b21; [457]), he debates it, at *but this is absurd*.

The problem (999b20), then, is whether all things that belong to the same species (for example, all men) have a single substance or form.

457. **But this is absurd** (999b21). Then he advances arguments on one side of the question to show that all things belonging to one species do not have a single form. He does this by means of two arguments,

the first of which runs thus. Things that belong to one species are many and different. Therefore, if all things that belong to one species have a single substance, it follows that those which have a single substance are many and different. But this is unreasonable.

458. **And at the same time** (999b23). Then he gives the second argument, which runs thus. That which is one and undivided in itself is not combined with something divided in order to constitute many things. But it is evident that matter is divided into different singular things. Hence, if substance in the sense of form is one and the same for all things, it will be impossible to explain how each of these singular things is a matter having a substance of the kind that is one and undivided, so that as a singular thing it is a concrete whole having two parts: a matter and a substantial form which is one and undivided.

459. Now he does not argue the other side of the question, because the very same arguments which were advanced above regarding the separateness of universals are applicable in the inquiry which follows it against the arguments just given. For if a separate universal exists, it must be held that things having the same species have a single substance numerically, because a universal is the substance of singular things. Now the truth of this question will be established in book 7 (1031a15; [1356]) of this work,

non esse aliud quam rem ipsam, nisi per accidens, ut ibi dicetur.

460. Deinde cum dicit *amplius autem* movet dubitationem de unitate principiorum in communi. Utrum scilicet principia rerum sint eadem numero, vel eadem specie et numero diversa: et circa hoc duo facit.

Primo ponit rationes ad ostendendum, quod sint eadem numero.

Secundo ad oppositum, ibi, *at vero* et cetera.

Circa primum, ponit tres rationes et praemittit dubitationem, dicens, quod idem potest quaeri universaliter de principiis rerum, quod quaesitum est de substantia, utrum scilicet principia rerum sint eadem numero.

461. Et inducit primam rationem, ad ostendendum, quod sint eadem numero. Non enim invenitur in principiatis nisi quod ex principiis habent: si igitur in principiis non inveniatur unum numero, sed solum unum specie, nihil erit in principiatis unum numero, sed solum unum specie.

462. Secunda ratio talis est: quia illud quod est ipsum unum vel ipsum ens, oportet quod sit unum numero. Dicit autem ipsum unum vel ipsum ens, unitatem aut ens abstractum. Si igitur principium rerum non sit unum numero, sed solum unum specie, sequetur, quod nihil sit ipsum unum et etiam ipsum ens, idest quod ens et unum non per se subsistant.

463. Tertia ratio est, quia scientia habetur de rebus per hoc, quod unum invenitur in multis, sicut homo communis invenitur in omnibus hominibus; non enim est scientia de singularibus, sed de uno quod invenitur in eis. Omnis autem scientia vel cognitio principiatorum dependet ex cognitione principiorum. Si igitur principia non sunt unum numero, sed solum unum specie, sequitur, quod scientia non sit de rebus.

464. Deinde cum dicit *at vero si* obiicit in contrarium tali ratione.

Si principia sunt unum numero, ita quod quodlibet principiorum in se consideratum sit unum, non erit dicere de principiis existentium, quod hoc modo se habent sicut principia sensibilium. Videmus enim in sensibilibus, quod diversorum sunt diversa principia secundum numerum, sed eadem secundum speciem; sicut et eorum quorum sunt principia, sunt diversa secundum numerum, sed eadem secundum speciem.

Sicut videmus quod diversarum syllabarum secundum numerum, quae conveniunt in specie, sunt principia eaedem literae secundum speciem, sed non secundum numerum. Si quis autem dicat quod non est ita

where it is shown that the whatness or essence of a thing is not other than the thing itself, except in an accidental way, as will be explained in that place.

460. *And again one might* (999b24). Here he raises a difficulty concerning the unity of principles in general: whether the principles of things are numerically the same, or only specifically the same and numerically distinct. And in regard to this he does two things.

First, he advances arguments to show that they are numerically the same.

Second (999b27; [464]), he argues on the other side of the question, at *but, on the other hand*.

In regard to the first (999b24) he gives three arguments. He introduces the problem by saying that the same question which was raised about substance can be raised about principles in general (that is, whether the principles of things are numerically the same).

461. He introduces the first argument to show that they are numerically the same. For things composed of principles merely contain what they receive from these principles. Therefore, if principles are not found to be one numerically but only specifically, the things composed of these principles will not be one numerically but only specifically.

462. The second argument runs thus. Unity itself or being itself must be numerically one. And by "unity itself" or "being itself," he means unity or being in the abstract. Hence, if the principles of things are not one numerically but only specifically, it will follow that neither unity itself nor being itself will subsist of itself.

463. The third argument is this. Science is had of things because there is found to be a one-in-many, as man in common is found in all men, for there is no science of singular things but of the unity found in them. Moreover, all science or cognition of things that are composed of principles depends on a knowledge of these principles. If, then, principles are not one numerically, but only specifically, it will follow that there is no science of beings.

464. *But, on the other hand* (999b27). Here he argues the opposite side of the question in the following fashion.

If principles are numerically one so that each of the principles considered in itself is one, it will be impossible to say that the principles of beings exist in the same way as the principles of sensible things. For we see that the principles of different sensible things are numerically different but specifically the same, just as the things of which they are the principles are numerically different but specifically the same.

We see, for example, that syllables which are numerically distinct but agree in species have letters as their principles, which are the same specifically but not numerically. And if anyone were to say that this is not true of the

in principiis entium, sed omnium entium principia sunt unum numero; sequetur quod nihil sit in rebus praeter elementa; quia quod est unum numero, est singulare. Sic enim appellamus singulare quod est unum numero, sicut universale quod est in multis. Quod autem est singulare, non multiplicatur nec invenitur nisi singulariter.

Si igitur ponatur quod omnium syllabarum essent principia eaedem literae numero, sequeretur quod illae literae nunquam possent multiplicari, ut scilicet essent duo aut plura: et sic non posset seorsum inveniri in syllaba ista BA, vel DA. Et eadem ratio est de aliis literis.

Pari igitur ratione si omnium entium sint principia eadem numero, sequetur quod nihil sit praeter principia: quod videtur inconveniens: quia cum principium alicuius sit, non erit principium nisi sit aliquid praeter ipsum.

465. Haec autem quaestio solvetur in duodecimo. Ibi enim ostendetur quod principia quae sunt intrinseca rebus, scilicet materia et forma, vel privatio, non sunt eadem numero omnium, sed analogia sive proportione. Principia autem separata, scilicet substantiae intellectuales, quarum suprema est Deus, sunt unum numero unaquaeque secundum seipsam. Id autem quod est ipsum unum et ens, Deus est; et ab ipso derivatur unitas secundum numerum in rebus omnibus.

Scientia autem est de his, non quia sint unum numero in omnibus, sed quia est unum in multis secundum rationem. Ratio autem quae est ad oppositum verificatur in principiis essentialibus, non autem in principiis separatis, cuiusmodi sunt agens et finis. Multa enim possunt produci ab uno agente vel movente et ordinari in unum finem.

principles of beings, but that the principles of all beings are the same numerically, it would follow that nothing exists in the world except the elements, because what is numerically one is a singular thing. For what is numerically one we call singular, just as we call universal what is in many. But what is singular is incapable of being multiplied, and is encountered only as a singular.

Therefore, if it is held that, numerically, the same letters are the principles of all syllables, it will follow that those letters could never be multiplied so that there could be two of them or more than two. Thus A could not be found in these two different syllables, BA or DA. And the argument is the same in the case of other letters.

Therefore, by the same reasoning, if the principles of all beings are numerically the same, it will follow that there is nothing besides these principles. But this seems to be untenable, because when a principle of anything exists it will not be a principle unless there is something else besides itself.

465. Now this question will be solved in book 12 [2464], for it will be shown there that the principles which things have (namely, matter, or privation, or form) are not numerically the same for all things, but analogically or proportionally the same. But those principles which are separate—namely, the intellectual substances, of which the highest is God—are each numerically one in themselves. Now that which is one in itself and being is God, and from him is derived the numerical unity found in all things.

And there is science of these, not because they are numerically one in all, but because in our conception there is a one in many. Moreover, the argument which is proposed in support of the opposite side of the question is true in the case of essential principles but not in that of separate ones, which is the genus to which the agent and final cause belong. For many things can be produced by one agent or efficient cause, and can be directed to one end.

LECTURE 11

Do corruptible and incorruptible things have the same principles?

1000a5 Non autem minor dubitatio modernis et prioribus relinquitur, utrum eadem corruptibilium et incorruptibilium sint principia, aut diversa. [466]

1000a7 Nam si eadem sint, quomodo haec quidem incorruptibilia, ilia vero corruptibilia? Et propter quam causam? [467]

1000a9 Qui quidem igitur circa Hesiodum, et omnes, qui theologi erant, solum apud ipsos persuasionem curaverunt, nos autem neglexerunt. Deos autem facientes principia, et ex deis esse facta, quae non gustaverunt necta et manna mortalia facta esse dicunt. [468]

1000a13 Palam quod haec omnia sibi nota dicentes, equidem de allatione harum causarum super nos dixerunt. [470]

Nam si gratia voluptatis ipsa tangunt, non est causa existendi nectar et manna. Si vero essendi, quomodo erunt sempitenii, cibo egentes?

1000a18 Sed de fabulose sophisticantibus non est dignum cum studio intendere. [471]

1000a19 A dicentibus vero per demonstrationem oportet sciscitari interrogantes, quare ex eisdem existentia, haec quidem sempiterna secundum naturam sunt, ilia vero corrumpuntur existentium? Quoniam autem nec causam dicunt, nec rationabile est sic se habere, palam quod nec eadem principia, nec causae ipsorum erunt. [472]

1000a24 Etenim quam existimabit aliquis utique maxime dicere ipsi confesse Empedocli, est et idem passus. Ponit enim quoddam principium causam corruptionis odium. [473]

οὐθενὸς δ' ἐλάττων ἀπορία παραλέλειπται καὶ τοῖς νῦν καὶ τοῖς πρότερον, πότερον αἱ αὐταὶ τῶν φθαρτῶν καὶ τῶν ἀφθάρτων ἀρχαί εἰσιν ἢ ἕτεραι.

εἰ μὲν γὰρ αἱ αὐταί, πῶς τὰ μὲν φθαρτὰ τὰ δὲ ἄφθαρτα, καὶ διὰ τίν' αἰτίαν;

οἱ μὲν οὖν περὶ Ἡσίοδον καὶ πάντες ὅσοι θεολόγοι {10} μόνον ἐφρόντισαν τοῦ πιθανοῦ τοῦ πρὸς αὐτούς, ἡμῶν δ' ὠλιγώρησαν (θεοὺς γὰρ ποιοῦντες τὰς ἀρχὰς καὶ ἐκ θεῶν γεγονέναι, τὰ μὴ γευσάμενα τοῦ νέκταρος καὶ τῆς ἀμβροσίας θνητὰ γενέσθαι φασίν,

δῆλον ὡς ταῦτα τὰ ὀνόματα γνώριμα λέγοντες αὐτοῖς· καίτοι περὶ αὐτῆς τῆς προσφορᾶς {15} τῶν αἰτίων τούτων ὑπὲρ ἡμᾶς εἰρήκασιν·

εἰ μὲν γὰρ χάριν ἡδονῆς αὐτῶν θιγγάνουσιν, οὐθὲν αἴτια τοῦ εἶναι τὸ νέκταρ καὶ ἡ ἀμβροσία, εἰ δὲ τοῦ εἶναι, πῶς ἂν εἶεν ἀΐδιοι δεόμενοι τροφῆς):

ἀλλὰ περὶ μὲν τῶν μυθικῶς σοφιζομένων οὐκ ἄξιον μετὰ σπουδῆς σκοπεῖν·

παρὰ δὲ τῶν δι' {20} ἀποδείξεως λεγόντων δεῖ πυνθάνεσθαι διερωτῶντας τί δή ποτ' ἐκ τῶν αὐτῶν ὄντα τὰ μὲν ἀΐδια τὴν φύσιν ἐστὶ τὰ δὲ φθείρεται τῶν ὄντων. ἐπεὶ δὲ οὔτε αἰτίαν λέγουσιν οὔτε εὔλογον οὕτως ἔχειν, δῆλον ὡς οὐχ αἱ αὐταὶ ἀρχαὶ οὐδὲ αἰτίαι αὐτῶν ἂν εἶεν.

καὶ γὰρ ὅνπερ οἰηθείη λέγειν {25} ἄν τις μάλιστα ὁμολογουμένως αὑτῷ, Ἐμπεδοκλῆς, καὶ οὗτος ταὐτὸν πέπονθεν· τίθησι μὲν γὰρ ἀρχήν τινα αἰτίαν τῆς φθορᾶς τὸ νεῖκος,

Again, there is a problem which has been neglected no less by the moderns than by their predecessors: whether the principles of corruptible and incorruptible things are the same or different.

For if they are the same, how is it that some things are incorruptible and others corruptible? And what is the cause?

The followers of Hesiod and all those who were called theologians paid attention only to what was plausible to themselves and have neglected us. For making the principles of things to be gods or generated from the gods, they say that whatever has not tasted nectar and ambrosia became mortal.

And it is clear that they are using these terms in a way known to themselves, but what they have said about the application of these causes is beyond our understanding.

For if it is for the sake of pleasure that the gods partake of these things, nectar and ambrosia are not the cause of their being. But if they partake of them to preserve their being, how will the gods be eternal in requiring food?

But with regard to those who have philosophized by using fables, it is not worth our while to pay any serious attention to them.

However, from those who make assertions by demonstration it is necessary to find out, by questioning them, why some things derived from the same principles are eternal in nature and others are corrupted. But since they mention no cause, and it is unreasonable that things should be as they say, it is clear that the principles and causes of these things will not be the same.

For the explanation which one will consider to say something most to the point is that of Empedocles, who has been subject to the same error. For he posits a certain principle, hate, which is the cause of corruption.

233

1000a28 Videbitur autem nihilominus et hoc generare extra unum. Nam omnia ex hoc alia sunt praeter Deum. Dicit ergo: *ex quibus omnia et quaecumque erant et arbores pullulaverunt et viri et feminae, bestiaeque et volucres, et aqua nutriti pisces, et dii longaevi.* Et praeter haec palam, quia si non esset in rebus, essent unum omnia, ut ait. *Nam quando convenerunt, tunc ultimum omnium stabit odium.* [474]

δόξειε δ᾽ ἂν οὐθὲν ἧττον καὶ τοῦτο γεννᾶν ἔξω τοῦ ἑνός· ἅπαντα γὰρ ἐκ τούτου τἆλλά ἐστι πλὴν ὁ θεός. λέγει γοῦν ἐξ ὧν πάνθ᾽ ὅσα τ᾽ ἦν ὅσα τ᾽ {30} ἔσθ᾽ ὅσα τ᾽ ἔσται ὀπίσσω, δένδρεά τ᾽ ἐβλάστησε καὶ ἀνέρες ἠδὲ γυναῖκες, θῆρές τ᾽ οἰωνοί τε καὶ ὑδατοθρέμμονες ἰχθῦς, καί τε θεοὶ δολιχαίωνες. καὶ χωρὶς δὲ τούτων δῆλον· {1000b1} εἰ γὰρ μὴ ἦν ἐν τοῖς πράγμασιν, ἓν ἂν ἦν ἅπαντα, ὡς φησίν· ὅταν γὰρ συνέλθῃ, "τότε δ᾽ ἔσχατον ἵστατο νεῖκος."

Yet even hate would seem to generate everything except the one. For all things except God are derived from this. Hence he says: *From which have blossomed forth all that was and is—trees, and men and women, and beasts and flying things, and water-nourished fish, and the long-lived gods.* And apart from these things it is evident that, if hate did not exist in the world, all things would be one, as he says: *For when they have come together, then hate will stand last of all.*

1000b3 Propter quod etiam accidit ipsi felicissimum Deum, minus prudentem aliis. Non enim cognoscit elementa omnia: nam odium non habet: notitia vero similis simili. Terram namque, ait, *per terram cognoscimus et per aquam aquam, et per affectum affectum, et adhuc odium per odium triste.* [476]

διὸ καὶ συμβαίνει αὐτῷ τὸν εὐδαιμονέστατον θεὸν ἧττον φρόνιμον εἶναι τῶν ἄλλων· οὐ γὰρ γνωρίζει {5} ἅπαντα· τὸ γὰρ νεῖκος οὐκ ἔχει, ἡ δὲ γνῶσις τοῦ ὁμοίου τῷ ὁμοίῳ. γαίῃ μὲν γάρ, (φησί,) γαῖαν ὀπώπαμεν, ὕδατι δ᾽ ὕδωρ, αἰθέρι δ᾽ αἰθέρα δῖον, ἀτὰρ πυρὶ πῦρ ἀΐδηλον, στοργὴν δὲ στοργῇ, νεῖκος δέ τε νείκεϊ λυγρῷ.

For this reason too it turns out that God, who is most happy, is less wise than other beings. For he does not know all the elements, because hate he does not have, and knowledge is of like by like. *For one knows earth by earth, water by water, and affection by affection, and hate by mournful hate.*

1000b8 Sed unde ratio haec etiam palam, quia accidit ei odium non magis corruptionis quam existendi causam. [476]

ἀλλ᾽ ὅθεν δὴ ὁ λόγος, τοῦτό γε φανερόν, ὅτι {10} συμβαίνει αὐτῷ τὸ νεῖκος μηθὲν μᾶλλον φθορᾶς ἢ τοῦ εἶναι αἴτιον·

But it is also clear (and this is where our discussion began) that hate no more turns out to be the cause of corruption than of being.

1000b11 Similiter autem nec amor existendi: colligens enim in unum corrumpit alia. [477]

ὁμοίως δ᾽ οὐδ᾽ ἡ φιλότης τοῦ εἶναι, συνάγουσα γὰρ εἰς τὸ ἓν φθείρει τὰ ἄλλα.

Nor, similarly, is love the cause of existence, for in blending things together into a unity it corrupts other things.

1000b12 Similiter quoque ipsius transmutationis causam nullam, nisi quia sic aptum natum fuit, loquitur. [478]

καὶ ἅμα δὲ αὐτῆς τῆς μεταβολῆς αἴτιον οὐθὲν λέγει ἀλλ᾽ ἢ ὅτι οὕτως πέφυκεν·

Moreover, he does not speak of the cause of change itself, except to say that it was naturally disposed to be so.

1000b14 *262. Sed itaque magnum odium in membris nutritum est, et ad honorem intendebat perfecto tempore, qui mutabilis dissolvit sacramentum.* Quare necessarium ens transmutari, causam vero necessitatis nullam ostendit. [479]

ἀλλ᾽ ὅτε δὴ μέγα νεῖκος ἐνὶ μελέεσσιν ἐθρέφθη, εἰς τιμάς {15} τ᾽ ἀνόρουσε τελειομένοιο χρόνοιο ὅς σφιν ἀμοιβαῖος πλατέος παρ᾽ ἐλήλαται ὅρκου· ὡς ἀναγκαῖον μὲν ὂν μεταβάλλειν· αἰτίαν δὲ τῆς ἀνάγκης οὐδεμίαν δηλοῖ.

But thus mighty hate was nourished among the members and rose to a position of honor when the time was fulfilled, which, being changeable, dissolved the bond. Hence change is a necessity, but he gives no reason for its necessity.

1000b17 Attamen tantum solum dicit confesse. Non enim existentium haec quidem corruptibilia, illa vero incorruptibilia facit; sed omnia corruptibilia praeter elementa. [481]

ἀλλ᾽ ὅμως τοσοῦτόν γε μόνος λέγει ὁμολογουμένως· οὐ γὰρ τὰ μὲν φθαρτὰ τὰ δὲ ἄφθαρτα ποιεῖ τῶν ὄντων ἀλλὰ πάντα {20} φθαρτὰ πλὴν τῶν στοιχείων.

Yet he alone speaks expressly to this extent. For he does not make some beings corruptible and others incorruptible, but makes all things corruptible except the elements.

Dicta vero dubitatio est, cur haec quidem, illa vero non, si ex eisdem sunt? Quod quidem igitur non utique erunt eadem principia, tot dicta sunt.

ἡ δὲ νῦν λεγομένη ἀπορία ἐστὶ διὰ τί τὰ μὲν τὰ δ᾽ οὔ, εἴπερ ἐκ τῶν αὐτῶν ἐστιν. ὅτι μὲν οὖν οὐκ ἂν εἴησαν αἱ αὐταὶ ἀρχαί, τοσαῦτα εἰρήσθω·

But the problem that has been stated is why some things are corruptible and others are not, if they come from the same principles. To this extent, then, it has been said that the principles of things will not be the same.

1000b23 Si vero diversa principia, una quidem dubitatio, utrum et incorruptibilia haec erunt, aut corruptibilia. Nam si corruptibilia, manifestum quia necessarium et

εἰ δὲ ἕτεραι ἀρχαί, μία μὲν ἀπορία πότερον ἄφθαρτοι καὶ αὗται ἔσονται ἢ φθαρταί· εἰ μὲν γὰρ φθαρταί, δῆλον ὡς {25} ἀναγκαῖον καὶ ταύτας ἔκ τινος εἶναι

But if the principles are different, one problem is whether they will be incorruptible or corruptible. For if they are corruptible, it is evident that they must

ea ex aliquibus esse: omnia enim corrumpuntur in ea ex quibus sunt. [483]

Quare contingit principiorum alia esse principia priora: hoc autem et impossibile, sive stet, sive in infinitum vadat. Amplius autem, quomodo erunt corruptibilia, si destruentur principia?

Si vero incorruptibilia, cur ex his quidem incorruptibilibus existentibus corruptibilia erunt, ex diversis vero incorruptibilia? Hoc enim non rationabile est; sed aut impossibile, aut multa ratione eget.

1000b32 Amplius autem nec conatus est aliquis diversa dicere, sed eadem omnium dicunt principia. Verum prima dubitatum concedunt, tamquam hoc parvum aliquid accipientes. [486]

(πάντα γὰρ φθείρεται εἰς ταῦτ᾽ ἐξ ὧν ἔστιν),

ὥστε συμβαίνει τῶν ἀρχῶν ἑτέρας ἀρχὰς εἶναι προτέρας, τοῦτο δ᾽ ἀδύνατον, καὶ εἰ ἵσταται καὶ εἰ βαδίζει εἰς ἄπειρον· ἔτι δὲ πῶς ἔσται τὰ φθαρτά, εἰ αἱ ἀρχαὶ ἀναιρεθήσονται;

εἰ δὲ ἄφθαρτοι, διὰ {30} τί ἐκ μὲν τούτων ἀφθάρτων οὐσῶν φθαρτὰ ἔσται, ἐκ δὲ τῶν ἑτέρων ἄφθαρτα; τοῦτο γὰρ οὐκ εὔλογον, ἀλλ᾽ ἢ ἀδύνατον ἢ πολλοῦ λόγου δεῖται.

ἔτι δὲ οὐδ᾽ ἐγκεχείρηκεν οὐδεὶς ἑτέρας, ἀλλὰ τὰς αὐτὰς ἁπάντων λέγουσιν ἀρχάς. {1001a1} ἀλλὰ τὸ πρῶτον ἀπορηθὲν ἀποτρώγουσιν ὥσπερ τοῦτο μικρόν τι λαμβάνοντες.

come from something, since all corrupted things are dissolved into the elements from which they come.

Hence it follows that there are other principles prior to these principles. But this is also unreasonable, whether the process stops or goes on to infinity. Further, how will corruptible things exist if their principles are destroyed?

But if they are incorruptible, why will corruptible things come from incorruptible principles, and incorruptible things from others? For this is unreasonable, and is either impossible or requires a great deal of reasoning.

Further, no one has attempted to say that these things have different principles, but all thinkers say that all things have the same principles. But they admit the first problem, considering it a trifling matter.

---

466. Postquam Philosophus inquisivit universaliter, utrum principia sint eadem numero omnia quae sunt unius speciei, vel eadem specie, hic inquirit utrum eadem numero sint principia corruptibilium et incorruptibilium: et circa hoc tria facit.

Primo proponit quaestionem.

Secundo inducit rationem ad ostendendum quod non sunt eadem principia corruptibilium et incorruptibilium, ibi, *nam si eadem* et cetera.

Tertio inducit rationes ad ostendendum quod non sunt diversa, ibi, *si vero diversa* et cetera.

Dicit ergo primo, quod quaedam dubitatio est, quae non minus relinquitur modernis philosophis Platonem sequentibus, quam fuit apud antiquos philosophos, qui etiam dubitaverunt, utrum corruptibilium et incorruptibilium sint eadem principia vel diversa.

467. Deinde cum dicit **nam si eadem** obiicit ad ostendendum quod non sunt eadem principia corruptibilium et incorruptibilium: et circa hoc tria facit.

Primo ponit rationem.

Secundo improbat solutionem positae rationis, quam poetae theologi adhibebant, ibi, *qui quidem* et cetera.

Tertio excludit solutionem quam adhibebant quidam philosophi naturales, ibi, *a dicentibus* et cetera.

Dicit ergo, quod si ponantur corruptibilium et incorruptibilium esse eadem principia, cum ex eisdem princi-

466. Having investigated in a general way whether all principles belonging to one species are numerically the same, the Philosopher inquires here whether the principles of corruptible and incorruptible things are numerically the same. In regard to this he does three things.

First (1000a5; [466]), he raises the question.

Second (1000a7; [467]), he introduces an argument to show that the principles of corruptible things and those of incorruptible things are not the same, at *for if they are the same*.

Third (1000b23; [483]), he introduces arguments to show that they are not different, at *but if the principles*.

He says first (1000a5), then, that there is a problem which has been neglected no less by the modern philosophers, who followed Plato, than by the ancient philosophers of nature, who also were puzzled about whether the principles of corruptible and incorruptible things are the same or different.

467. *For if they are the same* (1000a7). Here he advances an argument to show that the principles of corruptible things and of incorruptible things are not the same. In regard to this he does three things.

First (1000a7; [467]), he gives the argument.

Second (1000a9; [468]), he criticizes the solution of the proposed argument which the theological poets gave, at *the followers of Hesiod*.

Third (1000a19; [472]), he criticizes the solution which some philosophers of nature gave, at *however, from those who*.

He says first (1000a7), then, that if the principles of corruptible and of incorruptible things are held to be the

piis idem sequatur effectus, videtur quod omnia vel sint corruptibilia, vel omnia sint incorruptibilia. Relinquitur ergo quaestio quomodo quaedam sunt corruptibilia et quaedam incorruptibilia, et propter quam causam.

468. Deinde cum dicit *qui quidem* excludit solutionem poetarum theologorum.

Et primo ponit eorum solutionem.

Secundo obiicit contra praedictam positionem, ibi, *palam quod haec omnia sibi nota dicentes* et cetera.

Tertio se excusat a diligentiori improbatione huius positionis, ibi, *sed de fabulose* et cetera.

Circa primum considerandum est, quod apud Graecos, aut naturales philosophos, fuerunt quidam sapientiae studentes, qui deis se intromiserunt occultantes veritatem divinorum sub quodam tegmine fabularum, sicut Orpheus, Hesiodus et quidam alii: sicut etiam Plato occultavit veritatem philosophiae sub mathematicis, ut dicit Simplicius in commento *Praedicamentorum*. Dicit ergo, quod sectatores Hesiodi, et omnes, qui dicebantur theologi, curaverunt persuadere solis sibi, et nos alios spreverunt; quia scilicet veritatem, quam intellexerunt, taliter tradiderunt, quod eis solum possit esse nota. Si enim per fabulas veritas obumbretur, non potest sciri quid verum sub fabula lateat, nisi ab eo qui fabulam confixerit. Ii igitur Hesiodistae prima rerum principia deos nominaverunt; et dixerunt, quod illi de numero deorum, qui non gustaverunt de quodam dulci cibo, qui vocatur nectar vel manna, facti sunt mortales; illi vero qui gustaverunt, facti sunt immortales.

469. Potuit autem sub hac fabula aliquid veritatis occulte latere, ut scilicet per nectar et manna intelligatur ipsa suprema bonitas primi principii. Nam omnis dulcedo dilectionis et amoris ad bonitatem refertur. Omne autem bonum a primo bono derivatur. Potuit ergo esse intellectus eorum quod ex participatione propinqua summae bonitatis aliqua incorruptibilia reddantur, sicut quae perfecte participant divinum esse. Quaedam vero propter longe distare a primo principio, quod est non gustare manna et nectar, non possunt perpetuitatem conservare secundum idem numero, sed secundum idem specie: sicut dicit Philosophus in secundo *De generatione*. Sed utrum hoc intenderint occulte tradere, vel aliud, ex hoc dicto plenius percipi non potest.

470. Deinde cum dicit *palam quod* obiicit contra praedictam positionem: et dicit, quod praedicti Hesiodistae quid significare voluerint per ista nomina nectar et manna, fuit eis notum, sed non nobis. Et ideo quomodo afferantur istae causae ad istam quaestionem solvendam, et ad incorruptionem praestandam rebus, dixerunt su-

same, since from the same principles there follow the same effects, it seems that either all things are corruptible or all are incorruptible. Therefore, the question arises of how some things are corruptible and others incorruptible, and what the reason is.

468. *The followers of Hesiod* (1000a9). He criticizes the solution given by the theological poets.

First (1000a9; [468]), he gives their solution.

Second (1000a13; [470]), he argues against it, at *and it is clear that*.

Third (1000a18; [471]), he gives the reason why he does not criticize this position with more care, at *but with regard to those*.

Concerning the first (1000a9), it must be noted that there were among the Greeks, or philosophers of nature, certain students of wisdom (such as Orpheus, Hesiod, and certain others) who were concerned with the gods and hid the truth about the gods under a cloak of fables, just as Plato hid philosophical truth under mathematics (as Simplicius says in his *Commentary on the Categories*). Therefore, he says that the followers of Hesiod, and all those who were called theologians, paid attention to what was convincing to themselves and have neglected us, because the truth which they understood was treated by them in such a way that it could be known only to themselves. For if the truth is obscured by fables, then the truth which underlies these fables can be known only to the one who devised them. Therefore, the followers of Hesiod called the first principles of things gods, and said that those among the gods who have not tasted a certain delectable food called nectar or manna became mortal, whereas those who had tasted it became immortal.

469. But some part of the truth could lie hidden under this fable, provided that by nectar or manna is understood the supreme goodness itself of the first principle. For all the sweetness of love and affection is referred to goodness. But every good is derived from a first good. Therefore, the meaning of these words could be that some things are incorruptible by reason of an intimate participation in the highest good, as those which participate perfectly in the divine being. But certain things, because of their remoteness from the first principle, which is the meaning of "not tasting manna and nectar," cannot remain perpetually the same in number, but only in species, as the Philosopher says in *On Generation and Corruption* 2. But whether they intended to treat this obscurely, or something else, cannot be perceived any more fully from this statement.

470. *And it is clear* (1000a13). He argues against the aforesaid position. He says that the meaning which these followers of Hesiod wished to convey by the terms "nectar" or "manna" was known to them but not to us. Therefore, their explanation of the way in which these causes are meant to solve this question and preserve things from

pra nostrum intellectum. Si enim intelligantur ista verba secundum quod sonant, nullius efficaciae esse videntur. Dii enim, qui gustaverunt nectar et manna, aut gustaverunt propter delectationem, aut propter necessitatem essendi.

His enim de causis aliqui sumunt cibum. Siquidem sumpserunt ista propter delectationem, non possunt nectar et manna esse eis causa existendi, ita quod per hoc incorruptibiles reddantur: quia delectatio est quoddam consequens ad esse. Si autem propter necessitatem essendi praedicta sumpserunt, non erunt semper iterum cibo indigentes. Videtur ergo quod corruptibiles existentes prius tamquam cibo indigentes, per cibum facti sunt incorruptibiles. Quod iterum videtur inconveniens; quia cibus non nutrit in sua specie, nisi corruptus transeat in speciem nutriti. Quod autem est corruptibile, non potest alii incorruptionem praestare.

471. Deinde cum dicit *sed de fabulose* excusat se a diligentiori huius opinionis investigatione: et dicit quod de illis, qui philosophari coluerunt *fabulose*, veritatem scilicet sapientiae sub fabulis occultantes non est dignum cum studio intendere. Quia si quis contra dicta eorum disputaret secundum quod exterius sonant, ridiculosa sunt. Si vero aliquis velit de his inquirere secundum veritatem fabulis occultatam, immanifesta est. Ex quo accipitur quod Aristoteles disputans contra Platonem et alios huiusmodi, qui tradiderunt suam doctrinam occultantes sub quibusdam aliis rebus, non disputat secundum veritatem occultam, sed secundum ea quae exterius proponuntur.

472. Deinde cum dicit *a dicentibus* disputat contra responsionem quorumdam philosophorum naturalium. Et circa hoc tria facit.

Primo recitat rationem.

Secundo ponit responsionem, ibi, *etenim quam existimabit* et cetera.

Tertio improbat ipsam, ibi, *videbitur autem* et cetera.

Dicit ergo primo, quod praetermissis illis, qui sub fabulis veritatem tradiderunt, oportet a tradentibus veritatem per modum demonstrationis inquirere de quaestione praedicta: scilicet, si ex eisdem principiis sunt omnia existentia, quare quaedam existentium naturaliter sunt sempiterna, quaedam vero corrumpantur. Et quia nec ipsi causam dicunt quare hoc sit, nec rationabile est sic se habere, ut ex eisdem principiis existentium quaedam sint corruptibilia, quaedam sempiterna: vide-

corruption is beyond our understanding. For if these terms are understood in their literal sense, they appear to be inadequate, because the gods who tasted nectar or manna did so either for the sake of pleasure or because these things were necessary for their existence, since these are the reasons why men partake of food.

Now if they partook of them for the sake of pleasure, nectar and manna could not be the cause of their existence so as to make them incorruptible, because pleasure is something that follows on being. But if they partook of the aforesaid nourishment because they needed it to exist, they would not be eternal, having repeated need of food. Therefore, it seems that gods who are first corruptible, as it were, standing as they do in need of food, are made incorruptible by means of food. This also seems to be unreasonable, because food does not nourish a thing according to its species unless it is corrupted and passes over into the species of the one nourished. But nothing that is corruptible can be responsible for the incorruptibility of something else.

471. *But with regard to those* (1000a18). Here he gives his reason for not investigating this opinion with more care. He says that it is not worth our while to pay any attention to those who have philosophized *by using fables*, that is, by hiding philosophical truth under fables. For if anyone argues against their statements insofar as they are taken in a literal sense, these statements are ridiculous. But if one wishes to inquire into the truth hidden by these fables, it is not evident. Hence it is understood that Aristotle, in arguing against Plato and other thinkers of this kind who have treated their own doctrines by hiding them under something else, does not argue about the truth which is hidden, but about those things that are outwardly expressed.

472. *However, from those who make assertions* (1000a19). Then he argues against the answer given by some of the philosophers of nature, and in regard to this he does three things.

First (1000a19; [472]), he gives the argument.

Second (1000a24; [473]), he gives the answer, at *for the explanation*.

Third (1000a28; [474]), he criticizes it, at *yet even hate*.

Accordingly, he says, first (1000a19), that, having dismissed those who treated the truth by using fables, it is necessary to seek information about the aforesaid question from those who have treated the truth in a demonstrative way, by asking them why it is that, if all beings are derived from the same principles, some beings are eternal by nature and others are corrupted. And since these men give no reason why this is so, and since it is unreasonable that things should be as they say (namely, that, in the case of beings

tur manifeste sequi quod non sunt eadem principia nec causae corruptibilium et sempiternorum.

473. Deinde cum dicit *etenim quam* ponit quamdam solutionem: et dicit, quod ratio assignata circa praedictam dubitationem, quae maxime videtur esse conveniens ad quaestionem, est quam assignavit Empedocles: qui tamen idem passus est cum aliis: quia ratio quam assignavit, non est conveniens, sicut nec aliorum, ut ostendetur. Posuit enim quaedam principia communia corruptibilium et incorruptibilium; sed posuit quoddam principium esse causam specialem corruptionis, scilicet odium elementorum: ita scilicet quod adiunctio huius causae ad alia principia facit corruptionem in rebus.

474. Deinde cum dicit *videbitur autem* improbat praedictam rationem Empedoclis: et hoc tripliciter.

Primo quidem ostendendo, quod ratio ab eo assignata non convenit suae positioni.

Secundo ostendendo, quod non est sufficiens, ibi, *similiter quoque ipsius transmutationis* et cetera.

Tertio ostendendo quod non est ad propositum, ibi, *attamen tantum solum dicit* et cetera.

Circa primum tria facit.

Primo ostendit suam rationem non convenire aliis eius positionibus ex parte odii.

Secundo ex parte ipsius Dei, ibi, *propter quod* et cetera.

Tertio ex parte amoris, ibi, *similiter autem nec amor* et cetera.

Dicit ergo primo, quod inconvenienter Empedocles ponit odium esse causam corruptionis: quia non minus secundum eius positionem videtur esse causa generationis in omnibus rebus, nisi in una re tantum. Ponebat enim omnia alia essentialiter composita ex odio simul cum aliis principiis, nisi solus Deus, quem ponebat compositum esse ex aliis principiis praeter odium. Deum autem appellabat caelum, sicut supradictum est in primo, quod Xenophanes ad totum caelum respiciens, ipsum unum dicit esse Deum.

Ponebat autem Empedocles caelum esse compositum ex quatuor elementis, et ex amicitia: non autem ex lite sive ex odio, considerans indissolubilitatem caeli. Sed quantum ad alias res dicebat, quod omnia sunt ex odio quaecumque sunt, erunt vel fuerunt: sicut arbores pullulantes, et viri, et feminae, et bestiae quae sunt animalia terrestria: et vultures, quae sunt volantia diu viventia: et pisces nutriti in aqua, et dii longaevi.

Videtur autem hos deos vocare vel stellas, quas ponebat quandoque corrumpi, licet post longum tempus: vel

having the same principles, some should be corruptible and others eternal), it seems clearly to follow that corruptible and eternal things do not have the same principles or the same causes.

473. *For the explanation* (1000a24). Then he gives one solution. He says that the explanation given to the aforesaid question which seems to fit it best is the one which Empedocles gave, although he was subject to the same error as the others, because the explanation which he gave is no more adequate than theirs, as is about to be shown. For he maintained that corruptible and incorruptible things have certain common principles, but that a special principle, hate, causes the corruption of the elements in such a way that the coming together of this cause and another principle produces corruption in the world.

474. *Yet even hate* (1000a28). Here he criticizes Empedocles' argument, and he does this in three ways.

First (1000a28; [474]), he does this by showing that the argument which Empedocles gave is not in keeping with his position;

second (1000b12; [478]), by showing that it is not adequate, at *moreover, he does not*;

third (1000b17; [481]), by showing that it is not to the point, at *yet he alone speaks*.

In regard to the first, he does three things.

First, he shows that Empedocles' argument does not agree with his other views about hate;

second (1000b3; [476]), that it does not agree with his view about God himself, at *for this reason*;

and third (1000b11; [477]), that it does not agree with his view about love, at *nor, similarly*.

Accordingly, he says, first (1000a28), that Empedocles' position that hate is the cause of corruption is untenable, because according to his position hate also seems to be the cause of the generation of all things except one. For he held that everything else is composed essentially of hate along with the other principles, with the exception of God alone, whom he claimed to be composed of the other principles without hate. Moreover, he called the heavens God, as was stated above in book 1 (984b23; [101]), because Xenophanes, after reflecting upon the whole heavens, said that the one itself is God.

And Empedocles, considering the indestructibleness of the heavens, held that the heavens are composed of the four elements and love, but not of strife or hatred. But in the case of other things, he said that all those which are or were or will be come from hate, such as sprouting trees, and men and women, and beasts (which are terrestrial animals), and vultures (which are flying and long-lived animals), and fish (which are nourished in the water), and the long-lived gods.

And by the gods he seems to mean either the stars, which he held are sometimes corrupted (although after a

daemones quos ponebant Platonici esse animalia aerea. Vel etiam dii quos ponebant Epicurei in forma humana, sicut supra dictum est. Ex hoc ergo quod omnia animalia praeter unum sunt generata ex odio, potest haberi quod odium sit causa generationis.

475. Et praeter hoc etiam ex alia ratione. Manifestum est enim secundum positionem Empedoclis quod, si non esset odium in rebus, omnia essent unum. Odium enim est causa distinctionis secundum Empedoclem. Unde inducit verba Empedoclis dicentis, quod quando omnes res in unum conveniunt, ut puta quando fit chaos, tunc ultimum stabit odium separans et dissolvens. Unde litera Boetii habet: *ea enim convenit, tunc ultimam scit discordiam*. Et sic patet quod, cum esse mundi consistat in distinctione rerum, odium est causa generationis mundi.

476. Deinde cum dicit *propter quod* ponit secundam rationem sumptam ex parte Dei: et dicit, quod cum Empedocles poneret odium non esse de compositione Dei, accidit secundum rationes eius, quod Deus, qui est felicissimus secundum omnium dicta, et per consequens maxime cognoscens, sit minus prudens omnibus aliis cognoscentibus. Sequetur enim, secundum positionem Empedoclis, quod non cognoscat omnia elementa, quia non habet odium; unde non cognoscit ipsum. Cognoscit autem simile simili secundum opinionem Empedoclis qui dixit, quod per terram cognoscimus terram, per aquam cognoscimus aquam *et affectum*, idest amorem vel concordiam cognoscimus *per affectum*, idest amorem vel concordiam: et similiter *odium per odium*, quod est triste sive grave vel malum secundum literam Boetii, qui dicit *discordiam autem discordia malum*. Sic igitur patet, quod Aristoteles reputat inconveniens, et contra id quod ponitur Deus felicissimus, quod ipse ignoret aliquid eorum, quae nos scimus. Sed quia ista ratio videbatur esse praeter propositum, ideo ad principale propositum rediens, dicit, quod redeundo ad illud unde prius erat ratio, manifestum est quod accidit Empedocli quod odium non sit magis causa corruptionis quam existendi.

477. Deinde cum dicit *similiter autem* ponit tertiam rationem ex parte amoris: et dicit, quod similiter etiam amor non est causa generationis vel existendi, ut ipse ponebat, si alia eius positio attendatur. Dicebat enim quod cum omnia elementa in unum congregabuntur, tunc erit corruptio mundi. Et sic amor corrumpit omnia: ergo quantum ad totum mundum amor erat causa corruptionis, odium autem generationis. Quantum autem ad singulares odium erat causa corruptionis et amor generationis.

long period of time), or the demons, which the Platonists held to be ethereal animals. Or by the gods he also means those beings whom the Epicureans held to be of human form, as was stated above (997b5; [408]). Therefore, from the fact that all living things except one are generated from hate, it can be said that hate is the cause of generation.

475. And in addition to this there is another reason, for, according to Empedocles' position, it is evident that, if hate did not exist in the world, all things would be one, since hate is the reason why things are distinct. Hence he quotes Empedocles' words to the effect that, when all things come together into a unity (for example, when chaos comes into being), hate will stand last of all, separating and dissolving things. Hence the text of Boethius says: *when it comes together, then chaos knows the ultimate discord*. Thus it is clear that, since the being of the world consists in the distinction of things, hate is the cause of the world's generation.

476. *For this reason* (1000b3). Here he gives a second argument, which pertains to the deity. He says that, since Empedocles would hold that hate is not a constituent of the divine composition, it follows, according to his arguments, that God, who is said by all men to be most happy, and consequently most knowing, is less prudent than all other beings who have knowledge. For, according to Empedodes' position, it follows that God does not know the elements because he does not contain hate. Hence he does not know himself. And like knows like according to the opinion of Empedodes, who said that by earth we know earth, by water, water, and *by affection*, which is love or concord, we know *affection*, or love or concord. And in a similar way we know *hate by mournful hate*, which is sadness, whether unpleasant or evil, according to the text of Boethius, who says that *by evil discord we know discord*. It is evident, then, that Aristotle thought this untenable and contrary to the position that God is most happy, because he himself would not know some of the things that we know. And since this argument seemed to be beside the point, therefore, returning to his principal theme, he says (1000b8) that, in returning to the point from which the first argument began, it is evident, so far as Empedocles is concerned, that hate is no more a cause of corruption than of being.

477. *Nor, similarly, is love* (1000b11). Here he gives the third argument, which pertains to love. He says that in like manner love is not the cause of generation or being, as Empedocles claimed, if another position of his is considered. For he said that, when all the elements are combined into a unity, the corruption of the world will then take place. Thus love corrupts all things. Therefore, with respect to the world in general, love is the cause of corruption, whereas hate is the cause of generation. But with respect to singular things, hate is the cause of corruption and love of generation.

478. Deinde cum dicit *similiter quoque* ostendit quod ratio eius non fuit sufficiens. Dicebat enim quamdam transmutationem esse in rebus odii et amicitiae, ita scilicet quod amor quandoque omnia uniebat, et postmodum omnia odium separabat. Sed causam, quare sic transmutabatur, ut quodam tempore dominaretur odium, et alio tempore amor, nullam aliam dicebat, nisi quia sic aptum natum est esse.

479. Et ponit consequenter verba Empedoclis, quae, quia in Graeco metrice scripta sunt, habent aliquam difficultatem et diversitatem a communi modo loquendi. Sunt autem haec verba eius, *sed itaque magnum odium in membris nutritum est, et ad honorem intendebat perfecto tempore, qui mutabilis dissolvit sacramentum.* Litera vero Boetii sic habet *sed cum magna discordia in membris alita sit in honores: quia processit completo anno, qui illis mutatis amplo rediit sacramento.* Ad cuius intellectum notandum est, quod loquitur poetice de toto mundo, ad similitudinem unius animalis, in cuius membris et partibus primo quidem est magna convenientia, quam amorem nominabat sive concordiam: sed postea paulatim incipit aliqua dissonantia esse, quam dicit discordiam. Et similiter in partibus universi a principio erat magna concordia, sed postea paulatim nutritur odium quousque odium praecedat *ad honorem*, idest ad hoc quod dominetur super elementa. Quod quidem fit perfecto tempore quodam determinato, vel completo quodam anno, quem ponebat Empedocles: *qui*, scilicet odium et discordia, vel annus mutabilis existens dissolvit *sacramentum*, idest unionem praeexistentem elementorum, vel annus sive odium rediit amplo sacramento, quia quadam potentia et secreta virtute rediit ad dominandum in rebus.

480. Post quae verba Empedoclis Aristoteles faciens vim in hoc quod dixerat *mutabilis*, subiungit exponens quasi necessarium ens transmutari: quasi dicat: sic praedicta dixit Empedocles ac si necessarium sit esse transmutationem odii et amoris: sed nullam causam ostendit huius necessitatis. In uno enim animali est manifesta causa transmutationis et odii et amoris, propter motum caeli, qui causat generationem et corruptionem in rebus. Sed talis causa non potest assignari totius universi sic transmutati per amicitiam et litem. Unde patet, quod eius ratio fuit insufficiens.

481. Deinde cum dicit *attamen tantum* ostendit quod praedicta ratio Empedoclis non est ad propositum: et dicit quod hoc solum videtur dicere *confesse*, idest manifeste, quod non ponit quaedam existentium ex principiis esse corruptibilia, et quaedam non corruptibilia, sed omnia ponit esse corruptibilia praeter sola elementa. Et ita videtur evadere praedictam dubitatio-

478. *Moreover, he does* (1000b12). Here he shows that Empedocles' argument is not adequate. For Empedocles said that there exists in the world a certain alternation of hate and friendship, in such a way that at one time love unites all things and afterward hate separates them. But as to the reason why this alternation takes place, so that at one time hate predominates and at another time love, he said nothing more than that it was naturally disposed to be so.

479. And next he gives Empedocles' words, which, because they are written in Greek verse, are difficult and differ from the common way of speaking. These words are: *but thus mighty hate was nourished among the members and rose to a position of honor when the time was fulfilled, which, being changeable, dissolved the bond* (1000b14). But the text of Boethius runs thus: *but when mighty discord in the members was promoted to a place of honor, because it marched forward in a completed year, which, when these things have been changed, returns to a full bond.* Now in order to understand this it must be noted that he speaks poetically of the whole world as though it were a single living thing in whose members and parts there is found at first the greatest harmony, which he calls love or concord, and afterward there begins to exist little by little a certain dissonance, which he calls discord. And, similarly, in the parts of the universe at first there was maximum concord, and afterward hate was nourished little by little until it acquired *a position of honor*, that is, it acquired dominion over the elements. This comes about when a completed time is reached or a year is completed, as Empedocles held, *which* (hate or discord, or the year), being changeable, dissolves *the bond*, that is, the former union of the elements. Or the year or hate returns to a full bond because by a certain ability and hidden power it returns to predominate over things.

480. After these words of Empedocles, Aristotle, in giving the meaning of the word *changeable* which he used, explains it as though change were necessary. For he says that Empedocles made the foregoing statements as though it were necessary that there should be an alternation of hate and love, but he gives no reason for this necessity. For, in the case of this one living thing, it is evident that what causes the alternation of hate and love is the motion of the heavens which causes generation and corruption in the world. But no such cause can be assigned for why the whole should be changed in this way by love and hate. Hence it is clear that his argument was inadequate.

481. *Yet he alone* (1000b17). Here he shows that this argument of Empedocles is not to the point. He says that Empedocles seems to say *expressly*, or clearly, only that he does not hold that some of the things derived from these principles are corruptible and others incorruptible, but he holds that all things are corruptible with the exception of the elements alone. Thus he seems to avoid the forego-

nem, qua dubitabatur, quare quaedam sunt corruptibilia et quaedam non, si sunt ex eisdem principiis? Unde etiam patet, quod eius ratio non est ad propositum, quia interemit id de quo est dubitatio.

482. Sed potest quaeri quomodo hic dicit, quod Empedocles ponebat omnia esse corruptibilia praeter elementa, cum supra dixerit unum esse Deum, scilicet ex aliis principiis compositum praeter quam ex odio?

Sed dicendum, quod Empedocles ponebat duplicem corruptionem in rebus, sicut ex praedictis patet. Unam quidem secundum confusionem totius universi, quam faciebat amor; et ab hac corruptione nec ipsum Deum faciebat immunem, cum in eo poneret amorem, qui alia ei commiscebat. Aliam autem corruptionem ponebat singularium rerum, quarum principium est odium. Et hanc corruptionem excludebat a Deo per hoc, quod in eo odium non ponebat. Sic igitur Aristoteles epilogando concludit tot dicta esse ad ostendendum, quod non sunt eadem principia corruptibilium et incorruptibilium.

483. Deinde cum dicit *si vero* obiicit ad contrariam partem per duas rationes:

quarum prima est: si non sint eadem principia corruptibilium et incorruptibilium, relinquitur quaestio, utrum principia corruptibilium sint corruptibilia, an incorruptibilia. Si dicatur quod sint corruptibilia, ostendit hoc esse falsum duplici ratione.

Quarum prima est: omne corruptibile corrumpitur in ea ex quibus est: si igitur principia corruptibilium sunt corruptibilia, oportet iterum ponere alia principia ex quibus sint. Et hoc inconveniens est, nisi ponantur principia procedere in infinitum.

Ostensum autem est in secundo quod secundum nullum genus causae contingit in principiis procedere in infinitum. Similiter etiam est inconveniens si dicatur, quod fit status in principiis corruptibilibus; cum corruptio videatur esse per resolutionem in aliqua priora.

484. Secunda ratio est, quia si principia corruptibilium sint corruptibilia, oportet quod corrumpantur, quia omne corruptibile corrumpetur. Sed postquam sunt corrupta non possunt esse principia; quia quod corrumpitur vel corruptum est, non potest causare aliquid. Cum ergo corruptibilia semper causentur per successionem, non potest dici, quod principia corruptibilium sint corruptibilia.

485. Si autem dicatur, quod principia corruptibilium sunt incorruptibilia, manifestum est quod principia incorruptibilium sunt incorruptibilia. Relinquitur ergo

ing problem inasmuch as the question remains why some things are corruptible and some not, if they come from the same principles. Hence it is also clear that his argument is not to the point, because he neglects the very point that requires explanation.

482. But it can be asked how he can say here that Empedocles held all things to be corruptible except the elements, since Empedocles has said above that the one is God, that is, what is composed of the other principles except hate.

It must be noted, however, that Empedocles posited two processes of corruption in the world, as is clear from what was said above. He posited one with respect to the blending of the whole universe, which was brought about by love. From this process he did not make even God immune, because in God he placed love, which caused other things to be mixed with God. And he posited another process of corruption for singular things, and the principle of this process is hate. But he excluded this kind of corruption from God, seeing that he did not posit hate in God. In summing up, then, Aristotle concludes that this much has been said for the purpose of showing that corruptible and incorruptible things do not have the same principles.

483. *But if the principles* (1000b23). Here he argues the other side of the question, with two arguments.

The first is this. If the principles of corruptible and incorruptible things are not the same, the question arises of whether the principles of corruptible things are corruptible or incorruptible. If one says that they are corruptible, he proves that this is false by two arguments.

The first runs thus. Every corruptible thing is dissolved into the principles of which it is composed. If, then, the principles of corruptible things are corruptible, it will be necessary to hold also that there are other principles from which they are derived. But this is untenable, unless an infinite regress is posited.

Now it was shown in book 2 (994a1; [299]) that it is impossible to have an infinite regress in principles in any genus of cause. And it would be just as untenable for someone to say that this condition applies in the case of corruptible principles, since corruption seems to come about as a result of something being dissolved into prior principles.

484. The second argument runs thus. If the principles of corruptible things are corruptible, they must be corrupted, because every corruptible thing will be corrupted. But after they have been corrupted they cannot be principles, for what is corrupted or has been corrupted cannot cause anything. Therefore, since corruptible things are always caused in succession, the principles of corruptible things cannot be said to be corruptible.

485. Again, if it is said that the principles of corruptible things are incorruptible, evidently the principles of incorruptible things are incorruptible. Therefore, the question

quaestio, quare ex quibusdam incorruptibilibus principiis producantur effectus corruptibiles, et ex quibusdam effectus incorruptibiles. Hoc enim non videtur esse rationabile; sed aut est impossibile, aut indiget multa manifestatione.

486. Deinde cum dicit *amplius autem* secundam rationem ad principale propositum ponit, quae sumitur ex communi opinione omnium. Nullus enim conatus est hoc dicere, quod sint diversa principia corruptibilium et incorruptibilium; sed omnes dicunt eadem esse principia omnium. Et tamen id quod primo obiectum est, scilicet pro prima parte, ac si esset aliquid modicum omnes leviter transeunt, quod est concedere. Unde litera Boetii habet, *sed primum obiectum deglutiunt, sicut hoc parvum quoddam opinantes.*

487. Huius autem dubitationis solutio ponitur in duodecimo: ubi Philosophus ostendit prima quidem principia activa vel motiva esse eadem omnium sed quodam ordine. Nam prima quidem sunt principia simpliciter incorruptibilia et immobilia. Sunt autem secunda incorruptibilia et mobilia, scilicet caelestia corpora, quae per sui motum causant generationem et corruptionem in rebus. Principia autem intrinseca non sunt eadem numero corruptibilium et incorruptibilium, sed secundum analogiam. Nec tamen principia intrinseca corruptibilium, quae sunt materia et forma, sunt corruptibilia per se, sed solum per accidens. Sic enim corrumpitur materia et forma corruptibilium, ut habetur in primo *Physicorum.*

remains of why it is that, from certain incorruptible principles, corruptible effects are produced, and from certain others, incorruptible effects are produced. For this seems to be unreasonable and either is impossible or requires considerable explanation.

486. *Further, no one* (1000b32). Then, relative to his main thesis, he gives his second argument, which is drawn from the common opinions of all men. For no one has attempted to say that corruptible and incorruptible things have different principles, but all say that all things have the same principles. Yet, all pass lightly over the first argument, given in favor of the first part of the question, as though it were of little importance; but this is to acknowledge its truth. Hence the text of Boethius says: *but they swallow the first argument as though they considered it a minor matter.*

487. Now the solution to this problem is given in book 12 [2553], where the Philosopher shows that the first active or motive principles of all things are the same, but in a certain sequence. For the first principles of things are unqualifiedly incorruptible and immobile, whereas the second are incorruptible and mobile, that is, the celestial bodies, which cause generation and corruption in the world as a result of their motion. Now the intrinsic principles of corruptible things and of incorruptible things are the same, not numerically but analogically. Still the intrinsic principles of corruptible things, which are matter and form, are not corruptible in themselves, but only accidentally. For it is in this way that the matter and form of corruptible things are corrupted, as is stated in *Physics* 1.

LECTURE 12

Are unity and being the substance and principle of all things?

1001a4 Omnium autem ad considerandum difficillimum et ad cognoscendum veritatem maxime necessarium, utrum unum et ens substantiae entium sunt: et utrum ipsorum non alterum aliquid ens, hoc quidem unum, hoc autem quidem ens est. Aut oportet quaerere quid sit ipsum ens et unum, quasi subiecta alia natura. [488]

1001a8 Hi namque illo modo, illi hoc modo putant naturam se habere. [489]

Plato namque et Pythagorici non aliquid aliud ens nec unum, sed hoc ipsorum naturam esse quasi existente substantia ipsum unum esse et ens aliquid.

Aliis vero de natura ut Empedocles, ut ad aliquid notius reducens, dicit quod unum ens est: videbitur enim utique dicere hoc amorem esse, causa namque est hoc unum omnibus esse.

Alii vero ignem, alii aerem dicunt esse unum hoc et ens, ex quo entia esse et facta esse. Similiter et qui plura elementa ponunt. Necesse namque et his tot dicere ens et unum, quot principia dicunt esse.

1001a19 Accidit autem siquidem quis non ponit esse quamdam substantiam unum et ens, neque aliorum esse universalium nullum: haec namque universalia sunt maxime omnium. Si vero non est aliquid unum ipsum nec ipsum ens, vix aliorum aliquid erit praeter ea, quae dicta sunt, singula. Amplius autem non existente unius substantia, palam quia nec numerus erit quasi natura alia ab existentibus separata. Numerus enim unitates. Unitas vero quod vere unum aliquid est. Si autem est aliquid ipsum

πάντων δὲ καὶ θεωρῆσαι χαλεπώτατον καὶ πρὸς τὸ {5} γνῶναι τἀληθὲς ἀναγκαιότατον πότερόν ποτε τὸ ὂν καὶ τὸ ἓν οὐσίαι τῶν ὄντων εἰσί, καὶ ἑκάτερον αὐτῶν οὐχ ἕτερόν τι ὂν τὸ μὲν ἓν τὸ δὲ ὂν ἐστιν, ἢ δεῖ ζητεῖν τί ποτ᾽ ἐστὶ τὸ ὂν καὶ τὸ ἓν ὡς ὑποκειμένης ἄλλης φύσεως.

οἱ μὲν γὰρ ἐκείνως οἱ δ᾽ οὕτως οἴονται τὴν φύσιν ἔχειν.

Πλάτων {10} μὲν γὰρ καὶ οἱ Πυθαγόρειοι οὐχ ἕτερόν τι τὸ ὂν οὐδὲ τὸ ἓν ἀλλὰ τοῦτο αὐτῶν τὴν φύσιν εἶναι, ὡς οὔσης τῆς οὐσίας αὐτοῦ τοῦ ἑνὶ εἶναι καὶ ὄντι:

οἱ δὲ περὶ φύσεως, οἷον Ἐμπεδοκλῆς ὡς εἰς γνωριμώτερον ἀνάγων λέγει ὅ τι τὸ ἕν ἐστιν: δόξειε γὰρ ἂν λέγειν τοῦτο τὴν φιλίαν εἶναι (αἰτία {15} γοῦν ἐστιν αὕτη τοῦ ἓν εἶναι πᾶσιν),

ἕτεροι δὲ πῦρ, οἱ δ᾽ ἀέρα φασὶν εἶναι τὸ ἓν τοῦτο καὶ τὸ ὄν, ἐξ οὗ τὰ ὄντα εἶναί τε καὶ γεγονέναι. ὡς δ᾽ αὕτως καὶ οἱ πλείω τὰ στοιχεῖα τιθέμενοι: ἀνάγκη γὰρ καὶ τούτοις τοσαῦτα λέγειν τὸ ἓν καὶ τὸ ὂν ὅσας περ ἀρχὰς εἶναί φασιν.

συμβαίνει {20} δέ, εἰ μέν τις μὴ θήσεται εἶναί τινα οὐσίαν τὸ ἓν καὶ τὸ ὄν, μηδὲ τῶν ἄλλων εἶναι τῶν καθόλου μηθέν (ταῦτα γάρ ἐστι καθόλου μάλιστα πάντων, εἰ δὲ μὴ ἔστι τι ἓν αὐτὸ μηδ᾽ αὐτὸ ὄν, σχολῇ τῶν γε ἄλλων τι ἂν εἴη παρὰ τὰ λεγόμενα καθ᾽ ἕκαστα), ἔτι δὲ μὴ ὄντος τοῦ ἑνὸς οὐσίας, {25} δῆλον ὅτι οὐδ᾽ ἂν ἀριθμὸς εἴη ὡς κεχωρισμένη τις φύσις τῶν ὄντων (ὁ μὲν γὰρ ἀριθμὸς μονάδες, ἡ δὲ μονὰς ὅπερ ἕν τί ἐστιν): εἰ δ᾽ ἔστι τι αὐτὸ ἓν καὶ ὄν, ἀναγκαῖον οὐσίαν αὐτῶν εἶναι τὸ ἓν καὶ τὸ ὄν:

But the most difficult problem which has to be considered, and the one which is most necessary for a knowledge of the truth, is whether unity and being are the substance of existing things, and whether each of them is nothing else than unity and being. Or whether it is necessary to investigate what being and unity themselves are, as though there were some other nature which underlies them.

For some think that reality is of the former sort, and some of the latter.

For Plato and the Pythagoreans thought that being and unity were nothing else than themselves, and that this is their nature, their substance being simply unity and being. But among the other philosophers there are different opinions about the nature of unity.

Empedocles, for example, as though reducing it to something better known, says that unity is being; for he would seem to say that this is love, since this is the cause of why unity belongs to all things.

Others say that this unity and being of which existing things consist and have been made is fire, and others say it is air. And those who hold that there are many elements say the same thing; for they must also speak of unity and being in as many ways as they say there are principles.

But if anyone holds that unity and being are not substances, it will follow that no other universals are such, for these are the most universal of all. But if there is no one-in-itself or being-in-itself, there will hardly be any other things that exist apart from what are called singular things. Further, if unity is not a substance, evidently number will not exist as another reality separate from existing things, for number is of units, and a unit is truly something one. But if there is a one-in-itself and being-in-itself, the substance of these

unum et ens, necesse est substantiam ipsorum esse ipsum unum et ens: non enim aliquid universaliter praedicatur, sed haec ipsa. [490]

οὐ γὰρ ἕτερόν τι καθόλου κατηγορεῖται ἀλλὰ ταῦτα αὐτά.

must be unity itself and being itself. For nothing else is predicated universally of all things but these two.

1001a29 At vero si erit aliquid ens ipsum et ipsum unum, multa erat dubitatio quomodo erat diversum aliquod praeter haec. Dico autem, quomodo erunt uno plura entia? Quod enim diversum est ab ente, non est. Quare secundum Parmenidis rationem accidere necesse est, unum omnia esse entia et hoc esse ens. [493]

ἀλλὰ μὴν εἴ γ᾽ ἔσται {30} τι αὐτὸ ὂν καὶ αὐτὸ ἕν, πολλὴ ἀπορία πῶς ἔσται τι παρὰ ταῦτα ἕτερον, λέγω δὲ πῶς ἔσται πλείω ἑνὸς τὰ ὄντα. τὸ γὰρ ἕτερον τοῦ ὄντος οὐκ ἔστιν, ὥστε κατὰ τὸν Παρμενίδου συμβαίνειν ἀνάγκη λόγον ἓν ἅπαντα εἶναι τὰ ὄντα καὶ τοῦτο εἶναι τὸ ὄν.

But, on the other hand, if there is to be a one-in-itself and being-in-itself, there is great difficulty in seeing how there will be anything else besides these. I mean, how will there be more beings than one? For that which differs from being does not exist, Hence according to Parmenides' argument it must follow that all beings are one, and that this is being.

1001b1 Utrobique vero difficile: sive namque non sit ipsum unum substantia, sive sit unum idem, substantiam esse numerum est impossibile. [494]

ἀμφοτέρως δὲ δύσκολον: ἄν τε γὰρ μὴ ᾖ τὸ ἓν οὐσία ἄν τε ᾖ τὸ αὐτὸ ἕν, ἀδύνατον τὸν ἀριθμὸν οὐσίαν εἶναι.

But there is a difficulty in either case; for whether unity itself is not a substance, or whether there is a unity itself, it is impossible for number to be a substance.

Siquidem igitur non sit, dictum est prius propter quid: si autem fuerit, eadem est dubitatio et de ente. Ex aliquo namque et praeter ens, erit ipsum aliud unum. Nihil enim esse est necesse. Omnia autem entia, aut unum sunt aut multa, quorum est unumquodque.

ἐὰν μὲν οὖν μὴ ᾖ, εἴρηται πρότερον δι᾽ ὅ: ἐὰν δὲ ᾖ, ἡ αὐτὴ ἀπορία καὶ περὶ τοῦ ὄντος. ἐκ τίνος γὰρ {5} παρὰ τὸ ἓν ἔσται αὐτὸ ἄλλο ἕν; ἀνάγκη γὰρ μὴ ἓν εἶναι: ἅπαντα δὲ τὰ ὄντα ἢ ἕν ἢ πολλὰ ὧν ἓν ἕκαστον.

Now it has already been stated why this follows if unity is not a substance; but if it is, the same difficulty will arise with regard to being. For from something outside of being something else will be one; for it must be not one. But all beings are either one or many, each of which is a one.

1001b7 Amplius si indivisibile est ipsum unum, secundum Zenonis dignitatem, nihil utique erit. [496]

ἔτι εἰ ἀδιαίρετον αὐτὸ τὸ ἕν, κατὰ μὲν τὸ Ζήνωνος ἀξίωμα οὐθὲν ἂν εἴη

Further, if unity itself is indivisible, according to Zeno's axiom it will be nothing.

Quod enim nec additum nec ablatum facit maius nec minus, non ait esse hoc existentium: tamquam palam existente magnitudine ipso ente.

(ὃ γὰρ μήτε προστιθέμενον μήτε ἀφαιρούμενον ποιεῖ μεῖζον μηδὲ ἔλαττον, οὔ φησιν εἶναι τοῦτο τῶν ὄντων, {10} ὡς δηλονότι ὄντος μεγέθους τοῦ ὄντος:

For that which when added does not make a thing greater or when subtracted does not make it smaller, this, he says, does not belong to the realm of existing things, as though it were evident that whatever has being is a continuous quantity.

Et si magnitudo, corporalis. Hoc enim omnino ens.

καὶ εἰ μέγεθος, σωματικόν: τοῦτο γὰρ πάντῃ ὄν:

And if it is a continuous quantity, it is bodily; for this in every respect is a being.

Alia vero aliqualiter quidem addita facient maius, aliqualiter autem nihil ut superficies et linea. Punctus vero et unitas nullatenus.

τὰ δὲ ἄλλα πῶς μὲν προστιθέμενα ποιήσει μεῖζον, πῶς δ᾽ οὐθέν, οἷον ἐπίπεδον καὶ γραμμή, στιγμὴ δὲ καὶ μονὰς οὐδαμῶς):

But other quantities (for example, a surface and a line) will make a thing greater when added in one way, but in another way they will not. A point and a unit will do so in no way.

1001b13 Sed quoniam hic speculatur onerose, et contingit esse indivisibile, ut et sic ad illum aliqua habetur responsio: maius enim non faciet, sed plus additum tale. [498]

ἀλλ᾽ ἐπειδὴ οὗτος θεωρεῖ φορτικῶς, καὶ ἐνδέχεται εἶναι ἀδιαίρετόν τι {15} ὥστε [καὶ οὕτως] καὶ πρὸς ἐκεῖνόν τιν᾽ ἀπολογίαν ἔχειν (μεῖζον μὲν γὰρ οὐ ποιήσει πλεῖον δὲ προστιθέμενον τὸ τοιοῦτον):

But this philosopher speculates clumsily, and it is possible for a thing to be indivisible in such a way that some answer may be made against him; for when something of this kind is added it will not make a thing greater, but more.

1001b17 Sed quomodo ex uno tali, aut pluribus erit magnitudo? Simile namque est et lineam ex punctis esse dicere. [499]

ἀλλὰ πῶς δὴ ἐξ ἑνὸς τοιούτου ἢ πλειόνων τοιούτων ἔσται μέγεθος; ὅμοιον γὰρ καὶ τὴν γραμμὴν ἐκ στιγμῶν εἶναι φάσκειν.

Yet how will continuous quantity come from such a unity or from many of them? For this would be like saying that a line is made up of points.

1001b19 At vero et si quis ita putat ut factus sit, ut quidam dicunt ex uno ipso et alio non uno aliquo, numerus, nihil minus est quaerendum quare et quomodo. Quandoque quidem numerus, quandoque autem magnitudo erit quod factum est, si non unum inaequalitas et eadem natura erat. Nec enim quomodo ex uno et hac, nec quomodo ex numero aliquo et hac fient utique magnitudines, palam. [500]

ἀλλὰ μὴν καὶ εἴ τις οὕτως ὑπολαμβάνει ὥστε {20} γενέσθαι, καθάπερ λέγουσί τινες, ἐκ τοῦ ἑνὸς αὐτοῦ καὶ ἄλλου μὴ ἑνός τινος τὸν ἀριθμόν, οὐθὲν ἧττον ζητητέον διὰ τί καὶ πῶς ὁτὲ μὲν ἀριθμὸς ὁτὲ δὲ μέγεθος ἔσται τὸ γενόμενον, εἴπερ τὸ μὴ ἓν ἡ ἀνισότης καὶ ἡ αὐτὴ φύσις ἦν. οὔτε γὰρ ὅπως ἐξ ἑνὸς καὶ ταύτης οὔτε ὅπως ἐξ ἀριθμοῦ {25} τινὸς καὶ ταύτης γένοιτ᾿ ἂν τὰ μεγέθη, δῆλον.

But even if someone were to think that number has come, as some say, from unity itself and from something else that is not one, nonetheless it would be necessary to inquire as to why and how the thing which has come to be would sometimes be a number and sometimes a continuous quantity, if that not-one were inequality and the same nature in either case. For it is not clear how continuous quantities would be produced from unity and this principle, or from some number and this principle.

---

488. Postquam Philosophus inquisivit utrum principia sint eadem vel diversa, hic inquirit quomodo se habeat ipsum unum ad hoc quod sit principium: et circa hoc tria facit.

Primo inquirit, an ipsum unum sit principium.

Secundo inquirit an numeri, qui ex uno oriuntur vel consequuntur, sint principia rerum, ibi, *horum autem habita dubitatio* et cetera.

Tertio inquirit utrum species, quae sunt quaedam unitates separatae, sint principia, ibi, *omnino vero dubitabit aliquis* et cetera.

Et circa primum tria facit.

Primo movet dubitationem.

Secundo ponit opiniones ad utramque partem, ibi, *hi namque illo modo*.

Tertio ponit rationes ad utramque partem, ibi, *accidit autem si quidem* et cetera.

Dicit ergo primo, quod inter omnes alias quaestiones motas una est difficilior ad considerandum, propter efficaciam rationum ad utramque partem, in qua etiam veritatem cognoscere est maxime necessarium, quia ex hoc dependet iudicium de substantiis rerum.

Est ergo quaestio ista, utrum unum et ens sint substantiae rerum, ita scilicet quod neutrum eorum oporteat attribuere alicui alteri naturae quae quasi informetur unitate et entitate, sed potius ipsa unitas et esse rei sit eius substantia: vel e contrario oportet inquirere quid sit illud, cui convenit esse unum vel ens, quasi quaedam alia natura subiecta entitati et unitati.

489. Deinde cum dicit *hi namque* ponit opiniones ad utramque partem: et dicit, quod philosophorum quidam opinati sunt naturam rerum se habere uno modo, quidam alio. Plato enim et Pythagorici non posuerunt quod unum et ens advenirent alicui naturae, sed unum et ens essent natura rerum, quasi hoc ipsum quod est esse et unitas sit substantia rerum. Alii vero philosophi de naturalibus loquentes, attribuerunt unum et ens aliquibus

488. Having asked whether the principles of things are the same or different, the Philosopher now asks how unity itself could have the nature of a principle, and in regard to this he does three things.

First, he asks whether unity itself is a principle;

second (1001b26; [502]), he asks whether numbers, which arise or follow from unity, are the principles of things, at *and connected with these*;

third (1002b12; [515]), whether the forms, which are certain separate unities, are the principles of things, at *but in general one will wonder*.

In regard to the first he does three things.

First, he raises the question.

Second (1001a8; [489]), he gives the opinions on both sides, at *for some think*.

Third (1001a19; [490]), he advances arguments on both sides, at *but if anyone*.

He says first (1001a4) that, of all the different questions which have been raised, one is more difficult to consider because of the weight of the arguments on both sides, and that this question is also one about which it is necessary to know the truth, because our decision about the substances of things depends on it.

Now this question is whether unity and being are the substances of things not in such a way that either of them must be attributed to some other nature which would be informed, as it were, by unity and being, but rather such that the unity and being of a thing are its substance. Or, in an opposite way, whether it is necessary to ask what that thing is to which unity and being properly belong, as though there were some other nature which is their subject.

489. *For some think* (1001a8). Here he gives the opinions on each side of the question. He says that some philosophers thought that reality was of one kind, and some of another. For Plato and the Pythagoreans did not hold that unity and being are the attributes of some nature, but that they constitute the nature of things, as though being itself and unity itself were the substance of things. But some philosophers, in speaking about the natural world,

aliis naturis, sicut Empedocles reducit unum ad aliquid notius, quod dicebant esse unum et ens. Et hoc videtur esse amor, qui est causa unitatis in omnibus.

Alii vero philosophi naturales attribuerunt quibusdam causis elementaribus, sive ponerent unum primum, ut ignem vel aerem, sive etiam ponerent plura principia. Cum enim ponerent principia rerum materialia esse substantias rerum, oportebat quod in unoquoque eorum constituerent unitatem et entitatem rerum, ita quod quicquid aliquis poneret esse principium, ex consequenti opinaretur, quod per illud attribuitur omnibus esse et unum, sive poneret unum principium sive plura.

490. Deinde cum dicit *accidit autem* ponit rationes ad utramque partem.

Et primo ponit rationes pro opinione Platonis et Pythagorae.

Secundo ponit rationes in contrarium pro opinione naturalium, ibi, *at vero si erit* et cetera.

Circa primum, utitur tali divisione. Necesse est ponere quod vel ipsum unum et ens separatum sit quaedam substantia, vel non: si dicatur quod non est aliqua substantia quae sit unum et ens, sequuntur duo inconvenientia.

Quorum primum est, quod dicitur unum et ens quod sint maxime universalia inter omnia. Si igitur unum et ens non sunt separata quasi ipsum unum aut ens sit substantia quaedam, sic sequitur quod nullum universale sit separatum: et ita sequetur quod nihil erit in rebus nisi singularia: quod videtur esse inconveniens, ut in superioribus quaestionibus habitum est.

491. Aliud inconveniens est, quia numerus non est aliud quam unitates: ex unitatibus enim componitur numerus. Unitas enim nihil aliud est quam ipsum unum. Si igitur ipsum unum, non sit separatum quasi substantia per se existens, sequetur quod numerus non erat quaedam natura separata ab his quae sunt in materia. Quod potest probari esse inconveniens, secundum ea quae dicta sunt in superioribus. Sic ergo non potest dici quod unum et ens non sit aliqua substantia per se existens.

492. Si ergo detur alia pars divisionis, scilicet quod aliquid sit ipsum unum et ens separatum existens, necesse est quod ipsum sit substantia omnium eorum, de quibus dicitur unum et ens. Omne enim separatum existens, quod de pluribus praedicatur, est substantia eorum de quibus praedicatur. Sed nihil aliud praedicatur ita universaliter de omnibus sicut unum et ens; ergo unum et ens erit substantia omnium.

493. Deinde cum dicit *at vero* obiicit ad partem contrariam; et ponit duas rationes,

attributed unity and being to certain other natures, as Empedocles reduced the one to something better known, which he said is unity and being. (And this seems to be love, which is the cause of unity in the world.)

But other philosophers of nature attributed these to certain elementary causes, whether they posited one first principle, as fire or air, or more than one. Since they would hold that the material principles of things are the substances of things, it was necessary that each of these should constitute the unity and being of things. Thus whichever one of these anyone might hold to be a principle, he would logically think that through it being and unity would be attributed to all things, whether he posited one principle or more than one.

490. *But if anyone* (1001a19). Here he gives arguments on both sides of the question.

First, he gives arguments in support of the view of Plato and Pythagoras.

Second (1001a29; [493]), he gives arguments on the other side of the question, in support of the view of the philosophers of nature, at *but, on the other hand*.

In regard to the first (1001a19), he makes use of division as follows. It is necessary to hold either that unity and being, separate and existing apart, are a substance, or not. Now if it is said that unity and being are not a substance, two untenable consequences will follow.

The first of these is that unity and being are said to be the most universal of all; therefore, if unity and being are not separate in such a way that unity itself or being itself is a certain substance, it will then follow that no universal is separate. Thus it will follow that there is nothing in the world except singular things, which seems to be inappropriate, as has been stated in earlier questions [443].

491. The other untenable consequence is this. Number is nothing else than units, because number is composed of units (for a unit is nothing else than unity itself). Therefore, if unity itself is not separate as a substance existing of itself, it will follow that number will not be a reality separate from those things that are found in matter. This can be shown to be inappropriate in view of what has already been stated above. Hence it cannot be said that unity and being are not a substance which exists by itself.

492. Therefore, if the other part of the division is conceded, that there is something which is unity itself and being itself, and that this exists separately, it must be the substance of all those things of which unity and being are predicated. For everything that is separate and is predicated of many things is the substance of those things of which it is predicated. But nothing else is predicated of all things in as universal a way as unity and being. Therefore, unity and being will be the substance of all things.

493. *But, on the other hand* (1001a29). Then he argues the other side of the question, and he gives two arguments.

quarum secunda incipit ibi, *amplius si indivisibile* et cetera.

Circa primum duo facit.

Primo ponit rationem.

Secundo ostendit quomodo ex ratione inducta quaestio redditur difficilis, ibi, *utrobique vero difficile* et cetera.

Est ergo prima ratio talis. Si est aliquid, quod est ipsum ens et ipsum unum, quasi separatum existens, oportebit dicere quod idipsum sit unum quod ens. Sed quicquid est diversum ab ente non est; ergo sequetur secundum rationem Parmenidis, quod quicquid est praeter unum sit non ens. Et ita necesse erit omnia esse unum; quia non poterit poni quod id quod est diversum ab uno, quod est per se separatum, sit aliquod ens.

494. Deinde cum dicit *utrobique vero* ostendit quomodo ista ratio difficultatem facit in opinione Platonis ponentis numerum esse substantiam rerum: et dicit quod ex utraque parte sequitur difficultas contra eum, sive dicatur quod ipsum unum separatum sit substantia quaedam, sive quod non sit. Quodcumque enim horum ponatur, videtur impossibile esse, quod numerus sit substantia rerum. Quia si ponatur quod unum non sit substantia, dictum est prius, quare numerus non potest poni substantia.

495. Si autem ipsum unum fuerit substantia, oportet quod eadem dubitatio ponatur circa unum et ens. Aut enim praeter ipsum unum, quod est separatum per se existens, est aliud aliquod unum, aut non. Et si quidem non sit aliquod aliud unum, non erit iam multitudo, sicut Parmenides dicebat. Si autem sit aliquod aliud unum oportebit, quod illud aliud unum, cum non sit hoc ipsum quod est unum, quod sit materialiter ex aliquo quod est praeter ipsum unum, et per consequens praeter ens. Et sic necesse est ut illud aliquid, ex quo fit illud secundum unum, non sit ens. Et sic ex ipso uno quod est praeter ipsum unum, non potest constitui multitudo in entibus: quia omnia entia aut sunt unum, aut multa, quorum unumquodque est unum. Hoc autem unum est materialiter ex eo quod non est unum nec ens.

496. Deinde cum dicit *amplius si* ponit secundam rationem; et circa hoc tria facit.

Primo ponit rationem.

Secundo solvit eam, ibi, *sed quoniam* et cetera.

Tertio ostendit adhuc difficultatem remanere, ibi, *sed quomodo ex uno* et cetera.

Dicit ergo primo, quod si ipsum unum separatum sit indivisibile, sequitur secundum hoc, aliud, quod supponebat Zeno, quod nihil sit. Supponebat enim Zeno,

The second (1001b7; [496]) of these begins where he says, *further, if unity itself*.

In regard to the first he does two things.

First, he gives the argument.

Second (1001b1; [494]), he shows how the question is made difficult as a result of the argument given, at *but there is a difficulty in either case*.

The first (1001a29) argument, then, is as follows. If there is something which is itself being and unity as something existing separately, it will be necessary to say that unity is the very same thing as being. But that which differs from being is non-being. Therefore, it follows, according to the argument of Parmenides, that besides the one there is only non-being. Thus all things will have to be one, because it could not be held that that which differs from the one, which is *per se* separate, is a being.

494. *But there is a difficulty* (1001b1). Here he shows how this argument creates a difficulty in the case of the position of Plato, who held that number is the substance of things. He says that Plato faces a difficulty in either case, whether it is said that this separate one is a substance or not. For whichever view is held, it seems impossible that number should be the substance of things. For if it is held that unity is not a substance, it has already been stated (1001a29; [493]) why number cannot be held to be a substance.

495. But if unity itself is a substance, the same problem will arise with respect to both unity and being. For either there is some other unity besides this unity which exists separately of itself or there is not. And if there is no other, a multitude of things will not exist now, as Parmenides said. But if there is another unity, then that other unity, since it is not unity itself, must have as a material element something that is other than unity itself, and is consequently other than being. And that material element from which this second unity comes to be will have not to be a being. Thus a multitude of beings cannot be constituted from this unity which exists apart from unity itself, because all beings are either one or many, each of which is a one. But this one has as its material element something that is neither unity nor being.

496. *Further, if unity* (1001b7). Here he gives the second argument; and in regard to this he does three things.

First (1001b7; [496]), he gives the argument.

Second (1001b13; [498]), he criticizes it, at *but this philosopher*.

Third (1001b17; [499]), he shows that the difficulty remains, at *yet how will continuous quantity*.

He says first (1001b7), then, that if this separate unity is indivisible, there follows from this the other position that nothing exists, which Zeno assumed. For Zeno supposed

quod illud, quod additum non facit maius, et ablatum non facit minus, non est aliquid existentium.

Hoc autem supponit ac si idem sit ens quod magnitudo. Manifestum est enim quod non est magnitudo, illud scilicet quod additum non facit maius et subtractum non facit minus.

Sic ergo si omne ens esset magnitudo, sequeretur quod illud, quod non facit maius et minus additum et subtractum, non sit ens.

497. Et adhuc perfectius si aliquid velit hoc verificare, oportebit quod omne ens sit magnitudo corporalis. Corpus enim secundum quamcumque dimensionem additum et subtractum facit maius et minus. Aliae vero magnitudines, ut superficies et lineae, secundum aliquam dimensionem additam facerent maius, secundum autem aliquam non. Linea enim addita lineae secundum longitudinem facit maius, non autem secundum latitudinem. Superficies autem addita superficiei facit quidem maius secundum latitudinem et longitudinem, sed non secundum profunditatem. Punctus autem et unitas nullo modo faciunt maius vel minus. Sic ergo secundum principium Zenonis sequeretur quod punctus et unitas sint omnino non entia, corpus autem omnimodo ens, superficies et linea quodammodo entia et quodammodo non entia.

498. Deinde cum dicit *sed quoniam* solvit propositam rationem: et dicit, quod quia Zeno proponendo tale principium speculatur *onerose*, idest ruditer et grosse, ita quod secundum ipsum non contingit aliquid esse indivisibile, oportet quod aliqua responsio praedictae rationi detur, et si non sit ad rem, sit tamen ad hominem.

Dicemus autem quod unum etsi additum alteri non faciat maius, facit tamen plus. Et hoc sufficit ad rationem entis, quod faciat maius in continuis, et plus in discretis.

499. Deinde cum dicit *sed quomodo* ostendit difficultatem, quae adhuc remanet Platonicis post praedictam solutionem. Et inducit duas difficultates.

Quarum prima est, quia Platonici ponebant, quod illud unum indivisibile, non solum est causa numeri, qui est pluralitas quaedam, sed etiam est causa magnitudinis. Si igitur detur, quod unum additum faciat plus, quod videtur sufficere ad hoc quod unum sit causa numeri, quomodo poterit esse quod ex tali uno indivisibili, aut ex pluribus talibus, fiat magnitudo, ut Platonici posuerunt? Simile enim hoc videtur, si aliquis ponat lineam ex punctis. Nam unitas est indivisibilis sicut et punctus.

that that which when added does not make a thing greater and when taken away does not make it smaller is nothing in the real order.

But he makes this assumption on the grounds that continuous quantity is the same as being. For it is evident that this is not a continuous quantity—I mean that which, when added, does not make a thing greater and, when subtracted, does not make it smaller.

Therefore, if every being were a continuous quantity, it would follow that that which when added does not make a thing greater and when subtracted does not make it smaller is non-being.

497. And better still, if any particular thing were to bear this out, every being would have to be a bodily continuous quantity. For anything added to or subtracted from a body in any one of its dimensions makes the body greater or less. But other continuous quantities, such as lines and surfaces, become greater insofar as one dimension is added, whereas others do not. For line added to line in length causes increase in length but not in width, and surface added to surface causes increase in width and in length but not in depth. But a point and a unit do not become greater or less in any way. Hence according to Zeno's axiom it would follow that a point and a unit are non-beings in an absolute sense, whereas a body is a being in every respect, and surfaces and lines are beings in one respect and non-beings in another respect.

498. *But this philosopher* (1001b13). Here he criticizes the argument which has been given. He says that Zeno, by proposing such an axiom, speculated *clumsily*, or in an unskilled and rude manner, such that according to him there cannot be anything indivisible. And for this reason some answer must be given to the foregoing argument; and if not to the point at issue, at least to the man.

Now we say that, even though a unity when added to something else does not make it larger, it does cause it to be more. And this suffices for the notion of being, that it makes continuous things larger, and discreet things more.

499. *Yet how will* (1001b17). Then he states the difficulty which still faces the Platonists after the above solution. And he advances two difficulties.

The first of these is that the Platonists held that the one which is indivisible is the cause not only of number, which is a plurality, but also of continuous quantity. Therefore, if it is granted that when a one is added it makes a thing more, as would seem to suffice for the one which is the cause of number, how will it be possible for continuous quantity to come from an indivisible one of this kind, or from many such ones, as the Platonists held? For this would seem to be the same thing as to hold that a line is composed of points. For unity is indivisible just as a point is.

500. Secundam difficultatem ponit ibi *at vero* et dicit: si quis existimet ita, quod numerus sit effectus ex uno indivisibili, et ex aliquo alio quod non sit unum, sed participet unum sicut quaedam materialis natura, ut quidam dicunt; nihilominus remanet quaerendum propter quid, et per quem modum illud, quod fit ex illo uno formali et alia natura materiali, quae dicitur non unum, quandoque est numerus, quandoque autem est magnitudo.

Et praecipue si illud non unum materiale sit inaequalitas, quae significatur per magnum, et sit eadem natura. Non enim est manifestum quomodo ex hac inaequalitate quasi materia et uno formali fiant numeri; neque etiam quomodo ex aliquo numero formali et hac inaequalitate quasi materiali fiant magnitudines. Ponebant enim Platonici quod ex primo uno et ex prima dualitate fiebat numerus, ex quo numero et a qua inaequalitate materiali fiebat magnitudo.

501. Huius autem dubitationis solutio ab Aristotele in sequentibus traditur. Quod enim sit aliquod separatum, quod sit ipsum unum et ens, infra in duodecimo probabit, ostendens unitatem primi principii omnino separati, quod tamen non est substantia omnium eorum quae sunt unum, sicut Platonici putabant, sed est omnibus unitatis causa et principium.

Unum autem, secundum quod dicitur de aliis rebus, dicitur dupliciter.

Uno modo secundum quod convertitur cum ente: et sic unaquaeque res est una per suam essentiam, ut infra in quarto probabitur, nec aliquid addit unum supra ens nisi solam rationem indivisionis.

Alio modo dicitur unum secundum quod significat rationem primae mensurae, vel simpliciter, vel in aliquo genere.

Et hoc quidem si sit simpliciter minimum et indivisibile, est unum quod est principium et mensura numeri. Si autem non sit simpliciter minimum et indivisibile, nec simpliciter, sed secundum positionem erit unum et mensura, ut as in ponderibus, et diesis in melodiis, et mensura pedalis in lineis: et ex tali uno nihil prohibet componi magnitudinem: et hoc determinabit in decimo huius.

Sed quia Platonici aestimaverunt idem esse unum quod est principium numeri, et quod convertitur cum ente; ideo posuerunt unum quod est principium numeri, esse substantiam cuiuslibet rei, et per consequens numerum, inquantum ex pluribus substantialibus principiis, rerum compositarum substantia consistit vel constat.

500. *But even if someone* (1001b19). Here he gives the second difficulty. He says that if anyone were to think that the situation is such that number is the result of the indivisible one and of something else which is not one, but participates in the one as a kind of material nature (as some say), the question would still remain as to why and how that which comes from the one as form and from another material nature, which is called the not-one, is sometimes a number and sometimes a continuous quantity.

The difficulty would be most acute if that material not-one were inequality, as is implied in the continuously extended, and were to be the same reality. For it is not clear how numbers come from this inequality as matter and from the one as form. Nor again is it clear how continuous quantities come from some number as form and from this inequality as matter. For the Platonists held that number comes from a primary one and a primary two, and that, from this number and material inequality, continuous quantity is produced.

501. The solution of this problem is treated by Aristotle in the following books. For the fact that there is something separate, which is itself one and being, he will prove below in book 12 [2553], when he establishes the oneness of the first principle which is separate in an absolute sense, although it is not the substance of all things that are one, as the Platonists thought, but is the cause and principle of the unity of all things.

And insofar as unity is predicated of other things it is used in two ways.

In one way it is interchangeable with being, and in this way each thing is one by its very essence, as is proved below in book 4 [548]. Unity in this sense adds nothing to being except merely the notion of undividedness.

Unity is used in another way insofar as it has the character of a first measure, either in an absolute sense or with respect to some genus.

And this unity, if it is both a minimum in the absolute sense and indivisible, is the one which is the principle and measure of number. But if it is not both a minimum in an absolute sense and indivisible, it will not be a unit and measure in an absolute sense, as a pound in the case of weights and a half-tone in the case of melodies and a foot in the case of lengths. And nothing prevents continuous quantities from being composed of this kind of unity. He will establish this in book 10 [1940] of this work.

But because the Platonists thought that the one which is the principle of number and the one which is interchangeable with being are the same, they therefore held that the one which is the principle of number is the substance of each thing, and consequently that number, inasmuch as it is composed of many substantial principles, makes up or

Hanc autem quaestionem diffusius pertractabit in tertiodecimo et quartodecimo.

comprises the substance of composite things. But he will treat this question at greater length in books 13 and 14 of this work.

LECTURE 13

Is quantity the substance and principle of sensible things?

1001b26   Horum autem habita est dubitatio utrum numeri et corpora et superficies et puncta substantiae aliquae sunt, aut non. [502]

τούτων δ' ἐχομένη ἀπορία πότερον οἱ ἀριθμοὶ καὶ τὰ σώματα καὶ τὰ ἐπίπεδα καὶ αἱ στιγμαὶ οὐσίαι τινές εἰσιν ἢ οὔ.

And connected with these is the question of whether numbers and bodies and surfaces and points are substances, or not.

1001b28   Nam si non sunt, diffugit nos quidnam sit ipsum ens, et quaenam entium substantiae. Passiones enim, et motus, et ad aliquid, et dispositiones et orationes, nullius videntur substantiam significare. Dicuntur enim omnia de subiecto aliquo et nihil hoc aliquid. Quae vero maxime substantiam significare videntur aqua et ignis et terra, ex quibus corpora composita constant: horum calores quidem et frigiditates et similes passiones, non sunt substantiae. Corpus vero haec patiens, solum remanet ut ens aliquod et substantia aliqua existens. [503]

εἰ μὲν γὰρ μή εἰσιν, διαφεύγει τί τὸ ὂν καὶ τίνες αἱ οὐσίαι τῶν ὄντων: τὰ μὲν γὰρ πάθη καὶ αἱ κινήσεις {30} καὶ τὰ πρός τι καὶ αἱ διαθέσεις καὶ οἱ λόγοι οὐθενὸς δοκοῦσιν οὐσίαν σημαίνειν (λέγονται γὰρ πάντα καθ᾽ ὑποκειμένου τινός, καὶ οὐθὲν τόδε τι): ἃ δὲ μάλιστ᾽ ἂν δόξειε σημαίνειν οὐσίαν, ὕδωρ καὶ γῆ καὶ πῦρ καὶ ἀήρ, ἐξ ὧν τὰ σύνθετα σώματα συνέστηκε, {1002a1} τούτων θερμότητες μὲν καὶ ψυχρότητες καὶ τὰ τοιαῦτα πάθη, οὐκ οὐσίαι, τὸ δὲ σῶμα τὸ ταῦτα πεπονθὸς μόνον ὑπομένει ὡς ὄν τι καὶ οὐσία τις οὖσα.

For if they are not, we are in a quandary as to what being is, and what the substances of things are. For passions and motions and relations and dispositions and their complex conceptions do not seem to signify substance, because all are predicated of some subject, and no one of them is a particular thing. And those things that seem to signify substance most of all, as fire, water, and earth, of which composite bodies are constituted (their heat and cold and similar passions), are not substances. And it is only the body which undergoes these that remains as a being and is a substance.

1002a4   At vero corpus est minus substantia superficie et haec linea, et haec unitate et puncto: his enim definitur corpus. Et haec quidem sine corpore contingere videntur esse, corpus vero sine his impossibile. [504]

ἀλλὰ μὴν τό γε σῶμα ἧττον οὐσία τῆς ἐπιφανείας, {5} καὶ αὕτη τῆς γραμμῆς, καὶ αὕτη τῆς μονάδος καὶ τῆς στιγμῆς: τούτοις γὰρ ὥρισται τὸ σῶμα, καὶ τὰ μὲν ἄνευ σώματος ἐνδέχεσθαι δοκεῖ εἶναι τὸ δὲ σῶμα ἄνευ τούτων ἀδύνατον.

Yet a body is a substance to a lesser degree than a surface, and this than a line, and this in turn than a unit and a point. For a body is defined by means of these, and these seem to be capable of existing without a body, but that a body should exist without these is impossible.

1002a8   Propter quod multi quidem et priores substantiam et ens putabant corpus esse, alia vero huiusmodi passiones. Quare et principia corporum entium esse principia. Posteriores vero et sapientiores his, esse opinabantur numeros. Quemadmodum ergo dicebamus, si non sunt substantia haec, omnino nulla substantia est, neque ens nullum: non enim horum accidentia dignum est vocare entia. [506]

διόπερ οἱ μὲν πολλοὶ καὶ οἱ πρότερον τὴν οὐσίαν καὶ τὸ ὂν ᾤοντο τὸ σῶμα εἶναι τὰ δὲ ἄλλα {10} τούτου πάθη, ὥστε καὶ τὰς ἀρχὰς τὰς τῶν σωμάτων τῶν ὄντων εἶναι ἀρχάς: οἱ δ᾽ ὕστεροι καὶ σοφώτεροι τούτων εἶναι δόξαντες ἀριθμούς. καθάπερ οὖν εἴπομεν, εἰ μὴ ἔστιν οὐσία ταῦτα, ὅλως οὐδὲν ἐστιν οὐσία οὐδὲ ὂν οὐθέν: οὐ γὰρ δὴ τά γε συμβεβηκότα τούτοις ἄξιον ὄντα καλεῖν.

For this reason many of the natural philosophers, including the first, thought that substance and being are bodies, and that other things are attributes of this kind of thing, and hence too that the principles of bodies are the principles of beings. But the later philosophers, who were wiser than these, thought that the principles of things are numbers. Therefore, as we have said, if these are not substance, there is no substance or being at all, for the accidents of these things are not worthy to be called beings.

1002a15   At vero si hoc quidem confessum est, quia magis substantia sunt longitudines corporibus et puncta, haec autem non videmus qualium utique erunt corporum. Nam in sensibilibus impossibile esse, non utique erit substantia ulla. [507]

—ἀλλὰ μὴν εἰ τοῦτο μὲν ὁμολογεῖται, ὅτι μᾶλλον οὐσία τὰ μήκη τῶν σωμάτων καὶ αἱ στιγμαί, ταῦτα δὲ μὴ ὁρῶμεν ποίων ἂν εἶεν σωμάτων (ἐν γὰρ τοῖς αἰσθητοῖς ἀδύνατον εἶναι), οὐκ ἂν εἴη οὐσία οὐδεμία.

But if it is admitted that lengths and points are substances to a greater degree than bodies, and we do not see to what sort of bodies these belong (because it is impossible for them to exist in sensible bodies), there will then be no substance at all.

1002a18 Amplius autem haec omnia videntur dimensiones corporis: hoc quidem ad latitudinem, hoc vero ad profunditatem, aliud ad longitudinem. [508]

ἔτι δὲ φαίνεται ταῦτα πάντα διαιρέσεις ὄντα τοῦ σώματος, τὸ μὲν εἰς πλάτος {20} τὸ δ᾽ εἰς βάθος τὸ δ᾽ εἰς μῆκος.

Further, all of these seem to be dimensions of bodies, one according to width, another according to depth, and another according to length.

1002a20 Adhuc autem similiter est in solido quaecumque figura. Quare si nec in lapide Mercurius, nec medietas cubi in cubo sic ut segregata, igitur neque superficies, nam si quaecumque, et haec utique erat determinans medietatem: eadem enim ratio et in linea, et in puncto et in unitate. [509]

πρὸς δὲ τούτοις ὁμοίως ἔνεστιν ἐν τῷ στερεῷ ὁποιονοῦν σχῆμα: ὥστ᾽ εἰ μηδ᾽ ἐν τῷ λίθῳ Ἑρμῆς, οὐδὲ τὸ ἥμισυ τοῦ κύβου ἐν τῷ κύβῳ οὕτως ὡς ἀφωρισμένον: οὐκ ἄρα οὐδ᾽ ἐπιφάνεια (εἰ γὰρ ὁποιαοῦν, κἂν αὕτη ἂν ἦν ἡ ἀφορίζουσα τὸ ἥμισυ), ὁ δ᾽ {25} αὐτὸς λόγος καὶ ἐπὶ γραμμῆς καὶ στιγμῆς καὶ μονάδος,

Similarly, any figure whatever already exists in a solid. Hence if neither Mercury is in the stone, nor one half of a cube in a cube as something segregated, neither will surface exist in a solid. For if this were true of anything whatever, it would also be true of that which divides a thing in half. And the same argument would apply in the case of a line, a point, and a unit.

Quare si maxime quidem substantia est corpus, hoc autem magis ea, non sunt autem ea, nec substantiae aliquae, nos fugit quid est ipsum ens et quae substantia entium.

ὥστ᾽ εἰ μάλιστα μὲν οὐσία τὸ σῶμα, τούτου δὲ μᾶλλον ταῦτα, μὴ ἔστι δὲ ταῦτα μηδὲ οὐσίαι τινές, διαφεύγει τί τὸ ὂν καὶ τίς ἡ οὐσία τῶν ὄντων.

If, then, a body is substance in the highest degree, and these things are such to a greater degree than it is, and these do not exist and are not substances, it escapes our understanding as to what being itself is and what the substance of beings is.

1002a28 Nam cum dictis et circa generationem et corruptionem accidunt irrationabilia. Videtur enim substantia non ens prius, nunc esse, aut prius existens, posterius non esse, cum generatione et corruptione ea pati. [510]

πρὸς γὰρ τοῖς εἰρημένοις καὶ τὰ περὶ τὴν γένεσιν καὶ τὴν φθορὰν συμβαίνει ἄλογα. {30} δοκεῖ μὲν γὰρ ἡ οὐσία, ἐὰν μὴ οὖσα πρότερον νῦν ᾖ ἢ πρότερον οὖσα ὕστερον μὴ ᾖ, μετὰ τοῦ γίγνεσθαι καὶ φθείρεσθαι ταῦτα πάσχειν:

For along with what has been said there happen to be certain unreasonable views about generation and corruption. For if substance, not existing before, exists now, or does not exist afterwards when existing before, it seems to suffer these changes through generation and corruption.

Puncta vero et linea et superficies non contingit neque fieri et corrumpi, quandoque existentes, quandoque vero non existentes.

τὰς δὲ στιγμὰς καὶ τὰς γραμμὰς καὶ τὰς ἐπιφανείας οὐκ ἐνδέχεται οὔτε γίγνεσθαι οὔτε φθείρεσθαι, ὁτὲ μὲν οὔσας ὁτὲ δὲ οὐκ οὔσας.

But it is impossible for points and lines and surfaces either to come to be or to be destroyed, even though they sometimes exist and sometimes do not.

Nam quando copulantur aut distinguuntur corpora, simul quandoque quidem una copulatorum, quandoque duae divisorum fiunt: quia non compositorum est. Sed corruptum est, divisorumque sunt prius non existentes:

ὅταν γὰρ ἅπτηται ἢ διαιρῆται τὰ σώματα, {1002b1} ἅμα ὁτὲ μὲν μία ἁπτομένων ὁτὲ δὲ δύο διαιρουμένων γίγνονται: ὥστ᾽ οὔτε συγκειμένων ἔστιν ἀλλ᾽ ἔφθαρται, διῃρημένων τε εἰσὶν αἱ πρότερον οὐκ οὖσαι

For when bodies are joined or divided, whenever they are joined the two at once become one, and whenever they are divided, two are produced, because the one thing is no longer composed but has perished, and when they are divided, what did not exist before exists.

non enim indivisibile punctum divisum est in duo; et si generantur et corrumpuntur, ex aliquo generantur.

(οὐ γὰρ δὴ ἥ γ᾽ ἀδιαίρετος στιγμὴ διῃρέθη εἰς δύο), εἴ τε γίγνονται καὶ {5} φθείρονται, ἐκ τίνος γίγνονται;

For the indivisible point is not divided into two, and if things are generated and corrupted, they are generated from something.

1002b8 Similiter autem se habet circa nunc in tempore; non enim contingit fieri et corrumpi. Attamen videtur semper esse, non substantia aliqua existens. Similiter autem palam, quia se habet et circa puncta et lineas et superficies: eadem enim ratio. Nam omnia similiter aut termini aut divisiones sunt. [513]

παραπλησίως δ᾽ ἔχει καὶ περὶ τὸ νῦν τὸ ἐν τῷ χρόνῳ: οὐδὲ γὰρ τοῦτο ἐνδέχεται γίγνεσθαι καὶ φθείρεσθαι, ἀλλ᾽ ὅμως ἕτερον ἀεὶ δοκεῖ εἶναι, οὐκ οὐσία τις οὖσα. ὁμοίως δὲ δῆλον ὅτι ἔχει καὶ περὶ τὰς στιγμὰς καὶ τὰς γραμμὰς καὶ τὰ ἐπίπεδα: ὁ γὰρ {10} αὐτὸς λόγος: ἅπαντα γὰρ ὁμοίως ἢ πέρατα ἢ διαιρέσεις εἰσίν.

And it is similar with regard to the now in time, for this cannot be generated and corrupted. Yet it seems always to exist, although it is not a substance. It is also clear that this is true of points, lines, and surfaces, because the argument is the same. For they are all similarly either limits or divisions.

502. Postquam Philosophus inquisivit utrum unum et ens sint substantia rerum, hic inquirit utrum numerus et magnitudo sint substantia rerum: et circa hoc tria facit.

Primo movet dubitationem.

Secundo obiicit pro una parte, ibi, *nam si non sunt* et cetera.

Tertio obiicit ad contraria, ibi, *at vero si hoc quidem confessum est* et cetera.

Dicit ergo primo, quod dubitatio *habita*, idest consequens ad praemissam, est, utrum numeri et magnitudines, scilicet corpora et superficies et termini eorum, ut puncta, sint aliquae substantiae vel a rebus separatae, vel etiam sint substantiae ipsorum sensibilium, aut non. Dicit autem hanc dubitationem esse consequentem ad praemissam; quia in praemissa dubitatione quaerebatur utrum unum sit substantia rerum; unum autem est principium numeri; numerus autem videtur esse substantia magnitudinis; sicut et punctum, quod est principium magnitudinis, nihil aliud videtur quam unitas positionem habens, et linea dualitas positionem habens. Prima autem superficies est ternarius positionem habens, corpus autem quaternarius positionem habens.

503. Deinde cum dicit *nam si non* obiicit ad ostendendum quod praedicta sint substantiae rerum: et circa hoc duo facit.

Primo obiicit ad ostendendum quod praedicta sunt substantiae rerum.

Secundo ostendit quomodo philosophi praecedentes secuti fuerunt rationes primas, ibi, *propter quod multi*.

Circa primum duo facit.

Primo enim obiicit ad ostendendum quod corpus sit substantia rerum.

Secundo quod multo magis alia, ibi, *at vero corpus* et cetera.

Dicit ergo primo, quod si praedicta non sunt substantiae quaedam, fugiet a nobis quid sit substantialiter ens, et quae sunt substantiae entium. Manifestum est enim quod passiones et motus, et relationes, et dispositiones seu ordines, et orationes secundum quod voce proferuntur, prout ponuntur in genere quantitatis, non videntur alicuius significare substantiam, quia omnia huiusmodi videntur dici de aliquo subiecto, et nihil eorum significare *hoc aliquid*, idest aliquid absolutum et per se subsistens. Et hoc specialiter manifestum est in praemissis, qui non dicuntur absolute, sed eorum ratio in quadam relatione consistit. Inter omnia vero, quae maxime videntur significare substantiam, sunt ignis et terra et aqua, ex quibus componuntur corpora multa.

502. Having inquired whether unity and being are the substances of sensible things, the Philosopher now asks whether numbers and continuous quantities are the substances of sensible things; and in regard to this he does three things.

First (1001b26; [502]), he presents the question.

Second (1001b28; [503]), he argues in support of one side of the question, at *for if they are not*.

Third (1002a15; [507]), he argues on the other side, at *but if it is admitted*.

Accordingly he says, first, that **connected with these**, that is, following from the foregoing problem, there is the question of whether numbers and continuous quantities—bodies, surfaces, and their extremities, such as points—either are substances that are separate from sensible things or are the substances of sensible things themselves, or not. He says that this problem is a result of the foregoing one, because in the foregoing problem it was asked whether unity is the substance of things. Now unity is the principle of number. But number seems to be the substance of continuous quantity inasmuch as a point, which is a principle of continuous quantity, seems to be merely the number one having position, and a line to be the number two having position, and the primary kind of surface to be the number three having position, and a body to be the number four having position.

503. **For if they are not** (1001b28). Then he advances an argument to show that these are the substances of sensible things; and in regard to this he does two things.

First (1001b28; [503]), he introduces an argument to show that these are the substances of sensible things.

Second (1001b28; [506]), he shows how the early philosophers followed out the first arguments, at **for this reason**.

In regard to the first he does two things.

First, he advances an argument to show that body is the substance of things;

second (1002a4; [504]), to show that many other things are substances to an even greater degree, at **yet a body**.

He says first (1001b28) that, if these things are not substances, we are in a quandary as to what being is *per se* and what the substances of beings are. For it is evident that passions, motions, relations, dispositions (or arrangements), and their complex conceptions according as they are put into words do not seem to signify the substance of anything. For all things of this kind seem to be predicated of a subject as something belonging to the genus of quantity, and no one of them seems to signify **a particular thing**, that is, something that is complete and subsists of itself. This is especially evident in regard to the foregoing things, which are not said to be complete things but things whose nature consists in a kind of relation. But of all things those which especially seem to signify substance are fire, earth,

Praetermittit autem aerem, quia minus est sensibilis, unde aliqui opinati sunt aerem nihil esse. In his autem corporibus inveniuntur quaedam dispositiones, scilicet calor et frigus et aliae huiusmodi passiones vel passibiles qualitates, quae non sunt substantiae secundum praedicta. Unde relinquitur quod solum corpus sit substantia.

504. Deinde cum dicit **at vero**, procedit ulterius ad alia, quae etiam videntur magis esse substantia quam corpus: et dicit, quod corpus videtur minus esse substantia quam superficies, et superficies minus quam linea, et linea minus quam punctus aut unitas. Et hoc probat per duo media: quorum unum est; quia id, per quod aliquid definitur, videtur esse substantia eius: nam definitio significat substantiam. Sed corpus definitur per superficiem, et superficies per lineam, et linea per punctum, et punctus per unitatem, quia dicunt quod punctus est unitas positionem habens: ergo superficies est substantia corporis, et sic de aliis.

505. Secundum medium est, quia cum substantia sit primum in entibus, illud quod est prius, videtur esse magis substantia: sed superficies natura prior est corpore, quia superficies potest esse sine corpore non autem corpus sine superficie: ergo superficies est magis substantia quam corpus. Et idem potest argui de omnibus aliis per ordinem.

506. Deinde cum dicit **propter quod** ostendit quomodo philosophi praecedentes secuti fuerunt praedictas rationes; et dicit, quod propter praedictas rationes multi antiquorum philosophorum, et maxime illi, qui fuerunt priores, nihil opinabantur esse ens et substantiam nisi corpus, omnia vero alia esse quaedam accidentia corporis. Et inde est, quod quando volebant inquirere principia entium, inquirebant principia corporum, ut supra in primo circa opiniones antiquorum naturalium habitum est. Alii vero posteriores philosophi, qui reputabantur sapientiores praedictis philosophis, quasi altius attingentes ad principia rerum, scilicet Pythagorici et Platonici, opinati sunt numeros esse rerum substantias, inquantum scilicet numeri componuntur ex unitatibus. Unum autem videtur esse una substantia rerum.

Sic ergo videtur secundum praemissas rationes et philosophorum opiniones, quod si praedicta non sunt substantiae rerum, scilicet numeri et lineae et superficies et corpora, nihil erit ens. Non est enim dignum ut, si ista non sunt entia, quod accidentia eorum entia vocentur.

507. Deinde cum dicit **at vero** obiicit in contrarium: et ponit quatuor rationes:

quarum prima talis est. Si quis confitetur, quod longitudines et puncta sint magis substantiae quam corpora, sequetur quod, si huiusmodi non sint substantiae,

and water, of which many bodies are composed. But he omits air, because it is less perceptible, and this is the reason why some thought air to be nothing. But in these bodies there are found certain dispositions—namely, hot and cold and other passions and passible qualities of this kind—which are not substances according to what has been said. It follows, then, that body alone is substance.

504. *Yet a body* (1002a4). Here he proceeds to examine those things that appear to be substance to an even greater degree than a body. He says that a body seems to be a substance to a lesser degree than a surface, and a surface than a line, and a line than a point or a unit. He proves this in two ways, of which the first is as follows. That by which a thing is defined seems to be its substance, for a definition signifies substance. But a body is defined by a surface, a surface by a line, a line by a point, and a point by a unit, because they say that a point is a unit having position. Therefore, surface is the substance of body, and so on for the others.

505. The second argument runs as follows. Since substance is the primary kind of being, whatever is prior seems to be substance to a greater degree. But a surface is naturally prior to a body, because a surface can exist without a body but not a body without a surface. Therefore, a surface is substance to a greater degree than a body. The same reasoning can be applied to all the others in turn.

506. *For this reason* (1002a8). Then he shows how the earlier philosophers followed out the foregoing arguments. He says that it was because of the foregoing arguments that many of the ancient philosophers, especially the first, thought that body alone was being and substance, and that all other things were accidents of bodies. Hence when they wanted to study the principles of beings, they studied the principles of bodies, as was stated above in book 1 (983b6; [74]) with regard to the positions of the ancient natural philosophers. But the other philosophers, who came later and were reputed to be wiser than the aforesaid philosophers inasmuch as they dealt more profoundly with the principles of things (namely, the Pythagoreans and Platonists), were of the opinion that numbers are the substances of sensible things inasmuch as numbers are composed of units. And the unit seems to be one substance of things.

Hence, according to the foregoing arguments and opinions of the philosophers, it seems that, if these things—numbers, lines, surfaces, and bodies—are not the substances of things, there will be no being at all. For if these are not beings, it is unfitting that their accidents should be called beings.

507. *But if it is* (1002a15). Then he argues in support of the other side of the question; and he gives four arguments,

the first of which is as follows. If anyone were to admit that lengths and points are substances to a greater degree than bodies, then supposing that things of this sort are not

et corpora non sint substantiae; et per consequens nihil erit substantia, quia accidentia corporum non sunt substantiae, ut supra dictum est. Sed puncta et linea et superficies non sunt substantiae. Haec enim oportet aliquorum corporum esse terminos; nam punctus est terminus lineae, linea superficiei, et superficies corporis. Non autem videtur qualium corporum sint illae superficies, quae sunt substantiae, vel lineae, vel puncta. Manifestum enim est, quod lineae et superficies sensibilium corporum non sunt substantiae; variantur enim per modum aliorum accidentium circa idem subiectum. Sequetur ergo quod nihil erit substantia.

508. Secundam rationem ponit ibi, *amplius autem* quae talis est. Omnia praedicta videntur esse quaedam corporis dimensiones: vel secundum latitudinem, ut superficies: vel secundum profunditatem, ut corpus: vel secundum longitudinem, ut linea. Sed dimensiones corporis non sunt substantiae: ergo huiusmodi non sunt substantiae.

509. Tertiam rationem ponit ibi, *adhuc autem* quae talis est. In corpore solido simili modo inest, scilicet potentialiter, quaelibet figura, quae potest protrahi ex illo solido per aliquam dimensionem.

Sed manifestum est quod in quodam magno lapide nondum secto non inest *Mercurius* idest figura Mercurii, in actu, sed solum in potentia: ergo similiter *in cubo*, idest in corpore habente sex superficies quadratas, non inest medietas cubi, quae est quaedam alia figura, actu. Sed hoc modo est actu, quando iam cubus dividitur in duas medietates.

Et quia omnis protractio novae figurae in solido exciso fit secundum aliquam superficiem, quae terminat figuram, manifestum est quod nec etiam superficies talis erit in corpore in actu, sed solum in potentia: quia si quaecumque superficies praeter exteriorem essent in actu in corpore solido, pari ratione esset in actu superficies, quae terminat medietatem figurae.

Quod autem dictum est de superficie, intelligendum est in linea, puncto, unitate. Haec enim in continuo non sunt in actu, nisi solum quantum ad illa quae terminant continuum, quae manifestum est non esse substantiam corporis. Aliae vero superficies vel lineae non possunt esse corporis substantiae, quia non sunt actu in ipso. Substantia autem actu est in eo cuius est substantia.

Unde concludit quod inter omnia, maxime videtur esse substantia corpus; superficies autem et lineae magis videntur esse substantia quam corpus. Haec autem si non sunt entia in actu, nec sunt aliquae substantiae, videtur effugere cognitionem nostram, quid sit ens, et quae sit rerum substantia.

substances, it also follows that bodies are not substances. Consequently, no substance will exist, because the accidents of bodies are not substances, as has been stated above [503]. But points, lines, and surfaces are not substances. For these must be the limits of some bodies, because a point is the limit of a line, a line the limit of a surface, and a surface the limit of a body. But it is not evident to what sort of bodies these surfaces, lines, and points which are substances belong. For it is evident that the lines and surfaces of sensible bodies are not substances, because they are altered in the same way as the other accidents in reference to the same subject. Therefore, it follows that there will be no substance whatever.

508. *Further, all of these* (1002a18). Here he gives the second argument, which is as follows. All of the above-mentioned things seem to be certain dimensions of bodies, either according to width, as a surface, or according to depth, as a solid, or according to length, as a line. But the dimensions of a body are not substances. Therefore, things of this kind are not substances.

509. *Similarly, any figure* (1002a20). Here he gives a third argument, which is as follows. Any figure which can be educed from a solid body according to some dimension is present in that body in the same way, that is, potentially.

But in the case of a large piece of stone which has not yet been cut, it is evident that *Mercury*, that is, the figure of Mercury, is not present in it actually, but only potentially. Therefore, in like manner, *in a cube* (in a body having six square surfaces) one half of the cube, which is another figure, is not present actually; but it becomes actual in this way when a cube has already been divided into two halves.

And since every reduction of a new figure in a solid which has been cut is made according to some surface which limits a figure, it is also evident that such a surface will not be present in a body actually, but only potentially. For if each surface besides the external one were actually present in a solid body, then for the same reason the surface which limits one half of the figure would also be actually present in it.

But what has been said of a surface must also be understood of a line, a point, and a unit. For these are actually present in the continuum only insofar as they limit the continuum, and it is evident that these are not the substance of a body. But the other surfaces and lines cannot be the substance of a body, because they are not actually present in it, for a substance is actually present in the thing whose substance it is.

Hence he concludes that, of all of these, body especially seems to be substance, and that surfaces and lines seem to be substance to a greater degree than bodies. Now if these are not actual beings or substances, it seems to escape our comprehension as to what being is and what the substances of things are.

510. Quartam rationem ponit ibi *nam cum*,

et primo ponit ipsam.

Secundo manifestat eam in quodam simili, ibi, *similiter autem se habet* et cetera.

Dicit ergo primo, quod cum dictis inconvenientibus etiam irrationabilia accidunt ex parte generationis et corruptionis, ponentibus lineas et superficies esse substantias rerum.

Omnis enim substantia, quae prius non fuit et postea est, aut prius fuit et postea non est, videtur hoc pati cum generatione et corruptione. Et hoc manifeste apparet in omnibus his quae per motum causantur. Puncta autem et lineae et superficies quandoque quidem sunt, quandoque vero non sunt, et tamen non generantur nec corrumpuntur; ergo nec sunt substantiae.

511. Probat autem utrumque suppositorum. Primo quidem, quod quandoque sint et quandoque non sint. Contingit enim corpora prius divisa copulari in unum aut prius copulata dividi. Quando autem corpora primum divisa copulantur, fit una superficies duorum corporum, quia partes corporis continui copulantur ad unum communem terminum, qui est superficies una.

Quando vero corpus unum dividitur in duo, efficiuntur duae superficies. Quia non potest dici quod quando corpora duo componuntur, quod duae superficies eorum maneant, sed utraeque *corrumpuntur*, idest desinunt esse. Similiter quando corpora dividuntur, incipiunt esse de novo duae superficies prius non existentes.

Non enim potest dici quod superficies quae est indivisibilis secundum profunditatem, dividatur in superficies duas secundum profunditatem: aut linea, quae est indivisibilis secundum latitudinem, dividatur secundum latitudinem: aut punctum, quod omnino est indivisibile, quocumque modo dividatur.

Et sic patet quod ex uno non possent fieri duo in via divisionis: nec ex duobus praedictorum potest fieri unum in via compositionis. Unde relinquitur quod puncta et linea et superficies quandoque esse incipiant, et quandoque esse deficiant.

512. Consequenter probat secundum quod supponebatur, scilicet quod ista non generantur nec corrumpuntur. Omne enim quod generatur, ex aliquo generatur: et omne quod corrumpitur, in aliquid corrumpitur sicut in materiam. Sed non est dare aliquam materiam, ex qua ista generentur et in qua corrumpantur, propter eorum simplicitatem; ergo non generantur nec corrumpuntur.

510. *For along with what has been said* (1002a28). Here he gives the fourth argument.

First, he states it,

and second (1002b8; [513]), he clarifies it by using a similar case, at *and it is similar*.

Accordingly, he says, first (1002a28), that along with the other untenable consequences mentioned there also happen to be certain unreasonable views about generation and corruption on the part of those who hold that lines and surfaces are the substances of sensible things.

For every substance which at first did not exist and later does exist, or which first was and afterwards is not, seems to suffer this change by way of generation and corruption. This is most evident in the case of all those things that are caused by way of motion. But points and lines and surfaces sometimes are and sometimes are not. Yet they are not generated or corrupted. Neither, then, are they substances.

511. He then proves each assumption. The first of these is that they sometimes are and sometimes are not. For it happens that bodies which were at first distinct are afterwards united, and that those which were at first united are afterwards divided. For when bodies which were initially separated are united, one surface is produced for the two of them, because the parts of a continuous body are united in having one common boundary, which is one surface.

But when one body is divided into two, two surfaces are produced, because it cannot be said that when two bodies are brought together their surfaces remain intact, but that both *are corrupted*, or cease to be. In like manner, when bodies are divided, there begin to exist for the first time two surfaces which previously did not exist.

For it cannot be said that a surface, which is indivisible according to depth, is divided into two surfaces according to depth; or that a line, which is indivisible according to width, is divided according to width; or that a point, which is indivisible in every respect, is divided in any respect whatsoever.

Thus it is clear that two things cannot be produced from one thing by way of division, and that one thing cannot be produced from two of these things by way of combination. Hence it follows that points, lines, and surfaces sometimes begin to be and sometimes cease to be.

512. After having proved this, he proves the second assumption, namely, that these things are neither generated nor corrupted. For everything that is generated is generated from something, and everything that is corrupted is dissolved into something as its matter. But it is impossible to assign any matter whatever from which these things are generated and into which they are dissolved, because they are simple. Therefore, they are neither generated nor corrupted.

513. Deinde cum dicit *similiter autem* manifestat praedictam rationem in simili. Ita enim se habet nunc in tempore, sicut punctus in linea. Nunc autem non videtur generari et corrumpi: quia si generaretur vel corrumperetur, oporteret quod generatio et corruptio ipsius mensurarentur aliquo tempore vel instanti. Et sic mensura ipsius nunc, esset vel aliud nunc in infinitum, vel tempus, quod est impossibile.

Et licet nunc non generetur et corrumpatur, tamen videtur semper esse aliud et aliud nunc: non quidem quod differant secundum substantiam, sed secundum esse. Quia substantia ipsius nunc, respondet subiecto mobili. Variatio autem ipsius nunc secundum esse, respondet variationi motus, ut ostenditur in quarto *Physicorum*. Similiter ergo videtur se habere de puncto in comparatione ad lineam, et de linea in comparatione ad superficiem, et de superficie in comparatione ad corpus; scilicet quod non corrumpantur nec generentur, et tamen aliqua variatio attendatur circa huiusmodi.

Eadem enim ratio est de omnibus his: omnia enim huiusmodi similiter sunt termini, secundum quod in extremo considerantur, vel divisiones secundum quod sunt in medio. Unde, sicut secundum defluxum motus variatur nunc secundum esse, licet maneat idem secundum substantiam propter identitatem mobilis, ita etiam variatur punctus, nec fit aliud et aliud propter divisionem lineae, licet non corrumpatur nec generetur simpliciter. Et eadem ratio est de aliis.

514. Hanc autem quaestionem Philosophus pertractat in decimotertio et decimoquarto. Et veritas quaestionis huius est, quod huiusmodi mathematica non sunt substantiae rerum, sed sunt accidentia supervenientia substantiis. Deceptio autem quantum ad magnitudines provenit ex hoc, quod non distinguitur de corpore secundum quod est in genere substantiae, et secundum quod est in genere quantitatis. In genere enim substantiae est secundum quod componitur ex materia et forma, quam consequuntur dimensiones in materia corporali. Ipsae autem dimensiones pertinent ad genus quantitatis, quae non sunt substantiae, sed accidentia, quibus subiicitur substantia composita ex materia et forma. Sicut etiam supra dictum est, quod deceptio ponentium numeros esse substantias rerum, proveniebat ex hoc quod non distinguebant inter unum quod est principium numeri, et unum quod convertitur cum ente.

513. *And it is similar* (1002b8). Then he makes the foregoing argument clear by using a similar case. For the now in time stands in relation to time as a point to a line. But the now in time does not seem to be generated or corrupted, because if it were, its generation or corruption would have to be measured by some particular time or instant. Thus the measure of this now either would be another now, and so on to infinity, or would be time itself. But this is impossible.

And even though the now is not generated or corrupted, still each now always seems to differ, not substantially but existentially, because the substance of the now corresponds to the mobile subject. But the difference of the now in terms of existence corresponds to the variation in motion, as is shown in *Physics* 4. Therefore, the same thing seems to be true of a point in relation to a line, and of a line in relation to a surface, and of a surface in relation to a body, namely, that they are neither corrupted nor generated, although some variation is observable in things of this kind.

For the same holds true of all of these, because all things of this kind are, in like manner, limits if regarded as at the extremities, or divisions if they are found in between. Hence, just as the now varies existentially as motion flows by, although it remains substantially the same because the mobile subject remains the same, so also does the point vary. And it does not become different because of the division of a line, even though it is not corrupted or generated in an absolute sense. The same holds true of the others.

514. But the Philosopher will treat this question in books 13 and 14. And the truth of the matter is that mathematical entities of this kind are not the substances of things, but are accidents which accrue to substances. But this mistake about continuous quantities is due to the fact that no distinction is made between the sort of body which belongs to the genus of substance and the sort which belongs to the genus of quantity. For body belongs to the genus of substance according as it is composed of matter and form, and dimensions are a natural consequence of these in bodily matter. But dimensions themselves belong to the genus of quantity, and are not substances, but accidents whose subject is a body composed of matter and form. The same thing too was said above [500] about those who held that numbers are the substances of things, for their mistake came from not distinguishing between the one which is the principle of number and that which is interchangeable with being.

LECTURE 14

Are there separate forms which are the essences of sensible things?

1002b12 Omnino vero dubitabit aliquis, quare oportet quaerere quaedam praeter sensibilia, quae sunt intermedia, quas ponimus species. [515]

ὅλως δ' ἀπορήσειεν ἄν τις διὰ τί καὶ δεῖ ζητεῖν ἄλλ' ἄττα παρά τε τὰ αἰσθητὰ καὶ τὰ μεταξύ, οἷον ἃ τίθεμεν εἴδη.

But in general one will wonder why, in addition to sensible things and those which are intermediate, it is necessary to look for certain other things that we posit as the specific essences (or forms) of sensible things.

1002b14 Nam si ideo quia mathematica a praesentibus in aliquo quodam differunt, in esse vero plures similis speciei nihil differunt. Quare non erunt eorum principia numero determinata, quemadmodum nec praesentium literarum numero quidem omnium non sunt principia determinata, sed specie; nisi quis sumat huius syllabae, aut huius vocis: harum enim erunt et numero determinata. Similiter autem et in eis, quae sunt intermedia: infinita enim et illic sunt quae eiusdem speciei. [516]

εἰ γὰρ διὰ τοῦτο, ὅτι τὰ μὲν μαθηματικὰ {15} τῶν δεῦρο ἄλλῳ μέν τινι διαφέρει, τῷ δὲ πόλλ' ἄττα ὁμοειδῆ εἶναι οὐθὲν διαφέρει, ὥστ' οὐκ ἔσονται αὐτῶν αἱ ἀρχαὶ ἀριθμῷ ἀφωρισμέναι (ὥσπερ οὐδὲ τῶν ἐνταῦθα γραμμάτων ἀριθμῷ μὲν πάντων οὐκ εἰσὶν αἱ ἀρχαὶ ὡρισμέναι, εἴδει δέ, ἐὰν μὴ λαμβάνῃ τις τησδὶ τῆς συλλαβῆς {20} ἢ τησδὶ τῆς φωνῆς· τούτων δ' ἔσονται καὶ ἀριθμῷ ὡρισμέναι—ὁμοίως δὲ καὶ ἐπὶ τῶν μεταξύ· ἄπειρα γὰρ κἀκεῖ τὰ ὁμοειδῆ),

For if it is because the objects of mathematics differ in one respect from the things that are at hand, they do not differ in being from many things that are specifically the same. Hence the principles of sensible things will not be limited in number but only in species; unless one were to consider the principles of this particular syllable or word, for these are limited in number. And this is likewise true of the intermediate entities, for in their case too there are an infinite number of things that are specifically the same.

Quare, si non praeter sensibilia et mathematica, alia quaedam, qualia dicunt species ipsas quidam, non erit una numero et specie substantia. Nec principia entium numero existunt quanta aliqua, sed specie. Ergo si hoc est necessarium, et species necessarium est propter hoc esse. Etenim et si non bene dearticulant dicentes, sed hoc est quod volunt, et eos ea necesse est dicere: quia specierum singula substantia quaedam est, sed non secundum accidens.

ὥστ' εἰ μὴ ἔστι παρὰ τὰ αἰσθητὰ καὶ τὰ μαθηματικὰ ἕτερ' ἄττα οἷα λέγουσι τὰ εἴδη τινές, οὐκ ἔσται μία ἀριθμῷ ἀλλ' εἴδει οὐσία, οὐδ' αἱ ἀρχαὶ τῶν {25} ὄντων ἀριθμῷ ἔσονται ποσαί τινες ἀλλὰ εἴδει· εἰ οὖν τοῦτο ἀναγκαῖον, καὶ τὰ εἴδη ἀναγκαῖον διὰ τοῦτο εἶναι τιθέναι. καὶ γὰρ εἰ μὴ καλῶς διαρθροῦσιν οἱ λέγοντες, ἀλλ' ἔστι γε τοῦθ' ὃ βούλονται, καὶ ἀνάγκη ταῦτα λέγειν αὐτοῖς, ὅτι τῶν εἰδῶν οὐσία τις ἕκαστόν ἐστι καὶ οὐθὲν κατὰ συμβεβηκός.

Hence, if in addition to sensible substances and the objects of mathematics there are not certain other things, such as some call the forms, there will be no substance which is one both numerically and specifically. Nor will the principles of beings be limited in number, but only in species. Therefore, if this is necessary, it will also be necessary on this account that there should be forms. And even if those who speak of the forms do not express themselves clearly, although this is what they wanted to say, they must affirm that each of the forms is a substance, and that nothing accidental pertains to them.

1002b30 At vero si ponimus species esse et unum numero principia et non specie, diximus quae contingere necesse est impossibilia. [518]

ἀλλὰ μὴν εἴ γε θήσομεν τά τε εἴδη εἶναι καὶ ἓν ἀριθμῷ τὰς ἀρχὰς ἀλλὰ μὴ εἴδει, εἰρήκαμεν ἃ συμβαίνειν ἀναγκαῖον ἀδύνατα.

But if we hold that the forms exist, and that principles are one numerically but not specifically, we have stated the untenable conclusions that follow from this view.

---

515. Postquam Philosophus inquisivit utrum mathematica sint principia rerum sensibilium, hic inquirit utrum supra mathematica sint aliqua alia principia, puta quae dicuntur species, quae sunt substantiae et principia horum sensibilium. Et circa hoc tria facit.

515. Having inquired whether the objects of mathematics are the principles of sensible substances, the Philosopher now inquires whether in addition to the objects of mathematics there are certain other principles, such as those which we call forms, which are the substances and principles of sensible things. In regard to this, he does three things.

Primo movet dubitationem.

Secundo inducit rationem ad unam partem, ibi, *nam si ideo*.

Tertio obiicit ad partem contrariam, ibi, *at vero si ponimus* et cetera.

Dicit ergo primo, quod supposito quod mathematica non sint principia rerum sensibilium et eorum substantia, ulterius aliquis dubitabit quae est ratio quare praeter substantias sensibiles et praeter mathematica quae sunt media inter sensibilia et species, oportet iterum ponere tertium genus, scilicet ipsas *species*, idest ideas vel formas separatas.

516. Deinde cum dicit *nam si ideo* obiicit ad unam partem: et videtur haec esse ratio quare oportet species ponere praeter sensibilia et mathematica: quia mathematica *a praesentibus* idest a sensibilibus, quae in universo sunt, differunt quidem in aliquo, quia mathematica abstrahunt a materia sensibili;

non tamen differunt in hoc, sed magis conveniunt, quia sicut in sensibilibus inveniuntur plura numero differentia eiusdem speciei, utpote plures homines, aut plures equi, ita etiam in mathematicis inveniuntur plura numero differentia eiusdem speciei, puta plures trianguli aequilateri, et plures lineae aequales. Et si ita est, sequitur quod sicut principia sensibilium non sunt determinata secundum numerum, sed secundum speciem, ita etiam sit *in mediis* idest in mathematicis.

Manifestum est enim quod in sensibilibus propter hoc quod sunt plura individua unius speciei sensibilis, principia sensibilium non sunt determinata numero, sed specie, nisi forte accipiantur principia propria huius individui, quae sunt etiam in numero determinata et individualia.

Et ponit exemplum in vocibus. Manifestum est enim quod vocis literatae, literae sunt principia; non tamen sunt aliquo numero determinato individualium literarum, sed solum secundum speciem sunt determinatae literae secundum aliquem numerum, quarum aliae sunt vocales, et aliae consonantes: sed haec determinatio est secundum speciem, non secundum numerum. Non enim unum solum est A sed multa, et sic de aliis literis. Sed si accipiantur hae literae, quae sunt principia huius determinatae syllabae vel dictionis aut orationis, sic sunt determinatae numero.

Et eadem ratione, cum sint multa mathematica numero differentia in una specie, non poterunt esse mathematica principia mathematicorum determinata numero, sed determinata specie solum: puta si dicamus quod principia triangulorum sunt tria latera et tres anguli.

First, he presents the question.

Second (1002b14; [516]), he argues one side of the question, at *for if it is because*.

Third (1002b30; [518]), he argues the other side, at *but if we hold*.

Accordingly, he first says that, if one assumes that the objects of mathematics are not the principles of sensible things and their substances, one will next have the problem of why, in addition to both sensible things and the objects of mathematics (which are an intermediate genus between sensible things and the forms), it is necessary to posit a third genus of entities, namely, the *specific essences*, that is, the ideas or separate forms.

516. *For if it is because* (1002b14). Here he argues one side of the question. The reason why it is necessary to posit separate forms over and above sensible substances and the objects of mathematics seems to be that the objects of mathematics differ in one respect *from the things that are at hand*, that is, from sensible things, which exist in the universe. For the objects of mathematics abstract from sensible matter.

Yet in another respect they do not differ, but rather agree. For just as we find many sensible things that are specifically the same but numerically different, as many men or many horses, in a similar way we find many objects of mathematics which are specifically the same but numerically different, such as many equilateral triangles and many equal lines. And if this is true, it follows that, just as the principles of sensible things are not limited in number, but in species, the same thing is true *of the intermediate entities*—the objects of mathematics.

For, since in the case of sensible things there are many individuals of one sensible species, it is evident that the principles of sensible things are not limited in number, but in species—unless, of course, we can consider the proper principles of a particular individual thing, which are also limited in number and are individual.

He gives words as an example, for in the case of a word expressed in letters it is clear that the letters are its principles, yet there are not a limited number of individual letters taken numerically, but only a limited number taken specifically, some of which are vowels and some consonants. But this limitation is according to species and not according to number. For A is not only one, but many, and the same applies to other letters. But if we take those letters which are the principles of a particular syllable, whether written or spoken, then they are limited in number.

And for the same reason, since there are many objects of mathematics which are numerically different in one species, the mathematical principles of mathematical science could not be limited in number, but only in species. We might say, for example, that the principles of triangles are

Sed haec determinatio est secundum speciem: contingit enim quodlibet eorum in infinitum multiplicari.

Si igitur nihil esset praeter sensibilia et mathematica; sequeretur quod substantia speciei non esset una secundum numerum, et quod principia entium non essent determinata in aliquo numero, sed erunt determinata solum secundum speciem. Si ergo est necessarium quod sint determinata secundum numerum (alioquin contingeret esse principia rerum infinita numero), sequitur quod necesse sit species esse praeter mathematica et sensibilia.

517. Et hoc est quod Platonici volunt dicere, quod sequitur ex necessitate ad positiones eorum quod sit in singularium substantia species aliquid unum, cui non conveniat aliquid secundum accidens. Homini enim individuo convenit aliquid secundum accidens, scilicet album vel nigrum; sed homini separato, qui est species secundum Platonicos, nihil convenit per accidens, sed solum quod pertinet ad rationem speciei. Et quamvis hoc dicere intendant, *non tamen bene dearticulant*, idest non bene distinguunt.

518. Deinde cum dicit *at vero* obiicit in contrarium: et dicit, quod si ponamus species separatas esse, et quod principia rerum non sunt solum determinata specie, sed etiam numero, quaedam inconvenientia sequuntur, quae superius in quadam quaestione sunt tacta. Hanc autem dubitationem Philosophus determinat duodecimo et quartodecimo huius libri. Et veritas dubitationis est quod sicut mathematica non sunt praeter sensibilia, ita nec species rerum separatae praeter mathematica et sensibilia. Principia autem rerum efficientia et moventia sunt quidem determinata numero; sed principia rerum formalia quorum sunt multa individua unius speciei, non sunt determinata numero, sed solum specie.

three sides and three angles, but this limitation is according to species, for any of them can be multiplied to infinity.

Therefore, if there were nothing besides sensible things and the objects of mathematics, it would follow that the substance of a form would be numerically one, and that the principles of beings would not be limited in number, but only in species. Therefore, if it is necessary that they be limited in number (otherwise it would happen that the principles of things are infinite in number), it follows that there must be forms in addition to the objects of mathematics and sensible things.

517. This is what the Platonists wanted to say, because it necessarily follows from the things that they held that, in the case of the substance of sensible things, there is a single form to which nothing accidental belongs. For something accidental, such as whiteness or blackness, pertains to an individual man; but to this separate man, who is a form according to the Platonists, there pertains nothing accidental, but only what belongs to the definition of the species. And although they wanted to say this, they did not *express themselves clearly*; that is, they did not clearly distinguish things.

518. *But if we hold that* (1002b30). Then he counters with an argument for the other side of the question. He says that, if we hold that there are separate forms and that the principles of things are limited not only in species but also in number, certain impossible consequences will follow, which are touched on above in one of the questions [464]. But the Philosopher will deal with this problem in book 12 [2450] and book 14 of this work. And the truth of the matter is that, just as the objects of mathematics do not exist apart from sensible things, neither do forms exist apart from the objects of mathematics and from sensible substances. And while the efficient and moving principles of things are limited in number, the formal principles of things (of which there are many individuals in one species) are not limited in number, but only in species.

LECTURE 15

Do first principles exist actually or potentially, and
are they universal or singular?

1002b32 His autem affine est quaerere, utrum potestate sunt elementa, aut aliquo alio modo. [519]

And connected with these problems there is the question of whether the elements of things exist potentially or in some other way.

1002b34 Nam si aliter, prius aliquid erit principiis aliud. Prior enim erit potestas causa illa. Possibile autem non est necessarium illo modo se habere. [520]

If they exist in some other way, then there will be something else prior to first principles. For potency is prior to that cause, but the potential need not exist in that way.

1003a2 Si vero potestate sunt elementa, nihil entium esse convenit. Nam possibile est esse, quod nondum est ens: fit enim non ens. Nihil autem fit impossibilium esse. Has igitur dubitationes quaerere necesse est. [521]

But if the elements exist potentially, it is possible for nothing to exist, for even that which does not yet exist is capable of existing, because that which does not exist may come to be. But nothing that is incapable of existing may come to be. It is necessary, then, to investigate these problems.

1003a6 Et utrum universalia sint, aut ut dicimus singularia. [523]

And there is also the problem of whether principles are universals or singular things, as we maintain.

1003a7 Nam si universalia, non erunt substantiae. Nihil enim communium hoc aliquid significat, sed quale quid. Substantia vero hoc aliquid est. [524]

For if they are universals, they will not be substances, because a common term signifies not a particular thing, but what sort of thing, and a substance is a particular thing.

1003a9 Sed si est hoc aliquid, et ponitur quid communiter quod praedicatur, multa erit animalia Socrates ipseque homo et animal: si significat singulum hoc aliquid et unum. Si igitur universalia sint principia, ea contingunt. [526]

But if it is a particular thing, and is held to be the common whatness which is predicated of things, Socrates himself will be many animals: himself and man and animal. (That is, if each of these signifies a particular thing and a one.) If, then, the first principles of things are universals, these consequences will follow.

1003a13 Si autem non universalia, sed quasi singularia; non erunt scibilia. Universales enim sunt omnes scientiae. Quare erunt diversa priora principiis universaliter praedicata, si futura est eorum scientia. [527]

However, if they are not universals but have the nature of singular things, they will not be knowable, for all scientific knowledge is universal. Hence, if there is to be any scientific knowledge of first principles, there will have to be different principles which are predicated universally and are prior to first principles.

---

519. Postquam Philosophus inquisivit quae sunt principia, hic inquirit quomodo sunt.

Et primo utrum sint in potentia vel in actu.

519. Having inquired what the principles are, the Philosopher now asks how they exist.

First, he asks whether they exist potentially or actually;

Secundo utrum sint universalia vel singularia, ibi, *et utrum universalia* et cetera.

Circa primum tria facit.

Primo movet dubitationem.

Secundo obiicit ad unam partem, ibi, *nam si aliter* et cetera.

Tertio obiicit in contrarium, ibi, *si vero potestate* et cetera.

Quaerit ergo primo, utrum prima principia sint in potentia, vel *aliquo alio modo*, idest in actu. Et haec dubitatio inducitur propter antiquos naturales, qui ponebant sola principia materialia, quae sunt in potentia. Platonici autem ponentes species quasi principia formalia, ponebant eas esse in actu.

520. Deinde cum dicit *nam si aliter* probat quod principia sint in potentia. Si enim essent *aliter*, scilicet in actu, sequeretur quod aliquid esset prius principiis; potentia enim actu prius est. Quod patet ex hoc, quod prius est a quo non convertitur consequentia essendi: sequitur autem si est, quod possit esse; non autem ex necessitate sequitur, si est possibile, quod sit actu. Hoc autem est inconveniens quod aliquid sit prius primo principio; ergo impossibile quod primum principium sit aliter quam in potentia.

521. Deinde cum dicit *si vero* obiicit in contrarium; quia si principia rerum sint in potentia, sequitur quod nihil sit entium in actu; nam illud quod est possibile esse, nondum est ens. Et hoc probat per hoc quod id quod fit, non est ens; quod enim est, non fit. Sed nihil fit nisi quod possibile est esse; ergo omne quod est possibile esse, est non ens. Si igitur principia sint tantum in potentia, erunt non entia. Si autem principia non sint, nec effectus sunt: sequitur ergo quod contingit nihil esse in entibus. Et concludit epilogando quod secundum praedicta necessarium est dubitare de principiis propter praemissas rationes.

522. Haec autem quaestio determinabitur in nono huius, ubi ostendetur quod actus est simpliciter prior potentia, sed potentia est prior actu tempore in eo quod movetur de potentia ad actum. Et sic oportet primum principium esse in actu et non in potentia ut ostendit in duodecimo huius.

523. Deinde cum dicit *et utrum* inquirit utrum principia sint per modum universalium aut per modum singularium: et circa hoc tria facit.

Primo proponit dubitationem.

Secundo obiicit ad unam partem, ibi, *nam si universalia* et cetera.

second (1003a6; [523]), whether they are universals or singulars, at *and there is also the problem*.

In regard to the first he does three things.

First, he raises the question.

Second (1002b34; [520]), he argues one side, at *if they exist*.

Third (1003a2; [521]), he argues the opposite side, at *but if the elements*.

His first question (1002b32), then, is whether first principles exist potentially or *in some other way*, that is, actually. This problem is introduced because of the ancient philosophers of nature, who held that there are only material principles, which are in potency. But the Platonists, who posited separate forms as formal principles, claimed that they exist actually.

520. *If they exist* (1002b34). He proves that principles exist potentially. For if they were to exist *in some other way*, that is, actually, it would follow that there would be something prior to principles, for potency is prior to act. This is clear from the fact that one thing is prior to another when the sequence of their being cannot be reversed. For if a thing exists, it follows that it can be, but it does not necessarily follow that, if a thing is possible, it will exist actually. But it is impossible for anything to be prior to a first principle. Therefore, it is impossible for a first principle to exist in any other way than potentially.

521. *But if the elements* (1003a2). Here he argues the other side of the question. If the principles of things exist potentially, it follows that no beings exist actually, for that which exists potentially does not yet exist actually. He proves this on the grounds that that which is coming to be is not a being. For that which exists is not coming to be, but only that comes to be which exists potentially. Therefore, everything that exists potentially is non-being. Hence if principles exist only potentially, beings will not exist. But if principles do not exist, neither will their effects. It follows, then, that it is possible for nothing to exist in the order of being. And in summing this up he concludes that according to what has been said it is necessary to inquire about the principles of things for the reasons given.

522. This question will be answered in book 9 [1844] of this work, where it is shown that act is prior to potency in an unqualified sense, but that in anything moved from potency to act, potency is prior to act in time. Hence it is necessary that the first principles exist actually and not potentially, as is shown in book 12 [2500] of this work.

523. *And there is also the problem* (1003a6). Here he asks whether the principles of things exist as universals or as singular things, and in regard to this he does three things.

First, he presents the question.

Second (1003a7; [524]), he argues one side, at *for if they are universals*.

Tertio obiicit ad aliam, ibi, *si autem non universalia* et cetera.

Est ergo dubitatio, utrum principia sint universalia, vel existant per modum quorumdam singularium.

524. Deinde cum dicit *nam si* probat quod principia non sunt universalia tali ratione. Nullum communiter praedicatum de multis significat hoc aliquid, sed significat tale sive quale; non quidem secundum qualitatem accidentalem, sed secundum qualitatem substantialem; est enim quaedam substantialis qualitas, ut infra in quinto huius dicetur. Et ratio huius est quia hoc aliquid dicitur secundum quod in se subsistit; quod autem in se subsistit, non potest esse in multis ens, quod est de ratione communis. Quod enim in multis est, in se subsistens non est; nisi et ipsum esset multa, quod est contra rationem communis. Nam commune est, quod est unum in multis. Sic igitur patet, quod nullum communium significat hoc aliquid, sed significat formam in multis existentem.

525. Addit autem minorem, scilicet quod substantia significat hoc aliquid. Et hoc quidem verum est quantum ad primas substantias, quae maxime et proprie substantiae dicuntur, ut habetur in *Praedicamentis*: huiusmodi enim substantiae sunt in se subsistentes. Relinquitur ergo quod principia, si sunt universalia, non sunt substantiae. Et ita vel substantiarum non erunt aliqua principia, vel oportebit dicere quod non sint substantiae substantiarum principia.

526. Sed quia aliquis posset concedere quod aliquid communiter praedicatum significet hoc aliquid, consequenter diluitur cum dicit *sed si est*.

Ostendit quod inconveniens ex hoc sequitur. Si enim id quod communiter praedicatur sit hoc aliquid, sequeretur quod omne id de quo illud commune praedicatur, sit hoc aliquid quod est commune. Sed planum est, quod de Socrate praedicatur et homo et animal, quorum utrumque, scilicet homo et animal, est quoddam commune praedicatum. Unde si omne commune praedicatum sit hoc aliquid, sequitur quod Socrates sit tria hoc aliquid, quia Socrates est Socrates, quod est hoc aliquid: ipse etiam est homo, quod est secundum praedicta hoc aliquid: ipse etiam est animal, quod similiter est hoc aliquid. Erit ergo tria hoc aliquid. Et ulterius sequitur quod sit tria animalia: nam animal praedicatur de ipso et de homine et de Socrate.

Cum ergo hoc sit inconveniens, inconveniens est quod aliquid communiter praedicatum sit hoc aliquid. Haec igitur sunt inconvenientia quae sequuntur, si universalia sunt principia.

Third (1003a13; [527]), he argues the other side, at *however, if they are not universals*.

The problem (1003a6), then, is whether principles are universals or exist in the manner of singular things.

524. *For if they are* (1003a7). Then he proves that principles are not universals, by the following argument. No predicate common to many things signifies a particular thing, but rather signifies such and such a thing or of what sort a thing is. It does this not according to accidental quality, but according to substantial quality, as is stated below in book 5 (1020a33; [987]) of this work. The reason for this is that a particular thing is said to be such insofar as it subsists of itself. But that which subsists of itself cannot be something that exists in many, as belongs to the notion of common. For that which exists in many will not subsist of itself unless it is itself many. But this is contrary to the notion of common, because what is common is what is one-in-many. Hence it is clear that a particular thing does not signify anything common, but rather signifies a form existing in many things.

525. Further, he adds the minor premise, namely, that substance signifies a particular thing. And this is true of first substances, which are said to be substances in the full and proper sense, as is stated in the *Categories*. For substances of this kind are things that subsist of themselves. Thus it follows that, if principles are universals, they are not substances. Hence either there will be no principles of substances, or it will be necessary to say that the principles of substances are not substances.

526. But since it is possible for someone to affirm that some common predicate might signify this particular thing, he therefore criticizes this when he says, *but if it is* (1003a9).

He explains the untenable consequence resulting from this. For if a common predicate were a particular thing, it would follow that everything to which that common predicate is applied would be this particular thing which is common. But it is clear that both animal and man are predicated of Socrates, and that each of these—animal and man—is a common predicate. Hence, if every common predicate were a particular thing, it would follow that Socrates would be three particular things. For Socrates is Socrates, which is a particular thing, and he is also a man, which is a particular thing according to the above, and he is also an animal, which is similarly a particular thing. Hence he would be three particular things. Further, it would follow that there would be three animals; for animal is predicated of itself, of man, and of Socrates.

Therefore, since this is impossible, it is also impossible for a common predicate to be a particular thing. These, then, will be the impossible consequences which follow if principles are universals.

527. Deinde cum dicit *si autem* obiicit in contrarium. Cum enim omnes scientiae sint universales, non sunt singularium, sed universalium. Si igitur aliqua principia non sint universalia, sed singularia, non erunt scibilia secundum seipsa. Si ergo de eis debet aliqua scientia haberi, oportebit esse aliqua priora principia, quae sunt universalia. Sic igitur oportet prima principia esse universalia, ad hoc quod scientia habeatur de rebus; quia ignoratis principiis necesse est alia ignorare.

528. Haec autem quaestio determinatur in septimo huius; ubi ostenditur quod universalia non sunt substantiae, nec principia rerum. Non autem propter hoc sequitur, quod si principia et substantiae rerum sint singularia, quod eorum non possit esse scientia; tum quia res immateriales etsi sint singulariter subsistentes, sunt tamen etiam intelligibiles; tum etiam quia de singularibus est scientia secundum universales eorum rationes per intellectum apprehensas.

527. *However, if they are not* (1003a13). He argues the other side of the question. Since all sciences are universal, they are not concerned with singulars, but with universals. Therefore, if some principles were not universals, but were singular things, they would not be knowable in themselves. Hence, if any science were to be had of them, there would have to be certain prior principles, which would be universals. It is necessary, then, that first principles be universals in order that science may be had of things, because if principles remain unknown, other things must remain unknown.

528. This question will be answered in book 7 [1584] of this work, where it is shown that universals are neither substances nor the principles of things. However, it does not follow for this reason that, if the principles and substances of things were singulars, there could be no science of them: both because immaterial things, even though they subsist as singulars, are nevertheless also intelligible, and also because there is science of singulars according to their universal concepts which are apprehended by the intellect.

Book 4

The Subject of Metaphysics

Lecture 1

The proper subject of metaphysics

1003a21 Est autem scientia quaedam quae speculatur ens inquantum ens et quae hui insunt secundum se. [529]

ἔστιν ἐπιστήμη τις ἣ θεωρεῖ τὸ ὂν ᾗ ὂν καὶ τὰ τούτῳ ὑπάρχοντα καθ᾽ αὑτό.

There is a certain science which studies being as being and the attributes which necessarily belong to being.

1003a23 Haec autem nulli est in parte dictarum eadem. Aliarum enim nulla intendit universaliter de ente in uantum est ens, verum partem eius abscindentes aliquam, circa quidem hanc speculantur ipsum accidens: veluti scientiarum mathematicae. [532]

αὕτη δ᾽ ἐστὶν οὐδεμιᾷ τῶν ἐν μέρει λεγομένων ἡ αὐτή: οὐδεμία γὰρ τῶν ἄλλων ἐπισκοπεῖ καθόλου περὶ τοῦ ὄντος ᾗ ὄν, ἀλλὰ μέρος αὐτοῦ τι ἀποτεμόμεναι {25} περὶ τούτου θεωροῦσι τὸ συμβεβηκός, οἷον αἱ μαθηματικαὶ τῶν ἐπιστημῶν.

This science is not the same as any of the so-called particular sciences, for none of the other sciences attempt to study being as being in general, but rather, cutting off some part of it, they study the accidents of this part. This, for example, is what the mathematical sciences do.

1003a26 Quoniam autem principia et extremas quaerimus causas, palam, quia cuiusdam eas naturae secundum se esse necesse est. Si ergo et entium elementa quaerentes, ea quaesierunt principia, necesse et entis elementa esse non secundum accidens, sed inquantum sunt entia. Unde et nobis entis inquantum est ens, primae causae sunt accipiendae. [533]

ἐπεὶ δὲ τὰς ἀρχὰς καὶ τὰς ἀκροτάτας αἰτίας ζητοῦμεν, δῆλον ὡς φύσεώς τινος αὐτὰς ἀναγκαῖον εἶναι καθ᾽ αὑτήν. εἰ οὖν καὶ οἱ τὰ στοιχεῖα τῶν ὄντων ζητοῦντες ταύτας τὰς ἀρχὰς ἐζήτουν, ἀνάγκη καὶ τὰ {30} στοιχεῖα τοῦ ὄντος εἶναι μὴ κατὰ συμβεβηκὸς ἀλλ᾽ ᾗ ὄν: διὸ καὶ ἡμῖν τοῦ ὄντος ᾗ ὂν τὰς πρώτας αἰτίας ληπτέον.

Now since we are seeking the principles and ultimate causes of things, it is evident that these must be of themselves the causes of some nature. Hence, if those who sought the elements of beings sought these principles, they must be the elements of beings not in any accidental way, but inasmuch as they are beings. Therefore, the first causes of being as being must also be understood by us.

1003a33 Ens autem multis quidem dicitur modis; sed ad unum et ad unam naturam aliquam et non aequivoce. [534]

τὸ δὲ ὂν λέγεται μὲν πολλαχῶς, ἀλλὰ πρὸς ἓν καὶ μίαν τινὰ φύσιν καὶ οὐχ ὁμωνύμως

The term "being" is used in many senses, but with reference to one thing and to some one nature and not equivocally.

Sed quemadmodum salubre omne ad sanitatem, hoc quidem ad conservationem, id vero in actione, aliud quia et signum (ut urina) sanitatis, hoc autem quia illius est susceptibile.

ἀλλ᾽ ὥσπερ καὶ τὸ {35} ὑγιεινὸν ἅπαν πρὸς ὑγίειαν, τὸ μὲν τῷ φυλάττειν τὸ δὲ τῷ ποιεῖν τὸ δὲ τῷ σημεῖον εἶναι τῆς ὑγιείας τὸ δ᾽ ὅτι δεκτικὸν αὐτῆς,

Thus everything healthy is related to health, one thing because it preserves health, another because it causes it, another because it is a sign of it (like urine), and still another because it is receptive of it.

Et medicinale a medicina. Hoc enim habendo medicinas dicitur medicinale, illud vero susceptibile ad eam, aliud vero per actus existentium medicinae. Similiter autem alia sumemus his dicta.

{1003b1} καὶ τὸ ἰατρικὸν πρὸς ἰατρικήν (τὸ μὲν γὰρ τῷ ἔχειν ἰατρικὴν λέγεται ἰατρικὸν τὸ δὲ τῷ εὐφυὲς εἶναι πρὸς αὐτὴν τὸ δὲ τῷ ἔργον εἶναι τῆς ἰατρικῆς), ὁμοιοτρόπως δὲ καὶ ἄλλα ληψόμεθα λεγόμενα τούτοις,

The term "medical" is related in a similar way to the art of medicine, for one thing is called medical because it possesses the art of medicine, another because it is receptive of it, and still another because it is the act of those who have the art of medicine. We can take other words which are used in a way similar to these.

Ita vero et ens multipliciter dicitur quidem, sed omne ad primum principium.

{5} οὕτω δὲ καὶ τὸ ὂν λέγεται πολλαχῶς μὲν ἀλλ᾽ ἅπαν πρὸς μίαν ἀρχήν:

And similarly there are many senses in which the term "being" is used, but each is referred to a first principle.

Haec enim quia substantiae entia dicuntur, illa vero quia passiones substantiae dicuntur,

τὰ μὲν γὰρ ὅτι οὐσίαι, ὄντα λέγεται, τὰ δ᾽ ὅτι πάθη οὐσίας,

For some things are called beings because they are substances; others because they are passions of substances;

alia quia via ad substantiam aut corruptiones, aut privationes, aut qualitates, aut effectiva, aut generativa substantiae, aut ad substantiam dictorum, aut quorumdam horum negationes, aut substantiae.

τὰ δ᾽ ὅτι ὁδὸς εἰς οὐσίαν ἢ φθοραὶ ἢ στερήσεις ἢ ποιότητες ἢ ποιητικὰ ἢ γεννητικὰ οὐσίας ἢ τῶν πρὸς τὴν οὐσίαν λεγομένων, ἢ τούτων τινὸς {10} ἀποφάσεις ἢ οὐσίας:

others because they are a process toward substance, or corruptions or privations or qualities of substance, or because they are productive or generative principles of substance, or of things that are related to substance, or the negation of some of these or of substance.

Quare et non ens esse non ens dicimus.

διὸ καὶ τὸ μὴ ὂν εἶναι μὴ ὂν φαμεν.

For this reason too we say that non-being is non-being.

1003b11 Quemadmodum ergo salubrium omnium una est scientia, ita hoc etiam et in aliis. Non enim solum circa unum dictorum unius est scientiae speculari, sed ad unum dictorum naturam. Etenim ea modo quodam circa unum dicuntur. [544]

καθάπερ οὖν καὶ τῶν ὑγιεινῶν ἁπάντων μία ἐπιστήμη ἔστιν, ὁμοίως τοῦτο καὶ ἐπὶ τῶν ἄλλων. οὐ γὰρ μόνον τῶν καθ᾽ ἓν λεγομένων ἐπιστήμης ἐστὶ θεωρῆσαι μιᾶς ἀλλὰ καὶ τῶν πρὸς μίαν λεγομένων φύσιν: καὶ γὰρ ταῦτα τρόπον τινὰ {15} λέγονται καθ᾽ ἕν.

Therefore, just as there is one science of all healthy things, so too the same thing is true in other cases. For it is the office of one and the same science to study not only those things that are referred to one thing but also those which are referred to one nature. For those too in a sense are referred to one thing.

1003b15 Manifestum igitur quia entia unius est scientiae speculari inquantum entia. [545]

δῆλον οὖν ὅτι καὶ τὰ ὄντα μιᾶς θεωρῆσαι ᾗ ὄντα.

It is evident, then, that it is the function of one science to study beings as beings.

1003b16 Ubique vero proprie primi est scientia et ex quo alia pendent et propter quod dicuntur. Ergo si hoc est substantia, substantiarum oportet principia et causas habere philosophum ipsum. [546]

πανταχοῦ δὲ κυρίως τοῦ πρώτου ἡ ἐπιστήμη, καὶ ἐξ οὗ τὰ ἄλλα ἤρτηται, καὶ δι᾽ ὃ λέγονται. εἰ οὖν τοῦτ᾽ ἐστὶν ἡ οὐσία, τῶν οὐσιῶν ἂν δέοι τὰς ἀρχὰς καὶ τὰς αἰτίας ἔχειν τὸν φιλόσοφον.

But in every respect a science is concerned with what is primary, and that on which other things depend, and from which they derive their name. Hence, if this is substance, it must be of substances that the philosopher possesses the principles and causes.

1003b19 Omnis autem generis unius est sensus unus et scientia: ut grammatica una ens, omnes speculatur voces. Quapropter et entis inquantum est ens, quascumque species speculari unius est scientiae genere, et species specierum. [547]

ἅπαντος δὲ γένους καὶ αἴσθησις μία ἑνὸς {20} καὶ ἐπιστήμη, οἷον γραμματικὴ μία οὖσα πάσας θεωρεῖ τὰς φωνάς: διὸ καὶ τοῦ ὄντος ᾗ ὂν ὅσα εἴδη θεωρῆσαι μιᾶς ἐστὶν ἐπιστήμης τῷ γένει, τά τε εἴδη τῶν εἰδῶν.

Now, of every single genus of things, there is one sense and one science. For example, grammar, which is one science, studies all words. And for this reason too it belongs to a general science to study all species of being as being and the species of these species.

---

529. In praecedenti libro Philosophus disputative processit de illis, quae debent in hac scientia considerari: hic incipit procedere demonstrative determinando veritatem quaestionum prius motarum et disputatarum. Fuit autem in praecedenti libro disputatum tam de his quae pertinent ad modum huius scientiae, scilicet ad quae se extendit huius scientiae consideratio, quam etiam de his quae sub consideratione huius scientiae cadunt. Et quia prius oportet cognoscere modum scientiae quam procedere in scientia ad ea consideranda de

529. In the preceding book the Philosopher proceeded to treat dialectically the things that ought to be considered in this science. Here he begins to proceed demonstratively by establishing the true answer to those questions which have been raised and argued dialectically. In the preceding book he treated dialectically both the things that pertain to the method of this science, namely, those to which the consideration of this science extends, as well as those which fall under the consideration of this science. And because it is first necessary to know the method of a science before

quibus est scientia, ut in secundo libro dictum est: ideo dividitur haec pars in duas.

Primo dicit de quibus est consideratio huius scientiae.

Secundo dicit de rebus quae sub consideratione huius scientiae cadunt, in quinto libro, ibi, *principium dicitur aliud quidem* et cetera.

Prima in duas.

Primo subiectum stabilit huius scientiae.

Secundo procedit ad solvendum quaestiones motas in libro praecedenti de consideratione huius scientiae, ibi, *ens autem multis.*

Circa primum tria facit.

Primo supponit aliquam esse scientiam cuius subiectum sit ens.

Secundo ostendit quod ista non est aliqua particularium scientiarum, ibi, *haec autem* et cetera.

Tertio ostendit quod haec est scientia quae prae manibus habetur, ibi, *quoniam autem principia* et cetera.

Quia vero scientia non solum debet speculari subiectum, sed etiam subiecto per se accidentia: ideo dicit primo, quod est quaedam scientia, quae speculatur ens secundum quod ens, sicut subiectum, et speculatur *ea quae insunt enti per se*, idest entis per se accidentia.

530. Dicit autem *secundum quod est ens*, quia scientiae aliae, quae sunt de entibus particularibus, considerant quidem de ente, cum omnia subiecta scientiarum sint entia, non tamen considerant ens secundum quod ens, sed secundum quod est huiusmodi ens, scilicet vel numerus, vel linea, vel ignis, aut aliquid huiusmodi.

531. Dicit etiam *et quae huic insunt per se* et non simpliciter quae huic insunt, ad significandum quod ad scientiam non pertinet considerare de his quae per accidens insunt subiecto suo, sed solum de his quae per se insunt. Geometra enim non considerat de triangulo utrum sit cupreus vel ligneus, sed solum considerat ipsum absolute secundum quod habet tres angulos aequales et cetera. Sic igitur huiusmodi scientia, cuius est ens subiectum, non oportet quod consideret de omnibus quae insunt enti per accidens, quia sic consideraret accidentia quaesita in omnibus scientiis, cum omnia accidentia insint alicui enti, non tamen secundum quod est ens. Quae enim sunt per se accidentia inferioris, per accidens se habent ad superius, sicut per se accidentia hominis non sunt per se accidentia animalis.

Necessitas autem huius scientiae quae speculatur ens et per se accidentia entis, ex hoc apparet, quia huiusmodi non debent ignota remanere, cum ex eis aliorum

proceeding to consider the things with which it deals, as was explained in book 2 [335], this part is therefore divided into two members.

First, he speaks of the things that this science considers;

second [749], of those which fall under its consideration. He does this in book 5, at *in one sense the term "principle"* (1012b34).

The first part is divided into two members.

First, he establishes what the subject matter of this science is.

Second (1003a33; [534]), he proceeds to answer the questions raised in the preceding book about the things that this science considers, at *the term "being."*

In regard to the first he does three things.

First, he submits that there is a science whose subject is being.

Second (1003a23; [532]), he shows that it is not one of the particular sciences, at *this science is not the same*;

third (1003a26; [533]), he shows that it is the science with which we are now dealing, at *now since we are seeking.*

Now, because a science should investigate not only its subject but also the proper accidents of its subject, he therefore first says that there is a science which studies being as being, as its subject, and studies also *the attributes which necessarily belong to being*, that is, its proper accidents.

530. He says *as being* because the other sciences, which deal with particular beings, do indeed consider being (for all the subjects of the sciences are beings), yet they do not consider being as being, but as some particular kind of being (for example, number or line or fire or the like).

531. He also says *and the attributes which necessarily belong to being*, and not just those which belong to being, in order to show that it is not the business of this science to consider those attributes which belong accidentally to its subject, but only those which belong necessarily to it. For geometry does not consider whether a triangle is of bronze or of wood, but only considers it in an absolute sense according as it has three angles equal to two right angles. Hence a science of this kind, whose subject is being, must not consider all the attributes which belong accidentally to being, because then it would consider the accidents investigated by all sciences. For all accidents belong to some being, but not inasmuch as it is being. For those accidents which are the proper accidents of an inferior thing are related in an accidental way to a superior thing (for example, the proper accidents of man are not the proper accidents of animal).

Now the necessity of this science, which considers being and its proper accidents, is evident from this: such things should not remain unknown since the knowledge of other

dependeat cognitio; sicut ex cognitione communium dependet cognitio rerum propriarum.

532. Deinde cum dicit *haec autem* hic ostendit, quod ista scientia non sit aliqua particularium scientiarum, tali ratione. Nulla scientia particularis considerat ens universale inquantum huiusmodi, sed solum aliquam partem entis divisam ab aliis; circa quam speculatur per se accidens, sicut scientiae mathematicae aliquod ens speculantur, scilicet ens quantum. Scientia autem communis considerat universale ens secundum quod ens: ergo non est eadem alicui scientiarum particularium.

533. Deinde cum dicit *quoniam autem* hic ostendit, quod ista scientia, quae prae manibus habetur, habet ens pro subiecto, tali ratione. Omne principium est per se principium et causa alicuius naturae: sed nos quaerimus prima rerum principia et altissimas causas, sicut in primo dictum est: ergo sunt per se causa alicuius naturae. Sed non nisi entis. Quod ex hoc patet, quia omnes philosophi elementa quaerentes secundum quod sunt entia, quaerebant huiusmodi principia, scilicet prima et altissima; ergo in hac scientia nos quaerimus principia entis inquantum est ens: ergo ens est subiectum huius scientiae, quia quaelibet scientia est quaerens causas proprias sui subiecti.

534. Deinde cum dicit *ens autem* hic procedit ad solvendum quaestiones in praecedenti libro motas de consideratione huius scientiae: et dividitur in tres partes.

Primo solvit quaestionem, qua quaerebant, utrum huius scientiae esset consideratio de substantiis et accidentibus simul, et utrum de omnibus substantiis.

Secundo solvit quaestionem qua quaerebatur utrum huius scientiae esset considerare de omnibus istis, quae sunt unum et multa, idem et diversum, oppositum, contrarium et huiusmodi, ibi, *si igitur ens et unum* et cetera.

Tertio solvit quaestionem, qua quaerebatur utrum huius scientiae esset considerare demonstrationis principia, ibi, *dicendum est autem utrum unius* et cetera.

Circa primum tria facit.

Primo ostendit quod huius scientiae est considerare tam de substantiis quam de accidentibus.

Secundo quod principaliter de substantiis ibi, *ubique vero proprie* et cetera.

Tertio quod de omnibus substantiis, ibi, *omnis autem generis.*

Circa primum, utitur tali ratione. Quaecumque communiter unius recipiunt praedicationem, licet non univoce, sed analogice de his praedicetur, pertinent ad unius scientiae considerationem: sed ens hoc modo praedicatur de omnibus entibus: ergo omnia entia praedicatur de omnibus entibus: ergo omnia entia

things depends on them, just as the knowledge of proper objects depends on that of common objects.

532. *This science* (1003a23). Then he shows that this science is not one of the particular sciences, and he uses the following argument. No particular science considers universal being as such, but only some part of it separated from the others, and it studies the proper accidents of this part. For example, the mathematical sciences study one kind of being, quantitative being. But the common science considers universal being as being, and therefore it is not the same as any of the particular sciences.

533. *Now since* (1003a26). Here he shows that the science with which we are dealing has being as its subject, and he uses the following argument. Every principle is of itself the principle and cause of some nature. But we are seeking the first principles and ultimate causes of things, as was explained in book 1 [57], and therefore these are of themselves the causes of some nature. But this nature can only be the nature of being. This is clear from the fact that all philosophers, in seeking the elements of things inasmuch as they are beings, sought principles of this kind, namely, the first and ultimate ones. Therefore, in this science we are seeking the principles of being as being. Hence, being is the subject of this science, for any science seeks the proper causes of its subject.

534. *The term "being"* (1003a33). Then he proceeds to answer the questions raised in the preceding book about the things that this science considers, and this is divided into three parts.

First, he answers the question of whether this science considers substances and accidents together, and whether it considers all substances.

Second (1003b22; [548]), he answers the question of whether it belongs to this science to consider all of the following: one and many, same and different, opposites, contraries, and so forth, at *now although*.

Third (1005a19; [588]), he answers the question of whether it belongs to this science to consider the principles of demonstration, at *moreover, it is necessary*.

In regard to the first he does three things.

First, he shows that it is the office of this science to consider both substances and accidents.

Second (1003b16; [546]), he shows that this science is chiefly concerned with substances, at *but in every respect*.

Third (1003b19; [547]), he shows that it pertains to this science to consider all substances, at *now, of every*.

In regard to the first part he uses this kind of argument: those things that have one term predicated of them in common, not univocally but analogously, belong to the consideration of one science. But the term "being" is thus predicated of all beings. Therefore, all beings, both sub-

pertinent ad considerationem unius scientiae, quae considerat ens inquantum est ens, scilicet tam substantias quam accidentia.

535. In hac autem ratione primo ponit minorem.

Secundo maiorem, ibi, *quemadmodum ergo salubrium omnium*.

Tertio conclusionem, ibi, *manifestum igitur* et cetera.

Dicit ergo primo, quod ens sive quod est, dicitur multipliciter. Sed sciendum quod aliquid praedicatur de diversis multipliciter:

quandoque quidem secundum rationem omnino eamdem, et tunc dicitur de eis univoce praedicari, sicut animal de equo et bove.

Quandoque vero secundum rationes omnino diversas; et tunc dicitur de eis aequivoce praedicari, sicut canis de sidere et animali.

Quandoque vero secundum rationes quae partim sunt diversae et partim non diversae: diversae quidem secundum quod diversas habitudines important, unae autem secundum quod ad unum aliquid et idem istae diversae habitudines referuntur; et illud dicitur analogice praedicari, idest proportionaliter, prout unumquodque secundum suam habitudinem ad illud unum refertur.

536. Item sciendum quod illud unum ad quod diversae habitudines referuntur in analogicis, est unum numero, et non solum unum ratione, sicut est unum illud quod per nomen univocum designatur. Et ideo dicit quod ens etsi dicatur multipliciter, non tamen dicitur aequivoce, sed per respectum ad unum; non quidem ad unum quod sit solum ratione unum, sed quod est unum sicut una quaedam natura. Et hoc patet in exemplis infra positis.

537. Ponit enim primo unum exemplum, quando multa comparantur ad unum sicut ad finem, sicut patet de hoc nomine sanativum vel salubre. Sanativum enim non dicitur univoce de diaeta, medicina, urina et animali. Nam ratio sani secundum quod dicitur de diaeta, consistit in conservando sanitatem. Secundum vero quod dicitur de medicina, in faciendo sanitatem. Prout vero dicitur de urina, est signum sanitatis. Secundum vero quod dicitur de animali, ratio eius est, quoniam est receptivum vel susceptivum sanitatis. Sic igitur omne sanativum vel sanum dicitur ad sanitatem unam et eamdem. Eadem enim est sanitas quam animal suscipit, urina significat, medicina facit, et diaeta conservat.

538. Secundo ponit exemplum quando multa comparantur ad unum sicut ad principium efficiens. Aliquid enim dicitur medicativum, ut qui habet artem medicinae, sicut medicus peritus. Aliquid vero quia est bene

stances and accidents, belong to the consideration of one science which considers being as being.

535. Now in this argument he first gives the minor premise [535];

second (1003b11; [544]), the major premise, at *therefore, just as*;

third (1003b15; [545]), the conclusion, at *it is evident, then*.

He accordingly first says that the term "being," or what is, has several meanings. But it must be noted that a term is predicated of different things in various senses.

Sometimes it is predicated of them according to a meaning which is entirely the same, and then it is said to be predicated of them univocally, as "animal" is predicated of a horse and of an ox.

Sometimes it is predicated of them according to meanings which are entirely different, and then it is said to be predicated of them equivocally, as "dog" is predicated of a star and of an animal.

And sometimes it is predicated of them according to meanings which are partly different and partly not (different inasmuch as they imply different relationships, and the same inasmuch as these different relationships are referred to one and the same thing). Then it is said to be predicated analogously, or proportionally, according as each one by its own relationship is referred to that one same thing.

536. It must also be noted that the one thing to which the different relationships are referred in the case of analogical things is numerically one and not just one in meaning, which is the kind of oneness designated by a univocal term. Hence he says that, although the term "being" has several senses, still it is not predicated equivocally, but in reference to one thing—not to one thing which is one merely in meaning, but to one which is one as a single definite nature. This is evident in the examples given in the text.

537. First, he gives the example of many things being related to one thing as an end. This is clear in the case of the term "healthy" or "healthful." For the term "healthy" is not predicated univocally of food, medicine, urine, and an animal. The concept "healthy" as applied to food means something that preserves health; as applied to medicine, it means something that causes health; as applied to urine, it means something that is a sign of health; and as applied to an animal it means something that is the recipient or subject of health. Hence every use of the term healthy refers to one and the same health, for it is the same health which the animal receives, which urine signifies, which medicine causes, and which food preserves.

538. Second, he gives the example of many things being related to one thing as an efficient principle. For one thing is called medical because it possesses the art of medicine, like the skilled physician. Another is called medical be-

aptum ad habendum artem medicinae, sicut homines qui sunt dispositi ut de facili artem medicinae acquirant. Ex quo contingit quod ingenio proprio quaedam medicinalia operantur. Aliquid vero dicitur medicativum vel medicinale, quia eo opus est ad medicinam, sicut instrumenta quibus medici utuntur, medicinalia dici possunt, et etiam medicinae quibus medici utuntur ad sanandum. Et similiter accipi possunt alia quae multipliciter dicuntur, sicut et ista.

539. Et sicut est de praedictis, ita etiam et ens multipliciter dicitur. Sed tamen omne ens dicitur per respectum ad unum primum. Sed hoc primum non est finis vel efficiens sicut in praemissis exemplis, sed subiectum.

Alia enim dicuntur entia vel esse, quia per se habent esse sicut substantiae, quae principaliter et prius entia dicuntur.

Alia vero quia sunt passiones sive proprietates substantiae, sicut per se accidentia uniuscuiusque substantiae.

Quaedam autem dicuntur entia, quia sunt via ad substantiam, sicut generationes et motus.

Alia autem entia dicuntur, quia sunt corruptiones substantiae. Corruptio enim est via ad non esse, sicut generatio via ad substantiam. Et quia corruptio terminatur ad privationem, sicut generatio ad formam, convenienter ipsae etiam privationes formarum substantialium esse dicuntur.

Et iterum qualitates vel accidentia quaedam dicuntur entia, quia sunt activa vel generativa substantiae, vel eorum quae secundum aliquam habitudinem praedictarum ad substantiam dicuntur, vel secundum quamcumque aliam.

Item negationes eorum quae ad substantiam habitudinem habent, vel etiam ipsius substantiae esse dicuntur. Unde dicimus quod non ens est non ens. Quod non diceretur nisi negationi aliquo modo esse competeret.

540. Sciendum tamen quod praedicti modi essendi ad quatuor possunt reduci. Nam unum eorum quod est debilissimum, est tantum in ratione, scilicet negatio et privatio, quam dicimus in ratione esse, quia ratio de eis negociatur quasi de quibusdam entibus, dum de eis affirmat vel negat aliquid. Secundum quid autem differant negatio et privatio, infra dicetur.

541. Aliud autem huic proximum in debilitate est, secundum quod generatio et corruptio et motus entia dicuntur. Habent enim aliquid admixtum de privatione et negatione. Nam motus est actus imperfectus, ut dicitur tertio *Physicorum*.

cause it is naturally disposed to have the art of medicine, as men who are so disposed that they may acquire the art of medicine easily (and according to this some men can engage in medical activities as a result of a peculiar natural constitution). And another is called medical or medicinal because it is necessary for healing, as the instruments which physicians use can be called medical. The same thing is also true of the things called medicines, which physicians use in restoring health. Other terms which resemble these in having many senses can be taken in a similar way.

539. And just as the above-mentioned terms have many senses, so also does the term "being." Yet every being is called such in relation to one first thing, and this first thing is not an end or an efficient cause, as is the case in the foregoing examples, but a subject.

For some things are called beings, or are said to be, because they have being of themselves, as substances, which are called beings in the primary and proper sense.

Others are called beings because they are passions or properties of substances, as the proper accidents of any substance.

Others are called beings because they are processes toward substance, as generation and motion.

And others are called beings because they are corruptions of substances, for corruption is the process toward non-being just as generation is the process toward substance. And since corruption terminates in privation just as generation terminates in form, the very privations of substantial forms are fittingly called beings.

Again, certain qualities or certain accidents are called beings because they are productive or generative principles of substances or of those things that are related to substance according to one of the foregoing relationships or any other relationship.

And similarly the negations of those things that are related to substances, or even substance itself, are also called beings. Hence we say that non-being is non-being. But this would not be possible unless a negation possessed being in some way.

540. But it must be noted that the above-mentioned modes of being can be reduced to four. For one of them, which is the most imperfect (negation and privation) exists only in the mind. We say that these exist in the mind because the mind busies itself with them as kinds of being while it affirms or denies something about them. In what respect negation and privation differ will be treated below [564].

541. There is another mode of being inasmuch as generation and corruption are called beings, and this mode by reason of its imperfection comes close to the one given above. For generation and corruption have some admixture of privation and negation, because motion is an imperfect kind of act, as is stated in *Physics* 3.

542. Tertium autem dicitur quod nihil habet de non ente admixtum, habet tamen esse debile, quia non per se, sed in alio, sicut sunt qualitates, quantitates et substantiae proprietates.

543. Quartum autem genus est quod est perfectissimum, quod scilicet habet esse in natura absque admixtione privationis, et habet esse firmum et solidum, quasi per se existens, sicut sunt substantiae. Et ad hoc sicut ad primum et principale omnia alia referuntur. Nam qualitates et quantitates dicuntur esse, inquantum insunt substantiae; motus et generationes, inquantum tendunt ad substantiam vel ad aliquid praedictorum; privationes autem et negationes, inquantum removent aliquid trium praedictorum.

544. Deinde cum dicit *quemadmodum ergo* hic ponit maiorem primae rationis; dicens, quod est unius scientiae speculari non solum illa quae dicuntur *secundum unum*, idest secundum unam rationem omnino, sed etiam eorum quae dicuntur per respectum ad unam naturam secundum habitudines diversas. Et huius ratio est propter unitatem eius ad quod ista dicuntur; sicut patet quod de omnibus sanativis considerat una scientia, scilicet medicinalis, et similiter de aliis quae eodem modo dicuntur.

545. Deinde cum dicit *manifestum igitur* hic ponit conclusionem intentam quae per se est manifesta.

546. *Ubique vero* hic ponit quod haec scientia principaliter considerat de substantiis, etsi de omnibus entibus consideret, tali ratione. Omnis scientia quae est de pluribus quae dicuntur ad unum primum, est proprie et principaliter illius primi, ex quo alia dependent secundum esse, et propter quod dicuntur secundum nomen; et hoc ubique est verum. Sed substantia est hoc primum inter omnia entia. Ergo philosophus qui considerat omnia entia, primo et principaliter debet habere in sua consideratione principia et causas substantiarum; ergo per consequens eius consideratio primo et principaliter de substantiis est.

547. Deinde cum dicit *omnis autem* hic ostendit quod primi philosophi est considerare de omnibus substantiis, tali ratione. Omnium eorum qui sunt unius generis, est unus sensus et una scientia, sicut visus est de omnibus coloribus, et grammatica considerat omnes voces. Si igitur omnia entia sint unius generis aliquo modo, oportet quod omnes species eius pertineant ad considerationem unius scientiae quae est generalis: et species entium diversae pertineant ad species illius scientiae diversas.

Hoc autem dicit, quia non oportet quod una scientia consideret de omnibus speciebus unius generis secundum proprias rationes singularum specierum, sed se-

542. The third mode of being admits of no admixture of non-being, yet it is still an imperfect kind of being, because it does not exist of itself, but in something else (for example, qualities and quantities and the properties of substances).

543. The fourth mode of being is the one which is most perfect, namely, what has being in reality without any admixture of privation, and has firm and solid being inasmuch as it exists of itself. This is the mode of being which substances have. Now all the others are reduced to this as the primary and principal mode of being. For qualities and quantities are said to be inasmuch as they exist in substances; motions and generations are said to be inasmuch as they are processes tending toward substance or toward some of the foregoing; and negations and privations are said to be inasmuch as they remove some part of the preceding three.

544. *Therefore, just as* (1003b11). Here he gives the major premise of the first argument. He says that it is the office of one science to study not only those things that are referred *to one thing*, that is, to one common notion, but also those which are referred to one nature according to different relationships. And the reason for this is that the thing to which they are referred is one; just as it is clear that one science, medicine, considers all health-giving things. The same thing holds true of other things that are spoken of in the same way.

545. *It is evident* (1003b15). Then he draws his intended conclusion, which is clear by itself.

546. *But in every* (1003b16). Then he shows that this science, even though it considers all beings, is chiefly concerned with substances. He uses the following argument. Every science that deals with many things that are referred to one primary thing is properly and principally concerned with that primary thing on which other things depend for their being and from which they derive their name; this is true in every case. But substance is the primary kind of being. Hence the philosopher who considers all beings ought to consider primarily and chiefly the principles and causes of substances. Therefore, his consideration extends primarily and chiefly to substances.

547. *Now, of every* (1003b19). Then he shows by the following argument that it is the business of the first philosopher to consider all substances. There is one sense and one science of all things belonging to one genus. For example, sight is concerned with all colors, and grammar with all words. Therefore, if all beings somehow belong to one genus, all species of being must belong to the consideration of one science which is a general science, and different species of being must belong to the different species of that science.

He says this because it is not necessary for one science to consider all the species of one genus according to the special notes of every single species, but only inasmuch as

cundum quod conveniunt in genere. Secundum autem proprias rationes pertinent ad scientias speciales, sicut est in proposito. Nam omnes substantiae, inquantum sunt entia vel substantiae, pertinent ad considerationem huius scientiae: inquantum autem sunt talis vel talis substantia, ut leo vel bos, pertinent ad scientias speciales.

they agree generically. But according to their proper notions, the different species of one genus belong to the special sciences, as happens in the present case. For inasmuch as all substances are beings or substances, they belong to the consideration of this science, but inasmuch as they are a particular kind of substance, as a lion or an ox, they belong to the special sciences.

LECTURE 2

The divisions of being and unity

1003b22 Si igitur ens et unum idem et una natura, quia se adinvicem consequuntur ut principium et causa, sed non ut una ratione ostensa. Nihil autem differt, nec si similiter suscipimus, sed et prae opere magis. [548]

εἰ δὴ τὸ ὂν καὶ τὸ ἓν ταὐτὸν καὶ μία φύσις τῷ ἀκολουθεῖν ἀλλήλοις ὥσπερ ἀρχὴ καὶ αἴτιον, ἀλλ᾽ οὐχ ὡς ἑνὶ λόγῳ δηλούμενα {25} (διαφέρει δὲ οὐθὲν οὐδ᾽ ἂν ὁμοίως ὑπολάβωμεν, ἀλλὰ καὶ πρὸ ἔργου μᾶλλον):

Now, although being and unity are the same and are a single nature in the sense that they are associated like principle and cause, they are not the same in the sense that they are expressed by a single concept. Yet it makes no difference, even if we consider them to be the same; in fact, this will rather support our undertaking.

1003b26 Idem enim unus homo, et ens homo et homo: et non diversum aliquid ostenditur secundum repetitam dictionem, ipsum est homo, et homo, et unus homo. Palam autem, quia non separantur nec in generatione neque in corruptione. Similiter autem et in uno. Quare palam quia additio in his idem ostendit: et nihil aliud unum praeter ens. [550]

ταὐτὸ γὰρ εἷς ἄνθρωπος καὶ ἄνθρωπος, {27} καὶ ὢν ἄνθρωπος καὶ ἄνθρωπος, καὶ οὐχ ἕτερόν τι δηλοῖ κατὰ τὴν λέξιν ἐπαναδιπλούμενον τὸ εἷς ἄνθρωπος καὶ εἷς ὢν ἄνθρωπος (δῆλον δ᾽ ὅτι οὐ χωρίζεται οὔτ᾽ ἐπὶ γενέσεως οὔτ᾽ {30} ἐπὶ φθορᾶς), ὁμοίως δὲ καὶ ἐπὶ τοῦ ἑνός, ὥστε φανερὸν ὅτι ἡ πρόσθεσις ἐν τούτοις ταὐτὸ δηλοῖ, καὶ οὐδὲν ἕτερον τὸ ἓν παρὰ τὸ ὄν,

For "one man" and "human being" and "man" are the same thing; and nothing different is expressed by repeating the terms when we say, "This is a human being, a man, and one man." And it is evident that they are not separated either in generation or in corruption. The same holds true of what is one. Hence it is evident that any addition to these expresses the same thing, and that unity is nothing else than being.

1003b32 Amplius autem cuiuscumque substantia unum est non secundum accidens, similiter et quod ens aliquid. [554]

ἔτι δ᾽ ἡ ἑκάστου οὐσία ἕν ἐστιν οὐ κατὰ συμβεβηκός, ὁμοίως δὲ καὶ ὅπερ ὄν τι:

Further, the substance of each thing is one in no accidental way, and similarly it is something that is.

1003b33 Quare quotcumque unius sunt species, tot entis, et de quibus quidem est eiusdem scientiae genere speculari. Dico autem ut de eodem et simili et aliis talibus. Fere autem omnia referuntur contraria ad principium illud. Speculata sunt autem et ea a nobis in ecloga, idest explanatione, vel tractatione contrariorum. [561]

ὥσθ᾽ ὅσα περ τοῦ ἑνὸς εἴδη, τοσαῦτα καὶ τοῦ ὄντος: περὶ ὧν τὸ τί ἐστι τῆς {35} αὐτῆς ἐπιστήμης τῷ γένει θεωρῆσαι, λέγω δ᾽ οἷον περὶ ταὐτοῦ καὶ ὁμοίου καὶ τῶν ἄλλων τῶν τοιούτων. σχεδὸν δὲ πάντα ἀνάγεται τἀναντία εἰς τὴν ἀρχὴν ταύτην: {1004a1} τεθεωρήσθω δ᾽ ἡμῖν ταῦτα ἐν τῇ ἐκλογῇ τῶν ἐναντίων.

Hence there are as many species of being as there are of unity, of which it is the office of the same general science to treat. I mean, for example, sameness and likeness and other such attributes. And almost all contraries may be referred to this starting point. But these have been studied by us in our selection (that is, in our explanation or treatment) of contraries.

1004a2 Et tot partes sunt philosophiae quot substantiae. Quare aliquam esse primam necesse et habitam ipsis. Existunt enim recte genera ens et unum habentia. Quapropter et haec sequuntur scientiae. Est enim philosophus ut mathematicus dictus. Etenim ea partes habet et prima quaedam et secunda est scientia, et alia deinde in mathematicis. [563]

καὶ τοσαῦτα μέρη φιλοσοφίας ἔστιν ὅσαι περ αἱ οὐσίαι: ὥστε ἀναγκαῖον εἶναί τινα πρώτην καὶ ἐχομένην αὐτῶν. ὑπάρχει {5} γὰρ εὐθὺς γένη ἔχον τὸ ὂν [καὶ τὸ ἕν]: διὸ καὶ αἱ ἐπιστῆμαι ἀκολουθήσουσι τούτοις. ἔστι γὰρ ὁ φιλόσοφος ὥσπερ ὁ μαθηματικὸς λεγόμενος: καὶ γὰρ αὕτη ἔχει μέρη, καὶ πρώτη τις καὶ δευτέρα ἔστιν ἐπιστήμη καὶ ἄλλαι ἐφεξῆς ἐν τοῖς μαθήμασιν.

And there are just as many parts of philosophy as there are substances, so that there must be a first philosophy and one which is next in order to it. For being and unity are things that straightway have genera, and for this reason the sciences will correspond to these. For the term "philosopher" is used like the term "mathematician," for mathematics too has parts, and there is a first and a second science and then others, following these among the mathematical sciences.

548. Hic procedit ad ostendendum quod ad considerationem unius scientiae pertinent considerare huiusmodi communia, scilicet unum et multa, idem et diversum: et circa hoc duo facit.

Primo ostendit hoc de singulis per proprias rationes.

Secundo de omnibus simul per quasdam rationes communes, ibi, *et philosophi est de omnibus posse speculari.*

Circa primum duo facit.

Primo ostendit quod de omnibus hic considerare debet philosophus.

Secundo docet modum considerandi, ibi, *quare quoniam unum multipliciter* et cetera.

Circa primum duo facit.

Primo ostendit quod ad hanc scientiam pertineat considerare de uno et de speciebus unius.

Secundo quod ad eamdem scientiam pertineat considerare de omnibus oppositis, ibi, *quoniam autem unius est opposita considerare.*

Circa primum duo facit.

Primo enim ostendit quod huius scientiae est considerare de uno.

Secundo quod eius sit considerare de speciebus unius, ibi, *quare quotcumque unius.*

Dicit ergo primo, quod ens et unum sunt idem et una natura. Hoc ideo dicit, quia quaedam sunt idem numero quae non sunt una natura, sed diversae, sicut Socrates, et hoc album, et hoc musicum. Unum autem et ens non diversas naturas, sed unam significant. Hoc autem contingit dupliciter. Quaedam enim sunt unum quae consequuntur se adinvicem convertibiliter sicut principium et causa. Quaedam vero non solum convertuntur ut sint idem subiecto, sed etiam sunt unum secundum rationem, sicut vestis et indumentum.

549. Unum autem et ens significant unam naturam secundum diversas rationes. Unde sic se habent sicut principium et causa, sed non sicut tunica et vestis, quae sunt nomina penitus synonyma. Nihil tamen differt ad propositum, si similiter accipiamus ea dici, sicut illa quae sunt unum et subiecto et ratione. Sed hoc erit *magis prae opere*, idest magis utile ad hoc quod intendit.

Intendit enim probare quod unum et ens cadunt sub eadem consideratione, et quod habent species sibi correspondentes. Quod manifestius probaretur si unum et ens essent idem re et ratione, quam si sint idem re et non ratione.

548. Here he proceeds to show that the study of common attributes such as one and many and same and different belongs to the consideration of one and the same science, and in regard to this he does two things.

First, he shows that this is true of each attribute taken separately by arguing from proper or specific principles.

Second (1004a34; [570]), he shows that this is true of all attributes taken together by arguing from common principles, at *and it is also evident.*

In regard to the first he does two things.

First, he shows that the philosopher ought to investigate all these attributes.

Second (1004a22; [568]), he tells us how to investigate them, at *hence, since the term "one."*

In regard to the first he does two things.

First, he shows that it is the office of this science to consider unity and its species.

Second (1004a9; [564]), he shows that it is the office of one and the same science to consider all opposites, at *now, since it belongs to one science.*

In regard to the first he does two things.

First, he shows that it is the office of this science to consider unity.

Second (1003b33; [561]), he shows that it also belongs to it to examine the species of unity, at *hence there are as many.*

He therefore says first that being and unity are the same and are a single nature. He says this because some things are numerically the same which are not a single nature, but different natures (for example, Socrates, this white thing, and this musician). Now the terms "one" and "being" do not signify different natures, but a single nature. But things can be one in two ways: for some things are one which are associated as interchangeable things (like "principle" and "cause"), and some are interchangeable not only in the sense that they are one and the same numerically, but also in the sense that they are one and the same conceptually, like "garment" and "clothing."

549. Now the terms "one" and "being" signify one nature according to different concepts, and therefore they are like the terms "principle" and "cause," and not like the terms "tunic" and "garment," which are wholly synonymous. Yet it makes no difference to his thesis if we consider them to be used in the same sense, as those things that are one both numerically and conceptually. In fact, this will *rather support our undertaking*, that is, it will serve his purpose better.

For he intends to prove that unity and being belong to the same study, and that the species of the one correspond to those of the other. The proof of this would be clearer if unity and being were the same both numerically and conceptually, rather than just numerically and not conceptually.

550. Quod autem sint idem re, probat duabus rationibus,

quarum primam ponit ibi, *idem enim*, quae talis est. Quaecumque duo addita uni nullam diversitatem afferunt, sunt penitus idem: sed unum et ens addita homini vel cuicumque alii nullam diversitatem afferunt: ergo sunt penitus idem. Minor patet: idem enim est dictum homo, et unus homo. Et similiter est idem dictum, ens homo, vel quod est homo: et non demonstratur aliquid alterum cum secundum dictionem replicamus dicendo, est ens homo, et homo, et unus homo. Quod quidem probat sic.

551. Idem enim est generari et corrumpi hominem, et id quod est homo. Quod ex hoc patet, quia generatio est via ad esse, et corruptio mutatio ab esse ad non esse. Unde nunquam generatur homo, quin generetur ens homo: nec unquam corrumpitur homo, quin corrumpatur ens homo. Quae autem simul generantur et corrumpuntur sunt unum.

552. Et sicut dictum est quod ens et homo non separantur in generatione et corruptione, similiter apparet de uno. Nam cum generatur homo, generatur unus homo: et cum corrumpitur, similiter corrumpitur.

Unde manifestum est quod appositio in istis ostendit idem; et per hoc quod additur vel unum vel ens, non intelligitur addi aliqua natura supra hominem. Ex quo manifeste apparet, quod unum non est aliud praeter ens: quia quaecumque uni et eidem sunt eadem, sibi invicem sunt eadem.

553. Patet autem ex praedicta ratione, non solum quod sunt unum re, sed quod differunt ratione. Nam si non differrent ratione, essent penitus synonyma; et sic nugatio esset cum dicitur, ens homo et unus homo. Sciendum est enim quod hoc nomen homo, imponitur a quidditate, sive a natura hominis; et hoc nomen res imponitur a quidditate tantum; hoc vero nomen ens, imponitur ab actu essendi: et hoc nomen unum, ab ordine vel indivisione. Est enim unum ens indivisum. Idem autem est quod habet essentiam et quidditatem per illam essentiam, et quod est in se indivisum. Unde ista tria, res, ens, unum, significant omnino idem, sed secundum diversas rationes.

554. Deinde cum dicit *amplius autem* hic ponit secundam rationem ad idem; quae talis est.

Quaecumque duo praedicantur de substantia alicuius rei per se et non per accidens, illa sunt idem secundum rem: sed ita se habent unum et ens, quod

550. He proves that they are the same numerically by using two arguments.

He gives the first where he says, *for "one man"* (1003b26), and it runs as follows. Any two things that when added to some third thing cause no difference are wholly the same. But when one and being are added to man or to anything at all, they cause no difference. Therefore, they are wholly the same. The truth of the minor premise is evident, for it is the same thing to say "man" and "one man." And similarly it is the same thing to say "human being" and "the thing that is man," and nothing different is expressed when we repeat the terms in saying, "This is a human being, a man, and one man." He proves this as follows.

551. It is the same thing for man and the thing that is man to be generated and corrupted. This is evident from the fact that generation is a process toward being, and corruption a change from being to non-being. Hence a man is never generated without a human being being generated, nor is a man ever corrupted without a human being being corrupted. And those things that are generated and corrupted together are themselves one and the same.

552. And just as it has been said that being and man are not separated either in generation or in corruption, so too this is evident of what is one; for when a man is generated, one man is generated, and when a man is corrupted, one man is also corrupted.

It is clear, then, that the apposition of these expresses the same thing, and that, just because the term "one" or "being" is added to "man," it is not to be understood that some nature is added to man. And from this it is clearly apparent that unity does not differ from being, because any two things that are identical with some third thing are identical with each other.

553. It is also evident from the foregoing argument that unity and being are the same numerically but differ conceptually; for if this were not the case they would be wholly synonymous, and then it would be nonsense to say, "a human being," and "one man." For it must be borne in mind that the term "man" is derived from the quiddity or the nature of man, and the term "thing" from the quiddity only; but the term "being" is derived from the act of being, and the term "one" from order or lack of division (for what is one is an undivided being). Now what has an essence, and a quiddity by reason of that essence, and what is undivided in itself are the same. Hence these three—"thing," "being," and "one"—signify absolutely the same thing but according to different concepts.

554. *Further, the substance* (1003b32). Then he gives the second argument, which has to do with sameness or identity of subject. This argument is as follows.

Any two attributes which are predicated *per se* and not accidentally of the substance of each thing are the same in subject, or numerically. But unity and being are such

praedicantur per se et non secundum accidens de substantia cuiuslibet rei. Substantia enim cuiuslibet rei est unum per se et non secundum accidens. Ens ergo et unum significant idem secundum rem.

555. Quod autem ens et unum praedicentur de substantia cuiuslibet rei per se et non secundum accidens, sic potest probari. Si enim praedicarentur de substantia cuiuslibet rei per aliquod ens ei additum, de illo iterum necesse est praedicari ens, quia unumquodque est unum et ens.

Aut ergo iterum de hoc praedicatur per se, aut per aliquid aliud additum. Si per aliquid aliud, iterum esset quaestio de illo addito, et sic erit procedere usque ad infinitum. Hoc autem est impossibile: ergo necesse est stare in primo, scilicet quod substantia rei sit una et ens per seipsam, et non per aliquid additum.

556. Sciendum est autem quod circa hoc Avicenna aliud sensit. Dixit enim quod unum et ens non significant substantiam rei, sed significant aliquid additum. Et de ente quidem hoc dicebat, quia in qualibet re quae habet esse ab alio, aliud est esse rei, et substantia sive essentia eius: hoc autem nomen ens, significat ipsum esse. Significat igitur (ut videtur) aliquid additum essentiae.

557. De uno autem hoc dicebat, quia aestimabat quod illud unum quod convertitur cum ente, sit idem quod illud unum quod est principium numeri. Unum autem quod est principium numeri necesse est significare quamdam naturam additam substantiae: alioquin cum numerus ex unitatibus constituatur, non esset numerus species quantitatis, quae est accidens substantiae superadditum. Dicebat autem quod hoc unum convertitur cum ente, non quia significat ipsam rei substantiam vel entis, sed quia significat accidens quod inhaeret omni enti, sicut risibile quod convertitur cum homine.

558. Sed in primo quidem non videtur dixisse recte. Esse enim rei quamvis sit aliud ab eius essentia, non tamen est intelligendum quod sit aliquod superadditum ad modum accidentis, sed quasi constituitur per principia essentiae. Et ideo hoc nomen ens quod imponitur ab ipso esse, significat idem cum nomine quod imponitur ab ipsa essentia.

559. De uno autem non videtur esse verum, quod sit idem quod convertitur cum ente, et quod est principium numeri. Nihil enim quod est in determinato genere videtur consequi omnia entia. Unde unum quod determinatur ad speciale genus entis, scilicet ad genus

that they are predicated *per se* and not accidentally of the substance of each thing, for the substance of a thing is one in itself and not accidentally. Therefore, the terms "being" and "one" signify the same thing in subject.

555. That the terms "being" and "one" are predicated *per se* and not accidentally of the substance of each thing can be proved as follows. If being and one were predicated of the substance of each thing by reason of something added to it, being would have to be predicated also of the thing added, because anything at all is one and a being.

But then there would be the question of whether being is predicated of this thing (the one added) either *per se* or by reason of some other thing that is added to it in turn. And if the latter were the case, then the same question would arise once again regarding the last thing added, and so on to infinity. But this is impossible. Hence the first position must be held, namely, that a thing's substance is one and a being of itself and not by reason of something added to it.

556. But it must be noted that Avicenna felt differently about this; for he said that the terms "being" and "one" do not signify a thing's substance, but something added to it. He said this of "being" because, in the case of anything that derives its existence from something else, the existence of such a thing must differ from its substance or essence. But the term "being" signifies existence itself. Hence it seems that being or existence is something added to a thing's essence.

557. He spoke in the same way of "one," because he thought that the one which is interchangeable with being and the one which is the principle of number are the same. And the "one" which is the principle of number must signify a reality added to the substance; otherwise, number, since it is composed of ones, would not be a species of quantity, which is an accident added to substance. He said that this kind of "one" is interchangeable with "being," not in the sense that it signifies the very substance of a thing or being, but in the sense that it signifies an accident belonging to every being, just as the ability to laugh belongs to every man.

558. But in regard to the first point he does not seem to be right, for even though a thing's existence is other than its essence, it should not be understood to be something added to its essence after the manner of an accident, but something established, as it were, by the principles of the essence. Hence the term "being," which is applied to a thing by reason of its very existence, designates the same thing as the term applied to it by reason of its essence.

559. Nor does it seem to be true that the one or unity which is interchangeable with being and that which is the principle of number are the same, for nothing that pertains to some special genus of being seems to be characteristic of all beings. Hence the unity which is limited to a spe-

quantitatis discretae, non videtur posse cum ente universali converti. Si enim unum est proprium et per se accidens entis, oportet quod ex principiis causetur entis in quantum ens, sicut quodlibet accidens proprium ex principiis sui subiecti. Ex principiis autem communibus entis inquantum est ens, non intelligitur causari aliquod particulariter ens sufficienter. Unde non potest esse quod ens aliquod determinati generis et speciei sit accidens omnis entis.

560. Unum igitur quod est principium numeri, aliud est ab eo quod cum ente convertitur. Unum enim quod cum ente convertitur, ipsum ens designat, superaddens indivisionis rationem, quae, cum sit negatio vel privatio, non ponit aliquam naturam enti additam. Et sic in nullo differt ab ente secundum rem, sed solum ratione. Nam negatio vel privatio non est ens naturae, sed rationis, sicut dictum est.

Unum vero quod est principium numeri addit supra substantiam, rationem mensurae, quae est propria passio quantitatis, et primo invenitur in unitate. Et dicitur per privationem vel negationem divisionis, quae est secundum quantitatem continuam. Nam numerus ex divisione continui causatur. Et ideo numerus ad scientiam mathematicam pertinet, cuius subiectum extra materiam esse non potest, quamvis sine materia sensibili consideretur. Hoc autem non esset, si unum quod est principium numeri, secundum esse a materia separaretur in rebus immaterialibus existens, quasi cum ente conversum.

561. *Quare quotcumque* hic concludit quod philosophi est considerare de partibus unius, sicut de partibus entis.

Et primo hoc ostendit.

Secundo etiam ostendit, quod secundum diversas partes entis et unius, sunt diversae partes philosophiae, ibi, *et tot partes*.

Dicit ergo primo, quod ex quo unum et ens idem significant, et eiusdem sunt species eaedem, oportet quod tot sint species entis, quot sunt species unius, et sibi invicem respondentes.

Sicut enim partes entis sunt substantia, quantitas et qualitas et cetera, ita et partes unius sunt idem, aequale et simile. Idem enim unum in substantia est. Aequale, unum in quantitate. Simile, unum in qualitate. Et secundum alias partes entis possent sumi aliae partes unius, si essent nomina posita. Et sicut ad unam scientiam, scilicet ad philosophiam, pertinet consideratio de omnibus partibus entis, ita et de omnibus partibus unius, scilicet

cial genus of being—discrete quantity—does not seem to be interchangeable with universal being. For, if unity is a proper and *per se* accident of being, it must be caused by the principles of being as being, just as any proper accident is caused by the principles of its subject. But it is not reasonable that something having a particular mode of being should be adequately accounted for by the common principles of being as being. It cannot be true, then, that something which belongs to a definite genus and species is an accident of every being.

560. Therefore, the kind of unity which is the principle of number differs from that which is interchangeable with being; for the unity which is interchangeable with being signifies being itself, adding to it the notion of undividedness, which, since it is a negation or a privation, does not posit any reality added to being. Thus unity differs from being in no way numerically, but only conceptually; for a negation or a privation is not a real being, but a being of reason, as has been stated [540].

However, the kind of unity which is the principle of number adds to substance the notion of a measure, which is a special property of quantity and is found first in the unit. And it is described as the privation or negation of division which pertains to continuous quantity, for number is produced by dividing the continuous. Hence number belongs to mathematical science, whose subject cannot exist apart from sensible matter but can be considered apart from sensible matter. But this would not be so if the kind of unity which is the principle of number were separate from matter in being and existed among the immaterial substances, as is true of the kind of unity which is interchangeable with being.

561. *Hence there are as many* (1003b33). Then he concludes that it is the business of the philosopher to consider the parts of unity, just as it is to consider the parts of being.

First, he proves this;

second (1004a2), he shows that there are different parts of philosophy corresponding to the different parts of being and unity, at *and there are just*.

He first says that since being and unity signify the same thing, and the species of things that are the same are themselves the same, there must be as many species of being as there are of unity, and they must correspond to each other.

For just as the parts of being are substance, quantity, quality, and so on, in a similar way the parts of unity are sameness, equality, and likeness. For things are the same when they are one in substance, equal when they are one in quantity, and like when they are one in quality. And the other parts of unity could be taken from the other parts of being, if they were given names. And just as it is the office of one science, philosophy, to consider all parts of

eodem et simili et huiusmodi. Et ad hoc *principium*, scilicet unum, reducuntur omnia contraria *fere*.

562. Et hoc addit, quia in quibusdam non est ita manifestum. Et tamen hoc esse necesse est; quia cum in omnibus contrariis alterum habeat privationem inclusam, oportet fieri reductionem ad privativa prima, inter quae praecipue est unum. Et iterum multitudo, quae ex uno causatur, causa est diversitatis differentiae et contrarietatis, ut infra dicetur. Et haec dicit esse considerata *in ecloga*, idest in electione *contrariorum*, idest in tractatu, quae est pars electa ad tractandum de contrariis, scilicet in decimo huius.

563. *Et tot partes* hic ostendit partes philosophiae distingui secundum partes entis et unius; et dicit, quod tot sunt partes philosophiae, quot sunt partes substantiae, de qua dicitur principaliter ens et unum et de qua principalis est huius scientiae consideratio et intentio. Et, quia partes substantiae sunt ordinatae adinvicem, nam substantia immaterialis est prior substantia sensibili naturaliter; ideo necesse est inter partes philosophiae esse quamdam primam.

Illa tamen, quae est de substantia sensibili, est prima ordine doctrinae, quia a notioribus nobis oportet incipere disciplinam: et de hac determinatur in septimo et octavo huius.

Illa vero, quae est de substantia immateriali est prior dignitate et intentione huius scientiae, de qua traditur in duodecimo huius.

Et tamen quaecumque sunt prima, necesse est quod sint continua aliis partibus, quia omnes partes habent pro genere unum et ens. Unde in consideratione unius et entis diversae partes huius scientiae uniuntur, quamvis sint de diversis partibus substantiae; ut sic sit una scientia inquantum partes praedictae sunt consequentes *hoc*, id est unum et ens, sicut communia substantiae.

Et in hoc philosophus est similis mathematico. Nam mathematica habet diversas partes, et quamdam principaliter sicut arithmeticam, et quamdam secundario sicut geometriam, et alia consequenter se habent his, sicut perspectiva, astrologia et musica.

being, in a similar way it is the office of this same science to consider all parts of unity, such as sameness, likeness and so forth. And to this *starting point*, namely, unity, *almost* all contraries may be referred.

562. He adds this qualification because in some cases this point is not so evident. Yet it must be true; for since one member of every pair of contraries involves privation, they must be referred back to certain primary privatives, among which unity is the most basic. And plurality, which stems from unity, is the cause of otherness, difference, and contrariety, as will be stated below. He says that this has been treated *in our selection*, or extract, *of contraries*, that is, a treatise which is the part selected to deal with contraries, namely, book 10 [2000–21] of this work.

563. *And there are* (1004a2). Here he shows that the parts of philosophy are distinguished in reference to the parts of being and unity. He says that there are as many parts of philosophy as there are parts of substance, of which being and unity chiefly are predicated, and of which it is the principal intention or aim of this science to treat. And because the parts of substance are related to each other in a certain order (for immaterial substance is naturally prior to sensible substance), then among the parts of philosophy there must be a first part.

Now that part which is concerned with sensible substance is first in the order of instruction, because any branch of learning must start with things that are better known to us. He treats of this part in books 7 [1300] and 8 of this work.

But that part which has to do with immaterial substance is prior both in dignity and in the aim of this science. This part is treated in book 12 [2488] of this work.

Yet whatever parts are first must be continuous with the others, because all parts have unity and being as their genus. Hence all parts of this science are united in the study of being and unity, although they are about different parts of substance. Thus it is one science inasmuch as the foregoing parts are things that correspond to *these*, that is, to unity and being, as common attributes of substance.

In this respect the philosopher resembles the mathematician. For mathematical science has different parts, one of which is primary, as arithmetic, another secondary, as geometry, and others following these in order, as optics, astronomy, and music.

Lecture 3

One sciences treats unity, plurality, and all opposites

1004a9 Quoniam autem unius est opposita speculari, et uni opponitur pluralitas, et negationem et privationem unius est speculari: quia utrumque speculatur unum, cuius negatio aut privatio. Haec autem quae simpliciter dicitur, quia non inest illi, aut alicui generi. [564]

ἐπεὶ δὲ μιᾶς τἀντικείμενα {10} θεωρῆσαι, τῷ δὲ ἐνὶ ἀντίκειται πλῆθος—ἀπόφασιν δὲ καὶ στέρησιν μιᾶς ἐστι θεωρῆσαι διὰ τὸ ἀμφοτέρως θεωρεῖσθαι τὸ ἐν οὗ ἡ ἀπόφασις ἢ ἡ στέρησις (ἢ <γὰρ> ἁπλῶς λέγομεν ὅτι οὐχ ὑπάρχει ἐκεῖνο, ἤ τινι γένει:

Now, since it belongs to one science to study opposites, and plurality is the opposite of unity, to study negation and privation also belongs to one science, because in both cases the unity of which there is negation or privation is studied. But this is stated either absolutely, because an attribute is not present in a thing, or not absolutely, because it is not in some genus.

Huic igitur uni differentia adest praeter quod est in negatione. Illius enim absentia negatio est. In privatione vero subiecta quaedam fit natura, de qua dicitur privatio.

ἔνθα μὲν οὖν τῷ ἐνὶ ἡ διαφορὰ πρόσεστι παρὰ τὸ ἐν τῇ ἀποφάσει, ἀπουσία γὰρ {15} ἡ ἀπόφασις ἐκείνου ἐστί, ἐν δὲ τῇ στερήσει καὶ ὑποκειμένη τις φύσις γίγνεται καθ᾽ ἧς λέγεται ἡ στέρησις)

Therefore, this difference is present in unity over and above what is implied in negation; for negation is the absence of the thing in question. But in the case of privation there is an underlying subject of which the privation is predicated.

1004a16 Sed uni pluralitas opponitur. Quare opposita dictis diversumque et dissimile et inaequale et quaecumque alia dicuntur, aut secundum pluralitatem et unum, est dictae cognoscere scientiae. Quorum unum quidem contrarietas est. Differentia namque quaedam contrarietas est, et differentia diversitas. [567]

[τῷ δ᾽ ἐνὶ πλῆθος ἀντίκειται]—ὥστε καὶ τἀντικείμενα τοῖς εἰρημένοις, τό τε ἕτερον καὶ ἀνόμοιον καὶ ἄνισον καὶ ὅσα ἄλλα λέγεται ἢ κατὰ ταῦτα ἢ κατὰ πλῆθος καὶ τὸ ἕν, {20} τῆς εἰρημένης γνωρίζειν ἐπιστήμης: ὧν ἐστι καὶ ἡ ἐναντιότης: διαφορὰ γάρ τις ἡ ἐναντιότης, ἡ δὲ διαφορὰ ἑτερότης.

But plurality is the opposite of unity. Hence the opposites of the abovementioned concepts—otherness, unlikeness, inequality, and any others which are referred to plurality or unity—must come within the scope of the science mentioned above. And contrariety is one of these; for contrariety is a kind of difference, and difference is a kind of otherness.

1004a22 Quare quoniam unum multipliciter dicitur, et haec quidem multipliciter dicentur. Attamen unius omnia cognoscere. [568]

ὥστ᾽ ἐπειδὴ πολλαχῶς τὸ ἓν λέγεται, καὶ ταῦτα πολλαχῶς μὲν λεχθήσεται, ὅμως δὲ μιᾶς ἅπαντά ἐστι γνωρίζειν:

Hence, since the term "one" is used in many senses, the terms designating the foregoing opposites will also be used in many senses. Yet it is the business of one science to know them all.

Non enim si multipliciter alterius. Quare si nec secundum unum, nec ad unum rationes referuntur, tunc alterius.

οὐ γὰρ εἰ πολλαχῶς, ἑτέρας, ἀλλ᾽ εἰ μήτε καθ᾽ ἓν μήτε {25} πρὸς ἓν οἱ λόγοι ἀναφέρονται.

For if a term is used in many senses, it does not follow that it belongs to another science. If, therefore, terms are not used with one meaning and their concepts are not referred to one thing, then they belong to a different science.

Quoniam vero ad primum omnia referuntur, ut quaecumque unum dicuntur, ad primum unum, similiter dicendum est et de eodem et diverso et contrariis se habere. Ergo divisum quoties dicitur singulum, sic reducendum est ad primum in singulis praedicatis, quomodo ad illud dicitur. Hoc enim habendo il-

ἐπεὶ δὲ πάντα πρὸς τὸ πρῶτον ἀναφέρεται, οἷον ὅσα ἓν λέγεται πρὸς τὸ πρῶτον ἕν, ὡσαύτως φατέον καὶ περὶ ταὐτοῦ καὶ ἑτέρου καὶ τῶν ἐναντίων ἔχειν: ὥστε διελόμενον ποσαχῶς λέγεται ἕκαστον, οὕτως ἀποδοτέον πρὸς τὸ πρῶτον ἐν ἑκάστῃ κατηγορίᾳ πῶς πρὸς ἐκεῖνο {30} λέγεται: τὰ μὲν γὰρ τῷ ἔχειν ἐκεῖνο τὰ δὲ

But since all things are referred to some primary thing, as all things that are one are referred to a primary one, the same thing must hold true of sameness, otherness, and the contraries. It is necessary, then, to distinguish all the senses in which each term is used and then refer them back to the primary thing signified in

lud, illa vero faciendo illud, alia vero secundum alios dicentur modos.

τῷ ποιεῖν τὰ δὲ κατ' ἄλλους λεχθήσεται τοιούτους τρόπους.

each of the predicates in question to see how each is related to it. For one thing is given a particular predicate because it possesses it, another because it produces it, and others in other ways.

1004a31 Palam ergo, quod in quaestionibus dictum est quia uni est de his et de substantia sermonem habere: hoc autem erat unum dubitatorum. [569]

φανερὸν οὖν [ὅπερ ἐν ταῖς ἀπορίαις ἐλέχθη] ὅτι μιᾶς περὶ τούτων καὶ τῆς οὐσίας ἐστὶ λόγον ἔχειν (τοῦτο δ' ἦν ἐν τῶν ἐν τοῖς ἀπορήμασιν),

Hence it is evident, as has been stated in our problems, that it is the office of a single science to give an account of these predicates as well as of substance; and this was one of the problems (995b4, 997a15; [346, 393]).

---

564. Hic ostendit, quod considerare de oppositis pertinet ad scientiam istam: et circa hoc duo facit.

Primo ostendit, quod eius est considerare de negatione et privatione.
Secundo de contrariis, ibi, *sed uni* et cetera.

Dicit ergo, quod, cum ad unam scientiam pertineat considerare opposita, sicut ad medicinam considerare sanum et aegrum, et ad grammaticam congruum et incongruum: uni autem opponitur multitudo: necesse est, quod illius scientiae sit speculari negationem et privationem, cuius est speculari unum et multitudinem. Propter quod utriusque est considerare unum; scilicet ex utroque dependet unius consideratio, de cuius ratione est negatio et privatio. Nam sicut dictum est, unum est ens non divisum: divisio autem ad multitudinem pertinet, quae uni opponitur. Unde cuius est considerare unum, eius est considerare negationem vel privationem.

565. Negatio autem est duplex: quaedam simplex per quam absolute dicitur quod hoc non inest illi. Alia est negatio in genere, per quam aliquid non absolute negatur, sed infra metas alicuius generis;

sicut caecum dicitur non simpliciter, quod non habet visum, sed infra genus animalis quod natum est habere visum. Et haec adest differentia huic quod dico unum praeter *quod est in negatione*, idest per quam distat a negatione: quia negatio dicit tantum absentiam alicuius, scilicet quod removet, sine hoc quod determinet subiectum.

Unde absoluta negatio potest verificari tam de non ente, quod est natum habere affirmationem, quam de ente, quod est natum habere et non habet. Non videns enim potest dici tam chimaera quam lapis quam etiam homo. Sed in privatione est quaedam natura vel substantia determinata, de qua dicitur privatio: non enim

564. Here he shows that it is the office of this science to consider opposites; and in regard to this he does two things.

First, he shows that it is the office of this science to consider privation and negation;
second (1004a16; [567]), to consider contraries, at *but plurality*.

He accordingly says (1004a9) that, since it pertains to one science to consider opposites (for example, it belongs to medicine to consider health and sickness, and to grammar to consider agreement and disagreement), and since plurality is the opposite of unity, the study of privation and negation must belong to that science which deals with unity and plurality. For the consideration of both involves unity; that is, the study of unity, whose concept entails negation and privation, depends on both of these. For, as has been said above [553], what is one is an undivided being, and division relates to plurality, which is the opposite of unity. Hence the study of negation and privation belongs to that science whose business it is to consider unity.

565. Now there are two kinds of negation: simple negation, by which one thing is said absolutely not to be present in something else, and negation in a genus, by which something is denied of something else, not absolutely, but within the limits of some determinate genus.

For example, not everything that does not have sight is said absolutely to be blind, but something within the genus of an animal which is naturally fitted to have sight. And this difference is present in unity over and above *what is implied in negation*. In other words, it is something by which it differs from negation, because negation expresses only the absence of something (namely, what it removes) without stating a determinate subject.

Hence simple negation can be verified both of a non-being, which is not naturally fitted to have something affirmed of it, and of a being which is naturally fitted to have something affirmed of it and does not. For "unseeing" can be predicated of a chimera and of a stone and of a man. But in the case of privation there is a determinate nature

omne non videns potest dici caecum, sed solum quod est natum habere visum.

Et sic, cum negatio, quae in ratione unius includitur, sit negatio in subiecto (alias non ens, unum dici posset): patet, quod unum differt a negatione simpliciter, et magis trahit se ad naturam privationis, ut infra decimo huius habetur.

566. Sciendum est autem quod quamvis unum importet privationem implicitam, non tamen est dicendum quod importet privationem multitudinis: quia cum privatio sit posterior naturaliter eo cuius est privatio, sequeretur quod unum esset posterius naturaliter multitudine. Item quod multitudo poneretur in definitione unius.

Nam privatio definiri non potest nisi per suum oppositum, ut quid est caecitas? Privatio visus. Unde cum in definitione multitudinis ponatur unum (nam multitudo est aggregatio unitatum), sequitur quod sit circulus in definitionibus. Et ideo dicendum quod unum importat privationem divisionis, non quidem divisionis quae est secundum quantitatem, nam ista divisio determinatur ad unum particulare genus entis, et non posset cadere in definitione unius.

Sed unum quod cum ente convertitur importat privationem divisionis formalis quae fit per opposita, cuius prima radix est oppositio affirmationis et negationis.

Nam illa dividuntur adinvicem, quae ita se habent, quod hoc non est illud. Primo igitur intelligitur ipsum ens, et ex consequenti non ens, et per consequens divisio, et per consequens unum quod divisionem privat, et per consequens multitudo, in cuius ratione cadit divisio, sicut in ratione unius indivisio; quamvis aliqua divisa modo praedicto rationem multitudinis habere non possint nisi prius cuilibet divisorum ratio unius attribuatur.

567. *Sed uni pluralitas* hic ostendit quod philosophi est considerare contraria. Uni enim multitudo opponitur, ut dictum est. Opposita autem est unius scientiae considerare. Cum igitur ista scientia consideret unum et idem, aequale et simile, necesse est quod consideret opposita his, scilicet multum, alterum sive diversum, dissimile, et inaequale, et quaecumque alia reducuntur ad illa, sive etiam ad unum et pluralitatem. Et inter ista una est contrarietas. Nam contrarietas est quaedam differentia, eorum scilicet quae maxime differunt in eodem genere: differentia vero est quaedam alteritas sive diversitas, ut decimo huius habetur: igitur contrarietas pertinet ad considerationem huius scientiae.

or substance of which the privation is predicated, for not everything that does not have sight can be said to be blind, but only that which is naturally fitted to have sight.

Thus since the negation which is included in the concept of unity is a negation in a subject (otherwise a non-being could be called one), it is evident that unity differs from simple negation and rather resembles the nature of privation, as is stated below in book 10 [2069] of this work.

566. But it must be noted that, although unity includes an implied privation, it must not be said to include the privation of plurality. For, since a privation is subsequent in nature to the thing of which it is the privation, it would follow that unity would be subsequent in nature to plurality. And it would also follow that plurality would be given in the definition of unity, for a privation can be defined only by its opposite.

For example, if someone were to ask what blindness is, we would answer that it is the privation of sight. Hence, since unity is given in the definition of plurality (for plurality is an aggregate of units), it would follow that there would be circularity in definitions. Hence it must be said that unity includes the privation of division, although not the kind of division that belongs to quantity, for this kind of division is limited to one particular genus of being and cannot be included in the definition of unity.

But the unity which is interchangeable with being implies the privation of formal division, which comes about through opposites, and whose primary root is the opposition between affirmation and negation.

For those things are divided from each other which are of such a kind that one is not the other. Therefore, being itself is understood first, and then non-being, and then division, and then the kind of unity which is the privation of division, and then plurality, whose concept includes the notion of division just as the concept of unity includes the notion of undividedness. However, some of the things that have been distinguished in the foregoing way can be said to include the notion of plurality only if the notion of unity is first attributed to each of the things distinguished.

567. But plurality (1004a16). Here he shows that it is the business of the philosopher to consider contraries, or opposites. For plurality is the opposite of unity, as has been said [564], and it is the office of one science to consider opposites. Hence, since this science considers unity, sameness, likeness, and equality, it must also consider their opposites—plurality, otherness or diversity, unlikeness, inequality, and all other attributes which are reduced to these or even to unity and plurality. And contrariety is one of these, for contrariety is a kind of difference, namely, of things differing in the same genus. But difference is a kind of otherness or diversity, as is said in book 10 [2017]. Therefore, contrariety belongs to the consideration of this science.

568. *Quare quoniam* hic tradit modum, quo philosophus de his debet determinare: et dicit, quod cum omnia praedicta deriventur ab uno, et unum multipliciter dicatur, etiam omnia ista necesse est multipliciter dici: scilicet idem et diversum et alia huiusmodi. Sed tamen quamvis multipliciter dicantur omnia, tamen quae significantur per quodlibet horum nominum est cognoscere unius scientiae, scilicet philosophiae.

Non enim sequitur, quod si aliquid dicitur multipliciter, quod propter hoc sit alterius scientiae vel diversae. Diversa enim significata si neque dicuntur *secundum unum*, idest secundum unam rationem, scilicet univoce, nec ratione diversa referuntur ad unum, sicut est in analogicis: tunc sequitur, quod sit alterius, idest diversae scientiae de his considerare, vel ad minus unius per accidens. Sicut caeleste sidus, quod est canis, considerat astrologus, naturalis autem canem marinum et terrestrem. Haec autem omnia referuntur ad unum principium. Sicut enim quae significantur per hoc nomen unum, licet sint diversa, reducuntur tamen in unum primum significatum; similiter est dicendum de his nominibus, idem, diversum, contrarium, et huiusmodi.

Et ideo circa unumquodque istorum philosophus duo debet facere: videlicet primo dividere quot modis dicitur unumquodque. Et haec divisio consequenter assignatur in *unoquoque praedicato* idest in unoquoque istorum nominum de pluribus praedicatorum, ad quod primum dicatur; sicut quid est primum significatum huius nominis idem vel diversum et quomodo ad illud omnia alia referantur; aliquid quidem inquantum habet illud, aliquid autem inquantum facit illud, vel secundum alios huiusmodi modos.

569. Deinde cum dicit *palam ergo* inducit conclusionem ex omnibus praecedentibus; scilicet quod huius scientiae est ratiocinari de his communibus et de substantia: et hoc fuit unum quaesitum inter quaestiones in tertio disputatas.

568. *Hence, since* (1004a22). Then he deals with the method by which the philosopher ought to establish these things. He says that, since all of the above-mentioned opposites are derived from unity, and the term "one" is used in many senses, all of the terms designating these must also be used in many senses (namely, "same," "other," and so on). Yet even though all of these are used in many senses, it is still the work of one science, philosophy, to know the things signified by each of these terms.

For if some term is used in many senses, it does not therefore follow that it belongs to another or different science. For if the different things signified are not referred to *with one meaning*, or according to one concept (that is, univocally), or are not referred to one thing in different ways (as in the case of analogous things), then it follows that it is the office of another, that is, of a different, science to consider them. Or at least it is the office of one science accidentally, just as astronomy considers a star in the heavens, the dog star, and natural science considers a dog-fish and a dog. But all of these are referred to one starting point. For things signified by the term "one," even though diverse, are referred back to a primary thing signified as one; and we must also speak in the same way of the terms "same," "other," "contrary," and others of this kind.

Regarding each of these terms, then, the philosopher should do two things. First, he should distinguish the many senses in which each may be used; second, he should determine regarding *each of the predicates*, that is, each of the names predicated of many things, to what primary thing it is referred. For example, he should state what the first thing signified by the term "same" or "other" is, and how all the rest are referred to it—one inasmuch as it possesses it, another inasmuch as it produces it, or in other ways of this kind.

569. *Hence it is evident* (1004a31). He draws his conclusion from what has been said, namely, that it belongs to this science to reason about those common predicates and about substance. This was one of the problems investigated in the questions treated dialectically in book 3 [393].

LECTURE 4

Metaphysics' distinction from logic

1004a34 Et philosophi est de omnibus posse speculari. [570]

καὶ ἔστι τοῦ φιλοσόφου περὶ πάντων δύνασθαι θεωρεῖν.

And it is also evident that it is the function of the philosopher to be able to study all things.

Nam, si non philosophi, quis est qui investigat si idem Socrates et Socrates sedens, aut si unum uni contrarium, aut quid est contrarium, aut quoties dicitur? Similiter autem et de talibus.

{1004b1} εἰ γὰρ μὴ τοῦ φιλοσόφου, τίς ἔσται ὁ ἐπισκεψόμενος εἰ ταὐτὸ Σωκράτης καὶ Σωκράτης καθήμενος, ἢ εἰ ἓν ἑνὶ ἐναντίον, ἢ τί ἐστι τὸ ἐναντίον ἢ ποσαχῶς λέγεται; ὁμοίως δὲ καὶ περὶ τῶν ἄλλων τῶν τοιούτων.

For if it is not the function of the philosopher, who is it that will investigate whether Socrates and Socrates sitting are the same person, or whether one thing has one contrary, or what a contrary is, or how many meanings it has? And the same applies to other questions of this kind.

Quoniam ergo unius inquantum est unum, et entis inquantum est ens, eaedem secundum se passiones sunt, sed non inquantum numeri, aut lineae, aut ignis, palam quia illius scientiae et quid est in eis cognoscere et eorum accidentia.

{5} ἐπεὶ οὖν τοῦ ἑνὸς ᾗ ἓν καὶ τοῦ ὄντος ᾗ ὂν ταῦτα καθ᾽ αὐτά ἐστι πάθη, ἀλλ᾽ οὐχ ᾗ ἀριθμοὶ ἢ γραμμαὶ ἢ πῦρ, δῆλον ὡς ἐκείνης τῆς ἐπιστήμης καὶ τί ἐστι γνωρίσαι καὶ τὰ συμβεβηκότ᾽ αὐτοῖς.

Therefore, since these same things are the essential properties of unity as unity and of being as being, but not as numbers or lines or fire, evidently it is the office of this science to know both the quiddities of these and their accidents.

Et ideo non peccant qui de eis intendebant quasi non philosophantes, sed quia primum est substantia, de qua nihil audiunt. Quare sicut sunt et numeri et inquantum numeri propriae passiones sunt, ut imparitas et paritas, et mensuratio, aequalitas, excedentia et defectio, et ea quae secundum se et adinvicem insunt numeris, similiter autem et solido, et mobili et immobili, et levi et gravi sunt alia propria, sic entis inquantum est ens quaedam propria, et ea sunt de quibus est philosophi perscrutari veritatem.

καὶ οὐ ταύτῃ ἁμαρτάνουσιν οἱ περὶ αὐτῶν σκοπούμενοι ὡς οὐ φιλοσοφοῦντες, ἀλλ᾽ ὅτι πρότερον ἡ οὐσία, {10} περὶ ἧς οὐθὲν ἐπαΐουσιν, ἐπεὶ ὥσπερ ἔστι καὶ ἀριθμοῦ ᾗ ἀριθμὸς ἴδια πάθη, οἷον περιττότης ἀρτιότης, συμμετρία ἰσότης, ὑπεροχὴ ἔλλειψις, καὶ ταῦτα καὶ καθ᾽ αὑτοὺς καὶ πρὸς ἀλλήλους ὑπάρχει τοῖς ἀριθμοῖς (ὁμοίως δὲ καὶ στερεῷ καὶ ἀκινήτῳ καὶ κινουμένῳ ἀβαρεῖ τε καὶ βάρος {15} ἔχοντι ἔστιν ἕτερα ἴδια), οὕτω καὶ τῷ ὄντι ᾗ ὂν ἔστι τινὰ ἴδια, καὶ ταῦτ᾽ ἐστὶ περὶ ὧν τοῦ φιλοσόφου ἐπισκέψασθαι τὸ ἀληθές.

Therefore, those who have been studying these things do not err by being unphilosophical, but because substance, to which they pay no attention, is first. Now there are properties of number as number—for example, oddness and evenness, commensurability and equality, excess and defect—and these belong to numbers either in themselves or in relation to one another. And similarly there are properties of the solid, and of what is changeable and what is unchangeable, and of what is heavy and what is light. And in a similar fashion there are properties of being as being; these are the ones about which the philosopher has to investigate the truth.

1004b17 Signum autem. Dialectici namque et sophistae, eamdem subinduunt figuram philosopho, quia sophistae apparens est sophia et dialectici de omnibus disputant: omnibus autem commune ens est. Disputant autem et de his, scilicet quia sophistae sunt ea communia. Nam circa idem genus versatur et sophistica et dialectica cum philosophia. [572]

σημεῖον δέ· οἱ γὰρ διαλεκτικοὶ καὶ σοφισταὶ τὸ αὐτὸ μὲν ὑποδύονται σχῆμα τῷ φιλοσόφῳ· ἡ γὰρ σοφιστικὴ φαινομένη μόνον σοφία ἐστί, καὶ οἱ διαλεκτικοὶ {20} διαλέγονται περὶ ἁπάντων, κοινὸν δὲ πᾶσι τὸ ὂν ἐστιν, διαλέγονται δὲ περὶ τούτων δῆλον ὅτι διὰ τὸ τῆς φιλοσοφίας ταῦτα εἶναι οἰκεῖα. περὶ μὲν γὰρ τὸ αὐτὸ γένος στρέφεται ἡ σοφιστικὴ καὶ ἡ διαλεκτικὴ τῇ φιλοσοφίᾳ,

An indication of this is the following. Dialecticians and sophists assume the same guise as the philosopher, for sophistry is apparent wisdom, and dialecticians dispute about all things, and being is common to all things. But evidently they dispute about these matters because they are common to philosophy. For sophistry and dialectics are concerned with the same genus of things as philosophy.

1004b23 Sed differt ab hac quidem modo potestatis, ab illa vero vitae prohaeresi idest electione. Est autem dialectica tenta-

ἀλλὰ διαφέρει τῆς μὲν τῷ τρόπῳ τῆς δυνάμεως, τῆς δὲ τοῦ βίου {25} τῇ προαιρέσει· ἔστι δὲ ἡ διαλεκτικὴ πειρ-

But philosophy differs from the latter in the manner of its power, and from the former in the choice or selection of a

tiva, de quibus philosophia est sciens: sophistica quidem visa, ens vero non. [573]

ἀστικὴ περὶ ὧν ἡ φιλοσοφία γνωριστική, ἡ δὲ σοφιστικὴ φαινομένη, οὖσα δ᾽ οὔ.

way of life. For dialectics is in search of knowledge of what the philosopher actually knows, and sophistry has the semblance of wisdom but is not really such.

1004b27 Amplius contrariorum alia coelementatio, privatio, et omnia referuntur ad ens et ad non ens, et ad unum et ad pluralitatem: ut status unius et motus pluralitatis. [578]

ἔτι τῶν ἐναντίων ἡ ἑτέρα συστοιχία στέρησις, καὶ πάντα ἀνάγεται εἰς τὸ ὂν καὶ τὸ μὴ ὄν, καὶ εἰς ἓν καὶ πλῆθος, οἷον στάσις τοῦ ἑνὸς κίνησις δὲ τοῦ πλήθους·

Further, one corresponding member of each pair of contraries is privative, and all contraries are referred to being and to non-being and to unity and to plurality (for example, rest pertains to unity and motion to plurality).

1004b29 Entia vero et substantiam confitentur fere omnes ex contrariis componi. Omnes enim principia contraria dicunt. Hi namque impar et par, illi vero calidum et frigidum, alii finitum et infinitum, alii amorem et odium. [581]

δ᾽ ὄντα καὶ τὴν {30} οὐσίαν ὁμολογοῦσιν ἐξ ἐναντίων σχεδὸν ἅπαντες συγκεῖσθαι· πάντες γοῦν τὰς ἀρχὰς ἐναντίας λέγουσιν· οἱ μὲν γὰρ περιττὸν καὶ ἄρτιον, οἱ δὲ θερμὸν καὶ ψυχρόν, οἱ δὲ πέρας καὶ ἄπειρον, οἱ δὲ φιλίαν καὶ νεῖκος.

And almost all men admit that substance and beings are composed of contraries, for all say that principles are contraries. For some speak of the odd and even, others of the hot and cold, others of the limited and unlimited, and others of love and hate.

1004b33 Omnia vero alia reducta videntur ad unum et pluralitatem. Sumatur ergo illa reductio a nobis. Principia vero et omnia quae de aliis, ad unum et ens ut in genera ea cadunt. [582]

πάντα δὲ καὶ τἆλλα ἀναγόμενα φαίνεται εἰς τὸ ἓν καὶ πλῆθος (εἰλήφθω γὰρ ἡ ἀναγωγὴ ἡμῖν), {1005a1} αἱ δ᾽ ἀρχαὶ καὶ παντελῶς αἱ παρὰ τῶν ἄλλων ὡς εἰς γένη ταῦτα πίπτουσιν.

And all the other contraries seem to be reducible to unity and plurality. Therefore, let us take that reduction for granted. And all the principles which have to do with other things fall under unity and being as their genera.

1005a2 Palam igitur ex his, quia unius est scientiae ens inquantum est ens speculari. Omnia namque aut ex contrariis, aut contraria. Principia vero contrariorum unum et pluralitas: et ea unius scientiae, sive secundum unum dicantur, sive non, ut forsan habet veritas. [584]

φανερὸν οὖν καὶ ἐκ τούτων ὅτι μιᾶς ἐπιστήμης τὸ ὂν ᾗ ὂν θεωρῆσαι. πάντα γὰρ ἢ ἐναντία ἢ ἐξ ἐναντίων, ἀρχαὶ δὲ τῶν ἐναντίων τὸ ἓν {5} καὶ πλῆθος. ταῦτα δὲ μιᾶς ἐπιστήμης, εἴτε καθ᾽ ἓν λέγεται εἴτε μή, ὥσπερ ἴσως ἔχει καὶ τἀληθές.

It is clear from these discussions, then, that it is the office of one science to study being as being. For all beings are either contraries or composed of contraries, and the principles of contraries are unity and plurality. And these belong to one science, whether they are used in one sense or not. And perhaps the truth is that they are not.

Attamen etsi multipliciter dicatur unum, ad primum omnia dicentur et contraria similiter. Et propter hoc si ens et uniim non est universale idem in omnibus, aut separabile, ut forsan non est, sed hoc quidem ad unum, illud vero ad ea quae consequenter sunt.

ἀλλ᾽ ὅμως εἰ καὶ πολλαχῶς λέγεται τὸ ἕν, πρὸς τὸ πρῶτον τἆλλα λεχθήσεται καὶ τὰ ἐναντία ὁμοίως, [καὶ διὰ τοῦτο] καὶ εἰ μὴ ἔστι τὸ ὂν ἢ τὸ ἓν καθόλου καὶ ταὐτὸ ἐπὶ πάντων ἢ {10} χωριστόν, ὥσπερ ἴσως οὐκ ἔστιν ἀλλὰ τὰ μὲν πρὸς ἓν τὰ δὲ τῷ ἐφεξῆς.

Yet even if the term "one" is used in many senses, all will be referred to one primary sense. And the same is true of contraries. Hence, even if unity or being is not a universal and the same in all things or is something separate (as presumably it is not), still in some cases the thing will be referred to unity and in others it will be referred to what follows on unity.

1005a11 Et propter hoc non est geometriae speculari quid contrarium, aut perfectum, aut unum, aut ens, aut idem, aut diversum, nisi ex conditione. [586]

διὰ τοῦτο οὐ τοῦ γεωμέτρου θεωρῆσαι τί τὸ ἐναντίον ἢ τέλειον ἢ ἓν ἢ ὂν ἢ ταὐτὸν ἢ ἕτερον, ἀλλ᾽ ἢ ἐξ ὑποθέσεως.

And for this reason it is not the province of geometry to examine what a contrary is, or what the perfect is, or what unity is, or what sameness or otherness is, but to assume them.

1005a13 Quod quidem igitur unius scientiae est ens inquantum ens speculari, et quae insunt ei inquantum ens, manifestum. Et quia non solum substantiarum, sed accidentium eadem est theoria, et dictorum, et de priore et posteriore, et de

ὅτι μὲν οὖν μιᾶς ἐπιστήμης τὸ ὂν ᾗ ὂν θεωρῆσαι καὶ τὰ ὑπάρχοντα αὐτῷ ᾗ ὄν, δῆλον, καὶ ὅτι {15} οὐ μόνον τῶν οὐσιῶν ἀλλὰ καὶ τῶν ὑπαρχόντων ἡ αὐτὴ θεωρητική, τῶν τε εἰρημένων καὶ περὶ προτέρου καὶ ὑστέρου, καὶ γένους

It is evident, then, that it is the office of one science to study both being as being and the attributes which belong to being as being. And it is evident too that the same science studies not only substances but also their accidents, those mentioned

genere et specie et toto et parte et talibus aliis. [587]	καὶ εἴδους, καὶ ὅλου καὶ μέρους καὶ τῶν ἄλλων τῶν τοιούτων.	above and prior and subsequent, genus and species, whole and part, and others such as these.

570. Hic ostendit per rationes communes, quod de omnibus praedictis philosophus debet considerare.

Et primo ostendit propositum.

Secundo conclusionem inducit intentam, ibi, *quod quidem igitur* et cetera.

Circa primum duo facit.

Primo ostendit propositum.

Secundo ex dictis infert quoddam corollarium, ibi, *et propter hoc* et cetera.

Ostendit autem primum tribus rationibus.

Secunda ibi, *signum autem* et cetera.

Tertia ibi, *amplius autem* et cetera.

Prima ratio, talis est. Omnes dubitationes, quae possunt moveri, sunt in aliqua scientia solvendae: sed de praedictis communibus moventur quaedam quaestiones, sicut de eodem et de diverso movetur illa quaestio utrum sit idem Socrates, et Socrates sedens: et de contrariis movetur ista quaestio, utrum unum sit contrarium uni, et quot modis dicitur: ergo oportet, quod in aliqua scientia ista solvantur, quae consideret de eodem et contrario et aliis praedictis.

571. Et quod hoc pertineat ad philosophum et ad nullum alium, sic probat. Eius est considerare primas passiones entis, cuius est considerare ens secundum quod est ens. Sed praedicta omnia sunt per se accidentia entis et unius secundum quod huiusmodi. Sicut enim numerus, inquantum huiusmodi, habet proprias passiones, ut superfluum, aequale, commensuratum et huiusmodi, quorum quaedam insunt alicui numero absolute, ut par et impar, quaedam uni per comparationem ad alterum, ut aequale: et etiam substantia habet proprias passiones ut *firmum*, idest corpus, et alia huiusmodi. Similiter et ens inquantum ens, habet quaedam propria, quae sunt communia praedicta. Ergo consideratio eorum pertinet ad philosophum.

Et ideo tradentes philosophiam non peccaverunt de his tractando tamquam *non philosophantes*, idest tamquam ista non pertineant ad considerationem philosophiae; sed quia de his tractantes de substantia nihil audiunt, quasi substantiae omnino obliviscantur, cum tamen ipsa sit primum inter illa, de quibus philosophus debet considerare.

572. Deinde cum dicit *signum autem* hic ponit secundam rationem ad idem ostendendum, quae est per signum, quae talis est. Dialectici et sophistae induunt

570. Here he uses arguments based on common principles to prove what the philosopher ought to consider regarding all of the foregoing attributes.

First, he proves his thesis;

and second (1005a13; [587]), he introduces his intended conclusion, at *it is evident*.

In regard to the first part, he does two things.

First, he proves his thesis;

and second (1005a11; [586]), he draws a corollary from what has been said, at *and for this reason*.

He gives three arguments to prove his thesis.

The second (1004b17; [572]) begins where he says, *an indication of this*.

The third (1004b27; [578]) begins at *further, one corresponding*.

The first argument is as follows. All questions that can be raised must be answered by some science. But questions are raised about the common attributes mentioned above—for example, that raised about sameness and otherness (whether Socrates and Socrates sitting are the same), and that raised about contraries (whether one thing has one contrary, and how many meanings the term contrary has). Hence these questions must be answered by some science which considers sameness and contrariety and the other attributes mentioned above.

571. That this is the job of the philosopher and of no one else he proves thus. That science whose office is to consider being as being is the one which must consider the first properties of being. But all of the above-mentioned attributes are proper accidents of unity and being as such. For number as number has properties, such as excess, equality, commensurability, and so on, some of which belong to a number taken absolutely, as even and odd, and some to one number in relation to another, as equality. And even substance has proper attributes, as *the solid*, or body, and others of this kind. And in a similar way being as being has certain properties, which are the common attributes mentioned above; therefore, the study of them belongs to the philosopher.

Hence those dealing with philosophy have not erred in their treatment of these things *by being unphilosophical*, by considering them in a way that does not pertain to the investigations of philosophy, but because in treating them they pay no attention to substance, as though they were completely unmindful of it despite the fact that it is the first thing which the philosopher ought to consider.

572. *An indication* (1004b17). Then he gives a second argument to prove the same point. This argument employs an example and runs thus. Dialecticians and sophists

figuram eamdem philosopho, quasi similitudinem cum eo habentes: sed dialectici et sophistae disputant de praedictis: ergo et philosophi est ea considerare. Ad manifestationem autem primae ostendit quomodo dialectica et sophistica cum philosophia habeant similitudinem, et in quo differunt ab ea.

573. Conveniunt autem in hoc, quod dialectici est considerare de omnibus. Hoc autem esse non posset, nisi consideraret omnia secundum quod in aliquo uno conveniunt: quia unius scientiae unum subiectum est, et unius artis una est materia, circa quam operatur. Cum igitur omnes res non conveniant nisi in ente, manifestum est quod dialecticae materia est ens, et ea quae sunt entis, de quibus etiam philosophus considerat. Similiter etiam sophistica habet quamdam similitudinem philosophiae. Nam sophistica est *visa* sive apparens sapientia, non existens. Quod autem habet apparentiam alicuius rei, oportet quod aliquam similitudinem cum illa habeat. Et ideo oportet quod eadem consideret philosophus, dialecticus et sophista.

574. Differunt autem abinvicem. Philosophus quidem a dialectico secundum potestatem. Nam maioris virtutis est consideratio philosophi quam consideratio dialectici. Philosophus enim de praedictis communibus procedit demonstrative. Et ideo eius est habere scientiam de praedictis, et est cognoscitivus eorum per certitudinem. Nam certa cognitio sive scientia est effectus demonstrationis.

Dialecticus autem circa omnia praedicta procedit ex probabilibus; unde non facit scientiam, sed quamdam opinionem.

Et hoc ideo est, quia ens est duplex: ens scilicet rationis et ens naturae.

Ens autem rationis dicitur proprie de illis intentionibus, quas ratio adinvenit in rebus consideratis; sicut intentio generis, speciei et similium, quae quidem non inveniuntur in rerum natura, sed considerationem rationis consequuntur. Et huiusmodi, scilicet ens rationis, est proprie subiectum logicae.

Huiusmodi autem intentiones intelligibiles, entibus naturae aequiparantur, eo quod omnia entia naturae sub consideratione rationis cadunt. Et ideo subiectum logicae ad omnia se extendit, de quibus ens naturae praedicatur. Unde concludit, quod subiectum logicae aequiparatur subiecto philosophiae, quod est ens naturae.

Philosophus igitur ex principiis ipsius procedit ad probandum ea quae sunt consideranda circa huiusmodi communia accidentia entis. Dialecticus autem procedit ad ea consideranda ex intentionibus rationis, quae sunt

assume the same guise as the philosopher inasmuch as they resemble him in some respect. But the dialectician and sophist dispute about the above-mentioned attributes. Therefore, the philosopher should also consider them. In support of his first premise he shows how dialectics and sophistry resemble philosophy and how they differ from it.

573. Dialectics resembles philosophy in that it is also the office of the dialectician to consider all things. But this could not be the case unless he considered all things insofar as they agree in some one respect, because each science has one subject, and each art has one matter on which it operates. Therefore, since all things agree only in being, evidently the subject matter of dialectics is being and those attributes which belong to being. This is what the philosopher also investigates. And sophistry likewise resembles philosophy, for sophistry has *the semblance of wisdom*, or is apparent wisdom, without being wisdom. Now anything that takes on the appearance of something else must resemble it in some way. Therefore, the philosopher, the dialectician, and the sophist must consider the same thing.

574. Yet they differ from each other. The philosopher differs from the dialectician in power, because the consideration of the philosopher is more efficacious than that of the dialectician. For the philosopher proceeds demonstratively in dealing with the common attributes mentioned above, and thus it is proper to him to have scientific knowledge of these attributes. And he actually knows them with certitude, for certain or scientific knowledge is the effect of demonstration.

The dialectician, however, proceeds to treat all of the above-mentioned common attributes from probable premises, and thus he does not acquire scientific knowledge of them, but a kind of opinion.

The reason for this difference is that there are two kinds of beings: beings of reason and real beings.

The expression "being of reason" is applied properly to those notions which reason derives from the objects it considers—for example, the notions of genus, species, and the like, which are not found in reality but are a natural result of the consideration of reason. And this kind of being (a being of reason) constitutes the proper subject of logic.

But intellectual conceptions of this kind are equal in extension to real beings, because all real beings fall under the consideration of reason. Hence the subject of logic extends to all things to which the expression "real being" is applied. His conclusion is, then, that the subject of logic is equal in extension to the subject of philosophy, which is real being.

Now the philosopher proceeds from the principles of this kind of being to prove the things that have to be considered about the common accidents of this kind of being. But the dialectician proceeds to consider them from

extranea a natura rerum. Et ideo dicitur, quod dialectica est tentativa, quia tentare proprium est ex principiis extraneis procedere.

575. A sophista vero differt philosophus *prohaeresi*, idest electione vel voluptate, idest desiderio vitae. Ad aliud enim ordinat vitam suam et actiones philosophus et sophista. Philosophus quidem ad sciendum veritatem; sophista vero ad hoc quod videatur scire quamvis nesciat.

576. Licet autem dicatur, quod philosophia est scientia, non autem dialectica et sophistica, non tamen per hoc removetur quin dialectica et sophistica sint scientiae.

Dialectica enim potest considerari secundum quod est docens, et secundum quod est utens. Secundum quidem quod est docens, habet considerationem de istis intentionibus, instituens modum, quo per eas procedi possit ad conclusiones in singulis scientiis probabiliter ostendendas; et hoc demonstrative facit, et secundum hoc est scientia.

Utens vero est secundum quod modo adiuncto utitur ad concludendum aliquid probabiliter in singulis scientiis; et sic recedit a modo scientiae.

Et similiter dicendum est de sophistica; quia prout est docens tradit per necessarias et demonstrativas rationes modum arguendi apparenter. Secundum vero quod est utens, deficit a processu verae argumentationis.

577. Sed in parte logicae quae dicitur demonstrativa, solum doctrina pertinet ad logicam, usus vero ad philosophiam et ad alias particulares scientias quae sunt de rebus naturae.

Et hoc ideo, quia usus demonstrativae consistit in utendo principiis rerum, de quibus fit demonstratio, quae ad scientias reales pertinet, non utendo intentionibus logicis.

Et sic apparet, quod quaedam partes logicae habent ipsam scientiam et doctrinam et usum, sicut dialectica tentativa et sophistica; quaedam autem doctrinam et non usum, sicut demonstrativa.

578. *Amplius contrariorum* hic ponit tertiam rationem, quae talis est. Quaecumque reducuntur in unum et ens, debent considerari a philosopho, cuius est considerare unum et ens: sed omnia contraria reducuntur ad unum et ens: ergo omnia contraria sunt de consideratione philosophi, cuius est considerare unum et ens.

the conceptions of reason, which are extrinsic to reality. Hence it is said that dialectics is in search of knowledge, because in searching it is proper to proceed from extrinsic principles.

575. But the philosopher differs from the sophist *in the choice*, that is, in the selection, willing, or desire of a way of life. For the philosopher and sophist direct their life and actions to different things. The philosopher directs his to knowing the truth, whereas the sophist directs his so as to appear to know what he does not.

576. Now, although it is said that philosophy is scientific knowledge, and that dialectics and sophistry are not, this still does not do away with the possibility of dialectics and sophistry being sciences.

For dialectics can be considered both from the viewpoint of theory and from that of practice. From the viewpoint of theory it studies these conceptions and establishes the method by which one proceeds from them to demonstrate with probability the conclusions of the particular sciences. It does this demonstratively, and to this extent it is a science.

But from the viewpoint of practice it makes use of the above method so as to reach certain probable conclusions in the particular sciences, and in this respect it falls short of the scientific method.

The same must be said of sophistry, because, from the viewpoint of theory, it treats by means of necessary and demonstrative arguments the method of arguing to apparent truth. From the viewpoint of practice, however, it falls short of the process of true argumentation.

577. But that part of logic which is said to be demonstrative is concerned only with theory, and the practical application of it belongs to philosophy and to the other particular sciences, which are concerned with real beings.

This is because the practical aspect of the demonstrative part of logic consists in using the principles of things, from which proceeds demonstration (which properly belongs to the sciences that deal with real beings), and not in using the conceptions of logic.

Thus it appears that some parts of logic are at the same time scientific, theoretical, and practical, as exploratory dialectics and sophistry; and one is concerned with theory and not practice, namely, demonstrative logic.

578. *Further, one corresponding* (1004b27). Then he gives the third argument in support of his thesis. It runs as follows. Everything that is reducible to unity and being should be considered by the philosopher, whose function is to study unity and being. But all contraries are reducible to unity and being. Therefore, all contraries belong to the consideration of the philosopher, whose function is to study unity and being.

579. Quod autem omnia contraria reducantur ad unum et ens, ostendit quidem primo quantum ad ens hoc modo.

Inter duo contraria, quae a philosophis principia ponuntur, ut in primo habitum est, semper unum quidem est alteri correlativum, et ei coordinatum est, ut privatio. Quod ex hoc patet: quia semper alterum contrariorum est imperfectum respectu alterius, et sic quamdam perfectionis privationem alterius importat. Privatio autem est quaedam negatio, ut dictum est supra; et sic est non ens. Et sic patet quod omnia contraria reducuntur in ens et non ens.

580. Similiter etiam ostendit quod reducuntur in unum et multitudinem, per quoddam exemplum. Status enim sive quies reducitur in unitatem. Illud enim quiescere dicitur, quod uno modo se habet nunc et prius, ut in sexto *Physicorum* traditur. Motus autem ad multitudinem pertinet; quia quod movetur, diversimode se habet nunc et prius; quod multitudinem importat.

581. Deinde ibi *entia vero* ostendit alio modo, quod contraria reducuntur ad ens: quia principia et principiata sunt unius considerationis. Principia autem entium, inquantum huiusmodi, confitentur philosophi esse contraria. Omnes enim dicunt entia et substantias entium ex contrariis componi, ut in primo *Physicorum* dictum est, et primo huius.

Et quamvis in hoc conveniant quod entium principia sint contraria, differunt tamen quantum ad contraria quae ponunt. Quidam enim ponunt par et impar, sicut Pythagorici. Et alii calorem et frigus, sicut Parmenides. Quidam *finem* sive terminum *et infinitum*, idest finitum et infinitum, sicut idem Pythagoras. Nam pari et impari, finitum et infinitum attribuebant, ut in primo habitum est. Alii concordiam et discordiam, sicut Empedocles. Patet ergo quod contraria reducuntur in considerationem entis.

582. Deinde ulterius ibi *omnia vero* dicit, quod sicut praedicta contraria reducuntur ad ens, ita habent reduci ad unum et multitudinem. Quod apparet. Nam imparitas aliquid unitatis habet propter indivisionem: paritas autem ad naturam multitudinis pertinet propter suam divisionem. Sic autem finis sive terminus ad unitatem pertinet, quae est terminus omnis resolutionis: infinitum autem pertinet ad multitudinem, quae in infinitum augetur. Concordia etiam unitatis est manifeste. Discordia vero multitudinis. Calor autem ad unitatem pertinet, inquantum habet unire homogenea. Frigus autem ad multitudinem, inquantum habet ea separare. Nec solum ista contraria reducuntur sic in unum et multitudinem, sed etiam alia. Sed ista *reductio* sive introductio ad unum et multitudinem accipiatur sive *sumatur*, idest

579. Then he proves that all contraries are reducible to unity and being. He first does this with regard to being, and he proceeds thus.

Of any two contraries which the philosophers posited as the principles of things, as is said in book 1 (986b2; [132]), one contrary is always the correlative of the other and is related to it as its privation. This is clear from the fact that one of two contraries is always something imperfect when compared with the other, and thus implies some privation of the perfection of the other. But a privation is a kind of negation, as was stated above (1004a9; [564]), and thus is a non-being. Hence it is clear that all contraries are reducible to being and non-being.

580. He also shows by an example that all contraries are reducible to unity and plurality. For rest or repose is reducible to unity, since that is said to be at rest which is in the same condition now as it was before, as is stated in *Physics* 6. And motion is reducible to plurality, because whatever is in motion is in a different condition now than it was before, and this implies plurality.

581. *And almost all* (1004b29). Then he uses another argument to show that contraries are reducible to being. Both the principles of things and the things composed of them belong to the same study. But the philosophers admit that contraries are the principles of being as being, for all say that beings and the substances of beings are composed of contraries, as was stated in *Physics* 1 and book 1 (986b2; [132]) of this work.

Yet while they agree on this point—that the principles of beings are contraries—still they differ as to the contraries which they give. For some give the even and odd, as the Pythagoreans. Others, the hot and cold, as Parmenides. Others, *the limited*, or terminus, *and the unlimited*, that is, the finite and infinite, as did the same Pythagoreans, for they attributed limitedness and unlimitedness to the even and the odd, as is stated in book 1 (986a13; [124]). Still others gave friendship and strife, as Empedocles. Hence it is clear that contraries are reducible to the study of being.

582. *And all the other* (1004b33). He says that the above-mentioned contraries are reducible not only to being but also to unity and plurality. This is evident. For oddness by reason of its indivisibility is affiliated with unity, and evenness by reason of its divisibility has a natural connection with plurality. Thus, end or limit pertains to unity, which is the terminus of every process of resolution, and lack of limit pertains to plurality, which may be increased to infinity. Again, friendship also clearly pertains to unity, and strife to plurality. And heat pertains to unity inasmuch as it can unite homogeneous things, whereas cold pertains to plurality inasmuch as it can separate them. Further, not only these contraries are reducible in this way to unity and plurality, but so also are the others. Yet let us now accept or *take for granted* (that is, let us now assume) this *reduction*,

supponatur nunc a nobis, quia longum esset per singula contraria hoc discutere.

583. Deinde ostendit consequenter quod omnia contraria reducuntur ad unum et ens. Constat enim quod omnia tam principia quam quae sunt *de aliis*, idest principiata, inducunt in unum et ens tamquam in genera; non quod sint vere genera; sed ratione suae communitatis quamdam similitudinem generum habent. Si igitur contraria omnia sunt principia vel ex principiis, oportet quod ad unum et ens reducantur.

Sic igitur patet, quod dupliciter ostendit contraria reduci ad ens.

Primo per naturam privationis.

Secundo per hoc quod contraria sunt principia.

Quod vero reducantur ad unum, ostendit per exemplum et per quamdam reductionem.

Finaliter autem ostendit quod reducantur ad unum et ens inquantum sunt genera.

584. *Palam igitur* hic ostendit conversim, scilicet quod ista scientia considerat ens, quia considerat praedicta, tali ratione. Omnia entia reducuntur ad contraria; quia vel sunt contraria, vel sunt ex contrariis: contraria vero reducuntur ad unum et multitudinem, quia unum et multitudo sunt principia contrariorum: unum autem et multitudo sunt unius scientiae, scilicet philosophiae: ergo et eius est considerare ens secundum quod est ens.

Sciendum est tamen, quod praedicta omnia in unius scientiae considerationem cadunt, sive dicantur *secundum unum*, idest univoce, sive non, sicut fortasse verum est. Sed tamen quamvis unum dicatur multipliciter, omnia tamen alia, idest omnes significationes, reducuntur ad unam primam significationem. Et similiter est etiam de contrariis, quae dicuntur multipliciter, sed omnes significationes ad unam primam reducuntur.

Et propter hoc, si etiam unum et ens non est unum universale quasi genus existens, sicut supra ponebatur, sive dicamus quod universale sit unum in omnibus secundum opinionem nostram, sive quod sit aliquid separatum a rebus secundum opinionem Platonis, sicut fortassis non est verum: tamen dicuntur secundum prius et posterius: sicut et aliae significationes referuntur ad unum primum, et aliae se habent consequenter respectu illius primi. Utitur tamen adverbio dubitandi, quasi nunc supponens quae inferius probabuntur.

585. Sciendum tamen est quod hoc, quod dixit, omnia entia contraria esse vel ex contrariis, non posuit secundum suam opinionem, sed accepit quasi opinionem philosophorum antiquorum: entia enim immobilia nec sunt contraria, nec ex contrariis. Unde nec Plato circa sensibiles substantias immobiles posuit contrarietatem.

or introduction, to unity and plurality; to examine each set of contraries would be a lengthy undertaking.

583. Next he shows that all contraries are reducible to unity and being. For it is certain that all principles, inasmuch as they have to do **with other things**, that is, the things composed of them, fall under unity and being as their genera, not in the sense that they truly are genera, but in the sense that they bear some likeness to genera by reason of what they have in common. Hence, if all contraries are principles or things composed of principles, they must be reducible to unity and being.

Thus it is clear that he shows that contraries are reducible to being for two reasons:

first, because of the nature of privation;

second, by reason of the fact that contraries are principles.

He shows that they are reducible to unity by giving an example and by using a process of reduction.

Last, he shows that they are reducible to unity and being inasmuch as they have the character of genera.

584. *It is clear* (1005a2). Here he proves in a converse way that this science considers being because it considers the things mentioned above. His argument is this. All beings are reducible to contraries because they are either contraries or composed of contraries. And contraries are reducible to unity and plurality because unity and plurality are the principles of contraries. But unity and plurality belong to one science, philosophy. Therefore, it is the office of this science to consider being as being.

Yet it must be noted that all the contraries mentioned above fall under the consideration of one science whether they are used **in one sense**, that is, univocally, or not (as perhaps is the case). However, even if the term "one" is used in many senses, all the others (that is, all the other senses) are reducible to one primary sense. And the case is similar with contraries, which are said in many ways, yet all their significations are reduced to the first one.

Hence, even if unity or being is not one universal, like a genus, as was stated above (whether a universal is said to be a one-in-all, as we maintain, or something separate from things, as Plato thought, and as is presumably not the case), still each is used in a primary and a secondary sense. And the same holds true in the case of other terms, for some senses are referred to one primary sense, and others are secondary with respect to that primary sense. An adverb designating uncertainty is used inasmuch as we are now assuming things that will be proved below.

585. But nevertheless it must be borne in mind that the statement which he made—all beings are either contraries or composed of contraries—he did not give as his own opinion but as one which he took from the ancient philosophers. For unchangeable beings are not contraries or composed of contraries. And this is why Plato did not posit any

Fecit enim unitatem ex parte formae, contrarietatem ex parte materiae. Antiqui vero philosophi solummodo substantias sensibiles posuerunt, in quibus necesse est contrarietatem esse secundum quod mobiles sunt.

586. Deinde cum dicit *et propter* inducit quoddam corollarium ex praedictis; dicens, quod geometriae non est speculari de praedictis, quae sunt accidentia entis inquantum est ens, scilicet quid est contrarium, aut quid est perfectum, et huiusmodi.

Sed si consideret, hoc erit *ex conditione*, idest ex suppositione, quasi supponens ab aliquo priori philosopho, a quo sumit quantum est necessarium ad suam materiam. Et hoc quod dicitur de geometria, similiter est intelligendum in qualibet alia particulari scientia.

587. Deinde cum dicit *quod quidem* colligit quae sunt supra ostensa; dicens, manifestum esse, quod ad unam scientiam pertinet considerare ens secundum quod est ens, et ea quae per se illi insunt. Et per hoc patet, quod illa scientia non solum est considerativa substantiarum, sed etiam accidentium, cum de utrisque ens praedicetur. Et est considerativa eorum quae dicta sunt, scilicet eiusdem et diversi, similis et dissimilis, aequalis et inaequalis, negationis et privationis, et contrariorum; quae supra diximus esse per se entis accidentia. Et non solum est considerativa istorum, de quibus ostensum est singillatim propriis rationibus, quae cadunt in consideratione huius scientiae; sed etiam considerat de priori et posteriori, genere et specie, toto et parte, et aliis huiusmodi, pari ratione, quia haec etiam sunt accidentia entis inquantum est ens.

contrariety in the unchangeable sensible substances, for he attributed unity to form and contrariety to matter. But the ancient philosophers claimed that only sensible substances exist and that these must contain contrariety inasmuch as they are changeable.

586. *And for this reason* (1005a11). Then he draws a corollary from what has been said. He says that it is not the province of geometry to investigate the foregoing things, which are accidents of being as being—for example, to investigate what a contrary is, or what the perfect is, and so on.

But if a geometer were to consider them, he would *assume them*, or presuppose their truth, inasmuch as he would take them over from some prior philosopher from whom he accepts them insofar as they are necessary for his own subject matter. What is said about geometry must be understood to apply also in the case of any other particular science.

587. *It is evident* (1005a13). He now summarizes the points established above. He says that obviously the consideration of being as being and the attributes which belong to it of itself pertain to one science. Thus it is clear that that science considers not only substances but also accidents, since being is predicated of both. And it considers the things that have been discussed, which we said above are the proper accidents of being—namely, sameness and otherness, likeness and unlikeness, equality and inequality, privation and negation, and contraries. And it considers not only those things that fall under the consideration of this science, about which demonstration was made individually by means of arguments based on proper principles, but it in like manner also considers prior and subsequent, genus and species, whole and part, and other things of this kind, because these too are accidents of being as being.

LECTURE 5

Solution of difficulties on the principles of demonstration

1005a19 Dicendum autem, utrum unius, aut diversae scientiae, de vocatis in mathematicis dignitatibus et substantia. [588]

λεκτέον δὲ πότερον μιᾶς ἢ ἑτέρας ἐπιστήμης περί τε {20} τῶν ἐν τοῖς μαθήμασι καλουμένων ἀξιωμάτων καὶ περὶ τῆς οὐσίας.

Moreover, it is necessary to state whether it is the office of one science or of different sciences to inquire about those principles which are called axioms in mathematics, and about substance.

1005a21 Palam autem, quia unius est, et eius, quae est philosophi, quae de his perscrutatio. [589]

φανερὸν δὴ ὅτι μιᾶς τε καὶ τῆς τοῦ φιλοσόφου καὶ ἡ περὶ τούτων ἐστὶ σκέψις·

Now it is evident that it is the office of one science—that of the philosopher—to investigate these.

1005a22 Omnibus enim insunt existentibus, sed non generi alicui separatim ab aliis; et utuntur omnes, quia entis inquantum est ens. Unumquodque enim genus est ens: intantum vero utuntur, inquantum eis est sufficiens. Hoc autem est quantum continet genus, de quo demonstrationes ferunt. Quare quoniam manifestum est, quod inquantum sunt entia, insunt omnibus: (hoc enim eis est commune), de ente inquantum est ens cognoscentis et de eis est speculatio. [590]

ἅπασι γὰρ ὑπάρχει τοῖς οὖσιν ἀλλ᾽ οὐ γένει τινὶ χωρὶς ἰδίᾳ τῶν ἄλλων. καὶ χρῶνται μὲν πάντες, ὅτι τοῦ ὄντος ἐστὶν ᾗ ὄν, ἕκαστον δὲ τὸ γένος {25} ὄν· ἐπὶ τοσοῦτον δὲ χρῶνται ἐφ᾽ ὅσον αὐτοῖς ἱκανόν, τοῦτο δ᾽ ἐστὶν ὅσον ἐπέχει τὸ γένος περὶ οὗ φέρουσι τὰς ἀποδείξεις· ὥστ᾽ ἐπεὶ δῆλον ὅτι ᾗ ὄντα ὑπάρχει πᾶσι (τοῦτο γὰρ αὐτοῖς τὸ κοινόν), τοῦ περὶ τὸ ὂν ᾗ ὂν γνωρίζοντος καὶ περὶ τούτων ἐστὶν ἡ θεωρία.

For these principles apply to all beings and not to some genus distinct from the others. And all men employ them, because they pertain to being as being, for each genus is being. But they employ them just so far as to satisfy their needs, that is, so far as the genus contains the things about which they form demonstrations. Hence, since it is evident that these principles pertain to all things inasmuch as they are beings (for this is what they have in common), the investigation of them belongs to him who considers being as being.

1005a29 Unde nullus particulariter intendentium nititur dicere aliquid de eis, si vera aut non, neque geometra neque arithmeticus. [592]

διόπερ οὐθεὶς τῶν κατὰ μέρος ἐπισκοπούντων {30} ἐγχειρεῖ λέγειν τι περὶ αὐτῶν, εἰ ἀληθῆ ἢ μή, οὔτε γεωμέτρης οὔτ᾽ ἀριθμητικός,

Hence no one who is making a special inquiry attempts to say anything about their truth or falsity, neither the geometer nor the arithmetician.

1005a31 Nisi physicorum quidam merito hoc facientes. Soli namque putantur de tota natura intendere et de ente. Sed quoniam est adhuc physico aliquis superior, unum enim aliquod genus est natura entis, ipsius universalis et circa substantiam primam theorizantis, et de his erit perscrutatio. Est autem sophia sapientia quaedam physica, sed non prima. [593]

ἀλλὰ τῶν φυσικῶν ἔνιοι, εἰκότως τοῦτο δρῶντες· μόνοι γὰρ ᾤοντο περί τε τῆς ὅλης φύσεως σκοπεῖν καὶ περὶ τοῦ ὄντος. ἐπεὶ δ᾽ ἔστιν ἔτι τοῦ φυσικοῦ τις ἀνωτέρω (ἓν γάρ τι γένος τοῦ ὄντος ἡ φύσις), {35} τοῦ καθόλου καὶ τοῦ περὶ τὴν πρώτην οὐσίαν θεωρητικοῦ καὶ ἡ περὶ τούτων ἂν εἴη σκέψις· {1005b1} ἔστι δὲ σοφία τις καὶ ἡ φυσική, ἀλλ᾽ οὐ πρώτη.

However, some of the philosophers of nature have done this, and with reason; for they thought that they alone were inquiring about the whole of nature and about being. But since there is one kind of thinker who is superior to the philosopher of nature (for nature is only one genus of being), the investigation of these principles will belong to him who studies the universal and deals with first substance. The philosophy of nature is a kind of wisdom, but it is not the first.

1005b2 Quicumque vero conantur dicentium dicere quid de veritate quo oportet modo recipere, propter ignorantiam analyticorum hoc faciunt. Oportet enim de his pervenire scientes sed non audientes quaerere. [594]

ὅσα δ᾽ ἐγχειροῦσι τῶν λεγόντων τινὲς περὶ τῆς ἀληθείας ὃν τρόπον δεῖ ἀποδέχεσθαι, δι᾽ ἀπαιδευσίαν τῶν ἀναλυτικῶν τοῦτο δρῶσιν· δεῖ γὰρ περὶ τούτων {5} ἥκειν προεπισταμένους ἀλλὰ μὴ ἀκούοντας ζητεῖν.

And whatever certain ones of those who speak about the truth attempt to say concerning the way in which it must be accepted, they do this through ignorance of analytics. For they must know these principles in order to attain scientific knowledge and not be seeking them when they are learning a science.

1005b5   Quoniam igitur philosophi, et de omni substantia speculantis inquantum congruit, et de omnibus syllogisticis principiis est perscrutari, palam. [595]

ὅτι μὲν οὖν τοῦ φιλοσόφου, καὶ τοῦ περὶ πάσης τῆς οὐσίας θεωροῦντος ᾗ πέφυκεν, καὶ περὶ τῶν συλλογιστικῶν ἀρχῶν ἐστιν ἐπισκέψασθαι, δῆλον·

It is evident, then, that it is also the business of the philosopher—that is, of him who investigates all substance insofar as its nature permits—to investigate all syllogistic principles.

---

588. Hic solvit aliam quaestionem in tertio motam; scilicet utrum ad istam scientiam pertineat considerare prima principia demonstrationis. Et dividitur in duo.

Primo ostendit, quod eius est considerare universaliter de omnibus his principiis.

Secundo specialiter de primo eorum ibi, *congruit autem* et cetera.

Circa primum tria facit.

Primo movet quaestionem, quae est, utrum unius scientiae sit considerare de substantia et de principiis quae in scientiis mathematicis vocantur dignitates, aut est alterius et alterius scientiae considerare. Appropriat autem ista principia magis mathematicis scientiis, quia certiores demonstrationes habent, et manifestius istis principiis per se notis utuntur, omnes suas demonstrationes ad haec principia resolventes.

589. *Palam autem* secundo solvit: quae quidem solutio est, quia una scientia intendit de utrisque praedictis: et haec est philosophia, quae prae manibus habetur.

590. *Omnibus enim* tertio probat solutionem propositam: et circa hoc duo facit.

Primo probat propositum.

Secundo conclusionem principalem inducit, ibi, *quoniam igitur* et cetera.

Probat autem solutionem propositam dupliciter.

Primo per rationem.

Secundo per signum, ibi, *unde nullus* et cetera.

Ratio talis est. Quaecumque insunt omnibus entibus, et non solum alicui generi entium separatim ab aliis, haec pertinent ad considerationem philosophi: sed praedicta principia sunt huiusmodi: ergo pertinent ad considerationem philosophi. Minorem sic probat. Illa, quibus utuntur omnes scientiae, sunt entis inquantum huiusmodi: sed prima principia sunt huiusmodi: ergo pertinent ad ens inquantum est ens.

591. Rationem autem, quare omnes scientiae eis utuntur, sic assignat; quia unumquodque genus subiectum alicuius scientiae recipit praedicationem entis. Utuntur autem principiis praedictis scientiae particulares non secundum suam communitatem, prout se extendunt ad omnia entia, sed quantum sufficit eis: et hoc secundum continentiam generis, quod in scientia subiicitur, de quo ipsa scientia demonstrationes affert. Sicut

588. Here he answers another question raised in book 3 [387]: whether it belongs to this science to consider the first principles of demonstration. This is divided into two parts.

In the first he shows that it belongs to this science to make a general study of all these principles;

in the second [596], he shows that it also belongs to it to make a special study of the first of these principles, at *and it is fitting*.

In regard to the first he does three things.

First, he raises the question of whether it belongs to one or to different sciences to consider substance and the principles which are called axioms in the mathematical sciences. He assigns these principles more to the mathematical sciences because such sciences have more certain demonstrations and use these self-evident principles in a more manifest way inasmuch as they refer all of their demonstrations to them.

589. *Now it is evident* (1005a21). Second, he answers this question by saying that a single science investigates both of the foregoing things, and that this is the philosophy with which we are now concerned.

590. *For these principles* (1005a22). Third, he proves his proposed answer, and in regard to this he does two things.

First, he proves it.

Second (1005b5; [595]), he introduces his main conclusion, at *it is evident*.

Now he proves his proposed answer in two ways.

He does this first by an argument;

second (1005a29; [592]) by an example, at *hence no one*.

The argument is as follows. Whatever principles pertain to all beings, and not just to one genus of beings distinct from the others, belong to the consideration of the philosopher. But the above-mentioned principles are of this kind. Therefore, they belong to the consideration of the philosopher. He proves the minor premise as follows. Those principles which all sciences use pertain to being as being. But first principles are principles of this kind. Therefore, they pertain to being as being.

591. The reason which he gives for saying that all sciences use these principles is that the subject genus of each science has being predicated of it. Now the particular sciences do not use the foregoing principles insofar as they are common principles—that is, as extending to all beings—but insofar as they have need of them—that is, insofar as they extend to the things contained in the genus of beings which constitutes the subject of a particular science

ipsa philosophia naturalis utitur eis secundum quod se extendunt ad entia mobilia, et non ulterius.

592. Deinde cum dicit *unde nullus* probat quod dixerat, per signum.

Et primo inducit probationem.

Secundo excludit quorumdam errorem, ibi, *sed quoniam est adhuc*.

Dicit ergo primo, quod nullus intendens primo tradere scientiam alicuius particularis entis, conatus est aliquid dicere de primis principiis utrum sint vera aut non: nec geometra, aut arithmeticus, qui tamen istis principiis plurimum utuntur, ut supra dictum est. Unde patet quod consideratio dictorum principiorum ad hanc scientiam pertinet.

593. Deinde cum dicit *nisi physicorum* excludit errorem quorumdam: et circa hoc duo facit.

Primo excludit errorem eorum, qui de praedictis se intromittebant, cum ad eos non pertineret.

Secundo eorum, qui de eis alio modo volebant tractare quam de eis sit tractandum, ibi, *quicumque vero conantur* et cetera.

Dicit ergo primo, quod quamvis nulla scientiarum particularium de praedictis principiis se intromittere debeat, quidam tamen naturalium de his se intromiserunt; et hoc non sine ratione.

Antiqui enim non opinabantur aliquam substantiam esse praeter substantiam corpoream mobilem, de qua physicus tractat. Et ideo creditum est, quod soli determinent de tota natura, et per consequens de ente; et ita etiam de primis principiis quae sunt simul consideranda cum ente.

Hoc autem falsum est; quia adhuc est quaedam scientia superior naturali: ipsa enim natura, idest res naturalis habens in se principium motus, in se ipsa est unum aliquod genus entis universalis. Non enim omne ens est huiusmodi: cum probatum sit in octavo *Physicorum*, esse aliquod ens immobile. Hoc autem ens immobile superius est et nobilius ente mobili, de quo considerat naturalis.

Et quia ad illam scientiam pertinet consideratio entis communis, ad quam pertinet consideratio entis primi, ideo ad aliam scientiam quam ad naturalem pertinet consideratio entis communis; et eius etiam erit considerare huiusmodi principia communia. Physica enim est quaedam pars philosophiae: sed non prima, quae considerat ens commune, et ea quae sunt entis inquantum huiusmodi.

about which it makes demonstrations. For example, the philosophy of nature uses them insofar as they extend to changeable beings and no further.

592. *Hence no one* (1005a29). Then he proves what he had said by using an example.

First, he introduces the proof;

second (1005a31; [593]), he rejects a false notion held by some men, at *however, some of the philosophers*.

He accordingly first says that no one whose chief intention is to hand down scientific knowledge of some particular being has attempted to say anything about the truth or falsity of first principles. Neither the geometer nor the arithmetician does this, even though they make the greatest use of these principles, as was said above [588]. Hence it is evident that the investigation of these principles belongs to this science.

593. *However, some* (1005a31). Here he rejects the false notions held by some men, and in regard to this he does two things.

First, he rejects the false notion of those who occupied themselves with these principles even though they did not concern them.

Second (1005b2; [594]), he rejects the false notion of those who wanted to deal with these principles in a different way than they should be dealt with, at *and whatever certain ones*.

He accordingly first says that even though none of the particular sciences ought to deal with the above-mentioned principles, nevertheless some of the natural philosophers have dealt with them, and they did so not without reason.

For the ancients did not think that there was any substance besides the changeable bodily substance with which the philosophy of nature is concerned. Hence they believed that they alone established the truth about the whole of nature and therefore about being, and thus about first principles, which must be considered along with being.

But this is false, because there is still a science which is superior to the science of nature. For nature itself (that is, natural being), which has its own principle of motion, constitutes in itself one genus of universal being. But not every being is of this kind, because it has been proved in *Physics* 8 that an unchangeable being exists. Now this unchangeable being is superior to and nobler than changeable being, with which the philosophy of nature is concerned.

And since the consideration of common being belongs to that science which studies the primary kind of being, then the consideration of common being belongs to a different science than the philosophy of nature. And the consideration of common principles of this kind will also belong to this science. For the philosophy of nature is a part of philosophy, but not the first part, which considers common being and those attributes which belong to being as being.

594. Deinde cum dicit *quicumque vero* excludit alium errorem circa modum tractandi huiusmodi principia. Quidam enim tractabant de istis principiis volentes ea demonstrare: et quaecumque isti dixerunt de veritate praedictorum principiorum, quomodo oporteat ea recipere per vim demonstrationis, vel quomodo oporteat contingere veritatem in omnibus istis ita se habere, hoc fecerunt propter ignorantiam, vel propter imperitiam *analyticorum*, idest illius partis logicae, in qua ars demonstrandi traditur: quia oportet *scientes de his pervenire*, idest omnis scientia per demonstrationem acquisita ex his principiis causatur.

Sed non oportet *audientes*, idest discipulos instruendos in aliqua scientia, quaerere de his sicut de aliquibus demonstrandis. Vel secundum aliam literam *oportet de his pervenire scientes*, idest oportet, quod qui acquirunt scientiam per demonstrationem perveniant ad cognoscendum huiusmodi principia communia, et non quod quaerant ea sibi demonstrari.

595. Deinde cum dicit *quoniam igitur* concludit conclusionem principaliter intentam: scilicet quod philosophi erit considerare de omni substantia inquantum huiusmodi, et de primis syllogismorum principiis. Ad huius autem evidentiam sciendum, quod propositiones per se notae sunt, quae statim notis terminis cognoscuntur, ut dicitur primo *Posteriorum*. Hoc autem contingit in illis propositionibus, in quibus praedicatum ponitur in definitione subiecti, vel praedicatum est idem subiecto.

Sed contingit aliquam propositionem quantum in se est esse per se notam, non tamen esse per se notam omnibus, qui ignorant definitionem praedicati et subiecti. Unde Boetius dicit in libro *De hebdomadibus*, quod quaedam sunt per se nota sapientibus quae non sunt per se nota omnibus. Illa autem sunt per se nota omnibus, quorum termini in conceptionem omnium cadunt.

Huiusmodi autem sunt communia, eo quod nostra cognitio a communibus ad propria pervenit, ut dicitur in primo *Physicorum*. Et ideo istae propositiones sunt prima demonstrationum principia, quae componuntur ex terminis communibus, sicut totum et pars, ut, omne totum est maius sua parte; et sicut aequale et inaequale, ut, quae uni et eidem sunt aequalia, sibi sunt aequalia. Et eadem ratio est de similibus.

Et quia huiusmodi communes termini pertinent ad considerationem philosophi, ideo haec principia de consideratione philosophi sunt.

Determinat autem ea philosophus non demonstrando, sed rationes terminorum tradendo, ut quid totum

594. *And whatever* (1005b2). Then he rejects the other false notion, which concerns the way in which such principles should be treated. For some men investigated these principles with the aim of demonstrating them. And whatever they said about the truth of these principles—such as how they must be accepted as true by force of demonstration, or how the truth found in all these principles must be reached—they did through ignorance of, or lack of skill in, *analytics*, which is that part of logic in which the art of demonstration is treated. For *they must know these principles in order to attain scientific knowledge*; that is, every science acquired by demonstration depends on these principles.

But those who are *learning*, that is, the pupils who are being instructed in some science, must not seek these principles as something to be demonstrated. Or, according to another text, *those who have scientific knowledge must attain science from these principles*; that is, those who attain knowledge by demonstration must come to know common principles of this kind and not ask that they be demonstrated to them.

595. *It is evident* (1005b5). He draws the conclusion primarily intended, namely, that it will be the function of the philosopher to consider every substance as such and also the first syllogistic principles. In order to make this clear, it must be noted that self-evident propositions are those which are known as soon as their terms are known, as is stated in *Posterior Analytics* 1. This occurs in the case of those propositions in which the predicate is given in the definition of the subject, or is the same as the subject.

But it happens that one kind of proposition, even though it is self-evident in itself, is still not self-evident to all—namely, to those who are ignorant of the definition of both the subject and the predicate. Hence Boethius says in *De hebdomadibus* that there are some propositions which are self-evident to the learned but not to all. Now those are self-evident to all whose terms are comprehended by all.

And common principles are of this kind, because our knowledge proceeds from common principles to proper ones, as is said in *Physics* 1. Hence those propositions which are composed of such common terms as "whole" and "part" (for example, "every whole is greater than one of its parts") and of such terms as "equal" and "unequal" (for example, "things equal to one and the same thing are equal to each other") constitute the first principles of demonstration. And the same is true of similar terms.

Now, since common terms of this kind belong to the consideration of the philosopher, then it follows that these principles also fall within his scope.

But the philosopher does not establish the truth of these principles by way of demonstration, but by considering the

et quid pars et sic de aliis. Hoc autem cognito, veritas praedictorum principiorum manifesta relinquitur.

meaning of their terms, such as what a whole is and what a part is, and so forth. When the meaning of these terms becomes known, it follows that the truth of the above-mentioned principles becomes evident.

Lecture 6

The first principle of demonstration

1005b8 Congruit autem maxime cognoscentem circa unumquodque genus, habere dicere firmissima rei principia. Quare et de entibus, inquantum sunt entia, omnium firmissima. Est autem hic philosophus ipse. [596]

προσήκει δὲ τὸν μάλιστα γνωρίζοντα περὶ ἕκαστον γένος ἔχειν λέγειν τὰς βεβαιοτάτας ἀρχὰς {10} τοῦ πράγματος, ὥστε καὶ τὸν περὶ τῶν ὄντων ᾗ ὄντα τὰς πάντων βεβαιοτάτας. ἔστι δ᾽ οὗτος ὁ φιλόσοφος.

And it is fitting that the person who is best informed about each genus of things should be able to state the firmest principles of his subject. Hence he who understands beings as beings should be able to state the firmest principles of all things. This person is the philosopher.

1005b11 Et firmissimum omnium principiorum est, contra quod mentiri impossibile est, notissimum enim esse tale est necesse: nam, circa ea quae ignorant decipiuntur omnes. Et non conditionale. Quod enim necessarium habere quodcumque entium intelligentem, hoc non conditionale. Quod autem cognoscere est necessarium quodcumque cognoscentem et venire habenti est necesse. Quod quidem igitur tale principium omnium sit firmissimum, palam. [597]

βεβαιοτάτη δ᾽ ἀρχὴ πασῶν περὶ ἣν διαψευσθῆναι ἀδύνατον: γνωριμωτάτην τε γὰρ ἀναγκαῖον εἶναι τὴν τοιαύτην (περὶ γὰρ ἃ μὴ γνωρίζουσιν ἀπατῶνται πάντες) καὶ ἀνυπόθετον. {15} ἣν γὰρ ἀναγκαῖον ἔχειν τὸν ὁτιοῦν ξυνιέντα τῶν ὄντων, τοῦτο οὐχ ὑπόθεσις: ὃ δὲ γνωρίζειν ἀναγκαῖον τῷ ὁτιοῦν γνωρίζοντι, καὶ ἥκειν ἔχοντα ἀναγκαῖον. ὅτι μὲν οὖν βεβαιοτάτη ἡ τοιαύτη πασῶν ἀρχή, δῆλον:

And the firmest of all principles is that about which it is impossible to make a mistake, for such a principle must be both the best known (for all men make mistakes about things that they do not know) and not be hypothetical. For the principle which everyone must have who understands anything about beings is not hypothetical; and that which everyone must know who knows anything must be had by him when he comes to his subject. It is evident, then, that such a principle is the firmest of all.

1005b18 Quid vero sit illud, post hoc dicamus. Idem enim simul esse, et non esse in eodem, secundum idem, est impossibile: et quaecumque alia determinaremus, utique sint determinata ad logicas difficultates. Hoc autem omnium firmissimum est principium. Habet enim dictam determinationem. Impossibile namque quemcumque idem suscipere esse et non esse. Quemadmodum quidem quidam putant dicere Heraclitum. Non enim est necesse quae aliquis dicit, hoc et suscipere. [600]

τίς δ᾽ ἔστιν αὕτη, μετὰ ταῦτα λέγωμεν. τὸ γὰρ αὐτὸ ἅμα ὑπάρχειν τε καὶ μὴ {20} ὑπάρχειν ἀδύνατον τῷ αὐτῷ καὶ κατὰ τὸ αὐτό (καὶ ὅσα ἄλλα προσδιορισαίμεθ᾽ ἄν, ἔστω προσδιωρισμένα πρὸς τὰς λογικὰς δυσχερείας): αὕτη δὴ πασῶν ἐστι βεβαιοτάτη τῶν ἀρχῶν: ἔχει γὰρ τὸν εἰρημένον διορισμόν. ἀδύνατον γὰρ ὁντινοῦν ταὐτὸν ὑπολαμβάνειν εἶναι καὶ μὴ εἶναι, καθάπερ {25} τινὲς οἴονται λέγειν Ἡράκλειτον. οὐκ ἔστι γὰρ ἀναγκαῖον, ἅ τις λέγει, ταῦτα καὶ ὑπολαμβάνειν:

And let us next state what this principle is. It is that the same attribute cannot both belong and not belong to the same subject at the same time and in the same respect. Let us also stipulate any other qualifications that have to be laid down to meet dialectical difficulties. Now this is the firmest of all principles, since it answers to the definition given, for it is impossible for anyone to think that the same thing both is and is not, although some are of the opinion that Heraclitus speaks in this way (for what a man says he does not necessarily accept).

Si vero non contingit simul inesse eidem contraria (determinentur ergo nobis eadem, positione consueta), contraria vero est opinio opinioni, quae contradictionis: palam quia impossibile, simul suscipere eumdem esse et non esse idem: simul enim habebit contrarias opiniones, qui de hoc est mentitus. Quapropter omnes demonstrantes in hanc reducunt ultimam opinionem.

εἰ δὲ μὴ ἐνδέχεται ἅμα ὑπάρχειν τῷ αὐτῷ τἀναντία (προσδιωρίσθω δ᾽ ἡμῖν καὶ ταύτῃ τῇ προτάσει τὰ εἰωθότα), ἐναντία δ᾽ ἐστὶ δόξα δόξῃ ἡ τῆς ἀντιφάσεως, φανερὸν ὅτι ἀδύνατον ἅμα {30} ὑπολαμβάνειν τὸν αὐτὸν εἶναι καὶ μὴ εἶναι τὸ αὐτό: ἅμα γὰρ ἂν ἔχοι τὰς ἐναντίας δόξας ὁ διεψευσμένος περὶ τούτου. διὸ πάντες οἱ ἀποδεικνύντες εἰς ταύτην ἀνάγουσιν ἐσχάτην δόξαν: φύσει

But if it is impossible for contraries to belong simultaneously to the same subject (and let us then suppose that the same things are established here as in the usual proposition), and if one opinion which expresses the contradictory of another is contrary to it, evidently the same man at the same time cannot think that the same thing can both be and not be. One who is mistaken on this point will have contrary

Natura namque principium et aliarum dignitatum haec omnium.

γὰρ ἀρχὴ καὶ τῶν ἄλλων ἀξιωμάτων αὕτη πάντων.

opinions at the same time. And it is for this reason that all who make demonstrations reduce their argument to this ultimate position. For this is by nature the starting point of all the other axioms.

1005b35 Sunt autem quidam, qui, ut diximus, dicebant contingere idem esse et non esse, et existimare ita. Utuntur autem ratione hac multi eorum qui de natura. Nos autem nunc accipimus quasi impossibili existente simul esse et non esse, et per hoc ostendemus, quod firmissimum id principiorum est omnium. [606]

εἰσὶ δέ τινες οἵ, καθάπερ εἴπομεν, αὐτοί τε ἐνδέχεσθαί φασι τὸ αὐτὸ εἶναι καὶ μὴ εἶναι, {1006a1} καὶ ὑπολαμβάνειν οὕτως. χρῶνται δὲ τῷ λόγῳ τούτῳ πολλοὶ καὶ τῶν περὶ φύσεως. ἡμεῖς δὲ νῦν εἰλήφαμεν ὡς ἀδυνάτου ὄντος ἅμα εἶναι καὶ μὴ εἶναι, καὶ διὰ τούτου ἐδείξαμεν ὅτι βεβαιοτάτη {5} αὕτη τῶν ἀρχῶν πασῶν.

Now as we have said (1005b18), there are some who claimed that the same thing can both be and not be, and that this can be believed. And many of those who treat of nature adopt this theory. But now we take it to be impossible for a thing both to be and not be at the same time, and by means of this we shall show that this is the firmest of all principles.

1006a6 Dignantur autem et hoc demonstrate quidam propter apaedeusiam. Est enim apaedeusia non cognoscere, quorum oportet quaerere demonstrationem et quorum non oportet. [607]

ἀξιοῦσι δὴ καὶ τοῦτο ἀποδεικνύναι τινὲς δι᾽ ἀπαιδευσίαν: ἔστι γὰρ ἀπαιδευσία τὸ μὴ γιγνώσκειν τίνων δεῖ ζητεῖν ἀπόδειξιν καὶ τίνων οὐ δεῖ:

But some deem it fitting that even this principle should be demonstrated, and they do this through want of education. For not to know of what things one should seek demonstration and of what things one should not shows want of education.

Totaliter quidem enim omnium esse demonstrationem est impossibile: am in infinitum procederet, ut nec ita foret demonstratio. Si vero quorumdam non oportet demonstrationem quaerere, quod dignantur magis esse tale principium, non habent dicere.

ὅλως μὲν γὰρ ἁπάντων ἀδύνατον ἀπόδειξιν εἶναι (εἰς ἄπειρον γὰρ ἂν βαδίζοι, ὥστε μηδ᾽ οὕτως εἶναι ἀπόδειξιν), {10} εἰ δέ τινων μὴ δεῖ ζητεῖν ἀπόδειξιν, τίνα ἀξιοῦσιν εἶναι μᾶλλον τοιαύτην ἀρχὴν οὐκ ἂν ἔχοιεν εἰπεῖν.

For it is altogether impossible that there should be demonstration of all things, because there would then be an infinite regress so that there would still be no demonstration. But if there are some things of which it is not necessary to seek demonstration, these people cannot say what principle they think to be more indemonstrable.

1006a11 Est autem demonstrare elenchice et de hoc quia impossibile, si solum aliquid dicit qui dubitat. Si vero nihil, derisio est quaerere rationem ad nullam habentem rationem, inquantum non habet rationem. Similis enim plantae talis iam est. [608]

ἔστι δ᾽ ἀποδεῖξαι ἐλεγκτικῶς καὶ περὶ τούτου ὅτι ἀδύνατον, ἂν μόνον τι λέγῃ ὁ ἀμφισβητῶν: ἂν δὲ μηθέν, γελοῖον τὸ ζητεῖν λόγον πρὸς τὸν μηθενὸς ἔχοντα λόγον, ᾗ μὴ ἔχει: ὅμοιος {15} γὰρ φυτῷ ὁ τοιοῦτος ᾗ τοιοῦτος ἤδη.

But even in this case it is possible to show by refutation that this view is impossible, if only our opponent will say something. But if he says nothing, it is ridiculous to look for a reason against one who has no reason on the very point on which he is without reason. For such a man is really like a plant.

Elenchice autem demonstrare, dico utique differre et demonstrare. Quia demonstrat quidem quod in principio. Alterius autem tali existente causa, elenchus utique erit et non demonstratio.

τὸ δ᾽ ἐλεγκτικῶς ἀποδεῖξαι λέγω διαφέρειν καὶ τὸ ἀποδεῖξαι, ὅτι ἀποδεικνύων μὲν ἂν δόξειεν αἰτεῖσθαι τὸ ἐν ἀρχῇ, ἄλλου δὲ τοῦ τοιούτου αἰτίου ὄντος ἔλεγχος ἂν εἴη καὶ οὐκ ἀπόδειξις.

Now I say that demonstration by refutation is different from demonstration in the strict sense, because he who would demonstrate this principle in the strict sense would seem to beg the question. But when someone argues for the sake of convincing another, there will be refutation, not demonstration.

---

596. Hic ostendit principaliter, quod ad primum philosophum pertinet considerare de primo demonstrationis principio: et circa hoc duo facit.

Primo ostendit, quod eius est de ipso considerare.

596. He shows here that it is the first philosopher who is chiefly concerned with the first principle of demonstration; in regard to this he does two things.

First, he shows that it is the business of the first philosopher to consider this principle;

Secundo de ipso tractare incipit, ibi, *principium vero* et cetera.

Circa primum tria facit.

Primo ostendit, quod huius scientiae est considerare de primo demonstrationis principio.

Secundo ostendit quid sit illud, ibi, *et firmissimum* et cetera.

Tertio excludit quosdam errores circa idem principium, ibi, *sunt autem quidam* et cetera.

Utitur autem ad primum tali ratione. In unoquoque genere ille est maxime cognoscitivus, qui certissima cognoscit principia; quia certitudo cognitionis ex certitudine principiorum dependet. Sed primus philosophus est maxime cognoscitivus et certissimus in sua cognitione: haec enim erat una de conditionibus sapientis, ut in prooemio huius libri patuit, scilicet quod esset certissimus cognitor causarum; ergo philosophus debet considerare certissima et firmissima principia circa entia, de quibus ipse considerat sicut de genere sibi proprie subiecto.

597. Deinde cum dicit *et firmissimum* hic ostendit quid sit firmissimum sive certissimum principium: et circa hoc duo facit.

Primo dicit quae sunt conditiones certissimi principii.

Deinde adaptat eas uni principio, ibi, *quid vero sit* et cetera.

Ponit ergo primo, tres conditiones firmissimi principii.

Prima est, quod circa hoc non possit aliquis mentiri, sive errare. Et hoc patet, quia cum homines non decipiuntur nisi *circa ea quae ignorant*: ideo circa quod non potest aliquis decipi, oportet esse notissimum.

598. Secunda conditio est ut sit *non conditionale*, idest non propter suppositionem habitum, sicut illa, quae ex quodam condicto ponuntur.

Unde alia translatio habet: *et non subiiciantur*, idest non subiiciantur ea, quae sunt certissima principia. Et hoc ideo, quia illud, quod necessarium est habere intelligentem quaecumque entium *hoc non est conditionale*, idest non est suppositum, sed oportet per se esse notum.

Et hoc ideo, quia ex quo ipsum est necessarium ad intelligendum quodcumque, oportet quod quilibet qui alia est cognoscens, ipsum cognoscat.

599. Tertia conditio est, ut non acquiratur per demonstrationem, vel alio simili modo; sed adveniat quasi per naturam habenti ipsum, quasi ut naturaliter cognoscatur, et non per acquisitionem. Ex ipso enim lumine naturali intellectus agentis prima principia fiunt cognita, nec acquiruntur per ratiocinationes, sed solum per hoc

and second (1006a18; [611]), he begins to examine this principle, at *the starting point of all*.

In regard to the first he does three things.

First, he shows that it is the office of this science to consider the first principle of demonstration.

Second (1005b11; [597]), he indicates what this principle is, at *and the firmest*.

Third (1005b35; [606]), he rejects certain errors regarding this same principle, at *now as we have said*.

In regard to the first point he uses the following argument. In every genus of things, that man is best informed who knows the most certain principles, because the certitude of knowing depends on the certitude of principles. But the first philosopher is best informed and most certain in his knowledge. For this was one of the conditions of wisdom, as was made clear in the prologue of this work [35]—namely, that he who knows the causes of things has the most certain knowledge. Hence the philosopher ought to consider the most certain and firmest principles of beings, which he considers as the subject-genus proper to himself.

597. And the firmest (1005b11). Then he shows what the firmest or most certain principle is, and in regard to this he does two things.

First, he states the conditions for the most certain principle;

then (1005b18; [600]), he shows how they fit a single principle, at *and let us*.

He accordingly first gives the three conditions for the firmest principle.

The first is that no one can make a mistake or be in error regarding it. And this is evident, for since men make mistakes only *about things that they do not know*, then that principle about which no one can be mistaken must be the one which is best known.

598. The second condition is that it must *not be hypothetical*, that is, it must not be held as a supposition, as those things that are maintained through some kind of common agreement.

Hence another translation reads: *and they should not hold a subordinate place*, that is, those principles which are most certain should not be made dependent on anything else. And this is true, because whatever is necessary for understanding anything at all about being is *not hypothetical*, that is, it is not a supposition, but must be self-evident.

And this is true because whatever is necessary for understanding anything at all must be known by anyone who knows other things.

599. The third condition is that it is not acquired by demonstration or by any similar method, but comes in a sense by nature to the one having it inasmuch as it is naturally known and not acquired. For first principles become known through the natural light of the agent intellect, and they are not acquired by any process of reasoning, but by

quod eorum termini innotescunt. Quod quidem fit per hoc, quod a sensibilibus accipitur memoria et a memoria experimentorum et ab experimento illorum terminorum cognitio, quibus cognitis cognoscuntur huiusmodi propositiones communes, quae sunt artium et scientiarum principia. Manifestum est ergo quod certissimum principium sive firmissimum, tale debet esse, ut circa id non possit errari, et quod non sit suppositum et quod adveniat naturaliter.

600. Deinde cum dicit *quid vero* ostendit cui principio praedicta determinatio conveniat: et dicit, quod huic principio convenit tamquam firmissimo, quod est impossibile eidem simul inesse et non inesse idem: sed addendum est, et *secundum idem*: et etiam alia sunt determinanda circa hoc principium, quaecumque determinari contingit *ad logicas difficultates*, sine quibus videtur contradictio cum non sit.

601. Quod autem praedicta huic principio conveniant, sic ostendit. Impossibile enim est quemcumque *suscipere*, sive opinari, quod idem sit simul et non sit: quamvis quidam arbitrentur Heraclitum hoc opinatum fuisse. Verum est autem, quod Heraclitus hoc dixit, non tamen hoc potuit opinari. Non enim necessarium est, quod quicquid aliquis dicit, haec mente suscipiat vel opinetur.

602. Si autem aliquis diceret, quod contingeret aliquem opinari idem simul esse et non esse, sequitur hoc inconveniens, quod contingit contraria eidem simul inesse. Et haec *determinentur nobis*, idest ostendantur quadam propositione consueta et in logicis determinata.

Ostensum est enim in fine *Perihermenias*, quod opiniones sunt contrariae, non quae sunt contrariorum, sed quae sunt contradictionis per se loquendo. Hae enim non sunt contrariae opiniones primo et per se, ut si unus opinetur, quod Socrates est albus, et alius opinetur quod Socrates est niger. Sed, quod unus opinetur quod Socrates est albus, et alius opinetur quod Socrates non est albus.

603. Si igitur quis opinetur simul duo contradictoria esse vera, opinando simul idem esse et non esse, habebit simul contrarias opiniones: et ita contraria simul inerunt eidem, quod est impossibile.

Non igitur contingit aliquem circa haec interius mentiri et quod opinetur simul idem esse et non esse. Et propter hoc omnes demonstrationes reducunt suas propositiones in hanc propositionem, sicut in ultimam

having their terms become known. This comes about by reason of the fact that memory is derived from sensible things, experience from memory, and knowledge of those terms from experience. And when they are known, common propositions of this kind, which are the principles of the arts and sciences, become known. Hence it is evident that the most certain or firmest principle should be such that there can be no error regarding it, that it is not hypothetical, and that it comes naturally to the one having it.

600. *And let us next* (1005b18). Then he indicates the principle to which the above definition applies. He says that it applies to this principle as the one which is firmest: that it is impossible for the same attribute both to belong and not belong to the same subject at the same time. And it is necessary to add *in the same respect*; and any other qualifications that have to be given regarding this principle *to meet dialectical difficulties* must be laid down, since without these qualifications there would seem to be a contradiction when there is none.

601. That this principle must meet the conditions given above he shows as follows. It is impossible for anyone *to think*, or hold as an opinion, that the same thing both is and is not at the same time, although some believe that Heraclitus was of this opinion. But while it is true that Heraclitus spoke in this way, he could not think that this is true, for it is not necessary that everything that a person says he should mentally hold as opinion.

602. But if one were to say that it is possible for someone to think that the same thing both is and is not at the same time, this absurd consequence follows: contraries could belong to the same subject at the same time. And *let us then suppose that the same things are established here*, or shown, as in the usual proposition established in our logical treatises.

For it was shown at the end of *On Interpretation* that contrary opinions are not those which have to do with contraries, but those which have to do with contradictories, properly speaking. For when one person thinks that Socrates is white and another thinks that he is black, these are not contrary opinions in the primary and proper sense. But contrary opinions are had when one person thinks that Socrates is white and another thinks that he is not white.

603. Therefore, if someone were to think that two contradictories are true at the same time by thinking that the same thing both is and is not at the same time, he will have contrary opinions at the same time. Thus contraries will belong to the same thing at the same time. But this is impossible.

It is impossible, then, for anyone to be mistaken in his own mind about these things and to think that the same thing both is and is not at the same time. And it is for this reason that all demonstrations reduce their propositions to

opinionem omnibus communem: ipsa enim est naturaliter principium et dignitas omnium dignitatum.

604. Et sic patent aliae duae conditiones; quia inquantum in hanc reducunt demonstrantes omnia, sicut in ultimum resolvendo, patet quod non habetur ex suppositione. Inquantum vero est naturaliter principium, sic patet quod advenit habenti, et non habetur per acquisitionem.

605. Ad huius autem evidentiam sciendum est, quod, cum duplex sit operatio intellectus: una, qua cognoscit quod quid est, quae vocatur indivisibilium intelligentia: alia, qua componit et dividit: in utroque est aliquod primum:

in prima quidem operatione est aliquod primum, quod cadit in conceptione intellectus, scilicet hoc quod dico ens; nec aliquid hac operatione potest mente concipi, nisi intelligatur ens. Et quia hoc principium, impossibile est esse et non esse simul, dependet ex intellectu entis, sicut hoc principium, omne totum est maius sua parte, ex intellectu totius et partis: ideo hoc etiam principium est naturaliter primum in secunda operatione intellectus, scilicet componentis et dividentis.

Nec aliquis potest secundum hanc operationem intellectus aliquid intelligere, nisi hoc principio intellecto. Sicut enim totum et partes non intelliguntur nisi intellecto ente, ita nec hoc principium omne totum est maius sua parte, nisi intellecto praedicto principio firmissimo.

606. Deinde cum dicit *sunt autem* ostendit quomodo circa praedictum principium ab aliquibus est erratum: et circa hoc duo facit.

Primo tangit errorem illorum, qui contradicebant praedicto principio.

Secundo eorum, qui ipsum demonstrare volebant, ibi, *dignantur autem* et cetera.

Dicit ergo, quod quidam, sicut dictum est de Heraclito, dicebant quod contingit idem simul esse et non esse, et quod contingit hoc existimare. Et hac positione utuntur multi naturales, ut infra patebit:

sed nos nunc accipimus supponendo praedictum principium esse verum, scilicet quod impossibile sit idem esse et non esse, sed ex sui veritate ostendimus quod est certissimum. Ex hoc enim quod impossibile est esse et non esse, sequitur quod impossibile sit contraria simul inesse eidem, ut infra dicetur. Et ex hoc quod contraria non possunt simul inesse, sequitur quod homo non possit habere contrarias opiniones, et per consequens quod non possit opinari contradictoria esse vera, ut ostensum est.

this proposition as the ultimate opinion common to all, for this proposition is by nature the starting point and axiom of all axioms.

604. The other two conditions are therefore evident, because insofar as those making demonstrations reduce all their arguments to this principle as the ultimate one by referring them to it, evidently this principle is not based on an assumption. Indeed, insofar as it is by nature a starting point, it clearly comes unsought to the one having it and is not acquired by his own efforts.

605. Now for the purpose of making this evident it must be noted that, since the intellect has two operations—one by which it knows quiddities, which is called the understanding of indivisibles, and another by which it combines and separates—there is something first in both operations.

In the first operation, the first thing that the intellect conceives is being, and in this operation nothing else can be conceived unless being is understood. And because this principle—that it is impossible for a thing both to be and not be at the same time—depends on the understanding of being (just as the principle that every whole is greater than one of its parts depends on the understanding of whole and part), then this principle is by nature also the first in the second operation of the intellect (that is, in the act of combining and separating).

And no one can understand anything by this intellectual operation unless this principle is understood. For just as a whole and its parts are understood only by understanding being, in a similar way the principle that every whole is greater than one of its parts is understood only if the firmest principle is understood.

606. *Now as we have said* (1005b35). Then he shows how some men erred regarding this principle, and in regard to this he does two things.

First, he touches on the error of those who rejected the foregoing principle;

second (1006a6; [607]), he deals with those who wished to demonstrate it, at *but some*.

He accordingly says that some men, as was stated above about Heraclitus [601], said that the same thing can both be and not be at the same time, and that it is possible to hold this opinion. Many of the philosophers of nature adopt this position, as will be made clear below [665].

For our part, however, we now take as evident that the principle in question is true—the principle that the same thing cannot both be and not be—but from its truth we show that it is most certain. For from the fact that a thing cannot both be and not be it follows that contraries cannot belong to the same subject, as will be said below [663]. And from the fact that contraries cannot belong to a subject at the same time it follows that a man cannot have contrary opinions and, consequently, that he cannot think that contradictories are true, as has been shown [603].

607. Deinde cum dicit *dignantur autem* tangit errorem quorumdam, qui praedictum principium demonstrare volebant: et circa hoc duo facit.

Primo ostendit quod non possit demonstrari simpliciter.

Secundo quod aliquo modo potest demonstrari, ibi, *est autem demonstrare* et cetera.

Dicit ergo primo, quod quidam dignum ducunt, sive volunt demonstrare praedictum principium. Et hoc *propter apaedeusiam*, idest ineruditionem sive indisciplinationem. Est enim ineruditio, quod homo nesciat quorum oportet quaerere demonstrationem, et quorum non: non enim possunt omnia demonstrari.

Si enim omnia demonstrarentur, cum idem per seipsum non demonstretur, sed per aliud, oporteret esse circulum in demonstrationibus. Quod esse non potest: quia sic idem esset notius et minus notum, ut patet in primo *Posteriorum*. Vel oporteret procedere in infinitum.

Sed, si in infinitum procederetur, non esset demonstratio; quia quaelibet demonstrationis conclusio redditur certa per reductionem eius in primum demonstrationis principium: quod non esset si in infinitum demonstratio sursum procederet. Patet igitur, quod non sunt omnia demonstrabilia. Et si aliqua sunt non demonstrabilia, non possunt dicere quod aliquod principium sit magis indemonstrabile quam praedictum.

608. *Est autem* hic ostendit, quod aliquo modo potest praedictum principium demonstrari; dicens, quod contingit praedictum principium demonstrari argumentative. In Graeco habetur elenchice, quod melius transfertur redarguitive. Nam elenchus est syllogismus ad contradicendum. Unde inducitur ad redarguendum aliquam falsam positionem. Et propter hoc isto modo ostendi potest, quod impossibile sit idem esse et non esse. Sed solum si ille qui ex aliqua dubitatione negat illud principium, *dicit aliquid* idest aliquid nomine significat. Si vero nihil dicit, derisibile est quaerere aliquam rationem ad illum qui nulla utitur ratione loquendo. Talis enim in hac disputatione, qui nihil significat, similis erit plantae. Animalia enim bruta etiam significant aliquid per talia signa.

609. Differt enim demonstrare simpliciter principium praedictum, et demonstrare argumentative sive elenchice. Quia si aliquis vellet demonstrare simpliciter praedictum principium, videretur petere principium, quia non posset aliquid sumere ad eius demonstrationem, nisi aliqua quae ex veritate huius principii dependerent, ut ex praedictis patet. Sed quando demonstratio

607. *But some* (1006a6). Then he mentions the error of certain men who wished to demonstrate the above-mentioned principle; and in regard to this he does two things.

First, he shows that it cannot be demonstrated in the strict sense;

and second (1006a11; [608]), that it can be demonstrated in a way, at *but even in this case*.

Thus he says, first, that certain men deem it fitting, or they wish, to demonstrate this principle. They do this *through want of education*, that is, through lack of learning or instruction. For there is want of education when a man does not know what to seek demonstration for and what not to, since not all things can be demonstrated.

For if all things were demonstrable, then, since a thing is not demonstrated through itself but through something else, either demonstrations would be circular—and this cannot be true, because then the same thing would be both better known and less well known, as is clear in *Posterior Analytics* 1—or they would have to proceed to infinity.

But if there were an infinite regress in demonstrations, demonstration would be impossible, because the conclusion of any demonstration is made certain by reducing it to the first principle of demonstration. But this would not be the case if demonstration proceeded to infinity in an upward direction. It is clear, then, that not all things are demonstrable. And if some things are not demonstrable, these men cannot say that any principle is more indemonstrable than the above-mentioned one.

608. *But even in this case* (1006a11). Here he shows that the above-mentioned principle can be demonstrated in a certain respect. He says that it may be demonstrated by disproof. In Greek, the word is *elenchice*, which is better translated as "by refutation," for an *elenchus* is a syllogism that establishes the contradictory of a proposition, and so is introduced to refute some false position. And on these grounds it can be shown that it is impossible for the same thing both to be and not be. But this kind of argument can be employed only if the one who denies that principle because of difficulties *will say something*, that is, if he signifies something by a word. But if he says nothing, it is ridiculous to look for a reason against one who does not make use of reason in speaking, for in this dispute anyone who signifies nothing will be like a plant, for even brute animals signify something by such signs.

609. For it is one thing to give a strict demonstration of this principle, but another to demonstrate it argumentatively or by refutation. For if anyone wished to give a strict demonstration of this principle, he would seem to be begging the question, because any principle that he could take for the purpose of demonstrating this one would be one of those that depend on the truth of this principle, as

non erit talis, scilicet simpliciter, tunc est argumentatio sive elenchus et non demonstratio.

610. Alia litera sic habet et melius, *alterius autem cum huius causa sit, argumentatio erit, et non demonstratio*, idest cum huiusmodi processus a minus notis ad hoc magis notum principium fiat causa alterius hominis qui hoc negat, tunc poterit esse argumentatio sive elenchus, et non demonstratio, scilicet syllogismus contradicens ei poterit esse, cum id quod est minus notum simpliciter est concessum ab adversario, ex quo poterit procedi ad praedictum principium ostendendum quantum ad ipsum, licet non simpliciter.

is clear from what has been said above (1006a6; [607]). But when the demonstration is not of this kind (that is, demonstration in the strict sense), there will then be disproof or refutation at most.

610. Another text states this better by saying, *but when one argues for the sake of convincing another, there will then be refutation but not demonstration*. In other words, when a process of this kind from a less well known to a better known principle is employed for the sake of convincing another man who denies this, there will then be disproof or refutation but not demonstration—that is, it will be possible to have a syllogism which contradicts his view, since what is less known absolutely is admitted by the opponent, and thus it will be possible to proceed to demonstrate the above-mentioned principle so far as the man is concerned but not in the strict sense.

LECTURE 7

Contradictories cannot be true at the same time

1006a18 Principium vero ad omnia talia non velle, aut esse aliquid dicere, aut non esse. Hoc enim forsan utique quis opinabitur, quod a principio petere. Sed significare quidem aliquid et ipsi et alii. Hoc enim necesse est si dicat aliquid. Si enim non, cum tali utique non erit sermo, haec ipsi ad seipsum, nec ad alium. Si quis autem hoc dederit, erit demonstratio. Iam enim erit aliquid definitum, sed tamen non demonstrans, sed sustinens. Interimens enim rationem sustinet rationem. [611]

ἀρχὴ δὲ πρὸς ἅπαντα τὰ τοιαῦτα οὐ τὸ ἀξιοῦν ἢ εἶναί τι λέγειν {20} ἢ μὴ εἶναι (τοῦτο μὲν γὰρ τάχ' ἄν τις ὑπολάβοι τὸ ἐξ ἀρχῆς αἰτεῖν), ἀλλὰ σημαίνειν γέ τι καὶ αὐτῷ καὶ ἄλλῳ· τοῦτο γὰρ ἀνάγκη, εἴπερ λέγοι τι. εἰ γὰρ μή, οὐκ ἂν εἴη τῷ τοιούτῳ λόγος, οὔτ' αὐτῷ πρὸς αὐτὸν οὔτε πρὸς ἄλλον. ἂν δέ τις τοῦτο διδῷ, ἔσται ἀπόδειξις· ἤδη γάρ τι {25} ἔσται ὡρισμένον. ἀλλ' αἴτιος οὐχ ὁ ἀποδεικνὺς ἀλλ' ὁ ὑπομένων· ἀναιρῶν γὰρ λόγον ὑπομένει λόγον. ἔτι δὲ ὁ τοῦτο συγχωρήσας συγκεχώρηκέ τι ἀληθὲς εἶναι χωρὶς ἀποδείξεως [ὥστε οὐκ ἂν πᾶν οὕτως καὶ οὐχ οὕτως ἔχοι].

The starting point of all such discussions is not the desire that someone shall state that something either is or is not, for this might perhaps be thought to be begging the question, but that he shall state something significant both for himself and for someone else; for this he must do if he is to say anything. For if he does not, no discussion will be possible for such a person either with himself or with another. But if anyone will grant this, demonstration will be possible, for there will already be something definite. But this will not have the effect of demonstrating, but of upholding, for he who destroys reason upholds reason.

1006a26 Primum quidem igitur manifestum quod hoc quidem verum est quod significat nomen esse, aut non esse hoc. Quare neque utique omne sic et non sic se habebit. [612]

πρῶτον μὲν οὖν δῆλον ὡς τοῦτό γ' αὐτὸ ἀληθές, ὅτι σημαίνει τὸ {30} ὄνομα τὸ εἶναι ἢ μὴ εἶναι τοδί, ὥστ' οὐκ ἂν πᾶν οὕτως καὶ οὐχ οὕτως ἔχοι·

First of all, then, it is evident that this at least is true, that the term "to be" or "not to be" signifies something, such that not everything will be so and not so.

1006a31 Amplius si homo significat unum, sit hoc, animal bipes. [612]

ἔτι εἰ τὸ ἄνθρωπος σημαίνει ἕν, ἔστω τοῦτο τὸ ζῷον δίπουν.

Again, if the term "man" signifies one thing, let this be a two-footed animal.

1006a32 Dico autem unum significare hoc, si hoc est homo, si sit aliquid homo, hoc est hominem esse. Nihil autem differt nec si plura quis dicat significare: solum autem definita. Ponetur enim utique rationibus alterum nomen. [613]

λέγω δὲ τὸ ἓν σημαίνειν τοῦτο· εἰ τοῦτ' ἔστιν ἄνθρωπος, ἂν ᾖ τι ἄνθρωπος, τοῦτ' ἔσται τὸ ἀνθρώπῳ εἶναι (διαφέρει δ' οὐθὲν οὐδ' εἰ πλείω τις φαίη σημαίνειν μόνον δὲ ὡρισμένα, {1006b1} τεθείη γὰρ ἂν ἐφ' ἑκάστῳ λόγῳ ἕτερον ὄνομα·

Now, by "signifying one thing" I mean this. Granted that man is a two-footed animal, then if something is a man, this will be what being a man is. And it makes no difference even if someone were to say that this term signifies many things, provided that there are a definite number, for a different term might be assigned to each concept.

Dico autem, ut si non dicat hominem unum significare sed multa, quorum unius quidem una ratio, animal bipes. Sunt autem et aliae plures, sed definitae numero. Ponetur enim utique proprium nomen secundum unamquamque rationem.

λέγω δ' οἷον, εἰ μὴ φαίη τὸ ἄνθρωπος ἓν σημαίνειν, πολλὰ δέ, ὧν ἑνὸς μὲν εἷς λόγος τὸ ζῷον δίπουν, εἶεν δὲ καὶ ἕτεροι πλείους, ὡρισμένοι δὲ τὸν ἀριθμόν· {5} τεθείη γὰρ ἂν ἴδιον ὄνομα καθ' ἕκαστον τὸν λόγον·

I mean, for example, that if one were to say that the term "man" signifies not one thing but many, one of which would have a single concept, namely, two-footed animal, there might still be many others, if only there are a limited number. For a particular term might be assigned to each concept.

Si autem non ponatur, sed infinita significare dicat, palam quia non utique erit ratio. Nam non unum significare, nihil significare est. Non significantibus autem nominibus aufertur adinvicem disputare, secundum veritatem autem et ad seipsum. Nihil enim contingit intelligere nisi intelligentem

εἰ δὲ μή [τεθείη], ἀλλ' ἄπειρα σημαίνειν φαίη, φανερὸν ὅτι οὐκ ἂν εἴη λόγος· τὸ γὰρ μὴ ἓν σημαίνειν οὐθὲν σημαίνειν ἐστίν, μὴ σημαινόντων δὲ τῶν ὀνομάτων ἀνῄρηται τὸ διαλέγεσθαι πρὸς ἀλλήλους, κατὰ δὲ τὴν ἀλήθειαν καὶ πρὸς αὑτόν· {10} οὐθὲν γὰρ ἐνδέχεται νοεῖν μὴ νοοῦντα ἕν, εἰ δ' ἐνδέχεται, τεθείη ἂν

However, if this were not the case, but one were to say that a term signifies an infinite number of things, evidently reasoning would be impossible; for, not to signify one thing is to signify nothing. And if words signify nothing, there will be no discourse with another or even with ourselves. For it is impossible to

unum. Si autem contingit, ponatur huic rei nomen. Sit itaque sicut a principio dictum est, significans aliquid nomen et significans unum.

1006b13 Nec sic contingit hominem esse significare non esse hominem, si homo significat non solum de uno, sed et unum. Non enim hoc dignamur unum significare quod de uno, quoniam sic itaque musicus et album et homo unum significarent. Quare unum omnia erunt. Syonyma namque. Et non erunt esse et non esse idem, nisi secundum aequivocationem: ut si quem nos hominem vocamus, alii non hominem vocant. Dubitatum veto non hoc est, si contingit simul idem esse et non esse hominem secundum nomen, sed secundum rem. [616]

1006b22 Si autem non significet alterum homo et non homo, palam quia non esse hominem, non erit diversum ab esse hominem. Quare erit hominem esse non hominem esse. Unum enim erunt. Hoc enim significat esse unum, ut vestimentum et indumentum si ratio una. Si vero erunt unum, et unum significat hominem esse et non hominem. Sed ostensum est quod alteram significat. [619]

1006b28 Necesse itaque, si quidem est verum dicere quia homo, animal esse bipes: hoc enim erat quod significabat homo. Sed si hoc necesse, non contingit non esse hoc ipsum animal bipes: hoc enim significat necesse esse, impossibile non esse hominem. Non igitur contingit simul verum esse, dicere idem hominem esse et non esse hominem. Eadem autem ratio et de non esse hominem. [620]

1007a1 Nam hominem esse, et non hominem esse, alterum significat: si quidem album esse et hominem esse alteram; multum enim opponitur illud magis, quare significat diversum. Si autem et album dixerit idem significare et unum

ὄνομα τούτῳ τῷ πράγματι ἕν). ἔστω δή, ὥσπερ ἐλέχθη κατ᾽ ἀρχάς, σημαῖνόν τι τὸ ὄνομα καὶ σημαῖνον ἕν:

οὐ δὴ ἐνδέχεται τὸ ἀνθρώπῳ εἶναι σημαίνειν ὅπερ ἀνθρώπῳ μὴ εἶναι, εἰ τὸ ἄνθρωπος σημαίνει μὴ μόνον καθ᾽ ἑνὸς {15} ἀλλὰ καὶ ἕν (οὐ γὰρ τοῦτο ἀξιοῦμεν τὸ ἓν σημαίνειν, τὸ καθ᾽ ἑνός, ἐπεὶ οὕτω γε κἂν τὸ μουσικὸν καὶ τὸ λευκὸν καὶ τὸ ἄνθρωπος ἓν ἐσήμαινεν, ὥστε ἓν ἅπαντα ἔσται: συνώνυμα γάρ). καὶ οὐκ ἔσται εἶναι καὶ μὴ εἶναι τὸ αὐτὸ ἀλλ᾽ ἢ καθ᾽ ὁμωνυμίαν, ὥσπερ ἂν εἰ ὃν ἡμεῖς ἄνθρωπον {20} καλοῦμεν, ἄλλοι μὴ ἄνθρωπον καλοῖεν: τὸ δ᾽ ἀπορούμενον οὐ τοῦτό ἐστιν, εἰ ἐνδέχεται τὸ αὐτὸ ἅμα εἶναι καὶ μὴ εἶναι ἄνθρωπον τὸ ὄνομα, ἀλλὰ τὸ πρᾶγμα.

δὲ μὴ σημαίνει ἕτερον τὸ ἄνθρωπος καὶ τὸ μὴ ἄνθρωπος, δῆλον ὅτι καὶ τὸ μὴ εἶναι ἀνθρώπῳ τοῦ εἶναι ἀνθρώπῳ, ὥστ᾽ ἔσται τὸ ἀνθρώπῳ {25} εἶναι μὴ ἀνθρώπῳ εἶναι: ἓν γὰρ ἔσται. τοῦτο γὰρ σημαίνει τὸ εἶναι ἕν, τὸ ὡς λώπιον καὶ ἱμάτιον, εἰ ὁ λόγος εἷς: εἰ δὲ ἔσται ἕν, ἓν σημανεῖ τὸ ἀνθρώπῳ εἶναι καὶ μὴ ἀνθρώπῳ. ἀλλ᾽ ἐδέδεικτο ὅτι ἕτερον σημαίνει.

ἀνάγκη τοίνυν, εἴ τί ἐστιν ἀληθὲς εἰπεῖν ὅτι ἄνθρωπος, ζῷον εἶναι δίπουν {30} (τοῦτο γὰρ ἦν ὃ ἐσήμαινε τὸ ἄνθρωπος): εἰ δ᾽ ἀνάγκη τοῦτο, οὐκ ἐνδέχεται μὴ εἶναι <τότε> τὸ αὐτὸ ζῷον δίπουν (τοῦτο γὰρ σημαίνει τὸ ἀνάγκη εἶναι, τὸ ἀδύνατον εἶναι μὴ εἶναι [ἄνθρωπον]): οὐκ ἄρα ἐνδέχεται ἅμα ἀληθὲς εἶναι εἰπεῖν τὸ αὐτὸ ἄνθρωπον εἶναι καὶ μὴ εἶναι ἄνθρωπον. ὁ δ᾽ αὐτὸς λόγος καὶ ἐπὶ τοῦ μὴ εἶναι ἄνθρωπον:

τὸ γὰρ ἀνθρώπῳ εἶναι καὶ τὸ μὴ ἀνθρώπῳ εἶναι ἕτερον σημαίνει, εἴπερ καὶ τὸ λευκὸν εἶναι καὶ τὸ ἄνθρωπον εἶναι ἕτερον: πολὺ γὰρ ἀντίκειται ἐκεῖνο μᾶλλον, ὥστε σημαίνειν ἕτερον. εἰ δὲ καὶ {5} τὸ λευκὸν φήσει τὸ αὐτὸ καὶ ἓν

understand anything unless one understands one thing, but if this does happen, a term may be assigned to this thing. Let it be assumed, then, as we said at the beginning (1006a18), that a term signifies something, and that it signifies one thing.

It is impossible, then, that "being a man" should mean "not being a man," if the term "man" not only signifies something about one subject but also signifies one thing. For we do not think it fitting to identify "signifying one thing" with "signifying something about one subject," since the terms "musical," "white," and "man" would then signify one thing. And therefore all things would be one, because all would be synonymous. And it will be impossible to be and not to be the same thing, except in an equivocal sense, as occurs if one whom we call "man" others call "not-man." But the problem is not whether the same thing can at the same time be and not be a man in name, but whether it can in fact.

Now if "man" and "not-man" do not signify something different, it is evident that "not being a man" will not differ from "being a man." Thus "being a man" will be identical with "not being a man," for they will be one thing. For being one means this: being related as "clothing" and "garment" are if they are taken in the same sense. And if "being a man" and "not being a man" are to be one, they must signify one thing. But it has been shown that they signify different things.

Therefore, if it is true to say that something is a man, it must be a two-footed animal, for this is what the term "man" signifies. But if this is necessary, it is impossible for this very thing not to be a two-footed animal; for this is what "to be necessary" means, namely, unable not to be. Hence it cannot be true to say that the same thing is and is not a man at the same time. The same argument also applies to "not being a man."

For "being a man" and "not being a man" signify different things, since "being white" and "being a man" are different; for there is much greater opposition in the former case, so that they signify different things. And if one were to say

ratione, idem dicemus quod et prius dictum est, quod unum omnia sunt et non solum opposita. Si autem hoc non contingit, contingit quod dictum est. [622]

σημαίνειν, πάλιν τὸ αὐτὸ ἐροῦμεν ὅπερ καὶ πρότερον ἐλέχθη, ὅτι ἓν πάντα ἔσται καὶ οὐ μόνον τὰ ἀντικείμενα. εἰ δὲ μὴ ἐνδέχεται τοῦτο, συμβαίνει τὸ λεχθέν,

also that "white" signifies the same thing as "man" and is one in concept, we shall say the same thing as was said before (1006a32), namely, that all things are one, and not merely opposites. But if this is impossible, then what has been said will follow.

1007a8 Si respondeatur ad interrogatum. Si autem apponat interroganti simpliciter et negationes, non respondetur ad interrogatum. Nihil enim prohibet idem et hominem, et album et alia mille secundum pluralitatem. [623]

ἂν ἀποκρίνηται τὸ ἐρωτώμενον. ἐὰν δὲ προστιθῇ ἐρωτῶντος ἁπλῶς καὶ τὰς ἀποφάσεις, οὐκ ἀποκρίνεται {10} τὸ ἐρωτώμενον. οὐθὲν γὰρ κωλύει εἶναι τὸ αὐτὸ καὶ ἄνθρωπον καὶ λευκὸν καὶ ἄλλα μυρία τὸ πλῆθος·

That is to say, it will follow if our opponent answers the question. And if, in giving a simple answer to the question, he also adds the negations, he is not answering the question. For there is nothing to prevent the same thing from being man and white and a thousand other things numerically.

Attamen interroganti si verum est dicere hominem hoc esse, aut non respondendum est unum significatmn et non addendum quia et album et nigrum et magnum. Etenim impossibile infinita entis accidentia permeare. Aut igitur omnia permeantur aut nullum.

ἀλλ' ὅμως ἐρομένου εἰ ἀληθὲς εἰπεῖν ἄνθρωπον τοῦτο εἶναι ἢ οὔ, ἀποκριτέον τὸ ἓν σημαῖνον καὶ οὐ προσθετέον ὅτι καὶ λευκὸν καὶ μέγα. καὶ γὰρ ἀδύνατον ἄπειρά γ' ὄντα τὰ {15} συμβεβηκότα διελθεῖν· ἢ οὖν ἅπαντα διελθέτω ἢ μηθέν.

Still, if one asks whether it is or is not true to say that this is a man, his opponent should reply by stating something that means one thing and not add that it is also white or black or large. Indeed, it is impossible to enumerate the accidents of being, which are infinite in number; so therefore let him enumerate either all or none.

Similiter etiam si mil ies est homo idem et non homo, non est correspondendum interroganti si est homo: quia est simul et non homo, si non et alia quaecumque acciderant sunt correspondentia, quaecumque sunt aut non sunt. Si autem hoc non fecerit, non disputat.

ὁμοίως τοίνυν εἰ καὶ μυριάκις ἐστὶ τὸ αὐτὸ ἄνθρωπος καὶ οὐκ ἄνθρωπος, οὐ προσαποκριτέον τῷ ἐρομένῳ εἰ ἔστιν ἄνθρωπος, ὅτι ἐστὶν ἅμα καὶ οὐκ ἄνθρωπος, εἰ μὴ καὶ τἆλλα ὅσα συμβέβηκε προσαποκριτέον, ὅσα ἐστὶν ἢ μὴ ἔστιν· ἐὰν {20} δὲ τοῦτο ποιῇ, οὐ διαλέγεται.

Similarly, even if the same thing is a thousand times a man and a not-man, he must not, in answering the question of whether this is a man, add that it is also at the same time a not-man, unless he also gives all the other corresponding accidents, whatever are so or are not so. And if he does not do this, there will be no debate with him.

1007a20 Omnino vero destruunt qui hoc dicunt substantiam et quod quid erat esse: omnia namque accidere dicere eis est necesse et vere hominem esse aut animal, esse et non esse. Nam si quid fuerit quod est hominis esse, hoc non erit non hominem esse, aut non esse hominem. Etenim hae sunt negationes huius. Unum enim erat quod significabat nomen, et hoc erat alicuius substantia. Significare vero substantiam est quod non aliud aliquid esse ipsi. Si autem fuerit quod est esse hominem ipsi quod non hominem esse, esse hominem aliud erit. Quare dicere eos est necesse, quia nullius talis erit ratio, sed omnia secundum accidens. Hic enim determinata est substantia et accidens.

ὅλως δ' ἀναιροῦσιν οἱ τοῦτο λέγοντες οὐσίαν καὶ τὸ τί ἦν εἶναι. πάντα γὰρ ἀνάγκη συμβεβηκέναι φάσκειν αὐτοῖς, καὶ τὸ ὅπερ ἀνθρώπῳ εἶναι ἢ ζῴῳ εἶναι μὴ εἶναι. εἰ γὰρ ἔσται τι ὅπερ ἀνθρώπῳ εἶναι, τοῦτο οὐκ ἔσται μὴ ἀνθρώπῳ εἶναι ἢ μὴ εἶναι ἀνθρώπῳ {25} (καίτοι αὗται ἀποφάσεις τούτου)· ἓν γὰρ ἦν ὃ ἐσήμαινε, καὶ ἦν τοῦτό τινος οὐσία. τὸ δ' οὐσίαν σημαίνειν ἐστὶν ὅτι οὐκ ἄλλο τι τὸ εἶναι αὐτῷ. εἰ δ' ἔσται αὐτῷ τὸ ὅπερ ἀνθρώπῳ εἶναι ἢ ὅπερ μὴ ἀνθρώπῳ εἶναι ἢ ὅπερ μὴ εἶναι ἀνθρώπῳ, ἄλλο ἔσται, ὥστ' ἀναγκαῖον αὐτοῖς {30} λέγειν ὅτι οὐθενὸς ἔσται τοιοῦτος λόγος, ἀλλὰ πάντα κατὰ συμβεβηκός· τούτῳ γὰρ διώρισται οὐσία καὶ τὸ συμβεβηκός· τὸ γὰρ λευκὸν τῷ ἀνθρώπῳ συμβέβηκεν

And those who say this do away completely with substance or essence, for they must say that all attributes are accidents, and that there is no such thing as "being a man" or "being an animal." For if there is to be such a thing as "being a man," this will not be "being a not-man" or "not being a man"; in fact, these are the negations of it. For there was one thing which the term signified, and this was the substance of something. And to signify the substance of a thing is to signify that its being is not something else. And if being essentially a man is being essentially a not-man, then the being of man will be something else. Hence they are compelled to say that nothing will have such a concept as this, but that all attributes

Accidit enim album homini, quia est albus, sed non quod vere album. [624]

ὅτι ἔστι μὲν λευκὸς ἀλλ᾽ οὐχ ὅπερ λευκόν.

are accidental. For this distinguishes substance from accident; for white is an accident of man, because, while some man is white, he is not the essence of whiteness.

1007a33 Si vero omnia secundum accidens dicantur, nullum erit primum universale. Si autem semper accidens de subiecto aliquo significat praedicationem, in infinitum ergo necesse est ire: sed impossibile. Neque enim plura duobus complectitur. [629]

εἰ δὲ πάντα κατὰ συμβεβηκὸς λέγεται, οὐθὲν ἔσται πρῶτον τὸ καθ᾽ οὗ, εἰ ἀεὶ {35} τὸ συμβεβηκὸς καθ᾽ ὑποκειμένου τινὸς σημαίνει τὴν κατηγορίαν. {1007b1} ἀνάγκη ἄρα εἰς ἄπειρον ἰέναι. ἀλλ᾽ ἀδύνατον· οὐδὲ γὰρ πλείω συμπλέκεται δυοῖν·

Moreover, if all attributes are accidental predicates, there will be no first universal. And if the accidental always implies a predication about some subject, the process must go on to infinity. But this is impossible, for no more than two terms are combined in accidental predication.

Accidens enim accidenti non acciditi nisi quia ambo eidem accidunt. Dico autem ut album musico et homo albo: quia homini ambo accidunt, sed non Socrates musicus: itaque ambo accidunt alicui alteri.

τὸ γὰρ συμβεβηκὸς οὐ συμβεβηκότι συμβεβηκός, εἰ μὴ ὅτι ἄμφω συμβέβηκε ταὐτῷ, λέγω δ᾽ οἷον τὸ λευκὸν μουσικὸν καὶ τοῦτο λευκὸν {5} ὅτι ἄμφω τῷ ἀνθρώπῳ συμβέβηκεν. ἀλλ᾽ οὐχ ὁ Σωκράτης μουσικὸς οὕτω, ὅτι ἄμφω συμβέβηκεν ἑτέρῳ τινί.

For an accident is an accident of an accident only because both are accidents of the same subject. I mean, for example, that white is an accident of musical and musical of white only because both are accidental to man; but Socrates is not musical in the sense that both are accidental to something else.

Quoniam igitur haec quidem ita, illa vero illo modo dicuntur accidentia: quaecumque sic dicuntur ut album Socrati non contingit infinita esse in superius ut Socrati albo alterum aliquid accidens. Non enim fit unum aliquid ex omnibus.

ἐπεὶ τοίνυν τὰ μὲν οὕτως τὰ δ᾽ ἐκείνως λέγεται συμβεβηκότα, ὅσα οὕτως λέγεται ὡς τὸ λευκὸν τῷ Σωκράτει, οὐκ ἐνδέχεται ἄπειρα εἶναι ἐπὶ τὸ ἄνω, οἷον τῷ Σωκράτει τῷ λευκῷ {10} ἕτερόν τι συμβεβηκός· οὐ γὰρ γίγνεταί τι ἓν ἐξ ἁπάντων.

Therefore, since some accidents are predicated in the latter sense and some in the former sense, all those that are predicated in the same way as white is predicated of Socrates cannot form an infinite series in an upward direction so that there should be another accident of white Socrates. For no one thing results from all of these.

Nec itaque albo erit aliquod aliud accidens ut musicus: nihil enim magis hoc illi quam illud huic accidit. Et simul determinatum est, quia haec quidem ita accidunt, haec autem ut musicus Socrati:

οὐδὲ δὴ τῷ λευκῷ ἕτερόν τι ἔσται συμβεβηκός, οἷον τὸ μουσικόν· οὐθέν τε γὰρ μᾶλλον τοῦτο ἐκείνῳ ἢ ἐκεῖνο τούτῳ συμβέβηκεν, καὶ ἅμα διώρισται ὅτι τὰ μὲν οὕτω συμβέβηκε τὰ δ᾽ ὡς τὸ μουσικὸν Σωκράτει·

Nor again will white have another accident, such as musical, for this is no more an accident of that than that of this. And at the same time it has been established that some things are accidents in this sense and some in the sense that musical is an accident of Socrates.

quaecumque vero sic non accidenti accidunt per accidens, sed quaecumque illo modo: quare non omnia secundum accidens dicuntur: erit igitur aliquid etiam ut substantiam significans. Si autem hoc, ostensum est quia impossibile est simul praedicari contradictiones.

ὅσα δ᾽ οὕτως, οὐ {15} συμβεβηκότι συμβέβηκε συμβεβηκός, ἀλλ᾽ ὅσα ἐκείνως, ὥστ᾽ οὐ πάντα κατὰ συμβεβηκὸς λεχθήσεται. ἔσται ἄρα τι καὶ ὡς οὐσίαν σημαῖνον. εἰ δὲ τοῦτο, δέδεικται ὅτι ἀδύνατον ἅμα κατηγορεῖσθαι τὰς ἀντιφάσεις.

And whatever attributes are predicated accidentally in the latter sense are not accidents of accidents but only those predicated in the former sense. Not all attributes, then, are said to be accidents; and thus there must be some term which also signifies substance. And if this is so, then we have proved that contradictories cannot be predicated at the same time of the same subject.

---

611. Hic incipit elenchice disputare contra negantes praedictum principium: et dividitur in duas partes.

Primo disputat contra eos, qui dicunt contradictoria simul esse vera.

Secundo contra illos qui dicunt quod contingit ea simul esse falsa, *verum nec inter* et cetera.

611. Here he begins to argue by means of refutation against those who deny the foregoing principle, and this is divided into two parts.

In the first (1006a18; [611]), he argues against those who say that contradictories are true at the same time;

in the second (1011b23; [720]), against those who say that they are false at the same time, at *neither can there be.*

Circa primum duo facit.

Primo disputat contra praedictos errantes in communi.

Secundo ostendit quomodo in speciali sit disputandum contra diversos, ibi, *est autem non idem modus*.

Circa primum duo facit.

Primo disputat rationem negantium praedictum principium.

Secundo ostendit quod opinio Protagorae in idem redit cum praedicta positione, ibi, *est autem ab eadem* et cetera.

Circa primum ponit septem rationes.

Secunda ibi, *omnino vero destruunt*.

Tertia ibi, *amplius si contradictiones*.

Quarta ibi, *amplius autem circa omnia* et cetera.

Quinta ibi, *amplius igitur quomodo*.

Sexta ibi, *unde et maxime manifestum est*.

Septima ibi, *amplius quia si maxime*.

Circa primum duo facit.

Primo ostendit ex quo principio oporteat procedere contra negantes primum principium.

Secundo ex illo principio procedit, ibi, *primum quidem igitur manifestum* et cetera.

Dicit ergo primo, quod ad omnia talia inopinabilia non oportet accipere pro principio, quod aliquid velit supponere hoc determinate esse *vel non esse*, idest non oportet accipere pro principio aliquam propositionem, qua asseratur aliquid de re vel negetur ab ea: hoc enim esset quaerere principium ut prius dictum est. Sed oportet accipere pro principio, quod nomen significet aliquid, et ipsi qui profert, inquantum se loquentem intelligit, et alii qui eum audit.

Si autem hoc non concedit, tunc talis non habebit propositum nec secum, nec cum alio; unde superfluum erit cum eo disputare; sed cum hoc dederit, iam statim erit demonstratio contra eum: statim enim invenitur aliquid definitum et determinatum quod per nomen significatur distinctum a suo contradictorio, ut infra patebit. Sed tamen hoc non erit demonstrans praedictum principium simpliciter, sed tantum erit ratio sustinens contra negantes. Ille enim qui *destruit rationem*, idest sermonem suum, dicendo quod nomen nihil significat, oportet quod sustineat, quia hoc ipsum quod negat, proferre non potest nisi loquendo et aliquid significando.

612. Deinde cum dicit *primum quidem* procedit ex dicta suppositione ad propositum ostendendum.

In regard to the first, he does two things.

First, he argues in a general way against those who make the aforesaid errors.

Second (1009a16; [663]), he shows how we must argue specifically against different positions, at *but the same method*.

In regard to the first he does two things.

First, he argues dialectically against the reasoning of those who deny the foregoing principle.

Second (1009a6; [661]), he shows that Protagoras' opinion is fundamentally the same as the one just mentioned, at *the doctrine of Protagoras*.

In regard to the first point he gives seven arguments.

He gives the second (1007a20; [624]) at the words, *and those who*;

the third (1007b18; [636]) at, *furthermore, if all*;

the fourth (1008a8; [642]) at, *again, either this*;

the fifth (1008b2; [652]) at, *again, how*;

the sixth (1008b12; [654]) at, *it is most evident*;

and the seventh (1008b31; [659]) at, *further, even if all*.

In regard to the first he does two things.

First, he indicates the starting point from which one must proceed to argue against those who deny the first principle.

Second (1006a26; [612]), he proceeds to argue from that starting point, at *first of all, then*.

He therefore first says (1006a18) that, with respect to all such unreasonable positions, there is no need for us to take as a starting point that someone wishes to suppose that this thing definitely is *or is not*. In other words, it is not necessary to take as a starting point some proposition in which some attribute is either affirmed or denied of a subject (for this would be a begging of the question, as was said above (1006a11; [609]). But it is necessary to take as a starting point that a term signifies something both to the one who utters it, inasmuch as he himself understands what he is saying, and to someone else who hears him.

But if such a person does not admit this, he will not say anything meaningful, either for himself or for someone else, and it will then be idle to dispute with him. But when he has admitted this, a demonstration will at once be possible against him; for there is straightway found to be something definite and determinate which is signified by the term distinct from its contradictory, as will become clear below. Yet this will not strictly be a demonstration of the foregoing principle, but only an argument upholding this principle against those who deny it. For he who *destroys reason* (that is, his own intelligible expression) by saying that a term signifies nothing, must uphold its significance, because he can express what he denies only by speaking and by signifying something.

612. *First of all, then* (1006a26). He proceeds from the assumption he had made to prove what he intends.

Et primo singulariter in uno.

Secundo generaliter in omnibus, ibi, *amplius si homo* et cetera.

Dicit ergo primo, quod si nomen aliquid significat, primo hoc erit manifestum quod haec propositio erit vera, et eius contradictoria quam negat est falsa. Et sic ad minus hoc habemus, quia non omnis affirmatio est vera cum sua negatione.

613. Deinde cum dicit *dico autem* ostendit universaliter de omnibus, scilicet quod contradictoria non sint simul vera. Et circa hoc quatuor facit.

Primo ponit quaedam quae sunt necessaria ad propositum concludendum.

Secundo concludit propositum, ibi, *necesse itaque.*

Tertio probat quoddam quod supposuerat, ibi, *nam esse hominem* et cetera.

Quarto excludit quamdam cavillationem, ibi, *si autem respondeatur.*

Circa primum tria facit.

Primo ostendit quod nomen unum significat.

Secundo ex hoc ostendit ulterius quod hoc nomen homo, significet id quod est hominem esse, non autem id quod est non esse, ibi, *nec sic contingit* et cetera.

Tertio ostendit quod homo significat unum ibi, *si autem non significat* et cetera.

Dicit ergo primo, quod si homo significat aliquid unum, sit hoc unum, animal bipes. Hoc enim unum dicitur nomen significare, quod est definitio rei significatae per nomen; ut si est hominis esse *animal bipes*, idest si hoc est quod quid est homo, hoc erit significatum per hoc nomen homo.

614. Si autem dicat nomen plura significat, aut significabit finita, aut infinita. Si autem finita, nihil differt, secundum aliam translationem, ab eo quod ponitur significare unum, quia significat multas rationes diversarum rerum finitas, et singulis eorum possunt adaptari diversa nomina.

Ut si homo significet multa, et unius eorum sit ratio animal bipes, ponetur unum nomen secundum hanc rationem, quod est homo: et si sunt plures aliae rationes, ponentur alia plura nomina, dummodo rationes illae sint finitae. Et sic redibit primum quod nomen significet unum.

615. Si autem nomen non significat finitas rationes, sed infinitas, manifestum est quod nulla erit ratio sive disputatio. Quod sic patet.

First, he deals with one particular case;

second (1006a31), he treats all cases in a general way, at *again, if the term.*

He accordingly first says (1006a26) that, if a term signifies something, it will be evident first of all that this proposition will be true, and that its contradictory, which he denies, will be false. Thus this at least will be true: not every affirmation is true together with its negation.

613. *Now by "signifying"* (1006a32). Then he shows that this applies universally to all cases, namely, that contradictories are not true at the same time. In regard to this he does four things.

First, he makes certain assumptions which are necessary for drawing his intended conclusion.

Second (1006b28; [620]), he draws his conclusion, at *therefore, if it is true.*

Third (1007a1; [622]), he proves one assumption which he had made, at *for "being a man".*

Fourth (1007a8; [623]), he rejects a quibble, at *that is to say.*

In regard to the first he does three things.

First, he shows that a term signifies one thing;

second (1006b13; [616]), he shows from this that the term man signifies what being a man is, but not what it is not, at *it is impossible, then.*

Third (1006b22; [619]), he shows that the term man signifies one thing, at *now if "man".*

He accordingly first says (1006a32) that, if the term "man" signifies one thing, let this be two-footed animal. For a term is said to signify this one thing which is the definition of the thing signified by the term, so that if *two-footed animal* is the being of "man" (that is, if this is what the essence of man is), this will be what is signified by the term man.

614. But if one were to say that a term signifies many things, it will signify either a finite or an infinite number of them. But if it signifies a finite number, it will differ in no way, according to another translation, from the term which is assumed to signify one thing; for it signifies many finite concepts of different things and different terms can be fitted to each single concept.

For example, if the term "man" were to signify many concepts, and the concept two-footed animal is one of them, one term is assigned to the concept man. And if there are many other concepts, many other terms may be assigned so long as those concepts are finite in number. Thus he will be forced back to the first position, that a term signifies one thing.

615. But if a term does not signify a finite number of concepts, but rather an infinite number, evidently neither reasoning nor debate will be possible. This becomes clear as follows.

Quod enim non significat unum, nihil significat. Et hoc sic probatur. Nomina significant intellectus. Si igitur nihil intelligitur, nihil significatur. Sed si non intelligitur unum, nihil intelligitur; quia oportet quod qui intelligit ab aliis distinguat. Ergo si non significat unum, non significat. Sed si nomina non significant, tolletur disputatio, et quae est secundum veritatem et quae est ad hominem.

Ergo patet quod si nomina infinita significent, non erit ratio sive disputatio. Sed si contingit intelligere unum, imponatur ei nomen, et sic teneatur quod nomen significet aliquid.

616. Deinde cum dicit *nec sic contingit* ostendit secundum; scilicet quod hoc nomen homo non significet id quod est homini non esse: nomen enim significans unum, non solum significat unum subiecto, quod ideo dicitur unum quia de uno, sed id quod est unum simpliciter, scilicet secundum rationem. Si enim hoc vellemus dicere, quod nomen significat unum quia significat ea quae verificantur de uno, sic sequeretur quod musicum et album et homo unum significarent, quoniam omnia verificantur de uno. Et ex hoc sequeretur, quod omnia essent unum:

quia si album dicitur de homine, et propter hoc est unum cum eo, cum dicatur etiam de lapide, erit unum cum lapide. Et quae uni et eidem sunt eadem, sibi invicem sunt eadem. Unde sequeretur quod homo et lapis sit unum, et unius rationis. Et sic sequeretur quod omnia nomina sint *univoca*, idest unius rationis, vel *synonyma* secundum aliam literam, idest omnino idem significantia re et ratione.

617. Quamvis autem esse et non esse verificentur de eodem secundum negantes principium primum, tamen oportet quod alius sit hoc quod esse hominem et hoc quod est non esse; sicut aliud est ratione album et musicum, quamvis de eodem verificentur. Ergo patet quod esse et non esse non erunt idem ratione et re, quasi uno nomine significatum univoce.

618. Sciendum est autem quod esse hominem vel esse homini sive hominis, hic accipitur pro quod quid est hominis. Ex hoc ergo concluditur quod hoc quod dico homo, non significat hoc quod dico hominem non esse, sicut propriam rationem. Sed quia dixerat supra quod idem nomen potest plura significare secundum diversas rationes, ideo subiungit *nisi secundum aequivocationem*, ad determinandum quod homo univoce non significet esse hominem, et non esse hominem; sed aequivoce potest utrumque significare; ut si id quod vocamus hominem in una lingua, vocent alii non hominem

Any term that does not signify one thing signifies nothing. This is proved thus. Terms signify something understood, and therefore if nothing is understood, nothing is signified. But if one thing is not understood, nothing is understood, because anyone who understands anything must distinguish it from other things. If a term does not signify one thing, then it signifies nothing at all; if terms signify nothing, discourse will be impossible, both the kind which establishes truth and the kind which refutes an assertion.

Hence it is clear that, if terms signify an infinite number of things, neither reasoning nor dispute will be possible. But if it is possible to understand one thing, a term may be given to it. So let it be held then that a term signifies something.

616. *It is impossible* (1006b13). He proves the second point, namely, that the term "man" does not signify "not being a man." For a term that signifies one thing signifies not only what is one in subject (and is therefore said to be one because it is predicated of one subject), but what is one absolutely, that is, in concept. For if we wanted to say that a term signifies one thing because it signifies the attributes which are verified of one thing, it would then follow that the terms "musical," "white," and "man" all signify one thing, since all are verified of one thing. And from this it would follow that all things are one.

For if white is predicated of man and is therefore identical with him, then when it is also predicated of a stone it will be identical with a stone. And, since those things that are identical with one and the same thing are identical with each other, it would follow that a man and a stone are one thing and have one concept. Thus the result would be that all terms are *univocal*, that is, one in concept, or *synonymous*, as another text says, that is, meaning absolutely the same thing in subject and in concept.

617. Now, although being and non-being are verified of the same subject according to those who deny the first principle, still being a man and not being a man must differ in concept, just as white and musical differ in concept even though they are verified of the same subject. Hence it is evident that being and non-being cannot be the same in concept and in subject in the sense that they are signified by one univocal term.

618. Now it must be noted that the expression "being a man" or "to be a man" or "having the being of a man" is taken here for the quiddity of man, and therefore it is concluded from this that the term "man" does not signify not being a man as its proper concept. But because he had said above (1006a32; [614]) that the same term can signify many things according to different concepts, he therefore adds *except in an equivocal sense*, in order to make clear that the term "man" does not signify in a univocal sense both being a man and not being a man, but it can signify both in an equivocal sense (that is, in the sense that what

in alia lingua. Non enim est nostra disputatio si idem secundum nomen contingat esse et non esse, sed si idem secundum rem.

619. Deinde cum dicit *si autem* probat tertium, scilicet quod homo et non homo non significat idem, tali ratione. Homo significat hoc quod est esse hominem, et quod quid est homo: non homo autem significat non esse hominem, et quod quid est non homo. Si ergo homo et non homo non significant aliquid diversum, tunc id quod est esse homini non erit diversum ab hoc quod est non esse homini, vel non esse hominem. Et ita unum eorum praedicabitur de altero. Et erunt etiam secundum rationem unum. Cum enim dicimus aliqua unum significare, intelligimus quod significent rationem unam, sicut vestis et indumentum. Si igitur esse hominem et non esse hominem sunt hoc modo unum, scilicet secundum rationem, unum et idem erit illud quod significabit illud quod est esse hominem, et id quod est non esse hominem. Sed datum est vel demonstratum, quia diversum nomen est quod significat utrumque. Ostensum est enim quod hoc nomen homo significat hominem, et non significat non esse hominem: ergo patet quod esse hominem et non esse hominem, non sunt unum secundum rationem. Et sic patet propositum quod homo et non homo diversa significant.

620. Deinde cum dicit *necesse itaque* ostendit principale propositum ex prioribus suppositis, tali ratione. Necesse est quod homo sit animal bipes: quod patet ex praehabitis. Haec enim est ratio quam hoc nomen significat. Sed quod necesse est esse, non contingit non esse: hoc enim significat necessarium, scilicet non possibile non esse, vel non contingens non esse, vel impossibile non esse: ergo impossibile est sive non contingens vel non possibile hominem non esse animal bipes. Sic ergo patet quod non contingit utrumque verum esse affirmationem et negationem; scilicet quod si animal bipes, et quod non sit animal bipes. Et eadem ratio ex significationibus nominum sumpta potest accipi de non homine, quia necesse est non hominem esse non animal bipes, cum hoc significet nomen: ergo impossibile est esse animal bipes.

621. Ea autem, quae supra monstrata sunt, valent ad propositum: quia si consideretur quod homo et non homo idem significarent, vel quod hoc nomen homo significaret esse hominem et non esse hominem, posset adversarius negare istam: necesse est hominem esse animal bipes. Posset enim dicere, quod non magis necessarium est dicere hominem esse animal bipes, quam non esse animal bipes, si haec nomina homo et non homo idem significarent, vel si hoc nomen homo utrumque

619. *Now if "man"* (1006b22). Then he proves the third point. That the terms "man" and "not-man" do not signify the same thing, and he uses the following argument. The term "man" signifies being a man or what man is, and the term "not-man" signifies not being a man or what man is not. If, then, "man" and "not-man" do not signify something different, being a man will not differ from not being a man, or being a not-man, and therefore one of these will be predicated of the other. And they will also have one concept, for when we say that some terms signify one thing, we mean that they signify one concept, as the terms "clothing" and "garment" do. Hence, if being a man and not being a man are one in this way, that is, in concept, there will then be one concept which will signify both being a man and not being a man. But it has been granted or demonstrated that the term which signifies each is different; for it has been shown that the term "man" signifies man and does not signify not-man. Thus it is clear that being a man and not being a man do not have a single concept, and therefore the thesis that "man" and "not-man" signify different things becomes evident.

620. *Therefore, if it is true* (1006b28). Here he proves his main thesis from the assumptions made earlier, and he uses the following argument. A man must be a two-footed animal, as is true from the foregoing, for this is the concept which the term "man" signifies. But what is necessary cannot not be, for this is what the term necessary means—namely, unable not to be, or incapable of not being, or impossible not to be. Hence it is not possible, or incapable, or impossible for man not to be a two-footed animal. Therefore, it is evident that the affirmation and the negation cannot both be true—that is, it cannot be true that man is both a two-footed animal and not a two-footed animal. The same reasoning based on the meanings of terms can be understood to apply to what is not-man, because what is not-man must be not a two-footed animal, since this is what the term signifies. Therefore, it is impossible that a not-man should be a two-footed animal.

621. Now the things demonstrated above are useful to his thesis, because if someone were to think that the terms "man" and "not-man" might signify the same thing, or that the term "man" might signify both being a man and not being a man, his opponent could deny the proposition that man must be a two-footed animal. For he could say that it is no more necessary to say that man must be a two-footed animal than to say that he is not a two-footed animal, granted that the terms "man" and "not-man" signify the

significet, scilicet id quod est esse hominem, et id quod est non esse hominem.

622. Deinde cum dicit *nam hominem* hic probat quoddam quod supposuerat. Ad probandum autem quod hoc nomen, homo, non significat id quod est non esse hominem, assumpsit quod id quod est esse hominem, et id quod est non esse hominem, sint diversa, quamvis verificentur de eodem. Et hoc intendit hic probare tali ratione. Magis opponuntur esse hominem et non esse hominem quam homo et album: sed homo et album sunt diversa secundum rationem, licet sint idem subiecto; ergo et esse hominem et non esse hominem sunt diversa secundum rationem.

Minorem sic probat. Si enim omnia quae dicuntur de eodem sunt unum secundum rationem quasi significata uno nomine, sequitur quod omnia sunt unum, sicut supra dictum est et expositum. Si ergo hoc non contingit, continget illud quod dictum est, scilicet quod esse hominem et non esse hominem sunt diversa. Et per consequens sequitur ultima conclusio supradicta, scilicet quod homo sit animal bipes, et quod impossibile est ipsum esse non animal bipes.

623. Deinde cum dicit *si respondeatur* excludit quamdam cavillationem per quam praedictus processus posset impediri. Posset enim adversarius interrogatus, an necesse sit hominem esse animal bipes, non respondere affirmationem vel negationem, sed dicere, necesse est hominem esse animal bipes, et non esse animal bipes. Hoc autem excludit hic Philosophus dicens praedictam conclusionem sequi, dummodo velit respondere ad interrogatum simpliciter.

Si autem interroganti simpliciter de affirmatione, velit addere negationem in sua responsione, ut dictum est, non ad interrogatum responderet. Quod sic probat. Contingit enim unam et eamdem rem esse hominem et album et mille alia huiusmodi. Hic tamen si quaeratur, utrum homo sit albus, respondendum est tantum id quod uno nomine significatur. Nec sunt addenda alia omnia.

Verbi gratia: si quaeratur, utrum hoc sit homo, respondendum est, quod est homo. Et non est addendum quod est homo et albus et magnus et similia; quia oportet omnia quae accidunt alicui simul respondere, aut nullum. Omnia autem simul non possunt, cum sint infinita: infinita enim eidem accidunt ad minus secundum relationes ad infinita antecedentia et consequentia, et infinita non est pertransire.

In respondendo ergo, nullum eorum quae accidunt quaesito est respondendum, sed solum quod quaeritur. Licet ergo supponatur millies quod sit idem homo et non homo; cum tamen quaeritur de homine, non est respondendum de non homine, nisi respondeantur omnia

same thing, or granted that the term "man" signifies both of these, being a man and not being a man.

622. *For "being a man"* (1007a1). Then he proves one of the assumptions which he had made, for in order to prove that the term "man" does not signify not being a man, he assumed that being a man and not being a man are different, even though they might be verified of the same subject. His aim here is to prove this by the following argument. There is greater opposition between being a man and not being a man than between "man" and "white"; but "man" and "white" have different concepts, although they may be the same in subject. Therefore, being a man and not being a man also have different concepts.

He proves the minor thus. If all attributes which are predicated of the same subject have the same concept and are signified by one term, it follows that all are one, as has been stated and explained (1006b13; [616]). Now if this is impossible, the position we have maintained follows, namely, that being a man and not being a man are different. And for this reason the final conclusion given above will follow, namely, that man is a two-footed animal, and that it is impossible for him to be what is not a two-footed animal.

623. *That is to say* (1007a8). He rejects one quibble by which the foregoing process of reasoning could be obstructed. For when an opponent has been asked whether man must be a two-footed animal, he need not reply either affirmatively or negatively, but could say that man must be both a two-footed animal and not a two-footed animal. But the Philosopher rejects this here, saying that the foregoing conclusion follows so long as an opponent wishes to give a simple answer to the question.

But if in giving a simple answer to the question on the side of the affirmative he also wishes to include in his answer the negative aspect, he will not be answering the question. He proves this as follows. One and the same thing can be both a man and white and a thousand other things of this kind. Yet if it is asked here whether a man is white, we must give in our answer only what is signified by one word, and not add all the other attributes.

For example, if one asks whether this is a man, we must answer that it is a man, and not add that it is both a man and white and large and the like. For we must give either all of the accidents of a thing at once or none. But not all accidents can be given at once since they are infinite in number, for there are an infinite number of accidents belonging to one and the same thing by reason of its relationship to an infinite number of antecedents and consequents, and what is infinite in number cannot be traversed.

In answering the question, then, we must not give any of the attributes which are accidental to the thing about which the question is raised but only the attribute which is asked for. Hence, even if it is supposed a thousand times that man and not-man are the same, still, when the question

quae possunt homini accidere. Si enim hoc fieret, non esset disputandum, quia nunquam compleretur disputatio, cum impossibile sit infinita pertransire.

624. Deinde cum dicit *omnino vero* ponit secundam rationem, quae sumitur ex ratione praedicati substantialis et accidentalis: quae talis est. Si affirmatio et negatio verificantur de eodem, sequitur quod nihil praedicabitur in quid sive substantialiter, sed solum per accidens. Et sic in praedicatis per accidens erit procedere in infinitum. Sed hoc est impossibile: ergo primum.

625. Circa hanc rationem duo facit.
Primo ponit conditionalem.
Secundo probat destructionem consequentis, ibi, *si vero omnia secundum accidens* et cetera.
Circa primum sic procedit: dicens quod illi qui hoc dicunt, scilicet affirmationem et negationem simul esse vera, omnino destruunt *substantiam*, idest substantiale praedicatum, *et quod quid erat esse*, idest quod praedicatur in eo quod quid: necesse est enim eis dicere *quod omnia accidunt*, idest per accidens praedicantur, et quod non sit hominem esse aut animal esse, et quod non sit quod significet quid est homo, aut quid est animal.

626. Quod sic probat. Si aliquid est quod est hominem esse, idest quod quid est homo substantialiter, scilicet de homine praedicatum; illud non erit non esse hominem, nec erit esse non hominem. Huius enim quod est esse hominem sunt praedictae duae negationes; scilicet non esse hominem, vel esse non hominem. Patet ergo quod affirmatio et negatio non verificantur de eodem; quia scilicet de eo quod est esse hominem non verificatur non esse hominem, vel esse non hominem.

627. Conditionalem autem positam, quod si aliquid sit quod quid est homo, quod illud non sit non esse hominem, vel esse non hominem, sic probat. Propositum est enim supra et probatum quod hoc quod significat nomen est unum. Et iterum est positum quod illud quod significat nomen, est substantia rei, scilicet quod quid est res. Unde patet quod aliquid significat substantiam rei, et idem quod est significatum non est aliquid aliud. Si igitur illud quod est esse hominem, sive quod quid est homo, fuerit vel non esse hominem, vel esse non hominem, constat quidem quod erit alterum a se. Unde oportet dicere, quod non sit definitio significans quod quid est esse rei; sed sequetur ex hoc quod omnia praedicentur secundum accidens.

628. In hoc enim distinguitur substantia ab accidente, idest praedicatum substantiale ab accidentali, quia unumquodque est vere id quod praedicatur substantia-

is asked about man, the answer must not include anything about not-man, unless all those things that are accidental to man are given. And if this were done, no dispute would be possible, because it would never reach completion, since an infinite number of things cannot be traversed.

624. *And those who* (1007a20). Then he gives the second argument, and it is based on the notion of substantial and accidental predicates. This is his argument. If an affirmation and a negation are verified of the same subject, it follows that no term will be predicated quidditatively, or substantially, but only accidentally. Therefore, there will have to be an infinite regress in accidental predicates. But the consequent is impossible, and thus the antecedent must be impossible.

625. In this argument he does two things.
First, he gives a conditional proposition.
Second (1007a33; [629]), he gives a proof that destroys the consequent, at *moreover, if all*.
Regarding the first part he proceeds as follows. He says that those who state that an affirmation and a negation may be true at the same time completely do away with *substance*, that is, with a substantial predicate, *or essence*, that is, with an essential predicate. For they must say *that all attributes are accidents*, or accidental predicates, and that there is no such thing as being a man or being an animal, and that what the quiddity of man or the quiddity of animal signifies does not exist.

626. He proves this as follows. If there is something which is being a man, that is, which is the substantial essence of man, which is predicated of man, it will not be not being a man or being a not-man. For these two—not being a man and being a not-man—are the negations of being a man. It is clear, then, that an affirmation and a negation are not verified of the same subject, for not being a man or being a not-man is not verified of being a man.

627. And the assumption made—namely, that if there is such a thing as being a man, this will not be not being a man or being a not-man—he proves in the following way. It was posited and proved above that the thing which a term signifies is one. And it was also posited that the thing which a term signifies is the substance of something, namely, a thing's quiddity. Hence it is clear that some term signifies a thing's substance, and that the thing which was signified is not something else. Therefore, if the essence or quiddity of man should be either not being a man or being a not-man, it is quite clear that it would differ from itself. It would be necessary to say, then, that there is no definition signifying a thing's essence. But from this it would follow that all predicates are accidental ones.

628. For substance is distinguished from accident (that is, a substantial predicate is distinguished from an accidental one) in that each thing is truly what is predicated

liter de eo; et ita non potest dici illud quod praedicatur substantialiter esse non unum, quia quaelibet res non est nisi una. Sed homo dicitur albus, quia albedo vel album accidit ei. Non autem ita quod sit id quod vere est album vel albedo. Ergo non oportet quod id quod praedicatur per accidens sit unum tantum. Sed multa possunt per accidens praedicari. Substantiale vero praedicatum est unum tantum. Et sic patet, quod ita est esse hominem quod non est non esse hominem. Si autem utrumque fuerit, iam substantiale praedicatum non erit unum tantum, et sic non erit substantiale sed accidentale.

629. Deinde cum dicit *si vero* destruit consequens; ostendens hoc esse impossibile quod aliquid non praedicetur substantialiter, sed omnia accidentaliter; quia si omnia per accidens praedicentur, non erit aliquid praedicatum universale. (Dicitur autem hic praedicatum universale sicut in *Posterioribus*, secundum quod praedicatur de aliquo per se et secundum quod ipsum est). Hoc autem est impossibile: quia si semper aliquid praedicatur de altero per accidens, oportet quod accidentalis praedicatio procedat in infinitum, quod est impossibile hac ratione.

630. Praedicatio enim accidentalis non complectitur nisi duos modos.

Unus modus est secundum quod accidens de accidente praedicatur per accidens, et hoc ideo, quia ambo accidunt eidem subiecto, sicut album praedicatur de musico, quia ambo accidunt homini.

Alius modus est quo accidens praedicatur de subiecto, sicut Socrates dicitur musicus, non quia ambo accidunt alicui alteri subiecto, sed quia unum eorum accidit alteri.

Cum igitur sint duo modi praedicationis per accidens, in neutro contingit esse praedicationem in infinitum.

631. Constat enim quod illo modo, quo accidens praedicatur de accidente, non contingit abire in infinitum, quia oportet devenire ad subiectum. Iam enim dictum est, quod haec est ratio praedicationis huius, quia ambo praedicantur de uno subiecto; et sic descendendo a praedicato ad subiectum contingit invenire pro termino ipsum subiectum.

632. Sed illo modo praedicandi per accidens quo accidens praedicatur de subiecto, ut cum dicitur Socrates est albus, non contingit abire in infinitum in superius ascendendo a subiecto ad praedicatum, ita ut dicamus quod Socrati accidit album et quod Socrati albo accidit aliquod aliud. Hoc enim non posset esse nisi duobus modis.

Uno modo quia ex albo et Socrate fieret unum. Et sic sicut Socrates est unum subiectum albedinis, ita Socrates albus esset subiectum alterius accidentis. Hoc autem non potest esse, quia non fit aliquid unum ex omnibus

substantially of it. Thus it cannot be said that a substantial predicate is not one thing, for each thing exists only if it is one. But man is said to be white because whiteness or white is one of his accidents, although not in such a way that he is the very essence of white or whiteness. It is not necessary, then, that an accidental predicate should be one only, but there can be many accidental predicates. A substantial predicate, however, is one only; and thus it is clear that what being a man is, is not what not being a man is. But if a substantial predicate is both, it will no longer be one only, and thus will not be substantial, but accidental.

629. *Moreover, if all* (1007a33). He destroys the consequent, showing that it is impossible that all predicates should be accidental and none substantial, for if all were accidental, there would be no universal predicate. (And "universal predicate" here means the same thing as it does in the *Posterior Analytics*, namely, an attribute which is predicated of something in virtue of itself and in reference to what it itself is.) But this is impossible, for if one attribute is always predicated of another accidentally, there will be an infinite regress in accidental predication, which is impossible for this reason.

630. There are only two ways in which accidental predication occurs.

One way is when one accident is predicated accidentally of another, and this happens because both are accidents of the same subject (for example, when white is predicated of musical because both are accidents of man).

The other way is had when an accident is predicated of a subject (as when Socrates is said to be musical), not because both are accidents of some other subject, but because one of them is an accident of the other.

Hence, even though there are two ways in which accidents may be predicated, in neither way can there be an infinite regress in predication.

631. For it is clear that there cannot be an infinite regress in that way in which one accident is predicated of another, because one must reach some subject. For it has been stated already that the notion of this kind of predication is that both accidents are predicated of one subject. And thus by descending from a predicate to a subject, the subject itself can be found to be the terminus.

632. And there cannot be an infinite regress in an upward direction when an accident is predicated of a subject (as when Socrates is said to be white) by ascending from a subject to a predicate so as to say that white is an accident of Socrates and that some other attribute is an accident of white Socrates. For this could occur only in two ways.

One way would be that one thing would come from white and Socrates; and thus, just as Socrates is one subject of whiteness, in a similar way white Socrates would be one subject of another accident. But this cannot be so, because

quibuscumque praedicatis. Ex subiecto enim et accidente non fit unum simpliciter, sicut fit unum ex genere et differentia. Unde non potest dici quod Socrates albus, sit unum subiectum.

633. Alius modus esset quod sicut Socrates est subiectum albi, ita ipsi albo insit aliquid aliud accidens, ut musicum. Sed hoc etiam non potest esse, propter duo.

Primo, quia non erit aliqua ratio, quare musicum dicatur magis accidere albo quam e converso. Unde non erit ordo inter album et musicum, sed e converso respicient se adinvicem.

Secundo, quia simul cum hoc definitum est vel determinatum, quod iste est alius modus praedicandi per accidens in quo accidens praedicatur de accidente, ab illo modo quo accidens praedicatur de subiecto, et musicum de Socrate. In isto autem modo de quo nunc loquitur, non dicitur praedicatio accidentalis, quia accidens praedicetur de accidente; sed illo modo quo prius locuti sumus.

634. Sic igitur manifestum est, quod in accidentali praedicatione non est abire in infinitum: quare patet quod non omnia praedicantur secundum accidens. Et ulterius quod aliquid erit significans substantiam. Et ulterius quod contradictio non verificatur de eodem.

635. Sciendum autem est circa praedictam rationem, quod licet accidens non sit subiectum alterius, et sic non sit ordo accidentis ad accidens quantum ad rationem subiiciendi, est tamen ordo quantum ad rationem causae et causati. Nam unum accidens est causa alterius, sicut calidum et humidum dulcis et sicut superficies coloris. Subiectum enim per hoc quod subiicitur uni accidenti, est susceptivum alterius.

one thing does not come from all of these predicates. For what is one in an absolute sense does not come from a substance and an accident in the way that one thing comes from a genus and a difference. Hence it cannot be said that white Socrates is one subject.

633. The other way would be that, just as Socrates is the subject of whiteness, in a similar way, some other accident, such as musical, would have whiteness as its subject. But neither can this be so, and for two reasons.

First, there can be no special reason why musical should be said to be an accident of white rather than the reverse; neither white nor musical will be prior to the other, but they will rather be of equal rank.

Second, in conjunction with this, it has been established or determined at the same time that this way of predicating in which an accident is predicated of an accident differs from that in which an accident is predicated of a subject, as when musical is predicated of Socrates. But in the way of which he is now speaking, accidental predication does not mean that an accident is predicated of an accident, but it is to be so taken in the way we first described.

634. It is evident, then, that an infinite regress in accidental predication is impossible, and therefore that not all predications are accidental. And it is also evident that there will be some term which signifies substance, and that contradictories are not true of the same subject.

635. Now with regard to the argument given it must be noted that, even though one accident is not the subject of another, and thus one accident is not related to the other as its subject, still one is related to the other as cause and thing caused. For one accident is the cause of another. Heat and moistness, for example, are the cause of sweetness, and surface is the cause of color. For a subject is receptive of another accident because it is receptive of one.

LECTURE 8

Arguments against the foregoing position

1007b18 Amplius si contradictiones simul de eodem verae sunt omnes, palam quod omnia unum erunt. Erunt enim idem triremis et murus et homo, si de omni aliquid aut affirmare aut negate contingit. [636]

ἔτι εἰ ἀληθεῖς αἱ ἀντιφάσεις ἅμα κατὰ τοῦ αὐτοῦ πᾶσαι, δῆλον ὡς {20} ἅπαντα ἔσται ἕν. ἔσται γὰρ τὸ αὐτὸ καὶ τριήρης καὶ τοῖχος καὶ ἄνθρωπος, εἰ κατὰ παντός τι ἢ καταφῆσαι ἢ ἀποφῆσαι ἐνδέχεται,

Furthermore, if all contradictories are true of the same subject at the same time, it is evident that all things will be one. For the same thing will be a trireme, a wall, and a man, if it is possible either to affirm or to deny anything of everything.

1007b22 Quemadmodum est necesse dicentibus rationem Protagorae. Nam alicui si videatur non triremis homo, palam quia non triremis: quare et est, si contradictoria vera. Et fit itaque Anaxagorae simul res omnes esse, ut nihil vere sit unum. [637]

καθάπερ ἀνάγκη τοῖς τὸν Πρωταγόρου λέγουσι λόγον. εἰ γὰρ τῳ δοκεῖ μὴ εἶναι τριήρης ὁ ἄνθρωπος, δῆλον ὡς οὐκ ἔστι τριήρης· ὥστε καὶ ἔστιν, εἴπερ {25} ἡ ἀντίφασις ἀληθής. καὶ γίγνεται δὴ τὸ τοῦ Ἀναξαγόρου, ὁμοῦ πάντα χρήματα· ὥστε μηθὲν ἀληθῶς ὑπάρχειν.

And this is what must follow for those who agree with Protagoras' view. For if it appears to anyone that a man is not a trireme, it is evident that he is not a trireme; thus, if contradictories are true, he also is a trireme. And thus there arises the view of Anaxagoras that all things exist together at the same time, so that nothing is truly one.

Indefinitum igitur videntur dicere; et putantes dicere ens, de non ente dicunt. Nam potestate ens et non endelechia, indefinitum erit.

τὸ ἀόριστον οὖν ἐοίκασι λέγειν, καὶ οἰόμενοι τὸ ὂν λέγειν περὶ τοῦ μὴ ὄντος λέγουσι· τὸ γὰρ δυνάμει ὂν καὶ μὴ ἐντελεχείᾳ τὸ ἀόριστόν ἐστιν.

Hence they seem to be speaking about the indeterminate, and while they think they are speaking about being, they are speaking about non-being. For the indeterminate is what exists potentially and is not complete.

1007b29 Sed dicenda est ipsis de omni affirmatio et negatio. Inconveniens enim si unicuique sua quidem negatio inest, quae vero alterius quidem non inest ei. Dico autem ut verum est dicere hominem quia non homo, palam quod et non triremis. [639]

ἀλλὰ μὴν λεκτέον γ' αὐτοῖς κατὰ {30} παντὸς <παντὸς> τὴν κατάφασιν ἢ τὴν ἀπόφασιν· ἄτοπον γὰρ εἰ ἑκάστῳ ἡ μὲν αὐτοῦ ἀπόφασις ὑπάρξει, ἡ δ' ἑτέρου ὃ μὴ ὑπάρχει αὐτῷ οὐχ ὑπάρξει· λέγω δ' οἷον εἰ ἀληθὲς εἰπεῖν τὸν ἄνθρωπον ὅτι οὐκ ἄνθρωπος, δῆλον ὅτι καὶ ἢ τριήρης ἢ οὐ τριήρης.

But the affirmation and the negation of every predicate of every subject must be admitted by them, for it would be absurd if each subject should have its own negation predicated of it while the negation of something else which cannot be predicated of it should not be predicated of it. I mean that, if it is true to say that a man is not a man, evidently it is also true to say that he is not a trireme.

Ergo si affirmatio, necesse et negationem. Si autem existat affirmatio, negatio alia inerit magis quam illa quae sua.

εἰ μὲν οὖν ἡ κατάφασις, ἀνάγκη καὶ τὴν ἀπόφασιν· {35} εἰ δὲ μὴ ὑπάρχει ἡ κατάφασις, ἥ γε ἀπόφασις ὑπάρξει μᾶλλον ἢ ἡ αὐτοῦ.

Therefore, if the affirmation is predicable of him, so also must the negation be. But if the affirmation is not predicable of him, the negation of the other term will be predicable of him to a greater degree than his own negation.

Ergo et si illa inest, inerit quae et ipsius triremis. Si autem hoc, et affirmatio. Hoc ergo contingit hanc dicentibus rationem.

{1008a1} εἰ οὖν κἀκείνη ὑπάρχει, ὑπάρξει καὶ ἡ τῆς τριήρους· εἰ δ' αὕτη, καὶ ἡ κατάφασις. ταῦτά τε οὖν συμβαίνει τοῖς λέγουσι τὸν λόγον τοῦτον,

If, then, the latter negation is predicable of him, the negation of trireme will also be predicable of him, and if this is predicable of him, the affirmation will be too. This is what follows, then, for those who hold this view.

1008a3 Et quia non est necesse aut dicere aut negare. [640]

καὶ ὅτι οὐκ ἀνάγκη ἢ φάναι ἢ ἀποφάναι.

And it also follows for them that it is not necessary either to affirm or to deny.

Nam si verum est quia homo et non homo, palam quia nec homo nec non

εἰ γὰρ ἀληθὲς ὅτι ἄνθρωπος καὶ {5} οὐκ ἄνθρωπος, δῆλον ὅτι καὶ οὔτ' ἄνθρω-

For if it is true that the same thing is both a man and a not-man, evidently it will be

homo erit. Nam duorum duae negationes.

Si autem una ex utrisque illa, et una utique erit opposita.

1008a8 Amplius aut circa omnia ita se habet et est album et non est album, et ens et non ens, et circa alias dictiones et negationes modo simili, aut non, sed circa quasdam sic, circa quasdam autem non. Et siquidem non circa omnes, hae utique erunt confessae. [642]

Si vero circa omnes, iterum aut de quibuscumque dicere et negare et de quibuscumque negare et dicere: aut de quibus quidem dicere et negare, sed de quibuscumque negare, non de omnibus dicere.

Et si sic, erit aliquid firmiter non ens, et haec erit firma opinio. Et si ipsum non, firmum aliquid sit et notum, notior utique erit dictio quam opposita negatio.

Si vero negando similiter et quaecumque contingit negare dicere, necesse est de his aut dividentem verum dicere, ut quod album et iterum quod non album, aut non. Et siquidem on verum dividentem dicere, non dicet ea, et non erit nihil.

Non entia autem quomodo utique pronuntiabunt aut ibunt? Et omnia utique erunt unum (ut prius dictum est) et idem erit homo et Deus et triremis et ipsorum contradictiones.

Similiter si de unoquoque, nilul differret aliud ab alio. Namque si differret, erit hoc verum et proprium. Similiter autem si dividentem contingit verum esse, accidit quod dictum est.

Adhuc quia omnes dicent verum et omnes mentientur, et idem ipse seipsum falsum dicere confitetur. Simul autem

---

πος οὔτ' οὐκ ἄνθρωπος ἔσται: τοῖν γὰρ δυοῖν δύο ἀποφάσεις,

εἰ δὲ μία ἐξ ἀμφοῖν ἐκείνη, καὶ αὕτη μία ἂν εἴη ἀντικειμένη.

ἔτι ἤτοι περὶ ἅπαντα οὕτως ἔχει, καὶ ἔστι καὶ λευκὸν καὶ οὐ λευκὸν καὶ ὂν καὶ οὐκ ὄν, καὶ περὶ τὰς ἄλλας φάσεις καὶ {10} ἀποφάσεις ὁμοιοτρόπως, ἢ οὒ ἀλλὰ περὶ μέν τινας, περί τινας δ' οὔ.

καὶ εἰ μὲν μὴ περὶ πάσας, αὗται ἂν εἶεν ὁμολογούμεναι: εἰ δὲ περὶ πάσας, πάλιν ἤτοι καθ' ὅσων τὸ φῆσαι καὶ ἀποφῆσαι καὶ καθ' ὅσων ἀποφῆσαι καὶ φῆσαι, ἢ κατὰ μὲν ὧν φῆσαι καὶ ἀποφῆσαι, καθ' ὅσων δὲ ἀποφῆσαι {15} οὐ πάντων φῆσαι.

καὶ εἰ μὲν οὕτως, εἴη ἄν τι παγίως οὐκ ὄν, καὶ αὕτη βεβαία δόξα, καὶ εἰ τὸ μὴ εἶναι βέβαιόν τι καὶ γνώριμον, γνωριμωτέρα ἂν εἴη ἡ φάσις ἢ ἀντικειμένη:

εἰ δὲ ὁμοίως καὶ ὅσα ἀποφῆσαι φάναι, ἀνάγκη ἤτοι ἀληθὲς διαιροῦντα λέγειν, οἷον ὅτι {20} λευκὸν καὶ πάλιν ὅτι οὐ λευκόν, ἢ οὔ. καὶ εἰ μὲν μὴ ἀληθὲς διαιροῦντα λέγειν, οὐ λέγει τε ταῦτα καὶ οὐκ ἔστιν οὐθέν,

(τὰ δὲ μὴ ὄντα πῶς ἂν φθέγξαιτο ἢ βαδίσειεν;) καὶ πάντα δ' ἂν εἴη ἕν, ὥσπερ καὶ πρότερον εἴρηται, καὶ ταὐτὸν ἔσται καὶ ἄνθρωπος καὶ θεὸς καὶ τριήρης {25} καὶ αἱ ἀντιφάσεις αὐτῶν

(εἰ γὰρ ὁμοίως καθ' ἑκάστου, οὐδὲν διοίσει ἕτερον ἑτέρου: εἰ γὰρ διοίσει, τοῦτ' ἔσται ἀληθὲς καὶ ἴδιον): ὁμοίως δὲ καὶ εἰ διαιροῦντα ἐνδέχεται ἀληθεύειν, συμβαίνει τὸ λεχθέν,

πρὸς δὲ τούτῳ ὅτι πάντες ἂν ἀληθεύοιεν καὶ πάντες ἂν ψεύδοιντο, καὶ αὐτὸς αὑτὸν ὁμολογεῖ {30} ψεύδεσθαι. ἅμα δὲ

---

neither a man nor a not-man, for there are two negations of the two affirmations.

And if the former is taken as a single proposition composed of the two, the latter also will be a single proposition opposed to the former.

Again, either this is true of all things, and a thing is both white and not-white, and both being and not-being (and the same applies to other affirmations and negations), or it is not true of all but is true of some and not of others. And if not of all, the exceptions will be admitted.

But if it is true of all, then either the negation will be true of everything of which the affirmation is and the affirmation will be true of everything of which the negation is, or the negation will be true of everything of which the affirmation is true but the affirmation will not always be true of everything of which the negation is.

And if the latter is true, there will be something that certainly is not, and this will be an unshakable opinion. And if that it is not is something certain and knowable, more known indeed will be the opposite affirmation than the negation.

But if in denying something it is equally possible to affirm what is denied, it is necessary to state what is true about these things, either separately (for example, to say that a thing is white and that it is not-white) or not. And if it is not true to affirm them separately, then an opponent will not be saying what he professes to say, and nothing will exist.

But how could non-existent things speak or walk, as he does? Again, all things will be one, as has been said before (1006b13; [616]), and man, God, a trireme, and their contradictories will be the same.

Similarly, if this is true of each thing, one thing will differ in no respect from another, for if it differs, this difference will be something true and proper to it. And similarly if it is possible for each to be true separately, the results described will follow.

And to this we may add that all will speak the truth and all speak falsely, and that each man will admit of himself that he

palma quia de nullo est adhuc perscrutatio. Nihil enim dicit.

φανερὸν ὅτι περὶ οὐθενός ἐστι πρὸς τοῦτον ἡ σκέψις: οὐθὲν γὰρ λέγει.

is in error. And at the same time it is evident that up to this point the discussion is about nothing at all, because our opponent says nothing.

Nec enim ita, neque non ita dicit: sed ita et non ita et iterum haec negat ambo, quia nec ita nec non ita. Nam si non, iam utique erit aliquid determinatum.

οὔτε γὰρ οὕτως οὔτ' οὐχ οὕτως λέγει, ἀλλ' οὕτως τε καὶ οὐχ οὕτως: καὶ πάλιν γε ταῦτα ἀπόφησιν ἄμφω, ὅτι οὔθ' οὕτως οὔτε οὐχ οὕτως: εἰ γὰρ μή, ἤδη ἄν τι εἴη ὡρισμένον.

For he does not say that a thing is so or is not so, but that it is both so and not so. Again, he denies both of these and says that it is neither so nor not so. For if this were not the case there would already be some definite statement.

Amplius, si quando est affirmatio vera et negatio est falsa: et si haec vera, affirmatio falsa: non erit utique dicere simul idem affirmare et negare vere, sed forsan dicet utique aliquis hoc esse quod a principio positum est.

ἔτι εἰ ὅταν ἡ φάσις {35} ἀληθὴς ᾖ, ἡ ἀπόφασις ψευδής, κἂν αὕτη ἀληθὴς ᾖ, ἡ κατάφασις ψευδής, οὐκ ἂν εἴη τὸ αὐτὸ ἅμα φάναι καὶ ἀποφάναι ἀληθῶς. {1008b1} ἀλλ' ἴσως φαῖεν ἂν τοῦτ' εἶναι τὸ ἐξ ἀρχῆς κείμενον.

Further, if the negation is false when the affirmation is true, and if the affirmation is false when the negation is true, it will be impossible both to affirm and to deny the same thing truly at the same time. But perhaps someone will say that this was the contention from the very beginning.

---

636. Ponit tertiam rationem, quae sumitur ex uno et diverso: et est ratio talis. Si affirmatio et negatio verificantur simul de eodem, omnia sunt unum. Hoc autem est falsum; ergo et primum. Circa hanc rationem tria facit.

Primo ponit conditionalem et exemplificat, quia scilicet sequeretur si contradictiones simul verificantur de eodem, quod idem essent triremis, idest navis habens tres ordines remorum, et murus et homo.

637. Secundo cum dicit **quemadmodum est** ostendit quod idem inconveniens sequitur ad duas alias positiones.

Primo ad opinionem Protagorae, qui dicebat quod quicquid alicui videtur, hoc totum est verum; quia si alicui videtur quod homo non sit triremis, non erit triremis; et si alteri videtur quod sit triremis, erit triremis; et sic erunt contradictoria vera.

638. Secundo ad opinionem Anaxagorae, qui dicebat omnes res simul esse, quasi nihil sit vere unum ab aliis determinatum, sed omnia sint unum in quadam confusione. Dicebat enim, quod quodlibet sit in quolibet, sicut in primo *Physicorum* ostensum est.

Quod ideo accidebat Anaxagorae, quia ipse videtur loqui de ente indeterminato, idest quod non est determinatum in actu. Et cum putaret loqui de ente perfecto, loquebatur de ente in potentia, sicut infra patebit. Quod autem est in potentia et non **endelechia**, idest in actu, est indefinitum. Potentia enim non finitur nisi per actum.

636. Then he gives a third argument, which involves oneness and difference. The argument runs thus. If an affirmation and a negation are true of the same subject at the same time, all things will be one. But the consequent is false. Hence the antecedent must be false. In regard to this argument he does three things.

First (1007b18; [636]), he lays down a conditional proposition and gives an example, namely, that if contradictories are true of the same subject at the same time, it will follow that the same thing will be a trireme (which is a ship with three banks of oars), a wall, and a man.

637. **And this is what** (1007b22). Then he shows that the same impossible conclusion follows with regard to two other positions.

He does this first with regard to the opinion of Protagoras, who said that whatever seems so to anyone is wholly true for him, for if it seems to someone that a man is not a trireme, then he will not be a trireme; if it seems to someone else that a man is a trireme, he will be a trireme. Thus contradictories will be true.

638. Second, he does this with regard to the opinion of Anaxagoras, who said that all things exist together, so that nothing which is truly one is distinguished from other things, but all are one in a kind of mixture. For he said that everything is found in everything else, as has been shown in *Physics* 1.

This is the position which Anaxagoras adopted because he seems to be speaking about indeterminate being, that is, what has not been made actually determinate. And while he thought he was speaking about complete being, he was speaking about potential being, as will become clear below (1009a30; [667]). But the indeterminate is what exists potentially and is not **complete**, that is, actual. For potency is made determinate only by act.

639. Tertio cum dicit *sed dicenda* probat conditionalem primo propositam esse veram.

Et primo quantum ad hoc quod omnia affirmative dicta unum essent.

Secundo quantum ad hoc quod affirmationes a suis negationibus non distinguerentur in veritate et falsitate, ibi, *et quia non est necesse* et cetera.

Dicit ergo primo, quod illud primum est ab eis supponendum ex quo ponunt affirmationem et negationem simul verificari de eodem, quod de quolibet est affirmatio et negatio vera.

Constat enim quod de unoquoque magis videtur praedicari negatio alterius rei, quam negatio propria. Inconveniens enim esset si alicui inesset sua negatio et non inesset negatio alterius rei, per quam significatur quod illa res non inest ei:

sicut si verum est dicere quod homo non est homo, multo magis est verum dicere quod homo non est triremis. Patet ergo, quod de quocumque necessarium est praedicari negationem, quod praedicatur de eo affirmatio. Et ita per consequens praedicabitur negatio, cum affirmatio et negatio sint simul vera;

aut si non praedicabitur affirmatio, praedicabitur negatio alterius magis quam negatio propria. Sicut si triremis non praedicatur de homine, praedicabitur de eo non triremis, multo magis quam non homo. Sed ipsa negatio propria praedicatur, quia homo non est homo: ergo et negatio triremis praedicabitur de eo, ut dicatur quod homo non est triremis. Sed si praedicatur affirmatio, praedicabitur negatio, cum simul verificentur: ergo necesse est quod homo sit triremis et eadem ratione quodlibet aliud. Et sic omnia erunt unum. Hoc igitur contingit dicentibus hanc positionem, scilicet quod contradictio verificetur de eodem.

640. Deinde cum dicit *et quia non* deducit aliud inconveniens, quod scilicet non distinguatur negatio ab affirmatione in falsitate, sed utraque sit falsa.

Dicit ergo quod non solum praedicta inconvenientia sequuntur ad praedictam positionem, sed etiam sequitur quod non sit necessarium *affirmare et negare*, idest quod non sit necessarium affirmationem vel negationem esse veram, sed contingit utramque esse falsam. Et sic non erit distantia inter verum et falsum. Quod sic probat.

641. Si verum sit quod aliquid sit homo et non homo, verum est quod id non erit homo, nec erit non homo. Et hoc patet. Horum enim duorum quae sunt homo et non homo, sunt duae negationes, scilicet non homo et non non homo. Si autem ex primis duabus fiat una propositio, ut dicamus, Socrates non est homo nec non

639. *But the affirmation* (1007b29). Third, he proves that the first conditional proposition is true.

He first does this on the grounds that all things would have to be affirmed to be one;

second (1008a3; [640]), on the grounds that affirmations would not be distinguished from their negations from the viewpoint of truth and falsity, at *and it also follows*.

He accordingly first says (1007b29) that the first conditional proposition must be admitted by them inasmuch as they hold that an affirmation and a negation are true of the same subject at the same time because an affirmation and a negation are true of anything at all.

For it is clear that the negation of some other thing seems to be predicable of each thing to a greater degree than its own negation. For it would be absurd if some subject should have its own negation predicated of it and not the negation of something else by which it is signified that this other thing is not predicable of it.

For example, if it is true to say that a man is not a man, it is much truer to say that a man is not a trireme. Hence it is clear that anything of which a negation must be predicated must also have an affirmation predicated of it. Therefore, a negation will be predicated of it, since an affirmation and a negation are true at the same time.

If an affirmation is not predicated of it, the negation of the other term will be predicated of it to a greater degree than its own negation. For example, if the term "trireme" is not predicable of man, "non-trireme" will be predicated of him inasmuch as it may be said that a man is not a trireme. But if the affirmation is predicable, so also must the negation be, since they are verified of the same thing. A man, then, must be a trireme, and he must also be anything else on the same grounds. Hence all things must be one. Therefore, this is what follows for those who maintain the position that contradictories are true of the same subject.

640. *And it also follows* (1008a3). He now draws the other impossible conclusion which follows from this view, namely, that a negation will not be distinguished from an affirmation as regards falsity, but each will be false.

Thus he says that not only the foregoing impossible conclusions follow from the above-mentioned position, but also the conclusion that it is not necessary *either to affirm or to deny*, that is, it is not necessary that either the affirmation or the negation of a thing should be true, but each may be false. Thus there will be no difference between being true and being false. He proves this as follows.

641. If it is true that something is both a man and a not-man, it is also true that it is neither a man nor a not-man. This is evident. For of these two terms, "man" and "not-man," there are two negations, "not man" and "not not-man." And if one proposition were formed from the first two—for example, if one were to say that Socrates is

homo, sequitur quod nec affirmatio nec negatio sit vera, sed utraque falsa.

642. Deinde cum dicit *amplius autem* ponit quartam rationem quae sumitur ex certitudine cognitionis; et est talis. Si affirmatio et negatio simul verificantur, aut ita est in omnibus, aut ita est in quibusdam, et in quibusdam non: si autem non est verum in omnibus, illae, in quibus non est verum, erunt *confessae*, idest simpliciter et absolute concedendae, vel *erunt certae*, idest certitudinaliter verae secundum aliam translationem; idest in eis ita erit vera negatio, quod affirmatio erit falsa, vel e converso.

643. Si autem hoc est verum in omnibus, quod contradictio verificetur de eodem, hoc contingit dupliciter.

Uno modo quod de quibuscumque sunt verae affirmationes, sunt verae negationes, et e converso.

Alio modo quod de quibuscumque verificantur affirmationes, verificentur negationes, sed non e converso.

644. Et si hoc secundum sit verum, sequitur hoc inconveniens, quod aliquid firmiter vel certitudinaliter est non ens; et ita erit firma opinio, quae scilicet est de negativa; et hoc ideo, quia negativa semper est vera, eo quod quandocumque est affirmativa vera, est etiam negativa vera. Non autem affirmativa semper erit vera, quia positum est, quod non de quocumque est vera negativa, sit vera affirmativa; et ita negativa erit firmior et certior quam affirmativa: quod videtur esse falsum: quia dato quod non esse sit certum et notum, tamen semper erit certior affirmatio quam negatio ei opposita, quia veritas negativae semper dependet ex veritate alicuius affirmativae. Unde nulla conclusio negativa infertur, nisi in praemissis sit aliqua affirmativa. Conclusio vero affirmativa ex negativa non probatur.

645. Si autem dicatur primo modo, scilicet quod de quibuscumque est affirmare, ita de eis est negare; similiter de quibuscumque est negare, de eis est affirmare, ut scilicet affirmatio et negatio convertantur: hoc contingit dupliciter: quia si semper negatio et affirmatio sunt simul verae, aut erit divisim dicere de utraque quod sit vera, verbi gratia, quod sit divisim dicere quod haec est vera, homo est albus, iterum haec est vera, homo non est albus: aut non est divisum utramque dicere veram sed solum coniunctim, ut si dicamus quod haec copulativa sit vera, homo est albus et homo non est albus.

646. Et siquidem dicamus hoc secundo modo, ut scilicet non sit utraque vera divisim sed solum coniunctim, tunc sequuntur duo inconvenientia:

neither a man nor a not-man—it would follow that neither the affirmation nor the negation is true but, that both are false.

642. *Again, either this* (1008a8). Then he gives a fourth argument, and this is based on certitude in knowing. It runs thus. If an affirmation and a negation are true at the same time, either this is true of all things, or it is true of some and not of others. But if it is not true of all, then those of which it is true will be *admitted*, that is, they will be conceded simply and absolutely, or according to another translation *they will be certain*, or true with certainty—that is, in their case the negation will be true because the affirmation is false, or the reverse.

643. But if it is true in all cases that contradictories are verified of the same subject, this might happen in two ways.

In one way, for anything of which affirmations are true, negations are true, and the reverse.

In another way, for anything of which affirmations are true, negations are true, but not the reverse.

644. And if the second is true, this impossible conclusion will follow: there will be something that firmly or certainly is not, and so there will be an unshakable opinion regarding a negative proposition. And this will be the case because a negation is always true, since whenever an affirmation is true, its negation is also true. But an affirmation will not always be true, because it was posited that an affirmation is not true of anything at all of which a negation is true; thus, a negation will be more certain and knowable than an affirmation. But this seems to be false because, even though non-being is certain and knowable, an affirmation will always be more certain than its opposite negation. For the truth of a negation always depends on that of some affirmation. Hence a negative conclusion can be drawn only if there is some kind of affirmation in the premises. But an affirmative conclusion can never be drawn from negative premises.

645. Now if one were to speak in the first way, and say that, of anything of which an affirmation is true, the negation is also true, and similarly that, of anything of which the negation is true, the affirmation is also true, inasmuch as affirmation and negation are interchangeable, this might happen in two ways. For if an affirmation and a negation are both true at the same time, either it will be possible to state what is true of each separately (for example, to say that both "man is white" and "man is not white" are true, separately), or it will not be possible to state that each is true separately but only both together. For example, if we were to say that this copulative proposition, "man is white and man is not white," is true.

646. And if we were to speak in the second way and say that neither one is true separately, but only both together, two impossible conclusions would then follow.

quorum primum est, quod *non dicet ea*, idest quod non asseret nec affirmationem nec negationem, et quod ambae *erunt nihil*, idest quod ambae sunt falsae: vel secundum aliam translationem *et non erit nihil*, idest sequitur quod nihil sit verum, nec affirmatio nec negatio. Et si nihil est verum, nihil poterit dici nec intelligi. Quomodo enim aliquis pronuntiabit vel intelliget non entia? Quasi dicat, nullo modo.

647. Secundum inconveniens est, quia sequitur quod omnia sint unum, quod in priori ratione est dictum. Sequitur enim quod sit idem homo et Deus et triremis, et etiam contradictiones eorum, scilicet non homo et non Deus et non triremis. Et sic patet, quod si affirmatio et negatio simul dicuntur de unoquoque, tunc nihil differt unum ab alio. Si enim unum ab alio differret, oporteret quod aliquid diceretur de uno, quod non diceretur de alio. Et sic sequeretur quod aliquid esset verum determinate et proprium huic rei, quod non conveniret alteri. Et sic non de quolibet verificaretur affirmatio vel negatio. Constat autem quod ea quae nullo modo differunt, sunt unum; et ita sequetur omnia unum esse.

648. Si autem dicatur primo modo, scilicet quod non solum coniunctim est dicere affirmationem et negationem, sed etiam divisim, sequuntur quatuor inconvenientia:

quorum unum est, quod haec positio *significat ipsum dictum*, idest demonstrat hoc esse verum quod immediate est dictum. Unde alia litera habet *accidit quod dictum est*, scilicet quod omnia sunt unum; quia sic etiam similiter affirmatio et negatio de unoquoque dicetur, et non erit differentia unius ad aliud.

649. Secundum est quod omnes verum dicerent, quia quilibet vel dicit affirmationem vel negationem, et utraque est vera; et omnes mentientur, quia contradictorium eius quod quisque dicit, erit verum. Et idem etiam homo seipsum dicere falsum confitetur; quia cum dicit negationem esse veram, dicit se falsum dixisse cum dixit affirmationem.

650. Tertium est quia manifestum est quod adhuc non poterit esse perscrutatio vel disputatio. Non enim potest disputari cum aliquo qui nihil concedit. Ille enim nihil dicit, quia nec dicit absolute quod est ita, nec dicit quod non est ita; sed dicit quod est ita et non est ita. Et iterum ambo ea negat dicens quod nec est ita nec non ita, sicut ex praecedenti ratione apparet. Si enim non omnia ista neget, sequitur quod ipse noverit aliquid determinate verum; quod est contra positum. Vel secundum quod alia translatio habet, et planius, *iam utique erit determinatum*.

The first is that *an opponent will not be saying what he professes to say*, that is, he will assert neither the affirmation nor the negation of something, and *neither will exist*, or both will be false. Or, according to another text, *nothing will exist*, that is, it will follow that nothing is true, neither the affirmation nor the negation. And if nothing is true it will be impossible to understand or to express anything. For how can anyone understand or express non-being? As though to say, "in no way."

647. The second impossible conclusion would be that all things are one, as has been stated in a previous argument (1007b29; [639]). For it would follow that a man and God and a trireme, and also their contradictories, a not-man, not-God and a not-trireme, are the same. Thus it is clear that, if an affirmation and a negation are true of any subject at the same time, one thing will not differ from another. For if one were to differ from another, something would have to be predicated of the one which is not predicated of the other. Thus it would follow that something is definitely and properly true of this thing which does not fit the other. Therefore, an affirmation and a negation will not be true of anything whatever. But it is clear that things that differ in no way are one. Thus it would follow that all things are one.

648. But if one were to speak in the first way and say that it is possible for an affirmation and a negation to be true, not only together but also separately, four impossible conclusions will follow.

The first is that this position *indicates that this statement is true*, that is, it proves that the statement just made is true. Hence another text reads, *the results described will follow*, that is, all things will be one, because it will then be possible both to affirm and to deny each thing, and one will not differ from the other.

649. A second impossible conclusion is that all will speak the truth, because anyone at all must make either an affirmation or a negation, and each will be true. And each man will also admit of himself that he is wrong when he says that the affirmation is true, for, since he says that the negation is true, he admits that he was in error when he made the affirmation.

650. A third impossible conclusion is that up to this point there obviously could not be any investigation or dispute. For it is impossible to carry on a dispute with someone who admits nothing, because such a person really says nothing, since he does not say absolutely that something is so or is not so, but he says that it is both so and not so. And again he denies both of these, for he says that it is neither so nor not so, as is evident from the preceding argument. For if he does not deny all of these, he will know that something is definitely true, and this is contrary to his original position. Or, according to another translation which expresses this more clearly, *there would already be some definite statement*.

651. Quartum sequitur per definitionem veri et falsi. Verum enim est cum dicitur esse quod est vel non esse quod non est. Falsum autem est cum dicitur non esse quod est, aut esse quod non est. Ex quo patet per definitionem veri et falsi, quod quando affirmatio est vera, tunc negatio est falsa: tunc enim dicit non esse, quod est: et si negatio est vera, tunc affirmatio est falsa: tunc enim dicitur esse de eo quod non est. Non ergo contingit vere idem affirmare et negare. Sed forte adversarius ad hoc ultimum poterit dicere, quod hic est petitio principii. Qui enim ponit contradictionem simul esse veram, non recipit hanc definitionem falsi, scilicet quod falsum est dicere quod non est esse, vel quod est non esse.

651. A fourth impossible conclusion will follow because of the definition of the true and the false. For truth exists when one says that that which is is, or that that which is not is not. But falsity exists when one says that that which is, is not, or that which is not, is. Hence from the definition of the true and the false it is clear that, when an affirmation is true, its negation is false; for one then says that what is, is not. And when a negation is true, its affirmation is false; for what is not is then said to be. Therefore, it is impossible both to affirm and to deny the same thing truly. But perhaps an opponent could say that this last argument is begging the question, for he who claims that contradictories are true at the same time does not accept this definition of the false: the false is to say that that which is not is, or that that which is, is not.

LECTURE 9

Further refutations

1008b2 Amplius igitur quomodo aut habere existimans, aut non habere, mentitus est: qui autem ambo, verum dicit? Nam si verum dicit, quid utique erit quod dicitur, quia talis est entium natura? Si vero non verum dicit, magis verum dicit qui isto modo existimat: iam aliqualiter se habebunt entia et verum utique erit et non simul etiam non verum. Si autem similiter et omnes mentientur et vera dicunt: nec pronuntiandum est, nec dicendum est tali. Simul enim haec et non haec dicit. Si autem nihil suscipiat, sed similiter existimat et non existimat, et quid utique habebit differenter a plantis? [652]

1008b12 Unde et maxime manifestum est, quia nullus ita disponitur, nec aliorum, nec dicentium hanc rationem. Quare namque vadit domum et non quiescit putans ire? Nec statim diluculo vadit in puteum aut torrentem si contingat, sed videtur timens, tamquam non similiter putans non bonum esse incidere et bonum. Palam ergo quia hoc quidem melius existimat, hoc autem non melius. [654]

Si autem hoc in bono et non bono, necesse est et sic in aliis: et hoc quidem hominem, hoc autem non hominem: et hoc quidem dulce, illud vero non duice putare est necesse:

non enim existimant quando putant melius esse aquam bibere et hominem videre: deinde ea quaerit, quamvis oportebat si idem erat similiter homo et non homo.

Sed, secundum quod dictum est, nullus est qui non videatur haec quidem timens, illa vero non. Quare sicut videtur, omnes existimant habere simpliciter, sed non circa omnia, sed circa melius et deterius.

ἔτι ἄρα ὁ μὲν ἢ ἔχειν πως ὑπολαμβάνων ἢ μὴ ἔχειν διέψευσται, ὁ δὲ ἄμφω ἀληθεύει· εἰ γὰρ ἀληθεύει, τί ἂν εἴη τὸ λεγόμενον ὅτι τοιαύτη τῶν ὄντων ἡ {5} φύσις; εἰ δὲ μὴ ἀληθεύει, ἀλλὰ μᾶλλον ἀληθεύει ἢ ὁ ἐκείνως ὑπολαμβάνων, ἤδη πως ἔχοι ἂν τὰ ὄντα, καὶ τοῦτ’ ἀληθὲς ἂν εἴη, καὶ οὐχ ἅμα καὶ οὐκ ἀληθές. εἰ δὲ ὁμοίως ἅπαντες καὶ ψεύδονται καὶ ἀληθῆ λέγουσιν, οὔτε φθέγξασθαι οὔτ’ εἰπεῖν τῷ τοιούτῳ ἔσται· ἅμα γὰρ ταῦτά τε καὶ {10} οὐ ταῦτα λέγει. εἰ δὲ μηθὲν ὑπολαμβάνει ἀλλ’ ὁμοίως οἴεται καὶ οὐκ οἴεται, τί ἂν διαφερόντως ἔχοι τῶν γε φυτῶν;

ὅθεν καὶ μάλιστα φανερόν ἐστιν ὅτι οὐδεὶς οὕτω διάκειται οὔτε τῶν ἄλλων οὔτε τῶν λεγόντων τὸν λόγον τοῦτον. διὰ τί γὰρ βαδίζει Μέγαράδε ἀλλ’ οὐχ ἡσυχάζει, οἰόμενος {15} βαδίζειν δεῖν; οὐδ’ εὐθέως ἕωθεν πορεύεται εἰς φρέαρ ἢ εἰς φάραγγα, ἐὰν τύχῃ, ἀλλὰ φαίνεται εὐλαβούμενος, ὡς οὐχ ὁμοίως οἰόμενος μὴ ἀγαθὸν εἶναι τὸ ἐμπεσεῖν καὶ ἀγαθόν· δῆλον ἄρα ὅτι τὸ μὲν βέλτιον ὑπολαμβάνει τὸ δ’ οὐ βέλτιον.

εἰ δὲ τοῦτο, καὶ τὸ μὲν ἄνθρωπον τὸ δ’ οὐκ ἄνθρωπον {20} καὶ τὸ μὲν γλυκὺ τὸ δ’ οὐ γλυκὺ ἀνάγκη ὑπολαμβάνειν.

οὐ γὰρ ἐξ ἴσου ἅπαντα ζητεῖ καὶ ὑπολαμβάνει, ὅταν οἰηθεὶς βέλτιον εἶναι τὸ πιεῖν ὕδωρ καὶ ἰδεῖν ἄνθρωπον εἶτα ζητῇ αὐτά· καίτοι ἔδει γε, εἰ ταὐτὸν ἦν ὁμοίως καὶ ἄνθρωπος καὶ οὐκ ἄνθρωπος.

ἀλλ’ ὅπερ ἐλέχθη, οὐθεὶς ὃς οὐ {25} φαίνεται τὰ μὲν εὐλαβούμενος τὰ δ’ οὔ· ὥστε, ὡς ἔοικε, πάντες ὑπολαμβάνουσιν ἔχειν ἁπλῶς, εἰ μὴ περὶ ἅπαντα, ἀλλὰ περὶ τὸ ἄμεινον καὶ χεῖρον.

Again, how is that man wrong who judges that a thing is so or is not so, and is he right who judges both? For if the second is right, what will his statement mean except that such is the nature of beings? And if he is not right, he is more right than the one who holds the first view, and beings will already be of a certain nature, and this will be true, and not at the same time not true. But if all men are equally right and wrong, anyone who holds this view can neither mean nor state anything, for he will both affirm and not affirm these things at the same time. And if he makes no judgment but equally thinks and does not think, in what respect will he differ from plants?

It is most evident, then, that no one, either among those who profess this theory or any others, is really of this mind. For why does a man walk home and not remain where he is when he thinks he is going there? He does not at dawn walk directly into a well or into a brook if he happens on such, but he seems to be afraid of doing so because he does not think that to fall in is equally good and not good. Therefore, he judges that the one is better and the other not.

And if this is so in the case of what is good and what is not good, it must also be so in the case of other things. Thus he must judge that one thing is a man and another not a man, and that one thing is sweet and another not sweet.

For when he thinks that it is better to drink water and to see a man and then seeks these things, he does not make the same judgment about all of them, though this would be necessary if the same thing were equally a man and not a man.

But according to what has been said there is no one who does not seem to fear some things and not others. Hence, as it appears, all men make an unqualified judgment, and if not about all things, still about what is better or worse.

1008b27 Si autem non scientes, sed opinantes, multo magis curandum utique erit de veritate: quemadmodum infirmo existenti, quam sano de sanitate. Etenim opinans ad scientem, non salubriter disponitur ad veritatem. [658]

εἰ δὲ μὴ ἐπιστάμενοι {28} ἀλλὰ δοξάζοντες, πολὺ μᾶλλον ἐπιμελητέον ἂν εἴη τῆς ἀληθείας, ὥσπερ καὶ νοσώδει ὄντι ἢ ὑγιεινῷ τῆς ὑγιείας· {30} καὶ γὰρ ὁ δοξάζων πρὸς τὸν ἐπιστάμενον οὐχ ὑγιεινῶς διάκειται πρὸς τὴν ἀλήθειαν.

And if they do not have science but opinion, they ought to care all the more about the truth, just as one who is ill ought to care more about health than one who is well. For one who has opinion in contrast to one who has science is not healthily disposed toward the truth.

1008b31 Amplius autem quia si maxime sic se habent omnia et non sic, sed magis et minus inest in natura entium. Non enim similiter dicemus esse duo paria et tria; neque similiter mentitus est, qui quatuor esse pente, opinatus est, et qui mille. Si igitur non similiter, palam quia alter minus, quare magis verum dicit. Si igitur quod magis affinius, erit utique aliquid verum, cui affinius quod magis verum. Et utique si non est, sed iam aliquid est firmius et verius, et a ratione remoti utique erimus incondita et prohibente aliquid mente determinare. [659]

ἔτι εἰ ὅτι μάλιστα πάντα οὕτως ἔχει καὶ οὐχ οὕτως, ἀλλὰ τό γε μᾶλλον καὶ ἧττον ἔνεστιν ἐν τῇ φύσει τῶν ὄντων· οὐ γὰρ ἂν ὁμοίως φήσαιμεν εἶναι τὰ δύο ἄρτια καὶ τὰ τρία, οὐδ᾽ ὁμοίως διέψευσται ὁ τὰ {35} τέτταρα πέντε οἰόμενος καὶ ὁ χίλια. εἰ οὖν μὴ ὁμοίως, δῆλον ὅτι ἅτερος ἧττον, ὥστε μᾶλλον ἀληθεύει. εἰ οὖν τὸ μᾶλλον ἐγγύτερον, {1009a1} εἴη γε ἄν τι ἀληθὲς οὗ ἐγγύτερον τὸ μᾶλλον ἀληθές. κἂν εἰ μὴ ἔστιν, ἀλλ᾽ ἤδη γέ τι ἔστι βεβαιότερον καὶ ἀληθινώτερον, καὶ τοῦ λόγου ἀπηλλαγμένοι ἂν εἴημεν τοῦ ἀκράτου καὶ κωλύοντός τι τῇ διανοίᾳ {5} ὁρίσαι.

Further, even if all things are so and not so as much as you like, difference of degree still belongs to the nature of beings. For we should not say that two and three are equally even; and he who thinks that four is five is not equally as wrong as he who thinks that it is a thousand. Therefore, if they are not equally wrong, obviously one is less wrong and so more right. Hence, if what is truer is nearer to what is true, there must be some truth to which the truer is nearer. And even if there is not, still there is already something truer and more certain, and we shall be freed from that intemperate theory which prevents us from determining anything in our mind.

1009a6 Est autem et ab eadem opinione et Protagorae ratio et necesse similiter ipsas ambas aut esse, aut non esse. Nam si quae videntur omnia sunt vera et apparentia, necesse omnia simul vera et falsa. Multi namque contraria sibi invicem existimant et non eadem opinantes sibi ipsis mentiri putant. Quare necesse idem esse et non esse. Et si hoc est, necesse putat omnia esse vera; opposita namque invicem opinantur mentientes et verum dicentes: igitur entia si sic se habent, verum dicunt omnes. Quod quidem igitur ab eodem sunt intellectu utraeque rationes, palam. [661]

ἔστι δ᾽ ἀπὸ τῆς αὐτῆς δόξης καὶ ὁ Πρωταγόρου λόγος, καὶ ἀνάγκη ὁμοίως αὐτοὺς ἄμφω ἢ εἶναι ἢ μὴ εἶναι· εἴτε γὰρ τὰ δοκοῦντα πάντα ἐστὶν ἀληθῆ καὶ τὰ φαινόμενα, ἀνάγκη εἶναι πάντα ἅμα ἀληθῆ καὶ ψευδῆ (πολλοὶ γὰρ {10} τἀναντία ὑπολαμβάνουσιν ἀλλήλοις, καὶ τοὺς μὴ ταὐτὰ δοξάζοντας ἑαυτοῖς διεψεῦσθαι νομίζουσιν· ὥστ᾽ ἀνάγκη τὸ αὐτὸ εἶναί τε καὶ μὴ εἶναι), καὶ εἰ τοῦτ᾽ ἔστιν, ἀνάγκη τὰ δοκοῦντα εἶναι πάντ᾽ ἀληθῆ (τὰ ἀντικείμενα γὰρ δοξάζουσιν ἀλλήλοις οἱ διεψευσμένοι καὶ ἀληθεύοντες· εἰ οὖν ἔχει τὰ {15} ὄντα οὕτως, ἀληθεύσουσι πάντες). ὅτι μὲν οὖν ἀπὸ τῆς αὐτῆς εἰσι διανοίας ἀμφότεροι οἱ λόγοι, δῆλον·

The doctrine of Protagoras proceeds from the same opinion, and both of these views must be alike either true or not true. For if all things that seem or appear are true, everything must be at once true and false. For many men have opinions which are contrary to one another, and they think that those who do not have the same opinions as themselves are wrong. Consequently, the same thing must both be and not be. And if this is so, it is necessary to think that all opinions are true; for those who are wrong and those who are right entertain opposite opinions. If, then, beings are such, all men will speak the truth. Hence it is evident that both contraries proceed from the same way of thinking.

---

652. Hic ponit quintam rationem, quae sumitur ex veritatis ratione, quae talis est. Dictum est quod affirmatio et negatio simul vera ponuntur: ergo ille, qui suscipit sive opinatur *sic se habere*, idest affirmationem tantum *aut non sic se habere*, scilicet ille, qui opinatur negationem esse veram tantum, mentitus est: qui vero opinatur ambo simul, dicit verum.

Cum igitur verum sit quando ita est in re sicut est in opinione, vel sicut significatur voce, sequitur quod ipsum quod dicit erit aliquid determinatum in rebus,

652. Here he gives a fifth argument, which is based on the notion of truth, and it runs as follows. It has been stated that both the affirmation and the negation of something are held to be true at the same time. Therefore, he who judges or thinks that *a thing is so*, that the affirmation alone is true, *or is not so*, that the negation alone is true, is wrong; and he who judges that both are true at the same time is right.

Hence, since truth exists when something is such in reality as it is in thought, or as it is expressed in words, it follows that what a man expresses will be something defi-

scilicet quia entium natura talis erit qualis dicitur, ut non patiatur affirmationem et negationem simul. Vel secundum aliam literam *quia talis est entium natura*: quasi dicat, ex quo hoc quod dicitur est determinate verum, sequitur quod res habeat naturam talem.

Si autem dicatur quod ille qui existimat simul affirmationem et negationem, non opinatur verum, sed magis ille qui existimat illo modo, quod vel tantum affirmatio vel tantum negatio sit vera, adhuc manifestum est quod entia se habebunt in aliquo modo determinate. Unde alia translatio habet planius *quodammodo et hoc erit verum determinate, et non erit simul non verum* ex quo sola affirmatio vel negatio est vera.

653. Sed si omnes praedicti, scilicet et illi qui dicunt utramque partem contradictionis, et illi qui dicunt alteram *mentiuntur*, et omnes etiam verum dicunt; cum tali qui hoc ponit, non est disputandum nec aliquid dicendum ut disputetur cum eo; vel secundum aliam literam, *talis homo non asserit aliquid nec affirmat*. Sicut enim alia translatio dicit, *nec asserere nec dicere aliquid huiusmodi est*, quia similiter unumquodque et dicit et negat.

Et si ipse sicut similiter affirmat et negat exterius, ita et similiter interius opinatur et non opinatur, et nihil suscipit quasi determinate verum, in nullo videtur differre a plantis; quia etiam bruta animalia habent determinatas conceptiones.

Alius textus habet *ab aptis natis*: et est sensus, quia talis, qui nihil suscipit, nihil differt in hoc quod actu cogitat ab illis, qui apti nati sunt cogitare, et nondum cogitat actu; qui enim apti nati sunt cogitare de aliqua quaestione, neutram partem asserunt, et similiter nec isti.

654. Deinde cum dicit *unde et maxime* ponit sextam rationem, quae sumitur ab electione et fuga: et circa hoc duo facit.

Primo ponit rationem.

Secundo excludit quamdam cavillosam responsionem, ibi, *si autem non scientes* et cetera.

Dicit ergo primo, quod manifestum est quod nullus homo sic disponitur ut credat affirmationem et negationem simul verificari; nec illi qui hanc positionem ponunt, nec etiam alii.

Si enim idem esset ire domum et non ire, quare aliquis iret domum et non quiesceret, si putaret quod hoc ipsum quiescere, esset ire domum? Patet ergo, ex quo aliquis vadit et non quiescit, quod aliud putat esse ire et non ire.

nite in reality—that is, the nature of beings will be such as it is described to be, so that it will not be at once the subject both of an affirmation and of a negation. Or, according to another text, *beings will already be of a certain nature*, as if to say that, since the statement is definitely true, it follows that a thing has such a nature.

However, if one were to say that it is not he who judges that an affirmation and a negation are true at the same time that has a true opinion, but rather he who thinks that either the affirmation alone is true or the negation alone is true, it is evident that beings will already exist in some determinate way. Hence another translation says more clearly, *and in a sense this will be definitely true and not at the same time not true*, because either the affirmation alone is true or the negation alone is true.

653. But if all of those just mentioned, both those who affirm both parts of a contradiction and those who affirm one of the two, are *wrong*, and all are also right, it will be impossible to carry on a dispute with anyone who maintains this, or even to say anything that might provoke a dispute with him. Or according to another text, *such a man will not affirm or assert anything*. For, as another translation says, *he cannot assert or affirm anything of this kind*, because he equally affirms and denies anything at all.

And if this man takes nothing to be definitely true, and similarly thinks and does not think, just as he similarly affirms and denies something in speech, he seems to differ in no way from plants, because even brute animals have certain definite conceptions.

Another text reads, *from those disposed by nature*, and this means that such a one who admits nothing does not differ in what he is actually thinking from those who are naturally disposed to think but are not yet actually thinking. For those who are naturally disposed to think about any question do not affirm either part of it, and similarly neither do the others.

654. *It is most evident* (1008b12). Then he gives a sixth argument, which is based on desire and aversion. In regard to this he does two things.

First, he gives the argument.

Second (1008b27; [658]), he rejects an answer which is a quibble, at *and if they*.

He accordingly says, first (1008b12), that it is evident that no man is of such a mind as to think that both an affirmation and a negation can be verified of the same subject at the same time. Neither those who maintain this position nor any of the others can think in this way.

For if to go home were the same as not to go home, why would someone go home rather than remain where he is, if he were of the opinion that remaining is the same as going home? Therefore, from the fact that someone goes home and does not remain where he is, it is clear that he thinks that to go and not to go are different.

655. Et similiter si aliquis incedit per aliquam viam, quae forte directe vadit ad puteum vel ad torrentem, non recte incedit per viam illam, sed videtur timere casum in puteum aut in torrentem. Et hoc ideo, quia incidere in torrentem vel puteum non putat esse similiter bonum et non bonum, sed absolute putat esse non bonum.

Si autem putaret esse bonum sicut et non bonum, non magis vitaret quam eligeret. Cum ergo vitet et non eligat, palam est quod ipse suscipit sive opinatur quod unum sit melius, scilicet non incidere in puteum, quod novit esse melius.

656. Et si hoc est in non bono et bono, similiter necesse est esse in aliis, ut videlicet opinetur quod hoc sit homo, et illud non homo: et hoc sit dulce et illud non dulce.

Quod ex hoc patet, quia non omnia aequaliter quaerit et opinatur, cum ipse putet melius aquam bibere dulcem quam non dulcem, et melius videre hominem quam non hominem.

Et ex ista diversa opinione sequitur quod determinate quaerit unum et non aliud. Oporteret siquidem quod similiter utraque quaereret, scilicet dulce et non dulce, hominem et non hominem, si existimaret quod essent eadem contradictoria. Sed, sicut dictum est, nullus est qui non videatur hoc timere et illa non timere. Et sic per hoc ipsum quod homo afficitur diversimode ad diversa, dum quaedam timet et quaedam desiderat, oportet quod non existimet idem esse quodlibet et non esse.

657. Sic ergo patet quod omnes opinantur se habere veritatem vel in affirmativa tantum, vel in negativa, et non utraque simul. Et si non in omnibus, saltem in bonis et malis, vel in melioribus et in deterioribus. Ex hac enim differentia provenit quod quaedam quaeruntur et quaedam timentur.

658. Deinde cum dicit *si autem non* excludit quamdam cavillationem. Posset enim aliquis dicere quod homines quaedam desiderant tamquam bona, et alia fugiunt tamquam non bona, non quasi scientes veritatem, sed quasi opinantes, quod non idem sit bonum et non bonum, licet idem sit secundum rei veritatem.

Sed si hoc est verum, quod homines non sunt scientes, sed opinantes, multo magis debent curare ut addiscant veritatem. Quod sic patet; quia infirmus magis curat de sanitate quam sanus. Ille autem, qui opinatur non verum, non disponitur salubriter ad veritatem in comparatione ad scientem: habet enim se ad scientem

655. Similarly, if someone walks along a path which happens to lead directly to a well or a brook, he does not proceed straight along that path, but seems to fear that he will fall into the well or brook. This happens because he judges that to fall into a well or a brook is not equally good and not good, but he judges absolutely that it is not good.

However, if he were to judge that it is both good and not good, he would not avoid the above act any more than he would desire it. Therefore, since he avoids doing this and does not desire it, obviously he judges or thinks that the one course is better, namely, not to fall into the well, because he knows that it is better.

656. And if this is true of what is good and what is not good, the same thing must apply in other cases, so that clearly one judges that one thing is a man and another not a man, and that one thing is sweet and another not sweet.

This is evident from the fact that he does not seek all things to the same degree or make the same judgment about them, since he judges that it is better to drink water which is sweet than to drink that which is not sweet, and that it is better to see a man than to see something which is not a man.

And from this difference in opinion it follows that he definitely desires the one and not the other, for he would have to desire both equally (both the sweet and the not-sweet, and both man and not-man) if he thought that contradictories were the same. But, as has been said before (1008b12; [655]), there is no one who does not seem to avoid the one and not the other. So by the very fact that a man is differently disposed to various things inasmuch as he avoids some and desires others, he must not think that the same thing both is and is not.

657. It is evident, then that all men think that truth consists in affirmation alone or in negation alone and not in both at the same time. And if they do not think that this applies in all cases, they at least are of the opinion that it applies in the case of things that are good or evil, or of those which are better or worse. For this difference accounts for the fact that some things are desired and others are avoided.

658. *And if they* (1008b27). Then he rejects a quibble. For some one could say that men desire some things inasmuch as they are good and avoid others inasmuch as they are not good, not because they know the truth, but because they are of the opinion that the same thing is not both good and not good, although this amounts to the same thing in reality.

But if it is true that men do not have science but opinion, they ought to care all the more about learning the truth. This is made clear as follows: one who is ill cares more about health than one who is well. But one who has an untrue opinion, in comparison with one who has scientific knowledge, is not healthily disposed toward

sicut infirmus ad sanitatem. Defectus enim scientiae est opinio falsa, sicut aegritudo sanitatis.

Et sic patet, quod homines debent curare de veritate invenienda: quod non esset, si nihil esset verum determinate, sed simul aliquid verum et non verum.

659. Deinde cum dicit *amplius quia* ponit septimam rationem, quae sumitur ex diversis gradibus falsitatis. Dicit ergo, quod etsi maxime verum sit quod omnia sic se habeant et non sic, idest quod affirmatio et negatio sint simul vera, et omnia sint simul vera et falsa, sed tamen in natura entium oportet quod aliquid sit magis et minus verum. Constat enim quod non similiter se habet ad veritatem, quod duo sunt paria, et tria sunt paria: nec similiter se habet ad mendacium dicere quod *quatuor sunt pente* idest quinque, et quod sint mille. Si enim sunt falsa similiter, manifestum est quod alterum est minus falsum, scilicet dicere quatuor esse quinque, quam dicere quatuor esse mille. Quod autem est minus falsum, est verum magis vel propinquius vero, sicut et minus nigrum, quod est albo propinquius.

Patet ergo quod alter eorum magis dicit verum, idest magis appropinquat veritati, scilicet ille qui dicit quatuor esse quinque. Sed non esset aliquid affinius vero vel propinquius, nisi esset aliquid simpliciter verum, cui propinquius vel affinius esset magis verum et minus falsum. Relinquitur ergo quod aliquid oportet ponere esse absolute verum, et non omnia vera et falsa; quia sequitur ex hoc quod contradictio sit simul vera.

Et si per praedictam rationem non sequitur quod aliquid sit absolute verum, tamen iam habetur quod aliquid est verius et firmius sive certius alio. Et sic non eodem modo se habet ad veritatem et certitudinem affirmatio et negatio.

Et ita per hanc rationem et per alias praecedentes erimus liberati vel remoti a *ratione*, idest opinione *non mixta*, idest non temperata (unde alius textus habet, *distemperata*): tunc enim opinio est bene contemperata, quando praedicatum non repugnat subiecto: cum autem opinio implicat opposita, tunc non bene contemperatur. Talis autem est praedicta positio, quae dicit contradictionem verificari.

660. Item prohibet ne mente aliquid possimus definire vel determinare. Prima enim ratio distinctionis consideratur in affirmatione et negatione. Unde qui affirmationem et negationem unum esse dicit, omnem determinationem sive distinctionem excludit.

the truth, because he is in the same state with regard to scientific knowledge as a sick man is with regard to health. For a false opinion is a lack of scientific knowledge just as illness is a lack of health.

Thus it is evident that men ought to care about discovering the truth. However, this would not be the case if nothing were definitely true, but only if something were both true and not true at the same time.

659. *Further, even if all* (1008b31). Then he gives a seventh argument, which is based on the different degrees of falsity. He says that even if it should be most true that everything is so and not so, that an affirmation and its negation are true at the same time, still it is necessary that different degrees of truth should exist in reality. For obviously it is not equally true to say that two is even and that three is even; nor is it equally false to say that *four is five* and that it is a thousand. For if both are equally false, it is evident that one is less false: it is less false to say that four is five than to say that it is a thousand. But what is less false is truer, or nearer to the truth, just as that is also less black which is nearer to white.

Therefore, it is clear that one of them speaks more truly or comes nearer to the truth; this is the one who says that four is five. But nothing would be closer or nearer to the truth unless there were something which is absolutely true in relation to which the nearer or closer would be truer and less false. It follows, then, that it is necessary to posit something which is unqualifiedly true, and that not all things are both true and false, because otherwise it would follow from this that contradictories are true at the same time.

And even if it does not follow from the foregoing argument that there is something which is unqualifiedly true, still it has been stated already that one thing is truer and firmer or more certain than another (1008b31; [659]). Thus affirmation and negation are not related in the same way to truth and certitude.

Hence as a result of this argument and the others given above we shall be freed or liberated from *that theory*, that is, from this *non-mixed* opinion, or one that is not tempered (and for this reason another text has *intemperate*). For an opinion is well tempered when the predicate is not repugnant to the subject. But when an opinion involves opposite notions, it is not well tempered. And the position mentioned above, which says that contradictories can be true, is an opinion of this kind.

660. Further, this position prevents us from being able to define or settle anything in our mind. For the first notion of difference is considered in affirmation and negation. Hence he who says that an affirmation and a negation are one does away with all definiteness or difference.

661. Deinde cum dicit *est autem* ostendit quod opinio Protagorae reducitur in eamdem sententiam cum praedicta positione. Dicebat enim Protagoras, quod omnia, quae videntur alicui esse vera, omnia sunt vera. Et siquidem haec positio est vera, necesse est primam positionem esse veram, scilicet quod affirmatio et negatio sint simul vera.

Et per consequens, quod omnia sint simul vera et falsa, sicut ex hac positione sequitur, ut supra ostensum est. Quod sic ostendit. Multi enim homines opinantur sibi invicem contraria: et putant quod illi, qui non eadem opinantur quod ipsi, mentiantur, et e converso. Si ergo quidquid alicui videtur hoc est verum, sequitur quod utrique mentiantur, et verum dicant, quod idem sit et non sit. Et sic ad opinionem Protagorae sequitur quod contradictio simul verificetur.

662. Similiter etiam si hoc est verum quod contradictio simul verificetur, necessarium est opinionem Protagorae esse veram, scilicet quod omnia quae videntur aliquibus esse vera, sint vera. Constat enim quod aliqui habent diversas opiniones; quorum quidam sunt mentientes, et quidam sunt verum dicentes, quia opinantur sibi invicem opposita. Si ergo omnia opposita sunt simul vera, quod sequitur si contradictoria simul verificentur, necessario sequitur quod omnes dicant verum, et quod videtur alicui sit verum; et sic patet quod eiusdem sententiae vel intellectus vel rationis est utraque positio, quia ad unam sequitur alia de necessitate.

661. *The doctrine of Protagoras* (1009a6). Here he shows that the opinion of Protagoras is reduced to the same position as the one mentioned above. For Protagoras said that everything which seems to be true to anyone is true. And if this position is true, the first one must also be true, namely, that an affirmation and its negation are true at the same time.

Hence all things must be true and false at the same time inasmuch as this follows from this position, as has been shown above (1008b31; [659]). He proves this as follows. Many men have opinions which are contrary to one another, and they think that those who do not have the same opinions as themselves are wrong, and vice versa. If, then, whatever seems so to anyone is true, it follows that both are wrong and both are right, because the same thing is and is not. Hence, according to the opinion of Protagoras, it follows that both parts of a contradiction are true at the same time.

662. Similarly, if it is true that both parts of a contradiction are true at the same time, the opinion of Protagoras must be true, namely, that all things that seem true to anybody are true. For it is clear that people have different opinions, and some of these are false and others are true because they have opinions which are opposed to each other. If, then, all opposites are true at the same time (and this follows if contradictories are true at the same time), the result must be that all are right, and that what seems so to anyone is true. Thus it is clear that each position contains the same opinion, theory, or way of thinking, because one necessarily follows from the other.

LECTURE 10

Methods of refutation

1009a16 Est autem non idem modus homiliae ad omnes. Hi namque persuasione egent, illi vi. Quicumque enim dubitasse existimaverunt, horum bene curabilis ignorantia. Non enim ad orationem sed ad mentem obviatio est eorum. Quicumque vero orationis causa dicunt, horum argumentatio est medela et eius quae in voce orationis et eius quae in nominibus. [663]

ἔστι δ᾽ οὐχ ὁ αὐτὸς τρόπος πρὸς ἅπαντας τῆς ἐντεύξεως: οἱ μὲν γὰρ πειθοῦς δέονται οἱ δὲ βίας. ὅσοι μὲν γὰρ ἐκ τοῦ ἀπορῆσαι ὑπέλαβον οὕτως, τούτων εὔϊατος ἡ ἄγνοια (οὐ γὰρ πρὸς τὸν {20} λόγον ἀλλὰ πρὸς τὴν διάνοιαν ἡ ἀπάντησις αὐτῶν): ὅσοι δὲ λόγου χάριν λέγουσι, τούτων δ᾽ ἔλεγχος ἴασις τοῦ ἐν τῇ φωνῇ λόγου καὶ τοῦ ἐν τοῖς ὀνόμασιν.

But the same method of discussion is not applicable in all of these cases, because some men need persuasion and others force. For the ignorance of those who have formed their opinions as a result of difficulties is easily cured, because refutation is directed not against their words but against their thought. But the cure for all of those who argue for the sake of argument consists in refuting what they express in speech and in words.

1009a22 Venit autem dubitantibus haec opinio ex sensibilibus, quae quidem eius quod simul contradictiones et contraria existere, videntibus ex eodem facta contraria. [665]

ἐλήλυθε δὲ τοῖς διαπoροῦσιν αὕτη ἡ δόξα ἐκ τῶν αἰσθητῶν, ἡ μὲν τοῦ ἅμα τὰς ἀντιφάσεις καὶ τἀναντία ὑπάρχειν ὁρῶσιν ἐκ ταὐτοῦ {25} γιγνόμενα τἀναντία:

Those who have experienced difficulties have formed this opinion because of things observed in the sensible world—namely, the opinion that contradictories and contraries can both be true at the same time, inasmuch as they see that contraries are generated from the same thing.

Ergo si non contingit fieri non ens, praefuit similiter res ambo ens: ut et Anaxagoras mixtum omne in omni ait et Democritus. Etenim inane et plenum similiter secundum quamcumque existere partem; quamvis hoc quidem horum esse non ens, illud vero ens.

εἰ οὖν μὴ ἐνδέχεται γίγνεσθαι τὸ μὴ ὄν, προϋπῆρχεν ὁμοίως τὸ πρᾶγμα ἄμφω ὄν, ὥσπερ καὶ Ἀναξαγόρας μεμῖχθαι πᾶν ἐν παντί φησι καὶ Δημόκριτος: καὶ γὰρ οὗτος τὸ κενὸν καὶ τὸ πλῆρες ὁμοίως καθ᾽ ὁτιοῦν ὑπάρχειν μέρος, καίτοι τὸ μὲν ὂν τούτων εἶναι τὸ δὲ {30} μὴ ὄν.

Therefore, if it is impossible for non-being to come into being, the thing must have existed before as both contraries equally. This is Anaxagoras' view, for he says that everything is mixed in everything else. And Democritus is of the same opinion, for he holds that the void and the full are equally present in any part, and yet one of these is non-being and the other being.

1009a30 Igitur ex his ad suscipientes dicemus, quia modo quodam recte dicunt, et modo quodam ignorant. Ens enim dupliciter dicitur. Est ergo quomodo contingit fieri aliquid ex non ente, est autem quomodo non. Unde et simul idem esse ens et non ens, sed non secundum idem ens. Potentia namque contingit idem esse contraria, perfecte vero non. [667]

πρὸς μὲν οὖν τοὺς ἐκ τούτων ὑπολαμβάνοντας ἐροῦμεν ὅτι τρόπον μέν τινα ὀρθῶς λέγουσι τρόπον δέ τινα ἀγνοοῦσιν: τὸ γὰρ ὂν λέγεται διχῶς, ὥστ᾽ ἔστιν ὃν τρόπον ἐνδέχεται γίγνεσθαί τι ἐκ τοῦ μὴ ὄντος, ἔστι δ᾽ ὃν οὔ, καὶ ἅμα τὸ αὐτὸ εἶναι καὶ ὂν καὶ μὴ ὄν, ἀλλ᾽ οὐ κατὰ ταὐτὸ [ὄν]: δυνάμει {35} μὲν γὰρ ἐνδέχεται ἅμα ταὐτὸ εἶναι τὰ ἐναντία, ἐντελεχείᾳ δ᾽ οὔ.

Concerning those who base their opinions on these grounds, then, we say that in one sense they speak the truth, and that in another they do not know what they are saying. For being has two meanings, so that in one sense a thing can come to be from non-being and in another sense it cannot. Hence the same thing can both be and not be at the same time, but not in the same respect; for while the same thing can be potentially two contraries at the same time, it cannot perfectly in act.

1009a36 Amplius autem dignificemus ipsos existimare et aliam substantiam esse entium, cui nec motus existit, nec corruptio, nec generatio omnino. [668]

ἔτι δ᾽ ἀξιώσομεν αὐτοὺς ὑπολαμβάνειν καὶ ἄλλην τινὰ οὐσίαν εἶναι τῶν ὄντων ᾗ οὔτε κίνησις ὑπάρχει οὔτε φθορὰ οὔτε γένεσις τὸ παράπαν.

Further, we shall expect them to believe that among beings there is also another kind of substance to which neither motion nor generation nor corruption belongs in any way.

663. Postquam determinavit Philosophus et posuit rationes contra negantes primum principium, hic ostendit quomodo diversimode est procedendum, quo ad diversos, qui ex diversis viis in praedictum errorem devenerunt: et dividitur in duas partes.

Primo ostendit quod diversimode est procedendum contra diversos.

Secundo incipit procedere alio modo quam supra, ibi, *venit autem dubitantibus.*

Dicit ergo primo, quod non est idem modus *homiliae,* idest popularis allocutionis, vel *bonae constructionis,* secundum aliam translationem, idest ordinatae dispositionis *vel intercessionis,* sicut in Graeco habetur, idest persuasionis, ad omnes praedictas positiones, scilicet de veritate contradictionis et veritate eorum quae apparent.

Dupliciter enim aliqui incidunt in praedictas positiones.

Quidam enim ex dubitatione. Cum enim eis occurrunt aliquae sophisticae rationes, ex quibus videantur sequi praedictae positiones, et eas nesciunt solvere, concedunt conclusionem. Unde eorum ignorantia est facile curabilis. Non enim obviandum est eis vel occurrendum ad rationes quas ponunt, sed ad mentem, ut scilicet solvatur dubitatio de mentibus, per quam in huiusmodi opiniones inciderunt. Et tunc ab istis positionibus recedunt.

664. Alii vero praedictas positiones prosequuntur non propter aliquam dubitationem eos ad huiusmodi inducentem, sed solum *causa orationis,* idest ex quaedam protervia, volentes huiusmodi rationes impossibiles sustinere propter seipsas, quia contraria earum demonstrari non possunt. Et horum medela est argumentatio vel arguitio *quae est in voce orationis et in nominibus,* idest per hoc quod ipsa vox orationis aliquid significat. Significatio autem orationis a significatione nominum dependet. Et sic oportet ad hoc principium redire, quod nomina aliquid significant; sicut supra Philosophus usus est.

665. Deinde cum dicit *venit autem* quia superius obviavit super hoc ex significatione nominum, hic incipit obviare dubitantibus solvendo eorum dubitationes.

Et primo quantum ad illos, qui ponebant contradictoria esse simul vera.

Secundo quantum ad illos qui ponebant omnia apparentia esse vera, ibi, *similiter autem.*

Circa primum duo facit.

Primo ponit dubitationem quae movet quosdam ad concedendum contradictoria esse simul vera.

663. Having raised arguments against those who deny the first principle, and having settled the issue, here the Philosopher indicates how one must proceed differently against various men who adopted different versions of the above-mentioned error. This is divided into two parts.

In the first (1009a16; [663]), he shows that one must proceed differently against different men.

In the second (1009a22; [665]), he begins to proceed in a different way than he did above, at *those who have experienced.*

He accordingly says, first (1009a16), that the same method *of discussion,* that is, of popular address (or *of good grammatical construction,* according to another translation, or of well ordered argument *or intercession,* as is said in the Greek, that is, of persuasion), is not applicable to all of the foregoing positions—that is, to the position that contradictories can be true, and to the position that truth consists in appearances.

For some thinkers adopt the foregoing positions for two reasons.

Some do so because of some difficulty, for since certain sophistical arguments occur to them, from which the foregoing positions seem to follow, and they do not know how to solve them, they accept the conclusion. Hence their ignorance is easily cured. For one must not oppose them or attack the arguments which they give, but must appeal to their thought, clearing up the mental difficulties which have led them to form such opinions; then they will give up these positions.

664. Others adopt the foregoing positions not because of any difficulty which leads them to such things, but only because they want to argue *for the sake of argument,* that is, because of a certain insolence, inasmuch as they want to maintain impossible theories of this kind for their own sake, since the contrary of these cannot be demonstrated. The cure for these men is the refutation or rejection of *what they express in speech and in words,* that is, on the grounds that the word in a statement has some meaning. Now the meaning of a statement depends on the meaning of the words, such that it is necessary to return to the principle that words signify something. This is the principle which the Philosopher used above (1006a18; [611]).

665. *Those who* (1009a22). Since the Philosopher met the difficulties above on this point by considering the meaning of words, he begins here to meet those who are in difficulties by solving their problems.

First (1009a22), he deals with those who held that contradictories are true at the same time;

second (1009a38; [669]), he deals with those who held that everything which appears so is true, at *and similarly.*

In regard to the first he does two things.

First, he sets forth the difficulty which led some men to admit that contradictories are true at the same time.

Secundo solvit, ibi, *igitur ex his*.

Dicit ergo, quod opinio de hoc quod contradictio simul verificetur, quibusdam venit per modum dubitationis ex sensibilibus, in quibus apparet generatio et corruptio et motus. Videbatur enim quod ex aliquo uno fiebant contraria, sicut ex aqua fit et aer qui est calidus, et terra quae est frigida.

Sed omne quod fit, fit ex prius existente. Quod enim non est, non contingit fieri, cum ex nihilo nihil fiat. Oportet ergo quod res fuerit simul in se habens contradictionem; quia si ex uno et eodem fit calidum et frigidum, fit per consequens calidum et non calidum.

666. Propter hanc autem rationem Anaxagoras dixit quod omnia in omnibus miscentur. Ex hoc enim quod videbat quodlibet ex quolibet fieri, putabat quod nihil posset fieri ex alio nisi ante fuisset ibi. Et huic rationi videtur acquievisse Democritus. Posuit enim vacuum et plenum in qualibet parte corporis coniungi. Quae quidem se habent sicut ens et non ens. Nam plenum se habet sicut ens, vacuum vero sicut non ens.

667. Deinde cum dicit *igitur ex* solvit praedictam dubitationem dupliciter.

Primo sic, dicens quod sicut dictum est, illis qui ex dubitatione opinantur praedicta inconvenientia, obviandum est ad mentem.

Igitur *ad suscipientes*, idest opinantes contradictoria simul verificari, *ex his*, idest praedicta ratione dicimus, quod quodammodo recte dicunt, et quodammodo ignorant quid dicunt, inconvenienter loquentes.

Ens enim dupliciter dicitur; ens actu, et ens in potentia. Cum igitur dicunt quod ens non fit ex non ente, quodammodo verum dicunt, et quodammodo non. Nam ens fit ex non ente actu, ente vero in potentia.

Unde etiam aliquo modo idem potest esse simul ens et non ens, et aliquo modo non potest. Contingit enim quod idem sit contraria in potentia, non tamen *perfecte*, idest in actu. Si enim tepidum est in potentia calidum et frigidum, neutrum tamen in actu.

668. Deinde cum dicit *amplius autem* secundam solutionem ponit ibi, dicens, quod dignum dicimus, quod ipsi suscipiant vel opinentur aliquam substantiam esse

Second (1009a30; [667]), he clears up this difficulty, at *concerning those*.

He says, then, that the opinion on this point—that the parts of a contradiction may be true at the same time—was formed by some men as a result of a difficulty which arose with regard to sensible things, in which generation and corruption and motion are apparent. For it seemed that contraries were generated from the same thing: for example, air, which is warm, and earth, which is cold, both come from water.

But everything which is generated comes from something that existed before, for non-being cannot come into being, since nothing comes from nothing. A thing therefore had to have in itself contradictories simultaneously, because if both the hot and the cold are generated from one and the same thing, then it turns out to be hot and not-hot itself.

666. It was because of such reasoning that Anaxagoras claimed that everything is mixed in everything else. For from the fact that anything at all seemed to come from anything else, he thought that one thing could come from another only if it already existed in it. Democritus also seems to have agreed with this theory, for he claimed that the void and the full are combined in any part of a body. And these are like being and non-being, because the full has the character of being and the void the character of non-being.

667. *Concerning those* (1009a30). Here he solves the foregoing difficulty in two ways.

First, he says that the opinion of those who have adopted the foregoing absurd views because of some difficulty must be met by appealing to their thought, as has been stated (1009a16; [663]).

Therefore, *concerning those who base their opinions*, those who think that contradictories are true at the same time, *on these grounds*, that is, on the reasoning mentioned above, we say that in one sense they speak the truth and in another they do not know what they are saying since their statements are absurd.

For being has two meanings: actual being and potential being. Therefore, when they say that being does not come from non-being, in one sense they are right and in another they are not. For being does not come from actual being but from potential being.

Hence in one sense the same thing can be at the same time both being and non-being, and in another sense it cannot; for the same thing can be contraries potentially, but it cannot be both *perfectly in act*, that is, actually. For if something warm is potentially both hot and cold, it still cannot be actually both.

668. *Further, we shall* (1009a36). Then he gives the second solution. He says that we deem it fitting that they should accept or think that there is some kind of substance

cui nec insit motus, nec generatio, nec corruptio, quod probatum est octavo *Physicorum*. Tali autem substantiae non poterit concludi ex ratione praedicta, quod insint contraria, quia ex ea non fit aliquid.

Et haec solutio videtur procedere secundum Platonicos, qui propter mutabilitatem sensibilium coacti sunt ponere ideas immobiles, scilicet de quibus dentur definitiones, et fiant demonstrationes, et certa scientia habeatur; quasi de his sensibilibus propter eorum mutabilitatem et admixtionem contrarietatis in eis certa scientia esse non possit. Sed prima solutio sufficientior est.

to which neither motion nor generation nor corruption belongs, as is proved in *Physics* 8. Now one could not conclude to the existence of this kind of substance by reason of what has been said above, namely, that contraries belong to it, because nothing is generated from them.

This solution seems to be like the one reached by the Platonists, who, because of the changeable character of sensible things, were compelled to posit unchangeable separate forms (namely, those of which definitions are given, and demonstrations made, and certain knowledge is had) on the grounds that there could be no certain knowledge of sensible things because of their changeableness and the mixture of contrariety which they contain. But the first solution is a better one.

LECTURE 11

Why some considered appearances to be true

1009a38   Similiter autem et quae circa apparentia veritas quibusdam ex sensibilibus venit. Verum enim non pluralitate iudicari putant oportere, nec paucitate. Idem vero his gustantibus dulce videtur, illis vero amarum. Quare si omnes laboraverint, aut omnes desipuerint, duo autem vel tres sani sint, aut intellectum habent: hos quidem videri laborare et desipere, alios vero non. Amplius autem multis aliorum animalium contraria videri et nobis. Et ipsi autem unicuique ad seipsum non eadem secundum sensum semper videri. Quae igitur horum vera aut falsa non manifestum. Nihil enim magis haec quam illa vera, sed similiter. Propter quod Democritus ait, aut nihil esse verum, aut nobis non manifestum. [669]

—ὅμοιως δὲ καὶ ἡ περὶ τὰ φαινόμενα ἀλήθεια ἐνίοις ἐκ τῶν αἰσθητῶν ἐλήλυθεν. τὸ μὲν γὰρ ἀληθὲς οὐ πλήθει κρίνεσθαι οἴονται προσήκειν οὐδὲ ὀλιγότητι, τὸ δ' αὐτὸ τοῖς μὲν γλυκὺ γευομένοις δοκεῖν εἶναι τοῖς δὲ πικρόν, ὥστ' εἰ πάντες ἔκαμνον {5} ἢ πάντες παρεφρόνουν, δύο δ' ἢ τρεῖς ὑγίαινον ἢ νοῦν εἶχον, δοκεῖν ἂν τούτους κάμνειν καὶ παραφρονεῖν τοὺς δ' ἄλλους οὔ· ἔτι δὲ καὶ πολλοῖς τῶν ἄλλων ζῴων τἀναντία [περὶ τῶν αὐτῶν] φαίνεσθαι καὶ ἡμῖν, καὶ αὐτῷ δὲ ἑκάστῳ πρὸς αὐτὸν οὐ ταὐτὰ κατὰ τὴν αἴσθησιν ἀεὶ δοκεῖν. ποῖα οὖν τούτων ἀληθῆ {10} ἢ ψευδῆ, ἄδηλον· οὐθὲν γὰρ μᾶλλον τάδε ἢ τάδε ἀληθῆ, ἀλλ' ὁμοίως. διὸ Δημόκριτός γέ φησιν ἤτοι οὐθὲν εἶναι ἀληθὲς ἢ ἡμῖν γ' ἄδηλον.

And similarly the theory that truth consists in appearances comes to some thinkers from sensible things. For they think that the truth should not be judged by the large or small number who uphold some view, and they point out that the same thing appears to be sweet to some when they taste it and bitter to others. Hence, if all men were ill or all were mad, and only two or three were healthy or in possession of their wits, the latter would appear ill or mad and not the former. Further, they say that the impressions made upon many of the other animals are contrary to those made upon us, and that to the senses of each person things do not always appear to be the same. Therefore, it is not always evident which of these views is true or which is false, but both appear equally so. And it is for this reason that Democritus says that either nothing is true or it is not evident to us.

---

669. Postquam Philosophus solvit dubitationem, ex qua inducebantur antiqui ad ponendum contradictoria simul esse vera, hic removet illa, ex quibus aliqui inducebantur ad ponendum omne, quod apparet, esse verum. Dividitur autem pars ista in duas.

Primo ponit dubitationes, ex quibus aliqui movebantur ad praedictam positionem ponendam.

Secundo removet dubitationes praedictas, ibi, *nos autem et ad hanc orationem*.

Circa primum duo facit.

Primo ponit rationem eorum, ex qua movebantur ad ponendum omne, quod apparet, esse verum.

Secundo assignat causam praedictae rationis, ibi, *omnino vero propter existimare*.

Dicit ergo primo, quod sicut opinio, quae ponebat contradictoria simul esse vera, veniebat ex quibusdam sensibilibus, in quibus contingit contradictoria fieri ex aliquo uno, similiter *et veritas quae est circa apparentia*, idest opinio de veritate apparentium, venit ex quibusdam sensibilibus, illis scilicet qui non protervientes, sed dubitantes in hanc positionem incidunt.

Et hoc quia de eisdem sensibilibus inveniuntur contrariae opiniones diversorum. Et hoc tripliciter.

669. Having solved the difficulty which led the ancient philosophers to maintain that contradictories are true at the same time, the Philosopher now dispels the difficulty which led some thinkers to maintain that every appearance is true. This part is divided into two.

First (1009a38; [669]), he gives the difficulties which led some thinkers to hold the position mentioned above.

Second (1010a15; [685]), he dispels these difficulties, at *but in reply*.

In regard to the first he does two things.

First, he gives the reason which led these men to maintain that every appearance is true.

Second (1009b12; [672]), he explains why they reasoned in this way, at *and in general*.

He therefore first says (1009a38) that just as the opinion which maintained that contradictories are true at the same time came from certain sensible things in which it happens that contradictories come from the same thing, so too *the theory that truth consists in appearances*, or the opinion about the truth of appearances, is derived from certain sensible things, that is, by those who are not perverse but are drawn into this position because of difficulties.

This occurs because they find that different men hold contrary opinions about the same sensible things, and they give three reasons in support of their position.

Primo, quia quibusdam gustantibus videtur dulce, quod aliis videtur amarum esse. Et sic homines de omnibus sensibilibus contrariam opinionem habent.

Secundo, quia multa animalia contraria iudicant de sensibilibus nobis. Illud enim quod videtur sapidum bovi vel asino, mali saporis ab homine iudicatur.

Tertio, quia idem homo in diversis temporibus diversimode iudicat de sensibilibus. Quod enim nunc videtur sibi dulce et sapidum, alio tempore sibi videtur amarum et insipidum.

670. Nec potest assignari ratio certa per quam fiat manifestum, quae opinionum istarum sit vera, aut quae sit falsa; quia non magis una earum videtur vera uni, quam alteri altera. Ergo oportet quod aequaliter sint verae, vel aequaliter falsae. Et ideo dixit Democritus, quod aut nihil est determinate verum in rebus; aut si quid est verum, non est nobis manifestum. Cognitionem enim rerum accipimus per sensus. Iudicium autem sensus non est certum, cum non semper eodem modo iudicet. Unde nulla certitudo videtur nobis esse de veritate, ut possimus dicere, quod haec opinio determinate est vera et contraria determinate est falsa.

671. Sed quia posset aliquis dicere, contra hanc opinionem, quod aliqua regula potest sumi per quam discernitur inter contrarias opiniones quae earum sit vera, ut videlicet dicamus quod illud est verum iudicium de sensibilibus quod dant sani, non quod dant aegrotantes; et de veritate hoc est verum iudicium, quod dant sapientes et intelligentes, non autem quod dant insipientes vel stulti: ideo in principio removet istam responsionem per hoc, quod iudicium certum de veritate non convenienter potest sumi ex multitudine et paucitate, ut scilicet dicatur esse verum quod multis videtur, falsum autem quod videtur paucis; cum quandoque illud quod est pluribus opinabile, non sit simpliciter verum.

Sanitas autem et aegritudo, sive sapientia et stultitia, non videntur differre nisi secundum multitudinem et paucitatem. Si enim omnes vel plures essent tales quales sunt illi qui nunc reputantur desipientes vel stulti, illi reputarentur sapientes. Et qui nunc reputantur sapientes, reputarentur stulti. Et similiter est de sanitate et aegritudine. Non ergo credendum est magis iudicio sani et sapientis de falsitate et veritate, quam iudicio infirmi et insipientis.

First, they point out that the same thing appears to taste sweet to some and bitter to others, so that men have contrary opinions about all sensible things.

Second, they note that many animals make judgments about sensible things that are contrary to ours, for what seems tasty to the ox or to the ass is judged by man to be unpalatable.

Third, they say that the same man at different times makes different judgments about sensible things, for what now appears to be sweet and palatable to him at another time seems bitter or tasteless.

670. And no certain reason can be given that clearly indicates which of these opinions is true or which is false, because one of these seems no truer to one person than the other does to another person. Therefore, they must be equally true or equally false. Hence Democritus said that either nothing is definitely true or, if anything is true, it is not evident to us. Even though we acquire our knowledge of things through the senses, their judgment is not certain, since they do not always judge in the same way. Hence we do not seem to have any certainty regarding the truth so that we can say that this opinion is definitely true and its contrary definitely false.

671. But someone could say, in opposing this position, that some rule can be adopted whereby a person can discern among contrary opinions the one that is true. That is, we might say that the judgment which healthy people make about sensible things is right, and the one which sick people make is not; and that the judgment which wise and intelligent people make in matters of truth is right, and the one which foolish or ignorant people make is not. He rejects this reply at the very start on the grounds that no certain judgment about the truth of any theory can be fittingly based on the number, large or small, of persons who hold it, according to which that would be said to be true which seems so to many, and that to be false which seems so to a few. For sometimes what many believe is not simply true.

Now health and sickness or wisdom and foolishness do not seem to differ only by reason of the greater or smaller number of people involved. For if all or most persons were like those who are now thought to be ignorant or foolish, they would be considered wise, and those who are now thought to be wise would be considered foolish. The same applies in the case of health and sickness. Hence the judgment regarding truth and falsity of one who is healthy and wise is no more credible than the judgment of one who is ill and foolish.

LECTURE 12

Two reasons why some identify truth with appearances

1009b12 Omnino vero propter existimare prudentiam quidem sensum et hunc autem esse alterationem, quod videtur secundum sensum, ex necessitate verum dicunt. [672]

1009b15 Ex his enim Empedocles et Democritus et aliorum, ut est verisimile dicere, unusquisque talibus opinionibus facti sunt rei. [674]

Etenim Empedodes, permutantes habitum permutare dicit prudentiam. Ad apparens enim consilium augere hominibus: et in aliis dicit: quia quantum alteri transformati sunt, tantum ipsis et semper sapere altera affuit.

Parmenides vero enuntiat eodem modo. *Ut enim quicumque habuerunt membrorum complexionem multae flexionis, et hominibus intellectus inest. Idem enim est quod quidem sapit natura membrorum hominibus et omnibus et omni: quod enim plus est, intelligentia.*

Anaxagoras quoque pronuntiatione recordatur ad quosdam sociorum. Quia talia erant ipsis entia, qualia utique existimaverunt. Dicunt autem et Homerum hanc habentem, quia fecit Hectorem tamquam in extasi fuerit a plaga iacere aliud sapientem: tamquam sapientes quidem et desipientes, sed non secundum eadem. Palam ergo quod si uterque prudentiae, et entia simul sic et non sic se habent.

1009b33 Quare et gravissimum accidens est. Nam si qui maxime contingens verum viderunt (hi autem sunt maxime quaerentes ipsum et amantes) tales habent opiniones et talia enuntiant de veritate, quomodo non est dignum respuere philosophari conantes? Nam volantia prosequi erit utique veritatem inquirere. [680]

ὅλως δὲ διὰ τὸ ὑπολαμβάνειν φρόνησιν μὲν τὴν αἴσθησιν, ταύτην δ' εἶναι ἀλλοίωσιν, τὸ φαινόμενον κατὰ τὴν αἴσθησιν ἐξ ἀνάγκης ἀληθὲς εἶναί {15} φασιν:

ἐκ τούτων γὰρ καὶ Ἐμπεδοκλῆς καὶ Δημόκριτος καὶ τῶν ἄλλων ὡς ἔπος εἰπεῖν ἕκαστος τοιαύταις δόξαις γεγένηνται ἔνοχοι.

καὶ γὰρ Ἐμπεδοκλῆς μεταβάλλοντας τὴν ἕξιν μεταβάλλειν φησὶ τὴν φρόνησιν: πρὸς παρεὸν γὰρ μῆτις ἐναύξεται ἀνθρώποισιν. καὶ ἐν ἑτέροις δὲ λέγει {20} ὅτι ὅσσον <δ'> ἀλλοῖοι μετέφυν, τόσον ἄρ σφισιν αἰεὶ καὶ τὸ φρονεῖν ἀλλοῖα παρίστατο.

καὶ Παρμενίδης δὲ ἀποφαίνεται τὸν αὐτὸν τρόπον: ὡς γὰρ ἑκάστοτ' ἔχει κρᾶσιν μελέων πολυκάμπτων, τὼς νόος ἀνθρώποισι παρίσταται: τὸ γὰρ αὐτὸ ἔστιν ὅπερ φρονέει, μελέων φύσις ἀνθρώποισιν {25} καὶ πᾶσιν καὶ παντί: τὸ γὰρ πλέον ἐστὶ νόημα.

Ἀναξαγόρου δὲ καὶ ἀπόφθεγμα μνημονεύεται πρὸς τῶν ἑταίρων τινάς, ὅτι τοιαῦτ' αὐτοῖς ἔσται τὰ ὄντα οἷα ἂν ὑπολάβωσιν. φασὶ δὲ καὶ τὸν Ὅμηρον ταύτην ἔχοντα φαίνεσθαι τὴν δόξαν, ὅτι ἐποίησε τὸν Ἕκτορα, ὡς ἐξέστη ὑπὸ {30} τῆς πληγῆς, κεῖσθαι ἀλλοφρονέοντα, ὡς φρονοῦντας μὲν καὶ τοὺς παραφρονοῦντας ἀλλ' οὐ ταὐτά. δῆλον οὖν ὅτι, εἰ ἀμφότεραι φρονήσεις, καὶ τὰ ὄντα ἅμα οὕτω τε καὶ οὐχ οὕτως ἔχει.

ἦ καὶ χαλεπώτατον τὸ συμβαῖνόν ἐστιν: εἰ γὰρ οἱ μάλιστα τὸ ἐνδεχόμενον ἀληθὲς ἑωρακότες—οὗτοι {35} δ' εἰσὶν οἱ μάλιστα ζητοῦντες αὐτὸ καὶ φιλοῦντες—οὗτοι τοιαύτας ἔχουσι τὰς δόξας καὶ ταῦτα ἀποφαίνονται περὶ τῆς ἀληθείας, πῶς οὐκ ἄξιον ἀθυμῆσαι τοὺς φιλοσοφεῖν ἐγχειροῦντας; τὸ γὰρ τὰ πετόμενα διώκειν τὸ ζητεῖν ἂν εἴη τὴν ἀλήθειαν.

And in general, it is because these philosophers think that discretion is sensory perception, and that this in turn is alteration, that they say that what appears to the senses is necessarily true.

For it is for these reasons that both Empedocles and Democritus and, we may probably say, every one of the other philosophers became involved in such opinions.

For Empedocles also says that when men change their condition they change their knowledge, "for understanding varies in men in relation to what is seen," according to him. And elsewhere he says: "Insofar as they are changed into a different nature, to that extent it is proper for them always to think other thoughts."

And Parmenides also speaks in the same way: *for just as each has his mixture of many-jointed limbs, so intellect is present in men; for it is the same thing, the nature of the limbs, which exercises discretion in men—in all and in each; for that which is more is intellect.*

Anaxagoras is also recorded as saying to some of his companions that things were such to them as they thought them to be. And men also say that Homer maintained this view, because he made Hector, after he was stunned by the blow, think other thoughts—implying that people of sound and unsound mind both think, but not the same thoughts. It is evident, then, that if both of these states of mind are forms of knowledge, beings must also be so and not so at the same time.

Hence their conclusion happens to be the most serious one. For, if those who have seen most clearly the truth which it is possible for us to have (and these are those who seek and love it most) maintain such opinions and express such views about the truth, how is it unfitting that those who are trying to philosophize should abandon the attempt? For to seek the truth will be like chasing birds.

1010a1 Huius autem opinionis causa est, quia de entibus quidem veritatem intendebant. Entia vero putabant esse sensibilia solum. In his vero multa quae indeterminati natura consistit et quae entis, sicut diximus. Propter quod decenter quidem dicunt, non vera autem dicunt. Sic enim congruit magis dicere, quam sicut Epicharmus ad Xenophanem. [681]

—αἴτιον δὲ τῆς δόξης τούτοις ὅτι περὶ τῶν ὄντων μὲν τὴν ἀλήθειαν ἐσκόπουν, τὰ δ' ὄντα ὑπέλαβον εἶναι τὰ αἰσθητὰ μόνον: ἐν δὲ τούτοις πολλὴ ἡ τοῦ ἀορίστου φύσις ἐνυπάρχει καὶ ἡ τοῦ ὄντος οὕτως ὥσπερ εἴπομεν: {5} διὸ εἰκότως μὲν λέγουσιν, οὐκ ἀληθῆ δὲ λέγουσιν (οὕτω γὰρ ἁρμόττει μᾶλλον εἰπεῖν ἢ ὥσπερ Ἐπίχαρμος εἰς Ξενοφάνην).

Now the reason these men held this opinion is that, while they investigated the truth about beings, they thought that sensible things alone exist; and in these much of the nature of the indeterminate, that is, the kind of being which we have described (1009a30), is present. Hence, while they speak in a plausible way, they do not say what is true; for it is more plausible to speak as they do than as Epicharmus did to Xenophanes.

1010a7 Amplius autem omnem videntes hanc motam naturam, de permutante autem nihil verum dicimus: circa vero omnino semper permutans, non contingere verum dicere. [683]

ἔτι δὲ πᾶσαν ὁρῶντες ταύτην κινουμένην τὴν φύσιν, κατὰ δὲ τοῦ μεταβάλλοντος οὐθὲν ἀληθευόμενον, περί γε τὸ πάντη πάντως μεταβάλλον οὐκ ἐνδέχεσθαι ἀληθεύειν.

Again, since they saw that the whole of the natural world is in motion, and that we can say nothing true about what is undergoing change, they came to the conclusion that it is impossible to say anything true about what is always changing altogether.

Nam ex hac existimatione pullulavit opinio dictorum summa, quae est dicentium heraclizare, et qualem Cratylus habuit, qui tandem opinatus est nihil oportere dicere, sed digitum movebat solum, et Heraclitum increpavit dicentem, bis in eodem flumine non est intrare. Ipse enim existimavit nec semel.

{10} ἐκ γὰρ ταύτης τῆς ὑπολήψεως ἐξήνθησεν ἡ ἀκροτάτη δόξα τῶν εἰρημένων, ἡ τῶν φασκόντων ἡρακλειτίζειν καὶ οἵαν Κρατύλος εἶχεν, ὃς τὸ τελευταῖον οὐθὲν ᾤετο δεῖν λέγειν ἀλλὰ τὸν δάκτυλον ἐκίνει μόνον, καὶ Ἡρακλείτῳ ἐπετίμα εἰπόντι ὅτι δὶς τῷ αὐτῷ ποταμῷ οὐκ ἔστιν ἐμβῆναι: αὐτὸς {15} γὰρ ᾤετο οὐδ' ἅπαξ.

For it was from this view that the most extreme of the opinions mentioned above blossomed forth; that is, the opinion held by those who are said to Heraclitize, and such as Cratylus expressed, who finally thought that he should say nothing, but only moved his finger, and criticized Heraclitus for saying that it is impossible to step into the same river twice. For he himself thought that this could not be done even once.

---

672. Ostendit causam praedictae positionis.

Et primo ex parte sensus.

Secundo ex parte sensibilium, ibi, *huius autem opinionis causa* et cetera.
Circa primum tria facit.
Primo ponit causam praedictae positionis ex parte sensus.
Secundo recitat diversorum opiniones, quae in hanc causam concordaverunt, ibi, *ex his Empedocles* et cetera.

Tertio invehit contra eos, ibi, *quare gravissimum*.

Dicit ergo primo, quod antiqui hoc opinabantur, quod prudentia sive sapientia vel scientia non esset nisi sensus. Non enim ponebant differentiam inter sensum et intellectum. Cognitio autem sensus fit per quamdam alterationem sensus ad sensibilia: et ita quod sensus aliquid sentiat, provenit ex impressione rei sensibilis in sensum. Et sic semper cognitio sensus respondet naturae rei sensibilis, ut videtur. Oportet igitur, secundum eos, quod illud, quod videtur secundum sensum, sit

672. He gives the reason why these philosophers adopted the foregoing position.
First (1009b12; [672]), he shows how sensory perception provided one reason for adopting this position;
second (1010a1; [681]), how sensible objects provided another, at *now the reason*.
In regard to the first part he does three things.
First, he explains how sensory perception provided one reason for adopting this position.
Second (1009b15; [674]), he recounts the opinions of different men which have this reason as their common basis, at *for it is*.
Third (1009b33; [680]), he attacks these opinions, at *hence their conclusion*.

He accordingly first says (1009b12) that the ancients were of the opinion that discretion (that is, wisdom or science) is merely sensory perception, for they did not make any distinction between sense and intellect. Now sensory perception comes about through a certain alteration of a sense with reference to sensible objects. And so the fact that a sense perceives something results from the impression which a sensible thing makes on the sense. Thus a sensory perception always corresponds to the nature of the sensible

de necessitate verum. Cum autem coniunxerimus quod omnis cognitio est sensitiva, sequitur quod omne quod alicui apparet quocumque modo, sit verum.

673. Haec autem ratio non solum deficit in hoc, quod ponit sensum et intellectum idem, sed et in hoc quod ponit iudicium sensus nunquam falli de sensibilibus.

Fallitur enim de sensibilibus communibus et per accidens, licet non de sensibilibus propriis, nisi forte ex indispositione organi.

Nec oportet, quamvis sensus alteretur a sensibilibus, quod iudicium sensus sit verum ex conditionibus rei sensibilis. Non enim oportet quod actio agentis recipiatur in patiente secundum modum agentis, sed secundum modum patientis et recipientis. Et inde est quod sensus non est quandoque dispositus ad recipiendum formam sensibilis secundum quod est in ipso sensibili; quare aliter aliquando iudicat quam rei veritas se habeat.

674. Deinde cum dicit *ex his enim* recitat diversorum opiniones assentientium causis praedictis. Omnia autem dicta eorum, quae inducit, tendunt ad duo.

Quorum primum est, quod intellectus sit idem cum sensu.

Aliud est, quod omne quod videtur sit verum.

Dicit ergo, quod ex praedictis rationibus Empedocles et Democritus et singuli aliorum sunt facti rei talibus opinionibus, ut *est dicere verisimile*, idest sicut verisimiliter coniecturare possumus ex eorum dictis.

675. Dicit enim Empedocles quod illi, qui permutant *habitum*, idest dispositionem corporis, permutant etiam prudentiam; quasi intellectus cuius est prudentia, sequatur habitudinem corporis, sicut et sensus.

Nam prudentia crescit in hominibus *ad apparens*, idest per hoc quod aliquid de novo incipit apparere homini, profectus scientiae fit in homine: sed hoc fit per hoc quod dispositio corporis variatur. Alia translatio habet melius: *ad praesens enim voluntas vel consilium augetur hominibus*, quasi dicat: secundum dispositiones diversas praesentes, nova consilia, sive novae voluntates, sive novae prudentiae hominibus augentur; quasi consilium sive voluntas non sequatur aliquam vim intellectivam in homine, quae sit praeter sensum, sed solam dispositionem corporis quae variatur secundum praesentiam diversarum rerum.

object as it appears. Hence, according to these thinkers, whatever appears to the senses is necessarily true. Since we must add that all knowing is sensory, it follows that whatever appears in any way at all to anyone is true.

673. But this argument fails, not only because it holds that sense and intellect are the same, but also because it maintains that the judgment which a sense makes about sensible objects is never false.

For while a sense may make a mistake about common and accidental sensible objects, it does not do this with regard to its proper sensible object, except perhaps when the sensory organ is indisposed.

And even though a sense is altered by its sensible object, the judgment of a sense does not have to conform to the conditions of the sensible object, for it is not necessary that the action of an agent be received in the patient according to the mode of being of the agent, but only according to that of the patient or subject. This is why a sense sometimes is not disposed to receive the form of a sensible object according to the mode of being which the form has in the sensible object, and it therefore sometimes judges a thing to be otherwise than it really is.

674. *For it is* (1009b15). He presents the opinions which different men held for the reasons stated above. Now all of the statements of these men which he adduces imply two things:

first, that intellect is the same as sense;

second, that every appearance is true.

Thus he says that it is for the reasons mentioned above that Empedocles and Democritus and each of the other philosophers became involved in such opinions about reality *we may probably say*, that is, we can conjecture on the basis of their statements.

675. For Empedocles said that those who change *their condition*, or some bodily disposition, also change their understanding, implying that the intellect, to which knowledge belongs, depends on a condition of the body, just as a sense does.

For understanding increases in men *in relation to what is seen*; that is, an increase in knowledge takes place in a man by reason of the fact that something new begins to appear to him, and this comes about as a result of some change in a bodily disposition. Another translation states this more clearly, saying, *for purpose or decision develops in man in relation to what is at hand*—as if to say, according to the different dispositions which are actually present in men, new decisions or new purposes or new judgments develop in them. And the implication is that decision or purpose does not depend on any intellective power in man over and above the senses, but only on a disposition of the body, which is changed with the presence of different things.

In aliis autem libris suis dicit Empedocles quod quantum ad alterationem transformat, idest secundum quantitatem qua homo transformatur in alteram dispositionem corporis, tanta eis est semper cura inquit, id est quod tot curae sive sollicitudines seu prudentiae hominibus adveniunt. Quod quidem est difficile. Alia translatio melius sic habet. *Quia quantumcumque mutati fiant, intantum secundum ipsas semper sapere alia statutum est sive stultum.* Vel *ipsis affuit* secundum aliam literam: quasi dicat, quod quantumcumque homo mutatur in dispositione corporis, intantum semper alia sapientia, quasi alium intellectum et aliam sapientiam habens.

676. Deinde ponit opinionem Parmenidis ad idem; dicens, quod Parmenides de rerum veritate enuntiat eodem modo sicut Empedocles. Dicit enim quod sicut unusquisque habet dispositionem membrorum valde circumflexorum, vel *multae flexionis*, secundum aliam literam, ita intellectus hominibus: quasi dicat, quod in membris hominis est multa varietas et circumvolutio ad hoc quod talis membrorum dispositio adaptetur ad operationem intellectus, qui sequitur membrorum complexionem, secundum eum.

Ipse enim dicit quod idem est *quod curavit*, idest quod curam habet sive prudentiam de membris ex natura membrorum: et quod est *in omnibus*, idest in singulis partibus universi, et quod est *in omni*, idest in toto universo. Sed tamen aliter nominatur in toto universo, et in singulis partibus universi et etiam in homine.

Et hoc in toto universo, dicitur Deus. In singulis autem partibus universi, dicitur natura. In homine autem, dicitur intellectus. Et sic hoc habet plus in homine quam in aliis partibus universi, quia in homine illa virtus intelligit propter complexionem determinatam membrorum, non autem in aliis rebus.

In quo etiam datur intelligi quod intellectus sequitur complexionem corporis, et per consequens non differt a sensu. Alia translatio planius habet sic. *Idem enim quod quidam sapit membrorum, non est in hominibus et omnibus et omnium. Plus enim est intellectus.*

677. Deinde ponit opinionem Anaxagorae qui pronuntiavit ad quosdam suos socios vel amicos reducendo eis ad memoriam, quia talia sunt eis entia, qualia suscipiunt sive opinantur. Et hoc est secundum quod in illis dictis philosophorum tangitur, scilicet quod veritas sequatur opinionem.

But in other works of his, Empedocles says that to the extent that alteration occurs—that is, to the extent that men are changed to another bodily disposition—there is always thoughtfulness in them, or thought, concern, or planning arises in them proportionately. This translation is a difficult one to understand, but another states this notion more clearly, saying, *to the extent that men have been changed, to that extent they are always determined to think other thoughts or even foolish ones*. Or, according to another text, *it is proper for them always to think other thoughts*, as if to say that, insofar as a man is changed in some bodily disposition, to that extent his basic outlook is different—implying that he has a different understanding and a different outlook.

676. Then he gives Parmenides' opinion in this matter. He says that Parmenides speaks about the truth of things in the same way that Empedocles does, for Parmenides says that, just as each man has an arrangement of jointed members, or *of many-jointed limbs*, according to another text, so intellect is present in men, implying that there is a great deal of variety and circumvolution in the members of man in order that such an arrangement of members may be adjusted for the operation of the intellect, which depends on the way in which the members are combined, according to him.

For he says that it is the same thing *which cares for*, or which has the care or supervision of, the members because of the nature of the members, and which is *in each*, that is, in the individual parts of the universe, and *in all*, or in the whole universe. Yet insofar as it is present in the whole universe and in its individual parts and in men, it is designated by different names.

In the whole universe it is called God, in the individual parts it is called nature, and in men it is called thought. Thus it is present to a greater degree in man than it is in the other parts of the universe; for in man this power thinks as a result of the determinate way in which his members are combined, but this does not apply in the case of other things.

In this statement he also wants it understood that thought is a result of the way in which the body is composed, and thus does not differ from sensory perception. Another translation states this more clearly, saying, *for it is the same thing, the nature of the limbs, which exercises discretion in men—in all and in each; for that which is more is intellect*.

677. Then he gives the opinion of Anaxagoras, who expressed it to some of his companions and friends and had them commit it to memory—namely, that things are such to them as they take or believe them to be. This is the second point which is touched on in these statements of the philosophers, namely, that truth depends on opinion.

678. Deinde ponit opinionem Homeri, de quo dicunt, quod videbatur eamdem opinionem habere. Fecit enim in sua recitatione Hectorem iacere quasi in extasi a plaga sibi illata *aliud cunctantem*, idest aliud cogitantem quam prius, vel aliena sapientem, secundum aliam translationem, scilicet ab his quae prius sapuerat, quasi cunctantem quidem et non cunctantem, idest in illo strato, in quo iacebat percussus, esset sapiens et non sapiens: sed non quantum ad eadem; quia quantum ad illa, quae tunc sibi videbantur sapiens erat; quantum autem ad illa quae prius sapuerat et iam sapere desierat, non erat sapiens.

Alia translatio sic habet: *sapientes quidem et desipientes*: quasi dicat, fuit de Hectore qui sapiebat aliena post plagam, ita contingit et de aliis quod sunt simul sapientes et desipientes, non secundum eadem sed secundum diversa.

679. Ex omnibus autem praedictis philosophorum opinionibus concludit conclusionem intentam, scilicet quod si utraeque sint prudentiae, scilicet secundum quas homo existimat contraria mutatus de una dispositione in aliam; quod omne id quod existimatur sit verum. Non enim esset prudentia existimare falsum. Unde sequitur quod entia similiter se habeant sic et non sic.

680. Deinde cum dicit *quare et* invehit contra praedictos philosophos, dicens, quod gravissimum accidens est quod eis accidit. Nam si illi, qui maxime viderunt verum inquantum contingit ab homine posse videri, scilicet praedicti philosophi, qui etiam sunt maxime quaerentes et amantes verum, tales opiniones et tales sententias proferunt de veritate, quomodo non est dignum praedictos philosophos dolere de hoc, quod eorum studium frustratur, si veritas inveniri non potest?

Alia litera habet *quomodo non est dignum relinquere vel respuere philosophari conantes?* Idest quod homo non adhaereat his, qui volunt philosophari, sed eos contemnat. Nam si nullum verum potest ab homine de veritate sciri, quaerere veritatem est quaerere illud, quod non potest homo habere, sicut ille qui prosequitur vel fugat volatilia. Quanto enim magis prosequitur, tanto magis ab eo elongantur.

681. Deinde cum dicit *huius autem* assignat causam praemissae opinionis ex parte sensibilium; scilicet quae causa praedictae opinionis etiam ex parte sensibilium ponebatur. Nam, cum sensibile sit prius sensu naturaliter, oportet quod dispositio sensuum sequatur sensibilium dispositionem.

Assignat autem ex parte sensibilium duplicem causam;

678. Then he gives the view of Homer, who seemed to be of the same opinion according to what people said of him. For in his story he made Hector lie as in a trance from the blow which he had been dealt, and *think other thoughts*, that is, to think other thoughts than he had thought before, or, according to another text, to be of a different opinion from the one which he had before. It is as if in lingering and not lingering—that is, in the state in which he lay after being struck down—he would both think and not think, although not about the same thing. For he knew those things that then appeared to him, but not those which he had known before, and had then ceased to know.

Another translation expresses the idea thus, *implying that people of sound and unsound mind both think, but not the same thoughts*—as if to say that, just as this is true of Hector, who had strange opinions after the blow, so too it is possible for others to have sound and foolish opinions at the same, although not about the same things, but about different ones.

679. Now from all of the foregoing views of the philosophers he draws his intended conclusion that, if both of these states of mind constitute knowledge—that is, those states in which a man thinks contrary things when he is changed from one state to another—it follows that whatever anyone thinks is true. For knowing would not consist in thinking what is false. Hence it follows that beings are equally so and not so.

680. *Hence, their conclusion* (1009b33). Here he attacks the above-mentioned philosophers. He says that the conclusion which they drew is the most serious one. For if those who have seen the truth most clearly, insofar as it is possible for man to see it (namely, the foregoing philosophers, who are also the ones that love and seek it most of all), offer such opinions and views about the truth, how is it unfitting that these philosophers should grieve about the ineffectualness of their study if truth cannot be found?

Another text reads: *how is it unfitting that those who are trying to philosophize should abandon the attempt?* In other words, a man should not cling to those who want to philosophize, but despise them. For if a man can know nothing about the truth, to seek the truth is to seek something which he cannot attain. In fact, he resembles someone who chases or hunts birds, for the more he pursues them, the farther they get away from him.

681. *Now the reason* (1010a1). He indicates how sensible things influenced this opinion, that is, how they provided a basis for the above-mentioned position. Since sensible things are naturally prior to the senses, the dispositions of the senses must depend on those of sensible things.

He gives two ways in which sensible things provided a basis for this position.

quarum secunda ponitur, ibi, *amplius autem omnium* et cetera.

Dicit ergo primo, quod causa opinionis praedictorum philosophorum fuit, quia cum ipsi intenderent cognoscere veritatem de entibus, et videretur eis quod sola sensibilia entia essent, totius veritatis doctrinam diiudicaverunt ex natura sensibilium rerum. In rebus autem sensibilibus multum est de natura infiniti sive indeterminati, quia in eis est materia, quae quantum est de se non determinatur ad unum, sed est in potentia ad multas formas: et est in eis natura entis similiter ut diximus, videlicet quod esse rerum sensibilium non est determinatum, sed ad diversa se habens. Unde non est mirum si non determinatam cognitionem ingerit sensibus, sed huic sic, et alteri aliter.

682. Et propter hoc praedicti philosophi decenter sive verisimiliter loquuntur ratione praedicta. Non tamen verum dicunt in hoc quod ponunt nihil determinatum esse in rebus sensibilibus. Nam licet materia quantum est de se indeterminate se habeat ad multas formas, tamen per formam determinatur ad unum modum essendi. Unde cum res cognoscantur per suam formam magis quam per materiam, non est dicendum quod non possit haberi de rebus aliqua determinata cognitio. Et tamen quia verisimilitudinem aliquam habet eorum opinio, magis congruit dicere sicut ipsi dicebant, quam sicut dicit Epicharmus ad Xenophanem, qui forte dicebat omnia immobilia et necessaria esse, et per certitudinem sciri.

683. Deinde cum dicit *amplius autem* ponit secundam causam ex parte sensibilium sumptam; dicens quod philosophi viderunt *omnem hanc naturam*, scilicet sensibilem, *in motu esse*. Viderunt etiam *de permutante*, idest de eo quod movetur, quod nihil verum dicitur inquantum mutatur. Quod enim mutatur de albedine in nigredinem, non est album nec nigrum inquantum mutatur. Et ideo si natura rerum sensibilium semper permutatur, et *omnino*, idest quantum ad omnia, ita quod nihil in ea est fixum, non est aliquid determinate verum dicere de ipsa. Et ita sequitur quod veritas opinionis vel propositionis non sequatur modum determinatum essendi in rebus, sed potius id quod apparet cognoscendi; ut hoc sit esse verum unumquodque quod est alicui apparere.

684. Et quod ista fuerit eorum ratio, ex hoc patet. Nam ex hac susceptione sive opinione pullulavit opinio dictorum philosophorum summa vel *extrema*, idest quae invenit quid summum vel extremum huius sententiae, quae dicebat *heraclizare*, idest sequi opinionem Heracliti, vel sequentium Heraclitum secundum aliam

The second (1010a7) is treated at the words *again, since they*.

He accordingly first says that the reason why the foregoing philosophers adopted this position is this. Since they aimed to know the truth about beings, and it seemed to them that sensible things alone exist, they therefore based their doctrine about truth in general on the nature of sensible things. Now in sensible things, much of the nature of the infinite or indeterminate is present, because they contain matter, which is not in itself limited to one form, but is in potency to many. In these, the nature of being is also found, just as we have pointed out: the being of sensible things is not determinate, but is open to various determinations. It is not to be wondered at, then, if he does not assign a definite knowledge to the senses, but one kind of knowledge to one sense, and another kind to another sense.

682. And for this reason the above-mentioned philosophers use the foregoing argument plausibly or fittingly, though they are not right in claiming that there is nothing definite in sensible things. For even though matter in itself is indeterminately disposed for many forms, nevertheless by a form it is determined to one mode of being. Hence, since things are known by their form rather than by their matter, it is wrong to say that we can have no definite knowledge of them. Yet, since the opinion of these philosophers has some plausibility, it is more fitting to speak as they do than as Epicharmus did to Xenophanes, who seems to have said that all things are immovable, necessary, and known with certainty.

683. *Again, since they* (1010a7). He gives the second way in which sensible things provided a basis for this opinion. He says that the philosophers saw that *the whole of the natural world*—that is, the sensible world—*is in motion*, and they also saw that no attribute can be predicated of *what is undergoing change* insofar as it is being changed. For whatever is being changed insofar as it is being changed is neither white nor black. Hence, if the nature of sensible things is being changed always and *altogether*, that is, in all respects, such that there is nothing fixed in reality, it is impossible to make any statement about them that is definitely true. Thus it follows that the truth of an opinion or proposition does not depend on some determinate mode of being in reality, but rather on what appears to the knower, so that it is what appears to each individual that is true for him.

684. That such was their argument becomes clear as follows. For from this assumption or opinion there sprouted the most serious or *extreme* opinion of the philosophers of whom we have spoken—that is, the opinion which is found to be the most serious or extreme in this class. And this is the one which he called *to Heraclitize*, or following the

literam, idest qui dicebant se opinionem Heracliti sequi qui posuit omnia moveri, et per hoc nihil esse verum determinate.

Et hanc opinionem habuit Cratylus, qui ad ultimum ad hanc dementiam devenit, quod opinatus est quod non oportebat aliquid verbo dicere, sed ad exprimendum quod volebat, movebat solum digitum. Et hoc ideo, quia credebat quod veritas rei quam volebat enuntiare, primo transibat, quam oratio finiretur. Breviori autem spatio digitum movebat.

Iste autem Cratylus reprehendit vel increpavit Heraclitum. Heraclitus enim dixit quod non potest homo bis intrare in eodem flumine, quia antequam intret secundo, aqua quae erat fluminis iam defluxerat. Ipse autem existimavit, quod nec semel potest homo intrare in eumdem fluvium, quia ante etiam quam semel intret, aqua fluminis defluit et supervenit alia. Et ita non solum etiam non potest homo bis loqui de re aliqua antequam dispositio mutetur, sed etiam nec semel.

opinion of Heraclitus, or the opinion of those who were disciples of Heraclitus (according to another text), or of those who professed to follow the opinion of Heraclitus, who claimed that all things are in motion, and consequently that nothing is definitely true.

This opinion also was maintained by Cratylus, who finally arrived at such a pitch of madness that he thought that he should not express anything in words, but in order to express what he wanted he would only move his finger. He did this because he believed that the truth of the thing which he wanted to express would pass away before he had finished speaking. But he could move his finger in a shorter space of time.

This same Cratylus also reprimanded or rebuked Heraclitus. For Heraclitus said that a man cannot step into the same river twice, because before he steps in a second time the water of the river already has flowed by. But Cratylus thought that a man cannot step into the same river even once, because, even before he steps in once, the water then in the river flows by and other water replaces it. Thus a man is incapable not only of speaking twice about anything before his disposition is changed but even of speaking once.

LECTURE 13

Change in sensible things not opposed to their truth

1010a15 Nos autem et ad hanc rationem dicemus, quia permutans quando permutat habet quamdam ipsius veram rationem non existimari esse. [685]

ἡμεῖς δὲ καὶ πρὸς τοῦτον τὸν λόγον ἐροῦμεν ὅτι τὸ μὲν μεταβάλλον ὅτε μεταβάλλει ἔχει τινὰ αὐτοῖς λόγον μὴ οἴεσθαι εἶναι,

But in reply to this theory we shall also say that there is some reason why these men should think that what is changing, when it is changing, does not exist.

1010a17 Est etiam dubitatio. Abiiciens enim, habet aliquid eius quod abiicitur: et eius quod fit, iam necesse aliquid esse. [686]

καίτοι ἔστι γε ἀμφισβητήσιμον· τό τε γὰρ ἀποβάλλον ἔχει τι τοῦ ἀποβαλλομένου, καὶ τοῦ γιγνομένου ἤδη ἀνάγκη τι εἶναι,

Yet there is a problem here, for what is casting off some quality retains something of what is being cast off, and something of what is coming to be must already exist.

Omninoque si corrumpitur, existet aliquid ens. Et si fit, ex quo fit et a quo generatur necesse est esse, et hoc non esse in infinitum.

ὅλως {20} τε εἰ φθείρεται, ὑπάρξει τι ὄν, καὶ εἰ γίγνεται, ἐξ οὗ γίγνεται καὶ ὑφ᾽ οὗ γεννᾶται ἀναγκαῖον εἶναι, καὶ τοῦτο μὴ ἰέναι εἰς ἄπειρον.

And in general if a thing is ceasing to be, there must be something which is; and if a thing is coming to be, there must be something from which it comes to be and something by which it comes to be. This process cannot proceed to infinity.

1010a22 Sed haec praetermittentes, ita dicamus, quia non idem est permutans secundum quantitatem et secundum qualitatem. Secundum quantitatem igitur fit idem non manens. Sed secundum speciem omnia cognoscimus. [687]

ἀλλὰ ταῦτα παρέντες ἐκεῖνα λέγωμεν, ὅτι οὐ ταὐτό ἐστι τὸ μεταβάλλειν κατὰ τὸ ποσὸν καὶ κατὰ τὸ ποιόν· κατὰ μὲν οὖν τὸ ποσὸν ἔστω μὴ μένον, {25} ἀλλὰ κατὰ τὸ εἶδος ἅπαντα γιγνώσκομεν.

But setting aside these considerations, let us say that change in quantity and the change in quality are not the same. Let it be granted, then, that a thing does not remain the same in quantity, but it is by reason of its form that we know each thing.

1010a25 Amplius autem dignum increpare sic existimantes, quod sensibilium in minoribus numerum scientes sic habentem, de caelo toto similiter enuntiaverunt. Nam circa nos sensibilis locus in generatione et corruptione perseverat solum ens. Sed iste, ut ita dicatur, nulla pars est omnis. Quare iustius utique propter illa haec reveriti fuissent: quare propter hoc de illis erraverunt. [689]

ἔτι δ᾽ ἄξιον ἐπιτιμῆσαι τοῖς οὕτως ὑπολαμβάνουσιν, ὅτι καὶ αὐτῶν τῶν αἰσθητῶν ἐπὶ τῶν ἐλαττόνων τὸν ἀριθμὸν ἰδόντες οὕτως ἔχοντα περὶ ὅλου τοῦ οὐρανοῦ ὁμοίως ἀπεφήναντο· ὁ γὰρ περὶ ἡμᾶς τοῦ αἰσθητοῦ τόπος ἐν φθορᾷ καὶ γενέσει διατελεῖ {30} μόνος ὤν, ἀλλ᾽ οὗτος οὐθὲν ὡς εἰπεῖν μόριον τοῦ παντός ἐστιν, ὥστε δικαιότερον ἂν δι᾽ ἐκεῖνα τούτων ἀπεψηφίσαντο ἢ διὰ ταῦτα ἐκείνων κατεψηφίσαντο.

Again, those who hold this view deserve to be criticized, because what they saw in the case of a very small number of sensible things they asserted to be true also of the whole universe. For it is only that region of the sensible world about us which is always in process of generation and corruption. But this is, so to speak, not even a part of the whole, so that it would have been more just for them to have esteemed the changing because of the whole than to misjudge as they did the whole because of its changing part.

1010a32 Amplius autem palam quia ad hos eadem olim dictis dicemus. Quod enim est immobilis natura quadam, ostendendum ipsis et credendum est eis. [690]

ἔτι δὲ δῆλον ὅτι καὶ πρὸς τούτους ταὐτὰ τοῖς πάλαι λεχθεῖσιν ἐροῦμεν· ὅτι {34} γὰρ ἔστιν ἀκίνητός τις φύσις δεικτέον αὐτοῖς καὶ πειστέον {35} αὐτούς.

Further, it is evident that, in answering these men, we shall say the same things as we said before (1009a36). For we must show them and make them understand that there is a kind of nature which is immobile.

1010a35 Et etiam contingit simul dicentibus esse et non esse, quiescere magis dicere

καίτοι γε συμβαίνει τοῖς ἅμα φάσκουσιν εἶναι καὶ μὴ εἶναι ἠρεμεῖν μᾶλλον φάναι

And those who say that the same thing both is and is not at the same time can

omnia quam moveri. Non est enim in quod aliquid permutetur. Nam omnia insunt omnibus. [691]

πάντα ἢ κινεῖσθαι· οὐ γὰρ ἔστιν εἰς ὅ τι μεταβαλεῖ· ἅπαντα γὰρ ὑπάρχει πᾶσιν.

also say that all things are at rest rather than in motion. According to this view, there is nothing into which anything may be changed, since everything is already present in everything.

---

685. Disputat contra praedicta.

Et primo quantum ad hoc quod ponebant de mutabilitate rerum sensibilium.

Secundo quantum ad hoc quod dicebatur de apparentia sensuum, ibi, *de veritate vero quod non est.*

Circa primum, ponit sex rationes;

quarum prima talis est. Qui existimat non esse de eo quod non est, veram opinionem habet, et veram orationem profert si hoc enuntiat: sed quod mutatur, dum mutatur non est, nec illud ad quod mutatur, nec illud ex quo mutatur: ergo aliquid vere potest dici de eo quod mutatur.

Sic ergo possumus dicere contra praedictam *rationem* vel orationem, idest opinionem dicentem quod de eo quod mutatur nihil potest verum dici, quia *permutans*, idest quod mutatur, *quando permutat*, idest quando permutatur, habet quamdam orationem vel rationem veram *in eis*, idest secundum praedictorum opinionem *non existimari*, idest quod non existimetur aliquid ei inesse.

686. Deinde cum dicit *est etiam* secundam rationem ponit, quae talis est. Omne quod permutatur, habet iam aliquid de termino ad quem permutatur; quia quod mutatur, dum mutatur, partim est in termino ad quem, et partim in termino a quo, ut probatur in sexto *Physicorum*; vel secundum aliam literam *abiiciens habet aliquid eius quod abiicitur.*

Et ex hoc datur intelligi quod in eo quod movetur, sit aliquid de termino a quo: quia quamdiu aliquid movetur, tamdiu terminus a quo abiicitur; non autem abiiceretur nisi aliquid eius inesset subiecto mobili.

Et eius quod fit, necesse est iam aliquid esse: quia omne quod fit fiebat, ut probatur sexto *Physicorum*.

Patet etiam, quod si aliquid corrumpitur, quod adhuc aliquid sit; quia si omnino non esset, iam esset omnino in corruptum esse, et non in corrumpi. Similiter autem si aliquid generatur, oportet quod sit materia ex qua generatur, et agens a quo generatur. Hoc autem non est

685. He argues against the foregoing opinions.

First (1010a15; [685]), he argues against the views that were held about the changeable character of sensible things;

second (1010b1; [692]), against the statements that were made regarding sensory appearances, at *now concerning the truth.*

In regard to the first part (1010a15) he gives six arguments.

The first of these is as follows. He who thinks that what is not does not exist has a true opinion and makes a true statement if he expresses this. But what is being changed, while it is being changed, is neither that to which it is being changed nor that from which it is being changed. Thus some true statement can be made about a thing that is undergoing change.

Hence, in opposing the foregoing *theory* or account (that is, the opinion that no true statement can be made about anything which is changing), we can say that there is some ground or valid reason in their case, according to the opinion of the foregoing philosophers, for thinking *that what is changing*, or what is being changed, *when it is changing*, that is, while it is undergoing change, *does not exist.* In other words, there is some reason *why these men should think* that it has no being.

686. *Yet there is* (1010a17). Then he gives the second argument, and it runs thus. Everything which is being changed already has some part of the terminus to which it is being changed, because what is being changed, while it is being changed, is partly in the terminus to which it is being changed and partly in the terminus from which it is being changed, as is proved in *Physics* 6 (or, according to another text, *that which is casting off some quality retains something of what is being cast off*).

And by this statement we are given to understand that anything which is being moved retains some part of the terminus from which it is being moved, because so long as a thing is being moved it is casting off the terminus from which it is being moved, and it is possible to cast off only some quality which belongs to a mobile subject.

And something of what is coming to be must already exist, because everything which is coming to be was coming to be, as is proved in *Physics* 6.

And it is also evident that, if something is ceasing to be, there must be something which is, for if it did not exist in any way at all, it already would have ceased to be and would not be ceasing to be. Similarly, if something is coming to be, there must be a matter from which it is coming to be

possibile procedere in infinitum; quia ut probatur in secundo, nec in causis materialibus, nec in agentibus, in infinitum proceditur.

Sic igitur est magna dubitatio contra eos qui dicunt, quod de eo quod movetur nihil potest vere dici: tum quia in eo quod movetur et generatur est aliquid de termino ad quem: tum quia in omni generatione et motu oportet ponere aliquid ingenitum et immobile ex parte materiae et agentis.

687. Deinde cum dicit *sed haec* tertiam rationem ponit. Et haec ratio contradicit eis quantum ad causam, ex qua opinionem sumpserunt, quia omnia sensibilia semper moventur.

Moti enim sunt ad hoc dicendum ex his quae augentur. Viderunt enim quod aliquid per unum annum crescit secundum modicam quantitatem; et crediderunt quod motus augmenti esset continuus, ita quod quantitas, secundum quam attenditur augmentum divideretur proportionaliter secundum partes temporis, ita quod in qualibet parte fieret augmentum alicuius quantitatis, cuius proportio esset ad totam quantitatem, sicut proportio partis temporis ad totum tempus. Unde, cum iste motus sit insensibilis, existimaverunt similiter quod ea quae videntur quiescere, moventur, sed motu insensibili.

688. Dicit ergo contra illos, quod praetermissis illis, quae dicta sunt, patet quod non est idem motus secundum quantitatem, et secundum qualitatem vel formam. Et quamvis concedatur eis quod motus secundum quantitatem sit continuus in rebus, et quod omnia hoc motu semper insensibiliter moveantur, tamen secundum qualitatem vel formam non oportet quod propter hoc semper omnia moveantur. Et ita poterit haberi cognitio de rebus determinata; quia res magis cognoscuntur per suam speciem quam per suam quantitatem.

689. Deinde cum dicit *amplius autem* quartam rationem ponit, dicens, quod dignum est renuere sive increpare *sic existimantes*, idest opinantes, scilicet quod omnia sensibilia sunt semper in motu, propter hoc quod paucorum sensibilium numerum inveniunt sic se habentem, cum tamen plura sensibilia immobilia sint, nisi quantum ad motum localem.

Constat enim quod sola sensibilia quae sunt hic circa nos in sphaera activorum et passivorum, sunt in generatione et corruptione. Huiusmodi autem locus est quasi nihil respectu universi. Nam tota terra non habet sensibilem quantitatem respectu supremae sphaerae. Ideo se habet ad eam sicut centrum, sicut astrologi probant

and an agent by which it is coming to be. But this cannot go on to infinity, because, as is proved in book 2 (994a11; [301]), there cannot be an infinite regress either in the case of material causes or in that of efficient causes.

Hence a major problem faces those who say that no true statement can be made about anything which is being moved or generated, both because each thing which is being moved or generated has some part of the terminus to which it is being moved and because, in every process of generation or motion, there must be held to be something unproduced and unchangeable both on the part of the matter and on that of the agent.

687. *But setting aside* (1010a22). Then he gives the third argument, and this rejects the very ground on which these thinkers base their opinion that all sensible things are always in motion.

For they were led to make this statement because of things that increase as a result of growth. For they saw that a thing increases in quantity to a very small degree during one year, and they thought that the motion of growth was continuous, so that quantity, in which increase is observed, might be divided in proportion to the parts of time. Thus an increase in some part of quantity would take place in some part of time, and this part of quantity would be related to a whole quantity as some part of a period of time to the whole of that period. And since this kind of motion is imperceptible, they also thought that things that appear to be at rest are being moved, although by an imperceptible motion.

688. In opposing these thinkers, then, he says that even apart from the considerations which have been made, it is clear that change in quantity and in quality or form are not the same. And although they admit that change in quantity is continuous in reality, and that all things are always being moved imperceptibly by this motion, it is not therefore necessary for this reason that all things should be being moved in quality or form. Hence it will be possible to have a definite knowledge of things, because things are known by their form rather than by their quantity.

689. *Again, those who* (1010a25). Then he gives the fourth argument. He says that *those who hold this view*, that is, those who entertain the opinion that all sensible things are always being moved because they find a small number of sensible things of which this is true, deserve to be criticized. There are many sensible things that are capable of being moved only from the viewpoint of local motion.

For it is obvious that it is only the sensible things around us here in the sphere of active and passive things that are in process of generation and corruption. But this sphere or place amounts to nothing, so to speak, in comparison with the whole universe, for the entire earth has no sensible quantity in comparison with the outermost sphere. Hence

per hoc quod semper sex signa zodiaci super terram apparent.

Quod non esset, si terra aliquam partem caeli sensu notabilem a nobis occultaret. Stultum enim fuit de tota natura sensibili iudicare propter illa pauciora; immo tolerabilius fuisset quod tota natura sensibilis fuisset diiudicata secundum modum caelestium corporum, quae multum excedunt alia in quantitate.

690. Deinde cum dicit *amplius autem* quintam rationem ponit, dicens, quod contra haec dicenda sunt ea quae supra sunt dicta in hoc eodem libro; scilicet quod sit quaedam *natura immobilis*, scilicet natura primi motoris, ut probatum est in octavo *Physicorum*. Et hoc est dicendum contra eos, et ipsi debent hoc credere, sicut alibi probatum est. Et ideo non est verum, quod omnia sint semper in motu, et quod nihil vere de aliquo possit dici.

691. Deinde cum dicit *et etiam* sextam rationem ponit, dicens, quod illa positio, qua ponunt omnia moveri, repugnat primae eorum positioni, qua ponuntur contradictoria simul verificari de eodem: quia si aliquid simul est et non est, magis sequitur quod omnia quiescant quam quod omnia moveantur. Nihil enim permutatur ad hoc quod iam inest ei; sicut quod iam est album non mutatur ad albedinem.

Si autem idem contingit simul esse et non esse, omnia insunt omnibus, ut supra probatum est, quia omnia sunt unum. Et ita non erit in quod possit aliquid permutari.

this place is related to the universe as its central point, as the astronomers prove on the grounds that the six signs of the zodiac always appear above the earth.

But this would not be the case if the earth were to hide from us some part of the heavens which are perceived by the senses. For it would be foolish to make a judgment about the whole sensible world in the light of these few things. Indeed, it would have been more acceptable if the whole sensible world had been judged according to the motion of the celestial bodies, which far surpass the others in quantity.

690. *Further, it is evident* (1010a32). He gives the fifth argument. He says that we must also use the same arguments against these men as were used above in this same book. That is, we must show them that *there is a kind of nature which is immobile*, namely, that of the primary mover, as is proved in *Physics* 8. And this argument must be used against them, and they ought to accept it, as has been proved elsewhere (1009a36; [668]). It is not true, then, that all things are always in motion, and that it is impossible to make any true statement about anything.

691. *And those who say* (1010a35). He gives the sixth argument. He says that their position that all things are being moved is opposed to their first position—that contradictories are true of the same subject at the same time—because if something is and is not at the same time, it follows that all things are at rest rather than in motion. For nothing is being changed in terms of any attribute which already belongs to it (for example, what is already white is not being changed as regards whiteness).

But if it is possible for the same thing both to be and not be at the same time, all attributes will be present in all things, as has been proved above (1007b29; [639]), because all will be one. Hence there will not be anything to which a thing can be changed.

LECTURE 14

Truth does not consist in appearances

1010b1 De veritate autem, quod non omne apparens verum: primum quidem, quia neque sensus falsus proprii est: sed phantasia non idem sensui. [692]

—περὶ δὲ τῆς ἀληθείας, ὡς οὐ πᾶν τὸ φαινόμενον ἀληθές, πρῶτον μὲν ὅτι οὐδ' <εἰ> ἡ αἴσθησις <μὴ> ψευδὴς τοῦ γε ἰδίου ἐστίν, ἀλλ' ἡ φαντασία οὐ ταὐτὸν τῇ αἰσθήσει.

Now concerning the truth that not everything which appears is true, the following points must be taken into consideration. First, a sense is not false with regard to its proper object, but imagination is not the same as a sense.

1010b3 Deinde dignum mirari si hoc dubitatur, utrum tantae sunt magnitudines et colores tales quales a remotis videntur, aut quales de prope: [694]

εἶτ' ἄξιον θαυμάσαι εἰ τοῦτ' ἀποροῦσι, πότερον τηλικαῦτά ἐστι {5} τὰ μεγέθη καὶ τὰ χρώματα τοιαῦτα οἷα τοῖς ἄπωθεν φαίνεται ἢ οἷα τοῖς ἐγγύθεν,

Second, it is surprising if some should raise the question of whether magnitudes are as great and colors really such as they appear to those who are at a distance or to those who are close,

et utrum qualia sanis, aut qualia laborantibus.

καὶ πότερον οἷα τοῖς ὑγιαίνουσιν ἢ οἷα τοῖς κάμνουσιν,

and whether things are such as they appear to those who are healthy or to those who are ailing,

Et graviora, utrum qualia debilibus, aut qualia robustis.

καὶ βαρύτερα πότερον ἃ τοῖς ἀσθενοῦσιν ἢ ἃ τοῖς ἰσχύουσιν,

and whether heavy things are such as they appear to those who are weak or to those who are strong,

Et vera, utrum qualia dormientibus, aut qualia vigilantibus.

καὶ ἀληθῆ πότερον ἃ τοῖς καθεύδουσιν ἢ ἃ τοῖς ἐγρηγορόσιν.

and whether those things are true as they appear to those who are asleep or to those who are awake.

Quod quidem enim non putant palam. Nullus ergo si putaverit se de nocte Athenis esse ens in Lybia, vadit ad Odion.

ὅτι μὲν γὰρ οὐκ οἴονταί {10} γε, φανερόν· οὐθεὶς γοῦν, ἐὰν ὑπολάβῃ νύκτωρ Ἀθήνησιν εἶναι ὢν ἐν Λιβύῃ, πορεύεται εἰς τὸ ᾠδεῖον.

For it is clear that they do not think so. Therefore, no one who is in Lybia, having dreamed that he was in Athens, would go to the Odeon.

1010b11 Amplius autem de futuro, ut et Plato dicit nequaquam similiter propria medici opinio et ignorantis, velut de futuro sanum fore, aut non futuro. [700]

ἔτι δὲ περὶ τοῦ μέλλοντος, ὥσπερ καὶ Πλάτων λέγει, οὐ δήπου ὁμοίως κυρία ἡ τοῦ ἰατροῦ δόξα καὶ ἡ τοῦ ἀγνοοῦντος, οἷον περὶ τοῦ μέλλοντος ἔσεσθαι ὑγιοῦς ἢ μὴ μέλλοντος.

Again, concerning future things, as Plato says, the opinion of a physician and that of a person who is ignorant of the art of medicine are not of equal value as to whether someone will get well or not.

1010b14 Amplius autem et non similiter in sensibilibus propria alieni et proprii, aut propinqui et eius quod ipsius. Et de coloribus quidem visus non gustus; de chymis vero, gustus sed non visus. [701]

ἔτι δὲ ἐπ' αὐτῶν {15} τῶν αἰσθήσεων οὐχ ὁμοίως κυρία ἡ τοῦ ἀλλοτρίου καὶ ἰδίου ἢ τοῦ πλησίον καὶ τοῦ αὐτῆς, ἀλλὰ περὶ μὲν χρώματος ὄψις, οὐ γεῦσις, περὶ δὲ χυμοῦ γεῦσις, οὐκ ὄψις·

Again, in the case of the senses, the perception of a foreign object and that of a proper object, or that of a kindred object and that of the object of the sense concerned, are not of equal value. In the case of colors it is sight and not taste which passes judgment; in the case of flavors it is taste and not sight which does this.

1010b18 Quorum unusquisque in eodem tempore, circa idem nunquam dicit ita et non ita simul habere. Sed nec in altero tempore circa passionem dubitavit, sed circa id cui accidit passio. Dico autem, puta idem quidem videbitur vinum, aut mutatum vinum, aut corpore mutato, quandoque quidem dulce esse, quandoque autem non dulce. Sed quod non dulce, quale est quando fuerit, num-

ὧν ἑκάστη ἐν τῷ αὐτῷ χρόνῳ περὶ τὸ αὐτὸ οὐδέποτε φησιν ἅμα οὕτω καὶ οὐχ οὕτως ἔχειν. ἀλλ' οὐδὲ ἐν ἑτέρῳ {20} χρόνῳ περί γε τὸ πάθος ἠμφισβήτησεν, ἀλλὰ περὶ τὸ ᾧ συμβέβηκε τὸ πάθος. λέγω δ' οἷον ὁ μὲν αὐτὸς οἶνος δόξειεν ἂν ἢ μεταβαλὼν ἢ τοῦ σώματος μεταβαλόντος ὁτὲ μὲν εἶναι γλυκὺς ὁτὲ δὲ οὐ γλυκύς· ἀλλ' οὐ τό γε γλυκύ, οἷόν ἐστιν ὅταν ᾖ, οὐδεπώποτε μετέβαλεν,

And no one of these senses ever affirms at the same time about the same subject that it is simultaneously both so and not so. Nor at another time does it experience any difficulty about a modification, but only about the object of which the modification is an accident. I mean, for example, that the same wine, either as a result of a change in itself or in the body, might seem at one time sweet and at another

quam mutavit: sed semper de ipso verum dicit, et est ex necessitate existens tale dulce. [703]

ἀλλ᾽ ἀεὶ ἀληθεύει {25} περὶ αὐτοῦ, καὶ ἔστιν ἐξ ἀνάγκης τὸ ἐσόμενον γλυκὺ τοιοῦτον.

not, But sweetness, such as it is when it exists, has never changed; but one is always right about it, and sweetness itself is necessarily such as it is.

1010b26 Quamvis et hoc hae rationes omnes auferunt, quemadmodum et substantiam non esse ullius, ita nec ex necessitate nihil. Necessarium enim quod non contingit aliter et aliter se habere. Quare et siquidem ex necessitate, non habebit ita et non ita. [704]

καίτοι τοῦτο ἀναιροῦσιν οὗτοι οἱ λόγοι ἅπαντες, ὥσπερ καὶ οὐσίαν μὴ εἶναι μηθενός, οὕτω μηδ᾽ ἐξ ἀνάγκης μηθέν· τὸ γὰρ ἀναγκαῖον οὐκ ἐνδέχεται ἄλλως καὶ ἄλλως ἔχειν, ὥστ᾽ εἴ τι ἔστιν ἐξ ἀνάγκης, οὐχ ἕξει οὕτω τε καὶ {30} οὐχ οὕτως.

Yet all these theories destroy this, for just as things will have no substance, neither will they have any necessity, for that is necessary which cannot be in one way and in another. Hence, if anything is necessary, it will not be both so and not so.

1010b30 Et ex toto si est actu sensibile solum, nihil utique erit solum non existentibus animatis. Sensus enim non erit. Neque quidem igitur sensibilia esse, et neque sensationes forsan verum. Sentientis enim passio haec est. [705]

ὅλως τ᾽ εἴπερ ἔστι τὸ αἰσθητὸν μόνον, οὐθὲν ἂν εἴη μὴ ὄντων τῶν ἐμψύχων· αἴσθησις γὰρ οὐκ ἂν εἴη. τὸ μὲν οὖν μήτε τὰ αἰσθητὰ εἶναι μήτε τὰ αἰσθήματα ἴσως ἀληθές (τοῦ γὰρ αἰσθανομένου πάθος τοῦτό ἐστι),

And in general if only the sensible actually exists, there would be nothing if living things did not exist, for there would be no senses. Therefore, the position that neither sensible objects nor sensory perceptions would exist is perhaps true, for these are modifications of the one sensing.

Subiecta vero non esse quae sensum faciunt, et sine sensu, impossibile. Non enim sensus suimet est, sed aliquid alterum praeter sensum, quod prius esse sensu necesse est. Movens enim moto prius est natura. Et utique, si adinvicem dicantur haec ipsa, nihil minus.

τὸ δὲ τὰ ὑποκείμενα μὴ εἶναι, ἃ ποιεῖ τὴν αἴσθησιν, καὶ ἄνευ αἰσθήσεως, {35} ἀδύνατον. οὐ γὰρ δὴ ἥ γ᾽ αἴσθησις αὐτὴ ἑαυτῆς ἐστίν, ἀλλ᾽ ἔστι τι καὶ ἕτερον παρὰ τὴν αἴσθησιν, ὃ ἀνάγκη πρότερον εἶναι τῆς αἰσθήσεως· {1011a1} τὸ γὰρ κινοῦν τοῦ κινουμένου φύσει πρότερόν ἐστι, κἂν εἰ λέγεται πρὸς ἄλληλα ταῦτα, οὐθὲν ἧττον.

But that the underlying subjects which cause perception should not exist apart from perception is impossible, for a perception is not the perception of itself, but there is some other thing besides the perception which must be prior to the perception. For that which causes motion is naturally prior to that which is moved, and this is no less true if they are correlative terms.

---

692. Hic incipit procedere contra ipsam rationem de veritate apparentium: et circa hoc duo facit.

Primo improbat hanc opinionem.

Secundo inducit conclusionem intentam, ibi, *igitur quia cunctorum.*

Circa primum duo facit.

Primo disputat contra illos, qui praedictam positionem propter aliquam rationem vel dubitationem posuerunt.

Secundo contra protervientes, ibi, *sunt autem quidam.*

Circa primum ponit septem rationes.

Circa primam sic dicit. Ostensum est, quod non omnia sunt mutabilia, sed *de veritate quod non omne apparens sit verum*, ista consideranda sunt: quorum primum est quod sensus non est proprie causa falsitatis, sed phantasia, quae non est idem sensui: quasi dicat: diversitas iudiciorum, quae dantur de sensibilibus, non provenit ex sensu, sed ex phantasia, ad quam propter aliquod impedimentum naturae proveniunt deceptiones sensuum.

692. Here he begins to argue against the opinion that truth is equivalent to appearances; and in regard to this he does two things.

First (1010b1; [692]), he rejects this opinion.

Second (1011b13; [718]), he draws his intended conclusion, at *let this suffice.*

In regard to the first, he does two things.

First, he argues dialectically against those who held this opinion because of some theory or difficulty.

Second (1011a3; [708]), he argues against those who held this opinion because of insolence, at *now there are some.*

In regard to the first part (1010b1) he gives seven arguments.

The first of these is as follows. It has been shown (1010b1; [690]) that not all things are changeable, and *concerning the truth that not everything which appears is true*, these points must be considered. First, the proper cause of falsity is not the senses but the imagination, which is not the same as the senses. That is to say, the diversity of judgments made about sensible objects is not attributable to the senses, but to the imagination, in which errors are made about sensory perceptions because of some natural obstacle.

Phantasia autem non est eadem sensui, ut probatur tertio *De anima*, sed est motus factus a sensu secundum actum. Unde quod ipsi attribuerunt sensui istam diversitatem iudiciorum, per quam unus iudicatur falsum sentire de hoc, de quo alius verum sentit, non convenienter faciunt.

Alia translatio melius habet, *et primum quidem quia nec sensus falsus proprii est. Sed phantasia non idem est sensui*: quasi dicat, quod nullus sensus de proprio obiecto decipitur, sicut visus non decipitur de coloribus. Ex quo patet quod iudicium sensus de sensibili proprio est determinatum. Unde oportet determinatam veritatem esse in rebus.

693. Et si obiiciatur quod aliquando etiam circa sensibilia propria error accidit, respondet quod hoc non est ex sensu, sed ex phantasia, per cuius indispositionem aliquando contingit quod id quod per sensum accipitur, aliter ad ipsam perveniat quam sensu percipiatur, sicut patet in phreneticis in quibus organum phantasiae est laesum.

694. Deinde cum dicit *deinde dignum* secundam rationem ponit, circa quam sic dicit. *Dignum est admirari si aliqui de hoc quaerunt*, vel *dubitant*, secundum aliam literam, utrum magnitudines tales sint quales videntur a remotis, vel quales videntur a propinquis. Quasi enim per se verum est quod sensus propinquas magnitudines iudicat tales esse quales sunt, remotas autem minores quam sint, quia quod a remotiori videtur, videtur minus, ut in perspectiva probatur.

695. Et simile est si quis dubitat utrum colores sint tales quales videntur a remotis, vel quales videntur a propinquis. Constat enim quod virtus agentis quanto plus in remotis porrigitur in agendo, tanto deficientior eius invenitur effectus. Ignis enim minus calefacit quae distant, quam quae sunt propinqua. Unde et color corporis perfecti sensitivi non ita immutat perfecte in remoto ut in propinquo diaphanum. Et propter hoc verius est iudicium sensus de coloribus sensibilibus in propinquo quam in remoto.

696. Et simile est etiam si quis dubitat utrum aliqua talia sint *qualia videntur sanis, aut qualia videntur laborantibus*, idest infirmis. Sani enim habent organa sensuum bene disposita, et ideo species sensibilium in eis recipiuntur prout sunt, et propter hoc verum est iudicium sanorum de sensibilibus.

Now imagination is not the same as perception, as is proved in *On the Soul* 3, but is a motion produced as a result of actual sensing. Therefore, in attributing to the senses this diversity of judgments by which one person is considered to have a false perception of a particular object about which another has a true perception, they do not proceed as they should.

Another translation states this better, saying, *first, it must be understood that a sense is not false with regard to its proper object*, implying that no sense makes a mistake about its own proper object (for example, sight is not mistaken about colors). From this it is evident that the judgment which a sense makes about its proper sensible object is a definite one, so that there must be some definite truth in the world.

693. And if someone raises the objection that error sometimes arises even with regard to proper sensibles, his answer is that this is attributable not to the senses, but to the imagination; for when the imagination is subject to some sort of abnormality, it sometimes happens that the object apprehended by a sense enters the imagination in a way different from that in which it was apprehended by the sense. This is evident, for example, in the case of madmen, in whom the organ of imagination has been injured.

694. *Second, it is* (1010b3). Then he gives his second argument, and it runs thus. *It is surprising if some should raise the question*, or *be puzzled*, as another text says, as to whether continuous quantities are such as they appear to those who are at a distance or to those who are close at hand. For it is just about self-evidently true that a sense judges quantities which are close at hand to be such as they are and those which are far away to be smaller than they are, because what seems farther away appears small, as is proved in the science of optics.

695. The same thing applies if someone raises the question of whether colors are such as they appear to those who are close at hand, for it is evident that the farther an agent's power is extended when it acts, the more imperfect is its effect. Fire heats those things that are far away to a lesser degree than those which are close at hand. And for the same reason the color of a perfect sensible body does not change that part of the transparent medium which is far away from it as completely as it changes that part which is close to it. Hence the judgment of a sense is truer about sensible colors in things close at hand than it is about those in things far away.

696. The same thing is also true if someone asks *whether things are such as they appear to those who are healthy or to those who are ailing*, that is, to those who are ill. For healthy people have sensory organs which are well disposed, and therefore the forms of sensible things are received in them just as they are; and thus the judgment which healthy people make about sensible objects is true.

Organa vero infirmorum sunt indisposita. Unde non convenienter immutantur a sensibilibus. Et propter hoc eorum iudicium de eis non est rectum, ut patet in gustu: cuius organum quia in infirmis corruptis humoribus est infectum, ea quae sunt boni saporis eis insipida videntur.

697. Et simile iterum est utrum pondera sint ita gravia sicut videntur debilibus, vel sicut videntur robustis. Constat enim quod robusti de ponderibus iudicant secundum quod sunt. Non autem ita est in debilibus in quibus difficultas ad sustinendum pondus, non solum provenit ex magnitudine ponderis, quemadmodum in robustis, sed etiam ex paucitate virtutis. Unde etiam parva pondera eis magna videntur.

698. Simile est si aliqui dubitant utrum veritas sic se habeat sicut videtur dormientibus aut sicut videtur vigilantibus. In dormientibus enim ligati sunt sensus, et ita iudicium eorum de sensibilibus non potest esse liberum, sicut est iudicium vigilantium, quorum sensus sunt soluti. Supra autem dictum est quod mirandum est si dubitant, quia ex eorum actibus apparet quod non dubitant, nec existimant omnia praedicta iudicia aequaliter esse vera.

Si enim aliquis existens in Lybia in somnis videat se esse Athenis, vel aliquis existens Parisiis videat se esse in Hungaria in somnis, a somno surgens non talia operatur, qualia operaretur si in vigilia hoc percepisset. Iret enim ad Odion, idest ad locum quemdam qui est Athenis, si in vigilia se Athenis esse videret, quod non facit si hoc somniavit. Ergo patet quod putat similiter esse verum, quod videtur dormienti et vigilanti.

699. Similiter potest argui de aliis quaestionibus praedictis. Licet enim oretenus de talibus quaerant, tamen de eis in mente non dubitant. Unde patet rationem, esse nullam, qua ponebant omne quod videtur esse verum. Hoc enim ponebant, quia diversarum opinionum non potest accipi quae verior sit, sicut supra dictum est.

700. Deinde cum dicit *amplius autem* tertiam rationem ponit; dicens quod de futuris, sicut Plato dicebat, non similiter est *propria*, idest principalis firma et vera et digna credi opinio medici, et ignorantis medicinam, sicut de hoc futuro quod est infirmatum sanari vel non sanari. Nam medicus, qui scit causam sanitatis, potest aliqua signa sanitatis futurae praescire, quae nescit artis

But the organs of sick people are not properly disposed, and therefore they are not changed as they should be by sensible objects. Hence their judgment about such objects is not a true one. This is clear with regard to the sense of taste; for when the organ of taste in sick people has been rendered inoperative as a result of the humors being destroyed, things that have a good taste seem tasteless to them.

697. The same thing also applies regarding the question of whether things having weight are as heavy as they seem to those who are weak or to those who are strong; for it is clear that the strong judge about heavy things as they really are. But this is not the case with the weak, who find it difficult to lift a weight not only because of the heaviness of it (and this sometimes happens even with the strong), but also because of the weakness of their power, so that even less heavy things appear heavy to them.

698. The same thing again applies if the question is raised whether the truth is such as it appears to those who are asleep or to those who are awake. For the senses of those who are asleep are fettered, and thus their judgment about sensible things cannot be free like the judgment of those who are awake and whose senses are unfettered. For it has been pointed out above that it would be surprising if they should be perplexed, because it appears from their actions that they are not perplexed, and that they do not think that all of the above-mentioned judgments are equally true.

For if someone in Lybia seems in his dreams to be in Athens, or if someone in Paris seems in his dreams to be in Hungary, he does not when he awakens act in the same way that he would if he were to perceive this when he is awake. For if he were awake in Athens, he would go to the Odeon, which is a building in Athens; but he would not do this if he had merely dreamed it. It is clear, then, that he does not think that what appears to him when he is asleep and what appears when he is awake are equally true.

699. We can argue in the same way with regard to the other issues mentioned above, for even though men often raise questions about these issues, they are not in their own mind perplexed about them. Hence it is clear that their reason for holding to be true everything which appears is invalid, for they held this position because of the impossibility of deciding which of several opinions is the truer, as has been stated above (1009a16; [663]).

700. *Again, concerning future* (1010b11). Here he gives his third argument. He says that in the case of future events, as Plato points out, the opinion of a physician and that of a person who is ignorant of the art of medicine are not *of equal value*, that is, equally important, certain, true, or acceptable, as to the future possibility of some sick person being cured or not. For, while a physician knows the cause

medicinalis ignarus. Unde patet quod stulta est opinio, qua creditur omnes opiniones aequaliter esse veras.

701. Deinde cum dicit *amplius autem* quartam rationem ponit, quia in sensibilibus non similiter est *propria*, idest vera et credibilis iudicatio sensus de alieno sensibili, et de proprio.

Sicut visus non similiter iudicat de coloribus et gustus. Sed credendum est de coloribus iudicio visus. *Et de chymis*, idest saporibus, iudicio gustus. Unde si visus iudicet aliquid dulce esse, et gustus percipit idem esse amarum, credendum est magis gustui quam visui.

702. Et similiter etiam non est aequalis ponderis iudicium sensus de proprio sensibili, et de eo quod est proprio propinquum.

Propinqua autem propriis sensibilibus hic dicuntur sensibilia communia, ut magnitudo, numerus, et huiusmodi, circa quae magis decipitur sensus quam circa sensibilia propria, minus tamen quam circa sensibilia alterius sensus, vel circa ea quae sunt sensibilia per accidens. Et ita patet quod stultum est dicere omnia iudicia aequaliter esse vera.

703. Deinde cum dicit *quorum unusquisque* quintam rationem ponit; dicens, quod nullus sensus in eodem tempore simul dicit circa idem ita se habere et non habere. In eodem enim tempore non dicit visus aliquid esse album et non album, nec bicubitum et non bicubitum, nec dulce et non dulce.

Sed quamvis in diversis temporibus videatur iudicium sensus opposita de eodem iudicare, nunquam tamen dubitatio accidit ex iudicio circa passionem ipsam sensibilem, sed circa passionis subiectum,

verbi gratia, de eodem subiecto, scilicet vino, gustui quandoque videtur quod est dulce, et quandoque quod non est dulce. Quod provenit vel propter mutationem corporis sensibilis, vel instrumenti quod est infectum amaris humoribus; et sic quicquid gustat ei non dulce videtur; vel propter mutationem ipsius vini. Sed nunquam gustus mutat iudicium suum quin ipsam dulcedinem talem iudicet esse qualem perpendit in dulci, quando iudicavit eam esse dulcem; sed de ipsa dulcedine semper verum dicit, et semper eodem modo.

Unde si iudicium sensus est verum, sicut ipsi ponunt, sequitur etiam quod natura dulcis ex necessitate sit talis, et sic aliquid erit determinate verum in rebus. Sequitur

of health, this is unknown to someone who is ignorant of the art of medicine. It is clear, then, that the opinion which some held that all opinions are equally true is a foolish one.

701. *Again, in the case* (1010b14). He gives his fourth argument, which runs thus. In the case of sensible objects, the judgment which a sense makes about some sensible object foreign to it and that which it makes about its proper sensible object are not *of equal value*, that is, equally true and acceptable.

For example, sight and taste do not make the same sort of judgment about colors and flavors, but in the case of colors the judgment of sight must be accepted, *and in the case of flavors*, or savors, the judgment of taste must be accepted. Hence, if sight judges a thing to be sweet and taste judges it to be bitter, taste must be accepted rather than sight.

702. And in the same way, too, the judgment which a sense makes about its proper sensible object and the one which it makes about something akin to its proper object are not of equal value.

Now those things that are said here to be akin to proper sensible objects are called common sensibles (for example, size, number, and the like), about which a sense is deceived to a greater degree than it is about its proper sensible object, although it is deceived about them to a lesser degree than it is about the sensible objects of another sense or about things that are called accidental sensible objects. Hence it is clearly foolish to say that all judgments are equally true.

703. *And no one* (1010b18). He now gives his fifth argument. He says that no sense affirms at one instant of time that a thing is simultaneously both so and not so. For sight does not at the same moment affirm that something is white and not white or that it is two cubits and not two cubits or that it is sweet and not sweet.

But while a sense's power of judging may seem at different times to form opposite judgments about the same thing, still from this judgment no difficulty ever arises about the sensible modification itself, but only about the subject of this modification.

For example, if we take the same subject, wine, sometimes it appears to the sense of taste sweet and sometimes not. This happens either because of some change in the sentient body, that is, in the organ, which is infected by bitter humors so that whatever it tastes does not seem sweet to it, or else because of some change in the wine itself. But the sense of taste never changes its judgment without judging sweetness itself to be such as it considered it to be in the sweet thing when it judged it to be sweet; but about sweetness itself it always makes a true affirmation, and always does this in the same way.

Hence, if the judgment of a sense is true, as these men claimed, it also follows that the nature of sweetness is necessarily such as it is; thus something will be definitely true

etiam quod nunquam affirmatio vel negatio sunt simul vera, quia nunquam sensus simul dicit aliquid esse dulce et non dulce, ut dictum est.

704. Deinde cum dicit *quamvis et* sextam rationem ponit, dicens, quod praedictae rationes omnes vel opiniones sicut auferunt omnia substantialia praedicata, ut supra ostensum est, ita auferunt omnia praedicata necessaria. Sequitur enim quod nihil de altero praedicatur substantialiter aut necessario. Et quod non substantialiter, ex supra dictis patet.

Quod autem non necessario, sic probatur. Quia necessarium est, quod non contingit aliter se habere. Si ergo omne quod est, est sic vel aliter, secundum eos qui dicunt contradictoria simul esse vera, et oppositas opiniones, sequetur quod nihil sit necessarium in rebus.

705. Deinde cum dicit *et ex toto* septimam rationem ponit, dicens. Si omne apparens est verum, nec aliquid est verum nisi ex hoc ipso quod est apparens sensui, sequetur quod nihil est nisi inquantum sensibile est in actu. Sed si solum sic aliquid est, scilicet inquantum est sensibile, sequetur quod nihil sit si non erunt sensus. Et per consequens si non erunt animata vel animalia. Hoc autem est impossibile.

706. Nam hoc potest esse verum quod sensibilia inquantum sensibilia non sunt, idest si accipiantur prout sunt sensibilia in actu, quod non sunt sine sensibus. Sunt enim sensibilia in actu secundum quod sunt in sensu. Et secundum hoc omne sensibile in actu est quaedam passio sentientis, quae non potest esse si sentientia non sunt.

Sed quod ipsa sensibilia quae faciunt hanc passionem in sensu non sint, hoc est impossibile. Quod sic patet. Remoto enim posteriori, non removetur prius: sed res faciens passiones in sensu non est ipsemet sensus, quia sensus non est suimet, sed alterius, quod oportet esse prius sensu naturaliter, sicut movens moto naturaliter est prius. Visus enim non videt se sed colorem.

707. Et si contra hoc dicatur quod sensibile et sensus sunt relativa adinvicem dicta, et ita simul natura, et interempto uno interimitur aliud; nihilominus sequitur propositum; quia sensibile in potentia non dicitur relative ad sensum quasi ad ipsum referatur, sed quia sensus refertur ad ipsum, ut in quinto huius habetur. Patet igitur quod impossibile est dici quod ex hoc sunt aliqua

in reality. And it also follows that both an affirmation and a negation can never be true at the same time, because a sense never affirms that something is both sweet and not sweet at the same time, as has been stated.

704. *Yet all these* (1010b26). He gives the sixth argument. He says that, just as all of the above-mentioned theories or opinions destroy substantial predicates, as has been shown above (1007a20; [625]), in a similar way they destroy all necessary predicates. For it follows that nothing could ever be predicated of anything else either substantially or necessarily. That nothing could be predicated of anything else substantially is clear from what has been stated above.

That nothing could be predicated of anything else necessarily is proved as follows. That is necessary which cannot be otherwise than it is. Therefore, if everything which is can exist in one way or in another way, as is held by those who say that contradictories and opposite opinions are true at the same time, it follows that nothing is necessary in the world.

705. *And in general* (1010b30). Then he gives the seventh argument. He says that if everything which appears is true and a thing is true only insofar as it appears to the senses, it follows that a thing exists only insofar as it is actually being sensed. But if something exists only in this way—insofar as it is being sensed—then it follows that nothing would exist if the senses did not exist. This would follow if there were no animals or living things. But this is impossible.

706. For this can be true, that sensibles under the aspect of their sensibility do not exist. In other words, if they are considered under the aspect of sensibles actualized, they do not exist apart from the senses, for they are sensibles actualized insofar as they are present in a sense. And according to this every actualized sensible is a certain modification of the subject sensing, although this would be impossible if there were no sensory beings.

But that the sensible objects which cause this modification in a sense should not exist is impossible. This becomes clear as follows. When some subsequent thing is removed, it does not follow that a prior thing is removed. But the thing producing the modification in a sense is not the perception itself, because a perception is not the perception of itself but of something else, and this must be naturally prior to the perception just as a mover is prior to the thing which is moved. For sight does not see itself, but sees color.

707. And even if someone were to raise the objection that a sensible object and a sense are correlative, and thus naturally simultaneous, such that when one is destroyed the other is destroyed, Aristotle's thesis is still true. For what is potentially sensible is not said to be relative to a sense because it is referred to a sense, but because the sense is referred to it, as is stated in book 5 of this work (1021a26;

vera, quia sensui apparent. Quod ponunt illi qui ponunt omnia apparentia esse vera, ut ex praedictis patet.

[1027]). It is clearly impossible, then, to say that some things are true because they appear to the senses, yet this is what those men maintain who claim that all appearances are true, as is evident from the foregoing statements.

LECTURE 15

Contraries cannot belong to the same subject at the same time

1011a3 Sunt autem quidam qui dubitant, huiusmodi persuasorum, et has rationes solum dicentium. Quaerunt enim quis qui iudicat sanum, et omnino circa singula recte iudicantem. [708]

Tales veto dubitationes similes sunt dubitationi, utrum dormimus nunc, aut vigilamus? Possunt autem omnes dubitationes tales idem. Omnium enim rationem hi dignificant esse. Principium enim quaerunt et hoc per demonstrationem accipere. Quandoque vero quod non persuasi sunt, manifesti sunt in actibus. Sed secundum quod quidem diximus, haec eorum passio est. Rationem enim quaerunt, quorum non est ratio. Demonstrationis enim principium non est demonstratio. Hi quidem utique facile hoc credent. Est enim non difficile sumere.

1011a15 Qui vero vim in solo verbo quaerunt, impossibile quaerunt. Contraria namque dicere dignificant statim contraria dicentes. [711]

1011a18 Verum si non omnia sunt ad aliquid, sed quaedam secundum se, non erit utique omne quod apparet verum: nam quod apparet, alicui apparet. Quare qui omnia, quae apparent esse, vera dicit, omnia quae sunt facit ad aliquid. Propter quod et observandum vim in sermone quaerentibus, simul autem et sustinere sermonem dignificantibus, quod non quod apparet, est, sed quod apparet, cui apparet, et quando apparet, inquantum et ut. Si autem sustineant quidem sermonem, non sic autem sustineant, accidet ipsis contraria cito dicere: [712]

contingit enim secundum visum eisdem mel apparere, gustu vero non. Et

εἰσὶ δέ τινες οἳ ἀποροῦσι καὶ τῶν ταῦτα πεπεισμένων καὶ τῶν τοὺς λόγους τούτους μόνον λεγόντων: ζητοῦσι γὰρ {5} τίς ὁ κρινῶν τὸν ὑγιαίνοντα καὶ ὅλως τὸν περὶ ἕκαστα κρινοῦντα ὀρθῶς.

τὰ δὲ τοιαῦτα ἀπορήματα ὅμοιά ἐστι τῷ ἀπορεῖν πότερον καθεύδομεν νῦν ἢ ἐγρηγόραμεν, δύνανται δ᾿ αἱ ἀπορίαι αἱ τοιαῦται πᾶσαι τὸ αὐτό: πάντων γὰρ λόγον ἀξιοῦσιν εἶναι οὗτοι: ἀρχὴν γὰρ ζητοῦσι, καὶ ταύτην {10} δι᾿ ἀποδείξεως λαμβάνειν, ἐπεὶ ὅτι γε πεπεισμένοι οὐκ εἰσί, φανεροί εἰσιν ἐν ταῖς πράξεσιν. ἀλλ᾿ ὅπερ εἴπομεν, τοῦτο αὐτῶν τὸ πάθος ἐστίν: λόγον γὰρ ζητοῦσιν ὧν οὐκ ἔστι λόγος: ἀποδείξεως γὰρ ἀρχὴ οὐκ ἀπόδειξίς ἐστιν. οὗτοι μὲν οὖν ῥᾳδίως ἂν τοῦτο πεισθεῖεν (ἔστι γὰρ οὐ χαλεπὸν λαβεῖν):

οἱ δ᾿ ἐν τῷ λόγῳ τὴν βίαν μόνον ζητοῦντες ἀδύνατον ζητοῦσιν: ἐναντία γὰρ εἰπεῖν ἀξιοῦσιν, εὐθὺς ἐναντία λέγοντες.

εἰ δὲ μὴ ἔστι πάντα πρός τι, ἀλλ᾿ ἔνιά ἐστι καὶ αὐτὰ καθ᾿ αὑτά, οὐκ ἂν εἴη πᾶν τὸ φαινόμενον ἀληθές: τὸ γὰρ φαινόμενον τινί ἐστι φαινόμενον: ὥστε ὁ λέγων ἅπαντα τὰ {20} φαινόμενα εἶναι ἀληθῆ ἅπαντα ποιεῖ τὰ ὄντα πρός τι. διὸ καὶ φυλακτέον τοῖς τὴν βίαν ἐν τῷ λόγῳ ζητοῦσιν, ἅμα δὲ καὶ ὑπέχειν λόγον ἀξιοῦσιν, ὅτι οὐ τὸ φαινόμενον ἔστιν ἀλλὰ τὸ φαινόμενον ᾧ φαίνεται καὶ ὅτε φαίνεται καὶ ᾗ καὶ ὥς. ἂν δ᾿ ὑπέχωσι μὲν λόγον, μὴ οὕτω δ᾿ {25} ὑπέχωσι, συμβήσεται αὐτοῖς τἀναντία ταχὺ λέγειν.

ἐνδέχεται γὰρ τὸ αὐτὸ κατὰ μὲν τὴν ὄψιν μέλι φαίνεσθαι τῇ δὲ γεύσει μή, καὶ

Now there are some, both of those who have been convinced by theories of this kind and of those who merely state them, who raise a difficulty, for they ask who it is that judges a man to be healthy, and in general who it is that judges rightly in each particular case.

But such difficulties are like wondering whether we are now asleep or awake, and all such difficulties amount to the same thing. For these people think it fitting that there should be a reason for everything; for they are seeking a starting point, and they think they can get this by demonstration. Yet they make evident in their actions that sometimes they are not convinced. But according to what we have said, this is characteristic of them, for they are seeking a reason for things for which no reason can be given, because the starting point of demonstration is not demonstration. These men, then, might easily believe this truth, for it is not difficult to grasp.

But those who seek compulsion only in words are seeking the impossible. For they deem it right to speak as they do, and immediately say contrary things.

Yet if not all things are relative but some things are absolute, not everything which appears will be true, for that which appears appears to someone. Thus he who says that all things that appear are true, makes all things relative. Hence, those who look for compulsion in words, and think it fitting to maintain this view at the same time, must be careful to add that it is not what appears that is true, but what appears for him to whom it appears, and at the time when it appears, and in the manner in which it appears, and so on. And if they maintain their view but not in this way, it will soon happen that they are saying contrary things.

For it is possible that the same thing may appear to be honey to the sense of sight

oculis duobus existentibus, non eadem utrique visui, si sunt dissimiles.

τῶν ὀφθαλμῶν δυοῖν ὄντοιν μὴ ταὐτὰ ἑκατέρᾳ τῇ ὄψει, ἂν ὦσιν ἀνόμοιαι:

but not to the sense of taste, and that, since we have two eyes, things will not appear the same to each if their sight is unequal.

Quoniam ad dicentes propter iam dictas causas quod apparet verum esse et propter hoc similiter omnia esse vera et falsa: neque enim omnibus eadem apparere contingit. Nec enim accidunt semper eadem, sed multoties contraria secundum idem tempus.

ἐπεὶ πρός γε τοὺς διὰ τὰς πάλαι εἰρημένας αἰτίας τὸ φαινόμενον φάσκοντας {30} ἀληθὲς εἶναι, καὶ διὰ τοῦτο πάνθ᾽ ὁμοίως εἶναι ψευδῆ καὶ ἀληθῆ: οὔτε γὰρ ἅπασι ταὐτὰ φαίνεσθαι οὔτε ταὐτῷ ἀεὶ ταὐτά, ἀλλὰ πολλάκις τἀναντία κατὰ τὸν αὐτὸν χρόνον

Now, as we have stated, there are some who say, for the reasons already given (1009a38), that what appears is true, and that all things are therefore equally true and false, because they do not always appear the same to all men or to the same man (for they do not always happen to be the same), but often have contrary appearances at the same time.

Tactus enim duo dicit in digitorum varietate et visus unum: aut nullatenus idem et secundum idem sensui et similiter et in eodem tempore. Quare hoc utique erit verum.

(ἡ μὲν γὰρ ἁφὴ δύο λέγει ἐν τῇ ἐπαλλάξει τῶν δακτύλων ἡ δ᾽ ὄψις ἕν): ἀλλ᾽ οὔ τι τῇ αὐτῇ γε καὶ {35} κατὰ τὸ αὐτὸ αἰσθήσει καὶ ὡσαύτως καὶ ἐν τῷ αὐτῷ χρόνῳ, ὥστε τοῦτ᾽ ἂν εἴη ἀληθές.

For touch says there are two objects when the fingers are crossed, but sight says there is one. And in answering these men, we must say that what appears is true, but not for the same man and in the same way and at the same time, so that when these qualifications are added, what appears will be true.

Sed forsan ideo erat necesse dicere, non propter dubitationem, sed orationis causa dicentibus quia hoc non est verum, sed huic verum.

{1011b1} ἀλλ᾽ ἴσως διὰ τοῦτ᾽ ἀνάγκη λέγειν τοῖς μὴ δι᾽ ἀπορίαν ἀλλὰ λόγου χάριν λέγουσιν, ὅτι οὐκ ἔστιν ἀληθὲς τοῦτο ἀλλὰ τούτῳ ἀληθές.

But perhaps it is for this reason that those who argue thus, not because of some difficulty but for the sake of argument, must say that this is not true, but true for this person.

1011b4 Et sicut praedictum, est necesse ad aliquid facere omnia et ad opinionem et sensum. Quare nec factum est, nec erit nihil, nullo praeopinante. Si vero factum est, aut erit, palam quia non erunt omnia ad opinionem. [716]

καὶ ὥσπερ δὴ πρότερον εἴρηται, ἀνάγκη πρός τι ποιεῖν {5} ἅπαντα καὶ πρὸς δόξαν καὶ αἴσθησιν, ὥστ᾽ οὔτε γέγονεν οὔτ᾽ ἔσται οὐθὲν μηθενὸς προδοξάσαντος. εἰ δὲ γέγονεν ἢ ἔσται, δῆλον ὅτι οὐκ ἂν εἴη ἅπαντα πρὸς δόξαν.

And, as has been said before (1011a18), they must make everything relative both to opinion and to perception, so that nothing has come to be or will come to be unless someone has first formed an opinion about it. But if something has come to be or will come to be, it is evident that not all things depend on opinion.

1011b7 Amplius si unum ad unum, aut ad determinatum. Et si idem dimidium et aequale, sed non aequale ad duplum, neque dimidium ad aequale. [717]

ἔτι εἰ ἕν, πρὸς ἓν ἢ πρὸς ὡρισμένον: καὶ εἰ τὸ αὐτὸ καὶ ἥμισυ καὶ ἴσον, ἀλλ᾽ οὐ πρὸς τὸ διπλάσιόν γε τὸ ἴσον.

Further, if a thing is one, it is relative to one thing or to a determinate number; and if the same thing is both half and equal, still the equal is not relative to the double or the half to the equal.

Verum ad opinans si idem est homo et opinatum, non est homo opinans, sed opinatum. Si vero unumquodque fuerit ad opinans, ad infinita erit specie opinans.

πρὸς δὴ τὸ δοξάζον {10} εἰ ταὐτὸ ἄνθρωπος καὶ τὸ δοξαζόμενον, οὐκ ἔσται ἄνθρωπος τὸ δοξάζον ἀλλὰ τὸ δοξαζόμενον. εἰ δ᾽ ἕκαστον ἔσται πρὸς τὸ δοξάζον, πρὸς ἄπειρα ἔσται τῷ εἴδει τὸ δοξάζον.

If, then, in relation to the thinking subject, man and the object of thought are the same, man will not be the thinking subject, but the object of thought. And if each thing is relative to the thinking subject, the thinking subject will be relative to things infinite in species.

1011b13 Igitur quia cunctorum est opinio firmissima, non esse simul veras oppositas dictiones: et quid accidit ita

ὅτι μὲν οὖν βεβαιοτάτη δόξα πασῶν τὸ μὴ εἶναι ἀληθεῖς ἅμα τὰς ἀντικειμένας φάσεις, καὶ τί συμβαίνει τοῖς οὕτω {15}

Let this suffice, then, regarding the points under discussion. The firmest opinion of all is the one which asserts that opposite

dicentibus, et quare ita dicunt, tot sint dicta. [718]

λέγουσι, καὶ διὰ τί οὕτω λέγουσι, τοσαῦτα εἰρήσθω:

statements are not true at the same time; and the conclusions that follow for those who say that they are true; and why they speak as they do.

1011b15 Quoniam autem impossibile est contradictionem veram simul esse de eodem, palam quia nec contraria simul inesse eidem contingit. Contrariorum enim alterum est privatio. [719]

ἐπεὶ δ᾽ ἀδύνατον τὴν ἀντίφασιν ἅμα ἀληθεύεσθαι κατὰ τοῦ αὐτοῦ, φανερὸν ὅτι οὐδὲ τἀναντία ἅμα ὑπάρχειν ἐνδέχεται τῷ αὐτῷ: τῶν μὲν γὰρ ἐναντίων θάτερον στέρησίς ἐστιν οὐχ ἧττον, οὐσίας δὲ στέρησις:

But since it is impossible for contradictories to be true of the same subject at the same time, it is evident that contraries cannot belong to the same subject at the same time, for one of two contraries is a privation.

Non vero minus substantiae privatio negatio est ab aliquo genere determinato. Si igitur impossibile est simul affirmare et negare vere, impossibile est contraria simul inesse, sed vel quo ambo vel quo alterum: alterum vero simpliciter aut non.

ἡ δὲ στέρησις ἀπόφασίς ἐστιν ἀπό {20} τινος ὡρισμένου γένους: εἰ οὖν ἀδύνατον ἅμα καταφάναι καὶ ἀποφάναι ἀληθῶς, ἀδύνατον καὶ τἀναντία ὑπάρχειν ἅμα, ἀλλ᾽ ἢ πῇ ἄμφω ἢ θάτερον μὲν πῇ θάτερον δὲ ἁπλῶς.

But a privation is nothing less than the negation of substance from some determinate genus. Therefore, if it is impossible to affirm and deny something truly at the same time, it is also impossible for contraries to belong to the same subject at the same time, but either both belong in a certain respect, or the one in a certain respect and the other absolutely.

---

708. Disputat contra illos, qui praedictam rationem non ex ratione, sed ex pertinacia susceperunt: et circa hoc duo facit.

Primo ponit qualiter isti moventur ad hanc opinionem ponendam.

Secundo ostendit qualiter est resistendum, ibi, *qui vero vim in solo verbo* et cetera.

Dicit ergo primo, quod praeter praedictos qui in praedictam opinionem ex quibusdam dubitationibus inciderunt, sunt aliqui qui interrogant *persuasos in his*, scilicet opinionibus, idest deceptos, ut eos in deceptione detineant, et has solas rationes habent ad suam opinionem confirmandam.

Alia translatio habet: *sunt autem quidam qui deficiunt sive dubitant huiusmodi persuasorum has rationes solum dicentium.*

Et est sensus, quia quidam deceptorum, qui praedictam opinionem tenent, has solas dubitationes tenent, et his rationibus utuntur, quae infra dicentur.

Si enim dicatur eis quod inter contrarias opiniones credendum est magis sanis quam infirmis, et sapientibus quam ignorantibus, et vigilantibus quam dormientibus, ipsi iterato quaerunt quomodo possit diiudicari sanus per certitudinem ab infirmo, et vigilans a dormiente, et sapiens a stulto:

708. He argues against those who adopted the above-mentioned theory not because of any reason, but merely because they are obstinate, and in regard to this he does two things.

First (1011a3; [708]), he shows how these men were moved to adopt this opinion;

second (1011a15; [711]), how this opinion must be dealt with, at *but those who*.

He accordingly first says (1011a3) that besides the foregoing thinkers who adopted the above-mentioned opinion because of certain difficulties, there are some among *those who have been convinced by theories of this kind*, or opinions (that is, those who continue to deceive themselves and have only these arguments to support their view), who raise a question.

Another translation reads: *now there are some, both of those who have been convinced by theories of this kind and of those who merely state them, who are puzzled or raise a question.*

And this statement means that some of those who are puzzled, that is, some of those who hold the above-mentioned opinion, consider only these difficulties and use the arguments which are given below.

For if someone says to them that in the case of contrary opinions we should believe those persons who are healthy rather than those who are ill, and those who are wise rather than those who are ignorant, and those who are awake rather than those who are asleep, they will immediately ask how it is possible to distinguish with certainty between a healthy person and a sick one, and between one who is awake and one who is asleep, and between one who is wise and one who is foolish.

et breviter in omnibus diversitatibus opinionum quomodo potest discerni quis illorum iudicat recte in omnibus, cum quibusdam videatur aliquis esse sapiens qui aliis videtur stultus, et sic de aliis.

709. Sed istae dubitationes stultae sunt. Similes enim sunt illi dubitationi, qua dubitatur, utrum nunc dormiamus, an vigilemus. Horum enim omnium distinctio per se non est. Omnes autem dubitationes praedictae idem valent, quia ex eadem radice procedunt.

Volunt enim isti sophistae quod omnium possent accipi rationes demonstrativae. Patet enim quod ipsi quaerebant accipere aliquod principium, quod esset eis quasi regula ad discernendum inter infirmum et sanum, inter vigilantem et dormientem. Nec erant contenti istam regulam qualitercumque scire, sed eam volebant per demonstrationem accipere.

Ergo quod ipsi decepti sunt, manifestum est in eorum actibus secundum quod diximus. Ex quibus apparet quod positio eorum sit falsa. Nam si aequaliter efficax esset iudicium dormientis et vigilantis, eadem sequerentur in actibus hominum ex utroque iudicio; quod patet esse falsum.

Alia litera habet: *quandoque vero quod non persuasi sunt*: et est sententia convenientior praemissis. Ipsi enim licet hoc ponant et oretenus quaerant, non tamen mente in hoc decipiuntur quod credant similiter esse verum iudicium dormientis et vigilantis; quod ex eorum actibus patet, ut dictum est.

710. Sed quamvis non sint decepti ut in hoc dubitent, haec *tamen est passio eorum*, idest infirmitas mentis quod quaerunt rationem demonstrativam eorum quorum non est demonstratio. Nam *principium demonstrationis non est demonstratio*, idest de eo demonstratio esse non potest. Et hoc est eis facile ad credendum, quia non est hoc difficile sumere etiam per demonstrationem. Ratio enim demonstrativa probat quod non omnia demonstrari possunt, quia sic esset abire in infinitum.

711. Deinde cum dicit *qui vero* disputat contra istos, vel contra alios, qui nec hac ratione moventur ad ponendum omnia apparentia esse vera, quia non potest per demonstrationem accipi regula, per quam certitudinaliter possit discerni inter iudicantes vere et non vere, sed solum ex quadam protervia rationem praedictam ponunt. Et circa hoc tria facit.

Primo ostendit quod tales protervientes tendant ducere ad impossibile.

In short, regarding all differences of opinion, they will ask how it is possible to decide which one of these judges rightly in each particular case. For a man may seem to be wise to some and foolish to others, and the same applies in other cases.

709. But these questions are foolish, for they are similar to the question of whether we are now asleep or awake: the distinction between all of these is not *per se*. Yet all of the foregoing difficulties amount to the same thing, since they have a common root.

For these sophists desire that demonstrative arguments should be given for all things, for it is obvious that they wanted to take some starting point which would be for them a kind of rule whereby they could distinguish between those who are healthy and those who are ill, and between those who are awake and those who are asleep. And they were not content to know this rule in just any way at all, but wanted to acquire it by demonstration.

That these men were in error, then, becomes evident from their actions, according to what has been said. And from these considerations it appears that their position is false, for if the judgments of one who is asleep and of one who is awake were equally good, then the same thing would result from each judgment when men act. But this is clearly false.

Another text says, *yet they make evident in their actions that sometimes they are not convinced*, and this statement is the clearer one in the light of the things laid down above. For although these men maintain this view and raise such questions, still they are not deceived in their own mind so that they believe the judgment of one who is asleep and the judgment of one who is awake to be equally true. And this is clear from their actions, as has been pointed out.

710. But even though they are not deceived so as to be perplexed in this matter, *this is characteristic of them*, namely, this weakness of mind where they seek a demonstrative argument for things for which no demonstration can be given. For *the starting point of demonstration is not demonstration*; that is, there can be no demonstration of it. And this is easy for them to believe, because this too is not difficult to grasp by demonstration. For a demonstrative argument proves that not all things can be demonstrated, otherwise there would be an infinite regress.

711. *But those who* (1011a15). He now argues against the other philosophers, namely, against those who were not moved to maintain that all appearances are true on the grounds that no rule can be established demonstratively whereby it is possible to distinguish with certainty between those who judge rightly and those who do not, but who hold the above-mentioned theory or view only because they are insolent. In regard to this he does three things.

First (1011a15; [711]), he shows that such insolence tends to lead to an impossible conclusion.

Secundo qualiter resistendum est eis apparenter, ibi, *verum si non omnia*.

Tertio qualiter eis obviandum est secundum veritatem, ibi, *et sicut praedictum est* et cetera.

Dicit ergo primo, quod illi qui quaerunt *vim in solo verbo*, idest qui non moventur ex aliqua ratione, nec propter difficultatem alicuius dubitationis, nec propter defectum demonstrationis, sed solum verbis innituntur, et credunt quod omnia possunt dicere quae improbari non possunt, isti tales quaerunt ducere ad aliquod impossibile. Volunt enim ad hoc ducere, quod contraria sint simul vera, per hoc quod omnia apparentia sunt vera.

712. Deinde cum dicit *verum si* docet ex eorum positione eis resistere, et praedictum inconveniens evitare; dicens, quod nisi ponantur omnia quae sunt esse ad aliquod, non potest dici, quod omne apparens sit verum. Si enim sunt quaedam in rebus, quae secundum se habent esse absolutum, non per relationis sensum vel opinionem, non idem erit eis esse quod apparere: hoc enim dicit relationem ad sensum vel opinionem, quia apparens alicui apparet. Et ita oportebit quod non apparens sit verum. Patet igitur quod quicumque dicit omnia apparentia esse vera, facit omnia entia esse ad aliquid, scilicet in respectu ad opinionem vel sensum.

Et ideo contra praedictos sophistas, qui quaerunt vim in oratione, si aliquis dignetur eis *dare orationem*, idest concedere hanc positionem, quam ipsi ponunt, custodiendum sive observandum est eis ne deducantur ad concedendum contradictoria simul esse vera; quia non est dicendum absolute quod omne apparens est verum; sed quod apparet, est verum cui apparet, et quantum apparet, et quando apparet et sicut apparet: hoc enim licitum erat nobis apponere, ex quo res non habent esse absolutum, sed relativum tantum.

713. Ideo autem hoc observandum est volentibus hanc positionem concedere, quia si aliquis concedat eis quod omne apparens est verum, et ita non concedat cum praedictis determinationibus, sicut dictum est, sequeretur quod statim dicat contraria simul esse vera. Contingit enim quod idem secundum visum videtur mel propter similem colorem mellis, et secundum gustum non mel propter dissimilem saporem. Et similiter cum duo oculi sint dissimiles, non eadem est visio quae fit per utrumque oculum, vel non eadem videntur utrique visui qui fit per utrumque oculum.

Second (1011a18; [712]), he indicates the way in which it seems necessary to oppose them, at *yet if not all things*.

Third (1011b4; [716]), he explains how we must meet their argument from the viewpoint of truth, at *and, as has been*.

He accordingly first says (1011a15) that *those who seek compulsion merely in words*—that is, those who are not moved by any reason, or because of the difficulty involved in some problem, or because of some failure in demonstration, but depend solely on words and believe that they can say anything which cannot be disproved—such people as these want to argue to an impossible conclusion. For they want to adopt the principle that contraries are true at the same time on the grounds that all appearances are true.

712. *Yet if not all* (1011a18). Then he shows how we may oppose these men by using their own position and avoid the foregoing impossible conclusion. He says that, unless everything which exists is claimed to be relative, it cannot be said that every appearance is true. For if there are some things in the world which have absolute being and are not relative to perception or to opinion, being and appearing will not be the same. For appearing implies a relation to perception or to opinion, because that which appears, appears to someone; thus whatever is not an appearance must be true. It is clear, then, that whoever says that all appearances are true makes all beings relative to perception or to opinion.

Hence, in opposing the foregoing sophists who seek compulsion in words, we may say that, if anyone thinks it fitting *to maintain this view*, that is, to concede this opinion which they maintain, he must be careful or observant lest he be led to admit that contradictories are true at the same time. For it should not be said unqualifiedly that everything which appears is true, but that what appears is true for the one to whom it appears, and inasmuch as it appears, and when it appears, and in the manner in which it appears. We would be allowed to add these qualifications on the grounds that a thing does not have being in an absolute sense, but only relatively.

713. Now this should be noted by those who want to adopt this position, because if someone were to grant them that every appearance is true, and thus not admit the above-mentioned qualifications, as has been stated, it would follow immediately that he is saying that contraries are true at the same time. For it is possible that the same thing may appear to be honey to the sense of sight because its color resembles that of honey, and not appear to be honey to the sense of taste because it does not taste like honey. And similarly, when two eyes are unlike, the vision which is had through each is not the same, or the visual impressions which we get through each eye do not seem the same.

Ut si pupilla unius oculi infecta sit aliquo grosso vel nigro vapore, alia vero pura, videbuntur per oculum infectum omnia nigra vel obscura, per alium autem non. Ideo autem dico hoc esse custodiendum vel observandum, quia hoc est necessarium apud praedictos sophistas, qui dicunt ex causis praedictis omne apparens esse verum.

714. Et ex hoc sequi potest, quod omnia similiter sunt vera et falsa, propter hoc quod non omnibus eadem apparent, nec etiam eadem ad seipsum, cum multoties idem homo secundum idem tempus iudicet contraria secundum diversos sensus. Sicut visus iudicat esse unum, quod tactus iudicat esse duo propter variationem digitorum, qua contingit quod idem tangibile per diversa instrumenta tangibilia, scilicet tactus per diversos digitos, ad vim tactivam pervenit ac si essent duo tangibilia. Nullatenus autem eidem homini secundum eumdem sensum similiter et in eodem tempore, videtur quod hoc sit verum, scilicet contraria simul esse.

715. Ideo autem forsan est necessarium sic respondere praedictis sophistis, qui dicunt non propter dubitationem sed orationis causa, quasi ex protervia ipsam orationem propter seipsam concedentibus, quia hoc non est verum simpliciter, sed huic verum. Ex hoc enim non sequitur contradictoria simul esse vera. Esse enim huic verum, et non esse verum illi, non est contradictorium.

716. Deinde cum dicit *et sicut* docet resistere sophistis praedictis secundum veritatem, et non solum ad hominem; scilicet non concedendo falsam opinionem, quam ipsi ponunt. Et hoc duabus rationibus:

quarum prima sic dicit. Sicut dictum est prius, si omne apparens est verum, necesse *est facere omnia ad aliquid*, scilicet ad opinionem et sensum. Et ex hoc sequitur hoc inconveniens quod nihil sit, nec fiat, nullo opinante. Si autem hoc falsum est, quia multa sunt et fiunt de quibus nulla est opinio vel cognitio, sicut quae sunt in profundo maris vel in visceribus terrae, manifestum est quod non omnia sunt ad aliquid, idest ad opinionem et sensum. Et ita non omne apparens est verum.

717. Deinde cum dicit *amplius si* ponit secundam rationem, dicens, quod unum non refertur nisi ad unum; et non ad quodcumque unum, sed ad unum determinatum. Sicut patet quod sint idem subiecto dimidium et aequale; non tamen ad aequale dicitur duplum, sed magis ad dimidium. Aequale vero dicetur ad aequale. Et similiter si ipse homo qui est opinans sit etiam opinatus, non refertur homo ad opinans inquantum est opinans, sed inquantum est opinatus. Si igitur omnia

For example, if the pupil of one eye were infected by some gross or dark vapor, and the other were free of this, all things would seem dark or obscure through the infected eye but not through the good one. I say, then, that one must be careful or observant because this is necessary in confronting the foregoing sophists, who say, for the reasons given above (1011a3; [708]), that every appearance is true.

714. And from this position it would also follow that all things are equally true and false, because they do not appear the same to all men or even the same to one man, since the same man very often makes contrary judgments about the same thing at the same time on the basis of different senses. For example, sight judges that thing to be one which touch judges to be two, because when the fingers are crossed it happens that the same tangible object is sensed by different organs of touch; that is, the contact through different fingers affects the tactual power as though there were two tangible objects. But it does not seem to the same man through the same sense and in the same way and at the same time that contraries are true at once.

715. Therefore, it is perhaps necessary to use this answer against the above-mentioned sophists who argue thus not because of some difficulty but for the sake of argument (as though upholding this statement for its own sake because they are perverse)—namely, that this is not true absolutely, but true for this person. For it does not follow from this that contradictories are true at the same time, because it is not contradictory that something should be true for one person and not true for another.

716. *And, as has been said* (1011b4). He tells us that we should oppose the foregoing sophists from the standpoint of the truth and not just offer an argument *ad hominem*, namely, not by granting the false opinion which they maintain. And he does this by means of two arguments.

The first is this. As has been stated before, if everything which appears is true, they must *make everything relative* to perception or to opinion. Now from this the untenable position follows that nothing may exist or come to be if it is not thought of in some way. But if this is false (because many things are and come to be of which there is neither opinion nor knowledge, for example, things that exist in the depths of the sea or in the bowels of the earth), it is evident that not all things are relative to perception or to opinion. Hence not every appearance is true.

717. *Further, if a thing* (1011b7). He gives the second argument. He says that what is one is relative only to one thing, and not to any one thing at all but to a determinate one. For example, it is clear that the half and the equal may be the same in their subject, yet the double is not said to be relative to the equal but rather to the half. But equal is said to be relative to equal. Similarly, if man himself as a thinking subject is also the object of thought, man is not relative to the thinking subject as a thinking subject, but

entia inquantum sunt huiusmodi, referuntur ad opinans inquantum opinans est, sequetur quod hoc quod dico opinans non sit unum, cum ad unum non referatur nisi unum, sed infinita secundum speciem, cum infinita referantur ad ipsum; quod est impossibile. Unde non potest dici quod omnia relative dicantur ad opinans, nec per consequens quod omne apparens vel opinans sit verum.

718. Deinde cum dicit *igitur quia* concludit conclusionem suam intentam: et circa hoc duo facit.

Primo ponit ipsam principalem conclusionem.

Secundo inducit quoddam corollarium ex ea, ibi, *si igitur impossibile*.

Dicit ergo primo, quod ex praedictis patet, quod inter omnes opiniones vel sententias ista est firmissima, qua dicitur oppositas dictiones sive propositiones sive contradictiones non simul esse veras. Et etiam dictum est quae inconvenientia accidunt dicentibus eas simul esse veras, et ex qua causa moti sunt ad illa dicendum.

719. Deinde cum dicit *quoniam autem* concludit corollarium, dicens, ex dictis, quod quia impossibile est simul contradictionem verificari de eodem, manifestum est, quod nec etiam contraria eidem inesse possunt; quia manifestum est quod non minus in contrariis alterum eorum est privatio, quam in aliis oppositis, licet utrumque contrariorum sit natura aliqua; quod non est in affirmatione et negatione, vel in privatione et habitu. Alterum enim eorum est imperfectum respectu alterius, sicut nigrum respectu albi, et amarum respectu dulcis. Et sic habet privationem quamdam adiunctam.

Privatio autem est *aliqua negatio substantiae*, idest in aliquo subiecto determinato. Et est etiam ab aliquo genere determinato. Est enim negatio infra genus. Non enim omne non videns dicitur caecum, sed solum in genere videntium. Sic igitur patet quod contrarium includit privationem, et privatio est quaedam negatio. Si igitur impossibile est simul affirmare et negare, impossibile est contraria simul inesse eidem simpliciter, sed vel *ambo insunt quo*, idest secundum aliquid, sicut quando utrumque in potentia vel secundum partem, vel unum secundum quid et alterum simpliciter: sicut quando unum est in actu et alterum est in potentia; vel unum secundum plures et principaliores partes, alterum tantum secundum aliquam partem, sicut Aethiops est niger simpliciter et albus dente.

as the object of thought. If, then, all beings are relative to a thinking subject as such, it follows that what I call the thinking subject is not one, since one is relative only to one, but it is an infinite number of things in species, since an infinite number of things are related to it. But this is impossible. Hence it cannot be said that all things are said to be relative to a thinking subject, or that everything which appears so, or is thought to be so, is therefore true.

718. *Let this suffice* (1011b13). He now draws his intended conclusion, and in regard to this he does two things.

First, he draws his main conclusion;

second (1011b15; [719]), he derives a corollary from it, at *but since it is impossible*.

He accordingly first says (1011b13) that it is clear from the above statement that the most certain of all opinions or views is the one which states that opposite statements or propositions (that is, contradictory ones) are not true at the same time. And the impossible conclusions which face those who say that they are true at the same time and the reason which moved them to say this have also been explained.

719. *But since it is impossible* (1011b15). He draws the corollary. He says that since it is impossible from what has been said for two contradictories to be true of the same subject at the same time, it is also evident that contraries cannot belong to the same subject. For the privative character of one of two contraries is no less evident in the case of contraries than it is in the case of other opposites, although each of two contraries is a positive reality, for it does not consist in affirmation and negation or in privation and possession. For one of them is imperfect when compared with the other, as black when compared with white, and bitter with sweet; thus it has a kind of privation added to it.

But privation is *negation of substance*, that is, in some determinate subject. And it is also the deprivation of some determinate genus; for it is a negation within a genus. For not everything which does not see is said to be blind, but only that which is found in the genus of seeing things. It is clear, then, that a contrary includes privation, and that privation is a kind of negation. Hence, if it is impossible both to affirm and to deny something at the same time, it is also impossible for contraries to belong absolutely to the same subject at the same time, but either *both belong in a certain respect*, that is, relatively (as when both are present potentially or partially, or one is present in a certain respect and the other absolutely), or one is present in many and the more important parts, and the other only in some part (for example, an Ethiopian is black absolutely and white as regards his teeth).

LECTURE 16

Contradictories have no intermediate

1011b23 Verum nec inter contradictiones quicquam medium esse contingit; sed necessarium aut dicere aut negare unum de unoquoque. Palam autem, primum quidem definientibus quid verum est et falsum. Dicere namque ens non esse, aut non ens esse, falsum. Ens autem esse et non ens non esse, verum est. Quare qui dixerit ita esse aut non esse, verum dicet aut mentietur: sed neque ens dicet non esse, aut esse, neque non ens. [720]

1011b29 Amplius autem medium erit contradictionis, quemadmodum viride nigri et albi, quemadmodum neutrum hominis et equi. [722]

Siquidem igitur sic, non permutabitur. Nam ex bono in non bonum permutatur, aut ex hoc in bonum;

nunc autem semper apparet. Non est enim permutatio nisi in contraria et media. Si autem est medium, et sic utique erit aliqua in album non ex non albo generatio. Nunc autem non videtur.

1012a2 Amplius omne sententiale et intellectuale mens aut affirmat aut negat. Hoc autem ex definitione palam, quia verum dicit aut mentitur. Quando quidem sic componit dicens aut negans, verum didt: quando autem non sic, mentitur. [725]

1012a5 Amplius autem praeter omnes oportet esse contradictiones, nisi orationis causa dicatur. Quare nec verum dicit aliquis, nec non verum, et praeter ens et non ens, erit. Quare et praeter generationem et corruptionem, transmutatio quaedam erit. [726]

ἀλλὰ μὴν οὐδὲ μεταξὺ ἀντιφάσεως ἐνδέχεται εἶναι οὐθέν, ἀλλ' ἀνάγκη ἢ φάναι ἢ ἀποφάναι ἓν καθ' ἑνὸς ὁτιοῦν. {25} δῆλον δὲ πρῶτον μὲν ὁρισαμένοις τί τὸ ἀληθὲς καὶ ψεῦδος. τὸ μὲν γὰρ λέγειν τὸ ὂν μὴ εἶναι ἢ τὸ μὴ ὂν εἶναι ψεῦδος, τὸ δὲ τὸ ὂν εἶναι καὶ τὸ μὴ ὂν μὴ εἶναι ἀληθές, ὥστε καὶ ὁ λέγων εἶναι ἢ μὴ ἀληθεύσει ἢ ψεύσεται: ἀλλ' οὔτε τὸ ὂν λέγεται μὴ εἶναι ἢ εἶναι οὔτε τὸ μὴ ὄν.

ἔτι {30} ἤτοι μεταξὺ ἔσται τῆς ἀντιφάσεως ὥσπερ τὸ φαιὸν μέλανος καὶ λευκοῦ, ἢ ὡς τὸ μηδέτερον ἀνθρώπου καὶ ἵππου.

εἰ μὲν οὖν οὕτως, οὐκ ἂν μεταβάλλοι (ἐκ μὴ ἀγαθοῦ γὰρ εἰς ἀγαθὸν μεταβάλλει ἢ ἐκ τούτου εἰς μὴ ἀγαθόν),

νῦν δ' ἀεὶ φαίνεται (οὐ γὰρ ἔστι μεταβολὴ ἀλλ' ἢ εἰς τὰ ἀντικείμενα {35} καὶ μεταξύ): εἰ δ' ἔστι μεταξύ, καὶ οὕτως εἴη ἄν τις εἰς λευκὸν οὐκ ἐκ μὴ λευκοῦ γένεσις, νῦν δ' οὐχ ὁρᾶται.

ἔτι πᾶν τὸ διανοητὸν καὶ νοητὸν ἡ διάνοια ἢ κατάφησιν ἢ ἀπόφησιν—τοῦτο δ' ἐξ ὁρισμοῦ δῆλον—ὅταν ἀληθεύῃ ἢ ψεύδηται: ὅταν μὲν ὡδὶ συνθῇ φᾶσα ἢ ἀποφᾶσα, ἀληθεύει, {5} ὅταν δὲ ὡδί, ψεύδεται.

ἔτι παρὰ πάσας δεῖ εἶναι τὰς ἀντιφάσεις, εἰ μὴ λόγου ἕνεκα λέγεται: ὥστε καὶ οὔτε ἀληθεύσει {7} τις οὔτ' οὐκ ἀληθεύσει, καὶ παρὰ τὸ ὂν καὶ τὸ μὴ ὂν ἔσται, ὥστε καὶ παρὰ γένεσιν καὶ φθορὰν μεταβολή τις ἔσται.

Neither can there be an intermediate between contradictories, but of each subject it is necessary either to affirm or to deny one thing. This first becomes evident when people define what truth and falsity are. For to say that that which is, is not, or that which is not, is, is false; to say that which is, is, or that which is not, is not, is true. Hence he who affirms that something is or is not will say either what is true or what is false. But neither what is nor what is not is said to be or not to be.

Further, an intermediate between contradictories will be such either in the way that green is an intermediate between white and black, or as what is neither a man nor a horse is an intermediate between a man and a horse.

If it is of the latter sort, there will then be no change, for change is from what is good to what is not-good, or from the latter to the former.

But that this now occurs is always apparent, for change takes place only between opposites and intermediates. But if it is a true intermediate, then in this case there will be a kind of change to something white, but not from what is not-white. However, this is not now apparent.

Further, the mind either affirms or denies every sensible and intelligible object. This is clear from the definition, because it expresses what is true or what is false. Indeed, when the mind composes in this way by affirming or denying, it says what is true, and when it does it otherwise, it says what is false.

Again, there must be an intermediate in addition to all contradictories, unless one is arguing for the sake of argument. In that case one will say what is neither true nor false. And then there will be something else besides being and non-being; therefore, there will also be some kind of change besides generation and corruption.

1012a9 Amplius in quibuscumque generibus negatio contrarium inest, his etiam erit: ut in numeris, nec par nec impar numerus. Sed impossibile. Ex definitione vero palam. [728]

ἔτι ἐν ὅσοις γένεσιν ἡ ἀπόφασις τὸ ἐναντίον ἐπιφέρει, {10} καὶ ἐν τούτοις ἔσται, οἷον ἐν ἀριθμοῖς οὔτε περιττὸς οὔτε οὐ περιττὸς ἀριθμός· ἀλλ᾽ ἀδύνατον· ἐκ τοῦ ὁρισμοῦ δὲ δῆλον.

Again, there will also be an intermediate in all those genera of things in which the negation of a term implies its contrary. For example, in the genus of numbers, there will be a number which is neither even nor odd. But this is impossible, as is evident from the definition.

1012a12 Amplius in infinitum vadet, et non solum hemiolia quae sunt erunt, sed plura. Iterum enim est hoc negare ad dictionem et negationem, et hoc erit aliquid. Nam substantia est quaedam eius alia. [729]

ἔτι εἰς ἄπειρον βαδιεῖται, καὶ οὐ μόνον ἡμιόλια τὰ ὄντα ἔσται ἀλλὰ πλείω. πάλιν γὰρ ἔσται ἀποφῆσαι τοῦτο πρὸς τὴν φάσιν καὶ τὴν ἀπόφασιν, καὶ τοῦτ᾽ ἔσται τι· ἡ {15} γὰρ οὐσία ἐστί τις αὐτοῦ ἄλλη.

Further, there will be an infinite regress, and there will be things that are related not only as half again as much, but even more. For it will also be possible to deny the intermediate with reference both to its affirmation and to its negation. And this again will be something, for its substance is something different.

1012a15 Amplius quando interroganti si est album, dicit quoniam non: nihil aliud negavit quam ipsum esse. Negatio vero est quae non esse. [730]

ἔτι ὅταν ἐρομένου εἰ λευκόν ἐστιν εἴπῃ ὅτι οὔ, οὐδὲν ἄλλο ἀποπέφηκεν ἢ τὸ εἶναι· ἀπόφασις δὲ τὸ μὴ εἶναι.

Again, when one answers "no" to the question of whether a thing is white, he has denied nothing except that it is, and its not-being is a negation.

1012a17 Evenit autem quibusdam ea opinio sicut aliae inopinabilium. Quoniam enim solvere non possum orationes contentiosas, annuentes orationi, confirmant verum esse quod est syllogizatum. Hi quidem igitur propter talem causam dicunt. Illi vero propter omnium rationem inquirendam. [731]

ἐλήλυθε δ᾽ ἐνίοις αὕτη ἡ δόξα ὥσπερ καὶ ἄλλαι τῶν παραδόξων· ὅταν γὰρ λύειν μὴ δύνωνται λόγους ἐριστικούς, ἐνδόντες τῷ λόγῳ σύμφασιν ἀληθὲς {20} εἶναι τὸ συλλογισθέν. οἱ μὲν οὖν διὰ τοιαύτην αἰτίαν λέγουσιν, οἱ δὲ διὰ τὸ πάντων ζητεῖν λόγον.

Now some men have formed this opinion in the same way that other unreasonable opinions have been formed; for when they cannot refute eristic arguments, they assent to the argument and claim that the conclusion is true. Some men hold this view, then, for this reason, and others because they seek an explanation for everything.

1012a21 Principium autem ad hos omnes ex definitione. Definitio vero fit ex significare aliquid necessario res esse. Ratio namque cuius nomen est signum, definitio est rei. [733]

ἀρχὴ δὲ πρὸς ἅπαντας τούτους ἐξ ὁρισμοῦ. ὁρισμὸς δὲ γίγνεται ἐκ τοῦ σημαίνειν τι ἀναγκαῖον εἶναι αὐτούς· ὁ γὰρ λόγος οὗ τὸ ὄνομα σημεῖον ὁρισμὸς ἔσται.

The starting point to be used against all of these people is the definition, and the definition results from the necessity of them meaning something; for the concept, of which the word is a sign, is a definition.

1012a24 Videtur autem Heracliti quidem oratio dicens omnia esse et non esse, omnia vera facere. Quae vero Anaxagorae, esse aliquid medium contradictionis. Quare omnia falsa. Nam quando miscentur, nec bonum nec non bonum est mixtum. Quare nihil est dicere verum. [734]

ἔοικε δ᾽ ὁ μὲν Ἡρακλείτου {25} λόγος, λέγων πάντα εἶναι καὶ μὴ εἶναι, ἅπαντα ἀληθῆ ποιεῖν, ὁ δ᾽ Ἀναξαγόρου, εἶναί τι μεταξὺ τῆς ἀντιφάσεως, πάντα ψευδῆ· ὅταν γὰρ μιχθῇ, οὔτε ἀγαθὸν οὔτε οὐκ ἀγαθὸν τὸ μῖγμα, ὥστ᾽ οὐδὲν εἰπεῖν ἀληθές.

Now the statement of Heraclitus, which says that all things are and are not, seems to make all things true. And the statement of Anaxagoras that there is an intermediate between contradictories seems to make everything false, for when all things are mixed together, the mixture is neither good nor not good, so that it is impossible to say anything true.

---

720. Postquam disputavit contra ponentes contradictoria simul esse vera, hic disputat contra ponentes esse medium inter contradictionem: hi enim dicunt non semper alteram partem contradictionis esse veram. Et circa hoc duo facit.

Primo disputat contra ipsam positionem.

720. Having argued dialectically against those who maintain that contradictories are true at the same time, Aristotle now argues against those who maintain that there is an intermediate between contradictories; for these thinkers do not always say that the one or the other part of a contradiction is true. In regard to this he does two things.

First (1011b23; [720]), he argues against this position.

Secundo contra quasdam alias quaestiones inopinabiles, hanc et superiorem positionem comitantes, ibi, *his autem definitis.*

Circa primum duo facit.

Primo ponit rationes contra dictam positionem.

Secundo ostendit causam, quare aliqui moti sunt ad positionem illam ponendam, ibi, *evenit autem quibusdam* et cetera.

Circa primum ponit septem rationes:

dicens primo, quod sicut contradictoria non possunt simul esse vera, ita nec potest esse medium inter contradictionem; sed de unoquoque necessarium est aut affirmare aut negare.

721. Et hoc manifestum est primo ex definitione veri vel falsi: non enim aliud est magis falsum quam dicere non esse quod est, aut esse quod non est. Et nihil aliud est magis verum quam dicere esse quod est, aut non esse quod non est.

Patet igitur, quod quicumque dicit aliquid esse, aut dicit verum, aut dicit falsum: si dicit verum, oportet ita esse, quia verum est esse quod est. Si dicit falsum, oportet illud non esse, quia falsum nihil aliud est quam non esse quod est.

Et similiter si dicit hoc non esse, si dicit falsum, oportet esse; si verum, oportet non esse; ergo de necessitate aut affirmativa aut negativa est vera.

Sed ille, qui ponit medium inter contradictionem, non dicit quod necesse sit dicere de ente esse vel non esse, neque quod necesse sit de non ente. Et ita nec affirmans nec negans, de necessitate dicit verum vel falsum.

722. Deinde cum dicit *amplius autem* secundam rationem ponit; quae talis est. Medium inter duo aliqua accipi potest uno modo vel participatione utriusque extremi, quod est medium in eodem genere, sicut viride vel pallidum inter album et nigrum. Alio modo per abnegationem, quod etiam est diversum in genere, sicut inter hominem et equum, quod nec est homo, nec est equus, ut lapis.

Si ergo inter contradictoria est medium, aut hoc erit primo modo, aut secundo:

723. Si secundo modo, tunc nihil permutatur: quod sic patet. Omnis enim permutatio est ex non bono in bonum, aut ex bono in non bonum. Quare etiam cum est mutatio inter contraria, ut inter album et nigrum, est mutatio inter contradictorie opposita.

Second (1012a29; [736]), he argues against certain other unreasonable questions which follow from this position and from the one above, at *with these points*.

In regard to the first he does two things.

First, he raises arguments against the position mentioned.

Second (1012a17; [730]), he gives the reason why some thinkers have been moved to hold this position, at *now some men*.

In regard to the first part he gives seven arguments.

He first says (1011b23) that, just as contradictories cannot be true at the same time, neither can there be an intermediate between contradictories, but it is necessary either to affirm or to deny one or the other.

721. This first becomes evident from the definition of truth and falsity; for to say what is false is simply to say that that which is, is not or that that which is not is. And to say what is true is simply to say that that which is, is, or that that which is not, is not.

It is clear, then, that whoever says that something is says either what is true or what is false; if he says what is true, it must be so, because to say what is true is to say that what is is. And if he says what is false, it must not be so, because to say what is false is simply to say that what is, is not.

The same thing applies if he says that something is not, for if he says what is false, it must be; if he says what is true, it must not be. Therefore, either the affirmation or the negation is necessarily true.

But he who holds that there is an intermediate between contradictories does not claim that it is necessary to say that what is either is or is not; nor does he claim that it is necessary to speak in this way about what is not. Thus neither he who affirms nor he who denies need say what is true or what is false.

722. *Further, an intermediate* (1011b29). He gives the second argument, which runs thus. An intermediate between any two contradictories can be understood in one way as something that participates in each of the extremes, and this is an intermediate in the same genus—as green or yellow is an intermediate between white and black—or in another way as something that is the negation of each extreme, and such an intermediate is different in genus—for example, a stone, which is neither a man nor a horse, is an intermediate between a man and a horse.

Therefore, if there is an intermediate between contradictories, it will be such either in the first way or in the second.

723. If it is an intermediate in the second way, there will be no change. This becomes clear as follows. Every change is from what is not-good to what is good, or from what is good to what is not-good. Hence, since change is between contraries (for example, white and black), change must take place between things that are opposed as contradictories.

Nam nigrum est non album, ut ex praedictis patet. Secundum autem praedicta non posset fieri mutatio ex non bono in bonum, vel e converso: ergo nulla esset mutatio:

cum tamen semper hoc appareat vel videatur, quod ex non bono in bonum fiat mutatio, vel e converso. Quod autem omnis talis mutatio tollatur ex praedicta positione facta, sic patet. Non enim potest esse mutatio nisi inter contraria et media quae sunt unius generis: nec potest esse mutatio de uno extremo in alterum nisi per medium.

Si igitur est medium inter contradictoria per abnegationem, idest alterius generis, nulla poterit esse mutatio de extremo in medium, et ita per consequens de extremo in extremum.

724. Si autem primo modo, scilicet quod sit medium in contradictione quasi eiusdem generis, participatione utriusque, sicut pallidum inter album et nigrum, sequitur hoc inconveniens,

quod sit aliqua generatio quae terminetur ad album, et non fiat ex non albo; quia ad unum extremum non tantum fit mutatio ex alio extremo, sed etiam ex medio. Hoc autem non videtur esse verum, scilicet quod sit aliqua generatio terminata ad album quae non fiat ex non albo. Et sic patet quod nullo modo potest esse medium in contradictione.

725. Deinde cum dicit *amplius omne* tertiam rationem ponit, quae talis est. Intellectus in omni conceptione sua, qua sentit et intelligit, aut affirmat aliquid aut negat. Ex definitione autem veri et falsi apparet quod sive aliquis affirmet sive neget, oportet ut verum dicat, aut mentiatur: quia quando intellectus sic componit vel affirmando vel negando sicut est in re, dicit; quando autem non sic, mentitur. Et ita patet quod semper oportet quod sit vera vel affirmatio vel negatio; quia oportet quod aliqua opinio sit vera, et omnis opinio affirmatio est vel negatio:

unde oportet quod semper affirmatio vel negatio sit vera: et sic non est medium in contradictione.

726. Deinde cum dicit *amplius autem* quartam rationem ponit, quae talis est. Si in contradictione ponatur medium, oportet hoc in omnibus contradictionibus dicere, quod scilicet praeter omnes contradictiones sit aliquid verum quod est medium inter eas, nisi hoc dicat *aliquis orationis causa*, idest absque omni ratione, solum quia placet ei ita dicere. Sed hoc non potest verum esse in omnibus, quia verum et non verum sunt contradictoria quaedam. Et ita sequeretur quod aliquis

For black is not white, as is clear from the above statements. But according to the foregoing position there cannot be change from what is not-good to what is good, or the reverse. Hence there will be no change.

Yet it always appears or seems that change proceeds from what is not-good to what is good, or the reverse. That every change of this sort would be destroyed if the foregoing position is true becomes clear as follows. Change can take place only between contraries and intermediates which belong to the same genus. But there can be a change from one extreme to another only through an intermediate.

Therefore, if there is an intermediate between contradictories as the negation of both—that is, as something belonging to a different genus—it will be impossible for change to take place between an extreme and an intermediate, and therefore between one extreme and another.

724. And if it is an intermediate in the first way, such that the intermediate between contradictories belongs to the same genus by participating in both, as yellow is an intermediate between white and black, then an impossible conclusion follows.

There will be some process of generation which terminates in white and does not come from the not-white, because change proceeds not only from one extreme to another but also from an intermediate. But it does not seem to be true that there is any process of change terminating in the white which does not proceed from the not-white. Thus it is clear that there is no way at all in which there can be an intermediate between contradictories.

725. *Further, the mind* (1012a2). He gives the third argument, which runs thus. In every one of the conceptions by which the intellect knows or understands, it either affirms or denies something. Now from the definition of truth and falsity it seems that, whether one affirms or denies, he must say what is true or what is false. For when the intellect composes in this way, either by affirming or denying as the matter stands in reality, it expresses what is true, but when it does it otherwise, it expresses what is false. Thus it is clear that a true statement must always be either an affirmation or a negation, because some opinion must be true, and every opinion is either an affirmation or a negation.

Hence it must always be either an affirmation or a negation that is true. Thus there is no intermediate between contradictories.

726. *Again, there must* (1012a5). Then he gives the fourth argument, which runs thus. If one maintains that there must be an intermediate between contradictories, then it is necessary to say that, in the case of all contradictories, there must be besides the contradictories themselves something true which is an intermediate between them, unless this person is arguing *for the sake of argument*, that is, without any real reason, but only because it pleases him to speak in this way. But this cannot be true in all cases,

esset, qui nec verum diceret, nec non verum. Cuius contrarium patuit ex definitione veri et falsi.

727. Similiter, cum ens et non ens sint contradictoria, sequitur quod aliquid sit praeter ens et non ens. Et ita erit quaedam transmutatio praeter generationem et corruptionem. Nam generatio est transmutatio ad esse, et corruptio ad non esse; ergo in nulla contradictione erit medium.

728. Deinde cum dicit *amplius in* quintam rationem ponit, dicens, quod negatio in quibusdam generibus inest loco contrariae differentiae. Vel secundum aliam literam *negatio implet contrarium*, quia alterum contrariorum, quae necesse est esse in eodem genere, ex negatione rationem habet; sicut patet de pari et impari, iusto et iniusto. Si igitur inter affirmationem et negationem esset aliquod medium, in omnibus istis contrariis esset aliquod medium, cum affirmationem et negationem manifeste sequantur. Sicut in numero si esset aliquis numerus qui nec esset par nec impar. Hoc autem patet esse impossibile ex definitione paris et imparis. Nam par est quod potest dividi in aequalia. Impar vero quod non potest. Relinquitur ergo quod inter affirmationem et negationem non potest esse medium.

729. Deinde cum dicit *amplius in* sextam rationem ponit, quae talis est. Ponentes aliquid medium inter affirmationem et negationem, ponunt aliquod tertium praeter illa duo, quae ponunt omnes communiter, dicentes nihil inter ea esse medium.

Tria autem ad duo se habent in *hemiolia*, idest in sesquialtera proportione. Secundum igitur opinionem eorum qui ponunt inter affirmationem et negationem medium, in primo aspectu apparet quod omnia *erunt hemiolia*, idest in sesquialtera proportione ad ea quae ponuntur; quia non solum erunt affirmationes et negationes, sed etiam media.

Non solum autem hoc sequetur, sed etiam quod sint in infinitum plura. Constat enim quod omne quod contingit affirmare, contingit negare. Contingit autem affirmare haec tria esse, scilicet affirmationem, negationem, et medium; ergo contingit ista tria negare.

Et sicut negatio est aliud ab affirmatione, ita aliud erit quoddam quartum praeter tria praedicta. Erit enim eius

because the true and the not-true are contradictories. Thus it would follow that there is someone who says what is neither true nor false. But the opposite of this was made clear from the definition of truth and falsity.

727. Similarly, since being and non-being are contradictories, it will follow that there is something besides being and non-being, and thus there will be some kind of change besides generation and corruption. For generation is a change to being, and corruption a change to non-being. Therefore, there can be no intermediate between contradictories.

728. *Again, there will* (1012a9). He gives the fifth argument. He says that in some genera a negation takes the place of a contrary difference. Or, according to another text, *negation supplies the contrary*, because one of two contraries, which must be in the same genus, derives its definition from negation, as is clear in the case of the even and the odd, and the just and unjust. Therefore, if there is an intermediate between affirmation and negation, there will be some intermediate between all these contraries, since they obviously depend on affirmation and negation. For example, in the case of number, there will be some number which is neither even nor odd. But this is clearly impossible in the light of the definition of the even and the odd, for the even is what can be divided into equal numbers, and the odd is what cannot. Therefore, it follows that there cannot be an intermediate between affirmation and negation.

729. *Further, there will* (1012a12). He now gives the sixth argument: those who claim that there is an intermediate between an affirmation and a negation hold some third thing besides these two, which all posit in common, saying that there is nothing intermediate between them.

But three is related to two *as half again as much*, that is, in a proportion of one and a half to one. Therefore, according to the opinion of those who hold an intermediate between an affirmation and a negation, it appears at first sight that all things will be related *as half again as much*, that is, related to the things that are given in a proportion of one and a half to one, because there will be not only affirmations and negations but also intermediates.

And this is not the only conclusion that follows, but it also follows that there will be many more things in infinite regression. For it is evident that everything which can be affirmed can also be denied. But if it is possible to affirm that the following three things exist: an affirmation, a negation and an intermediate, it is then also possible to deny these three.

And just as a negation differs from an affirmation, in a similar way there will also be some fourth thing which

substantia et ratio alia a praedictis, sicut et negationis alia ab affirmatione.

Item ista quatuor contingit negare, et horum negatio erit verum, et sic in infinitum. Erunt igitur plura in infinitum quam modo ponantur. Quod videtur inconveniens.

730. Deinde cum dicit *amplius quando* septimam rationem ponit, quae talis est. Si quis interrogaret utrum homo vel aliquid aliud sit album, oportet quod respondens vel assentiat vel non assentiat: et si assentiat, planum est quod dicit affirmationem esse veram; si autem non assentiat respondendo non, constat quod negat. Nec negat aliquid aliud quam illud quod ille interrogavit; et ipsa negatio est non esse, quia negativa. Relinquitur igitur, quod respondens ad quaestionem, vel necesse habet concedere affirmationem, vel proferre negativam; et ita inter haec duo non est medium.

731. Deinde cum dicit *evenit autem* ostendit causam quare quidam in hanc opinionem incidunt: et circa hoc tria facit.

Primo enim ostendit quare quidam hanc opinionem posuerunt.

Secundo modum disputandi contra eos, ibi, *principium autem ad hos omnes*.

Tertio ad quas opiniones philosophorum praedictae opiniones sequuntur, ibi, *videtur autem Heracliti*.

Dicit ergo primo, quod praedicta opinio evenit quibusdam, sicut et aliae opiniones inopinabilium, ex duplici causa:

quarum prima est, quia quando aliqui non possunt solvere *orationes contentiosas*, idest rationes litigiosas sive sophisticas factas eis ab aliis vel a seipsis, consentiunt rationi probanti, et concedunt conclusionem, dicentes verum esse quod syllogizatum est. Et ulterius ipsam nituntur confirmare aliquas alias rationes adinveniendo.

732. Secunda est propter hoc, quod quidam volunt inquirere rationem probantem de omnibus; et ideo illa quae probari non possunt, nolunt concedere, sed negant. Prima autem principia quae sunt omnium conceptiones communes probari non possunt; et ideo eas negant, per hoc in positiones inopinabiles incidentes.

733. Deinde cum dicit *principium autem* ostendit ex quo principio debeat procedi contra tales opiniones; et dicit quod ex definitione veri vel falsi vel aliquorum aliorum nominum, sicut ex supra dictis rationibus patet. Necesse est enim eis concedere definitiones rerum, si ponunt quod nomina aliquid significent. Nam ratio

differs from the three mentioned; for it will have a substance and intelligible structure different from those just mentioned, in the same way that a negation has a different substance and intelligible structure from an affirmation.

And it is possible to deny these four, and the negations of these will be true, and so on to infinity. Hence there will be infinitely more things than have just been posited. This seems absurd.

730. *Again, when one* (1012a15). He gives the seventh argument, which runs as follows. If someone were to ask whether a man or some other thing is white, the one answering him must say either "yes" or "no." If he says "yes," it is plain that he says that the affirmation is true; but if he does not affirm this, but says "no," it is clear that he denies this. Now the only thing which he denies is what he was asked, and the negation of this is non-being because it is negative. Therefore, it follows that, when he answers this question, he must of necessity either admit the affirmative or assert the negative. Hence there is no intermediate between these two.

731. *Now some men* (1012a17). He gives the reason why some men adopt this opinion, and in regard to this he does three things.

First, he shows why some men have held this opinion.

Second (1012a21; [733]), he explains how one can argue dialectically against them, at *the starting point*.

Third (1012a24; [734]), he notes the philosophical views on which the foregoing opinions depend, at *now the statement*.

He accordingly first says (1012a17) that the foregoing opinion, like other unreasonable opinions, is adopted by certain thinkers for one of two reasons.

The first is this: when some men cannot refute *eristic arguments*, that is, disputatious or sophistical arguments, which are presented to them either by others or by themselves, they agree with the one giving the argument and assent to the conclusion, saying that what has been shown is true. And then they try to confirm this by devising other arguments.

732. The second reason why men adopt this position is that some men want to discover an argument to prove everything, and therefore whatever cannot be proved they do not want to affirm, but deny. But first principles, which are the common conceptions of all men, cannot be proved. Hence these men deny them, and thereby adopt unreasonable views.

733. *The starting point* (1012a21). He indicates the starting point from which one must proceed to argue against such opinions. He says that the starting point is derived from the definitions of truth and falsity, or from the definitions of other terms, as is clear from the arguments given above. For men must admit the definitions of things if

quam nomen significat est definitio rei. Si autem non concedunt omnia significare aliquid, tunc non differunt a plantis, sicut supra dictum est.

734. Deinde cum dicit *videtur autem* ostendit ad quas opiniones praedictae positiones consequuntur: et dicit quod ad positionem Heracliti, qui dicebat omnia moveri simul, et per consequens esse et non esse. Et quia id quod movetur habet non esse admixtum cum esse, sequitur quod omnia sunt vera.

735. Ad positionem vero Anaxagorae sequitur quod aliquid sit medium contradictionis. Ipse enim ponebat quod quodlibet miscetur cum quolibet, propter hoc quod quodlibet fit ex quolibet. De permixto autem neutrum extremorum potest dici; sicut colores medii nec sunt albedo nec nigredo. Unde illud quod est mixtum, nec est bonum nec non bonum, nec album nec non album. Et sic est aliquid medium contradictionis. Et per consequens sequitur omnia esse falsa. Nihil enim secundum communem opinionem ponimus nisi affirmationem et negationem. Unde si affirmatio et negatio sunt falsa, sequitur omnia falsa esse.

they hold that words signify something, for the intelligible expression of a thing which a word signifies is a thing's definition. But if they do not admit that all words signify something, they do not differ from plants, as has been said above (1008b2; [652]).

734. *Now the statement* (1012a24). Here he gives the opinion on which the foregoing opinions depend. He says that these opinions stem from the position of Heraclitus, who said that all things are in motion, and therefore that they both are and are not at the same time. And since what is being moved has non-being mixed with being, it follows that everything is true.

735. And from the position of Anaxagoras it follows that there is an intermediate between contradictories, for he held that everything is mixed with everything, because everything comes from everything. But neither of the extremes can be predicated of the mixture—for example, intermediate colors are neither whiteness nor blackness. Hence the mixture is neither good nor not-good, neither white nor not-white; thus there is an intermediate between contradictories. It follows, then, that everything is false, for according to the common opinion, we posit nothing but affirmation and negation. Hence, if both an affirmation and its negation are false, it follows that everything is false.

LECTURE 17

Nothing is both true and false, or both at rest and in motion

1012a29   His autem definitis, palam quia et univoce dicta, et de omnibus, impossibile est esse, sicut quidam dicunt. [737]

Hi quidem dicentes nihil verum esse. Nihil enim prohibere dicunt sic omnia esse, sicut diametrum commensurabilem esse. Illi vero omnia vera.

Fere namque hae orationes eaedem ipsius Heracliti. Nam qui dicit quod omnia sunt vera et omnia falsa, extra orationes has utrumque dicit. Quare si sunt impossibilia illa, et ea esse est impossibile.

1012b2   Amplius autem palam quia contradictiones sunt, quas non est possibile simul esse veras nec falsas omnes. Et hoc quidem putabitur magis contingere ex dictis. [739]

1012b5   Sed ad omnes tales orationes quaerere oportet, quemadmodum in superioribus orationibus dictum est, an esse aliquid, aut non esse, sed significare aliquid. Quare ex definitione disputare oportet, accipientes quid significat verum aut falsum. Sed si nihil aliud verum dicere quam negare falsum, impossibile omnia falsa esse. Necesse est enim contradictionis partem alteram esse veram. [740]

1012b11   Amplius si omne aut dicere aut negare est necesse, utraque falsa esse est impossibile. Altera namque pars contradictionis est falsa. [741]

1012b13   Contingit autem quod famatum est omnibus talibus rationibus ipsas seipsas destruere. Nam qui omnia vera dicit, orationis suae contrariam veram facit. Quare et suam non veram. Contraria enim non dicit ipsam esse veram. Qui vero omnia falsa, et ipse seipsum. [742]

Sed si auferant hic quidem contrariam, quia non vera sola: ille vero suam pro-

διωρισμένων δὲ τούτων φανερὸν ὅτι καὶ τὰ μοναχῶς {30} λεγόμενα καὶ κατὰ πάντων ἀδύνατον ὑπάρχειν ὥσπερ τινὲς λέγουσιν,

οἱ μὲν οὐθὲν φάσκοντες ἀληθὲς εἶναι (οὐθὲν γὰρ κωλύειν φασὶν οὕτως ἅπαντα εἶναι ὥσπερ τὸ τὴν διάμετρον σύμμετρον εἶναι), οἱ δὲ πάντ᾽ ἀληθῆ.

σχεδὸν γὰρ οὗτοι οἱ λόγοι οἱ αὐτοὶ τῷ Ἡρακλείτου· ὁ γὰρ λέγων {35} ὅτι πάντ᾽ ἀληθῆ καὶ πάντα ψευδῆ, καὶ χωρὶς λέγει τῶν λόγων ἑκάτερον τούτων, {1012b1} ὥστ᾽ εἴπερ ἀδύνατα ἐκεῖνα, καὶ ταῦτα ἀδύνατον εἶναι.

ἔτι δὲ φανερῶς ἀντιφάσεις εἰσὶν ἃς οὐχ οἷόν τε ἅμα ἀληθεῖς εἶναι—οὐδὲ δὴ ψευδεῖς πάσας· καίτοι δόξειέ γ᾽ ἂν μᾶλλον ἐνδέχεσθαι ἐκ τῶν εἰρημένων.

ἀλλὰ πρὸς πάντας τοὺς τοιούτους λόγους αἰτεῖσθαι δεῖ, καθάπερ ἐλέχθη καὶ ἐν τοῖς ἐπάνω λόγοις, οὐχὶ εἶναί τι ἢ μὴ εἶναι ἀλλὰ σημαίνειν τι, ὥστε ἐξ ὁρισμοῦ διαλεκτέον λαβόντας τί σημαίνει τὸ ψεῦδος ἢ τὸ ἀληθές. εἰ δὲ μηθὲν ἄλλο τὸ ἀληθὲς φάναι ἢ <ὃ> ἀποφάναι· ψεῦδός ἐστιν, ἀδύνατον {10} πάντα ψευδῆ εἶναι· ἀνάγκη γὰρ τῆς ἀντιφάσεως θάτερον εἶναι μόριον ἀληθές.

ἔτι εἰ πᾶν ἢ φάναι ἢ ἀποφάναι ἀναγκαῖον, ἀδύνατον ἀμφότερα ψευδῆ εἶναι· θάτερον γὰρ μόριον τῆς ἀντιφάσεως ψεῦδός ἐστιν.

συμβαίνει δὴ καὶ τὸ θρυλούμενον πᾶσι τοῖς τοιούτοις λόγοις, αὐτοὺς {15} ἑαυτοὺς ἀναιρεῖν. ὁ μὲν γὰρ πάντα ἀληθῆ λέγων καὶ τὸν ἐναντίον αὐτοῦ λόγον ἀληθῆ ποιεῖ, ὥστε τὸν ἑαυτοῦ οὐκ ἀληθῆ (ὁ γὰρ ἐναντίος οὔ φησιν αὐτὸν ἀληθῆ), ὁ δὲ πάντα ψευδῆ καὶ αὐτὸς αὑτόν.

ἐὰν δ᾽ ἐξαιρῶνται ὁ μὲν τὸν ἐναντίον ὡς οὐκ ἀληθὴς μόνος ἐστίν, ὁ δὲ τὸν αὑτοῦ

With these points settled it is evident that the theories which have been expressed univocally and about all things cannot be true as some affirm them to be.

Now some say that nothing is true (for they say that there is nothing to prevent all statements from being like the statement that the diagonal of a square is commensurable with one of its sides), and others say that everything is true.

These views are almost the same as that of Heraclitus, for he who says that all things are true and all false admits both views apart from his own words. Hence, if those are impossible, these also must be impossible.

Further, it is evident that there are contradictories which cannot be true at the same time. Nor can they all be false, though this would seem more possible from what has been said.

But in opposing all such views it is necessary to postulate, as has been stated in the above discussion (1006a18), not that something is or is not, but that a word signifies something. Hence it is necessary to argue from a definition once we have accepted what truth and falsity mean. But if to say what is true is merely to deny what is false, not everything can be false. For one part of a contradiction must be true.

Again, if everything must be either affirmed or denied, both cannot be false, for one part of a contradiction is false.

And the view commonly expressed applies to all such theories: they destroy themselves. For he who says that everything is true makes the contrary of his own statement true, and thus makes his own not true, for the contrary denies that it is true. And he who says that everything is false makes his own statement false.

But if the former makes an exception of the contrary statement, saying that it

priam, quia non falsa: nihilominus infinitas accidit eis quaerere orationes
veras et falsas. Nam qui veram orationem dicit, verus est. Et hoc in infinitum
vadit.

ὡς οὐ ψευδής, {20} οὐδὲν ἧττον ἀπείρους συμβαίνει αὐτοῖς αἰτεῖσθαι λόγους
ἀληθεῖς καὶ ψευδεῖς: ὁ γὰρ λέγων τὸν
ἀληθῆ λόγον ἀληθῆ ἀληθής, τοῦτο δ'
εἰς ἄπειρον βαδιεῖται.

alone is not true, and the latter makes
an exception of his own statement, saying
that it is not false, still they will have to
consider the truth and falsity of an infinite number of statements. For he who
says that a true statement is true is right,
and this process will go on to infinity.

1012b22 Palam autem quia neque qui omnia
quiescere dicunt, vera dicunt, nec qui
omnia moveri. [744]

φανερὸν δ' ὅτι οὐδ' οἱ πάντα ἠρεμεῖν
λέγοντες ἀληθῆ λέγουσιν οὐδ' οἱ πάντα
κινεῖσθαι.

Now it is evident that those who say that
all things are at rest do not speak the
truth, and neither do those who say that
all things are in motion.

1012b24 Nam si quiescunt omnia, semper eadem vera et falsa erunt: videtur autem
hoc transmutatum. Nam qui dicit, is
quidem aliquando non erat, et iterum
non erit. [745]

εἰ μὲν γὰρ ἠρεμεῖ πάντα, ἀεὶ ταὐτὰ ἀληθῆ καὶ {25} ψευδῆ ἔσται, φαίνεται δὲ
τοῦτο μεταβάλλον (ὁ γὰρ λέγων ποτὲ
αὐτὸς οὐκ ἦν καὶ πάλιν οὐκ ἔσται):

For if all things are at rest, the same thing
will always be true and false. But this
seems to be something that changes, for
he who makes a statement at this time
was not and again will not be.

1012b26 Si vero omnia moventur, nihil erit verum; ergo omnia falsa. Sed hoc osten-
sum est quia impossibile. [746]

εἰ δὲ πάντα κινεῖται, οὐθὲν ἔσται ἀληθές:
πάντα ἄρα ψευδῆ: ἀλλὰ δέδεικται ὅτι
ἀδύνατον.

And if all things are in motion, nothing
will be true, and so everything will be
false. But it has been shown that this is
impossible.

1012b28 Amplius autem ens permutari est necesse. Nam ex aliquo in aliquid fit permutatio. [747]

ἔτι ἀνάγκη τὸ ὂν μεταβάλλειν: ἔκ τινος
γὰρ εἴς τι ἡ μεταβολή.

Further, it must be some being which is
changed, for change is from something to
something.

1012b29 Sed nec omnia quiescunt aut moventur
aliquando, semper autem nihil. Etenim
est aliquid quod semper movet quae
moventur, et primum movens immobile ipsum. [748]

ἀλλὰ μὴν οὐδὲ πάντα ἠρεμεῖ {30} ἢ
κινεῖται ποτέ, ἀεὶ δ' οὐθέν: ἔστι γάρ τι
ὃ ἀεὶ κινεῖ τὰ κινούμενα, καὶ τὸ πρῶτον
κινοῦν ἀκίνητον αὐτό.

But it is not true that all things are at rest
or in motion sometimes, and nothing always; for there is something which always
moves the things that are being moved,
and the first mover is itself immovable.

---

736. Disputat contra quasdam positiones, quae ad
praedicta consequuntur.

Et primo contra quosdam, qui destruunt principia
logicae.

Secundo contra quosdam, qui destruunt principia
physicae, ibi, *palam autem quia neque qui omnia* et
cetera.

Philosophus enim primus debet disputare contra negantes principia singularium scientiarum, quia omnia
principia firmantur super hoc principium, quod affirmatio et negatio non sunt simul vera, et quod nihil est
medium inter ea.

Illa autem sunt propriissima huius scientiae, cum
sequantur rationem entis, quod est huius philosophiae
primum subiectum. Verum autem et falsum pertinent
proprie ad considerationem logici; consequuntur enim
ens in ratione de quo considerat logicus: nam verum et
falsum sunt in mente, ut in sexto huius habetur.

Motus autem et quies sunt proprie de consideratione
naturalis, per hoc quod natura definitur quod est principium motus et quietis. Ad errorem autem qui accidit

736. He argues dialectically against certain positions
which stem from those mentioned above.

First (1012a29; [736]), he argues against certain men
who destroy the principles of logic;

and second (1012b22; [744]), against certain men who
destroy the principles of natural philosophy, at *now it is
evident*.

For first philosophy should argue dialectically against
those who deny the principles of the particular sciences,
because all principles are based on the principle that an
affirmation and a negation are not true at the same time,
and that there is no intermediate between them.

Now these principles are the most specific principles of
this science, since they depend on the concept of being,
which is the primary subject of this branch of philosophy.
But the true and the false belong specifically to the study
of logic, for they depend on the kind of being which is
found in the mind, with which logic deals; for truth and
falsity exist in the mind, as is stated in book 6 of this work
(1027b25; [1231]).

Motion and rest, on the other hand, belong properly to
the study of natural philosophy, because nature is defined
as a principle of motion and of rest. Now the error made

circa esse et non esse, sequitur error circa verum et fal-sum: nam per esse et non esse verum et falsum definitur, ut supra habitum est. Nam verum est cum dicitur esse quod est, vel non esse quod non est. Falsum autem, e converso. Similiter autem ex errore, qui est circa esse vel non esse, sequitur error qui est circa moveri et quiescere. Nam quod movetur, inquantum huiusmodi, nondum est. Quod autem quiescit, est. Et ideo destructis errori-bus circa esse et non esse, ex consequenti destruuntur errores circa verum et falsum, quietem et motum.

737. Circa primum duo facit.

Primo ponit opiniones falsas circa verum et falsum.

Secundo reprobat eas, ibi, *amplius autem palam* et cetera.

Dicit ergo, quod *definitis*, idest determinatis prae-dictis quae erant dicenda contra praedictas inopinabiles opiniones, manifestum est quod impossibile est quod quidam dixerunt quod *univoce*, idest uno modo sen-tentiandum est de omnibus, ut dicamus omnia similiter esse falsa vel similiter esse vera.

Quidam enim dixerunt nihil esse verum, sed omnia esse falsa, et quod nihil prohibet quin dicamus omnia sic esse falsa, sicut illa est falsa, diameter est commensura-bilis lateri quadrati, quod est falsum.

Alii vero dixerunt quod omnia sunt vera. Et huius-modi orationes consequuntur ad opinionem Heracliti, sicut dictum est. Ipse enim dixit simul esse et non esse, ex quo sequitur omnia esse vera.

738. Et ne forte aliquis diceret quod praeter has opi-niones est etiam tertia, quae dicit quod omnia simul sunt vera et falsa, quasi tacitae obiectioni respondens di-cit, quod qui hoc ponit, utrumque praedictorum ponit. Unde si duae primae opiniones sunt impossibiles, illam tertiam oportet esse impossibilem.

739. Deinde cum dicit *amplius autem* ponit rationes contra praedictas opiniones; quarum prima talis. Con-stat quasdam esse contradictiones quas impossibile est simul esse veras nec simul falsas, sicut verum et non verum, ens et non ens. Et hoc magis potest sciri ex dictis. Si igitur harum contradictionum necesse est alteram esse veram et alteram falsam, non omnia sunt vera nec omnia sunt falsa.

740. Deinde cum dicit *sed ad omnes* secundam ra-tionem ponit, dicens, quod ad *istas orationes*, idest posi-

about truth and falsity is a result of the error made about being and non-being, for truth and falsity are defined by means of being and non-being, as has been said above. For there is truth when one says that what is, is, or that what is not, is not. Falsity is defined in the opposite way. And similarly the error made about rest and motion is a result of the error made about being and non-being, for what is in motion as such does not yet exist, whereas what is at rest already is. Hence, when the errors made about being and non-being have been removed, the errors made about truth and falsity and rest and motion will then also be removed.

737. Regarding the first part of this division he does two things.

First (1012a29; [737]), he gives the erroneous opinions about truth and falsity.

Second (1012b2; [739]), he criticizes these opinions, at *further, it is evident*.

Thus he says (1012a29) that, *with these points settled*, that is, with the foregoing points established which have to be used against the paradoxical positions mentioned above, it is obviously impossible that the views of some men should be true, namely, that we must form an opinion *univocally* (or think in the same way) about all things, so that we should say that all things are equally true or equally false.

For some thinkers said that nothing is true but every-thing false, and that there is nothing to prevent us from saying that all statements are just as false as the statement (which is false) that the diameter of a square is commensu-rate with one of its sides.

But others have said that all things are true. Statements of the latter kind are a result of the opinion of Heraclitus, as has been pointed out (1010a7; [684]). For he said that a thing is and is not at the same time, and from this it follows that everything is true.

738. And lest perhaps someone might say that besides these opinions there is also a third one, which states that everything is both true and false at the same time, he replies, as though meeting a tacit objection, that anyone who maintains this opinion also maintains both of the fore-going ones. Hence, if the first two opinions are impossible, the third must also be impossible.

739. *Further, it is evident* (1012b2). Then he presents arguments against the foregoing opinions, and the first of these is as follows: it is evident that there are certain con-tradictories which cannot be true at the same time or false at the same time, for example, the true and not-true, being and non-being. This can be better understood from what has been said. Therefore, if one of these two contradictories must be false and the other true, not all things can be true or all false.

740. *But in opposing* (1012b5). He gives the second argu-ment. He says that in opposing *all such views*, or positions,

tiones, non **oportet quaerere**, idest petere concedendum aliquid esse vel non esse in rebus, quemadmodum supra dictum est; quia hoc videtur petere principium. Sed hoc petendum est, quod detur nomina aliquid significare; quo non dato, disputatio tollitur. Hoc autem dato, oportet ponere definitiones, sicut iam supra dictum est.

Et ideo ex definitionibus contra eos disputare oportet, et praecipue in proposito, accipiendo definitionem falsi. Si autem non est aliud verum, quam illud affirmare, quod falsum est negare, et e converso: et similiter falsum non aliud est quam affirmare id quod negare est verum, et e converso: sequitur quod impossibile sit omnia esse falsa; quia necesse erit vel affirmationem vel negationem esse veram. Patet enim, quod verum nihil est aliud quam dicere esse quod est, vel non esse quod non est. Falsum autem, dicere non esse quod est, vel esse quod non est. Et ideo patet, quod verum est dicere illud esse, quod falsum est non esse; vel non esse, quod falsum est esse. Et falsum est dicere id esse, quod verum est non esse; vel non esse quod verum est esse. Et ita, ex definitione veri vel falsi, patet quod non sunt omnia falsa. Et ratione eadem patet quod non omnia sunt vera.

741. Deinde cum dicit **amplius si** tertiam rationem ponit, quae talis est. Constat ex praedictis, quod necesse est de quolibet aut affirmare aut negare, cum nihil sit medium in contradictione. Igitur impossibile est omnia falsa esse. Et eadem ratione probatur quod impossibile est omnia esse vera, per hoc quod ostensum est, quod non est simul affirmare et negare.

742. Deinde cum dicit **contingit autem** quartam rationem ponit, quae talis est. Ad omnes praedictas orationes, idest positiones, contingit hoc inconveniens quod seipsas destruunt. Et hoc **est famatum**, idest famosum ab omnibus dictum. Unde alius textus habet, **accidit autem et id vulgare**. Quod sic probat. Ille enim, qui dicit omnia esse vera, facit opinionem contrariam suae opinioni esse veram; sed contraria suae opinionis est quod sua opinio non sit vera: ergo qui dicit omnia esse vera, dicit suam opinionem non esse veram, et ita destruit suam opinionem. Et similiter manifestum est quod ille, qui dicit omnia esse falsa, dicit etiam seipsum dicere falsum.

743. Et quia posset aliquis dicere quod dicens omnia vera excipit aut aufert ab universalitate suam contrariam, et similiter, qui dicit omnia esse falsa excipit suam opinionem: ideo hanc responsionem excludit; et dicit, quod si ille qui dicit omnia esse vera, excipiat suam contrariam, dicens solam eam esse non veram, et dicens

it is necessary to postulate, or request, not that someone should admit that something either is or is not in reality, as has been stated above (1006a18; [611]), because this seems to be begging the question, but that he should admit that a word signifies something. Now if this is not granted, the dispute comes to an end; but if it is granted, it is then necessary to give definitions, as has already been stated above (1006a18; [611]).

Hence we must argue against these thinkers by proceeding from definitions, and in the case of the present thesis we must do this especially by considering the definition of falsity. Now if truth consists merely in affirming what it is false to deny, and vice versa, it follows that not all statements can be false, because either the affirmation or the negation of something must be true. For obviously truth consists simply in saying that what is is, or in saying that what is not is not; and falsity consists in saying that what is, is not, or in saying that what is not is. Hence it is clear that it is true to say that that is of which it is false that it is not, or to say that that is not of which it is false that it is; it is false to say that that is of which it is true that it is not, or to say that that is not of which it is true that it is. Thus from the definition of truth and falsity it is clear that not all things are false. And for the same reason it is clear that not all things are true.

741. *Again, if everything* (1012b11). Here he gives the third argument, which runs thus: it is clear from what has been said above that we must either affirm or deny something of each thing, since there is no intermediate between contradictories. It is impossible, then, for everything to be false. And by the same reasoning it is proved that it is impossible for everything to be true, by reason of the fact that it is impossible both to affirm and to deny something at the same time.

742. *And the view* (1012b13). He gives the fourth argument. All of the foregoing statements, or opinions, face this unreasonable result: they destroy themselves. This is **the view commonly expressed**, that is, a frequently heard statement made by all; thus another text says, **it happens that it is commonly held**. He proves this view as follows. Anyone who says that everything is true makes the contrary of his own opinion true. But the contrary of his own opinion is that his own opinion is not true. Therefore, he who says that everything is true says that his own opinion is not true; thus he destroys his own opinion. Similarly it is evident that he who says that everything is false also says that his own opinion is false.

743. And because someone could say that he who claims that everything is true makes an exception of the one contrary to his own statement or bars it from what holds universally (and the same thing applies to one who says that everything is false), he therefore rejects this answer. He says that if the one who says that everything is true

omnia esse falsa excipiat suam opinionem dicens quod ipsa sola non est falsa, nihilominus sequitur quod contingat eis *quaerere*, idest repetere infinitas esse orationes veras contra ponentes omnia esse falsas, et infinitas falsas contra ponentes omnia vera esse. Si enim detur una opinio vera, sequetur infinitas esse veras.

Et si detur una opinio falsa, sequetur infinitas esse falsas. Si enim haec positio vel opinio est vera: Socrates sedet, ergo et haec erit vera: Socratem sedere est verum. Et si illa est vera, ulterius haec erit vera, Socratem sedere esse verum est verum, et sic in infinitum. Semper enim qui dicit de oratione vera quod sit vera, verus est. Et qui dicit de oratione falsa quod sit vera, falsus est. Et hoc potest procedere in infinitum.

744. Deinde cum dicit *palam autem* disputat contra opiniones destruentes principia naturae, scilicet motum et quietem: et circa hoc tria facit.

Primo tangit falsitatem harum opinionum; dicens, quod ex praedictis est manifestum, quod nec opinio dicens omnia moveri, nec opinio dicens omnia quiescere, vera est.

745. Deinde cum dicit *nam si quiescunt* secundo ostendit has opiniones esse falsas.

Et primo ostendit quod opinio sit falsa, quae ponit omnia quiescere: quia si omnia quiescunt, tunc nihil removetur a dispositione, in qua aliquando est; et ideo quicquid est verum, semper erit verum, et quicquid est falsum, semper est falsum. Sed hoc videtur inconveniens: transmutatur enim veritas et falsitas propositionis. Nec hoc est mirum: quia homo, qui opinatur vel profert propositionem, aliquando non erat, postmodum fuit, et iterum non erit.

746. Secundo ostendit esse falsam opinionem quae ponit omnia moveri, duabus rationibus.

Quarum primam ponit ibi, *si vero omnia*. Quae talis est. Si omnia moventur et nihil est quiescens, nihil erit verum in rebus: quia quod est verum, iam est; quod autem movetur nondum est: ergo oportet omnia esse falsa: quod est impossibile, ut ostensum est.

747. Deinde cum dicit *amplius autem* secundam rationem ponit, quae talis est. Omne quod permutatur, necessario est ens; quia omne quod permutatur, ex aliquo in aliud permutatur; et omne quod in aliquo permutatur, inest ei quod permutatur. Unde non oportet dicere quod quicquid est in re permutata, mutetur, sed quod aliquid sit manens; et ita non omnia moventur.

makes his own contrary opinion an exception, saying that it alone is not true, and if the one who says that everything is false makes his own opinion an exception, saying that it alone is not false, nonetheless it follows that they will be able *to consider*, or bring forward, an infinite number of true statements against those who hold that all are false, and an infinite number of false statements against those who hold that all are true.

For granted that one opinion is true, it follows that an infinite number are true. And granted that one opinion is false, it follows that an infinite number are false. For if the position, or opinion, that Socrates is sitting is true, then the opinion that it is true that Socrates is sitting will also be true, and so on to infinity. For he who says that a true statement is true is always right; and he who says that a false statement is true is always wrong, and this can proceed to infinity.

744. *Now it is* (1012b22). He argues against those who destroy the principles of nature, namely, motion and rest, and in regard to this he does three things.

First, he mentions the falsity of these opinions, saying that it is evident, from what has been said above, that neither the opinion which states that everything is in motion nor the one which states that everything is at rest is true.

745. *For if all things* (1012b24). Second, he shows that these opinions are false.

First of all, he shows that the opinion which holds that everything is at rest is false. For if everything were at rest, nothing would then be changed from the state in which it sometimes is. Hence, whatever is true would always be true, and whatever is false would always be false. But this seems to be absurd, for the truth and falsity of a proposition is changeable. Nor is this to be wondered at, because the man who has an opinion or makes a statement at one time was not and now is and again will not be.

746. Second, he uses two arguments to show that the opinion which holds that all things are in motion is false.

He gives the first (1012b26) where he says, *and if all things*. It is as follows. If all things are in motion and nothing is at rest, nothing will be true in the world, for what is true already exists, but what is in motion does not yet exist. Hence everything must be false. But this is impossible, as has been shown (1012b5; [740]).

747. *Further, it must be* (1012b28). He gives the second argument, and it runs thus. Everything that is undergoing change is necessarily a being, because everything that is being changed is being changed from something to something else, and everything that is being changed in something else belongs to the subject that is undergoing change. Hence it is not necessary to say that everything in the subject undergoing change is being changed, but that there is something which remains. Hence not everything is in motion.

748. Deinde cum dicit *sed nec omnia* tertiam rationem ponit, excludens quamdam falsam opinionem, quae posset occasionari ex praedictis. Posset enim aliquis credere quod, quia non omnia moventur nec omnia quiescunt, quod ideo omnia quandoque moventur et quandoque quiescunt. Et hoc removens, dicit, quod non est verum quod omnia quandoque quiescant et quandoque moveantur. Sunt enim quaedam mobilia, quae semper moventur; scilicet corpora super caelestia; et est quoddam movens, scilicet primum, quod semper est immobile, et semper eodem modo se habet, ut probatum est octavo *Physicorum*.

748. *But it is not* (1012b29). He gives the third argument, and it disposes of a false opinion which could arise from what has been said above. Since not all things are in motion, nor all at rest, someone could therefore think that all things are sometimes in motion and sometimes at rest. In disposing of this opinion he says that it is not true that all things are sometimes in motion and sometimes at rest, for there are certain movable things that are always being moved, namely, the celestial bodies above us, and there is a mover, namely, the first, which is always immovable and ever in the same state, as has been proved in *Physics* 8.

Book 5

Definitions

Lecture 1

The definition of "principle"

1012b34 Principium dicitur aliud quidem unde aliquis rem moveat primum, ut longitudinis et viae, hinc quidem principium ipsum, e converse vero diversum. [749]

ἀρχὴ λέγεται ἡ μὲν ὅθεν ἄν τις τοῦ πράγματος {35} κινηθείη πρῶτον, οἷον τοῦ μήκους καὶ ὁδοῦ ἐντεῦθεν μὲν αὕτη ἀρχή, ἐξ ἐναντίας δὲ ἑτέρα:

In one sense the term "principle" means that from which someone first moves something; for example, in the case of a line or a journey, if the motion is from here, this is the principle, but if the motion is in the opposite direction, this is something different.

Est aliud unde optime fiet unumquodque, ut doctrinae. Nam non a primo et rei principio inchoandum est aliquando, sed unde opportunius discat.

{1013a1} ἡ δὲ ὅθεν ἂν κάλλιστα ἕκαστον γένοιτο, οἷον καὶ μαθήσεως οὐκ ἀπὸ τοῦ πρώτου καὶ τῆς τοῦ πράγματος ἀρχῆς ἐνίοτε ἀρκτέον ἀλλ᾽ ὅθεν ῥᾷστ᾽ ἂν μάθοι:

In another sense, principle means that from which a thing best comes into being, as the starting point of instruction. For sometimes it is not from what is first or from the starting point of the thing that one must begin, but from that from which one learns most readily.

Aliud unde primum generator in existente, ut navis sedile et domus fundamentum, et animalium alii cor, alii cerebrum, alii quodcumque talium suscipiunt.

ἡ δὲ ὅθεν πρῶτον γίγνεται ἐνυπάρχοντος, οἷον ὡς πλοίου {5} τρόπις καὶ οἰκίας θεμέλιος, καὶ τῶν ζῴων οἱ μὲν καρδίαν οἱ δὲ ἐγκέφαλον οἱ δ᾽ ὅ τι ἂν τύχωσι τοιοῦτον ὑπολαμβάνουσιν:

Again, "principle" means that first inherent thing from which something is brought into being, as the keel of a ship and the foundation of a house, and as some suppose the heart to be the principle in animals, and others the brain, and others anything else of the sort.

Aliud autem unde fit primum non existente, et unde primum motus natus est initiari et permutatio, ut puer ex patre et matre et bellum ex convitio.

ἡ δὲ ὅθεν γίγνεται πρῶτον μὴ ἐνυπάρχοντος καὶ ὅθεν πρῶτον ἡ κίνησις πέφυκεν ἄρχεσθαι καὶ ἡ μεταβολή, οἷον τὸ τέκνον ἐκ τοῦ πατρὸς καὶ τῆς μητρὸς καὶ ἡ μάχη {10} ἐκ τῆς λοιδορίας:

In another sense it means that non-inherent first thing from which something comes into being; and that from which motion and change naturally first begins, as a child comes from its father and mother, and a fight from abusive language.

Aliud secundum cuius voluntatem moventur mobilia et mutantur mutabilia, ut civitatum principatus, et potestates, et imperia et tyrannides. Principia dicuntur et artes et architectonicae maxime.

ἡ δὲ οὗ κατὰ προαίρεσιν κινεῖται τὰ κινούμενα καὶ μεταβάλλει τὰ μεταβάλλοντα, ὥσπερ αἵ τε κατὰ πόλεις ἀρχαὶ καὶ αἱ δυναστεῖαι καὶ αἱ βασιλεῖαι καὶ τυραννίδες ἀρχαὶ λέγονται καὶ αἱ τέχναι, καὶ τούτων αἱ ἀρχιτεκτονικαὶ μάλιστα.

In another sense "principle" means that according to whose will movable things are moved and changeable things are changed—in states, for example, princely, magistral, imperial, or tyrannical power are all principles. And so also are the arts, especially the architectonic arts, called "principles."

Amplius unde cognoscibilis res primum et id principium rei dicitur, ut demonstrationum suppositiones.

ἔτι ὅθεν γνωστὸν τὸ πρᾶγμα {15} πρῶτον, καὶ αὕτη ἀρχὴ λέγεται τοῦ πράγματος, οἷον τῶν ἀποδείξεων αἱ ὑποθέσεις.

And that from which a thing can first be known is also called a "principle" of that thing, as the postulates of demonstrations.

Toties autem et causae dicuntur. Omnes enim causae principia.

ἰσαχῶς δὲ καὶ τὰ αἴτια λέγεται: πάντα γὰρ τὰ αἴτια ἀρχαί.

And causes are also spoken of in the same number of senses, for all "causes" are "principles."

1013a17 Omnium igitur principiorum est commune primum omne unde aut est, aut fit, aut cognoscitur. Horum autem haec quidem inexistentia sunt, illa vero extra. Quapropter natura principium et elementum est et mens et praevoluntas et substantia, et quod est cuius causa. Multorum enim et cognitionis et motus principium est bonum et malum. [761]

πασῶν μὲν οὖν κοινὸν τῶν ἀρχῶν τὸ πρῶτον εἶναι ὅθεν ἢ ἔστιν ἢ γίγνεται ἢ γιγνώσκεται: τούτων δὲ αἱ μὲν ἐνυπάρχουσαί εἰσιν αἱ δὲ {20} ἐκτός. διὸ ἥ τε φύσις ἀρχὴ καὶ τὸ στοιχεῖον καὶ ἡ διάνοια καὶ ἡ προαίρεσις καὶ οὐσία καὶ τὸ οὗ ἕνεκα: πολλῶν γὰρ καὶ τοῦ γνῶναι καὶ τῆς κινήσεως ἀρχὴ τἀγαθὸν καὶ τὸ καλόν.

Therefore, it is common to all principles to be the first thing from which a thing either is, comes to be, or is known. And of these some are intrinsic and others extrinsic. And for this reason nature is a principle, and so also is an element, and mind, purpose, substance, and the final cause. For good and evil are the principles of both the knowledge and the motion of many things.

---

749. In praecedenti libro determinavit Philosophus quid pertineat ad considerationem huius scientiae; hic incipit determinare de rebus, quas scientia ista considerat. Et quia ea quae in hac scientia considerantur, sunt omnibus communia, nec dicuntur univoce, sed secundum prius et posterius de diversis, ut in quarto libro est habitum;

ideo prius distinguit intentiones nominum, quae in huius scientiae consideratione cadunt.

Secundo incipit determinare de rebus, quae sub consideratione huius scientiae cadunt, in sexto libro, qui incipit, ibi, *principia et causae*.

Cuiuslibet autem scientiae est considerare subiectum, et passiones, et causas; et ideo hic quintus liber dividitur in tres partes.

Primo determinat distinctiones nominum quae significant causas;

secundo, illorum nominum quae significant subiectum huius scientiae vel partes eius, ibi, *unum dicitur aliud secundum accidens*.

Tertio nominum quae significant passiones entis inquantum est ens, ibi, *perfectum vero dicitur* et cetera.

Prima in duas.
Primo distinguit nomina significantia causas.

Secundo quoddam nomen significans quoddam quod consequitur ad causam, scilicet necessarium. Nam causa est ad quam de necessitate sequitur aliud, ibi, *necessarium dicitur sine quo non contingit*.

Prima dividitur in duas.
Primo distinguit nomina significantia causas generaliter.

749. Having established in the preceding book the things that pertain to the consideration of this science, here the Philosopher begins to deal with the things that this science considers. And since the attributes considered in this science are common to all things, they are not predicated of various things univocally, but in a prior and subsequent way, as has been stated in book 4 [535].

Therefore, first [751], he distinguishes the meanings of the terms which come under the consideration of this science.

Second [751], he begins to deal with the things that come under the consideration of this science. He does this in the book 6, which begins with the words, *the principles and causes* (1025b3).

Now, since it is the office of each science to consider both its subject and the properties and causes of its subject, this fifth book is accordingly divided into three parts.

First, he establishes the various senses of the terms which signify causes;

second (1015b16; [843]), the various senses of the terms which signify the subject or parts of the subject of this science, at *the term "one"*;

third (1021b12; [1034]), the various senses of the terms which signify the properties of being as being, at *that thing is said to be perfect*.

The first part is divided into two members.

First, he distinguishes the various senses in which the term "cause" is used.

Second (1015a20; [827]), he explains the meaning of a term which signifies something associated with a cause—the term "necessary"—for a cause is that on which something else follows of necessity, at *necessary means*.

The first part is divided into two members.

First, he distinguishes the various senses of the terms which signify cause in a general way.

Secundo distinguit quoddam nomen, quod significat quamdam causam in speciali, scilicet hoc nomen natura, ibi, *natura vero dicitur* et cetera.

750. Prima dividitur in tres.

Primo distinguit hoc nomen, principium.

Secundo hoc nomen, causa, ibi, *causa vero dicitur*.

Tertio hoc nomen, elementum, ibi, *elementum vero dicitur*.

Procedit autem hoc ordine, quia hoc nomen principium communius est quam causa: aliquid enim est principium, quod non est causa; sicut principium motus dicitur terminus a quo. Et iterum causa est in plus quam elementum. Sola enim causa intrinseca potest dici elementum.

Circa primum duo facit.

Primo ponit significationes huius nominis principium.

Secundo reducit omnes ad unum commune, ibi, *omnium igitur principiorum*.

751. Sciendum est autem, quod principium et causa licet sint idem subiecto, differunt tamen ratione. Nam hoc nomen principium ordinem quemdam importat; hoc vero nomen causa, importat influxum quemdam ad esse causati.

Ordo autem prioris et posterioris invenitur in diversis; sed secundum id, quod primo est nobis notum, est ordo inventus in motu locali, eo quod ille motus est sensui manifestior. Sunt autem trium rerum ordines sese consequentes; scilicet magnitudinis, motus, et temporis. Nam secundum prius et posterius in magnitudine est prius et posterius in motu; et secundum prius et posterius in motu est prius et posterius in tempore, ut habetur quarto *Physicorum*.

Quia igitur principium dicitur quod in aliquo ordine, et ordo qui attenditur secundum prius et posterius in magnitudine, est prius nobis notus, secundum autem quod res sunt nobis notae secundum hoc a nobis nominantur, ideo hoc nomen principium secundum propriam sui inquisitionem significat id quod est primum in magnitudine, super quam transit motus. Et ideo dicit, quod principium dicitur illud *unde aliquis rem primo moveat*, idest aliqua pars magnitudinis, a qua incipit motus localis.

Vel secundum aliam literam, *unde aliquid rei primo movebitur*, idest ex qua parte rei aliquid incipit primo moveri. Sicut in longitudine et in via quacumque, ex illa parte est principium, unde incipit motus. Ex parte vero opposita sive contraria, est *diversum* vel alterum, idest finis vel terminus. Sciendum est, quod ad hunc modum

Second (1014b16; [808]), he gives the meaning of the term which signifies a special kind of cause, namely, the term "nature," at *nature means*.

750. The first part is divided into three members.

First, he gives the various meanings of the term "principle";

second (1013a24; [763]), of the term "cause," at *in one sense the term "cause"*;

and third (1014a26; [795]), of the term "element," at *the inherent principle*.

He follows this order because the term "principle" is more common than the term "cause," for something may be a principle and not be a cause—for example, the principle of motion is said to be the point from which motion begins. Again, a cause is found in more things than an element is, for only an intrinsic cause can be called an element.

In regard to the first he does two things.

First, he gives the meanings of the term "principle."

Second (1013a17; [761]), he reduces all of these to one common notion, at *therefore, it is common*.

751. Now, it should be noted that, although a principle and a cause are the same in subject, they nevertheless differ in meaning; for the term "principle" implies an order or sequence, whereas the term "cause" implies some influence on the being of the thing caused.

Now an order of priority and posteriority is found in different things, but according to what is first known by us, order is found in local motion, because that kind of motion is more evident to the senses. Further, order is found in three kinds of things, one of which is naturally associated with the other—namely, continuous quantity, motion, and time. For insofar as there is priority and posteriority in continuous quantity, there is priority and posteriority in motion; and insofar as there is priority and posteriority in motion, there is priority and posteriority in time, as is stated in *Physics* 4.

Therefore, because a principle is said to be what is first in any order, and the order which is considered according to priority and posteriority in continuous quantity is first known by us (and things are named by us insofar as they are known to us), for this reason the term "principle," properly considered, designates what is first in a continuous quantity over which motion passes. Hence he says that a principle is said to be *that from which someone first moves something*, that is, any part of a continuous quantity from which local motion begins.

Or, according to another reading, *some part of a thing from which motion will first begin*, that is, some part of a thing from which it first begins to be moved (for example, in the case of a line, and in that of any kind of journey, the principle is the point from which motion begins). But the opposite or contrary point is *something different* or other,

pertinet principium motus et principium temporis ratione iam dicta.

752. Quia vero motus non semper incipit a principio magnitudinis, sed ab ea parte unde est unicuique in promptu magis ut moveatur, ideo ponit secundum modum, dicens, quod alio modo dicitur principium motus *unde unumquodque fiet maxime optime*, idest unusquisque incipit optime moveri. Et hoc manifestat per simile, in disciplinis scilicet in quibus non semper incipit aliquis addiscere ab eo quod est principium simpliciter et secundum naturam, *sed ab eo unde aliquid facilius sive opportunius valet addiscere*, idest ab illis, quae sunt magis nota quo ad nos, quae quandoque posteriora sunt secundum naturam.

753. Differt autem hic modus a primo. Nam in primo modo ex principio magnitudinis designatur principium motus. Hic autem ex principio motus designatur principium in magnitudine.

Et ideo etiam in illis motibus, qui sunt super magnitudines circulares non habentes principium, accipitur aliquod principium a quo optime vel opportune movetur mobile secundum suam naturam.

Sicut in motu primi mobilis principium est ab oriente. In motibus etiam nostris non semper incipit homo moveri a principio viae, sed quandoque a medio, vel a quocumque termino, unde est ei opportunum primo moveri.

754. Ex ordine autem, qui consideratur in motu locali, fit nobis etiam notus ordo in aliis motibus; et ideo sequuntur significationes principii, quae sumuntur secundum principium in generatione vel fieri rerum. Quod quidem principium dupliciter se habet. Aut enim est *inexistens*, idest intrinsecum; vel *non est inexistens*, idest extrinsecum.

755. Dicitur ergo primo modo principium illa pars rei, quae primo generatur, et ex qua generatio rei incipit; sicut in navi fit primo sedile vel carina, quae est quasi navis fundamentum, super quod omnia ligna navis compaginantur. Similiter quod primo in domo fit, est fundamentum.

In animali vero primo fit cor secundum quosdam, et secundum alios cerebrum, aut aliud tale membrum. Animal enim distinguitur a non animali, sensu et motu.

namely, the end or terminus. It should also be noted that a principle of motion and a principle of time belong to this kind for the reason just given.

752. But because motion does not always begin from the starting point of a continuous quantity but from that part from which the motion of each thing begins most readily, he therefore gives a second meaning of "principle," saying that we speak of a principle of motion in another way *as that from which a thing best comes into being*, that is, the point from which each thing begins to be moved most easily. He makes this clear by an example, for in the disciplines, one does not always begin to learn from something that is a beginning in an absolute sense and by nature, *but from that from which one learns most readily*, that is, from those things that are better known to us, even though they are sometimes more remote by their nature.

753. Now this sense of "principle" differs from the first. For in the first sense a principle of motion gets its name from the starting point of a continuous quantity, whereas here the principle of continuous quantity gets its name from the starting point of motion.

Hence in the case of those motions which are over circular continuous quantities and have no starting point, the principle is also considered to be the point from which the movable body is best or most fittingly moved according to its nature.

For example, in the case of the first thing moved, the starting point is in the east. The same thing is true in the case of our own movements; for a man does not always start to move from the beginning of a road but sometimes from the middle, or from any terminus at all from which it is convenient for him to start moving.

754. Now from the order considered in local motion we come to know the order in other motions. And for this reason we have the senses of "principle" based upon the principle of generation or coming to be of things. But this is taken in two ways; for it is either *inherent*, that is, intrinsic, or *non-inherent*, that is, extrinsic.

755. In the first way, then, "a principle" means that part of a thing which is first generated and from which the generation of the thing begins; for example, in the case of a ship the first thing to come into being is the base or keel, which is in a certain sense the foundation on which the whole superstructure of the ship is raised. And, similarly, in the case of a house the first thing that comes into being is the foundation.

And in the case of an animal the first thing that comes into being, according to some, is the heart, and according to others, the brain or some such member of the body. For an animal is distinguished from a non-animal by reason of sensation and motion.

Principium autem motus apparet esse in corde. Operationes autem sensus maxime manifestantur in cerebro. Et ideo qui consideraverunt animal ex parte motus, posuerunt cor principium esse in generatione animalis.

Qui autem consideraverunt animal solum ex parte sensus, posuerunt cerebrum esse principium; quamvis etiam ipsius sensus primum principium sit in corde, etsi operationes sensus perficiantur in cerebro.

Qui autem consideraverunt animal inquantum agit vel secundum aliquas eius operationes, posuerunt membrum adaptatum illi operationi, ut hepar vel aliud huiusmodi, esse primam partem generatam in animali. Secundum autem Philosophi sententiam, prima pars est cor, quia a corde omnes virtutes animae per corpus diffunduntur.

756. Alio autem modo dicitur principium, unde incipit rei generatio, quod tamen est extra rem; et hoc quidem manifestatur in tribus.

Primo quidem in rebus naturalibus, in quibus principium generationis dicitur, unde primum natus est motus incipere in his quae fiunt per motum, sicut in his quae acquiruntur per alterationem, vel per aliquem alium motum huiusmodi. Sicut dicitur homo fieri magnus vel albus.

Vel unde incipit permutatio, sicut in his quae non per motum, sed per solam fiunt mutationem; ut patet in factione substantiarum, sicut puer est ex patre et matre qui sunt eius principium, et bellum ex convitio, quod concitat animos hominum ad bellum.

757. Secundo etiam manifestat in rebus agibilibus sive moralibus aut politicis, in quibus dicitur principium id, ex cuius voluntate vel proposito moventur et mutantur alia; et sic dicuntur principatus in civitatibus illi qui obtinent potestates et imperia, vel etiam tyrannides in ipsis. Nam ex eorum voluntate fiunt et moventur omnia in civitatibus. Dicuntur autem potestates habere homines, qui in particularibus officiis in civitatibus praeponuntur, sicut iudices et huiusmodi. Imperia autem illi, qui universaliter quibuscumque imperant, ut reges. Tyrannides autem obtinent, qui per violentiam et praeter iuris ordinem ad suam utilitatem civitates et regnum detinent.

758. Tertium exemplum ponit in artificialibus, quia artes etiam simili modo principia esse dicuntur artificiatorum, quia ab arte incipit motus ad artificii constructionem. Et inter has maxime dicuntur principia architectonicae, quae a principio **nomen habent**, idest

Now the principle of motion appears to be in the heart, and sensory operations are most evident in the brain. Hence those who considered an animal from the viewpoint of motion held that the heart is the principle in the generation of an animal.

But those who considered an animal only from the viewpoint of the senses held that the brain is this principle, yet the first principle of sensation is also in the heart even though the operations of the senses are completed in the brain.

And those who considered an animal from the viewpoint of operation, or according to some of its activities, held that the organ which is naturally disposed for that operation—as the liver or some other such part—is the first part which is generated in an animal. But, according to the view of the Philosopher, the first part is the heart, because all of the soul's powers are diffused throughout the body by means of the heart.

756. In the second way, "a principle" means that from which a thing's process of generation begins but which is outside the thing. This is made clear in the case of three kinds of things.

The first is that of natural beings, in which the principle of generation is said to be the first thing from which motion naturally begins in those things that come about through motion, as those which come about through alteration or through some similar kind of motion—for example, a man is said to become large or white.

Or it is said to be that from which a complete change begins, as in the case of those things that are not a result of motion but come into being through mutation alone. This is evident in the case of substantial generation—for example, a child comes from its father and mother, who are its principles, and a fight comes from jeers, which stir men's souls to quarrel.

757. The second kind in which this is made clear is human acts, whether ethical or political, in which that by whose will or intention others are moved or changed is called a principle. Thus those who hold civil, imperial, or even tyrannical power in states are said to have the principal places; for it is by their will that all things come to pass or are put into motion in states. Those men are said to have civil power who are put in command of particular offices in states, as judges and persons of this kind. Those are said to have imperial power who govern everyone without exception, as kings. And those hold tyrannical power who, through violence and disregard for law, keep royal power within their grip for their own benefit.

758. He gives as the third kind things made by art, for the arts too in a similar way are called principles of artificial things, because the motion necessary for producing an artifact begins from an art. And of these arts, the architectonic, which **derive their name** from the word principle, that is,

principales artes dictae. Dicuntur enim artes architectonicae quae aliis artibus subservientibus imperant, sicut gubernator navis imperat navifactivae, et militaris equestri.

759. Ad similitudinem autem ordinis, qui in motibus exterioribus consideratur, attenditur etiam quidam ordo in rerum cognitione; et praecipue secundum quod intellectus noster quamdam similitudinem motus habet, discurrens de principiis in conclusiones. Et ideo alio modo dicitur principium, unde res primo innotescit; sicut dicimus principia demonstrationum *esse suppositiones*, idest dignitates et petitiones.

760. His etiam modis et causae dicuntur quaedam principia. *Nam omnes causae sunt quaedam principia.* Ex causa enim incipit motus ad esse rei, licet non eadem ratione causa dicatur et principium, ut dictum est.

761. Deinde cum dicit *omnium igitur* reducit omnes praedictos modos ad aliquid commune; et dicit quod commune in omnibus dictis modis est, ut dicatur principium illud, quod est primum, aut in esse rei, sicut prima pars rei dicitur principium, aut in fieri rei, sicut primum movens dicitur principium, aut in rei cognitione.

762. Sed quamvis omnia principia in hoc, ut dictum est, conveniant, differunt tamen, quia quaedam sunt intrinseca, quaedam extrinseca, ut ex praedictis patet. Et ideo natura potest esse principium et elementum, quae sunt intrinseca. Natura quidem, sicut illud a quo incipit motus: elementum autem sicut pars prima in generatione rei. *Et mens*, idest intellectus, *et praevoluntas*, idest propositum, dicuntur principia quasi extrinseca.

Et iterum quasi intrinsecum dicitur principium *substantia rei*, idest forma quae est principium in essendo, cum secundum eam res sit in esse.

Et secundum etiam praedicta, finis cuius causa fit aliquid, dicitur etiam esse principium. Bonum enim, quod habet rationem finis in prosequendo, et malum in vitando, in multis sunt principia cognitionis et motus, sicut in omnibus quae aguntur propter finem. In naturalibus enim, et moralibus et artificialibus, praecipue demonstrationes ex fine sumuntur.

those called principal arts, are said to be principles in the highest degree. For by "architectonic arts" we mean those which govern subordinate arts, as the art of the navigator governs the art of ship-building, and the military art governs the art of horsemanship.

759. Again, in likeness to the order considered in external motions, a certain order may also be observed in our apprehensions of things, and especially insofar as our act of understanding, by proceeding from principles to conclusions, bears a certain resemblance to motion. Therefore, in another way that is said to be a principle from which a thing first becomes known. For example, we say that *postulates*, that is, axioms and assumptions, are principles of demonstrations.

760. Causes are also said to be principles in these ways, *for all causes are principles*. For the motion that terminates in a thing's being begins from some cause, although it is not designated a cause and a principle from the same point of view, as was pointed out above [750].

761. *Therefore, it is* (1013a17). Then he reduces all of the abovementioned senses of principle to one that is common. He says that all of the foregoing senses have something in common inasmuch as that is said to be a principle which comes first either with reference to a thing's being (as the first part of a thing is said to be a principle), or with reference to its coming to be (as the first mover is said to be a principle), or with reference to the knowing of it.

762. But while all principles agree in the respect just mentioned, they nevertheless differ, because some are intrinsic and others extrinsic, as is clear from the above. Hence nature and element, which are intrinsic, can be principles—nature as that from which motion begins, and element as the first part in a thing's generation. *And mind*, or intellect, *and purpose*, or a man's intention, are said to be as extrinsic principles.

Again, *a thing's substance*, that is, its form, which is its principle of being, is called an intrinsic principle, since a thing has being by its form.

Again, according to what has been said, that for the sake of which something comes to be is said to be one of its principles. For the good, which has the character of an end in the case of pursuing, and evil, which is an end in that of shunning, are principles of the knowledge and motion of many things—that is, all those which are done for the sake of some end. For in the realm of nature, in that of moral acts, and in that of artifacts, demonstrations make special use of the final cause.

LECTURE 2

The definition of "cause"

1013a24 Causa vero dicitur uno quidem modo ex quo fit aliquid ut inexistente, ut aes statuae, et argentum phialae et horum genera. [772]

Alio vero species et exemplum. Haec autem ratio ipsius quod quid erat esse, et huius genera, ut diapason, duo ad unum et totaliter numerus et partes quae in ratione.

Amplius unde principium permutationis primum aut quietis, ut consiliator est causa et pater pueri et omnino efficiens facti, et permutans permutati.

Amplius ut finis. Hoc autem est quod est cuius causa, ut ambulandi sanitas: nam quare ambulavit, dicimus ut sanetur. Et dicentes ita, putamus reddidisse causam.

Et quaecumque movente alio fiunt infra finem, ut attenuatio, aut purgatio, aut pharmacia, aut organa. Haec namque omnia finis causa fiunt. Differunt autem ab invicem tamquam entia haec quidem, ut organa, illa vero, ut opera.

1013b3 Ergo causae fere toties dicuntur. [772]

1013b4 Accidit autem multoties dictis causis multas eiusdem causas esse, non secundum accidens, ut statuae, effector statuae, et aes, non secundum aliud aliquid, sed inquantum statua. Verum non eodem modo; sed hoc quidem ut materia, illud vero ut unde motus. [773]

αἴτιον λέγεται ἕνα μὲν τρόπον ἐξ οὗ γίγνεταί τι ἐνυπάρχοντος, {25} οἶον ὁ χαλκὸς τοῦ ἀνδριάντος καὶ ὁ ἄργυρος τῆς φιάλης καὶ τὰ τούτων γένη:

ἄλλον δὲ τὸ εἶδος καὶ τὸ παράδειγμα, τοῦτο δ᾽ ἐστὶν ὁ λόγος τοῦ τί ἦν εἶναι καὶ τὰ τούτου γένη (οἶον τοῦ διὰ πασῶν τὸ δύο πρὸς ἓν καὶ ὅλως ὁ ἀριθμός) καὶ τὰ μέρη τὰ ἐν τῷ λόγῳ.

ἔτι ὅθεν ἡ {30} ἀρχὴ τῆς μεταβολῆς ἡ πρώτη ἢ τῆς ἠρεμήσεως, οἶον ὁ βουλεύσας αἴτιος, καὶ ὁ πατὴρ τοῦ τέκνου καὶ ὅλως τὸ ποιοῦν τοῦ ποιουμένου καὶ τὸ μεταβλητικὸν τοῦ μεταβάλλοντος.

ἔτι ὡς τὸ τέλος: τοῦτο δ᾽ ἐστὶ τὸ οὗ ἕνεκα, οἶον τοῦ περιπατεῖν ἡ ὑγίεια. διὰ τί γὰρ περιπατεῖ; φαμέν. ἵνα ὑγιαίνῃ. καὶ {35} εἰπόντες οὕτως οἰόμεθα ἀποδεδωκέναι τὸ αἴτιον.

καὶ ὅσα δὴ κινήσαντος ἄλλου μεταξὺ γίγνεται τοῦ τέλους, {1013b1} οἶον τῆς ὑγιείας ἡ ἰσχνασία ἢ ἡ κάθαρσις ἢ τὰ φάρμακα ἢ τὰ ὄργανα: πάντα γὰρ ταῦτα τοῦ τέλους ἕνεκά ἐστι, διαφέρει δὲ ἀλλήλων ὡς ὄντα τὰ μὲν ὄργανα τὰ δ᾽ ἔργα.

τὰ μὲν οὖν αἴτια σχεδὸν τοσαυταχῶς λέγεται,

συμβαίνει δὲ πολλαχῶς {5} λεγομένων τῶν αἰτίων καὶ πολλὰ τοῦ αὐτοῦ αἴτια εἶναι οὐ κατὰ συμβεβηκός (οἶον τοῦ ἀνδριάντος καὶ ἡ ἀνδριαντοποιητικὴ καὶ ὁ χαλκὸς οὐ καθ᾽ ἕτερόν τι ἀλλ᾽ ἢ ἀνδριάς: ἀλλ᾽ οὐ τὸν αὐτὸν τρόπον ἀλλὰ τὸ μὲν ὡς ὕλη τὸ δ᾽ ὡς ὅθεν ἡ κίνησις),

In one sense the term "cause" means that from which, as something intrinsic, a thing comes to be, as the bronze of a statue and the silver of a goblet, and the genera of these.

In another sense it means the form and pattern of a thing, that is, the intelligible expression of the quiddity and its genera (for example, the ratio of two to one and number in general are the cause of an octave chord), and the parts which are included in the intelligible expression.

Again, that from which the first beginning of change or of rest comes is a cause: for example, an adviser is a cause, and a father is the cause of a child, and in general a maker is a cause of the thing made, and a changer a cause of the thing changed.

Further, a thing is a cause inasmuch as it is an end, or that for the sake of which something is done; for example, health is the cause of walking. For if we are asked why someone took a walk, we answer, "in order to be healthy," and in saying this we think we have given the cause.

And whatever occurs on the way to the end under the motion of something else is also a cause. For example, reducing, purging, drugs, and instruments are causes of health, for all of these exist for the sake of the end, although they differ from each other inasmuch as some are instruments and others are processes.

These, then, are nearly all the ways in which causes are spoken of.

And since there are several senses in which causes are spoken of, it turns out that there are many causes of the same thing, and not in an accidental way. For example, both the maker of a statue and the bronze are causes of a statue not in any other respect but insofar as it is a statue. However, they are not causes in the same way, but the one as matter and the other as the source of motion.

1013b9 Et adinvicem causae sunt, ut dolor causa est sanitatis, et sanitas causa est dolendi: sed non eodem modo. Verum hoc quidem, ut finis; illud vero, ut principium motus. [774]

καὶ ἀλλήλων αἴτια (οἷον τὸ πονεῖν {10} τῆς εὐεξίας καὶ αὕτη τοῦ πονεῖν: ἀλλ᾽ οὐ τὸν αὐτὸν τρόπον ἀλλὰ τὸ μὲν ὡς τέλος τὸ δ᾽ ὡς ἀρχὴ κινήσεως).

And there are things that are causes of each other. Pain, for example, is a cause of health, and health is a cause of pain, although not in the same way, but one as an end and the other as a source of motion.

1013b11 Amplius autem idem quandoque contrariorum est causa. Quod enim praesens, huius est causa, hoc absens, causamur quandoque de contrario. Ut absentia gubernatoris deperditionis navis, cuius erat praesentia causa salutis. Utraque vero, et praesentia et privatio, causae sunt quasi moventes. [776]

ἔτι δὲ ταὐτὸ τῶν ἐναντίων ἐστίν: ὃ γὰρ παρὸν αἴτιον τουδί, τοῦτ᾽ ἀπὸν αἰτιώμεθα ἐνίοτε τοῦ ἐναντίου, οἷον τὴν ἀπουσίαν τοῦ κυβερνήτου τῆς ἀνατροπῆς, οὗ ἦν ἡ παρουσία αἰτία τῆς {15} σωτηρίας: ἄμφω δέ, καὶ ἡ παρουσία καὶ ἡ στέρησις, αἴτια ὡς κινοῦντα.

Further, the same thing is sometimes the cause of contraries, for that which, when present, is the cause of some particular thing, we sometimes blame for the contrary when it is absent. Thus the cause of the loss of a ship is the absence of the pilot whose presence is the cause of the ship's safety. And both of these—the absence and the presence—are moving causes.

---

763. Hic Philosophus distinguit quot modis dicitur causa. Et circa hoc duo facit.

Primo assignat species causarum.
Secundo modos causarum, ibi, *modi vero causarum.*

Circa primum duo facit.
Primo enumerat diversas species causarum.
Secundo reducit eas ad quatuor, ibi, *omnes vero causae dictae.*

Circa primum duo facit.
Primo enumerat diversas species causarum.
Secundo manifestat quaedam circa species praedictas, ibi, *accidit autem multoties* et cetera.

Dicit ergo primo, quod uno modo dicitur causa id ex quo fit aliquid, et est ei *inexistens,* idest intus existens. Quod quidem dicitur ad differentiam privationis, et etiam contrarii. Nam ex contrario vel privatione dicitur aliquid fieri sicut ex non inexistente, ut album ex nigro vel album ex non albo.

Statua autem fit ex aere, et phiala ex argento, sicut ex inexistente. Nam cum statua fit, non tollitur ratio aeris, nec si fit phiala, tollitur ratio argenti. Et ideo aes statuae, et argentum phialae sunt causa per modum materiae.

Et horum genera, quia cuiuscumque materia est species aliqua, materia est eius genus, sicut si materia statuae est aes, eius materia erit metallum, et mixtum, et corpus, et sic de aliis.

764. Alio autem modo dicitur causa, species et exemplum, id est exemplar; et haec est causa formalis, quae comparatur dupliciter ad rem.

763. Here the Philosopher distinguishes the various senses in which the term "cause" is used, and in regard to this he does two things.

First, he enumerates the species of causes.
Second (1013b29; [783]), he gives the modes of causes, at *now the modes.*

In regard to the first part, he does two things.
First, he enumerates the various species of causes.
Second (1013b16; [777]), he reduces them to four, at *all the causes.*

In regard to the first part he does two things.
First, he enumerates the different species of causes.
Second (1013b4; [773]), he clarifies certain things about the species of causes, at *and since.*

He accordingly first says that in one sense the term "cause" means that from which a thing comes to be and is *something intrinsic,* or something which exists within the thing. This is said to distinguish it from a privation and also from a contrary, for a thing is said to come from a privation or from a contrary as from something which is not intrinsic (for example, white is said to come from black or from not-white).

But a statue comes from bronze and a goblet from silver as from something which is intrinsic, for the nature of bronze is not destroyed when a statue comes into being, nor is the nature of silver destroyed when a goblet comes into being. Therefore, the bronze of a statue and the silver of a goblet are causes in the sense of matter.

He adds, *and the genera of these,* because if matter is the species of anything it is also its genus. For example, if the matter of a statue is bronze, its matter will also be metal, compound, and body. The same holds true of other things.

764. In another sense, "cause" means the form and pattern of a thing, that is, its exemplar. This is the formal cause, which is related to a thing in two ways.

Uno modo sicut forma intrinseca rei; et haec dicitur species.

Alio modo sicut extrinseca a re, ad cuius tamen similitudinem res fieri dicitur; et secundum hoc, exemplar rei dicitur forma. Per quem modum ponebat Plato ideas esse formas.

Et, quia unumquodque consequitur naturam vel generis vel speciei per formam suam, natura autem generis vel speciei est id quod significat definitio, dicens quid est res, ideo forma est ratio ipsius *quod quid erat esse*, idest definitio per quam scitur quid est res.

Quamvis enim in definitione ponantur aliquae partes materiales, tamen id quod est principale in definitione, oportet quod sit ex parte formae. Et ideo haec est ratio quare forma est causa, quia perficit rationem quidditatis rei. Et sicut id quod est genus materiae, est etiam materia, ita etiam genera formarum sunt formae rerum; sicut forma consonantiae diapason, est proportio duorum ad unum. Quando enim duo soni se habent adinvicem in dupla proportione, tunc est inter eos consonantia diapason, unde dualitas est forma eius. Nam proportio dupla ex dualitate rationem habet. Et, quia numerus est genus dualitatis, ideo ut universaliter loquamur, etiam numerus est forma diapason, ut scilicet dicamus quod diapason est secundum proportionem numeri ad numerum.

Et non solum tota definitio comparatur ad definitum ut forma, sed etiam partes definitionis, quae scilicet ponuntur in definitione in recto. Sicut enim animal gressibile bipes est forma hominis, ita animal, et gressibile, et bipes. Ponitur autem interdum materia in definitione, sed in obliquo; ut cum dicitur, quod anima est actus corporis organici physici potentia vitam habentis.

765. Tertio modo dicitur causa unde primum est principium permutationis et quietis; et haec est causa movens, vel efficiens. Dicit autem, *motus, aut etiam quietis*, quia motus naturalis et quies naturalis in eamdem causam reducuntur, et similiter quies violenta et motus violentus. Ex eadem enim causa ex qua movetur aliquid ad locum, quiescit in loco.

Sicut consiliator est causa. Nam ex consiliatore incipit motus in eo, qui secundum consilium agit ad rei conservationem. Et similiter *pater est causa filii*. In quibus duobus exemplis duo principia motus tetigit ex quibus omnia fiunt, scilicet propositum in consiliatore, et naturam in patre. Et universaliter omne faciens est causa facti per hunc modum, et permutans permutati.

In one way, it stands as the intrinsic form of a thing, and in this respect it is called the formal "principle" of a thing.

In another way, it stands as something which is extrinsic to a thing but is that in likeness to which it is made, and in this respect an exemplar is also called a thing's form. It is in this sense that Plato held the ideas to be forms.

Moreover, because it is from its form that each thing derives its nature (whether of its genus or of its species), and the nature of its genus or of its species is what is signified by the definition (which expresses its quiddity), the form of a thing is therefore the intelligible expression of its *quiddity*—that is, the formula by which its quiddity is known.

For even though certain material parts are given in the definition, still it is from a thing's form that the principal part of the definition comes. The reason why the form is a cause, then, is that it completes the intelligible expression of a thing's quiddity. And just as the genus of a particular matter is also matter, in a similar way the genera of forms are the forms of things—for example, the form of the octave chord is the ratio of two to one. For when two notes stand to each other in the ratio of two to one, the interval between them is one octave. Hence two-ness is its form, for the ratio of two to one derives its meaning from two-ness. And because number is the genus of two-ness, we may therefore say in a general way that number is also the form of the octave, inasmuch as we may say that the octave chord involves the ratio of one number to another.

And not only is the whole definition related to the thing defined as its form, but so also are the parts of the definition, that is, those which are given directly in the definition. For just as two-footed animal capable of walking is the form of man, so also are animal, capable of walking, and two-footed. But sometimes matter is given indirectly in the definition, as when the soul is said to be the act of a physical organic body having life potentially.

765. In a third sense, "cause" means that from which the first beginning of change or of rest comes—that is, a moving or efficient cause. He says *of change or of rest*, because natural motion and rest are traced back to the same cause, and the same is true of violent motion and rest. For that cause by which something is moved to a place is the same as that by which it is made to rest there.

An adviser is an example of this kind of cause, for it is as a result of an adviser that motion begins in the one who acts upon his advice for the sake of safeguarding something. And in a similar way *a father is the cause of a child*. In these two examples, Aristotle touches upon the two principles of motion from which all things come to be, namely, purpose in the case of an adviser, and nature in the case of a father. And in general every maker is a cause of the thing made, and every changer a cause of the thing changed.

766. Sciendum est autem quod secundum Avicennam quatuor sunt modi causae efficientis; scilicet perficiens, disponens, adiuvans, et consilians. Perficiens autem dicitur causa efficiens, quae ultimam rei perfectionem causat, sicut quod inducit formam substantialem in rebus naturalibus, vel artificialem in artificialibus, ut aedificator domus.

767. Disponens autem quod non inducit ultimam formam perfectivam, sed tantummodo praeparat materiam ad formam; sicut ille, qui dolat ligna et lapides, dicitur domum facere. Et haec non proprie dicitur efficiens domus; quia id, quod ipse facit, non est domus nisi in potentia. Magis tamen proprie erit efficiens, si inducat ultimam dispositionem ad quam sequitur de necessitate forma; sicut homo generat hominem non causans intellectum, qui est ab extrinseco.

768. Adiuvans autem dicitur causa secundum quod operatur ad principalem effectum. In hoc tamen differt ab agente principali, quia principale agens agit ad finem proprium, adiuvans autem ad finem alienum;

sicut qui adiuvat regem in bello, operatur ad finem regis. Et haec est dispositio causae secundariae ad primam; nam causa secunda operatur propter finem primae causae in omnibus agentibus per se ordinatis, sicut militaris propter finem civilis.

769. Consilians autem differt ab efficiente principali, inquantum dat finem et formam agendi. Et haec est habitudo primi agentis per intellectum ad omne agens secundum, sive sit naturale, sive intellectuale. Nam primum agens intellectuale in omnibus dat finem et formam agendi secundo agenti, sicut architector navis navim operanti, et primus intellectus toti naturae.

770. Ad hoc autem genus causae reducitur quicquid facit aliquid quocumque modo esse, non solum secundum esse substantiale, sed secundum accidentale; quod contingit in omni motu. Et ideo non solum dicit quod faciens sit causa facti, sed etiam mutans mutati.

771. Quarto modo dicitur causa finis; hoc autem est cuius causa aliquid fit, sicut sanitas est causa ambulandi. Et quia de fine videbatur minus quod esset causa, propter hoc quod est ultimum in esse, unde etiam ab aliis prioribus philosophis haec causa est praetermissa, ut in primo libro praehabitum est, ideo specialiter probat de fine quod sit causa.

766. Moreover, it should be noted that according to Avicenna, there are four modes of efficient cause—namely, perfective, dispositive, auxiliary, and advisory. An efficient cause is said to be perfective inasmuch as it causes the final perfection of a thing, as the one who induces a substantial form in natural things or artificial forms in things made by art, as a builder induces the form of a house.

767. An efficient cause is said to be dispositive if it does not induce the final form that perfects a thing, but only prepares the matter for that form, as one who hews timbers and stones is said to build a house. This cause is not properly said to be the efficient cause of a house, because what he produces is only potentially a house. But he will be more properly an efficient cause if he induces the ultimate disposition on which the form necessarily follows. For example, man generates man without causing his intellect, which comes from an extrinsic cause.

768. And an efficient cause is said to be auxiliary insofar as it contributes to the principal effect. Yet it differs from the principal efficient cause in that the principal efficient cause acts for its own end, whereas an auxiliary cause acts for an end which is not its own.

For example, one who assists a king in war acts for the king's end. And in this way a secondary cause is disposed for a primary cause. For in the case of all efficient causes which are directly subordinated to each other, a secondary cause acts because of the end of a primary cause—for example, the military art acts because of the end of the political art.

769. And an advisory cause differs from a principal efficient cause inasmuch as it specifies the end and form of the activity. This is the way in which the first agent acting by intellect is related to every secondary agent, whether it be natural or intellectual. For in every case a first intellectual agent gives to a secondary agent its end and its form of activity. For example, the naval architect gives these to the shipwright, and the first intelligence does the same thing for everything in the natural world.

770. Further, to this genus of cause is reduced everything that makes anything to be in any manner whatsoever, not only as regards substantial being, but also as regards accidental being, which occurs in every kind of motion. Hence he says not only that the maker is the cause of the thing made, but also that the changer is the cause of the thing changed.

771. In a fourth sense, "cause" means a thing's end, or that for the sake of which something is done, as health is the cause of walking. And since it is less evident that the end is a cause in view of the fact that it comes into being last of all—which is also the reason why this cause was overlooked by the earlier philosophers, as was pointed out in book 1 [1771]—he therefore gives a special proof that an end is a cause.

Nam haec quaestio quare, vel propter quid, quaerit de causa: cum enim quaeritur quare, vel propter quid quis ambulat, convenienter respondentes dicimus, ut sanetur. Et sic respondentes opinamur reddere causam. Unde patet quod finis est causa.

Non solum autem ultimum, propter quod efficiens operatur, dicitur finis respectu praecedentium; sed etiam omnia intermedia quae sunt inter primum agens et ultimum finem, dicuntur finis respectu praecedentium; et eodem modo dicuntur causa unde principium motus respectu sequentium:

sicut inter medicinam, quae est primum agens in hoc ordine, et sanitatem quae est ultimus finis, sunt ista media: scilicet attenuatio, quae est propinquissima sanitati in his, qui superabundant in humoribus, et purgatio, per quam acquiritur attenuatio, *et pharmacia*, idest medicina laxativa, et ex qua purgatio causatur, et *organa* idest instrumenta quibus medicina vel pharmacia praeparatur et ministratur. Huiusmodi etiam omnia sunt propter finem; et tamen unum eorum est finis alterius. Nam attenuatio est finis purgationis, et purgatio pharmaciae.

Haec autem intermedia posita differunt adinvicem in hoc, quaedam eorum sunt organa, sicut instrumenta quibus medicina praeparatur et ministratur, et ipsa medicina ministrata qua natura utitur ut instrumento; quaedam vero sunt opera, idest operationes, sive actiones, ut purgatio et attenuatio.

772. Concludit ergo quod *causae toties dicuntur*, idest quatuor modis. Et addit *fere* propter modos causarum quos infra ponet. Vel etiam ideo, quia illae eaedem species non eadem ratione in omnibus inveniuntur.

773. Deinde cum dicit *accidit autem* ponit quaedam, quae consequuntur circa causas ex praedictis; et sunt tria:

quorum primum est, quod quia causa multis modis dicitur, contingit multas causas esse unius rei non secundum accidens, sed secundum se. Quod enim secundum accidens multae sint causae unius rei, hoc difficile non videbatur; quia rei, quae est causa per se alicuius effectus, multa possunt accidere, qua omnia illius effectus possunt etiam causa per accidens dici:

sed, quod causae per se sint multae unius, hoc fit manifestum ex hoc, quod causae multipliciter dicuntur. Statuae enim causa per se et non per accidens est factor statuae, et aes; sed non eodem modo. Hoc enim est impossibile quod eiusdem secundum idem genus, sint

For to ask why or for what reason is to ask about a cause, because when we are asked why or for what reason someone walks, we reply properly by answering that he does so in order to be healthy. And when we answer in this way we think that we are stating the cause. Hence it is evident that the end is a cause.

Moreover, not only the ultimate reason for which an agent acts is said to be an end with respect to those things that precede it, but everything that is intermediate between the first agent and the ultimate end is also said to be an end with respect to the preceding agents. And similarly those things are said to be causes from which motion arises in subsequent things.

For example, between the art of medicine (which is the first efficient cause in this order) and health (which is the ultimate end), there are these intermediates: reducing, which is the most proximate cause of health in those who have a superfluity of humors; purging, by means of which reducing is brought about; *drugs*, or laxative medicine, by means of which purging is accomplished; and *instruments*, that is, the instruments by which medicine or drugs are prepared and administered. And all such things exist for the sake of the end, although one of them is the end of another. For reducing is the end of purging, and purging is the end of medicines.

However, these intermediates differ from each other in that some are instruments—namely, the instruments by means of which medicine is prepared and administered (and the administered medicine itself is something which nature employs as an instrument)—and some, such as purging and reducing, are processes, that is, operations or activities.

772. He concludes, then, that *these are the ways in which causes are spoken of* (1013b3), that is, the four ways. And he adds *nearly all* because of the modes of causes which he gives below. Or he also adds this because the same species of causes are not found for the same reason in all things.

773. *And since* (1013b4). Then he indicates certain points which follow from the things said above about the causes, and there are three of these.

The first is that since the term "cause" is used in many senses, there may be several causes of one thing not accidentally but properly. For the fact that there are many causes of one thing accidentally presents no difficulty, because many things may be accidents of something that is the proper cause of some effect, and all of these can be said to be accidental causes of that effect.

But that there are several proper causes of one thing becomes evident from the fact that causes are spoken of in various ways. For the maker of a statue is a proper cause and not an accidental cause of a statue, and so also is the bronze, but not in the same way. For it is impossible that

multae causae per se eodem ordine; licet possint esse plures causae hoc modo, quod una sit proxima, alia remota: vel ita, quod neutrum sit causa sufficiens, sed utrumque coniunctim; sicut patet in multis, qui trahunt navem. Sed in proposito diversis modis ista duo sunt causa statuae: aes quidem ut materia, artifex vero ut efficiens.

774. Secundum ponit ibi, *et adinvicem* dicit, quod etiam contingit, quod aliqua duo adinvicem sibi sunt causae: quod impossibile est in eodem genere causae. Manifestum vero fit multipliciter dictis causis. Sicut dolor ex incisione vulneris est causa sanitatis, ut efficiens sive principium motus: sanitas autem est causa illius doloris, ut finis. Secundum enim idem genus causae aliquid esse causam et causatum est impossibile.

Alia litera habet melius *laborare causa est euexiae*, idest bonae dispositionis, quae causatur ex labore moderato, qui ad digestionem confert et superfluos humores consumit.

775. Sciendum est autem, quod cum sint quatuor causae superius positae, earum duae sibi invicem correspondent, et aliae duae similiter.

Nam efficiens et finis sibi correspondent invicem, quia efficiens est principium motus, finis autem terminus.

Et similiter materia et forma: nam forma dat esse, materia autem recipit.

Est igitur efficiens causa finis, finis autem causa efficientis.

Efficiens est causa finis quantum ad esse quidem, quia movendo perducit efficiens ad hoc, quod sit finis. Finis autem est causa efficientis non quantum ad esse, sed quantum ad rationem causalitatis.

Nam efficiens est causa inquantum agit: non autem agit nisi causa finis. Unde ex fine habet suam causalitatem efficiens.

Forma autem et materia sibi invicem sunt causa quantum ad esse. Forma quidem materiae inquantum dat ei esse actu; materia vero formae inquantum sustentat ipsam. Dico autem utrumque horum sibi invicem esse causam essendi vel simpliciter vel secundum quid. Nam forma substantialis dat esse materiae simpliciter. Forma autem accidentalis secundum quid, prout etiam forma est. Materia etiam quandoque non sustentat formam secundum esse simpliciter, sed secundum quod est

there should be many proper causes of the same thing within the same genus and in the same order. Nevertheless, there can be many causes, provided that one is proximate and another remote, or that neither of them is of itself a sufficient cause, but both together. An example would be many men rowing a boat. Now in the case in point these two things are causes of a statue in different ways: the bronze as matter, and the artist as efficient cause.

774. *And there are* (1013b9). Then he sets down the second fact that may be drawn from the foregoing discussion. He says that it may also happen that any two things may be the cause of each other, although this is impossible in the same genus of cause. But it is evident that this may happen when causes are spoken of in different senses. For example, the pain resulting from a wound is a cause of health as an efficient cause or source of motion, whereas health is the cause of pain as an end. For it is impossible that a thing should be both a cause and something caused.

Another text states this better, saying that *exercise is the cause of physical fitness*, that is, of the good disposition caused by moderate exercise, which promotes digestion and uses up superfluous humors.

775. Now it must be borne in mind that although four causes are given above, two of these are related to one another, and so also are the other two.

For the efficient cause and the final cause are related to each other, because the efficient cause is the starting point of motion and the final cause is its terminus.

There is a similar relationship between matter and form. For form gives being, and matter receives it.

Hence the efficient cause is the cause of the final cause, and the final cause is the cause of the efficient cause.

The efficient cause is the cause of the final cause inasmuch as it makes the final cause exist, for the efficient cause brings about the final cause by causing motion. But the final cause is the cause of the efficient cause not in the sense that it makes it be, but inasmuch as it is the reason for the causality of the efficient cause.

For an efficient cause is a cause inasmuch as it acts, and it acts only because of the final cause. Hence the efficient cause derives its causality from the final cause.

And form and matter are mutual causes of being: form is a cause of matter inasmuch as it gives actual being to matter, and matter is a cause of form inasmuch as it supports form in being. And I say that both of these together are causes of being either in an unqualified sense or with some qualification. For substantial form gives being absolutely to matter, whereas accidental form, inasmuch as it is a form, gives being in a qualified sense. And matter sometimes does not support a form in being in an unqualified

forma huius, habens esse in hoc, sicut se habet corpus humanum ad animam rationalem.

776. Tertium ponit ibi, *amplius autem* dicit, quod idem contrariorum contingit esse causam. Quod etiam difficile videbatur vel impossibile, si similiter ad utrumque referatur; sed dissimiliter est causa utriusque. Illud enim, quod per sui praesentiam est causa huius, quando est absens *causamur* idest accusamus ipsum *de contrario*, idest dicimus ipsum esse causam contrarii. Sicut patet, quod gubernator per sui praesentiam est causa salutis navis, dicimus eius absentiam esse causam perditionis. Ne autem putetur quod hoc sit referendum ad diversa genera causarum sicut et priora duo, ideo subiungit quod utrumque istorum reducitur ad idem genus causae, scilicet ad causam moventem. Eodem enim modo oppositum est causa oppositi, quo haec est causa huius.

sense, but according as it is the form of this particular thing and has being in this particular thing. This is what happens in the case of the human body in relation to the rational soul.

776. *Further, the same thing* (1013b11). Then he gives the third conclusion that may be drawn from the foregoing discussion. He says that the same thing can be the cause of contraries. This would also seem to be difficult or impossible if it were related to both in the same way. But it is the cause of each in a different way. For that which, when present, is the cause of some particular thing, this when absent *we blame*, or hold responsible, *for the contrary*. For example, it is evident that by his presence the pilot is the cause of a ship's safety, and we say that his absence is the cause of the ship's loss. And lest someone might think that this is to be attributed to different genera of causes, just as the preceding two were, he therefore adds that both of these may be reduced to the same genus of cause—the moving cause. For an opposite cause causes an opposite effect in the same way that the original cause caused its own effect.

LECTURE 3

All causes reduced to four

1013b16 Omnes vero causae dictae in quatuor modos cadunt manifestissimos. Nam elementa syllabarum et materia artificialium et ignis et terra et talia omnia corporum, et partes totius et suppositiones conclusionis, ut ex quo causae sunt. [777]

Harum autem haec quidem quasi subiectum, ut partes. Illa vero ut quod quid erat esse, ut totum, compositio et species. Sperma vero et medicus et consiliator, et omnino efficiens, omnia sunt unde principium permutationis aut status.

Alia vero ut finis et bonum aliorum. Nam quod cuius causa, optimum, et finis aliorum vult esse. Nihil autem differt dicere sive bonum, sive apparens bonum. Causae igitur hae sunt, et tot specie.

1013b29 Modi vero causarum numero quidem sunt multi, capitulatum vero et hi pauciores. Dicunitur enim causae multipliciter. Et earum conspecialium prius et posterius altera alia, ut sanitatis medicus et artifex, diapason duplum et numerus, et semper quae singularium sunt continentia. [783]

Amplius autem ut accidens et horum genera, velut statuae aliter Polycletus, et aliter statuae factor, quia accidit statuae factori Polycletum esse:

et continentia accidens, ut homo causa statuae, aut et totaliter animal, quia Polycletus homo est et animal.

Sunt etiam et accidentium aliis remotiora et propinquiora, ut si album et

ἅπαντα δὲ τὰ νῦν εἰρημένα αἴτια εἰς τέτταρας τρόπους πίπτει τοὺς φανερωτάτους. τὰ μὲν γὰρ στοιχεῖα τῶν συλλαβῶν καὶ ἡ ὕλη τῶν σκευαστῶν καὶ τὸ πῦρ καὶ ἡ γῆ καὶ τὰ τοιαῦτα πάντα τῶν σωμάτων καὶ τὰ {20} μέρη τοῦ ὅλου καὶ αἱ ὑποθέσεις τοῦ συμπεράσματος ὡς τὸ {21} ἐξ οὗ αἴτιά ἐστιν:

τούτων δὲ τὰ μὲν ὡς τὸ ὑποκείμενον, οἷον τὰ μέρη, τὰ δὲ ὡς τὸ τί ἦν εἶναι, τό τε ὅλον καὶ ἡ σύνθεσις καὶ τὸ εἶδος. τὸ δὲ σπέρμα καὶ ὁ ἰατρὸς καὶ ὁ βουλεύσας καὶ ὅλως τὸ ποιοῦν, πάντα ὅθεν ἡ ἀρχὴ τῆς μεταβολῆς {25} ἢ στάσεως.

τὰ δ᾽ ὡς τὸ τέλος καὶ τἀγαθὸν τῶν ἄλλων: τὸ γὰρ οὗ ἕνεκα βέλτιστον καὶ τέλος τῶν ἄλλων ἐθέλει εἶναι: διαφερέτω δὲ μηδὲν αὐτὸ εἰπεῖν ἀγαθὸν ἢ φαινόμενον ἀγαθόν. τὰ μὲν οὖν αἴτια ταῦτα καὶ τοσαῦτά ἐστι τῷ εἴδει,

τρόποι δὲ τῶν αἰτίων ἀριθμῷ μέν {30} εἰσι πολλοί, κεφαλαιούμενοι δὲ καὶ οὗτοι ἐλάττους. λέγονται γὰρ αἴτια πολλαχῶς, καὶ αὐτῶν τῶν ὁμοειδῶν προτέρως καὶ ὑστέρως ἄλλο ἄλλου, οἷον ὑγιείας ὁ ἰατρὸς καὶ ὁ τεχνίτης, καὶ τοῦ διὰ πασῶν τὸ διπλάσιον καὶ ἀριθμός, καὶ ἀεὶ τὰ περιέχοντα ὁτιοῦν τῶν καθ᾽ ἕκαστα.

ἔτι δ᾽ ὡς τὸ συμβεβηκὸς {35} καὶ τὰ τούτων γένη, οἷον ἀνδριάντος ἄλλως Πολύκλειτος καὶ ἄλλως ἀνδριαντοποιός, ὅτι συμβέβηκε τῷ ἀνδριαντοποιῷ Πολυκλείτῳ εἶναι:

{1014a1} καὶ τὰ περιέχοντα δὲ τὸ συμβεβηκός, οἷον ἄνθρωπος αἴτιος ἀνδριάντος, ἢ καὶ ὅλως ζῷον, ὅτι ὁ Πολύκλειτος ἄνθρωπος ὁ δὲ ἄνθρωπος ζῷον.

ἔστι δὲ καὶ τῶν συμβεβηκότων ἄλλα ἄλλων πορρώτερον καὶ {5} ἐγγύτερον,

All the causes mentioned fall under one of the four kinds that are most evident. For the elements of syllables, the matter of things made by art, fire, earth, and all such elements of bodies, the parts of a whole, and the premises of a conclusion are all causes in the sense of that from which things are made.

But of these some are causes as a subject (like parts), and others as the essence (like the whole, the composition and the species); but the seed, the physician, the adviser, and in general every agent are sources of change or of rest.

But the others are causes as the end and the good of other things. For that for the sake of which other things come to be is the greatest good and the end of other things. And it makes no difference whether we say that it is a good or an apparent good. These, then, are the causes, and this the number of their species.

Now the modes of causes are many in number, but these become fewer when summarized. For causes are spoken of in many senses, and of those that belong to the same species, some are prior and some subsequent. For example, both the physician and one possessing an art are causes of health, and both the ratio of two to one and number are causes of the octave chord; and always those that contain singulars.

Further, a thing may be a cause in the sense of an accident, and the genera that contain these—for example, in one sense the cause of a statue is Polyclitus and in another a sculptor, because it is accidental that a sculptor should be Polyclitus.

And the universals which contain accidents are causes—for example, man is the cause of a statue, and even generally animal, because Polyclitus is a man and an animal.

And of accidental causes some are more remote and some more proximate than

musicum causa dicuntur statuae, et non solum Polycletus aut homo.

Praeter omnia autem et proprie dicta et secundum accidens, haec quidem ut potentia dicuntur, illa vero ut agentia, ut aedificationis aedificator, aut aedificans.

Similiter autem dicentur, et in quibus causae sunt causae dictis, ut huius statuae, aut statuae, aut omnino imaginis, aut aeris, aut aeris huius, aut omnino materiae: et in accidentibus similiter.

Amplius autem complexa et ea et illa dicuntur; ut nec Polycletus, nec statuae factor, sed Polycletus statuae factor.

Attamen ea omnia sunt pluralitate sex, sed dupliciter dicta. Aut enim ut singulare, aut ut genus. Et secundum se, aut secundum accidens, aut ut genus accidentis. Aut ut ea complexa, aut simpliciter dicta. Amplius autem ut agentia, aut secundum potentiam. Differunt autem intantum, quod agentia quidem singularia simul sunt et non sunt cum his quorum sunt causae; ut hic medens cum hoc convalescente, et hic aedificator cum hoc aedificio. Quae vero sunt secundum potentiam, non semper. Corrumpitur enim non simul aedificium et aedificator.

οἷον εἰ ὁ λευκὸς καὶ ὁ μουσικὸς αἴτιος λέγοιτο τοῦ ἀνδριάντος, ἀλλὰ μὴ μόνον Πολύκλειτος ἢ ἄνθρωπος.

παρὰ πάντα δὲ καὶ τὰ οἰκείως λεγόμενα καὶ τὰ κατὰ συμβεβηκός, τὰ μὲν ὡς δυνάμενα λέγεται τὰ δ' ὡς ἐνεργοῦντα, οἷον τοῦ οἰκοδομεῖσθαι οἰκοδόμος ἢ οἰκοδομῶν οἰκοδόμος.

{10} ὁμοίως δὲ λεχθήσεται καὶ ἐφ' ὧν αἴτια τὰ αἴτια τοῖς εἰρημένοις, οἷον τοῦδε τοῦ ἀνδριάντος ἢ ἀνδριάντος ἢ ὅλως εἰκόνος, καὶ χαλκοῦ τοῦδε ἢ χαλκοῦ ἢ ὅλως ὕλης: καὶ ἐπὶ τῶν συμβεβηκότων ὡσαύτως.

ἔτι δὲ συμπλεκόμενα καὶ ταῦτα κἀκεῖνα λεχθήσεται, οἷον οὐ Πολύκλειτος οὐδὲ ἀνδριαντοποιὸς {15} ἀλλὰ Πολύκλειτος ἀνδριαντοποιός.

ἀλλ' ὅμως ἅπαντά γε ταῦτ' ἐστὶ τὸ μὲν πλῆθος ἕξ, λεγόμενα δὲ διχῶς: ἢ γὰρ ὡς τὸ καθ' ἕκαστον ἢ ὡς τὸ γένος, ἢ ὡς τὸ συμβεβηκὸς ἢ ὡς τὸ γένος τοῦ συμβεβηκότος, ἢ ὡς συμπλεκόμενα ταῦτα ἢ ὡς ἁπλῶς λεγόμενα, πάντα δὲ ἢ ὡς {20} ἐνεργοῦντα ἢ κατὰ δύναμιν. διαφέρει δὲ τοσοῦτον, ὅτι τὰ μὲν ἐνεργοῦντα καὶ τὰ καθ' ἕκαστον ἅμα ἔστι καὶ οὐκ ἔστι καὶ ὧν αἴτια, οἷον ὅδε ὁ ἰατρεύων τῷδε τῷ ὑγιαζομένῳ καὶ ὅδε ὁ οἰκοδόμος τῷδε τῷ οἰκοδομουμένῳ, τὰ δὲ κατὰ δύναμιν οὐκ ἀεί: φθείρεται γὰρ οὐχ ἅμα ἡ οἰκία καὶ ὁ {25} οἰκοδόμος.

others. Thus what is white and what is musical might be said to be the causes of a statue, and not just Polyclitus or man.

Again, in addition to all of these—both proper causes and accidental causes—some are said to be causes potentially and some actually, as a builder and one who is building.

And the distinctions which have been made will apply in like manner to the effects of these causes—for example, to this statue, or to a statue, or to an image generally, or to this bronze, or to bronze, or to matter in general. And the same applies to accidental effects.

Again, both proper and accidental causes may be spoken of together, so that the cause of a statue may be referred to as neither Polyclitus nor a sculptor, but the sculptor Polyclitus.

But while all these varieties of causes are six in number, each is spoken of in two ways. For causes are either singular or generic; either proper or accidental (or generically accidental); or spoken of in combination or singly; or again either active or potential causes. But they differ in this respect: active causes (that is, singular causes) exist or cease to exist simultaneously with their effects, as this particular one who is healing with this particular person who is being healed, and as this particular builder with this particular thing which is being built. But this is not always true of potential causes, for the builder and the thing built do not cease to exist at the same time.

777. Hic Philosophus reducit omnes causas in quatuor modos causarum praedictos; dicens, quod omnia quae dicuntur causae, incidunt in praedictos quatuor modos. Dicuntur enim *elementa*, idest literae, causae syllabarum, et materia artificialium dicitur esse causa factorum per artem, et ignis et terra et huiusmodi omnia simplicia corpora, dicuntur esse causae corporum mixtorum. Et partes dicuntur esse causa totius. *Et suppositiones*, idest propositiones praemissae, ex quibus propositis syllogizatur, dicuntur esse causa conclusionis. Et in omnibus istis est una ratio causae, secundum quod dicitur causa illud ex quo fit aliquid, quod est ratio causae materialis.

777. Here the Philosopher reduces all causes to the kinds of causes mentioned above (1013b16), saying that all those things that are called "causes" fall into one of the four kinds mentioned above. For *elements*, or letters, are said to be the causes of syllables; and the matter of artificial things is said to be their cause; and fire and earth and all simple bodies of this kind are said to be the causes of compounds. And parts are said to be the causes of a whole, and *premises*, that is, propositions previously set down from which conclusions are drawn, are said to be the causes of the conclusion. And in all of these cases, cause has a single formal aspect according as "cause" means that from which a thing is produced, and this is the formal aspect of material cause.

778. Sciendum est autem, quod propositiones dicuntur esse materia conclusionis, non quidem secundum quod sub tali forma existunt, vel secundum virtutem earum; (sic enim magis se habent in ratione causae efficientis); sed quantum ad terminos, ex quibus componuntur. Nam ex terminis praemissarum componitur conclusio, scilicet ex maiori et ex minori extremitate.

779. Inter ea autem ex quibus res integratur, aliquid se habet per modum subiecti, sicut partes et alia quae praedicta sunt; alia vero se habent ut *quod quid erat esse*, scilicet totum, et compositio, et species, quae pertinent ad rationem formae, secundum quam quidditas rei completur. Sciendum est enim, quod quandoque una res simpliciter est alicuius materia, sicut argentum phialae; et tunc forma correspondens tali materiae potest dici species. Quandoque autem plures adinvicem adunatae sunt materia alicuius rei. Quod quidem contingit tripliciter. Quandoque enim adunantur secundum ordinem tantum, sicut homines in exercitu, vel domus in civitate; et sic pro forma respondet totum, quod designatur nomine exercitus vel civitatis. Quandoque autem non solum adunantur ordine, sed contactu et colligatione, sicut apparet in partibus domus; et tunc respondet pro forma compositio. Quandoque autem super hoc additur alteratio componentium, quod contingit in mixtione; et tunc forma est ipsa mixtio, quae tamen est quaedam compositionis species. Ex quolibet autem trium horum sumitur quod quid est rei, scilicet ex compositione et specie et toto: sicut patet si definiretur exercitus, domus et phiala. Sic ergo habemus duos modos causae.

780. Secundum autem aliam rationem dicitur causa sperma et medicus et consiliator, et universaliter omne faciens, ex eo scilicet quod sunt principia motus et quietis. Unde iam hoc est aliud genus causae, propter aliam rationem causandi. Ponit autem sperma in hoc genere causae, quia secundum eius sententiam sperma vim habet activam, menstruum autem mulieris cedit in materiam concepti.

781. Quarta vero ratio causandi est secundum quod aliqua dicuntur causae per modum finis et boni respectu aliorum. Illud enim cuius causa fit aliquid, est optimum inter alia *et vult esse* idest habet aptitudinem ut sit aliorum finis.

Quia vero posset aliquis obiicere quod non semper bonum est finis, cum quandoque aliqui inordinate agentes malum finem sibi constituant, ideo respondet, quod nihil ad propositum differt dicere quod simpliciter sit bonum vel apparens bonum. Qui enim agit, agit per se loquendo propter bonum; hoc enim intendit; per acci-

778. Now it must be noted that propositions are said to constitute the matter of a conclusion, not inasmuch as they exist under such a form, or according to their force (for in this way they would rather have the formal aspect of an efficient cause), but with reference to the terms of which they are composed. For a conclusion is constituted of the terms contained in the premises, that is, of the major and minor terms.

779. And of those things of which something is composed, some are like a subject (for example, parts and the other things mentioned above), but some are like *the essence* (for example, the whole, the composition, and the species, which have the character of a form by which a thing's essence is made complete). For it must be borne in mind that sometimes one thing is the matter of something else in an unqualified sense (for example, silver of a goblet), and then the form corresponding to such a matter can be called the species. But sometimes many things taken together constitute the matter of a thing, and this may occur in three ways. For sometimes things are united merely by their arrangement, as the men in an army or the houses in a city; then the whole has the role of a form, which is designated by the term "army" or "city." And sometimes things are united not just by arrangement alone but by contact and a bond, as is evident in the parts of a house; then their composition has the role of a form. And sometimes the alteration of the component parts is added to the above, as occurs in the case of a compound; then the compound state itself is the form, and this is still a kind of composition. And a thing's essence is derived from any one of these three— the composition, species, or whole—as becomes clear when an army, a house, or a goblet is defined. Thus we have two kinds of cause.

780. But the seed, the physician, and the adviser, and in general every agent, are called causes for a different reason, namely, because they are the sources of motion and rest. Hence this is now a different genus of cause because of a different formal aspect of causality. He puts seed in this genus of cause because he is of the opinion that the seed has active power, whereas a woman's menstrual fluid has the role of the matter of the offspring.

781. There is a fourth formal aspect of causality inasmuch as some things are said to be causes in the sense of the end and good of other things. For that for the sake of which something else comes to be is the greatest good *and the end* of other things; that is, it is naturally disposed to be their end.

But because someone could raise the objection that an end is not always a good, since certain agents sometimes inordinately set up an evil as their end, he therefore replies that it makes no difference to his thesis whether we speak of what is good without qualification or of an apparent good. For one who acts does so, properly speaking, because of

dens autem propter malum, inquantum accidit ei quod existimat bonum esse. Nullus enim agit propter aliquid intendens malum.

782. Sciendum autem est, quod licet finis sit ultimus in esse in quibusdam, in causalitate tamen est prior semper. Unde dicitur causa causarum, quia est causa causalitatis in omnibus causis. Est enim causa causalitatis efficientis, ut iam dictum est. Efficiens autem est causa causalitatis et materiae et formae. Nam facit per suum motum materiam esse susceptivam formae, et formam inesse materiae. Et per consequens etiam finis est causa causalitatis et materiae et formae;

et ideo potissimae demonstrationes sumuntur a fine, in illis in quibus agitur aliquid propter finem, sicut in naturalibus, in moralibus et artificialibus. Concludit igitur, quod praedicta sunt causae, et quod causae secundum tot species distinguuntur.

783. Deinde cum dicit *modi vero* distinguit modos causarum. Est autem distinctio causae per species et per modos. Nam distinctio per species est penes diversas rationes causandi; et ideo est quasi divisio per differentias essentiales species constituentes.

Divisio autem per modos est penes diversas habitudines causae ad causatum. Et ideo est in his quae habent eamdem rationem causandi, sicut per se et per accidens, remotum et propinquum.

Unde est quasi per differentias accidentales non diversificantes speciem.

784. Dicit ergo, quod multi sunt modi causarum, sed pauciores inveniuntur quando *capitulatim*, idest quodam compendio comprehenduntur. Per se enim et per accidens sunt duo modi; tamen reducuntur ad unum capitulum, secundum quod est eadem consideratio de utroque.

Et similiter est de aliis modis oppositis. Causae enim multis modis dicuntur, non solum quantum ad diversas species causae, sed etiam quantum ad causas conspeciales, quae scilicet reducuntur ad unam speciem causae.

785. Dicitur enim una prior, et altera posterior. Prius autem et posterius in causis invenitur dupliciter.

Uno modo in causis diversis numero adinvicem ordinatis, quarum una est prima et remota, et alia secunda et propinqua; sicut in causis efficientibus homo generat hominem ut causa propinqua et posterior, sol autem ut

a good, for this is what he has in mind. And one acts for the sake of an evil accidentally inasmuch as he happens to think that it is good. For no one acts for the sake of something with evil in view.

782. Moreover, it must be noted that, even though the end is the last thing to come into being in some cases, it is always prior in causality. Hence it is called the "cause of causes," because it is the cause of the causality of all causes. For it is the cause of efficient causality, as has already been pointed out [775]; and the efficient cause is the cause of the causality of both the matter and the form, because by its motion it causes matter to be receptive of form and makes form exist in matter. Therefore, the final cause is also the cause of the causality of both the matter and the form.

Hence in those cases in which something is done for an end (as occurs in the realm of natural things, in that of moral matters, and in that of art), the most forceful demonstrations are derived from the final cause. Therefore, he concludes that the foregoing are causes, and that causes are distinguished into this number of species.

783. *Now the modes* (1013b29). Then he distinguishes between the modes of causes. And causes are distinguished into species and into modes. For the division of causes into species is based on different formal aspects of causality, and is therefore equivalently a division based on essential differences, which constitute species.

But the division of causes into modes is based on the different relationships between causes and things caused, and therefore pertains to those causes which have the same formal aspect of causality, as proper and accidental causes, or remote and proximate causes.

Therefore, this division is equivalently a division based on accidental differences, which do not constitute different species.

784. He accordingly says that there are many modes of causes, but that these are found to be fewer in number when *summarized*, that is, when brought together under one head. For even though proper causes and accidental causes are two modes, they are still reduced to one head insofar as both may be considered from the same point of view.

The same thing is true of the other different modes. For many different modes of causes are spoken of, not only with reference to the different species of causes, but also with reference to causes of the same species, namely, those which are reduced to one species of cause.

785. For one cause is said to be prior and another subsequent, and causes are prior or subsequent in two ways.

In one way, when there are many distinct causes which are related to each other, one of which is primary and remote, and another secondary and proximate. For example, in the case of efficient causes man generates man as a

causa prior et remota: et similiter potest considerari in aliis speciebus causarum.

Alio modo in una et eadem causa numero secundum ordinem rationis qui est inter universale et particulare. Nam universale naturaliter est prius, particulare posterius.

786. Praetermittit autem primum modum, et accipit secundum. In secundo enim modo immediate effectus ab utraque causa existit, scilicet priori et posteriori, quod in primo non convenit. Unde dicit, quod sanitatis causa est medicus et artifex in genere causae efficientis. Artifex quidem ut universale, et prius; medicus vero ut particulare, sive speciale, et posterius.

Similiter etiam in causis formalibus dupliciter est causa formalis: ut diapason duplum, vel proportio dupla, vel dualitas est causa formalis, ut speciale et posterius; numerum autem, vel proportio numeri ad numerum vel ad unum, ut universale et prius. Et ita *semper ea quae continent singularia*, scilicet universalia, dicuntur causae priores.

787. Alia divisio est causarum, secundum quod aliquid dicitur esse causa per se et per accidens. Sicut enim causa per se dividitur in universale et particulare, sive in prius et posterius, ita etiam causa per accidens. Unde non solum ipsae causae accidentales dicuntur causae per accidens, sed etiam ipsarum genera. Ut statuae factor, statuae causa est per se; Polycletus autem per accidens est causa, inquantum accidit ei factorem statuae esse. Et sicut Polycletus est causa statuae per accidens, ita omnia universalia *continentia accidens*, idest causam per accidens, dicuntur per accidens causae; sicut homo et animal, quae sub se continent Polycletum, qui est homo et animal.

788. Et sicut causarum per se quaedam sunt propinquae, quaedam remotae, ut dictum est, ita et inter causas per accidens. Nam Polycletus est causa statuae magis propinqua quam album et musicum. Magis enim remotus modus praedicationis per accidens est, cum accidens praedicatur de accidente, quam cum accidens praedicatur de subiecto. Accidens enim non praedicatur de accidente, nisi quia ambo praedicantur de subiecto. Unde magis remotum est ut attribuatur uni accidenti quod est alterius, sicut musico quod est aedificatoris,

proximate and subsequent cause, but the sun as a prior and remote cause. The same thing can be considered in the case of the other species of causes.

In another way, when the cause is numerically one and the same, but is considered according to the sequence which reason sets up between the universal and the particular, for the universal is naturally prior and the particular subsequent.

786. But he omits the first way and considers the second. For in the second way, the effect is the immediate result of both causes, that is, of both the prior and subsequent cause. But this cannot happen in the first way. Hence he says that the cause of health is both the physician and one possessing an art, who belong to the genus of efficient cause: one possesses an art as a universal and prior cause, and the physician possessing it as a particular, or special, and subsequent cause.

The same thing is true of the formal cause, since this cause may also be considered in two ways: for example, for an octave chord "double," or the ratio of 2:1, or the number two, is a formal cause as one that is special and subsequent, whereas number, or the ratio of one number to another or to the unit, is like a universal and prior cause. And in this way too *always those that contain singulars*, that is, universals, are said to be prior causes.

787. Causes are distinguished in another way inasmuch as one thing is said to be a proper cause and another an accidental cause. For just as proper causes are divided into universal and particular, or into prior and subsequent, so also are accidental causes. Therefore, not only accidental causes themselves are called such, but so also are the genera that contain these. For example, a sculptor is the proper cause of a statue, and Polyclitus is an accidental cause inasmuch as he happens to be a sculptor. And just as Polyclitus is an accidental cause of a statue, in a similar way all universals *which contain accidents*, that is, accidental causes, are said to be accidental causes (for example, man and animal, which contain under themselves Polyclitus, who is a man and an animal).

788. And just as some proper causes are proximate and some remote, as was pointed out above, so also is this the case with accidental causes. For Polyclitus is a more proximate cause of a statue than what is white or what is musical. For an accidental mode of predication is more remote when an accident is predicated of an accident than when an accident is predicated of a subject. For one accident is predicated of another only because both are predicated of a subject. Hence when something pertaining to one accident is predicated of another, as when something

quam quod attribuatur subiecto quod est accidentis, sicut Polycleto quod est aedificatoris.

789. Sciendum autem est, quod aliquid potest dici causa per accidens alterius dupliciter.

Uno modo ex parte causae; quia scilicet illud quod accidit causae, dicitur causa per accidens, sicut si album dicatur causa domus.

Alio modo ex parte effectus; ut scilicet aliquid dicatur causa per accidens alicuius, quod accidit ei quod est effectus per se. Quod quidem potest esse tripliciter.

Uno modo, quia habet ordinem necessarium ad effectum, sicut remotio impedimenti habet ordinem necessarium ad effectum. Unde removens prohibens dicitur movens per accidens; sive illud accidens sit contrarium, sicut cholera prohibet frigiditatem, unde scamonaea dicitur infrigidare per accidens, non quia causet frigiditatem sed quia tollit impedimentum frigiditatis, quod est ei contrarium, scilicet choleram: sive etiam si non sit contrarium, sicut columna impedit motum lapidis, unde removens columnam dicitur per accidens movere lapidem superpositum

alio modo, quando accidens habet ordinem ad effectum, non tamen necessarium, nec ut in pluribus, sed ut in paucioribus, sicut inventio thesauri ad fossionem in terra. Et hoc modo fortuna et casus dicuntur causae per accidens.

Tertio, quando nullum ordinem habent, nisi forte secundum existimationem; sicut si aliquis dicat se esse causam terraemotus, quia eo intrante domum accidit terraemotus.

790. Tertia distinctio est, secundum quod prae omnibus his vel praeter omnia haec, quae dicuntur esse secundum se sive per se, et secundum accidens, quaedam sunt causae in potentia, quaedam ut agentia, idest in actu. Sicut aedificationis causa est aedificator in potentia. Hoc enim sonat habitum vel officium. Vel aedificans actu.

791. Et eisdem modis, quibus dividuntur causae, possunt dividi causata in quibus vel quorum causae sunt causae. Potest enim dividi causatum per prius et posterius sive particulare et universale; sicut si dicamus, quod statuae factor est causa huius statuae, quod est posterius, aut statuae, quod est universalius et prius, aut imaginis, quod est adhuc universalius. Et similiter aliquid est causa formalis huius aeris, aut aeris, quod est universalius,

pertaining to a builder is predicated of a musician, this mode of predication is more remote than one in which something is predicated of the subject of an accident, as when something pertaining to a builder is predicated of Polyclitus.

789. Now it must be borne in mind that one thing can be said to be the accidental cause of something else in two ways.

In one way, from the viewpoint of the cause, because whatever is accidental to a cause is itself called an accidental cause—for example, when we say that something white is the cause of a house.

In another way, from the viewpoint of the effect, inasmuch as one thing is said to be an accidental cause of something else because it is accidental to the proper effect. This can happen in three ways.

The first is that the thing has a necessary connection with the effect. Thus that which removes an obstacle is said to be a mover accidentally. This is the case whether that accident is a contrary, as when bile prevents coolness (and thus scammony is said to produce coolness accidentally, not because it causes coolness, but because it removes the obstacle preventing coolness, namely, bile, which is its contrary), or even if it is not a contrary, as when a pillar hinders the movement of a stone which rests upon it, so that one who removes the pillar is said to move the stone accidentally.

In a second way, something is accidental to the proper effect when the accident is connected with the effect neither necessarily nor in the majority of cases but seldom, as the discovery of a treasure is connected with digging in the soil. It is in this way that fortune and chance are said to be accidental causes.

In a third way, things are accidental to the effect when they have no connection except perhaps in the mind, as when someone says that he is the cause of an earthquake because an earthquake took place when he entered the house.

790. And besides the distinction of all things into causes in themselves or proper causes and accidental causes, there is a third division of causes inasmuch as some things are causes potentially and some actually, that is, actively. For example, the cause of building is a builder in a state of potency (for this designates his habit or office), or one who is actually building.

791. And the same distinctions which apply to causes can apply to the effects of which these causes are the causes. For effects, whether particular or universal, can be divided into prior and subsequent, as a sculptor may be called the cause of this statue, which is subsequent; or of a statue, which is more universal and prior; or of an image, which is still more universal. And similarly something is the formal cause of this particular bronze; or of bronze,

aut materiae, quod est adhuc universalius. Et similiter potest dici in accidentalibus, scilicet in effectibus per accidens. Nam statuae factor qui est causa statuae, est etiam causa gravis vel albi vel rubei quae accidunt ex parte materiae, et non sunt ab hoc agente causata.

792. Ulterius ponit quartam distinctionem causae, quae est in simplex et in compositum; ut simplex causa dicatur secundum quod accipitur causa statuae per se totum ut statuae factor, sive per accidens tantum, scilicet Polycletus. Composita autem secundum quod utrumque simul accipitur, ut dicatur causa statuae Polycletus statuae factor.

793. Est autem alius modus quo causae possunt dici compositae, secundum quod plures causae concurrunt ad unius rei constitutionem; sicut plures homines ad trahendum navem, vel plures lapides, ut sint materia domus. Sed hoc praetermisit, quia nullum illorum est causa, sed pars causae.

794. His autem modis positis, colligit istorum modorum numerum, dicens, quod isti modi causarum sunt sex et variantur dupliciter, et ita efficiuntur duodecim.

Hi enim modi sex sunt aut singulare, aut genus, quod superius dixit prius et posterius. Et secundum se et per accidens, ad quod etiam reducitur genus accidentis, nam genus accidentis est causa per accidens. Et iterum per complexum et simplex.

Hi autem sex modi ulterius dividuntur per potentiam et per actum, et sunt duodecim. Ideo autem oportet omnes istos modos per potentiam et actum dividi, quia potentia et actus diversificant habitudinem causae ad effectum.

Nam causae in actu particulares sunt simul et tolluntur cum suis effectibus, sicut hic medicans cum hoc convalescente, et hic aedificans cum hoc aedificato: non enim potest aliquid actu aedificari, nisi sit actu aedificans.

Sed causae secundum potentiam non semper removentur cum effectibus; sicut domus et aedificator non simul corrumpuntur. In quibusdam tamen contingit, quod remota actione efficientis tollitur substantia effectus, sicut in his quorum esse est in fieri, vel quorum causa non solum est effectui causa fiendi sed essendi. Unde remota illuminatione solis ab aere, tollitur lumen. Dicit autem *causas singulares*, quia actus singularium sunt, ut in primo huius habitum est.

which is more universal; or of matter, which is still more universal. The same things can be said of accidental effects, that is, of things produced by accident. For a sculptor who is the cause of a statue is also the cause of the heaviness, whiteness, or redness which are in it as accidents from the matter; these are not caused by this agent.

792. Again, he gives a fourth division of causes, namely, the division into simple causes and composite causes. A cause is said to be simple when in the case of a statue, for example, the proper cause alone is considered, as a sculptor, or when an accidental cause alone is considered, as Polyclitus. But a cause is said to be composite when both are taken together, for example, when we say that the cause of a statue is the sculptor Polyclitus.

793. There is moreover another way in which causes are said to be composite, namely, when several causes act together to produce one effect—for example, when many men act together in order to row a boat, or when many stones combine in order to constitute the matter of a house. But he omits the latter way because no one of these things taken in itself is the cause, but a part of the cause.

794. And having given these different modes of causes, he brings out their number, saying that these modes of causes are six in number, and that each of these have two alternatives so that twelve result.

For these six modes are either singular or generic (or, as he called them above, prior and subsequent); either proper or accidental (to which the genus of the accident is also reduced, for the genus to which an accident belongs is an accidental cause); and again, either composite or simple.

Now these six modes are further divided by potency and act, and thus are twelve in number. Now the reason why all these modes must be divided by potency and act is that potency and act distinguish the connection between cause and effect.

For active causes are at one and the same time particulars and cease to exist along with their effects—for example, this act of healing ceases with this act of recovering health, and this act of building with this thing being built (for a thing cannot be actually being built unless something is actually building).

But potential causes do not always cease to exist when their effects cease; for example, a house and a builder do not cease to exist at one and the same time. In some cases, however, it does happen that when the action of the efficient cause ceases the substance of the effect ceases. This occurs in the case of those things whose being consists in coming to be, or whose cause is not only the cause of their coming to be but also of their being. For example, when the sun's illumination is removed from the atmosphere, light ceases to be. He says *singular causes*, because acts belong to singular things, as was stated in book 1 of this work [21].

LECTURE 4

The definition of "element"

1014a26 Elementum vero dicitur ex quo aliquid componitur primo inexistente indivisibile specie in aliam speciem, [795]

ut vocis elementa, ex quibus componitur vox, et in quae dividitur ultima, illa vero non in alias voces ab eis specie diversas; sed et si dividantur, particulae sunt conformes, ut aquae particulae sunt aqua, sed non syllabae.

Similiter autem et corporum elementa dicunt, dicentes, in quae dividuntur corpora, ultima, et illa non in alia specie differentia corpora, et sive unum, sive plura talia, ea elementa dicuntur.

Similiter vero et quae sunt diagrammatum dicuntur elementa, et ex toto quae sunt demonstrationum. Nam primae demonstrationes in pluribus demonstrationibus existentes, esse demonstrationum elementa dicuntur. Sum autem tales syllogismi primi per unum medium ex tribus terminis.

1014b3 Et transferentes elementum vocant hinc quodcumque unum ens et parvum, quod ad multa est utile. Quapropter parvum et simplex et indivisibile dicitur elementum. Unde evenit maxime universalia elementa esse, qui unumquodque eorum unum ens et simplex multis inest, aut omnibus, aut plurimis. Et unum et punctum principia quibusdam videntur esse. Quoniam ergo vocata genera sunt universalia et indivisibilia (una enim est eorum ratio), elementa genera dicunt aliqui. Et magis quam differentiam, quoniam universale magis genus: nam cui differentia inest, et genus id sequitur; sed cui genus, non omnino differentia. [802]

στοιχεῖον λέγεται ἐξ οὗ σύγκειται πρώτου ἐνυπάρχοντος ἀδιαιρέτου τῷ εἴδει εἰς ἕτερον εἶδος,

οἷον φωνῆς στοιχεῖα ἐξ ὧν σύγκειται ἡ φωνὴ καὶ εἰς ἃ διαιρεῖται ἔσχατα, ἐκεῖνα δὲ μηκέτ' εἰς ἄλλας φωνὰς ἑτέρας τῷ {30} εἴδει αὐτῶν, ἀλλὰ κἂν διαιρῆται, τὰ μόρια ὁμοειδῆ, οἷον ὕδατος τὸ μόριον ὕδωρ, ἀλλ' οὐ τῆς συλλαβῆς.

ὁμοίως δὲ καὶ τὰ τῶν σωμάτων στοιχεῖα λέγουσιν οἱ λέγοντες εἰς ἃ διαιρεῖται τὰ σώματα ἔσχατα, ἐκεῖνα δὲ μηκέτ' εἰς ἄλλα εἴδει διαφέροντα: καὶ εἴτε ἓν εἴτε πλείω τὰ τοιαῦτα, {35} ταῦτα στοιχεῖα λέγουσιν.

παραπλησίως δὲ καὶ τὰ τῶν διαγραμμάτων στοιχεῖα λέγεται, καὶ ὅλως τὰ τῶν ἀποδείξεων: αἱ γὰρ πρῶται ἀποδείξεις καὶ ἐν πλείοσιν ἀποδείξεσιν ἐνυπάρχουσαι, {1014b1} αὗται στοιχεῖα τῶν ἀποδείξεων λέγονται: εἰσὶ δὲ τοιοῦτοι συλλογισμοὶ οἱ πρῶτοι ἐκ τῶν τριῶν δι' ἑνὸς μέσου.

καὶ μεταφέροντες δὲ στοιχεῖον καλοῦσιν ἐντεῦθεν ὃ ἂν ἓν ὂν καὶ μικρὸν ἐπὶ πολλὰ ᾖ χρήσιμον, {5} διὸ καὶ τὸ μικρὸν καὶ ἁπλοῦν καὶ ἀδιαίρετον στοιχεῖον λέγεται. ὅθεν ἐλήλυθε τὰ μάλιστα καθόλου στοιχεῖα εἶναι, ὅτι ἕκαστον αὐτῶν ἓν ὂν καὶ ἁπλοῦν ἐν πολλοῖς ὑπάρχει ἢ πᾶσιν ἢ ὅτι πλείστοις, καὶ τὸ ἓν καὶ τὴν στιγμὴν ἀρχάς τισι δοκεῖν εἶναι. ἐπεὶ οὖν τὰ καλούμενα γένη {10} καθόλου καὶ ἀδιαίρετα (οὐ γὰρ ἔστι λόγος αὐτῶν), στοιχεῖα τὰ γένη λέγουσί τινες, καὶ μᾶλλον ἢ τὴν διαφορὰν ὅτι καθόλου μᾶλλον τὸ γένος: ᾧ μὲν γὰρ ἡ διαφορὰ ὑπάρχει, καὶ τὸ γένος ἀκολουθεῖ, ᾧ δὲ τὸ γένος, οὐ παντὶ ἡ διαφορά.

The inherent principle of which a thing is first composed and which is not divisible into another species is called an element.

For example, the elements of a word are the parts of which a word is composed, into which it is ultimately divided, and which are not further divided into other words specifically different from them. But if they are divided, their parts are alike, as the parts of water are water—but this is not true of the syllable.

Similarly, people who speak of the elements of bodies mean the component parts into which bodies are ultimately divided and which are not divided into other bodies specifically different. And whether such parts are one or many, they call them elements.

And similarly, the parts of diagrams are called elements, and in general the parts of demonstrations. For the primary demonstrations which are contained in many other demonstrations are called the elements of demonstrations, and such are the primary syllogisms which are composed of three terms and proceed through one middle term.

Some transfer the meaning of the term "element" to mean anything which is one and small and useful for many purposes, and thus anything which is small and simple and indivisible is called an element. Hence it follows that the most universal things are elements, because each of them, being one and simple, is found in many things, either in all or in most of them. And to some the unit and the point seem to be principles. Therefore, since what are called genera are universal and indivisible (for their formal character is one), some men call the genera elements, and these more than a difference, since a genus is more universal. For where the difference is present the genus also follows, but the difference is not always present where the genus is.

1014b14 Omnium autem commune est elementum cuiuslibet, quod primum est cuique. [807]

ἁπάντων δὲ κοινὸν τὸ εἶναι στοιχεῖον ἑκάστου τὸ {15} πρῶτον ἐνυπάρχον ἑκάστῳ.

And in all these cases it is common for the element of each thing to be the primary component of each thing.

---

795. Hic distinguit hoc nomen elementum. Circa quod duo facit.

Primo assignat diversos modos elementi.

Secundo ostendit quid in omnibus sit commune, ibi, **omnium autem commune**.

Circa primum duo facit.

Primo ostendit quomodo elementum proprie dicatur.

Secundo quomodo dicatur transumptive, ibi, **et transferentes elementum** et cetera.

Ponit ergo primo, quamdam elementi descriptionem; ex qua colligi potest, quod quatuor sunt de ratione elementi.

Quorum primum est, ut sit causa sicut ex quo: per quod patet, quod elementum ponitur in genere causae materialis.

796. Secundum est, quod sit principium ex quo aliquid fiat primo. Cuprum enim est ex quo fit statua; non tamen est elementum, quia habet aliquam aliam materiam ex qua fit.

797. Tertium est, quod sit inexistens sive intrinsecum: per quod differt elementum ab omni eo ex quo fit aliquid sicut ex transeunte, sive sit privatio, aut contrarium, sive materia contrarietati et privationi subiecta, quae est materia transiens. Ut cum dicimus, quod homo musicus fit ex homine non musico, vel musicum ex non musico. Elementa enim oportet manere in his quorum sunt elementa.

798. Quartum est, quod habeat aliquam speciem, quae non dividatur in diversas species: per quod differt elementum a materia prima, qua nullam speciem habet, et etiam ab omnibus materiis, quae in diversas species resolvi possunt, sicut sanguis et huiusmodi.

Propter hoc dicit, quod elementum est ex quo aliquid componitur, quantum ad primum.

Primo, quantum ad secundum.

Inexistente, quantum ad tertium.

Indivisibili specie in aliam speciem, quantum ad quartum.

799. Hanc autem definitionem manifestat in quatuor, in quibus utimur nomine elementi.

Dicimus enim ipsas literas esse elementa vocis, quia ex eis omnis vox componitur, et primo. Quod ex hoc patet, quia omnes voces in literas resolvuntur, sicut in ultima. Quod est enim ultimum in resolutione, oportet esse primum in compositione. Literae autem non resolvuntur ulterius in alias voces specie diversas. Sed, si ali-

795. Here he distinguishes the different senses of the term "element," and in regard to this he does two things.

First, he gives the different senses in which the term "element" is used.

Second (1014b14; [807]), he indicates what all of them have in common, at **and in all these**.

In regard to the first he does two things.

First, he explains how the term "element" is used in its proper sense;

second (1014b3; [802]), how it is used in transferred senses, at **people also use**.

First, he gives a sort of description of an element, and from this one can gather the four ideas contained in its definition.

The first is that an element is a cause in the sense of that from which a thing comes to be; from this it is clear that an element is placed in the genus of material cause.

796. The second is that an element is the principle from which something first comes to be. For copper is that from which a statue comes to be, but it is still not an element because it has some matter from which it comes to be.

797. The third is that an element is inherent or intrinsic. For this reason it differs from everything of a transitory nature from which a thing comes to be, whether it be a privation or a contrary or the matter subject to contrariety and privation, which is transitory. For example, when we say that a musical man comes from a non-musical man, or that the musical comes from the non-musical. For elements must remain in the things of which they are the elements.

798. The fourth is that an element has a species which is not divisible into different species. Thus an element differs from first matter, which has no species, and also from every sort of matter which is capable of being divided into different species, as blood and things of this kind.

Hence he says, as to the first idea, that an element is that of which a thing is composed;

as to the second, that it is that of which a thing is **first** composed;

as to the third, that it is **an inherent principle**;

and to as the fourth, that it is **not divisible into another species**.

799. He illustrates this definition of element in four cases in which we use the term "element."

For we say that letters are the elements of a word because every word is composed of them, and of them primarily. This is evident from the fact that all words are divided into letters as ultimate things, for what is last in the process of dissolution must be first in the process of composition. But letters are not further divided into other

quo modo dividantur, particulae in quas fit divisio, erunt *conformes*, idest unius speciei, sicut omnes particulae aquae sunt aqua. Dividitur autem litera secundum tempora prolationis, prout litera longa dicitur habere duo tempora, brevis vero unum. Nec tamen partes, in quas sic dividuntur literae, sunt diversae secundum speciem vocis. Non est autem ita de syllaba: nam eius partes sunt diversae secundum speciem: alius enim sonus est secundum speciem, quem facit vocalis et consonans, ex quibus syllaba componitur.

800. Secundum exemplum ponit in corporibus naturalibus, in quibus etiam quaedam dicimus elementa quorumdam. Illa enim dicuntur corporum esse elementa, in quae ultimo resolvuntur omnia corpora mixta: et per consequens ea sunt, ex quibus primo componuntur huiusmodi corpora. Ipsa autem corpora, quae elementa dicuntur, non dividuntur in alia corpora specie differentia, sed in partes consimiles, sicut quaelibet pars aquae est aqua. Et quicumque posuerunt tale corpus esse unum, scilicet in quod omnia resolvuntur, et ipsum non resolvitur in alia, dixerunt unum esse elementum. Quidam vero aquam, quidam autem aerem, quidam autem ignem. Qui vero posuerunt plura talia corpora, dixerunt etiam esse elementa plura. Sciendum est, quod cum in definitione elementi ponatur, quod non dividitur in diversa secundum speciem, non est intelligendum de partibus in quas aliquid dividitur divisione quantitatis: sic enim lignum esset elementum, quia quaelibet pars ligni est lignum: sed de divisione, quae fit secundum alterationem, sicut corpora mixta resolvuntur in simplicia.

801. Tertium exemplum ponit in demonstrationibus; in quibus etiam utimur nomine elementi, sicut dicitur liber elementorum Euclidis. Et dicit, quod modo simili et propinquo dictis dicuntur elementa, quae *sunt diagrammatum*, idest descriptionum geometralium elementa. Et non solum hoc potest dici in geometria, sed universaliter in omnibus demonstrationibus. Illae enim demonstrationes, quae existunt in tribus terminis tantum, dicuntur esse aliorum elementa. Nam ex his componuntur aliae demonstrationes, et in ea resolvuntur.

Quod sic patet. Secunda enim demonstratio accipit pro principio conclusionem primae demonstrationis, inter cuius terminos intelligitur medium, quod fuit primae demonstrationis principium. Et sic secunda demonstratio erit ex quatuor terminis; prima ex tribus tantum, tertia vero ex quinque, quarta ex sex, et sic quaelibet demonstratio unum terminum addit. In quo manifestum est demonstrationes primas in postremis includi: ut si sit haec demonstratio prima: omne B est A:

words which are specifically different. Yet if they should be divided in any way, the parts in which the division results would be *alike*, that is, specifically the same, just as all parts of water are water. Now letters are divided according to the amount of time required to pronounce them, inasmuch as a long letter is said to require two periods of time, and a short letter one. But while the parts into which letters are so divided do not differ as the species of words do, this is not the case with a syllable, for its parts are specifically different, since the sounds which a vowel and a consonant make (of which a syllable is composed) are specifically different.

800. He gives as a second example natural bodies, certain of which we also call the elements of certain others. For those things into which all compounds are ultimately divided are called their elements; therefore, they are the things of which bodies of this kind are composed. But those bodies which are called elements are not divisible into other bodies which are specifically different, but into like parts, as any part of water is water. And all those who held for one such body into which every body is divided and which is itself incapable of being further divided said that there is one element. Some said that it is water, some air, and some fire. But those who posited many such bodies also said there are many elements. Now it should be borne in mind that when it is set down in the definition of an element that an element is not divisible into different species, this should not be understood of the parts into which a thing is divided in a quantitative division (for wood would then be an element, since any part of wood is wood), but in a division made by alteration, as compounds are divided into simple bodies.

801. As a third example he gives the order of demonstrations, in which we also employ the word element. For example, we speak of Euclid's *Elements*. And he says that, in a way similar and close to those mentioned, those things that *are parts of diagrams*, or the constituents of geometrical figures, are called elements. This can be said not only of the demonstrations in geometry but universally of all demonstrations. For those demonstrations which have only three terms are called the elements of other demonstrations, because the others are composed of them and resolved into them.

This is shown as follows. A second demonstration takes as its starting point the conclusion of a first demonstration, whose terms are understood to contain the middle term which was the starting point of the first demonstration. Thus the second demonstration will proceed from four terms; the first from three only; the third from five; and the fourth from six. Thus each demonstration adds one term. So it is clear that first demonstrations are included in subsequent ones, as when this first demonstration, "Every

omne C est B: ergo omne C est A: hoc includetur in hac, omne C est A: omne D est C: ergo omne D est A. Et ulterius ista in alia, quae concludit, omne E est A: ut quasi videatur esse ad hanc ultimam conclusionem unus syllogismus ex pluribus syllogismis compositus plura media habens, ut dicatur sic, omne B est A: et omne C est B: et omne D est C: et omne E est D: ergo omne E est A. Prima igitur demonstratio, quae habebat unum medium et solum tres terminos, est simplex et non resolvitur in aliam demonstrationem, sed omnes aliae resolvuntur in ipsam. Et ideo syllogismi primi, qui fiunt ex terminis tribus per unum medium, elementa dicuntur.

802. Deinde cum dicit *et transferentes* ostendit quomodo elementum dicatur transumptive; dicens, quod ex hac praemissa ratione et significatione elementi transtulerunt quidam hoc nomen elementum ad significandum aliquid, quod est unum, et parvum, et ad multa utile. Ex hoc enim quod elementum est indivisibile in diversas species, acceperunt quod sit unum. Ex eo vero quod est primum, quod sit simplex. Ex eo vero, quod ex elementis alia componuntur, acceperunt quod sit utile ad multa. Unde hanc rationem elementi constituerunt, ut elementum dicerent omne illud, quod est parvum in quantitate, et simplex, quasi ex aliis non compositum, et indivisibile in diversa.

803. Hac autem ratione elementi constituta, per transumptionem contingebat eis ut duos modos elementorum adinvenirent; quorum primus est, ut ea quae sunt maxime universalia, dicerent elementa. Universale enim est unum secundum rationem, et est simplex, quia eius definitio non componitur ex diversis, et est in multis, et sic est ad multa utile, sive sit in omnibus, sicut unum et ens; sive in pluribus, sicut alia genera. Per eamdem vero rationem contingebat eis secundo, quod punctum et unitatem dicerent esse principia vel elementa, quia utrumque eorum est unum simplex et ad multa utile.

804. Sed in hoc a vera ratione elementi defecerunt, quia universalia non sunt materia, ex quibus componuntur particularia, sed praedicant eorum substantiam. Similiter et punctus non est materia linearum; non enim linea ex punctis componitur.

805. Hac autem transumptiva elementi ratione constituta, patet solutio cuiusdam quaestionis in tertio libro disputatae; scilicet quid sit magis elementum, utrum genus vel species, et utrum genus magis quam differentia. Patet enim consequi quod genera magis sunt elementa, quia genera magis sunt universalia et indivisibilia. Non enim est ratio eorum et definitio, quam oporteat componi ex genere et differentia; sed definitiones proprie dantur de speciebus. Et si aliquod genus definitur,

B is A, every C is B, therefore every C is A," is included in this demonstration, "Every C is A, every D is C, therefore every D is A." This again is included in the demonstration whose conclusion is that every E is A, so that for this final conclusion there seems to be one syllogism composed of several syllogisms having several middle terms. This may be expressed thus: "Every B is A, every C is B, every D is C, every E is D, therefore every E is A." Hence a first demonstration, which has one middle term and only three terms, is simple and not reducible to another demonstration, whereas all other demonstrations are reducible to it. Hence first syllogisms, which come from three terms by way of one middle term, are called elements.

802. *People also use* (1014b3). Here he shows how the term "element" is used in a transferred sense. He says that some men, on the basis of the foregoing notion or meaning of element, have used the term in a transferred sense to signify anything that is one and small and useful for many purposes. For from the fact that an element is indivisible they understood that it is one, and from the fact that it is first they understood that it is simple, and from the fact that other things are composed of elements they understood that an element is useful for many purposes. Hence they set up this definition of an element in order that they might say that everything which is smallest in quantity and simple (inasmuch as it is not composed of other things) and incapable of division into different species is an element.

803. But when they had set up this definition of element, it turned out that by using it in a transferred sense they had invented two senses of element. First, they called the most universal things elements, for a universal is one in definition and is simple (because its definition is not composed of different parts) and is found in many things, and thus is useful for many purposes, whether it be found in all things, as unity and being are, or in most things, as the other genera. And by the same reasoning it came about that they called points and units "principles" or "elements" because each of them is one simple thing and useful for many purposes.

804. But in this respect they fell short of the true notion of a principle, because universals are not the matter of which particular things are composed, but predicate their very substance. And similarly, points are not the matter of a line, for a line is not composed of points.

805. Now with this transferred notion of element established, the solution to a question disputed in book 3 [431–36] becomes clear—namely, whether a genus or a species is more an element, and whether a genus or a difference is more an element. For it clearly follows that genera are elements to a greater degree because genera are more universal and indivisible. For there is no concept or definition of them which must be composed of genera and differences, but it is species which are properly defined. And if a genus

non definitur inquantum est genus, sed inquantum est species; et ideo species dividitur in diversa, et propter hoc non habent rationem elementi. Genus autem non dividitur in diversa: et ideo dixerunt genera esse elementa magis quam species. Alia translatio habet **una enim est eorum ratio** idest indivisibilis, quia genera, etsi non habeant definitionem, tamen id quod significatur per nomen generis, est quaedam conceptio intellectus simplex, quae ratio dici potest.

806. Et sicut genus est magis elementum quam species, quia est simplicius; ita etiam magis quam differentia, licet ipsa simplex sit, quia genus est universalius. Quod ex hoc patet: quia cuicumque inest differentia, inest genus, cum per se differentiae non transcendant genus: non tamen oportet quod ad omne id sequatur differentia cui convenit genus.

807. Ultimo autem dicit, quod omnibus praedictis modis elementi hoc est commune, esse primum in unoquoque, sicut dictum est.

is defined, it is not defined insofar as it is a genus but insofar as it is a species. Hence a species is divided into different parts and thus does not have the character of an element. But a genus is not divisible into different parts, and therefore they said that genera are elements more than species. Another translation reads, **for their formal character is one**, that is, indivisible, because even though genera do not have a definition, still what is signified by the term "genus" is a simple conception of the intellect which can be called a definition.

806. And just as a genus is more an element than a species is because it is simpler, in a similar way it is more an element than a difference is, even though a difference is simple, because a genus is more universal. This is clear from the fact that anything which has a difference has a genus (since *per se* differences do not transcend a genus), but not everything which has a genus necessarily has a difference.

807. Last of all, he says that all of the foregoing senses of element have this notion in common: an element is the primary component of each being (as has been stated).

Lecture 5

The definition of "nature"

1014b16 Natura vero dicitur uno quidem modo nascentium generatio, ut si quis porrigens dicat naturam. [808]

Uno vero modo, ex quo generatur primum generatum inexistente.

Amplius unde motus primus in quolibet natura entium, et est in eo inquantum id existit. Nasci vero dicuntur quaecumque augmentum habent per alterum in tangendo et simul et aliquid esse apte, ut embryo.

Differt autem connascentia a tactu. Hic enim nihil praeter tactum diversum esse necesse est. Insimul vero ante existentibus est aliquid unum idem in ambobus, quod facit pro tactu simul apte esse, et unum esse secundum quantitatem et continuitatem, sed non secundum qualitatem.

Amplius autem natura dicitur ex quo primo aut est aut fit aliquid entium natura, cum informe sit et immutabile a sua propria potestate, ut statuae, et vasorum aereorum, aes natura dicitur, et ligneorum, lignum; similiter autem in aliis; ex his enim unumquodque, salvata prima materia. Hoc enim modo et existentium natura elementa dicunt naturam, alii ignem, alii terram, alii aquam, alii aerem, alii aliquid aliud tale dicentes, alii quaedam horum, alii omnia ea.

Amplius alio modo dicitur natura, existentium natura substantia, ut dicentes naturam primam esse compositionem, ut Empedocles dicit, *quod natura nullius est entium, sed solum mixtio et permutatio permixtorum natura in hominibus nominatur.* Quapropter et quaecumque natura sunt, aut fiunt, iam existente ex quo apta nata sunt fieri aut esse, non dicimus naturam habere, si

φύσις λέγεται ἕνα μὲν τρόπον ἡ τῶν φυομένων γένεσις, οἷον εἴ τις ἐπεκτείνας λέγοι τὸ υ,

ἕνα δὲ ἐξ οὗ φύεται πρώτου τὸ φυόμενον ἐνυπάρχοντος:

ἔτι ὅθεν ἡ κίνησις ἡ πρώτη ἐν ἑκάστῳ τῶν φύσει ὄντων ἐν αὐτῷ ᾗ αὐτὸ {20} ὑπάρχει: φύεσθαι δὲ λέγεται ὅσα αὔξησιν ἔχει δι᾽ ἑτέρου τῷ ἅπτεσθαι καὶ συμπεφυκέναι ἢ προσπεφυκέναι ὥσπερ τὰ ἔμβρυα:

διαφέρει δὲ σύμφυσις ἁφῆς, ἔνθα μὲν γὰρ οὐδὲν παρὰ τὴν ἁφὴν ἕτερον ἀνάγκη εἶναι, ἐν δὲ τοῖς συμπεφυκόσιν ἔστι τι ἓν τὸ αὐτὸ ἐν ἀμφοῖν ὃ ποιεῖ ἀντὶ τοῦ {25} ἅπτεσθαι συμπεφυκέναι καὶ εἶναι ἓν κατὰ τὸ συνεχὲς καὶ ποσόν, ἀλλὰ μὴ κατὰ τὸ ποιόν.

ἔτι δὲ φύσις λέγεται ἐξ οὗ πρώτου ἢ ἔστιν ἢ γίγνεταί τι τῶν φύσει ὄντων, ἀρρυθμίστου ὄντος καὶ ἀμεταβλήτου ἐκ τῆς δυνάμεως τῆς αὐτοῦ, οἷον ἀνδριάντος καὶ τῶν σκευῶν τῶν χαλκῶν ὁ χαλκὸς ἡ {30} φύσις λέγεται, τῶν δὲ ξυλίνων ξύλον: ὁμοίως δὲ καὶ ἐπὶ τῶν ἄλλων: ἐκ τούτων γάρ ἐστιν ἕκαστον διασωζομένης τῆς πρώτης ὕλης: τοῦτον γὰρ τὸν τρόπον καὶ τῶν φύσει ὄντων τὰ στοιχεῖά φασιν εἶναι φύσιν, οἱ μὲν πῦρ οἱ δὲ γῆν οἱ δ᾽ ἀέρα οἱ δ᾽ ὕδωρ οἱ δ᾽ ἄλλο τι τοιοῦτον λέγοντες, οἱ δ᾽ {35} ἔνια τούτων οἱ δὲ πάντα ταῦτα.

ἔτι δ᾽ ἄλλον τρόπον λέγεται ἡ φύσις ἡ τῶν φύσει ὄντων οὐσία, οἷον οἱ λέγοντες τὴν φύσιν εἶναι τὴν πρώτην σύνθεσιν, {1015a1} ἢ ὥσπερ Ἐμπεδοκλῆς λέγει ὅτι φύσις; οὐδενός ἐστιν ἐόντων, ἀλλὰ μόνον μῖξίς τε διάλλαξίς τε μιγέντων ἔστι, φύσις δ᾽ ἐπὶ τοῖς ὀνομάζεται ἀνθρώποισιν. διὸ καὶ ὅσα φύσει ἔστιν ἢ γίγνεται, ἤδη ὑπάρχοντος ἐξ οὗ πέφυκε γίγνεσθαι ἢ εἶναι, οὔπω φαμὲν {5} τὴν

Nature means, in one sense, the generation of things that are born, as if one were to pronounce the word "nature" long.

And in another sense it means the immanent principle from which anything generated is first produced.

Again, it means the source of the primary motion in any beings which are by nature, and it is in each inasmuch as it is such. Now all those things are said to be born that grow through something else by touching and by existing together, or by being naturally joined, as in the case of embryos.

But being born together differs from touching, for in the latter case there need be nothing but contact. But in things that are naturally joined together there is some one same thing in both, instead of contact, which causes them to be one, and which makes them to be one in quantity and continuity but not in quality.

Again, nature means the primary thing of which a natural being is composed or from which it comes to be, when it is unformed and immutable by its own power. For example, the bronze of a statue or of bronze articles is said to be their nature, and the wood of wooden things, and the same applies in the case of other things. For each thing comes from these though its primary matter is preserved. For it is also in this sense that men speak of the elements of natural beings as their nature; some calling it fire, others earth, others water, others air, and others something similar to these, whereas others call all of them nature.

In still another sense, nature means the substance of things that are by nature, as those who say that nature is the primary composition of a thing. As Empedocles says, *Of nothing that exists is there nature, but only the mixing and separating-out of what has been mixed.* Nature is but the name men give to these. For this reason we do not say that things that are or come to be by nature have a nature, even when

non habent speciem et formam. Ergo natura quidem quod ex utrisque est, ut animalia et eorum partes.

φύσιν ἔχειν ἐὰν μὴ ἔχῃ τὸ εἶδος καὶ τὴν μορφήν. φύσει μὲν οὖν τὸ ἐξ ἀμφοτέρων τούτων ἐστίν, οἷον τὰ ζῷα καὶ τὰ μόρια αὐτῶν:

that from which they can be or come to be is already present, so long as they do not have their form or species. Hence that which is composed of both of these exists by nature, as animals and their parts.

1015a7 Natura autem prima materia; et haec dupliciter: aut quae ad id prima, aut ex toto prima: ut operum aereorum, ad ipsa quidem primum aes: totaliter vero forsan aqua, si omnia liquescentia aqua. [821]

φύσις δὲ ἤ τε πρώτη ὕλη (καὶ αὕτη διχῶς, ἢ ἡ πρὸς αὐτὸ πρώτη ἢ ἡ ὅλως πρώτη, οἷον τῶν χαλκῶν ἔργων πρὸς αὐτὰ μὲν πρῶτος ὁ χαλκός, ὅλως δ᾽ {10} ἴσως ὕδωρ, εἰ πάντα τὰ τηκτὰ ὕδωρ)

Again, "nature" is the primary matter of a thing, and this in two senses: either what is primary with respect to this particular thing, or primary in general; for example, the primary matter of bronze articles is bronze, but in general it is perhaps water, if everything capable of being liquefied is water.

Et species et substantia. Haec autem finis generationis. Metaphora vero iam et omnino omnis substantia natura dicitur propter hanc, quia et natura substantia quaedam est.

καὶ τὸ εἶδος καὶ ἡ οὐσία: τοῦτο δ᾽ ἐστὶ τὸ τέλος τῆς γενέσεως. μεταφορᾷ δ᾽ ἤδη καὶ ὅλως πᾶσα οὐσία φύσις λέγεται διὰ ταύτην, ὅτι καὶ ἡ φύσις οὐσία τίς ἐστιν.

And nature is also a thing's form or substance, the terminus of the process of generation. But metaphorically speaking, every substance in general is called "nature" because of form or species, for the nature of a thing is also a kind of substance.

1015a13 Ex dictis igitur prima natura et proprie dicta est substantia, quae principium motus habentium in se inquantum ea. Materia namque, quia huius est susceptibilis, esse dicitur natura. [824]

ἐκ δὴ τῶν εἰρημένων ἡ πρώτη φύσις καὶ κυρίως λεγομένη ἐστὶν ἡ οὐσία ἡ τῶν ἐχόντων {15} ἀρχὴν κινήσεως ἐν αὑτοῖς ἢ αὑτά: ἡ γὰρ ὕλη τῷ ταύτης δεκτικὴ εἶναι λέγεται φύσις,

Hence, from what has been said, "nature" in its primary and proper sense is the substance of those things that have within themselves as such the source of their motion. For matter is called nature because it is receptive of this.

Et generationes et generari, quia sunt ab ea motus. Et principium motus natura existentium idipsum est existens, aut potestate, aut perfectione.

καὶ αἱ γενέσεις καὶ τὸ φύεσθαι τῷ ἀπὸ ταύτης εἶναι κινήσεις. καὶ ἡ ἀρχὴ τῆς κινήσεως τῶν φύσει ὄντων αὕτη ἐστίν, ἐνυπάρχουσά πως ἢ δυνάμει ἢ ἐντελεχείᾳ.

And processes of generation and growth are called nature because they are motions proceeding from it. And nature is the source of motion in those things that are by nature, and it is something present in them either potentially or perfectly in act.

---

808. Hic distinguit hoc nomen natura: cuius quidem consideratio, licet non videatur ad primum philosophum, sed magis ad naturalem pertinere, ideo tamen hic hoc nomen natura distinguitur, quia natura secundum sui quamdam acceptionem de omni substantia dicitur, ut patebit. Et per consequens cadit in consideratione philosophi primi, sicut et substantia universalis. Circa hoc autem duo facit.

Primo distinguit diversos modos, quibus natura dicitur.

Secundo reducit omnes ad unum primum, ibi, *ex dictis igitur*.

Circa primum duo facit.

Primo ponit quinque modos principales.

Secundo ponit duos alios adiunctos duobus ultimis, ibi, *natura autem prima materia*.

808. Here he gives the different meanings of the term "nature." And even though an investigation of the term "nature" appears not to belong to first philosophy, but rather to the philosophy of nature, he nevertheless gives the different meanings of this term here, because according to one of its common meanings, nature is predicated of every substance, as he will make clear. Hence it falls under the consideration of first philosophy, just as universal substance does. In regard to this he does two things.

First [808], he distinguishes the different senses in which the term "nature" is used.

Second (1015a13; [824]), he reduces all of these to one primary notion, at **hence, from what**.

In regard to the first he does two things.

First, he gives five principal senses in which the term "nature" is used.

Second (1015a7; [821]), he gives two additional senses connected with the last two of these, at **again, nature**.

Dicit ergo primo, quod natura dicitur uno modo generatio generatorum, vel ut alia litera habet melius, *nascentium*. Non enim omnia generata nascentia dici possunt; sed solum in viventibus, sicut in plantis, sive in animalibus, et in partibus eorum. Non autem generatio rerum non viventium potest dici natura proprie loquendo secundum communem usum vocabuli, sed solum generatio viventium; ut dicatur natura ipsa nativitas vel ipsa nascentia, quod ipsum nomen sonare videtur. *Ut si quis porrigens dicat naturam*. Litera ista corrupta est. Quod ex alia translatione patet, quae sic habet *ut si quis producens dicat ypsilon*. Physis enim, quod apud Graecos naturam significat, si pro generatione viventium accipiatur, habet primum ypsilon productum; si vero pro principio, sicut communiter utitur, habet primum ypsilon breve. Posset tamen per hanc literam intelligi quod hoc nomen natura de generatione viventium dicatur secundum quamdam porrectionem idest extensionem.

809. Ex hoc autem quod ipsa nativitas primo natura dicta est, secutus est modus secundus, ut scilicet generationis principium, ex quo aliquid generatur, sive ex quo illud, quod nascitur generatur primo, sicut ex intrinseco principio, dicatur natura.

810. Et per similitudinem nativitatis ad alios motus, ulterius processit huius nominis significatio, ut natura tertio modo dicatur id, unde est principium motus in quolibet entium secundum naturam, dummodo sit in eo inquantum huiusmodi, et non per accidens. Sicut in medico, qui infirmatur, inest principium sanationis, scilicet ars medicinae, non tamen inquantum est infirmus, sed inquantum medicus. Sanatur autem non inquantum est medicus, sed inquantum infirmus: et sic principium motus non est in eo inquantum movetur. Et haec est definitio naturae posita in secundo *Physicorum*.

811. Et, quia de nascentibus mentionem fecit, ostendit quid sit proprie *nasci*, ut habet alia litera, loco cuius haec litera improprie habet *generari*. Differt enim generatio in viventibus a generatione inanimatorum, quia inanimatum generatur, non ut coniunctum sive unitum generanti, ut ignis ab igne, et aqua ab aqua.

In viventibus autem fit generatio per quamdam unionem ad generationis principium. Et, quia additio quanti ad quantum facit augmentum, ideo in generatione viventium videtur esse quoddam augmentum, sicut est cum ex arbore nascitur fructus, aut folium. Et ideo dicit, quod nasci dicuntur quaecumque *augmentum habent*, idest quoddam augmentum cum generationis principio.

He accordingly first says that in one sense "nature" means the process of generation of things that are generated, or according to another text which states this in a better way, *of things that are born*. For not everything that is generated can be said to be born, but only living things (for example, plants and animals and their parts). The generation of non-living things cannot be called "nature," properly speaking, according to the common use of the term, but only the generation of living things inasmuch as "nature" may mean the nativity or birth of a thing. *As if one were to pronounce the word "nature" long*. This text is corrupt. This is clear from another translation, which says: *as if one were to pronounce the letter "upsilon" long*. For *physis*, which means "nature" in Greek, if it is used to mean the generation of living things, is pronounced with a long upsilon; but if it is used for a principle, as it ordinarily is, it is pronounced with a short upsilon. Yet even from this text it can be understood that the term "nature" means the generation of living things by a certain lengthening or extension of usage.

809. Again, from the fact that "nature" was first used to designate the birth of a thing, there followed a second use of the term, such that "nature" came to mean the principle of generation from which a thing comes to be, or that from which (as from an intrinsic principle) something born is first generated.

810. And as a result of the likeness between birth and other kinds of motion, the meaning of the term "nature" has been extended farther, so that in a third sense it means the source from which motion begins in any being according to its nature, provided that it is present in it insofar as it is such a being and not accidentally. For example, the principle of health, which is the medical art, is not present in a physician who is ill insofar as he is ill, but insofar as he is a physician. And he is not healed insofar as he is a physician, but insofar as he is ill; and thus the source of motion is not in him insofar as he is moved. This is the definition of "nature" given in *Physics* 2.

811. And because he mentioned things that are born, he also shows what it means in the proper sense *to be born*, as another text says, and in place of which this text incorrectly says *to be generated*. For the generation of living things differs from that of non-living things, because a non-living thing is not generated by being joined or united to its generator, as fire is generated by fire and water by water.

But the generation of a living thing comes about through some kind of union with the principle of generation. And because the addition of quantity to quantity causes growth, therefore in the generation of living things there seems to be a certain growth, as when a tree puts forth foliage and fruit. Hence he says that those things are said to be born which *grow*, that is, have some growth with the principle of generation.

812. Differt autem hoc augmentum a specie motus quae augmentum dicitur, qua moventur iam nata. Nam in augmento aliquid augetur in seipso per hoc, quod id quod additur transit in substantiam eius cui additur, sicut nutrimentum in substantiam nutriti:

id autem, quod nascitur apponitur ei ex quo nascitur, tamquam alterum et diversum, non sicut in eius substantiam transiens. Et ideo dicit, quod habet augmentum *per diversum* sive per alterum: quasi dicat, quod hoc augmentum fit per appositionem alicuius alterius, vel diversi.

813. Sed appositio augmentum faciens potest intelligi dupliciter. Uno modo *tangendo*, idest per solum contactum. Alio modo per hoc *quod est simul* idest aliqua duo simul producuntur adinvicem coaptata, sicut brachium et nervus et *aliquid esse apte*, idest quod aliquid adaptetur ad alterum iam praeexistens, sicut capilli capiti, et dentes gingivis.

Loco autem huius alia litera habet melius *connasci* et *adnasci*. In hac autem generatione viventium non solum fit appositio per tactum, sed etiam per quamdam coaptationem sive connascentiam; ut patet in embryonibus, qui non solum tanguntur in matrice, sed etiam alligantur in principio suae generationis.

814. Ostendit autem quid inter duo praedicta differat; dicens, quod *conflatio*, idest colligatio sive *connascentia*, ut alia litera habet, differt a tactu, quia in tactu non est necessarium aliquid esse praeter tangentia, quod ea faciat unum.

In colligatis autem sive coaptatis sive connatis vel adnatis oportet esse quid unum in ambobus *quod pro tactu*, idest loco tactus faciat ea simul *apta esse* idest coaptata vel ligata sive simul nasci. Intelligendum est autem quod id, quod facit ea unum, facit esse unum secundum quantitatem et continuitatem, et non secundum qualitatem; quia ligamentum non alterat ligata a suis dispositionibus.

815. Ex hoc autem apparet, quia quod nascitur semper est coniunctum ei ex quo nascitur. Ideo natura numquam dicit principium extrinsecum, sed secundum omnes suas acceptiones dicit principium intrinsecum.

816. Ex hac autem tertia ratione naturae sequitur quarta. Si enim principium motus rerum naturalium natura dicitur, principium autem motus rerum naturalium quibusdam videbatur esse materia, consequens fuit ut materia natura diceretur, quae quidem est principium

812. But this kind of growth differs from that species of motion which is called "growth," by which things that are already born are moved or changed. For a thing that grows within itself does so because the part added passes over into the substance of that thing, as food passes over into the substance of the one nourished.

But anything that is born is added to the thing from which it is born as something other and different, and not as something that passes over into its substance. Hence he says that it grows *through something distinct* or something else, as if to say that this growth comes about through the addition of something that is other or different.

813. But addition that brings about growth can be understood to take place in two ways: in one way, *by touching*, that is, by contact alone; in another way, *by existing together*, that is, by the fact that two things are produced together and naturally connected with each other, as the arms and sinews; *and by being joined*, that is, by the fact that something is naturally adapted to something else already existing, as hair to the head and teeth to the gums.

In place of this another text reads, more appropriately, *by being born together with*, and *by being connected with at birth*. Now in the generation of living things, addition comes about not only by contact, but also by a kind of joining together or natural connection, as is evident in the case of embryos, which are not only in contact in the womb, but are also bound to it at the beginning of their generation.

814. Further, he indicates the difference between these two, saying that *being fused*, that is, being bound together, or *being connected at birth*, as another text says, differs from contact, because in the case of contact there need be nothing besides the things in contact which makes them one.

But in the case of things that are bound together, whether naturally connected or born together and joined at birth, there must be some one thing *instead of contact*, that is, in the place of contact, which causes them *to be naturally joined*, that is, joined or bound together or born together. Moreover, it must be understood that the thing which causes them to be one makes them one in quantity and continuity but not in quality. For a bond does not alter the things bound from their own dispositions.

815. And from this it is evident that anything that is born is always connected with the thing from which it is born. Hence "nature" never means an extrinsic principle, but in every sense in which it is used, it is taken to mean an intrinsic principle.

816. And from this third meaning of "nature" there follows a fourth. For if the source of motion in natural bodies is called their nature, and it seemed to some that the principle of motion in natural bodies is matter, it was for this reason that matter came to be called nature, which is

rei, et quantum ad esse et quantum ad fieri. Ipsa etiam absque omni forma consideratur, nec a seipsa movetur, sed ab alio. Et ideo dicit quod natura dicitur ex quo aliquod entium primo est aut fit.

817. Quod ideo dicit, quia materia essendi et fiendi est principium. Ex quo, dico, *existente inordinato* idest absque forma. Unde alia litera habet *cum informe sit*. In quibusdam enim ipse ordo habetur pro forma, sicut in exercitu et civitate. Ex quo, dico, *immutabili ex sua potestate*, idest, quod moveri non potest per suam potestatem, sed secundum potestatem sui superioris agentis. Nam materia non movet seipsam ad formam, sed movetur a superiori exteriori agente. Sicut si diceremus aes materiam statuae et vasorum aereorum, et ligna ligneorum, si huiusmodi vasa, naturalia corpora essent. Similiter est in omnibus aliis quae ex materia sunt vel fiunt. Unumquodque enim eorum fit ex sua materia, ea salvata. Dispositiones autem formae non salvantur in generatione; una enim forma introducitur altera abiecta. Et propter hoc formae videbantur esse quibusdam accidentia, et sola materia substantia et natura, ut dicitur secundo *Physicorum*.

818. Et hoc ideo, quia similiter existimabant formam et materiam in rebus naturalibus, sicut in rebus artificialibus, in quibus formae sunt accidentia, et sola materia substantia.

Unde isto modo naturales dixerunt elementa esse materiam existentium secundum naturam, vel aquam, vel aerem, vel ignem aut terram, quam nullus elementum naturalium posuit solam, sed aliqui non naturales, ut in primo libro est habitum.

Quidam autem posuerunt aliqua eorum esse elementa et naturam rerum, sicut Parmenides. Quidam vero omnia quatuor, sicut Empedocles. Quidam vero aliquid aliud, sicut Heraclitus vaporem.

819. Quia vero motus rerum naturalium magis causatur ex forma quam ex materia, ideo supervenit quintus modus quo ipsa forma dicitur natura. Et sic alio modo natura dicitur *ipsa substantia*, idest forma rerum existentium secundum naturam, sicut naturam rerum dixerunt esse ipsam compositionem mixtorum; sicut Empedocles dixit, quod non est aliquid entium absolutum, sed solummodo commutatio seu relaxatio vel commixtio permixtorum, secundum aliam translationem, natura apud homines dicitur. Dicuntur enim quae sunt permixtionis diversae, naturam diversam habere.

taken as a principle of a thing, both as to its being and as to its becoming. And it is also considered to be without any form, and is not moved by itself, but by something else. He accordingly says that nature is spoken of as that primary thing of which any being is composed or from which it comes to be.

817. He says this because matter is a principle both of being and of becoming. Hence he says that *it is without order*, that is, form, and for this reason another text says *when it is unformed*. In the case of some things, their order (or arrangement) is regarded as their form, as in the case of an army or of a city. From this, he says that it is *immutable by its own power*: it cannot be moved by its own power, but by that of a higher agent. For matter does not move itself to acquire a form but is moved by a higher and extrinsic agent. For instance, we might say that bronze is the nature of a statue or of bronze vessels or wood of wooden, as if such vessels were natural bodies. The same is true of everything else that is composed of or comes to be from matter, for each comes to be from its matter, though this is preserved. But in the process of generation, the dispositions of a form are not preserved; for when one form is introduced, another is cast out. And for this reason it seemed to some thinkers that forms are accidents and that matter alone is substance and nature, as he points out in the *Physics* 2.

818. They held this view because they considered the matter and form of natural bodies in the same way as they did the matter and form of things made by art, in which forms are merely accidents and matter alone is substance.

It was in this sense that the philosophers of nature said that the elements are the matter of things that come to be by nature, that is, water, air, fire, or earth, which no philosopher has held to be the element of natural beings all by itself, although some of those who were not philosophers of nature did hold this, as was stated in book 1 [134].

And some philosophers, such as Parmenides, held that some of these are the elements and natures of things; others, such as Empedocles, held that all four are the elements of things; but others held that something different is the element of things, such as Heraclitus held of vapor.

819. Now, because motion is caused in natural bodies by the form rather than by the matter, he therefore adds a fifth sense in which the term "nature" is used: that in which it means the form of a thing. Hence in another sense "nature" means *the substance of things*, that is, the form of things, which are by nature. It was in this sense that some said that the nature of things is the composition of mixed bodies, as Empedocles said that there is nothing absolute in the world, but that only the alteration or loosening (or mixing, according to another text) of what has been mixed is called "nature" by men. For they said that things composed of different mixtures have different natures.

820. Ad ponendum autem formam esse naturam, hac ratione inducebantur, quia quaecumque sunt et fiunt naturaliter non dicuntur habere naturam, existente materia ex qua nata sunt fieri vel esse, nisi habeant speciem propriam et formam, per quam speciem consequantur. Videtur autem nomen speciei poni pro forma substantiali, et forma pro figura quae consequitur speciem, et est signum speciei. Si igitur forma est natura, nec aliquid potest dici habere naturam nisi quando habet formam, illud ergo quod compositum est ex materia et forma *dicitur esse natura*, idest secundum naturam, ut animalia et partes eorum, sicut caro et os et huiusmodi.

821. Deinde cum dicit *natura autem* ponit duos modos adiunctos duobus ultimis praecedentibus, quorum primus additur quarto modo quo materia dicebatur natura. Et dicit, quod materia dicitur natura non quaecumque, sed prima.

Quod potest intelligi dupliciter aut quantum ad id quod est genus; aut ex toto vel simpliciter prima. Sicut operum artificialium quae fiunt ex aere, prima materia secundum genus illud est aes. Prima vero simpliciter est aqua. Nam omnia quae liquescunt calido et indurantur frigido sunt aquea magis, ut dicitur quarto *Meteororum*.

822. Secundus modus adiacet quinto modo praedicto quo forma dicebatur natura. Et secundum hunc modum non solum forma partis dicitur natura, sed species ipsa est forma totius. Ut si dicamus quod hominis natura non solum est anima, sed humanitas et substantia quam significat definitio.

Secundum hoc enim Boetius dicit, quod natura est unumquodque informans specifica differentia. Nam specifica differentia est, quae complet substantiam rei et dat ei speciem.

Sicut autem forma vel materia dicebatur natura, quia est principium generationis, quae secundum primam nominis impositionem natura dicitur; ita species et substantia dicitur natura, quia est finis generationis. Nam generatio terminatur ad speciem generati, quae resultat ex unione formae et materiae.

823. Et ex hoc secundum quamdam metaphoram et nominis extensionem omnis substantia dicitur natura; quia natura quam diximus quae est generationis terminus, substantia quaedam est. Et ita cum eo quod natura dicitur, omnis substantia similitudinem habet. Et hunc

820. Now they were led to hold that form is nature by this process of reasoning. Whatever things exist or come to be by nature are not said to have a nature, even though the matter from which they are naturally disposed to be or to come to be is already present, unless they have a proper species and a form through which they acquire their species. Now the term "species" seems to be given in place of substantial form and the term "form" in place of figure, which is a natural result of the species and a sign of it. Hence, if form is nature, a thing cannot be said to have a nature unless it has a form. Therefore, that which is composed of matter and form *is said to be by nature*, according to nature, as animals and the parts of animals, such as flesh and bones and the like.

821. *Again, nature* (1015a7). Then he gives two meanings of nature which are connected with the last two preceding ones, and the first of these is added to the fourth sense of nature, in which it means the matter of a thing. And he says that not every kind of matter is said to be the nature of a thing but only first matter.

This can be understood in two senses: either with reference to something generic, or with reference to something that is first absolutely or without qualification. For example, the first matter generically of artificial things produced from bronze is bronze, but their first matter without qualification is water, for all things that are liquefied by heat and solidified by cold have the character of water, as he says in *Meteorology* 4.

822. He links up the second of these additional meanings with the fifth sense of "nature" mentioned above, according to which "nature" means form. And in this sense, not only is the form of a part called "nature," but the species is the form of the whole. For example, we might say that the nature of man is not only a soul but humanity and the substance signified by the definition.

For it is from this point of view that Boethius says that the nature of a thing is the specific difference which informs each thing, because the specific difference is the principle that completes a thing's substance and gives it its species.

And just as form or matter is called nature because it is a principle of generation, which is the meaning of nature according to the original use of the term, in a similar way the species or substance of a thing is called its nature because it is the end of the process of generation. For the process of generation terminates in the species of the thing generated, which is a result of the union of matter and form.

823. And because of this, every substance is called "nature" according to a kind of metaphorical and extended use of the term, for the nature which we spoke of as the terminus of generation is a substance. Thus every substance is similar to what we call nature. Boethius also gives this

modum etiam ponit Boetius. Ratione autem istius modi distinguitur hoc nomen natura inter nomina communia. Sic enim commune est sicut et substantia.

824. Deinde dum dicit *ex dictis* reducit omnes modos praedictos ad unum. Sciendum est autem, quod reductio aliorum modorum ad unum primum, fieri potest dupliciter. Uno modo secundum ordinem rerum. Alio modo secundum ordinem, qui attenditur quantum ad nominis impositionem.

Nomina enim imponuntur a nobis secundum quod nos intelligimus, quia nomina sunt intellectuum signa. Intelligimus autem quandoque priora ex posterioribus. Unde aliquid per prius apud nos sortitur nomen, cui res nominis per posterius convenit: et sic est in proposito. Quia enim formae et virtutes rerum ex actibus cognoscuntur, per prius ipsa generatio vel nativitas, naturae nomen accepit, et ultimo forma.

825. Sed secundum rerum ordinem, formae prius competit ratio naturae, quia, ut dictum est, nihil dicitur habere naturam, nisi secundum quod habet formam.

826. Unde patet ex dictis, quod *primo et proprie natura dicitur substantia*, idest forma rerum habentium in se principium motus inquantum huiusmodi. Materia enim dicitur esse natura, quia est formae susceptibilis. Et generationes habent nomen naturae, quia sunt motus procedentes a forma, et iterum ad formas. Et idipsum, scilicet forma est principium motus rerum existentium secundum naturam, aut in actu, aut in potentia. Forma enim non semper facit motum in actu, sed quandoque in potentia tantum: sicut quando impeditur motus naturalis ab aliquo exteriori prohibente, vel etiam quando impeditur actio naturalis ex materiae defectu.

meaning of the term. Moreover, it is because of this meaning that the term "nature" is distinguished from other common terms. For it is common in this way just as substance also is.

824. *Hence, from what* (1015a13). Then he reduces all of the foregoing senses of the term "nature" to one common notion. But it must be noted that the reduction of the other senses to one primary sense can happen in two ways: in one way, with reference to the order which things have; and in another way, with reference to the order which is observed in giving names to things.

For names are given to things according as we understand them, because names are signs of what we understand; and sometimes we understand prior things from subsequent ones. Hence something that is prior for us receives a name which subsequently fits the object of that name. And this is what happens in the present case, for, since the forms and powers of things are known from their activities, the process of generation or birth of a thing is the first to receive the name of "nature," and the last is the form.

825. But with reference to the order which things have in reality, the concept of "nature" primarily fits the form, because, as has been said [808], nothing is said to have a nature unless it has a form.

826. Hence from what has been said it is evident that *in its primary and proper sense "nature" is the substance*, that is, the form, of those things that have within themselves as such the source of their motion. For matter is called "nature" because it is receptive of form, and processes of generation get the name of "nature" because they are motions proceeding from a form and terminating in further forms. And this form is the principle of motion in those things that are by nature, either potentially or actually. For a form is not always the cause of actual motion, but sometimes only of potential motion, as when a natural motion is prevented by an external obstacle, or even when a natural action is prevented by a defect in the matter.

LECTURE 6

The definition of "necessary"

1015a20 Necessarium dicitur sine quo non contingit esse aut vivere quasi concausali. Ut spirare et cibus animalium est necessarium. Nam sine his esse est impossibile. [827]

1015a22 Et sine quibus homini bonum non contingit esse aut fieri, aut aliquid malum expellere aut privari. Veluti bibere pharmacum necessarium, ut non laboret; et ad Aeginam navigare ut pecuniam recipiat. [828]

1015a26 Amplius vim faciens et vis. Sed hoc est praeter impetum et praevoluntatem impediens et prohibens. Vim enim faciens necessarium dicitur. Quapropter triste etiam, sicut Evenus ait, *omnis enim res necessaria lamentabilis est facta.* Et vis necessitas quaedam, ut Sophocles dicit. *Sed vis ea me facere cogit.* Et videtur necessitas aliquid inculpabile esse recte. Contrarium enim est motui secundum praevoluntatem et secundum excogitationem. [829]

1015a33 Amplius quod non contingit aliter se habere, necessarium dicimus sic se habere. [832]

1015a35 Et secundum hoc necessarium et alia dicuntur omnia necessaria. Vim enim patiens necessarium dicitur aut facere aut pati tunc quando non contingit secundum impetum propter coagens quasi ea necessitate existente propter quam non contingit aliter. [836]

Et in concausalibus vivendi et boni similiter. Nam, cum non contingit hic quidem bonum, illic vero vivere et esse sine aliquibus, ea necessaria, et causa necessitas quaedam est haec.

1015b6 Amplius demonstratio necessariorum est, quia non contingit aliter se habere quod demonstratum est simpliciter.

ἀναγκαῖον λέγεται οὗ ἄνευ οὐκ ἐνδέχεται ζῆν ὡς συναιτίου (οἷον τὸ ἀναπνεῖν καὶ ἡ τροφὴ τῷ ζῴῳ ἀναγκαῖον, ἀδύνατον γὰρ ἄνευ τούτων εἶναι),

καὶ ὧν ἄνευ τὸ ἀγαθὸν μὴ ἐνδέχεται ἢ εἶναι ἢ γενέσθαι, ἢ τὸ κακὸν ἀποβαλεῖν ἢ στερηθῆναι (οἷον τὸ πιεῖν τὸ φάρμακον ἀναγκαῖον {25} ἵνα μὴ κάμνῃ, καὶ τὸ πλεῦσαι εἰς Αἴγιναν ἵνα ἀπολάβῃ τὰ χρήματα).

ἔτι τὸ βίαιον καὶ ἡ βία· τοῦτο δ᾽ ἐστὶ τὸ παρὰ τὴν ὁρμὴν καὶ τὴν προαίρεσιν ἐμποδίζον καὶ κωλυτικόν, τὸ γὰρ βίαιον ἀναγκαῖον λέγεται, διὸ καὶ λυπηρόν (ὥσπερ καὶ Εὔηνός φησι πᾶν γὰρ ἀναγκαῖον πρᾶγμ᾽ ἀνιαρὸν {30} ἔφυ), καὶ ἡ βία ἀνάγκη τις (ὥσπερ καὶ Σοφοκλῆς λέγει ἀλλ᾽ ἡ βία με ταῦτ᾽ ἀναγκάζει ποιεῖν), αἱ δοκεῖ ἡ ἀνάγκη ἀμετάπειστόν τι εἶναι, ὀρθῶς· ἐναντίον γὰρ τῇ κατὰ τὴν προαίρεσιν κινήσει καὶ κατὰ τὸν λογισμόν.

ἔτι τὸ μὴ ἐνδεχόμενον ἄλλως ἔχειν ἀναγκαῖόν φαμεν οὕτως {35} ἔχειν·

καὶ κατὰ τοῦτο τὸ ἀναγκαῖον καὶ τἆλλα λέγεταί πως ἅπαντα ἀναγκαῖα· τό τε γὰρ βίαιον ἀναγκαῖον λέγεται ἢ ποιεῖν ἢ πάσχειν τότε, {1015b1} ὅταν μὴ ἐνδέχηται κατὰ τὴν ὁρμὴν διὰ τὸ βιαζόμενον, ὡς ταύτην ἀνάγκην οὖσαν δι᾽ ἣν μὴ ἐνδέχεται ἄλλως,

καὶ ἐπὶ τῶν συναιτίων τοῦ ζῆν καὶ τοῦ ἀγαθοῦ ὡσαύτως· ὅταν γὰρ μὴ ἐνδέχηται ἔνθα {5} μὲν τὸ ἀγαθὸν ἔνθα δὲ τὸ ζῆν καὶ τὸ εἶναι ἄνευ τινῶν, ταῦτα ἀναγκαῖα καὶ ἡ αἰτία ἀνάγκη τίς ἐστιν αὕτη.

ἔτι ἡ ἀπόδειξις τῶν ἀναγκαίων, ὅτι οὐκ ἐνδέχεται ἄλλως ἔχειν, εἰ ἀποδέδεικται ἁπλῶς· τούτου δ᾽ αἴτια τὰ πρῶτα, εἰ ἀδ-

"Necessary" means that without which, as a contributing cause, a thing cannot be or live. For example, breathing and food are necessary to an animal because it cannot exist without them.

And it also means that without which the good for man cannot be or come to be, and that without which one cannot get rid of or remain free of some evil; for example, the drinking of some drug is necessary in order that one may not be sick, and sailing to Aegina is necessary in order that one may collect money.

Again, it means what applies force, and force itself, and this is something which hinders and prevents, in opposition to desire and choice. For that which applies force is said to be necessary, and for this reason anything necessary is also said to be lamentable. As Evenus says, *Every necessary thing is mournful.* And force is a kind of necessity, as Sophocles says, *But force compels me to do this.* And necessity seems to be something blameless, and rightly so, for it is contrary to motion, which stems from choice and from knowledge.

Again, we say that anything which cannot be otherwise is necessarily so.

And from this sense of the term "necessary" all the other senses are derived. For whatever is forced is said either to do or to undergo something necessary when it cannot do something according to its inclination as a result of force, as if there were some necessity by reason of which the thing could not be otherwise.

The same thing applies to the contributing causes of life and of good. For when in the one case good, and in the other life or being, is impossible without certain contributing causes, these are necessary; and this cause is a kind of necessity.

Further, demonstration belongs to necessary things, because whatever has been demonstrated in the strict sense cannot

Huius autem causa est quae prima sunt: si impossibile est aliter se habere, ex quibus est syllogismus. [838]

ύνατον ἄλλως ἔχειν ἐξ ὧν ὁ συλλογισμός.

be otherwise. The reason for this is the principles, for the principles from which a syllogism proceeds cannot be otherwise.

1015b9 Horum quidem itaque altera causa essendi necessaria est, aliorum vero nulla: sed propterea alia sunt ex necessitate. Quare primum et proprie necessarium ipsum simplex est. Hoc enim habere non contingit pluribus modis. Quare nec aliter et aliter; iam enim plus haberet. Ergo, si qua sunt sempiterna et immobilia, nihil illis est violentum, nec praeter naturam. [839]

τῶν μὲν {10} δὴ ἕτερον αἴτιον τοῦ ἀναγκαῖα εἶναι, τῶν δὲ οὐδέν, ἀλλὰ διὰ ταῦτα ἕτερά ἐστιν ἐξ ἀνάγκης. ὥστε τὸ πρῶτον καὶ κυρίως ἀναγκαῖον τὸ ἁπλοῦν ἐστίν· τοῦτο γὰρ οὐκ ἐνδέχεται πλεοναχῶς ἔχειν, ὥστ᾽ οὐδὲ ἄλλως καὶ ἄλλως· ἤδη γὰρ πλεοναχῶς ἂν ἔχοι. εἰ ἄρα ἔστιν ἄττα ἀΐδια καὶ ἀκίνητα, {15} οὐδὲν ἐκείνοις ἐστὶ βίαιον οὐδὲ παρὰ φύσιν.

Now, of necessary things, some have something else as the cause of their necessity and others do not, but it is because of them that other things are necessary. Hence what is necessary in the primary and proper sense is what is simple, for this cannot be in more ways than one. Therefore, it cannot be in one state and in another; otherwise, there would be more ways than one. If, then, there are any beings which are eternal and immobile, in them nothing forced or contrary to nature is found.

---

827. Postquam Philosophus distinxit nomina, quae significant causas, hic distinguit nomen quod significat aliquid pertinens ad orationem causae; scilicet necessarium. Causa enim est ad quam de necessitate sequitur aliud. Et circa hoc duo facit.

Primo distinguit modos necessarii.

Secundo reducit omnes ad unum primum, ibi, *et secundum hoc necessarium.*

Ponit autem in prima parte quatuor modos necessarii.

Primus est, secundum quod dicitur aliquid necessarium, sine quo non potest aliquid vivere aut esse; quod licet non sit principalis causa rei, est tamen quaedam concausa. Sicut respirare est necessarium animali respiranti, quia sine respiratione vivere non potest. Ipsa enim respiratio, etsi non sit causa vitae, est tamen concausa, inquantum cooperatur ad contemperamentum caloris, sine quo non est vita. Et similiter est de cibo, sine quo animal vivere non potest, inquantum cooperatur ad restaurationem deperditi, et impedit totalem consumptionem humidi radicalis, quod est causa vitae. Igitur huiusmodi dicuntur necessaria, quia sine eis impossibile est esse.

828. Secundum modum ponit ibi, *et sine* dicit, quod secundo modo dicuntur necessaria, sine quibus non potest esse vel fieri bonum aliquod, vel vitari aliquod malum, vel expelli; sicut **bibere pharmacum**, idest medicinam laxativam, dicimus esse necessarium, non quia sine hoc vivere animal non possit; sed ad expellendum, scilicet hoc malum quod est infirmitas, vel etiam vitandum. Est enim hoc necessarium **ut non laboret**, idest ut non infirmetur aliquis. Similiter **navigare ad Aeginam**, scilicet ad illum locum, est necessarium, non quia sine

827. Having distinguished the different senses of the terms which signify causes, the Philosopher now gives the different senses of a term which designates something pertaining to the notion of cause, that is, the term "necessary." For a cause is that from which something else follows of necessity. In regard to this he does two things.

First, he distinguishes the different senses of the term "necessary."

Second (1015a35; [836]), he reduces all of these to one primary sense, at **and from this sense.**

In the first part he gives four senses in which the term "necessary" is used.

First, it means that without which a thing cannot be or live; and even when this is not the principal cause of a thing, it is still a contributing cause. Breathing, for example, is necessary to an animal which breathes, because it cannot live without this. And while breathing is not the principal cause of life, nonetheless it is still a contributing cause inasmuch as it helps to restore what is lost and prevents the total consumption of moisture, which is a cause of life. Hence things of this kind are said to be necessary because it is impossible for things to exist without them.

828. **And it also means** (1015a22). Then he gives a second sense in which things are said to be necessary. He says that in a second way those things are said to be necessary without which some good cannot be or come about, or some evil avoided or expelled. For example, we say that **the drinking of some drug**, a laxative medicine, is necessary, not because an animal cannot live without it, but because it is required to expel something, namely, an evil or illness, or even to avoid it. For this is necessary **in order that one may not be in distress**, that is, to avoid being ill. And similarly

hoc non possit homo esse; sed quia sine hoc non potest acquirere aliquod bonum, idest pecuniam. Unde dicitur, quod necessaria est talis navigatio, ut aliquis pecuniam recipiat.

829. Tertium modum ponit ibi, *amplius vim* dicit quod id quod infert violentiam, et etiam ipsa violentia necessarii nomen accepit; nam violentia necessaria dicitur, et qui vim patitur dicitur de necessitate id facere ad quod cogitur.

Quid autem sit faciens vim, manifestat in naturalibus, et in voluntariis. In naturalibus quidem est impetus, sive inclinatio ad aliquem finem, cui respondet voluntas in natura rationali; unde et ipsa naturalis inclinatio appetitus dicitur.

Utrumque autem, scilicet et impetum naturalis inclinationis, et propositum voluntatis, contingit impediri et prohiberi. Impediri quidem, in prosecutione motus iam incepti. Prohiberi autem, ne etiam motus incipiat. Illud ergo dicitur esse violentum, *quod est praeter impetum*, idest praeter inclinationem rei naturalis, et est *impediens praevoluntatem*, idest propositum in prosecutione motus voluntarii iam incepti, et prohibens etiam ne incipiat.

Alia litera habet *et hoc est secundum ormin*, idest secundum impetum. Violentia enim est cum aliquid agit secundum impetum exterioris agentis, contra voluntatem vim passi. Violentum autem est secundum impetum vim faciens.

830. Ex hac autem violenti definitione duas conclusiones inducit.

Quarum prima est, quod omne violentum est triste sive flebile. Quod probat per cuiusdam poetae sive doctoris dictum; dicens, quod omnis res necessaria sive violenta est tristis sive lamentabilis: necessitas enim est quaedam violentia; sicut Sophocles poeta dicit: *violentia me facere coegit ea*, idest necessitas. Dictum est enim, quod violentia est impediens voluntatem. Ea autem, qua voluntati sunt contraria, contristant. Tristitia enim est de his quae nobis nolentibus accidunt.

831. Secunda conclusio est, quod necessitas recte dicitur, quod est inculpabilis et irreprehensibilis. Dicitur enim quod necessitas magis meretur veniam quam increpationem. Et hoc ideo, quia non inculpamur nisi de his quae voluntarie facimus, de quibus etiam rationabiliter increpamur. Necessitas autem violentiae est contraria voluntati et excogitationi, ut dictum est; et ideo rationabilius dicitur, quod violenta non sunt culpabilia.

sailing to Aegina, that is, to a definite place, is necessary not because a man cannot exist without this, but because he cannot acquire some good—namely, money—without doing this. Hence, such a voyage is said to be necessary in order to collect a sum of money.

829. *Again, it means* (1015a26). Here he gives a third sense in which things are said to be necessary. He says that anything which exerts force, and even force itself, is termed "necessary." For force is said to be necessary, and one who is forced is said to do of necessity whatever he is compelled to do.

He shows what is meant by something that exerts force both in the case of natural beings and in that of beings endowed with will. In natural beings, there is a desire for or an inclination toward some end or goal, to which the will of a rational nature corresponds; and for this reason a natural inclination is itself called an appetite.

For both of these—the desire of a natural inclination and the intention of the will—can be hindered and prevented. They are hindered in carrying out a motion already begun, and prevented from initiating motion. Therefore, that is said to be forced *which is done in opposition to desire*, against the inclination of a natural being; and it is *something that hinders choice*, that is, the end intended in executing a voluntary motion already begun, and also something that prevents it from beginning.

Another text says, *and this is according to impetuousness*, that is, according to impulse. For force is found when something is done through the impulse of an external agent and is opposed to the will and power of the subject. And that is forced which is done as a result of an impulse applying force.

830. Now from this definition of the forced he draws two conclusions.

The first is that everything forced is sad or mournful. He proves this by using the statement of a certain poet or teacher, saying that everything which is necessary or forced is sad or lamentable; for force is a kind of necessity, as the poet Sophocles says: *force*, that is, necessity, *compelled me to do this*. For it has been said that force is something which hinders the will; and things that are opposed to the will cause sorrow, because sorrow has to do with things that happen to us against our will.

831. The second conclusion is that anything which is necessary is rightly said to be without blame or reproach. For it is said that necessity deserves forgiveness rather than blame; and this is true because we deserve to be blamed only for the things that we do voluntarily and for which we may also be reasonably rebuked. But the kind of necessity which pertains to force is opposed to the will and to reason, as has been stated [829]; thus it is more reasonable to say that things done by force are not subject to blame.

832. Quartum modum ponit ibi, *amplius quod* dicit, quod necessarium etiam dicimus sic se habere, quod non contingit aliter se habere: et hoc est necessarium absolute. Prima autem necessaria sunt secundum quid.

833. Differt autem necessarium absolute ab aliis necessariis: quia necessitas absoluta competit rei secundum id quod est intimum et proximum ei; sive sit forma, sive materia, sive ipsa rei essentia;

sicut dicimus animal necesse esse corruptibile, quia hoc consequitur eius materiam inquantum ex contrariis componitur. Dicimus etiam animal necessario esse sensibile, quia consequitur eius formam: et animal necessario esse substantiam animatam sensibilem, quia est eius essentia.

834. Necessarium autem secundum quid et non absolute est, cuius necessitas dependet ex causa extrinseca. Causa autem extrinseca est duplex; scilicet finis et efficiens. Finis autem est, vel ipsum esse absolutum, et ab hoc fine necessitas sumpta pertinet ad primum modum; vel bene esse, sive aliquod bonum habere, et ab hoc fine sumitur necessitas secundi modi.

835. Necessitas autem quae est a movente exteriori, pertinet ad tertium modum. Nam violentia est quando aliquid movetur ab exteriori agente ad aliud ad quod ex propria natura aptitudinem non habet. Si enim secundum suam naturam ordinetur ad hoc quod recipiat motum ab exteriori agente, tunc motus non erit violentus, sed naturalis. Sicut patet de motu caelestium orbium a substantiis separatis, et de motu inferiorum corporum a superioribus.

836. Deinde cum dicit *et secundum* reducit omnes modos ad unum: et circa hoc tria facit.

Primo ostendit quod omnes modi necessitatis, qui in rebus inveniuntur ad hunc ultimum modum pertinent.

Secundo ostendit, quod secundum ultimum modum accipitur necessarium in demonstrativis, ibi, *amplius demonstratio*.

Tertio infert quoddam corollarium ex praemissis, ibi, *horum quidem itaque*.

Dicit ergo primo, quod secundum istum ultimum modum necessarii, omnes alii modi aliqualiter dicuntur. Quod primo ostendit in tertio modo. Illud enim quod vim patitur, de necessitate dicitur aliquid facere vel pati, propter hoc quod non contingit secundum proprium impetum aliquid agere propter violentiam agentis, quae est quaedam necessitas propter quam non contingit aliter se habere.

832. *Again, we say* (1015a33). He gives a fourth sense in which things are said to be necessary. He says that being in such a state that it cannot be otherwise we also call "necessary," and this is what is necessary in an absolute sense. Things necessary in the first senses, however, are necessary in a relative sense.

833. Now whatever is absolutely necessary differs from the other types of necessity, because absolute necessity belongs to a thing by reason of something that is intimately and closely connected with it, whether it be the form or the matter or the very essence of a thing.

For example, we say that an animal is necessarily corruptible because this is a natural result of its matter inasmuch as it is composed of contraries; we say that an animal is necessarily capable of sensing because this is a result of its form; and we also say that an animal is necessarily a living sensible substance because this is its essence.

834. However, the necessity of something which is necessary in a relative sense and not absolutely depends on an extrinsic cause. And there are two kinds of extrinsic causes—the end and the agent. Either the end is existence taken absolutely—and the necessity taken from this end pertains to the first kind—or it is well disposed existence or the possession of some good, and necessity of the second kind is taken from this end.

835. Again, the necessity which comes from an external agent pertains to the third kind of necessity. For force exists when a thing is moved by an external agent to something which it has no aptitude for by its own nature. For if something is disposed by its own nature to receive motion from an external agent, such motion will not be forced but natural. This is evident in the motion of the celestial bodies by separate substances, and in that of lower bodies by higher ones.

836. *And from this* (1015a35). Here he reduces all of the senses in which things are necessary to one, and in regard to this he does three things.

First (1015a35; [836]), he shows that all the types of necessity found in reality pertain to this last type.

Second (1015b6; [838]), he shows that necessity in matters of demonstration is taken in this last sense, at *further, demonstration*.

Third (1015b9; [839]), he draws a corollary from what has been set down above, at *now, of necessary things*.

He accordingly says, first, that all the other senses of the term "necessary" are somehow referred to this last sense. He first makes this clear with reference to the third way in which things are said to be necessary. For whatever is forced is said to do or to undergo something of necessity on the grounds that it cannot act through its own power because of the force exerted on it by an agent. This is a kind of necessity by which it cannot be otherwise than it is.

837. Et similiter ostendit hoc in primo et secundo modo, in quibus necessitas sumitur ex causis vivendi vel essendi simpliciter, quantum ad primum modum: vel ex causis boni, quantum ad secundum modum. Sic enim in aliis modis necessarium dicebatur, sine quo non poterat esse ex una parte bonum, et ex alia parte vivere et esse.

Et sic illa causa, sine qua non contingit vivere vel esse, vel bonum habere, vel malo carere, necessitas dicitur; quasi ex hoc sit prima ratio necessarii, quia impossibile est aliter se habere.

838. Deinde cum dicit *amplius demonstratio* ostendit quod secundum ultimum modum accipitur necessarium in demonstrativis, et quantum ad conclusiones, et quantum ad principia. Demonstratio enim dicitur esse necessariorum, et dicitur esse ex necessariis. Necessariorum quidem esse dicitur, quia illud, quod simpliciter demonstratur, non contingit aliter se habere. Dicitur autem *simpliciter demonstratum* ad eius differentiam quod demonstratur in demonstratione quae est ad aliquem, et non simpliciter; quod in quarto libro dixit demonstrare ad hominem arguentem. In talibus enim demonstrationibus, quae sunt ad aliquem, contingit etiam impossibile concludi ex aliquibus impossibilibus positis. Sed, quia causae conclusionis in demonstrationibus sunt praemissae, cum demonstratio simpliciter scire faciat, quod non est nisi per causam, oportet etiam principia, ex quibus est syllogismus, esse necessaria quae impossibile sint aliter se habere. Nam ex causa non necessaria non potest sequi effectus necessarius.

839. Deinde cum dicit *horum quidem* concludit ex praemissis tres conclusiones se invicem sequentes:

quarum prima est, quod ex quo in demonstrationibus praemissae sunt causae conclusionis, et utraque sunt necessaria, sequitur quod aliqua sunt necessaria dupliciter. Quaedam quidem quorum altera sit causa necessitatis; quaedam vero quorum nulla sit causa necessitatis; et talia sunt necessaria propter seipsa. Et hoc est contra Democritum, qui dicebat quod necessariorum non sunt quaerendae causae, ut habetur in octavo *Physicorum*.

840. Secunda conclusio, quia, cum oporteat esse unum primum necessarium, a quo alia necessitatem habent, quia in causis non est procedere in infinitum, ut in secundo ostensum est, oportet hoc primum necessarium, quod etiam maxime proprie est necessarium, quia est omnibus modis necessarium, quod ipsum sit simplex. Ea enim, quae sunt composita, sunt mutabilia, et ita pluribus modis se possunt habere: quae autem

837. Then he shows that the same thing is true of the first and second ways in which things are said to be necessary: in the first way with reference to the causes of living and being absolutely, and in the second with reference to the causes of good. For the term "necessary" was so used in these other ways: in one way to designate that without which a thing cannot be well off, and in the other to designate that without which a thing cannot live or exist.

Hence that cause without which a thing cannot live or exist or possess a good or avoid an evil is said to be necessary, the supposition being that the primary notion of the necessary derives from the fact that something cannot be otherwise.

838. *Further, demonstration* (1015b6). Then he shows that the necessary in matters of demonstration is taken from this last sense, and this applies both to principles and to conclusions. For demonstration is said to be about necessary things, and to proceed from necessary things. It is said to be about necessary things because what is demonstrated in the strict sense cannot be otherwise. He says *demonstrated in the strict sense* in order to distinguish this from what is demonstrated by the kind of demonstration which refutes an opponent and does not strictly demonstrate. In book 4 [609], he called this an *ad hominem* argument. In demonstrations of this kind which refute an opponent we conclude to the impossible from certain impossible premises. But since in demonstrations the premises are the causes of the conclusion, for demonstrations in the strict sense are productive of science, and this is had only by way of a cause, the principles from which a syllogism proceeds must also be necessary, and thus cannot be otherwise than they are. For a necessary effect cannot come from a non-necessary cause.

839. *Now of necessary things* (1015b9). Here he draws three conclusions from the points set down above, one of which follows from the other.

The first is that, since in demonstrations the premises are the causes of the conclusion and both of these are necessary, it follows that some things are necessary in one of two ways. For there are some things whose necessity is caused by something else, and there are others whose necessity has no cause; such things are necessary of themselves. This is said against Democritus, who claimed that we must not look for the causes of necessary things, as is stated in *Physics* 8.

840. The second conclusion is that, since there must be one first necessary being from which other beings derive their necessity (for there cannot be an infinite regress in causes, as was shown in book 2 [301]), this first necessary being, which is also necessary in the most proper sense because it is necessary in all ways, must be simple. For composite things are changeable and thus can be in more ways than one. But things that can be in more ways than

pluribus modis habere se possunt, possunt se habere aliter et aliter; quod est contra rationem necessarii. Nam necessarium est, quod est impossibile aliter se habere. Unde oportet, quod primum necessarium non aliter et aliter se habeat, et per consequens nec pluribus modis. Et ita oportet ipsum esse simplex.

841. Tertia conclusio est, quod, cum violentum sit quod movetur ab aliquo exteriori agente praeter naturam propriam, principia autem necessaria sunt simplicia et immobilia, ut ostensum est, necessarium est ut si sunt aliqua sempiterna et immobilia sicut sunt substantiae separatae, quod in illis non sit aliquid violentum nec praeter naturam. Et hoc dicit, ne deceptio accidat in nomine necessitatis, cum dicitur de substantiis immaterialibus, nec per hoc intelligitur aliqua violentia in eis esse.

one can be now in one way and now in another, and this is opposed to the notion of necessity; for that is necessary which cannot be otherwise. Hence the first necessary being must not be now in one way and now in another, and consequently cannot be in more ways than one. Thus he must be simple.

841. The third conclusion is that, since the forced is something which is moved by an external agent in opposition to its own nature, and necessary principles are simple and unchangeable, as has been shown (1015b9; [840]), therefore if there are certain eternal and unchangeable beings, as the separate substances are, in them there must be nothing forced or contrary to their nature. He says this lest a mistake should be made in the case of the term "necessity," since it is predicated of immaterial substances without implying on this account that anything forced is found in them.

LECTURE 7

The kinds of accidental and essential unity

1015b16 Unum dicitur aliud autem secundum accidens, aliud secundum se. Secundum accidens quidem, ut Coriscus et musicus, et Coriscus musicus. Idem enim est dicere Coriscus et musicus, et Coriscus musicus, et musicum et iustum, et musicus iustus Coriscus. [843]

ἓν λέγεται τὸ μὲν κατὰ συμβεβηκὸς τὸ δὲ καθ᾽ αὑτό, κατὰ συμβεβηκὸς μὲν οἷον Κορίσκος καὶ τὸ μουσικόν, καὶ Κορίσκος μουσικός (ταὐτὸ γὰρ εἰπεῖν Κορίσκος καὶ τὸ μουσικόν, καὶ Κορίσκος μουσικός), καὶ τὸ μουσικὸν καὶ τὸ {20} δίκαιον, καὶ μουσικὸς <Κορίσκος> καὶ δίκαιος Κορίσκος:

The term "one" is used both of what is accidentally one and of what is essentially one. A thing is said to be accidentally one, for example, when we say "Coriscus" and "musical" and "musical Coriscus." For to say "Coriscus" and "musical" and "musical Coriscus" amounts to the same thing; and this is also true when we say "just" and "musical" and "just musical Coriscus."

Omnia namque ea unum dicuntur secundum accidens. Iustum quidem et musicum, quia uni substantiae accidunt: musicus vero et Coriscus, quia alterum alteri accidit. Similiter autem et modo quodam musicus Coriscus cum Corisco unum, quia altera partium alteri accidit earum quae sunt in oratione: ut musicum Corisco et musicus Coriscus iusto Corisco, quia utriusque pars eidem uni accidit.

πάντα γὰρ ταῦτα ἓν λέγεται κατὰ συμβεβηκός, τὸ μὲν δίκαιον καὶ τὸ μουσικὸν ὅτι μιᾷ οὐσίᾳ συμβέβηκεν, τὸ δὲ μουσικὸν καὶ Κορίσκος ὅτι θάτερον θατέρῳ συμβέβηκεν: ὁμοίως δὲ τρόπον τινὰ καὶ ὁ μουσικὸς Κορίσκος τῷ Κορίσκῳ ἓν ὅτι θάτερον {25} τῶν μορίων θατέρῳ συμβέβηκε τῶν ἐν τῷ λόγῳ, οἷον τὸ μουσικὸν τῷ Κορίσκῳ: καὶ ὁ μουσικὸς Κορίσκος δικαίῳ Κορίσκῳ ὅτι ἑκατέρου μέρος τῷ αὐτῷ ἑνὶ συμβέβηκεν ἕν.

For all of these are said to be accidentally one—just and musical because they are accidents of one substance, and musical and Coriscus because the one is an accident of the other. And similarly, in a sense, musical Coriscus is one with Coriscus, because one of the parts of this expression is an accident of the other. Thus musical is an accident of Coriscus and musical Coriscus is an accident of just Coriscus, because one part of each expression is an accident of one and the same subject.

Nihil enim differt quam Corisco musicum accidere. Similiter autem sive in genere, sive in universalis alicuius nominibus dicatur accidens, ut quia homo idem et musicus homo.

ὡσαύτως δὲ κἂν ἐπὶ γένους κἂν ἐπὶ τῶν καθόλου τινὸς ὀνομάτων λέγηται τὸ συμβεβηκός, οἷον ὅτι ἄνθρωπος τὸ αὐτὸ {30} καὶ μουσικὸς ἄνθρωπος:

For it makes no difference whether musical is an accident of Coriscus or of just Coriscus. The same thing also holds true if an accident is predicated of a genus or of any universal term—for example, when one says that man and musical man are the same.

Aut enim quia homini uni existenti substantiae accidit musicum: aut quia ambo singularium alicui accidunt, ut Corisco. Tamen non eodem modo ambo insunt. Sed hoc quidem forsan ut genus et substantia, illud vero ut habitus aut passio substantiae. Ergo quaecumque secundum accidens dicuntur unum, hoc modo dicuntur.

ἢ γὰρ ὅτι τῷ ἀνθρώπῳ μιᾷ οὔσῃ οὐσίᾳ συμβέβηκε τὸ μουσικόν, ἢ ὅτι ἄμφω τῶν καθ᾽ ἕκαστόν τινι συμβέβηκεν, οἷον Κορίσκῳ. πλὴν οὐ τὸν αὐτὸν τρόπον ἄμφω ὑπάρχει, ἀλλὰ τὸ μὲν ἴσως ὡς γένος καὶ ἐν τῇ οὐσίᾳ τὸ δὲ ὡς ἕξις ἢ πάθος τῆς οὐσίας. ὅσα μὲν {35} οὖν κατὰ συμβεβηκὸς λέγεται ἕν, τοῦτον τὸν τρόπον λέγεται:

For this occurs either because musical is an accident of man, which is one substance, or because both are accidents of some singular thing, for example, Coriscus. Yet both do not belong to it in the same way, but one perhaps as the genus and substance, and the other as a habit or modification of the substance. Therefore, whatever things are said to be accidentally one are said to be such in this way.

1015b36 Secundum se vero unum dictorum alia dicuntur natura continuitatis, ut onus vinculo, et lignum cum visco. Et linea et si flexa sit, continua autem, una dici-

τῶν δὲ καθ᾽ ἑαυτὰ ἓν λεγομένων τὰ μὲν λέγεται τῷ συνεχῆ εἶναι, οἷον φάκελος δεσμῷ καὶ ξύλα κόλλῃ: {1016a1} καὶ γραμμή, κἂν κεκαμμένη ᾖ, συνεχὴς δέ, μία

But in the case of things that are said to be essentially one, some are said to be such by nature of their continuity—for example, a bundle becomes one by means

tur: sicut et partium singulae, ut tibia et brachium. [848]

λέγεται, ὥσπερ καὶ τῶν μερῶν ἕκαστον, οἷον σκέλος καὶ βραχίων.

of a binding, and pieces of wood become one by means of glue. And a continuous line, even if it is bent, is said to be one, just as each member is, such as a leg or an arm.

Ipsorum autem magis unum natura continua quam arte. Continuum vero dicitur, cuius motus unus secundum se et non possibile aliter. Unus autem unius indivisibilis. Indivisibilis autem secundum tempus.

αὐτῶν δὲ τούτων μᾶλλον ἓν τὰ φύσει συνεχῆ ἢ τέχνῃ. {5} συνεχὲς δὲ λέγεται οὗ κίνησις μία καθ᾽ αὑτὸ καὶ μὴ οἷόν τε ἄλλως· μία δ᾽ οὗ ἀδιαίρετος, ἀδιαίρετος δὲ κατὰ χρόνον.

And of these things themselves, those which are continuous by nature are one to a greater degree than those which are continuous by art. And that is said to be continuous whose motion is essentially one and cannot be otherwise. And motion is one when it is indivisible in time.

1016a7 Secundum se autem continua, quaecumque non tactu sunt unum. Nam si ponis se tangentia ligna, non dices haec unum esse, nec lignum, nec corpus, nec aliud continuum ullum. Quae itaque omnino sunt continua, unum dicuntur, quamvis reflexionem habeant. [856]

καθ᾽ αὑτὰ δὲ συνεχῆ ὅσα μὴ ἁφῇ ἕν· εἰ γὰρ θείης ἁπτόμενα ἀλλήλων ξύλα, οὐ φήσεις ταῦτα εἶναι ἓν οὔτε ξύλον οὔτε σῶμα οὔτ᾽ ἄλλο συνεχὲς οὐδέν. τά τε δὴ ὅλως συνεχῆ {10} ἓν λέγεται κἂν ἔχῃ κάμψιν,

Again, all those things are essentially continuous which are one not merely by contact; for if you place pieces of wood so that they touch each other, you will not say that they are one, either one board or one body or any other continuous thing. Hence those things that are continuous throughout are said to be one even though they are bent.

Adhuc magis quae non habent reflexionem, ut tibia aut femur vel crus, quia contingit non unum esse motum cruris. Et recta quam reflexa magis unum. Reflexam vero et angulum habentem, unam et non unam dicimus, quia contingit et non simul esse motum eius et simul. Rectae vero semper simul; et nulla pars habens magnitudinem, haec quidem movetur, haec vero quiescit, quemadmodum reflexae.

καὶ ἔτι μᾶλλον τὰ μὴ ἔχοντα κάμψιν, οἷον κνήμη ἢ μηρὸς σκέλους, ὅτι ἐνδέχεται μὴ μίαν εἶναι τὴν κίνησιν τοῦ σκέλους. καὶ ἡ εὐθεῖα τῆς κεκαμμένης μᾶλλον ἕν· τὴν δὲ κεκαμμένην καὶ ἔχουσαν γωνίαν καὶ μίαν καὶ οὐ μίαν λέγομεν, ὅτι ἐνδέχεται καὶ μὴ ἅμα τὴν {15} κίνησιν αὐτῆς εἶναι καὶ ἅμα· τῆς δ᾽ εὐθείας ἀεὶ ἅμα, καὶ οὐδὲν μόριον ἔχον μέγεθος τὸ μὲν ἠρεμεῖ τὸ δὲ κινεῖται, ὥσπερ τῆς κεκαμμένης.

And those which are not bent are one to an even greater degree; for example, the lower leg or the thigh is one to a greater degree than the leg, because the motion of the leg may not be one. And a straight line is one to a greater degree than a bent line. But what is bent and angular we refer to as either one or not one, because its motion may be either simultaneous or not. But the motion of a straight line is always simultaneous, and no part of it which has extension is at rest when another moves, as in a bent line.

1016a17 Amplius alio modo dicitur, eo quod subiectum sit specie indifferens. Indifferens vero, ut quorum indivisibilis species secundum sensum. Subiectum autem primum, aut ultimum ad finem. Vinum enim unum dicitur et aqua una, inquantum indivisibile secundum speciem. Et liquores omnes unum dicuntur, ut oleum, vinum et fluida, quia omnium ultimum subiectum idem. Nam aqua aut aere omnia haec fiunt. [859]

ἔτι ἄλλον τρόπον ἓν λέγεται τῷ τὸ ὑποκείμενον τῷ εἴδει εἶναι ἀδιάφορον· ἀδιάφορον δ᾽ ὧν ἀδιαίρετον τὸ εἶδος κατὰ τὴν αἴσθησιν· τὸ δ᾽ ὑποκείμενον {20} ἢ τὸ πρῶτον ἢ τὸ τελευταῖον πρὸς τὸ τέλος· καὶ γὰρ οἶνος εἷς λέγεται καὶ ὕδωρ ἕν, ᾗ ἀδιαίρετον κατὰ τὸ εἶδος, καὶ οἱ χυμοὶ πάντες λέγονται ἕν (οἷον ἔλαιον οἶνος) καὶ τὰ τηκτά, ὅτι πάντων τὸ ἔσχατον ὑποκείμενον τὸ αὐτό· ὕδωρ γὰρ ἢ ἀὴρ πάντα ταῦτα.

Again, a thing is said to be one in another sense because its underlying subject is uniform in species; and it is uniform in species as those things whose form is indivisible from the viewpoint of sensory perception. And the underlying subject is either one that is primary or one that is last in relation to the end. For wine is said to be one and water is said to be one inasmuch as they are indivisible in species. And all liquids are said to be one, as oil, wine, and fluids, because the ultimate subject of all is the same (for all of these are made up of water or of air).

1016a24 Dicuntur autem unum, et quorum genus unum differens oppositis differentiis; et haec dicuntur omnia unum quod subiicitur differentiis: ut homo, canis et equus, unum quidem, quia om-

λέγεται δ᾽ ἓν καὶ ὧν τὸ γένος ἓν {25} διαφέρον ταῖς ἀντικειμέναις διαφοραῖς—καὶ ταῦτα λέγεται πάντα ἓν ὅτι τὸ γένος ἓν τὸ ὑποκείμενον ταῖς διαφοραῖς (οἷον ἵππος ἄνθρωπος κύων

And those things are said to be one whose genus is one and differs by opposite differences. And all these things are said to be one because the genus, which is the subject of the differences, is one—for ex-

nia animalia. Et modo propinquissimo, sicut materia una. [861]

Haec autem quandoque quidem ita unum dicuntur, quandoque vero genere superiore; quod idem dicitur, si sint ultimae species generis superiores his. Ut isosceles et isopleurus sunt una et eadem figura quia ambo triangulus; sed trianguli non iidem.

1016a32 Amplius autem unum dicuntur, quorumcumque ratio quae quod quid erat esse dicit, indivisibilis est ad aliam significantem quid erat esse rei. Ipsa enim secundum se omnis ratio divisibilis. Sic enim augmentatum et diminutum unum sunt, quia ratio una, sicut in superficiebus quae specie una. [864]

1016b1 Omnino vero quorum intelligentia indivisibilis intelligetis quid erat esse, et non potest separari neque tempore, neque loco, neque ratione, maxime haec unum: et horum quaecumque substantia. [865]

ἕν τι ὅτι πάντα ζῷα), καὶ τρόπον δὴ παραπλήσιον ὥσπερ ἡ ὕλη μία.

ταῦτα δὲ ὁτὲ μὲν οὕτως ἕν λέγεται, ὁτὲ δὲ τὸ ἄνω γένος ταὐτὸν λέγεται {30} —ἂν ᾗ τελευταῖα τοῦ γένους εἴδη—τὸ ἀνωτέρω τούτων, οἷον τὸ ἰσοσκελὲς καὶ τὸ ἰσόπλευρον ταὐτὸ καὶ ἓν σχῆμα ὅτι ἄμφω τρίγωνα: τρίγωνα δ' οὐ ταὐτά.

ἔτι δὲ ἓν λέγεται ὅσων ὁ λόγος ὁ τὸ τί ἦν εἶναι λέγων ἀδιαίρετος πρὸς ἄλλον τὸν δηλοῦντα [τί ἦν εἶναι] τὸ πρᾶγμα (αὐτὸς γὰρ καθ' αὑτὸν {35} πᾶς λόγος διαιρετός). οὕτω γὰρ καὶ τὸ ηὐξημένον καὶ φθῖνον ἕν ἐστιν, ὅτι ὁ λόγος εἷς, ὥσπερ ἐπὶ τῶν ἐπιπέδων ὁ τοῦ εἴδους.

ὅλως δὲ ὧν ἡ νόησις ἀδιαίρετος ἡ νοοῦσα τὸ τί ἦν εἶναι, καὶ μὴ δύναται χωρίσαι μήτε χρόνῳ μήτε τόπῳ μήτε λόγῳ, μάλιστα ταῦτα ἕν, καὶ τούτων ὅσα οὐσίαι:

ample, man, dog, and horse are one because all are animals—and it is such in a way closest to that in which matter is one.

And sometimes these things are said to be one in this way, and sometimes in their higher genus, which is said to be the same if those which are higher than these are the last species of the genus. For example, the isosceles and the equilateral triangle are one and the same figure because both are triangles, but they are not the same triangles.

Further, any two things are said to be one when the definition expressing the essence of one is indistinguishable from that signifying the essence of the other. For in itself every definition is divisible. And what has increased and what has decreased are one in this way, because their definition is one. An example of this is found in plane figures, which are one in species.

And those things are altogether one and in the highest degree whose concept, which grasps their essence, is indivisible and cannot be separated either in time or in place or in its intelligible structure; and of these, all those which are substances are especially such.

---

842. Postquam Philosophus distinxit nomina quae significant causas, hic distinguit nomina quae significant id quod est subiectum aliquo modo in ista scientia. Et dividitur in duas partes.

Primo ponit sive distinguit nomina, quae significant subiectum huius scientiae.

Secundo ea, quae significant partes subiecti, ibi, *eadem dicuntur.*

Subiectum autem huius scientiae potest accipi, vel sicut communiter in tota scientia considerandum, cuiusmodi est ens et unum: vel sicut id de quo est principalis intentio, ut substantia.

Et ideo primo distinguit hoc nomen unum.

Secundo hoc nomen ens, ibi, *ens dicitur* et cetera.

Tertio hoc nomen substantia, ibi, *substantia dicitur* et cetera.

Circa primum duo facit.

842. Having given the various senses of the terms which signify causes, the Philosopher now proceeds to do the same thing with those terms which signify in some way the subject of this science. This is divided into two parts.

In the first (1015b16; [843]), he gives or distinguishes the different senses of the terms which signify the subject of this science;

and in the second (1017b27; [908]) he distinguishes the different senses of the terms which signify the parts of this subject, at *things are said to be the same.*

Now the subject of this science can be taken either as that which has to be considered generally in the whole science, and as such it is unity and being, or as that with which this science is chiefly concerned, and this is substance.

Therefore, first (1015b16), he gives the different senses of the term "one";

second (1017a7; [885]), of the term "being," at *the term "being"*;

and third (1017b10; [898]), of the term "substance," at *the term "substance."*

In regard to the first part of this division, he does two things.

Primo distinguit unum in per se et per accidens; et ostendit quot modis dicitur unum per accidens.

Secundo quot modis dicitur unum per se, ibi *secundum se vero unum* et cetera.

843. Dicit ergo, quod unum dicitur et per se et per accidens. Per accidens autem unum docet considerare primo in terminis singularibus;

et hoc dupliciter. Uno modo secundum quod accidens comparatur ad subiectum. Alio modo secundum quod unum accidens comparatur ad aliud.

In utroque autem istorum tria est accipere; scilicet unum compositum et duo simplicia. Si enim unum per accidens accipiatur secundum comparationem accidentis ad subiectum, sic sunt ista tria: primum est Coriscus, secundum est musicus, tertium Coriscus musicus. Et haec tria sunt unum per accidens. Nam idem subiecto est Coriscus et musicus.

Et similiter, quando comparatur accidens ad accidens, tria est accipere; quorum primum est musicum, secundum est iustum, tertium est musicus iustus Coriscus. Et omnia praedicta dicuntur esse unum secundum accidens; tamen alia et alia ratione.

844. Iustum enim et musicum, quae sunt duo simplicia in secunda acceptione, dicuntur unum per accidens, quia accidunt uni subiecto. Musicus vero et Coriscus, quae sunt duo simplicia in prima acceptione, dicuntur unum per accidens, quia *alterum eorum*, scilicet musicum *accidit alteri*, scilicet Corisco.

Et similiter quantum ad aliquid musicus Coriscus cum Corisco, quod est compositum cum uno simplicium, in prima acceptione dicuntur unum per accidens, quia inter partes istas quae sunt in hac oratione, idest in hoc termino complexo, scilicet Coriscus musicus, altera pars termini complexi, scilicet musicus, accidit alteri parti per se signatae, scilicet Corisco. Et eadem ratione potest dici, quod musicus Coriscus est unum cum iusto Corisco, quae sunt duo composita in secunda acceptione, quia ambae partes utriusque compositi accidunt uni, scilicet Corisco.

Si enim idem est musicus et musicus Coriscus, et iustus et iustus Coriscus, cuicumque accidit musicum accidit musicus Coriscus; et quicquid accidit Corisco accidit Corisco iusto.

Unde, si musicum accidit Corisco, sequitur, quod musicus Coriscus accidit iusto Corisco. Et sic nihil dif-

First, he makes a distinction between what is one *per se* and what is accidentally one, and he also indicates the various senses in which things are said to be accidentally one.

Second (1015b36; [848]), he notes the various senses in which things are said to be one *per se*, at **but in the case**.

843. He says (1015b16), then, that the term "one" signifies both what is one *per se* and what is accidentally one. And he tells us that what is accidentally one we should consider first in the case of singular terms.

Now singular terms can be accidentally one in two ways: in one way according as an accident is related to a subject; in another way according as one accident is related to another.

And in both cases, three things have to be considered—one composite thing and two simple ones. For if what is accidentally one is considered to be such according as an accident is related to a subject, then there are (for example) these three things: first, Coriscus; second, musical; and third, musical Coriscus. And these three are accidentally one; for Coriscus and what is musical are the same in subject.

Similarly, when an accident is related to an accident, three terms must be considered: first, musical; second, just; and third, just musical Coriscus. And all these are said to be accidentally one, but for different reasons.

844. For just and musical, which are two simple terms in the second way, are said to be accidentally one because both are accidents of one and the same subject. But musical and Coriscus, which are two simple terms in the first way, are said to be accidentally one because **the one**, namely, musical, **is an accident of the other**, namely, of Coriscus.

And similarly in regard to the relationship of musical Coriscus to Coriscus (which is the relationship of a composite term to one of two simple terms), these are said to be accidentally one in the first way, because in this expression, that is, in the complex term "musical Coriscus," one of the parts, namely, musical, is an accident of the other, which is designated as a substance, namely, Coriscus. And for the same reason it can be said that musical Coriscus is one with just Coriscus, which are two composites in the second way, because two of the parts of each composite are accidents of one subject, Coriscus.

For if musical and musical Coriscus, and just and just Coriscus, are the same, then whatever is an accident of musical is also an accident of musical Coriscus; and whatever is an accident of Coriscus is also an accident of just Coriscus.

Hence, if musical is an accident of Coriscus, it follows that musical Coriscus is an accident of just Coriscus. There-

fert dicere musicum Coriscum accidere iusto Corisco, quam musicum accidere Corisco.

845. Quia vero huiusmodi praedicata per accidens per prius praedicantur de singularibus, et per posterius de universalibus, cum tamen e converso sit de praedicatis per se, manifestat consequenter in terminis universalibus quod in singularibus ostenderat; dicens, quod similiter accipitur unum per accidens, si aliquod accidens dicatur cum aliquo nomine alicuius generis, vel cuiuscumque universalis, sicut accipitur unum per accidens in praedictis, quando accidens adiungitur nomini singulari; sicut cum dicitur, quod homo et musicus homo sunt unum per accidens, licet quantum ad aliquid differant.

846. Singulares enim substantiae nec sunt in subiecto, nec de subiecto praedicantur. Unde tantum substant et nihil eis substat. Substantiae quidem universales dicuntur de subiecto, sed non sunt in subiecto. Unde non substant accidentibus, et eis aliquid substat. Cum ergo accidens adiungitur particulari substantiae, non potest esse alia ratio dicti, nisi quia accidens inest substantiae particulari, ut quia musicum inest Corisco cum dicitur Coriscus musicus.

847. Sed, cum dicitur homo musicus, potest esse duplex ratio dicti.

Aut enim hoc dicitur, quia musicum accidit homini, per quod significatur substantia, et ex hoc competit sibi quod possit substare accidenti.

Aut hoc ideo dicit, quia ambo, scilicet homo et musicus, insunt alicui singulari, sicut Corisco: sicut musicum dicebatur iustum, quia eidem singulari insunt, et eodem modo, scilicet per accidens.

Sed forsan hoc non eodem modo; sed universalis substantia inest singulari ut genus, sicut hoc nomen animal; aut si non sit genus, saltem est in substantia subiecti, idest ut substantiale praedicatum, sicut hoc nomen homo.

Sed aliud, scilicet musicum, non est ut genus vel essentiale praedicatum, sed ut habitus vel passio subiecti, vel qualecumque accidens.

Ponit autem haec duo, habitum et passionem, quia quaedam accidentia sunt manentia in subiecto, sicut habitus, qui sunt difficile mobiles; quaedam autem sunt accidentia pertranseuntia et non manentia, sicut passiones. Patet igitur quod isti sunt modi, quibus aliqua dicuntur unum per accidens.

fore, it makes no difference whether we say that musical Coriscus is an accident of just Coriscus, or that musical is an accident of Coriscus.

845. But because accidental predicates of this kind are first applied to singular things and then to universals (although the reverse is true of essential predicates), he therefore makes clear that what he showed in the case of singular terms also applies in that of universal terms. He says that if an accident is used along with the name of a genus or of any universal term, accidental unity is taken in the same way as it is in the above cases when an accident is joined to a singular term—for example, when it is said that "man" and "musical man" are accidentally one, although they differ in some respect.

846. For singular substances are neither present in a subject nor predicated of a subject, such that, while they are the subject of other things, they themselves do not have a subject. Now universal substances are predicated of a subject but are not present in a subject, such that, while they are not the subjects of accidents, they have something as their subject. Hence, when an accident is joined to a singular substance, the expression stating this can only mean that an accident belongs to a singular substance, as musical belongs to Coriscus when Coriscus is said to be musical.

847. But when we say "musical man," the expression can mean one of two things:

either that musical is an accident of man, by which substance is designated, and from this it derives its ability to be the subject of an accident;

or it means that both of these, man and musical, belong to some singular thing (for example, Coriscus) in the way that musical was predicated of just, because these two belong to the same singular thing and in the same way (accidentally).

But perhaps the one term does not belong to the other in the same way, but in the way that universal substance belongs to the singular as a genus, like the term "animal," or if it is not a genus, it at least belongs to the substance of the subject, that is, as an essential predicate, like the term "man."

But the other term, "musical," does not have the character of a genus or essential predicate, but that of a habit or modification of the subject, or whatever sort of accident it may be.

He gives these two, habit and modification, because there are some accidents which remain in their subject, such as habits, which are moved with difficulty, and others which are not permanent, but transient, such as modifications. It is clear, then, that these are the ways in which things are said to be accidentally one.

848. Deinde cum dicit *secundum se* ponit modos unius per se; et circa hoc duo facit.

Primo ostendit quot modis dicitur unum.

Secundo quot modis dicuntur multa, ibi, *palam autem, et quia multa.*
Circa primum duo facit.
Primo distinguit modos unius naturaliter, idest secundum conditiones in rebus inventas.

Secundo vero logice, idest secundum intentiones logicales, ibi, *amplius autem alia* et cetera.

Circa primum duo facit.
Primo distinguit modos unius.

Secundo vero ponit quamdam proprietatem consequentem ad unum, ibi, *uni vero esse, est principium.*
Circa primum duo facit.
Primo ponit modos unius.

Secundo reducit eos omnes ad unum, ibi, *universaliter enim quaecumque.*
Ponit autem in prima parte quinque modos unius.

849. Quorum primus est, quod eorum quae secundum se dicuntur unum, quaedam dicuntur unum esse *natura continuitatis,* idest essendo continua: vel eo quod sunt *continua,* sicut dicit alia translatio.
Sed continua dicuntur aliqua dupliciter. Quaedam enim sunt continua, sicut dicit alia litera, per aliud, quaedam secundum se.
850. Prosequitur ergo primo continua secundum aliud, dicens, quod continua per aliud sunt, sicut onus lignorum continuum est ratione ligaminis vel vinculi: et hoc modo ligna adinvicem conviscata dicuntur unum per viscum.

Quod etiam contingit dupliciter: quia quandoque continuatio alligatorum fit secundum lineam rectam, quandoque autem secundum lineam indirectam, sicut est linea reflexa angulum continens, quae fit ex contactu duarum in una superficie, quarum applicatio non est directa.

Per hunc enim modum partes animalis dicuntur unum et continuum. Sicut tibia, quae habet reflexionem, et angulum continet ad genu, dicitur una et continua, et similiter brachium.
851. Sed, cum talis continuatio, quae est per aliud, possit esse vel fieri naturaliter et arte, magis unum sunt

848. *But in the case* (1015b36). Then he gives the ways in which things are one *per se*, and in regard to this he does two things.
First, he indicates the different senses in which the term "one" is used;
and second (1017a3), the different senses in which the term "many" is used, at *moreover, it is evident.*
In regard to the first he does two things.
First, he gives the different senses in which things are one from the viewpoint of nature, that is, according to the conditions found in reality;
second (1016b31), from the viewpoint of logic, that is, according to the considerations of logic, at *further, some things.*
In regard to the first he does two things.
First, he distinguishes the different senses in which things are said to be one.
Second (1016b17), he indicates a property which accompanies unity, at *but the essence of oneness.*
In regard to the first he does two things.
First, he sets down the different senses in which things are said to be one.
Second (1016b3), he reduces all of them to a single sense, at *for in general.*
In the first part he gives five senses in which the term one is used.
849. The first is this: some of the things that are said to be essentially one are such *by nature of their continuity,* that is, by being continuous, or because they are *continuous,* as another translation says.
But things are said to be continuous in two ways: as another text says, some things are continuous by reason of something other than themselves, and some in themselves.
850. First, he proceeds to deal with those things that are continuous by reason of something other than themselves. He says that there are things that are continuous as a result of something else, as a bundle of sticks is continuous by means of a cord or binding; in this way likewise pieces of wood glued together are said to be one by means of the glue.
Now there are also two ways in which this occurs, because the continuity of things that are fastened together sometimes takes the form of a straight line, and sometimes that of a line which is not straight. This is the case, for example, with a bent line having an angle, which results from the contact of two lines in one surface in such a way that they are not joined in a straight line.
And it is in this way that the parts of an animal are said to be one and continuous; for example, the leg, which is bent, and contains an angle at the knee, is said to be one and continuous; and it is the same with the arm.
851. But since this kind of continuity which comes about by reason of something else can exist or come to be

quae sunt continua per naturam, quam quae sunt continua per artem:

quia in his quae sunt continua per naturam, illud
unum, per quod fit continuatio, non est extraneum a
natura rei quae per ipsum continuatur, sicut accidit in
his quae sunt unum per artificium, in quibus vinculum,
vel viscus, vel aliquid tale est omnino extraneum a natura colligatorum. Et ita ea quae sunt naturaliter colligata,
prius accedunt ad ea quae sunt secundum se continua,
quae sunt maxime unum.

852. Et ad evidentiam huius, definit continuum, dicens, quod *continuum dicitur id cuius est secundum
se unus motus tantum, et non est possibile aliter.* Non
enim possibile est in continuo, ut diversae partes diversis
motibus moveantur, sed totum continuum movetur uno
motu. Dicit autem *secundum se*, quia possibile est ut
continuum moveatur uno modo per se, et uno alio vel
pluribus per accidens; sicut si homo movetur in navi
per se contra motum navis, movetur nihilominus motu
navis per accidens.

853. Ad hoc autem quod sit unus motus, oportet
quod sit indivisibilis: et hoc dico secundum tempus, ut
videlicet simul dum movetur una pars continui, moveatur et alia. Non enim contingit in continuo quod una
pars moveatur et alia quiescat, vel quod una quiescat et
alia moveatur, ut sic motus diversarum partium continui
sint in diversis partibus temporis.

854. Ideo autem hic definit Philosophus continuum
per motum et non per unitatem termini, ad quem partes continui coniunguntur, sicut in *Praedicamentis* et in
libro *Physicorum* habetur, quia ex ista definitione potest
sumi diversus gradus unitatis in diversis continuis, sicut
postea patebit, non autem ex definitione ibi data.

855. Sciendum est autem, quod hoc quod hic dicitur,
quod motus continui indivisibilis est secundum tempus,
non est contrarium ei quod probatur in sexto *Physicorum*, scilicet, quod tempus motus dividitur secundum
partes mobilis. Hic enim loquitur Philosophus quantum
ad motum absolute, quia scilicet non ante incipit moveri
una pars continui quam alia: ibi autem loquitur referendo ad aliquod signum, quod signatur in magnitudine, per quam fit motus. Illud enim signum, quod est
prior pars magnitudinis, in priori tempore transitur, licet etiam in illa priori parte temporis aliae partes mobilis
continui moveantur.

856. Deinde cum dicit *secundum se* prosequitur de
illis quae sunt secundum se continua, dicens, quod illa

both by nature and by art, those things that are continuous
by nature are one to a greater degree than those which are
continuous by art.

For the unity that accounts for the continuity of things
that are continuous by nature is not extrinsic to the nature
of the thing which is made continuous by it, as happens in
the case of things that are one by art, in which the binding
or glue or something of the sort is entirely extrinsic to the
nature of the things that are joined together. Hence those
things that are joined by nature hold the first place among
those which are essentially continuous, which are one in
the highest degree.

852. In order to make this clear he defines the "continuous." He says that *that is said to be continuous whose
motion is essentially one and cannot be otherwise.* For the
different parts of any continuous thing cannot be moved by
different motions, but the whole continuous thing is moved
by one motion. He says *essentially* because a continuous
thing can be moved in one way *per se* and in another or
others accidentally. For example, if a man in a ship moves
against the motion of the ship *per se*, he is still moved
accidentally by the motion of the ship.

853. Now in order for motion to be one it must be indivisible, and by this I mean from the viewpoint of time, in
the sense that at the same time that one part of a continuous
thing is moved another is also moved. For it is impossible
that one part of a continuous thing should be in motion
and another at rest, or that one part should be at rest and
another in motion, so that the motion of the different parts
should take place in different parts of time.

854. Therefore, the Philosopher defines the continuous
here by means of motion, and not by means of the oneness of the boundary at which the parts of the continuous
things are joined, as is stated in the *Categories* and in
the *Physics*, because from this definition he can consider
different grades of unity in different continuous things (as
will be made clear later on [856]), but he cannot do this
from the definition given there.

855. Moreover, it should be noted that what is said here
about the motion of a continuous thing being indivisible
from the viewpoint of time is not opposed to the point
proved in *Physics* 6, that the time of a motion is divided
according to the parts of the thing moved. For here the
Philosopher is speaking of motion in an unqualified sense,
because one part of a continuous thing does not begin to be
moved before another part does, but there he is speaking of
some designation which is made in the continuous quantity
over which motion passes. For that designation, which is
the first part of a continuous quantity, is traversed in a
prior time, although in that prior time other parts of the
continuous thing that is in motion are also moved.

856. *Again, all those* (1016a7). Then he proceeds to deal
with things that are *per se* continuous. He says that those

sunt secundum se continua quae non dicuntur unum per contactum. Quod sic probat. Illa enim, quae se tangunt, ut duo ligna, non dicuntur unum lignum, nec unum corpus, nec unum aliquid aliud quod pertineat ad genus continui. Et sic patet quod alia est unitas continuorum, et alia tangentium. Quae enim sunt se tangentia non habent unitatem continuitatis per seipsa, sed per aliquod vinculum quod ea coniungit. Sed illa quae sunt continua, dicuntur unum secundum se, quamvis habeant reflexionem. Duae enim lineae reflexae continuantur ad unum communem terminum, qui est punctus in loco ubi constituitur angulus.

857. Sed tamen magis sunt unum quae per se sunt continua sine reflexione. Cuius ratio est, quia linea recta non potest habere nisi unum motum in omnibus partibus suis. Linea vero reflexa potest habere unum motum, et duos motus. Potest enim intelligi linea reflexa tota moveri in unam partem: et iterum potest intelligi quod una parte quiescente, alia pars, quae cum parte quiescente continet angulum, appropinquet per suum motum ad partem quiescentem, sicut quando tibia vel crus applicatur ad coxam, quae hic dicitur femur. Unde utrumque eorum, scilicet tibia vel coxa, sunt magis unum quam *scelos*, ut habetur in Graeco, idest quam id quod est compositum ex tibia et coxa.

858. Sciendum autem, quod litera quae habet *curvitatem* loco *reflexionis*, falsa est. Constat enim quod partes lineae curvae angulum non continentes, oportet quod simul moveantur et simul quiescant, sicut partes lineae rectae; quod non accidit in reflexa, ut dictum est.

859. Secundum modum ponit ibi, *amplius alio* dicit, quod secundo modo dicitur unum, non tantum ratione continuae quantitatis, sed ex eo quod subiectum totum est indifferens forma secundum speciem. Quaedam enim esse possunt continua quae tamen in subiecto sunt diversa secundum speciem; sicut si continuetur aurum argento, vel aliqua huiusmodi. Et tunc talia duo erunt unum si attendatur sola quantitas, non autem si attendatur natura subiecti. Si vero totum subiectum continuum sit unius formae secundum speciem, erit unum et secundum rationem quantitatis et secundum rationem naturae.

860. Subiectum autem dicitur esse indifferens secundum speciem, quando eadem species sensibilis non dividitur, ita quod sint diversae formae sensibiles in diversis partibus subiecti, sicut quandoque contingit quod unius corporis sensibilis una pars est alba, et alia nigra.

Hoc autem subiectum indifferens potest accipi dupliciter. Uno modo subiectum primum. Alio modo subiectum finale sive ultimum, ad quod pervenitur in fine divisionis.

things are *per se* continuous which are said to be one not by contact. He proves this as follows: things that touch each other, as two pieces of wood, are not said to be one piece of wood or one body or any other kind of one which belongs to the genus of the continuous. Hence it is evident that the oneness of things that are continuous differs from that of things that touch each other. For those things that touch each other do not have any unity of continuity of themselves, but by reason of some bond which unites them; but those things that are continuous are said to be *per se* one even though they are bent. For two bent lines are continuous in relation to one common boundary, which is the point at which the angle is formed.

857. Yet those things are one to a greater degree which are *per se* continuous and without a bend. The reason is that a straight line can have only one motion in all of its parts, whereas a bent line can have one or two motions. For the whole of a bent line can be understood to be moved in one part; and it can also be understood that, when one part is at rest, the other part, which makes an angle with the part at rest, can come closer by its motion to the unmoved part, for example, when the lower leg or shin is bent in the direction of the upper leg, which here is called the thigh. Hence each of these—the shin and thigh—is one to a greater degree than *the scelos*, as the Greek text says, that is, the whole composed of the shin and thigh.

858. Further, it must be noted that the text which reads *curved* instead of *bent* is false. For, since the parts of a curved line do not contain an angle, it is evident that they must be in motion together or at rest together, just as the parts of a straight line are; but this does not happen in the case of a bent line, as has been stated [857].

859. *Again, a thing* (1016a17). Here he gives the second way in which things are one. He says that a thing is said to be one in a second way not merely by reason of continuous quantity, but because of the fact that the whole subject is uniform in species. For some things can be continuous even though they differ in species—for example, when gold is continuous with silver or something of this kind. And then two such things will be one if quantity alone is considered, but not if the nature of the subject is considered. But if the whole continuous subject is uniform in species, it will be one both from the viewpoint of quantity and from that of nature.

860. Now a subject is said to be uniform in species when the same sensible form is not divided in such a way that there are different sensible forms in different parts of the subject, as it sometimes happens, for example, that one part of a sensible body is white and another black.

And this subject, which does not differ in species, can be taken in two ways: in one way as the first subject, and in another as the last or ultimate subject which is reached at the end of a division.

Sicut patet quod totum vinum dicitur unum esse, quia partes eius communicant in uno primo subiecto quod est indifferens secundum speciem. Et similiter est de aqua. Omnes enim liquores sive humores dicuntur unum in uno ultimo. Nam oleum et vinum et omnia huiusmodi resolvuntur ultimo in aquam vel aerem, qui in omnibus est radix humiditatis.

861. Tertium modum ponit ibi, *dicuntur autem* dicit, quod aliqua dicuntur unum, quorum genus est unum, oppositis differentiis divisum. Et ille modus habet aliquam similitudinem cum praecedenti. Ibi enim aliqua dicebantur esse unum, quia genus subiectum est unum: hic etiam aliqua dicuntur esse unum, quia eorum genus, quod est subiectum differentiis, est unum;

sicut homo et equus et canis dicuntur unum, quia communicant in animali, quasi in uno genere, subiecto differentiis. Differt tamen hic modus a praedicto, quia in illo modo subiectum erat unum non distinctum per formas; hic autem genus subiectum est unum distinctum per diversas differentias quasi per diversas formas.

862. Et sic patet quod propinquissimo modo dicuntur aliqua esse unum genere, et similiter sicut aliqua dicuntur esse unum materia. Nam illa etiam quae dicuntur esse unum materia, distinguuntur per formas. Genus enim, licet non sit materia, quia non praedicaretur de specie, cum materia sit pars, tamen ratio generis sumitur ab eo quod est materiale in re; sicut ratio differentiae ab eo quod est formale.

Non enim anima rationalis est differentia hominis, cum de homine non praedicetur; sed habens animam rationalem, quod significat hoc nomen rationale. Et similiter natura sensitiva non est genus hominis, sed pars. Habens etiam naturam sensitivam, quod nomine animalis significatur, est hominis genus. Similiter ergo et propinquus modus est quo aliqua sunt unum materia et unum genere.

863. Sed sciendum est, quod unum ratione generis dicitur dupliciter.

Quandoque enim aliqua dicuntur ita unum in genere sicut dictum est, quia scilicet eorum unum est genus qualitercumque.

Quandoque vero non dicuntur aliqua esse unum in genere, nisi in genere superiori, quod cum adiunctione unitatis vel identitatis praedicatur de ultimis speciebus generis inferioris, quando sunt aliquae aliae superiores species supremi generis, in quarum una infinitae species conveniunt.

Sicut figura est unum genus supremum continens sub se multas species, scilicet circulum, triangulum, quadratum, et huiusmodi. Et triangulus etiam conti-

It is evident, for example, that a whole amount of wine is said to be one because its parts are parts of one common subject which is undifferentiated specifically. The same is true of water. For all liquids or moist things are said to be one insofar as they have a single ultimate subject. For oil and wine and the like are ultimately dissolved into water or air, which is the root of moistness in all things.

861. *And those things* (1016a24). Then he indicates the third way in which things are said to be one. He says that those things are said to be one whose genus is one, even though it is divided by opposite differences. And this way resembles the preceding one; for some things were said to be one in the preceding way because their subject genus is one, and now some things are said to be one because their genus, which is the subject of differences, is one.

For example, a man and a horse and a dog are said to be one because they have animality in common as one genus, which is the subject of differences. Yet this way differs from the preceding, because in the preceding way the subject was one thing which was not differentiated by forms; but here the subject genus is one thing which is differentiated by various differences, as though by various forms.

862. Thus it is evident that some things are said to be one in genus in a most proximate sense, and in a way similar to that in which some things are said to be one in matter. For those things that are said to be one in matter are also differentiated by forms. For even though a genus is not matter, because it would then not be predicated of a species (since matter is part of a thing), still the notion of a genus is taken from what is material in a thing, just as the notion of a difference is taken from what is formal.

For the rational soul is not the difference of man (since it is not predicated of man), but something having a rational soul (for this is what the term "rational" signifies). Similarly, sensory nature is not the genus of man, but a part. But something having a sensory nature, which the term "animal" signifies, is the genus of man. In a similar fashion, then, the way in which things are one in matter is closely related to that in which they are one in genus.

863. But it must be borne in mind that to be one in generic character has two meanings.

For sometimes some things are said to be one in genus, as has been stated, because they belong to one genus of any sort whatever.

But sometimes some things are said to be one in genus only in reference to a higher genus, which, along with the designation "one" or "the same," is predicated of the last species of a lower genus when there are other higher species in one of which the lower species agree.

For example, figure is one supreme genus which has many species under it—namely, circle, triangle, square, and the like. And triangle also has different species, namely, the

net diversas species, scilicet aequilaterum, qui dicitur isopleurus, et triangulum duorum aequalium laterum, qui dicitur aequitibiarum vel isosceles. Isti igitur duo trianguli dicuntur una figura, quod est genus remotum, sed non unus triangulus, quod est genus proximum. Cuius ratio est, quia hi duo trianguli non differunt per differentias quibus dividitur figura. Differunt autem per differentias quibus dividitur triangulus. Idem autem dicitur a quo aliquid non differt differentia.

864. Quartum modum ponit ibi, *amplius autem* dicit quod unum etiam dicuntur, quaecumque ita se habent quod definitio unius, quae est ratio significans quid est esse, non dividitur a definitione alterius, quae significat etiam quid est esse eius.

Ipsa enim definitio, scilicet secundum se, oportet quod sit divisibilis, cum constet ex genere et differentia. Sed potest esse quod definitio unius sit indivisibilis a definitione alterius, quando duo habent unam definitionem;

sive illae definitiones significent totum hoc quod est in definito, sicut tunica et indumentum: et tunc sunt simpliciter unum, quorum definitio est una: sive illa communis definitio non totaliter comprehendat rationem duorum, quae in ea conveniunt, sicut bos et equus conveniunt in una definitione animalis. Unde numquam sunt unum simpliciter, sed secundum quid, in quantum scilicet utrumque eorum est animal.

Et similiter augmentum et diminutio conveniunt in una definitione generis, quia utraque est motus secundum quantitatem. Similiter in omnibus superficiebus est una definitio huius speciei quae est superficies.

865. Quintum modum ponit ibi, *omnino vero* dicit, quod *omnino* idest perfecte et maxime *sunt unum, quorum intellectus intelligens quidditatem eorum est omnino indivisibilis*, sicut simplicia, quae non componuntur ex principiis materialibus et formalibus.

Unde intellectus accipiens quidditatem eorum, non comprehendit ea, quasi componens definitionem eorum ex diversis principiis; sed magis per modum negationis, sicut punctus est, cuius pars non est: vel etiam per modum habitudinis ad composita, sicut si dicatur quod unitas est principium numeri. Et, quia talia habent intellectum indivisibilem in seipsis, ea autem quae sunt quocumque modo divisa, possunt intelligi separatim, ideo sequitur quod huiusmodi sunt inseparabilia, et secundum tempus, et secundum locum, et secundum rationem.

equilateral, which is called isopleural, and the triangle with two equal sides, which is called equal-legged or isosceles. Hence these two triangles are said to be one figure, which is their remote genus, but not one triangle, which is their proximate genus. The reason for this is that these two triangles do not differ by any differences which divide figure, but by differences which divide triangle. And the term "same" means that from which something does not differ by a difference.

864. He now describes the fourth way in which things are said to be one, at *further, any two* (1016a32a). He says that things are also said to be one when the definition of one (which is the concept signifying its quiddity) is not distinguished from the definition of the other (which also signifies its quiddity).

For while every definition must be divisible or distinguishable in itself (or essentially), since it is composed of genus and difference, it is possible for the definition of one thing to be indistinguishable from that of another when the two have one definition.

And this applies whether those definitions signify the whole of the thing defined, as tunic and clothing (and then things whose definition is one are one in an absolute sense), or whether that common definition does not totally comprehend the intelligible structure of the two things that have it in common, as an ox and a horse have in common the one definition of animal. Hence they are never one in an absolute sense, but only in a relative sense inasmuch as each is an animal.

The same applies in the case of increase and decrease, for there is one common definition of the genus, because each is a motion relating to quantity. And the same thing is true of plane figures, for there is one definition of the species, plane figure.

865. *And those things* (1016b1). He gives the fifth way in which things are one. He says that *those things are altogether one* (that is, perfectly and in the highest degree), *whose concept, which grasps their essence, is altogether indivisible*—like simple things, which are not composed of material and formal principles.

Hence the concept which embraces their quiddity does not comprehend them in such a way as to form a definition of them from different principles, but rather grasps them negatively, as happens in the case of a point, which has no parts. Or it even comprehends them by relating them to composite things, as happens, for example, when someone defines the unit as the principle of number. And because such things have in themselves an indivisible concept, and things that are divided in any way at all can be understood separately, it therefore follows that such things are indivisible both in time and in place and in their intelligible structure.

Et propter hoc sunt maxime unum; praecipue illud quod est indivisibile in genere substantiae. Nam quod est indivisibile in genere accidentis, etsi ipsum in se non sit compositum, est tamen alteri compositum, idest subiecto in quo est. Indivisibilis autem substantia, neque secundum se composita est, nec alteri componitur.

Vel ly substantia, potest esse ablativi casus. Et tunc est sensus, quod licet aliqua dicantur unum quia sunt indivisibilia secundum locum vel tempus vel rationem, tamen inter ea illa maxime dicuntur unum, quae non dividuntur secundum substantiam. Et redit in eumdem sensum cum priore.

Hence these things are one in the highest degree, and especially those which are indivisible in the genus of substance. For even though what is indivisible in the genus of accident is not composite in itself, nonetheless it does form a composite with something else, namely, the subject in which it inheres. But an indivisible substance neither is composite in itself nor forms a composite with something else.

Or the term "substance" can be taken in the ablative case, and then the sense is that, even though some things are said to be one because they are indivisible in time and in place and in definition, still those things among them that are indivisible in substance are said to be one in the highest degree. This sense is reduced to the preceding one.

LECTURE 8

The definition of "one"

1016b3 Universaliter enim quaecumque non habent divisionem, inquantum non habent, sic unum dicuntur. [866]

καθόλου γὰρ ὅσα μὴ ἔχει διαίρεσιν, ᾗ μὴ ἔχει, ταύτῃ ἓν λέγεται,

For in general those things that do not admit of division are said to be one insofar as they do not admit of division.

Ut si inquantum homo non habet divisionem, unus homo.

{5} οἷον εἰ ᾗ ἄνθρωπος μὴ ἔχει διαίρεσιν, εἷς ἄνθρωπος,

Thus, if two things do not admit of division insofar as they are man, they are one man;

Si vero inquantum animal, unum animal.

εἰ δ᾽ ᾗ ζῷον, ἓν ζῷον,

if they do not admit of division insofar as they are animal, they are one animal;

Et si inquantum magnitudo, una magnitudo.

εἰ δὲ ᾗ μέγεθος, ἓν μέγεθος.

and if they do not admit of division insofar as they have continuous quantity, they are one continuous quantity.

Plura quidem igitur unum dicuntur per alterum aliquid facere, aut pati, aut habere, aut aliquid esse unum. Quae autem unum primo dicuntur, quorum substantia una. Una vero aut continuatione, aut specie, aut ratione.

τὰ μὲν οὖν πλεῖστα ἓν λέγεται τῷ ἕτερόν τι ἢ ποιεῖν ἢ ἔχειν ἢ πάσχειν ἢ πρός τι εἶναι ἕν, τὰ δὲ πρώτως λεγόμενα ἓν ὧν ἡ οὐσία μία, μία δὲ ἢ συνεχείᾳ ἢ εἴδει ἢ λόγῳ·

Hence many things are said to be one because they do or undergo or have or are related to some other thing which is one. But those things are said to be one in a primary sense whose substance is one, and they are one either by continuity or in species or in intelligible structure.

Etenim numeramus ut plura, aut quae non continua, aut quorum non una species, aut quorum ratio non una.

καὶ γὰρ {10} ἀριθμοῦμεν ὡς πλείω ἢ τὰ μὴ συνεχῆ ἢ ὧν μὴ ἓν τὸ εἶδος ἢ ὧν ὁ λόγος μὴ εἷς.

For we count as "many" those things that are not continuous, or those whose form is not one, or those whose intelligible structure is not one.

1016b11 Amplius autem, est quidem ut quodcumque unum continuitate dicimus esse, si sit quantum et continuum: est autem ut non: si non aliquod totum sit. Hoc autem si non speciem habeat unam. [870]

ἔτι δ᾽ ἔστι μὲν ὡς ὁτιοῦν ἕν φαμεν εἶναι ἂν ᾖ ποσὸν καὶ συνεχές, ἔστι δ᾽ ὡς οὔ, ἂν μή τι ὅλον ᾖ, τοῦτο δὲ ἂν μὴ τὸ εἶδος ἔχῃ ἕν·

Again, in one sense we say that anything at all is one by continuity if it is quantitative and continuous, and in another sense we say that a thing is not one unless it is a whole, unless it has one form.

Ut videntes utique non dicemus similiter unum qualitercumque partes compositas calceamenti, nisi propter continuitatem, sed si sit ut calceamentum sit, et speciem habeat aliquam, iam unum. Quapropter et quae circuli, maxime una linearum, quia tota et perfecta est.

οἷον οὐκ ἂν φαῖμεν ὁμοίως ἓν ἰδόντες ὁπωσοῦν τὰ μέρη συγκείμενα τοῦ ὑποδήματος, {15} ἐὰν μὴ διὰ τὴν συνέχειαν, ἀλλ᾽ ἐὰν οὕτως ὥστε ὑπόδημα εἶναι καὶ εἶδός τι ἔχειν ἤδη ἕν· διὸ καὶ ἡ τοῦ κύκλου μάλιστα μία τῶν γραμμῶν, ὅτι ὅλη καὶ τέλειός ἐστιν.

Thus, in looking at the parts of a shoe which are put together in any way at all, we would not say that they are one except by reason of their continuity, but if they are put together in such a way as to be a shoe and to have a certain form, there would then be one thing. And for this reason, among lines, the circular line is one in the highest degree because it is whole and complete.

1016b17 Uni vero esse est principium alicui numero esse. Prima namque mensura principium. Nam quo primo cognoscimus, hoc est prima mensura cuiuslibet generis. Principium ergo cognoscibilis circa quodlibet, unum. [872]

τὸ δὲ ἑνὶ εἶναι ἀρχῇ τινί ἐστιν ἀριθμοῦ εἶναι· τὸ γὰρ πρῶτον μέτρον ἀρχή, ᾧ γὰρ πρώτῳ γνωρίζομεν, τοῦτο πρῶτον μέτρον {20} ἑκάστου γένους· ἀρχὴ οὖν τοῦ γνωστοῦ περὶ ἕκαστον τὸ ἕν.

But the essence of oneness is to be a principle of some number, for the first measure is a principle, because that by which we first come to know each genus of things is its first measure. Unity, then, is the first principle of what is knowable about each genus.

Non idem autem in omnibus generibus unum. Hoc quidem enim est dioesis, illis autem vocalis aut consonans; gravitatis autem alterum, et in motu aliud: ubique vero unum aut quantitate aut specie, indivisibile.

Secundum quantum quidem igitur, et inquantum quantum, indivisibile: quod quidem omnino et sine positione, dicitur unitas. Quod autem omnino et positionem habens, punctum.

Quod autem secundum unum, linea. Quod autem secundum duo, superficies. Omnino vero et tripliciter divisibile secundum quantitatem, corpus. Facta autem conversione, dualiter quidem divisibile superficies, unice autem linea, nullatenus divisibile secundum quantitatem punctus et unitas. Hoc quidem non habens positionem unitas. Illud vero habens positionem, punctus.

1016b31 Amplius autem alia secundum numerum sunt unum, alia secundum speciem, alia secundum genus, alia secundum analogiam. Numero quidem, quorum materia una. Specie, quorum ratio est una. Genere, quorum eadem figura praedicationis. Secundum proportionem, quaecumque se habent ut aliud ad aliud. Semper itaque posteriora, praecedentia sequuntur. [876]

Ut quaecum que numero, specie unum: sed quaecumque specie, non omnia numero. Sed genere omnia unum, quaecumque et specie: quaecumque vero genere, non omnia specie, sed proportione: et quaecumque unum proportione, non omnia genere.

1017a3 Palam autem et quia multa opposita dicuntur uni. Nam alia non existendo continua. Alia in habendo materiam divisibilem secundum speciem, aut primam aut ultimam. Alia in habendo rationes plures, quod quid erat esse dicentes. [881]

οὐ ταὐτὸ δὲ ἐν πᾶσι τοῖς γένεσι τὸ ἕν. ἔνθα μὲν γὰρ δίεσις ἔνθα δὲ τὸ φωνῆεν ἢ ἄφωνον· βάρους δὲ ἕτερον καὶ κινήσεως ἄλλο. πανταχοῦ δὲ τὸ ἓν ἢ τῷ ποσῷ ἢ τῷ εἴδει ἀδιαίρετον.

τὸ μὲν οὖν κατὰ τὸ ποσὸν ἀδιαίρετον, {25} τὸ μὲν πάντη καὶ ἄθετον λέγεται μονάς, τὸ δὲ πάντη καὶ θέσιν ἔχον στιγμή,

τὸ δὲ μοναχῆ γραμμή, τὸ δὲ διχῆ ἐπίπεδον, τὸ δὲ πάντη καὶ τριχῆ διαιρετὸν κατὰ τὸ ποσὸν σῶμα· καὶ ἀντιστρέψαντι δὴ τὸ μὲν διχῆ διαιρετὸν ἐπίπεδον, τὸ δὲ μοναχῆ γραμμή, τὸ δὲ μηδαμῆ διαιρετὸν κατὰ {30} τὸ ποσὸν στιγμὴ καὶ μονάς, ἡ μὲν ἄθετος μονὰς ἡ δὲ θετὸς στιγμή.

ἔτι δὲ τὰ μὲν κατ᾽ ἀριθμόν ἐστιν ἕν, τὰ δὲ κατ᾽ εἶδος, τὰ δὲ κατὰ γένος, τὰ δὲ κατ᾽ ἀναλογίαν, ἀριθμῷ μὲν ὧν ἡ ὕλη μία, εἴδει δ᾽ ὧν ὁ λόγος εἷς, γένει δ᾽ ὧν τὸ αὐτὸ σχῆμα τῆς κατηγορίας, κατ᾽ ἀναλογίαν δὲ ὅσα ἔχει ὡς {35} ἄλλο πρὸς ἄλλο. ἀεὶ δὲ τὰ ὕστερα τοῖς ἔμπροσθεν ἀκολουθεῖ,

οἷον ὅσα ἀριθμῷ καὶ εἴδει ἕν, ὅσα δ᾽ εἴδει οὐ πάντα ἀριθμῷ· {1017a1} ἀλλὰ γένει πάντα ἓν ὅσαπερ καὶ εἴδει, ὅσα δὲ γένει οὐ πάντα εἴδει ἀλλ᾽ ἀναλογία· ὅσα δὲ ἀναλογίᾳ οὐ πάντα γένει.

φανερὸν δὲ καὶ ὅτι τὰ πολλὰ ἀντικειμένως λεχθήσεται τῷ ἑνί· τὰ μὲν γὰρ τῷ μὴ συνεχῆ εἶναι, τὰ δὲ τῷ διαιρετὴν {5} ἔχειν τὴν ὕλην κατὰ τὸ εἶδος, ἢ τὴν πρώτην ἢ τὴν τελευταίαν, τὰ δὲ τῷ τοὺς λόγους πλείους τοὺς τί ἦν εἶναι λέγοντας.

But this unity or unit is not the same in all genera, for in one it is the lesser half tone, and in another it is the vowel or consonant; in the case of weight, the unit is different; and in that of motion, different still. But in all cases, what is one is indivisible either in quantity or in species.

Thus a unit is indivisible in quantity as quantity in every way and has no position; and a point is indivisible in every way and has position.

A line is divisible in one dimension, a surface in two, and a body in three. And conversely, that which is divisible in two dimensions is a surface, in one is a line, and quantitatively indivisible in every way is a point and a unit. If it has no position, it is a unit, and if it has position, it is a point.

Further, some things are one in number, some in species, some in genus, and some analogically or proportionally. Those things are one in number which have one matter; in species, which have one intelligible structure; in genus, which have the same figure of predication; and proportionally, which are related to each other as some third thing is to a fourth. And the latter types of unity always follow the former.

Thus things that are one in number are one in species, but not all which are one in species are one in number; and all which are one in species are one in genus, but not all which are one in genus are one in species, although they are all one proportionally. And not all which are one proportionally are one in genus.

Moreover, it is evident that things are said to be many in a way opposite to that in which they are one. For some things are many because they are not continuous; others, because their matter, either the first or ultimate, is divisible in species; and others because they have many conceptions expressing their essence.

866. Hic Philosophus reducit omnes modos ad unum primum; et circa hoc duo facit.

Primo ponit reductionem praedictam.
Secundo super modos positos ponit alium modum unitatis, ibi, *amplius autem* et cetera.

Dicit ergo primo, quod ex hoc patet, quod illa quae sunt penitus indivisibilia, maxime dicuntur unum: quia ad hunc modum omnes alii modi reducuntur, quia universaliter hoc est verum, quod quaecumque non habent divisionem, secundum hoc dicuntur unum, inquantum divisionem non habent. Sicut quae non dividuntur in eo quod est homo, dicuntur unum in homine, sicut Socrates et Plato. Et quae non dividuntur in ratione animalis, dicuntur unum in animali. Et quae non dividuntur in magnitudine vel mensura, dicuntur unum secundum magnitudinem, sicut continua.

867. Et ex hoc potest accipi etiam numerus et diversitas modorum unius suprapositorum; quia unum aut est indivisibile simpliciter, aut indivisibile secundum quid. Siquidem simpliciter, sic est ultimus modus, qui est principalis. Si autem est indivisibile secundum quid, aut secundum quantitatem tantum, aut secundum naturam. Si secundum quantitatem, sic est primus modus. Si secundum naturam, aut quantum ad subiectum, aut quantum ad divisionem quae se tenet ex parte formae. Si quantum ad subiectum, vel quantum ad subiectum reale, et sic est secundus modus. Vel quantum ad subiectum rationis, et sic est tertius modus. Indivisibilitas autem formae, quae est indivisibilitas rationis, idest definitionis, facit quartum modum.

868. Ex his autem modis ulterius aliqui alii modi derivantur. Plurima autem sunt, quae dicuntur unum, ex eo quod faciunt unum; sicut plures homines dicuntur unum, ex hoc quod trahunt navem. Et etiam dicuntur aliqua unum, ex eo quod unum patiuntur; sicut multi homines sunt unus populus, ex eo quod ab uno rege reguntur. Quaedam vero dicuntur unum ex eo quod habent aliquid unum, sicut multi possessores unius agri sunt unum in dominio eius. Quaedam etiam dicuntur unum ex hoc quod sunt aliquid unum; sicut multi homines albi dicuntur unum, quia quilibet eorum albus est.

869. Sed respectu omnium istorum modorum secundariorum, primo dicuntur unum illa quae sunt unum secundum suam substantiam, de quibus supra dictum est in quinque modis suprapositis.

866. Here the Philosopher reduces all senses in which things are said to be one to one primary sense, and in regard to this he does two things.

First, he makes this reduction;
second (1016b11; [870]), he adds another to those senses in which things are said to be one, which have already been given, at *again, in one sense.*

He accordingly first says that it is evident from what precedes that things that are indivisible in every way are said to be one in the highest degree. For all the other senses in which things are said to be one are reducible to this sense, because it is universally true that those things that do not admit of division are said to be one insofar as they do not admit of division. For example, those things that are undivided insofar as they are man are said to be one in humanity, as Socrates and Plato; those which are undivided in the notion of animality are said to be one in animality; and those which are undivided from the viewpoint of extension or measure are said to be one in quantity, as continuous things.

867. And from this we can also derive number and the types of unity given above, because what is one is indivisible either in an absolute sense or in a qualified one. If it is indivisible in an absolute sense, it is the last type of unity, which is a principle; but if it is indivisible in a qualified sense, it is so either in quantity alone or in nature. If it is indivisible in quantity, then it is the first type. If it is indivisible in nature, it is so either in reference to its subject or to the division which depends upon the form. If it is divisible in reference to its subject, it is so either in reference to a real subject, and then it is the second type, or to a logical subject, and then it is the third type. And indivisibility of form, which is indivisibility of intelligible structure, or definition, constitutes the fourth type.

868. Now, from these senses of the term "one," certain others are again derived. Thus there are many things that are said to be one because they are doing one thing. For example, many men are said to be one insofar as they are rowing a boat. And some things are said to be one because they are subject to one thing—for example, many men constitute one people because they are ruled by one king. And some are said to be one because they possess one thing—for example, many owners of a field are said to be one in their ownership of it. And some things are also said to be one because they are something which is one—for example, many men are said to be one because each of them is white.

869. But considering all of these secondary senses in which things are said to be one, which have already been stated in the five ways given above, we can say that those things are one in the primary sense which are one in their substance.

Una namque substantia est, aut ratione continuitatis, sicut in primo modo: aut propter speciem subiecti, sicut in secundo modo, et etiam in tertio, prout unitas generis aliquid habet simile cum unitate speciei: aut etiam propter rationem, sicut in quarto et in quinto modo.

Et quod adhuc ex his modis aliqua dicantur unum, patet per oppositum. Aliqua enim sunt numero plura, vel numerantur ut plura, quia non sunt continua, vel quia non habent speciem unam, vel quia non conveniunt in una ratione.

870. Deinde cum dicit *amplius autem* addit alium modum a supradictis, qui non sumitur ex ratione indivisionis sicut praedicti, sed magis ex ratione divisionis; et dicit, quod quandoque aliqua dicuntur unum propter solam continuitatem, quandoque vero non, nisi sit aliquod totum et perfectum; quod quidem contingit quando habet aliquam unam speciem, non quidem sicut subiectum homogeneum dicitur unum specie quod pertinet ad secundum modum positum prius, sed secundum quod species in quadam totalitate consistit requirens determinatum ordinem partium;

sicut patet quod non dicimus unum aliquid, ut artificiatum, quando videmus partes calceamenti qualitercumque compositas, nisi forte secundum quod accipitur unum pro continuo; sed tunc dicimus esse unum omnes partes calceamenti, quando sic sunt compositae, quod sit calceamentum et habeat aliquam unam speciem, scilicet calceamenti.

871. Et ex hoc patet, quod linea circularis est maxime una; quia non solum habet continuitatem, sicut linea recta; sed etiam habet totalitatem et perfectionem, quod non habet linea recta. Perfectum est enim et totum, cui nihil deest: quod quidem contingit lineae circulari. Non enim potest sibi fieri additio, sicut fit lineae rectae.

872. Deinde cum dicit *uni vero* ponit quamdam proprietatem consequentem unum; et dicit, quod ratio unius est in hoc, quod sit principium alicuius numeri. Quod ex hoc patet, quia unum est prima mensura numeri, quo omnis numerus mensuratur: mensura autem habet rationem principii, quia per mensuram res mensuratae cognoscuntur, res autem cognoscuntur per sua propria principia. Et ex hoc patet, quod unum est principium noti vel cognoscibilis circa quodlibet, et est in omnibus principium cognoscendi.

873. Hoc autem unum, quod est principium cognoscendi, non est idem in omnibus generibus. In genere enim consonantiarum est unum, quod est diesis, quod est minimum in consonantiis. Diesis enim est semito-

For a thing is one in substance either by reason of its continuity, as in the first way; or because of the species of the subject, as in the second way; and again in the third way because the unity of the genus is somewhat similar to the unity of the species; or also because of the intelligible structure, as in the fourth and fifth ways.

That some things are said to be one in these ways is clear from the opposite of one. For things are many in number—that is, they are counted as many—either because they are continuous, or because they do not have one species, or because they do not have one common intelligible structure.

870. *Again, in one sense* (1016b11). Then he gives an additional sense in which the term "one" is used, which differs from the preceding ones. This sense is not derived from the notion of indivision, as the foregoing are, but rather from the notion of division. He says that sometimes some things are said to be one because of continuity alone, and sometimes they are said to be one only if they constitute a whole and something complete. Now this happens when the thing has one form, not in the sense that a homogeneous subject is said to have one form, which pertains to the second type given above, but in the sense that the form consists in a kind of totality requiring a definite order of parts.

Thus it is clear that we do not say that a thing is one—for example, some artifact such as a shoe—when we see the parts put together in any way at all (unless perhaps it is taken to be one insofar as it is continuous), but we say that all parts of a shoe are one when they are united in such a way that the thing is a shoe and has one form—that of a shoe.

871. And from this it is clear that a circular line is one in the highest degree. For a circular line is not only continuous like a straight line, but also has a totality and completeness which a straight line does not have; for that is complete and whole which lacks nothing. Now this characteristic belongs to a circular line; for nothing can be added to a circular line, but something can be added to a straight one.

872. *But the essence* (1016b17). Then he indicates a property which flows from oneness or unity. He says that the essence of one consists in being the principle of some number. This is clear from the fact that the unit is the primary numerical measure by which every number is measured. Now a measure has the character of a principle, because measured things are known by their measure, and things are known by their proper principles. And it is clear from this that unity is the first principle of what is known or knowable about each thing, and that it is the principle of knowing in everything.

873. But this unity which is the principle of knowing is not the same in all genera of things. For in the genus of musical sounds it is the lesser half tone, which is the smallest thing in this genus; for a lesser half tone is less than

nium minus. Dividitur enim tonus in duo semitonia inaequalia, quorum unus dicitur diesis.

In vocibus autem unum primum et minimum est litera vocalis, aut consonans; et magis vocalis quam consonans, ut in decimo dicetur.

Et in gravitatibus sive ponderibus est aliquid minimum, quod est mensura, scilicet uncia, vel aliquid aliud huiusmodi.

Et in motibus est una prima mensura, quae mensurat alios motus, scilicet motus simplicissimus et velocissimus, sicut est motus diurnus.

874. In omnibus tamen istis hoc est commune, quod illud, quod est prima mensura, est indivisibile secundum quantitatem, vel secundum speciem.

Quod igitur est in genere quantitatis unum et primum, oportet quod sit indivisibile et secundum quantitatem.

Si autem sit omnino indivisibile et secundum quantitatem et non habeat positionem, dicitur unitas. Punctus vero est id, quod est omnino indivisibile secundum quantitatem et tamen habet positionem. Linea vero est quod est divisibile secundum unam dimensionem tantum: superficies vero secundum duas. Corpus autem est omnibus modis divisibile secundum quantitatem, scilicet secundum tres dimensiones. Et hae descriptiones convertuntur. Nam omne quod duabus dimensionibus dividitur, est superficies, et sic de aliis.

875. Sciendum est autem quod esse mensuram est propria ratio unius secundum quod est principium numeri. Hoc autem non est idem cum uno quod convertitur cum ente, ut in quarto dictum est.

Ratio enim illius unius in sola indivisione consistit: huiusmodi autem unius in mensuratione. Sed tamen haec ratio mensurae, licet primo conveniat uni quod est principium numeri, tamen per quamdam similitudinem derivatur ad unum in aliis generibus, ut in decimo huius Philosophus ostendet.

Et secundum hoc ratio mensurae invenitur in quolibet genere. Haec autem ratio mensurae consequitur rationem indivisionis, sicut habitum est. Et ideo unum non omnino aequivoce dicitur de eo quod convertitur cum ente, et de eo quod est principium numeri; sed secundum prius et posterius.

876. Deinde cum dicit *amplius autem* ponit aliam divisionem unius, quae est magis logica; dicens, quod *quaedam sunt unum numero, quaedam specie, quaedam genere, quaedam analogia.*

a half tone, since a tone is divided into two unequal half tones, one of which is called a lesser half tone.

And in words, the first and smallest unity is the vowel or consonant, and the vowel to a greater degree than the consonant, as will be stated in book 10 (1053b24; [1971]).

And in heavy things or weights, there is some smallest thing which is their measure (the ounce or something of this kind).

And in motions, there is one first measure which measures the other motions—namely, the simplest and swiftest motion, which is the diurnal motion.

874. Yet all of these have this feature in common: the first measure is indivisible in quantity or in species.

Hence, in order that something be one and first in the genus of quantity it must be indivisible, and indivisible in quantity.

It is called a "unit" if it is indivisible in every way and has no position, and a "point" if it is altogether indivisible in quantity but has position. A line is something divisible in one dimension only; a surface, in two; and a body, in all three dimensions. And these descriptions are reversible; for everything that is divisible in two dimensions is a surface, and so on with the others.

875. Again, it must be noted that being a measure is the distinctive characteristic of unity insofar as it is the principle of number. But this unity or one is not the same as that which is interchangeable with being, as has been stated in book 4 (1003b32; [557]).

For the concept of the latter kind of unity involves only being undivided, but that of the former kind involves being a measure. But even though this character of a measure belongs to the unity which is the principle of number, still by a kind of likeness it is transferred to the unity found in other genera of things, as the Philosopher will show in book 10 of this work (1052a15; [1921]).

And according to this, the character of a measure is found in any genus. But this character of a measure is a natural consequence of the notion of undividedness, as has been explained (1016b17; [872]). Hence the term "one" is not predicated in a totally equivocal sense of the unity which is interchangeable with being and of that which is the principle of number, but it is predicated of one primarily and of the other secondarily.

876. *Further, some things* (1016b31). Then he gives another way of dividing unity, and this division is rather from the viewpoint of logic. He says that *some things are one in number, some in species, some in genus, and some analogically.*

Numero quidem sunt unum, quorum materia est una. Materia enim, secundum quod stat sub dimensionibus signatis, est principium individuationis formae. Et propter hoc ex materia habet singulare quod sit unum numero ab aliis divisum.

877. Specie autem dicuntur unum, *quorum una est ratio*, idest definitio. Nam nihil proprie definitur nisi species, cum omnis definitio ex genere et differentia constet. Et si aliquod genus definitur, hoc est inquantum est species.

878. Unum vero genere sunt, *quae conveniunt in figura praedicationis*, idest quae habent unum modum praedicandi. Alius enim est modus quo praedicatur substantia, et quo praedicatur qualitas vel actio; sed omnes substantiae habent unum modum praedicandi, inquantum praedicantur non ut in subiecto existentes.

879. Proportione vero vel analogia sunt unum quaecumque in hoc conveniunt, quod hoc se habet ad illud *sicut aliud ad aliud*. Et hoc quidem potest accipi duobus modis,

vel in eo quod aliqua duo habent diversas habitudines ad unum; sicut sanativum de urina dictum habitudinem significat signi sanitatis; de medicina vero, quia significat habitudinem causae respectu eiusdem.

Vel in eo quod est eadem proportio duorum ad diversa, sicut tranquillitatis ad mare et serenitatis ad aerem. Tranquillitas enim est quies maris et serenitas aeris.

880. In istis autem modis unius, semper posterius sequitur ad praecedens et non convertitur. Quaecumque enim sunt unum numero, sunt specie unum et non convertitur. Et idem patet in aliis.

881. Deinde cum dicit *palam autem* ex modis unius accipit modos multorum; et dicit, quod multa dicuntur per oppositum ad unum. Et ideo quot modis dicitur unum, tot modis dicuntur multa; quia quoties dicitur unum oppositorum, toties dicitur et reliquum. Unde aliqua dicuntur multa propter hoc, quod non sunt continua. Quod est per oppositum ad primum modum unius.

882. Alia dicuntur multa *propter hoc quod materiam habent divisam secundum speciem*, sive intelligamus de materia *prima*, idest proxima, aut de finali sive *ultima*, in quam ultimo fit resolutio. Per divisionem quippe proximae materiae dicuntur multa vinum et oleum: per divisionem vero materiae remotae, vinum et lapis. Et si materia accipiatur tam pro materia naturae quam pro

Those things are one in number which have one matter, for insofar as matter has certain designated dimensions, it is the principle by which a form is individuated. And for this reason a singular thing is numerically one and divided from other things as a result of matter.

877. Those things are said to be one in species *which have one intelligible structure*, or definition, for the only thing that is defined in a proper sense is the species, since every definition is composed of a genus and a difference. And if any genus is defined, this happens in so far as it is a species.

878. Those things are one in genus *which have the same figure of predication*, that is, which have one way of being predicated. For the way in which substance is predicated and that in which quality or action is predicated are different, but all substances have one way of being predicated inasmuch as they are not predicated as something which is present in a subject.

879. And those things are proportionally or analogically one which agree in this respect: one is related to another *as some third thing is to a fourth*. Now this can be taken in two ways.

First, in the sense that any two things are related in different ways to one third thing. For example, the term "healthy" is predicated of urine because it signifies the relationship of a sign of health to health itself, and of medicine because it signifies the relationship of a cause to the same health.

Or it may be taken in the sense that the proportion of two things to two other things is the same. For example, tranquility is to the sea as serenity is to the air, for tranquility is a state of rest in the sea, and serenity is a state of rest in the air.

880. Now with regard to the ways in which things are one, the latter types of unity always follow the former, and not the reverse, for those things that are one in number are one in species, but not the other way about. The same thing is clear in the other cases.

881. *Moreover, it is evident* (1017a3). From the ways in which things are said to be one he now derives the ways in which things are said to be many. He says that things are said to be many in just as many ways as they are said to be one, because in the case of opposite terms, one is used in as many ways as the other. Hence some things are said to be many because they are not continuous, which is the opposite of the first way in which things are one.

882. Other things are said to be many *because their matter is divisible in species*, whether we understand by matter *the first*, that is, their proximate matter, or the final *or ultimate* matter into which they are ultimately dissolved. Indeed, it is by the division of their proximate matter that wine and oil are said to be many, and by the division of their remote matter that wine and a stone are said to be

materia rationis, scilicet pro genere quod habet simili-tudinem materiae, hic modus multitudinis sumitur per oppositum ad secundum et tertium modum unius.

883. Alia vero dicuntur multa quae habent rationes, quod quid est esse dicentes, plures. Et hoc sumitur per oppositum ad quartum modum.

884. Quod autem opponitur quinto modo, nondum habet rationem pluralitatis nisi secundum quid et in potentia. Non enim ex hoc quod aliquid est divisibile propter hoc est multa nisi in potentia.

many. And if matter be taken both for real matter and for conceptual matter—that is, for a genus, which resembles matter—"many" in this sense is taken as the opposite of the second and third ways in which things are said to be one.

883. And still other things are said to be many when the conceptions which express their essence are many. And "many" in this sense is taken as the opposite of the fourth way in which things are said to be one.

884. But the opposite of the fifth way in which things are one does not have the notion of many except in a qualified sense and potentially, for the fact that a thing is divisible does not make it many except potentially.

LECTURE 9

Division of being into accidental and essential

1017a7 Ens dicitur hoc quidem secundem accidens, illud vero secundum se. [885]

1017a8 Secundum accidens quidem, ut iustum musicum esse dicimus, et hominem musicum, et musicum hominem. Similiter autem dicentes ut musicum aedificare, quia accidit aedificatori musicum esse, aut musico aedificatorem. Hoc enim esse hoc significat accidere hoc huic. [886]

Si autem et in dictis, quando hominem musicum dicimus, et musicum hominem, aut album musicum, aut hunc album. Hoc quidem, quia ambo eidem accidunt: illud vero, quia enti accidit hoc: aliud autem musicum hominem, quia huic musicum accidit.

Sic autem dicitur et album esse, quia cui accidit ille est. Quae quidem igitur secundum accidens esse dicuntur, sic dicuntur aut eo quod eidem enti ambo insunt, aut quia enti illud inest, aut quia ipsum est cui inest, de quo ipsum praedicatur.

1017a22 Secundum se vero esse dicuntur, quaecumque significant figuras praedicationis. Quoties enim dicitur, toties esse significat. [889]

Quoniam ergo praedicatorum, alia quid est significant, alia quale, alia quantum, alia ad aliquid, alia facere, alia pati, alia ubi, alia quando: horum unicuique idem esse significat.

Nihil enim refert, homo convalescens est, aut homo convalescit: vel homo vadens est aut secans, vel hominem vadere aut secare. Similiter autem et in aliis.

τὸ ὂν λέγεται τὸ μὲν κατὰ συμβεβηκὸς τὸ δὲ καθ' αὑτό,

κατὰ συμβεβηκὸς μέν, οἷον τὸν δίκαιον μουσικὸν εἶναί φαμεν καὶ τὸν ἄνθρωπον μουσικὸν καὶ τὸν μουσικὸν {10} ἄνθρωπον, παραπλησίως λέγοντες ὡσπερεὶ τὸν μουσικὸν οἰκοδομεῖν ὅτι συμβέβηκε τῷ οἰκοδόμῳ μουσικῷ εἶναι ἢ τῷ μουσικῷ οἰκοδόμῳ (τὸ γὰρ τόδε εἶναι τόδε σημαίνει τὸ συμβεβηκέναι τῷδε τόδε),

οὕτω δὲ καὶ ἐπὶ τῶν εἰρημένων· τὸν γὰρ ἄνθρωπον ὅταν μουσικὸν λέγωμεν καὶ τὸν μουσικὸν ἄνθρωπον, {15} ἢ τὸν λευκὸν μουσικὸν ἢ τοῦτον λευκόν, τὸ μὲν ὅτι ἄμφω τῷ αὐτῷ συμβεβήκασι, τὸ δ' ὅτι τῷ ὄντι συμβέβηκε, τὸ δὲ μουσικὸν ἄνθρωπον ὅτι τούτῳ τὸ μουσικὸν συμβέβηκεν

(οὕτω δὲ λέγεται καὶ τὸ μὴ λευκὸν εἶναι, ὅτι ᾧ συμβέβηκεν, ἐκεῖνο ἔστιν)· τὰ μὲν οὖν κατὰ συμβεβηκὸς {20} εἶναι λεγόμενα οὕτω λέγεται ἢ διότι τῷ αὐτῷ ὄντι ἄμφω ὑπάρχει, ἢ ὅτι ὄντι ἐκείνῳ ὑπάρχει, ἢ ὅτι αὐτὸ ἔστιν ᾧ ὑπάρχει οὗ αὐτὸ κατηγορεῖται·

καθ' αὑτὰ δὲ εἶναι λέγεται ὅσαπερ σημαίνει τὰ σχήματα τῆς κατηγορίας· ὁσαχῶς γὰρ λέγεται, τοσαυταχῶς τὸ εἶναι σημαίνει.

ἐπεὶ οὖν τῶν {25} κατηγορουμένων τὰ μὲν τί ἐστι σημαίνει, τὰ δὲ ποιόν, τὰ δὲ ποσόν, τὰ δὲ πρός τι, τὰ δὲ ποιεῖν ἢ πάσχειν, τὰ δὲ πού, τὰ δὲ ποτέ, ἑκάστῳ τούτων τὸ εἶναι ταὐτὸ σημαίνει·

οὐθὲν γὰρ διαφέρει τὸ ἄνθρωπος ὑγιαίνων ἐστὶν ἢ τὸ ἄνθρωπος ὑγιαίνει, οὐδὲ τὸ ἄνθρωπος βαδίζων ἐστὶν ἢ τέμνων τοῦ ἄνθρωπος {30} βαδίζει ἢ τέμνει, ὁμοίως δὲ καὶ ἐπὶ τῶν ἄλλων.

The term "being" signifies both accidental being and essential being.

Accidental being is designated when we say, for example, that the just person is musical, and that the man is musical, and that the musician is a man. And the same thing applies when we say that the musician builds, because it is accidental to a builder to be a musician, or to a musician to be a builder. For to say that this is that means that this is an accident of that.

And so it is in the cases given, for when we say that the man is musical, and that the musician is a man, or that what is musical is white, in the latter case we mean that both are accidents of the same thing, and in the former that the attribute is accidental to the being. But when we say that what is musical is a man, we mean that musical is an accident of this person.

And in this sense too white is said to exist, because the thing of which it is an accident exists. Therefore, those things that are said to be in an accidental sense are said to be such either because both belong to the same being, or because the attribute belongs to the being, or because the thing to which it belongs and of which it is itself predicated, itself exists.

On the other hand, those things are said to be essentially which signify the figures of predication, for being is signified in just as many ways as predications are made.

Therefore, since some of these predications signify what a thing is, others what it is like, others how much, others how related, others what it does, others what it undergoes, others where, and others when, to each of these there corresponds a mode of being which signifies the same thing.

For there is no difference between "The man is recovering" and "The man recovers," or between "The man is walking" or "cutting" and "The man walks" or "cuts." And the same is true in other cases.

1017a31 Amplius autem et esse significat, quia verum; non esse, quia non verum, sed falsum. Similiter in afiirmatione et negatione, ut quod est Socrates musicus, quia hoc verum: aut quod non est Socrates albus, quia verum est. Hoc autem non est, diameter incommensurabilis, quia falsum. [895]

ἔτι τὸ εἶναι σημαίνει καὶ τὸ ἔστιν ὅτι ἀληθές, τὸ δὲ μὴ εἶναι ὅτι οὐκ ἀληθὲς ἀλλὰ ψεῦδος, ὁμοίως ἐπὶ καταφάσεως καὶ ἀποφάσεως, οἷον ὅτι ἔστι Σωκράτης μουσικός, ὅτι ἀληθὲς τοῦτο, ἢ ὅτι ἔστι Σωκράτης οὐ λευκός, ὅτι ἀληθές· τὸ δ' οὐκ {35} ἔστιν ἡ διάμετρος σύμμετρος, ὅτι ψεῦδος.

Again, "being" signifies that something is true, and non-being signifies that something is not true, but false. This also holds true of affirmation and negation. For example, to say that Socrates is musical means that this is true. Or to say that Socrates is not white means that this is true. But to say that the diagonal of a square is not incommensurable with a side means that this is false.

1017a35 Amplius esse significat et ens, hoc quidem potestate dicibili, illud vero actu. Horum enim dictorum terminorum esse dicimus, et quod potestate est dicibile terminorum, et quod est actu. [897]

ἔτι τὸ εἶναι σημαίνει καὶ τὸ ὂν τὸ μὲν δυνάμει ῥητὸν τὸ δ' ἐντελεχείᾳ τῶν εἰρημένων τούτων· ὁρῶν τε γὰρ εἶναί φαμεν καὶ τὸ δυνάμει ὁρῶν καὶ τὸ ἐντελεχείᾳ,

Again, "to be," and "being," signifies that some of the things mentioned are potentially and others actually. For in the case of the terms mentioned we predicate being both of what is said to be potentially and of what is said to be actually.

Et scire similiter et potens uti scientia, et utens. Et quiescens et cum iam inest quies et potens quiescere.

καὶ [τὸ] ἐπίστασθαι ὡσαύτως καὶ τὸ δυνάμενον χρῆσθαι τῇ ἐπιστήμῃ καὶ τὸ {5} χρώμενον, καὶ ἠρεμοῦν καὶ ᾧ ἤδη ὑπάρχει ἠρεμία καὶ τὸ δυνάμενον ἠρεμεῖν.

And similarly we say both of one who is capable of using scientific knowledge and of one who is actually using it that he knows. And we say that that is at rest which is already so or capable of being so.

Similiter autem et in substantiis. Etenim Mercurium in lapide dicimus esse, et medietatem lineae et frumentum nondum perfectum. Quando vero potens et quando non, in aliis determinandum.

ὁμοίως δὲ καὶ ἐπὶ τῶν οὐσιῶν· καὶ γὰρ Ἑρμῆν ἐν τῷ λίθῳ φαμὲν εἶναι, καὶ τὸ ἥμισυ τῆς γραμμῆς, καὶ σῖτον τὸν μήπω ἁδρόν. πότε δὲ δυνατὸν καὶ πότε οὔπω, ἐν ἄλλοις διοριστέον.

And this also applies in the case of substances, for we say that Mercury is in the stone, and half of the line in the line, and we call that grain which is not yet ripe. But when a thing is potential and when not must be settled elsewhere (1048b37; [1832]).

---

885. Hic Philosophus distinguit quot modis dicitur ens. Et circa hoc tria facit.

Primo distinguit ens in ens per se et per accidens.

Secundo distinguit modos entis per accidens, ibi, *secundum accidens quidem* et cetera.
Tertio modos entis per se, ibi, *secundum se vero.*

Dicit ergo, quod ens dicitur quoddam secundum se, et quoddam secundum accidens. Sciendum tamen est quod illa divisio entis non est eadem cum illa divisione qua dividitur ens in substantiam et accidens. Quod ex hoc patet, quia ipse postmodum, ens secundum se dividit in decem praedicamenta, quorum novem sunt de genere accidentis. Ens igitur dividitur in substantiam et accidens, secundum absolutam entis considerationem, sicut ipsa albedo in se considerata dicitur accidens, et homo substantia. Sed ens secundum accidens prout hic sumitur, oportet accipi per comparationem accidentis ad substantiam. Quae quidem comparatio significatur hoc verbo, est, cum dicitur, homo est albus. Unde hoc totum, homo est albus, est ens per accidens. Unde patet quod divisio entis secundum se et secundum accidens,

885. Here the Philosopher gives the various senses in which the term "being" is used, and in regard to this he does three things.

First (1017a7), he divides being into being *per se* and being *per accidens.*

Second (1017a8; [886]), he distinguishes between the types of accidental being, at *accidental being.*

Third (1017a22; [889]), he distinguishes between the types of being *per se,* at *on the other hand.*

He says, then, that while things are said to be both *per se* and accidentally, it should be noted that this division of being is not the same as that whereby being is divided into substance and accident. This is clear from the fact that he later divides being *per se* into the ten predicaments, nine of which belong to the genus of accident [889]. Hence being is divided into substance and accident insofar as it is considered in an absolute sense—for example, whiteness considered in itself is called an accident, and man a substance. But accidental being, in the sense in which it is taken here, must be understood by comparing an accident with a substance; and this comparison is signified by the term "is" when (for example) it is said that the man is white. Hence this whole, "The man is white," is an accidental being. It is clear, then, that the division of being into *per se* being and being *per*

attenditur secundum quod aliquid praedicatur de aliquo per se vel per accidens. Divisio vero entis in substantiam et accidens attenditur secundum hoc quod aliquid in natura sua est vel substantia vel accidens.

886. Deinde cum dicit *secundum accidens* ostendit quot modis dicitur ens per accidens; et dicit, quod tribus:

quorum unus est, quando accidens praedicatur de accidente, ut cum dicitur, iustus est musicus.

Secundus, cum accidens praedicatur de subiecto, ut cum dicitur, homo est musicus.

Tertius, cum subiectum praedicatur de accidente, ut cum dicitur musicus est homo.

Et, quia superius iam manifestavit quomodo causa per accidens differt a causa per se, ideo nunc consequenter per causam per accidens manifestat ens per accidens.

887. Et dicit, quod sicut assignantes causam per accidens dicimus quod musicus aedificat, eo quod musicum accidit aedificatori, vel e contra, constat enim *quod hoc esse hoc*, idest musicum aedificare, nihil aliud significat quam *hoc accidere huic*, ita est etiam in praedictis modis entis per accidens, quando dicimus hominem esse musicum, accidens praedicando de subiecto: vel musicum esse hominem, praedicando subiectum de accidente: vel album esse musicum, vel e converso, scilicet musicum esse album, praedicando accidens de accidente.

In omnibus enim his, esse, nihil aliud significat quam accidere. *Hoc quidem*, scilicet quando accidens de accidente praedicatur, significat quod ambo accidentia accidunt eidem subiecto: *illud vero*, scilicet cum accidens praedicatur de subiecto, dicitur esse, *quia enti* idest subiecto accidit accidens.

Sed musicum esse hominem dicimus, quia huic, scilicet praedicato, accidit musicum, quod ponitur in subiecto. Et est quasi similis ratio praedicandi, cum subiectum praedicatur de accidente, et accidens de accidente.

Sicut enim subiectum praedicatur de accidente ea ratione, quia praedicatur subiectum de eo, cui accidit accidens in subiecto positum; ita accidens praedicatur de accidente, quia praedicatur de subiecto accidentis. Et propter hoc, sicut dicitur musicum est homo, similiter dicitur musicum esse album, quia scilicet illud cui accidit esse musicum, scilicet subiectum, est album.

888. Patet igitur, quod *ea, quae dicuntur esse secundum accidens, dicuntur* triplici ratione:

accidens is based on the fact that one thing is predicated of another either *per se* or accidentally. But the division of being into substance and accident is based on the fact that a thing is in its own nature either a substance or an accident.

886. Then he indicates the various senses in which a thing is said to be accidentally. He says that this occurs in three ways:

first, when an accident is predicated of an accident, as when it is said that someone just is musical;

second, when an accident is predicated of a subject, as when it is said that the man is musical;

and third, when a subject is predicated of an accident, as when it is said that the musician is a man.

And since he has shown above [787] how an accidental cause differs from a cause *per se*, he therefore now shows that an accidental being is a result of an accidental cause.

887. He says that, in giving an accidental cause, we say that the musician builds, because it is accidental to a builder to be a musician, or vice versa. For it is evident that the statement *this is that*, namely, "The musician is a builder," simply means that *this is an accident of that*. The same is true of the foregoing senses of accidental being when we say that the man is musical by predicating an accident of a subject, or when we say that what is white is musical, or conversely that what is musical is white, by predicating an accident of an accident.

For in all of these cases "is" signifies merely accidental being. *In the latter case*, when an accident is predicated of an accident, "is" signifies that both accidents are accidental to the same subject, *and in the former*, when an accident is predicated of a subject, "is" signifies *that the attribute is accidental to the being*, that is, to the subject.

But when we say that what is musical is a man, we mean that musical is an accident of this person, that is, that musical, which holds the position of a subject, is an accident of the predicate. And the reason for making the predication is similar in a sense when a subject is predicated of an accident and when an accident is predicated of an accident.

For a subject is predicated of an accident by reason of the fact that the subject is predicated of that to which the accident, which is expressed in the subject, is accidental; and in a similar fashion an accident is predicated of an accident because it is predicated of the subject of an accident. And for this reason the attribute "musical" is predicated not only of man but also of white, because that of which the attribute musical is an accident (that is, the subject) is white.

888. It, is evident, then, that *those things that are said to be in an accidental sense are said to be such* for three reasons.

aut eo *quod ambo*, scilicet subiectum et praedicatum, *insunt eidem*, sicut cum accidens praedicatur de accidente,

aut *quia illud*, scilicet praedicatum, ut musicum, *inest enti*, idest subiecto, quod dicitur esse musicum; et hoc est cum accidens praedicatur de subiecto;

aut *quia illud*, scilicet subiectum in praedicato positum, est illud cui inest accidens, de quo accidente illud, scilicet subiectum, praedicatur. Et hoc est scilicet cum subiectum praedicatur de accidente, ut cum dicimus, musicum est homo.

889. Deinde cum dicit *secundum se* distinguit modum entis per se: et circa hoc tria facit.

Primo distinguit ens, quod est extra animam, per decem praedicamenta, quod est ens perfectum.

Secundo ponit alium modum entis, secundum quod est tantum in mente, ibi, *amplius autem et esse significat*.

Tertio dividit ens per potentiam et actum: et ens sic divisum est communius quam ens perfectum. Nam ens in potentia, est ens secundum quid tantum et imperfectum, ibi, *amplius esse significat et ens*.

Dicit ergo primo, quod illa dicuntur esse secundum se, quaecumque significant figuras praedicationis. Sciendum est enim quod ens non potest hoc modo contrahi ad aliquid determinatum, sicut genus contrahitur ad species per differentias. Nam differentia, cum non participet genus, est extra essentiam generis. Nihil autem posset esse extra essentiam entis, quod per additionem ad ens aliquam speciem entis constituat: nam quod est extra ens, nihil est, et differentia esse non potest. Unde in tertio huius probavit Philosophus, quod ens, genus esse non potest.

890. Unde oportet, quod ens contrahatur ad diversa genera secundum diversum modum praedicandi, qui consequitur diversum modum essendi; quia *quoties ens dicitur*, idest quot modis aliquid praedicatur, *toties esse significatur*, idest tot modis *significatur aliquid esse*. Et propter hoc ea in quae dividitur ens primo, dicuntur esse praedicamenta, quia distinguuntur secundum diversum modum praedicandi. Quia igitur eorum quae praedicantur, quaedam significant quid, idest substantiam, quaedam quale, quaedam quantum, et sic de aliis; oportet quod unicuique modo praedicandi, esse significet idem; ut cum dicitur homo est animal, esse significat substantiam. Cum autem dicitur, homo est albus, significat qualitatem, et sic de aliis.

891. Sciendum enim est quod praedicatum ad subiectum tripliciter se potest habere.

First, *because both*, namely, the subject and predicate, *belong to the same being* (as when an accident is predicated of an accident).

Second, *because the attribute*, that is, the predicate (such as musical) *belongs to the being*, that is, to the subject which is said to be musical (and this occurs when an accident is predicated of a subject).

Third, *because the thing*, the subject which is expressed in the predicate *to which belongs the accident of which it* (the subject) *is itself predicated, itself exists*. (This occurs when a subject is predicated of an accident, as when we say that what is musical is a man.)

889. *On the other hand* (1017a22). Here he distinguishes between the types of being *per se*, and in regard to this he does three things.

First, he divides the kind of being which lies outside the mind, which is complete being, by the ten predicaments.

Second (1017a31; [895]), he gives another type of being, inasmuch as being exists only in the mind, at *again, "being" signifies*.

Third (1017a35; [897]), he divides being by potency and act—and being divided in this way is more common than complete being, for potential being is being only imperfectly and in a qualified sense, at *again, "to be."*

He says, first (1017a22), that all those things that signify the figures of predication are said to be essentially. For it must be noted that being cannot be narrowed down to some definite thing in the way in which a genus is narrowed down to a species by means of differences. Since a difference does not participate in a genus, it lies outside the essence of a genus. But there could be nothing outside the essence of being which could constitute a particular species of being by adding to being; for what is outside of being is nothing, and this cannot be a difference. Hence, in book 3 of this work [433], the Philosopher proved that being cannot be a genus.

890. Being must then be narrowed down to diverse genera on the basis of a different mode of predication, which flows from a different mode of being; for *being is signified*, that is, something is signified to be, *in just as many ways* (or in as many senses) *as predications are made*. And for this reason, those things into which being is first divided are called "predicaments," because they are distinguished on the basis of different ways of predicating. Therefore, since some predicates signify what (or substance), some signify what kind, some signify how much, and so on, there must be a mode of being corresponding to each type of predication. For example, when it is said that a man is an animal, "is" signifies substance; when it is said that a man is white, "is" signifies quality, and so on.

891. For it should be noted that a predicate can be referred to a subject in three ways.

Uno modo cum est id quod est subiectum, ut cum dico, Socrates est animal. Nam Socrates est id quod est animal. Et hoc praedicatum dicitur significare substantiam primam, quae est substantia particularis, de qua omnia praedicantur.

892. Secundo modo ut praedicatum sumatur secundum quod inest subiecto: quod quidem praedicatum, vel inest ei per se et absolute, ut consequens materiam, et sic est quantitas: vel ut consequens formam, et sic est qualitas: vel inest ei non absolute, sed in respectu ad aliud, et sic est ad aliquid.

Tertio modo ut praedicatum sumatur ab eo quod est extra subiectum: et hoc dupliciter.

Uno modo ut sit omnino extra subiectum: quod quidem si non sit mensura subiecti, praedicatur per modum habitus, ut cum dicitur, Socrates est calceatus vel vestitus. Si autem sit mensura eius, cum mensura extrinseca sit vel tempus vel locus, sumitur praedicamentum vel ex parte temporis, et sic erit quando: vel ex loco, et sic erit ubi, non considerato ordine partium in loco, quo considerato erit situs.

Alio modo ut id a quo sumitur praedicamentum, secundum aliquid sit in subiecto, de quo praedicatur.

Et si quidem secundum principium, sic praedicatur ut agere. Nam actionis principium in subiecto est.

Si vero secundum terminum, sic praedicabitur ut in pati. Nam passio in subiectum patiens terminatur.

893. Quia vero quaedam praedicantur, in quibus manifeste non apponitur hoc verbum est, ne credatur quod illae praedicationes non pertineant ad praedicationem entis, ut cum dicitur, homo ambulat, ideo consequenter hoc removet, dicens quod in omnibus huiusmodi praedicationibus significatur aliquid esse. Verbum enim quodlibet resolvitur in hoc verbum est, et participium. Nihil enim differt dicere, homo convalescens est, et homo convalescit, et sic de aliis. Unde patet quod quot modis praedicatio fit, tot modis ens dicitur.

894. Nec est verum quod Avicenna dicit, quod praedicata, quae sunt in generibus accidentis, principaliter significant substantiam, et per posterius accidens, sicut hoc quod dico album et musicum. Nam album ut in praedicamentis dicitur, solam qualitatem significat. Hoc autem nomen album significat subiectum ex consequenti, inquantum significat albedinem per modum accidentis. Unde oportet, quod ex consequenti includat

This occurs in one way when the predicate states what the subject is, as when I say that Socrates is an animal, for Socrates is the thing which is an animal. And this predicate is said to signify first substance (that is, a particular substance), of which all attributes are predicated.

892. A predicate is referred to a subject in a second way when the predicate is taken as being in the subject, and this predicate is in the subject either *per se* and absolutely and as something flowing from its matter, and then it is quantity, or as something flowing from its form, and then it is quality; or it is not present in the subject absolutely but with reference to something else, and then it is relation.

A predicate is referred to a subject in a third way when the predicate is taken from something extrinsic to the subject, and this occurs in two ways.

In one way, that from which the predicate is taken is totally extrinsic to the subject; and if this is not a measure of the subject, it is predicated after the manner of attire, as when it is said that Socrates is shod or clothed. But if it is a measure of the subject, then, since an extrinsic measure is either time or place, either the predicament is taken in reference to time, and so it will be "when," or it is taken in reference to place and the order of parts in place is not considered, and it will be "where," but if this order is considered, it will be position.

In another way, that from which the predicate is taken, though outside the subject, is nevertheless from a certain point of view in the subject of which it is predicated.

And if it is from the viewpoint of the principle, then it is predicated as an action, for the principle of action is in the subject.

But if it is from the viewpoint of its terminus, then it will be predicated as a passion, for a passion is terminated in the subject which is being acted upon.

893. But since there are some predications in which the verb "is" is clearly not used (for example, when it is said that a man walks), lest someone think that these predications do not involve the predication of being, Aristotle subsequently rejects this notion, saying that in all predications of this kind something is signified to be. For every verb is reduced to the verb "is" plus a participle. For there is no difference between the statements "The man is recovering" and "The man recovers" (and it is the same in other cases). It is clear, then, that "being" is used in as many ways as we make predications.

894. And there is no truth in Avicenna's statement that predicates which belong to the genus of accidents primarily signify substance and secondarily accidents, as the terms "white" and "musical." For the term "white," as it is used in the categories, signifies quality alone. Now the term "white" implies a subject inasmuch as it signifies whiteness after the manner of an accident, so that it must by implication include the subject in its notion, because the being of an

in sui ratione subiectum. Nam accidentis esse est inesse. Albedo enim etsi significet accidens, non tamen per modum accidentis, sed per modum substantiae. Unde nullo modo consignificat subiectum. Si enim principaliter significaret subiectum, tunc praedicata accidentalia non ponerentur a Philosopho sub ente secundum se, sed sub ente secundum accidens. Nam hoc totum, quod est homo albus, est ens secundum accidens, ut dictum est.

895. Deinde cum dicit *amplius autem* ponit alium modum entis, secundum quod esse et est, significant compositionem propositionis, quam facit intellectus componens et dividens. Unde dicit, quod esse significat veritatem rei. Vel sicut alia translatio melius habet *quod esse significat quia aliquod dictum est verum*.

Unde veritas propositionis potest dici veritas rei per causam. Nam ex eo quod res est vel non est, oratio vera vel falsa est. Cum enim dicimus aliquid esse, significamus propositionem esse veram. Et cum dicimus non esse, significamus non esse veram; et hoc sive in affirmando, sive in negando.

In affirmando quidem, sicut dicimus quod Socrates est albus, quia hoc verum est. In negando vero, ut Socrates non est albus, quia hoc est verum, scilicet ipsum esse non album. Et similiter dicimus, quod non est diameter incommensurabilis lateri quadrati, quia hoc est falsum, scilicet non esse ipsum non commensurabilem.

896. Sciendum est autem quod iste secundus modus comparatur ad primum, sicut effectus ad causam. Ex hoc enim quod aliquid in rerum natura est, sequitur veritas et falsitas in propositione, quam intellectus significat per hoc verbum est prout est verbalis copula. Sed, quia aliquid, quod est in se non ens, intellectus considerat ut quoddam ens, sicut negationem et huiusmodi, ideo quandoque dicitur esse de aliquo hoc secundo modo, et non primo. Dicitur enim, quod caecitas est secundo modo, ex eo quod vera est propositio, qua dicitur aliquid esse caecum; non tamen dicitur quod sit primo modo vera. Nam caecitas non habet aliquod esse in rebus, sed magis est privatio alicuius esse.

Accidit autem unicuique rei quod aliquid de ipsa vere affirmetur intellectu vel voce. Nam res non refertur ad scientiam, sed e converso. Esse vero quod in sui natura unaquaeque res habet, est substantiale. Et ideo, cum dicitur, Socrates est, si ille est primo modo accipiatur, est de praedicato substantiali. Nam ens est superius ad unumquodque entium, sicut animal ad hominem. Si autem accipiatur secundo modo, est de praedicato accidentali.

accident consists in being in something. For even though whiteness signifies an accident, it still does not signify this after the manner of an accident, but after that of a substance. Hence it implies a subject in no way. For if it were to signify a subject primarily, then the Philosopher would not put accidental predicates under essential being, but under accidental being. For the whole statement "The man is white" is a being in an accidental sense, as has been stated [886].

895. *Again, "being" signifies* (1017a31). Then he gives another sense in which the term "being" is used, inasmuch as the terms "being" and "is" signify the composition of a proposition, which the intellect makes when it combines and separates. He says that being signifies the truth of a thing, or as another translation better expresses it, *"being" signifies that some statement is true*.

Thus the truth of a thing can be said to determine the truth of a proposition after the manner of a cause; for a discourse is true or false by reason of the fact that a thing is or is not. For when we say that something is, we signify that a proposition is true; and when we say that something is not, we signify that it is not true. And this applies both to affirmation and to negation.

It applies to affirmation as when we say that Socrates is white because this is true, and to negation as when we say that Socrates is not white because this is true (namely, that he is not white). And in a similar way we say that the diagonal of a square is not incommensurable with a side, because its being incommensurable is false.

896. Now it must be noted that this second way in which "being" is used is related to the first as an effect is to a cause. For from the fact that something is in reality, it follows that there is truth and falsity in a proposition, and the intellect signifies this by the term "is" taken as a verbal copula. But since the intellect considers as a kind of being something which is in itself a non-being, such as a negation and the like, therefore sometimes being is predicated of something in this second way and not in the first. For blindness is said to be in the second way on the grounds that the proposition in which something is said to be blind is true. However, it is not said to be true in the first way; for blindness does not have any being in reality, but is rather a privation of some being.

Now it is accidental to a thing that an attribute should be affirmed of it truly in thought or in word, for reality is not referred to knowledge, but the reverse. But the act of being which each thing has in its own nature is substantial. Therefore, when it is said that Socrates is, if the "is" is taken in the first way, it belongs to substantial predicates, for being is a higher predicate with reference to any particular being, as animal with reference to man. But if it is taken in the second way, it belongs to accidental predicates.

897. Deinde cum dicit *amplius esse* ponit distinctionem entis per actum et potentiam; dicens, quod ens et esse significant aliquid dicibile vel effabile in potentia, vel dicibile in actu. In omnibus enim praedictis terminis, quae significant decem praedicamenta, aliquid dicitur in actu, et aliquid in potentia. Et ex hoc accidit, quod unumquodque praedicamentum per actum et potentiam dividitur.

Et sicut in rebus, quae extra animam sunt, dicitur aliquid in actu et aliquid in potentia, ita in actibus animae et privationibus, quae sunt res rationis tantum.

Dicitur enim aliquis scire, quia potest uti scientia, et quia utitur: similiter quiescens, quia iam inest ei quiescere, et quia potest quiescere.

Et non solum hoc est in accidentibus, sed etiam in substantiis. *Etenim Mercurium*, idest imaginem Mercurii *dicimus esse in lapide* in potentia, *et medium lineae dicitur esse in linea* in potentia. Quaelibet enim pars continui est potentialiter in toto. Linea vero inter substantias ponitur secundum opinionem ponentium mathematica esse substantias, quam nondum reprobaverat. Frumentum etiam quando nondum est perfectum, sicut quando est in herba, dicitur esse in potentia. Quando vero aliquid sit in potentia, et quando nondum est in potentia, determinandum est in aliis, scilicet in nono huius.

897. *Again, "to be," and "being"* (1017a35). Here he gives the division of being into the actual and the potential. He says that "to be," and "being," signifies something which is expressible or utterable potentially or actually. For in the case of all of the foregoing terms which signify the ten predicaments, something is said to be so actually and something else potentially; and from this it follows that each predicament is divided by act and potency.

And just as in the case of things that are outside the mind some are said to be actually and some potentially, so also is this true in the case of the mind's activities, and in that of privations, which are only conceptual beings.

For one is said to know both because he is capable of using scientific knowledge and because he is using it; similarly, a thing is said to be at rest both because rest belongs to it already and because it is capable of being at rest.

And this is true not only of accidents but also of substances. *For we say that Mercury* (that is, the image of Mercury), *is in the stone* potentially; *and half of the line is in the line* potentially, for every part of a continuum is potentially in the whole. And the line is included among substances according to the opinion of those who hold that the objects of mathematics are substances—an opinion which he has not yet disproved. And when grain is not yet ripe—for example, when it is still in blade—it is said to be potentially. Just when, however, something is potential and when it is no longer such must be established elsewhere—namely, in book 9 of this work [1832].

LECTURE 10

The definition of "substance"

1017b10 Substantia dicitur, et simplicia corpora, ut terra et ignis et aqua et quaecumque talia. Et universaliter corpora. Et ex his constantia, et animalia, et daemonia et partes horum. Haec autem omnia dicuntur substantia, quia non de subiecto dicuntur, sed de his alia. [898]

1017b14 Alio vero modo quodcumque fuerit causa existendi inexistens in talibus, quaecumque non dicuntur de subiecto, ut anima in animali. [899]

1017b18 Amplius quaecumque particulae existentes sunt in talibus terminantes et hoc aliquid significantes, quibus destructis destruitur totum: ut superficie corpus, (ut quidam dicunt) et superficies linea. Et totaliter numerus videtur quibusdam esse talis. Nam eo destructo, nihil esse et terminate omnia. [900]

1017b21 Amplius quod quid erat esse cuius ratio est definitio; et haec substantia videtur uniuscuiusque. [902]

1017b23 Accidit itaque secundum duos modos substantiam dici: subiectum ultimum, quod non adhuc de alio dicitur: et quodcumque hoc aliquid ens, et separabile fuerit. Tale vero uniuscuiusque forma et species. [903]

οὐσία λέγεται τά τε ἁπλᾶ σώματα, οἷον γῆ καὶ πῦρ καὶ ὕδωρ καὶ ὅσα τοιαῦτα, καὶ ὅλως σώματα καὶ τὰ ἐκ τούτων συνεστῶτα ζῷά τε καὶ δαιμόνια καὶ τὰ μόρια τούτων· ἅπαντα δὲ ταῦτα λέγεται οὐσία ὅτι οὐ καθ᾽ ὑποκειμένου λέγεται ἀλλὰ κατὰ τούτων τὰ ἄλλα.

ἄλλον δὲ {15} τρόπον ὃ ἂν ᾖ αἴτιον τοῦ εἶναι, ἐνυπάρχον ἐν τοῖς τοιούτοις ὅσα μὴ λέγεται καθ᾽ ὑποκειμένου, οἷον ἡ ψυχὴ τῷ ζῴῳ.

ἔτι ὅσα μόρια ἐνυπάρχοντά ἐστιν ἐν τοῖς τοιούτοις ὁρίζοντά τε καὶ τόδε τι σημαίνοντα, ὧν ἀναιρουμένων ἀναιρεῖται τὸ ὅλον, οἷον ἐπιπέδου σῶμα, ὥς φασί τινες, καὶ ἐπίπεδον {20} γραμμῆς· καὶ ὅλως ὁ ἀριθμὸς δοκεῖ εἶναί τισι τοιοῦτος (ἀναιρουμένου τε γὰρ οὐδὲν εἶναι, καὶ ὁρίζειν πάντα):

ἔτι τὸ τί ἦν εἶναι, οὗ ὁ λόγος ὁρισμός, καὶ τοῦτο οὐσία λέγεται ἑκάστου.

συμβαίνει δὴ κατὰ δύο τρόπους τὴν οὐσίαν λέγεσθαι, τό θ᾽ ὑποκείμενον ἔσχατον, ὃ μηκέτι κατ᾽ ἄλλου λέγεται, καὶ ὃ {25} ἂν τόδε τι ὂν καὶ χωριστὸν ᾖ· τοιοῦτον δὲ ἑκάστου ἡ μορφὴ καὶ τὸ εἶδος.

The term "substance" means the simple bodies, such as earth, fire, water, and the like, and in general bodies and the things composed of them, both animals and demons and their parts. All of these are called substances because they are not predicated of a subject, but other things are predicated of them.

In another sense, "substance" means that which, being present in such things as are not predicated of a subject, is the cause of their being, as the soul in an animal.

Again, "substance" means those parts which, being present in such things, limit them and designate them as individuals and as a result of whose destruction the whole is destroyed—for example, body is destroyed when surface is, as some say, and surface when line is. And in general it seems to some that number is of this nature, for (according to them) if it is destroyed, nothing will exist, and it limits all things.

Again, the quiddity of a thing, whose intelligible expression is the definition, also seems to be the substance of each thing.

It follows, then, that the term "substance" is used in two senses. It means the ultimate subject, which is not further predicated of something else; and it means anything which is a particular being and capable of existing apart. The form and species of each thing is said to be of this nature.

---

898. Hic ostendit quot modis dicitur substantia: et circa hoc duo facit.

Primo ponit diversos modos substantiae.

Secundo reducit omnes ad duos, ibi, ***accidit itaque***.

Circa primum ponit quatuor modos;

quorum primus est secundum quod substantiae particulares dicuntur substantiae, sicut ***simplicia corpora***, ut terra et ignis et aqua et huiusmodi.

898. Aristotle now explains the various senses in which the term "substance" is used; and in regard to this he does two things.

First, he gives the various senses in which the term "substance" is used.

Second (1017b23; [903]), he reduces all of these to two, at ***it follows***.

In treating the first part he gives four senses of the term "substance."

First, it means particular substances, such as ***the simple bodies***: earth, fire, water, and the like.

Et universaliter omnia corpora, etiam si non sint simplicia, sicut mixta similium partium, ut lapis, sanguis, caro, et huiusmodi.

Et iterum *animalia* quae constant et huiusmodi corporibus sensibilibus, *et partes eorum*, ut manus et pedes et huiusmodi, *et daemonia*, idest idola, quae in templis posita colebantur pro diis. Vel *daemonia* dicit quaedam animalia rationabilia secundum Platonicos, quae Apuleius sic definit: *Daemones sunt animalia corpore aerea, mente rationalia, animo passiva, tempore aeterna.* Haec enim omnia praedicta dicuntur substantia, quia non dicuntur de alio subiecto, sed alia dicuntur de his. Et haec est descriptio primae substantiae in praedicamentis.

899. Secundum modum ponit ibi *alio vero* dicit quod alio modo dicitur substantia quae est causa essendi praedictis substantiis quae non dicuntur de subiecto; non quidem extrinseca sicut efficiens, sed intrinseca eis, ut forma. Sicut dicitur anima substantia animalis.

900. Deinde cum dicit *amplius quaecumque* ponit tertium modum, secundum opinionem Platonicorum et Pythagoricorum, dicens, quod quaecumque particulae sunt in praedictis substantiis, quae sunt termini earum, et significant hoc aliquid secundum opinionem eorum, in quibus destructis destruitur totum, dicuntur etiam substantiae. Sicut superficie destructa destruitur corpus, ut quidam dicunt, et destructa linea destruitur superficies. Patet etiam, quod superficies est terminus corporis, et linea terminus superficiei. Et secundum dictorum positionem, linea est pars superficiei, et superficies pars corporis. Ponebant enim corpora componi ex superficiebus et superficies ex lineis, et lineas ex punctis. Unde sequebatur, quod punctum sit substantia lineae, et linea superficiei, et sic de aliis. Numerus autem secundum hanc positionem videtur esse substantia totaliter omnium rerum, quia remoto numero nihil remanet in rebus: quod enim non est unum, nihil est. Et similiter quae non sunt plura, non sunt. Numerus etiam invenitur terminare omnia, eo quod omnia mensurantur per numerum.

901. Iste autem modus non est verus. Nam hoc quod communiter invenitur in omnibus, et sine quo res esse non potest, non oportet quod sit substantia rei, sed potest esse aliqua proprietas consequens rei substantiam vel principium substantiae. Provenit etiam eis error specialiter quantum ad unum et numerum, eo quod non distinguebant inter unum quod convertitur cum ente, et unum quod est principium numeri.

902. Quartum modum ponit ibi *amplius quod* dicit quod etiam quidditas rei, quam significat definitio, dicitur substantia uniuscuiusque. Haec autem quidditas

And in general it means all bodies, even though they are not simple, that is, compound bodies of like parts, such as stones, blood, flesh, and the like.

Again, it means **animals**, which are composed of such sensible bodies, **and their parts** (such as hands and feet and so on), **and demons**, the idols set up in temples and worshipped as gods. Or by **demons** he means certain animals which the Platonists claimed are capable of reasoning, and which Apuleius defines thus: *demons are animals composed of an ethereal body, rational in mind, passive in soul, and eternal in time.* Now all of the foregoing things are called substances because they are not predicated of another subject but other things are predicated of them. This is the description of first substance given in the *Categories*.

899. *In another sense* (1017b14). He says that in another sense "substance" means the cause of the being of the foregoing substances which are not predicated of a subject, and it is not extrinsic to them like an efficient cause, but is intrinsic like a form. It is in this sense that the soul is called the substance of an animal.

900. *Again, "substance"* (1017b18). He gives a third meaning of "substance," which is the one used by the Platonists and Pythagoreans. He says that all those parts of the foregoing substances which constitute their limits and designate them as individuals (according to the opinion of these thinkers), and by whose destruction the whole is destroyed, are also termed "substances." For example, body is destroyed when surface is, as some say, and surface when line is. It is also clear that surface is the limit of body and line the limit of surface. And, according to the opinion of the philosophers just mentioned, the line is a part of surface and surface a part of body. For they held that bodies are composed of surfaces, surfaces of lines, and lines of points; and thus it would follow that the point is the substance of the line, the line the substance of the surface, and so on for the rest. And, according to this position, number seems to constitute the entire substance of all things, because when number is destroyed, nothing remains in the world; for what is not one is nothing. And similarly things that are not many are non-existent. And number is also found to limit all things, because all things are measured by number.

901. But this sense of substance is not a true one. For that which is found to be common to all things and is something without which they cannot exist does not necessarily constitute their substance, but it can be some property flowing from the substance or from a principle of the substance. These philosophers also fell into error especially regarding unity and number because they failed to distinguish between the unity which is interchangeable with being and that which is the principle of number.

902. *Again, the quiddity* (1017b21). He says that the quiddity of each thing, which the definition signifies, is also called its substance. Now the quiddity or essence of a thing,

sive rei essentia, cuius definitio est ratio, differt a forma quam dixit esse substantiam in secundo modo, sicut differt humanitas ab anima. Nam forma est pars essentiae vel quidditatis rei. Ipsa autem quidditas vel essentia rei includit omnia essentialia principia. Et ideo genus et species dicuntur esse substantia eorum, de quibus praedicantur, hoc ultimo modo. Nam genus et species non significant tantum formam, sed totam rei essentiam.

903. Deinde cum dicit *accidit itaque* reducit dictos modos substantiae ad duos; dicens, quod ex praedictis modis considerari potest, quod substantia duobus modis dicitur:

quorum unus est secundum quod substantia dicitur id quod ultimo subiicitur in propositionibus, ita quod de alio non praedicetur, sicut substantia prima. Et hoc est, quod est hoc aliquid, quasi per se subsistens, et quod est separabile, quia est ab omnibus distinctum et non communicabile multis. Et quantum ad haec tria differt substantia particularis ab universali.

Primo quidem, quia substantia particularis non praedicatur de aliquo inferiori, sicut universalis.

Secundo, quia substantia universalis non subsistit nisi ratione singularis quae per se subsistit.

Tertio, quia substantia universalis est in multis, non autem singularis, sed est ab omnibus separabilis et distincta.

904. Sed *etiam forma et species uniuscuiusque rei, dicitur tale*, idest substantia. In quo includit et secundum et quartum modum. Essentia enim et forma in hoc conveniunt quod secundum utrumque dicitur esse illud quo aliquid est. Sed forma refertur ad materiam, quam facit esse in actu; quidditas autem refertur ad suppositum, quod significatur ut habens talem essentiam. Unde sub uno comprehenduntur forma et species, idest sub essentia rei.

905. Tertium autem modum praetermittit, quia falsus est, vel quia reducibilis est ad formam, quae habet rationem termini. Materiam vero, quae substantia dicitur, praetermittit, quia non est substantia in actu. Includitur tamen in primo modo, quia substantia particularis non habet quod sit substantia et quod sit individua in rebus materialibus, nisi ex materia.

whose intelligible expression is the definition, differs from a form, which he identified with the second meaning of substance, just as humanity differs from a soul. For a form is part of a thing's essence or quiddity, but the essence or quiddity itself of a thing includes all its essential principles. It is in this last sense, then, that genus and species are said to be the substance of the things of which they are predicated, for genus and species do not signify the form alone, but the whole essence of a thing.

903. *It follows* (1017b23). Then he reduces the foregoing senses of "substance" to two. He says that from the above-mentioned ways in which the term "substance" is used we can understand that it has two meanings.

It means the ultimate subject in propositions, and thus is not predicated of something else. This is first substance, which means a particular thing which exists of itself and is capable of existing apart because it is distinct from everything else and cannot be common to many. And a particular substance differs from universal substance in these three respects:

first, a particular substance is not predicated of inferiors, whereas a universal substance is;

second, universal substance subsists only by reason of a particular substance, which subsists of itself;

and third, universal substance is present in many things, whereas a particular substance is not, but is distinct from everything else and capable of existing apart.

904. And *the form and species of each thing is said to be of this nature*, that is, substance. In this he includes the second and fourth senses of substance; for essence and form have this idea in common: both are said to be that by which something is. However, form, which causes a thing to be actual, is related to matter, whereas quiddity or essence is related to the suppositum, which is signified as having such and such an essence. Hence the form and species are comprehended under one thing—a being's essence.

905. He omits the third sense of substance because it is a false one, or because it is reducible to form, which has the character of a limit. And he omits matter, which is called substance, because it is not substance actually. However, it is included in the first sense of substance, because a particular substance is a substance and is individuated in the world of material things only by means of matter.

LECTURE 11

How things are the same essentially and accidentally

1017b27 Eadem dicuntur, secundum accidens, quidem, ut album et musicum idem, quia eidem accidunt. Et homo et musicum quia alterum alteri accidit. Sed et musicum homo, quia musicum homini accidit. Et utrique hoc, et horum utrumque illi. [908]

ταὐτὰ λέγεται τὰ μὲν κατὰ συμβεβηκός, οἷον τὸ λευκὸν καὶ τὸ μουσικὸν τὸ αὐτὸ ὅτι τῷ αὐτῷ συμβέβηκε, καὶ ἄνθρωπος καὶ μουσικὸν ὅτι θάτερον θατέρῳ συμβέβηκεν, {30} τὸ δὲ μουσικὸν ἄνθρωπος ὅτι τῷ ἀνθρώπῳ συμβέβηκεν: ἑκατέρῳ δὲ τοῦτο καὶ τούτῳ ἑκάτερον ἐκείνων,

Things are said to be the same accidentally; for example, "white" and "musical" are the same because they are accidents of the same subject. And "man" and "musical" are the same because the one is an accident of the other. And "musical" is the same as "man" because it is an accident of a man. And the composite is the same as each of these simple terms, and each the same as it.

Etenim homini musico, et homo et musicus idem dicitur et his illud. Quapropter et omnia ea universaliter non dicuntur. Non enim verum dicere, quia omnis homo idem et musicum. Nam universalia secundum se existunt, et accidentia non secundum se, sed in singularibus simpliciter dicuntur. Idem enim videtur Socrates musicus et Socrates esse. Nam Socrates non in multis. Quapropter non omnis Socrates dicitur, quemadmodum omnis homo. Et haec quidem sic dicuntur eadem.

καὶ γὰρ τῷ ἀνθρώπῳ τῷ μουσικῷ καὶ ὁ ἄνθρωπος καὶ τὸ μουσικὸν ταὐτὸ λέγεται, καὶ τούτοις ἐκεῖνο (διὸ καὶ πάντα ταῦτα καθόλου οὐ λέγεται: οὐ γὰρ ἀληθὲς εἰπεῖν ὅτι πᾶς ἄνθρωπος ταὐτὸ {35} καὶ τὸ μουσικόν: τὰ γὰρ καθόλου καθ᾽ αὑτὰ ὑπάρχει, τὰ δὲ συμβεβηκότα οὐ καθ᾽ αὑτά: {1018a1} ἀλλ᾽ ἐπὶ τῶν καθ᾽ ἕκαστα ἁπλῶς λέγεται: ταὐτὸ γὰρ δοκεῖ Σωκράτης καὶ Σωκράτης εἶναι μουσικός: τὸ δὲ Σωκράτης οὐκ ἐπὶ πολλῶν, διὸ οὐ πᾶς Σωκράτης λέγεται ὥσπερ πᾶς ἄνθρωπος): καὶ τὰ μὲν οὕτως {5} λέγεται ταὐτά,

For both "man" and "musical" are said to be the same as "musical man," and this the same as they. And for this reason none of these predications are universal. For it is not true to say that every man is the same as the musical, for universal predicates are essential, whereas accidental predicates are not, but are said of singulars in an unqualified sense. For "Socrates" and "musical Socrates" seem to be the same because Socrates is not found in many. And for this reason we do not say "every Socrates" as we say "every man." Some things, then, are said to be the same in this way.

1018a5 Alia vero secundum se quemadmodum et unum. Etenim quorum materia una, aut specie, aut numero, eadem dicuntur, et quorum substantia una. [911]

τὰ δὲ καθ᾽ αὑτὰ ὁσαχῶσπερ καὶ τὸ ἕν: καὶ γὰρ ὧν ἡ ὕλη μία ἢ εἴδει ἢ ἀριθμῷ ταὐτὰ λέγεται καὶ ὧν ἡ οὐσία μία,

And others are said to be the same essentially, and in the same number of ways in which they are said to be one. For those things whose matter is one in species or in number and those whose substance is one are said to be the same.

Quare palam quia identitas unio quaedam est plurium essendi, aut quando utitur uno ut pluribus, veluti quando dicit idem eidem idem: nam ut duobus utitur eodem.

ὥστε φανερὸν ὅτι ἡ ταυτότης ἑνότης τίς ἐστιν ἢ πλειόνων τοῦ εἶναι ἢ ὅταν χρῆται ὡς πλείοσιν, οἷον ὅταν λέγῃ αὐτὸ αὑτῷ ταὐτόν: ὡς δυσὶ γὰρ χρῆται αὑτῷ.

Hence it is evident that sameness is a kind of unity of the being of many things or of one thing taken as many—for example, when a person says that something is the same as itself, he uses the same thing as though it were two.

---

906. Postquam Philosophus distinxit nomina, quae significant subiectum huius scientiae, hic distinguit nomina, quae significant partes eorum, quae sunt subiecta huius scientiae: et dividitur in partes duas.

In prima distinguit nomina, quae significant partes unius.

In secunda, nomina, quae significant partes entis; hoc ibi, ***potestas dicitur.*** Substantia enim quae etiam

906. Having given the various senses of the terms which signify the subject of this science, here the Philosopher gives those which signify the parts of such things as constitute the subject of this science. This is divided into two parts.

In the first (1017b27; [906]), he gives the various senses of the terms which signify the parts of unity;

in the second (1019a15; [954]), those which signify the parts of being, at ***in one sense.*** For substance, which is also

posita est subiectum huius scientiae, est unum solum praedicamentum non divisum in multa praedicamenta.

Prima dividitur in duas.

In prima distinguit nomina, quae significant partes unius.

In secunda, nomina, quae significant, aliquod consequens ad rationem unius, scilicet prius et posterius. Nam unum esse, est principium esse, ut supra dictum est. Et hoc ibi, *priora et posteriora dicuntur*.

907. Prima dividitur in duas.

In prima distinguit nomina, quae significant primas partes unius et eius oppositi, scilicet multitudinis.

In secunda distinguit nomina, quae significant quasdam secundarias partes, ibi, *opposita dicuntur*.

Partes autem unius sunt idem, quod est unum in substantia: et simile, quod est unum in qualitate: et aequale, quod est unum in quantitate. Et e contrario partes multitudinis sunt diversum, dissimile et inaequale.

Circa primum duo facit.

Primo distinguit hoc nomen idem, et ea quae ei opponuntur.

Secundo distinguit hoc nomen simile et dissimile oppositum eius, ibi, *similia dicuntur*. De aequali autem, et eius opposito, mentionem hic non facit, quia in eis multiplicitas non est ita manifesta.

Circa primum tria facit.

Primo distinguit hoc nomen idem.

Secundo hoc nomen diversum, ibi, *diversa vero dicuntur*.

Tertio hoc nomen differens, ibi, *differentia vero*.

Circa primum duo facit.

Primo ponit modos eiusdem per accidens.

Secundo eiusdem per se, ibi, *alia vero secundum se*.

908. Dicit ergo quod aliqua dicuntur eadem per accidens tribus modis.

Uno modo sicut duo accidentia; ut album et musicum dicuntur idem, quia accidunt eidem subiecto.

Secundo modo, quando praedicatum dicitur idem subiecto in quantum de eo praedicatur; ut cum dicitur, homo est musicus, quae dicuntur idem, *quia accidit musicum homini*, idest praedicatum subiecto.

Tertio modo dicuntur idem per accidens, quando subiectum dicitur esse idem accidenti quasi de eo praedicatum:

posited as the subject of this science, is a single category which is not divided into many categories.

The first part is divided into two sections.

In the first, he gives the various senses of the terms which signify the parts of unity;

in the second (1018b9; [936], those which signify something that flows from the notion of unity, namely, prior and subsequent, at *things are said to be*. For to be one is to be a principle or starting point, as has been explained above (1016b17; [872]).

907. The first part is divided into two sections.

In the first he gives the various senses of the terms which signify the primary parts of unity and of its opposite, plurality;

in the second (1018a20; [922]), he gives those which signify certain secondary parts of unity, at *by "opposites."*

Now the parts of unity are sameness (which is unity in substance), likeness (which is unity in quality) and equality (which is unity in quantity). And, opposed to these, the parts of plurality are otherness, unlikeness, and inequality.

In regard to the first he does two things.

First, he gives the various senses in which the term "same" is used, and the senses of its opposite.

Second (1018a15; [918]), he gives the various senses of the term "like," and of its opposite, "unlike," at *things are said to be "like."* He makes no mention here, however, of the term "equal" and its opposite, because in the case of these terms, plurality is not so evident.

In regard to the first part he does three things.

First, he gives the various senses of the term "same";

second (1018a9; [913]), of the term "other," or "diverse," at *things are said to be "other"*;

and third (1018a12; [916]), of the term "different," at *things are said to be "diverse."*

In regard to the first he does two things.

First, he gives the ways in which things are said to be accidentally the same;

second (1018a5; [911]), he gives those in which things are said to be *per se* the same, at *and others*.

908. He says that things are said to be accidentally the same in three ways.

In one way, they are the same in the sense that two accidents are; thus "white" and "musical" are said to be the same because they are accidents of the same subject.

Things are accidentally the same in a second way when a predicate is said to be the same as a subject inasmuch as it is predicated of it; thus when it is said that the man is musical, these (man and musical) are said to be the same because musical *is an accident of a man*, that is, the predicate is an accident of the subject.

And things are accidentally the same in a third way when the subject is said to be the same as an accident inasmuch as it is predicated of it.

ut cum dicitur, musicus est homo, significatur quod homo sit idem musico. Quod enim praedicatur de aliquo, significatur idem esse illi. Et haec ratio identitatis est, quia subiectum accidit praedicato.

909. Praeter hos autem modos eiusdem per accidens, in quibus sumitur accidens per se et subiectum per se, sunt alii modi in quibus accipitur accidens cum subiecto compositum. Et in hoc variantur duo modi:

quorum unus significatur, quando accidens simpliciter praedicatur de composito ex accidente et subiecto. Et tunc significatur hoc, scilicet accidens esse idem utrique simul accepto; sicut musico homini, musicum.

Alius modus significatur quando compositum praedicatur de subiecto simplici, ut cum dicitur, homo est homo musicus.

Tunc enim *illi*, idest subiecto simplici, significatur esse idem horum utrumque simul acceptum, scilicet hoc quod dicitur homo musicus. Et similis ratio est, si accidens accipitur ut simplex, et subiectum cum compositione; ut si dicamus, musicus est homo musicus, aut e converso, quia et homini musico, quod est compositum, dicuntur idem per accidens et homo et musicum, quando haec duo de illo uno praedicantur, et e converso.

910. Ex hoc autem concludit ulterius conclusionem, quod in omnibus praedictis modis praedicandi, in quibus idem per accidens praedicatur, non praedicatur aliquod nomen universaliter. Non enim est verum dicere, quod omnis homo sit idem musico. Quod sic patet. Ea enim sola de universalibus praedicantur universaliter, quae secundum se insunt eidem. Propter hoc enim modus praedicandi, qui est universaliter praedicari, convenit cum conditione subiecti, quod est universale, quia praedicatum per se de subiecto praedicatur. Sed accidentia non praedicantur secundum se de universalibus, sed ratione singularium. Et ideo de universalibus non praedicantur universaliter. Sed de singularibus praedicantur simpliciter, quia idem videtur esse subiecto Socrates et Socrates musicus; non tamen praedicantur de singulari universaliter, quia de nullo potest praedicari aliquid universaliter quod non est universale. Socrates autem non est universale: nam non est in multis. Et ideo non praedicatur universaliter aliquid de Socrate, ut dicatur, omnis Socrates sicut omnis homo. Igitur quae diximus sic dicuntur eadem, scilicet per accidens, ut dictum est.

911. Deinde cum dicit *alia vero* ponit modos eiusdem per se; et dicit, quod aliqua dicuntur eadem secundum se eisdem modis, quibus dicitur unum per se.

For example, when it is said that the musical thing is a man, it is understood that the man is the same as the musical thing; for what is predicated of some subject is identified with that subject. And "sameness" in this sense means that the subject is an accident of the predicate.

909. Now besides these ways in which things are accidentally the same (wherein an accident and a subject are taken in themselves), there are also others, in which an accident is taken in conjunction with a subject. And when this occurs two senses of the term "same" have to be distinguished.

One of these is signified when an accident taken singly is predicated of the composite of subject and accident; then the meaning is that the accident is the same as both of the simple terms taken together (for example, "musical" is the same as "musical man").

The other is signified when the composite of accident and subject is predicated of the subject taken singly, as when we say that the man is a musical man;

and then both of these (the composite "musical man") are signified as being the same as this, as the subject taken singly. The same notion applies if an accident is taken singly and a subject is taken in combination with the accident. This would be the case, for example, if we were to say that what is musical is a musical man, or the reverse, for both "man" and "musical" are said to be accidentally the same as "musical man," which is the composite when these two are predicated of that one thing (and vice versa).

910. From this he draws the further conclusion that, in all of the foregoing modes of predication in which things are said to be accidentally the same, no term is predicated universally. For it is not true to say that every man is the same as what is musical. This becomes clear as follows: only those attributes which belong *per se* to the same subject are predicated universally of universals; for a predicate is predicated *per se* of a subject because the mode of predication, which is a universal one, agrees with the condition of the subject, which is universal. However, accidents are not predicated *per se* of universals, but only by reason of singular things; thus they are not predicated universally of universals. But while accidents are predicated in an unqualified sense of singular things (for Socrates and musical Socrates seem to be the same in subject), they are not predicated universally of singular things, for nothing can be predicated universally of something that is not universal. But Socrates is not universal, because he is not present in many. Hence nothing can be predicated of Socrates so that we should say "every Socrates" as we say "every man." The things of which we have spoken, then, are said to be one in this way—that is, accidentally—as has been stated.

911. *And others* (1018a5). Then he gives the ways in which things are said to be *per se* the same. He says that things are said to be *per se* the same in the same number of

Omnes enim modi, quibus aliqua unum per se dicuntur, reducuntur ad duos:

quorum unus est secundum quod dicuntur unum illa, quorum materia est una; sive accipiamus materiam eamdem secundum speciem, sive secundum numerum; ad quod pertinet secundus et tertius modus unius.

Alio modo dicuntur unum, quorum substantia est una: vel ratione continuitatis, quod pertinet ad primum modum: vel propter unitatem et indivisibilitatem rationis, quod pertinet ad quartum et quintum. Unde et his modis dicuntur aliqua esse idem.

912. Ex hoc autem ulterius concludit, quod identitas est unitas vel unio; aut ex eo quod illa quae dicuntur idem, sunt plura secundum esse, et tamen dicuntur idem in quantum in aliquo uno conveniunt. Aut quia sunt unum secundum esse, sed intellectus utitur eo ut pluribus ad hoc quod relationem intelligat. Nam non potest intelligi relatio nisi inter duo extrema. Sicut cum dicitur aliquid esse idem sibiipsi. Tunc enim intellectus utitur eo quod est unum secundum rem, ut duobus. Alias eiusdem ad seipsum relationem designare non posset.

Unde patet, quod si relatio semper requirit duo extrema, et in huiusmodi relationibus non sunt duo extrema secundum rem sed secundum intellectum solum, relatio identitatis non erit relatio realis, sed rationis tantum, secundum quod aliquid dicitur idem simpliciter.

Secus autem est, quando aliqua duo dicuntur esse idem vel genere vel specie. Si enim identitatis relatio esset res aliqua praeter illud quod dicitur idem, res etiam, quae relatio est, cum sit idem sibi, pari ratione haberet aliam relationem, quae sibi esset idem, et sic in infinitum.

Non est autem possibile in rebus in infinitum procedere. Sed in his quae sunt secundum intellectum nihil prohibet. Nam cum intellectus reflectatur super suum actum, intelligit se intelligere. Et hoc ipsum potest etiam intelligere, et sic in infinitum.

ways in which they are said to be *per se* one. Now all of the ways in which things are said to be *per se* one are reduced to two.

Thus, in one sense, things are said to be essentially one because their matter is one, whether we take the matter to be the same in species or in number. The second and third ways in which things are one are reduced to this.

And, in another sense, things are said to be one because their substance is one, whether by reason of continuity, which pertains to the first way in which things are one, or by reason of the unity and indivisibility of their intelligible structure, which pertains to the fourth and fifth ways. Therefore, some things are said to be the same in these ways too.

912. From this he further concludes that sameness is a unity or union. For either things that are said to be the same are many in being but are said to be the same inasmuch as they agree in some respect, or they are one in being but the intellect uses this as many in order to understand a relationship (for a relationship can be understood only between two extremes). This is what happens, for example, when we say that something is the same as itself, for the intellect then uses something which is one in reality as though it were two, otherwise it could not designate the relationship of a thing to itself.

Hence it is clear that, if a relationship always requires two extremes, and in relations of this kind there are not two extremes in reality but only in the mind, then the relationship of sameness according to which something is said to be absolutely the same will not be a real relation, but only a conceptual relation.

This is not the case, however, when any two things are said to be the same either in genus or in species. For if the relationship of sameness were something in addition to what we designate by the term "same," then since this reality, which is a relation, is the same as itself, it would have to have, for a like reason, something that is also the same as itself—and so on to infinity.

Now, while it is impossible to proceed to infinity in the case of real beings, nothing prevents this from taking place in the case of things that have being in the mind. For, since the mind may reflect on its own act, it can understand that it understands, and it can also understand this act in turn, and so on to infinity.

LECTURE 12

"Diverse," "different," "like," "contrary," and "diverse in species"

1018a9 Diversa vera dicuntur quorum aut species plures, aut materia, aut ratio substantiae: et omnino opposite eidem dicitur diversum. [913]

ἕτερα {10} δὲ λέγεται ὧν ἢ τὰ εἴδη πλείω ἢ ἡ ὕλη ἢ ὁ λόγος τῆς οὐσίας: καὶ ὅλως ἀντικειμένως τῷ ταὐτῷ λέγεται τὸ ἕτερον.

Things are said to be "other" or "diverse" of which either the forms or the matter or the intelligible structure of the essence is many; and in general the term "other" has senses opposite to those of "same."

1018a12 Differentia vero dicuntur quaecumque diversa sunt, idem aliquid entia: et non solum in numero, sed specie, aut genere, aut proportione. Amplius quorum diversum genus, et contraria et quaecumque habent in substantia diversitatem. [916]

διάφορα δὲ λέγεται ὅς᾿ ἕτερά ἐστι τὸ αὐτό τι ὄντα, μὴ μόνον ἀριθμῷ ἀλλ᾿ ἢ εἴδει ἢ γένει ἢ ἀναλογίᾳ: ἔτι ὧν ἕτερον τὸ γένος, καὶ τὰ ἐναντία, καὶ ὅσα ἔχει ἐν τῇ οὐσίᾳ {15} τὴν ἑτερότητα.

Things are said to be "different" which, while being diverse, are the same in some respect, and not merely in number, but in species or in genus or proportionally. And so also are those things whose genus is not the same, and contraries, and all those things that have diversity or otherness in their essence.

1018a15 Similia dicuntur quae idem sunt passa. Et plura idem patientia aut diversa. Et quorum qualitas una. [918]

ὅμοια λέγεται τά τε πάντῃ ταὐτὸ πεπονθότα, καὶ τὰ πλείω ταὐτὰ πεπονθότα ἢ ἕτερα, καὶ ὧν ἡ ποιότης μία:

Things are said to be "like" which undergo the same modifications, or undergo more of the same than of different modifications, or whose quality is one.

1018a17 Et secundum quae alterari contingit horum contrariorum quod plura habet, aut magis proprium, hoc est simile. Opposite vero similibus, dissimilia. [920]

καὶ καθ᾿ ὅσα ἀλλοιοῦσθαι ἐνδέχεται τῶν ἐναντίων, τούτων τὸ πλείω ἔχον ἢ κυριώτερα ὅμοιον τούτῳ. ἀντικειμένως δὲ τοῖς ὁμοίοις τὰ ἀνόμοια.

And whatever has a greater number or the more important of those contraries in reference to which alteration is possible is said to be like something else. And things are said to be "unlike" in ways opposite to those in which they are like.

1018a20 Opposita dicuntur contraria, contradictio, et ad aliquid, et privatio, et habitus. [922]

ἀντικείμενα λέγεται ἀντίφασις καὶ τἀναντία καὶ τὰ πρός τι καὶ στέρησις καὶ ἕξις

By "opposites" we mean contraries, contradictories, relatives, privation, and possession.

1018a21 Et ex quibus et in quae ultima, ut generationes et corruptiones. [923]

καὶ ἐξ ὧν καὶ εἰς ἃ ἔσχατα αἱ γενέσεις καὶ φθοραί:

And opposites also mean the ultimate parts of which things are composed and into which they are dissolved, as in processes of generation and corruption.

Et quaecumque non contingunt simul adesse amborum susceptibili, ea opponi dicuntur, aut ea ex quibus sunt.

καὶ ὅσα μὴ ἐνδέχεται ἅμα παρεῖναι τῷ ἀμφοῖν δεκτικῷ, ταῦτα ἀντικεῖσθαι λέγεται ἢ αὐτὰ ἢ ἐξ ὧν ἐστίν.

And those things that cannot be present at the same time in a subject which is receptive of them are called opposites: either they themselves or the things of which they are composed.

Nam pallidum et album simul eidem non insunt. Unde ex quibus sunt haec opponuntur.

φαιὸν γὰρ καὶ λευκὸν ἅμα τῷ {25} αὐτῷ οὐχ ὑπάρχει: διὸ ἐξ ὧν ἐστιν ἀντίκειται.

Gray and white, for example, are not present at the same time in the same subject, and therefore the things of which they are composed are opposites.

1018a25 Contraria dicuntur quae non possunt simul adesse eidem differentium secundum genus. Et quae plurimum differunt eorum quae sunt in eodem genere. Et quae plurimum differunt eorum, quae sunt in eodem susceptibili.

ἐναντία λέγεται τά τε μὴ δυνατὰ ἅμα τῷ αὐτῷ παρεῖναι τῶν διαφερόντων κατὰ γένος, καὶ τὰ πλεῖστον διαφέροντα τῶν ἐν τῷ αὐτῷ γένει, καὶ τὰ πλεῖστον διαφέροντα τῶν ἐν ταὐτῷ δεκτικῷ, καὶ τὰ πλεῖστον διαφέροντα τῶν ὑπὸ τὴν αὐτὴν

By "contraries" we mean those attributes which, differing in genus, cannot be present at the same time in the same subject; also, those which differ most in the same genus, those which differ most in the same subject, those which differ most

Et quae plurimum differunt eorum, quae sub eadem potestate. Et quorum differentia maxima aut simpliciter, aut secundum genus, aut secundum speciem. [925]

{30} δύναμιν, καὶ ὧν ἡ διαφορὰ μεγίστη ἢ ἁπλῶς ἢ κατὰ γένος ἢ κατ᾽ εἶδος.

among those which come under the same power, and things that differ most either absolutely or in genus or in species.

1018a31 Alia vero contraria dicuntur, haec quidem talium habitu, alia talium susceptione, alia existendo aut activa aut passiva talium, alia agentia, alia patientia, aut expulsiones, aut acceptiones, aut habitus, aut privationes talium. [928]

τὰ δ᾽ ἄλλα ἐναντία λέγεται τὰ μὲν τῷ τὰ τοιαῦτα ἔχειν, τὰ δὲ τῷ δεκτικὰ εἶναι τῶν τοιούτων, τὰ δὲ τῷ ποιητικὰ ἢ παθητικὰ εἶναι τῶν τοιούτων, ἢ ποιοῦντα ἢ πάσχοντα, ἢ ἀποβολαὶ ἢ λήψεις, ἢ ἕξεις ἢ στερήσεις {35} εἶναι τῶν τοιούτων.

Other things are called contraries either because they have contrary attributes or because they are receptive of them. Others because they are capable of causing them or undergoing them, or because they are actually causing them or undergoing them, or because they are rejections or acquisitions or possessions or privations of such attributes.

1018a35 Sed quoniam ens et unum multipliciter dicuntur, sequi est necesse, et alia quaecumque secundum ea dicuntur. Quare idem, et diversum, et contrarium, est diversum secundum unamquamque categoriam. [930]

ἐπεὶ δὲ τὸ ἓν καὶ τὸ ὂν πολλαχῶς λέγεται, ἀκολουθεῖν ἀνάγκη καὶ τἆλλα ὅσα κατὰ ταῦτα λέγεται, ὥστε καὶ τὸ ταὐτὸν καὶ τὸ ἕτερον καὶ τὸ ἐναντίον, ὥστ᾽ εἶναι ἕτερον καθ᾽ ἑκάστην κατηγορίαν.

But since the term "being" and the term "one" are used in many ways, all other terms which are used in relation to them must follow upon them, so that the terms "same," "diverse," and "contrary" vary according to each category.

1018a38 Diversa vero specie dicuntur quaecumque eiusdem generis existentia non sunt subalterna. Et quaecumque sub eodem genere existentia differentiam habent. Et quaecumque in substantia contrarietatem habent. [931]

ἕτερα δὲ τῷ εἴδει λέγεται ὅσα τε ταὐτοῦ γένους ὄντα μὴ ὑπάλληλά ἐστι, {1018b1} καὶ ὅσα ἐν τῷ αὐτῷ γένει ὄντα διαφορὰν ἔχει, καὶ ὅσα ἐν τῇ οὐσίᾳ ἐναντίωσιν ἔχει·

Those things are said to be diverse (or other) in species which belong to the same genus but are not subalternate. And so are those which belong to the same genus and have a difference; and also those which have contrariety in their substance.

Contraria enim diversa sunt specie ab invicem, aut omnia, aut dicta primum. Et quorumcumque in finali generis specie rationes diversae,

καὶ τὰ ἐναντία ἕτερα τῷ εἴδει ἀλλήλων ἢ πάντα ἢ τὰ λεγόμενα πρώτως, καὶ ὅσων ἐν τῷ {5} τελευταίῳ τοῦ γένους εἴδει οἱ λόγοι ἕτεροι

For contraries differ from each other in species, either all of them, or those which are called such in a primary sense; and so are those things whose intelligible structures differ in the lowest species of the genus

ut homo et equus individua genere, et rationes eorum diversae. Et quaecumque in eadem substantia differentiam habent. Eadem vero specie opposite his dicta.

(οἷον ἄνθρωπος καὶ ἵππος ἄτομα τῷ γένει οἱ δὲ λόγοι ἕτεροι αὐτῶν), καὶ ὅσα ἐν τῇ αὐτῇ οὐσίᾳ ὄντα ἔχει διαφοράν. ταὐτὰ δὲ τῷ εἴδει τὰ ἀντικειμένως λεγόμενα τούτοις.

(for example, man and horse do not differ in genus but their intelligible structures are different); and those attributes which belong to the same substance and have a difference. Things that are the same in species are said to be such in ways opposite to those just given.

---

913. Hic ostendit quot modis dicitur diversum; et dicit, quod diversa dicuntur aliqua tripliciter.

Dicuntur enim aliqua diversa specie, quorum species sunt plures, sicut asinus et bos.

Quaedam vero dicuntur diversa numero, quia differunt secundum materiam, sicut duo individua unius speciei.

Quaedam vero dicuntur diversa secundum *rationem substantiae*, idest definitionem declarantem substantiam rei. Contingit enim quaedam esse idem numero,

913. Here he explains the various ways in which the term "diverse" (or "other") is used, and he gives three senses.

Thus some things are said to be diverse in species because their species are many, as an ass and an ox;

others are said to be diverse in number because their matters differ, as two individuals of one species;

and others are said to be diverse because *the intelligible structure of the essence*, that is, the definition designating their substance, is different. For some things may be the

scilicet subiecti, sed diversa ratione, sicut Socrates et hoc album.

914. Et quia plures modi diversitatis accipi possunt, sicut quod dicatur diversum genere et diversum propter continui divisionem, ideo subiungit, quod diversum dicitur oppositum totaliter ad idem. Cuilibet enim modo eius, quod est idem, opponitur aliquis modus eius quod est diversum. Et propter hoc, quot modis dicitur idem, tot modis diversum.

915. Et tamen alii modi unius, vel eius quod est idem, possunt reduci ad istos hic tactos. Diversitas enim generis includitur in diversitate speciei. Diversitas vero continuitatis in diversitate materiae, eo quod partes quantitatis se habent per modum materiae ad totum.

916. Deinde cum dicit *differentia vero* hic distinguit quot modis dicitur hoc nomen differens. Assignat autem duos modos:

quorum primus est, quod aliquid proprie dicitur differens secundum quod aliqua duo quae sunt *aliquid idem entia*, idest in aliquo uno convenientia, sunt diversa: sive conveniant in aliquo uno secundum numerum, sicut Socrates sedens a Socrate non sedente: sive conveniant in aliquo uno specie, sicut Socrates et Plato in homine: sive in aliquo uno genere, sicut homo et asinus in animali: sive in aliquo uno secundum proportionem, sicut quantitas et qualitas in ente.

Ex quo patet, quod differens omne est diversum, sed non convertitur. Nam illa diversa, quae in nullo conveniunt, non possunt proprie dici differentia, quia non differunt aliquo alio, sed seipsis. Differens autem dicitur, quod aliquo alio differt.

Secundus modus est prout differens communiter sumitur pro diverso; et sic differentia dicuntur etiam illa, quae habent diversum genus, et in nullo communicant.

917. Deinde docet quibus conveniat esse differens secundum primum modum qui est proprius. Cum enim oporteat ea, quae proprie dicuntur differentia, in uno aliquo convenire; ea vero, quae conveniunt in specie, non distinguuntur nisi per accidentales differentias, ut Socrates albus vel iustus, Plato niger vel musicus; quae vero conveniunt in genere et sunt diversa secundum speciem, differunt differentiis substantialibus: illa propriissime dicuntur differentia, quae sunt eadem genere et diversa secundum speciem. Omne autem genus dividitur in contrarias differentias; non autem omne genus dividitur in contrarias species. Coloris enim species sunt contrariae, scilicet album, nigrum: et differentiae

same in number, that is, from the viewpoint of matter, but diverse in their intelligible structure, as Socrates and this white man.

914. And since many modes of diversity can be considered (for example, diversity in genus and the diversity resulting from the division of the continuous), he therefore adds that the term "diverse" means the very opposite of "the same"; for to every way in which things are the same there corresponds an opposite way in which they are diverse. Hence things are said to be diverse in the same number of senses in which they are said to be the same.

915. Yet the other ways in which things are said to be one, that is, the same, can be reduced to those stated here. For diversity of genus is included in diversity of species, and diversity of quantity is included in diversity of matter, because the parts of a quantity have the character of matter in relation to the whole.

916. *Things are said to be "different"* (1018a12). Then he gives the various senses in which the term "different" is used, and there are two of them.

First, any two things are said properly to be different which, while being diverse, are *the same in some respect*, that is, they have some one thing in common. And this is so whether they have some one thing in common numerically, as Socrates sitting and Socrates not sitting; or whether they have some one thing in common specifically, as Socrates and Plato have man in common; or whether they have a common genus, as man and ass share in the genus animal; or whether they share in some one thing proportionally, as quantity and quality both share in being.

And from this it is evident that everything different is diverse, but not the reverse. For diverse things that agree in no respect cannot properly be called different, because they do not differ in some other respect, but only in themselves. But that is said to be different which differs in some particular respect.

The term "different" is used in a second way when it is taken commonly in place of the term "diverse," and then those things are also said to be different which belong to diverse genera and have nothing in common.

917. Next, he indicates the kind of things that admit of difference in the first way, which is the proper one. Now those things that are said properly to differ must agree in some respect. Those which agree in species differ only by accidental differences—for example, Socrates insofar as he is white or just differs from Plato insofar as he is black or musical. And those things that agree in genus and are diverse in species differ by substantial differences. And since this is so, then those things are said to differ most properly which are the same in genus and diverse in species. For every genus is divided into contrary differences, but not every genus is divided into contrary species. Thus the species of color, white and black, are contraries,

etiam, scilicet congregativum et disgregativum. Animalis autem differentiae quidem sunt contrariae, scilicet rationale et irrationale sed species animalis, ut homo et equus et cetera non sunt contrariae. Illa igitur, quae propriissime dicuntur differentia, sunt quae vel sunt species contrariae, sicut album et nigrum: vel sunt species unius generis non contrariae, sed habentia contrarietatem in substantia ratione contrarii differentiarum quae sunt de substantia specierum.

918. Deinde cum dicit *similia dicuntur* ostendit quot modis dicitur simile. Circa hoc autem duo facit.

Nam primo assignat quot modis dicitur simile.

Secundo quot modis dicitur dissimile, ibi, *opposita vero*.

Circa primum duo facit.

Primo ostendit quot modis dicitur simile.

Secundo quomodo dicatur aliquid maxime simile, ibi, *et secundum quae alterari*.

Ponit autem tres modos similitudinis. Constat enim quod unum in qualitate facit simile. Passio autem est affinis qualitati, eo quod praecipue passio in mutatione qualitatis, quae est alteratio, attenditur. Unde et quaedam species qualitatis est passio et passibilis qualitas. Et propter hoc similitudo non solum attenditur secundum convenientiam in qualitate, sed secundum convenientiam in passione. Quod quidem potest esse dupliciter. Aut ex parte passionis, aut ex parte eius ad quod passio terminatur.

919. Sic igitur tripliciter aliqua sunt similia.

Uno modo, quia patiuntur idem, sicut duo ligna, quae comburuntur, possunt dici similia.

Alio modo ex hoc solo, quod patiuntur aliqua plura, similia dicuntur, sive patiuntur idem, sive diversa: sicut duo homines, quorum unus fustigatur, et alter incarceratur, dicuntur similes in patiendo.

Tertio modo dicuntur similia quorum una est qualitas; sicut duo albi, et duo sidera in caelo habentia similem splendorem aut virtutem.

920. Deinde cum dicit *et secundum* ostendit unde aliquid maxime dicatur simile. Quando enim sunt plures contrarietates, secundum quas attenditur alteratio, illud, quod secundum plures illarum contrarietatum est alicui simile, dicitur magis proprie simile. Sicut allium, quod est calidum et siccum, dicitur magis proprie simile igni, quam saccharum, quod est calidum et humidum. Et idem est inter duo quorum utrumque est simile alicui tertio secundum unam qualitatem tantum: illud quod

and so are their differences, expanding and contracting. And the differences of animal—rational and irrational—are contraries, but the species of animal—such as man, horse, and the like—are not. Therefore, things that are said to differ most properly are either those which are contrary species, as white and black, or those species of one genus which are not contrary but have contrariety in their essence because of the contrariety of differences which belong to the essence of the species.

918. *Things are said to be "like"* (1018a15). Here he points out the various ways in which the term "like" is used, and in regard to this he does two things.

First, he indicates the various ways in which this term is used;

second (1018a20; [922]), he gives those senses in which the term "unlike" is used, at *by opposites*.

In regard to the first he does two things.

First, he gives the ways in which the term "like" is used;

second (1018a17; [920]), he explains how one thing is said to be most like another, at *and whatever*.

He gives three ways in which things are like. Now it is evident that oneness in quality causes likeness. Further, passion is associated with quality, because passion is most noticeable in the case of qualitative change or alteration; thus one species of quality is called passion or passible quality. Hence things are observed to be like not only insofar as they have a common quality but also insofar as they undergo or suffer something in common. And this can be taken from two points of view: either from that of the passion, or from that of the subject in which the passion is terminated.

919. Some things are like, then, for three reasons.

First, they undergo or suffer the same thing—for example, two pieces of wood which are consumed by fire can be said to be like.

Second, several things are like merely because they are affected or undergo something, whether this be the same or different—for example, two men, one of whom is beaten and the other imprisoned, are said to be like in that they both undergo something or suffer.

Third, those things are said to be like which have one quality—for example, two white things are alike in whiteness, and two stars in the heaven are alike in brightness or in power.

920. *And whatever* (1018a17). Then he shows how one thing is said to be most like some other thing. For when there are several contraries of the sort which are observed to be alterable, whatever resembles some other thing in having the more important of these contraries is said to be more properly like that thing. For example, garlic, which is hot and dry, is said to be more properly like fire than sugar, which is hot and moist. The same holds true of any two things that are like some third thing in terms of only one

est simile secundum qualitatem magis sibi propriam, magis proprie dicitur simile ei: sicut aer magis proprie similis est igni, quam terra. Aer enim assimilatur igni in calore, quae est qualitas sibi propria, magis quam siccitas in qua assimilatur sibi terra.

921. Consequenter dicit, quod dissimilia dicuntur per oppositum ad similia.

922. Deinde cum dicit **opposita dicuntur** hic distinguit secundarias partes pluralitatis, quae scilicet continentur sub differenti et diverso, quae sunt partes primae: et circa hoc tria facit.

Primo ostendit quot modis dicuntur opposita.

Secundo quot modis dicuntur contraria, ibi, **contraria dicuntur**.

Tertio quot modis dicuntur diversa specie, ibi, **diversa vero specie**.

Circa primum duo facit.

Primo enim dicit quot modis dicuntur opposita; quia quatuor modis; scilicet contradictoria, contraria, privatio et habitus, et ad aliquid.

Aliquid enim contraponitur alteri vel opponitur aut ratione dependentiae, qua dependet ab ipso, et sic sunt opposita relative. Aut ratione remotionis, quia scilicet unum removet alterum. Quod quidem contingit tripliciter.

Aut enim totaliter removet nihil relinquens, et sic est negatio.

Aut relinquit subiectum solum, et sic est privatio.

Aut relinquit subiectum et genus, et sic est contrarium. Nam contraria non sunt solum in eodem subiecto, sed etiam in eodem genere.

923. Secundo ibi **et ex quibus** ponit duos modos, secundum quos potest cognosci, quod aliqua sunt opposita:

quorum primus est per comparationem ad motum. Nam in quolibet motu vel mutatione, terminus a quo, opponitur termino ad quem. Et ideo ex quibus est motus, et in quae est motus, sunt opposita, ut patet in generationibus. Nam generatio albi est ex non albo, et ignis ex non igne.

924. Secundo modo per comparationem ad subiectum. Nam illa, quae non possunt inesse simul eidem susceptibili, oportet quod adinvicem opponantur, vel ipsa, vel ea in quibus sunt. Non enim potest idem corpus simul esse album et nigrum, quae sunt contraria. Homo vero et asinus non possunt de eodem dici, quia habent in suis rationibus differentias oppositas, scilicet rationale et irrationale. Et similiter pallidum et album; quia pallidum componitur ex nigro, quod est oppositum albo.

quality; for whatever resembles some other thing in terms of some quality which is more proper to itself is said to be more properly like that thing. For example, air is more properly like fire than earth, for air is like fire in reference to warmth, which is a quality proper to fire itself to a greater degree than dryness, in reference to which earth is like air.

921. Then he states that things are said to be "unlike" in ways opposite to those in which they are "like."

922. *By "opposites"* (1018a20). Here he distinguishes between the secondary parts of plurality, that is, those contained under difference and diversity, which are its primary parts, and in regard to this he does three things.

First, he gives the various ways in which the term "opposite" is used;

second (1018a25; [925]), those in which the term "contrary" is used, at *by contraries*;

third (1018a38; [931]), those in which things are said to be diverse or other in species, at *those things are said to be*.

In regard to the first he does two things.

First (1018a20), he gives the various ways in which we speak of opposites, and there are four of these: contradictories, contraries, privation and possession, and relatives.

For one thing is contraposed or opposed to another either by reason of dependence, that is, insofar as one depends on another, and then they are opposed as relatives; or by reason of removal, because one removes another. This occurs in three ways:

either one thing removes another entirely and leaves nothing, and then there is negation;

or the subject alone remains, and then there is privation;

or the subject and genus remain, and then there is contrariety. For there are contraries not only in the same subject but also in the same genus.

923. *And opposites* (1018a21). Second, he gives two ways in which things can be recognized as opposites.

The first of these pertains to motion, for in any motion or change the terminus-from-which is the opposite of the terminus-to-which. Hence those things from which motion begins and those in which it ends are opposites. This is evident in processes of generation; for the white is generated from the not-white, and fire is generated from what is not-fire.

924. The second pertains to the subject. For those attributes which cannot belong at the same time to the same subject must be the opposite of each other, either they themselves or the things in which they are present. For the same body cannot be at the same time both white and black, which are contraries; nor can the terms "man" and "ass" be predicated of the same thing, because their intelligible structures contain opposite differences, that is, rational and irrational. The same holds true of gray and

Et notandum, quod signanter dicit, *eidem susceptibili*: quia quaedam non possunt alicui eidem subiecto simul inesse, non propter oppositionem quam habeant adinvicem, sed quia subiectum non est susceptibile utriusque; sicut albedo et musica non possunt simul inesse asino, possunt autem simul inesse homini.

925. Deinde cum dicit *contraria dicuntur* hic ostendit quot modis contraria dicuntur: et circa hoc tria facit.

Quorum primum est, quod assignat modos, quibus aliqua principaliter dicuntur contraria: inter quos ponit unum primum improprium: scilicet quod aliqua dicuntur contraria, quae non possunt simul adesse eidem, licet differant secundum genus: proprie enim contraria sunt quae sunt unius generis: sicut si diceretur, quod gravitas et motus circularis non sunt in eodem subiecto.

926. Alium modum ponit proprium secundum quod contraria dicuntur in aliquo convenientia. Conveniunt enim contraria in tribus: scilicet in eodem genere, et in eodem subiecto, et in eadem potestate. Et ideo notificat secundum ista tria, illa quae sunt vere contraria; dicens, quod illa, quae plurimum differunt eorum quae sunt in eodem genere, dicuntur contraria, sicut album et nigrum in genere coloris. Et iterum illa, quae plurimum differunt in eodem susceptibili existentia, sicut sanum et aegrum in animali. Et iterum, quae plurimum differunt in eadem potestate contenta, sicut congruum et incongruum in grammatica. Potestates enim rationabiles ad opposita sunt. Dicit autem *plurimum* ad differentiam mediorum inter contraria, quae etiam conveniunt in eodem genere, subiecto et potestate, non tamen sunt plurimum differentia.

927. Unde subiungit universalem rationem, secundum quam aliqua dicuntur contraria; quia scilicet eorum differentia est maxima, vel simpliciter, vel in eodem genere, vel in eadem specie.

Simpliciter quidem, sicut in motu locali extrema sunt maxime distantia, sicut punctus orientis et occidentis, quae sunt extrema diametri totius orbis.

In eodem genere, sicut specificae differentiae, quae dividunt genus.

In eadem specie, sicut accidentales differentiae contrariae per quae differunt individua eiusdem speciei.

928. Secundum ponit ibi, *alia vero* et ostendit qualiter aliqua secundario modo dicuntur contraria, propter hoc quod habent habitudinem ad ea quae principaliter sunt contraria;

white, because gray is composed of black, which is the opposite of white. And we should note that he expressly says, *in the same subject*, for certain things cannot exist at the same time in the same subject not because they are opposed to each other, but because the subject is not receptive of the one or the other; for example, whiteness and music cannot exist at the same time in an ass, but they can exist at the same time in a man.

925. *By "contraries"* (1018a25). Then he states the various ways in which the term "contrary" is used, and in regard to this he does three things.

First, he gives the principal ways in which things are said to be contrary. Among these he first includes one improper usage of the term, whereby some attributes are called contraries which, while differing in genus, cannot belong at the same time to the same subject. Properly speaking, contraries are attributes which belong to one genus. An example of this would be found if we were to say that heaviness and circular motion cannot belong to the same subject.

926. Then he gives a second usage of the term, which is a proper one, according to which contraries are said to be things that agree in some respect. For contraries agree in three respects: in reference to the same genus, or to the same subject, or to the same power. Then he uses these three to reveal the things that are real contraries. He says that those attributes which differ most in the same genus are called contraries, as white and black in the genus of color; and those which differ most in the same subject, as health and disease in an animal; and those which differ most in reference to the same power, as what is correct and what is incorrect in reference to grammar; for rational powers extend to opposites. He says *most* in order to differentiate contraries from the intermediate attributes which lie between them, which also agree in the same genus, subject, and power, yet do not differ to the greatest degree.

927. Hence he adds the universal notion involved in things that are designated as "contraries," namely, that contraries are things that differ most either absolutely or in the same genus or in the same species.

They differ *absolutely*, for example, in the case of local motion, where the extremes are separated most widely, as the most easterly and westerly points of the whole universe, which are the limits of its diameter.

And they differ *in the same genus*, as the specific differences which divide a genus;

and *in the same species*, as contrary differences of an accidental kind by which individuals of the same species differ from each other.

928. *Other things* (1018a31). Here he shows in what respect some things are said to be contraries in a secondary way because they are related to those things that are contraries in the primary way.

scilicet quia vel habent contraria in actu, sicut ignis et aqua dicuntur contraria, quia alterum est calidum et alterum frigidum;

vel quia sunt susceptibilia contrariorum in potentia, sicut sanativum et aegrotativum.

Vel quia sunt activa vel passiva contrariorum in potentia, ut calefactivum et infrigidativum, calefactibile et infrigidabile.

Vel quia sunt contrariorum agentia et patientia in actu, sicut calefaciens et infrigidans, calefactum et infrigidatum.

Vel quia sunt expulsiones, sive abiectiones, sive acceptiones contrariorum, vel etiam habitus aut privationes eorum. Nam privatio albi opposita est privationi nigri, sicut habitus habitui.

929. Patet ergo quod tangit triplicem habitudinem circa contraria.

Una quae est subiecti in actu, vel in potentia.

Alia quae est activi et passivi in actu et potentia.

Tertia quae est generationis et corruptionis, vel secundum se, vel quantum ad eorum terminos, qui sunt habitus et privatio.

930. Tertium ponit ibi *sed quoniam* et ostendit qua de causa praedicta dicuntur multipliciter. Quia enim unum et ens dicuntur multipliciter, oportet quod ea quae dicuntur secundum ea, multipliciter dicantur; sicut idem et diversum, quae consequuntur unum et multa, et contrarium, quod sub diverso continetur. Et ita oportet, quod diversum dividatur secundum decem praedicamenta, sicut ens et unum.

931. *Diversa vero* hic ostendit quot modis dicantur aliqua diversa specie: et ponit quinque modos:

quorum primus est, quando aliqua sunt in eodem genere, et non sunt subalterna, sicut scientia et albedo sub qualitate, licet non contra se dividantur oppositis differentiis.

932. Secundus est, quando sunt ea in eodem genere, et dividuntur contra invicem per aliquam differentiam; sive differentiae sint contrariae, sive non, ut bipes et quadrupes.

933. Tertius modus est, quando sua subiecta habent contrarietatem, utpote quae dividuntur per differentias contrarias; sive ipsa sint contraria, ut album et nigrum, quae dividuntur per congregativum et disgregativum; sive non, ut homo et asinus, quae dividuntur per rationale et irrationale. Contraria enim oportet esse diversa specie, vel omnia, vel illa quae principaliter dicuntur esse contraria.

For some things are contraries because they actually possess contraries, as fire and water are called contraries because one is hot and the other cold.

Others, because they are the potential recipients of contraries, as what is receptive of health and of disease.

Others, because they are potentially causing contraries or undergoing them, as what is capable of heating and of cooling and what is able to be heated and to be cooled.

Still others are contraries because they are actually causing contraries or undergoing them, as what is heating and cooling or being heated and being cooled.

Finally, others are so because they are expulsions or rejections or acquisitions of contraries, or even possessions or privations of them. For the privation of white is the opposite of the privation of black, just as the possession of the former is the opposite of that of the latter.

929. It is evident, then, that he touches on a threefold relationship of contraries to things:

one is to a subject which is either in act or in potency;

another is to something that is active or passive in act or in potency;

and a third is to processes of generation and corruption, either to the processes themselves or to their termini, which are possession and privation.

930. *But since the term* (1018a35). He gives a third way in which the term "contrary" is used, and he also shows why the foregoing terms are used in many ways. For since the terms "one" and "being" have several meanings, the terms which are based upon them must also have several meanings; for example, "same" and "diverse" (which flow from "one" and "many"), and "contrary," which is contained under "diverse." Hence "diverse" must be divided according to the ten categories, just as "being" and "one" are.

931. *Those things* (1018a38). He now explains the various ways in which things are said to be diverse (or other) in species, and he gives five of these.

First, they belong to the same genus and are not subalternate—for example, science and whiteness both come under quality, yet they are not distinguished from each other by opposite differences.

932. Second, they belong to the same genus and are distinguished from each other by some difference, whether such differences are contrary or not, as two-footed and four-footed.

933. Third, their subjects contain contrariety; that is, those things that are distinguished by contrary differences, whether the subjects are contrary themselves (as white and black, which are distinguished by the differences "expanding" and "contracting") or not (as "man" and "ass," which are distinguished by the differences "rational" and "irrational"). For contraries must differ in species, either all of them or those which are called contraries in the primary sense.

934. Quartus modus est, quando sunt diversae species ultimae, eaedemque specialissimae in aliquo genere, ut homo et equus. Magis enim proprie dicuntur specie differre, quae solum specie differunt, quam quae specie et genere.

935. Quintus modus est, quando aliqua accidentia sunt in eodem subiecto, et tamen differunt adinvicem, eo quod impossibile est plura accidentia unius speciei in eodem subiecto esse. Eadem vero specie dicuntur per oppositum ad praedicta.

934. Fourth, the lowest species are diverse and are the last in some genus, as man and horse. For those things that differ only in species are said more properly to differ in species than those which differ both in species and in genus.

935. Fifth, they are accidents in the same subject yet differ from each other, for many accidents of one and the same kind cannot exist in the same subject. And things are said to be "the same in species" in ways opposite to those given above.

Lecture 13

How things are prior and subsequent

1018b9 Priora et posteriora dicuntur quaedam quidem tamquam existente aliquo primo principio in singulo genere, quod propinquius principio alicui determinato, aut simpliciter et natura, aut ad aliquid, aut ad ubi, aut ab aliquibus. [936]

1018b12 Ut hoc quidem secundum locum in existendo propinquius, aut natura alicui determinato loco, ut medio, aut ultimo, aut sicut evenit. Quod vero remotius, posterius. [938]

1018b14 Alia secundum tempus. Haec quidem enim eo quod remotiora ab ipso nunc, ut in factis. Priora namque troica medis, quia remotiora ab ipso nunc. [940]

Alia affiniora ipsi nunc ut in futuris. Prius enim Nemea Pythion, quia propinquius nunc: et ipso nunc ut principio et primo usi sunt.

1018b19 Alia secundum motum. Propinquius enim primo moventi est prius. Ut puer viro. Principium autem, et id quoddam simpliciter est. Alia secundum potestatem. Excedens enim potestate prius est, et quod est potentius. Tale vero est, cuius secundum praevoluntatem sequi est necesse alterum, et posterius, quia non movente illo non moveatur, et movente moveatur: et est praevoluntas principium. [942]

1018b26 Alia secundum ordinem; et ea sunt quaecumque ad aliquid unum determinatum distant secundum rationem, [944]

ut parastata, et tritostata, et paranitae nitis.

πρότερα καὶ ὕστερα λέγεται ἔνια μέν, ὡς ὄντος τινὸς {10} πρώτου καὶ ἀρχῆς ἐν ἑκάστῳ γένει, τῷ ἐγγύτερον <εἶναι> ἀρχῆς τινὸς ὡρισμένης ἢ ἁπλῶς καὶ τῇ φύσει ἢ πρός τι ἢ ποὺ ἢ ὑπό τινων,

οἶον τὰ μὲν κατὰ τόπον τῷ εἶναι ἐγγύτερον ἢ φύσει τινὸς τόπου ὡρισμένου (οἶον τοῦ μέσου ἢ τοῦ ἐσχάτου) ἢ πρὸς τὸ τυχόν, τὸ δὲ πορρώτερον ὕστερον:

τὰ δὲ κατὰ {15} χρόνον (τὰ μὲν γὰρ τῷ πορρώτερον τοῦ νῦν, οἶον ἐπὶ τῶν γενομένων, πρότερον γὰρ τὰ Τρωϊκὰ τῶν Μηδικῶν ὅτι πορρώτερον ἀπέχει τοῦ νῦν:

τὰ δὲ τῷ ἐγγύτερον τοῦ νῦν, οἶον ἐπὶ τῶν μελλόντων, πρότερον γὰρ Νέμεα Πυθίων ὅτι ἐγγύτερον τοῦ νῦν τῷ νῦν ὡς ἀρχῇ καὶ πρώτῳ χρησαμένων):

τὰ {20} δὲ κατὰ κίνησιν (τὸ γὰρ ἐγγύτερον τοῦ πρώτου κινήσαντος πρότερον, οἶον παῖς ἀνδρός: ἀρχὴ δὲ καὶ αὕτη τις ἁπλῶς): τὰ δὲ κατὰ δύναμιν (τὸ γὰρ ὑπερέχον τῇ δυνάμει πρότερον, καὶ τὸ δυνατώτερον: τοιοῦτον δ' ἐστὶν οὗ κατὰ τὴν προαίρεσιν ἀνάγκη ἀκολουθεῖν θάτερον καὶ τὸ ὕστερον, ὥστε μὴ κινοῦντός {25} τε ἐκείνου μὴ κινεῖσθαι καὶ κινοῦντος κινεῖσθαι: ἡ δὲ προαίρεσις ἀρχή):

τὰ δὲ κατὰ τάξιν (ταῦτα δ' ἐστὶν ὅσα πρός τι ἓν ὡρισμένον διέστηκε κατά τινα λόγον,

οἶον παραστάτης τριτοστάτου πρότερον καὶ παρανήτη νήτης:

Things are said to be prior and subsequent insofar as there is some primary thing or principle in each genus; for prior means what is nearer to some principle determined either in an absolute sense and by nature, or relatively, or in reference to place, or in certain other ways.

For example, a thing is prior in place because it is nearer either to some naturally determined place, as the middle or last, or to one that depends on chance. And what is farther away is subsequent.

Other things are prior in time. For some are prior because they are farther away from the present, as in the case of things that have taken place. Thus the Trojan war is prior to that of the Medes because it is farther away from the present.

And others are prior in time because they are nearer to the present, as in the case of future events; for the Nemean games are prior to the Pythian because they are nearer to the present, provided that the present is taken as the principle or primary point.

Other things are prior in motion, for what is nearer to a first mover is prior (for example, the boy is prior to the man). And this too is a kind of principle in an absolute sense. Other things are prior in power, for whatever surpasses another in power, or is more powerful, is prior. And such is that according to whose will another thing necessarily follows subsequently, because if the one does not move, the other is not moved, and if it does move, the other is moved—and will is a principle.

Other things are prior in arrangement, and these are the things that have a different place in relation to some one determinate thing according to some plan.

For example, one who stands second is prior to one who stands third, and among the strings of the lyre the paranete is prior to the nete.

Hic quidem enim, qui sumitur; illic autem, quae media, principium. Ergo ea priora dicuntur hoc modo.

ἔνθα μὲν γὰρ ὁ κορυφαῖος ἔνθα δὲ ἡ μέση ἀρχή): ταῦτα μὲν οὖν πρότερα {30} τοῦτον λέγεται τὸν τρόπον,

For in the one case it is the leader who is taken as the principle or starting point, and in the other it is the middle string. These things, then, are said to be prior in this way.

1018b30 Alio vero modo quod cognitione est prius, ut simpliciter prius. Horum autem aliter: et quae secundum rationem, et quae secundum sensum. Nam secundum rationem universalia priora, secundum autem sensum singularia. [946]

ἄλλον δὲ τρόπον τὸ τῇ γνώσει πρότερον ὡς καὶ ἁπλῶς πρότερον. τούτων δὲ ἄλλως τὰ κατὰ τὸν λόγον καὶ τὰ κατὰ τὴν αἴσθησιν. κατὰ μὲν γὰρ τὸν λόγον τὰ καθόλου πρότερα κατὰ δὲ τὴν αἴσθησιν τὰ καθ' ἕκαστα:

In another way, whatever is prior in knowledge is considered to be prior in an absolute sense. And of such things, some are prior in a different way, for some are prior in reference to reason, and others in reference to the senses. For universals are prior in reference to reason, but singulars in reference to the senses.

1018b34 Et secundum rationem accidens toto prius, ut musicum, musico homine. Non est enim ratio tota sine parte; et non contingit musicum esse non existente aliquo musico. [948]

καὶ κατὰ τὸν λόγον δὲ τὸ συμβεβηκὸς τοῦ ὅλου {35} πρότερον, οἷον τὸ μουσικὸν τοῦ μουσικοῦ ἀνθρώπου: οὐ γὰρ ἔσται ὁ λόγος ὅλος ἄνευ τοῦ μέρους: καίτοι οὐκ ἐνδέχεται μουσικὸν εἶναι μὴ ὄντος μουσικοῦ τινός.

And in the intelligible structure, the attribute is prior to the whole, as "musical" is prior to "musical man." For the intelligible structure is not complete without one of its parts, and "musical man" cannot exist unless there is someone who is musical.

1018b37 Amplius priora dicuntur priorum passiones, ut rectitudo laevitate. Hoc enim lineae secundum se passio, illud vero superficiei. Alia quidem sic dicuntur priora et posteriora. [949]

ἔτι πρότερα λέγεται τὰ τῶν προτέρων πάθη, οἷον εὐθύτης λειότητος: τὸ μὲν γὰρ γραμμῆς καθ' αὑτὴν πάθος τὸ δὲ ἐπιφανείας. {1019a1} τὰ μὲν δὴ οὕτω λέγεται πρότερα καὶ ὕστερα,

Again, the attributes of prior things are said to be prior, as straightness is prior to smoothness, for the former is a property of a line considered in itself, and the latter a property of surface. Some things, then, are said to be prior and subsequent in this way.

1019a2 Alia vero secundum naturam et secundum substantiam, quaecumque contingit esse sine aliis, et alia non sine illis. Qua divisione usus est Plato. Et quoniam esse multipliciter dicitur, primum quidem subiectum prius, propter quod substantia prius. [950]

τὰ δὲ κατὰ φύσιν καὶ οὐσίαν, ὅσα ἐνδέχεται εἶναι ἄνευ ἄλλων, ἐκεῖνα δὲ ἄνευ ἐκείνων μή: ᾗ διαιρέσει ἐχρήσατο Πλάτων. (ἐπεὶ δὲ τὸ εἶναι {5} πολλαχῶς, πρῶτον μὲν τὸ ὑποκείμενον πρότερον, διὸ ἡ οὐσία πρότερον,

But others are said to be prior in nature and in substance, namely, all those things that can exist without others, although others cannot exist without them. And this is the division which Plato used. And since the term "being" is used in many ways, the first subject is prior, and therefore substance is prior.

Deinde aliter quae sunt potestate et perfectione. Nam alia potestate priora, alia perfectione: ut secundum potestatem quidem dimidietas, toto: et pars, toto: et materia, quam substantia. Secundum perfectionem vero, posterius. Nam dissoluta, secundum actum erunt.

ἔπειτα ἄλλως τὰ κατὰ δύναμιν καὶ κατ' ἐντελέχειαν: τὰ μὲν γὰρ κατὰ δύναμιν πρότερά ἐστι τὰ δὲ κατὰ ἐντελέχειαν, οἷον κατὰ δύναμιν μὲν ἡ ἡμίσεια τῆς ὅλης καὶ τὸ μόριον τοῦ ὅλου καὶ ἡ ὕλη τῆς οὐσίας, κατ' {10} ἐντελέχειαν δ' ὕστερον: διαλυθέντος γὰρ κατ' ἐντελέχειαν ἔσται.)

Things that exist potentially and those which exist actually are prior in various ways, for some things are prior in being potential, and others in being actual. For example, half a line is prior to the whole, a part is prior to its whole, and matter is prior to substance. But according to perfection they are subsequent, for when the whole has been dissolved, its parts exist actually.

1019a11 Modo itaque quodam, omnia prius et posterius dicta secundum haec dicuntur. [953]

τρόπον δή τινα πάντα τὰ πρότερον καὶ ὕστερον λεγόμενα κατὰ ταῦτα λέγεται:

In a sense, then, all things that are prior and subsequent are said to be such in this last way.

Alia namque secundum generationem quae sine aliis esse contingit, ut to-

τὰ μὲν γὰρ κατὰ γένεσιν ἐνδέχεται ἄνευ τῶν ἑτέρων εἶναι, οἷον τὸ ὅλον τῶν μο-

For some things can exist without others so far as the process of generation is con-

tum partibus. Alia secundum corruptionem, ut pars toto. Similiter autem et alia.

ρίων, τὰ δὲ κατὰ φθοράν, οἶον τὸ μόριον τοῦ ὅλου. ὁμοίως δὲ καὶ τἆλλα.

cerned (as the whole without the parts), and some again without others so far as the process of corruption is concerned (as the parts without the whole). The same thing applies in other cases.

---

936. Postquam distinxit nomina, quae significant partes unius, hic distinguit nomina significantia ordinem, scilicet prius et posterius. Unum enim quemdam ordinem importat, eo quod uni esse est principium esse, ut supra dictum est. Et circa hoc duo facit.

Primo assignat rationem communem prioris et posterioris.

Secundo distinguit diversos modos prioris et posterioris secundum communem rationem, ibi, *ut hoc quidem secundum locum.*

Dicit ergo primo, quod significatio prioris dependet a significatione principii. Nam principium in unoquoque genere est id, quod est primum in genere. Prius autem dicitur, quod est propinquius alicui determinato principio.

Huiusmodi autem ordo principii, et eius, quod est principio propinquum, potest attendi multipliciter. Aut enim aliquid est principium et primum simpliciter et secundum naturam, sicut pater est principium filii. Aut est principium *ad aliquid,* idest per ordinem ad aliquid extrinsecum; sicut dicitur id, quod est secundum se posterius, esse prius quantum ad aliquid; vel quantum ad cognitionem, vel perfectionem, vel dignitatem, vel aliquo tali modo. Vel etiam dicitur aliquid esse principium et prius quantum ad ubi. Aut etiam aliquibus aliis modis.

937. Deinde cum dicit *ut hoc* distinguit modos diversos, quibus dicitur aliquid prius et posterius. Et quia prius et posterius dicuntur in ordinem ad principium aliquod, principium autem est, ut supra dictum est, quod est primum in esse, aut in fieri, aut in cognitione: ideo pars ista dividitur in partes tres.

In prima dicit quomodo dicitur aliquid esse prius secundum motum et quantitatem; nam ordo in motu, sequitur ordinem in quantitate. Per prius enim et posterius in magnitudine, est prius et posterius in motu, ut dicitur in quarto *Physicorum.*

Secundo ostendit, quomodo aliquid dicitur prius altero in cognitione, ibi, *alio vero modo.*

Tertio, quomodo dicitur aliquid altero prius in essendo, idest secundum naturam, ibi, *alia vero secundum naturam.*

Circa primum duo facit.

936. Having given the various senses of the terms which signify the parts of unity, here Aristotle gives those which signify order, namely, "prior" and "subsequent." For unity implies a certain order, because the essence of unity consists in being a principle, as was stated above [872]. In regard to this he does two things.

First, he indicates the common meaning of the terms "prior" and "subsequent";

second (1018b12; [938]), he gives the various senses in which these terms are commonly taken, at *for example, a thing.*

He accordingly first says that the meaning of the term "prior" depends on that of the term "principle" (or starting point); for the principle in each genus of things is what is first in that genus, and the term "prior" means what is nearest to some determinate principle.

Now the relationship between a principle of this kind and something which is near it can be considered from several points of view. For something is a principle or primary thing either in an absolute sense and by nature (as a father is a principle of a child), or *relatively,* in relation to some extrinsic thing (for example, something that is subsequent by nature is said to be prior in relation to something else). Things that are prior in this last sense are such either in reference to knowledge or to perfection or to dignity, or in some such way. Or a thing is also said to be a principle and to be prior in reference to place, or even in certain other ways.

937. Then, when he says *for example, a thing*, he gives the various ways in which things are said to be prior and subsequent. And since the terms "prior" and "subsequent" are used in reference to some principle, and a principle is what is first either in being or in becoming or in knowledge (as has been stated above (1012b28; [761]), this part is therefore divided into three sections.

In the first, he explains how a thing is said to be prior in motion and in quantity, because the order found in motion flows from that found in quantity. For the prior and subsequent in motion depends on the prior and subsequent in continuous quantity, as is stated in *Physics* 4.

Second (1018b30; [946]), he shows how one thing is said to be prior to another in knowledge, at *in another way.*

Third (1019a2; [950]), he explains how one thing is said to be prior to another in being, that is, in nature, at *but others.*

In regard to the first he does two things.

Primo ostendit quomodo aliquid sit prius et posterius secundum quantitatem in rebus continuis.

Secundo, quomodo in rebus discretis, ibi, *alia secundum ordinem*.

938. Et circa primum ponit tres modos.

Primus modus attenditur secundum ordinem in loco; sicut aliquid dicitur esse prius secundum locum in hoc, quod est propinquius alicui loco determinato; sive ille locus determinatus accipiatur ut medium in aliqua magnitudine, sive ut extremum. Potest enim in ordine locali accipi ut principium, centrum mundi, ad quod feruntur gravia: ut sic ordinemus elementa, dicentes terram esse primum, aquam secundum et cetera. Et potest etiam accipi ut principium etiam ipsum caelum, ut si dicamus ignem esse primum, aerem secundum, et sic deinceps.

939. Propinquitas autem ad principium in loco, quidquid sit illud, potest esse dupliciter.

Uno modo secundum ordinem naturalem: sicut aqua propinquior est medio naturaliter quam aer, aer vero propinquior extremo, scilicet caelo.

Alio modo *sicut evenit*, idest secundum quod ordinantur aliqua in loco a casu, vel a quacumque causa praeter naturam; sicut in lapidibus superpositis invicem in acervo, supremus est prior uno ordine, et alio est prior infimus. Et sicut id quod est propinquius principio, est prius, ita quod remotius a principio, est posterius.

940. *Alia secundum tempus* secundus modus attenditur secundum ordinem temporis; quem ponit, dicens, quod alia dicuntur priora secundum tempus, et diversimode.

Quaedam namque dicuntur priora, eo quod sunt remotiora a praesenti nunc, ut accidit *in factis*, idest in praeteritis. Bella enim Troiana dicuntur priora bellis Medis et Persicis, quibus Xerses rex Persarum et Medorum Graeciam expugnavit, quia remotiora sunt a praesenti nunc. Quaedam vero dicuntur priora, quia sunt affiniora vel propinquiora ipsi nunc; sicut dicitur quod prius est Menelaus Pyrrho, quia propinquius alicui nunc praesenti, respectu cuius utrumque erat futurum. Videtur autem haec litera falsa esse, quia utrumque erat praeteritum tempore Aristotelis quando haec sunt scripta. In Graeco autem habetur, quod prius est Nemea Python, quae quidem erant duae nundinae vel duo fe-

First, he shows how one thing is said to be prior and another subsequent in quantity in the case of continuous things;

second (1018b26; [944]), how one thing is prior and another subsequent in the case of discrete things, at *other things are prior in arrangement*.

938. In treating the first member of this division he gives three ways in which things are prior.

The first has to do with place. For example, a thing is said to be prior in place inasmuch as it is nearer to some determinate place, whether that place be the middle point in some continuous quantity or an extreme. For the center of the world, to which heavy bodies gravitate, can be taken as the principle (or starting point) of the order involving place, and then we put the elements in the following order, saying that earth is first, water second, and so on. Or the outermost sphere can be taken as the principle, and then we say that fire is first, air second, and so on.

939. Now nearness to a principle of place, whatever it may be, can be taken in two ways.

In one way, with reference to an order naturally determined, as water is naturally nearer to the middle of the universe than air, and air nearer to the extreme, the outermost sphere.

In another way, with reference to an order *that depends on chance*, that is, insofar as some things have a certain order purely as a result of chance, or on some other cause than nature. For example, in the case of stones which lie on top of one another in a heap, the highest is prior according to one order, and the lowest according to another. And just as what is nearest to a principle is prior, in a similar way what is farther away from a principle is subsequent.

940. *Other things are prior in time* (1018b14). Things are understood to be prior and subsequent in a second way with reference to the order in time. And he now describes this order, saying that other things are said to be prior in time, and this in various ways.

For some things are prior because they are farther away from the present, as occurs *in the case of things that have taken place*, past events. For the Trojan wars are said to be prior to those of the Medes and the Persians (in which Xerxes, the king of the Persians and Medes, fought against the Greeks), because they are farther away from the present. And some things are said to be prior because they are closer or nearer to the present. For example, Menelaus is said to be prior to Pyrrho because he is nearer to some present moment in reference to which each was future. But this text seems to be false, because both of them lived before the time of Aristotle, when these words were written. And it is said in the Greek that the Nemean are prior

sta, quorum unum erat propinquius illi nunc quo haec scripta sunt, cum tamen utrumque esset futurum.

941. Patet autem quod in hoc utimur ipso nunc, ut principio et primo in tempore; quia per propinquitatem vel remotionem respectu eius, dicimus aliquid esse prius vel posterius. Et hoc necessarium est dicere secundum ponentes aeternitatem temporis. Non enim potest accipi hac positione facta, aliquod principium in tempore, nisi ab aliquo nunc, quod est medium praeteriti et futuri, ut ex utraque parte tempus in infinitum procedat.

942. *Alia secundum motum* tertius modus est secundum ordinem in motu: et hoc primo ponit quantum ad naturalia; dicens, quod aliqua dicuntur esse priora secundum ordinem in motu. Illud enim, quod est propinquius primo moventi, est prius; sicut puer est prius viro, quia est propinquior primo, scilicet generanti. Et hoc etiam prius dicitur per propinquitatem ad aliquod principium. Id enim, scilicet movens et generans, est principium quodammodo, non qualitercumque, sicut in loco accidebat, sed simpliciter et secundum naturam.

Secundo ponit hunc ordinem motus etiam in rebus voluntariis; dicens, quod quaedam priora dicuntur secundum potestatem, sicuti homines, qui sunt in potestatibus constituti. Ille enim, qui excedit potestate, et qui est potentior, dicitur esse prior. Et hic est ordo dignitatis.

943. Patet autem, quod hic ordo etiam est secundum motum, quia potentius et potestate excedens est secundum *cuius praevoluntatem*, idest propositum, *necesse est sequi aliquid*, quod est eo posterius in movendo; ita scilicet quod non movente illo potentiori vel priori, non moveatur posterius, et movente moveatur.

Sicut se habet princeps in civitate. Nam ex eius imperio moventur alii ad exequendum imperata; eo vero non imperante, non moventur. Et patet, quod hoc etiam prius dicitur propter propinquitatem ad aliquod principium. Nam *praevoluntas*, idest propositum imperantis, hic accipitur ut principium, cui propinquiores sunt, et per consequens priores per quos propositum et imperium principis ad subditos defertur.

944. Deinde cum dicit *alia secundum ordinem* ponit modum secundum ordinem in rebus discretis; dicens, quod alia dicuntur priora secundum ordinem, qui invenitur in aliquibus rebus tantummodo quodam ordine associatis sibi, non per continuitatem, ut in praeceden-

to the Pythian, these being two holidays or feasts, one of which was nearer to the moment at which these words were written, although both were future.

941. Now it is clear that in this case we are using the present as a principle or starting point in time, because we say that something is prior or subsequent on the grounds that it is nearer to or farther away from the present. And those who hold that time is eternal must say this. For, when this is supposed, the only principle or starting point of time which can be taken is one that relates to some present moment, which is the middle point between the past and the future, inasmuch as time might proceed to infinity in both directions.

942. *Other things are prior in motion* (1018b19). The term "prior" is used in a third way with reference to the order in motion, and he first shows how this applies to natural things. He says that some things are said to be prior in the order found in motion; for what is nearer to a first cause of motion is prior. A boy, for example, is prior to a man because he is nearer to his primary mover, the one begetting him. And the latter is also said to be prior because of his nearness to some principle. For that— the one moving and begetting—is in a sense a principle, though not in just any way at all (as happened in the case of place), but in an absolute sense and by nature.

Second, he also mentions this order of motion in the realm of the voluntary, saying that some things are said to be prior in power, as men who are placed in positions of authority. For one who surpasses another in power, or is more powerful, is said to be prior. This is the order of dignity.

943. Now it is evident that this order also involves motion; for one who is more powerful, or surpasses another in power, is one *according to whose will* (or intention) *another thing necessarily follows*, because it is through him that some subsequent thing is put in motion. Hence, when the more powerful or prior does not move, no subsequent thing moves; but when the former moves, the latter is also moved.

This is the position of a prince in a state, for it is by his authority that others are moved to carry out the things that he commands, and if he does not command them they do not move. And it is clear that the term "prior" is used here too because of the nearness of a thing to some principle. For *the will*, that is, the intention, of the ruler is taken here as a principle, and those who are nearer to the ruler, and therefore prior, are the ones through whom his commands are made known to his subjects.

944. *Other things are prior in arrangement* (1018b26). He now explains how a thing is prior in the order found among discrete things. He says that some things are said to be prior in order only because they have some kind of arrangement, and not because of continuity, as happened in

tibus accidebat. Huiusmodi autem sunt, quae distant ab aliquo uno determinato secundum aliquam rationem determinatam, ut parastata, tritostata. Parastata est prius tritostata. Parastata dicitur ille, qui stat iuxta aliquem, puta regem. Tritostata autem ille, qui stat tertius ab eo.

Unde alia litera habet, *praestans, tertio stante prius est*. Patet autem, quod alia ratio distantiae est distare ut secundum, vel tertium. Et similiter paranitae sunt priores nitis. In chordis enim hypatae dicuntur quae sunt graves, nitae vero acutae dicuntur, mediocres autem vocantur mesae. Paranitae autem dicuntur quae sunt iuxta nitas mesis propinquiores.

945. Patet etiam, quod hic dicitur etiam esse aliquid prius per propinquitatem ad aliquod principium. Sed differenter in utroque praedictorum exemplorum: quia in illis, scilicet parastata et tritostata, accipitur principium id quod est verum initium et extremum, scilicet ille, qui est summus inter alios vel vertex aliorum, ut rex vel aliquis alius talis. Sed in chordis accipitur ut principium, medium, et media chorda quae dicitur mesa, cui propinquiores dicuntur paranitae, et per hoc priores dicuntur nitis. Ista ergo dicuntur priora per hunc modum, scilicet per ordinem quantitatis vel continuae vel discretae.

946. Secundo ibi *alio vero* ostendit quomodo aliquid dicitur prius altero in cognitione. Illud autem prius est cognitione, quod etiam prius est simpliciter, non secundum quid, sicut erat in loco: nam res per sua principia cognoscitur. Sed, cum cognitio sit duplex, scilicet intellectus vel rationis, et sensus, aliter dicimus aliqua priora secundum rationem, et aliter secundum sensum.

947. Ponit autem tres modos, secundum quos aliquid est prius ratione sive cognitione intellectiva;

quorum primus est secundum quod universalia sunt priora singularibus, licet in cognitione sensitiva accidat e converso. Ibi enim singularia sunt priora. Ratio enim est universalium, sensus autem singularium. Unde sensus non cognoscit universalia nisi per accidens, inquantum cognoscit singularia, de quibus universalia praedicantur. Cognoscit enim hominem inquantum cognoscit Socratem, qui est homo. E contrario autem intellectus cognoscit Socratem inquantum cognoscit hominem. Semper autem quod est per se est prius eo quod est per accidens.

948. Secundum modum ponit *et secundum* dicit, quod secundum rationem prius est *accidens quam totum*, idest quam compositum ex subiecto et accidente;

the previous cases. And things of this kind have a different place in relation to some one determinate thing from a given point of view, as one who stands second and one who stands third—the one who stands second being prior to the one who stands third. By "one who stands second" is meant one who stands next to someone, such as a king; and by "one who stands third" is meant one who stands third from the king.

Hence another text reads, *the leader is prior to the one who stands third*. It is evident, then, that things are understood to have different places inasmuch as one is second and another third. And in a similar way the paranete is prior to the nete, for among the strings of the lyre the low-pitched string is called the hypate; the high-pitched, the nete; and the middle, the mese. And the paranete refers to that which is next to the nete and nearer to the mese.

945. It is also evident that something is said to be prior here because of its nearness to some principle, although this happens differently in both of the examples given above. For in the former case—that of one who stands second and one who stands third—the thing which is taken as a principle is a real starting point and extreme, namely, the one who is highest among them, or the chief of the others, as a king or some other person of this kind. But in the case of the strings of the lyre, it is the middle string, termed the mese, that is taken as the principle. Since those which are nearer to this are called the paranete, the paranete are therefore said to be prior to the nete. These things are said to be prior in this way, then, by the order in quantity, whether continuous or discrete.

946. *In another way* (1018b30). Here he shows how one thing is said to be prior to another in knowledge. Now what is prior in knowledge is also prior in an absolute sense and not in a qualified one, as was the case with place; for a thing is known through its principles. But since knowledge is twofold—intellectual or rational, and sensory—we say that things are prior in one way in reference to reason, and in another in reference to the senses.

947. He gives three ways in which something is prior in reference to reason or intellectual knowledge:

first, there is the way in which universals are prior to singulars, although the opposite occurs in the case of sensory knowledge because singulars are prior there. For reason has to do with universals and the senses with singulars; thus the senses know universals only accidentally inasmuch as they know the singular of which the universals are predicated. For a sense knows man inasmuch as it knows Socrates, who is a man, and in the opposite way the intellect knows Socrates inasmuch as it knows man. But what is *per se* is always prior to what is *per accidens*.

948. *And in the intelligible structure* (1018b34). Here he gives the second way in which a thing is prior in reference to reason. He says that in the intelligible structure *the at-*

et musicus homo cognosci non potest sine ratione huius partis, quod est musicum.

Eodem modo quaecumque alia simplicia sunt priora secundum rationem compositis, cum in sensu sit e converso. Nam sensui primo composita offeruntur.

949. Tertium modum ponit ibi *amplius priora* dicit, quod priora dicuntur etiam secundum rationem, passiones, sicut rectitudo habetur prior levitate. Rectitudo enim est per se passio lineae, levitas autem superficiei, linea vero naturaliter est prior superficie. Secundum autem sensum prior est superficies linea, et passiones compositorum passionibus simplicium. Haec igitur dicuntur priora per hunc modum, scilicet per ordinem cognoscendi.

950. Deinde cum dicit *alia vero* ponit modos, quibus dicitur aliquid prius secundum ordinem in essendo: et circa hoc duo facit.

Primo ponit tres modos, quibus dicitur aliquid esse prius in essendo.

Secundo reducit eos ad unum, ibi, *modo itaque quodam*.

Dicit ergo primo, quod quaedam dicuntur esse priora, *secundum naturam et substantiam*, idest secundum naturalem ordinem in essendo. Et hoc tripliciter.

Primo ratione communitatis aut dependentiae: secundum quod priora dicuntur, quae possunt esse sine aliis et illa non possunt esse sine eis. Et hoc est prius a quo non convertitur essendi consequentia, ut dicitur in *Praedicamentis*. Et *hac divisione*, idest isto modo prioris et posterioris contra alios diviso usus est Plato. Voluit enim quod propter hoc universalia essent priora in essendo quam singularia, et superficies quam corpora, et lineae quam superficies, et numerus quam omnia alia.

951. Secundus modus attenditur secundum ordinem substantiae ad accidens. Quia enim ens multipliciter dicitur, et non univoce, oportet, quod omnes significationes entis reducantur ad unam primam, secundum quam dicitur ens, quod est subiectum aliorum entium per se existens. Et propter hoc primum subiectum dicitur esse prius: unde substantia prius est accidente.

952. Tertius modus attenditur secundum divisionem entis in actum et potentiam. Nam uno modo dicitur aliquid esse prius secundum potentiam et alio modo secundum actum: secundum potentiam quidem dimidium rei est prius re ipsa, et quaelibet pars toto, et materia *quam substantia*, idest quam forma.

Haec enim omnia sic comparantur ad ea, respectu quorum sic dicuntur priora, ut potentia ad actum: se-

tribute is prior to the whole, to the composite of subject and attribute; thus "musical man" cannot be known without grasping the meaning of the part "musical."

And in the same way all other simple things are prior in intelligibility to the composite, although the opposite is true from the viewpoint of the senses, for it is composite things that are first offered to the senses.

949. *Again, the attributes* (1018b37). Then he gives the third way. He says that the attributes of prior things are also said to be prior from the viewpoint of reason, as straightness is said to be prior to smoothness. For straightness is an essential property of a line, and smoothness a property of a surface, and a line is naturally prior to a surface. But from the viewpoint of the senses, a surface is prior to a line, and the attributes of composite things are prior to those of simple ones. These things, then, are said to be prior in this way—namely, according to the order in knowing.

950. *But others* (1019a2). He then gives the ways in which a thing is said to be prior according to the order in being, and in regard to this he does two things.

First, he gives three ways in which a thing is said to be prior in being;

and second (1019a11; [953]), he reduces them to one, at *in a sense, then*.

He says, first, that some things are said to be prior in being, that is, *in nature and in substance*, or according to the natural order in being. And this is so for three reasons.

First, priority is attributed because of community or dependence, and according to this those things are said to be prior which can exist without others, although others cannot exist without them. And one thing is prior to another when the sequence of their being cannot be reversed, as is stated in the *Categories*. *This is the division*, the mode of division of prior and subsequent, which Plato used against others, for it was because of community or dependence that he wanted universals to be prior in being to singular things, surfaces prior to bodies, lines to surfaces, and numbers to all other things.

951. Second, things are said to be prior in being because of the relationship of substance to accident. For since the term "being" is used in many senses and not univocally, all senses of "being" must be reduced to one primary sense, according to which being is said to be the subject of other things and to subsist of itself. Hence the first subject is said to be prior, and thus substance is prior to accident.

952. Third, things are said to be prior in being inasmuch as being is divided into the actual and the potential. For a thing is said to be prior in one way potentially and in another actually. A thing is said to be prior potentially in the sense that half a line is prior to an entire line, and any part to its whole, and matter *to substance*, that is, to form.

For all of the first things mentioned in these instances are related to the others, to which they are said to be prior,

cundum actum vero dicuntur praedicta esse posteriora. Nam praedicta non efficiuntur in actu nisi per dissolutionem. Resoluto enim toto in partes, incipiunt partes esse in actu.

953. Deinde cum dicit *modo itaque* concludit, quod omnes modi prioris et posterioris possunt reduci ad hos ultimos modos, et praecipue ad primum, prout prius dicitur quod potest esse sine aliis, et non e converso.

Quaedam enim possunt esse sine aliis secundum generationem, per quem modum totum est prius partibus: quia, quando iam totum generatum est, partes non sunt in actu, sed in potentia. Quaedam vero contingit esse sine aliis secundum corruptionem, sicut pars sine toto, quando est iam totum corruptum et dissolutum in partes. Et similiter etiam alii modi prioris et posterioris ad hunc modum reduci possunt. Constat enim, quod priora non dependent a posterioribus, sicut e converso. Unde omnia priora aliquo modo possunt esse sine posterioribus, et non e converso.

as something potential to something actual. However, from the viewpoint of act the first things mentioned are said to be subsequent, since they become actual only by the dissolution of some whole. For when a whole is dissolved into its parts, the parts then begin to exist actually.

953. *In a sense, then* (1019a11). Here he concludes that all of the ways in which the terms "prior" and "subsequent" are used can be reduced to the last one given, and especially to the first of these inasmuch as the term "prior" means something which can exist without other things, but not the reverse.

For from the viewpoint of generation some things can exist without others, and it is in this way that a whole is prior to its parts; for when a whole has been generated, its parts do not exist actually but only potentially. And from the viewpoint of corruption some things can exist without others—for example, the parts can exist without the whole after the whole has been corrupted and dissolved into its parts. And in the same way too the other senses of "prior" and "subsequent" can be reduced to this sense. For it is certain that prior things do not depend upon subsequent ones, but the reverse. Hence all prior things can exist without subsequent ones, but not the reverse.

LECTURE 14

"Potency," "capable," "incapable," "possible," and "impossible"

1019a15 Potestas dicitur alia quidem principium motus aut mutationis in diverso, inquantum diversum, ut aedificativa potestas est quae non existit in aedificato. Sed ars medicinalis est potentia et existit in sanato, sed non inquantum sanatum est. Ergo totaliter principium permutationis aut motus dicitur potestas in diverso, inquantum diversum. [954]

δύναμις λέγεται ἡ μὲν ἀρχὴ κινήσεως ἢ μεταβολῆς ἡ ἐν ἑτέρῳ ἢ ᾗ ἕτερον, οἷον ἡ οἰκοδομικὴ δύναμίς ἐστιν ἣ οὐχ ὑπάρχει ἐν τῷ οἰκοδομουμένῳ, ἀλλ᾽ ἡ ἰατρικὴ δύναμις οὖσα ὑπάρχοι ἂν ἐν τῷ ἰατρευομένῳ, ἀλλ᾽ οὐχ ᾗ ἰατρευόμενος. ἡ μὲν οὖν ὅλως ἀρχὴ μεταβολῆς ἢ κινήσεως λέγεται δύναμις {20} ἐν ἑτέρῳ ἢ ᾗ ἕτερον,

In one sense the term "potency" or "power" means the principle of motion or change in some other thing as other; for example, the art of building is a potency which is not present in the thing built; but the art of medicine is a potency and is present in the one healed, but not inasmuch as he is healed. In general, then, "potency" means the principle of change or motion in some other thing as other.

1019a20 Alia diverso inquantum diversum. [956]

ἡ δ᾽ ὑφ᾽ ἑτέρου ἢ ᾗ ἕτερον

Or it means the principle of a thing's being moved or changed by some other thing as other.

Nam secundum quam patiens patitur aliquid, quandoque quidem si quodcumque pati sit possibile, dicimus esse potens pati.

(καθ᾽ ἣν γὰρ τὸ πάσχον πάσχει τι, ὁτὲ μὲν ἐὰν ὁτιοῦν, δυνατὸν αὐτό φαμεν εἶναι παθεῖν,

For, by reason of that principle by which a patient undergoes some change, we sometimes say that it has the potency of passion if it is possible for it to undergo any change at all.

Quandoque vero non secundum omnem passionem, sed si secundum excellentiorem.

ὁτὲ δ᾽ οὐ κατὰ πᾶν πάθος ἀλλ᾽ ἂν ἐπὶ τὸ βέλτιον):

But sometimes we do not say this by reason of every change which a thing can undergo, but only if the change is for the better.

1019a23 Amplius alia bene hoc perficiendi aut secundum praevoluntatem. Nam quandoque solum progredientes aut dicentes, non bene vero, aut non ut maluerunt, non dicimus posse dicere aut vadere. Similiter autem et in pati. [959]

ἔτι ἡ τοῦ καλῶς τοῦτ᾽ ἐπιτελεῖν ἢ κατὰ προαίρεσιν: ἐνίοτε γὰρ τοὺς μόνον ἂν πορευθέντας ἢ εἰπόντας, μὴ {25} καλῶς δὲ ἢ μὴ ὡς προείλοντο, οὔ φαμεν δύνασθαι λέγειν ἢ βαδίζειν: ὁμοίως δὲ καὶ ἐπὶ τοῦ πάσχειν.

And in another sense, "potency" means the ability or power to do this particular thing well or according to intention. For sometimes we say of those who can merely walk or talk but not well or as they planned that they cannot walk or talk. And the same applies to things that are undergoing change.

1019a26 Amplius quicumque habitus, secundum quos impassibilia omnino et immutabilia, aut non facile in peius mobilia potestates dicuntur. [960]

ἔτι ὅσαι ἕξεις καθ᾽ ἃς ἀπαθῆ ὅλως ἢ ἀμετάβλητα ἢ μὴ ῥᾳδίως ἐπὶ τὸ χεῖρον εὐμετακίνητα, δυνάμεις λέγονται:

Further, all states in virtue of which things are altogether unsusceptible to change or immutable, or are not easily changed for the worse, are called "potencies" or "powers."

Franguntur autem et conteruntur, curvantur et omnino corrunpuntur, non per potentiam, sed per non potentiam et alicuius defectionem.

κλᾶται μὲν γὰρ καὶ συντρίβεται καὶ κάμπτεται καὶ ὅλως φθείρεται οὐ τῷ {30} δύνασθαι ἀλλὰ τῷ μὴ δύνασθαι καὶ ἐλλείπειν τινός:

For things are broken and crushed and bent and in general destroyed not because they have a potency, but because they do not have one and are deficient in some way.

Impassibilia vero talium, quae vix et paulatim patiuntur propter potentiam et posse aliquo modo habere.

ἀπαθῆ δὲ τῶν τοιούτων ἃ μόλις καὶ ἠρέμα πάσχει διὰ δύναμιν καὶ τῷ δύνασθαι καὶ τῷ ἔχειν πώς.

And things are not susceptible to such processes when they are hardly or slightly affected by them because they have the potency and the ability to be in some definite state.

1019a32 Dicta vero potestate, toties et possible dicetur: [961]

λεγομένης δὲ τῆς δυνάμεως τοσαυτα-χῶς, καὶ τὸ δυνατὸν

And since the term "potency" is used in these senses, the term "capable" or "potent" will be used in the same number of senses.

uno quidem modo, quod habet motus principium, aut mutationis. Etenim stativum possibile quoddam in diverso, inquantum est diversum. Alio vero modo siquidem ab eo aliud potestatem habet talem.

ἕνα μὲν τρόπον λεχθήσεται τὸ ἔχον κιν-ήσεως ἀρχὴν ἢ μεταβολῆς (καὶ γὰρ {35} τὸ στατικὸν δυνατόν τι) ἐν ἑτέρῳ ἢ ᾗ ἕτερον, ἕνα δ᾽ ἐὰν ἔχῃ τι αὐτοῦ ἄλλο δύναμιν τοιαύτην,

Thus, in one sense, whatever has within itself the source of the motion or change which takes place in some other thing as other (for even something that brings another to rest is potent in a sense) is said to be capable. And in another sense, that which receives such a potency or power from it is said to be capable.

1019b1 Alio si habet permutari in quolibet secundum potestatem sive in peius, sive in melius. Etenim corruptibile, esse videtur possibile corrumpi: aut utique non corrumpi, si erat impossibile. [962]

ἕνα δ᾽ ἐὰν ἔχῃ μεταβάλλειν ἐφ᾽ ὁτιοῦν δύναμιν, εἴτ᾽ ἐπὶ τὸ χεῖρον εἴτ᾽ ἐπὶ τὸ βέλτιον (καὶ γὰρ τὸ φθειρόμενον δοκεῖ δυνατὸν εἶναι φθείρεσθαι, ἢ οὐκ ἂν φθαρῆναι εἰ ἦν ἀδύνατον·

And in still another sense a thing is said to be capable if it has the potency of being changed in some way, whether for the worse or for the better. For anything which is corrupted seems to be capable of being corrupted, since it would not have been corrupted if it had been incapable of it.

Nunc autem quamdam dispositionem habet et causam talis passionis et principium. Aliquando quidem igitur per habere aliquid videtur, aliquando per privari, tale esse.

νῦν δὲ ἔχει τινὰ {5} διάθεσιν καὶ αἰτίαν καὶ ἀρχὴν τοῦ τοιούτου πάθους· ὁτὲ μὲν δὴ τῷ ἔχειν τι δοκεῖ, ὁτὲ δὲ τῷ ἐστερῆ-σθαι τοιοῦτον εἶναι·

But as matters stand, it already has a certain disposition and cause and principle to undergo such change. Hence sometimes a thing seems to be such (that is, capable) because it has something, and sometimes because it is deprived of something.

1019b6 Sed, si privatio est habitus aliquo modo in habendo, omnia utique erunt aliquid. Ens vero dictum aequivoce. Quare in habendo privationem aliquam et principium, est possibile: et habendo huiusmodi privationem, si contingit habere privationem. [964]

εἰ δ᾽ ἡ στέρησίς ἐστιν ἕξις πως, πάντα τῷ ἔχειν ἂν εἴη τι, [εἰ δὲ μὴ] ὥστε τῷ τε ἔχειν ἕξιν τινὰ καὶ ἀρχήν ἐστι δυνατὸν [ὁμ-ωνύμως] καὶ τῷ ἔχειν τὴν τούτου στέρη-σιν, εἰ ἐνδέχεται {10} ἔχειν στέρησιν, <εἰ δὲ μή, ὁμωνύμως>·

But if privation is in a sense a having, all things will be capable or potent by having something. But "being" is used in two different senses. Hence a thing is capable both by having some privation and principle and by having the privation of this, if it can have a privation.

1019b10 Alio in non habendo ipsius potestatem aut principium in alio, inquantum est aliud, corruptivum. [965]

ἕνα δὲ τῷ μὴ ἔχειν αὐτοῦ δύναμιν ἢ ἀρχὴν ἄλλο ἢ ᾗ ἄλλο φθαρτικήν.

And in another sense a thing is capable because there is no potency or power in some other thing as other which can corrupt it.

1019b11 Amplius autem ea omnia aut ex solo accidere fieri aut non fieri, aut bene. [966]

ἔτι δὲ ταῦτα πάντα ἢ τῷ μόνον ἂν συμβῆναι γενέσθαι ἢ μὴ γενέσθαι, ἢ τῷ καλῶς.

Again, all these things are capable either because they merely might happen to come into being or not, or because they might do so well.

Nam in inanimatis est talis potestas ut in organis. Alia enim dicunt posse sonare lyram, alia non, si est non bene sonans.

καὶ γὰρ ἐν τοῖς ἀψύχοις ἔνεστιν ἡ τοιαύ-τη δύναμις, οἷον ἐν τοῖς ὀργάνοις· τὴν μὲν γὰρ δύνασθαί φασι {15} φθέγγεσθαι λύραν, τὴν δ᾽ οὐδέν, ἂν ᾖ μὴ εὔφωνος.

For this sort of potency or power is found in inanimate things such as instruments. For men say that one lyre can produce a sound, and that another cannot, if it does not have a good tone.

1019b15 Impotentia autem est privatio potentiae et talis principii sublatio quaedam, qualis dicta est, aut omnino, aut in apto nato aut quando aptum natum est iam

ἀδυναμία δὲ ἐστὶ στέρησις δυνάμεως καὶ τῆς τοιαύτης ἀρχῆς οἷα εἴρηται, ἢ ὅλως ἢ τῷ πεφυκότι ἔχειν, ἢ καὶ ὅτε πέφυ-κεν ἤδη ἔχειν· οὐ γὰρ ὁμοίως ἂν φαῖεν

Incapacity, on the other hand, is a privation of capacity, a kind of removal of such a principle as has been described, either altogether, or in the case of something

habere. Non enim similiter dicuntur impossibile generare puerum et virum et eunuchum. [967]

ἀδύνατον εἶναι γεννᾶν παῖδα καὶ ἄνδρα καὶ εὐνοῦχον.

which is naturally disposed to have it, or when it is already naturally disposed to have it and does not. For it is not in the same way that a boy, a man, and a eunuch are said to be incapable of begetting.

1019b19 Amplius autem secundum potentiam utramque est impotentia opposita ei quae solum mobili, et ei quae bene mobili. [969]

ἔτι δὲ καθ᾽ ἑκατέραν {20} δύναμιν ἔστιν ἀδυναμία ἀντικειμένη, τῇ τε μόνον κινητικῇ καὶ τῇ καλῶς κινητικῇ.

Again, there is an incapacity corresponding to each kind of capacity, both to that which can merely produce motion and to that which can produce it well.

1019b21 Impossibilia vero haec quidem secundum impotentiam eam dicuntur; alia, alio modo, ut possibile et impossibile. [970]

καὶ ἀδύνατα δὴ τὰ μὲν κατὰ τὴν ἀδυναμίαν ταύτην λέγεται, τὰ δὲ ἄλλον τρόπον, οἷον δυνατόν τε καὶ ἀδύνατον,

And some things are said to be incapable according to this sense of "incapacity," but others in a different sense, namely, as possible and impossible.

Impossibile quidem, cuius contrarium de necessitate est verum; ut diametrum commensurabilem esse impossibile, quia falsum tale, cuius contrarium non solum verum, sed et necesse, non commensurabilem esse.

ἀδύνατον μὲν οὗ τὸ ἐναντίον ἐξ ἀνάγκης ἀληθές (οἷον τὸ τὴν διάμετρον σύμμετρον εἶναι {25} ἀδύνατον ὅτι ψεῦδος τὸ τοιοῦτον οὗ τὸ ἐναντίον οὐ μόνον ἀληθὲς ἀλλὰ καὶ ἀνάγκη [ἀσύμμετρον εἶναι]:

"Impossible" means that of which the contrary is necessarily true; thus it is impossible that the diagonal of a square should be commensurable with a side, because such a statement is false of which the contrary is not only true but also necessarily so—that is, that the diagonal is not commensurable.

Ergo commensurabile non solum falsum, sed ex necessitate falsum.

τὸ ἄρα σύμμετρον οὐ μόνον ψεῦδος ἀλλὰ καὶ ἐξ ἀνάγκης ψεῦδος):

Therefore, that the diagonal is commensurable is not only false, but necessarily false.

1019b27 Contrarium vero huic possibile, quando non necesse est contrarium falsum esse. Ut sedere hominem possibile, non enim ex necessitate non sedere falsum. Ergo possibile est uno modo sicut dictum est, quod non ex necessitate falsum significat, alio modo verum esse, alio contingens verum iam. [972]

τὸ δ᾽ ἐναντίον τούτῳ, τὸ δυνατόν, ὅταν μὴ ἀναγκαῖον ᾖ τὸ ἐναντίον ψεῦδος εἶναι, οἷον τὸ καθῆσθαι ἄνθρωπον δυνατόν: οὐ {30} γὰρ ἐξ ἀνάγκης τὸ μὴ καθῆσθαι ψεῦδος. τὸ μὲν οὖν δυνατὸν ἕνα μὲν τρόπον, ὥσπερ εἴρηται, τὸ μὴ ἐξ ἀνάγκης ψεῦδος σημαίνει, ἕνα δὲ τὸ ἀληθές [εἶναι], ἕνα δὲ τὸ ἐνδεχόμενον ἀληθὲς εἶναι.

And the contrary of this—the possible—is when the contrary is not necessarily false. For example, it is possible that a man should be seated, because it is not necessarily false that he should not be seated. Hence the term "possible" means, in one sense (as has been stated), whatever is not necessarily false; and in another sense, whatever is true; and in still another, whatever may be true.

1019b33 Secundum metaphoram autem quae in geometria dicitur potentia. Haec quidem igitur possibilia non secundum potentiam. [974]

κατὰ μεταφορὰν δὲ ἡ ἐν γεωμετρίᾳ λέγεται δύναμις. ταῦτα μὲν οὖν τὰ δυνατὰ οὐ κατὰ δύναμιν:

And what is called "a power" in geometry is called such metaphorically. These senses of "capable," then, do not refer to potency.

1019b35 Quae vero secundum potentiam omnia dicuntur ad primam unam, et ea est principium mutationis in alio inquantum aliud. [975]

τὰ δὲ λεγόμενα κατὰ δύναμιν πάντα λέγεται πρὸς τὴν πρώτην [μίαν]: {1020a1} αὕτη δ᾽ ἐστὶν ἀρχὴ μεταβολῆς ἐν ἄλλῳ ἢ ᾗ ἄλλο.

But those senses which do refer to potency are all used in reference to the one primary sense of potency, namely, a principle of change in some other thing inasmuch as it is other.

Alia namque dicuntur possibilia, haec quidem eorum in habendo aliquid aliud talem potentiam, illa vero in non habendo, alia in sic habendo. Similiter autem et impossibilia.

τὰ γὰρ ἄλλα λέγεται δυνατὰ τῷ τὰ μὲν ἔχειν αὐτῶν ἄλλο τι τοιαύτην δύναμιν τὰ δὲ μὴ ἔχειν τὰ δὲ ὡδὶ ἔχειν. ὁμοίως δὲ καὶ τὰ ἀδύνατα.

And other things are said to be "capable" in a passive sense—some because some other thing has such power over them, some because it does not, and some because it has it in a special way. The same applies to the term "incapable."

Quare propria definitio primae potentiae erit principium permutationis in alio inquantum aliud.	ὥστε ὁ κύριος ὅρος {5} τῆς πρώτης δυνάμεως ἂν εἴη ἀρχὴ μεταβλητικὴ ἐν ἄλλῳ ἢ ᾗ ἄλλο.	Hence the proper definition of the primary kind of potency will be a principle of change in some other thing as other.

954. Postquam distinxit nomina significantia partes unius, hic incipit distinguere nomina significantia partes entis.

Et primo secundum quod ens dividitur per actum et potentiam.

Secundo, prout dividitur ens in decem praedicamenta, ibi, *quantum vero dicitur quod est divisibile.*

Circa primum distinguit hoc nomen potentia vel potestas. Nomen autem actus praetermittit, quia eius significationem sufficienter explicare non poterat, nisi prius natura formarum esset manifesta, quod faciet in octavo et nono. Unde statim in nono simul determinat de potentia et actu. Dividitur ergo pars ista in partes duas:

in prima ostendit quot modis dicitur potentia.

In secunda reducit omnes ad unum primum, ibi, *quae vero secundum potentiam.*

Circa primum duo facit.

Primo distinguit hoc nomen, potentia.

Secundo hoc nomen, impotentia, ibi, *impotentia autem.*

Circa primum duo facit.

Primo ponit modos potentiae.

Secundo modos possibilis, ibi, *dicta vero potestate.*

955. Ponit ergo in prima parte quatuor modos potentiae vel potestatis.

Quorum primus est, quod potentia dicitur principium motus et mutationis in alio inquantum est aliud. Est enim quoddam principium motus vel mutationis in eo quod mutatur, ipsa scilicet materia: vel aliquod principium formale, ad quod consequitur motus, sicut ad formam gravis vel levis sequitur motus sursum aut deorsum. Sed huiusmodi principium non potest dici de potentia activa, ad quam pertinet motus ille. Omne enim quod movetur ab alio movetur. Neque aliquid movet seipsum nisi per partes, inquantum una pars eius movet aliam, ut probatur in octavo *Physicorum.*

Potentia igitur, secundum quod est principium motus in eo in quo est, non comprehenditur sub potentia activa, sed magis sub passiva. Gravitas enim in terra non est principium ut moveat, sed magis ut moveatur. Potentia igitur activa motus oportet quod sit in alio ab eo quod movetur, sicut aedificativa potestas non est in ae-

954. Having treated the various senses of the terms which signify the parts of unity, here Aristotle begins to treat those which signify the parts of being.

He does this first according as being is divided by act and potency;

second (1020a7; [977]), according as it is divided by the ten categories, at *"quantity" means.*

In regard to the first, he gives the various senses in which the term "potency" or "power" is used. But he omits the term "act," because he could explain its meaning adequately only if the nature of forms had been made clear first, and he will do this in books 8 [1703] and 9 [1823]. Hence in book 9 he immediately settles the question about potency and act together. This part, then, is divided into two members.

In the first he explains the various senses in which the term "potency" is used;

in the second (1019b35; [975]), he reduces all of them to one primary sense, at *but those senses.*

In regard to the first he does two things.

First, he gives the various senses in which the term "potency" is used;

and second (1019b15; [967]), the various senses in which the term incapacity is used, at *incapacity, on the other hand.*

In treating the first he does two things.

First, he gives the senses in which the term "potency" is used;

second (1019a32; [961]), those in which the term capable or potent is used, at *and since the term.*

955. In dealing with the first part, then, he gives four senses in which the term "potency" or "power" is used.

First, "potency" means an active principle of motion or change in some other thing as other. For there is some principle of motion or change in the thing changed, namely, the matter, or some formal principle on which the motion depends, as upward or downward motion is a result of the forms of lightness or heaviness. But a principle of this kind cannot be designated as the active power on which this motion depends. For everything which is moved is moved by another, and a thing moves itself only by means of its parts inasmuch as one part moves another, as is proved in *Physics* 8.

Hence, insofar as a potency is a principle of motion in the thing where motion is found, it is not included under active power, but under passive potency. For heaviness in earth is not a principle causing motion, but rather one which causes it to be moved. Hence active power must be present in some other thing than the one moved—for ex-

dificato, sed magis in aedificante. Ars autem medicinalis, quamvis sit potentia activa, quia per eam medicus curat, contingit tamen quod sit in aliquo sanato, non inquantum est sanatum, sed per accidens, inquantum accidit eidem esse medicum et sanatum. Sic igitur universaliter loquendo, potestas dicitur uno modo principium mutationis aut motus in alio, inquantum est aliud.

956. Secundum modum ponit ibi, *alia diverso* dicit, quod quodam alio modo dicitur potestas principium motus vel mutationis ab altero inquantum est aliud. Et haec est potentia passiva, secundum quam patiens aliquid patitur.

Sicut enim omne agens et movens, aliud a se movet, et in aliud a se agit; ita omne patiens, ab alio patitur: et omne motum, ab alio movetur. Illud enim principium, per quod alicui competit ut moveatur vel patiatur ab alio, dicitur potentia passiva.

957. Posse autem pati ab alio dicitur dupliciter.

Aliquando quidem, quicquid sit illud, quod aliquid potest pati, dicimus ipsum esse possibile ad illud patiendum, sive sit bonum, sive malum.

Aliquando vero non dicitur aliquid potens ex eo quod potest pati aliquod malum, sed ex hoc quod potest pati aliquod excellentius.

Sicut, si aliquis potest vinci, non dicimus potentem; sed si aliquis potest doceri vel adiuvari, dicimus eum potentem. Et hoc ideo, quia posse pati aliquem defectum quandoque attribuitur impotentiae; et posse non pati idem, attribuitur potentiae, ut infra dicetur.

958. Alia tamen litera habet, *aliquando autem non secundum omnem passionem, sed utique in contrarium.* Quod quidem sic debet intelligi. Improprie enim dicitur pati, quicquid recipit aliquam perfectionem ab aliquo, sicut intelligere dicitur quoddam pati. Proprie autem pati dicitur quod recipit aliquid cum sui transmutatione ab eo quod est ei naturale.

Unde et talis passio dicitur esse abiiciens a substantia. Hoc autem non potest fieri nisi per aliquod contrarium. Unde, quando aliquid patitur, secundum quod est contrarium suae naturae vel conditioni, proprie pati dicitur. Secundum quod etiam aegritudines passiones dicuntur. Quando vero aliquis recipit id quod est ei con-

ample, the power of building is not in the thing being built but rather in the builder. And while the art of medicine is an active power, since the physician heals by means of it, it may also be found in the one who is healed not inasmuch as he is healed, but accidentally, inasmuch as the physician and the one who is healed happen to be the same. So therefore, generally speaking, "potency" or "power" means in one sense a principle of motion or change in some other thing as other.

956. *Or it means* (1019a20). Here he gives a second sense in which the term "potency" is used. He says that in another sense the term "potency" means the principle whereby something is moved or changed by another thing as other. Now this is passive potency, and it is by reason of it that a patient undergoes some change.

For just as every agent or mover moves something other than itself and acts in something other than itself, so too every patient is acted upon by something other than itself— that is, everything moved is moved by another. For that principle whereby one thing is properly moved or acted upon by another is called "passive potency."

957. Now there are two ways in which we can say that a thing has the potency to be acted upon by another.

Sometimes we attribute such a potency to something, whatever it may be, because it is able to undergo some change, whether it be good or bad.

And sometimes we say that a thing has such a potency not because it can undergo something evil, but because it can be changed for the better.

For example, we do not say that one who can be overpowered has a potency in this last sense, but we do attribute such a potency to one who can be taught or helped. And we speak thus because sometimes an ability to be changed for the worse is attributed to incapacity, and the ability not to be changed in the same way is attributed to potency, as will be said below [965].

958. Another text reads, *sometimes this is not said of every change which a thing undergoes but of change to a contrary*. This should be understood thus: whatever receives a perfection from something else is said in an improper sense to undergo a change, and it is in this sense that to understand is said to be a kind of passion. But that which receives along with a change in itself something other than what is natural to it is said to undergo a change in a proper sense.

Hence such passion is also said to be a removing of something from a substance. But this can come about only by way of some contrary. Therefore, when a thing is acted upon in a way contrary to its own nature or condition, it is said in a proper sense to undergo a change or to be passive. And in this sense even illnesses are called passions. But

veniens secundum suam naturam, magis dicitur perfici quam pati.

959. Tertium modum ponit ibi *amplius alia* dicit, quod alia potestas dicitur, quae est principium faciendi aliquid non quocumque modo, sed bene, aut secundum *praevoluntatem*, idest secundum quod homo disponit. Quando enim aliqui progrediuntur vel loquuntur, sed non bene, aut non secundum quod volunt, dicuntur non posse loqui aut progredi.

Et *similiter est in pati*. Dicitur enim aliquid posse pati illud quod bene potest pati.

Sicut dicuntur aliqua ligna combustibilia, quia de facili comburuntur, et incombustibilia, quae non possunt de facili comburi.

960. Quartum modum ponit ibi *amplius quicumque* dicit, quod etiam potestates dicuntur omnes habitus sive formae vel dispositiones, quibus aliqua dicuntur vel redduntur omnino impassibilia, vel immobilia, aut non de facili mobilia in peius.

Quod enim in peius mutentur, sicut quod frangantur, vel curventur, vel conterantur, vel qualitercumque corrumpantur, non inest corporibus per aliquam potentiam, sed magis per impotentiam et defectum alicuius principii, quod corrumpenti resistere non potest. Nunquam enim corrumpitur aliquid nisi propter victoriam corrumpentis supra ipsum. Quod quidem contingit ex debilitate propriae virtutis.

Illis vero, quae non possunt tales defectus pati, *aut vix aut paulatim*, idest tarde vel modicum patiuntur, accidit eis propter potentiam, et in eo quod habent *aliquo modo posse*, idest cum quadam perfectione, ut non superentur a contrariis.

Et per hunc modum dicitur in *Praedicamentis*, quod durum vel sanativum significat potentiam naturalem non patiendi a corrumpentibus. Molle autem et aegrotativum impotentiam.

961. Deinde cum dicit *dicta vero* ponit modos possibilis correspondentes praedictis modis potestatis. Primo autem modo potestatis respondent duo modi possibilis.

Secundum potestatem enim activam aliquid dicitur potens agere dupliciter. Uno modo, quia ipse per seipsum agit immediate. Alio modo, quia agit mediante altero, cui potentiam suam communicat, sicut rex agit per ballivum.

when a thing receives something which is fitting to it by reason of its nature, it is said to be perfected rather than passive.

959. *And in another sense* (1019a23). He now gives a third sense in which the term "potency" is used. He says that in another sense "potency" means the principle of performing some act, not in any way at all, but well or according to *intention*, that is, according to what a man plans. For when men walk or talk but not well or as they planned to do, we say that they do not have the ability to walk or to talk.

And *the same applies to things that are undergoing change*, for a thing is said to be able to undergo something if it can undergo it well.

For example, some pieces of wood are said to be combustible because they can be burned easily, and others are said to be incombustible because they cannot be burned easily.

960. *Further, all states* (1019a26). He gives a fourth sense in which the term "potency" is used. He says that we designate as potencies all habits or forms or dispositions by which some things are said or made to be altogether incapable of being acted upon or changed, or to be not easily changed for the worse.

For when bodies are changed for the worse, as those which are broken or bent or crushed or destroyed in any way at all, this does not happen to them because of some ability or potency, but rather because of some inability and the weakness of some principle which does not have the power of resisting the thing which destroys them. For a thing is destroyed only because of the victory which the destroyer wins over it, and this is a result of the weakness of its proper active power.

For those things that cannot be affected by defects of this kind, or can *hardly or slightly* be affected by them (that is, they are affected slowly or to a small degree) are such *because they have the potency and the ability to be in some definite state*; that is, they have a certain perfection which prevents them from being overcome by contraries.

And, as is said in the *Categories*, it is in this way that "hard" or "healthy" signifies a natural power which a thing has of resisting change by destructive agents. But "soft" and "sickly" signify incapacity or lack of power.

961. *And since the term* (1019a32). Here he gives the senses of the term "capable" or "potent" which correspond to the above senses of "potency." And there are two senses of "capable" which correspond to the first sense of "potency."

For according to its active power, a thing is said to be capable of acting in two ways: in one way, because it acts immediately of itself; in another way, because it acts through something else to which it communicates its power, as a king acts through a bailiff.

Dicit ergo, quod, cum potentia tot modis dicatur, possibile etiam et potens pluribus modis dicetur. Uno quidem modo, quod habet principium activum mutationis in seipso *sicut stativum vel sistitivum*, idest id quod facit aliud stare, dicitur esse potens ad sistendum aliquid aliud diversum ab eo. Alio vero modo, quando ipse non immediate operatur, sed aliud habet ab eo talem potestatem, ut possit immediate agere.

962. Deinde cum dicit *alio si* secundo ponit secundum modum respondentem secundo modo potentiae, idest potentiae passivae; dicens, quod alio modo a praedicto dicitur possibile sive potens, quod potest mutari in aliquid, quicquid sit illud; scilicet sive possit mutari in peius, sive in melius.

Et secundum hoc, aliquid dicitur corruptibile, quia *potest corrumpi*, quod est in peius mutari: vel non corruptibile, quia potest non corrumpi, si sit impossibile illud ipsum corrumpi.

963. Oportet autem illud, quod est possibile ad aliquid patiendum, habere in se quamdam dispositionem, quae sit causa et principium talis passionis; et illud principium vocatur potentia passiva.

Principium autem passionis potest inesse alicui passibili dupliciter.

Uno modo per hoc, quod habet aliquid; sicut homo est possibilis pati infirmitatem propter abundantiam alicuius inordinati humoris in ipso.

Alio vero modo est aliquid potens pati per hoc, quod privatur aliquo, quod posset repugnare passioni; sicut si homo dicatur potens infirmari propter subtractionem fortitudinis et virtutis naturalis.

Et haec duo oportet esse in quolibet potente pati. Nunquam enim aliquid pateretur, nisi esset in eo subiectum, quod esset receptivum dispositionis, vel formae, quae per passionem inducitur; et nisi esset debilitas virtutis in patiente ad resistendum actioni agentis.

964. Hi enim duo modi principii patiendi possunt reduci in unum, quia potest privatio significari ut habitus. Et sic sequetur, quod privari sit habere privationem. Et ita uterque modus erit in aliquid habendo. Quod autem privatio possit significari ut habitus, et ut aliquid habitum, ex hoc contingit, quod ens aequivoce dicitur. Et secundum unum modum et privatio et negatio dicitur ens, ut habitum est in principio quarti. Et sic sequitur quod etiam negatio et privatio possunt significari

Hence he says that, since the term "potency" is used in this number of senses, the term "capable" or "potent" must also be used in the same number of senses. Thus in one sense it means something which has an active principle of change in itself, as what *brings another to rest* or to a stop; that is, what causes some other thing to stand still is said to be capable of bringing something different from itself to a state of rest. And it is used in another sense when a thing does not act directly, but another thing receives such power from it that it can act directly.

962. *And in still another* (1019b1). Next, he gives a second sense in which the term "capable" is used, and this corresponds to the second sense of the term "potency," namely, passive potency. He says that, in a different way from the foregoing, a thing is said to be capable or potent when it can be changed in some respect, whatever it may be, that is, whether it can be changed for the better or for the worse.

And in this sense a thing is said to be corruptible because it is *capable of being corrupted*, which is to undergo change for the worse, or it is not corruptible because it is capable of not being corrupted, assuming that it is impossible for it to be corrupted.

963. And what is capable of being acted upon in some way must have within itself a certain disposition which is the cause and principle of its passivity, and this principle is called "passive potency."

But such a principle can be present in the thing acted upon for two reasons.

First, this is because it possesses something; for example, a man is capable of suffering from some disease because he has an excessive amount of some inordinate humor.

Second, a thing is capable of being acted upon because it lacks something which could resist the change. This is the case, for example, when a man is said to be capable of suffering from some disease because his strength and natural power have been weakened.

Now both of these must be present in anything which is capable of being acted upon, for a thing would never be acted upon unless it both contained a subject which could receive the disposition or form induced in it as a result of the change and also lacked the power of resisting the action of an agent.

964. Now these two ways in which the principle of passivity is spoken of can be reduced to one, because privation can be designated as "a having." Thus it follows that to lack something is to have a privation, and so each way will involve the having of something. Now the designation of privation as a having and as something had follows from the fact that "being" is used in two different ways; and both privation and negation are called being in one of these ways, as has been pointed out at the beginning of book

ut habitus. Et ideo possumus universaliter dicere, quod aliquid possibile sit pati propter hoc quod habet in se quemdam habitum et quoddam principium passionis; cum etiam privari sit habere aliquid, si contingat privationem habere.

965. Deinde cum dicit *alio in* tertium modum ponit hic; et respondet quarto modo potentiae, secundum quod potentia dicebatur inesse alicui, quod non potest corrumpi, vel in peius mutari. Dicit ergo, quod alio modo dicitur possibile vel potens, inquantum non habet potestatem vel principium aliquod ad hoc quod corrumpatur. Et hoc dico ab alio inquantum est aliud; quia secundum hoc aliquid dicitur potens et vigorosum, quod ab exteriori vinci non potest, ut corrumpatur.

966. Deinde cum dicit *amplius autem* quartum modum ponit, qui respondet tertio modo potentiae, secundum quem dicebatur potentia ad bene agendum vel patiendum. Dicit ergo, quod secundum praedictos modos, qui pertinent ad agendum vel patiendum, potest dici aliquid potens vel ex eo solum, quod aliquid accidit fieri vel non fieri, vel ex eo quod accidit etiam bene fieri.

Sicut etiam dicitur potens agere, quia potest bene et faciliter agere, vel quia potest agere simpliciter. Et similiter potens pati et corrumpi, quia de facili hoc pati potest.

Et iste modus potestatis etiam invenitur in rebus inanimatis *ut in organis*, idest in lyra et musicis instrumentis. Dicitur enim quod aliqua lyra potest sonare, quia bene sonat; alia non potest sonare, quia non bene sonat.

967. Deinde cum dicit *impotentia autem* ostendit quot modis dicitur impotentia; et circa hoc duo facit.

Primo distinguit hoc nomen impotentia.

Secundo hoc nomen impossibile, ibi, *impossibilia vero*.

Circa primum duo facit.

Primo enim ostendit communem rationem huius nominis impotentia.

Secundo ostendit quot modis dicatur, ibi, *amplius autem*.

Dicit ergo primo, quod impotentia est privatio potentiae. Ad rationem autem privationis duo requiruntur; quorum primum est remotio habitus oppositi. Id autem, quod opponitur impotentiae, est potentia. Unde, cum

4 [564]. Hence it follows that negation and privation can also be designated as "havings." We can say, then, that in general something is capable of passion because it contains a kind of "having" and a certain principle that enables it to be acted upon—for even to lack something is to have something, if a thing can have a privation.

965. *An in another sense* (1019b10). Here he gives a third sense in which the term "capable" is used, and this sense corresponds to the fourth sense of "potency" inasmuch as a potency was said to be present in something which cannot be corrupted or changed for the worse. Thus he says that in another sense a thing is said to be capable because it does not have some potency or principle which enables it to be corrupted. And I mean by some other thing as other. For a thing is said to be potent or powerful in the sense that it cannot be overcome by something external so as to be corrupted.

966. *Again, all these* (1019b11). He gives a fourth sense in which the term "capable" is used, and this corresponds to the third sense of "potency" inasmuch as "potency" designated the ability to act or be acted upon well. He says that according to the foregoing senses of potency which pertain both to acting and to being acted upon, a thing can be said to be capable either because it merely happens to come into being or not or because it happens to come into being well.

For a thing is said to be capable of acting either because it can simply act or because it can act well and easily. And in a similar way a thing is said to be capable of being acted upon and corrupted because it can be acted upon easily.

And this sense of "potency" is also found in inanimate things *such as instruments*, in the case of the lyre and other musical instruments. For one lyre is said to be able to produce a tone because it has a good tone, and another is said not to because its tone is not good.

967. *Incapacity* (1019b15). Then he gives the different senses of the term "incapacity," and in regard to this he does two things.

First, he gives the various senses in which we speak of incapacity;

second (1019b21; [970]), he treats the different senses in which the term "impossible" is used, at *and some things*.

In treating the first part he does two things.

First, he gives the common meaning of the term "incapacity."

Second (1019b19; [969]), he notes the various ways in which it is used, at *again, there is*.

He accordingly says, first, that incapacity is the privation of potency. Now two things are required in the notion of privation, and the first of these is the removal of an opposite state. But the opposite of incapacity is potency.

potentia sit quoddam principium, impotentia erit sublatio quaedam talis principii, qualis dicta est esse potentia.

Secundum quod requiritur, est quod privatio proprie dicta sit circa determinatum subiectum et determinatum tempus. Improprie autem sumitur absque determinatione subiecti et temporis. Non enim caecum proprie dicitur nisi quod est aptum natum habere visum, et quando est natum habere visum.

968. Impotentia autem sic dicta dicit remotionem potentiae, *aut omnino*, idest universaliter, ut scilicet omnis remotio potentiae impotentia dicatur, sive sit aptum natum habere, sive non: aut dicitur remotio in eo quod est aptum natum habere quandocumque, aut solum tunc quando aptum natum est habere.

Non enim similiter accipitur impotentia, cum dicimus puerum non posse generare, et cum virum et eunuchum simul. Puer enim dicitur impotens generare, quia subiectum est aptum ad generandum, non tamen pro illo tempore. Vir autem eunuchus dicitur impotens ad generandum, quia pro illo tempore esset quidem aptus, non tamen potest, quia caret principiis activis generationis. Unde hic magis salvatur ratio privationis. Mulus autem vel lapis dicitur impotens ad generandum, quia non potest nec etiam habet aptitudinem in subiecto existentem.

969. Deinde cum dicit *amplius autem* dat intelligere impotentiae modos per oppositum ad modos potentiae. Sicut enim potentia est duplex, scilicet activa et passiva: et iterum utraque aut ad agendum et patiendum simpliciter, aut ad bene agendum et patiendum; ita secundum utramque potentiam est impotentia opposita.

Et *solum mobili et bene mobili* idest potentiae activae, quae est ad movendum simpliciter, vel bene movendum: et potentiae passivae, quae est ad moveri simpliciter, vel bene moveri.

970. Deinde cum dicit *impossibilia vero* ostendit quot modis dicitur impossibile: et circa hoc duo facit.

Primo distinguit modos impossibilis.

Secundo reducit illos modos ad unum, ibi, *quae vero secundum*.
Circa primum tria facit.
Primo dicit, quod uno modo dicuntur aliqua impossibilia secundum quod habent impotentiam praedictam,

Therefore, since potency is a kind of principle, incapacity will be the removal of that kind of principle which potency has been described to be.

The second thing required is that privation properly speaking must belong to a definite subject and at a definite time; and it is taken in an improper sense when taken without a definite subject and without a definite time. For, properly speaking, only that is said to be blind which is naturally fitted to have sight and at the time when it is naturally fitted to have it.

968. And he says that incapacity, such as it has been described, is the removal of a potency: *either altogether*, that is, universally, in the sense that every removal of a potency is called incapacity, whether the thing is naturally disposed to have the potency or not; or from something which is naturally fitted to have it at some time or other; or only at the time when it is naturally fitted to have it.

For incapacity is not taken in the same way when we say that a boy is incapable of begetting and when we say this of a man and of a eunuch. For to say that a boy is incapable of begetting means that, while the subject is naturally fitted to beget, it cannot beget before the proper time. But to say that a eunuch is incapable of begetting means that, while he was naturally fitted to beget at the proper time, he cannot beget now, for he lacks the active principles of begetting. Hence incapacity here retains the notion of privation. But a mule or a stone is said to be incapable of begetting because neither can do so, and also because neither has any real aptitude for doing so.

969. *Again, there is* (1019b19). Then he explains the various senses of "incapacity" by contrasting them with the senses of "potency." For just as potency is twofold—active and passive—and both refer either to acting and being acted upon simply, or to acting and being acted upon well, in a similar fashion there is an opposite sense of "incapacity" corresponding to each type of potency.

That is to say, there is a sense of "incapacity" corresponding *both to that which can merely produce motion and to that which can produce it well*, namely, to active potency, which is the potency to simply move a thing or to move it well, and to passive potency, which is the potency to simply be moved or to be moved well.

970. *And some things* (1019b21). Then he explains the various senses in which the term "impossible" is used, and in regard to this he does two things.

First, he gives the various senses in which the term "impossible" is used;

second (1019b35; [975]), he reduces them to one, at *but those senses*.

In regard to the first he does three things.

First, he says that in one sense some things are said to be impossible because they have the foregoing inca-

quae opponitur potentiae. Et huiusmodi modus in quatuor dividitur, sicut et impotentia.

971. Ideo cum dicit *alio modo*, ponit alium modum, quo dicuntur aliqua impossibilia, non propter privationem alicuius potentiae, sed propter repugnantiam terminorum in propositionibus. Cum enim posse dicatur in ordine ad esse, sicut ens dicitur non solum quod est in rerum natura, sed secundum compositionem propositionis, prout est in ea verum vel falsum; ita possibile et impossibile dicitur non solum propter potentiam vel impotentiam rei: sed propter veritatem et falsitatem compositionis vel divisionis in propositionibus. Unde impossibile dicitur, cuius contrarium est verum de necessitate, ut diametrum quadrati esse commensurabilem eius lateri, est impossibile, quia hoc tale est falsum, cuius contrarium non solum est verum, sed etiam necessarium, quod quidem est non commensurabilem esse. Et propter hoc esse commensurabilem est falsum de necessitate, et hoc est impossibile.

972. Tertio ibi, *contrarium vero* manifestat quid sit possibile oppositum impossibili secundo modo dicto. Impossibile enim opponitur possibili secundo modo dicto, sicut dictum est. Dicit ergo, quod possibile contrarium huic secundo impossibili est, cuius contrarium non est de necessitate falsum: sicut sedere hominem est possibile, quia non sedere, quod est eius oppositum, non est de necessitate falsum.

973. Ex quo patet, quod ille modus possibilis in tres modos dividitur.

Dicitur enim uno modo possibile quod falsum est, sed non ex necessitate: sicut hominem sedere dum non sedet, quia eius oppositum non est verum ex necessitate.

Alio modo dicitur possibile quod est verum, sed non de necessitate, quia eius oppositum non est falsum de necessitate, sicut Socratem sedere dum sedet.

Tertio modo dicitur possibile, quia licet non sit verum, tamen contingit in proximo verum esse.

974. Deinde cum dicit *secundum metaphoram* ostendit quomodo potentia sumatur metaphorice; et dicit, in geometria dicitur potentia secundum metaphoram. Potentia enim lineae in geometria dicitur quadratum lineae per hanc similitudinem: quia sicut ex eo quod est in potentia fit illud quod est in actu, ita ex ductu alicuius lineae in seipsam, resultat quadratum ipsius.

Sicut si diceremus, quod ternarius potest in novenarium, quia novenarius consurgit ex ductu ternarii in

pacity which is opposed to potency. And "impossible" in this sense is used in four ways corresponding to those of "incapacity."

971. Accordingly, when he says *in a different sense*, he gives another way in which some things are said to be impossible. And they are said to be such not because of the privation of some potency, but because of the opposition existing between the terms in propositions. For since potency is referred to being, then just as being is predicated not only of things that exist in reality but also of the composition of a proposition inasmuch as it contains truth and falsity, in a similar fashion the terms "possible" and "impossible" are predicated not only of real potency and incapacity, but also of the truth and falsity found in the combining or separating of terms in propositions. Hence the term "impossible" means that of which the contrary is necessarily true. For example, it is impossible that the diagonal of a square should be commensurable with a side, because such a statement is false whose contrary is not only true, but necessarily so—namely, that it is not commensurable. Hence the statement that it is commensurable is necessarily false. And this is impossible.

972. *And the contrary* (1019b27). Here he shows that the possible is the opposite of the impossible in the second way mentioned, for the impossible is opposed to the possible in the second way mentioned. He says, then, that "the possible," as the contrary of this second sense of "the impossible," means that whose contrary is not necessarily false. For example, it is possible that a man should be seated, because the opposite of this—that he should not be seated—is not necessarily false.

973. From this it is clear that this sense of "possible" has three usages.

For in one way it designates what is false but is not necessarily so—for example, it is possible that a man should be seated while he is not seated, because the opposite of this is not necessarily true.

In another way, "possible" designates what is true but is not necessarily so because its opposite is not necessarily false—for example, that Socrates should be seated while he is seated.

And in a third way it means that, although a thing is not true now, it may be true later on.

974. *And what is called a "power"* (1019b33). He shows how the term "power" is used metaphorically. He says that in geometry the term "power" is used metaphorically. For in geometry the square of a line is called its "power" by reason of the following likeness, namely, that just as from something in potency something actual comes to be, in a similar way, from multiplying a line by itself, its square results.

It would be the same if we were to say that the number three is capable of becoming the number nine, because

seipsum. Nam ter tria sunt novem. Sicut autem impossibile secundo modo acceptum non dicitur secundum aliquam impotentiam, ita et modi possibilis ultimo positi, non dicuntur secundum aliquam potentiam, sed secundum similitudinem, vel secundum modum veri et falsi.

975. Deinde cum dicit *quae vero* reducit omnes modos possibilis et impossibilis ad unum primum: et dicit, quod possibilia, quae dicuntur secundum potentiam, omnia dicuntur per respectum ad unam primam potentiam, quae est prima potentia activa, de qua supra dictum est, quod est principium mutationis in alio inquantum est aliud. Nam omnia alia possibilia dicuntur per respectum ad istam potentiam. Aliquid enim dicitur possibile per hoc, quod aliquid aliud habet potentiam activam in ipsum, secundum quod dicitur possibile secundum potentiam passivam. Quaedam vero dicuntur possibilia in non habendo aliquid aliud talem potentiam in ipsa: sicut quae dicuntur potentia, quia non possunt corrumpi ab exterioribus agentibus. Quaedam vero potentia *in sic habendo*, idest in hoc quod habent potentiam, ut bene aut faciliter agant vel patiantur.

976. Et sicut omnia possibilia, quae dicuntur secundum aliquam potentiam, reducuntur ad unam primam potentiam; ita omnia impossibilia, quae dicuntur secundum aliquam impotentiam, reducuntur ad unam primam impotentiam, quae est opposita primae potentiae. Patet igitur, quod propria definitio potentiae primo modo dictae est principium permutationis in alio inquantum est aliud, quod est ratio potentiae activae.

from multiplying the number three by itself the number nine results, for three times three makes nine. And just as the term "impossible" taken in the second sense does not correspond to any incapacity, in a similar way the senses of the term "possible" which were given last do not correspond to any potency, but they are used figuratively or in the sense of the true and the false.

975. *But those senses* (1019b35). He now reduces all senses of "capable" and "incapable" to one primary sense. He says that those senses of the term "capable" or "potent" which correspond to potency all refer to one primary kind of potency—the first active potency which was described above [955] as the principle of change in some other thing as other, because all the other senses of "capable" or "potent" are referred to this kind of potency. For a thing is said to be capable by reason of the fact that some other thing has active power over it, and in this sense it is said to be capable according to passive potency. And some things are said to be capable because some other thing does not have power over them, as those which are said to be capable because they cannot be corrupted by external agents. And others are said to be capable because they have it *in some special way*, that is, because they have the power or potency to act or be acted upon well or easily.

976. And just as all things that are said to be capable because of some potency are reduced to one primary potency, in a similar way all things that are said to be incapable because of some impotency are reduced to one primary incapacity, which is the opposite of the primary potency. It is clear, then, that the proper notion of potency in the primary sense is this: a principle of change in some other thing as other. This is the notion of active potency or power.

LECTURE 15

The definition of "quantity"

1020a7 Quantum vero dicitur quod est divisibile in ea quae insunt, quorum utrumque aut singulum, unum aliquid, et hoc aliquid, aptum natum est esse. [977]

ποσὸν λέγεται τὸ διαιρετὸν εἰς ἐνυπάρχοντα ὧν ἑκάτερον ἢ ἕκαστον ἕν τι καὶ τόδε τι πέφυκεν εἶναι.

"Quantity" means what is divisible into constituent parts, both or one of which is by nature a one and a particular thing.

1020a8 Multitudo ergo quantum aliquid si fuerit munerabilis. Magnitudo, si fuerit mensurabilis. [978]

πλῆθος μὲν οὖν ποσόν τι ἐὰν ἀριθμητὸν ᾖ, μέγεθος δὲ ἂν μετρητὸν ᾖ.

Therefore, "plurality" or "multitude" is a kind of quantity if it is numerable; and so also is "magnitude" or "continuous quantity" if it is measurable.

Dicitur autem multitudo quidem, quod est divisibile potestate in non continua. Magnitudo autem quod in continua. Mensura vero, alia in unum continuum, longitudine: alia in duo, latitudine: alia in tria, profunditate.

λέγεται δὲ πλῆθος μὲν τὸ διαιρετὸν δυνάμει εἰς μὴ συνεχῆ, μέγεθος δὲ τὸ εἰς συνεχῆ: μεγέθους δὲ τὸ μὲν ἐφ᾽ ἓν συνεχὲς μῆκος τὸ δ᾽ ἐπὶ δύο πλάτος τὸ δ᾽ ἐπὶ τρία βάθος.

"Plurality" means what is potentially divisible into non-continuous parts, and "magnitude" means what is divisible into continuous parts. Again, of the kinds of magnitude, what is continuous in one dimension is length; in two, breadth; and in three, depth.

Horum autem pluralitas quidem finita, numerus: sed longitudo, linea: latitudo, superficies: et profundum, corpus.

τούτων δὲ πλῆθος μὲν τὸ πεπερασμένον ἀριθμὸς μῆκος δὲ γραμμὴ πλάτος δὲ ἐπιφάνεια βάθος δὲ σῶμα.

And of these, limited plurality is number; limited length, a line; limited breadth, a surface; and limited depth, a body.

1020a14 Amplius autem alia dicuntur secundum se quanta, alia secundum accidens: ut linea quantum aliquid secundum se, musicum vero secundum accidens. [979]

ἔτι τὰ {15} μὲν λέγεται καθ᾽ αὑτὰ ποσά, τὰ δὲ κατὰ συμβεβηκός, οἷον ἡ μὲν γραμμὴ ποσόν τι καθ᾽ ἑαυτό, τὸ δὲ μουσικὸν κατὰ συμβεβηκός.

Again, some things are said to be quantitative essentially and others accidentally. For example, a line is quantitative essentially, but the musical accidentally.

1020a17 Eorum vero quae sunt secundum se, alia secundum substantiam sunt, ut linea quantum quid. Nam in ratione quid est dicente, quantum quid existit. Alia passiones et habitus talis sunt substantiae; ut multum et paucum et productum et breve: et latum et strictum, et profundum et humile, et grave et leve, et alia talia. Sunt autem magnum et parvum, et maius et minus, secundum se et ad invicem dicta, quanti passiones secundum se. Transferuntur etiam et ad alia ea nomina. [980]

τῶν δὲ καθ᾽ αὑτὰ τὰ μὲν κατ᾽ οὐσίαν ἐστίν, οἷον ἡ γραμμὴ ποσόν τι (ἐν γὰρ τῷ λόγῳ τῷ {19} τί ἐστι λέγοντι τὸ ποσόν τι ὑπάρχει), τὰ δὲ πάθη καὶ ἕξεις {20} τῆς τοιαύτης ἐστὶν οὐσίας, οἷον τὸ πολὺ καὶ τὸ ὀλίγον, καὶ μακρὸν καὶ βραχύ, καὶ πλατὺ καὶ στενόν, καὶ βαθὺ καὶ ταπεινόν, καὶ βαρὺ καὶ κοῦφον, καὶ τὰ ἄλλα τὰ τοιαῦτα. ἔστι δὲ καὶ τὸ μέγα καὶ τὸ μικρὸν καὶ μεῖζον καὶ ἔλαττον, καὶ καθ᾽ αὑτὰ καὶ πρὸς ἄλληλα λεγόμενα, τοῦ {25} ποσοῦ πάθη καθ᾽ αὑτά: μεταφέρονται μέντοι καὶ ἐπ᾽ ἄλλα ταῦτα τὰ ὀνόματα.

And of those things that are quantitative essentially, some are such by reason of their substance, as a line is quantitative quidditatively. For in the definition expressing its quiddity some kind of quantity is found. Others are properties and states of this kind of substance, such as much and little, long and short, broad and narrow, deep and shallow, heavy and light, and the like. And large and small, and larger and smaller, whether they are spoken of per se or in relation to each other, are properties of quantity. And these terms are also transferred to other things.

1020a26 Secundum accidens vero dictarum quantitatum aliae sic dicuntur, sicut dictum est, quia musicum quantum est, et album, per esse quantum aliquid cui insunt. [984]

τῶν δὲ κατὰ συμβεβηκὸς λεγομένων ποσῶν τὰ μὲν οὕτως λέγεται ὥσπερ ἐλέχθη ὅτι τὸ μουσικὸν ποσὸν καὶ τὸ λευκὸν τῷ εἶναι ποσόν τι ᾧ ὑπάρχουσι,

But of things that are quantitative accidentally, some are said to be such in the sense in which the musical and the white are quantitative: because the subject to which they belong is quantitative.

Alia ut motus et tempus. Etenim haec quanta quaedam dicuntur et continua,

τὰ δὲ ὡς κίνησις καὶ χρόνος: καὶ γὰρ ταῦτα πός᾽ ἄττα λέγεται {30} καὶ συνεχῆ

Others are said to be quantitative in the sense in which motion and time are, for

quia illa sunt divisibilia, quorum sunt hae passiones.	τῷ ἐκεῖνα διαιρετὰ εἶναι ὧν ἐστὶ ταῦτα πάθη.	these too are said to be in a sense quantitative and continuous because the things of which they are the properties are divisible.
Dico autem non quod movetur, sed quo motum est. Nam per esse quantum illud et motus est quantus. Tempus vero per ipsum, scilicet motum.	λέγω δὲ οὐ τὸ κινούμενον ἀλλ' ὃ ἐκινήθη· τῷ γὰρ ποσὸν εἶναι ἐκεῖνο καὶ ἡ κίνησις ποσή, ὁ δὲ χρόνος τῷ ταύτην.	And I mean not the thing which is moved, but the space through which it is moved. For since space is quantitative, motion is also quantitative; through motion, time is also quantitative.

977. Quoniam ens non solum dividitur in potentiam et actum, sed etiam in decem praedicamenta, postquam Philosophus distinxit hoc nomen potentia, hic incipit distinguere nomina, quae significant praedicamenta.

Et primo nomen quantitatis.
Secundo nomen qualitatis, ibi, *quale autem*.

Tertio distinguit modos ad aliquid, ibi, *ad aliquid dicuntur*.

Alia vero praedicamenta praetermittit, quia sunt determinata ad aliquod genus rerum naturalium; ut patet praecipue de agere et pati, et de ubi et quando.

Circa primum tria facit.

Primo ponit rationem quantitatis; dicens, quod quantum dicitur quod est divisibile in ea quae insunt. Quod quidem dicitur ad differentiam divisionis mixtorum. Nam corpus mixtum resolvitur in elementa, quae non sunt actu in mixto, sed virtute tantum. Unde non est ibi tantum divisio quantitatis; sed oportet quod adsit aliqua alteratio, per quam mixtum resolvitur in elementa. Et iterum addit, quod utrumque aut singulum, est natum esse *unum aliquid*, hoc est aliquid demonstratum. Et hoc dicit ad removendum divisionem in partes essentiales, quae sunt materia et forma. Nam neutrum eorum aptum natum est esse unum aliquid per se.

978. Secundo ibi, *multitudo ergo* ponit species quantitatis; inter quas primae sunt duae; scilicet multitudo sive pluralitas, et magnitudo sive mensura. Utrumque autem eorum habet rationem quanti, inquantum multitudo numerabilis est et magnitudo est mensurabilis. Mensuratio enim propria pertinet ad quantitatem. Definitur autem multitudo sic.

Multitudo est, quod est divisibile secundum potentiam in partes non continuas. Magnitudo autem quod est divisibile in partes continuas. Quod quidem contingit tripliciter: et secundum hoc sunt tres species magnitudinis. Nam, si sit divisibile secundum unam tantum dimensionem in partes continuas, erit longitudo. Si autem in duas, latitudo. Si autem in tres, profunditas. Ulterius autem, quando pluralitas vel multitudo est finita, dicitur numerus. Longitudo autem finita, dicitur

977. Since being is divided not only into potency and act but also into the ten categories, having given the different senses of the term "potency" [954–60], the Philosopher begins here to give the different senses of the terms which designate the categories.

First, he considers the term "quantity";

second (1020a33; [987]), the term "quality," at *quality means*.

Third (1020b26; [1001]), he gives the different meanings of the term "relative," at *some things*.

He omits the other categories because they are limited to one genus of natural beings, as is especially evident of action and passion, and of place and time.

In regard to the first he does three things.

First, he gives the meaning of "quantity." He says that "quantity" means what is divisible into constituent parts. Now this is said to distinguish this kind of division from that of compounds. For a compound is dissolved into the elements, and these are not present in it actually but only virtually. Hence, in the latter case, there is not just division of quantity, but there must also be some alteration by means of which a compound is dissolved into its elements. He adds that both or one of these constituents is by nature *a one*, that is, something which is pointed out. He says this in order to exclude the division of a thing into its essential parts, which are matter and form; for neither one of these is fitted by nature to be a particular thing of itself.

978. *Therefore, plurality* (1020a8). Second, he gives the kinds of quantity, and of these there are two primary kinds: plurality or multitude, and magnitude or measure. And each of these has the character of something quantitative inasmuch as plurality is numerable and magnitude is measurable. For measuring pertains properly to quantity.

However, plurality is defined as what is divisible potentially into parts which are not continuous, and magnitude as what is divisible into parts which are continuous. Now this occurs in three ways, and therefore there are three kinds of magnitude. For if magnitude is divisible into continuous parts in one dimension only, it will be length; if into two, width; and if into three, depth. Again, when plurality or multitude is limited, it is called number. And a limited length is called a line; a limited width, surface;

linea. Latitudo finita, corpus. Si enim esset multitudo infinita, non esset numerus; quia quod infinitum est, numerari non potest. Similiter, si esset longitudo infinita, non esset linea. Linea enim est longitudo mensurabilis. Et propter hoc in ratione lineae ponitur, quod eius extremitates sunt duo puncta. Simile est de superficie et corpore.

979. Tertio ibi, *amplius autem* distinguit modos quantitatis; et circa hoc tria facit.

Primo distinguit quantum in id quod est quantum per se, sicut linea, et in id quod est quantum per accidens, sicut musicum.

980. Secundo ibi, *eorum vero* distinguit quantum per se; quod quidem duplex est.

Quaedam enim significantur per modum substantiae et subiecti, sicut linea, vel superficies, vel numerus. Quodlibet enim istorum substantialiter est quantum, quia in definitione cuiuslibet ponitur quantitas. Nam linea est quantitas continua secundum longitudinem divisibilis, finita: et similiter est de aliis.

981. Quaedam vero per se pertinent ad genus quantitatis, et significantur per modum habitus vel passionis talis substantiae, scilicet lineae, quae est substantialiter quantitas, vel aliarum similium quantitatum: sicut multum et paucum significantur ut passiones numeri: et productum et breve, ut passiones lineae: et latum et strictum, ut passiones superficiei: et profundum et humile sive altum, ut passiones corporis: et similiter grave et leve, secundum opinionem illorum, qui dicebant multitudinem superficierum vel atomorum esse causam gravitatis in corporibus, paucitatem vero eorumdem, causam levitatis. Sed secundum veritatem grave et leve non pertinent ad quantitatem, sed ad qualitatem, ut infra ponet. Et similiter est de aliis talibus.

982. Quaedam etiam sunt, quae communiter cuiuslibet quantitatis continuae passiones sunt, sicut magnum et parvum, maius et minus; sive haec dicantur *secundum se*, idest absolute, sive dicantur *ad invicem*, sicut aliquid dicitur magnum et parvum respective, sicut in *Praedicamentis* habetur. Ista autem nomina, quae significant passiones quantitatis per se, transferuntur etiam ad alia quam ad quantitates. Dicitur enim albedo magna et parva, et alia huiusmodi.

983. Sciendum autem est, quod quantitas inter alia accidentia propinquior est substantiae. Unde quidam quantitates esse substantias putant, scilicet lineam et numerum et superficiem et corpus. Nam sola quantitas habet divisionem in partes proprias post substantiam. Albedo enim non potest dividi, et per consequens nec intelligitur individuare nisi per subiectum. Et inde est,

and a limited depth, body. For if multitude were unlimited, number would not exist, because what is unlimited cannot be numbered. Similarly, if length were unlimited, a line would not exist, because a line is a measurable length (and this is why it is stated in the definition of a line that its extremities are two points). The same things holds true of surface and of body.

979. *Again, some things* (1020a14). Third, he gives the different ways in which things are quantitative; and in regard to this he does three things.

First, he draws a distinction between what is *per se* quantitative, as a line, and what is accidentally quantitative, as the musical.

980. *And of those* (1020a17). Second, he gives the different senses in which things are *per se* quantitative, and there are two of these.

For some things are said to be such after the manner of a substance or subject, as line, surface, or number; for each of these is essentially quantitative because quantity is given in the definition of each. For a line is a limited quantity divisible in length. The same is true of the other dimensions.

981. And other things belong *per se* to the genus of quantity and are signified after the manner of a state or property of such substance, that is, of a line, which is *per se* quantitative, or of other similar kinds of quantity. For example, much and little are signified as properties of number; long and short, as properties of a line; broad and narrow, as properties of surface; and high and low or deep, as properties of body. And the same is true of heavy and light according to the opinion of those who said that having many surfaces, or atoms, causes bodies to be heavy, and having few causes them to be light. But the truth of the matter is that heavy and light do not pertain to quantity but to quality, as he states below [993]. The same thing is true of other such attributes as these.

982. There are also certain attributes which are common properties of any continuous quantity, as large and small, and larger and smaller—whether these are taken *per se*, that is, absolutely, or *in relation to each other*, just as something is said to be large and small relatively (as is stated in the *Categories*). But these terms which signify the properties of quantity pure and simple are also transferred to other things besides quantities. For whiteness is said to be large and small, and so also are other accidents of this kind.

983. But it must be borne in mind that of all the accidents, quantity is closest to substance. Hence some men think that quantities, such as line, number, surface, and body, are substances. For next to substance only quantity can be divided into distinctive parts. For whiteness cannot be divided, and therefore it cannot be understood to be individuated except by its subject. And it is for this reason

quod in solo quantitatis genere aliqua significantur ut subiecta, alia ut passiones.

984. Tertio ibi, *secundum accidens* distinguit modos quantitatis per accidens: et ponit duos modos quantitatis per accidens:

quorum unus est secundum quod aliqua dicuntur quanta per accidens ex hoc solo, quod sunt accidentia alicuius quanti, sicut album et musicum per hoc quod sunt accidentia alicuius subiecti, quod est quantum.

985. Alio modo dicuntur aliqua quanta per accidens non ratione subiecti, in quo sunt, sed eo quod dividuntur secundum quantitatem ad divisionem alicuius quantitatis;

sicut motus et tempus, quae dicuntur quaedam quanta et continua, propterea quod ea, quorum sunt, sunt divisibilia, et ipsa dividuntur ad divisionem eorum. Tempus enim est divisibile et continuum propter motum; motus autem propter magnitudinem; non quidem propter magnitudinem eius quod movetur, sed propter magnitudinem eius in quo aliquid movetur. Ex eo enim quod illa magnitudo est quanta, et motus est quantus. Et propter hoc quod motus est quantus, sequitur tempus esse quantum. Unde haec non solum per accidens quantitates dici possunt, sed magis per posterius, inquantum quantitatis divisionem ab aliquo priori sortiuntur.

986. Sciendum est autem, quod Philosophus in *Praedicamentis* posuit tempus quantitatem per se, cum hic ponat ipsum quantitatem per accidens;

quia ibi distinxit species quantitatis secundum diversas rationes mensurae. Aliam enim rationem mensurae habet tempus, quod est mensura extrinseca, et magnitudo, quae est mensura intrinseca. Et ideo ponitur ibi ut alia species quantitatis. Hic autem considerat species quantitatis quantum ad ipsum esse quantitatis.

Et ideo illa, quae non habent esse quantitatis nisi ex alio, non ponit hic species quantitatis, sed quantitates per accidens, ut motum et tempus.

Motus autem non habet aliam rationem mensurae quam tempus et magnitudo. Et ideo nec hic nec ibi ponitur quantitatis species. Locus autem ponitur ibi species quantitatis, non hic, quia habet aliam rationem mensurae, sed non aliud esse quantitatis.

that only in the genus of quantity are some things designated as subjects and others as properties.

984. *But of things* (1020a26). Then he gives the different senses in which things are said to be accidentally quantitative. These senses are two.

In one sense, things are said to be accidentally quantitative only because they are accidents of some quantity; for example, white and musical are said to be quantitative because they are accidents of a subject which is quantitative.

985. In another sense, some things are said to be accidentally quantitative, not because of the subject in which they exist, but because they are divided quantitatively as a result of the division of some quantity.

For example, motion and time (which are said to be quantitative and continuous because of the subjects to which they belong) are divisible and are themselves divided as a result of the division of the subjects to which they belong. For time is divisible and continuous because of motion, and motion is divisible because of magnitude—not because of the magnitude of the thing which is moved, but because of the magnitude of the space through which it is moved. For, since that magnitude is quantitative, motion is also quantitative; and since motion is quantitative, it follows that time is quantitative. Hence these can be said to be quantitative not merely accidentally but rather subsequently, inasmuch as they receive quantitative division from something prior.

986. However, it must be noted that in the *Categories* the Philosopher held that time is *per se* quantitative, while here he holds that it is accidentally quantitative.

There he distinguished between the species of quantity from the viewpoint of the different kinds of measure. For time, which is an external measure, has the character of one kind of measure, and continuous quantity, which is an internal measure, has a different one. Hence in the *Categories* time is given as another species of quantity, whereas here he considers the species of quantity from the viewpoint of the being of quantity.

Therefore, those things that receive their quantitative being only from something else he does not give here as species of quantity, but as things that are accidentally quantitative, as motion and time.

But motion has no other manner of measure than time and magnitude. Hence neither in this work nor in the *Categories* does he give it as a species of quantity. Place, however, is given there as a species of quantity. But it is not given as such here because it has a different manner of measure, although not a different quantitative being.

LECTURE 16

The definition of "quality"

1020a33 Quale, uno quidem mode dicitur differentia substantiae: ut quale quid homo? Quia animal bipes, equus quadrupes: et circulus qualis? Quia quaedam figura, quia agonion est, quasi differentia secundum substantiam qualitate existente. Uno quidem itaque modo haec dicitur qualitas differentia substantiae. [987]

[τὸ] ποιὸν λέγεται ἔνα μὲν τρόπον ἡ διαφορὰ τῆς οὐσίας, οἷον ποιόν τι ἄνθρωπος ζῷον ὅτι δίπουν, ἵππος δὲ τετράπουν, {35} καὶ κύκλος ποιόν τι σχῆμα ὅτι ἀγώνιον, ὡς τῆς διαφορᾶς τῆς κατὰ τὴν οὐσίαν ποιότητος οὔσης: {1020b1} —ἔνα μὲν δὴ τρόπον τοῦτον λέγεται ἡ ποιότης διαφορὰ οὐσίας,

"Quality" (the qualified, or of what sort) means in one sense substantial difference. For example, how is man's quiddity qualified? As a two-footed animal. How is a horse's? As a four-footed animal. A circle's? As a figure which is non-angular, as if substantial difference were quality. In this one sense, then, "quality" means substantial difference.

1020b1 Alio vero modo ut immobilia et mathematica, sicut numeri quales quidem sunt, quemadmodum compositi, et non solum ad unum entes, sed quorum imitatio superficies et solidum. Hi vero sunt quoties quanti, aut quoties quot quanti: [989]

ἔνα δὲ ὡς τὰ ἀκίνητα καὶ τὰ μαθηματικά, ὥσπερ οἱ ἀριθμοὶ ποιοί τινες, οἷον οἱ σύνθετοι καὶ μὴ μόνον ἐφ᾽ ἓν ὄντες ἀλλ᾽ ὧν μίμημα {5} τὸ ἐπίπεδον καὶ τὸ στερεόν (οὗτοι δ᾽ εἰσὶν οἱ ποσάκις ποσοὶ ἢ ποσάκις ποσάκις ποσοί),

In another sense the term applies to immobile things and to mathematical objects, as numbers are of a certain type—for example, those that are compound, and not only those of one dimension but also those of which surface and solid are the counterpart (for there are numbers that are so many times so much and so many times so many times so much).

et totaliter quod praeter quantitatem existit substantia. Nam substantia cuiuslibet, quod semel: ut ipsorum sex, non bis tres sunt, sed semel. Sex enim, semel sex.

καὶ ὅλως ὃ παρὰ τὸ ποσὸν ὑπάρχει ἐν τῇ οὐσίᾳ: οὐσία γὰρ ἑκάστου ὃ ἅπαξ, οἷον τῶν ἓξ οὐχ ὃ δὶς ἢ τρὶς εἰσὶν ἀλλ᾽ ὃ ἅπαξ: ἓξ γὰρ ἅπαξ ἕξ.

And in general it means what is present in substance besides quantity. For the substance of each number is what it is once—for example, the substance of six is not twice three, but six taken once, for six times one is six.

1020b8 Amplius quaecumque passiones sunt earum, quae moventur, substantiarum, ut calor et frigiditas, albedo et nigredo, gravitas et levitas, et quaecumque talia secundum quae dicuntur mutari corpora permutantium. [993]

ἔτι ὅσα πάθη τῶν κινουμένων οὐσιῶν, οἷον θερμότης καὶ ψυχρότης, {10} καὶ λευκότης καὶ μελανία, καὶ βαρύτης καὶ κουφότης, καὶ ὅσα τοιαῦτα, καθ᾽ ἃ λέγονται καὶ ἀλλοιοῦσθαι τὰ σώματα μεταβαλλόντων.

Again, all the modifications of substances which are moved, such as heat and cold, whiteness and blackness, heaviness and lightness, and any other attributes of this sort according to which the bodies of changing things are said to be altered, are called qualities.

1020b12 Amplius secundum virtutem et vitium, et omnino bonum et malum. [994]

ἔτι κατ᾽ ἀρετὴν καὶ κακίαν καὶ ὅλως τὸ κακὸν καὶ ἀγαθόν.

Further, the term "quality" is used of virtue and vice, and in general of good and evil.

1020b13 Fere vero secundum duos modos dicitur quale, et horum quoddam maxime secundum priorem. Nam prima qualitas, substantiae differentia. Eius vero quaedam et quae in numeris qualitas, pars: nam differentia quaedam substantiarum est, sed aut non motorum, aut non inquantum mota. [996]

σχεδὸν δὴ κατὰ δύο τρόπους λέγοιτ᾽ ἂν τὸ ποιόν, καὶ τούτων ἔνα τὸν κυριώτατον: πρώτη μὲν γὰρ {15} ποιότης ἡ τῆς οὐσίας διαφορά (ταύτης δέ τι καὶ ἡ ἐν τοῖς ἀριθμοῖς ποιότης μέρος: διαφορὰ γάρ τις οὐσιῶν, ἀλλ᾽ ἢ οὐ κινουμένων ἢ οὐχ ᾗ κινούμενα),

The senses of "quality," then, come down to two, and one of these is more basic than the other. For the primary kind of quality is substantial difference. And the quality found in number is a part of this, for this is a substantial difference, but either of things that are not moved or of things not insofar as they are moved.

Hae autem passiones motorum inquantum sunt mota et motuum differentiae. Virtus autem et vitium passionum pars quaedam est. Differentias enim ostendunt motus et actus, secundum quos

τὰ δὲ πάθη τῶν κινουμένων ᾗ κινούμενα, καὶ αἱ τῶν κινήσεων διαφοραί. ἀρετὴ δὲ καὶ κακία τῶν παθημάτων μέρος τι: διαφορὰς γὰρ δηλοῦσι τῆς {20} κινήσεως καὶ τῆς ἐνεργείας, καθ᾽ ἃς ποιοῦσιν ἢ

The others, however, are the modifications of things that are moved inasmuch as they are moved, and are the differences of motions. And virtue and vice are parts of these modifications, for they indicate

faciunt vel patiuntur bene aut prave, quae sunt in motu.

Possibile namque sic moveri aut agere, bonum: quod vero non sic sed contrarie, pravum. Maxime vero bonum et malum significant quale in animatis, et horum maxime in habentibus prohaeresim.

πάσχουσι καλῶς ἢ φαύλως τὰ ἐν κινήσει ὄντα:

τὸ μὲν γὰρ ὡδὶ δυνάμενον κινεῖσθαι ἢ ἐνεργεῖν ἀγαθὸν τὸ δ᾽ ὡδὶ καὶ ἐναντίως μοχθηρόν. μάλιστα δὲ τὸ ἀγαθὸν καὶ τὸ κακὸν σημαίνει τὸ ποιὸν ἐπὶ τῶν ἐμψύχων, καὶ τούτων μάλιστα ἐπὶ τοῖς ἔχουσι {25} προαίρεσιν.

clearly the differences of the motion or activity according to which things in motion act or are acted upon well or badly.

For what is capable of being moved or of acting in this way is good, and what cannot do so but acts in a contrary way is bad. And good and bad signify quality especially in the case of living things, and especially in those which have the power of choice.

---

987. Hic distinguit modos qualitatis: et circa hoc duo facit.

Primo ponit quatuor modos qualitatis.

Secundo reducit eos ad duos, ibi, *fere vero secundum duos modos*.

Dicit ergo primo, quod unus modus qualitatis est secundum quod qualitas dicitur *differentia substantiae*, idest differentia, per quam aliquid ab altero substantialiter differt, quae intrat in definitionem substantiae. Et propter hoc dicitur, quod differentia praedicatur in quale quid. Ut si quaeratur, quale animal est homo? Respondemus quod bipes: et quale animal equus? Respondemus quod quadrupes: et qualis figura est circulus? Respondemus quod *agonion*, id est sine angulo; ac si ipsa differentia substantiae qualitas sit. Uno igitur modo ipsa differentia substantiae qualitas dicitur.

988. Hunc autem modum qualitatis Aristoteles in *Praedicamentis* praetermisit, quia non continetur sub praedicamento qualitatis, de quo ibi agebat. Hic autem agit de significationibus huius nominis, qualitas.

989. Secundum ponit ibi, *alio vero* dicit, quod alius modus qualitatis vel qualis est secundum quod immobilia et mathematica dicuntur qualia. Mathematica enim abstrahunt a motu, ut in sexto huius dicetur. Mathematica enim sunt numeri, et magnitudines; et in utrisque utimur nomine qualis. Dicimus enim superficies esse quales, inquantum sunt quadratae vel triangulares. Et similiter numeri dicuntur quales, inquantum sunt compositi. Dicuntur autem numeri compositi, qui communicant in aliquo numero mensurante eos; sicut senarius numerus et novenarius mensurantur ternario, et non solum ad unitatem comparationem habent, sicut ad mensuram communem. Numeri autem incompositi, vel primi in sua proportione dicuntur, quos non mensurat alius numerus communis, nisi sola unitas.

990. Dicuntur etiam numeri quales ad similitudinem superficiei *et solidi*, idest corporis. Secundum quidem imitationem superficiei, inquantum numerus ducitur in

987. Here he gives the various senses in which the term "quality" is used, and in regard to this he does two things.

First, he gives four senses of the term "quality";

and second (1020b13; [996]), he reduces them to two, at *the senses of quality*.

He accordingly says, first, that the term quality is used in one sense as *substantial difference*, the difference by which one thing is distinguished substantially from another and which is included in the definition of the substance. And for this reason it is said that a difference is predicated as a substantial qualification. For example, if one were to ask what sort of animal man is, we would answer that he is two-footed. If one were to ask what sort of animal a horse is, we would answer that it is four-footed. If one were to ask what sort of figure a circle is, we would answer that it is *non-angular*, without angles. It is as if a substantial difference were quality. In one sense, then, quality means substantial difference.

988. Now Aristotle omits this sense of "quality" in the *Categories* because it is not contained under the category of quality, which he deals with there. But here he is dealing with the meaning of the term "quality."

989. *In another sense* (1020b1). Here he gives a second sense in which the term "quality" is used. He says that the term "quality" or "qualified" is used in another sense insofar as immobile things and the objects of mathematics are said to be qualified in a certain way. For the objects of mathematics are abstracted from motion, as is stated in book 6 of this work [1161]. Such objects are numbers and continuous quantities, and of both we use the term "quality." Thus we say that surfaces are qualified as being square or triangular. And similarly numbers are said to be qualified as being compound. Those numbers are said to be compound which have some common number that measures them—for example, the number six and the number nine are measured by the number three, and are not merely referred to one as a common measure. But those which are measured by no common number other than one are called uncompounded or first in their proportion.

990. Numbers are also spoken of as having quality in a metaphor taken from surface and from *solid*, that is, body. They are considered like a surface inasmuch as one number

numerum, vel eumdem vel alium; ut cum dicitur bis tria, vel ter tria. Et hoc est quod dicit *quoties quanti*. Nam designatur quasi una dimensio in hoc quod dicitur *tria*, quasi vero secunda dimensio, hoc quod dicitur *bis tria*, vel etiam *ter tria*.

991. Ad imitationem vero solidi, quando est duplex ductus, vel eiusdem numeri in seipsum, vel diversorum numerorum in unum, ut cum dicitur ter tria ter, vel bis tria bis, vel bis tria quater. Et hoc est quod dicit *quoties quot quanti*. Sic enim considerantur in numero quasi tres dimensiones ad modum solidi. In hac autem numerorum ordinatione, aliquid consideratur per modum substantiae; sicut hoc quod dico tria, vel quicumque numerus qui in alium ducitur. Aliquid vero per modum quantitatis; sicut ipse ductus unius numeri in alterum, vel in se ipsum; ut cum dico bis tria, binarius significatur per modum quantitatis mensurantis, ternarius vero per modum substantiae. Id ergo, quod existit in substantia numeri praeter ipsam quantitatem, quae est numeri substantia, dicitur qualitas eius, ut hoc quod significatur per hoc quod dicitur bis vel ter.

992. Alia litera habet *secundum quantitatem*; et tunc substantia numeri dicitur ipse numerus simpliciter prolatus, ut quod dico tria. Quantitas autem secundum quam attenditur eius qualitas, dicitur ipsa multiplicatio numeri in numerum. Et huic concordat litera sequens, quae dicit, quod substantia cuiuslibet numeri est id quod semel dicitur. Sicut substantia senarii est quod dicitur semel sex, non quod dicitur bis tria, vel ter duo: sed hoc pertinet ad eius qualitatem. Dicere enim numerum esse superficialem vel solidum sive quadratum, sive cubicum, significat eum esse qualem. Hic autem modus qualitatis est quarta species in *Praedicamentis* posita.

993. Tertio ponit ibi, *amplius quaecumque* dicit, quod etiam qualitates dicuntur passiones substantiarum mobilium, secundum quas corpora per alterationem mutantur, ut calidum, frigidum, et huiusmodi. Et hic modus pertinet ad tertiam speciem qualitatis in *Praedicamentis* positam.

994. Quartum ponit ibi, *amplius secundum* dicit quod qualitas sive quale dicitur quarto modo secundum quod aliquid disponitur per virtutem et vitium, vel qualitercumque per bonum et malum, sicut per scientiam et ignorantiam, sanitatem et aegritudinem, et huiusmodi. Et haec est prima species qualitatis in *Praedicamentis* posita.

995. Praetermittit autem inter hos modos secundam qualitatis speciem, quia magis comprehenditur sub potentia, cum non significetur nisi ut principium passioni

is multiplied by another, either by the same number or by a different one, as in the phrase "twice three" or "three times three." And this is what he means by *so many times so much*; for something like one dimension is designated by saying *three*, and a sort of second dimension by saying *twice three* or *three times three*.

991. Numbers are considered like a solid when there is a twofold multiplication, either of the same number by itself, or of different numbers by one; as in the expression "three times three times three" or "two times three times two" or "two times three times four." And this is what he means by *so many times so many times so much*. For we treat of three dimensions in a number in somewhat the same way as in a solid, and in this arrangement of numbers there is something which is treated as a substance, like three, or any other number that is multiplied by another. And there is something else which is treated as quantity, as the multiplication of one number by another or by itself. Thus when I say "twice three," the number two is signified after the manner of a measuring quantity, and the number three after the manner of a substance. Therefore, what belongs to the substance of number besides quantity itself, which is the substance of number, is called a quality of it, as what is meant in saying twice or three times.

992. Another text reads *according to quantity*, and then the substance of number is said to be the number itself expressed in an unqualified sense, as "three." And insofar as we consider the quality of a quantity, this is designated by multiplying one number by another. The rest of the text agrees with this, saying that the substance of any number is what it is said to be once. For example, the substance of six is six taken once, and not three taken twice or two taken three times; this pertains to its quality. For to speak of a number in terms of surface or solid, whether square or cubic, is to speak of its quality. And this type of quality is the fourth kind given in the *Categories*.

993. *Again, all the modifications* (1020b8). Then he gives the third sense in which "quality" is used. He says that "quality" also means the modifications of mobile substances according to which bodies are changed through alteration, as heat and cold and accidents of this kind. And this sense of "quality" belongs to the third kind of quality given in the *Categories*.

994. Next he gives the fourth sense in which "quality" is used. He says that "quality" or "qualified" is used in a fourth sense insofar as something is disposed by virtue or vice, or in whatever way it is well or badly disposed, as by knowledge or ignorance, health or sickness, and the like. This is the first kind of quality given in the *Categories*.

995. Now he omits the second of these senses of quality because it is contained rather under "power," since it is signified only as a principle which resists modification. But

resistens; sed propter modum denominandi ponitur in *Praedicamentis* inter species qualitatis. Secundum autem modum essendi magis continetur sub potentia, sicut et supra posuit.

996. Deinde cum dicit *fere vero* reducit quatuor positos modos ad duos; dicens, quod quale dicitur aliquid fere secundum duos modos, inquantum alii duo de quatuor reducuntur ad alios duos. Horum autem unus principalissimus est primus modus, secundum quem differentia substantiae dicitur qualitas, quia per eum aliquid significatur informatum et qualificatum.

997. Et ad hunc modum reducitur qualitas, quae est in numeris, et in mathematicis aliis, sicut quaedam pars. Huiusmodi enim qualitates sunt quasi quaedam differentiae substantiales mathematicorum. Nam ipsa significantur per modum substantiae potius quam alia accidentia, ut in capitulo de quantitate dictum est. Sunt autem huiusmodi qualitates differentiae substantiarum *aut non motarum, aut non inquantum sunt motae*: et hoc dicit, ut ostendat quantum ad propositum non differre, utrum mathematica sint quaedam substantiae per se existentes secundum esse, ut dicebat Plato, a motu separatae; sive sint in substantiis mobilibus secundum esse, sed separatae secundum rationem. Primo enim modo essent qualitates non motorum. Secundo autem, motorum, sed non inquantum sunt mota.

998. Secundus modus principalis est, ut passiones motorum inquantum mota, et etiam differentiae motuum dicantur qualitates. Quae quidem dicuntur differentiae motuum, quia alterationes differunt secundum huiusmodi qualitates, sicut calefieri et infrigidari secundum calidum et frigidum.

999. Et ad hunc modum reducitur ille modus secundum quem vitium et virtus dicitur qualitas. Hic enim modus est quasi quaedam pars illius. Virtus enim et vitium ostendunt quasdam differentias motus et actus secundum bene et male. Nam virtus est, per quam se aliquis habet bene ad agendum et patiendum; vitium autem secundum quod male. Et simile est de aliis habitibus, sive intellectualibus, ut scientia, sive corporalibus, ut sanitas.

1000. Sed tamen bene et male maxime pertinet ad qualitatem in rebus animatis; et praecipue in habentibus *prohaeresim* idest electionem. Et hoc ideo, quia bonum habet rationem finis. Ea vero, quae agunt per electionem, agunt propter finem. Agere autem propter finem maxime competit rebus animatis. Res enim inanimatae agunt vel moventur propter finem, non tamquam cognoscentes finem, neque tamquam se agentes ad finem; sed potius ab alio diriguntur, qui eis naturalem inclina-

it is given in the *Categories* among the kinds of quality because of the way in which it is named. However, according to its mode of being it is contained rather under power, as he also held above [960].

996. *The senses of quality* (1020b13). Then he reduces the four senses of "quality" so far given to two, saying that a thing is said to be qualified in a certain way in two senses, inasmuch as two of these four senses are reduced to the other two. The most basic of these senses is the first one, according to which "quality" means substantial difference, because by means of it a thing is designated as being informed and qualified.

997. The quality found in numbers and in other objects of mathematics is reduced to this as a part. For qualities of this kind are in a sense the substantial differences of mathematical objects, because they are signified after the manner of substance to a greater degree than the other accidents, as was stated in the chapter on quantity [980]. Further, qualities of this kind constitute substantial differences, *either of things that are not moved or of things not insofar as they are moved*. He says this in order to show that it makes no difference to his thesis whether the objects of mathematics are self-subsistent substances, as Plato claimed, and are separate from motion, or whether they exist in substances which are mobile in reality but separate in thought. For in the first sense they would not be qualities of things that are moved; but in the second sense they would be, but not inasmuch as they are moved.

998. The second basic sense in which "quality" is used is that in which the modifications of things that are moved as such, and also the differences of things that are moved, are called qualities. They are called the differences of motions because alterations differ in terms of such qualities, as becoming hot and becoming cold differ in terms of heat and cold.

999. The sense in which virtue and vice are called qualities is reduced to this last sense, for it is in a way a part of this sense. For "virtue" and "vice" indicate certain differences of motion and activity based on good or bad performance. For virtue is that by which a thing is well disposed to act or be acted upon, and vice is that by which a thing is badly disposed. The same is true of other habits, whether they are intellectual, like science, or bodily, like health.

1000. But the terms "well" and "badly" relate chiefly to quality in living things, and especially in those having *election*, that is, choice. And this is true because good has the role of an end or goal. So those things that act by choice act for an end. Now to act for an end belongs particularly to living things. For non-living things act or are moved for an end not inasmuch as they know the end, or inasmuch as they themselves act for an end, but rather inasmuch as they are directed by something else which gives them their

tionem dedit, sicut sagitta dirigitur in finem a sagittante. Res autem irrationales animatae cognoscunt quidem finem et appetunt ipsum appetitu animali, et movent seipsa localiter ad finem tamquam iudicium habentes de fine; sed appetitus finis, et eorum quae sunt propter finem, determinatur eis ex naturali inclinatione. Propter quod sunt magis acta quam agentia. Unde nec in eis est iudicium liberum. Rationalia vero in quibus solum est electio, cognoscunt finem, et proportionem eorum, quae sunt in finem ipsum. Et ideo sicut seipsa movent ad finem, ita etiam ad appetendum finem, vel ea quae sunt propter finem, ex quo est in eis electio libera.

natural inclination, just as an arrow is directed toward its goal by an archer. And non-rational living things apprehend an end or goal and desire it by an appetite of the soul, and they move locally toward some end or goal inasmuch as they have discernment of it; but their appetite for an end, and for those things that exist for the sake of the end, is determined for them by a natural inclination. Hence they are acted upon rather than act, and thus their judgment is not free. But rational beings, in whom alone choice exists, know both the end and the proportion of the means to the end. Therefore, just as they move themselves toward the end, so also do they move themselves to desire the end and the means; for this reason they have free choice.

LECTURE 17

The definition of "relative"

1020b26 Ad aliquid dicuntur alia per se, ut duplum ad dimidium, et triplum ad tertiam partem, et totaliter multiplicatum ad multiplicati partem, et continens ad contentum. Alia ut calefactivum ad calefactibile, et sectivum ad secabile, et omne activum ad passivum. Alia ut mensurabile ad mensuram, et scibile ad scientiam, et sensibile ad sensum. [1001]

πρός τι λέγεται τὰ μὲν ὡς διπλάσιον πρὸς ἥμισυ καὶ τριπλάσιον πρὸς τριτημόριον, καὶ ὅλως πολλαπλάσιον πρὸς πολλοστημόριον καὶ ὑπερέχον πρὸς ὑπερεχόμενον· τὰ δ᾽ ὡς τὸ θερμαντικὸν πρὸς τὸ θερμαντὸν καὶ τὸ τμητικὸν πρὸς τὸ {30} τμητόν, καὶ ὅλως τὸ ποιητικὸν πρὸς τὸ παθητικόν· τὰ δ᾽ ὡς τὸ μετρητὸν πρὸς τὸ μέτρον καὶ ἐπιστητὸν πρὸς ἐπιστήμην καὶ αἰσθητὸν πρὸς αἴσθησιν.

Some things are said to be relative directly, as double to half and triple to a third part. And in general what is multiplied to a part of what is multiplied, and what includes to what is included in it. And in another sense, as what heats to what can be heated, and what cuts to what can be cut. And in general everything active to everything passive. And in another sense as what is measurable to a measure, and what is knowable to knowledge, and what is sensible to sense.

1020b32 Dicuntur autem prima quidem secundum numerum, aut simpliciter, aut determinate ad eos, aut ad unum, ut duplum ad dimidium, ut numerus determinatus. [1006]

λέγεται δὲ τὰ μὲν πρῶτα κατ᾽ ἀριθμὸν ἢ ἁπλῶς ἢ ὡρισμένως, πρὸς αὐτοὺς ἢ πρὸς ἕν (οἷον τὸ μὲν διπλάσιον πρὸς ἕν ἀριθμὸς ὡρισμένος,

The first things that are said to be relative numerically are such either without qualification, or in some definite relation to them, or to unity, as double is related to half as a definite number.

Multiplex vero secundum numerum ad unum, sed non determianatum, ut hunc aut hunc. Sed hemiolum ad subhemiolum, secundum numerum ad numerum determinatum.

τὸ δὲ πολλαπλάσιον {35} κατ᾽ ἀριθμὸν πρὸς ἕν, οὐχ ὡρισμένον δέ, οἷον τόνδε ἢ τόνδε· {1021a1} τὸ δὲ ἡμιόλιον πρὸς τὸ ὑφημιόλιον κατ᾽ ἀριθμὸν πρὸς ἀριθμὸν ὡρισμένον·

And the multiple is related numerically to the unit, but not in a definite numerical relation such as this or that. But what is one and a half times as great as something else is related to it in a definite numerical relation to a number.

Et superparticulare ad subparticulare secundum indeterminatum, ut multiplex ad numerum. Continens autem ad contentum omnino indeterminatum secundum numerum: numerus enim commensurabilis. Secundum non commensurabilem autem numerum dicuntur.

τὸ δ᾽ ἐπιμόριον πρὸς τὸ ὑπεπιμόριον κατὰ ἀόριστον, ὥσπερ τὸ πολλαπλάσιον πρὸς τὸ ἕν· τὸ δ᾽ ὑπερέχον πρὸς τὸ ὑπερεχόμενον ὅλως ἀόριστον κατ᾽ ἀριθμόν· {5} ὁ γὰρ ἀριθμὸς σύμμετρος, κατὰ μὴ συμμέτρου δὲ ἀριθμὸς οὐ λέγεται,

And the superparticular is related to the subparticular in an indefinite relation, as what is multiple is related to a number. And what includes is related to what is included in it as something altogether indefinite in number, for number is commensurable.

Continens enim ad contentum tantum quid est, et amplius; sed hoc indeterminatum. Quodcumque enim evenit, aut aequale est, aut non aequale. Haec igitur ad aliquid omnia secundum numerum dicuntur, et numeri passiones.

τὸ δὲ ὑπερέχον πρὸς τὸ ὑπερεχόμενον τοσοῦτόν τέ ἐστι καὶ ἔτι, τοῦτο δ᾽ ἀόριστον· ὁπότερον γὰρ ἔτυχέν ἐστιν, ἢ ἴσον ἢ οὐκ ἴσον)· ταῦτά τε οὖν τὰ πρός τι πάντα κατ᾽ ἀριθμὸν λέγεται καὶ ἀριθμοῦ πάθη,

For what includes is related to what is included in it according to so much and something more; but this something more is indefinite. For whatever the case may be, it is either equal or not equal to it. Therefore, all these relations are said to be numerical and are properties of number.

1021a9 Et amplius aequale et simile, et idem secundum alium modum. Haec enim secundum unum dicuntur omnia. Eadem namque quorum una est substantia. Similia vero quorum qualitas est una. Aequalia vero quorum quantitas

καὶ ἔτι τὸ ἴσον καὶ {10} ὅμοιον καὶ ταὐτὸ κατ᾽ ἄλλον τρόπον (κατὰ γὰρ τὸ ἕν λέγεται πάντα, ταὐτὰ μὲν γὰρ ὧν μία ἡ οὐσία, ὅμοια δ᾽ ὧν ἡ ποιότης μία, ἴσα δὲ ὧν τὸ ποσὸν ἕν· τὸ δ᾽ ἕν τοῦ ἀριθμοῦ ἀρχὴ καὶ μέτρον, ὥστε ταῦτα πάντα

Further, "equal," "like," and "same" are said to be relative, but in a different way, because all these terms are referred to unity. For those things are the same whose substance is one; and those are alike whose quality is one; and those are

est una. Unum vero est numeri principium et metrum. Quare ea omnia dicuntur ad aliquid secundum numerum quidem, non tamen eodem modo. [1022]

πρός τι λέγεται κατ' ἀριθμὸν μέν, οὐ τὸν αὐτὸν δὲ τρόπον):

equal whose quantity is one. And unity is the principle and measure of number. Hence all these are said to be relative numerically, yet not in the same way.

1021a14 Activa vero et passiva secundum potentiam activam et passivam sunt, et actiones potentiarum; [1023]

τὰ δὲ {15} ποιητικὰ καὶ παθητικὰ κατὰ δύναμιν ποιητικὴν καὶ παθητικὴν καὶ ἐνεργείας τὰς τῶν δυνάμεων,

Active and passive things are relative in virtue of active and passive potencies and the operations of potencies;

ut calefactivum ad calefactibile, quia potest; et iterum calefaciens ad calefactum, et secans ad sectum, tamquam agentia.

οἷον τὸ θερμαντικὸν πρὸς τὸ θερμαντὸν ὅτι δύναται, καὶ πάλιν τὸ θερμαῖνον πρὸς τὸ θερμαινόμενον καὶ τὸ τέμνον πρὸς τὸ τεμνόμενον ὡς ἐνεργοῦντα.

for example, what can heat is relative to what can be heated, because it can heat it; and what is heating is relative to what is being heated; and what is cutting to what is being cut, inasmuch as they are doing these things.

Eorum vero, quae sunt secundum numerum, non sunt actiones, nisi quemadmodum in aliis dictum est: quae autem secundum motum, actiones non existunt. Istorum autem, quae secundum potentiam et secundum tempus iam dicuntur ad aliquid, ut faciens ad quod fit, et facturum ad faciendum.

τῶν δὲ κατ' ἀριθμὸν οὐκ εἰσὶν ἐνέργειαι ἀλλ' {20} ἢ ὃν τρόπον ἐν ἑτέροις εἴρηται: αἱ δὲ κατὰ κίνησιν ἐνέργειαι οὐχ ὑπάρχουσιν. τῶν δὲ κατὰ δύναμιν καὶ κατὰ χρόνους ἤδη λέγονται πρός τι οἷον τὸ πεποιηκὸς πρὸς τὸ πεποιημένον καὶ τὸ ποιῆσον πρὸς τὸ ποιησόμενον.

But of those things that are relative numerically there are no operations, except in the sense stated elsewhere; and operations which imply motion are not found in them. Moreover, of things that are relative potentially, some are said to be relative temporally also, as what makes to what is made, and what will make to what will be made.

Sic enim pater, filii dicitur pater: hoc quidem enim fecit, illud autem passum quid est. Amplius quaedam secundum privationem potentiae, ut impossibile, et quaecumque sic dicuntur, ut invisibile.

οὕτω γὰρ καὶ πατὴρ υἱοῦ λέγεται πατήρ: τὸ μὲν γὰρ πεποιηκὸς τὸ δὲ πεπονθός {25} τί ἐστιν. ἔτι ἔνια κατὰ στέρησιν δυνάμεως, ὥσπερ τὸ ἀδύνατον καὶ ὅσα οὕτω λέγεται, οἷον τὸ ἀόρατον.

For in this way a father is said to be the father of his son, because the former has acted, whereas the latter has been acted upon. Again, some things are said to be relative according to the privation of potency—for example, "the incapable" and other terms used in this way, as "the invisible."

1021a26 Ergo secundum numerum et potentiam dicta ad aliquid, omnia sunt ad aliquid, eo quod ipsum, quod est alterius dicitur quid est, sed non eo quod aliud ad aliud. [1026]

τὰ μὲν οὖν κατ' ἀριθμὸν καὶ δύναμιν λεγόμενα πρός τι πάντα ἐστὶ πρός τι τῷ ὅπερ ἐστὶν ἄλλου λέγεσθαι αὐτὸ ὅ ἐστιν, ἀλλὰ μὴ τῷ ἄλλο πρὸς ἐκεῖνο:

Therefore, things that are said to be relative numerically and potentially are all relative because the subject of the reference is itself referred to something else, not because something else is referred to it.

Mensurabile vero et scibile, et intellectuale, eo quod aliud dicitur ad ipsum, ad aliquid dicuntur, sed non eo, quod illa ad aliud. Nam intellectuale significat quod ipsius est intellectus.

τὸ δὲ μετρητὸν καὶ τὸ ἐπιστητὸν καὶ τὸ {30} διανοητὸν τῷ ἄλλο πρὸς αὐτὸ λέγεσθαι πρός τι λέγονται. τό τε γὰρ διανοητὸν σημαίνει ὅτι ἔστιν αὐτοῦ διάνοια,

But what is measurable and knowable and thinkable are said to be relative because in each case something else is referred to them, not because they are referred to something else. For by "what is thinkable" is meant that of which there may be a thought.

Non est autem intellectus ad hoc cuius est intellectus. Bis enim idem diceretur.

οὐκ ἔστι δ' ἡ διάνοια πρὸς τοῦτο οὗ ἐστι διάνοια (δὶς γὰρ ταὐτὸν εἰρημένον ἂν εἴη),

However, a thought is not relative to the one whose thought it is, for then the same thing would be expressed twice.

Et similiter alicuius visus est visus, et non cuius est visus, quamvis sit verum hoc dicere; sed ad colorem, aut ad aliquid tale.

ὁμοίως δὲ καὶ τινός ἐστιν ἡ ὄψις ὄψις, οὐχ οὗ ἐστὶν ὄψις (καίτοι γ' ἀληθὲς τοῦτο εἰπεῖν) ἀλλὰ πρὸς χρῶμα ἢ πρὸς ἄλλο τι τοιοῦτον.

And similarly sight is relative to that of which it is the sight and not to the one whose sight it is (although it is true to say this); but it is relative to color or to something of this sort.

Illo vero modo bis diceretur, quia est visus cuius est visus. Ergo secundum se dicta ad aliquid, sic dicuntur.

1021b4 Illa vero, quia sua genera sunt talia, ut medicina ad aliquid, quia suum genus scientia videtur aliquid esse. Amplius quaecumque secundum habentia dicuntur ad aliquid; ut aequalitas, quia aequale, et similitudo, quia simile. [1030]

1021b8 Alia vero secundum accidens: ut homo ad aliquid, quia ei accidit duplum esse, et hoc est ad aliquid; ut album, quia ei accidit album et duplum esse. [1032]

ἐκείνως δὲ δὶς τὸ αὐτὸ λεχθήσεται, ὅτι ἐστὶν οὗ ἐστὶν ἡ ὄψις. {1021b1} τὰ μὲν οὖν καθ᾽ ἑαυτὰ λεγόμενα πρός τι τὰ μὲν οὕτω λέγεται,

τὰ δὲ ἂν τὰ {5} γένη αὐτῶν ᾖ τοιαῦτα, οἷον ἡ ἰατρικὴ τῶν πρός τι ὅτι τὸ γένος αὐτῆς ἡ ἐπιστήμη δοκεῖ εἶναι πρός τι· ἔτι καθ᾽ ὅσα τὰ ἔχοντα λέγεται πρός τι, οἷον ἰσότης ὅτι τὸ ἴσον καὶ ὁμοιότης ὅτι τὸ ὅμοιον·

τὰ δὲ κατὰ συμβεβηκός, οἷον ἄνθρωπος πρός τι ὅτι συμβέβηκεν αὐτῷ διπλασίῳ εἶναι, {10} τοῦτο δ᾽ ἐστὶ τῶν πρός τι· ἢ τὸ λευκόν, εἰ τῷ αὐτῷ συμβέβηκε διπλασίῳ καὶ λευκῷ εἶναι.

But then the same thing would be said twice: that sight is of the one whose sight it is. Things that are said to be relative directly, then, are spoken of in this way.

And other things are said to be relative because their genera are such; for example, medicine is relative because its genus, science, seems to be relative. Furthermore, of this type are all things that are said to be relative by reason of their subject; for example, equality is said to be relative because equal is relative, and likeness, because like is relative.

But other things are said to be relative indirectly, as man is relative because he happens to be double, and this is relative; or the white is said to be relative because the same thing happens to be white and double.

1001. Hic determinat Philosophus de ad aliquid: et circa hoc duo facit.

Primo ponit modos eorum, quae sunt ad aliquid secundum se.

Secundo eorum, quae sunt ad aliquid ratione alterius, ibi, *illa vero quia sua genera*.

Circa primum duo facit.

Primo enumerat modos eorum, quae secundum se ad aliquid dicuntur.

Secundo prosequitur de eis, ibi, *dicuntur autem prima*.

Ponit ergo tres modos eorum, quae ad aliquid dicuntur:

quorum primus est secundum numerum et quantitatem, sicut duplum ad dimidium, et triplum ad tertiam partem, et *multiplicatum*, idest multiplex, ad partem *multiplicati*, idest ad submultiplex, *et continens ad contentum*. Accipitur autem continens pro eo, quod excedit secundum quantitatem. Omne enim excedens secundum quantitatem continet in se illud quod exceditur. Est enim hoc et adhuc amplius; sicut quinque continet in se quatuor, et tricubitum continet in se bicubitum.

1002. Secundus modus est prout aliqua dicuntur ad aliquid secundum actionem et passionem, vel potentiam activam et passivam; sicut calefactivum ad calefactibile, quod pertinet ad actiones naturales, et sectivum ad sectibile, quod pertinet ad actiones artificiales, et universaliter omne activum ad passivum.

1003. Tertius modus est secundum quod mensurabile dicitur ad mensuram. Accipitur autem hic mensura et mensurabile non secundum quantitatem (hoc

1001. Here the Philosopher establishes the meaning of the "relative" or "relation," and in regard to this he does two things.

First, he gives the senses in which things are said to be relative directly;

second (1021b4; [1030]), those in which things are said to be relative indirectly, at *and other things*.

In regard to the first he does two things.

First, he enumerates the senses in which things are said to be relative directly.

Second (1020b32; [1006]), he proceeds to deal with these, at *the first things*.

He accordingly first gives three senses in which things are said to be relative directly.

The first of these has to do with number and quantity, as double to half and triple to a third, and *what is multiplied*, that is, the multiple, to a part *of what is multiplied*, the submultiple, *and what includes to what is included in it*. But what includes is here taken for what is greater in quantity. For everything which is greater in quantity includes within itself that which it exceeds. For it is this and something more: for example, five includes within itself four, and three cubits include two.

1002. The second sense is that in which some things are said to be relative according to action and passion, or to active and passive potency. For example, in the realm of natural actions, as what can heat to what can be heated; in the realm of artificial actions, as what can cut to what can be cut; and in general as everything active to everything passive.

1003. The third sense of "relation" is that in which something measurable is said to be relative to a measure. Here "measure" and "measurable" are not taken quantitatively

enim ad primum modum pertinet, in quo utrumque ad utrumque dicitur: nam duplum dicitur ad dimidium, et dimidium ad duplum), sed secundum mensurationem esse et veritatis.

Veritas enim scientiae mensuratur a scibili. Ex eo enim quod res est vel non est, oratio scita vera vel falsa est, et non e converso. Et similiter est de sensibili et sensu.

Et propter hoc non mutuo dicuntur mensura ad mensurabile et e converso, sicut in aliis modis, sed solum mensurabile ad mensuram. Et similiter etiam imago dicitur ad id cuius est imago, tamquam mensurabile ad mensuram. Veritas enim imaginis mensuratur ex re cuius est imago.

1004. Ratio autem istorum modorum haec est. Cum enim relatio, quae est in rebus, consistat in ordine quodam unius rei ad aliam, oportet tot modis huiusmodi relationes esse, quot modis contingit unam rem ad aliam ordinari. Ordinatur autem una res ad aliam, vel secundum esse, prout esse unius rei dependet ab alia, et sic est tertius modus. Vel secundum virtutem activam et passivam, secundum quod una res ab alia recipit, vel alteri confert aliquid; et sic est secundus modus. Vel secundum quod quantitas unius rei potest mensurari per aliam; et sic est primus modus.

1005. Qualitas autem rei, inquantum huiusmodi, non respicit nisi subiectum in quo est. Unde secundum ipsam una res non ordinatur ad aliam, nisi secundum quod qualitas accipit rationem potentiae passivae vel activae, prout est principium actionis vel passionis. Vel ratione quantitatis, vel alicuius ad quantitatem pertinentis; sicut dicitur aliquid albius alio, vel sicut dicitur simile, quod habet unam aliquam qualitatem. Alia vero genera magis consequuntur relationem, quam possint relationem causare. Nam quando consistit in aliquali relatione ad tempus. Ubi vero, ad locum. Positio autem ordinem partium importat. Habitus autem relationem habentis ad habitum.

1006. Deinde cum dicit *dicuntur autem* prosequitur tres modos enumeratos;

et primo prosequitur primum.
Secundo prosequitur secundum, ibi, *activa vero et passiva*.
Tertio tertium, ibi, *ergo secundum numerum*.

Circa primum duo facit.
Primo ponit relationes quae consequuntur numerum absolute.

(for this pertains to the first sense, in which either one is said to be relative to the other, since double is said to be relative to half and half to double), but according to the measurement of being and truth.

For the truth of knowledge is measured by the knowable object. For it is because a thing is so or is not so that a statement is known to be true or false, and not the reverse. The same thing applies in the case of a sensible object and sensation.

And for this reason a measure and what is measurable are not said to be related to each other reciprocally, as in the other senses, but only what is measurable is related to its measure. And in a similar fashion too an image is related to that of which it is the image as what is measurable is related to its measure. For the truth of an image is measured by the thing whose image it is.

1004. These senses are explained as follows. Since a real relation consists in the bearing of one thing upon another, there must be as many relations of this kind as there are ways in which one thing can bear upon another. Now one thing bears upon another either in being, inasmuch as the being of one thing depends on another, and then we have the third sense; or according to active or passive power, inasmuch as one thing receives something from another or confers it upon the other, and then we have the second sense; or according as the quantity of one thing can be measured by another, and then we have the first sense.

1005. But the "quality" as such of a thing pertains only to the subject in which it exists. Therefore, from the viewpoint of quality, one thing bears upon another only inasmuch as quality has the character of an active or passive power, which is a principle of action or of being acted upon. Or it is related by reason of quantity or of something pertaining to quantity, as one thing is said to be whiter than another, or as that which has the same quality as another is said to be like it. But the other genera of things are a result of relation rather than a cause of it. For the category "when" consists in a relation to time, and the category "where" in a relation to place. And "posture" implies an arrangement of parts, and "having," the relation of the thing having to the things had.

1006. *The first things* (1020b32). Then he proceeds to deal with the three senses of "relation" which have been enumerated.

First, he considers the first sense.
Second (1021a14; [1023]), he treats the second sense, at *active and passive*.
Third (1021a26; [1026]), he attends to the third sense, at *therefore, things*.
In regard to the first he does two things.
First, he describes the relations which are based simply on number;

Secundo ponit relationes quae consequuntur unitatem absolute, ibi, *et amplius aequale*.

Dicit ergo, quod primus modus relationum, qui est secundum numerum, distinguitur hoc modo: quia vel est secundum comparationem numeri ad numerum, vel numeri ad unum. Et secundum comparationem ad utrumque dupliciter: quia vel est secundum comparationem numeri indeterminate ad numerum, aut ad unum determinate. Et hoc est quod dicit, quod prima, quae dicuntur ad aliquid secundum numerum, aut dicuntur *simpliciter*, idest universaliter, vel indeterminate, aut determinate. Et utrolibet modo *ad eos*, scilicet numeros. *Aut ad unum*, idest ad unitatem.

1007. Sciendum est autem, quod omnis mensuratio, quae est in quantitatibus continuis, aliquo modo derivatur a numero. Et ideo relationes, quae sunt secundum quantitatem continuam, etiam attribuuntur numero.

1008. Sciendum est etiam, quod proportio numeralis dividitur primo in duas; scilicet aequalitatis, et inaequalitatis. Inaequalitatis autem sunt duae species; scilicet excedens et excessum, et magis et minus. Inaequale autem excedens in quinque species dividitur.

1009. Numerus enim maior quandoque respectu minoris est multiplex; quando scilicet aliquoties continet ipsum, sicut sex continet duo ter. Et si quidem contineat ipsum bis, dicitur duplum; sicut duo ad unum vel quatuor ad duo. Si ter, triplum. Si quater, quadruplum. Et sic inde.

1010. Quandoque vero numerus maior continet totum numerum minorem semel, et insuper unam aliquam partem eius. Et tunc dicitur superparticularis. Et si quidem contineat totum et medium, vocatur sesquialterum, sicut tria ad duo. Si autem tertiam, sesquitertius, sicut quatuor ad tria. Si quartam, sesquiquartus, sicut quinque ad quatuor. Et sic inde.

1011. Quandoque numerus maior continet minorem totum semel; et insuper non solum unam partem, sed plures partes. Et sic dicitur superpartiens. Et si quidem contineat duas partes, dicitur superbipartiens, sicut quinque se habent ad tria. Si vero tres, dicitur supertripartiens, sicut septem se habent ad quatuor. Si autem quatuor, sic est superquadripartiens; et sic se habet novem ad quinque. Et sic inde.

1012. Quandoque vero numerus maior continet totum minorem pluries, et insuper aliquam partem eius; et tunc dicitur multiplex superparticularis. Et si quidem contineat ipsum bis et mediam partem eius, dicitur duplum sesquialterum, sicut quinque ad duo. Si autem ter et mediam partem eius, vocabitur triplum sesquialterum, sicut se habent septem ad duo. Si autem quater et dimidiam partem eius, dicitur quadruplum sesquialterum, sicut novem ad duo. Possent etiam ex

second (1021a9; [1022]), he treats those which are based simply on unity, at *further, "equal."*

He first says that the first way in which things are relative, which is numerical, is divided inasmuch as the relation is based on the ratio of one number to another or on that of a number to unity. And in either case it may be taken in two ways, for the number which is referred to another number or to unity in the ratio on which the relation is based is either definite or indefinite. This is his meaning in saying that the first things that are said to be relative numerically are said to be such *without qualification*, that is, in general or indefinitely, *or in some definite relation to them*. And in both ways *to them*, namely, to numbers, *or to unity*, that is, to the unit.

1007. Now it should be borne in mind that every measure which is found in continuous quantities is derived in some way from number. Hence relations which are based on continuous quantity are also attributed to number.

1008. It should also be borne in mind that numerical ratios are divided first into two species, that of equality and that of inequality. And there are two species of inequality: the larger and smaller, and the more and less. And the larger is divided into five species.

1009. For a number is larger whenever it is multiple with respect to a smaller number, when it includes it many times, as six includes two three times. And if it includes it twice, it is called double, as two in relation to one, or four to two. And if it includes it three times, it is called triple; if four times, quadruple, and so on.

1010. But sometimes a larger number includes a whole smaller number once and some part of it besides, and then it is said to be superparticular. If it includes a whole smaller number and a half of it besides, it is called sesquialteral, as three to two; and if a third part besides, it is called sesquitertian, as four to three; and if a fourth part besides, it is called sesquiquartan, as five to four; and so on.

1011. Sometimes a larger number includes a whole smaller number once and not merely one part but many parts besides, and then it is called superpartient. And if it includes two parts, it is called superbipartient, as five to three. Again, if it includes three parts, then it is called supertripartient, as seven to four; and if it includes four parts, it is superquadripartient, and then it is related as nine to five; and so on.

1012. Sometimes a larger number includes a whole smaller number many times and some part of it besides, and then it is called multiple superparticular. If it includes it two and a half times, it is called double sesquialteral, as five to two. If it includes it three and a half times, it is called triple sesquialteral, as seven to two. And if it includes it four and a half times, it is called quadruple sesquialteral, as nine to two. And the species of this kind of ratio can also be considered in the case of the superparticular, inasmuch as

parte superparticularis huiusmodi proportionis species sumi, ut dicatur duplex sesquitertius, quando maior numerus habet minorem bis et tertiam partem eius, sicut se habent septem ad tria: vel duplex sesquiquartus, sicut novem ad quatuor, et sic de aliis.

1013. Quandoque etiam numerus maior habet minorem totum pluries, et etiam plures partes eius, et tunc dicitur multiplex superpartiens. Et similiter proportio potest dividi secundum species multiplicitatis, et secundum species superpartientis, si dicatur duplum superbipartiens, quando habet maior numerus totum minorem bis et duas partes eius, sicut octo ad tria. Vel etiam triplum superbipartiens, sicut undecim ad tres. Vel etiam duplum supertripartiens, sicut undecim ad quatuor. Habet enim totum bis, et tres partes eius.

1014. Et totidem species sunt ex parte inaequalitatis eius qui exceditur. Nam numerus minor dicitur submultiplex, subparticularis, subpartiens, submultiplex subparticularis, submultiplex subpartiens, et sic de aliis.

1015. Sciendum autem quod prima species proportionis, scilicet multiplicitas, consistit in comparatione unius numeri ad unitatem. Quaelibet enim eius species invenitur primo in aliquo numero respectu unitatis. Duplum primo invenitur in binario respectu unitatis. Et similiter proportio tripli in ternario respectu unitatis, et sic de aliis. Primi autem termini in quibus invenitur aliqua proportio, dant speciem ipsi proportioni. Unde in quibuscumque aliis terminis consequenter inveniatur, invenitur in eis secundum rationem primorum terminorum. Sicut proportio dupla primo invenitur inter duo et unum. Unde ex hoc proportio recipit rationem et nomen. Dicitur enim proportio dupla proportio duorum ad unum.

Et propter hoc, si etiam unus numerus respectu alterius numeri sit duplus, tamen hoc est secundum quod minor numerus accipit rationem unius, et maior rationem duorum. Sex enim se habet in dupla proportione ad tria, inquantum tria se habent ad sex ut unum ad duo. Et simile est in tripla proportione, et in omnibus aliis speciebus multiplicitatis. Et ideo dicit, quod ista relatio dupli, est per hoc quod numerus determinatus, scilicet duo, *refertur ad unum*, idest ad unitatem.

1016. Sed hoc quod dico, multiplex, importat relationem numeri ad unitatem; sed non alicuius determinati numeri, sed numeri in universali. Si enim determinatus numerus accipiatur ut binarius vel ternarius, esset una species multiplicitatis, ut dupla vel tripla. Sicut autem duplum se habet ad duo, et triplum ad tria, quae sunt numeri determinati, ita multiplex ad multiplicitatem, quia significat numerum indeterminatum.

we speak of the double sesquitertian ratio when a greater number includes a smaller number two and a third times, as seven to three; or of the double sesquiquartan, as nine to four (and so on).

1013. Sometimes too a larger number includes a whole smaller number many times and many parts of it besides, and then it is called multiple superpartient. And similarly a ratio can be divided from the viewpoint of the species of multiplicity, and from that of the species of the superpartient, provided that we may speak of a double superbipartient, when a greater number includes a whole smaller number twice and two parts of it, as eight to three; or even of triple superbipartient, as eleven to three; or even of double supertripartient, as eleven to four. For it includes a whole number twice and three parts of it besides.

1014. And there are just as many species of inequality in the case of a smaller number. For a smaller number is called submultiple, subpartient, submultiple superparticular, submultiple superpartient, and so on.

1015. But it must be noted that the first species of ratio—namely, multiplicity—consists in the relation of one number to the unit. For any species of it is found first in the relation of some number to the unit. Double, for example, is found first in the relation of two to the unit. And similarly a triple ratio is found in the relation of three to the unit, and so on in other cases. But the first terms in which any ratio is found give species to the ratio itself. Hence in whatever other terms it is subsequently found, it is found in them according to the ratio of the first terms. For example, the double ratio is found first between two and the unit. It is from this, then, that the ratio receives its meaning and name, for a double ratio means the ratio of two to the unit.

And it is for this reason too that we use the term in other cases; for even though one number is said to be double another, this happens only inasmuch as a smaller number takes on the role of the unit and a larger number the role of two, for six is related to three in a double ratio inasmuch as six is to three as two is to one. And it is similar in the case of a triple ratio, and in all other species of multiplicity. Hence he says that the relation of double is a result of the fact that a definite number, two, *is referred to unity*, to the unit.

1016. But the term "multiple" implies the relation of a number to the unit, not of any definite number, but of number in general. For if a definite number were taken, as two or three, there would be one species of multiplicity, as double or triple. And just as the double is related to two and the triple to three, which are definite numbers, so too the multiple is related to multiplicity, because it signifies an indefinite number.

1017. Aliae autem proportiones non possunt attendi secundum numerum ad unitatem, scilicet neque proportio superparticularis, neque superpartiens, neque multiplex superparticularis, neque multiplex superpartiens. Omnes enim hae proportionum species attenduntur secundum quod maior numerus continet minorem semel, vel aliquoties; et insuper unam vel plures partes eius. Unitas autem partem habere non potest: et ideo nulla harum proportionum potest attendi secundum comparationem numeri ad unitatem, sed secundum comparationem numeri ad numerum. Et sic est duplex, vel secundum numerum determinatum, vel secundum numerum indeterminatum.

1018. Si autem secundum numerum determinatum, sic *est hemiolum*, idest sesquialterum, aut *subhemiolum*, idest supersesquialterum. Proportio enim sesquialtera primo consistit in his terminis, scilicet ternario et binario; et sub ratione eorum in omnibus aliis invenitur. Unde quod dicitur hemiolum vel sesquialterum importat relationem determinati numeri ad determinatum numerum, scilicet trium ad duo.

1019. Quod vero dicitur superparticulare, refertur ad subparticulare, non secundum determinatos numeros, sicut etiam multiplex refertur ad unum, sed secundum numerum indeterminatum. Primae enim species inaequalitatis superius numeratae accipiuntur secundum indeterminatos numeros, ut multiplex, superparticulare, superpartiens et cetera. Species vero istorum accipiuntur secundum numeros determinatos, ut duplum, triplum, sesquialterum, sesquitertium, et sic de aliis.

1020. Contingit enim aliquas quantitates continuas habere proportionem adinvicem, sed non secundum aliquem numerum, nec determinatum, nec indeterminatum. Omnium enim quantitatum continuarum est aliqua proportio; non tamen est proportio numeralis. Quorumlibet enim duorum numerorum est una mensura communis, scilicet unitas, quae aliquoties sumpta, quemlibet numerum reddit. Non autem quarumlibet quantitatum continuarum invenitur esse una mensura communis; sed sunt quaedam quantitates continuae incommensurabiles: sicut diameter quadrati est incommensurabilis lateri. Et hoc ideo, quia non est proportio eius ad latus, sicut proportio numeri ad numerum, vel numeri ad unum.

1021. Cum ergo dicitur in quantitatibus, quod haec est maior illa, vel se habet ad illam ut continens ad contentum, non solum haec ratio non attenditur secundum aliquam determinatam speciem numeri, sed nec etiam quod sit secundum numerum, quia omnis numerus est alteri commensurabilis. Omnes enim numeri habent unam communem mensuram, scilicet unitatem.

1017. Other ratios, however, cannot be reduced to the relation of a number to the unit: either a superparticular ratio, or a superpartient, or a multiple superparticular, or a multiple superpartient. For all of these species of ratios are based on the fact that a larger number includes a smaller number once, or some part of it, and one or several parts of it besides. But the unit cannot have a part, and therefore none of these ratios can be based on the relation of a number to the unit but on the relation of one number to another. Thus the double ratio is either that of a definite number or that of an indefinite number.

1018. And if it is that of a definite number, then *it is what is one and a half times as great*, that is, sesquialteral, or *that which it exceeds*, supersesquialteral. For a sesquialteral ratio consists first in the terms three and two, and it is found in all other cases in the ratio of these. Hence what is called one and a half times as great, or sesquialteral, implies the relation of one definite number to another—namely, of three to two.

1019. But the relation which is called superparticular is relative to the subparticular not according to any definite number, as the multiple is relative also to the unit, but according to an indefinite number. For the first species of inequality given above [1008] are taken according to indefinite numbers—for example, the multiple, superparticular, superpartient, and so on. But the species of these are taken according to definite numbers, as double, triple, sesquialteral, sesquiquartan, and so on.

1020. Now it happens that some continuous quantities have a ratio to each other which does not involve any number, either definite or indefinite. For there is some ratio between all continuous quantities, although it is not a numerical ratio. For there is one common measure of any two numbers—namely, the unit—which, when taken many times, yields a number. But no common measure of all continuous quantities can be found, since there are certain incommensurable continuous quantities, as the diameter of a square is incommensurable with one of its sides. The reason is that there is no ratio between it and one of its sides like the ratio of one number to another or of a number to the unit.

1021. Therefore, when it is said in the case of quantities that this quantity is greater than that one, or is related to that one as what includes is related to what is included in it, not only is this ratio not considered according to any definite species of number, but it is not even considered according to number at all, because every number is commensurable with another. For all numbers have one common measure, which is the unit.

Sed continens et contentum non dicuntur secundum aliquam commensurationem numeralem. Continens enim ad contentum dicitur, quod est tantum, et adhuc amplius. Et hoc est indeterminatum, utrum sit commensurabile, vel non commensurabile. Quantitas enim qualiscumque accipiatur, vel est aequalis, vel inaequalis. Unde, si non est aequalis, sequitur quod sit inaequalis et continens, etiam si non sit commensurabilis. Patet igitur quod omnia praedicta dicuntur ad aliquid secundum numerum, et secundum passiones numerorum, quae sunt commensuratio, proportio, et huiusmodi.

1022. Deinde cum dicit *et amplius* ponit relativa, quae accipiuntur secundum unitatem, et non per comparationem numeri ad unum vel ad numerum; et dicit quod alio modo a praedictis dicuntur relative, aequale, simile, et idem. Haec enim dicuntur secundum unitatem. Nam eadem sunt, quorum substantia est una. Similia, quorum qualitas est una. Aequalia, quorum quantitas est una.

Cum autem unum sit principium numeri et mensura, patet etiam, quod haec dicuntur ad aliquid *secundum numerum*, idest secundum aliquid ad genus numeri pertinens; non eodem modo tamen haec ultima cum primis. Nam primae relationes erant secundum numerum ad numerum, vel secundum numerum ad unum; hoc autem secundum unum absolute.

1023. Deinde cum dicit *activa vero* prosequitur de secundo modo relationum, quae sunt in activis et passivis:

et dicit, quod huiusmodi relativa sunt relativa dupliciter. Uno modo secundum potentiam activam et passivam; et secundo modo secundum actus harum potentiarum, qui sunt agere et pati; sicut calefactivum dicitur ad calefactibile secundum potentiam activam et passivam.

Nam calefactum est, quod potest calefacere; calefactibile vero, quod potest calefieri. Calefaciens autem ad calefactum, et secans ad id quod secatur, dicuntur relative secundum actus praedictarum potentiarum.

1024. Et differt iste modus relationum a praemissis. Quae enim sunt secundum numerum, non sunt aliquae actiones nisi secundum similitudinem, sicut multiplicare, dividere et huiusmodi, ut etiam in aliis dictum est, scilicet in secundo *Physicorum*; ubi ostendit, quod mathematica abstrahunt a motu, et ideo in eis esse non possunt huiusmodi actiones, quae secundum motum sunt.

But what includes and what is included in it are not spoken of according to any numerical measure, for it is what is so much and something more that is said to have the relation of what includes to what is included in it. And this is indefinite, whether it be commensurable or incommensurable, for whatever quantity may be taken, it is either equal or unequal. If it is not equal, then it follows that it is unequal and includes something else, even though it is not commensurable. Hence it is clear that all of the above-mentioned things are said to be relative according to number and to the properties of numbers, which are commensuration, ratio, and the like.

1022. *Further, "equal"* (1021a9). He now treats those relative terms which have a reference to unity or oneness and are not based on the relation of one number to another or to the unit. He says that "equal," "like," and "same" are said to be relative in a different way than the foregoing. For these are called such in reference to unity. For those things are the "same" whose substance is one; and those are "alike" whose quality is one; and those are "equal" whose quantity is one.

Now since unity is the principle and measure of number, it is also clear that the former terms are said to be *relative numerically*, that is, in reference to something belonging to the genus of number. But these last terms are not said to be relative in the same way as the first. For the first relations seen are those of number to number, or of a number to the unit; but this relation has to do with unity in an absolute sense.

1023. *Active and passive* (1021a14). Here he proceeds to treat the second type of relations, which pertains to active and passive things.

He says that relative beings of this kind are relative in two ways: in one way according to active and passive potency; in a second way according to the actualizations of these potencies, which are action and passivity (for example, what can heat is said to be relative to what can be heated in virtue of active and passive potency).

For it is what is capable of heating that can heat, and it is what is capable of being heated that can become hot. Again, what is heating in relation to what is heated, and what is cutting in relation to what is being cut, are said to be relative according to the operations of the aforesaid potencies.

1024. Now this type of relation differs from those previously given; for those which are numerical are operations only figuratively—for example, to multiply, to divide, and so forth. This has also been stated in *Physics* 2, where he shows that the objects of mathematics abstract from motion, and therefore they cannot have operations of the kind that have to do with motion.

1025. Sciendum etiam est quod eorum relativorum, quae dicuntur secundum potentiam activam et passivam, attenditur diversitas secundum diversa tempora. Quaedam enim horum dicuntur relative secundum tempus praeteritum, sicut quod fecit, ad illud quod factum est; ut pater ad filium, quia ille genuerit, iste genitus est; quae differunt secundum fecisse, et passum esse. Quaedam vero secundum tempus futurum, sicut facturus refertur ad faciendum. Et ad hoc genus relationum reducuntur illae relationes, quae dicuntur secundum privationem potentiae, ut impossibile et invisibile. Dicitur enim aliquid impossibile huic vel illi; et similiter invisibile.

1026. Deinde cum dicit *ergo secundum* prosequitur de tertio modo relationum; et dicit quod in hoc differt iste tertius modus a praemissis, quod in praemissis, unumquodque dicitur relative ex hoc, quod ipsum ad aliud refertur; non ex eo quod aliud referatur ad ipsum. Duplum enim refertur ad dimidium, et e converso; et similiter pater ad filium, et e converso; sed hoc tertio modo aliquid dicitur relative ex eo solum, quod aliquid refertur ad ipsum; sicut patet, quod sensibile et scibile vel intelligibile dicuntur relative, quia alia referuntur ad illa. Scibile enim dicitur aliquid, propter hoc, quod habetur scientia de ipso. Et similiter sensibile dicitur aliquid quod potest sentiri.

1027. Unde non dicitur relative propter aliquid quod sit ex eorum parte, quod sit qualitas, vel quantitas, vel actio, vel passio, sicut in praemissis relationibus accidebat; sed solum propter actiones aliorum, quae tamen in ipsa non terminantur.

Si enim videre esset actio videntis perveniens ad rem visam, sicut calefactio pervenit ad calefactibile; sicut calefactibile refertur ad calefaciens, ita visibile referretur ad videntem. Sed videre et intelligere et huiusmodi actiones, ut in nono huius dicetur, manent in agentibus, et non transeunt in res passas; unde visibile et scibile non patitur aliquid, ex hoc quod intelligitur vel videtur.

Et propter hoc non ipsamet referuntur ad alia, sed alia ad ipsa. Et simile est in omnibus aliis, in quibus relative aliquid dicitur propter relationem alterius ad ipsum, sicut dextrum et sinistrum in columna. Cum enim dextrum et sinistrum designent principia motuum in rebus animatis, columnae et alicui inanimato attribui non possunt, nisi secundum quod animata aliquo modo se habeant ad ipsam, sicut columna dicitur dextra, quia homo est ei sinister.

1025. It should also be noted that among relative terms based on active and passive potency, we find diversity from the viewpoint of time. For some of these terms are predicated relatively with regard to past time, as what has made something to what has been made—for instance, a father in relation to his son, because the former has begot and the latter has been begotten—and these differ as what has acted and what has been acted upon. And some are used with respect to future time, as when what will make is related to what will be made. And those relations which are based on privation of potency, as the "impossible" and the "invisible," are reduced to this genus of relations. For something is said to be impossible for this person or for that one, and the invisible is spoken of in the same way.

1026. *Therefore, things* (1021a26). Next he proceeds to deal with the third type of relations. He says that this third type differs from the foregoing in this way: each of the foregoing things is said to be relative because each is referred to something else, not because something else is referred to it. For double is related to half, and vice versa; in a similar way a father is related to his son, and vice versa. But something is said to be relative in this third way because something is referred to it. It is clear, for example, that the sensible and the knowable or intelligible are said to be relative because other things are related to them, for a thing is said to be knowable because knowledge is had of it. And similarly something is said to be sensible because it can be sensed.

1027. Hence they are not said to be relative because of something which pertains to them—such as quality, quantity, action, or passion—as was the case in the foregoing relations, but only because of the action of other things, although these are not terminated in them.

For if seeing were the action of the one seeing as extending to the thing seen, as heating extends to the thing which can be heated, then just as what can be heated is related to the one heating, so would what is visible be related to the one seeing. But to see and to understand and actions of this kind, as is stated in book 9 [1788] of this work, remain in the things acting and do not pass over into those which are acted upon. Hence what is visible or what is knowable is not acted upon by being known or seen.

And on this account, these are not referred to other things, but others to them. The same is true in all other cases in which something is said to be relative because something else is related to it, as right and left in the case of a pillar. For since right and left designate starting points of motion in living things, they cannot be attributed to a pillar or to any non-living thing except insofar as living things are related to a pillar in some way. It is in this sense that one speaks of a right-hand pillar because a man stands to the left of it.

Et simile est de imagine respectu exemplaris, et denario, quo fit pretium emptionis. In omnibus autem his tota ratio referendi in duobus extremis, pendet ex altero. Et ideo omnia huiusmodi quodammodo se habent ut mensurabile et mensura. Nam ab eo quaelibet res mensuratur, a quo ipsa dependet.

1028. Sciendum est autem, quod quamvis scientia secundum nomen videatur referri ad scientem et ad scibile, dicitur enim scientia scientis, et scientia scibilis, et intellectus ad intelligentem et intelligibile; tamen intellectus secundum quod ad aliquid dicitur, non ad hoc cuius est sicut subiecti dicitur: sequeretur enim quod idem relativum bis diceretur. Constat enim quoniam intellectus dicitur ad intelligibile, sicut ad obiectum.

Si autem diceretur ad intelligentem, bis diceretur ad aliquid; et cum esse relativi sit ad aliud quodammodo se habere, sequeretur quod idem haberet duplex esse. Et similiter de visu patet quod non dicitur ad videntem, sed ad obiectum quod est color *vel aliquid aliud tale*. Quod dicit propter ea, quae videntur in nocte non per proprium colorem, ut habetur in secundo *De anima*.

1029. Quamvis et hoc recte posset dici, scilicet quod visus sit videntis. Refertur autem visus ad videntem, non inquantum est visus, sed inquantum est accidens, vel potentia videntis. Relatio enim respicit aliquid extra, non autem subiectum nisi inquantum est accidens. Et sic patet, quod isti sunt modi, quibus aliqua dicuntur secundum se ad aliquid.

1030. Deinde cum dicit *illa vero* ponit tres modos, quibus aliqua dicuntur ad aliquid non secundum se, sed secundum aliud.

Quorum primus est, quando aliqua dicuntur ad aliquid propter hoc quod sua genera sunt ad aliquid, sicut medicina dicitur ad aliquid, quia scientia est ad aliquid. Dicitur enim, quod medicina est scientia sani et aegri. Et isto modo refertur scientia per hoc quod est accidens.

1031. Secundus modus est, quando aliqua abstracta dicuntur ad aliquid, quia concreta habentia illa abstracta ad aliud dicuntur; sicut aequalitas et similitudo dicuntur ad aliquid, quia simile et aequale ad aliquid sunt. Aequalitas autem et similitudo secundum nomen non dicuntur ad aliquid.

1032. Tertius modus est, quando subiectum dicitur ad aliquid, ratione accidentis; sicut homo vel album dicitur ad aliquid, quia utrique accidit duplum esse; et hoc modo caput dicitur ad aliquid, eo quod est pars.

The same holds true of an image in relation to the original, and of a denarius, by means of which one fixes the price of a sale. And in all these cases the whole basis of relation between two extremes depends on something else. Hence all things of this kind are related in somewhat the same way as what is measurable and its measure. For everything is measured by the thing on which it depends.

1028. Now it must be borne in mind that even though verbally knowledge would seem to be relative to the knower and to the object of knowledge (for we speak both of the knowledge of the knower and of the knowledge of the thing known), and thought to the thinker and to what is thought, nevertheless a thought as predicated relatively is not relative to the one whose thought it is as its subject, for it would follow that the same relative term would then be expressed twice. For it is evident that a thought is relative to what is thought about as to its object.

Again, if it were relative to the thinker, it would then be called relative twice; and since the very existence of what is relative is to be relative in some way to something else, it would follow that the same thing would have two acts of existence. Similarly, in the case of sight it is clear that sight is not relative to the seer, but to its object, which is color, *or something of this sort*. (He says this because of the things that are seen at night but not by means of their proper color, as is stated in *On the Soul* 2.)

1029. And although it is correct to say that sight is of him who sees, sight is not related to the seer formally as sight, but as an accident or power of the seer. For a relation has to do with something external, but a subject does not, except insofar as it is an accident. It is clear, then, that these are the ways in which some things are said to be relative directly.

1030. *And other things* (1021b4). He now gives three ways in which some things are said to be relative not directly, but indirectly.

The first of these is that in which things are said to be relative because their genera are relative, as medicine is said to be relative because science is relative. For medicine is called the science of health and sickness. And science is relative in this way because it is an accident.

1031. The second way is that in which certain abstract terms are said to be relative because the concrete things to which these abstract terms apply are relative to something else. For example, equality and likeness are said to be relative because the like and the equal are relative. But equality and likeness are not considered relative as words.

1032. The third way is that in which a subject is said to be relative because of an accident. For example, a man or some white thing is said to be relative because each happens to be double; and in this way, a head is said to be relative because it is a part.

LECTURE 18

The definition of "perfect"

1021b12 Perfectum vero dicitur, unum quidem, extra quod non est accipere ullam quidem particulam: ut tempus perfectum singulorum, extra quod non est accipere tempus aliquod, quod sit huius temporis pars. Et quae sunt, secundum virtutem et eius quod bene, non habentia hyperbolem ad genus. Ut perfectus medicus, et perfectus fistulator, quando secundum speciem propriae virtutis in nullo deficiunt. Sic autem transferentes ad mala dicimus sycophantam perfectum et latronem perfectum, quoniam et honos dicimus eos, ut latronem bonum, sycophantam bonum. Est enim virtus perfectio quaedam. Quodlibet enim perfectum, et substantia omnis tunc perfecta, quando secundum speciem propriae virtutis in nulla deficit parte secundum naturam mensurae. [1034]

τέλειον λέγεται ἓν μὲν οὗ μὴ ἔστιν ἔξω τι λαβεῖν μηδὲ ἓν μόριον (οἷον χρόνος τέλειος ἑκάστου οὗτος οὗ μὴ ἔστιν ἔξω λαβεῖν χρόνον τινὰ ὃς τούτου μέρος ἐστὶ τοῦ χρόνου), καὶ τὸ {15} κατ᾽ ἀρετὴν καὶ τὸ εὖ μὴ ἔχον ὑπερβολὴν πρὸς τὸ γένος, οἷον τέλειος ἰατρὸς καὶ τέλειος αὐλητὴς ὅταν κατὰ τὸ εἶδος τῆς οἰκείας ἀρετῆς μηθὲν ἐλλείπωσιν (οὕτω δὲ μεταφέροντες καὶ ἐπὶ τῶν κακῶν λέγομεν συκοφάντην τέλειον καὶ κλέπτην τέλειον, ἐπειδὴ καὶ ἀγαθοὺς λέγομεν αὐτούς, οἷον κλέπτην {20} ἀγαθὸν καὶ συκοφάντην ἀγαθόν· καὶ ἡ ἀρετὴ τελείωσίς τις· ἕκαστον γὰρ τότε τέλειον καὶ οὐσία πᾶσα τότε τελεία, ὅταν κατὰ τὸ εἶδος τῆς οἰκείας ἀρετῆς μηδὲν ἐλλείπῃ μόριον τοῦ κατὰ φύσιν μεγέθους):

That thing is said to be perfect (or complete) outside of which it is impossible to find even a single part. For example, the perfect time of each thing is that outside of which it is impossible to find any time which is a part of it. And those things are perfect whose power and goodness admit of no further degree in their species—for example, we speak of a perfect physician and a perfect flute player when they lack nothing pertaining to the form of their particular power. And thus in transferring this term to bad things, we speak of a perfect slanderer and a perfect thief, since we also call them good, as a good slanderer and a good thief. For any power is a perfection, since each thing is perfect and every substance is perfect when, in the line of its particular power, it lacks no part of its natural measure.

1021b23 Amplius quibus est finis studiosus, ea dicuntur perfecta. Etenim secundum habere finem perfecta. Quare quoniam finis ultimorum aliquis est, et ad prava transferentes dicimus perfecte perdi, et perfecte corrumpi, quando nihil deest corruptioni et malo, sed in ultimo est. Quapropter mors secundum metaphoram dicitur finis, quia ambo ultima. Finis autem et cuius causa ultimum. [1039]

ἔτι οἷς ὑπάρχει τὸ τέλος, σπουδαῖον <ὄν>, ταῦτα λέγεται τέλεια: κατὰ γὰρ τὸ ἔχειν τὸ {25} τέλος τέλεια, ὥστ᾽ ἐπεὶ τὸ τέλος τῶν ἐσχάτων τί ἐστι, καὶ ἐπὶ τὰ φαῦλα μεταφέροντες λέγομεν τελείως ἀπολωλέναι καὶ τελείως ἐφθάρθαι, ὅταν μηδὲν ἐλλείπῃ τῆς φθορᾶς καὶ τοῦ κακοῦ ἀλλ᾽ ἐπὶ τῷ ἐσχάτῳ ᾖ: διὸ καὶ ἡ τελευτὴ κατὰ μεταφορὰν λέγεται τέλος, ὅτι ἄμφω ἔσχατα: τέλος δὲ {30} καὶ τὸ οὗ ἕνεκα ἔσχατον.

Further, those things are said to be perfect which have a goal or end worth seeking. For things are perfect which have attained their goal. Hence, since a goal is something final, we also say, in transferring the term perfect to bad things, that a thing has been perfectly spoiled and perfectly corrupted when nothing pertaining to its corruption and evil is missing, but it is at its final point. And for this reason death is described metaphorically as an end, for both of these are final things. But an end is a final purpose.

1021b30 Secundum se dicta quidem igitur perfecta toties dicuntur. Alia quidem, quia secundum bene in nullo deficiunt, nec hyperbolem habent, nec extra aliquid accipiunt. Alia omnino secundum quod non habent hyperbolem, in unoquoque genere, nec aliquid est extra. [1040]

τὰ μὲν οὖν καθ᾽ αὑτὰ λεγόμενα τέλεια τοσαυταχῶς λέγεται, τὰ μὲν τῷ κατὰ τὸ εὖ μηδὲν ἐλλείπειν μηδ᾽ ἔχειν ὑπερβολὴν μηδὲ ἔξω τι λαβεῖν, τὰ δ᾽ {33} ὅλως κατὰ τὸ μὴ ἔχειν ὑπερβολὴν ἐν ἑκάστῳ γένει μηδ᾽ εἶναί τι ἔξω:

Things that are said to be perfect in themselves, then, are said to be such in all of these senses—some because they lack no part of their goodness and admit of no further degree and have no part outside; others in general inasmuch as they admit of no further degree in any genus and have no part outside.

1022a1 Alia vero iam secundum ipsa, aut in faciendo aliquid tale aut habendo, aut

τὰ δὲ ἄλλα ἤδη κατὰ ταῦτα τῷ ἢ ποιεῖν τι τοιοῦτον ἢ ἔχειν ἢ ἁρμόττειν τούτῳ ἢ

And other things are now termed perfect in reference to these, either because they

cognoscendo tali, aut in aliqualiter dici ad primo dicta perfecta. [1043]

ἀμῶς γέ πως λέγεσθαι πρὸς τὰ πρώτως λεγόμενα τέλεια.

make something such, or have something such, or know something such, or because they are somehow referred to things that are said to be perfect in the primary senses.

1033. Postquam Philosophus distinxit nomina, quae significant causas, et subiectum, et partes subiectorum huius scientiae; hic incipit distinguere nomina quae significant ea quae se habent per modum passionis; et dividitur in duas partes.

In prima distinguit nomina ea quae pertinent ad perfectionem entis.

In secunda distinguit nomina quae pertinent ad entis defectum, ibi, *falsum dicitur uno modo*.

Circa primum duo facit.

Primo distinguit nomina significantia ea quae pertinent ad perfectionem entis.

Secundo pertinentia ad totalitatem.

Perfectum enim et totum, aut sunt idem, aut fere idem significant, ut dicitur in tertio *Physicorum*.

Secunda ibi, *ex aliquo esse dicitur*.

Circa primum duo facit.

Primo distinguit hoc nomen perfectum.

Secundo distinguit quaedam nomina, quae significant quasdam perfectiones perfecti, ibi, *terminus dicitur*.

Circa primum duo facit.

Primo ponit modos, quibus aliqua dicuntur perfecta secundum se.

Secundo modos, quibus aliqua dicuntur perfecta per respectum ad alia, ibi, *alia vero*.

Circa primum duo facit.

Primo ponit tres modos quibus aliquid secundum se dicitur perfectum.

Secundo ostendit quomodo secundum hos modos aliqua diversimode perfecta dicuntur, ibi, *secundum se dicta quidem igitur*.

1034. Dicit ergo primo, quod perfectum uno modo dicitur, extra quod non est accipere aliquam eius particulam; sicut homo dicitur perfectus, quando nulla deest ei pars. Et dicitur tempus perfectum, quando non est accipere extra aliquid quod sit temporis pars; sicut dicitur dies perfectus, quando nulla pars diei deest.

1035. Alio modo dicitur aliquid perfectum secundum virtutem; et sic dicitur aliquid perfectum, quod non habet *hyperbolem*, idest superexcellentiam vel superabundantiam ad hoc quod aliquid bene fiat secun-

1033. Having treated the various senses of the terms which signify the causes, the subject, and the parts of the subject of this science, here the Philosopher begins to treat the various senses of the terms which designate attributes having the character of properties. This is divided into two parts.

In the first he gives the various senses of the terms which refer to the perfection or completeness of being.

In the second (1024b17; [1128]), he treats those which refer to a lack of being, at *false means*.

In regard to the first he does two things.

First, he gives the different senses of the terms which designate attributes pertaining to the perfection of being;

second [1085], he treats those which designate the wholeness of being.

For the terms "perfect" and "whole" have the same or nearly the same meaning, as is said in the *Physics* 3.

He considers the second part of this division where he says, *to come from something* (1023a26).

In regard to the first part he does two things.

First, he treats the various senses of the term "perfect."

Second (1022a4; [1044]), he treats the various senses of the terms which signify certain conditions of that which is perfect, at *the term "limit."*

In regard to the first he does two things.

First, he considers the senses in which things are said to be perfect in themselves;

and second (1022a1; [1043]), he treats those in which things are said to be perfect by reason of something else, at *and other things*.

In regard to the first he does two things.

First, he gives three senses in which a thing is said to be perfect in itself.

Second (1021b30; [1040]), he shows how, according to these senses, a thing is said to be perfect in different ways, at *things that are said*.

1034. He accordingly first says that in one sense, that thing is said to be perfect outside of which it is impossible to find any of its parts. For example, a man is said to be perfect when no part of him is missing, and a period of time is said to be perfect when none of its parts can be found outside of it. For example, a day is said to be perfect or complete when no part of it is missing.

1035. A thing is said to be perfect in another sense with reference to some ability. Thus a thing is said to be perfect which admits of *no further degree*—that is, excess or superabundance—from the viewpoint of good performance in

dum genus illud, et similiter nec defectum. Hoc enim dicimus bene se habere, ut dicitur in secundo *Ethicorum*, quod nihil habet nec plus nec minus quam debet habere. Et sic dicitur perfectus medicus et perfectus fistulator, quando non deficit ei aliquid, quod pertineat ad speciem propriae virtutis, secundum quam dicitur, quod hic est bonus medicus, et ille bonus fistulator. Virtus enim cuiuslibet est quae bonum facit habentem, et opus eius bonum reddit.

1036. Secundum autem hunc modum utimur translative nomine perfecti etiam in malis. Dicimus enim perfectum *sycophantam*, idest calumniatorem, et perfectum latronem, quando in nullo deficit ab eo quod competit eis inquantum sunt tales. Nec est mirum si in istis quae magis sonant defectum, utimur nomine perfectionis; quia etiam cum sint mala, utimur in eis nomine bonitatis per quamdam similitudinem. Dicimus enim bonum furem et bonum calumniatorem, quia sic se habent in suis operationibus, licet malis, sicut boni in bonis.

1037. Et quod aliquid dicatur perfectum per comparationem ad virtutem propriam, provenit quia virtus est quaedam perfectio rei. Unumquodque enim tunc est perfectum quando nulla pars magnitudinis naturalis, quae competit ei secundum speciem propriae virtutis, deficit ei. Sicut autem quaelibet res naturalis, habet determinatam mensuram naturalis magnitudinis secundum quantitatem continuam, ut dicitur in secundo *De anima*, ita etiam quaelibet res habet determinatam quantitatem suae virtutis naturalis. Equus enim habet quantitatem dimensivam determinatam secundum naturam cum aliqua latitudine. Est enim aliqua quantitas, ultra quam nullus equus protenditur in magnitudine. Et similiter est aliqua quantitas, quam non transcendit in parvitate. Ita etiam ex utraque parte determinatur aliquibus terminis quantitas virtutis equi. Nam aliqua est virtus equi, qua maior in nullo equo invenitur: et similiter est aliqua tam parva, qua nulla est minor.

1038. Sicuti igitur primus modus perfecti accipiebatur ex hoc quod nihil rei deerat de quantitate dimensiva sibi naturaliter determinata, ita hic secundus modus accipitur ex hoc quod nihil deest alicui de quantitate virtutis sibi debitae secundum naturam. Uterque autem modus perfectionis attenditur secundum interiorem perfectionem.

1039. *Amplius quibus* tertium modum ponit per respectum ad exterius; dicens, quod illa dicuntur tertio modo perfecta *quibus inest finis*, idest quae iam consecuta sunt suum finem; si tamen ille finis fuerit *studiosus*, idest bonus:

some particular line and is not deficient in any respect. For we say that that thing is in a good state which has neither more nor less than it ought to have, as is said in *Ethics* 2. Thus a man is said to be a perfect physician or a perfect flute player when he lacks nothing pertaining to the particular power by which he is said to be a good physician or a good flute player. For the ability which each thing has is what makes its possessor good and renders his work good.

1036. And it is in this sense that we also transfer the term "perfect" to bad things. For we speak of a perfect *slanderer*, or scandal monger, and a perfect thief, when they lack none of the qualities proper to them as such. Nor is it surprising if we use the term "perfect" of those things that rather designate a defect, because even when things are bad we predicate the term good of them in an analogous sense. For we speak of a good thief and a good scandalmonger because even though they are evil, in their operations they are disposed like good men towards good operations.

1037. The reason why a thing is said to be perfect in the line of its particular power is that an power is a perfection of a thing. For each thing is perfect when no part of the natural magnitude which belongs to it according to the form of its proper power is missing. Moreover, just as each natural being has a definite measure of natural magnitude in continuous quantity, as is stated in *On the Soul* 2, so too each thing has a definite amount of its own natural ability. For example, a horse has by nature a definite dimensive quantity, within certain limits; for there is both a maximum quantity and minimum quantity beyond which no horse can go in size. And in a similar way the quantity of active power in a horse has certain limits in both directions. For there is some maximum power of a horse which is not in fact surpassed in any horse; similarly, there is some minimum which never fails to be attained.

1038. Therefore, just as the first sense of the term "perfect" was based on the fact that a thing lacks no part of the dimensive quantity which it is naturally determined to have, in a similar way this second sense of the term is based on the fact that a thing lacks no part of the quantity of power which it is naturally determined to have. And each of these senses of the term has to do with internal perfection.

1039. *Further, those things* (1021b23). Here he gives the third sense in which the term "perfect" is used, and it pertains to external perfection. He says that in a third way those things are said to be perfect *which have a goal*, that is, which have already attained their end, but only if that end is *worth seeking*, or good.

sicut homo, quando iam consequitur beatitudinem. Qui autem consequitur finem suum in malis, magis dicitur deficiens quam perfectus; quia malum est privatio perfectionis debitae. In quo patet, quod mali, quando suam perficiunt voluntatem, non sunt feliciores, sed miseriores.

Quia vero omnis finis est quoddam ultimum, ideo per quamdam similitudinem transferimus nomen perfectum ad ea, quae perveniunt ad ultimum, licet illud sit malum. Sicut dicitur aliquid perfecte perdi, vel corrumpi, quando nihil deest de corruptione vel perditione rei. Et per hanc metaphoram, mors dicitur finis, quia est ultimum. Sed finis non solum habet quod sit ultimum, sed etiam quod sit cuius causa fit aliquid. Quod non contingit morti vel corruptioni.

1040. Deinde cum dicit *secundum se* ostendit quomodo aliqua diversimode se habeant ad praedictos modos perfectionis; et dicit, quod quaedam dicuntur secundum se perfecta: et hoc dupliciter.

Alia quidem universaliter perfecta, quia nihil omnino deficit eis absolute, nec aliquam habent **hyperbolem**, idest excedentiam, quia a nullo videlicet penitus in bonitate exceduntur, nec aliquid extra accipiunt, quia nec indigent exteriori bonitate. Et haec est conditio primi principii, scilicet Dei, in quo est perfectissima bonitas, cui nihil deest de omnibus perfectionibus in singulis generibus inventis.

1041. Alia dicuntur perfecta in aliquo genere, ex eo quod quantum ad illud genus pertinet, nec **habent hyperbolem**, idest excedentiam, quasi aliquid eis deficiat eorum, quae illi generi debentur; nec aliquid eorum, quae ad perfectionem illius generis pertinent, est extra ea, quasi eo careant; sicut homo dicitur perfectus, quando iam adeptus est beatitudinem.

1042. Et sicut fit haec distinctio quantum ad secundum modum perfectionis supra positum, ita potest fieri quantum ad primum, ut tangitur in principio *Caeli et mundi*. Nam quodlibet corpus particulare est quantitas perfecta secundum suum genus, quia habet tres dimensiones, quibus non sunt plures. Sed mundus dicitur perfectus universaliter, quia omnino nihil extra ipsum est.

1043. Deinde cum dicit *alia vero* ponit modum, secundum quem aliqua dicuntur perfecta per respectum ad aliud: et dicit, quod alia dicuntur perfecta *secundum ipsa*, idest per comparationem ad perfecta, quae sunt secundum se perfecta. Vel ex eo, quod faciunt aliquid perfectum aliquo priorum modorum; sicut medicina est perfecta, quia facit sanitatem perfectam. Aut ex eo, quod habent aliquid perfectum; sicut homo dicitur perfectus,

A man, for instance, is called perfect when he has already attained happiness. But someone who has attained some evil goal is said to be deficient rather than perfect, because evil is a privation of the perfection which a thing ought to have. Thus it is evident that when evil men accomplish their will, they are not happier, but sadder.

And since every goal or end is something final, for this reason we transfer the term "perfect" somewhat figuratively to those things that have reached some final state, even though it be evil. For example, a thing is said to be perfectly spoiled or corrupted when nothing pertaining to its ruin or corruption is missing. And by this metaphor death is called an end, because it is something final. However, an end is not only something final, but also that for the sake of which a thing comes to be. This does not apply to death or corruption.

1040. *Things that are said to be* (1021b30). Here he shows how things are perfect in different ways according to the foregoing senses of perfection. He says that some things are said to be perfect in themselves, and this occurs in two ways.

For some things are altogether perfect because they lack absolutely nothing at all; they neither have any *further degree* (that is, excess), because there is nothing which surpasses them in goodness, nor receive any good from outside, because they have no need of any external goodness. This is the condition of the first principle, God, in whom the most perfect goodness is found, and to whom none of all the perfections found in each genus of things are lacking.

1041. Some things are said to be perfect in some particular line because **they do not admit of any further degree**, or excess, **in their genus**, as though they lacked anything proper to that genus. Nor is anything that belongs to the perfection of that genus external to them, as though they lacked it—just as a man is said to be perfect when he has already attained happiness.

1042. And not only is this distinction made with reference to the second sense of "perfection" given above, but it can also be made with reference to the first sense of the term, as is mentioned at the beginning of *On the Heavens*. For any individual body is a perfect quantity in its genus, because it has three dimensions, which are all there are. But the world is said to be universally perfect because there is absolutely nothing outside of it.

1043. *And other things* (1022a1). He now gives the sense in which some things are said to be perfect by reason of their relation to something else. He says that other things are said to be perfect **in reference to these**, that is, in reference to things that are perfect in themselves, either because they make something perfect in one of the preceding ways, as medicine is perfect because it causes perfect health; or because they have some perfection, as a man is said to

qui habet perfectam scientiam. Aut repraesentando tale perfectum; sicut illa, quae habent similitudinem ad perfecta; ut imago dicitur perfecta, quae repraesentat hominem perfecte. Aut qualitercumque aliter referantur ad ea, quae dicuntur per se perfecta primis modis.

be perfect who has perfect knowledge; or because they represent such a perfect thing, as things that bear a likeness to those that are perfect (as, for example, an image which represents a man perfectly is said to be perfect); or in any other way in which they are referred to things that are said to be perfect in themselves in the primary senses.

LECTURE 19

"Limit," "according to which," and "in itself"

1022a4 Terminus dicitur quod est cuiuslibet ultimum, et extra quod nihil est accipere primi, et infra quod omnia primi. [1044]

πέρας λέγεται τό τε ἔσχατον ἑκάστου καὶ οὗ ἔξω μηδὲν {5} ἔστι λαβεῖν πρώτου καὶ οὗ ἔσω πάντα πρώτου,

The term "limit" means the extremity of anything, that beyond which nothing of that being can be found, and that within which everything belonging to it is contained.

1022a5 Et quaecumque fuerit species magnitudinis, aut habentis magnitudinem: et finis cuiusque. [1045]

καὶ ὃ ἂν ᾖ εἶδος μεγέθους ἢ ἔχοντος μέγεθος, καὶ τὸ τέλος ἑκάστου

And "limit" means the form, whatever it may be, of a continuous quantity or of something having continuous quantity. It also means the goal or end of each thing.

Tale vero ad quod motus et actus, et non a quo. Et quandoque ambo; et a quo et in quod.

(τοιοῦτον δ᾽ ἐφ᾽ ὃ ἡ κίνησις καὶ ἡ πρᾶξις, καὶ οὐκ ἀφ᾽ οὗ—ὁτὲ δὲ ἄμφω, καὶ ἀφ᾽ οὗ καὶ ἐφ᾽ ὃ καὶ τὸ οὗ ἕνεκα),

And such too is that *toward* which motion and action proceed, and not that *from* which they proceed. And sometimes it is both, not only that from which but also that to which.

Et cuius causa. Et substantia cuiuslibet, et quod quid erat esse cuique. Cognitionis enim hic terminus: sed si cognitionis, et rei.

καὶ ἡ οὐσία ἡ ἑκάστου καὶ τὸ τί ἦν εἶναι ἑκάστῳ· τῆς γνώσεως γὰρ τοῦτο {10} πέρας· εἰ δὲ τῆς γνώσεως, καὶ τοῦ πράγματος.

And it means the reason for which something is done, and also the substance or essence of each. For this is the limit or terminus of knowledge—and if of knowledge, also of the thing.

1022a10 Quare palam, quia quoties principia dicuntur, toties terminus, et adhuc amplius. Principium enim terminus quidam est, sed terminus non omnis principium. [1049]

ὥστε φανερὸν ὅτι ὁσαχῶς τε ἡ ἀρχὴ λέγεται, τοσαυταχῶς καὶ τὸ πέρας, καὶ ἔτι πλεοναχῶς· ἡ μὲν γὰρ ἀρχὴ πέρας τι, τὸ δὲ πέρας οὐ πᾶν ἀρχή.

Hence it is clear that the term "limit" has as many meanings as the term "principle" has, and even more. For a principle is a limit, but not every limit is a principle.

1022a14 Et secundum quod dicitur multipliciter. Uno quidem modo species et substantia cuiusque rei: ut secundum quod bonum per se bonum. [1050]

τὸ καθ᾽ ὃ λέγεται πολλαχῶς, ἕνα μὲν τρόπον τὸ εἶδος {15} καὶ ἡ οὐσία ἑκάστου πράγματος, οἷον καθ᾽ ὃ ἀγαθός, αὐτὸ ἀγαθόν,

The phrase "according to which" has several meanings. In one sense it means the species or substance of each thing; for example, that according to which a thing is good is goodness itself.

Alio vero in quo primum aptum natum est fieri, ut color in superficie.

ἕνα δὲ ἐν ᾧ πρώτῳ πέφυκε γίγνεσθαι, οἷον τὸ χρῶμα ἐν τῇ ἐπιφανείᾳ.

And in another sense it means the first subject in which an attribute is naturally disposed to come into being, as color in surface.

Primo quidem ergo dictum, secundum quod species est. Secundo autem ut materia cuiusque, et subiectum cuiusque primum. Omnino vero ipsum secundum quod pariter et causa existit.

τὸ μὲν οὖν πρώτως λεγόμενον καθ᾽ ὃ τὸ εἶδός ἐστι, δευτέρως δὲ ὡς ἡ ὕλη ἑκάστου καὶ τὸ ὑποκείμενον ἑκάστῳ πρῶτον. ὅλως δὲ τὸ καθ᾽ ὃ ἰσαχῶς καὶ {20} τὸ αἴτιον ὑπάρξει·

Therefore, in its primary sense, "that according to which" is the form; in its secondary sense it is the matter of each thing and the first subject of each. And in general "that according to which" is used in the same way as a reason.

Nam secundum quod venit, aut cuius causa venit, dicitur et secundum quod paralogizatum est, aut syllogizatum, aut qua causa syllogismi sunt, aut paralogismi.

κατὰ τί γὰρ ἐλήλυθεν ἢ οὗ ἕνεκα ἐλήλυθε λέγεται, καὶ κατὰ τί παραλελόγισται ἢ συλλελόγισται, ἢ τί τὸ αἴτιον τοῦ συλλογισμοῦ ἢ παραλογισμοῦ.

For we speak of that according to which he comes, or the reason of his coming; and that according to which he has reasoned incorrectly or simply reasoned, or the reason why he has reasoned or reasoned incorrectly.

Amplius secundum quod secundum positionem dicitur: ut secundum quod stetit, aut secundum quod vadit: ea namque omnino positionem significant et locum.

1022a24 Quare secundum se dici multipliciter est necesse. Unum enim secundum se quod quid erat esse unicuique, ut Callias et quod quid erat esse Calliam. Alia vero quaecumque in eo quod quid est existunt, ut animal Callias secundum se: nam in ratione inest animal. Animal enim quoddam est Callias. [1054]

Amplius autem si in ipso ostensum est primo, aut in eius aliquo, ut superficies alba secundum se, et vivum secundum se homo. Anima namque pars est quaedam hominis, in qua prima est ipsum vivere. Amplius cuius non est alia causa. Hominis enim multae sunt causae, animal, bipes: attamen secundum se homo est homo. Amplius quaecumque soli insunt, et inquantum soli, eo quod separatum, secundum se.

ἔτι δὲ τὸ καθ' ὃ τὸ κατὰ θέσιν λέγεται, καθ' ὃ ἕστηκεν ἢ καθ' ὃ βαδίζει· πάντα γὰρ ταῦτα τόπον σημαίνει καὶ θέσιν.

ὥστε καὶ {25} τὸ καθ' αὑτὸ πολλαχῶς ἀνάγκη λέγεσθαι. ἓν μὲν γὰρ καθ' αὑτὸ τὸ τί ἦν εἶναι ἑκάστῳ, οἷον ὁ Καλλίας καθ' αὑτὸν Καλλίας καὶ τὸ τί ἦν εἶναι Καλλίᾳ· ἓν δὲ ὅσα ἐν τῷ τί ἐστιν ὑπάρχει, οἷον ζῷον ὁ Καλλίας καθ' αὑτόν· ἐν γὰρ τῷ λόγῳ ἐνυπάρχει τὸ ζῷον· ζῷον γάρ τι ὁ Καλλίας.

ἔτι {30} δὲ εἰ ἐν αὑτῷ δέδεκται πρώτῳ ἢ τῶν αὑτοῦ τινί, οἷον ἡ ἐπιφάνεια λευκὴ καθ' ἑαυτήν, καὶ ζῇ ὁ ἄνθρωπος καθ' αὑτόν· ἡ γὰρ ψυχὴ μέρος τι τοῦ ἀνθρώπου, ἐν ᾗ πρώτῃ τὸ ζῆν. ἔτι οὗ μὴ ἔστιν ἄλλο αἴτιον· τοῦ γὰρ ἀνθρώπου πολλὰ αἴτια, τὸ ζῷον, τὸ δίπουν, ἀλλ' ὅμως καθ' αὑτὸν ἄνθρωπος ὁ ἄνθρωπός {35} ἐστιν. ἔτι ὅσα μόνῳ ὑπάρχει καὶ ᾗ μόνον δι' αὑτὸ κεχωρισμένον καθ' αὑτό.

Further, "that according to which" is used in reference to place, as according to (or next to) which he stands, or according to (or along) which he walks. For in general these signify position and place.

Hence the phrase "in itself" must be used in many senses. For in one sense it means the quiddity of each thing, as Callias and the quiddity of Callias. And in another sense it means everything that is found in the quiddity of a thing. For example, Callias is an animal in himself, because animal belongs to his definition (for Callias is an animal).

Again, it is used of a thing when something has been manifested in it as its first subject or in some part of it—for example, a surface is white in itself, and a man is alive in himself. For the soul is a part of man in which life is first present. Again, it means a thing which has no other cause. For there are many causes of man—such as animal and two-footed—yet man is man in himself. Further, it means any attributes that belong to a thing alone and inasmuch as they belong to it alone, because whatever is separate is in itself.

1044. Hic prosequitur de nominibus, quae significant conditiones perfecti. Perfectum autem, ut ex praemissis patet, est terminatum et absolutum, non dependens ab alio, et non privatum, sed habens ea, quae sibi secundum suum genus competunt.

Et ideo primo ponit hoc nomen terminus.

Secundo hoc quod dicitur per se, ibi, *et secundum quod dicitur.*
Tertio hoc nomen habitus, ibi, *habitus vero dicitur.*

Circa primum tria facit.

Primo ponit rationem termini; dicens, quod terminus dicitur quod est ultimum cuiuslibet rei, ita quod nihil de primo terminato est extra ipsum terminum; et omnia quae sunt eius, continentur intra ipsum. Dicit autem *primi* quia contingit id, quod est ultimum primi, esse principium secundi; sicut nunc quod est ultimum praeteriti, est principium futuri.

1045. *Et quaecumque* secundo ponit quatuor modos, quibus dicitur terminus;

quorum primus est secundum quod in qualibet specie magnitudinis, finis magnitudinis, vel habentis magnitudinem, dicitur terminus; sicut punctus dicitur

1044. Here Aristotle proceeds to examine the terms which signify the conditions necessary for perfection. Now what is perfect or complete, as is clear from the above, is what is determinate and absolute, independent of anything else, and not deprived of anything, but having whatever befits it in its own line.

Therefore, first, he deals with the term "limit" (which is a boundary or terminus);
second (1022a14; [1050]), with the phrase "in itself," at *the phrase according to which*;
third (1022b4; [1062]), with the term "having," at *"having" means.*

In regard to the first he does three things.

First, he gives the meaning of "limit." He says that "limit" means the last part of anything, such that no part of what is first limited lies outside this limit, and all things that belong to it are contained within it. He says *first* because the last part of a first thing may be the starting point of a second thing—for example, the now of time, which is the last point of the past, is the beginning of the future.

1045. *And limit means the form* (1022a5). Second, he gives four senses in which the term "limit" is used.

The first of these applies to any kind of continuous quantity insofar as the terminus of a continuous quantity, or of a thing having continuous quantity, is called a limit—

terminus lineae, et superficies corporis, vel etiam lapidis habentis quantitatem.

1046. Secundus modus est similis primo, secundum quod unum extremum motus vel actionis dicitur terminus, hoc scilicet ad quod est motus, et non a quo: sicut terminus generationis est esse, non autem non esse; quamvis quandoque ambo extrema motus dicantur terminus largo modo, scilicet a quo, et in quod; prout dicimus, quod omnis motus est inter duos terminos.

1047. Tertius modus dicitur terminus, cuius causa fit aliquid; hoc enim est ultimum intentionis, sicut terminus secundo modo dictus est ultimum motus vel operationis.

1048. Quartus modus est secundum quod substantia rei, quae est essentia et definitio significans quod quid est res, dicitur terminus. Est enim terminus cognitionis. Incipit enim cognitio rei ab aliquibus signis exterioribus quibus pervenitur ad cognoscendum rei definitionem; quo cum perventum fuerit, habetur perfecta cognitio de re.

Vel dicitur terminus cognitionis definitio, quia infra ipsam continentur ea, per quae scitur res. Si autem mutetur una differentia, vel addatur, vel subtrahatur, iam non erit eadem definitio. Si autem est terminus cognitionis, oportet quod sit rei terminus, quia cognitio fit per assimilationem cognoscentis ad rem cognitam.

1049. Deinde cum dicit *quare palam* concludit comparationem termini ad principium; dicens, quod quoties dicitur principium, toties dicitur terminus, et adhuc amplius; quia omne principium est terminus, sed non terminus omnis est principium. Id enim ad quod motus est, terminus est, et nullo modo principium est: illud vero a quo est motus, est principium et terminus, ut ex praedictis patet.

1050. Deinde cum dicit *et secundum* hic determinat de per se: et circa hoc tria facit.

Primo determinat de hoc, quod dicitur secundum quod; quod est communius quam secundum se.

Secundo concludit modos eius, quod dicitur secundum se, ibi, *quare secundum se.*

Tertio, quia uterque dictorum modorum secundum aliquem modum significat dispositionem, determinat de nomine dispositionis, ibi, *dispositio.*

Circa primum ponit quatuor modos eius quod dicitur secundum quod;

for example, a point is called the limit of a line, and a surface the limit of a body, or also of a stone, which has quantity.

1046. The second sense of "limit" is similar to the first inasmuch as one extreme of a motion or action is called a limit—that is, that toward which there is motion, and not that from which there is motion, as the limit of generation is being and not non-being. Sometimes, however, both extremes of motion are called limits in a broad sense, both that from which and that to which, inasmuch as we say that every motion is between two limits or extremes.

1047. In a third sense, "limit" means that for the sake of which something comes to be, for this is the terminus of an intention, just as "limit" in the second sense meant the terminus of a motion or an operation.

1048. In a fourth sense, "limit" means the substance of a thing, that is, the essence of a thing or the definition signifying what a thing is. For this is the limit or terminus of knowledge, because knowledge of a thing begins with certain external signs from which we come to know a thing's definition, and when we have arrived at it, we have complete knowledge of the thing.

Or the definition is called the limit or terminus of knowledge because under it are contained the ideas by which the thing is known. And if one difference is changed, added, or subtracted, the definition will not remain the same. Now if the definition is the limit of knowledge, it must also be the limit of the thing, because knowledge is had through the assimilation of the knower to the thing known.

1049. *Hence it is clear* (1022a10). Here he concludes by comparing a limit with a principle, saying that limit has as many meanings as principle has, and even more, because every principle is a limit but not every limit is a principle. For that toward which there is motion is a limit, but it is not in any way a principle, whereas that from which there is motion is both a principle and a limit, as is clear from what was said above [1046].

1050. *The phrase "according to which"* (1022a14). Here he deals with the phrase "in itself," and in regard to this he does three things.

First, he lays down the meaning of the phrase "according to which," which is more common than the phrase "in itself."

Second (1022a24; [1054]), he draws his conclusion as to the ways in which the phrase "in itself" is used, at *hence the phrase.*

Third (1022b1; [1058]), he establishes the meaning of the term "disposition," because each of the senses in which we use the phrases mentioned above somehow signifies disposition, at *"disposition" means the order.*

In regard to the first, he gives four senses in which the phrase "according to which" is used.

quorum primus est, prout *species*, idest forma, et *substantia rei*, idest essentia, est id, secundum quod aliquid esse dicitur; sicut secundum Platonicos, *per se bonum*, idest idea boni, est illud, secundum quod aliquid bonum dicitur.

1051. Secundus modus est, prout subiectum, in quo primo aliquid natum est fieri, dicitur secundum quod, sicut color primo fit in superficie; et ideo dicitur, quod corpus est coloratum secundum superficiem. Hic autem modus differt a praedicto, quia praedictus pertinet ad formam, et hic pertinet ad materiam.

1052. Tertius modus est, prout universaliter quaelibet causa dicitur secundum quod. Unde toties dicitur secundum quod quoties et causa.

Idem enim est quaerere secundum quod venit, et cuius causa venit; similiter secundum quod paralogizatum, aut syllogizatum est, et qua causa facti sunt syllogismi.

1053. Quartus modus est prout secundum quod significat positionem et locum; sicut dicitur, iste *stetit secundum hunc*, idest iuxta hunc, et ille *vadit secundum hunc*, idest iuxta hunc; quae omnia significant positionem et locum. Et hoc manifestius in Graeco idiomate apparet.

1054. Deinde cum dicit *quare secundum* concludit ex praedictis, quatuor modos dicendi per se, vel secundum se.

Quorum primus est, quando definitio significans quid est esse uniuscuiusque, dicitur ei inesse secundum se, sicut Callias *et quod quid erat esse Calliam*, idest et essentia rei, ita se habent quod unum inest secundum se alteri. Non autem solum tota definitio dicitur de definito secundum se; sed aliquo modo etiam quaecumque insunt in definitione dicente quid est, praedicantur de definito secundum se, sicut Callias est animal secundum se.

Animal enim inest in ratione Calliae. Nam Callias est quoddam animal; et poneretur in eius definitione, si singularia definitionem habere possent. Et hi duo modi sub uno comprehenduntur. Nam eadem ratione, definitio et pars definitionis per se de unoquoque praedicantur. Est enim hic primus modus per se, qui ponitur in libro *Posteriorum*; et respondet primo modo eius quod dicitur secundum quod, superius posito.

1055. Secundus modus est, quando aliquid ostenditur esse in aliquo, sicut in primo subiecto, cum inest ei per se. Quod quidem contingit dupliciter:

The first has to do with the *species*, that is, the form, or *the substance of each thing*, or its essence, inasmuch as this is that according to which something is said to be. For example, according to the Platonists, *the good itself* (that is, the idea of the good) is that according to which something is said to be good.

1051. This phrase has a second meaning, insofar as the subject in which some attribute is naturally disposed to first come into being is termed "that according to which," as color first comes into being in surface; therefore, it is said that a body is colored according to its surface. Now this sense differs from the preceding one, because the preceding sense pertains to form, but this last sense pertains to matter.

1052. There is a third sense in which this phrase is used, inasmuch as any cause or reason in general is said to be "that according to which." Hence the phrase "according to which" is used in the same number of senses as the term reason.

For it is the same thing to ask, "According to what does he come?," and "For what reason does he come?" And in like manner it is the same to ask, "According to what has he reasoned incorrectly or simply reasoned," and "For what reason has he reasoned?'

1053. This phrase "according to which" is used in a fourth sense inasmuch as it signifies position and place, as in the statement, *according to which he stands*, (or next to which), and, *according to which he walks* (or along which he walks). Both of these signify place and position, as appears more clearly in the Greek idiom.

1054. *Hence the phrase* (1022a24). From what has been said above he draws four senses in which the phrase "in itself" or "of itself" is used.

The first of these is found when the definition, which signifies the quiddity of each thing, is said to belong to each in itself, as Callias *and the quiddity of Callias*, that is, the essence of the thing, are such that one belongs to the other "in itself." And not only the whole definition is predicated of the thing defined in itself, but so too (in a way) everything which belongs to the definition, which expresses the quiddity, is predicated of the thing defined in itself. For example, Callias is an animal in himself.

For animal belongs in the definition of Callias, because Callias is an individual animal, and this would be given in his definition if individual things could have a definition. And these two senses are included under one, because both the definition and a part of the definition are predicated of each thing in itself for the same reason. For this is the first type of essential predication given in the *Posterior Analytics*; and it corresponds to the first sense given above [1050] in which we use the phrase "according to which."

1055. This phrase is used in a second sense when something is shown to be in something else as in a first subject, when it belongs to it of itself. This can happen in two ways.

quia vel primum subiectum accidentis est ipsum totum subiectum de quo praedicatur (sicut superficies dicitur colorata vel alba secundum seipsam. Primum enim subiectum coloris est superficies, et ideo corpus dicitur coloratum ratione superficiei).

Vel etiam aliqua pars eius; sicut homo dicitur vivens secundum se, quia aliqua pars eius est primum subiectum vitae, scilicet anima. Et hic est secundus modus dicendi per se in *Posterioribus* positus, quando scilicet subiectum ponitur in definitione praedicati. Subiectum enim primum et proprium, ponitur in definitione accidentis proprii.

1056. Tertius modus est prout secundum se esse dicitur illud, cuius non est aliqua alia causa; sicut omnes propositiones immediatae, quae scilicet per aliquod medium non probantur. Nam medium in demonstrationibus propter quid est causa, quod praedicatum insit subiecto. Unde, licet homo habeat multas causas, sicut animal et bipes, quae sunt causae formales eius; tamen huius propositionis, homo est homo, cum sit immediata, nihil est causa; et propter hoc homo est homo secundum se. Et ad hunc modum reducitur quartus modus dicendi per se in *Posterioribus* positus, quando effectus praedicatur de causa; ut cum dicitur interfectus interiit propter interfectionem, vel infrigidatum infriguit vel refriguit.

1057. Quartus modus est, prout illa dicuntur secundum se inesse alicui, quae ei soli inquantum soli insunt.

Quod dicit ad differentiam priorum modorum, in quibus non dicebatur secundum se inesse ex eo quod est soli inesse. Quamvis etiam ibi aliquid soli inesset, ut definitio definito. Hic autem secundum se dicitur ratione solitudinis. Nam hoc quod dico secundum se, significat aliquid separatum; sicut dicitur homo secundum se esse, quando solus est. Et ad hunc reducitur tertius modus in *Posterioribus* positus, et quartus modus dicendi secundum quod, qui positionem importabat.

First, the first subject of an accident is the whole subject itself of which the accident is predicated, as a surface is said to be colored or white in itself (for the first subject of color is surface, and therefore a body is said to be colored by reason of its surface).

Second, the subject of the accident is some part of the subject, just as a man is said to be alive in himself because part of him (the soul) is the first subject of life. This is the second type of essential predication given in the *Posterior Analytics*, namely, that in which the subject is given in the definition of the predicate. For the first and proper subject is given in the definition of a proper accident.

1056. This phrase is used in a third sense when something having no cause is spoken of as "in itself," like all immediate propositions—that is, those which are not proved by a middle term. For in *a priori* demonstrations, the middle term is the cause of the predicate's belonging to the subject. Hence, although man has many causes—for example, animal and two-footed, which are his formal cause—still nothing is the cause of the proposition "Man is man," since it is an immediate one. For this reason man is man in himself. And to this sense is reduced the fourth type of essential predication given in the *Posterior Analytics*, the case in which an effect is predicated of a cause (as when it is said that the slain man perished by slaying, or that the thing cooled was made cold or chilled by cooling).

1057. This phrase is used in a fourth sense inasmuch as those things are said to belong to something "in themselves" which belong to it alone and precisely as belonging to it alone.

He says this in order to differentiate this sense of "in itself" from the preceding senses, in which it was not said that a thing belongs to something in itself because it belongs to it alone—though in that sense too something would belong to it alone, as the definition to the thing defined. But here something is said to be in itself by reason of its exclusiveness. For "in itself" signifies something separate, as a man is said to be by himself when he is alone. And to this sense is reduced the third sense given in the *Posterior Analytics*, and the fourth sense of the phrase "according to which," which implies position.

Lecture 20

"Disposition," "having," "affection," "privation," and "to have"

1022b1 Dispositio dicitur habentis partes ordo, aut secundum locum, aut secundum potentiam, aut secundum speciem. Positionem enim oportet quamdam esse, sicut et ipsum hoc nomen dispositio ostendit. [1058]

διάθεσις λέγεται τοῦ ἔχοντος μέρη τάξις ἢ κατὰ τόπον ἢ κατὰ δύναμιν ἢ κατ᾽ εἶδος· θέσιν γὰρ δεῖ τινὰ εἶναι, ὥσπερ καὶ τοὔνομα δηλοῖ ἡ διάθεσις.

"Disposition" means the order of what has parts, either as to place or as to potency or as to species. For there must be a certain position, as the term disposition itself makes clear.

1022b4 Habitus vero dicitur uno quidem modo tamquam actio quaedam habentis et habiti, ut actus quidam, aut motus. Nam quando hoc quidem facit, illud vero fit, est factio intermedia. Et ita inter habentem indumentum, et habitum indumentum, intermedius est habitus. [1062]

ἕξις δὲ λέγεται ἕνα μὲν τρόπον οἷον ἐνέργειά τις τοῦ {5} ἔχοντος καὶ ἐχομένου, ὥσπερ πρᾶξίς τις ἢ κίνησις (ὅταν γὰρ τὸ μὲν ποιῇ τὸ δὲ ποιῆται, ἔστι ποίησις μεταξύ· οὕτω καὶ τοῦ ἔχοντος ἐσθῆτα καὶ τῆς ἐχομένης ἐσθῆτος ἔστι μεταξὺ ἕξις):

"Having" means in one sense a certain action of the haver and of what is had, as a sort of act or motion. For when one thing makes and another is made, the making is intermediate. And likewise between one having clothing and the clothing had, the having is intermediate.

Ergo palam quia non convenit habere habitum: in infinitum enim vadit, si habiti fuerit habere habitum.

ταύτην μὲν οὖν φανερὸν ὅτι οὐκ ἐνδέχεται ἔχειν ἕξιν (εἰς ἄπειρον γὰρ βαδιεῖται, εἰ τοῦ ἐχομένου ἔσται ἔχειν τὴν {10} ἕξιν),

It is accordingly clear that it is not reasonable to have a having; for if it were possible to have the having of what is had, this would go on to infinity.

Alio vero modo habitus dispositio dicitur, secundum quam bene et male disponitur dispositum, et aut secundum se, aut ad aliud; ut sanitas est habitus quidam et dispositio est talis.

ἄλλον δὲ τρόπον ἕξις λέγεται διάθεσις καθ᾽ ἣν ἢ εὖ ἢ κακῶς διάκειται τὸ διακείμενον, καὶ ἢ καθ᾽ αὑτὸ ἢ πρὸς ἄλλο, οἷον ἡ ὑγίεια ἕξις τις· διάθεσις γάρ ἐστι τοιαύτη.

In another sense, "having" means a certain disposition whereby the thing disposed is well or badly disposed, in relation either to itself or to something else—for example, health is a sort of having and is such a disposition.

Amplius habitus quidem dicitur, si est pars dispositionis talis. Quapropter et partium virtus habitus est quidam.

ἔτι ἕξις λέγεται ἂν ᾖ μόριον διαθέσεως τοιαύτης· διὸ καὶ ἡ τῶν μερῶν ἀρετὴ ἕξις τίς ἐστιν.

Again, the term "having" is used if there is a part of such a disposition. And for this reason any virtue pertaining to the powers of the soul is a sort of having.

1022b15 Passio dicitur uno quidem modo qualitas secundum quam alterari contingit, ut album et nigrum, dulce et amarum, gravitas et levitas, et quaecumque sunt talia. Alio vero modo horum actiones et alterationes. Amplius horum magis nocivae alterationes et motus. Et maxime lamentabiles et nocivae. Amplius magnitudines exultationum et lamentationum passiones dicuntur. [1065]

πάθος λέγεται ἕνα μὲν τρόπον ποιότης καθ᾽ ἣν ἀλλοιοῦσθαι ἐνδέχεται, οἷον τὸ λευκὸν καὶ τὸ μέλαν, καὶ γλυκὺ καὶ πικρόν, καὶ βαρύτης καὶ κουφότης, καὶ ὅσα ἄλλα τοιαῦτα· ἕνα δὲ αἱ τούτων ἐνέργειαι καὶ ἀλλοιώσεις ἤδη. ἔτι τούτων μᾶλλον αἱ βλαβεραὶ ἀλλοιώσεις καὶ κινήσεις, {20} καὶ μάλιστα αἱ λυπηραὶ βλάβαι. ἔτι τὰ μεγέθη τῶν συμφορῶν καὶ λυπηρῶν πάθη λέγεται.

"Passion" means, in one sense, the quality according to which alteration occurs, as white and black, sweet and bitter, heavy and light, and all other such attributes. And in another sense, it means the actualizations and alterations of these; of these, particularly harmful operations and motions, most especially those which are painful and injurious. Again, great rejoicing and grieving are called passions.

1022b22 Privatio dicitur, uno quidem modo si non habet aliquid aptorum natorum haberi, etsi non sit id natum habere, ut oculis privari dicitur planta. [1070]

στέρησις λέγεται ἕνα μὲν τρόπον ἂν μὴ ἔχῃ τι τῶν πεφυκότων ἔχεσθαι, κἂν μὴ αὐτὸ ᾖ πεφυκὸς ἔχειν, οἷον φυτὸν ὀμμάτων ἐστερῆσθαι λέγεται·

The term "privation" is used in one sense when a thing does not have one of those attributes which it is suitable for some things to have, even though that particular thing would not naturally have it. In this sense, a plant is said to be deprived of eyes.

Alio vero si aptum natum habere, aut ipsum, aut genus, non habet. Ut aliter

ἕνα δὲ ἂν πεφυκὸς {25} ἔχειν, ἢ αὐτὸ ἢ τὸ γένος, μὴ ἔχῃ, οἷον ἄλλως ἄνθρωπος

And it is used in another sense when a thing is naturally disposed to have some-

homo caecus visu privari dicitur, et talpa; hoc quidem secundum genus, illud vero secundum se.

ὁ τυφλὸς ὄψεως ἐστέρηται καὶ ἀσπάλαξ, τὸ μὲν κατὰ τὸ γένος τὸ δὲ καθ' αὑτό.

thing, either in itself or according to its genus, and does not have it. A man and a mole, for example, are deprived of sight, but in different ways: the latter according to its genus and the former in itself.

Amplius si aptum natum, et quando aptum natum est habere, et non habet:

ἔτι ἂν πεφυκὸς καὶ ὅτε πέφυκεν ἔχειν μὴ ἔχῃ:

Again, we speak of privation when a thing is by nature such as to have a certain perfection and does not have it even when it is naturally disposed to have it.

caecitas enim privatio quaedam est, sed caecus non est secundum omnem aetatem, sed in qua aptum natum est habere, si non habet.

ἡ γὰρ τυφλότης στέρησίς τις, τυφλὸς δ' οὐ κατὰ πᾶσαν ἡλικίαν, ἀλλ' ἐν ᾗ πέφυκεν ἔχειν, ἂν μὴ ἔχῃ.

For blindness is a privation, although a man is not blind at every age but only if he does not have sight at the age when he is naturally disposed to have it.

Similiter autem et in quo, et secundum quid, et ad quod, et ut, si non habet, aptum natum.

{30} ὁμοίως δὲ καὶ ἐν ᾧ ἂν ᾖ <πεφυκὸς> καὶ καθ' ὃ καὶ πρὸς ὃ καὶ ὥς, ἂν μὴ ἔχῃ [πεφυκός].

And similarly, we speak of privation when a thing does not have what it is naturally disposed to have, in reference to where, and to what part, and to the object in relation to which, and in the manner in which it may have it.

Amplius cuiusque per vim ablatio privatio dicitur.

ἔτι ἡ βιαία ἑκάστου ἀφαίρεσις στέρησις λέγεται.

Again, the removal of anything by force is called a privation.

1022b33 Et quoties ab eo quod A privativa particula negationes dicuntur, toties et privationes dicuntur. Nam inaequale, non habere aequalitatem aptum quidem natum dicitur. [1074]

καὶ ὁσαχῶς δὲ αἱ ἀπὸ τοῦ <α> ἀποφάσεις λέγονται, τοσαυταχῶς καὶ αἱ στερήσεις λέγονται: ἄνισον μὲν γὰρ τῷ μὴ ἔχειν ἰσότητα πεφυκὸς λέγεται,

And in all instances in which negations are expressed by the privative particle,[4] privations are expressed. For a thing is said to be unequal because it does not have the equality which it is naturally fitted to have.

Invisibile vero et eo quod non habere omnino colorem et eo quod turpiter. Et sine pede, et non habere omnino pedes, et ex eo quod turpes.

ἀόρατον δὲ {35} καὶ τῷ ὅλως μὴ ἔχειν χρῶμα καὶ τῷ φαύλως, καὶ ἄπουν καὶ τῷ μὴ ἔχειν ὅλως πόδας καὶ τῷ φαύλους.

And a thing is said to be invisible either because it has no color at all or because its color is deficient, and a thing is said to be footless either because it lacks feet altogether or because its feet are imperfect.

Amplius et eo quod parum habeat, ut non ignitum: hoc autem est turpiter aliquo modo habere.

ἔτι καὶ τῷ μικρὸν ἔχειν, οἷον τὸ ἀπύρηνον: {1023a1} τοῦτο δ' ἐστὶ τὸ φαύλως πως ἔχειν.

Again, we use the term "privation" of a thing when it has something to a very small degree—for example, "unfired"—and this means to have it in a deficient way.

Amplius non facile, aut non bene; ut insecabile, non solum quia non secatur, sed quia non facile, aut quia non bene.

ἔτι τῷ μὴ ῥαδίως ἢ τῷ μὴ καλῶς, οἷον τὸ ἄτμητον οὐ μόνον τῷ μὴ τέμνεσθαι ἀλλὰ καὶ τῷ μὴ ῥαδίως ἢ μὴ καλῶς.

And "privation" also designates what is not had easily or well. For example, a thing is uncuttable not only because it cannot be cut, but because it cannot be cut easily or well.

Amplius non habere omnino. Caecus enim non dicitur monoculus, sed qui in ambobus non habet visum. Propter quod non omnis homo bonus aut malus aut iustus aut iniustus est, sed est medium.

ἔτι τῷ πάντῃ μὴ ἔχειν: τυφλὸς γὰρ οὐ λέγεται ὁ {5} ἑτερόφθαλμος ἀλλ' ὁ ἐν ἀμφοῖν μὴ ἔχων ὄψιν: διὸ οὐ πᾶς ἀγαθὸς ἢ κακός, ἢ δίκαιος ἢ ἄδικος, ἀλλὰ καὶ τὸ μεταξύ.

And we use the term "privation" of what is not had in any way. For it is not only a one-eyed man that is said to be blind, but one who lacks sight in both eyes. And for this reason, not every man is good or bad, just or unjust, but there is an intermediate state.

---

4. In English, privatives can be signified by un- or in- (for example, "incapable" or "unfit").

1023a8   Habere multipliciter dicitur. [1080]

Uno quidem modo deducere secundum suam naturam, aut secundum suum impetum. Propter quod febris dicitur habere hominem, et tyranni civitatem et vestimentum induti.

Alio in quo utique aliquid extiterit ut susceptibile, ut aes habet speciem statuae et infirmitatem corpus.

Alio ut continens contentum. Nam in quo est, contentum aliquod haberi ab hoc dicitur, ut lagenam habere humidum dicimus, et civitatem homines, et naves nautas. Sic autem et totum habere partes.

Amplius et prohibens secundum suum impetum aliquid movere aut operari, habere dicitur hoc ipsum, ut columnae ponderosa superposita, ut poetae Atlantem faciunt habere caelum tamquam casurum super terram, quemadmodum physiologorum quidam dicunt. Hoc autem modo, continens dicitur quae continet habere, quasi separata secundum suum impetum singula. Et in aliquo aliquid esse simili modo dicitur; et consequenter ipsi habere.

τὸ ἔχειν λέγεται πολλαχῶς,

ἕνα μὲν τρόπον τὸ ἄγειν κατὰ τὴν αὐτοῦ φύσιν ἢ κατὰ τὴν αὐτοῦ ὁρμήν, διὸ {10} λέγεται πυρετός τε ἔχειν τὸν ἄνθρωπον καὶ οἱ τύραννοι τὰς πόλεις καὶ τὴν ἐσθῆτα οἱ ἀμπεχόμενοι:

ἕνα δ' ἐν ᾧ ἄν τι ὑπάρχῃ ὡς δεκτικῷ, οἷον ὁ χαλκὸς ἔχει τὸ εἶδος τοῦ ἀνδριάντος καὶ τὴν νόσον τὸ σῶμα:

ἕνα δὲ ὡς τὸ περιέχον τὰ περιεχόμενα: ἐν ᾧ γάρ ἐστι περιέχοντι, ἔχεσθαι ὑπὸ {15} τούτου λέγεται, οἷον τὸ ἀγγεῖον ἔχειν τὸ ὑγρόν φαμεν καὶ τὴν πόλιν ἀνθρώπους καὶ τὴν ναῦν ναύτας, οὕτω δὲ καὶ τὸ ὅλον ἔχειν τὰ μέρη.

ἔτι τὸ κωλῦον κατὰ τὴν αὐτοῦ ὁρμήν τι κινεῖσθαι ἢ πράττειν ἔχειν λέγεται τοῦτο αὐτό, οἷον καὶ οἱ κίονες τὰ ἐπικείμενα βάρη, καὶ ὡς οἱ ποιηταὶ {20} τὸν Ἄτλαντα ποιοῦσι τὸν οὐρανὸν ἔχειν ὡς συμπεσόντ' ἂν ἐπὶ τὴν γῆν, ὥσπερ καὶ τῶν φυσιολόγων τινές φασιν: τοῦτον δὲ τὸν τρόπον καὶ τὸ συνέχον λέγεται ἃ συνέχει ἔχειν, ὡς διαχωρισθέντα ἂν κατὰ τὴν αὐτοῦ ὁρμὴν ἕκαστον. καὶ τὸ ἔν τινι δὲ εἶναι ὁμοτρόπως λέγεται καὶ ἑπομένως τῷ {25} ἔχειν.

"To have" has many meanings.

In one sense it means to treat something according to one's own nature or to one's own impulse. For this reason a fever is said to possess a man, and tyrants are said to possess cities, and people who are clothed are said to possess clothing.

And in another sense a thing is said to have something when this is present in the subject which receives it. Thus bronze has the form of a statue, and a body of disease.

And whatever contains something else is said to have or to hold it, for that which is contained is said to be held by the container. For example, we say that a bottle holds a liquid, and a city men, and a ship sailors. It is in this way too that a whole has parts.

Again, whatever prevents a thing from moving or from acting according to its own impulse is said to hold it, as pillars hold the weight imposed on them. It is in this sense that the poets make Atlas hold the heavens (as if otherwise it would fall on the earth, as certain of the physicists also say). And it is in this sense that that which holds something together is said to hold what it holds together, because otherwise it would be separated, each according to its own impulse. And to be in something is expressed in a similar way and corresponds to the meanings of "to have."

1058. Quia uno modo secundum quod positionem significat, ideo consequenter Philosophus prosequitur de nomine dispositionis; et ponit rationem communem huius nominis dispositio, dicens, quod dispositio nihil est aliud quam ordo partium in habente partes. Ponit autem modos quibus dicitur dispositio: qui sunt tres.

Quorum primus est secundum ordinem partium in loco. Et sic dispositio sive situs est quoddam praedicamentum.

1059. Secundus modus est, prout ordo partium attenditur secundum potentiam sive virtutem; et sic dispositio ponitur in prima specie qualitatis. Dicitur enim aliquid hoc modo esse dispositum, utputa secundum sanitatem vel aegritudinem, ex eo quod partes eius habent ordinem in virtute activa vel passiva.

1058. Because the phrase "according to which" signifies in one sense position, the Philosopher therefore proceeds to examine next [1058] the term "disposition." He gives the common meaning of this term, saying that a disposition is nothing else than the order of parts in a thing which has parts. He also gives the senses in which the term "disposition" is used; and there are three of these.

The first designates the order of parts in place, and in this sense disposition or posture is a special category.

1059. "Disposition" is used in a second sense inasmuch as the order of parts is considered in reference to potency or active power, and then disposition is placed in the first species of quality. For a thing is said to be disposed in this sense—for example, according to health or sickness—because its parts have an order in its active or passive power.

1060. Tertius modus est, prout ordo partium attenditur secundum speciem et figuram totius; et sic dispositio sive situs ponitur differentia in genere quantitatis. Dicitur enim quod quantitas alia est habens positionem, ut linea, superficies, corpus et locus; alia non habens, ut numerus et tempus.

1061. Ostendit etiam quod hoc nomen dispositio, ordinem significet. Significat enim positionem, sicut ipsa nominis impositio demonstrat: de ratione autem positionis est ordo.

1062. *Habitus vero* hic prosequitur de nomine habitus;

et primo distinguit ipsum nomen habitus.

Secundo quaedam nomina quae habent propinquam considerationem ad hoc nomen, ibi, *passio dicitur*.

Ponit ergo primo duos modos, quibus hoc nomen dicitur.

Quorum primus est aliquid medium inter habentem et habitum. Habere enim, licet non sit actio, significat tamen per modum actionis.

Et ideo inter habentem et habitum intelligitur habitus esse medius, et quasi actio quaedam; sicut calefactio intelligitur esse media inter calefactum et calefaciens; sive illud medium accipiatur ut actus, sicut quando calefactio accipitur active; sive ut motus, sicut quando calefactio accipitur passive.

Quando enim hoc facit, et illud fit, est media factio. In Graeco habetur poiesis, quod factionem significat. Et siquidem ulterius procedatur ab agente in patiens, est medium factio activa, quae est actus facientis.

Si vero procedatur a facto in facientem, sic est medium factio passiva, quae est motus facti.

Ita etiam inter hominem habentem vestem, et vestem habitam, est medius habitus; quia si consideretur procedendo ab homine ad vestem, erit ut actio, prout significatur in hoc quod dicitur habere: si vero e converso, erit ut passio motus, prout significatur in hoc quod dicitur haberi.

1063. Quamvis autem habitus intelligatur esse medius inter hominem et vestem, inquantum habet eam; tamen manifestum est, quod non contingit inter ipsum habitum et habentem esse aliud medium, quasi adhuc sit alius habitus medius inter habentem et ipsum medium habitum.

Sic enim procederetur in infinitum, si dicatur quod convenit habere habitum *habiti*, idest rei habitae. Homo

---

1060. "Disposition" is used in a third sense according as the order of parts is considered in reference to the form and figure of the whole; then disposition or position is held to be a difference in the genus of quantity. For it is said that one kind of quantity has position (like line, surface, body, and place), but that another has not (like number and time).

1061. He also points out that the term "disposition" signifies order, for it signifies position, as the derivation itself of the term makes clear, and order is involved in the notion of position.

1062. *"Having" means* (1022b4). He now proceeds to examine the term "having."

First, he gives the different senses of the term "having."

Second (1022b15; [1065]), he gives the different senses of certain other terms which are closely connected with this one, at *"passion" means*.

He accordingly first gives the two senses in which the term "having" is used.

First, it designates something intermediate between the haver and the thing had. Now even though having is not an action, nonetheless it signifies something after the manner of an action.

Therefore, "having" is understood to be something intermediate between the haver and the thing had and to be a sort of action, just as heating is understood to be something intermediate between the thing being heated and the heater, whether what is intermediate be taken as an action (as when heating is taken in an active sense), or as a motion (as when heating is taken in a passive sense).

For when one thing makes and another is made, the making stands between them. In Greek, the term *poiesis* is used, and this signifies making. Moreover, if one goes from the agent to the patient, the intermediate is making in an active sense, and this is the action of the maker.

But if one goes from the thing made to the maker, then the intermediate is making in a passive sense, and this is the motion of the thing being made.

And between a man having clothing and the clothing had, the having is also an intermediate, for if we consider it by going from the man to his clothing, it will be like an action, as is expressed under the form "to have." But if we consider it in the opposite way, it will be like the undergoing of a motion, as is expressed under the form "to be had."

1063. Now, although having is understood to be intermediate between a man and his clothing inasmuch as he has it, nonetheless it is evident that there cannot be another intermediate between the having and the thing had, as though there were another having midway between the haver and the intermediate having.

For if one were to say that it is possible to have the having *of what is had* (that is, of the thing had), an infinite

enim habet *rem habitam*, idest vestem. Sed illum habitum rei habitae non habet homo, alio medio habitu, sicut homo faciens facit factum factione media; sed ipsam mediam factionem non facit aliqua alia factione media.

Et propter hoc etiam relationes, quibus subiectum refertur ad aliud, non referuntur ad subiectum aliqua alia relatione media, nec etiam ad oppositum; sicut paternitas neque ad patrem neque ad filium refertur aliqua alia relatione media: et si aliquae relationes mediae dicantur, sunt rationis tantum, et non rei. Habitus autem sic acceptus est unum praedicamentum.

1064. Secundo modo dicitur habitus dispositio, secundum quam aliquid disponitur bene et male; sicut sanitate aliquid disponitur bene, aegritudine male. Utroque autem, scilicet aegritudine et sanitate, aliquid disponitur bene vel male dupliciter; scilicet aut secundum se aut per respectum ad aliquid. Sicut sanum est quod est bene dispositum secundum se; robustum autem quod est bene dispositum ad aliquid agendum. Et ideo sanitas est habitus quidam, quia est talis dispositio qualis dicta est.

Et non solum habitus dicitur dispositio totius, sed etiam dispositio partis, quae est pars dispositionis totius; sicuti bonae dispositiones partium animalis, sunt partes bonae habitudinis in toto animali.

Et virtutes etiam partium animae, sunt quidam habitus; sicut temperantia concupiscibilis, et fortitudo irascibilis, et prudentia rationalis.

1065. Deinde cum dicit *passio dicitur* hic prosequitur de illis quae consequuntur ad habitum;

et primo de his quae se habent ad ipsum per modum oppositionis.

Secundo de eo quod se habet ad ipsum per modum effectus, scilicet de habere, quod ab habitu denominatur, ibi, *habere multipliciter dicitur.*

Habitui autem opponitur aliquid, scilicet passio, sicut imperfectum perfecto. Privatio autem oppositione directa.

Unde primo determinat de passione.
Secundo de privatione, ibi, *privatio dicitur.*

Ponit ergo primo, quatuor modos, quibus passio dicitur.

Uno modo dicitur qualitas, secundum quam fit alteratio, sicut album et nigrum et huiusmodi. Et haec est tertia species qualitatis. Probatum enim est in septimo

regress would then result. For the man has **the thing had**, his clothing, but he does not have the having of the thing had by way of another intermediate having. It is like the case of a maker, who makes the thing made by an intermediate making, but does not make the intermediate making itself by way of some other intermediate making.

It is for this reason too that the relations by which a subject is related to something else are not related to the subject by some other intermediate relation and also not to the opposite term. Paternity, for example, is not related to a father or to a son by some other intermediate relation. And if some relations are said to be intermediate, they are merely conceptual relations and not real ones. "Having" in this sense is taken as one of the categories.

1064. In a second sense, the term "having" means the disposition whereby something is well or badly disposed—for example, a thing is well disposed by health and badly disposed by sickness. Now by each of these, health and sickness, a thing is well or badly disposed in two ways: either in itself or in relation to something else. Thus a healthy thing is one that is well disposed in itself, and a robust thing is one that is well disposed for doing something. Health is a kind of having, then, because it is a disposition such as has been described.

And "having," or "habit," designates not only the disposition of a whole but also that of a part, which is a part of the disposition of the whole. For example, the good dispositions of an animal's parts are themselves parts of the good disposition of the whole animal.

The virtues pertaining to the parts of the soul are also habits. For example, temperance is a habit of the concupiscible part, fortitude a habit of the irascible part, and prudence a habit of the rational part.

1065. *Passion*. Here he proceeds to treat the terms which are associated with "having."

First, he deals with those which are associated as an opposite;

and second (1023a8; [1080]), he considers something which is related to it as an effect, namely, "to have," which derives its name from "having," at *"to have" has many meanings*.

Now there is something which is opposed to having as the imperfect is opposed to the perfect, and this is "passion" (being affected). And "privation" is opposed by direct opposition.

Hence, first [1065], he deals with passion;

second (1022b22; [1070]), with privation, at *the term "privation."*

He accordingly first gives four senses of the term "passion."

In one sense it means the quality according to which alteration takes place, such as white and black and the like. And this is the third species of quality, for it has been

Physicorum, quod in sola tertia specie qualitatis potest esse alteratio.

1066. Secundus modus est, secundum quod huiusmodi actiones qualitatis et alterationis, quae fiunt secundum eas, dicuntur passiones; et sic passio est unum praedicamentum, ut calefieri et infrigidari et huiusmodi.

1067. Tertio modo dicuntur passiones, non quaelibet alterationes, sed quae sunt nocivae, et ad malum terminatae, et quae sunt lamentabiles, sive tristes: non enim dicitur aliquid pati secundum hunc modum quod sanatur, sed quod infirmatur; vel etiam cuicumque aliquod nocumentum accidit: et hoc rationabiliter. Patiens enim per actionem agentis sibi contrarii, trahitur a sua dispositione naturali in dispositionem similem agenti. Et ideo magis proprie dicitur pati, cum subtrahitur aliquid de eo quod sibi congruebat, et dum agitur in ipso contraria dispositio, quam quando fit e contrario. Tunc enim magis dicitur perfici.

1068. Et quia illa, quae sunt modica, quasi nulla reputantur, ideo quarto modo dicuntur passiones, non quaecumque nocivae alterationes, sed quae habent magnitudinem nocumenti, sicut magnae calamitates et magnae tristitiae. Quia etiam excedens laetitia fit nociva, cum quandocumque propter excessum laetitiae aliqui mortui sint et infirmati; et similiter superabundantia prosperitatis in nocumentum vertitur his qui ea bene uti nesciunt: ideo alia litera habet **magnitudines lamentationum et exultationum passiones dicuntur**. Cui concordat alia litera, quae dicit **magnitudines dolorum et prosperorum**.

1069. Sciendum est autem, quod quia haec tria, scilicet dispositio, habitus, et passio, non significant genus praedicamenti, nisi secundum unum modum significationis, ut ex praehabitis patet, ideo non posuit ea cum aliis partibus entis, scilicet quantitate, qualitate et ad aliquid. In illis enim vel omnes vel plures modi ad genera praedicamenti, significata per illa nomina, pertinebant.

1070. *Privatio dicitur* hic distinguit modos, quibus dicitur privatio;

et quia privatio includit in sua ratione negationem et aptitudinem subiecti, ideo primo distinguit modos privationis ex parte aptitudinis.

Secundo ex parte negationis, ibi, *et quoties.*

Et circa primum ponit quatuor modos.

Primus modus est, secundum quod aptitudo consideratur ex parte rei privatae, non ex parte subiecti. Dicitur enim hoc modo privatio, quando ab aliquo non

proved in *Physics* 7 that there can be alteration only in the third species of quality.

1066. "Passion" is used in another sense according as the actualizations of this kind of quality and alteration, which comes about through them, are called passions. And in this sense "passion" is one of the categories (for example, being heated and cooled and other motions of this kind).

1067. In a third sense, "passion" means not any kind of alteration at all, but those which are harmful and terminate in some evil, and which are lamentable or sorrowful, for a thing is not said to suffer insofar as it is healed, but insofar as it is made ill. Or it also designates anything harmful that befalls anything at all, and with good reason. For a patient, by the action of some agent which is contrary to it, is drawn from its own natural disposition to one similar to that of the agent. Hence, a patient is said more properly to suffer when some part of something fitting to it is being removed while its disposition is being changed into a contrary one rather than when the reverse occurs. For then it is said rather to be perfected.

1068. And because things that are not very great are considered as nothing, therefore, in a fourth sense, "passion" means not any kind of harmful alteration whatsoever, but those which are extremely injurious, as great calamities and great sorrows. And because excessive pleasure becomes harmful (for sometimes people have died or become ill as a result of it), and because too great prosperity is turned into something harmful to those who do not know how to make good use of it, therefore another text reads **great rejoicing and grieving are called passions**. And still another text agrees with this, saying, **very great sorrows and prosperities**.

1069. Now it should be noted that because these three—"disposition," "habit" or "having," and "passion"—signify one of the categories only in one of the senses in which they are used, as is evident from what was said above, he therefore did not place them with the other parts of being (quantity, quality, and relation). For either all or most of the senses in which they were used pertained to the category signified by these terms.

1070. *The term "privation"* (1022b22). Here he gives the different senses in which the term "privation" is used.

And since privation includes in its intelligible structure both negation and the fitness of some subject to possess some attribute, he therefore first gives the different senses of "privation" which refer to this fitness or aptitude for some attribute.

Second (1022b33; [1074]), he treats the various senses of negation, at *and in all instances.*

In regard to the first he gives four senses of "privation."

The first has to do with this natural fitness taken in reference to the attribute of which the subject is deprived, and not in reference to the subject itself. For we speak

habetur id quod natum est haberi, licet hoc quod ipso caret non sit natum habere;

sicut planta dicitur privari oculis, quia oculi nati sunt haberi, licet non a planta.

In his vero, quae a nullo nata sunt haberi, non potest dici aliquid privari, sicut oculus visu penetrante per corpora opaca.

1071. Secundus modus attenditur secundum aptitudinem subiecti. Hoc enim modo dicitur privari hoc solum quod natum est illud habere, aut *secundum se*, aut *secundum genus* suum:

secundum se, sicut homo caecus dicitur privari visu, quem natus est habere secundum se. Talpa autem dicitur privari visu, non quia ipsa secundum se sit nata habere visum; sed quia genus eius, scilicet animal, natum est habere visum.

Multa enim sunt a quibus aliquid non impeditur ratione generis, sed ratione differentiae; sicut homo non impeditur quin habeat alas ratione generis, sed ratione differentiae.

1072. Tertius modus attenditur ex parte circumstantiarum. Unde hoc modo dicitur aliquid privari aliquo, si non habet ipsum habitum cum *natum sit habere*. Sicut caecitas, quae est quaedam privatio, et tamen animal non dicitur caecum *secundum omnem aetatem*, sed solum si non habeat visum in illa aetate in qua natum est habere; unde canis non dicitur caecus ante nonum diem.

Et sicut est de hac circumstantia quando, ita est et de aliis circumstantiis, scilicet *in quo*, ut in loco; sicut nox dicitur privatio lucis in loco ubi nata est esse lux, non in cavernis, ad quas lumen solis pervenire non potest;

et secundum quid, sicut homo non dicitur edentulus, si non habet dentes in manu; sed si non habet secundum illam partem, secundum quam natus est habere; *et ad quod*, sicut homo non dicitur parvus, vel deficientis staturae si non est magnus respectu montis, vel respectu cuiuscumque alterius rei, ad cuius comparationem non est natus habere magnitudinem: et sic homo non dicitur tardus esse motu, si non currat ita velociter sicut lepus vel ventus; vel ignorans, si non intelligit sicut Deus.

1073. Quartus modus est secundum quod *ablatio cuiuslibet rei per violentiam*, dicitur privatio. Violentum enim est contra impetum naturalem, ut habitum est su-

of a privation in this sense when some attribute which is naturally fitted to be had is not had, even though the subject which lacks it is not designed by nature to have it.

For example, a plant is said to be deprived of eyes because eyes are naturally designed to be had by something, although not by a plant.

But in the case of those attributes which a subject is not naturally fitted to have, the subject cannot be said to be deprived of them—for example, that the eye by its power of vision should penetrate an opaque body.

1071. A second sense of the term "privation" is noted in reference to a subject's fitness to have some attribute. For in this sense, "privation" refers only to some attribute which a thing is naturally fitted to have either *in itself* or *according to its genus*.

An example of having it *in itself* is when a blind person is said to be deprived of sight, which he is naturally fitted to have in himself. And a mole is said to be deprived of sight not because it is naturally fitted to have it, but because the genus, animal, to which the mole belongs, is so fitted.

For there are many attributes which a thing is not prevented from having by reason of its genus, but by reason of its differences—for example, a man is not prevented from having wings by reason of his genus, but by reason of his difference.

1072. A third sense of the term "privation" is noted in reference to circumstances. And in this sense a thing is said to be deprived of something if it does not have it when it is *naturally disposed to have it*. This is the case, for example, with the privation "blindness," for an animal is not said to be blind *at every age*, but only if it does not have sight at an age when it is naturally disposed to have it. Hence a dog is not said to be blind before the ninth day.

And what is true of the circumstance of "when" also applies to other circumstances, as *to where*, or place. Thus "night" means the privation of light in a place where light may naturally exist, but not in caverns, which the sun's rays cannot penetrate.

And it applies *to what part*, as a man is not said to be toothless if he does not have teeth in his hand, but only if he does not have them in that part in which they are naturally disposed to exist; and *to the object in relation to which*, as a man is not said to be small or imperfect in stature if he is not large in comparison with a mountain or with any other thing with which he is not naturally comparable in size. Hence a man is not said to be slow in moving if he does not run as fast as a hare or move as fast as the wind; nor is he said to be ignorant if he does not understand as God does.

1073. "Privation" is used in a fourth sense inasmuch as *the removal of anything by violence* is called a privation. For what is forced is contrary to natural impulse, as has

pra. Et ita *ablatio per violentiam* est respectu eius quod quis natus est habere.

1074. Deinde cum dicit *et quoties* distinguit modos privationis ex parte negationis. Graeci enim utuntur hac praepositione a in compositionibus ad designandas negationes et privationes, sicut nos utimur hac praepositione in. Dicit ergo quod quoties dicuntur negationes designatae ab hac praepositione a posita in principio dictionis per compositionem, toties dicuntur etiam privationes. Dicitur enim inaequale uno modo, quod non habet aequalitatem, si aptum natum est habere; et invisibile, quod non habet colorem; et sine pede, quod non habet pedes.

1075. Secundo modo dicuntur huiusmodi negationes non per hoc quod est omnino non habere; sed per hoc quod est prave vel turpiter habere; sicut dicitur non habere colorem, quia habet malum colorem vel turpem; et non habere pedes, quia habet parvos vel turpes.

1076. Tertio modo significatur aliquid privative vel negative ex hoc, quod est parum habere; sicut dicitur in Graeco apirenon, idest non ignitum, ubi est modicum de igne: et hic modus quodammodo continetur sub secundo, quia parum habere est quodammodo prave et turpiter habere.

1077. Quarto modo dicitur aliquid privative vel negative, ex eo quod non est facile, vel non bene; sicut aliquid dicitur insecabile, non solum quia non secatur, sed quia non facile, aut non bene.

1078. Quinto modo dicitur aliquid negative vel privative, ex eo quod est omnino non habere. Unde monoculus non dicitur caecus, sed ille qui in ambobus oculis caret visu.

1079. Ex hoc inducit quoddam corollarium; scilicet quod inter bonum et malum, iustum et iniustum, est aliquid medium. Non enim ex quocumque defectu bonitatis efficitur aliquis malus, sicut Stoici dicebant ponentes omnia peccata esse paria; sed quando multum a virtute recedit, et in contrarium habitum inducitur. Unde in secundo *Ethicorum* dicitur: ex eo quod homo recedit parum a medio virtutis, non vituperatur.

1080. Deinde cum dicit *habere multipliciter* hic ponit quatuor modos eius, quod est habere:

quorum primus est, secundum quod habere aliquid est ducere illud secundum suam naturam in rebus naturalibus, aut secundum suum impetum in rebus voluntariis. Et hoc modo febris dicitur habere hominem, quia homo traducitur a naturali dispositione in dispositionem febrilem. Et hoc modo habent tyranni civitates, quia secundum voluntatem et impetum tyrannorum res civitatum aguntur. Et hoc etiam modo induti dicuntur habere vestimentum, quia vestimentum coaptatur indu-

been said above [829]; thus *the removal of anything by violence* has reference to something that a person is naturally fitted to have.

1074. *And in all* (1022b33). Then he gives the different senses of "privation" which involve negation: for the Greeks use the prefix *a-* or *an-* when compounding words to designate negations and privations, just as we use the prefix *in-* or *un-*. Therefore, he says that in every case in which one expresses negations designated by the prefix *a-* or *an-*, used in composition at the beginning of a word, privations are designated. For "unequal" means in one sense what lacks equality, provided that it is naturally such as to have it; and "invisible" means what lacks color; and "footless" means what lacks feet.

1075. Negations of this kind are used in a second sense to indicate not what is not had at all but what is had badly or in an ugly way. For example, a thing is said to be colorless because it has a bad or unfitting color, and a thing is said to be footless because it has defective or deformed feet.

1076. In a third sense an attribute is signified privatively or negatively because it is had to a small degree. For example, the term *apirenon* (unignited) is used in the Greek text, and it signifies a situation where the smallest amount of fire exists. And in a way, this sense is contained under the second, because to have something to a small degree is in a way to have it defectively or unfittingly.

1077. Something is designated as a privation or negation in a fourth sense because it is not done easily or well; for example, something is said to be uncuttable not only because it is not cut, but because it is not cut easily or well.

1078. And something is designated as a privation or negation in a fifth sense because it is not had in any way at all. Hence it is not a one-eyed person who is said to be blind, but one who lacks sight in both eyes.

1079. From this he draws a corollary, namely, that there is some intermediate between good and evil, between just and unjust. For a person does not become evil when he lacks goodness to any degree at all, as the Stoics said (for they held all sins to be equal), but when he deviates widely from virtue and is brought to a contrary habit. Hence it is said in *Ethics* 2 that a man is not to be blamed for deviating a little from virtue.

1080. *"To have"* (1023a8). Then he gives four ways in which the term "to have" (to possess or hold) is used:

first, to have a thing is to treat it according to one's own nature in the case of natural things, or according to one's own impulse in the case of voluntary matters. Thus a fever is said to possess a man because he is brought from a normal state to one of fever. And in the same sense, tyrants are said to possess cities, because civic business is carried out according to the will and impulse of tyrants. And in this sense too those who are clothed are said to possess or have clothing, because clothing is fitted to the one who wears

to ut accipiat figuram eius. Et ad hunc modum reducitur etiam habere possessionem, quia homo re possessa utitur secundum suam voluntatem.

1081. Secundus modus est, prout illud, in quo existit aliquid ut in proprio susceptibili, dicitur habere illud; sicut aes habet speciem statuae, et corpus habet infirmitatem. Et sub hoc modo comprehenditur habere scientiam, quantitatem, et quodcumque accidens, vel quamcumque formam.

1082. Tertius modus est, secundum quod continens dicitur habere contentum, et contentum haberi a continente;

sicut dicimus quod lagena *habet humidum*, idest humorem aliquem, ut aquam vel vinum; et quod civitas habet homines, et navis nautas. Et secundum hunc modum etiam dicitur quod totum habet partes. Totum enim continet partem, sicut et locus locatum. In hoc enim differt locus a toto, quia locus est divisus a locato, non autem totum a partibus. Unde locatum est sicut pars divisa, ut habetur in quarto *Physicorum*.

1083. Quartus modus est secundum quod aliquid dicitur habere alterum, ex eo, quod prohibet ipsum operari vel moveri secundum suum impetum;

sicut columnae dicuntur habere corpora ponderosa imposita super eas, quia prohibent ea descendere deorsum secundum inclinationem. Et hoc etiam modo poetae dixerunt quod Atlas habet caelum. Fingunt enim poetae quod Atlas est quidam gigas qui sustinet caelum ne cadat super terram.

Quod etiam quidam naturales dicunt, qui ponebant quod caelum quandoque corrumpetur et resolutum cadet super terram. Quod patet praecipue ex opinione Empedoclis, qui posuit mundum infinities corrumpi et infinities generari. Habuit autem poetica fictio ex veritate originem. Atlas quidem magnus astrologus, subtiliter motus caelestium corporum perscrutatus est, ex quo fictio processit quod ipse caelum sustineret.

Differt autem hic modus a primo. Nam in primo habens, habitum cogebat sequi secundum suum impetum, et sic erat causa motus violenti.

Hic autem habens, prohibet habitum moveri motu naturali, unde est causa quietis violentae.

Ad hunc autem modum reducitur tertius modus quo continens dicitur habere contenta; ea ratione quia aliter contenta suo proprio impetu singula separarentur abinvicem, nisi continens prohiberet; sicut patet in lagena

it so that it takes on his figure. And to have possession of a thing is also reduced to this sense of "to have," because anything that a man possesses he uses as he wills.

1081. "To have" is used in a second way inasmuch as that in which some attribute exists as its proper subject is said to have it. It is in this sense that bronze has the form of a statue, and a body has disease. And to have a science or quantity or any accident or form is included under this sense.

1082. "To have" is used in a third way (to hold) when a container is said to have or to hold the thing contained, and the thing contained is said to be held by the container.

For example, we say that a bottle has or *holds a liquid* (that is, some fluid) such as water or wine, and that a city has men, and a ship, sailors. It is in this sense too that a whole is said to have parts, for a whole contains a part just as a place contains the thing in place. But a place differs from a whole in this respect: a place may be separated from the thing which occupies it, whereas a whole may not be separated from its parts. Hence, anything that occupies a place is like a separate part, as is said in *Physics* 4.

1083. "To have" is used in a fourth way (to hold up) inasmuch as one thing is said to hold another because it prevents it from operating or being moved according to its own impulse.

It is in this sense that pillars are said to hold up the heavy bodies placed upon them, because they prevent these bodies from falling down in accordance with their own inclination. And in this sense too the poets said that Atlas holds up the heavens, for the poets supposed Atlas to be a giant who prevents the heavens from falling on the earth.

And certain natural philosophers also say this, holding that the heavens will at some time be corrupted and fall in dissolution upon the earth. This is most evident in the opinions expressed by Empedocles, for he held that the world is destroyed an infinite number of times and comes into being an infinite number of times. And the fables of the poets have some basis in reality, for Atlas, who was a great astronomer, made an accurate study of the motion of the celestial bodies, and from this arose the story that he holds up the heavens.

But this sense of the term "to have" differs from the first. For, according to the first, as was seen, the thing having compels the thing had to follow by reason of its own impulse, and thus is the cause of forced motion.

But here the thing having prevents the thing had from being moved by its own natural motion, and thus is the cause of forced rest.

The third sense of "having," according to which a container is said to have or hold the thing contained, is reduced to this sense, because the individual parts of the thing contained would be separated from each other by their own

continente aquam, quae prohibet partes abinvicem separari.

1084. Dicit autem in fine, quod esse *in aliquo* similiter dicitur sicut et habere; et modi essendi in aliquo consequuntur ad modos habendi. Octo autem modi essendi in aliquo in quarto *Physicorum* positi sunt:

quorum duo, scilicet secundum quod totum integrale est in partibus et e converso:

duo etiam, scilicet secundum quod totum universale est in partibus, et e converso,

et alius modus secundum quod locatum est in loco, consequuntur ad tertium modum habendi, secundum quod totum habet partes, et locus locatum.

Modus autem secundum quod aliquid dicitur esse in aliquo, ut in efficiente vel movente, sicut quae sunt regni in rege, consequitur primum modum habendi hic positum.

Modus autem essendi in, secundum quod forma est in materia, reducitur ad secundum modum habendi hic positum. Modus autem quo aliquid est in fine, reducitur ad modum habendi quartum hic positum; vel etiam ad primum, quia secundum finem moventur et quiescunt ea quae sunt ad finem.

peculiar impulse if the container did not prevent this. This is clear, for example, in the case of a bottle containing water, inasmuch as the bottle prevents the parts of the water from being separated.

1084. In closing he says that the phrase *to be in* a thing is used in the same way as "to have," and the ways of being in a thing correspond to those of having a thing. Now the eight ways of being in a thing have been treated in *Physics* 4.

Two of these are as follows: that in which an integral whole is in its parts, and the reverse of this.

Two others are the way in which a universal whole is in its parts, and vice versa.

And another is that in which a thing in place is in a place, and this corresponds to the third sense of "having," according to which a whole has parts, and a place has the thing which occupies it.

But the way in which a thing is said to be in something as in an efficient cause or mover (as the things belonging to a kingdom are in the king) corresponds to the first sense of "having" given here [1080].

And the way in which a thing is in an end or goal is reduced to the fourth sense of "having" given here [1083], or also to the first, because those things that are related to an end are moved or at rest because of it.

LECTURE 21

"To come from something," "part," "whole," and "mutilated"

1023a26 Ex aliquo esse dicitur uno quidem modo ex quo est ut materia: et hoc dupliciter: [1085]

τὸ ἔκ τινος εἶναι λέγεται ἕνα μὲν τρόπον ἐξ οὗ ἐστιν ὡς ὕλης, καὶ τοῦτο διχῶς,

"To come from something" means in one sense to come from something as matter, and this in two ways:

aut secundum genus primum, aut secundum ultimam speciem, ut sunt quaedam, tamquam omnia liquabilia ex aqua, est autem veluti ex aere statua.

ἢ κατὰ τὸ πρῶτον γένος ἢ κατὰ τὸ ὕστατον εἶδος, οἷον ἔστι μὲν ὡς ἅπαντα τὰ τηκτὰ ἐξ ὕδατος, ἔστι δ᾽ ὡς ἐκ χαλκοῦ ὁ ἀνδριάς:

in reference either to the first genus or to the ultimate species; for example, all liquefiable things come from water, and a statue comes from bronze.

Alio vero ex primo movente principio, ut ex quo pugna? Ex convitio: id enim est principium pugnae.

ἕνα δ᾽ ὡς ἐκ τῆς {30} πρώτης κινησάσης ἀρχῆς (οἷον ἐκ τίνος ἡ μάχη; ἐκ λοιδορίας, ὅτι αὕτη ἀρχὴ τῆς μάχης):

And in another sense it means to come from a thing as a first moving principle. For example, from what did the fight come? From a jeer, because this was the cause of the fight.

Alio ex composito ex materia et forma; ut ex toto partes, et ex *Iliade* versus, et ex domo lapides.

ἕνα δ᾽ ἐκ τοῦ συνθέτου ἐκ τῆς ὕλης καὶ τῆς μορφῆς, ὥσπερ ἐκ τοῦ ὅλου τὰ μέρη καὶ ἐκ τῆς Ἰλιάδος τὸ ἔπος καὶ ἐκ τῆς οἰκίας οἱ λίθοι:

In another sense it means to come from the composite of matter and form, as parts come from a whole, and a verse from the *Iliad*, and stones from a house.

Finis enim est forma, perfectum vero habens finem. Hoc autem tamquam ex parte speciei species, ut homo ex bipede, et syllaba ex elemento.

τέλος μὲν γάρ ἐστιν ἡ μορφή, τέλειον δὲ τὸ ἔχον τέλος. {35} τὰ δὲ ὡς ἐκ τοῦ μέρους τὸ εἶδος, οἷον ἄνθρωπος ἐκ τοῦ δίποδος καὶ ἡ συλλαβὴ ἐκ τοῦ στοιχείου:

For the form is an end or goal, and what is in possession of its end is complete. And one thing comes from another in the sense that a species comes from a part of a species, and man from two-footed, and a syllable from an element.

Aliter enim hoc, et statua ex aere: nam ex sensibili materia est composita substantia. Sed et species ex speciei materia.

ἄλλως γὰρ τοῦτο καὶ ὁ ἀνδριὰς ἐκ χαλκοῦ: {1023b1} ἐκ τῆς αἰσθητῆς γὰρ ὕλης ἡ συνθετὴ οὐσία, ἀλλὰ καὶ τὸ εἶδος ἐκ τῆς τοῦ εἴδους ὕλης.

For this is different from the way in which a statue comes from bronze, because a composite substance comes from sensible matter, but a species also comes from the matter of a species.

Haec quidem igitur sic dicuntur.

τὰ μὲν οὖν οὕτω λέγεται,

These are the senses, then, in which some things are said to "come from" something.

1023b3 Alia vero, si secundum partem aliquam horum aliquis existit modorum, [1090]

τὰ δ᾽ ἐὰν κατὰ μέρος τι τούτων τις ὑπάρχῃ τῶν τρόπων,

But other things are said to come from something if they come from a part of that thing in any of the aforesaid senses.

ut ex patre et matre puer, et ex terra plantae, quia ex aliqua parte eorum.

οἷον ἐκ πατρὸς καὶ μητρὸς τὸ τέκνον {5} καὶ ἐκ γῆς τὰ φυτά, ὅτι ἔκ τινος μέρους αὐτῶν.

For example, a child comes from its father and mother, and plants come from the earth, because they come from some part of them.

1023b5 Alia vero prius quidem tempore, tu ex die nox, ex serenitate hyems, quia hoc post hoc. [1091]

ἕνα δὲ μεθ᾽ ὃ τῷ χρόνῳ, οἷον ἐξ ἡμέρας νὺξ καὶ ἐξ εὐδίας χειμών, ὅτι τοῦτο μετὰ τοῦτο:

And some things come from others only because they come one after the other in time, as night comes from day, and a storm from a calm.

Horum autem, alia quia habent transmutationem adinvicem, ita dicuntur, ut quae nunc sunt dicta. Alia quia secundum tempus solum, ut ex aequi-

τούτων δὲ τὰ μὲν τῷ ἔχειν μεταβολὴν εἰς ἄλληλα οὕτω λέγεται, ὥσπερ καὶ τὰ νῦν εἰρημένα, τὰ δὲ τῷ κατὰ τὸν χρόνον ἐφεξῆς μόνον, οἷον ἐξ ἰσημερίας {10} ἐγ-

And some of these are so described only because they admit of change into each other, as in the cases just mentioned, and some only because they follow one an-

noctio fit navigatio, quia post aequinoctium.

ένετο ὁ πλοῦς ὅτι μετ᾽ ἰσημερίαν ἐγένετο,

other in time, as a voyage is made from the equinox because it takes place after the equinox.

Sic festivitates sunt, ut ex Dionysiis Thargelia, quia post Dionysia.

καὶ ἐκ Διονυσίων Θαργήλια ὅτι μετὰ τὰ Διονύσια.

And feasts come one from another in this way, as the Thargelian from the Dionysian, because it comes after the Dionysian.

1023b12 Pars dicitur quidem uno modo, in quam dividitur utique quantum quocumque modo. Semper enim ablatum a quanto ut quantum est, pars dicitur illius; ut trium duo pars quodammodo dicuntur. [1093]

μέρος λέγεται ἕνα μὲν τρόπον εἰς ὃ διαιρεθείη ἂν τὸ ποσὸν ὁπωσοῦν (ἀεὶ γὰρ τὸ ἀφαιρούμενον τοῦ ποσοῦ ᾖ ποσὸν μέρος λέγεται ἐκείνου, οἷον τῶν τριῶν τὰ δύο μέρος λέγεταί {15} πως),

"Part" means in one sense that into which a quantity is divided in any way, for what is subtracted from a quantity is always called a part of it. For example, the number two is said in a sense to be a part of the number three.

Alio vero modo, quae talia mensurant solum. Propter quod trium, duo sunt ut dicitur pars, sunt autem ut non.

ἄλλον δὲ τρόπον τὰ καταμετροῦντα τῶν τοιούτων μόνον: διὸ τὰ δύο τῶν τριῶν ἔστι μὲν ὡς λέγεται μέρος, ἔστι δ᾽ ὡς οὔ.

And in another sense "part" means only such things as measure a whole. And for this reason the number two is said in a sense to be a part of the number three, and in another, not.

Amplius et in quae dividitur utique species sine quantitate, et ea partes huius dicuntur: quare species, generis dicuntur esse partes.

ἔτι εἰς ἃ τὸ εἶδος διαιρεθείη ἂν ἄνευ τοῦ ποσοῦ, καὶ ταῦτα μόρια λέγεται τούτου: διὸ τὰ εἴδη τοῦ γένους φασὶν εἶναι μόρια.

Again, those things into which a species is divided irrespective of quantity are also called parts of this species, and it is for this reason that species are said to be parts of a genus.

Amplius in quae dividitur aliquid, aut ex quibus componitur totum, aut species, aut habens speciem, ut sphaerae aereae, aut cubi aerei, aes pars est: hoc autem est materia in qua species. Et angulus pars.

ἔτι εἰς ἃ διαιρεῖται ἢ ἐξ ὧν σύγκειται {20} τὸ ὅλον, ἢ τὸ εἶδος ἢ τὸ ἔχον τὸ εἶδος, οἷον τῆς σφαίρας τῆς χαλκῆς ἢ τοῦ κύβου τοῦ χαλκοῦ καὶ ὁ χαλκὸς μέρος (τοῦτο δ᾽ ἐστὶν ἡ ὕλη ἐν ᾗ τὸ εἶδος) καὶ ἡ γωνία μέρος.

Again, "parts" means those things into which a whole is divided or of which a whole is composed, whether the whole is a species or the thing having the species, as bronze is a part of a bronze sphere or of a bronze cube (for this is the matter in which the form inheres). An angle also is a part.

Amplius quae sunt in ratione unumquodque ostendente, et ea partes sunt totius. Propter quod et genus speciei pars dicitur; aliter autem species, generis pars.

ἔτι τὰ ἐν τῷ λόγῳ τῷ δηλοῦντι ἕκαστον, καὶ ταῦτα μόρια τοῦ ὅλου: διὸ τὸ γένος τοῦ εἴδους καὶ μέρος λέγεται, ἄλλως δὲ τὸ {25} εἶδος τοῦ γένους μέρος.

And those elements contained in the intelligible expression, which manifests what each thing is, are also parts of a whole. And for this reason the genus is also called a part of the species, although in another respect the species is called a part of the genus.

1023b26 Totum dicitur cuius nulla partium deest, ex quibus dicitur totum natura: et continens contenta: unde unum aliquid sunt illa. [1098]

ὅλον λέγεται οὗ τε μηθὲν ἄπεστι μέρος ἐξ ὧν λέγεται ὅλον φύσει, καὶ τὸ περιέχον τὰ περιεχόμενα ὥστε ἕν τι εἶναι ἐκεῖνα:

"Whole" means that from which none of the things of which it is said to consist by nature are missing, and that which contains the things contained in such a way that they form one thing.

1023b28 Hoc autem dupliciter. Aut enim ut unumquodque unum, aut ut ex his unum. [1099]

τοῦτο δὲ διχῶς: ἢ γὰρ ὡς ἕκαστον ἕν ἢ ὡς ἐκ τούτων τὸ ἕν.

But this occurs in two ways: either inasmuch as each is the one in question, or inasmuch as one thing is constituted of them.

1023b29 Universale quidem enim et quod totaliter, dicitur ut aliquid ens unum sicut universale, quasi multa continens, quia praedicatur de unoquoque, et unum

τὸ μὲν γὰρ καθόλου, καὶ τὸ ὅλως λεγόμενον {30} ὡς ὅλον τι ὄν, οὕτως ἐστὶ καθόλου ὡς πολλὰ περιέχον τῷ κατηγορεῖσθαι καθ᾽ ἑκάστου καὶ ἓν ἅπαντα

For a whole is a universal, or what is predicated in general as being some one thing as a universal is one, in the sense that it contains many things, because it is

omnia sunt et unumquodque: ut homo, et equus, et deus, quia omnia animalia. [1100]

1023b32 Continuum vero et finitum, quando unum aliquid ex pluribus est quae insunt, maxime quidem potestate. Sin autem et energia. [1101]

1023b34 Horum vero eorumdem magis quae sunt natura, quam arte talia; quemadmodum et in uno dicimus, tamquam existente totalitate unione aliqua. [1104]

1024a1 Amplius quanto habente principium et medium et ultimum, quorum quidem non facit positio differentiam, omne dicitur; [1105]

quorum vero facit totum,

et quaecumque ambo dicuntur et omne et totum.

Sunt autem ea quorum natura quidem eadem manet transpositione, forma vero non, ut cera et vestis. Etenim omne et totum dicuntur. Habent enim ambo. Alia vero et quaecumque sunt humida, et numerus omne quidem dicuntur; totus vero numerus, et tota aqua non dicitur, nisi metaphorice. Omnia vero dicuntur in quibus omne, ut in uno: in his omnia, ut in diversis: omnis hic numerus, omnes hae unitates.

1024a11 Colobon vero dicitur quantum non quodlibet, sed partibile oportet illud esse, et totum. Nam duo non sunt coloba, altero ablato uno. Non enim aequale colobonion et reliquum unquam est. Nec totaliter numerus ullus. Etenim substantiam oportet manere. Si calix colobos, adhuc oportet esse calicem. Sed numerus non est idem parte sublata. Adhuc et quae sunt partium dissimilium. Nec haec omnia. Numerus enim est ut dissimiles habeat partes, ut dualitatem et trinitatem. Sed et totaliter quorum positio non facit diffe-

εἶναι ὡς ἕκαστον, οἷον ἄνθρωπον ἵππον θεόν, διότι ἅπαντα ζῷα:

τὸ δὲ συνεχὲς καὶ πεπερασμένον, ὅταν ἕν τι ἐκ πλειόνων ᾖ, ἐνυπαρχόντων μάλιστα μὲν δυνάμει, εἰ δὲ μή, ἐνεργείᾳ.

τούτων {35} δ᾽ αὐτῶν μᾶλλον τὰ φύσει ἢ τέχνῃ τοιαῦτα, ὥσπερ καὶ ἐπὶ τοῦ ἑνὸς ἐλέγομεν, ὡς οὔσης τῆς ὁλότητος ἑνότητός τινος.

ἔτι τοῦ ποσοῦ ἔχοντος δὲ ἀρχὴν καὶ μέσον καὶ ἔσχατον, ὅσων μὲν μὴ ποιεῖ ἡ θέσις διαφοράν, πᾶν λέγεται,

ὅσων δὲ ποιεῖ, ὅλον.

ὅσα δὲ ἄμφω ἐνδέχεται, καὶ ὅλα καὶ πάντα:

ἔστι δὲ ταῦτα ὅσων ἡ μὲν φύσις ἡ αὐτὴ μένει τῇ μεταθέσει, ἡ {5} δὲ μορφὴ οὔ, οἷον κηρὸς καὶ ἱμάτιον: καὶ γὰρ ὅλον καὶ πᾶν λέγεται: ἔχει γὰρ ἄμφω. ὕδωρ δὲ καὶ ὅσα ὑγρὰ καὶ ἀριθμὸς πᾶν μὲν λέγεται, ὅλος δ᾽ ἀριθμὸς καὶ ὅλον ὕδωρ οὐ λέγεται, ἂν μὴ μεταφορᾷ. πάντα δὲ λέγεται ἐφ᾽ οἷς τὸ πᾶν ὡς ἐφ᾽ ἑνί, ἐπὶ τούτοις τὸ πάντα ὡς ἐπὶ διῃρημένοις: {10} πᾶς οὗτος ὁ ἀριθμός, πᾶσαι αὗται αἱ μονάδες.

κολοβὸν δὲ λέγεται τῶν ποσῶν οὐ τὸ τυχόν, ἀλλὰ μεριστόν τε δεῖ αὐτὸ εἶναι καὶ ὅλον. τά τε γὰρ δύο οὐ κολοβὰ θατέρου ἀφαιρουμένου ἑνός (οὐ γὰρ ἴσον τὸ καλόβωμα καὶ τὸ λοιπὸν οὐδέποτ᾽ ἐστίν) οὐδ᾽ ὅλως ἀριθμὸς οὐδείς: καὶ {15} γὰρ τὴν οὐσίαν δεῖ μένειν: εἰ κύλιξ κολοβός, ἔτι εἶναι κύλικα: ὁ δὲ ἀριθμὸς οὐκέτι ὁ αὐτός. πρὸς δὲ τούτοις κἂν ἀνομοιομερῆ ᾖ, οὐδὲ ταῦτα πάντα (ὁ γὰρ ἀριθμὸς ἔστιν ὡς καὶ ἀνόμοια ἔχει μέρη, οἷον δυάδα τριάδα), ἀλλ᾽ ὅλως ὧν μὴ ποιεῖ ἡ θέσις διαφορὰν οὐδὲν κολοβόν, οἷον ὕδωρ ἢ πῦρ, {20}

predicated of each, and all of them taken singly are that one thing, as man, horse, and god, because all are living things.

A whole is something continuous and limited when one thing is constituted of many parts which are present in it, particularly when they are present potentially; but if not, even when they are present in activity.

And of these same things, those which are wholes by nature are such to a greater degree than those which are wholes by art, as we also say of a thing that is one (1015b36; [848]), inasmuch as wholeness is a kind of unity.

Again, since a quantity has a beginning, a middle point, and an end, those quantities to which position makes no difference we designate by the term "all,"

but those to which position makes a difference we designate by the term "whole."

and those to which both descriptions apply we designate by both terms—all and whole.

Now these are the things whose nature remains the same in being rearranged but whose shape does not, as wax and a garment; for both "all" and "whole" are predicated of them, since they verify both. But water and all moist things and number have "all" applied to them, although water and number are called wholes only in a metaphorical sense. But those things of which the term "every" is predicated with reference to one have the term "all" predicated of them with reference to several— for example, all this number, all these units.

It is not any quantity at all that is said to be "mutilated," but it must be a whole and also divisible into parts. For two things are not mutilated when one is taken away from the other, because the mutilated part is never equal to the remainder. And in general no number is mutilated, for its substance must remain. If a goblet is mutilated, it must still be a goblet; but a number is not the same when a part is taken away. Again, all things composed of unlike parts are not said to be mutilated. For a number is like something having unlike parts, as two and three.

rentiam; nullum enim colobon, ut aqua aut ignis; sed oportet talia esse, quae in substantia positionem habeant. Amplius continua. Nam harmonia est ex his quae sunt dissimilium partium et positionem habent, sed colobon non est. [1109]

1024a22 Adhuc autem nec quaelibet tota, nec cuiusque particulae privatione coloba. Non enim nec quae sunt propria substantiae, nec quae sunt ubique entia; [1117]

ut si perforaretur calix, non colobon, sed si auris calicis, aut extremitas aliqua. Et homo non si carnem aut splenem, sed si extremitatem.

Et hanc non omnem, sed quae non habet generationem ablatam a toto. Quapropter calvi non colobi.

ἀλλὰ δεῖ τοιαῦτα εἶναι ἃ κατὰ τὴν οὐσίαν θέσιν ἔχει. ἔτι συνεχῆ· ἡ γὰρ ἁρμονία ἐξ ἀνομοίων μὲν καὶ θέσιν ἔχει, κολοβὸς δὲ οὐ γίγνεται.

πρὸς δὲ τούτοις οὐδ' ὅσα ὅλα, οὐδὲ ταῦτα ὁτουοῦν μορίου στερήσει κολοβά. οὐ γὰρ δεῖ οὔτε τὰ κύρια τῆς οὐσίας οὔτε τὰ ὁπουοῦν ὄντα·

οἷον ἂν τρυπηθῇ ἡ {25} κύλιξ, οὐ κολοβός, ἀλλ' ἂν τὸ οὖς ἢ ἀκρωτήριόν τι, καὶ ὁ ἄνθρωπος οὐκ ἐὰν σάρκα ἢ τὸν σπλῆνα, ἀλλ' ἐὰν ἀκρωτήριόν τι,

καὶ τοῦτο οὐ πᾶν ἀλλ' ὃ μὴ ἔχει γένεσιν ἀφαιρεθὲν ὅλον. διὰ τοῦτο οἱ φαλακροὶ οὐ κολοβοί.

And in general those things to which position makes no difference, such as water and fire, are not mutilated; but they must have position in their substance. And they must be continuous, for a harmony is made up of unlike parts and has position but is not mutilated.

Further, neither is every whole mutilated by the privation of every part. For the parts which are removed must not be things that are proper to the substance or things that exist anywhere at all.

For example, a goblet is not mutilated if a hole is made in it, but only if an ear or some extremity is removed; and a man is not mutilated if his flesh or spleen is removed, but only if an extremity is removed.

And this means not any extremity whatever, but those which cannot regenerate when removed from the whole. Hence to have one's head shaven is not a mutilation.

1085. Hic incipit prosequi de his quae pertinent ad rationem totius et partis.

Et primo de his quae pertinent ad partem.

Secundo de his, quae pertinent ad totum, ibi, ***totum dicitur.***

Et quia ex partibus constituitur totum; ideo circa primum duo facit.

Primo ostendit quot modis dicitur aliquid esse ex aliquo.

Secundo quot modis dicitur pars, ibi, ***pars dicitur uno quidem modo.***

Circa primum tria facit.

Primo ponit modos, quibus aliquid ex aliquo fieri dicitur proprie et primo.

Secundo quo modo fit aliquid ex aliquo, sed non primo, ibi, ***alia vero si secundum partem.***

Tertio quo modo fit aliquid ex aliquo non proprie, ibi, ***alia vero.***

Circa primum ponit quatuor modos.

Quorum primus est, secundum quod aliquid dicitur esse ex aliquo, ut ex materia. Quod quidem contingit dupliciter.

1085. Here he begins to treat the things that pertain to the notion of whole and part.

First, he deals with those which pertain to the notion of part;

and second (1023b26; [1098]), with those which pertain to the notion of whole, at ***"whole" means.***

And because a whole is constituted of parts, he therefore does two things in dealing with the first member of this division.

First, he explains the various ways in which a thing is said to come from something;

second (1023b12; [1093]), he considers the different senses in which the term part is used, at ***"part" means.***

In regard to the first he does three things.

First, he considers the ways in which a thing is said to come from something in the primary and proper sense.

Second [1090], he indicates the ways in which one thing comes from another but not in the primary sense, at ***but other things.***

Third [1091], he considers the ways in which one thing comes from another but not in the proper sense, at ***and some things.***

In dealing with the first part he gives four ways in which a thing is said to come from something.

First, a thing is said to come from something as from matter, and this can happen in two ways.

Uno modo secundum quod accipitur *materia primi generis*, scilicet communis; sicut aqua est materia omnium liquabilium, quae omnia dicuntur esse ex aqua.

Alio modo *secundum speciem ultimam*, idest specialissimam; sicut haec species, quae est statua, dicitur fieri ex aere.

1086. Secundo modo dicitur aliquid fieri ex alio ut *ex primo principio movente*, sicut pugna ex convitio, quod est principium movens animum convitiati ad pugnandum. Et sic etiam dicitur, quod domus est ex aedificante, et sanitas ex medicina.

1087. Tertio modo dicitur fieri ex aliquo, sicut simplex, *ex composito ex materia et forma*. Et hoc est in via resolutionis, sicut dicimus quod partes fiunt ex toto, *et versus ex Iliade*, idest ex toto tractatu Homeri de Troia; resolvitur enim *Ilias* in versus, sicut totum in partes. Et similiter dicitur quod lapides fiunt ex domo.

Ratio autem huius est, quia forma est finis in generatione. Perfectum enim dicitur quod habet finem, ut supra habitum est. Unde patet, quod perfectum est quod habet formam.

Quando igitur ex toto perfecto fit resolutio partium, est motus quasi a forma ad materiam; sicut e converso, quando partes componuntur, est motus a materia in formam. Et ideo haec praepositio ex quae principium designat, utrobique competit: et in via compositionis, quia determinat principium materiale; et in via resolutionis, quia significat principium formale.

1088. Quarto modo dicitur aliquod fieri ex aliquo sicut *species ex parte speciei*.

Pars autem speciei potest accipi dupliciter: aut secundum rationem, aut secundum rem.

Secundum rationem, sicut bipes est pars hominis, quia est pars definitionis eius, quamvis secundum rem non sit pars, quia aliter non praedicaretur de toto. Toti enim homini competit habere duos pedes.

Secundum rem vero, sicut *syllaba est ex elemento*, idest ex litera sicut ex parte speciei. Hic autem quartus modus differt a primo. Nam ibi dicebatur aliquid esse ex parte materiae sicut statua ex aere. Nam haec substantia quae est statua, est composita ex sensibili materia tamquam ex parte substantiae. Sed haec species componitur ex parte speciei.

1089. Sunt enim partium, quaedam partes speciei, et quaedam partes materiae.

In one way, inasmuch as matter is taken to be *the matter of the first genus* (that is, common matter), as water is the matter of all liquids and liquables, all of which are said to come from water.

In another way, *in reference to the ultimate species* (that is, the lowest species), as the species of statue is said to come from bronze.

1086. In a second way a thing is said to come from something as *from a first moving principle*, as a fight comes from a jeer, which is the principle moving the soul of the taunted person to fight. And it is in this way too that a house is said to come from a builder, and health from the medical art.

1087. In a third way, one thing is said to come from another as something simple *comes from the composite of matter and form*. This pertains to the process of dissolution, and it is in this way that we say parts come from a whole, *and a verse from the Iliad* (that is, from the whole treatise of Homer about Troy). For the *Iliad* is divided into verses as a whole is divided into parts. And it is in the same way that stones are said to come from a house.

The reason for this is that the form is the goal or end in the process of generation, for it is what has attained its end that is said to be perfect or complete, as was explained above (1021b23; [1039]). Hence it is evident that that is perfect which has a form.

Therefore, when a perfect whole is broken down into its parts, there is motion in a sense from form to matter; and in a similar way when parts are combined, there is an opposite motion from matter to form. Hence the preposition "from," which designates a beginning, applies to both processes: both to the process of composition (because it signifies a material principle), and to that of dissolution (because it signifies a formal principle).

1088. In a fourth way, a thing is said to come from something as *a species comes from a part of a species*.

And "part of a species" can be taken in two ways: in reference either to the conceptual order or to the real order.

It is taken in reference to the conceptual order when we say (for example) that two-footed is a part of man, because while it is part of his definition, it is not a real part, otherwise it would not be predicated of the whole. For it is proper to the whole man to have two feet.

And it is taken in reference to the real order when we say (for example) that *a syllable comes from an element*, or letter, as from a part of the species. But here the fourth way in which the term is used differs from the first. In the first way, a thing was said to come from a part of matter, as a statue comes from bronze. For this substance—a statue—is composed of sensible matter as a part of its substance. But this species is composed of part of the species.

1089. For some parts are parts of a species and some are parts of matter.

Partes quidem speciei dicuntur, a quibus dependet perfectio speciei, et sine quibus esse non potest species. Unde et tales partes in definitione totius ponuntur, sicut anima et corpus in definitione animalis, et angulus in definitione trianguli, et litera in definitione syllabae.

Partes vero materiae dicuntur ex quibus species non dependet, sed quodammodo accidunt speciei; sicut accidit statuae quod fiat ex aere, vel ex quacumque materia. Accidit etiam circulo quod dividatur in duos semicirculos: et angulo recto, quod angulus acutus sit eius pars.

Unde huiusmodi partes non ponuntur in definitione totius speciei, sed potius e converso, ut in septimo huius erit manifestum. Sic ergo patet quod sic quaedam dicuntur ex aliquo fieri primo et proprie.

1090. Aliqua vero dicuntur ex aliquo fieri non primo, sed secundum partem. Et hoc secundum *quaecumque praedictorum modorum*; sicut puer dicitur fieri ex patre, sicut principio motivo, et matre sicut ex materia; quia quaedam pars patris movet, scilicet sperma, et quaedam pars matris est materia, scilicet menstruum. Et plantae fiunt ex terra; non tamen quidem ex toto, sed ex aliqua eius parte.

1091. Alio vero modo dicitur fieri aliquid ex aliquo non proprie, scilicet ex hoc ipso quod importat solum ordinem; et sic aliquid fieri dicitur ex aliquo, post quod fit, sicut *nox fit ex die*, idest post diem: et *imber ex serenitate*, idest post serenitatem. Hoc autem dicitur dupliciter.

Quandoque enim inter ea, quorum unum dicitur fieri ex altero, attenditur ordo secundum motum, et non solum secundum tempus; quia vel sunt duo extrema eiusdem motus, ut cum dicitur quod album fit ex nigro: vel consequuntur aliqua extrema motus, sicut nox et dies consequuntur diversa ubi solis. Et similiter hiems et aestas. Unde in quibusdam dicitur hoc fieri post hoc, quia habent transmutationem adinvicem, ut in praedictis patet.

1092. Quandoque vero attenditur ordo secundum tempus tantum; sicut dicitur quod *ex aequinoctio fit navigatio*, idest post aequinoctium. Haec enim duo extrema non sunt duo extrema unius motus, sed ad diversos motus pertinent. Et similiter dicitur, ex Dionysiis fiunt Thargelia, quia fiunt post Dionysia. Haec autem

Those which are called parts of a species are those on which the perfection of the species depends and without which it cannot be a species. And it is for this reason that such parts are placed in the definition of the whole, as body and soul are placed in the definition of an animal, and an angle in the definition of a triangle, and a letter in the definition of a syllable.

And those parts which are called parts of matter are those on which the species does not depend but are in a sense accidental to the species—for example, it is accidental to a statue that it should come from bronze or from any particular matter at all. And it is also accidental that a circle should be divided into two semi-circles, and that a right angle should have an acute angle as part of it.

Parts of this sort, then, are not placed in the definition of the whole species but rather the other way around, as will be shown in book 7 of this work [1542]. Hence it is clear that in this way some things are said to come from others in the primary and proper sense.

1090. But some things are said to come from something not in the primary sense but according to a part of that thing in *any of the aforesaid senses*. For example, a child is said to come from its father as an efficient principle, and from its mother as matter, because a certain part of the father (the sperm) causes motion and a certain part of the mother has the character of matter (the menstrual fluid). And plants come from the earth, although not from the whole of it but from some part.

1091. And in another way a thing is said to come from something in an improper sense, namely, from the fact that this implies order or succession alone. In this way one thing is said to come from another in the sense that it comes after it, as *night comes from day* (that is, after the day), *and a storm from a calm* (that is, after a calm). And this is said in reference to two things.

For in those cases in which one thing is said to come from another, order is sometimes noted in reference to motion and not merely to time. For either they are the two extremes of the same motion, as when it is said that white comes from black, or they are a result of different extremes of the motion, as night and day are a result of different locations of the sun. And the same thing applies to winter and summer. Hence in some cases one thing is said to come from another because one is changed into the other, as is clear in the above examples.

1092. But sometimes order or succession is considered in reference to time alone; for example, it is said that *a voyage is made from the equinox*, that is, after the equinox. For these two extremes are not extremes of a single motion, but pertain to different motions. And similarly it is said that the Thargelian festival comes from the Dionysian because

sunt quaedam festa, quae apud gentiles celebrabantur, quorum unum erat prius et aliud posterius.

1093. Deinde cum dicit *pars dicitur* hic ponit quatuor modos, quibus aliquid dicitur esse pars.

Primo modo pars dicitur, in quam dividitur aliquid secundum quantitatem: et hoc dupliciter.

Uno enim modo quantumcumque fuerit quantitas minor, in quam quantitas maior dividitur, dicitur eius pars. Semper enim id quod aufertur a quantitate, dicitur pars eius; sicut duo aliquo modo sunt partes trium.

Alio modo dicitur solum pars quantitas minor, quae mensurat maiorem. Et sic duo non sunt pars trium; sed sic duo sunt pars quatuor, quia bis duo sunt quatuor.

1094. Secundo modo ea dicuntur partes, in quae dividitur aliquid sine quantitate: et per hunc modum species dicuntur esse partes generis. Dividitur enim in species, non sicut quantitas, in partes quantitatis. Nam tota quantitas non est in una suarum partium. Genus autem est in qualibet specierum.

1095. Tertio modo dicuntur partes, in quas dividitur, aut ex quibus componitur aliquod totum; sive sit species, sive aliquid habens speciem, scilicet individuum. Sunt enim, sicut dictum est, quaedam partes speciei, et quaedam partes materiae, quae sunt partes individui. Aes enim est pars sphaerae aereae, aut cubi aerei, sicut materia, in qua species est recepta. Unde aes non est pars speciei, sed pars habentis speciem. Est autem cubus corpus contentum ex superficiebus quadratis. Angulus autem est pars trianguli sicut speciei, sicut supra dictum est.

1096. Quarto modo dicuntur partes, quae ponuntur in definitione cuiuslibet rei, quae sunt partes rationis sicut animal et bipes sunt partes hominis.

1097. Ex quo patet, quod genus quarto modo est pars speciei: aliter vero, scilicet secundo modo, species est pars generis. In secundo enim modo sumebatur pars pro parte subiectiva totius universalis; in aliis autem tribus pro parte integrali. Sed in primo pro parte quantitatis, in aliis autem duobus pro parte substantiae; ita tamen, quod pars secundum tertium modum est pars rei; sive sit pars speciei, sive pars individui. Quarto autem modo est pars rationis.

it comes after the Dionysian. (These are two feasts which were celebrated among the gentiles, one of which preceded the other in time.)

1093. *"Part" means* (1023b12). He now gives four senses in which something is said to be a part.

In one sense, "part" means that into which a thing is divided from the viewpoint of quantity, and this can be taken in two ways.

For in one way, no matter how much smaller that quantity may be into which a larger quantity is divided, it is called a part of this quantity. For anything that is taken away from a quantity is always called a part of it—for example, the number two is in a sense a part of the number three.

And, in another way, only a smaller quantity which measures a larger one is called a part. In this sense the number two is not a part of the number three, but a part of the number four, because two times two equals four.

1094. In a second sense, "parts" means those things into which something is divided irrespective of quantity, and it is in this sense that species are said to be parts of a genus. For a genus is divided into species, but not as a quantity is divided into quantitative parts. For a whole quantity is not in each one of its parts, but a genus is in each one of its species.

1095. In a third sense, "parts" means those things into which some whole is divided or of which it is composed, whether the whole is a species or the thing having a species (the individual). For, as has been pointed out already [1089], there are parts of the species and parts of matter, and these (species and matter) are parts of the individual. Hence bronze is a part of a bronze sphere or of a bronze cube as the matter in which the form is received, and thus bronze is not a part of the form, but of the thing having the form. And a cube is a body composed of square surfaces. And an angle is part of a triangle as part of its form, as has been stated above [1099].

1096. In a fourth sense, "parts" means those things that are placed in the definition of anything, and these are parts of its intelligible structure—for example, animal and two-footed are parts of man.

1097. From this it is clear that a genus is part of a species in this fourth sense, but that a species is part of a genus in a different sense, in the second sense. For in the second sense, a part was taken as a subjective part of a universal whole, whereas in the other three senses, it was taken as an integral part. And in the first sense it was taken as a part of quantity, and in the other two senses as a part of substance, yet in such a way that a part in the third sense means a part of a thing (whether it be a part of the species or of the individual). But in the fourth sense, it is a part of the intelligible structure.

1098. Deinde cum dicit *totum dicitur* hic prosequitur de his quae pertinent ad totum.

Et primo de toto in communi.

Secundo de toto quodam, scilicet de genere, ibi, *genus dicitur.*

Circa primum duo facit.

Primo prosequitur de ipso nomine totius.

Secundo de eius opposito, scilicet de colobon, ibi, *colobon autem dicitur.*

Circa primum tria facit.

Primo ponit rationem communem totius, quae consistit in duobus.

Primo in hoc quod perfectio totius integratur ex partibus. Et significat hoc, cum dicit quod *totum dicitur cui nulla suarum partium deest, ex quibus* scilicet partibus *dicitur totum natura*, idest totum secundum suam naturam constituitur.

Secundum est quod partes uniuntur in toto. Et sic dicit quod totum *continens est contenta*, scilicet partes, ita quod illa contenta sunt aliquid unum in toto.

1099. Secundo ibi, *hoc autem* ponit duos modos totius; dicens quod totum dicitur dupliciter;

aut ita quod unumquodque contentorum a toto continente, sit *ipsum unum*, scilicet ipsum totum continens, quod est in toto universali de qualibet suarum partium praedicato.

Aut ex partibus constituatur unum, ita quod non quaelibet partium sit unum illud. Et haec est ratio totius integralis, quod de nulla suarum partium integralium praedicatur.

1100. Tertio ibi, *universale quidem* exponit praedictos modos totius;

et primo primum, dicens quod universale *et quod totaliter* idest quod communiter praedicatur, dicitur quasi sit aliquod unum totum ex hoc quod praedicatur de unoquoque, sicut universale, quasi multa continens ut partes, in eo quod praedicatur de unoquoque. Et omnia illa sunt unum in toto universali, ita quod unumquodque illorum est illud unum totum. Sicut animal continet hominem et equum et deum, quia *omnia sunt animalia*, idest quia animal praedicatur de unoquoque. Deum autem hic dicit aliquod corpus caeleste, ut solem vel lunam, quae antiqui animata corpora esse dicebant et deos putabant. Vel animalia quaedam aerea, quae Platonici dicebant esse daemones, et pro diis colebantur a gentibus.

1101. Secundo ibi, *continuum vero* exponit modum secundum totius qui pertinet ad totum integrale; et circa hoc duo facit.

Primo ponit rationem communem huius totius, et praecipue de toto quod dividitur in partes quantitativas,

1098. *"Whole" means* (1023b26). He proceeds to treat the things that pertain to a whole.

First, he considers a whole in a general way;

second (1024a29; [1119]), he deals with a particular kind of whole, namely, a genus, at *the term "genus."*

In regard to the first part he does two things.

First, he proceeds to deal with the term "whole";

second (1024a11; [1109]), with its opposite, "mutilated," at *it is not any quantity at all.*

In regard to the first he does three things.

First, he states the common meaning of "whole," which involves two things.

The first is that the perfection of a whole is derived from its parts. He indicates this when he says *a whole means that from which none of the things*—that is, the parts—*of which it is said to consist by nature*—that is, of which the whole is composed according to its own nature—*are missing.*

The second is that the parts become one in the whole. Thus he says that a whole is *that which contains the things contained*, namely, the parts, in such a way that the things contained in the whole are some one thing.

1099. *But this occurs* (1023b28). Second, he notes two ways in which a thing is a whole. He says that a thing is said to be a whole in two ways.

First, in the sense that each of the things contained by the containing whole is *the one in question*, that is, the containing whole, which is in the universal whole that is predicated of any one of its own parts.

Second, in the sense that it is one thing composed of parts in such a way that none of the parts are that one thing. This is the notion of an integral whole, which is not predicated of any of its own integral parts.

1100. *For a whole* (1023b29). Third, he explains the foregoing senses of "whole."

First, he explains the first sense. He says that a whole is a universal *or what is predicated in general*, that is, a common predicate, as being some one thing—just as the universal, which contains many parts, is predicated of each of its parts. And all of these are one in a universal whole in such a way that each of them is that one whole. For example, "living thing" contains man and horse and god, because *all are living things*, since "living thing" is predicated of each. By a "god" he means here a celestial body, such as the sun or the moon, which the ancients said were living bodies and considered to be gods. Or he means certain ethereal living beings, which the Platonists called demons, and which were worshipped by the pagans as gods.

1101. *A whole is something* (1023b32). Second, he explains the meaning of "whole" in the sense of an integral whole; and in regard to this he does two things.

First, he gives the common meaning of this kind of whole, and particularly of that which is divided into quan-

quod est manifestius; dicens, quod aliquid dicitur *continuum et finitum*, idest perfectum et totum. Nam infinitum non habet rationem totius, sed partis, ut dicitur in tertio *Physicorum*; quando scilicet unum aliquod fit ex pluribus quae insunt toti. Et hoc dicit ad removendum modum quo aliquid fit ex aliquo sicut ex contrario.

1102. Partes autem ex quibus constituitur totum dupliciter possunt esse in toto. Uno modo in potentia, alio modo in actu.

Partes quidem sunt in potentia in toto continuo; actu vero in toto non continuo, sicut lapides actu sunt in acervo. Magis autem est unum, et per consequens magis totum, continuum, quam non continuum. Et ideo dicit quod oportet partes inesse toti, maxime quidem in potentia sicut in toto continuo. Et si non in potentia, saltem *energia*, idest in actu. Dicitur enim energia, interior actio.

1103. Licet autem magis sit totum quando partes sunt in eo in potentia, quam quando sunt actu, tamen si respiciamus ad partes, magis sunt ipsae partes, quando sunt actu, quam quando sunt in potentia.

Unde alia litera habet *maxime quidem perfectione et actu. Sin autem, et potestate*. Et subiungit etiam quod prius dictum est *et maxime potestate. Sin autem, et energia*.

Unde videtur quod translator duas invenit literas et utramque transtulit, et errore factum est, sic ut coniungantur ambae quasi una litera. Et hoc patet ex alia translatione quae non habet nisi alterum tantum. Sic enim dicit *continuum autem et finitum est, cum unum aliquod sit ex pluribus inhaerentibus, maxime quod potentia*. Si autem non, actu sunt.

1104. Secundo ibi, *horum vero* ostendit duas diversitates in isto secundo modo totius:

quarum prima est, quod continuorum quaedam sunt continua per artem, quaedam per naturam. Et illa quae sunt continua per naturam, magis sunt *talia*, idest tota, quam quae sunt per artem. Sicut de uno dictum est supra; scilicet quod illa quae sunt continua per naturam, magis sunt unum, ac si totalitas sit aliqua unio: ex quo patet quod, quod est magis unum, est magis totum.

1105. Deinde cum dicit *amplius quanto* secundam diversitatem ponit. Cum enim ita sit quod in quantitate sit ordo partium, quia est ibi principium, medium et ultimum, in quo ratio positionis consistit, oportet quod omnia tota ista continuam habeant positionem in suis

titative parts, which is more evident to us. He says that a whole is something *continuous and limited*, perfect or complete. For what is unlimited does not have the character of a whole, but of a part, as is said in *Physics* 3, when one thing is composed of many parts which are present in it. He says this in order to exclude the sense in which one thing comes from another as from a contrary.

1102. Now the parts of which a whole is composed can be present in it in two ways: in one way potentially, and in another actually.

Parts are potentially present in a whole which is continuous, and actually present in a whole which is not continuous, as stones are actually present in a heap. But that which is continuous is one to a greater degree, and therefore is a whole to a greater degree, than that which is not continuous. Hence he says that parts must be present in a whole, especially potential parts, as they are in a continuous whole; and if not potentially, then at least *in activity*, or actually. For "activity" means interior action.

1103. Now, although a thing is a whole to a greater degree when its parts are present potentially than when they are present actually, nonetheless if we look to the parts, they are parts to a greater degree when they exist actually than when they exist potentially.

Hence another text reads, *especially when they are present perfectly and actually; but otherwise, even when they are present potentially*. And it also adds the words given above: *particularly when they are present potentially; but if not, even when they are present in activity*.

Hence it seems that the translator found two texts, which he translated, and then made the mistake of combining them so as to make one text. This is clear from another translation, which contains only one of these statements; for it reads as follows: *and a whole is continuous and limited when some one thing is composed of many intrinsic parts, especially when they are present potentially*; but if not, when they are present actually.

1104. *And of these same things* (1023b34). Second, he indicates two differences within this second sense of "whole."

The first is that some continuous things are such by art and some by nature. Those which are continuous by nature are *such* (wholes), to a greater degree than those which are such by art. And since we spoke in the same way above [848] about things that are one, saying that things that are continuous by nature are one to a greater degree (as though wholeness were oneness), it is clear from this that anything which is one to a greater degree is a whole to a greater degree.

1105. *Again, since a quantity* (1024a1). He gives the second difference. For since it is true that there is an order of parts in quantity, because a quantity has a beginning, a middle point, and an end, and the notion of position involves these, the positions of the parts in all these quantities

partibus. Sed ad positionem partium totum continuum tripliciter se invenitur habere. Quaedam enim tota sunt in quibus diversa positio partium non facit diversitatem, sicut patet in aqua. Qualitercumque enim transponantur partes aquae, nihil differunt: et similiter est de aliis humidis, sicut de oleo, vino et huiusmodi. In his autem significatur totum per hoc quod dicitur omne, non autem ipso nomine totius. Dicimus enim, omnis aqua, vel omne vinum, vel omnis numerus; non autem totus, nisi secundum metaphoram: et hoc forte est secundum proprietatem Graeci idiomatis. Nam apud nos dicitur proprie.

1106. Quaedam vero sunt in quibus positio differentiam facit, sicut in homine, et in quolibet animali, et in domo et huiusmodi. Non enim est domus qualitercumque partes ordinentur, sed secundum determinatum ordinem partium: et similiter nec homo nec animal; et in his dicimus totum, et non omne. Dicimus enim de uno solo animali loquentes, totum animal, non omne animal.

1107. Quaedam vero sunt in quibus contingunt ambo, quia positio quodammodo facit differentiam in eis. In his autem dicimus utrumque, scilicet et omne et totum; et ista sunt in quibus facta transpositione partium manet eadem materia, sed non eadem forma sive figura;

ut patet in cera, cuius qualitercumque transponantur partes, nihilominus est cera, licet non eiusdem figurae: et similiter est de vestimento, et de omnibus quae sunt similium partium, retinentium diversam figuram. Humida enim, etsi sunt similium partium, non tamen figuram possunt habere propriam, quia non terminantur terminis propriis, sed alienis: et ideo transpositio in eis nihil variat quod sit ex parte eorum.

1108. Ratio autem huius diversitatis est, quia omne, distributivum est: et ideo requirit multitudinem in actu, vel in potentia propinqua: et quia ea sunt similium partium, dividuntur in partes consimiles toti, fitque ibi multiplicatio totius.

Nam si quaelibet pars aquae est aqua, in unaquaque aqua sunt multae aquae, licet in potentia; sicut in uno numero sunt multae unitates in actu. Totum vero significat collectionem partium in aliquo uno: et ideo in illis proprie dicitur totum in quibus, ex omnibus partibus acceptis simul, fit unum perfectum, cuius perfectio nulli partium competit, sicut domus et animal. Unde omne animal, non dicitur de uno animali, sed de pluribus:

must be continuous. But if we consider the position of the parts, a whole is found to be continuous in three ways. For there are some wholes which are unaffected by a difference of position in their parts. This is evident in the case of water, for it makes no difference how the parts of water are interchanged. The same thing is true of other liquids, as oil and wine and the like. And in these things, a whole is signified by the term "all" and not by the term "whole." For we say all the water or all the wine or all the numbers, but not the whole, except metaphorically. (This perhaps applies to the Greek idiom, but in Latin it is a proper way of speaking.)

1106. And there are some things to which the position of the parts does make a difference—for example, a man and any animal and a house and the like. For a thing is not a house if its parts are arranged in just any way at all, but only if they have a definite arrangement; and of these we use the term "whole" and not the term "all." And similarly a thing is not a man or an animal if its parts are arranged in just any way at all. For when we speak of only one animal, we say "the whole animal," and not "all the animal."

1107. And there are some things to which both of these apply, because in a sense the position of their parts accounts for their differences. Of these we use both terms ("all" and "whole"). And these are the things in which the matter, but not the form or shape, remains the same when the parts are interchanged.

This is clear, for example, in the case of wax, for no matter how its parts are interchanged, the wax still remains, but it does not have the same shape. The same is true of a garment and of all things that have like parts and take on a different shape. For even though liquids have like parts, they cannot have a shape of their own, because they are not limited by their own boundaries, but by those of other things. Hence when their parts are interchanged, no change occurs in anything that is proper to them.

1108. The reason for this difference is that the term "all" is distributive and therefore requires an actual multitude or one in proximate potency to act. And because those things have like parts, they are divided into parts entirely similar to the whole, and in that manner multiplication of the whole takes place.

For if every part of water is water, then in each part of water there are many waters, although they are present potentially, just as in one number there are many units actually. But "a whole" signifies a collection of parts into some one thing; therefore, in those cases in which the term "whole" is properly used, one complete thing is made from all the parts taken together, and the perfection of the whole belongs to none of the parts. A house and an animal are examples of this. Hence, "every animal" is not said of one animal, but of many.

et ideo in fine dicit, quod in illis totis in quibus dicitur omne, ut de uno referente ad totum, potest dici omnia in plurali, ut in diversis referendo ad partes:

sicut dicitur, omnis hic numerus et omnes hae unitates et omnis haec aqua, demonstrato toto, et omnes hae aquae, demonstratis partibus.

1109. Deinde cum dicit *colobon vero* hic determinat de eo, quod est oppositum toti, quod est colobon, pro quo alia translatio habet *diminutum membro*, sed non usquequaque convenienter. Nam colobon non dicitur solum in animalibus, in quibus solis sunt membra. Videtur autem esse colobon quod nos dicimus truncatum. Unde Boetius transtulit *mancum*, id est 'defectivum.' Est ergo intentio Philosophi ostendere quid requiratur ad hoc quod aliquid dicatur colobon.

Et primo quid requiratur ex parte totius;

secundo quid requiratur ex parte partis deficientis, ibi, *adhuc autem neque quaelibet.*

1110. Ad hoc autem, quod aliquod totum dici possit colobon, septem requiruntur.

Primum est, ut illud totum sit quantum habens partes in quas dividatur secundum quantitatem. Non enim totum universale potest dici colobon si una species eius auferatur.

1111. Secundum est quod non quodlibet quantum potest dici colobon, sed oportet quod *sit partibile*, idest distinctionem habens, et *totum*, idest ex diversis partibus integratum. Unde ultimae partes, in quas aliquod totum resolvitur, licet habeant quantitatem, non possunt dici colobae, sicut caro vel nervus.

1112. Tertium est, quod duo non sunt coloba, vel aliquid habens duas partes, si altera earum auferatur. Et hoc ideo quia nunquam *colobonium*, idest quod aufertur a colobon, est aequale residuo, sed semper oportet residuum esse maius.

1113. Quartum est, quod numerus nullus potest esse colobus quotcumque partes habeat; quia substantia colobi manet parte subtracta; sicut si calix truncetur, adhuc manet calix; sed numerus non manet idem, ablata quacumque parte. Quaelibet enim unitas addita vel subtracta, variat numeri speciem.

1114. Quintum est, quia oportet quod habeat partes dissimiles. Ea enim, quae sunt similium partium, non possunt dici coloba, quia ratio totius salvatur in qualibet parte: unde, si auferatur aliqua partium, altera pars non dicitur coloba. Nec tamen omnia, quae sunt dissimilium partium, possunt dici coloba: numerus enim non po-

Therefore, at the end of this part of his discussion he says that those wholes of which the term "every" is used—as is done of one thing when reference is made to a whole—can have the plural term "all" used of them, as is done of several things when reference is made to them as parts.

For example, one says "all this number," and "all these units," and "all this water," when the whole has been indicated, and "all these waters" when the parts have been indicated.

1109. *It is not any quantity* (1024a11). Here he clarifies the issue about the opposite of "whole," which is "mutilated." In place of this, another translation reads *diminished by a member*, but this translation does not always fit. For the term "mutilated" is used only of animals, which alone have members. Now "mutilated" seems to mean "cut off," and thus Boethius translated it *maimed*, that is, "defective." Hence the Philosopher's aim here is to show what is required in order that a thing may be said to be mutilated.

First, he gives what is required on the side of the whole;

second (1024a22; [1117]), what is required on the side of the part which is missing, at *further, neither.*

1110. Now in order that a whole can be said to be mutilated, seven things are required.

First, the whole must be a quantified being having parts into which it may be divided quantitatively. For a universal whole cannot be said to be mutilated if one of its species is removed.

1111. Second, not every kind of quantified being can be said to be mutilated, but it must be one that is *divisible into parts*, that is, capable of being separated, and be *a whole*, something composed of different parts. Hence the ultimate parts into which any whole is divided, such as flesh and sinew, cannot be said to be mutilated even though they have quantity.

1112. Third, two things are not mutilated—that is, anything having two parts—if one of them is taken away from the other. And this is true because a *mutilated part*, whatever is taken away from the mutilated thing, is never equal to the remainder, but the remainder must always be larger.

1113. Fourth, no number can be mutilated, no matter how many parts it may have, because the substance of the mutilated thing remains after the part is taken away. For example, when a goblet is mutilated it still remains a goblet, but a number does not remain the same no matter what part of it is taken away. For when a unit is added to or subtracted from a number, it changes the species of the number.

1114. Fifth, the thing mutilated must have unlike parts. For those things that have like parts cannot be said to be mutilated, because the nature of the whole remains verified in each part. Hence, if any of the parts are taken away, the others are not said to be mutilated. Not all things having unlike parts, however, can be said to be mutilated. A

test dici colobus, ut dictum est, quamvis quodammodo habeat dissimiles partes, sicut duodenarius habet pro partibus dualitatem et trinitatem. Aliquo tamen modo omnis numerus habet partes similes, prout omnis numerus ex unitatibus constituitur.

1115. Sextum est quod nullum eorum potest dici colobon, in quibus positio non facit differentiam, sicut aqua aut ignis. Oportet enim coloba talia esse, quod in suae ratione substantiae habeant determinatam positionem, sicut homo vel domus.

1116. Septimum est quod oportet esse continua coloba. Harmonia enim musicalis non potest dici coloba voce vel chorda subtracta, licet sit dissimilium partium: quia constituitur ex vocibus gravibus, et acutis; et licet partes eius habeant determinatam positionem: non enim qualitercumque voces graves et acutae ordinatae, talem constituunt harmoniam.

1117. Deinde cum dicit **adhuc autem** ostendit quae sunt conditiones colobi ex parte partis diminutae; et ponit tres: dicens quod sicut non quaelibet tota possunt dici coloba, ita nec cuiuslibet particulae ablatione potest aliquid dici colobon.

Oportet enim primo quod pars ablata non sit pars substantiae principalis, quae scilicet rei substantiam constituit, et sine qua substantia esse non possit; quia, ut supra dictum est, colobon oportet manere ablata parte. Unde homo non potest dici colobus, capite abscisso.

1118. Secundo, ut pars subtracta non sit ubique, sed sit in extremitate. Unde si perforatur calix circa medium aliqua parte eius ablata, non potest dici colobus; sed, si accipiatur **auris calicis**, idest particula, quae est ad similitudinem auris, aut quaecumque alia extremitas. Et similiter homo non dicitur colobus, si amittat aliquid de carne, vel in tibia, vel in brachio, vel circa medium corporis; aut si amittens splenem, vel aliquam eius partem; sed si amittat aliquam eius extremitatem, ut manum aut pedem.

Tertio vero, ut non omni particula in extremitate existente ablata, aliquid dicatur colobum; sed, si sit talis pars, quae non regeneratur iterum, si tota auferatur, sicut manus, aut pes. Capillus autem totus incisus iterum regeneratur. Unde per eorum subtractionem, licet in extremitate sint, non dicitur colobus. Et propter hoc calvi non dicuntur colobi.

number cannot, as has been stated, even though in a sense it has unlike parts—for example, the number twelve has the number two and the number three as parts of it. Yet in a sense every number has like parts because every number is constituted of units.

1115. Sixth, none of those things in which the position of the parts makes no difference can be said to be mutilated—for example, water or fire. For mutilated things must be such that the intelligible structure of their substance contains the notion of a determinate arrangement of parts, as in the case of a man or of a house.

1116. Seventh, mutilated things must be continuous. For a musical harmony cannot be said to be mutilated when a note or a chord is taken away, even though it is made up of low- and high-pitched sounds, and even though its parts have a determinate position. For it is not any low- and high-pitched sounds arranged in any way at all that constitute such a harmony.

1117. **Further, neither is** (1024a22). Then he indicates the conditions which must prevail with regard to the part cut off in order that a thing may be mutilated; there are three of these. He says that just as not every kind of whole can be said to be mutilated, so neither can there be mutilation by the removal of every part.

First, the part which is removed must not be a principal part of the substance—that is, one which constitutes the substance of the thing and without which the substance cannot be—because the thing that is mutilated must remain when a part is removed, as has been stated above [1113]. Hence a man cannot be said to be mutilated when his head has been cut off.

1118. Second, the part removed should not be everywhere, but in some extremity. Thus, if a goblet is perforated about the middle by removing some part of it, it cannot be said to be mutilated. But this is said if someone removes **the ear of a goblet**, that is, a part which is similar to an ear, or any other extremity. Similarly, a man is not said to be mutilated if he loses some of his flesh from his leg or from his arm or from his waist, or if he loses his spleen or some part of it, but if he loses one of his extremities, such as a hand or a foot.

Third, a thing is not said to be mutilated if just any part that is an extremity is removed, but if it is such a part which does not regenerate if the whole of it is removed, as a hand or a foot. But if a whole head of hair is cut off, it grows again. So if such parts are removed, the man is not said to be mutilated, even though they are extremities. And for this reason people with shaven heads are not said to be mutilated.

LECTURE 22

"Genus," "falsity," and "accident"

1024a29 Genus dicitur hoc quidem si sit generatio continua speciem habentium eamdem, ut dicitur, donec utique genus hominum sit; quia dum est generatio eorum continua. [1119]

γένος λέγεται τὸ μὲν ἐὰν ᾖ ἡ γένεσις συνεχὴς τῶν τὸ {30} εἶδος ἐχόντων τὸ αὐτό, οἷον λέγεται ἕως ἂν ἀνθρώπων γένος ᾖ, ὅτι ἕως ἂν ᾖ ἡ γένεσις συνεχὴς αὐτῶν:

The term "genus" (or "race") is used if there is a continuous generation of things having the same species. For example, "as long as the genus of man lasts" means "while there is continuous generation of men."

Istud vero a quo sunt primo movente ad esse. Sic enim dicuntur Hellines genere et Iones, quia illi ab Helline, illi ab Ione generante.

τὸ δὲ ἀφ᾽ οὗ ἂν ὦσι πρώτου κινήσαντος εἰς τὸ εἶναι: οὕτω γὰρ λέγονται Ἕλληνες τὸ γένος οἱ δὲ Ἴωνες, τῷ οἱ μὲν ἀπὸ Ἕλληνος οἱ δὲ ἀπὸ Ἴωνος εἶναι πρώτου γεννήσαντος:

And the term also designates that from which things are first brought into being. For it is in this way that some men are called Hellenes by race and others Ionians, because the former come from Hellen and the latter from Ion as the ones who begot them.

Et magis qui a generante quam qui a materia. Dicuntur enim et a femina genere, ut a Pleia.

καὶ μᾶλλον οἱ ἀπὸ {35} τοῦ γεννήσαντος ἢ τῆς ὕλης (λέγονται γὰρ καὶ ἀπὸ τοῦ θήλεος τὸ γένος, οἷον οἱ ἀπὸ Πύρρας).

Again, the term is applied to the members of the genus more from the begetter than from the material principle. For some people are also said to derive their race from the female, as those who come from Pleia.

Amplius autem, ut superficies figurarum genus superficialium, et solidum solidorum. Figurarum enim unaquaeque haec superficies quidem talis, hoc autem solidum tale. Hoc autem est subiectum differentiis.

{1024b1} ἔτι δὲ ὡς τὸ ἐπίπεδον τῶν σχημάτων γένος τῶν ἐπιπέδων καὶ τὸ στερεὸν τῶν στερεῶν: ἕκαστον γὰρ τῶν σχημάτων τὸ μὲν ἐπίπεδον τοιονδὶ τὸ δὲ στερεόν ἐστι τοιονδί: τοῦτο δ᾽ ἐστὶ τὸ ὑποκείμενον ταῖς διαφοραῖς.

Further, the term is used in the sense that the plane is called the genus of plane figures, and the solid the genus of solid figures. For each of the figures is either a plane of such and such a kind or a solid of such and such a kind; and this is the subject underlying the differences.

Amplius ut in rationibus quod primum inest, et dicitur in eo quod quid est, hoc genus, cuius differentiae dicuntur qualitates. Genus igitur toties dicitur, aliud quidem secundum generationem continuam speciei, aliud quidem secundum primum movens eiusdem speciei, aliud ut materia. Cuius enim differentia, et qualitas est, hoc est subiectum quod dicimus materiam.

ἔτι ὡς ἐν τοῖς λόγοις τὸ πρῶτον ἐνυπάρχον, ὃ {5} λέγεται ἐν τῷ τί ἐστι, τοῦτο γένος, οὗ διαφοραὶ λέγονται αἱ ποιότητες. τὸ μὲν οὖν γένος τοσαυταχῶς λέγεται, τὸ μὲν κατὰ γένεσιν συνεχῆ τοῦ αὐτοῦ εἴδους, τὸ δὲ κατὰ τὸ πρῶτον κινῆσαν ὁμοειδές, τὸ δ᾽ ὡς ὕλη: οὗ γὰρ ἡ διαφορὰ καὶ ἡ ποιότης ἐστί, τοῦτ᾽ ἔστι τὸ ὑποκείμενον, ὃ λέγομεν ὕλην.

Again, "genus" means the primary element present in definitions, which is predicated quidditatively of the thing whose differences are called "qualities." The term "genus," then, is used in all these senses: in one as the continuous generation of a species; in another as the primary mover of the same species; and in another as matter. For that to which the difference or quality belongs is the subject which we call "matter."

1024b9 Diversa vero genere dicuntur, quorum diversum primum est subiectum, et non resolvitur alterum in alterum, nec ambo in idem, ut species et materia diversum genere. Et quaecumque secundum diversam figuram categoriae entis dicuntur. Alia namque quid significant entium. Alia quale quid. Alia aliud, ut

ἕτερα {10} δὲ τῷ γένει λέγεται ὧν ἕτερον τὸ πρῶτον ὑποκείμενον καὶ μὴ ἀναλύεται θάτερον εἰς θάτερον μηδ᾽ ἄμφω εἰς ταὐτόν, οἷον τὸ εἶδος καὶ ἡ ὕλη ἕτερον τῷ γένει, καὶ ὅσα καθ᾽ ἕτερον σχῆμα κατηγορίας τοῦ ὄντος λέγεται (τὰ μὲν γὰρ τί ἐστι σημαίνει τῶν ὄντων τὰ δὲ ποιόν τι τὰ δ᾽ ὡς διῄρηται {15} πρότερον): οὐδὲ

Things are said to be "diverse" (or "other") in species whose first subject is diverse and cannot be resolved one into the other or both into the same thing. For example, form and matter are diverse in genus. And all things that are predicated according to a different categorical figure of being are diverse in genus.

521

divisum est prius. Nec enim ea resolvuntur nec in invicem, nec in unum aliquod. [1124]

γὰρ ταῦτα ἀναλύεται οὔτ᾽ εἰς ἄλληλα οὔτ᾽ εἰς ἕν τι.

For some signify the quiddity of beings, others quality, and others something else, in the sense of our previous distinctions. For they are not analyzed into each other or into some one thing.

1024b17 Falsum dicitur uno modo ut res falsa; et huius hoc quidem per non componi, aut per impossibile esse componi. [1128]

τὸ ψεῦδος λέγεται ἄλλον μὲν τρόπον ὡς πρᾶγμα ψεῦδος, καὶ τούτου τὸ μὲν τῷ μὴ συγκεῖσθαι ἢ ἀδύνατον εἶναι συντεθῆναι

"False" means in one sense what is false as a thing, and that either because it is not combined or is incapable of being combined.

Sicut dicitur diametrum esse commensurabilem, aut te sedere: horum enim falsum hoc quidem semper, illud vero quandoque: sic enim non entia haec.

(ὥσπερ λέγεται τὸ τὴν διάμετρον εἶναι {20} σύμμετρον ἢ τὸ σὲ καθῆσθαι: τούτων γὰρ ψεῦδος τὸ μὲν ἀεὶ τὸ δὲ ποτέ: οὕτω γὰρ οὐκ ὄντα ταῦτα),

For example, the statement that the diagonal is commensurable or that you are sitting belong to this kind. For the former is always false and the latter is sometimes so, since it is in these senses that these things are non-beings.

Alia vero, quae sunt quidem entia et apta nata sunt videri, aut non qualia sunt, aut quae non sunt, ut schiagraphia, et somnia. Ea namque sunt aliquid quidem, sed non quorum faciunt phantasiam.

τὰ δὲ ὅσα ἔστι μὲν ὄντα, πέφυκε μέντοι φαίνεσθαι ἢ μὴ οἷά ἐστιν ἢ ἃ μὴ ἔστιν (οἷον ἡ σκιαγραφία καὶ τὰ ἐνύπνια: ταῦτα γὰρ ἔστι μέν τι, ἀλλ᾽ οὐχ ὧν ἐμποιεῖ τὴν φαντασίαν):

But there are things that exist and are fitted by nature to appear either other than they are or as things that do not exist, as a shadowgraph and dreams. For these in fact are something, but not that of which they cause an image in us.

Res ergo falsae dicuntur, aut quia non sunt, aut quia ab eis phantasia non entis est.

πράγματα {25} μὲν οὖν ψευδῆ οὕτω λέγεται, ἢ τῷ μὴ εἶναι αὐτὰ ἢ τῷ τὴν ἀπ᾽ αὐτῶν φαντασίαν μὴ ὄντος εἶναι:

Therefore, things are said to be false either because they do not exist or because the image derived from them is not of something real.

1024b26 Ratio vero falsa est, quae non entium inquantum falsa. Unde omnis ratio falsa, alterius quam cuius est vera; ut quae circuli, falsa trigoni. [1130]

λόγος δὲ ψευδὴς ὁ τῶν μὴ ὄντων, ᾗ ψευδής, διὸ πᾶς λόγος ψευδὴς ἑτέρου ἢ οὗ ἐστιν ἀληθής, οἷον ὁ τοῦ κύκλου ψευδὴς τριγώνου.

A "false notion," inasmuch as it is false, is the notion of something non-existent. Hence every notion is false when applied to something other than that of which it is true—for example, the notion of a circle is false when applied to a triangle.

Cuiuslibet autem ratio est quidem quasi una quae est eius quod quid erat esse: est et quasi multae: quoniam idem aliqualiter ipsum et ipsum passum, ut Socrates et Socrates musicus.

ἑκάστου δὲ λόγος ἔστι μὲν ὡς εἷς, ὁ τοῦ τί ἦν εἶναι, ἔστι δ᾽ ὡς {30} πολλοί, ἐπεὶ ταὐτό πως αὐτὸ καὶ αὐτὸ πεπονθός, οἷον Σωκράτης καὶ Σωκράτης μουσικός

Now of each thing there is in a sense one notion, which is its essence, but there are also in a sense many, since the thing itself and the thing with a modification are in a sense the same, as Socrates and musical Socrates.

Sed falsa ratio nullius est simpliciter ratio. Quapropter Antisthenes opinatus est fatue, nihil dignatus dici nisi propria ratione semper unum de uno. Ex quibus accidit non esse contradicere. Fere autem nec mentiri.

(ὁ δὲ ψευδὴς λόγος οὐθενός ἐστιν ἁπλῶς λόγος): διὸ Ἀντισθένης ᾤετο εὐή- θως μηθὲν ἀξιῶν λέγεσθαι πλὴν τῷ οἰκείῳ λόγῳ, ἓν ἐφ᾽ ἑνός: ἐξ ὧν συνέβαι- νε μὴ εἶναι ἀντιλέγειν, σχεδὸν δὲ μηδὲ ψεύδεσθαι.

But a false notion is absolutely speaking not the notion of anything. And it is for this reason that Antisthenes entertained a silly opinion when he thought that nothing could be expressed except by its proper notion—one term always for one thing. From this it would follow that there can be no contradiction and almost no error.

Est autem unumquodque dicere non solum sua ratione, sed et ea quae alterius. Falso quidem et omnino. Est au-

ἔστι {35} δ᾽ ἕκαστον λέγειν οὐ μόνον τῷ αὐτοῦ λόγῳ ἀλλὰ καὶ τῷ ἑτέρου, ψευδῶς μὲν καὶ παντελῶς, ἔστι δ᾽ ὡς καὶ

It is possible, however, to express each thing not only by its own notion, but also by that which belongs to something else

tem et vere; sicut octo dupla dualitatis ratione. Haec igitur ita dicuntur falsa.

ἀληθῶς, ὥσπερ τὰ ὀκτὼ διπλάσια τῷ τῆς δυάδος λόγῳ. {1025a1} τὰ μὲν οὖν οὕτω λέγεται ψευδῆ,

not only falsely but also truly, as eight may be said to be double through the notion of two. These are the ways, then, in which things are said to be false.

1025a2 Sed et homo falsus, quia talium rationum electivus non propter aliud aliquid, nisi propter idipsum. Et in aliis talium factor rationum; sicut res dicimus esse falsas quaecumque falsam faciunt phantasiam. [1135]

ἄνθρωπος δὲ ψευδὴς ὁ εὐχερὴς καὶ προαιρετικὸς τῶν τοιούτων λόγων, μὴ δι' ἕτερόν τι ἀλλὰ δι' αὐτό, καὶ ὁ ἄλλοις ἐμποιητικὸς τῶν τοιούτων λόγων, {5} ὥσπερ καὶ τὰ πράγματά φαμεν ψευδῆ εἶναι ὅσα ἐμποιεῖ φαντασίαν ψευδῆ.

A false man is one who chooses such thoughts not for any other reason but for themselves and one who is the cause of such thoughts in others, just as we say that those things are false which produce a false image or impression.

1025a6 Quare in Hippia oratio refutatur, quae eadem vera et falsa. Potentem enim mentiri accipit falsum, hic autem sciens et prudens. [1137]

διὸ ὁ ἐν τῷ Ἱππίᾳ λόγος παρακρούεται ὡς ὁ αὐτὸς ψευδὴς καὶ ἀληθής. τὸν δυνάμενον γὰρ ψεύσασθαι λαμβάνει ψευδῆ (οὗτος δ' ὁ εἰδὼς καὶ ὁ φρόνιμος):

Hence, the speech in the *Hippias* which says that the same man is true and false is refuted, for it assumes that that man is false who is able to deceive, even though he is knowing and prudent.

1025a8 Amplius volentem turpia meliorem: et hoc falsum accipit per inductionem. [1138]

ἔτι τὸν ἑκόντα φαῦλον βελτίω. τοῦτο δὲ ψεῦδος {10} λαμβάνει διὰ τῆς ἐπαγωγῆς

And further, it assumes that one who is capable of willing evil things is better. And this false opinion is arrived at by way of induction.

Nam voluntate claudicans, non voluntarie dignior, claudicantem imitari dicimus.

—ὁ γὰρ ἑκὼν χωλαίνων τοῦ ἄκοντος κρείττων—τὸ χωλαίνειν τὸ μιμεῖσθαι λέγων,

For one who limps voluntarily is better than one who does so involuntarily; and by "limping" we mean imitating a limp.

Quoniam sic claudus voluntarie, indignior forsan sicut in more et hoc.

ἐπεὶ εἴ γε χωλὸς ἑκών, χείρων ἴσως, ὥσπερ ἐπὶ τοῦ ἤθους, καὶ οὗτος.

For if a man were to limp voluntarily, he would be worse in this way, just as he would be in the case of moral character.

1025a14 Accidens est quod inest alicui, et est verum dicere, non tamen ex necessitate, nec secundum magis: ut si quis fodiens plantae fossam, thesaurum inveniat: hoc quidem accidens fodienti foveam invenire thesaurum. Nec enim ex necessitate hoc ex hoc, aut post hoc: nec ut secundum magis, si quis plantat inveniet thesaurum. Et quis utique musicus est albus; sed quoniam nec ex necessitate, nec ut secundum magis hoc fit, accidens esse dicimus. Sed quoniam inest aliquid alicui, et horum quaedam et alicubi et quandoque, quodcumque extiterit quidem sed non quia nunc aut hoc, accidens erit. [1139]

συμβεβηκὸς λέγεται ὃ ὑπάρχει μέν τινι καὶ ἀληθὲς {15} εἰπεῖν, οὐ μέντοι οὔτ' ἐξ ἀνάγκης οὔτε <ὡς> ἐπὶ τὸ πολύ, οἷον εἴ τις ὀρύττων φυτῷ βόθρον εὗρε θησαυρόν. τοῦτο τοίνυν συμβεβηκὸς τῷ ὀρύττοντι τὸν βόθρον, τὸ εὑρεῖν θησαυρόν: οὔτε γὰρ ἐξ ἀνάγκης τοῦτο ἐκ τούτου ἢ μετὰ τοῦτο, οὔθ' ὡς ἐπὶ τὸ πολὺ ἄν τις φυτεύῃ θησαυρὸν εὑρίσκει. καὶ μουσικός γ' {20} ἄν τις εἴη λευκός: ἀλλ' ἐπεὶ οὔτε ἐξ ἀνάγκης οὔθ' ὡς ἐπὶ τὸ πολὺ τοῦτο γίγνεται, συμβεβηκὸς αὐτὸ λέγομεν. ὥστ' ἐπεὶ ἔστιν ὑπάρχον τι καὶ τινί, καὶ ἔνια τούτων καὶ ποῦ καὶ ποτέ, ὅ τι ἂν ὑπάρχῃ μέν, ἀλλὰ μὴ διότι τοδὶ ἦν ἢ νῦν ἢ ἐνταῦθα, συμβεβηκὸς ἔσται.

An "accident" is what attaches to anything and which it is true to affirm is so, although not necessarily or for the most part. For example, if someone discovers a treasure while digging a hole for a plant, the discovery of the treasure is an accident to the digger. For the one does not necessarily come from the other or come after it, nor does it happen for the most part that someone will find a treasure when he digs a hole to set out a plant. And a musician may be white, but since this does not happen necessarily or for the most part, we say that it is accidental. But since something belongs to something, and some belong somewhere and at some time, then whatever attaches to a subject, but not because it is now or here, will be an accident.

Nec est aliqua causa determinata accidentis, sed contingens, vel quia forte. Hoc autem indeterminatum. Accidit enim alicui Aeginam venire; sed, si non propter hoc advenit ut illuc veniat, sed ab hieme expulsus, aut a latronibus captus, evenit quidem et est accidens. At non inquantum ipsum, sed inquan-

οὐδὲ δὴ αἴτιον ὡρισμένον οὐδὲν {25} τοῦ συμβεβηκότος ἀλλὰ τὸ τυχόν: τοῦτο δ' ἀόριστον. συνέβη τῳ εἰς Αἴγιναν ἐλθεῖν, εἰ μὴ διὰ τοῦτο ἀφίκετο ὅπως ἐκεῖ ἔλθῃ, ἀλλ' ὑπὸ χειμῶνος ἐξωσθεὶς ἢ ὑπὸ λῃστῶν ληφθείς. γέγονε μὲν δὴ ἢ ἔστι τὸ συμβεβηκός, ἀλλ' οὐχ ᾗ αὐτὸ ἀλλ' ᾗ ἕτερον: ὁ γὰρ χειμὼν αἴτιος τοῦ

Nor does an accident have any determinate cause, but only a contingent or chance cause—that is, an indeterminate one. For it was by accident that someone came to Aegina, and if he did not come there in order to get there, but because he was driven there by a storm or was captured by pirates, the event has occurred

tum alterum. Hiems enim est causa non quo navigabat veniendi, et hoc erat Aegina.

μὴ ὅπου ἔπλει ἐλθεῖν, {30} τοῦτο δ᾽ ἦν Αἴγινα.

and is an accident, though not of itself, but by reason of something else. For the storm is the cause of his coming to the place to which he was not sailing, and this was Aegina.

Dicitur et aliter accidens, et quaecumque in unoquoque secundum se non in substantia entia. Veluti in triangulo duos rectos habere. Et eadem quidem contingit sempiterna esse. Illorum veto nullum. Huius autem ratio in aliis.

λέγεται δὲ καὶ ἄλλως συμβεβηκός, οἷον ὅσα ὑπάρχει ἑκάστῳ καθ᾽ αὑτὸ μὴ ἐν τῇ οὐσίᾳ ὄντα, οἷον τῷ τριγώνῳ τὸ δύο ὀρθὰς ἔχειν. καὶ ταῦτα μὲν ἐνδέχεται ἀΐδια εἶναι, ἐκείνων δὲ οὐδέν. λόγος δὲ τούτου ἐν ἑτέροις.

And in another sense, "accident" means whatever belongs to each thing of itself but not in its substance—for example, it is an accident of a triangle to have its angles equal to two right angles. And these same accidents may be eternal, but none of the others can be. But an account of this has been given elsewhere.

1119. Hic determinat de quodam toto, scilicet de genere.

Et primo ostendit quot modis dicitur genus.

Secundo quot modis dicuntur aliqua diversa, ibi, *diversa vero genere*.

Dicit ergo primo, quod genus dicitur quatuor modis.

Primo generatio continua aliquorum habentium eamdem speciem. Sicut dicitur dum erit *genus hominum*, idest dum durabit generatio continua hominum. Iste est primus modus positus in Porphyrio, scilicet multitudo habentium relationem adinvicem et ad unum principium.

1120. Secundo modo dicitur genus illud a quo *primo movente ad esse*, idest a generante procedunt aliqua; sicut dicuntur Hellenes genere, quia descendunt a quodam Hellene nomine, et aliqui dicuntur Iones genere, quia descendunt a quodam Ione, sicut a primo generante. Magis autem denominantur aliqui a patre, qui est generans, quam a matre, quae dat materiam in generatione: et tamen aliqui denominantur genere a matre, sicut a quadam femina nomine Pleia, dicuntur aliquae Pleiades. Et iste est secundus modus generis in Porphyrio positus.

1121. Tertio modo dicitur genus, sicut superficies est genus figurarum superficialium, *et solidum*, idest corpus, dicitur esse genus figurarum solidarum, idest corporearum. Genus autem hoc non est quod significat essentiam speciei, sicut animal est genus hominis; sed quod est proprium subiectum, specie differentium accidentium. Superficies enim est subiectum omnium figurarum superficialium. Et habet similitudinem cum genere; quia proprium subiectum ponitur in definitione accidentis, sicut genus in definitione speciei. Unde subiectum proprium de accidente praedicatur ad similitudinem generis. *Unaquaeque enim figurarum haec*

1119. Here he gives his views about a particular kind of whole, namely, a genus.

First, he gives the different senses in which the term "genus" is used;

second (1024b9; [1124]), he treats the different senses in which things are said to be diverse (or other) in genus, at *things are said*.

He accordingly says, first, that the term "genus" is used in four senses.

First, it means the continuous generation of things that have the same species. For example, it is said, *as long as* "*the genus of man lasts*, meaning while the continuous generation of men will last. This is the first sense of genus given in Porphyry: a multitude of things having a relation to each other and to one principle.

1120. In a second sense, "genus" ("race") means that from which *things are first brought into being*—that is, some things proceed from a begetter. For example, some men are called Hellenes by race because they are descendants of a man called Hellen, and some are called Ionians by race because they are descendants of a certain Ion as their first begetter. Now people are more commonly named from their father, who is their begetter, than from their mother, who produces the matter of generation, although some derive the name of their race from the mother. For example, some are named from a certain woman called Pleia. This is the second sense of genus given in Porphyry.

1121. The term "genus" is used in a third sense when the surface or the plane is called the genus of plane figures, *and the solid*, or body, is called the genus of solid figures, or bodies. This sense of "genus" is not the one that signifies the essence of a species, as animal is the genus of man, but the one that is the proper subject in the species of different accidents. For surface is the subject of all plane figures. And it bears some likeness to a genus, because the proper subject is given in the definition of an accident just as a genus is given in the definition of a species. Hence the proper subject of an accident is predicated like a genus. *For each of the figures*, that is, plane figures, is such and such

quidem, idest superficialis, est talis superficies. ***Hoc autem***, idest figura solida, est tale solidum, ac si figura sit differentia qualificans superficiem vel solidum. Superficies enim se habet ad figuras superficiales, et solidum ad solidas, sicut genus quod subiicitur contrariis. Nam differentia praedicatur in eo quod quale. Et propter hoc, sicut cum dicitur animal rationale significatur tale animal, ita cum dicitur superficies quadrata, significatur talis superficies.

1122. Quarto modo genus dicitur, quod primo ponitur in definitione, et praedicatur in eo quod quid, et differentiae sunt eius qualitates. Sicut in definitione hominis primo ponitur animal, et bipes sive rationale, quod est quaedam substantialis qualitas hominis.

1123. Patet ergo quod tot modis dicitur genus. Uno modo secundum generationem continuam in eadem specie, quod pertinet ad primum modum. Alio modo secundum primum movens, quod pertinet ad secundum. Alio modo sicut materia, quod pertinet ad tertium et quartum modum.

Hoc enim modo se habet genus ad differentiam, sicut subiectum ad qualitatem. Et ideo patet quod genus praedicabile, et genus subiectum, quasi sub uno modo comprehenduntur, et utrumque se habet per modum materiae. Licet enim genus praedicabile non sit materia, sumitur tamen a materia, sicut differentia a forma. Dicitur enim aliquid animal ex eo quod habet naturam sensitivam. Rationale vero ex eo, quod habet rationalem naturam, quae se habet ad sensitivam sicut forma ad materiam.

1124. Deinde cum dicit *diversa vero* hic ostendit quot modis dicuntur aliqua diversa genere; et ponit duos modos respondentes ultimis duobus modis generis. Primi enim duo modi non multum pertinent ad philosophicam considerationem.

Primo igitur modo dicuntur aliqua genere diversa, quia eorum primum subiectum est diversum. Sicut primum subiectum colorum est superficies, primum autem subiectum saporum est humor. Unde quantum ad genus subiectum, sapor et color sunt diversa genere.

1125. Oportet autem quod duo diversa subiecta, talia sint, quorum unum non resolvatur in alterum. Solidum enim quodammodo resolvitur in superficies. Unde figurae solidi, et figurae superficiales non sunt diversorum generum. Et iterum oportet quod ambo non resolvantur in aliquod idem. Sicut species et materia sunt diversa genere, si secundum suam essentiam considerentur, quod nihil est commune utrique. Et similiter corpora caelestia et inferiora sunt diversa genere, inquantum non habent materiam communem.

1126. Alio modo dicuntur diversa genere, quae dicuntur *secundum diversam figuram categoriae*, idest

a surface. ***And this***, a solid figure, is such and such a solid, as though the figure were a difference qualifying surface or solid. For surface is related to plane (or surface) figures, and solid to solid figures, as a genus, which is the subject of contraries; and difference is predicated in the sense of quality. And for this reason, just as when we say "rational animal" such and such an animal is signified, so too when we say "square surface," such and such a surface is signified.

1122. In a fourth sense, "genus" means the primary element given in a definition, which is predicated quidditatively, and differences are its qualities. For example, in the definition of man, "animal" is given first and then "two-footed" or "rational," which is a certain substantial quality of man.

1123. It is evident, then, that the term "genus" is used in so many different senses: in one sense as the continuous generation of the same species, and this pertains to the first sense; in another as the first moving principle, and this pertains to the second sense; and in another as matter, and this pertains to the third and fourth senses.

For a genus is related to a difference in the same way as a subject is to a quality. Hence it is evident that genus as a predicable and genus as a subject are included in a way under one meaning, and that each has the character of matter. For even though genus as a predicable is not matter, still it is taken from matter as difference is taken from form. For a thing is called an animal because it has a sentient nature, and it is called rational because it has a rational nature, which is related to sentient nature as form is to matter.

1124. ***Things are said*** (1024b9). Here he explains the different senses in which things are said to be "diverse" (or other) in genus, and he gives two senses of this corresponding to the last two senses of "genus." For the first two senses are of little importance for the study of philosophy.

In the first sense, then, some things are said to be diverse in genus because their first subject is diverse. For example, the first subject of color is surface, and the first subject of flavors is something moist. Hence, with regard to their subject genus, flavor and color are diverse in genus.

1125. Further, the two different subjects must be such that one of them is not reducible to the other. Now a solid is in a sense reducible to surfaces, and therefore solid figures and plane figures do not belong to diverse genera. Again, they must not be reducible to the same thing. For example, form and matter are diverse in genus if they are considered according to their own essence, because there is nothing common to both. And in a similar way the celestial bodies and lower bodies are diverse in genus inasmuch as they do not have a common matter.

1126. In another sense, those things are said to be diverse in genus which are predicated *according to a different*

praedicationis entis. Alia namque entia significant quid est, alia quale, alia aliis modis, sicut divisum est prius, ubi tractavit de ente. Istae enim categoriae nec resolvuntur invicem, quia una non continetur sub alia. Nec resolvuntur in unum aliquid, quia non est unum aliquod genus commune ad omnia praedicamenta.

1127. Patet autem ex dictis quod aliqua continentur sub uno praedicamento, et sunt unum genere hoc modo secundo, quae tamen sunt diversa genere primo modo. Sicut corpora caelestia et elementaria, et colores, et sapores.

Primus autem modus diversitatis secundum genus consideratur magis a naturali, et etiam a philosopho, quia est magis realis.

Secundus autem modus consideratur a logico, quia est rationis.

1128. Deinde cum dicit *falsum dicitur* hic distinguit nomina, quae significant defectum entis, vel ens incompletum.

Et primo hoc nomen falsum.

Secundo hoc nomen accidens.

Circa primum tria facit.
Primo ostendit quomodo dicatur falsum in rebus.

Secundo quomodo in definitionibus, ibi, *ratio vero falsa*.

Tertio quomodo sit falsum in hominibus, ibi, *sed et homo falsus*.

Dicit ergo primo, quod falsum dicitur uno modo in rebus, per hoc quod oratio significans rem non congrue componitur. Quod quidem contingit dupliciter.

Uno modo per hoc, quod aliquid componitur quod non debet componi, sicut est in falsis contingentibus.

Alio modo per hoc quod est impossibile componi, sicut est in falsis impossibilibus.

Si enim dicamus diametrum esse commensurabilem quadrati lateri, est falsum impossibile, quia impossibile est commensurabile componi diametro. Si autem dicatur te sedere, te stante, est falsum contingens, quia praedicatum non inest subiecto, licet non sit impossibile inesse. Unde unum istorum, scilicet impossibile, est falsum semper; sed aliud, scilicet contingens, non est falsum semper. Sic igitur falsa dicuntur, quae omnino sunt non entia. Nam oratio tunc esse falsa dicitur, quando non est id quod oratione significatur.

categorical figure of being, that is, of the predication of being. For some things signify quiddity, some quality, and some signify in other ways, which are given in the division made above where he dealt with being [889–94]. For these categories are not reducible one to the other, because one is not included under the other. Nor are they reducible to some one thing, because there is not some one common genus for all the categories.

1127. Now it is clear from what has been said that some things are contained under one category and are in one genus in this second sense, although they are diverse in genus in the first sense. Examples of this are the celestial bodies and elemental bodies, and colors and flavors.

The first way in which things are diverse in genus is considered rather by the natural scientist and also by the philosopher, because it is more real.

But the second way in which things are diverse in genus is considered by the logician, because it is conceptual.

1128. *"False" means* (1024b17). Here he gives the various senses of the terms which signify a lack of being or incomplete being.

First, he gives the senses in which the term "false" is used.

Second [1139], he deals with the various senses of "accident."

In regard to the first he does three things.

First, he shows how the term "false" is used of real things;

second (1024b26; [1130]), how it is used of definitions, at a *"false notion"*;

third (1025a2; [1135]), how men are said to be false, at *a false man*.

He accordingly first says that the term "false" is applied in one sense to real things inasmuch as a statement signifying a reality is not properly composed. And there are two ways in which this can come about.

In one way, by forming a proposition which should not be formed; this is what happens, for instance, in the case of false contingent propositions.

In another way, by forming a proposition about something impossible, and this is what happens in the case of false impossible propositions.

For if we say that the diagonal of a square is commensurable with one of its sides, it is a false impossible proposition; for it is impossible to combine "commensurable" and "diagonal." And if someone says that you are sitting while you are standing, it is a false contingent proposition; for the predicate does not attach to the subject, although it is not impossible for it to do so. Hence one of these—the impossible—is always false, but the other—the contingent—is not always so. Therefore, those things are said to be false which are non-beings in their entirety, for a statement is said to be false when what is signified by the statement is nonexistent.

1129. Secundo modo dicitur falsum in rebus ex eo, quod aliqua quidem sunt entia in se, sed tamen sunt apta nata videri aut qualia non sunt, aut quae non sunt, sicut *schiagraphia*, idest umbrosa descriptio. Umbrae enim quandoque videntur res, quarum sunt umbrae, sicut umbra hominis videtur homo. Et eadem ratio est de somniis, quae videntur res verae, tamen non sunt nisi rerum similitudines. Et similiter dicitur aurum falsum, quod habet similitudinem auri veri.

Differt autem hic modus a primo: quia in primo dicebatur aliquod falsum, ex eo quod non erat. Hic autem dicuntur aliqua falsa quae quidem in se sunt aliquid, sed non sunt illa *quorum faciunt phantasiam*, idest quorum habent apparentiam. Patet ergo quod res dicuntur falsae, aut quia non sunt, aut quia ab eis est apparentia eius quod non est.

1130. Deinde cum dicit *ratio vero* ostendit quomodo est falsum in definitionibus: et dicit quod *ratio*, idest definitio, inquantum est falsa, est non entium.

Dicit autem *inquantum est falsa*, quia definitio dicitur falsa dupliciter.
Aut secundum se; et sic non est definitio alicuius, sed penitus non entis.

Aut est definitio vera in se, sed falsa est prout attribuitur alteri quam proprio definito, et sic dicitur falsa inquantum non est eius.

1131. Unde patet, quod omnis definitio, quae est vera definitio alicuius rei, est falsa definitio alterius; ut definitio quae est vera de circulo, est falsa de triangulo. Definitio autem cuiuslibet rei significans quod quid est, quodam modo est una tantum unius, et quodam modo sunt multae unius.
Aliquo enim modo ipsum subiectum per se sumptum, et *ipsum passum*, idest cum passione sumptum, est idem, sicut Socrates et Socrates musicus.

Aliquo modo non: est enim idem per accidens, sed non per se. Patet autem, quod eorum sunt definitiones diversae. Alia enim est definitio Socratis et Socratis musici; et tamen ambae sunt quodammodo eiusdem.

1132. Sed illa definitio, quae est falsa secundum se, non potest esse definitio alicuius rei. Definitio autem falsa secundum se vel simpliciter, dicitur ex eo, quod una pars definitionis non potest stare cum altera; sicut si diceretur, animal inanimatum.

1129. The term "false" is applied to real things in a second way inasmuch as some things, though beings in themselves, are fitted by nature to appear to be either other than they are or as things that do not exist, as *a shadow-graph*, a delineation in shadow. For sometimes shadows appear to be the things of which they are the shadows, as the shadow of a man appears to be a man. The same applies to dreams, which seem to be real things yet are only the likenesses of things. And one speaks in the same way of false gold, because it bears a resemblance to real gold.

Now this sense differs from the first, because in the first sense things were said to be false because they did not exist, but here things are said to be false because, while being something in themselves, they are not the things *of which they cause an image*, that is, which they resemble. It is clear, then, that things are said to be false either because they do not exist or because there arises from them the appearance of what does not exist.

1130. A *"false notion"* (1024b26). He indicates how the term "false" applies to definitions. He says that *a notion*, or a definition, is of something non-existent inasmuch as it is false.

Now he says *inasmuch as it is false* because a definition is said to be false in two ways.
Either it is a false definition in itself, and then it is not the definition of anything, but has to do entirely with the nonexistent;
or it is a true definition in itself but false inasmuch as it is attributed to something other than the one properly defined, and then it is said to be false inasmuch as it does not apply to the thing defined.

1131. It is clear, then, that every definition which is a true definition of one thing is a false definition of something else. For example, the definition which is true of a circle is false when applied to a triangle. Now, for one thing there is, in one sense, only one definition signifying its quiddity; in another sense there are many definitions for one thing.
For in one sense the subject taken in itself and *the thing with a modification*, that is, taken in conjunction with a modification, are the same, as Socrates and musical Socrates.

But in another sense they are not, for it is the same thing accidentally but not in itself. And it is clear that they have different definitions. For the definition of "Socrates" and that of "musical Socrates" are different, although in a sense both are definitions of the same thing.

1132. But a definition which is false in itself cannot be a definition of anything. And a definition is said to be false in itself, or unqualifiedly false, by reason of the fact that one part of it cannot stand with the other. Such a definition would be had, for example, if one were to say, "inanimate living thing."

1133. Patet autem ex hoc, quod stulta fuit opinio Antisthenis. Volebat enim, quod quia voces sunt signa rerum, quod sicut res non habet aliam essentiam nisi propriam, ita in propositione nihil posset praedicari de aliquo, nisi propria eius definitio, ut simpliciter vel semper de uno subiecto dicatur unum praedicatum. Et ex hoc sequitur, quod non sit contradictio; quia, si de homine praedicatur animal, quod est in eius ratione, non poterit de ipso praedicari non animal; et ita non poterit formari negativa propositio. Et ex hac positione etiam sequitur, quod non contingit aliquem mentiri: quia propria definitio rei vere praedicatur de re. Unde, si de nullo potest praedicari nisi propria definitio, nulla propositio erit falsa.

1134. Est autem eius opinio falsa, quia contingit praedicari de unoquoque non solum suam definitionem, sed etiam alterius. Quod quando fit, universaliter et omnino, est falsa praedicatio. Aliquo tamen modo potest esse vera praedicatio; sicut octo dicuntur dupla, inquantum habent rationem dualitatis, quia ratio dupli est ut se habeat sicut duo ad unum. Octo autem, inquantum sunt duplum, sunt quodammodo duo, quia dividuntur in duo aequalia. Haec ergo dicuntur falsa modo praedicto.

1135. Deinde cum dicit *sed homo* ostendit quomodo falsum dicatur de homine: et circa hoc duo facit.

Primo ponit duos modos, quibus homo dicitur falsus:

quorum primus est, quod homo dicitur falsus, qui est promptus vel gaudens in huiusmodi rationibus, scilicet falsis, et qui est electivus talium rationum non propter aliquod aliud, sed propter se. Unicuique enim habenti habitum fit delectabilis et in promptu operatio, quae est secundum habitum illum; et sic habens habitum operatur secundum habitum illum, non propter aliquod extrinsecum. Sicut luxuriosus fornicatur propter delectationem coitus: si autem fornicetur propter aliquid aliud, puta ut furetur, magis est fur quam luxuriosus. Similiter et qui eligit falsum dicere, propter lucrum, magis est avarus quam falsus.

1136. Secundus modus est prout homo dicitur falsus, qui facit aliis falsas rationes; quasi consimili modo sicut supra dicebamus res esse falsas quae faciunt falsam phantasiam. Patet autem ex praemissis, quod falsum pertinet ad non ens; ex quo homo dicitur falsus per respectum ad rationes falsas: et ratio dicitur falsa, inquantum est non entis.

1137. Secundo ibi, *quare in* excludit ex praemissis duas falsas opiniones:

1133. Again, it is clear from this that Antisthenes' opinion was foolish. For since words are the signs of things, he maintained that just as a thing does not have any essence other than its own, so too in a proposition nothing can be predicated of a subject but its own definition, so that only one predicate absolutely or always may be used of one subject. And from this position it follows that there is no such thing as a contradiction, because if "animal," which is included in his notion, is predicated of man, "non-animal" can not be predicated of him, and thus a negative proposition cannot be formed. And from this position it also follows that one cannot speak falsely, because the proper definition of a thing is truly predicated of it. Hence, if only a thing's own definition can be predicated of it, no proposition can be false.

1134. But his opinion is false, because of each thing we can predicate not only its own definition but also the definition of something else. And when this occurs in a universal or general way, the predication is false. Yet in a way there can be a true predication. For example, eight is said to be double inasmuch as it has the character of duality, because the character of duality is to be related as two is to one. But inasmuch as it is double, eight is in a sense two, because it is divided into two equal quantities. These things, then, are said to be false in the foregoing way.

1135. Then, at *a false man* (1025a2), he shows how the term "false" may be predicated of a man, and in regard to this he does two things.

First, he gives two ways in which a man is said to be false.

In one way, a man is said to be false if he is ready to think, or takes pleasure in thinking, thoughts of this kind—that is, false ones—and chooses such thoughts not for any other reason but for themselves. For anyone who has a habit finds the operation relating to that habit to be pleasurable and readily performed, and thus one who has a habit acts in accordance with that habit and not for the sake of anything extrinsic. For example, a debauched person commits fornication because of the pleasure resulting from coition, but if he commits fornication for some other end—for instance, that he may steal—he is more of a thief than a lecher. And similarly one who chooses to speak falsely for the sake of money is more avaricious than false.

1136. In a second way, a man is said to be false if he causes false notions in others, in much the same way as we said above that things are false which cause a false image or impression. For it is clear from what has been said that the false has to do with the non-existent. Hence a man is said to be false inasmuch as he makes false statements, and a notion is said to be false inasmuch as it is about something nonexistent.

1137. *Hence, the speech* (1025a6). Second, he excludes two false opinions from what has been laid down above.

de quarum prima concludit ex praemissis, dicens, quod ex quo falsus homo est electivus et factivus falsarum opinionum, rationabiliter refutatur et reprobatur in Hippia, qui est liber quidam Platonis, oratio quaedam, quae dicebat, eamdem rationem esse veram et falsam. Haec enim opinio accipiebat illum hominem esse falsum qui potest mentiri; et sic, cum idem homo possit mentiri et verum dicere, idem homo esset verus et falsus. Similiter eadem oratio esset vera et falsa, quia eadem oratio vera et falsa potest esse, ut haec, Socrates sedet, eo sedente est vera, non sedente, est falsa. Constat autem, quod hic inconvenienter accipit, quia etiam homo sciens et prudens potest mentiri; non tamen est falsus, quia non est factivus vel electivus falsarum rationum vel opinionum, ex qua ratione dicitur homo falsus, ut dictum est.

1138. Deinde cum dicit *amplius volentem* secundam falsam opinionem excludit. Dicebat haec opinio, quod homo, qui facit turpia et prava volens, melior est eo qui facit nolens, quod est falsum. Nam quilibet vitiosus ex hoc definitur quod est promptus vel electivus malorum. Et tamen hoc falsum vult accipere per quamdam inductionem ex simili. Ille enim qui claudicat voluntarie, melior et dignior est eo, qui, claudicat non voluntarie. Et ita dicit, quod prava agere imitatur hoc quod est claudicare, ut scilicet sit eadem ratio de utroque. Et hoc quodammodo verum est. Nam claudicans voluntarie deterior est quantum ad morem, licet sit perfectior quantum ad virtutem gressivam. Et similiter qui agit prava voluntarie, deterior est quantum ad morem, licet forte non sit deterior quantum ad aliquam aliam potentiam. Sicut ille qui dicit falsum voluntarie, licet sit peior secundum morem, est tamen intelligentior eo qui credit se verum dicere, cum falsum dicat non voluntarie.

1139. Deinde cum dicit *accidens est* hic ultimo, distinguit nomen accidentis: et ponit duos modos, quibus dicitur hoc nomen accidens:

quorum primus est, quod accidens dicitur id quod inest alicui, et quod contingit vere affirmare, non tamen ex necessitate, nec *secundum magis* idest ut in pluribus, sed ut in paucioribus; sicut, si aliquis fodiens aliquam fossam ad plantandum aliquam plantam, inveniat thesaurum. Hoc ergo, quod est fodientem fossam invenire thesaurum, est quoddam accidens. Neque enim unum est causa alterius ex necessitate, ut hoc sit ex hoc necessario.

Neque etiam de necessitate se comitantur, ut hoc sit post hoc, sicut dies consequitur noctem, quamvis unum non sit causa alterius.

Neque etiam secundum magis hoc contingit, sive ut in pluribus, hoc contingit, ut ille qui plantat, inveniat

He draws the first of these from the points made above. He says that since a false man is one who chooses and creates false opinions, one may logically refute or reject a statement made in the *Hippias*, one of Plato's works, which said that the same notion is both true and false. For this opinion considered that man to be false who is able to deceive, so that, being able both to deceive and to speak the truth, the same man is both true and false. And similarly the same statement will be both true and false, because the same statement is able to be both true and false—for example, the statement "Socrates sits" is true when he is seated, but is false when he is not seated. Now it is evident that this is taken unwarrantedly, because even a man who is prudent and knowing is able to deceive, but he is not false because he does not cause or choose false notions or opinions, and this is the reason why a man is said to be false, as has been stated [1135].

1138. *And further* (1025a8). Then he rejects the second false opinion. This opinion maintained that a man who does base things and wills evil is better than one who does not. But this is false. For anyone is defined as being evil on the grounds that he is ready to do or to choose evil things. Yet this opinion wishes to accept this sense of "false" on the basis of a sort of induction from a similar case. For one who voluntarily limps is better and nobler than one who limps involuntarily. Hence he says that to do evil is like limping inasmuch as the same notion applies to both. And in a sense this is true, for one who limps voluntarily is worse as regards his moral character, although he is more perfect as regards his power of walking. And similarly one who voluntarily does evil is worse as regards his moral character, although perhaps he is not worse as regards some other power. For example, even though that man is more evil, morally speaking, who voluntarily says what is false, still he is more intelligent than one who believes that he speaks the truth when he in fact speaks falsely, though not willfully.

1139. *An "accident"* (1025a14). Here, finally, he gives the different senses in which the term "accident" is used, and there are two of these.

First, "an accident" means anything that attaches to a thing and is truly affirmed of it, although not necessarily or *for the most part*, that is, in the majority of cases, but in a minority; for example, if one were to find a treasure while digging a hole to set out a plant. Hence, finding a treasure while digging a hole is an accident. For the one is not necessarily the cause of the other such that the one necessarily comes from the other.

Neither do they necessarily accompany each other such that the latter comes after the former as day follows night, even though the one is not the cause of the other.

Neither does it happen for the most part, or in the majority of cases, that this should occur, that is, that one who

thesaurum. Et simili modo musicus dicitur esse albus, sed tamen hoc non est ex necessitate, nec fit ut in pluribus; ideo dicimus hoc per accidens. Differt autem hoc exemplum a primo. Nam in primo exemplo sumebatur accidens quantum ad fieri; in secundo vero quantum ad esse.

1140. Quia ergo sicut aliquid inest alicui subiecto determinate, ita et aliquid consideratur *esse alicubi*, idest in aliquo loco determinato, et *quandoque*, idest in aliquo tempore determinato, in omnibus contingit inesse per accidens, si non insit secundum quod huiusmodi. Sicut si album dicitur de musico, hoc est per accidens, quia non inest musico inquantum huiusmodi. Et similiter si sit abundantia pluviae in aestate, hoc est per accidens, quia non accidit in aestate inquantum est aestas; et similiter si grave sit sursum, hoc est per accidens, non enim est in tali loco secundum quod talis locus est, sed per aliquam causam extraneam.

1141. Et sciendum, quod accidentis hoc modo dicti, non est aliqua causa determinata, *sed contingens*, idest qualiscumque contingat, vel *quia forte*, idest causa fortuita, quae est causa indeterminata. Sicut accidit alicui quod *veniat Aeginam*, idest ad illam villam, *si non propter hoc advenit ut illuc veniat*, idest si non propter hoc incepit moveri ut ad hunc terminum perveniret, sed ab aliqua extranea causa illuc adductus est, sicut quia impulsus est ab hieme concitante tempestatem in mari, aut etiam captus est a latronibus, et illuc perductus praeter intentionem. Unde patet, quod hoc est per accidens, et causari potest ex diversis causis; sed tamen quod iste navigans ad hunc locum perveniat non est *inquantum ipsum*, idest inquantum erat navigans, cum intenderet ad alium locum navigare; sed hoc contingit *inquantum alterum*, idest secundum aliquam aliam causam extraneam. Hiems enim est causa veniendi *quo non navigabat*, idest ad Aeginam, aut latrones, aut aliquid aliud huiusmodi.

1142. Secundo modo dicitur accidens, quod inest alicui secundum se, et tamen non est de substantia eius. Et hic est secundus modus dicendi per se, ut supra dictum est. Nam primus erat prout secundum se dicitur de aliquo quod in eius definitione ponitur, ut animal de homine, quod nullo modo est accidens. Sed triangulo inest per se duos rectos habere, et non est de substantia eius; unde est accidens.

1143. Differt autem hic modus a primo, quia accidentia hoc secundo modo contingit esse sempiterna. Semper enim triangulus habet tres angulos aequales duobus rectis. Accidentium vero secundum primum modum,

sets out a plant finds a treasure. And similarly a musician is said to be white, although this is not necessarily so nor does it happen for the most part. Hence our statement is accidental. But this example differs from the first, for in the first example the term "accident" is taken in reference to becoming, and in the second example it is taken in reference to being.

1140. Now, just as something belongs to some definite subject, so too it is considered *to belong somewhere*, that is, in some definite place, *and at some time*, at some definite time. And therefore it happens to belong to all of these accidentally if it does not belong to them by reason of their own nature—for example, when white is predicated of a musician, this is accidental, because white does not belong to a musician as such. And similarly if there is an abundance of rain in summer, this is accidental, because it does not happen in summer insofar as it is summer. And again if what is heavy is high up, this is accidental, for it is not in such a place inasmuch as the place is such, but because of some external cause.

1141. And it should be borne in mind that there is no determinate cause of the kind of accident here mentioned, *but only a contingent cause*, whatever one there happens to be, or *a chance cause*, a fortuitous one, which is an indeterminate cause. For example, it was an accident that someone *came to Aegina*, that is, to that city, *if he did not come there in order to get there*, that is, if he began to head for that city not in order that he might reach it but because he was forced there by some external cause; for example, because he was driven there by the winter wind which caused a tempest at sea, or even because he was captured by pirates and was brought there against his will. It is clear, then, that this is accidental and that it can be brought about by different causes. Yet the fact that he reaches this place in sailing occurs *not of itself*, that is, inasmuch as he was sailing (since he intended to sail to another place), but *by reason of something else*, another external cause. For a storm (or pirates, or something of this kind) is the cause of his coming to the place *to which he was not sailing*, to Aegina.

1142. In a second sense, "accident" means whatever belongs to each thing of itself but is not in its substance. This is the second mode of essential predication, as was noted above [1055]. For the first mode exists when something is predicated *per se* of something which is given in its definition, as animal is predicated of man, which is not an accident in any way. Now it belongs *per se* to a triangle to have two right angles, but this does not belong to its substance. Hence it is an accident.

1143. This sense of accident differs from the first, because accidents in this second sense can be perpetual. For a triangle always has three angles equal to two right angles. But none of those things that are accidents in the first sense

nullum contingit esse sempiternum, quia sunt semper ut in paucioribus: et huius ratio habetur in aliis, sicut infra in sexto huius, et in secundo *Physicorum*. Accidens ergo secundum primum modum opponitur ad secundum se. Accidens vero secundo modo opponitur ad substantialiter. Et haec de quinto.

can be perpetual, because they are always such as occur in the minority of cases. The discussion of this kind of accident is undertaken in another place—for example, in book 6 of this work [1172], and in *Physics* 2. "Accident" in the first sense, then, is opposed to what exists in itself; but "accident" in the second sense is opposed to what is substantial. This completes book 5.

Book 6

The Method of Investigating Being

Lecture 1

The method of investigating being as being

1025b3 Principia et causae quaeruntur entium: palam autem quia inquantum entia. [1145]

αἱ ἀρχαὶ καὶ τὰ αἴτια ζητεῖται τῶν ὄντων, δῆλον δὲ ὅτι ᾗ ὄντα.

The principles and causes of beings are the object of our search, and it is evident that we must investigate the principles and causes of beings as beings.

Est enim aliqua causa sanitatis et convalescentiae. Sunt autem et mathematicorum principia et elementa et causae,

ἔστι γάρ τι αἴτιον ὑγιείας καὶ εὐεξίας, καὶ τῶν {5} μαθηματικῶν εἰσιν ἀρχαὶ καὶ στοιχεῖα καὶ αἴτια,

For there is a cause of health and of its recovery, and there are also principles and elements and causes of the objects of mathematics.

et totaliter omnis scientia intellectualis participans aliquid intellectus circa causas et principia est aut certiora, aut simpliciora.

καὶ ὅλως δὲ πᾶσα ἐπιστήμη διανοητικὴ ἢ μετέχουσά τι διανοίας περὶ αἰτίας καὶ ἀρχάς ἐστιν ἢ ἀκριβεστέρας ἢ ἁπλουστέρας.

And in general, every intellectual science, to whatever degree it participates in intellect, deals with principles and causes: either with those which are more certain or with those which are simpler.

1025b7 Sed et omnes illae circa unum quid et genus aliquod circumscriptae de hoc tractant; sed non de ente simpliciter, nec inquantum est ens. [1147]

ἀλλὰ πᾶσαι αὗται περὶ ὄν τι καὶ γένος τι περιγραψάμεναι περὶ τούτου πραγματεύονται, ἀλλ' οὐχὶ περὶ ὄντος ἁπλῶς οὐδὲ ᾗ {10} ὄν,

But all these sciences single out some one thing, or some particular genus, and confine their investigations to this, but they do not deal with being in an unqualified sense, or as being.

Nec de ipso quod quid est ullam faciunt mentionem. Sed ex hoc aliae quidem sensu facientes ipsum manifestum, aliae per suppositionem accipientes quod quid est, sic secundum se quae insunt generi circa quod sunt, demonstrant, aut magis necessarie, aut infirmius.

οὐδὲ τοῦ τί ἐστιν οὐθένα λόγον ποιοῦνται, ἀλλ' ἐκ τούτου, αἱ μὲν αἰσθήσει ποιήσασαι αὐτὸ δῆλον αἱ δ' ὑπόθεσιν λαβοῦσαι τὸ τί ἐστιν, οὕτω τὰ καθ' αὑτὰ ὑπάρχοντα τῷ γένει περὶ ὅ εἰσιν ἀποδεικνύουσιν ἢ ἀναγκαιότερον ἢ μαλακώτερον·

Nor do they make any mention of the whatness itself of things. But proceeding from this, some making it evident by means of the senses and others taking the whatness by assuming it, they demonstrate with greater necessity or more weakly the essential attributes of the genus of things with which they deal.

Quapropter palam quia non est demonstratio substantiae, nec eius quod quid est ex tali inductione, sed alius modus est ostensionis.

διόπερ φανερὸν ὅτι οὐκ ἔστιν ἀπόδειξις οὐσίας οὐδὲ τοῦ τί ἐστιν {15} ἐκ τῆς τοιαύτης ἐπαγωγῆς, ἀλλά τις ἄλλος τρόπος τῆς δηλώσεως.

For this reason it is evident that there is no demonstration of a thing's substance or whatness from such an inductive method, but there is another method of making it known.

Similiter autem nec si est aut non est genus circa quod versantiur, nihil dicunt propter eiusdem esse scientiae ipsum quod quid est manifestum facere, et hoc si est.

ὁμοίως δὲ οὐδ' εἰ ἔστιν ἢ μὴ ἔστι τὸ γένος περὶ ὃ πραγματεύονται οὐδὲν λέγουσι, διὰ τὸ τῆς αὐτῆς εἶναι διανοίας τό τε τί ἐστι δῆλον ποιεῖν καὶ εἰ ἔστιν.

And similarly they say nothing about the existence or non-existence of the genus of things with which they deal, because it belongs to the same science to show what a thing is and whether it exists.

1025b18 Quoniam vero physica scientia est circa genus quoddam entis, nam circa talem est substantiam, in qua est principium motus et quietis in ea, palam quia nec activa nec factiva est. [1152]

Factivarum enim, in faciente principium, aut intellectus, aut ars, aut potentia quaedam. Activarum vero in agente prohaeresis. Idem enim agibile et eligibile.

Quare, si omnis scientia, aut activa, aut factiva, aut theorica, physica theorica quaedam est. Sed theorica circa tale ens, quod est possibile moveri; et circa substantiam, quae est secundum rationem, ut secundum magis non separabile solum.

1025b28 Oportet autem quod quid erat esse, et rationem quomodo est, non latere, quia sine hoc quaerere nihil est facere. [1156]

Definientium autem et ipsorum quod quid est, hoc quidem ita fit ut simum, illa vero ut concavum. Differunt autem ea, quia simum conceptum est cum materia; est enim simus nasus concavus, concavitas vero sine materia sensibili. Sed omnia physica similiter simo dicuntur, ut nasus, oculus, facies, caro, os, totaliter animal. Folium, radix, cortex, totaliter planta. Nullius enim sine motu ratio eorum, sed semper habet materiam. Palam quomodo oportet in physicis ipsum quid est quaerere et definire. Ideoque et de anima aliqua speculari est physici, quaecumque non sine materia est. Ergo quia physica theorica, manifestum est ex his.

1026a7 Sed est et mathematica theorica. Sed si immobilium et separabilium, adhuc non manifestum. [1160]

Quia tamen mathematica inquantum sunt immobilia, et inquantum separabilia speculatur, palam.

ἐπεὶ δὲ καὶ ἡ φυσικὴ ἐπιστήμη τυγχάνει οὖσα περὶ γένος τι τοῦ ὄντος (περὶ {20} γὰρ τὴν τοιαύτην ἐστὶν οὐσίαν ἐν ᾗ ἡ ἀρχὴ τῆς κινήσεως καὶ στάσεως ἐν αὐτῇ), δῆλον ὅτι οὔτε πρακτική ἐστιν οὔτε ποιητική

(τῶν μὲν γὰρ ποιητῶν ἐν τῷ ποιοῦντι ἡ ἀρχή, ἢ νοῦς ἢ τέχνη ἢ δύναμίς τις, τῶν δὲ πρακτῶν ἐν τῷ πράττοντι, ἡ προαίρεσις: τὸ αὐτὸ γὰρ τὸ πρακτὸν καὶ προαιρετόν),

{25} ὥστε εἰ πᾶσα διάνοια ἢ πρακτικὴ ἢ ποιητικὴ ἢ θεωρητική, ἡ φυσικὴ θεωρητική τις ἂν εἴη, ἀλλὰ θεωρητικὴ περὶ τοιοῦτον ὂν ὅ ἐστι δυνατὸν κινεῖσθαι, καὶ περὶ οὐσίαν τὴν κατὰ τὸν λόγον ὡς ἐπὶ τὸ πολὺ ὡς οὐ χωριστὴν μόνον.

δεῖ δὲ τὸ τί ἦν εἶναι καὶ τὸν λόγον πῶς ἐστὶ μὴ λανθάνειν, ὡς ἄνευ γε {30} τούτου τὸ ζητεῖν μηδέν ἐστι ποιεῖν.

ἔστι δὲ τῶν ὁριζομένων καὶ τῶν τί ἐστι τὰ μὲν ὡς τὸ σιμὸν τὰ δ᾽ ὡς τὸ κοῖλον. διαφέρει δὲ ταῦτα ὅτι τὸ μὲν σιμὸν συνειλημμένον ἐστὶ μετὰ τῆς ὕλης (ἔστι γὰρ τὸ σιμὸν κοίλη ῥίς), ἡ δὲ κοιλότης ἄνευ ὕλης αἰσθητῆς. {1026a1} εἰ δὴ πάντα τὰ φυσικὰ ὁμοίως τῷ σιμῷ λέγονται, οἷον ῥὶς ὀφθαλμὸς πρόσωπον σὰρξ ὀστοῦν, ὅλως ζῷον, φύλλον ῥίζα φλοιός, ὅλως φυτόν (οὐθενὸς γὰρ ἄνευ κινήσεως ὁ λόγος αὐτῶν, ἀλλ᾽ ἀεὶ ἔχει ὕλην), δῆλον πῶς δεῖ ἐν τοῖς φυσικοῖς τὸ τί ἐστι ζητεῖν καὶ ὁρίζεσθαι, {5} καὶ διότι καὶ περὶ ψυχῆς ἐνίας θεωρῆσαι τοῦ φυσικοῦ, ὅση μὴ ἄνευ τῆς ὕλης ἐστίν. ὅτι μὲν οὖν ἡ φυσικὴ θεωρητική ἐστι, φανερὸν ἐκ τούτων:

ἀλλ᾽ ἔστι καὶ ἡ μαθηματικὴ θεωρητική: ἀλλ᾽ εἰ ἀκινήτων καὶ χωριστῶν ἐστί, νῦν ἄδηλον,

ὅτι μέντοι ἔνια μαθήματα ᾗ ἀκίνητα καὶ ᾗ χωριστὰ {10} θεωρεῖ, δῆλον.

And since the philosophy of nature is concerned with some genus of being (for it deals with that kind of substance in which there is a principle of motion and rest), it is evident that it is neither a practical nor a productive science.

For the principle of productive sciences is in the maker, whether it be intellect or art or some kind of power; but the principle of practical sciences is *prohaeresis* in the agent, for the object of action and that of choice are the same.

Thus if every science is either practical, productive, or theoretical, the philosophy of nature will be a theoretical science. But it will be theoretical of that kind of being which is subject to motion, and of that kind of substance which is inseparable in its intelligible structure for the most part only.

Now the essence and the conceptual expression of the way in which a thing exists must not remain unknown, because without this our investigation will be unfruitful.

And regarding things defined, or their whatness, some are like snub and others like concave. And these differ, because snub is conceived with sensible matter (for snub is a concave nose), whereas concave is conceived without sensible matter. But all physical things are spoken of like the snub—for example, nose, eye, face, flesh, bone, and animal in general; leaf, root, bark, and plant in general. For the definition of none of these is without motion but always includes matter. Thus it is clear how we must investigate and define the essence in the case of physical things, and why it also belongs to the natural philosopher to speculate about one kind of soul, that which does not exist without matter. From these facts, then, it is evident that the philosophy of nature is a theoretical science.

But mathematics is also a theoretical science, although it is not yet evident whether it deals with things that are immobile and separable from matter.

However, it is evident that mathematics speculates about things insofar as they are immobile and insofar as they are separable from matter.

1026a10 Si vero est immobile aliquid et sempiternum et separabile, palam quia est theoricae id nosse, non tamen physicae. [1162]

εἰ δέ τί ἐστιν ἀΐδιον καὶ ἀκίνητον καὶ χωριστόν, φανερὸν ὅτι θεωρητικῆς τὸ γνῶναι,

Now if there is something which is immobile, eternal, and separable from matter, evidently a knowledge of it belongs to a theoretical science.

Nam de mobilibus quibusdam est physica. Sed nec mathematicae, sed prioris ambarum.

οὐ μέντοι φυσικῆς γε (περὶ κινητῶν γάρ τινων ἡ φυσική) οὐδὲ μαθηματικῆς, ἀλλὰ προτέρας ἀμφοῖν.

However, it does not belong to the philosophy of nature (for this science deals with certain mobile things), or to mathematics, but to a science prior to both.

Physica namque circa inseparabilia forsan quidem, sed non immobilia.

ἡ μὲν γὰρ φυσικὴ περὶ ἀχώριστα[5] μὲν ἀλλ᾽ οὐκ ἀκίνητα,

For the philosophy of nature deals with things that are inseparable from matter but not immobile.

Mathematicae autem quaedam circa immobilia, sed et inseparabilia forsan, verum quasi in materia.

τῆς δὲ μαθηματικῆς ἔνια {15} περὶ ἀκίνητα μὲν οὐ χωριστὰ δὲ ἴσως ἀλλ᾽ ὡς ἐν ὕλῃ:

And some mathematical sciences deal with things that are immobile but presumably do not exist separately, but are present, as it were, in matter.

Prima vero circa separabilia et immobilia. Necesse vero communes quidem causas sempiternas, et maxime has: hae namque causae manifestis sensibilium sunt.

ἡ δὲ πρώτη καὶ περὶ χωριστὰ καὶ ἀκίνητα. ἀνάγκη δὲ πάντα μὲν τὰ αἴτια ἀΐδια εἶναι, μάλιστα δὲ ταῦτα: ταῦτα γὰρ αἴτια τοῖς φανεροῖς τῶν θείων.

First philosophy, however, deals with things that are both separable from matter and immobile. Now common causes must be eternal, and especially these, since they are the causes of the sensible things visible to us.

1026a17 Quare tres erunt philosophiae theoricae: mathematica, physica et theologia. [1166]

ὥστε τρεῖς ἂν εἶεν φιλοσοφίαι θεωρητικαί, μαθηματική, φυσική, θεολογική

Hence there will be three theoretical philosophies: mathematics, philosophy of nature, and theology.

1026a19 Non enim immanifestum, si alicubi divinum existit, in tali existit natura. [1167]

(οὐ γὰρ {20} ἄδηλον ὅτι εἴ που τὸ θεῖον ὑπάρχει, ἐν τῇ τοιαύτῃ φύσει ὑπάρχει),

For it is obvious that if the divine exists anywhere, it exists in this kind of nature.

1026a22 Et honorabilissimam scientiarum oportet circa honorabilissimum genus esse: ergo theoricae aliis scientiis desiderabiliores sunt. [1168]

καὶ τὴν τιμιωτάτην δεῖ περὶ τὸ τιμιώτατον γένος εἶναι. αἱ μὲν οὖν θεωρητικαὶ τῶν ἄλλων ἐπιστημῶν αἱρετώταται, αὕτη δὲ τῶν θεωρητικῶν.

And the most honorable of the sciences must deal with the most honorable genus of things. Therefore, the theoretical sciences are more desirable than the other sciences.

1026a23 Dubitabit autem aliquis, utrum prima philosophia sit universalis, aut circa aliquod genus, aut naturam unam. Non enim idem modus, nec in mathematicis; quia geometria et astrologia circa aliquam naturam sunt: illa vero universaliter omnium est communis. [1169]

ἀπορήσειε γὰρ ἄν τις πότερόν ποθ᾽ ἡ πρώτη φιλοσοφία καθόλου ἐστὶν ἢ περί τι γένος {25} καὶ φύσιν τινὰ μίαν (οὐ γὰρ ὁ αὐτὸς τρόπος οὐδ᾽ ἐν ταῖς μαθηματικαῖς, ἀλλ᾽ ἡ μὲν γεωμετρία καὶ ἀστρολογία περί τινα φύσιν εἰσίν, ἡ δὲ καθόλου πασῶν κοινή):

But someone will raise the question of whether first philosophy is universal or deals with some particular genus, that is, one kind of reality. For not even in the mathematical sciences is the method the same, because both geometry and astronomy deal with a particular kind of nature, whereas the first science is universally common to all.

1026a27 Si igitur non est aliqua diversa substantia praeter natura consistentes, physica erit prima scientia. [1170]

εἰ μὲν οὖν μὴ ἔστι τις ἑτέρα οὐσία παρὰ τὰς φύσει συνεστηκυίας, ἡ φυσικὴ ἂν εἴη πρώτη ἐπιστήμη:

Therefore, if there is no substance other than those which exist in the way that natural substances do, the philosophy of nature will be the first science.

Sed, si est aliqua substantia immobilis, ea prior, et philosophia prima et universalis sic.

εἰ δ᾽ ἔστι τις οὐσία ἀκίνητος, {30} αὕτη προτέρα καὶ φιλοσοφία πρώτη, καὶ καθόλου οὕτως ὅτι πρώτη:

But if there is an immobile substance, this substance will be prior, and first philosophy will be the first science, and thus will be universal.

---

5. Ross's edition reads χωριστὰ here.

Et quia prima et de ente inquantum est ens, eius utique est speculari, et quod quid est, et quae insunt inquantum ens.	καὶ περὶ τοῦ ὄντος ᾗ ὂν ταύτης ἂν εἴη θεωρῆσαι, καὶ τί ἐστι καὶ τὰ ὑπάρχοντα ᾗ ὄν.	And because it will be first and about being, it will be the function of this science to investigate both what being is and what the attributes are which belong to it as being.

1144. Postquam Philosophus in quarto huius ostendit, quod haec scientia considerat de ente et de uno, et de his quae consequuntur ad ens inquantum huiusmodi, et quod omnia ista dicuntur multipliciter, et in quinto huius eorum multiplicitatem distinxit, hic incipit de ente determinare, et de aliis quae consequuntur ad ens. Dividitur autem pars ista in duas.

In prima ostendit per quem modum haec scientia debet determinare de ente.

In secunda incipit de ente determinare, scilicet in principio septimi, ibi, *ens dicitur multipliciter*.

Prima pars dividitur in duas.

In prima ostendit modum tractandi de entibus, qui competit huic scientiae per differentiam ad alias scientias.

In secunda removet a consideratione huius scientiae ens aliquibus modis dictum, secundum quos modos ens non intenditur principaliter in hac scientia, ibi, *sed quoniam ens simpliciter*.

Prima autem pars dividitur in duas.

In prima parte ostendit differentiam huius scientiae ad alias, per hoc, quod considerat principia entis inquantum est ens.

Secundo, quantum ad modum tractandi de huiusmodi principiis, ibi, *quoniam vero physica*.

Circa primum duo facit.

1145. Primo ostendit quomodo haec scientia convenit cum aliis in consideratione principiorum; dicens, quod ex quo ens est subiectum in huiusmodi scientia, ut in quarto ostensum est, et quaelibet scientia debet inquirere principia et causas, sui subiecti, quae sunt eius inquantum huiusmodi, oportet quod in ista scientia inquirantur principia et causae entium, inquantum sunt entia. Ita etiam est et in aliis scientiis. Nam sanitatis et convalescentiae est aliqua causa, quam quaerit medicus. Et similiter etiam mathematicorum sunt principia et elementa et causae, ut figurae et numeri et aliarum huiusmodi quae perquirit mathematicus.

Et universaliter omnis scientia intellectualis qualitercumque participet intellectum: sive sit solum circa intelligibilia, sicut scientia divina; sive sit circa ea quae sunt aliquo modo imaginabilia, vel sensibilia in particulari, in

1144. Having shown in book 4 [535] of this work that this science considers being and unity and those attributes which belong to being as such, and that all of these are used in several senses, and having distinguished the number of these in book 5 [843, 885] of this work, here the Philosopher begins to establish the truth about being and those attributes which belong to being. This part is divided into two sections.

In the first, he explains the method by which this science should establish what is true about being.

In the second (1028a10; [1247]), he begins to settle the issue about being. He does this at the beginning of book 7, at *the term "being" is used in many senses*.

The first part is divided into two sections.

In the first he explains the method of treating beings which is proper to this science by showing how it differs from the other sciences.

In the second (1026a33; [1170]), he excludes certain senses of being from the investigation of this science, namely, those senses which are not the chief concern of this science, at *being, in an unqualified sense*.

The first part is again divided into two sections.

In the first he shows how this science differs from the others because it considers the principles of being as being.

In the second (1025b18; [1152]), he shows how this science differs from the others in its method of treating principles of this kind, at *and since the philosophy of nature*.

In regard to the first he does two things.

1145. First, he shows how this science agrees with the other sciences in its study of principles. He says that, since being is the subject of this kind of science, as has been shown in book 4 [529–30], and every science must investigate the principles and causes which belong to its subject inasmuch as it is this kind of thing, we must investigate in this science the principles and causes of beings as beings. And this is also what occurs in the other sciences. For there is a cause of health and of its recovery which the physician seeks. And similarly there are also principles, elements, and causes of the objects of mathematics, like figure and number and other things of this kind which the mathematician investigates.

And in general every intellectual science, to whatever degree it participates in intellect, must always deal with causes and principles. This is the case whether it deals with purely intelligible things, as divine science does, or with

universali autem intelligibilia, et etiam sensibilia prout de his est scientia, sicut in mathematica et in naturali;

sive etiam ex universalibus principiis ad particularia procedant, in quibus est operatio, sicut in scientiis practicis: semper oportet quod talis scientia sit circa causas et principia.

1146. Quae quidem principia aut sunt certiora quo ad nos sicut in naturalibus, quia sunt propinquiora sensibilibus, aut simpliciora et priora secundum naturam, sicut est in mathematicis. Cognitiones autem quae sunt sensitivae tantum, non sunt per principia et causas, sed per hoc quod ipsum sensibile obiicitur sensui. Discurrere enim a causis in causata vel e contrario, non est sensus, sed solum intellectus. Vel certiora principia dicit ea quae sunt magis nota et exquisita. Simplicia autem ea, quae magis superficialiter exquiruntur, sicut est in scientiis moralibus, quorum principia sumuntur ex his quae sunt ut in pluribus.

1147. Secundum ibi, *sed et omnes* ostendit differentiam aliarum scientiarum ad istam quantum ad considerationem principiorum et causarum; dicens, quod omnes istae scientiae particulares, de quibus nunc facta est mentio, sunt circa unum aliquod particulare genus entis, sicut circa numerum vel magnitudinem, aut aliquid huiusmodi. Et *tractat unaquaeque circumscripte de suo genere subiecto*, idest ita de isto genere, quod non de alio: sicut scientia quae tractat de numero, non tractat de magnitudine. Nulla enim earum determinat *de ente simpliciter*, idest de ente in communi, nec etiam de aliquo particulari ente inquantum est ens. Sicut arithmetica non determinat de numero inquantum est ens, sed inquantum est numerus. De quolibet enim ente inquantum est ens, proprium est metaphysici considerare.

1148. Et, quia eiusdem est considerare de ente inquantum est ens, et *de eo quod quid est*, idest de quiddidate rei, quia unumquodque habet esse per suam quiddditatem, ideo etiam aliae scientiae particulares *nullam mentionem*, idest determinationem faciunt de eo *quod quid est*, idest de quiddidate rei, et de definitione, quae ipsam significat. *Sed ex hoc*, idest ex ipso quod quid est ad alia procedunt, utentes eo quasi demonstrato principio ad alia probanda.

1149. Ipsum autem quod quid est sui subiecti aliae scientiae faciunt esse manifestum per sensum; sicut scientia, quae est de animalibus, accipit quid est animal per id quod apparet *sensui*, idest per sensum et motum, quibus animal a non animali discernitur. Aliae vero scientiae *accipiunt quod quid est sui subiecti, per suppositionem* ab aliqua alia scientia, sicut geometria

those which are in some way imaginable or sensible in particular but intelligible in general, or even with sensible things inasmuch as there is science of them (as occurs in the case of mathematics and in that of the philosophy of nature).

Or again whether they proceed from universal principles to particular cases in which there is activity, as occurs in the practical sciences, it is always necessary that such sciences deal with principles and causes.

1146. Now these principles are either more certain to us (like the natural sciences) because they are closer to sensible things, or they are simpler and prior in nature (as occurs in the mathematical sciences). But cognitions which are only sensory are not the result of principles and causes, but of the sensible object itself acting upon the senses. For to proceed from causes to effects or the reverse is not an activity of the senses, but only of the intellect. Or "more certain principles" means those which are better known and more deeply probed, and "simple" means those which are studied in a more superficial way, as occurs in the moral sciences, whose principles are derived from those things that occur in the majority of cases.

1147. *But all these* (1025b7). Second, he shows how the other sciences differ from this science in their study of principles and causes. He says that all these particular sciences which have now been mentioned are about one particular genus of being—such as number, continuous quantity, or something of this kind—and each *confines its investigations to its subject genus*, dealing with this genus and not with another—for example, the science that deals with number does not deal with continuous quantity. For no one of the other sciences deals *with being in an unqualified sense* (with being in general) or even with any particular being as being. For example, arithmetic does not deal with number as being, but as number. For to consider each being as being is proper to metaphysics.

1148. And since it belongs to the same science to consider both being and *the whatness* or quiddity, because each thing has being by reason of its quiddity, therefore the other particular sciences make *no mention of*—that is, they do not investigate—*the whatness* or quiddity of a thing and the definition signifying it. *But proceeding from this*, the whatness itself of a thing, to other things, they use this as an already established principle for the purpose of proving other things.

1149. Now some sciences make the whatness of their subject evident by means of the senses, as the science which treats of animals understands what an animal is by means of what is apparent to *the senses*, that is, by means of sensation and local motion, by which animal is distinguished from non-animal. And other sciences *take the whatness of their subject by assuming it* from some other science,

accipit quid est magnitudo a philosopho primo. Et sic ex ipso quod quid est noto per sensum vel per suppositionem, demonstrant scientiae proprias passiones, quae secundum se insunt generi subiecto, circa quod sunt. Nam definitio est medium in demonstratione propter quid. Modus autem demonstrationis est diversus; quia quaedam demonstrant magis necessarie, sicut mathematicae scientiae, quaedam vero *infirmius*, idest non de necessitate; sicut scientiae naturales, in quibus multae demonstrationes sumuntur ex his quae non semper insunt, sed frequenter.

1150. Alia translatio habet loco *suppositionis, conditionem*. Et est idem sensus. Nam quod supponitur, quasi ex conditione accipitur: et quia principium demonstrationis est definitio, palam est ex tali inductione, quod *demonstratio non est de substantia rei*, idest de essentia eius; nec de definitione, quae significat quid est res; sed est aliquis alius modus, quo definitiones ostenduntur; scilicet divisione, et aliis modis, qui ponuntur in secundo *Posteriorum*.

1151. Et sicut nulla scientia particularis determinat quod quid est, ita etiam nulla earum dicit de genere subiecto, circa quod versatur, est, aut non est. Et hoc rationabiliter accidit; quia eiusdem scientiae est determinare quaestionem an est, et manifestare quid est. Oportet enim quod quid est accipere ut medium ad ostendendum an est. Et utraque est consideratio philosophi, qui considerat ens inquantum ens. Et ideo quaelibet scientia particularis supponit de subiecto suo, quia est, et quid est, ut dicitur in primo *Posteriorum*; et hoc est signum, quod nulla scientia particularis determinat de ente simpliciter, nec de aliquo ente inquantum est ens.

1152. Deinde cum dicit *quoniam vero* ostendit differentiam huius scientiae ad alias, quantum ad modum considerandi principia entis inquantum est ens. Et quia ab antiquis scientia naturalis credebatur esse prima scientia, et quae consideraret ens inquantum est ens, ideo ab ea, quasi a manifestiori incipiens,

primo ostendit differentiam scientiae naturalis a scientiis practicis.

Secundo differentiam eius a scientiis speculativis, in quo ostenditur modus proprius considerationis huius scientiae, ibi, *oportet autem quod quid erat esse*.

Dicit ergo primo, quod scientia naturalis non est circa ens simpliciter, sed circa quoddam genus entis; scilicet circa substantiam naturalem, quae habet in se principium motus et quietis: et ex hoc apparet quod

as geometry learns what continuous quantity is from first philosophy. Thus, beginning from the whatness itself of a thing, which has been made known either by the senses or by assuming it from some other science, these sciences demonstrate the proper attributes which belong *per se* to the subject genus with which they deal; for a definition is the middle term in a causal demonstration. But the method of demonstration differs, because some sciences demonstrate with greater necessity, as the mathematical sciences, and others *more weakly*, that is, without necessity, like the sciences of nature, whose demonstrations are based on things that do not pertain to something always but for the most part.

1150. Another translation has *condition* in place of *assumption*, but the meaning is the same, for what is assumed is taken as though by stipulation. And since the starting point of demonstration is definition, it is evident that from this kind of inductive method *there is no demonstration of a thing's substance* (that is, of its essence, or of the definition signifying its whatness) but there is some other method by which definitions are made known, such as the method of division and the other methods that are given in *Posterior Analytics* 2.

1151. And just as no particular science settles the issue about the whatness of things, neither does any one of them discuss the existence or nonexistence of the subject genus with which it deals. This is understandable, because it belongs to the same science to settle the question of a thing's existence and to make known its whatness. For in order to prove that a thing exists, its whatness must be taken as the middle term of the demonstration. Now both of these questions belong to the investigation of the philosopher who considers being as being. Therefore, every particular science assumes the existence and whatness of its subject, as is stated in *Posterior Analytics* 1. This is indicated by the fact that no particular science establishes the truth about being in an unqualified sense, or about any being as being.

1152. *And since the philosophy of nature* (1025b18). Here he shows how this science differs from the other sciences in its method of considering the principles of being as being. And since the philosophy of nature was considered by the ancients to be the first science and the one which would consider being as being, therefore, beginning with it as with what is more evident,

The first shows (1025b18) how the philosophy of nature differs from the practical sciences;

second (1025b28), how it differs from the speculative sciences, showing also the method of study proper to this science, at *now the essence*.

He first says (1025b18) that the philosophy of nature does not deal with being in an unqualified sense, but with some particular genus of being—that is, with natural substance, which has within itself a principle of motion and

neque est activa, neque factiva. Differunt enim agere et facere: nam agere est secundum operationem manentem in ipso agente, sicut est eligere, intelligere et huiusmodi: unde scientiae activae dicuntur scientiae morales. Facere autem est secundum operationem, quae transit exterius ad materiae transmutationem, sicut secare, urere, et huiusmodi: unde scientiae factivae dicuntur artes mechanicae.

1153. Quod autem scientia naturalis non sit factiva, patet; quia principium scientiarum factivarum est in faciente, non in facto, quod est artificiatum; sed principium motus rerum naturalium est in ipsis rebus naturalibus.

Hoc autem principium rerum artificialium, quod est in faciente, est primo intellectus, qui primo artem adinvenit;

et secundo ars, quae est habitus intellectus;

et tertio aliqua potentia exequens, sicut potentia motiva, per quam artifex exequitur conceptionem artis.

Unde patet, quod scientia naturalis non est factiva.

1154. Et per eamdem rationem patet quod non est activa. Nam principium activarum scientiarum est in agente, non in ipsis actionibus, sive moribus. Hoc autem principium est *prohaeresis*, idest electio. *Idem enim est agibile et eligibile.* Sic ergo patet, quod naturalis scientia non sit activa neque factiva.

1155. Si igitur omnis scientia est aut activa, aut factiva, aut theorica, sequitur quod naturalis scientia theorica sit. Ita tamen est *theorica*, idest speculativa circa determinatum genus entis, *quod scilicet est possibile moveri*. Ens enim mobile est subiectum naturalis philosophiae. Et est solum circa *talem substantiam*, idest quidditatem et essentiam rei, quae *secundum rationem non est separabilis* a materia, ut in pluribus; et hoc dicit propter intellectum, qui aliquo modo cadit sub consideratione naturalis philosophiae, et tamen substantia eius est separabilis. Sic patet, quod naturalis scientia est circa determinatum subiectum, quod est ens mobile; et habet determinatum modum definiendi, scilicet cum materia.

1156. Deinde cum dicit *oportet autem* hic ostendit differentiam naturalis scientiae ad alias speculativas quantum ad modum definiendi: et circa hoc duo facit.

Primo ostendit differentiam praedictam.

Secundo concludit numerum scientiarum theoricarum, ibi *quare*.

Circa primum tria facit.

Primo ostendit modum proprium definiendi naturalis philosophiae; dicens, quod ad cognoscendum diffe-

rest. From this it is evident that it is neither a practical nor a productive science. For action and production differ, because action is an operation that remains in the agent itself, as choosing, understanding, and the like. (For this reason the practical sciences are called moral sciences.) But production is an operation that passes over into some matter in order to change it, as cutting, burning, and the like. (For this reason the productive sciences are called mechanical arts.)

1153. Now it is evident that the philosophy of nature is not a productive science, because the principle of productive sciences is in the maker and not in the thing made, which is the artifact. But the principle of motion in natural bodies is within these natural bodies.

Further, the principle of things made by art, which is in the maker, is first, the intellect which discovers the art;

second, the art, which is an intellectual habit;

third, some executive power, such as the motive power by which the artisan executes the work conceived by his art.

Hence it is evident that the philosophy of nature is not a productive science.

1154. And for this reason it is evident that it is not a practical science; for the principle of practical sciences is in the agent, not in the actions or customary operations themselves. This principle is *prohaeresis*, or choice, *for the object of action and that of choice are the same*. Hence it is evident that the philosophy of nature is neither a practical nor a productive science.

1155. If, then, every science is either practical, productive, or theoretical, it follows that the philosophy of nature is a theoretical science. Yet it is *theoretical*, or speculative, of a special genus of being, namely, that *which is subject to motion*. For mobile being is the subject matter of the philosophy of nature. And it deals only with *that kind of substance*, that is, the quiddity or essence of a thing, *which is inseparable in its intelligible structure* from matter, for the most part. He adds this because of the intellect, which comes in a sense within the scope of the philosophy of nature, although its substance is separable from matter. Thus it is clear that the philosophy of nature deals with some special subject, which is mobile being, and that it has a special way of defining things, namely, with matter.

1156. *Now the essence* (1025b28). Here he shows how the philosophy of nature differs from the other speculative sciences in its method of defining things, and in regard to this he does two things.

First, he explains this difference.

Second (1026a17; [1166]), he draws a conclusion about the number of theoretical sciences, at *hence there will be*.

In regard to the first he does three things.

First, he exposes the method of defining things that is proper to the philosophy of nature. He says that in order

rentiam scientiarum speculativarum adinvicem, oportet non latere quidditatem rei, et *rationem* idest definitionem significantem ipsam, quomodo est assignanda in unaquaque scientia. Quaerere enim differentiam praedictam *sine hoc*, idest sine cognitione modi definiendi, nihil facere est. Cum enim definitio sit medium demonstrationis, et per consequens principium sciendi, oportet quod ad diversum modum definiendi, sequatur diversitas in scientiis speculativis.

1157. Sciendum est autem, quod eorum quae diffiniuntur, quaedam definiuntur sicut definitur simum, quaedam sicut definitur concavum; et haec duo differunt, quia definitio simi est accepta cum materia sensibili. Simum enim nihil aliud est quam nasus curvus vel concavus. Sed concavitas definitur sine materia sensibili. Non enim ponitur in definitione concavi vel curvi aliquod corpus sensibile, ut ignis aut aqua, aut aliquod corpus huiusmodi. Dicitur enim concavum, cuius medium exit ab extremis.

1158. Omnia autem naturalia simili modo definiuntur sicut simum, ut patet in partibus animalis tam dissimilibus, ut sunt nasus, oculus et facies, quam similibus, ut sunt caro et os; et etiam in toto animali. Et similiter in partibus plantarum quae sunt folium, radix et cortex; et similiter in tota planta. Nullius enim praedictorum definitio potest assignari sine motu: sed quodlibet eorum habet materiam sensibilem in sui definitione, et per consequens motum. Nam cuilibet materiae sensibili competit motus proprius. In definitione enim carnis et ossis, oportet quod ponatur calidum et frigidum aliquo modo contemperatum; et similiter in aliis. Et ex hoc palam est quis est modus inquirendi quidditatem rerum naturalium, et definiendi in scientia naturali, quia scilicet cum materia sensibili.

1159. Et propter hoc etiam de anima, quaedam speculatur naturalis, quaecumque scilicet non definitur sine materia sensibili. Dicitur enim in secundo *De anima*, quod anima est actus primus corporis physici organici potentia vitam habentis. Anima autem secundum quod non est actus talis corporis non pertinet ad considerationem naturalis, si qua anima potest a corpore separari. Manifestum est ergo ex praedictis quod physica est quaedam scientia theorica, et quod habet determinatum modum definiendi.

1160. Secundo ibi, *sed est et mathematica* ostendit modum proprium mathematicae; dicens quod etiam mathematica est quaedam scientia theorica. Constat enim, quod neque est activa, neque factiva; cum mathematica consideret ea quae sunt sine motu, sine quo actio et factio esse non possunt. Sed utrum illa de quibus considerat mathematica scientia, sint mobilia et separabilia a materia secundum suum esse, adhuc non est

to understand how the speculative sciences differ from each other, the quiddity of a thing and the way in which *the conceptual expression*—that is, the definition signifying it—should be expressed in each science, must not remain unknown. For in seeking the aforesaid difference *without this* (without knowing how to define things), our search would be unfruitful. For since a definition is the middle term in a demonstration, and is therefore the starting-point of knowing, the difference between the speculative sciences must depend on the different ways of defining things.

1157. Now concerning things that are defined, it must be noted that some are defined like snub and others like concave. And these two differ because the definition of snub includes sensible matter (since "snub" is merely a curved or concave nose), whereas concavity is defined without sensible matter. For some sensible body, such as fire or water or the like, is not included in the definition of concave or curved. For that is said to be concave whose middle curves away from the ends.

1158. Now all natural things are defined in a way similar to snub, as is evident both of those parts of an animal which are unlike—for example, nose, eye and face—and of those which are alike—for example, flesh and bone—and also of the whole animal. And the same is true of the parts of plants—for example, leaf, root, and bark—and also of the whole plant. For no one of these can be defined without motion, but each includes sensible matter in its definition, and therefore motion, because every kind of sensible matter has its own kind of motion. Thus, in the definition of flesh and bone, it is necessary that the hot and cold be held to be suitably mixed in some way; the same is true of other things. From this it is evident what the method is which the philosophy of nature uses in investigating and defining the quiddity of natural things: it involves sensible matter.

1159. And for this reason the philosophy of nature also investigates one kind of soul—the kind that is not defined without sensible matter. For in *On the Soul* 2, he says that a soul is the first act of a natural organic body having life potentially. But if any soul can exist separately from a body, then insofar as it is not the act of such a body, it does not fall within the scope of the philosophy of nature. Therefore, it is evident from the above that the philosophy of nature is a theoretical science, and that it has a special method of defining things.

1160. *But mathematics* (1026a7). Second, he shows the method proper to mathematics. He says that mathematics is also a speculative science. For evidently it is neither a practical nor a productive science, since it considers things that are devoid of motion, without which action and production cannot exist. But whether those things that mathematical science considers are immobile and separable from matter in their being is not yet clear. For some men, the

manifestum. Quidam enim posuerunt numeros et magnitudines et alia mathematica esse separata et media inter species et sensibilia, scilicet Platonici, ut in primo et tertio libro habitum est; cuius quaestionis veritas nondum est ab eo perfecte determinata; determinabitur autem infra.

1161. Sed tamen hoc est manifestum, quod scientia mathematica speculatur quaedam inquantum sunt immobilia et inquantum sunt separata a materia sensibili, licet secundum esse non sint immobilia vel separabilia. Ratio enim eorum est sine materia sensibili, sicut ratio concavi vel curvi. In hoc ergo differt mathematica a physica, quia physica considerat ea quorum definitiones sunt cum materia sensibili. Et ideo considerat non separata, inquantum sunt non separata. Mathematica vero considerat ea, quorum definitiones sunt sine materia sensibili. Et ideo, etsi sunt non separata ea quae considerat, tamen considerat ea inquantum sunt separata.

1162. Tertio ibi, *si vero est* ostendit modum proprium scientiae huius; dicens quod, si est aliquid immobile secundum esse, et per consequens sempiternum et separabile a materia secundum esse, palam est, quod eius consideratio est theoricae scientiae, non activae vel factivae, quarum consideratio est circa aliquos motus.

Et tamen consideratio talis entis non est physica. Nam physica considerat de quibusdam entibus, scilicet de mobilibus. Et similiter consideratio huius entis non est mathematica; quia mathematica non considerat separabilia secundum esse, sed secundum rationem, ut dictum est. Sed oportet quod consideratio huius entis sit alterius scientiae prioris ambabus praedictis, scilicet physica et mathematica.

1163. Physica enim est circa inseparabilia et mobilia, et mathematica quaedam circa immobilia, quae tamen non sunt separata a materia secundum esse, sed solum secundum rationem, secundum vero esse sunt in materia sensibili. Dicit autem *forsan*, quia haec veritas nondum est determinata. Dicit autem quasdam mathematicas esse circa immobilia, sicut geometriam et arithmeticam; quia quaedam scientiae mathematicae applicantur ad motum sicut astrologia. Sed prima scientia est circa separabilia secundum esse, et quae sunt omnino immobilia.

1164. Necesse vero est communes causas esse sempiternas. Primas enim causas entium generativorum oportet esse ingenitas, ne generatio in infinitum procedat; et maxime has, quae sunt omnino immobiles et

Platonists, held that numbers, continuous quantities, and other mathematical objects are separate from matter and midway between the forms and sensible things, as is stated in book 1 [157] and in book 3 [350]. But the answer to this question has not yet been fully established by him, but will be established later on.

1161. However, it is evident that mathematical science studies some things insofar as they are immobile and separate from matter, although they are neither immobile nor separable from matter in being. For their intelligible structure—for example, that of concave or curved—does not contain sensible matter. Hence mathematical science differs from the philosophy of nature in this respect, that while the philosophy of nature considers things whose definitions contain sensible matter (and thus it considers what is not separate insofar as it is not separate), mathematical science considers things whose definitions do not contain sensible matter. And thus even though the things that it considers are not separate from matter, it nevertheless considers them insofar as they are separate.

1162. *Now if there is something* (1026a10). Third, he exposes the method proper to this science. He says that if there is something whose being is immobile, and therefore eternal and separable from matter in being, it is evident that the investigation of it belongs to a theoretical science and not to a practical or productive one, whose investigations have to do with certain kinds of motion.

However, the study of such being does not belong to the philosophy of nature, for the philosophy of nature deals with certain kinds of beings (namely, mobile ones). Nor likewise does the study of this being belong to mathematics, because mathematics does not consider things that are separable from matter in being but only in their intelligible structure, as has been stated [1161]. But the study of this being must belong to another science which is prior to both of these—that is, prior to the philosophy of nature and to mathematics.

1163. For the philosophy of nature deals with things that are mobile and inseparable from matter, and mathematics deals with certain immobile things, though these are not separate from matter in being, but only in their intelligible structure, since in reality they are found in sensible matter. And he says *presumably* because this truth has not yet been established. Further, he says that some mathematical sciences deal with immobile things, as geometry and arithmetic, because some mathematical sciences are applied to motion, as astronomy. But the first science deals with things that are separable from matter in being and are altogether immobile.

1164. Now common causes must be eternal, because the first causes of beings which are generated must not themselves be generated, otherwise the process of generation would proceed to infinity. This is true especially of those

immateriales. Hae namque causae immateriales et immobiles sunt causae sensibilibus manifestis nobis, quia sunt maxime entia, et per consequens causae aliorum, ut in secundo libro ostensum est. Et per hoc patet, quod scientia quae huiusmodi entia pertractat, prima est inter omnes, et considerat communes causas omnium entium. Unde sunt causae entium secundum quod sunt entia, quae inquiruntur in prima philosophia, ut in primo proposuit. Ex hoc autem apparet manifeste falsitas opinionis illorum, qui posuerunt Aristotelem sensisse, quod Deus non sit causa substantiae caeli, sed solum motus eius.

1165. Advertendum est autem, quod licet ad considerationem primae philosophiae pertineant ea quae sunt separata secundum esse et rationem a materia et motu, non tamen solum ea; sed etiam de sensibilibus, inquantum sunt entia, philosophus perscrutatur. Nisi forte dicamus, ut Avicenna dicit, quod huiusmodi communia de quibus haec scientia perscrutatur, dicuntur separata secundum esse, non quia semper sint sine materia; sed quia non de necessitate habent esse in materia, sicut mathematica.

1166. Deinde cum dicit *quare tres* concludit numerum scientiarum theoricarum; et circa hoc tria facit.

Primo concludit ex praemissis, quod tres sunt partes philosophiae theoricae, scilicet mathematica, physica et theologia, quae est philosophia prima.

1167. Deinde cum dicit *non enim* secundo assignat duas rationes quare haec scientia dicatur theologia. Quarum prima est, quia *manifestum est, quod si alicubi*, idest in aliquo genere rerum existit aliquod divinum, quod existit in tali natura, scilicet entis immobilis et a materia separati, de quo considerat ista scientia.

1168. Deinde cum dicit *et honorabilissimam* secundam rationem ponit quae talis est. Honorabilissima scientia est circa honorabilissimum genus entium, in quo continentur res divinae: ergo, cum haec scientia sit honorabilissima inter omnes, quia est honorabilior theoricis, ut prius ostensum est—quae quidem sunt honorabiliores practicis, ut in primo libro habitum est—manifestum est, quod ista scientia est circa res divinas; et ideo dicitur theologia, quasi sermo de divinis.

causes which are altogether immobile and immaterial. For those immaterial and immobile causes are the causes of the sensible things evident to us, because they are beings in the highest degree, and therefore are the cause of other things, as was shown in book 2 [290]. From this it is evident that the science which considers beings of this kind is the first of all the sciences and the one which considers the common causes of all beings. Hence there are causes of beings as beings, which are investigated in first philosophy, as he proposed in book 1 [36]. And from this it is quite evident that the opinion of those who claimed that Aristotle thought that God is not the cause of the substance of the heavens, but only of their motion, is false.[6]

1165. However, we must remember that, even though things that are separate from matter and motion in being and in their intelligible structure belong to the study of first philosophy, still the philosopher investigates not only these but also sensible things inasmuch as they are beings. This is so unless perhaps we may say, as Avicenna does, that common things of the kind which this science considers are said to be separate from matter in being not because they are always without matter, but because they do not necessarily have being in matter, as the objects of mathematics do.

1166. *Hence there will be* (1026a17). He draws a conclusion as to the number of theoretical sciences. And in regard to this he does three things.

First, he concludes from what has been laid down above that there are three parts of theoretical philosophy: mathematics, the philosophy of nature, and theology (which is first philosophy).

1167. *For it is obvious* (1026a19). Second, he gives two reasons why this science is called "theology." The first of these is that *it is obvious that if the divine exists anywhere*, if something divine exists in any genus of things, it exists in such a nature, namely, in the genus of being which is immobile and separate from matter, which this science studies.

1168. *And the most honorable* (1026a22). He gives the second reason why this science is called theology, which is as follows. The most honorable science deals with the most honorable genus of beings, and this is the one in which divine beings are contained. Therefore, since this science is the most honorable of the sciences because it is the most honorable of the theoretical sciences, as was shown before [64]—and these are more honorable than the practical sciences, as was stated in book 1 [35]—it is evident that this science deals with divine beings. Therefore, it is called theology inasmuch as it is a discourse about divine beings.

---

6. Cf. *De unitate intellectus contra Averroistas.*

1169. Deinde cum dicit *dubitabit autem* tertio movetur quaedam quaestio circa praedeterminata:

et primo movet eam, dicens, quod aliquis potest dubitare, utrum prima philosophia sit universalis quasi considerans ens universaliter, aut eius consideratio sit circa aliquod genus determinatum et naturam unam. Et hoc non videtur. Non enim est unus modus huius scientiae et mathematicarum; quia geometria et astrologia, quae sunt mathematicae, sunt circa aliquam naturam determinatam; sed philosophia prima est universaliter communis omnium. Et tamen e converso videtur, quod sit alicuius determinatae naturae, propter hoc quod est separabilium et immobilium, ut dictum est.

1170. Deinde cum dicit *si igitur* secundo solvit, dicens quod si non est aliqua alia substantia praeter eas quae consistunt secundum naturam, de quibus est physica, physica erit prima scientia. Sed, si est aliqua substantia immobilis, ista erit prior substantia naturali; et per consequens philosophia considerans huiusmodi substantiam, erit philosophia prima. Et quia est prima, ideo erit universalis, et erit eius speculari de ente inquantum est ens, et de eo quod quid est, et de his quae sunt entis inquantum est ens: eadem enim est scientia primi entis et entis communis, ut in principio quarti habitum est.

1169. *But someone will* (1026a23). Third, he raises a question about a point already established.

First, he states the question, saying that someone can inquire whether first philosophy is universal inasmuch as it considers being in general, or whether it investigates some particular genus or a single nature. Now this does not seem to be the case. For this science and the mathematical sciences do not have one and the same method, because geometry and astronomy, which are mathematical sciences, deal with a special nature, whereas first philosophy is universally common to all. Yet the reverse seems to be true—namely, that it deals with a special nature, because it is concerned with things that are separable from matter and immobile, as has been stated [1163].

1170. *Therefore, if* (1026a27). Second, he answers this question, saying that, if there is no substance other than those which exist in the way that natural substances do, with which the philosophy of nature deals, the philosophy of nature will be the first science. But if there is some immobile substance, this will be prior to natural substance, and therefore the philosophy of nature, which considers this kind of substance, will be first philosophy. And since it is first, it will be universal; and it will be its function to study being as being, both what being is and what the attributes are which belong to being as being. For the science of the primary kind of being and that of being in general are the same, as has been stated at the beginning of book 4 [533].

LECTURE 2

Being as the object of metaphysics

1026a33 Sed quoniam ens simpliciter dictum dicitur multipliciter, quorum unum quidem accidens, et aliud quasi verum et non ens quasi falsum; praeter haec autem sunt figurae categoriae, ut quid, quale, quantum, ubi, quando, et si quod aliud significat hoc modo; amplius praeter ea omnia, quod est potestate et actu. [1171]

ἀλλ᾽ ἐπεὶ τὸ ὂν τὸ ἁπλῶς λεγόμενον λέγεται πολλαχῶς, ὧν ἓν μὲν ἦν τὸ κατὰ συμβεβηκός, ἕτερον δὲ τὸ {35} ὡς ἀληθές, καὶ τὸ μὴ ὂν ὡς τὸ ψεῦδος, παρὰ ταῦτα δ᾽ ἐστὶ τὰ σχήματα τῆς κατηγορίας (οἷον τὸ μὲν τί, τὸ δὲ ποιόν, τὸ δὲ ποσόν, τὸ δὲ πού, τὸ δὲ ποτέ, καὶ εἴ τι ἄλλο σημαίνει τὸν τρόπον τοῦτον), {1026b1} ἔτι παρὰ ταῦτα πάντα τὸ δυνάμει καὶ ἐνεργείᾳ·

Being, in an unqualified sense, is said of many things, of which one is the accidental, and another the true (and "non-being" may signify the false). Besides these there are the categorical figures—for example, the what, of what sort, how much, where, when, and anything else which signifies in this way. Besides all of these, there is the potential and the actual.

1026b2 Quoniam itaque multipliciter dicitur ens, primum de eo quod secundum accidens est dicendum est, quia nulla est circa id speculatio. Signum autem. Nulla enim scientia studiosa est de eo, nec practica, nec theorica. [1172]

ἐπεὶ δὴ πολλαχῶς λέγεται τὸ ὄν, πρῶτον περὶ τοῦ κατὰ συμβεβηκός λεκτέον, ὅτι οὐδεμία ἐστὶ περὶ αὐτὸ θεωρία. σημεῖον δέ· οὐδεμιᾷ γὰρ ἐπιστήμῃ ἐπιμελὲς {5} περὶ αὐτοῦ οὔτε πρακτικῇ οὔτε ποιητικῇ οὔτε θεωρητικῇ.

Since being is said in many ways, then, we must speak first of the accidental, because there is no speculation about it. And this is indicated by the fact that there is no science, either practical or speculative, that investigates it.

Non enim faciens domum, facit quaecumue simul accidunt domui factae. Infinita enim sunt. His enim voluptuosam, illis vero nocivam, aliis utilem, nihil enim prohibet factam, et alteram, ut est dicere, ab omnibus entibus, quorum nullius est aedificativa factiva. Eodem vero modo nec geometer speculatur sic accidentia figuris, nec si alterum est trigonum, et trigonum duos rectos habens.

οὔτε γὰρ ὁ ποιῶν οἰκίαν ποιεῖ ὅσα συμβαίνει ἅμα τῇ οἰκίᾳ γιγνομένῃ (ἄπειρα γάρ ἐστιν· τοῖς μὲν γὰρ ἡδεῖαν τοῖς δὲ βλαβερὰν τοῖς δ᾽ ὠφέλιμον οὐθὲν εἶναι κωλύει τὴν ποιηθεῖσαν, καὶ ἑτέραν ὡς εἰπεῖν πάντων τῶν ὄντων· ὧν οὐθενός {10} ἐστιν ἡ οἰκοδομικὴ ποιητική), τὸν αὐτὸν δὲ τρόπον οὐδ᾽ ὁ γεωμέτρης θεωρεῖ τὰ οὕτω συμβεβηκότα τοῖς σχήμασιν, οὐδ᾽ εἰ ἕτερόν ἐστι τρίγωνον καὶ τρίγωνον δύο ὀρθὰς ἔχον.

For one who builds a house does not simultaneously cause all traits that are accidental to the completed house, since these are infinite in number. For nothing prevents the completed house from being pleasant to some, harmful to others, useful to others, and different, as I may say, from all other things, none of which the art of building produces. And similarly neither does the geometrician speculate about things that are accidents of figures in this way, nor whether a triangle differs from a triangle having two right angles.

1026b12 Et hoc rationabiliter accidit. Quemadmodum enim nomine solum accidens est. [1176]

καὶ τοῦτ᾽ εὐλόγως συμπίπτει· ὥσπερ γὰρ ὄνομά τι μόνον τὸ συμβεβηκός ἐστιν.

And this is understandable, because the accidental is in a sense being only in name.

1026b14 Unde Plato modo quodam non male sophistica circa non ens ordinavit. Sunt enim sophistarum rationes circa accidens, ut est dicere maxime omnium. Utrum diversum aut idem musicum et grammaticum, et musicus Coriscus et Coriscus. Et si omne quod est, et non semper, factum est. Quare si musicus ens grammaticus est factus, et grammaticus ens musicus, et quaecumque aliae rationum tales sunt. Videtur enim accidens propinquum non enti. [1177]

διὸ Πλάτων τρόπον τινὰ οὐ κακῶς τὴν σοφιστικὴν {15} περὶ τὸ μὴ ὂν ἔταξεν. εἰσὶ γὰρ οἱ τῶν σοφιστῶν λόγοι περὶ τὸ συμβεβηκὸς ὡς εἰπεῖν μάλιστα πάντων, πότερον ἕτερον ἢ ταὐτὸν μουσικὸν καὶ γραμματικόν, καὶ μουσικὸς Κορίσκος καὶ Κορίσκος, καὶ εἰ πᾶν ὃ ἂν ᾖ, μὴ ἀεὶ δέ, γέγονεν, ὥστ᾽ εἰ μουσικὸς ὢν γραμματικὸς γέγονε, καὶ γραμματικὸς {20} ὢν μουσικός, καὶ ὅσοι δὴ ἄλλοι τοιοῦτοι τῶν λόγων εἰσίν· φαίνεται γὰρ τὸ συμβεβηκὸς ἐγγύς τι τοῦ μὴ ὄντος.

Hence, in a way, Plato was not wrong when he said that sophistry deals with non-being. For the arguments of the sophists, as I may say, are concerned chiefly with the accidental—whether the musical and the grammatical are the same or different; whether musical Coriscus and Coriscus are the same; whether everything which is but has not always been has come to be (so that if one who is musical has become grammatical, then one who is grammatical has become musical); and all other such arguments. For the accidental seems to be close to non-being.

1026b22 Palam autem et ex his rationibus. Nam alio modo entium, generatio est et corruptio. Eorum vero quae sunt secundum accidens, non est. [1179]

δῆλον δὲ καὶ ἐκ τῶν τοιούτων λόγων: τῶν μὲν γὰρ ἄλλον τρόπον ὄντων ἔστι γένεσις καὶ φθορά, τῶν δὲ κατὰ συμβεβηκὸς οὐκ ἔστιν.

Now this is also clear from these arguments: there is generation and corruption of those things that are in another way, but not of those things that are by accident.

1026b24 Attamen dicendum est amplius de accidente inquantum contingit, quae eius natura, et propter quam causam est. Simul enim forsan palam erit, et quare eius non est scientia. [1180]

ἀλλ᾽ ὅμως λεκτέον ἔτι περὶ τοῦ συμβεβηκότος {25} ἐφ᾽ ὅσον ἐνδέχεται, τίς ἡ φύσις αὐτοῦ καὶ διὰ τίν᾽ αἰτίαν ἔστιν: ἅμα γὰρ δῆλον ἴσως ἔσται καὶ διὰ τί ἐπιστήμη οὐκ ἔστιν αὐτοῦ.

Yet concerning the accidental, it is necessary to state further (so far as it is possible) what its nature is and by what cause it exists. Perhaps at the same time it will also become evident why there is no science of it.

1026b27 Quoniam igitur in entibus sunt haec quidem semper similiter se habentia et ex necessitate, non secundum vim dicta, sed secundum quod dicimus in non contingere aliter, illa vero ex necessitate quidem non sunt, nec semper, sed quasi secundum magis, hoc principium et haec causa eius est, quod est accidens esse. [1182]

ἐπεὶ οὖν ἐστὶν ἐν τοῖς οὖσι τὰ μὲν ἀεὶ ὡσαύτως ἔχοντα καὶ ἐξ ἀνάγκης, οὐ τῆς κατὰ τὸ βίαιον λεγομένης ἀλλ᾽ ἣν λέγομεν τῷ μὴ ἐνδέχεσθαι ἄλλως, τὰ δ᾽ {30} ἐξ ἀνάγκης μὲν οὐκ ἔστιν οὐδ᾽ ἀεί, ὡς δ᾽ ἐπὶ τὸ πολύ, αὕτη ἀρχὴ καὶ αὕτη αἰτία ἐστὶ τοῦ εἶναι τὸ συμβεβηκός:

Therefore, since there are some beings which always are in the same way and of necessity (not necessity in the sense of compulsion, but in the sense of that which cannot be otherwise) and others which are neither of necessity nor always, but for the most part, this is the principle and this the cause of the accidental.

1026b31 Quod enim nec semper, nec quasi secundum magis est, hoc dicimus esse accidens: ut sub cane si fuerit hiems et frigus, hoc accidere dicimus, sed non si aestuatio et calor; quia hoc quidem semper aut secundum magis, illud vero non. [1184]

ὃ γὰρ ἂν ᾖ μήτ᾽ ἀεὶ μήθ᾽ ὡς ἐπὶ τὸ πολύ, τοῦτό φαμεν συμβεβηκὸς εἶναι. οἷον ἐπὶ κυνὶ ἂν χειμὼν γένηται καὶ ψῦχος, τοῦτο συμβῆναί φαμεν, ἀλλ᾽ οὐκ ἂν πνῖγος καὶ ἀλέα, ὅτι {35} τὸ μὲν ἀεὶ ἢ ὡς ἐπὶ τὸ πολὺ τὸ δ᾽ οὔ.

For that which is neither always nor for the most part we call the accidental. For example, if there should be wintry and cold weather during the dog days, we say that this is accidental; but not if the weather is sultry and hot, because the latter occurs either always or for the most part, whereas the former does not.

Et hominem album esse accidit; nec enim semper nec secundum magis; animal vero non secundum accidens.

καὶ τὸν ἄνθρωπον λευκὸν εἶναι συμβέβηκεν (οὔτε γὰρ ἀεὶ οὔθ᾽ ὡς ἐπὶ τὸ πολύ), ζῷον δ᾽ οὐ κατὰ συμβεβηκός.

And it is accidental for a man to be white, for this is so neither always nor for the most part, but it is not accidental for him to be an animal.

Et aedificatorem sanitatem facere, accidens; quia non est natus hoc facere aedificator, sed medicus: sed accidit medicum esse aedificatorem.

καὶ τὸ ὑγιάζειν δὲ τὸν οἰκοδόμον συμβεβηκός, {1027a1} ὅτι οὐ πέφυκε τοῦτο ποιεῖν οἰκοδόμος ἀλλὰ ἰατρός, ἀλλὰ συνέβη ἰατρὸν εἶναι τὸν οἰκοδόμον.

And it is accidental if a builder produces health, because it is not a builder but a physician who is naturally fitted to do this, but it is accidental for a builder to be a physician.

Et opsopios voluptatem coniectans, faciet utique alicui salubre, sed non secundum opsopoieticam:

καὶ ὀψοποιὸς ἡδονῆς στοχαζόμενος ποιήσειεν ἄν τι ὑγιεινόν, ἀλλ᾽ οὐ κατὰ τὴν ὀψοποιητικήν:

Again, a confectioner, preparing something pleasing, may produce something health-giving, but not according to the confectioner's art.

quapropter accidens dicimus et est ut facit, simpliciter autem non. Aliorum enim aliae quandoque potentiae factivae sunt; horum vero nulla est ars, nec potentia determinata. Nam secundum accidens entium aut factorum causa est secundum accidens.

διὸ συνέβη, φαμέν, καὶ {5} ἔστιν ὡς ποιεῖ, ἁπλῶς δ᾽ οὔ. τῶν μὲν γὰρ ἄλλων [ἐνίοτε] δυνάμεις εἰσὶν αἱ ποιητικαί, τῶν δ᾽ οὐδεμία τέχνη οὐδὲ δύναμις ὡρισμένη: τῶν γὰρ κατὰ συμβεβηκὸς ὄντων ἢ γιγνομένων καὶ τὸ αἴτιόν ἐστι κατὰ συμβεβηκός.

Hence we say that it was accidental. And while there is a sense in which he produces it, he does not produce it in a primary and proper sense. For there are other powers which sometimes are productive of other things, but there is no art or determinate power which is productive of the accidental, for the cause of things that are or come to be by accident is also accidental.

1027a8 Quare quoniam quidem non omnia ex necessitate sunt et semper, aut entia, aut quae fiunt, sed plurima secundum magis, necesse est quod secundum accidens ens, ut nec semper, nec secundum magis albus musicus est. Quoniam vero fit aliquando, secundum accidens erit; si autem non, omnia erunt ex necessitate. [1186]

Quare materia erit causa contingens propter quam ut in pluribus aliter accidentis. Principium autem hoc oportet sumere, utrum nihil est nec semper, nec secundum magis? Aut hoc impossibile?

Est igitur aliquid praeter hoc quod utrumque contingit et secundum accidens. Sed utrum hoc quod in pluribus et quod semper, nulli insunt, aut sunt quaedam sempiterna? De his quidem igitur posterius perscrutandum est.

ὥστ' ἐπεὶ οὐ πάντα ἐστὶν ἐξ ἀνάγκης καὶ ἀεὶ ἢ ὄντα ἢ γιγνόμενα, ἀλλὰ τὰ {10} πλεῖστα ὡς ἐπὶ τὸ πολύ, ἀνάγκη εἶναι τὸ κατὰ συμβεβηκὸς ὄν· οἷον οὔτ' ἀεὶ οὔθ' ὡς ἐπὶ τὸ πολὺ ὁ λευκὸς μουσικός ἐστιν, ἐπεὶ δὲ γίγνεταί ποτε, κατὰ συμβεβηκὸς ἔσται (εἰ δὲ μή, πάντ' ἔσται ἐξ ἀνάγκης)·

ὥστε ἡ ὕλη ἔσται αἰτία ἡ ἐνδεχομένη παρὰ τὸ ὡς ἐπὶ τὸ πολὺ ἄλλως τοῦ συμβεβηκότος. {15} ἀρχὴν δὲ τηνδὶ ληπτέον, πότερον οὐδέν ἐστιν οὔτ' αἰεὶ οὔθ' ὡς ἐπὶ τὸ πολύ. ἢ τοῦτο ἀδύνατον;

ἔστιν ἄρα τι παρὰ ταῦτα τὸ ὁπότερ' ἔτυχε καὶ κατὰ συμβεβηκός. ἀλλὰ πότερον τὸ ὡς ἐπὶ τὸ πολύ, τὸ δ' ἀεὶ οὐθενὶ ὑπάρχει, ἢ ἔστιν ἄττα ἀΐδια; περὶ μὲν οὖν τούτων ὕστερον σκεπτέον,

Hence, since not all things are or come to be of necessity and always, but most things occur for the most part, the accidental must exist—for example, a white man is neither always nor for the most part musical. But since this occurs only occasionally, it must be accidental, otherwise everything would be of necessity.

Hence matter will be the contingent cause of the accidental, which happens otherwise than usually occurs. And we must take as our starting point this question: Is there nothing that is neither always nor for the most part, or is this impossible?

There is, then, besides these something which is contingent and accidental. But then there is the question: does that which occurs for the most part and that which occurs always, have no existence, or are there some beings which are eternal? These questions must be investigated later (1071b3).

1027a19 Quod autem scientia non est accidentia, palam. Scientia namque omnis, aut est eius quod semper, aut eius quod secundum magis. Etenim quomodo docebitur aut docebit alium? [1189]

Oportebit enim definiri, aut per semper, aut per magis, ut quia utile melicratum febricitanti, ut secundum magis.

Quod autem praeter hoc, non habebit dicere. Quando puta nova luna. Aut enim semper, aut in pluribus, et quod nova luna. Accidens autem est praeter hoc.

Quid quidem igitur est accidens, et propter quam causam, et quia scientia non est eius, dictum est.

ὅτι δ' {20} ἐπιστήμη οὐκ ἔστι τοῦ συμβεβηκότος φανερόν· ἐπιστήμη μὲν γὰρ πᾶσα ἢ τοῦ ἀεὶ ἢ τοῦ ὡς ἐπὶ τὸ πολύ—πῶς γὰρ ἢ μαθήσεται ἢ διδάξει ἄλλον;

δεῖ γὰρ ὡρίσθαι ἢ τῷ ἀεὶ ἢ τῷ ὡς ἐπὶ τὸ πολύ, οἷον ὅτι ὠφέλιμον τὸ μελίκρατον τῷ πυρέττοντι ὡς ἐπὶ τὸ πολύ—

τὸ δὲ παρὰ τοῦτο οὐχ ἕξει λέγειν, {25} πότε οὔ, οἷον νουμηνίᾳ· ἢ γὰρ ἀεὶ ἢ ὡς ἐπὶ τὸ πολὺ καὶ τὸ τῇ νουμηνίᾳ· τὸ δὲ συμβεβηκός ἐστι παρὰ ταῦτα.

τί μὲν οὖν ἐστι τὸ συμβεβηκὸς καὶ διὰ τίν' αἰτίαν καὶ ὅτι ἐπιστήμη οὐκ ἔστιν αὐτοῦ, εἴρηται.

However, it is evident that there is no science of the accidental, for all scientific knowledge is of that which is always or for the most part; otherwise how could one be taught or teach anyone else?

For a thing must be defined either as being so always or for the most part—for example, honey-water is beneficial in most cases to those with a fever.

But with regard to what happens in the other cases, it will be impossible to state when they occur, for example, at the new moon. For whatever happens at the new moon also happens either always or for the most part, but the accidental is contrary to this.

We have explained, then, what the accidental is, and by what cause it exists, and that there is no science of it.

1171. Hic ostendit de quibus entibus principaliter haec scientia tractare intendit; et circa hoc tria facit.

Primo repetit modos quibus aliquid dicitur ens.
Secundo determinat naturam entis secundum duos modos de quibus principaliter non intendit, ibi, *quoniam itaque multipliciter dicitur ens.*

1171. Here Aristotle indicates with what beings this science chiefly intends to deal; and in regard to this he does three things.

First, he recalls the ways in which things are said to be.
Second (1026b2; [1172]), he establishes the nature of the two kinds of being with which he is not chiefly concerned, at *since being.*

Tertio ostendit quod de his modis entis principaliter non intendit, ibi, *quoniam autem complexio*.

Dicit ergo primo, quod *ens simpliciter*, idest universaliter dictum, *dicitur multipliciter*, ut in quinto est habitum.

Uno modo dicitur aliquid ens secundum accidens.

Alio modo dicitur ens, idem quod verum propositionis; et non ens, idem quod falsum.

Tertio modo dicitur ens quod continet sub se figuras praedicamentorum, ut quid, quale, quantum et cetera.

Quarto modo praeter praedictos omnes, quod dividitur per potentiam et actum.

1172. Deinde cum dicit *quoniam itaque* determinat de modis entis quos praetermittere intendit.

Et primo de ente per accidens.

Secundo de ente quod est idem quod verum, ibi, *quod autem ut verum* et cetera.

Circa primum duo facit.

Primo ostendit quod de ente per accidens non potest esse aliqua scientia.

Secundo determinat ea quae sunt consideranda circa ens per accidens, ibi, *attamen dicendum est* et cetera.

Dicit ergo primo, quod, cum *ens multipliciter dicatur*, ut dictum est, primo dicendum est de ente per accidens; ut quod minus habet de ratione entis, primo a consideratione huius scientiae excludatur. Hoc autem dicendum est de eo, quod nulla speculatio cuiuscumque scientiae potest esse circa ipsum. Et hoc probat dupliciter.

1173. Primo per signum; dicens, signum esse huius quod de ente per accidens non possit esse speculatio, quia *nulla scientia quantumcumque sit studiosa* aut *meditativa*, ut alia translatio habet, idest diligenter inquisitiva eorum quae ad ipsam pertinent, invenitur esse de ente per accidens. Sed nec etiam practica quae dividitur per activam et factivam, ut supra dictum est, neque scientia theorica.

1174. Et hoc manifestat primo in practicis scientiis, quia ille qui facit domum, si facit eam, non facit ea quae insunt domui factae, nisi per accidens, cum illa sint infinita, et sic non possunt cadere sub arte. Nihil enim prohibet domum factam esse istis *voluptuosam*, idest delectabilem, illis scilicet qui in ea prospere vivunt: aliis autem *nocivam* qui scilicet occasione domus aliquod detrimentum incurrunt. Et aliis *utilem* qui in domo aliquod emolumentum conquirunt, et etiam esse *alteram* et dissimilem omnibus entibus. Nullius autem

Third (1027b29; [1241]), he shows that it is not his chief aim to consider these two kinds of being, at *but since combination*.

Accordingly he says, first, that *being, in an unqualified sense* (that is, in a universal sense), *is said of many things*, as has been stated in book 5 [885].

In one sense, "being" means what is accidental.

In another sense, it means the same thing as the truth of a proposition (and "non-being" the same as the falseness of a proposition).

In a third sense, being is predicated of the things contained under the categorical figures—for example, the what, of what sort, how much, and so on.

In a fourth sense, in addition to all of the above, being applies to what is divided by potency and act.

1172. *Since being* (1026b2). Here he deals with the senses of being which he intends to exclude from this science.

First [1172], he deals with accidental being;

second (1027b17; [1223]), with being which is identical with the true, at *again, being in the sense*.

In regard to the first he does two things.

First, he shows that there can be no science of the accidental.

Second (1026b24; [1180]), he establishes the things that must be considered about accidental being, at *yet concerning the accidental*.

He first says that *since being is said in many ways*, as has been stated [1171], it is necessary first of all to speak of accidental being, so that anything which has the character of being in a lesser degree may first be excluded from the study of this science. And with regard to this kind of being it must be said that no speculation of any science can be concerned with it. He proves this in two ways.

1173. He does this first by giving a concrete indication. He says that the impossibility of there being any speculation about accidental being is indicated by the fact that *no science, howsoever investigative* it may be (or *thoughtful*, as another translation says)—that is, no matter how carefully it investigates the objects which come within its scope—is found to deal with accidental being. No practical science (and this is divided into the science of action and productive science, as was said above [1152]) is concerned with it, nor even any speculative science.

1174. He first makes this evident in the case of the practical sciences. For one who builds a house, granted that he builds it, is only an accidental cause of those things that are accidental to the completed house, since these are infinite in number and thus cannot come within the scope of art. For nothing prevents the completed house from being *pleasant* or delightful to those who dwell there happily, *harmful* to those who suffer some misfortune occasioned by it, *useful* to those who acquire some profit from it, and also *different* from and unlike all other things. But the art

eorum, quae per accidens insunt domui, factiva est ars aedificativa; sed solum est factiva domus, et eorum quae per se insunt domui.

1175. Et deinde ostendit idem in scientiis speculativis: quia simili modo nec geometria *speculatur ea quae sunt accidentia figuris sic*, idest per accidens, sed solum illa quae accidunt figuris per se. Speculatur enim hoc quod triangulus est *habens duos rectos*, idest tres angulos aequales duobus rectis; sed non speculatur, si aliquid alterum, utputa lignum vel aliquid huiusmodi, est trigonum. Haec enim per accidens conveniunt triangulo.

1176. Secundo ibi, *et hoc* probat idem per rationem; dicens, quod rationabiliter hoc accidit quod scientia non speculatur de ente per accidens; quia scientia speculatur de his quae sunt entia secundum rem; ens autem secundum accidens est ens quasi solo nomine, inquantum unum de alio praedicatur. Sic enim unumquodque est ens inquantum unum est. Ex duobus autem, quorum unum accidit alteri, non fit unum nisi secundum nomen; prout scilicet unum de altero praedicatur, ut cum musicum dicitur esse album, aut e converso. Non autem ita, quod aliqua res una constituatur ex albedine et musico.

1177. *Unde Plato* quod autem ens per accidens sit quasi solo nomine ens, probat dupliciter.

Primo per auctoritatem Platonis.

Secundo per rationem.

Dicit ergo, quod propter hoc quod ens per accidens quodammodo est ens solo nomine, ideo Plato quodammodo non male fecit cum ordinando diversas scientias circa diversa substantia, ordinavit scientiam sophisticam circa non ens. Rationes enim sophisticorum maxime sunt circa accidens. Secundum enim fallaciam accidentis fiunt maxime latentes paralogismi.

1178. Et ideo dicitur in primo *Elenchorum*, quod secundum accidens faciunt syllogismos contra sapientes; ut patet in istis paralogismis, in quibus dubitatur utrum diversum an idem sit musicum et grammaticum. Ut fiat talis paralogismus. Musicum est aliud a grammatico; musicum autem est grammaticum, ergo musicum est alterum a se. Musicum enim est aliud a grammatico, per se loquendo; sed musicus est grammaticus per accidens. Unde non est mirum si sequitur inconveniens, non distincto quod est per accidens ab eo quod est per se.

Et similiter si sic dicatur: Coriscus est alterum a Corisco musico: sed Coriscus est Coriscus musicus; ergo

of building does not produce any of the things that are accidental to a house, but only produces a house and the things that are essential to it.

1175. Then he shows that the same thing is true in the case of the speculative sciences, because similarly neither does geometry *speculate about those things that are accidents of figures in this way* (that is, accidentally), but only about those attributes which belong *per se* to figures. For it speculates about a triangle being a figure *having two right angles*, that is, having its three angles equal to two right angles. But it does not speculate whether a triangle is anything else, such as wood or something of the sort, because these things pertain to a triangle accidentally.

1176. *And this is understandable* (1026b12). Second, he proves the same thing by means of an argument. He says it is reasonable that no science should speculate about accidental being, because a science studies those things that are being in a real sense, but accidental being is in a sense being only in name, inasmuch as one thing is predicated of another. For each thing is a being insofar as it is one. But from any two things that are accidentally related to each other there comes to be something that is one only in name, only inasmuch as one is predicated of the other— for example, when the musical is said to be white, or the converse. But this does not happen in such a way that some one thing is constituted from whiteness and the musical.

1177. *Hence, in a way* (1026b14). He proves in two ways that accidental being is in a sense being only in name.

He first does this on the authority of Plato;

second [1179], by an argument.

He says that since accidental being is in a sense being only in name, Plato in a way was not wrong when he assigned sophistical science to the realm of non-being in allotting different sciences to different kinds of substance. For the arguments of the sophists are concerned chiefly with the accidental, since hidden paralogisms have the fallacy of accident as their principal basis.

1178. Therefore, in the first book of the *Sophistical Refutations*, it is said that in arguing against wise men, the sophists construct syllogisms that are based on the accidental. This is evident, for example, in these paralogisms in which the question is raised whether the musical and the grammatical are the same or different. Let us construct such a paralogism: the musical differs from the grammatical; but the musical is the grammatical; hence the musical differs from itself. For the musical differs from the grammatical *per se* speaking, but the musical is the grammatical by accident. Little wonder, then, that an absurd conclusion follows, for what is accidental is not distinguished from what is essential.

And it would be similar if we were to speak thus: Coriscus differs from musical Coriscus; but Coriscus is

Coriscus est aliud a se. Hic etiam non distinguitur quod est per accidens ab eo quod est per se.

Et similiter si dicatur: omne quod est et non fuit semper, est factum: sed musicus ens est grammaticus et non fuit semper: ergo sequitur quod musicus ens grammaticus sit factus, et grammaticus ens musicus. Quod quidem est falsum; quia nulla generatio terminatur ad hoc quod est grammaticum esse musicum; sed una ad hoc quod est grammaticum esse, alia ad hoc quod est musicum esse.

Patet etiam, quod in hac ratione, prima est vera de eo quod est per se, sed in secunda assumitur quod est ens per accidens. Et similiter est in omnibus talibus rationibus, quae sunt secundum fallaciam accidentis. Videtur enim ens per accidens, esse propinquum non enti. Et ideo sophistica, quae est circa apparens et non existens, est praecipue circa ens per accidens.

1179. *Palam autem* secundo probat idem per rationem, dicens, quod etiam ex his rationibus, quibus utuntur sophistae, palam est, quod ens per accidens est propinquum non enti. Nam eorum, quae sunt entia alio modo quam per accidens, est generatio et corruptio: sed entis per accidens non est neque generatio neque corruptio. Musicum enim una generatione fit, et grammaticum alia. Non est autem una generatio grammatici musici, sicut animalis bipedis, vel sicut hominis risibilis. Unde patet, quod ens per accidens non vere dicitur ens.

1180. Deinde cum dicit *attamen dicendum* determinat de ente per accidens secundum quod est possibilis de eo determinatio. Quamvis enim ea, quibus convenit esse per accidens, non cadant sub consideratione alicuius scientiae, tamen ratio huius quod est esse per accidens, per aliquam scientiam considerari potest. Sicut etiam licet id quod est infinitum, secundum quod est infinitum, sit ignotum, tamen de infinito secundum quod infinitum aliqua scientia tractat. Et circa hoc duo facit.

Primo determinat ea, quae sunt consideranda circa ens per accidens.

Secundo excludit quamdam opinionem, per quam removetur ens per accidens, ibi, *quod autem sint principia et esse* et cetera.

1181. Circa primum duo facit.

Primo dicit, quod est dicendum de ente per accidens inquantum contingit de ipso tractare, tria; scilicet quae est eius natura, et quae est eius causa; et ex his erit tertium manifestum, quare eius non potest esse scientia.

musical Coriscus; therefore Coriscus differs from himself. Here too no distinction is drawn between what is accidental and what is essential.

And it would be the same if we were to say: everything that is and has not always been, has come to be; but the musical is grammatical and has not always been so; therefore it follows that the musical has become grammatical and that the grammatical has become musical. But this is false, because no process of generation terminates in the grammatical being musical, but one process of generation terminates in a man being grammatical and another in a man being musical.

It is also evident that, in this argument, the first statement is true of something that has being *per se*, whereas in the second, something is assumed that has being only by accident. And it is similar in all such argument based on the fallacy of accident. For accidental being seems to be close to non-being. Therefore sophistics, which is concerned with the apparent and nonexistent, deals chiefly with the accidental.

1179. *Now this is also clear* (1026b22). Second, he proves the same thing by an argument. He says that it is also evident from these arguments of the sophists that the accidental is close to non-being. For there is generation and corruption of those things that are beings in a different way than the accidental is, but there is neither generation nor corruption of the accidental. For the musical comes to be by one process of generation and the grammatical by another, but there is not one process of generation of the grammatical musical as there is of two-footed animal or of risible man. Hence it is evident that accidental being is not called being in any true sense.

1180. *Yet concerning the accidental* (1026b24). He now establishes the truth about accidental being insofar as it is possible to do so. For even though those things that are properly accidental do not come within the scope of any science, still the nature of the accidental can be considered by some science. This is also what happens in the case of the infinite, for even though the infinite as infinite remains unknown, still some science treats of the infinite as infinite. In regard to this he does two things.

First, he settles the issue regarding those points which should be investigated about accidental being.

Second (1027a29; [1191]), he rejects an opinion that would abolish accidental being, at *now it is evident.*

1181. In regard to the first he does two things.

First (1026b24), he says that there are three points which must be discussed about accidental being insofar as it is possible to treat of it: what its nature is, and what causes it, and (as the these make evident) why there can be no science of it.

1182. Deinde cum dicit *quoniam igitur* prosequitur tria praedicta.

Et primo quae sit causa entis per accidens; dicens, quod quia in entibus quaedam sunt semper similiter se habentia ex necessitate (non quidem secundum quod necessitas ponitur pro violentia, sed prout necessitas dicitur secundum quam non contingit aliter se habere, ut hominem esse animal); quaedam vero non sunt ex necessitate, nec semper, sed sunt *secundum magis*, idest ut in pluribus. Et *hoc*, scilicet ens ut in pluribus, est causa et principium quod aliquid sit per accidens. In rebus enim quae sunt semper, non potest esse aliquid per accidens; quia solum quod est per se potest esse necessarium et sempiternum, ut etiam in quinto habitum est. Unde relinquitur, quod solum in contingentibus potest esse ens per accidens.

1183. Contingens autem ad utrumlibet, non potest esse causa alicuius inquantum huiusmodi. Secundum enim quod est ad utrumlibet, habet dispositionem materiae, quae est in potentia ad duo opposita: nihil enim agit secundum quod est in potentia. Unde oportet quod causa, quae est ad utrumlibet, ut voluntas, ad hoc quod agat, inclinetur magis ad unam partem, per hoc quod movetur ab appetibili, et sic sit causa ut in pluribus. Contingens autem ut in paucioribus est ens per accidens cuius causa quaeritur. Unde relinquitur, quod causa entis per accidens sit contingens ut in pluribus, quia eius defectus est ut in paucioribus. Et hoc est ens per accidens.

1184. Secundo ibi, *quod enim* ostendit naturam entis per accidens, dicens: ideo dico quod id quod est in pluribus est causa entis per accidens, quia quod non est semper neque secundum magis, hoc dicimus esse per accidens. Et hoc est defectus eius quod est in pluribus, ut si *fuerit hiems* idest tempus pluviosum et frigus *sub cane*, idest in diebus canicularibus, *hoc dicimus esse per accidens*. Non tamen si tunc *fuerit aestuatio*, idest siccitas *et calor*. Hoc enim est semper vel ut in pluribus, sed illud non.

Et similiter dicimus hominem esse album per accidens, quia hoc non est semper nec in pluribus. Hominem vero per se dicimus esse animal, non per accidens, quia hoc est semper.

Et similiter aedificator facit sanitatem per accidens, quia aedificator non est aptus natus facere sanitatem inquantum huiusmodi, sed solus medicus. Aedificator autem facit sanitatem inquantum accidit eum esse medicum;

et similiter *opsopios*, idest cocus *coniectans*, idest intendens facere *voluptatem*, idest delectationem in cibo, faciendo aliquem cibum bene saporatum, facit aliquid salubre. Cibus enim bonus et delectabilis quandoque est

1182. *Therefore, since there are* (1026b27). He discusses these three points.

First, he shows what the cause of the accidental is. He says that there are some beings that always are in the same way and of necessity (not in the sense in which necessity is taken to mean compulsion, but in the sense of that which cannot be otherwise than it is, as "Man is an animal"). There are other beings that are neither always nor of necessity, but *for the most part*, meaning in the majority of cases, and *this* (what occurs in the majority of cases), is the principle and the cause of the accidental. For in the case of those things that always are, there can be nothing accidental, because only that which exists of itself can be necessary and eternal, as is also stated in book 5 [839]. Hence it follows that accidental being can be found only in the realm of contingent things.

1183. But that which is contingent, or open to opposites, cannot as such be the cause of anything. For insofar as it is open to opposites it has the character of matter, which is in potency to two opposites; for nothing acts insofar as it is in potency. Hence a cause that is open to opposites in the way that the will is, in order that it may act, must be inclined more to one side than to the other by being moved by the appetible object, and thus be a cause in the majority of cases. But that which takes place in only a few instances is the accidental, and it is this whose cause we seek. Hence it follows that the cause of the accidental is what occurs in the majority of cases, because this fails to occur in only a few instances. And this is what is accidental.

1184. *For that which* (1026b31). Second, he exposes the nature of accidental being, and he speaks thus. That which exists for the most part is the cause of the accidental, because we call that accidental which is neither always nor for the most part. And this is the absence of what occurs for the most part, so that *if there should be wintry*, that is, rainy, *and cold weather during the dog days* (that is, in the days of the dog star), *we say that this is accidental*. But we do not say this *if the weather is sultry*, that is, dry, *and hot* during that time, for the latter occurs always or almost always, but the former does not.

Similarly, we say that it is accidental for a man to be white, because this is so neither always nor for the most part. But we say that man is an animal *per se*, not accidentally, because this is so always.

And similarly a builder causes health accidentally, because a builder inasmuch is he is a builder is not naturally fitted to cause health, but only a physician can do this. However, a builder may cause health inasmuch as he happens to be a physician.

Similarly, *a confectioner*, or cook, who is aiming to *prepare something pleasing* or delightful in the line of food, may make something health-giving when he prepares a tasty dish. For food that is good and delightful sometimes

utilis ad sanitatem. *Sed hoc non est secundum artem opsopoieticam*, idest pulmentariam, quod faciat salubre, sed quod faciat delectabile. Et propter hoc dicimus hoc accidere.

1185. Et notandum quod in primo exemplo fuit ens per accidens secundum concursum in eodem tempore.

In secundo per concursum in eodem subiecto, sicut album cum homine.

In tertio secundum concursum in eadem causa agente, sicut aedificator et medicus.

In quarto secundum concursum in eodem effectu, sicut in pulmento salubre et delectabile. Quamvis autem cocus faciat pulmentum delectabile, tamen hoc fit per accidens salubre. Cocus quidem facit modo quodam salubre secundum quid; sed simpliciter non facit, quia ars operatur per intentionem.

Unde quod est praeter intentionem artis, non fit ab arte per se loquendo. Et ideo ens per accidens, quod est praeter intentionem artis, non fit ab arte. Aliorum enim entium, quae sunt per se, sunt quandoque aliquae potentiae factivae determinatae; sed entium per accidens nulla ars neque potentia determinata est factiva.

Eorum enim quae sunt aut fiunt secundum accidens, oportet esse causam secundum accidens, et non determinatam. Effectus enim et causa proportionantur adinvicem; et ideo effectus per accidens habet causam per accidens, sicut effectus per se causam per se.

1186. Et quia supra dixerat quod ens ut in pluribus est causa entis per accidens, consequenter cum dicit *quare quoniam* ostendit qualiter ex eo quod est in pluribus, est ens per accidens; dicens, quod, quia non omnia ex necessitate et semper existunt et fiunt, *sed plurima sunt secundum magis*, idest ut in pluribus, ideo necesse est esse quod est secundum accidens, quod neque est semper neque secundum magis, ut hoc quod dico, albus est musicus.

Quia tamen aliquando fit, licet non semper nec ut in pluribus, sequitur quod fit per accidens. Si enim non fieret aliquando id quod est in paucioribus, tunc id quod est in pluribus nunquam deficeret, sed esset semper et ex necessitate, et ita omnia essent sempiterna et necessaria; quod est falsum.

Et, quia defectus eius quod est ut in pluribus, est propter materiam, quae non subditur perfecte virtuti agenti ut in pluribus, ideo *materia est causa accidentis*

promotes health. *But it is not according to the confectioner's art*, the culinary art, that he produces something health-giving, but something delightful. And for this reason we say that this is accidental.

1185. And it should be noted that in the first example the accidental came about insofar as two things happen to occur at the same time;

in the second, insofar as two things happen to be present in the same subject, as white and man;

in the third, insofar as the same efficient cause happens to be a twofold agent, as a builder and a physician;

finally, in the fourth, insofar as the effect happens to be twofold, as health and pleasure in the case of food—for while a cook prepares a pleasing dish, nevertheless this happens to be health-giving by accident. In fact, a cook prepares something health-giving only in a secondary sense, not in a primary and proper sense, because an art operates through knowledge.

Hence whatever lies outside the knowledge of an art is not produced primarily and properly by that art. Therefore, the accidental, which lies outside the knowledge of an art, is not produced by art. For there are certain determinate powers which sometimes are productive of other beings which have being in the proper sense of the term, but there is no art or determinate power that is productive of beings in an accidental sense.

Now, the cause of those things that are or come to be by accident must be an accidental cause and not a proper cause. For effect and cause are proportionate to each other, and therefore whatever is an accidental effect has only an accidental cause, just as an effect in the proper sense has a cause in the proper sense.

1186. And since he had said above [1182] that the cause of the accidental is what occurs for the most part, therefore when he says, *hence, since not all*, he shows how the accidental exists as a result of what occurs for the most part. He says that since not all things are or come to be always and of necessity, *but most things occur for the most part*, that is, in the majority of cases, therefore the accidental must exist; and this is what does not occur always or for the most part, as when I say, "The white man is musical."

Yet because this sometimes happens, although not always or in the majority of cases, it follows that this comes about by accident. For if that which occurs only occasionally were never to occur, then that which occurs in the majority of cases would never fail to occur, but would be always and of necessity. Thus all things would be eternal and necessary. But this is false.

And since that which occurs in the majority of cases fails to occur because of matter (which is not completely subject to the active power of the agent, as happens in the

aliter quam ut in pluribus, scilicet accidentis ut in paucioribus: causa inquam non necessaria, sed *contingens*.

1187. Habito autem, quod non omnia sunt necessaria, sed aliquid est nec semper nec secundum magis, principium hoc oportet hic sumere, utrum nihil sit nec semper, nec secundum magis. Sed hoc patet esse impossibile; quia, cum id quod est ut in pluribus, sit causa entis per accidens, oportet esse et id quod est semper, et id quod est ut in pluribus. Igitur quod est praeter utrumque dictorum, est ens secundum accidens.

1188. Sed utrum iterum id quod est ut in pluribus inest alicui, quod autem est semper nulli inest, aut etiam sunt aliqua sempiterna, considerandum est posterius in duodecimo; ubi ostendet quasdam substantias esse sempiternas.

Sic igitur per primam quaestionem quaeritur, utrum omnia sint per accidens.

Per secundam vero, utrum omnia possibilia, et nihil sempiternum.

1189. Deinde cum dicit *quod autem* ostendit tertium praemissorum; scilicet quod scientia non sit de ente per accidens. Quod quidem dicit esse palam ex hoc, quod omnis scientia est aut eius quod est semper, aut eius quod est in pluribus. Unde cum ens per accidens nec sit semper, nec sit in pluribus, de eo non poterit esse scientia.

Primam sic probat. Non enim potest aliquis doceri ab alio, vel docere alium, de eo quod nec est semper, nec ut frequenter. Hoc enim de quo est doctrina oportet esse definitum aut per hoc quod est semper, aut per hoc quod est in pluribus. Sicut quod *melicratum*, idest mixtum ex aqua et melle, utile est febricitantibus, determinatum est ut in pluribus.

1190. Sed quod est *praeter hoc*, idest praeter id quod est semper et magis, non potest dici quando fiat, sicut quod fiat in tempore novilunii. Quia quod determinatur fieri in tempore novilunii, vel est semper, vel ut in pluribus.

Vel potest esse hoc quod dicitur de nova luna aliud exemplum, eius scilicet quod determinatur semper; et quod addit, *aut in pluribus fit*, addit, propter differentiam eius per accidens, quod nec sic nec sic est. Unde subdit quod *accidens sit praeter hoc*, scilicet praeter ens semper et ens ut magis. Et haec minor est rationis principalis superius positae.

majority of cases), then *matter is the cause of the accidental, which happens otherwise than usually occurs*, that is, which happens only occasionally. This cause, I say, is not a necessary cause, but a *contingent* one.

1187. Granted that not all things are necessary, but that there is something which is neither always nor for the most part, then we must take as our starting-point the question of whether there is nothing that is neither always nor for the most part. But obviously this is impossible, for, since that which occurs for the most part is the cause of the accidental, then both that which always is and that which is for the most part must exist. Hence anything besides the things just mentioned is an accidental being.

1188. However, the question of whether that which occurs for the most part is found in some being, and of whether that which occurs always is not found in any being, or of whether there are some things that are eternal, must be dealt with later in book 12 [2488], where he will show that there are some substances that are eternal.

Hence in the first question he asks whether all things are accidental;

and in the second, whether all things are contingent and nothing is eternal.

1189. *However, it is evident* (1027a19). Here he establishes the third point, namely, that there is no science of the accidental. He says that this is evident from the fact that every science is concerned with what is either always or for the most part. Therefore, since the accidental occurs neither always nor for the most part, there will be no science of it.

He proves the first thus: one cannot be taught by another or teach another about something which does not occur either always or for the most part, for anything that may be taught must be defined on the grounds that it is so either always or for the most part. For example, that *honey-water* (a mixture of honey and water) is beneficial to those with a fever is defined as something that occurs for the most part.

1190. But as to *what happens in the other cases*, that is, in the case of things that are neither always nor for the most part, it cannot be said when they will occur (for example) at the time of the new moon. For whatever is destined to happen at that time also happens either always or for the most part.

Or his statement about the new moon can be another example of something that is defined as occurring always, and he adds the phrase, *or for the most part*, because of the way in which the accidental differs, since it does not occur in either of these ways. Hence he adds that *the accidental is contrary to this*, contrary to what occurs always or for the most part. And this is the minor premise of the principal argument used above.

Ulterius autem epilogando dicit quod dictum est, quid est ens per accidens, et quae est causa eius, et quod de eo non potest esse scientia.

In bringing his discussion to a close, he mentions the points which have been explained, namely, what the accidental is, and what its cause is, and that there can be no science of it.

LECTURE 3

Accidental being

1027a29 Quod autem sint principia et causae generabilia et corruptibilia sine generari et corrumpi, palam. [1191]

Si enim non hoc, ex necessitate omnia erunt, si eius quod fit et corrumpitur, non secundum accidens causam aliquam necesse est esse.

Utrum enim erit hoc, aut non? Si hoc fiat, erit. Si autem non, non. Hoc autem, si aliud.

Et ita manifestum quia semper tempore ablato a finito tempore, venit usque ad nunc.

Quare hic moritur infirmitate aut vi, si exit, aut si facit; sed hoc, si aliud;

et ita veniet ad quod nunc est. Aut in factotum aliquid, ut si sitit. Hoc autem, si comedit mordicantia. Sed hoc, aut est, aut non.

Quare ex necessitate morietur, aut non morietur.

Similiter autem et si supersiliat aliquis ad facta, eadem ratio. Iam enim est hoc in aliquo, dico autem factum.

Ex necessitate ergo omnia erunt, quae sunt futura, et moriturum fore viventem. Iam enim aliquid factum est ut contraria in eodem corpore;

sed si infirmitate aut vi, nondum, nisi hoc factum fuerit.

ὅτι δ᾽ εἰσὶν ἀρχαὶ καὶ αἴτια γενητὰ καὶ φθαρτὰ {30} ἄνευ τοῦ γίγνεσθαι καὶ φθείρεσθαι, φανερόν.

εἰ γὰρ μὴ τοῦτ᾽, ἐξ ἀνάγκης πάντ᾽ ἔσται, εἰ τοῦ γιγνομένου καὶ φθειρομένου μὴ κατὰ συμβεβηκὸς αἴτιόν τι ἀνάγκη εἶναι.

πότερον γὰρ ἔσται τοδὶ ἢ οὔ; ἐάν γε τοδὶ γένηται· εἰ δὲ μή, οὔ. τοῦτο δὲ ἐὰν ἄλλο.

καὶ οὕτω δῆλον ὅτι ἀεὶ χρόνου ἀφαιρουμένου ἀπὸ πεπερασμένου χρόνου ἥξει ἐπὶ τὸ νῦν,

{1027b1} ὥστε ὁδὶ ἀποθανεῖται [νόσῳ ἢ] βίᾳ, ἐάν γε ἐξέλθῃ· τοῦτο δὲ ἐὰν διψήσῃ· τοῦτο δὲ ἐὰν ἄλλο·

καὶ οὕτως ἥξει εἰς ὃ νῦν ὑπάρχει, ἢ εἰς τῶν γεγονότων τι. οἷον ἐὰν διψήσῃ· τοῦτο δὲ εἰ ἐσθίει δριμέα· {5} τοῦτο δ᾽ ἤτοι ὑπάρχει ἢ οὔ·

ὥστ᾽ ἐξ ἀνάγκης ἀποθανεῖται ἢ οὐκ ἀποθανεῖται.

ὁμοίως δὲ κἂν ὑπερπηδήσῃ τις εἰς τὰ γενόμενα, ὁ αὐτὸς λόγος· ἤδη γὰρ ὑπάρχει τοῦτο ἔν τινι, λέγω δὲ τὸ γεγονός·

ἐξ ἀνάγκης ἄρα πάντα ἔσται τὰ ἐσόμενα, οἷον τὸ ἀποθανεῖν τὸν ζῶντα· ἤδη γάρ τι γέγονεν, {10} οἷον τὰ ἐναντία ἐν τῷ αὐτῷ. ἀλλ᾽ εἰ νόσῳ ἢ βίᾳ, οὔπω, ἀλλ᾽ ἐὰν τοδὶ γένηται.

δῆλον ἄρα ὅτι μέχρι τινὸς βαδίζει ἀρχῆς, αὕτη δ᾽ οὐκέτι εἰς ἄλλο.

Now it is evident that there are principles and causes which are generable and corruptible that are without generation and corruption.

For if this were not the case, everything would be of necessity—that is, if there must be some cause, and not an accidental one, of that which is generated and corrupted.

We ask: "Will this thing exist or not?" It will if some second thing happens, but if the latter does not, neither will the former. And this second thing will happen if some third thing does.

And thus it is evident that when time is continually taken away from a limited period of time, one will finally come to the present moment.

Hence this man will die either from illness or violence if he goes out, and he will do this if he gets thirsty, and this will happen if something else does.

And in this way one will come to what exists now, or to something that has already happened—for example, he will go out if he gets thirsty, and this will happen if he eats highly seasoned food, and this is either the case or not.

Therefore, it will be from necessity that he dies or does not die.

And similarly if one jumps back to something that has already happened, the same argument applies, for this—I mean what has already happened—is already present in something.

Therefore, everything that will be will be of necessity—for example, one who lives shall die—because some part of the process has already been completed, as the presence of contraries in the same body.

But whether he will die from illness or violence has not yet been determined, unless something else will have happened.

1027b11 Palam ergo quia usque ad aliquod vadit principium, hoc autem non adhuc ad aliud. Erit ergo eius quodcumque evenit ipsum, et causa ipsius generationis nulla. [1201]

ἔσται οὖν ἡ τοῦ ὁπότερ᾽ ἔτυχεν αὕτη, καὶ αἴτιον τῆς γενέσεως αὐτῆς ἄλλο οὐθέν.

It is evident, then, that this process goes back to some principle, but that this does not go back to anything else. Therefore, this will be the principle of everything that happens by chance, and there will be no cause of its generation.

1027b14 Sed ad principium quale et causam qualem reductio talis? Utrum ut ad materiam, aut ad quod cuius gratia, aut ut ad movens, maxime perscrutandum. Ergo de ente secundum accidens praetermittatur. Determinatum est enim sufficienter. [1202]

ἀλλ᾽ εἰς ἀρχὴν ποίαν καὶ αἴτιον ποῖον ἡ ἀναγωγὴ ἡ {15} τοιαύτη, πότερον ὡς εἰς ὕλην ἢ ὡς εἰς τὸ οὗ ἕνεκα ἢ ὡς εἰς τὸ κινῆσαν, μάλιστα σκεπτέον.

But to what kind of principle and what kind of cause such a process of reduction leads, whether to matter or to a final cause or to a cause of motion, must be given careful consideration. Let us dismiss accidental being, then, for it has been dealt with at sufficient length.

1191. Postquam Philosophus determinavit de ente per accidens, hic excludit quamdam opinionem, per quam tollitur totum ens per accidens. Quidam enim posuerunt, quod quicquid fit in mundo habet aliquam causam per se; et iterum quod qualibet causa posita, necesse est sequi effectum eius. Unde sequebatur quod per quamdam connexionem causarum omnia ex necessitate acciderent, et nihil esset per accidens in rebus.

Et ideo hanc opinionem Philosophus intendit destruere: et circa hoc tria facit.

Primo enim destruit praedictam opinionem.

Secundo infert quamdam conclusionem ex praedictis, ibi, *palam ergo quia usque ad aliquod* et cetera.

Tertio movet quamdam quaestionem quae ex praedictis occasionatur, ibi, *sed ad principium quale.*

Dicit ergo primo, quod palam erit ex sequentibus quod principia et causae generationis et corruptionis aliquorum *sunt generabilia et corruptibilia*, idest contingit generari et corrumpi sine generatione et corruptione, idest sine hoc quod sequatur generatio et corruptio. Non enim oportet, quod si generatio alicuius rei vel corruptio est causa generationis aut corruptionis rei alterius, quod posita generatione vel corruptione causae, de necessitate sequatur generatio vel corruptio effectus: quia quaedam causae sunt agentes ut in pluribus: unde eis positis, adhuc potest impediri effectus per accidens, sicut propter indispositionem materiae, vel propter occursum contrarii agentis, vel propter aliquid huiusmodi.

1192. Sciendum tamen, quod Avicenna probat in sua *Metaphysica*, quod nullus effectus sit possibilis in comparatione ad suam causam, sed solum necessarius. Si enim posita causa, possibile est effectum non poni, et poni, id autem quod est in potentia inquantum huiusmodi reducitur in actum per aliquod ens actu, oportebit ergo quod aliquid aliud a causa faciat ibi sequi effectum in actu. Causa igitur illa non erat sufficiens. Et hoc videtur contra id, quod Philosophus hic dicit.

1191. Having drawn his conclusions concerning accidental being, the Philosopher now rejects an opinion that would completely abolish this kind of being. For some men held that whatever comes to pass in the world has some proper cause, and again that, given any cause, its effect necessarily follows. Hence, as a result of the connection between causes it would follow that everything in the world happens of necessity and nothing by chance.

Therefore, the Philosopher's aim is to destroy this position, and in regard to this he does three things.

First, he destroys this position.

Second (1027b11; [1201]), he draws a conclusion from his discussion, at *it is evident.*

Third (1027b14; [1202]), he poses a question that arises out of this discussion, at *but to what kind of principle.*

He first says that it will be evident from the following remarks that the principles and causes of the generation and corruption of some things *are generable and corruptible* (that is, they are capable of being generated and corrupted) without generation and corruption—that is, generation and corruption actually taking place. For if the generation or corruption of one thing is the cause of the generation or corruption of another, it is not necessary that the generation or corruption of the effect necessarily follows when the generation or corruption of the cause takes place, because some causes are active only for the most part. Therefore, granted that these causes exist, their effect can be hindered accidentally, either because the matter is not disposed, or because an opposing agent interferes, or because of some such reason.

1192. Yet it must be noted that Avicenna proves in his *Metaphysics* that no effect is possible in relation to its own cause, but only necessary. For if when the cause is posited, it is possible for its effect not to follow, and it does follow (and the potential as such is made actual by some actual being), then something else besides this cause will have to cause the actual effect to follow. Therefore, this cause was not sufficient. This appears to be contrary to what the Philosopher says here.

1193. Sed sciendum, quod dictum Avicennae intelligi debet, supposito quod nullum impedimentum causae adveniat. Necesse est enim causa posita sequi effectum, nisi sit impedimentum, quod quandoque contingit esse per accidens. Et ideo Philosophus dicit, quod non est necessarium generationem sequi vel corruptionem, positis causis generationis vel corruptionis.

1194. Si enim non est verum hoc quod dictum est, sequetur, quod omnia erunt ex necessitate, si tamen cum hoc quod dictum est, quod posita causa necesse est sequi effectum, ponatur etiam alia positio, scilicet quod cuiuslibet quod fit et corrumpitur, necesse sit esse aliquam causam per se et non per accidens. Ex his enim duabus propositionibus, sequitur omnia esse de necessitate. Quod sic probat.

1195. Si enim quaeratur de aliquo, utrum sit futurum vel non, sequitur ex praedictis, quod alterum sit de necessitate verum: quia si omne quod fit habet causam per se suae factionis, qua posita necesse est ipsum fieri, sequetur quod res illa, de qua quaeritur utrum sit futura, fiat, si sit hoc quod ponitur causa eius; et si illud non fuerit, quod non fiat. Et similiter oportet dicere, quod ista causa erit futura, si aliquod aliud quod est causa eius, erit futurum.

1196. Constat autem, quod tempus quantumcumque futurum accipiatur, sive post centum annos, sive post mille, est finitum, incipiendo a praesenti nunc usque ad illum terminum. Cum autem generatio causae praecedat tempore generationem effectus, oportet quod procedendo ab effectu ad causam auferamus aliquid de tempore futuro, et appropinquemus magis ad praesens. Omne autem finitum consumitur aliquoties ablato quodam ab ipso. Et ita sequitur quod procedendo ab effectu ad causam, et iterum ab illa causa ad eius causam, et sic deinceps, auferatur totum tempus futurum cum sit finitum, et ita perveniatur ad ipsum nunc.

1197. Quod quidem patet in hoc exemplo. Si enim omnis effectus habet aliquam causam per se, ad quam de necessitate sequitur, oportet quod iste de necessitate moriatur, vel per infirmitatem, vel per violentiam, si exit domum suam. Exitus enim a domo eius invenitur causa esse mortis eius, vel violentiae; puta si exiens domum invenitur a latronibus et occiditur; vel per infirmitatem; puta si exiens de domo ex aestu incurrit febrem et moritur. Et eodem modo hoc erit ex necessitate, scilicet quod exeat domum ad hauriendum aquam si sitit. Nam sitis invenitur esse causa ut exeat domum ad hauriendum aquam. Similiter per eamdem rationem hoc erit de necessitate, scilicet quod sitiat, si aliquid aliud erit quod est causa sitis:

1193. But it must be noted that Avicenna's statement should be understood to apply only if we assume that no obstacle interferes with the cause. For, given the cause, its effect must follow unless there is some obstacle, and sometimes this occurs accidentally. Hence the Philosopher says that generation and corruption need not follow when the causes of generation and corruption are posited.

1194. For if this statement were not true, it would follow that all things would be of necessity, granted that along with this statement, "Given the cause the effect must follow," another position is also maintained—namely, that there must be some proper cause, and not merely an accidental one, of each thing which is generated and corrupted. For from these two propositions it follows that all things are of necessity. He proves this as follows.

1195. If it is asked whether a thing will be or not, it follows from the above remarks that one or the other is true of necessity. For if everything that is generated has a proper cause which produces it, and if given the cause its effect must follow, then it follows that that thing about which it was asked whether it will exist or not will come to be if its cause is held to exist. And if that cause will not exist, neither will its effect. Similarly, it will be necessary to say that this cause will exist if some other thing which is its cause will exist.

1196. Further, it is evident that regardless of the amount of future time that may be taken, whether after a hundred or a thousand years, the amount of time beginning from the present moment up to that point is limited. However, since the generation of a cause is prior in time to the generation of its effect, then, by proceeding from effect to cause, we must subtract some part of future time and come closer to the present. But every limited thing is used up by having some part of it constantly taken away. Thus by proceeding from an effect to its cause and again from that cause to its cause and so on in this way, it follows that the whole period of future time is used up, since it is limited, and in this way the present moment is reached.

1197. This is clear in the following example. If every effect has some proper cause from which it follows of necessity, then this man must die of necessity from either illness or violence if he leaves the house. For his leaving the house is found to be the cause of his death by either violence (for example, if on leaving the house he is discovered by robbers and is killed) or illness (for example, if on leaving the house he contracts a fever from the heat and dies). And in the same way it will also happen of necessity that he leaves the house in order to draw water from a well if he is thirsty, for thirst is the cause of his leaving the house in order to draw water. And similarly by the same argument it will also happen of necessity that he is thirsty if there is something else which causes his thirst.

et ita sic procedens de effectu ad causam perveniet ad aliquod *quod nunc est*, idest in aliquod praesens, vel in *aliquod factorum*, idest in aliquod praeteritorum. Sicut si dicamus quod sitis erit si comedit mordicantia vel salsa, quae faciunt sitim: hoc autem, scilicet quod comedat salsa vel non comedat, est in praesenti. Et ita sequitur quod *praedictum futurum*, scilicet quod iste moriatur vel non moriatur, ex necessitate erit.

1198. Cum enim quaelibet conditionalis vera sit necessaria, oportet quod ex quo antecedens est positum, quod consequens ex necessitate ponatur. Sicut haec est vera, si Socrates currit, movetur. Posito ergo quod currat, necesse erit ipsum moveri, dum currit. Si autem quilibet effectus habet causam per se, ex qua de necessitate sequitur, oportet quod sit illa conditionalis vera, cuius antecedens est causa et consequens effectus.

Et licet inter causam, quae nunc est praesens, et effectum qui erit futurus, quandoque sint plurima media, quorum unumquodque est effectus respectu praecedentium, et causa respectu sequentium; tamen sequitur de primo ad ultimum, quod conditionalis sit vera cuius antecedens est praesens et eius consequens quandoque futurum. Sicut hic, si comedit salsa, occidetur. Antecedens autem ponitur, ex quo praesens est; ergo de necessitate erit quod occidatur. Et ita omnia alia futura erunt necessaria, quorum causae proximae vel remotae, sunt praesentes.

1199. Et similis ratio est si aliquis procedens ab effectibus ad causas, supersiliat *ad facta*, idest ad praeterita, hoc est dicere si reducat effectus futuros in aliquam causam praeteritam non praesentem; quia hoc quod praeteritum est iam est secundum aliquem modum. Hoc autem dico inquantum est factum vel praeteritum. Licet enim vita Caesaris non sit nunc ut in praesenti, est tamen in praeterito. Verum enim est Caesarem vixisse. Et ita nunc est ponere verum esse antecedens conditionalis, in cuius antecedente est causa praeterita, et in consequente est causa futura.

Et sic sequetur, cum omnes effectus futuros oporteat redigere in tales causas praesentes vel praeteritas, quod omnia futura ex necessitate eveniant. Sicut nos dicimus quod viventem fore moriturum est necessarium absolute, quia sequitur de necessitate ad aliquid quod iam factum est, scilicet duo contraria esse in eodem corpore per commixtionem. Haec enim conditionalis est vera: si aliquod corpus est compositum ex contrariis, corrumpetur.

1200. Hoc autem est impossibile, quod omnia futura ex necessitate eveniant. Ergo illa duo sunt impossibilia, ex quibus hoc sequebatur; scilicet quod quilibet effec-

Thus, by proceeding from effect to cause in this way one comes to **what exists now**, to some present thing or to **something that has already happened**, some past event. For example, if we were to say that a man will be thirsty if he eats highly seasoned or salty food which makes him thirsty, his eating or not eating salty food is in the present. Thus it follows that **the aforesaid future event**, namely, that this man will die or not die, will happen of necessity.

1198. For since every conditional proposition is a necessary one, then granted the antecedent, the consequent must follow. For example, this conditional proposition is true: "If Socrates runs, he moves." Therefore, granted that he runs, he must be moving so long as he runs. But if any effect has a proper cause from which it follows of necessity, then that conditional proposition must be true of which the antecedent is the cause and the consequent is the effect.

And although there are sometimes several intermediates between a cause which exists at the present moment and an effect which will exist in the future (each of which is an effect in relation to those preceding it and a cause in relation to those following it), nevertheless it follows from first to last that any conditional proposition is true whose antecedent is present and whose consequent exists at some future time—for example, the proposition: "If a man eats salty food, he will be killed." Now the antecedent refers to what is present, and therefore it will be by necessity that he is killed. And in this way all other future events whose proximate or remote causes exist in the present will be necessary.

1199. The same argument applies if one, in proceeding from effects to causes, jumps back **to something that has already happened**, or to past events, that is to say, if one traces future effects back to some past cause that is not present. For that which is past nevertheless still is in some sense. I say this insofar as it has occurred, or is past. For even though Caesar's life is not now, in the present, nevertheless it is in the past, because it is true that Caesar has lived. Thus it is possible to hold as true now the antecedent of a conditional proposition in whose antecedent clause there is a past cause and in whose consequent clause there is a future effect.

And thus, since all future effects must be traced back to such present or past causes, it follows that all future events happen of necessity. For example, we say that it is absolutely necessary that one now living is going to die, because this follows of necessity in reference to something that has already come to pass, namely, that there are two contraries in the same body by reason of its composition; for this conditional proposition is true: "If a body is composed of contraries, it will be corrupted."

1200. But it is impossible that all future events should happen of necessity. Therefore, the two premises from which this conclusion would follow are impossible—

tus habeat causam per se, et quod causa posita necesse sit effectum poni. Quia ex hoc ipso sequeretur quod iam dictum est, quod quorumlibet effectuum futurorum essent aliquae causae iam positae. Sicut corruptionis animalis, iam sunt aliquae causae positae. Sed quod iste homo moriatur per infirmitatem vel violentiam, nondum habet aliquam causam positam ex qua de necessitate sequatur.

1201. Deinde cum dicit *palam ergo* infert quamdam conclusionem ex praedictis; dicens: ergo ex quo non quodlibet, quod fit, habet causam per se, palam, quod in futuris contingentibus, effectus futuri reductio ad causam per se, vadit usque ad aliquod principium; quod quidem principium non reducitur in aliquod principium adhuc per se, sed ipsum erit cuius causa *erit quodcumque evenit*, idest causa casualis, et illius causae casualis non erit aliqua alia causa; sicut iam praedictum est, quod ens per accidens non habet causam neque generationem. Verbi gratia, quod iste occidatur a latronibus habet causam per se quia vulneratur; et hoc etiam habet causam per se, quia a latronibus invenitur; sed hoc non habet nisi causam per accidens. Hoc enim quod iste qui negotiatur, ad negotium vadens, inter latrones incidat, est per accidens, ut ex praedictis patet. Unde eius non oportet ponere aliquam causam. Ens enim per accidens, ut supra dictum est, non habet generationem, et ita eius generationis causam per se quaerere non oportet.

1202. Deinde cum dicit *sed ad principium* movet quamdam quaestionem occasionatam ex dictis. Dixit enim supra immediate, quod causae entium per accidens reducuntur usque ad aliquod principium, cuius non est ponere aliam causam. Et ideo hic inquirit de hac reductione, vel anagoge, quod idem est, ad *quale principium et ad qualem causam debeat fieri*, idest ad quod genus causae vel principii: scilicet utrum ad aliquam causam primam, quae sit causa sicut materia; aut ad aliquam, quae sit causa sicut finis, cuius gratia aliquid fit; aut ad aliquam, quae sit causa sicut movens.

Praetermittit autem de causa formali, quia quaestio hic habetur de causa generationis rerum, quae fiunt per accidens. In generatione autem, forma non habet causalitatem, nisi per modum finis. Finis enim et forma in generatione incidunt in idem numero. Hanc autem quaestionem hic motam non solvit: sed supponit eius solutionem ab eo quod est determinatum in secundo *Physicorum*. Ibi enim ostensum est quod fortuna et casus, quae sunt causae eorum quae fiunt per accidens, reducuntur ad genus causae efficientis. Ergo concludit ex praemissis, quod praetermittendum est loqui de ente

namely, that any effect has a proper cause, and that, given the cause, its effect must follow. For from this would follow the position already mentioned, namely, that there are some causes already posited for any future effect. (For example, some causes have already been posited for the corruption of an animal.) But no cause has yet been posited from which it will follow of necessity that this man will die either from illness or violence.

1201. *It is evident* (1027b11). He draws a conclusion from the foregoing discussion. He says that since not everything which comes to be has a proper cause, it is therefore evident that, in the case of future contingent events, the reduction of a future effect to some proper cause goes back to some principle, and that this principle is not reduced to some other proper principle, but will be the cause of *everything that happens by chance*—that is, an accidental cause—and that there will be no other cause of that accidental cause, just as we have already said [1184] that accidental being has no cause and is not generated. For example, the cause of this man being killed by robbers is a proper cause, because he is wounded by robbers, and this also has a proper cause, because he is found by the robbers—but this finding has only an accidental cause. For if, on his way to work, this man is wounded by robbers, this is accidental, as is evident from the foregoing, and therefore it is not necessary to posit a cause for this. For that which is accidental is not generated, and thus it is not necessary to look for some proper cause which produces it, as was said above.

1202. *But to what kind of principle* (1027b14). Here he poses a question arising out of the foregoing discussion; for he has just said above that the causes of those beings which are accidental are ultimately reduced to some principle for which it is impossible to give another cause. Hence he inquires here about this process of reduction or *anagoge*, which means the same as *to what kind of principle and what kind of cause such a process of reduction leads*, that is, to what genus of cause or principle, whether to some first cause which is a material cause, or to one which is a final cause (or that for the sake of which a thing comes to be), or to one which is a mover.

He omits the formal cause because the question here involves the cause responsible for the generation of things that come to be by accident. But in the process of generation, a form has no causal role except that of an end, because in the process of generation the end and the form are identical. Now he does not answer the question which is raised here, but assumes its solution from what has been established in *Physics* 2. For it was shown there that fortune and chance, which are the causes of things that come to be by accident, are reduced to the genus of efficient cause. Hence he concludes from the above that we must omit any

per accidens, ex quo determinatum est sufficienter secundum id quod de eo determinari potest.

1203. Attendendum est autem quod ea quae Philosophus hic tradit, videntur removere quaedam, quae secundum philosophiam ab aliquibus ponuntur, scilicet fatum et providentiam. Vult enim hic Philosophus, quod non omnia quae fiunt, reducantur in aliquam causam per se, ex qua de necessitate sequantur: alias sequeretur, quod omnia essent ex necessitate, et nihil per accidens esset in rebus. Illi autem, qui ponunt fatum, dicunt, contingentia, quae hic fiunt, quae videntur per accidens, esse reducibilia in aliquam virtutem corporis caelestis, per cuius actionem ea quae secundum se considerata per accidens fieri videntur, cum quodam ordine producantur. Et similiter illi, qui ponunt providentiam, ea quae aguntur hic, dicunt esse ordinata secundum ordinem providentiae.

1204. Ex utraque igitur positione duo videntur sequi, quae sunt contraria his, quae hic Philosophus determinat:

quorum primum est: in rebus nihil fit per accidens neque a fortuna neque a casu. Quae enim secundum aliquem ordinem procedunt, non sunt per accidens. Sunt enim vel semper vel in maiori parte.

Secundum autem est, quod omnia ex necessitate eveniant. Si enim omnia ex necessitate eveniunt quorum causa vel ponitur in praesenti, vel iam est posita in praeterito, ut ratio Philosophi procedit, eorum autem quae sunt sub providentia vel fato causa ponitur in praesenti, et iam posita est in praeterito, eo quod providentia est immutabilis et aeterna, motus etiam caeli est invariabilis: videtur sequi quod ea quae sunt sub providentia vel fato, ex necessitate contingant. Et ita, si omnia quae hic aguntur, fato et providentia subduntur, sequitur quod omnia ex necessitate proveniant. Videtur ergo quod secundum intentionem Philosophi non sit ponere neque providentiam neque fatum.

1205. Ad horum autem evidentiam considerandum est, quod quanto aliqua causa est altior, tanto eius causalitas ad plura se extendit. Habet enim causa altior proprium causatum altius quod est communius et in pluribus inventum. Sicut in artificialibus patet quod ars politica, quae est supra militarem, ad totum statum communitatis se extendit. Militaris autem solum ad eos, qui in ordine militari continentur. Ordinatio, autem quae est in effectibus ex aliqua causa tantum se extendit quantum extendit se illius causae causalitas. Omnis enim causa per se habet determinatos effectus, quos secundum aliquem ordinem producit. Manifestum igitur est, quod effectus relati ad aliquam inferiorem causam nullum ordinem habere videntur, sed per accidens sibi ipsis coincidunt; qui si referantur ad superiorem causam

discussion of accidental being, because the truth concerning it has been established as completely as it is possible to do so.

1203. It must be noted, however, that the doctrine of the Philosopher set forth here seems to do away with certain things that some thinkers hold in philosophy, namely, fate and providence. For here the force of the Philosopher's argument is that not all that occurs may be traced back to some proper cause from which it follows of necessity, otherwise it would follow that everything in the world would be of necessity and nothing by accident. But those who posit fate say that the contingent events occurring here, which appear to be accidental, can be traced back to some power of a celestial body, whose action produces in a certain order those things that, viewed in themselves, seem accidental. And similarly those who posit providence say that whatever occurs here is ordained by the order of providence.

1204. From both of these positions, then, there seem to follow two conclusions which are opposed to what the Philosopher establishes here.

The first is that nothing in the world happens accidentally either by fortune or by chance, for those things that occur in a certain order are not accidental, since they occur either always or for the most part.

The second is that all things happen of necessity. For if all those things whose cause is placed in the present or has been placed in the past occur of necessity, as the Philosopher's argument maintains, and if the cause of those things that come under providence or fate is placed in the present or has already been placed in the past (because providence is unchangeable and eternal, and the motion of the heavens is also invariable), it seems to follow that those things that come under providence or fate happen of necessity. Thus if everything that occurs here is subject to fate and providence, it follows that everything happens of necessity. Therefore, according to the mind of the Philosopher, it seems impossible to posit either fate or providence.

1205. In clearing up this difficulty, it must be noted that the higher a cause, the more extensive is its causality, for a higher cause produces its own proper higher effect, which is more general and extends to many things. For example, in the case of the arts, it is evident that the political art, which is higher than the military art, has jurisdiction over the entire political community, whereas the military art has jurisdiction only over those things that fall within the military sphere. But the order found in the effects of a cause extends only so far as the causality of that cause extends, for every cause in the proper sense has definite effects which it produces in a certain order. It is evident, then, that when effects are referred to lower causes, they seem to be unrelated and to coincide with each other accidentally, but that when they are referred to some higher common cause,

communem, ordinati inveniuntur, et non per accidens coniuncti, sed ab una per se causa simul producti sunt.

1206. Sicut floritio huius herbae vel illius, si referatur ad particularem virtutem, quae est in hac planta vel in illa, nullum ordinem habere videtur—immo videtur esse accidens—quod hac herba florente illa floreat. Et hoc ideo, quia causa virtutis huius plantae extendit se ad floritionem huius, et non ad floritionem alterius: unde est quidem causa, quod haec planta floreat, non autem quod simul cum altera. Si autem ad virtutem corporis caelestis, quae est causa communis, referatur, invenitur hoc non esse per accidens, quod hac herba florente illa floreat, sed esse ordinatum ab aliqua prima causa hoc ordinante, quae simul movet utramque herbam ad floritionem.

1207. Invenitur autem in rebus triplex causarum gradus.

Est enim primo causa incorruptibilis et immutabilis, scilicet divina;

sub hac secundo est causa incorruptibilis, sed mutabilis; scilicet corpus caeleste;

sub hac tertio sunt causae corruptibiles et mutabiles. Hae igitur causae in tertio gradu existentes sunt particulares, et ad proprios effectus secundum singulas species determinatae: ignis enim generat ignem, et homo generat hominem, et planta plantam.

1208. Causa autem secundi gradus est quodammodo universalis, et quodammodo particularis.

Particularis quidem, quia se extendit ad aliquod genus entium determinatum, scilicet ad ea quae per motum in esse producuntur; est enim causa movens et mota.

Universalis autem, quia non ad unam tantum speciem mobilium se extendit causalitas eius, sed ad omnia, quae alterantur et generantur et corrumpuntur: illud enim quod est primo motum, oportet esse causam omnium consequenter mobilium.

1209. Sed causa primi gradus est simpliciter universalis: eius enim effectus proprius est esse: unde quicquid est, et quocumque modo est, sub causalitate et ordinatione illius causae proprie continetur.

1210. Si igitur ea quae hic sunt contingentia, reducamus in causas proximas particulares tantum, inveniuntur multa fieri per accidens, tum propter concursum duarum causarum,

quarum una sub altera non continetur, sicut cum praeter intentionem occurrunt mihi latrones. (Hic enim concursus causatur ex duplici virtute motiva, scilicet mea et latronum).

they are found to be related and not accidentally connected but to be produced simultaneously by one proper cause.

1206. For example, if the blossoming of one plant is referred to a particular power in this plant and the blossoming of a second plant is referred to a particular power in that plant, there seems to be no reason (indeed, it seems to be accidental) why the first plant should blossom when the second does. And this is true, because the cause of the power of the first plant extends to the blossoming of this plant and not to that of the second, so that while it causes the first plant to blossom, it does not cause it to blossom at the same time as the second. But if this is attributed to the power of a celestial body, which is a universal cause, then we find that the first plant blossoms when the second does not by accident, but by the direction of some first cause, which ordains this and moves each plant to blossom at the same time.

1207. Now we find three grades of causes in the world.

First, there is a cause which is incorruptible and immutable (namely, the divine cause);

second, beneath this there are causes which are incorruptible but mutable (namely, the celestial bodies);

and third, beneath this there are those causes which are corruptible and mutable. Therefore, causes in this third grade are particular causes and are determined to proper effects of the same kind—for example, fire generates fire, man generates man, and plants generate plants.

1208. Now a cause belonging to the second grade is in one sense universal and in another particular.

It is particular because it extends to some special genus of beings, namely, to those which are generated by motion; for it is both a cause of motion and something that is moved.

And it is universal because its causality extends not only to one species of changeable things, but to everything that is altered, generated, and corrupted; for that which is first moved must be the cause of everything that is subsequently moved.

1209. But the cause belonging to the first grade is universal without qualification, because its proper effect is existence. Hence whatever exists, and in whatever way it exists, comes properly under the causality and direction of that cause.

1210. If, then, we attribute all contingent events here to particular causes only, many things will be found to occur accidentally. This will be so for a number of reasons.

First, because of the conjunction of two causes, one of which does not come under the causality of the other, as when robbers attack me without my intending this; for this meeting is caused by a twofold motive power, namely, mine and that of the robbers.

Tum etiam propter defectum agentis, cui accidit debilitas, ut non possit pervenire ad finem intentum; sicut cum aliquis cadit in via propter lassitudinem.

Tum etiam propter indispositionem materiae, quae non recipit formam intentam ab agente, sed alterius modi sicut accidit in monstruosis partibus animalium.

1211. Haec autem contingentia, si ulterius in causam caelestem reducantur, multa horum invenientur non esse per accidens; quia causae particulares etsi non continentur sub se invicem, continentur tamen sub una causa communi caelesti; unde concursus earum potest habere aliquam unam causam caelestem determinatam.

Quia etiam virtus corporis caelestis et incorruptibilis est et impassibilis, non potest exire aliquis effectus ordinem causalitatis eius propter defectum vel debilitatem ipsius virtutis. Sed quia agit movendo, et omne tale agens requirit materiam determinatam et dispositam, potest contingere quod in rebus naturalibus virtus caelestis non consequatur suum effectum propter materiae indispositionem; et hoc erit per accidens.

1212. Quamvis igitur multa, quae videntur esse per accidens reducendo ipsa ad causas particulares, inveniantur non esse per accidens reducendo ipsa ad causam communem universalem, scilicet virtutem caelestem, tamen etiam hac reductione facta, inveniuntur esse aliqua per accidens, sicut superius est habitum a Philosopho. Quando enim agens aliquod inducit effectum suum ut in pluribus, et non semper, sequetur, quod deficiat in paucioribus, et hoc per accidens est. Si igitur corpora caelestia effectos suos inducunt in inferiora corpora, ut in pluribus, et non semper, propter materiae indispositionem, sequetur, quod ipsum sit per accidens, quod virtus caelestis effectum suum non consequatur.

1213. Licet etiam ex hoc inveniantur aliqua per accidens, facta reductione ad corpus caeleste: quia in istis inferioribus sunt aliquae causae agentes, quae possunt per se agere absque impressione corporis caelestis, scilicet animae rationales, ad quas non pertingit virtus corporis caelestis (cum sint formae corporibus non subiectae), nisi forte per accidens, inquantum scilicet ex impressione corporis caelestis fit aliqua immutatio in corpore, et per accidens in viribus animae, quae sunt actus quarumdam partium corporis, ex quibus anima rationalis inclinatur ad agendum,

licet nulla necessitas inducatur, cum habeat liberum dominium super passiones, ut eis dissentiat. Illa igitur, quae in his inferioribus inveniuntur per accidens fieri reducendo ad has causas, scilicet animas rationales, prout non sequuntur inclinationem, quae est ex impressione

Second, because of some defect in the agent, who is so weak that he cannot attain the goal at which he aims—for example, when someone falls on the road because of fatigue.

Third, because of the indisposition of the matter, which does not receive the form intended by the agent, but another kind of form. This is what occurs, for example, in the case of the deformed parts of animals.

1211. But if these contingent events are traced back further to a celestial body, we find that many of them are not accidental; because even though particular causes are not contained under each other, they are nevertheless contained under one common celestial cause. Hence their concurrence can be attributed to one definite celestial cause.

Again, since the power of a celestial body is incorruptible and impassible, no effect can escape from the sphere of its causality because of any defect or weakness of its power. But since it acts by moving, and since every agent of this kind requires a matter which is properly determined or disposed, then in the case of natural beings it can happen that the power of a celestial body fails to produce its effect because the matter is not disposed, and this will be accidental.

1212. Therefore, even though many things that seem to be accidental when traced back to these particular causes are found not to be accidental when traced back to a common universal cause (namely, to a celestial body), yet even when this reduction has been made, some things are found to be accidental, as the Philosopher stated above [1201]. For when an agent produces its effect for the most part but not always, it follows that it fails in a few instances, and this is accidental. If, then, the celestial bodies cause their effects in these lower bodies for the most part but not always, because the matter is not properly disposed, then it follows that when the power of a celestial body fails to produce its effect, this happens accidentally.

1213. There is also another reason why things happen accidentally even if causality is traced back to a celestial body. In the sphere of lower bodies, there are some efficient causes which can act of themselves without the influence of a celestial body. These causes are rational souls, to which the power of a celestial body does not extend (since they are not forms subjected to bodies), except in an accidental way, that is, inasmuch as the influence of a celestial body produces some change in the human body, and accidentally in the powers of the soul which are the acts of certain parts of the body, by which the rational soul is disposed to act.

However, no necessity is involved, since the soul's dominion over the passions is free inasmuch as it may not assent to them. Therefore, in the sphere of lower bodies, whatever things are found to happen accidentally when reduced to these causes—that is, rational souls, insofar as

caelesti, non invenientur per se fieri per reductionem ad virtutem corporis caelestis.

1214. Et sic patet, quod positio fati, quae est quaedam dispositio inhaerens rebus inferioribus ex actione corporis caelestis, non removet omnia ea quae sunt per accidens.

1215. Sed si ulterius ista contingentia reducantur in causam altissimam divinam, nihil inveniri poterit, quod ab ordine eius exeat, cum eius causalitas extendat se ad omnia inquantum sunt entia. Non potest igitur sua causalitas impediri per indispositionem materiae; quia et ipsa materia, et eius dispositiones non exeunt ab ordine illius agentis, quod est agens per modum dantis esse, et non solum per modum moventis et alterantis. Non enim potest dici, quod materia praesupponatur ad esse, sicut praesupponitur ad moveri, ut eius subiectum; quinimo est pars essentiae rei.

Sicut igitur virtus alterantis et moventis non impeditur ex essentia motus, aut ex termino eius, sed ex subiecto, quod praesupponitur; ita virtus dantis esse non impeditur a materia, vel a quocumque, quod adveniat qualitercumque ad esse rei. Ex quo etiam patet, quod nulla causa agens potest esse in istis inferioribus, quae eius ordini non subdatur.

1216. Relinquitur igitur quod omnia, quae hic fiunt, prout ad primam causam divinam referuntur, inveniuntur ordinata et non per accidens existere; licet per comparationem ad alias causas per accidens esse inveniantur. Et propter hoc secundum fidem Catholicam dicitur, quod nihil fit temere sive fortuito in mundo, et quod omnia subduntur divinae providentiae. Aristoteles autem hic loquitur de contingentibus quae hic fiunt, in ordine ad causas particulares, sicut per eius exemplum apparet.

1217. Nunc autem restat videre quomodo positio fati et providentiae non tollit a rebus contingentiam, quasi omnia ex necessitate eveniant. Et de fato quidem manifestum est per ea quae dicta sunt. Iam enim est ostensum, quod licet corpora caelestia et eorum motus et actiones quantum in ipsis est necessitatem habeant, tamen effectus eorum in istis inferioribus potest deficere, vel propter indispositionem materiae, vel propter animam rationalem quae habet liberam electionem sequendi inclinationes, quae sunt ex impressione caelesti, vel non sequendi: et ita relinquitur, quod huiusmodi effectus non ex necessitate, sed contingenter proveniant. Non enim positio causae caelestis est positio causae talis, ad quam de necessitate sequatur effectus, sicut ad com-

they do not follow the inclination produced by the influence of a celestial body—will not be found to be generated in any essential way by being traced back to the power of a celestial body.

1214. Thus it is evident that to posit fate, which is a certain disposition present in lower bodies as a result of the action of a celestial body, is not to do away with everything that happens by chance.

1215. But if these contingent events are traced back further to the highest, divine cause, it will be impossible to find anything that lies outside its sphere of influence, since its causality extends to all things insofar as they are beings. Hence its causal activity cannot be thwarted as a result of the matter being indisposed, because matter itself and its dispositions do not lie outside the domain of this agent, since he is the agent who gives things their being and not merely moves and changes them. For it cannot be said that matter is presupposed as the subject of being as it is presupposed as the subject of motion; it is rather part of the essence of a thing.

Therefore, just as the power of changing and moving is not hindered by the essence of motion or its terminus, but by the subject which is presupposed, in a similar fashion the power of the one giving being is not hindered by matter or anything which accrues in any way to the being of a thing. From this it is also evident that, in the sphere of lower bodies, no efficient cause can be found which is not subject to the control of this first cause.

1216. It follows, then, that everything which occurs here, insofar as it is related to the first divine cause, is found to be ordained by it and not to be accidental, although it may be found to be accidental in relation to other causes. This is why the Catholic faith says that nothing in the world happens by chance or fortuitously, and that everything is subject to divine providence. But in this place, Aristotle is speaking of those contingent events which occur here as a result of particular causes, as is evident from his example.

1217. It now remains to see how the affirming of fate and providence does not eliminate contingency from the world, as though all things were to happen of necessity. From the things that have been said above it is evident that fate does not do away with contingency. For it has been shown already that, even though the celestial bodies and their motions and activities are necessary, nevertheless their effects in these lower bodies can fail either because the matter is not disposed or because the rational soul may freely choose to follow or not follow the inclinations produced in it by the influence of a celestial body. Thus it follows that effects of this sort do not happen of necessity, but contingently. For to posit a celestial cause is not to posit a cause of such a kind that its effect follows of necessity, as

positionem ex contrariis sequitur mors animalis, ut in litera tangitur.

1218. Sed de providentia maiorem habet difficultatem. Providentia enim divina falli non potest. Haec enim duo sunt incompossibilia, quod aliquid sit provisum a Deo, et non fiat: et ita videtur, quod ex quo providentia iam ponitur, quod eius effectum necesse sit sequi.

1219. Sed sciendum est, quod ex eadem causa dependet effectus, et omnia quae sunt per se accidentia illius effectus. Sicut enim homo est a natura, ita et omnia eius per se accidentia, ut risibile, et mentis disciplinae susceptibile. Si autem aliqua causa non faciat hominem simpliciter sed hominem talem, eius non erit constituere ea quae sunt per se accidentia hominis, sed solum uti eis. Politicus enim facit hominem civilem; non tamen facit eum mentis disciplinae susceptibilem, sed hac eius proprietate utitur ad hoc quod homo fiat civilis.

1220. Sicut autem dictum est, ens inquantum ens est, habet causam ipsum Deum: unde sicut divinae providentiae subditur ipsum ens, ita etiam omnia accidentia entis inquantum est ens, inter quae sunt necessarium et contingens. Ad divinam igitur providentiam pertinet non solum quod faciat hoc ens, sed quod det ei contingentiam vel necessitatem. Secundum enim quod unicuique dare voluit contingentiam vel necessitatem, praeparavit ei causas medias, ex quibus de necessitate sequatur, vel contingenter. Invenitur igitur uniuscuiusque effectus secundum quod est sub ordine divinae providentiae necessitatem habere. Ex quo contingit quod haec conditionalis est vera, si aliquid est a Deo provisum, hoc erit.

1221. Secundum autem quod effectus aliquis consideratur sub ordine causae proximae, sic non omnis effectus est necessarius; sed quidam necessarius et quidam contingens secundum analogiam suae causae. Effectus enim in suis naturis similantur causis proximis, non autem remotis, ad quarum conditionem pertingere non possunt.

1222. Sic ergo patet, quod cum de divina providentia loquimur, non est dicendum solum, hoc est provisum a Deo ut sit, sed hoc est provisum a Deo, ut contingenter sit, vel ut necessario sit. Unde non sequitur secundum rationem Aristotelis hic inductam, quod ex quo divina providentia est posita, quod omnes effectus sint necessarii; sed necessarium est effectus esse contingenter, vel de necessitate. Quod quidem est singulare in hac causa, scilicet in divina providentia. Reliquae enim causae non constituunt legem necessitatis vel contingentiae, sed constituta a superiori causa utuntur. Unde causalitati cuiuslibet alterius causae subditur solum quod eius effectus sit. Quod autem sit necessario vel contingenter, depen-

the death of an animal is a result of its being composed of contraries, as he mentions in the text.

1218. But there is greater difficulty with regard to providence, because divine providence cannot fail; for these two statements are incompatible, namely, that something is foreknown by God and that it does not come to pass. Hence it seems that, once providence is posited, its effect follows of necessity.

1219. But it must be noted that an effect and all of its proper accidents depend on one and the same cause; for just as a man is from nature, so also are his proper accidents, such as risibility and susceptibility to mental instruction. However, if some cause does not produce man in an absolute sense, but such and such a man, it will not be within the power of this cause to produce the proper attributes of man, but only to make use of them. For while the statesman makes man a citizen, he does not make him susceptible to mental instruction. Rather, he makes use of this property in order to make a citizen of him.

1220. Now, as has been pointed out [1215], being as being has God himself as its cause. Hence, just as being itself is subject to divine providence, so also are all the accidents of being as being, among which are found necessity and contingency. Therefore, it belongs to divine providence not only to produce a particular being but also to give it contingency or necessity, for insofar as God wills to give contingency or necessity to anything, he has prepared for it certain intermediate causes from which it follows either of necessity or contingently. Hence the effect of every cause is found to be necessary insofar as it comes under the control of providence. And from this it follows that this conditional proposition is true: "If anything is foreknown by God, it will be."

1221. However, insofar as any effect is considered to come under its proximate cause, not every effect is necessary, but some are necessary and some contingent in proportion to their cause. For effects are likened in their nature to their proximate causes, but not to their remote causes, whose state they cannot attain.

1222. It is evident, then, that when we speak of divine providence, we must say that this thing is foreseen by God not only insofar as it is, but also insofar as it is either contingent or necessary. Therefore, just because divine providence is held to exist, it does not follow, according to the argument which Aristotle gives here, that every effect happens of necessity, but only that it must be either contingent or necessary. In fact, this applies solely in the case of this cause (that is, divine providence), because the remaining causes do not establish the law of necessity or contingency, but make use of this law established by a higher cause. Hence the only thing that is subject to the causality of any other cause is that its effect exist. But that it be either

det ex causa altiori, quae est causa entis inquantum est ens; a qua ordo necessitatis et contingentiae in rebus provenit.

necessary or contingent depends on a higher cause, which is the cause of being as being, and the one from which the order of necessity and of contingency originates in the world.

LECTURE 4

Kinds of being not investigated by metaphysics

1027b17 Quod autem ut verum, ens; et non ens, ut falsum, quoniam secundum compositionem et divisionem, totaliter autem circa partitionem contradictionis. Verum quidem enim affirmationem contradictionis in composito habet, negationem vero in disiuncto. Sed falsum huius partitionis contradictionem. [1223]

περὶ μὲν οὖν τοῦ κατὰ συμβεβηκὸς ὄντος ἀφείσθω (διώρισται γὰρ ἱκανῶς): τὸ δὲ ὡς ἀληθὲς ὄν, καὶ μὴ ὂν ὡς ψεῦδος, ἐπειδὴ παρὰ σύνθεσίν ἐστι καὶ διαίρεσιν, τὸ δὲ σύνολον {20} περὶ μερισμὸν ἀντιφάσεως (τὸ μὲν γὰρ ἀληθὲς τὴν κατάφασιν ἐπὶ τῷ συγκειμένῳ ἔχει τὴν δ' ἀπόφασιν ἐπὶ τῷ διῃρημένῳ, τὸ δὲ ψεῦδος τούτου τοῦ μερισμοῦ τὴν ἀντίφασιν:

Again, being in the sense of the true and non-being in the sense of the false are not to be considered, since such being depends on combination and separation, and these taken together form both parts of a contradiction. For truth resides in the affirmation of one side of a contradiction when there is combination, and in negation when there is separation. But falsity consists in the reverse of this division.

1027b23 Quomodo autem quod simul aut quod separatim intelligere accidit, alius sermo. [1227]

πῶς δὲ τὸ ἅμα ἢ τὸ χωρὶς νοεῖν συμβαίνει, ἄλλος λόγος,

But how the intellect happens to understand things that are combined and separated, whether together or separately, pertains to another discussion;

Dico autem quod simul et separatim, non ut eo consequenter, sed in unum aliquid fieri.

λέγω δὲ τὸ ἅμα καὶ τὸ χωρὶς ὥστε μὴ τὸ ἐφεξῆς {25} ἀλλ' ἕν τι γίγνεσθαι):

and by "understanding things together or separately," I mean understanding them not successively but insofar as they form a unity.

1027b25 Non est autem verum et falsum in rebus, ut quod quid bonum verum, quod autem malum falsum, sed in mente. Circa vero simplicia et quid est nec in mente est. Igitur quaecumque oportet speculari circa sic ens et non ens, posterius perscrutandum est. [1230]

οὐ γάρ ἐστι τὸ ψεῦδος καὶ τὸ ἀληθὲς ἐν τοῖς πράγμασιν, οἷον τὸ μὲν ἀγαθὸν ἀληθὲς τὸ δὲ κακὸν εὐθὺς ψεῦδος, ἀλλ' ἐν διανοίᾳ, περὶ δὲ τὰ ἁπλᾶ καὶ τὰ τί ἐστιν οὐδ' ἐν διανοίᾳ: ὅσα μὲν οὖν δεῖ θεωρῆσαι περὶ τὸ οὕτως ὂν καὶ μὴ ὄν, ὕστερον ἐπισκεπτέον:

For what is true and what is false are not in things themselves, so that what is good is true and what is evil is false, but only in the mind. And with regard to simple concepts and the whatness of things, there is neither truth nor falsity in the mind. Hence everything that must be investigated about being and non-being in this sense must be considered later on (1051a34).

1027b29 Quoniam autem complexio et divisio est in mente et non in rebus. Quod autem ita ens, alterum ens a propriis: aut enim quia quid est, aut quia quale, aut quia quantum, aut si quid aliud copulat aut dividit mens. Quod quidem ut accidens, et quod ut verum ens, praetermittendum. [1241]

ἐπεὶ δὲ ἡ συμπλοκή {30} ἐστιν καὶ ἡ διαίρεσις ἐν διανοίᾳ ἀλλ' οὐκ ἐν τοῖς πράγμασι, τὸ δ' οὕτως ὂν ἕτερον ὂν τῶν κυρίως (ἢ γὰρ τὸ τί ἐστιν ἢ ὅτι ποιὸν ἢ ὅτι ποσὸν ἤ τι ἄλλο συνάπτει ἢ ἀφαιρεῖ ἡ διάνοια), τὸ μὲν ὡς συμβεβηκὸς καὶ τὸ ὡς ἀληθὲς ὂν ἀφετέον—

But since combination and separation exist in thought and not in things, and being in this sense is different from being in the proper senses (for these are either what a thing is, or of what sort, or how much, or anything else that the mind combines or separates), then being in the sense of what is accidental and being in the sense of what is true must be omitted from this science.

Causa enim huius quidem indefinita, illius vero mentis aliqua passio, et utraque circa reliquum genus entis, et non extra ostendunt entem aliquam naturam entis. Quapropter ea quidem praetermittantur. Perscrutanda vero sunt ipsius entis causae et principia, inquantum ens. Palam autem in

τὸ γὰρ αἴτιον τοῦ μὲν ἀόριστον τοῦ δὲ τῆς διανοίας τι πάθος, {1028a1} καὶ ἀμφότερα περὶ τὸ λοιπὸν γένος τοῦ ὄντος, καὶ οὐκ ἔξω δηλοῦσιν οὖσάν τινα φύσιν τοῦ ὄντος—διὸ ταῦτα μὲν ἀφείσθω, σκεπτέον δὲ τοῦ ὄντος αὐτοῦ τὰ αἴτια καὶ τὰς ἀρχὰς ᾗ ὄν. [φανερὸν δ' ἐν οἷς διωρισάμεθα περὶ {5} τοῦ ποσαχῶς

For the cause of the former is the indeterminate, and of the latter some positive state of mind. Both of these pertain to the remaining genus of being and do not indicate the existence of any definite kind of being outside of the mind. For this reason, then, let us exclude them from our study, and let us look for the causes and

quibus determinavimus de eo quoties unumquodque dicitur, quia multipliciter dicitur ens.

λέγεται ἕκαστον, ὅτι πολλαχῶς λέγεται τὸ ὄν.]

principles of being as being. Now, from our discussions of the different meanings of words, it is evident that "being" is used in several senses (1017a7).

1223. Postquam determinavit Philosophus de ente per accidens, hic determinat de ente, quod significat veritatem propositionis: et circa hoc duo facit.

Primo determinat qualiter dicatur huiusmodi ens.

Secundo removet ipsum a principali consideratione huius scientiae, ibi, *quoniam autem complexio* et cetera.
Circa primum tria facit.
Primo ostendit qualiter huiusmodi ens dicatur.
Secundo respondet cuidam quaestioni, ibi, *quomodo autem quod simul* et cetera.
Tertio manifestat quoddam quod dixerat, ibi, *non est autem verum et falsum in rebus* et cetera.
Dicit ergo *quod ens quoddam dicitur quasi verum*, idest quod nihil aliud significat nisi veritatem. Cum enim interrogamus si homo est animal, respondetur quod est; per quod significatur, propositionem praemissam esse veram. Et eodem modo non ens significat quasi falsum. Cum enim respondetur, non est, significatur quod proposita oratio sit falsa. Hoc autem ens, quod dicitur quasi verum, et non ens, quod dicitur quasi falsum, consistit circa compositionem et divisionem. Voces enim incomplexae neque verum neque falsum significant; sed voces complexae, per affirmationem aut negationem veritatem aut falsitatem habent. Dicitur autem hic affirmatio compositio, quia significat praedicatum inesse subiecto. Negatio vero dicitur hic divisio, quia significat praedicatum a subiecto removeri.

1224. Et cum voces sint signa intellectuum, similiter dicendum est de conceptionibus intellectus. Quae enim sunt simplices, non habent veritatem neque falsitatem, sed solum illae quae sunt complexae per affirmationem vel negationem.

1225. Et quia praedictum ens et non ens, scilicet verum et falsum, consistit in compositione et divisione, ideo similiter consistit circa partitionem contradictionis. Unaquaeque enim contradictionum partiuntur sibi invicem verum et falsum; ita quod altera pars est vera, et altera pars est falsa. Cum enim contradictio ex affirmatione et negatione constituatur, utraque autem harum ex praedicato sit et subiecto, praedicatum et subiectum dupliciter se possunt habere. Aut enim sunt coniuncta in rerum natura, sicut homo et animal; aut sunt disiuncta, ut homo et asinus.

1226. Si ergo formantur duae contradictiones: una ex terminis coniunctis, ut, homo est animal, homo non est animal; alia ex terminis disiunctis, ut, homo est asinus,

---

1223. Having drawn his conclusions about accidental being, the Philosopher now settles the issue about the being which signifies the truth of a proposition, and in regard to this he does two things.
First (1027b17; [1223]), he determines the meaning of this kind of being.
Second (1027b29; [1241]), he excludes it from the principal study of this science, at *but since combination*.
In regard to the first he does three things.
First, he determines the meaning of this kind of being.
Second (1027b23; [1227]), he answers a question, at *but how the intellect*.
Third (1027b25; [1230]), he clarifies a statement which he had made, at *for what is true*.
He says, then, that *in one sense being means what is true*, that is, it signifies nothing else than truth. For when we ask whether man is an animal, the answer is that he is, by which it is meant that this proposition is true. And in the same way, "non-being" signifies in a sense what is false, for when one answers that he is not, it is meant that the statement made is false. Now this being which means what is true, and non-being which means what is false, depend on combination and separation; for simple terms signify neither truth nor falsity, whereas complex terms have truth and falsity through affirmation or negation. And here affirmation is called combination because it signifies that a predicate belongs to a subject, whereas negation is called separation because it signifies that a predicate does not belong to a subject.

1224. Further, since words are the signs of concepts, we must speak in the same way about the concepts of the intellect; for those which are simple do not have truth and falsity, but only those which are complex through affirmation or negation.

1225. And since the being and non-being just mentioned—the true and the false—depend on combination and separation, they therefore also depend on the division of a contradiction. For each part of a contradiction separates the true and the false from each other such that one part is true and the other is false. For, since a contradiction is constituted of an affirmation and a negation, and each of these is constituted of a predicate and a subject, then a predicate and a subject can be related to each other in two ways; because they are either connected in reality, as man and animal, or are unconnected, as man and ass.

1226. Hence, if two contradictions are formed, one from connected terms, as "Man is an animal" and "Man is not an animal," and another from unconnected terms, as "Man is

---

homo non est asinus, utramque contradictionem inter se condividunt verum et falsum; ita quod verum pro parte sua *habet affirmationem in composito*, idest in terminis coniunctis, et *negationem in disiuncto*, idest in terminis disiunctis. Hae enim duae sunt verae, homo est animal et homo non est asinus. Sed falsum pro sua parte habet *contradictionem partitionis*, idest contradictoria eorum, quae cedunt in partem veri. Habet enim falsum pro sua parte negationem in coniuncto, et affirmationem in disiuncto. Hae enim duae sunt falsae, homo non est animal, et homo est asinus.

1227. Deinde cum dicit *quomodo autem* removet quamdam dubitationem, quae posset occasionari ex dictis. Dixerat enim quod verum et falsum consistunt in compositione et divisione, vocum quidem secundario, intellectus autem primo et principaliter: omnis autem compositio vel divisio plurium est: et ideo potest esse dubium, quomodo ista quae componuntur et dividuntur, intellectus intelligat: utrum scilicet simul, aut separatim. Sed dicit, quod hoc pertinet ad alium sermonem, scilicet ad librum *De anima*.

1228. Et quia simul dupliciter dicitur,

quandoque enim significat unitatem, sicut dicimus simul esse secundum tempus quae sunt in uno et eodem instanti:

quandoque vero significat coniunctionem et vicinitatem eorum quae consequenter se habent, sicut dicimus duos homines esse simul secundum locum, quorum loca sunt coniuncta et consequenter se habentia, et secundum tempus, quae se tempore consequuntur:

ideo exponit quaestionem motam, qua quaesivit utrum simul aut separatim intelligat intellectus ea quae componuntur et dividuntur: dicens, quod non intelligit simul secundum quod aliqua dicuntur esse simul, ut consequenter se habent; sed secundum quod aliqua dicuntur esse simul in eo quod fit aliquid unum.

1229. Et in hoc innuitur solutio quaestionis. Si enim intellectus intelligat hominem et animal unumquodque secundum se, ut sunt duo quaedam, intelligit ea consequenter duabus conceptionibus simplicibus, non formans ex eis affirmationem neque negationem. Cum autem ex eis format compositionem vel divisionem, intelligit ambo ut unum, inquantum scilicet ex eis aliquod unum fit: sicut etiam partes cuiuslibet totius intelligit intellectus ut unum, intelligendo ipsum totum. Non enim intelligit domum intelligendo prius fundamentum et postea parietem et postea tectum; sed omnia ista intelligit simul, inquantum ex eis fit unum. Similiter intelligit

an ass" and "Man is not an ass," then truth and falsity divide each contradiction between themselves, so that the true on its side *resides in affirmation when there is combination*, that is, in connected terms, and *in negation when there is separation*, that is, in unconnected terms. For these two propositions, "Man is an animal" and "Man is not an ass," are true. But the false on its side resides in *the reverse of this division*, that is, in the contradictory of those statements which fall on the side of the true, because it consists in the negating of connected terms and in the affirming of unconnected terms; for these two propositions "Man is not an animal" and "Man is an ass" are false.

1227. *But how the intellect* (1027b23). Here he dismisses a problem that could arise from the foregoing remarks. For he said that the true and the false consist secondarily in the combination and separation of words, but primarily and properly in the combination and separation which the intellect makes. Now every combination and separation involves a plurality, and therefore the problem can arise of how the intellect understands things that are combined and separated, whether together or separately. But he says that this pertains to another discussion, namely, to *On the Soul*.

1228. Now "together" is used in two senses.

For sometimes it signifies a unity, as when we say that those things that exist at one and the same instant are together in time;

and sometimes it signifies the connection and proximity of things that succeed each other, as when we say that two men are together in place when their places are joined and next to each other, and in time when their times succeed each other.

And since this is so, he therefore answers the proposed question which asks whether the intellect understands things that are combined or separated, together or separately, by saying that it does not understand them together according as some things are said to be together insofar as they succeed each other, but according as they are said to be together insofar as they form one thing.

1229. And in this way he indicates the solution of this question. For if the intellect understands a man and an animal as they are in themselves, as two distinct things, it understands them successively by two simple concepts without forming an affirmation or a negation from them. But when it combines or separates them, it understands them both as one thing, according as one thing is constituted from them, just as the intellect also understands the parts of a whole as one thing by understanding the whole itself. For the intellect does not understand a house by understanding first the foundation and then the walls and then the roof, but it understands all of these together

praedicatum et subiectum simul, inquantum ex eis fit unum, scilicet affirmatio et negatio.

1230. Deinde cum dicit *non est autem*. Manifestat quoddam quod dixerat scilicet quod verum et falsum sint in compositione et divisione. Quod quidem probat per modum cuiusdam divisionis. Eorum enim, quae dicuntur voce, quaedam sunt in rebus extra animam, quaedam autem sunt in anima tantum. Album enim et nigrum sunt extra animam; sed rationes horum sunt in anima tantum.

Posset autem aliquis credere, quod verum et falsum sint etiam in rebus sicut bonum et malum; ita quod verum sit quoddam bonum, et falsum sit quoddam malum: hoc enim oporteret si verum et falsum essent in rebus. Verum enim quamdam perfectionem naturae significat, falsum vero defectum.

Omnis autem perfectio in rebus existens, ad perfectionem et bonitatem naturae pertinet, defectus vero et privatio ad malitiam.

1231. Sed ipse hoc negat; dicens, quod verum et falsum non sunt in rebus, ita quod verum rationis sit quoddam bonum naturae, et falsum sit quoddam malum; sed *sunt tantum in mente*, idest in intellectu.

1232. Intellectus autem habet duas operationes,

quarum una vocatur indivisibilium intelligentia, per quam intellectus format simplices conceptiones rerum intelligendo quod quid est uniuscuiusque rei.

Alia eius operatio est per quam componit et dividit.

1233. Verum autem et falsum, etsi sint in mente, non tamen sunt circa illam operationem mentis, qua intellectus format simplices conceptiones, et quod quid est rerum. Et hoc est quod dicit, quod *verum et falsum, circa simplicia et quod quid est, nec in mente est*. Unde relinquitur per locum a divisione, quod ex quo non est in rebus, nec est in mente circa simplicia et quod quid est, quod sit circa compositionem et divisionem mentis primo et principaliter; et secundario vocis, quae significat conceptionem mentis.

Et ulterius concludit, quod *quaecumque oportet speculari circa ens et non ens sic dictum*, scilicet prout ens significat verum, et non ens falsum, *posterius perscrutandum est*, scilicet in fine noni et etiam in libro *De anima*, et in logicalibus. Tota enim logica videtur esse de ente et non ente sic dicto.

insofar as one thing is constituted from them. And in a similar way it understands a predicate and a subject together insofar as one judgment is constituted from them, namely, an affirmation or a negation.

1230. *For what is true* (1027b25). He explains a statement which he had made to the effect that truth and falsity consist in combination and separation, and he proves this by means of the process of division. For some of the things signified by a word are found in things outside of the mind, but others are found only in the mind. For white and black are found outside of the mind, but their concepts are found only in the mind.

Now, someone might think that the true and the false are also found in things, just as good and evil are, so that the true is a kind of good and the false a kind of evil. For this would be necessary if truth and falsity were found in things, since truth signifies a certain perfection of nature, and falsity a defect.

Moreover, every perfection existing in things pertains to the perfection and goodness of their nature, whereas every defect and privation pertains to evil.

1231. But he denies this, saying that the true and the false are not found in things in such a way that what is true on the part of reason is a kind of natural good, and what is false a kind of evil, but *they are only in the mind*, or intellect.

1232. The intellect, however, has two operations.

One of these is called the understanding of indivisibles, and this is the operation by which the intellect forms simple concepts of things by understanding the whatness of each one of them.

The other operation is that by which the intellect combines and separates.

1233. Now, while truth and falsity are in the mind, they do not pertain to that operation by which the mind forms simple concepts and the whatness of things. This is what he means when he says *with regard to simple concepts and the whatness of things, there is neither truth nor falsity in the mind*. Hence, as a result of this process of division, it follows that, since truth and falsity are neither in things nor in the mind when it apprehends simple concepts and the whatness of things, they must pertain primarily and principally to the combination and separation which the mind makes, and secondarily to that of words, which signify the mind's conceptions.

Further, he concludes that *everything which must be considered about being and non-being in this sense*, namely, insofar as being signifies the true, and non-being the false, *must be considered later on*, meaning at the end of book 9 [1895], and also in *On the Soul*, and in his works on logic. For the whole of logic seems to be devoted to the being and non-being spoken of in this way.

1234. Sciendum est autem, quod cum quaelibet cognitio perficiatur per hoc quod similitudo rei cognitae est in cognoscente; sicut perfectio rei cognitae consistit in hoc quod habet talem formam per quam est res talis, ita perfectio cognitionis consistit in hoc, quod habet similitudinem formae praedictae.

Ex hoc autem, quod res cognita habet formam sibi debitam, dicitur esse bona; et ex hoc, quod aliquem defectum habet, dicitur esse mala. Et eodem modo ex hoc quod cognoscens habet similitudinem rei cognitae, dicitur habere veram cognitionem: ex hoc vero, quod deficit a tali similitudine, dicitur falsam cognitionem habere. Sicut ergo bonum et malum designant perfectiones, quae sunt in rebus: ita verum et falsum designant perfectiones cognitionum.

1235. Licet autem in cognitione sensitiva possit esse similitudo rei cognitae, non tamen rationem huius similitudinis cognoscere ad sensum pertinet, sed solum ad intellectum. Et ideo, licet sensus de sensibili possit esse verus, tamen sensus veritatem non cognoscit, sed solum intellectus: et propter hoc dicitur quod verum et falsum sunt in mente.

1236. Intellectus autem habet apud se similitudinem rei intellectae, secundum quod rationes incomplexorum concipit; non tamen propter hoc ipsam similitudinem diiudicat, sed solum cum componit vel dividit. Cum enim intellectus concipit hoc quod est animal rationale mortale, apud se similitudinem hominis habet; sed non propter hoc cognoscit se hanc similitudinem habere, quia non iudicat hominem esse animal rationale et mortale: et ideo in hac sola secunda operatione intellectus est veritas et falsitas, secundum quam non solum intellectus habet similitudinem rei intellectae, sed etiam super ipsam similitudinem reflectitur, cognoscendo et diiudicando ipsam. Ex his igitur patet, quod veritas non est in rebus, sed solum in mente, et etiam in compositione et divisione.

1237. Et si res dicatur aliquando falsa, vel etiam definitio, hoc erit in ordine ad affirmationem et ad negationem. Dicitur enim res falsa, ut in fine quinti habitum est, aut quae non est omnino, sicut diametrum commensurabilem; aut quia est quidem, sed est apta nata videri aliter quam sit. Et similiter definitio dicitur falsa aut quia nullius, vel quia assignatur alteri quam ei cuius est. In omnibus enim his modis patet quod falsum in rebus vel in definitionibus dicitur, ratione falsae enunciationis de ipsis.

1238. Et similiter patet de vero. Nam res dicitur vera, quando habet propriam formam, quae ei ostenditur

1234. Now it must be noted that any kind of knowing attains its completion as a result of the likeness of the thing known existing in the knowing subject. Therefore, just as the completion of the thing known depends upon this thing having the kind of form which makes it to be such and such a thing, in a similar fashion the completion of the act of knowing depends upon the knowing subject having the likeness of this form.

Moreover, just as the thing known is said to be good because it has the form which it ought to have, and evil because it is defective in some way, in a similar fashion the knowledge of the knowing subject is said to be true because this subject possesses a likeness of the thing known, and false because its knowledge falls short of such a likeness. Therefore, just as good and evil designate perfections of things, in a similar way truth and falsity designate perfections of knowledge.

1235. But even though in sensory perception there can be a likeness of the thing known, nevertheless it does not belong to the senses to know the formality of this likeness, but only to the intellect. Hence, even though the senses can be true in relation to sensible objects, they still cannot know the truth, but only the intellect can do this. And this is why it is said that truth and falsity are in the mind.

1236. And although the intellect has within itself a likeness of the things known according as it forms concepts of incomplex things, it does not for that reason make a judgment about this likeness. This occurs only when it combines or separates. For when the intellect forms a concept of "mortal rational animal," it has within itself a likeness of man, but it does not for that reason know that it has this likeness, since it does not judge that "Man is a mortal rational animal." There is truth and falsity, then, only in this second operation of the intellect, according to which it not only possesses a likeness of the thing known but also reflects on this likeness by knowing it and by making a judgment about it. Hence it is evident from this that truth is not found in things, but only in the mind, and that it depends upon combination and separation.

1237. And if a thing is sometimes said to be false, and the same applies to a definition, this will be so in reference to affirmation and negation. For a false thing, as is said at the end of book 5 [1128], means one that does not exist in any way (for example, the commensurability of a diagonal) or one that exists but is naturally disposed to appear otherwise than it is. Similarly, a definition is said to be false either because it is not the definition of any existing thing or because it is assigned to something other than that of which it is the definition. For it is evident that falsity is said to be in things or in definitions in all of these ways by reason of a false statement made about them.

1238. The same thing is evident in the case of truth. For a thing is said to be true when it has the proper form which

inesse. Et definitio vera, quae vere competit ei cui assignatur.

1239. Patet etiam quod nihil prohibet verum esse quoddam bonum, secundum quod intellectus cognoscens accipitur ut quaedam res. Sicut enim quaelibet alia res dicitur bona sua perfectione, ita intellectus cognoscens, sua veritate.

1240. Apparet etiam ex his quae hic dicuntur, quod verum et falsum, quae sunt obiecta cognitionis, sunt in mente. Bonum vero et malum, quae sunt obiecta appetitus, sunt in rebus. Item quod, sicut cognitio perficitur per hoc quod res cognitae sunt in cognoscente, ita appetitus quicumque perficitur per ordinem appetentis ad res appetibiles.

1241. Deinde cum dicit *quoniam autem* excludit ens verum et ens per accidens a principali consideratione huius doctrinae; dicens, quod compositio et divisio, in quibus est verum et falsum, est in mente, et non in rebus. Invenitur siquidem et in rebus aliqua compositio; sed talis compositio efficit unam rem, quam intellectus recipit ut unum simplici conceptione.

Sed illa compositio vel divisio, qua intellectus coniungit vel dividit sua concepta, est tantum in intellectu, non in rebus. Consistit enim in quadam duorum comparatione conceptorum; sive illa duo sint idem secundum rem, sive diversa. Utitur enim intellectus quandoque uno ut duobus compositionem formans; sicut dicitur, homo est homo: ex quo patet quod talis compositio est solum in intellectu, non in rebus. Et ideo illud, quod est ita ens sicut verum in tali compositione consistens, est alterum ab his quae proprie sunt entia, quae sunt res extra animam, quarum unaquaeque est *aut quod quid est*, idest substantia, aut quale, aut quantum, aut aliquod incomplexum, quod mens copulat vel dividit.

1242. Et ideo utrumque est praetermittendum; scilicet et ens per accidens, et ens quod significat verum; quia huius, scilicet entis per accidens, causa est indeterminata, et ideo non cadit sub arte, ut ostensum est. Illius vero, scilicet entis veri, causa est *aliqua passio mentis*, idest operatio intellectus componentis et dividentis. Et ideo pertinet ad scientiam de intellectu.

1243. Et alia ratio est, quia *utrumque*, scilicet ens verum et ens per accidens, sunt circa aliquod genus entis, non circa ens simpliciter per se quod est in rebus; et non ostendunt aliquam aliam naturam entis existentem extra per se entia. Patet enim quod ens per accidens est ex concursu accidentaliter entium extra animam,

is shown to be present in it, and a definition is said to be true when it really fits the thing to which it is assigned.

1239. It is also evident that nothing prevents truth from being a kind of good insofar as the knowing intellect is taken as a thing. For just as every other thing is said to be good because of its perfection, in a similar fashion the intellect which knows is said to be good because of its truth.

1240. It is also evident from the statements made here that the true and the false, which are objects of knowing, are found in the mind, but that good and evil, which are the objects of appetite, are found in things. And it is also evident that, just as the act of knowing attains its completion as a result of the things known existing in the knowing subject, in a similar fashion every appetite attains its completion as a result of the ordering of the appetitive subject to its appetible objects.

1241. *But since combination* (1027b29). Here he excludes being in the sense of the true and being in the sense of the accidental from the principal consideration of this science. He says that combination and separation, on which truth and falsity depend, are found in the mind and not in things, and that if any combination is also found in things, such combination produces a unity which the intellect understands as one by a simple concept.

But that combination or separation by which the intellect combines or separates its concepts is found only in the intellect and not in things. For it consists in a certain comparison of two concepts, whether these two are identical or distinct in reality. For sometimes the intellect uses one concept as two when it forms a combination, as when we say "Man is man," and it is clear from this that such a combination is found only in the intellect and not in things. Therefore, whatever is a being in the sense of the true, and consists in such a combination, differs from those things that are beings in the proper sense and are realities outside of the mind, each of which is *either what a thing is* (that is, substance), or of what sort, or how much, or any of the simple concepts which the mind combines or separates.

1242. Therefore, both being in the sense of the accidental and being in the sense of the true must be excluded from this science. For the cause of the former—being in the sense of the accidental—is the indeterminate, and therefore it does not come within the scope of art, as has been shown [1174]. The cause of the latter—being in the sense of the true—is *some positive state of mind*, the operation of the intellect combining and separating, and therefore it belongs to that science which studies the intellect.

1243. Another reason for excluding them is that, while *both of these*, namely, being in the sense of the true and accidental being, belong to some genus of being, they do not belong to being in the proper sense, which is found in reality. Nor do they designate another kind of being distinct from beings in the proper sense. For it is evident that

quorum unumquodque est per se. Sicut grammaticum musicum licet sit per accidens, tamen et grammaticum et musicum est per se ens, quia utrumque per se acceptum, habet causam determinatam. Et similiter intellectus compositionem et divisionem facit circa res, quae sub praedicamentis continentur.

1244. Unde si determinetur sufficienter illud genus entis quod continetur sub praedicamento, manifestum erit et de ente per accidens, et de ente vero. Et propter hoc huiusmodi entia praetermittuntur. Sed perscrutandae sunt causae et principia ipsius entis per se dicti, inquantum est ens. De quo palam est ex his quae determinavimus in quinto libro; ubi dictum est, quoties unumquodque talium nominum dicitur, quod ens dicitur multipliciter, sicut infra in principio septimi sequetur.

accidental being is a result of the coincidental connection of beings which exist outside the mind, each of which is a being of itself. For even though the grammatical musical has being only accidentally, nevertheless both grammatical and musical are beings in the proper sense, because each of these taken by itself has a definite cause. Similarly, the intellect combines and separates those things that are contained in the categories.

1244. If, then, the genus of being contained in the categories is sufficiently dealt with, the nature of accidental being and being in the sense of the true will be evident. And for this reason we must exclude these types of being and investigate the causes and principles of beings as beings in the proper sense. This is also evident from what has been established in book 5 [885], where, in discussing the different senses of such terms, it was stated that being is used in many senses, as follows below at the beginning of book 7 [1240].